The Oxford Handbook of Education and Training in Professional Psychology

OXFORD LIBRARY OF PSYCHOLOGY

Editor in Chief PETER E. NATHAN

The Oxford Handbook of Education and Training in Professional Psychology

Edited by

W. Brad Johnson

Nadine J. Kaslow

OXFORD
UNIVERSITY PRESS

OXFORD
UNIVERSITY PRESS

Oxford University Press is a department of the University of Oxford.
It furthers the University's objective of excellence in research, scholarship,
and education by publishing worldwide.

Oxford   New York
Auckland   Cape Town   Dar es Salaam   Hong Kong   Karachi
Kuala Lumpur   Madrid   Melbourne   Mexico City   Nairobi
New Delhi   Shanghai   Taipei   Toronto

With offices in
Argentina   Austria   Brazil   Chile   Czech Republic   France   Greece
Guatemala   Hungary   Italy   Japan   Poland   Portugal   Singapore
South Korea   Switzerland   Thailand   Turkey   Ukraine   Vietnam

Oxford is a registered trademark of Oxford University Press
in the UK and certain other countries.

Published in the United States of America by
Oxford University Press
198 Madison Avenue, New York, NY 10016

© Oxford University Press 2014

Library of Congress Cataloging-in-Publication Data
The Oxford handbook of education and training in professional psychology / edited by W. Brad Johnson and Nadine J. Kaslow.
pages cm.–(Oxford library of psychology)
ISBN 978-0-19-987401-9
1. Psychology—Study and teaching (Graduate)—Handbooks, manuals, etc.   2. Psychologists—Training of—Handbooks, manuals,
etc.   3. Psychology—Study and teaching (Internship)—Handbooks, manuals, etc.   I. Johnson, W. Brad. II. Kaslow, Nadine J.
BF77.O94 2013
150.71'1—dc23
2013031622

9 7 8 6 5 4 3 2 1
Printed in the United States of America
on acid-free paper

SHORT CONTENTS

The *Oxford Library of Psychology*, a landmark series of handbooks, is published by Oxford University Press, one of the world's oldest and most highly respected publishers, with a tradition of publishing significant books in psychology. The ambitious goal of the *Oxford Library of Psychology* is nothing less than to span a vibrant, wide-ranging field and, in so doing, to fill a clear market need.

Encompassing a comprehensive set of handbooks, organized hierarchically, the *Library* incorporates volumes at different levels, each designed to meet a distinct need. At one level are a set of handbooks designed broadly to survey the major subfields of psychology; at another are numerous handbooks that cover important current focal research and scholarly areas of psychology in depth and detail. Planned as a reflection of the dynamism of psychology, the *Library* will grow and expand as psychology itself develops, thereby highlighting significant new research that will impact on the field. Adding to its accessibility and ease of use, the *Library* will be published in print and, later on, electronically.

The *Library* surveys psychology's principal subfields with a set of handbooks that capture the current status and future prospects of those major subdisciplines. This initial set includes handbooks of social and personality psychology, clinical psychology, counseling psychology, school psychology, educational psychology, industrial and organizational psychology, cognitive psychology, cognitive neuroscience, methods and measurements, history, neuropsychology, personality assessment, developmental psychology, and more. Each handbook undertakes to review one of psychology's major subdisciplines with breadth, comprehensiveness, and exemplary scholarship. In addition to these broadly conceived volumes, the *Library* also includes a large number of handbooks designed to explore, in depth, more specialized areas of scholarship and research, such as stress, health and coping, anxiety and related disorders, cognitive development, or child and adolescent assessment. In contrast to the broad coverage of the subfield handbooks, each of these latter volumes focuses on an especially productive, more highly focused line of scholarship and research. Whether at the broadest or most specific level, however, all the *Library* handbooks offer synthetic coverage that reviews and evaluates the relevant past and present research and anticipates research in the future. Each handbook in the *Library* includes introductory and concluding chapters written by its editor to provide a roadmap to the handbook's table of contents and to offer informed anticipations of significant future developments in that field.

An undertaking of this scope calls for handbook editors and chapter authors who are established scholars in the areas about which they write. Many of the nation's and world's most productive and best-respected psychologists have agreed to edit *Library* handbooks or write authoritative chapters in their areas of expertise.

For whom has the *Oxford Library of Psychology* been written? Because of its breadth, depth, and accessibility, the *Library* serves a diverse audience, including graduate students in psychology and their faculty mentors, scholars, researchers, and practitioners in psychology and related fields. Each will find in the *Library* the information they seek on the subfield or focal area of psychology in which they work or are interested.

Befitting its commitment to accessibility, each handbook includes a comprehensive index, as well as extensive references to help guide research. Because the *Library* was designed from its inception as an online as well as a print resource, its structure and contents will be readily and rationally searchable online. Further, once the *Library* is released online, the handbooks will be regularly and thoroughly updated.

In summary, the *Oxford Library of Psychology* will grow organically to provide a thoroughly informed perspective on the field of psychology, one that reflects both psychology's dynamism and its increasing interdisciplinarity. Once published electronically, the *Library* is also destined to become a uniquely valuable interactive tool, with extended search and browsing capabilities. As you begin to consult this handbook, we sincerely hope you will share our enthusiasm for the more than 500-year tradition of Oxford University Press for excellence, innovation, and quality, as exemplified by the *Oxford Library of Psychology.*

Peter E. Nathan
Editor-in-Chief
Oxford Library of Psychology

ABOUT THE EDITORS

W. Brad Johnson

W. Brad Johnson is professor of psychology in the Department of Leadership, Ethics and Law at the United States Naval Academy, and a faculty associate in the Graduate School of Education at Johns Hopkins University. He currently serves as senior professor for the Naval Academy's Lead Division. A clinical psychologist and former lieutenant commander in the Navy's Medical Service Corps, Dr. Johnson served as a psychologist at Bethesda Naval Hospital and the Medical Clinic at Pearl Harbor where he was the division head for psychology. He is a fellow of the American Psychological Association and recipient of the Johns Hopkins University Teaching Excellence Award. He has served as chair of the American Psychological Association's Ethics Committee and as president of the Society for Military Psychology. Dr. Johnson is the author of numerous publications including 11 books, in the areas of mentoring, professional ethics, and counseling.

Nadine J. Kaslow

Nadine J. Kaslow, Ph.D., ABPP, is a professor with tenure, Emory University School of Medicine Department of Psychiatry and Behavioral Sciences; chief psychologist, Grady Health System; vice chair of the Department of Psychiatry and Behavioral Sciences; and director of the Postdoctoral Fellowship Program in Professional Psychology at Emory University School of Medicine. She holds a joint appointment in the Departments of Psychology, Pediatrics, and Emergency Medicine, and the Rollins School of Public Health. In 2012, she received an honorary degree (Doctor of Humane Letters) from Pepperdine University, where she also gave the commencement address. At Emory, she is past president of the university senate and past chair of the faculty council and former special assistant to the provost. Dr. Kaslow received her doctorate at the University of Houston and completed her internship and postdoctoral fellowship training at the University of Wisconsin. Prior to joining the faculty at Emory University in 1990, Dr. Kaslow was an assistant professor in the Departments of Psychiatry, Child Study Center, and Pediatrics at Yale University School of Medicine.

President-elect of the American Psychological Association (APA), she serves as the editor of the *Journal of Family Psychology*. She is past president of APA's Society of Clinical Psychology (Division 12), Society of Family Psychology (Division 43), and Division of Psychotherapy (Division 29), as well as the American Board of Clinical Psychology, the American Board of Professional Psychology, Family Process Institute, and the Wynne Center for Family Research. From 1998–2002, Dr. Kaslow was the chair of the Association of Psychology Postdoctoral and Internship Centers, and she is now a board member emeritus of this organization. In 2002, she chaired the multinational 2002 Competencies Conference: Future Directions in Education and Credentialing in Professional Psychology. Dr. Kaslow was a Fellow in the 2003–2004 Class of the Executive Leadership in Academic Medicine (ELAM) Program for Women, a fellow in the 2004 Woodruff Leadership Academy, and a primary-care public-policy fellow through the United States Public Health Service–Department of Health and Human Services.

CONTRIBUTORS

Elizabeth M. Altmaier
Department of Psychological and Quantitative
    Foundations
University of Iowa
Iowa City, IA

Jeff Baker
University of Texas Medical Branch
Galveston, TX

Jeffrey E. Barnett
Department of Psychology
Loyola University Maryland
Baltimore, MD

Stephen H. Behnke
Director, Office of Ethics
American Psychological Association
Washington, D.C.

Debora J. Bell
Department of Psychology
University of Missouri-Columbia
Columbia, MO

Samantha L. Bernecker
Department of Psychology
University of Massachusetts Amherst
Amherst, MA

Clark D. Campbell
Rosemead School of Psychology
Biola University
La Mirada, CA

Robin L. Cautin
Department of Psychology
Manhattanville College
Purchase, NY

Michael J. Constantino
Department of Psychology
University of Massachusetts Amherst
Amherst, MA

Jennifer A. Erickson Cornish
Graduate School of Professional Psychology
University of Denver
Denver, CO

David R. Cox
American Board of Professional Psychology
Chapel Hill, NC

Stephen T. DeMers
Association of State and Provincial
    Psychology Boards
Peachtree City, GA

Nancy S. Elman
School of Education
University of Pittsburgh
Pittsburgh, PA

Carol A. Falender
Department of Psychology
Pepperdine University
Los Angeles, CA

Eugene W. Farber
School of Medicine
Emory University
Atlanta, GA

Ruth E. Fassinger
College of Graduate and Professional Studies
John F. Kennedy University
Pleasant Hill, CA

Molly Fechter-Leggett
Stanford Youth Solutions
Sacramento, CA

Linda Forrest
College of Education
University of Oregon
Eugene, OR

Nadya A. Fouad
Department of Educational Psychology
University of Wisconsin-Milwaukee
Milwaukee, WI

Myrna L. Friedlander
Division of Counseling Psychology
School of Education
University at Albany
Albany, NY

Ian D. Goncher
Department of Behavioral Health Services
Johnstown, PA

Catherine L. Grus
American Psychological Association
Washington, D.C.

Robert L. Hatcher
Department of Psychology
City University of New York
New York, NY

Estee M. Hausman
Department of Psychological Sciences
University of Missouri-Columbia
Columbia, MO

Allison B. Hill
School of Medicine
Emory University
Atlanta, GA

Jacqueline B. Horn
Private Practice
Sacramento, CA

Christina E. Jeffrey
Texas A & M University
College Station, TX

W. Brad Johnson
Department of Leadership, Ethics, and Law
United States Naval Academy
Annapolis, MD

Jeffrey H. Kahn
Department of Psychology
Illinois State University
Normal, IL

Nadine J. Kaslow
School of Medicine
Emory University
Atlanta, GA

W. Gregory Keilin
The University of Texas at Austin
Austin, TX

Nicholas Ladany
School of Education and Counseling
  Psychology
Santa Clara University
Santa Clara, CA

Dorian A. Lamis
School of Medicine
Emory University
Atlanta, GA

Stephen R. McCutcheon
Veterans Affairs, Puget Sound Health
  Care System
Seattle, WA

Lynett Henderson Metzger
Graduate School of Professional Psychology
University of Denver
Denver, CO

Joseph R. Miles
Department of Psychology
University of Tennessee, Knoxville
Knoxville, TN

Lavita I. Nadkarni
Graduate School of Professional Psychology
University of Denver
Denver, CO

Greg J. Neimeyer
Department of Psychology
University of Florida
Gainesville, FL

Christopher E. Overtree
Department of Psychology
University of Massachusetts Amherst
Amherst, MA

Jesse Owen
College of Education and Human Development
University of Louisville
Louisville, KY

Roger L. Peterson
Department of Clinical Psychology
Antioch University New England
Keene, NH

Kelley Quirk
University of Louisville
Louisville, KY

Charles R. Ridley
Department of Psychology
Texas A & M University
College Station, TX

Emil Rodolfa
University of California, Davis
Davis, CA

Ronald H. Rozensky
Department of Clinical and Health Psychology
University of Florida
Gainesville, FL

Lewis Z. Schlosser
Department of Professional Psychology and
  Family Therapy
Seton Hall University
South Orange, NJ

Ann Schwartz
School of Medicine
Emory University
Atlanta, GA

Edward P. Shafranske
Graduate School of Education and Psychology
Pepperdine University
Los Angeles, CA

David S. Shen-Miller
College of Education
Tennessee State University
Nashville, TN

Jennifer M. Taylor
Department of Psychology
University of Florida
Gainesville, FL

Wendy L. Vincent
Commonwealth Psychology Associates
Newton, MA

Carol Webb
Department of Psychiatry and Behavioral
Sciences
Emory University
Atlanta, GA

Christina K. Wilson
School of Medicine
Emory University
Atlanta, GA

Erica H. Wise
Clinical Psychology Program
University of North Carolina – Chapel Hill
Chapel Hill, NC

CONTENTS

On Developing Professional Psychologists: The State of the Art and a Look Ahead

W. Brad Johnson *and* Nadine J. Kaslow

Abstract

Education and training in professional psychology have a rich history. In the last half century, the scientific and theoretical literature bearing on training future psychologists has dramatically accelerated. This chapter introduces the *Oxford Handbook of Education and Training in Professional Psychology*, the most comprehensive treatment of the topic to date. This handbook covers the full spectrum of historical developments, salient issues, current standards, and emerging trends in professional psychology education and training. We summarize the contributions of chapter authors—all luminaries in the discipline, and highlight the current state of the art in distinct domains of psychology education and training. We conclude this chapter with several bold predictions for the future of training in psychology.

Key Words: professional psychology, competence, education, training

Formal efforts to educate and train professional psychologists date to the start of the 20th century when psychologists working in applied settings such as government, education, and health care recognized a need to articulate training standards in their new profession. Today, there are hundreds of accredited doctoral training programs in professional psychology in the U. S. and Canada (http://www.apa.org/education/grad/applying.aspx) and thousands of internship and postdoctoral fellowship training programs. Although scholarly literature on graduate and postgraduate education and training in psychology has been rapidly accumulating for several decades; and although thousands of psychologists are employed full-time as faculty members and clinical supervisors in graduate, practicum, internship, and postdoctoral training programs; and a journal focused on *Training and Education in Professional Psychology;* until now there has been no single reference work for psychologists engaged in training and educating professional psychologists. Enter,

the *Oxford Handbook of Education and Training in Professional Psychology.*

This handbook covers the full spectrum of historical developments, salient issues, current standards, and emerging trends in professional psychology education and training. The handbook focuses on doctoral and postdoctoral training for psychologists in the health-service professions. Because competencies are moving to the forefront in the design of educational and training programs and the evaluation of trainee performance, models and standards for competency are a pervasive theme throughout the chapters. Although certain training issues, such as curriculum content and sequence of training experiences, often are in-flux or under review by various associations, this volume captures the current state of education and training while emphasizing emerging trends and forecasting future directions.

Professional psychology training program leaders and directors may easily feel overloaded by the substantial and varied duties required of their roles. Kenkel (this volume) observes that training program leaders often are tasked with the following responsibilities: (a) recruiting, reviewing, and selecting trainees; (b) advising and monitoring trainee progress; (c) developing and implementing training program curriculum, policies, and procedures; (d) selecting and supervising training faculty and staff; (e) shaping and monitoring the training program climate and culture; (f) representing the training program to external constituencies and review bodies; and (g) ensuring sufficient financial resources in the context of long-term planning. Of course, this list offers only a partial glimpse of the duties weighing on both program leaders, faculty, and supervising psychologists in the day-to-day work of preparing the next generation of psychologists. This handbook was launched with the guiding vision of helping training psychologists to better understand, appreciate, and conceptualize the work of training professional psychologists. We hope that it promotes competence and inspires excellence within the community of training psychologists (Johnson, Barnett, Elman, Forrest, & Kaslow, 2012).

The 30 chapters that follow have been clustered into five parts:

Part 1. Overview and Evolution of Education and Training in Psychology (2–6)
Part 2. Competence and Competencies in Professional Psychology (7–14)
Part 3. Trainee Selection, Development, and Evaluation (15–22)
Part 4. Culture and Context in Education and Training (23–27)
Part 5. Emerging Trends in Education and Training (28–31)

Each chapter is authored by one or more luminaries in the field of training. Readers will note that the table of contents constitutes a veritable "who's who" of scholars in the domain of professional psychology education and training. Each chapter incorporates a comprehensive literature review with an emphasis on evidence-based and competency-focused professional psychology education and training, articulates the current state of the art in a distinct training domain, and each concludes with prescient predictions for the future of training in psychology.

In the balance of this introductory chapter we set the stage and offer a preview of the highlights to come. We provide a brief overview of the literature on professional psychology education and training followed by a series of bold predictions regarding the future of training.

Evolution of Education and Training in Psychology

Benjamin (2007) observed that a profession comprises "specialized knowledge involving intensive training; high standards of practice, usually supported by a code of ethics; continuing education so that practitioners stay current with the latest developments in the profession; and provision of service to the public" (p. 155). Cautin and Baker (this volume) reflect that the 100-year evolution of psychology as a profession has been shaped by its application to everyday life. G. Stanley Hall (1894) first promoted psychology as an applied discipline, but it was not until 1917 and the founding of the American Association of Clinical Psychologists that there was a concerted effort to organize professional psychology (Routh, 1994). Yet, for most of the early 20th century, psychology promulgated no standard training guidelines, and the training of psychologists remained largely unsystematic and informal (Cautin & Baker, this volume).

It was the aftermath of World War II, the addition of 16 million new veterans to the Veterans' Administration (VA) system, and the VA's subsequent urgent request for more well-trained clinical psychologists that finally galvanized psychology to begin articulating standards for use in evaluating training programs and facilities. Under the leadership of David Shakow (1942), various committees began to formulate psychology's first professional training standards (e.g., American Psychological Association [APA] Committee on Training in Clinical Psychology). Simultaneously, the VA initiated a training program in 1946, under the leadership of James Miller, in which psychologists would perform diagnostic, therapeutic, and research functions. It was Miller who established the doctoral degree as the minimum requirement for aspiring psychologists in the VA. At the urging of the VA, the APA established the Committee on Training in Clinical Psychology (CTCP) to formulate a standard training program in clinical psychology for use in early efforts at peer evaluations of training entities. APA soon organized the Boulder Conference on Graduate Education in Psychology at which a common model of professional training—the scientist-practitioner model, or "Boulder Model"—was affirmed (Raimy, 1950). Cautin and Baker note that the Boulder Model designated the core skills that professional psychologists should demonstrate as well as the nature of both clinical and research training required to help trainees achieve competence in the role of professional psychologist.

Subsequent conferences articulated training models in other specialties, such as counseling psychology (e.g., Ann Arbor Conference—1948, Northwestern Conference—1951) and school psychology (Thayer Conference—1954).

Training Models in Professional Psychology

Bell and Hausman (this volume) observe that since 1949, training models have defined training in professional psychology, often providing a clear identity for graduate programs yet simultaneously fracturing the field in various ways. Today, there are three predominant models of doctoral education in professional psychology, the *scientist-practitioner*, *practitioner-scholar*, and *clinical scientist* models.

The Boulder Conference and its 70 resolutions established the scientist-practitioner model of training. Several of these resolutions became the foundation for all of professional psychology (e.g., inclusion of both research and applied training, foundations in the broader field of psychology, ethics training, attention to student qualifications, and faculty involvement: Bell & Housman, this volume). Explicit and ongoing integration of research and practice has remained the hallmark of scientist-practitioner training over the years (Raimy, 1950).

The practitioner-scholar (or scholar-practitioner) model, an alternative to the scientist-practitioner approach, was formulated at the Vail (Colorado) Conference in 1973 (Korman, 1973) and resulted in the development of the PsyD degree. This model prepares trainees primarily for careers in professional practice, emphasizes comprehensive clinical experiences beginning early in training, and offers science training focused on translating research and theory into practice. The *local-clinical scientist model*, represents a more recent evolution of this research into practice model at the level of the individual psychologist's local practice.

Finally, the clinical-scientist model (McFall, 1991) places greater emphasis than the other models on science and research in doctoral training, with a focus on preparing trainees for science-based careers. Use of the term "clinical-scientist" represents an attempt to address perceived weaknesses in prior training models by placing scientific methods and evidence at the core of education and training (Bell & Housman, this volume). Central to this model is a commitment to contribute to scientific knowledge in all one's professional activities, both research and applied.

In terms of demonstrable outcomes associated with programs espousing different training models, research is preliminary at best. Various efforts to compare doctoral programs by degree type (PhD versus PsyD) have yielded several trends (Rozensky, this volume). First, PsyD doctoral programs, particularly those located in specialized schools that do not provide broad academic programing, tend to admit much larger proportions of applicants while utilizing less stringent admissions criteria (Sayette, Norcross, & Dimoff, 2011). Second professional psychologists trained in PhD programs pass the Examination for Professional Practice of Psychology (EPPP) national licensing exam at a rate at a higher rate (82%) than those trained in PsyD programs (69%) (Schaffer et al., 2012). Finally, Graham and Kim (2011) reported that students enrolled in PhD programs, compared to those in PsyD programs, were significantly more likely to receive an APA-accredited internship and eventually become board certified. More and better evidence is required regarding the outcomes of training programs by training model.

Theoretical Orientation in Training Programs

Farber (this volume) reminds us that clinical theories have had a significant influence on professional psychology education and training. Proficiency in using one or more theoretical models of psychological functioning in order to understand clients/patients, formulate a diagnosis, and select and apply an appropriate intervention is central to engaging in theoretically-grounded clinical work (Wampold, 2010). Therefore, fostering the development of theoretical knowledge is often a key priority in professional psychology training. Farber highlights the benefits and liabilities of strong allegiance to a single theoretical approach within training programs. Readers will appreciate the essential tension between theoretical indoctrination and the broad charge to imbue trainees with a broad and general education in professional psychology (APA Commission on Accreditation, 2009). Training psychologists must provide trainees with common and essential knowledge in psychology (Peterson, Vincent, & Fechter-Leggett, this volume), while integrating this core curriculum with any program-specific theoretical model(s).

Competence and Competencies in Professional Psychology

The past decade has ushered in a somewhat dramatic shift to what Roberts, Borden, Christiansen, and Lopez (2005) described as a *culture of competence*. There is growing consensus about the core competencies within professional psychology (Kaslow, 2004; Kaslow et al., 2004). Competency-based training in professional psychology focuses on ensuring that trainees develop specific competencies during their education and applied training (Fouad & Grus, this volume). This approach represents a shift from earlier models of training that emphasized merely counting hours of supervised experience or completing a specified curriculum (Nelson, 2007). Fouad and Grus describe how the focus of training has turned to trainee learning outcomes and further, how training programs can be held accountable to demonstrate that trainees are competent to practice psychology. They note that the context for competency-based training stems from a convergence of three movements: (a) a zeitgeist of accountability for professionals to benefit the public and demonstrate consistent quality care outcomes (APA, 2010; Institute of Medicine, 2003); (b) a move within health-service provider education toward outcome-based education and learner-based outcomes (Nelson, 2007); and (c) concerns about the cost of professional training in psychology.

Competency-based education and training clarifies and measures the acquisition of knowledge, skills, and attitudes and their integration across a range of foundational and functional competency domains (Donovan & Ponce, 2009; Fouad et al., 2009; Kaslow et al., 2009). Foundational competencies refer to fundamental professional knowledge, structures, and skill sets (Fouad & Grus) and include, but are not limited to, professionalism, reflective practice, ethical and legal standards, and relationships (Rodolfa et al., 2005). Functional competencies in professional psychology include assessment, intervention, consultation, research and evaluation, supervision, administration, and advocacy (Rodolfa et al., 2005). Benchmarks that characterize competence in knowledge, attitude, and skill are now in place for the prepracticum, practicum, and internship levels of psychology training (Fouad et al., 2009), as well as specialty credentialing and maintenance of competence (Baker & Cox, this volume).

McCutcheon and Keilin (this volume) discuss the internship in professional psychology, from inception to the current questions, quandaries, and conflicts linked to internship year. A critical element in the sequence of training professional psychologists, the internship has been referred to as a capstone, and more recently, the *keystone experience* for health-service psychologists (McCutcheon, 2011). McCutcheon and Keilin note that the internship year remains broad and general in emphasis (Zlotlow, Nelson & Peterson, 2011); it is intended to promote intermediate to advanced knowledge, skills, and attitudes in a broad spectrum of foundational and functional competencies.

Beyond the internship, there is growing recognition of the value of supervised postdoctoral training for the purpose of solidifying professional competence and professional identity. Wilson, Hill, Lamis, and Kaslow (this volume) reflect that the postdoctoral movement in professional psychology occurred in response to myriad factors, including the proliferation of practice competencies and the emergence of specialties within psychology (Kaslow & Webb, 2011). But there are other salient reasons for trainers to encourage and trainees to pursue postdoctoral training. These include: (a) enhanced career marketability; (b) the fact that most jurisdictions require postdoctoral experience for licensure; (c) the linkage between postdoctoral training and specialization; and (d) the reality that many psychology trainees are viewed as not fully prepared for independent practice until they have completed a supervised postdoctoral experience (Rodolfa, Ko, & Petersen, 2004).

Competence in the consumption and application of research, as well as the production of original research, is another essential component of training in professional psychology. Kahn and Schlosser (this volume) reflect that training students to be proficient in research is central to the philosophy of most doctoral training models within professional psychology. Beginning with the Boulder Conference and continuing today, the integration of science and practice has been an indispensable facet of applied psychology training (e.g., Bieschke, Fouad, Collins, & Halonen, 2004). There are research components nested within the Competency Benchmarks document (Fouad et al., 2009). These elements of scientific mindedness include critical scientific thinking, valuing and applying scientific methods to professional practice, and independently applying scientific methods to practice (Fouad et al., 2009).

Kahn and Schlosser show that a graduate program's research training environment (RTE) is not only key to influencing trainees' research skills, but an effective RTE also will lead trainees to be more interested in research, value research more, be more motivated to engage in research, and have a greater sense of self-efficacy concerning research (Gelso, 1993). Research training is not limited to doctoral programs. Phillips, Szymanski, Ozegovic, & Briggs-Phillips (2004) developed the Internship Research Training Environment Scale (IRTES) to assess the RTE during the internship year. Salient predictors of strong internship RTEs included strong mentoring, research role modeling, and recognition and encouragement for research. If research competencies are desired in professional psychologists, then effective RTEs must be integrated into all phases of psychologists' training.

The evolving association between training programs and licensing and credentialing bodies constitutes a final link in the competency continuum. Licensing boards in psychology define the nature and scope of practice (APA, 2011) and credential-qualified health-care psychologists. In order to solidify and reinforce psychology's burgeoning competency benchmarks, DeMers, Webb, and Horn (this volume) note that a collaborative and mutually respectful relationship between the training and credentialing communities is essential. Both communities are committed to ensuring trainee competence for entry into the profession, Additionally, those psychologists engaged in licensing and other forms of credentialing are equally concerned that credentialed psychologists maintain competence beyond initial licensure and throughout their careers (Johnson et al., 2012).

Trainee Selection, Development, and Evaluation
Trainee Selection and Evaluation

Owen, Quirk, and Rodolfa (this volume) remind us that trainee selection—beginning at the level of graduate school matriculation—carries significant implications for graduate and training programs, the profession, and the public. Current training candidate assessment strategies (e.g., Graduate Record Exam, letters of recommendation, interviews) offer some selection utility but several of these selection approaches have dubious validity, reliability, and fidelity. Owen and colleagues provide an important service to the profession by proposing several promising trainee selection alternatives. These include the constructs of facilitative interpersonal skills (FIS: Anderson, Ogles, Patterson, Lambert & Vermeersch, 2009) and cognitive complexity (Owen & Lindley, 2010). Facilitative interpersonal skills refer to an individual's ability to effectively and accurately communicate and interpret messages as well as the ability to persuade others in helpful ways. Cognitive complexity facilitates mastery of many of the core competencies in professional psychology.

Once admitted to a doctoral program, a trainee must embark on a journey of consistent evaluation that will typically extend through postdoctoral training, licensure, and often, terminating only at the moment of board certification. Trainee evaluation processes have been dramatically impacted by the competency movement, with competency benchmarks—incorporating cognitive, relational, affective, moral, behavioral, and integrative dimensions—now applied to all phases of training (e.g., Kaslow et al., 2009; Kaslow, Falendar & Grus, 2012; Kerns, Berry, Frantsve, & Linton, 2009) from doctoral program screening (Kenkel, 2009) to postlicensure determinations of fitness to practice (Kerns et al., 2009). In this volume, Shen-Miller notes that in matters of trainee evaluation, the best training programs begin with clear definitions and transparent communication regarding what will be evaluated, followed by specific feedback from multiple raters (including one's self) that identifies (a) areas for growth and self-improvement, (b) a timeline for change and improvement, and (c) specific ways to improve performance (Kenkel, 2009). Like Kennedy and Lingard (2007), Shen-Miller argues that trainee assessment and feedback should be dynamic, ongoing, and ever-evolving in the life of any training program. A persistent focus on trainee evaluation is essential to ensuring quality of care and client/patient safety.

Trainee Mentoring and Supervision

Perhaps no facet of training in psychology has more to do with the development from novice trainee to professional psychologist than clinical supervision. According to Falender and Shafranske (this volume), supervision, a core competency in professional psychology, involves learning how to apply science-informed knowledge to solve clinical problems, ongoing socialization to the profession, transmitting and strengthening values and ethics, and enhancing respect and appreciation for all persons. Excellent supervision promotes attitudes and skills in self-assessment and spurs commitment to life-long learning. Of course, the paramount function of supervision in the course of psychology training is protection of the public. Perhaps not surprisingly, Falendar and Shafranske identify discernible challenges to the implementation of competency-based clinical supervision within training programs and the need for transformational leadership to ensure such implementation (Kaslow et al., 2012). For instance, the shift from a development-through-osmosis model of supervision to one rooted in planful development competencies has been quite slow at times. A competency-based approach to supervision places far greater focus on the process of supervisor assessment of supervisee preparedness to execute clinical tasks with clients/patients.

In addition to astute supervisors, training psychologists increasingly are called to become intentional and deliberate mentors for graduate students, interns, and postdoctoral residents (Johnson, 2007; Kaslow & Mascaro, 2007). The most effective mentorships in psychology training environments have been distinguished by focal characteristics including positive emotional valence, increasing mutuality, deliberate focus on the trainee's career and professional identity development, and a host of career and psychosocial functions (Johnson, 2007). Johnson (this volume) proposes the Mentoring Relationship Continuum Model as a strategy for integrating various trainer-trainee developmental relationships under a single mentoring relationship umbrella. According to Johnson, as any developmental training relationship evolves along the mentoring continuum, it may be characterized by more and more of the qualities of mentoring. Recognizing that no single training relationship is likely to meet the full spectrum of trainee developmental needs, Johnson further proposes a mentoring constellation or developmental network approach to conceptualizing mentoring. In this model, a *mentoring constellation* is the set of relationships an individual has with the people who take an active interest in and action to advance the individual's career by assisting with both personal and professional development (Higgins & Thomas, 2001).

Ethics and Professionalism

In their various roles as teachers and supervisors, training psychologists will inevitably serve as salient role models, demonstrating in their day-to-day interactions with trainees what it means to be a professional psychologist. Barnett and Goncher (this volume) and Grus and Kaslow (this volume) explore the weighty responsibility for personally modeling ethical behavior and professionalism as trainers intentionally acculturate trainees into the profession. Knapp and VanderCreek (2006) refer to the myriad teaching moments outside the classroom and supervision session as *implicit* or *underground* curricula that "refer to the institutional atmosphere within the program" (p. 216). When it comes to ethics acculturation, Handlesman, Gottlieb, and Knapp (2005) note that psychology is a culture with its own traditions, values, and ethical expectations; training faculty will communicate much of this culture through their daily interactions with others. Barnett and Goncher note that the important work of ethics acculturation in professional psychology requires creating a culture of ethics, modeling self-care and wellness, appropriately managing boundaries with trainees, promoting integrity in research and publication, maintaining and developing one's own clinical competence, and working through ethical challenges and dilemmas in a transparent way, always with an eye toward modeling the ethical consultation and decision-making process for trainees.

Often entwined with ethics, professionalism is a core element of personal identity and character that develops over the course of one's professional life (Passi, Doug, Peile, Thistlethwaite, & Johnson, 2010). Grus and Kaslow (this volume) offer one of the first systematic efforts to review and integrate the literature on professionalism from the professional psychology literature. They describe professionalism as behavior and comportment that reflect the values and attitudes of psychology (Fouad et al., 2009). Salient elements of professionalism include: (a) integrity—honesty, personal responsibility, and adherence to professional values; (b) deportment; (c) accountability; (4) concern for the welfare of others; and (5) professional identity. A necessary, though not sufficient, competency for the effective practice of psychology (Cruess, Cruess, & Steinert, 2009; Lesser et al., 2010; Pellegrino, 2002), professionalism *can* be taught. In fact, it is imperative that trainers help trainees to make a life-long commitment to refining professionalism over the course of their professional development (Lesser et al., 2010).

When Training Goes Awry

Although the large majority of trainer-trainee relationships are productive and positive and most training environments are conducive to effective education and professional development, this is not always the case. Kaslow, Johnson, and Schwartz (this volume) note that difficulties at the level of the trainee, the trainer, the training relationship, peers in the training milieu, or the training context itself can easily undermine the efficacy of training. When training goes awry, evidence sometimes points to trainer behavior that is inadequate or even harmful (Ellis, 2010). Survey findings indicate that when training relationships become dysfunctional, faculty and supervisors sometimes contribute directly to the difficulty (Clark, Harden, & Johnson, 2000; Nelson et al., 2008). For instance, if trainers exhibit shortcomings with multicultural competence, this may diminish both the process and outcome of supervisory relationships (Inman, 2006).

At times, training relationships suffer when trainees evidence problems of professional competence. Forrest and Elman (this volume) find that professional psychology has made great strides in understanding problems of professional competence within the evolving culture of competency and further in conceptualizing the individual trainee with problems of professional competence as located within a larger training ecology or system. According to Forrest and Campbell (2012), the competency movement has made a critical contribution to addressing the complexities present in evaluating clinical competence —particularly when problems develop. In many cases, trainers and peers report that the most common and troubling problems of professional competence in training settings include defensiveness, lack of self-reflection, and deficits in empathy. Recently, the inclusion of interpersonal relationships and professionalism as core competencies in the professional psychology benchmarks has provided a way to clearly address these problems of professional competence (Forrest, Elman, & Shen Miller, 2008). Moving forward, Forrest and Elman advocate that the profession cease using the term "impairment" in relation to problems of professional competence, that work continues on developing a typology of common categories of competence problems in trainees, and that the individual competency framework be expanded and applied to the broader training ecology.

When problems of professional competence rise to the level of requiring *remedial* or *disciplinary* interventions, a complex array of ethical concerns and legal requirements often come to bear such that trainers may feel bewildered regarding an appropriate course of action. Behnke (this volume) addresses 25 essential questions for training psychologists to consider when trainees require either (a) interventions designed to assist the trainee to enhance competence and move toward graduation (remedial), or (b) interventions designed to terminate a trainee (disciplinary). In these cases, trainers must be conversant with the ethical and legal issues bearing on liability, remediation plans, privacy, confidentiality, and disclosures.

Culture and Context in Education and Training

Several excellent chapters in this volume provide a contextual perspective on professional training including modern trends in diversity education and current strategies for promoting cultural competence (c.f., Metzger, Cornish, & Ndkarni, this volume). Cultural competence in the context of training may be defined as the deliberate incorporation of cultural data in the training relationship. The purpose of the incorporation is to determine, facilitate, evaluate, and sustain positive professional outcomes for the trainee (Ridley, Mollen, & Kelly, 2011). Ladany and Friedlander (this volume) provide a framework for understanding how psychology educators and trainers can enhance gender competencies in trainees. Essential elements of self-awareness related to gender competence include: (a) self-reflective practice, (b) gender identity, and (c) gender-based countertransference (Boswell & Castonguay, 2007). Miles and Fassinger (this volume) urge psychology trainers to play intentional roles in producing knowledge and inculcating trainee competence bearing on sexual orientation, gender identity, and mental health. Training psychologists are situated to ensure that new psychologists provide mental health services and develop policies that promote the welfare of lesbian, gay, bisexual, and transgender (LGBT) individuals and families. These authors craft their chapter around APA's (2012) revised Guidelines for Psychological Practice with lesbian, gay, and bisexual clients, and specifically guideline 19, "Psychologists strive to include lesbian, gay, and bisexual issues in professional education and training" (p. 25).

Ridley and Jeffrey (this volume) take on the linkage between diversity and power in the trainer-trainee relationship as they address the current state of race and ethnicity in professional psychology training. Although White trainers and trainees continue to outnumber minority trainers and trainees, the gap is gradually shrinking (APA, 2008). In addition to describing essential competencies bearing on race and diversity, Ridley and Jeffrey (this volume) offer a typology of problems in training programs related to race. These include: (a) avoiding discussion of racial differences, (b) stereotypes and attributions, (c) cultural incompetence (Foo-Kune & Rodolfa, 2013), (d) uncritical acceptance of privilege (King, 1991), and (e) downright denial of racial differences. Becoming a culturally competent trainer requires careful self-reflection and often deliberate personal work in each of these domains.

Finally, Campbell (this volume) addresses the unique role of religious-distinctive training programs. Because few programs currently include religious or spiritual issues in the training curriculum (Hage, Hopson, Siegel, Payton, & DeFanti, 2006) and because training directors of many APA-accredited programs report little interest in offering focused training in this area (Russell & Yarhouse, 2006), religious-distinctive programs seek to prepare psychologists with focused competency in service to religious communities, including the delivery of mental health services that integrate or accommodate client/patient religious or spiritual beliefs and practices. In addition, with the data emerging on the salience of religion and spirituality as related to the psychological well-being of many individuals, the value of attending to this form of diversity in all training programs as a component of cultural competence is underscored.

The Road Ahead: The Future of Training in Professional Psychology

Rozensky (this volume) highlights a variety of trends likely to influence the success of the professional psychology workforce moving forward. Although social, political, and economic factors will continue to shape the evolution of health-care professions broadly, Rozensky cautions that psychologists must be particularly attentive to the following trends (among many others): (a) ever-increasing diversity in the population we serve; (b) rapid changes in the health-care system; (c) increasing emphasis on accountability, evidence-based treatments, and demonstration of medical-cost offset; (d) interprofessionalism; and (e) matters of supply and demand for professional psychologists. According to Rozensky, it is of paramount importance that training programs are transparent with applicants about how each of these trends may shape career options and expectations.

We conclude this introduction to the *Oxford Handbook of Education and Training in Professional Psychology* by distilling some of the most farsighted and evidence-supported predictions offered by authors of the following 30 chapters. Although there is always some risk inherent in forecasting the future of a profession, we are particularly confident that contributors to this volume are in the best position to offer valuable projections about the road ahead. We now offer 10 salient trends in professional psychology training. Each trend is part observation, part prediction, and part recommendation. We hope these trends help to both set the stage for the important contributions contained in the handbook and offer training psychologists a glimpse of the road ahead.

Models of Doctoral Training Will Be Integrated and Streamlined

Although the PhD was established as the degree associated with the scientist-practitioner model over 60 years ago (Raimy, 1950), and the PsyD stipulated as the degree of choice for Vail-model practitioner programs (Korman, 1973), professional psychology currently struggles with some confusion regarding degree and training model distinctions (Bell & Housman, this volume). For instance, some practitioner-scholar programs grant the PhD degree and certain scientist-practitioner model programs offer the PsyD. On the upside, distinct training models in professional psychology provide coherent frameworks for program emphasis and trainee competencies. On the downside, the often muddled contours between degrees and training models pose an obstacle to the promotion of professional psychology as a coherent health-care profession. Bell and Housman reflect that the evolution of training models within psychology has been neither necessary nor sufficient. In fact, training psychologists are at risk for spending more time debating the merits of nuanced distinctions among models (see Bieschke et al., 2011) and far too little time focusing on the shared values, principles, and foci across models.

The fact remains that consumers and allied health-care professionals are often unaware of and utterly unconcerned about the training model employed by a psychologist's training programs. Rather, our clients/patients and colleagues hope that we will be competent, ethical, and professional. Just as the field of psychotherapy has begun a growing movement toward evidence-based integration and consolidation (Collins, Leffingwell, & Belar, 2007; Norcross, 2005), so too should professional psychology education and training begin a process of integration and parsimonious consolidation, always with an eye toward core competencies required for the effective practice of professional psychology.

The Practical Training Sequence Will Be Revisioned and Refined

Several of the authors in this volume address the controversies and complexities centering on supervised practical training in professional psychology. At present, doctoral students experience considerable pressure to accrue substantial numbers of supervised practicum hours at the predoctoral level. Of course, number of hours accrued may say little about established competence for more advanced training (Kaslow & Keilin, 2006). To the extent that practicum hours serve as one indicator of preparation and competence, it will be increasingly important that accrediting bodies and training programs attend to the quality of practicum experiences (Fouad & Grus, this volume; Schaffer & Rodolfa, 2011). A related concern has to do with the internship imbalance and the question of whether the internship in professional psychology should be shifted to a postdoctoral experience (McCutcheon & Keilin, this volume). If practicum experiences are extensive, well-supervised, scrutinized during program accreditation, and linked to a clear process of competency assessment, then perhaps trainees will be better served financially and professionally if the doctoral degree is awarded prior to the formal internship. However, such a shift in timing has many significant downsides, related to continued concerns about readiness for independent practice without such experience as well the credibility of the profession if less education and training is required. Whatever the approach to sequencing training experiences, the current scarcity of both internship and postdoctoral residency opportunities in professional psychology requires concerted attention (Hogg & Olvey, 2007). As McCutcheon and Keilin reflect, discussions of the imbalance between trainees and available training positions inevitably touch upon issues of equity, quality, opportunity, identity, social justice, and the very health and future of professional psychology. But this problem also must be contextualized in a large context, namely challenges associated with multiple transitions in the education, training, credentialing, and career employment guideline.

An Increasing Focus on Competence and Professionalism

The culture of competence—including accurate and multi-method assessment of competence—will continue to define professional psychology moving forward (Fouad et al., 2009; Kaslow et al., 2009). In light of the steadily evolving and increasing knowledge base in psychology (Neimeyer, Taylor, & Rozensky, 2012), psychology competency benchmarks must be frequently updated and used reliably in both formative and summative assessments of trainees. Fouad and Grus (this volume) challenge training psychologists to move beyond merely identifying and assessing competencies to clearly establishing the link between this process and improved client or patient well-being. We further challenge psychologists to move beyond individualistic conceptions of trainee competence and begin to incorporate larger contextual influences when evaluating competence (e.g., agency setting, case complexity, trainee caseload) (Schulte & Daly, 2009). Finally, we predict that professionalism will become more

clearly conceptualized, more precisely operationalized, and more thoughtfully assessed at all levels of professional psychology training (see Grus & Kaslow, this volume). Inevitably intertwined with competence, professionalism manifests in both specific competencies and in more macro or big-picture notions of what it means to be a professional psychologist.

Specialization Will Loom Large in the Future of the Profession

Roberts (2006) described the "essential tension" between broad and general training in psychology on one hand and specialization on the other. It is increasingly evident that doctoral training programs cannot provide both the foundational training required by the Commission on Accreditation (CoA) and high-quality specialty training in focused areas of professional practice (Baker & Cox, this volume). Professional psychology must acknowledge the need for specialty training, while making difficult decisions about where precisely to locate specialty training in the professional psychology training sequence (Altmaier, this volume). Should specialty training be confined to internship and postdoctoral programs? How will specialized programs be regarded by accreditation bodies? Should psychology fully adopt the model of board certification so long effective in medicine? Whatever the answers to these questions, it is clear that psychology must find a coherent solution to the increasing complexity and requirement for specialized competence in professional practice.

Trainee Selection Must Become More Rigorous and Effective

Several authors in this volume raise concerns and recommend alternatives to current strategies for vetting training program applicants. Although the competency benchmarks (Busseri, Tyler, & King, 2005; Fouad et al., 2009) have refined the profession's approach to assessing trainee competence following matriculation, current approaches to determining which applicants merit entrée into the profession are less well developed. For instance, Owen, Quirk, and Rodolfa (this volume) surmise that reliance on GRE scores and letters of recommendation leaves much to be desired. In the future, program leaders must do more to reliably and validly ascertain whether an applicant possesses the requisite ethical-mindedness, psychological fitness, and interpersonal facility required for the acquisition of competence in psychology.

Trainer Selection and Preparation Must Become More Rigorous and Effective

It is unreasonable to assume that all psychologists demonstrate the necessary and sufficient motivation and competence to cultivate positive and effective developmental relationships with trainees. When training goes awry, trainer competence problems are occasionally responsible for this (Kaslow et al., this volume). Moreover, even when training psychologists demonstrate potential for excellence as a supervisor, teacher, and mentor, they are likely to encounter unique conundrums and tensions related to their dual roles as educator/supervisor—including advocacy and collegial friendship with trainees—and gatekeeper for the profession (Johnson, 2007). For these reasons, training programs must do more to increase the rigor and reliability of selection and hiring strategies for new faculty/supervisors, while doing more to prepare new training psychologists for their roles. Currently, evidence of robust research funding or numerous publications may serve as primary hiring criteria for program faculty, whereas evidence of a relevant clinical experience may be a primary measure of readiness to supervise. Of course, neither of these criteria have any demonstrated connection to competence as a training psychologist (Kaslow et al., 2007; 2009). Johnson (this volume) recommends that training programs become much more deliberate about selecting, training, and supervising psychologists with the interest, aptitude, and interpersonal competence required of excellent advising, supervising, and role-modeling.

Training in Psychology Increasingly Will Be Shaped by Technology and Innovation

Constantino, Overtree, and Bernecker (this volume) address both technological advances and paradigmatic challenges to professional psychology training (Kazdin & Blasé, 2011). As psychology moves forward, some of the direct technological innovations likely to have a tremendous impact on training new psychologists include: (a) use of streaming video for therapeutic, teaching, and mentoring purposes; (b) video conferencing to enhance the value and frequency of clinical supervision; and (c) moment-to-moment outcome monitoring capability in training clinics. Some of the most intriguing non-technology-based innovations in training will include: (a) integrating research infrastructures directly into the psychotherapy training mission; and (b) migration toward common-factors psychotherapy training (Norcross, 2011).

In addition, with the advances in technology and social media, trainers must focus more of their attention on providing education and supervision related to the roles(s) of social media in the practice of psychology. More consideration needs to be given to pertinent ethical, practical, and professionalism related issues (APA Practice Organization, 2010; Gabbard et al., 2011).

Licensing and Credentialing Organizations Must Confront Several Quandaries

The profession of psychology must address several questions and quandaries related to licensure and credentialing of psychologists. As DeMers and colleagues (this volume) suggest, many of these unresolved concerns will have direct bearing on training. For instance, although APA and the Canadian Psychological Association (CPA) have promulgated standards of accreditation of training programs that adhere to the doctoral standard (APA Commission on Accreditation, 2009), the doctoral standard is not universally accepted by state and provincial licensing boards as the training standard. Psychology must further address the growth of online delivery for graduate education courses, and even entire degree programs. DeMers and colleagues raise excellent and troubling questions regarding whether the physical presence of a trainee within a training environment is essential for developing all facets of competence required of a professional psychologist. Within psychology, there is also growing concerns about a perceived lack of communication between trainers stationed at various levels within the training sequence (doctoral program, practicum site, internship program, postdoctoral program; Johnson et al., 2008), such that gatekeeping efforts are hampered and consistent tracking of trainee competence is inconsistent at best. Finally, there is considerable discussion and debate regarding telepractice, and, by extension, *teletraining*, across accreditation and credentialing bodies. Very few psychology licensing laws currently address the question of long-distance supervision.

There Will Be Increasing Rapprochement between Religious and LGBT Training Psychologists

Miles and Fassinger (this volume), like many in the profession, express concern that religious-distinctive programs are empowered—by a footnote in the accreditation guidelines—to exclude faculty and prospective students whose sexual or gender orientation and related behavior (e.g., open LGBT relationships) is considered incongruent with religious institutional faith statements. As professional psychology continues to develop an appreciation for the complex identities and identity interactions among trainers and trainees, as training psychologists continue to identify components of the cultural diversity competency, as the profession places greater emphasis on social justice and advocacy during education and training, and as attitudes in the population continue to shift, we anticipate greater cooperation and even collaboration between religious-distinctive training programs (Campbell, this volume) and the broader profession that values full inclusivity. The current APA Accreditation Guidelines (APA, 2009) require that accredited training programs ensure a supportive and encouraging learning environment appropriate for the training of diverse individuals and the provision of training opportunities for a broad spectrum of individuals. Importantly, the guidelines prohibit actions that would restrict program access on grounds that are irrelevant to success in graduate training. We encourage religious-distinctive program directors to take the lead in ensuring that their graduates are competent to work ethically and effectively with LGBT persons, to work at changing institutional policies that unfairly restrict employment or admission for LGBT faculty and trainees, and to promote collaborative scholarship on the interface of religion, spirituality, sexual orientation, and gender identity.

Training Psychologists Will Better Prepare Trainees for Career-Long Professional Development and Communitarian Engagement

Neimeyer and Taylor (this volume) urge greater commitment and accountability when it comes to lifelong learning and continuing professional development following initial licensure. How can training psychologists more effectively inculcate trainees with an ethic of accountability for one's ongoing competence and professional growth? How can continuing education and self-assessment of competence become more evidence-based and reliable? These questions link nicely to recent calls for collegial engagement as one salient mechanism for ensuring ongoing professional competence (Johnson et al., 2012; Johnson, Elman, Forrest, Robiner, Rodolfa, & Schaffer, 2013) Johnson and colleagues (2012) have advocated that individual notions of accountability for ongoing competence must be augmented with interdependent and collectivistic (communitarian) perspectives on ethics generally and competence specifically. We predict that psychologists functioning

with a communitarian perspective would feel some sense of accountability for the competence and well-functioning of their colleagues; show less reticence, and suffer less shame about exposing imperfections, emotional distress, and need for assistance with colleagues; and share a concern for the common good that would include all those served by their professional community, not just their own individual clients/patients or students/supervisees (Johnson et al., 2012). In the future, we predict that training psychologists will infuse communitarian ideals into all facets of the training culture. This will include preparing trainees to deliberately construct personal *competence constellations* or clusters of relationships people who take an active interest in and action to advance the trainee's well-being and professional competence (Johnson et al., 2013).

References

American Psychological Association, Office of Minority Affairs (2008). *A portrait of success and challenge—Progress report: 1997–2005*. Washington, DC: Author.

American Psychological Association (2010). Ethical principles of psychologists and code of conduct. Retrieved from: http://www.apa.org/ethics/code/index.aspx

American Psychological Association (2011). Model act of state licensure of psychologists. *American Psychologist, 66*, 214–226. doi: 10.1037/a0022655

American Psychological Association. (2012). Guidelines for psychological practice with lesbian, gay, and bisexual clients. *American Psychologist, 67*, 10–42. doi: 10.1037/a0024659

American Psychological Association, Commission on Accreditation. (2009). *Guidelines and principles for accreditation of program in professional psychology*. Washington, DC: APA. Retrieved January 3, 2013, from: http://www.apa.org/ed/accreditation/about/policies/guiding-principles.pdf

American Psychological Association. (2012). Guidelines for psychological practice with lesbian, gay, and bisexual clients. *American Psychologist, 67*, 10–42. doi: 10.1037/a0024659

American Psychological Association, Commission on Accreditation. (2009). *Guidelines and principles for accreditation of program in professional psychology*. Washington, DC: APA. Retrieved January 3, 2013, from: http://www.apa.org/ed/accreditation/about/policies/guiding-principles.pdf

American Psychological Association Practice Organization. (Summer, 2010). *Telehealth: Legal basics for psychologists. Good Practice*. Washington, DC: Author. 2–7.

Anderson, T., Ogles, B. M., Patterson, C. L., Lambert, M. J., & Vermeersch, D. A. (2009). Therapist effects: Facilitative interpersonal skills as a predictor of therapist success. *Journal of Clinical Psychology, 65*, 1–14.

Benjamin, L. T., Jr. (2007). *A brief history of modern psychology*. Malden, MA: Blackwell.

Bieschke, K. J., Bell, D., Davis, C. III, Hatcher, R., Peterson, R., & Rodolfa, E. R. (2011). Forests, grazing areas, water supplies, and the internship imbalance problem: Redefining the paradigm to implement effective change. *Training and Education in Professional Psychology, 5*, 123–125. doi: 10.1037/a0024902

Bieschke, K. J., Fouad, N. A., Collins, F. L., & Halonen, J. S. (2004). The scientifically-minded psychologist: Science as a core competency. *Journal of Clinical Psychology, 60,* 713–723. doi: 10.1002/jclp.20012

Boswell, J. F., & Castonguay, L. G. (2007). Psychotherapy training: Suggestions for core ingredients and future research. *Psychotherapy: Theory, Research, Practice, Training, 44,* 378–383. doi:10.1037/0033-3204.44.4.378

Busseri, M. A., Tyler, J. D., & King, A. R. (2005). An exploratory examination of student dismissals and prompted resignations from clinical psychology Ph.D. training. *Professional Psychology: Research and Practice, 36,* 441–445. doi: 10.1037/0735-7028.36.4.441

Clark, R. A., Harden, S. L., & Johnson, W. B. (2000). Mentor relationships in clinical psychology doctoral training: Results of a national survey. *Teaching of Psychology, 27,* 262–268. doi: 10.1207/S15328023TOP2704_04

Collins, F. L., Leffingwell, T. R., & Belar, C. D. (2007). Teaching evidence-based practice: Implications for psychology. *Journal of Clinical Psychology, 63,* 657–670. doi: 10.1002/jclp.20378

Cruess, R. L., Cruess, S. R., & Steinert, Y. (Eds.). (2009). *Teaching medical professionalism.* Cambridge: Cambridge University Press.

Donovan, R. A., & Ponce, A. N. (2009). Identification and measurement of core competencies in professional psychology: Areas for consideration. *Training and Education in Professional Psychology, 3(Suppl.),* S46–S49. doi: 10.1037/a0017302

Ellis, M. V. (2010). Bridging the science and practice of clinical supervision: Some discoveries, some misconceptions. *The Clinical Supervisor, 29,* 95–116. doi: 10.1080/07325221003741910

Foo-Kune, N. W. R. & Rodolfa, E. R. (2013). Putting the benchmarks into practice: Multiculturally competent supervisors—effective supervision. *The Counseling Psychologist, 41*(1), 121–130. doi:10.1177/0011000012453944

Forrest, L., & Campbell, L. F. (2012). Emerging trends in counseling psychology education and training. In N. Fouad, J. Carter, & L. Subich [Eds.]. *APA handbook o of counseling psychology: Theories, research and methods.* (Vol. I, pp. 119–154). Washington, DC: APA Press.

Forrest, L., Elman, N. S., & Shen Miller, D. S. (2008). Psychology trainees with competence problems: From individual to ecological conceptualizations. *Training and Education in Professional Psychology, 2,* 183–192.

Fouad, N. A., Grus, C. L., Hatcher, R. L., Kaslow, N. J., Hutchings, P. S., Madson, M. B., Collins, F. L., Jr., Crossman, R. E. (2009). Competency benchmarks: A model for understanding and measuring competence in professional psychology across training levels. *Training and Education in Professional Psychology, 3* (Suppl.), S5–S26. doi: 10.1037/a0015832

Gabbard, G. O., Roberts, L. W., Crisp-Han, H., Ball, V., Hobday, G., & Rachal, F. (2011). *Professionalism in psychiatry.* Washington, DC: American Psychiatric Publications.

Gelso, C. J. (1993). On the making of a scientist-practitioner: A theory of research training in professional psychology. *Professional Psychology: Research and Practice, 24,* 468–476. doi: 10.1037/0735-7028.24.4.468

Graham, J. M., & Kim, Y. H. (2011). Predictors of doctoral student success in professional psychology: characteristics of students, programs, and universities. *Journal of Clinical Psychology, 67,* 340–54. doi: 10.1002/jclp.20767

Hage, S. M., Hopson, A., Siegel, M., Payton, G., & DeFanit, E. (2006). Multicultural training in spirituality: An interdisciplinary review. *Counseling and Values, 50,* 217–235. doi: 10.1002/j.2161-007X.2006.tb00058.x

Hall, G. S. (1894). The new psychology as a basis of education. *Forum, 17,* 710–720.

Higgins, M. C., & Thomas, D. A. (2001). Constellations and careers: Toward understanding the effects of multiple developmental relationships. *Journal of Organizational Behavior, 22,* 223–247. doi: 10.1002/job.66

Hogg, A., & Olvey, C. D. V. (2007). State psychological association creates a postdoctoral residency and internship training program. *Professional Psychology: Research and Practice, 38,* 705–713. doi: 10.1037/0735-7028.38.6.705

Inman, A. G. (2006). Supervisor multicultural competence and its relation to supervisory process and outcome. *Journal of Marital and Family Therapy, 32,* 73–85. doi: 10.1111/j.1752-0606.2006.tb01589.x

Institute of Medicine (2003). *Health Professions Education: A Bridge to Quality.* Washington DC: The National Academies Press.

Johnson, W. B. (2007). *On being a mentor: A guide for higher education faculty.* Mahwah, NJ:: Erlbaum.

Johnson, W. B., Barnett, J. E., Elman, N. S., Forrest, L., & Kaslow, N. J. (2012). The competent community: Toward a vital reformulation of professional ethics. *American Psychologist, 67,* 557–569. doi: 10.1037/a0027206

Johnson, W. B., Barnett, J. E., Elman, N. S., Forrest, L., & Kaslow, N. J. (in press). The competence constellation: A developmental network model for psychologists. *Professional Psychology: Research and Practice.*

Johnson, W. B., Elman, N. S., Forrest, L., Robiner, W. N., Rodolfa, E., & Schaffer, J. B. (2008). Addressing professional competence problems in trainees: Some ethical considerations. *Professional Psychology: Research and Practice, 39,* 589–599. doi: 10.1037/a0014264

Kaslow, N. J. (2004). Competencies in professional psychology. *American Psychologist, 59,* 774–781. doi:10.1037/0003-066X.59.8.774

Kaslow, N. J., Borden, K. A., Collins, F. A., Jr., Forrest, L., Illfelder-Kaye, J., Nelson, P. D., & Willmuth, M. E. (2004). Competencies conference: Future directions in education and credentialing in professional psychology. *Journal of Clinical Psychology, 60,* 699–712. doi:10.1002/jclp.20016

Kaslow, N. J., Falender, C. A., & Grus, C. (2012). Valuing and practicing competency-based supervision: A transformational leadership perspective. *Training and Education in Professional Psychology, 6,* 47–54. doi: 10.1037/a0026704

Kaslow, N. J., Grus, C. L., Campbell, L. F., Fouad, N. A., Hatcher, R. L., Rodolfa, E. R. (2009). Competency assessment toolkit for professional psychology. *Training and Education in Professional Psychology, 3* (Suppl.), S27–S45. doi: 10.1037/a0015833

Kaslow, N. J. & Keilin, W. G. (2006). Internship training in clinical psychology: Looking into our crystal ball. *Clinical Psychology Science and Practice, 13,* 242–248. doi: 10.1111/j.1468-2850.2006.00031.x

Kaslow, N. J., & Mascaro, N. A. (2007). Mentoring interns and postdoctoral residents in academic health sciences center. *Journal of Clinical Psychology in Medical Settings, 14,* 191–196. doi: 10.1007/s10880-007-9070-y

Kaslow, N. J., Rubin, N. J., Bebeau, M., Leigh, I. W., Lichtenberg, J., Nelson, P. D.,...Smith, I. L. (2007). Guiding principles and recommendations for the assessment of competence. *Professional Psychology: Research and Practice, 38(5)*, 441–451. doi: 10.1037/0735-7028.38.5.441

Kaslow, N. J., & Webb, C. (2011). Internship and postdoctoral residency. In J. C. Norcross, G. R. Vandebos & D. K. Friedheim (Eds.), *History of psychotherapy: Continuity and change* (2nd edition, pp. 640–650). Washington D.C.: American Psychological Association.

Kazdin, A. E., & Blase, S. L. (2011). Rebooting psychotherapy research and practice to reduce the burden of mental illness. *Perspectives on Psychological Science, 6*, 21–37. doi:10.1177/1745691610393527

Kennedy, T. J. T., & Lingard, L. A. (2007). Questioning competence: A discourse analysis of attending physicians' use of questions to assess trainee competence. *Academic Medicine, 82(10, Supplement)*, S12–S15.

Kenkel, M. B. (2009). Adopting a competency model for professional psychology: Essential elements and resources. *Training and Education in Professional Psychology, 3*(4S), S59–62.

Kerns, R. D., Berry, S., Frantsve, L. M. E., & Linton, J. C. (2009). Life-long competency development in clinical health psychology. *Training and Education in Professional Psychology, 3*(4), 212–217. doi: 10.1037/a0016753

King, J. E. (1991). Dysconscious racism: Ideology, identity, and the miseducation of teachers. *Journal of Negro Education, 60*(2), 133–146.

Knapp, S. J., & VandeCreek, L. D. (2006). *Practical ethics for psychologists: A positive approach*. Washington, DC: American Psychological Association.

Korman, M. (Ed.) 1973. *Levels and patterns of professional training in psychology*. Washington, DC: American Psychological Association.

Lesser, C. S., Lucey, C. R., Egener, B., Braddock, C. H., Linas, S. L., & Levinson, W. (2010). A behavioral and systems view of professionalism. *JAMA, 304*, 2732–2737. doi: 10.1001/jama.2010.1864

McCutcheon, S. R. (2011). The internship crisis: An uncommon urgency to build a common solution. *Training and Education in Professional Psychology, 5*, 144–148. doi:10.1037/a0024896

McFall, R. M. (1991). Manifesto for a science of clinical psychology. *The Clinical Psychologist, 44*, 75–88.

Neimeyer, G. J., Taylor, J. M. & Rozensky, R. H. (2012). The diminishing durability of knowledge in professional psychology: A Delphi poll of specialties and proficiencies. *Professional Psychology: Research and Practice, 43*, 364–371.

Nelson, M. L., Barnes, K. L., Evans, A. L., & Triggiano, P. J. (2008). Working with conflict in clinical supervision: Wise supervisors' perspectives. *Journal of Counseling Psychology, 55*, 172–184. doi: 10.1037/0022-0167.55.2.172

Nelson, P. D. (2007). Striving for competence in the assessment of competence: Psychology's professional education and credentialing journey of public accountability. *Training and Education in Professional Psychology, 1*(1), 3–12. doi:10.1037/1931-3918.1.1.3

Norcross, J. C. (2005). A primer on psychotherapy integration. In J. C. Norcross & M. R. Goldfried (Eds.), *Handbook of Psychotherapy Integration* (2nd ed., pp. 3–23). New York: Oxford University Press.

Norcross, J. (Ed.). (2011). *Psychotherapy relationships that work: Evidence-based responsiveness* (2nd ed.). New York: Oxford University Press.

Owen, J., & Lindley, L. D. (2010). Therapists' cognitive complexity: review of theoretical models and development of an integrated approach for training. *Training and Education in Professional Psychology, 4*, 128–137.

Passi, V., Doug, M., Peile, E., Thistlethwaite, J., & Johnson, N. (2010). Developing medical professionalism in future doctors: A systematic review. *International Journal of Medical Education, 1*, 19–29. doi: 10.5116/ijme.4bda.ca2a

Pellegrino, E. D. (2002). Professionalism, profession and the virtues of the good physician. *Mount Sinai Journal of Medicine, 69*, 378–384.

Phillips, J. C., Szymanski, D. M., Ozegovic, J. J., Briggs-Phillips, M. (2004). Preliminary examination and measurement of the internship research training environment. *Journal of Counseling Psychology, 51*, 240–248. doi:10.1037/0022-0167.51.2.240

Raimy, V. C. (Ed.). (1950). *Training in clinical psychology*. Englewood Cliffs, NJ: Prentice Hall.

Ridley, C. R., Mollen, D., & Kelly, S. M. (2011). Beyond microskills: Toward a model of counseling competence. *The Counseling Psychologist, 39*(6), 825–864. doi:10.1177/0011000010378440

Roberts, M. C. (2006). Essential tension: Specialization with broad and general training in psychology. *American Psychologist, 61*, 862–870.

Roberts, M. C., Borden, K. A., Christiansen, M. D., & Lopez, S. J. (2005). Fostering a culture shift: Assessment of competence in the education and careers of professional psychologists. *Professional Psychology: Research and Practice, 36*, 355–361. Doi: 10.1037/0735-7028.36.4.355.

Rodolfa, E., Bent, R., Eisman E., Nelson, P., Rehm, L., & Ritchie, P. (2005). A cube model for competency development: Implications for psychology educators and regulators. *Professional Psychology: Research and Practice, 36*, 347–354. doi: 10.1037/0735-7028.36.4.347

Rodolfa, E. R., Ko, S. F., & Petersen, L. (2004). Psychology training directors' views of trainees' readiness to practice independently. *Professional Psychology: Research and Practice, 35*, 397–404.

Routh, D. K. (1994). *Clinical psychology since 1917: Science, practice, and organization*. New York: Plenum.

Russell, S. R., & Yarhouse, M. A. (2006). Religion/spirituality within APA-accredited psychology predoctoral internships. *Professional Psychology: Research and Practice, 37*, 430–436. doi: 10.1037/0735-7028.37.4.430

Sayette, M. A., Norcross, J. C., & Dimoff, J. D. (2011).The heterogeneity of clinical psychology Ph.D. programs and the distinctiveness of APCS programs. *Clinical Psychology: Science and Practice, 18*, 4–11. doi.org/10.1111/j.1468-2850.2010.01227.x

Schaffer, J. B. & Rodolfa, E. R. (2011). Intended and unintended consequences of state practicum licensure regulation. *Training and Education in Professional Psychology, 5*, 222–228, doi: 0.1037/a0024998.

Schulte, A. C., & Daly III, E. J. (2009). Operationalizing and evaluating professional competencies in psychology: Out with the old, in with the new? *Training and Education in Professional Psychology, 3*(4, Suppl), S54–S58

Shakow, D. (1942). The training of the clinical psychologist. *Journal of Consulting Psychology, 6*, 277–288.

Wampold, B. E. (2010). *The basics of psychotherapy: An introduction to theory and practice*. Washington, DC: American Psychological Association.

Zlotlow, S. F., Nelson, P. D., & Peterson, R. L. (2011). The history of broad and general education in scientific psychology: The foundation for professional psychology education and training. *Training and Education in Professional Psychology, 5*, 1–8. doi: 10.1037/a0022529

Overview and Evolution of Education and Training in Psychology

PART

1

Overview and Evolution of Education and Training in Psychology

A History of Education and Training in Professional Psychology

Robin L. Cautin *and* David B. Baker

Abstract

The education and training in professional psychology have origins dating to the beginning of the 20th century, as psychologists working in various applied settings, such as in government, industry, education, and health care, recognized the need to articulate education and training standards for their burgeoning profession. Amid intradisciplinary and interdisciplinary resistance, attempts to define such standards were made by psychologists in an effort to differentiate themselves from a variety of pseudo-psychological practitioners, all of whom represented themselves as psychological experts. Formal developments in the education and training of professional psychologists advanced rapidly during and immediately following World War II, as the federal government, recognizing the acute need for mental health professionals and the relative shortage thereof, invested significantly in the creation of a substantial mental health workforce. One of the most important developments in this regard was the 1949 Boulder Conference on Graduate Education in Clinical Psychology, which delivered to professional psychology the scientist-practitioner (Boulder) model of training. Its critics notwithstanding, this model has served as a significant frame of reference for the ongoing examination and discussion of the education and training of professional psychologists.

Key Words: Boulder conference, education and training, professional psychology, scientist practitioner, scholar-practitioner

Education and training in professional psychology have origins dating back to the beginning of the 20th century, when the new science of psychology found its way from Europe to America. The new laboratory-based psychology sought to apply the objective methods of science to understanding the mind. Psychological laboratories founded at a handful of American universities utilized experimental methods to analyze a variety of phenomena of consciousness. Studies of sensation and perception, reaction time, and memory were common subjects of empirical study. At the same time, there was an equal interest in applying psychological science to various areas with practical import, such as advertising, the measurement of individual differences,

and the identification and treatment of educational, behavioral and emotional problems.

Applied psychologists were eager to identify themselves with the new psychological science, as it would affirm their credibility and professionalism, as well as differentiate them from pseudo-psychological practitioners claiming to offer help and healing. Such pseudo-professionals, variously termed mental healers, spiritualists, or phrenologists, were popular with the American public at the end of the 19th century and practiced with virtually no regard for clearly articulated standards of education and training (Benjamin & Baker, 2004).

Benjamin (2007) observed that a profession comprises "specialized knowledge involving intensive training; high standards of practice, usually supported by a code of ethics; continuing education so that practitioners stay current with the latest developments in the profession; and provision of a service to the public" (p. 155). Early applied American psychologists understood the need that they define for themselves standards of education and training so that their work would be identified with the professional practice of psychology. This chapter focuses on those efforts and describes the history of education and training in professional psychology in America.

The history of education and training in professional psychology mirrors the fieldx's protracted struggle for scientific legitimacy and professional standing. Challenged by colleagues who narrowly conceived of psychology's mission as the furtherance of psychology as a science, to the virtual exclusion of practice, and by psychiatrists who would vehemently defend the boundaries of their field, professional psychologists battled both intradisciplinary and interdisciplinary tensions in their quest for professional identity and status. Efforts to delineate education and training standards in professional psychology put into sharp focus these struggles. Owing to various social, economic, and political tides, and to the influence of key individuals, professional psychology would ultimately secure its place in the world of mental health professionals.

Origins of Professional Psychology: Applications of Psychological Science

The founding of psychological science in the late 19th century is commonly associated with Wilhelm Wundt (1832–1920), who in 1879 at the University of Leipzig established a research laboratory that has since been considered the birthplace of psychology. Establishing a clear demarcation between mental philosophy and the new psychological science, Wundt employed strict experimental techniques, such as experimental introspection and the psychophysical methods developed by Weber and Fechner, to study the structures and processes of consciousness. He published copious reports on a range of topics, most notably sensation and perception (Balance & Evans, 1975). Wundt is remembered for his evangelism for experimentalism; his prolificacy; and the training of over 150 students, about 30 of whom went on to establish early psychological laboratories at American Universities (Benjamin, 2007).

Contrary to the notion that the first psychologists were interested solely in advancing a pure science with no regard for the practical, some of the most prominent among them strongly advocated

for psychology's application to real-world problems, most notably in education. G. Stanley Hall (1844–1924), the founder of the American Psychological Association (APA), published an article in 1883 that described the scarcity of knowledge among Boston school children. The study's methodological flaws notwithstanding, the paper lent momentum to the country's growing concerns about the quality of education in America. Hall was a pioneer in the Child Study Movement (Davidson & Benjamin, 1987), a national effort to apply newly established scientific understanding of child development to the task of educational reform (Hall, 1883). In 1891 he founded the journal *Pedagogical Seminary* to print the findings of child study research, and he continued to evangelize for the new science to his colleagues and to the public. In the summary of an article published in a popular magazine, Hall (1894) wrote, "The one chief and immediate field of application for all this work [psychology] is its application to education, considered as the science of human nature and the art of developing it to its fullest nature." (p. 718) Ultimately, the lofty goals of the Child Study Movement were hardly achieved, and by 1910 it had virtually lost its impact on psychology and education. But the movement served to introduce the American public to the new psychology and its potential for addressing real-world problems.

The anthropometrics testing program at Columbia University in the 1890s, under the directorship of James McKeen Cattell (1860–1944), also may be considered an early application of the new psychological science, despite the fact that it was ultimately revealed to lack predictive validity and was subsequently discontinued. Indeed, Cattell (1890) coined the term "mental test;" mental testing or assessment would become the hallmark of American psychology in the 20th century. Inspired by the work of Francis Galton (1822–1911), Cattell's testing program entailed the vast accumulation of sensory acuity and reaction time data from hundreds of students. Cattell's efforts were based on the assumption that these data represented accurate and reliable measurements of mental faculties and would thus be useful for pedagogical purposes (Cattell, 1893). But Clark Wissler (1901), one of Cattell's graduate students, demonstrated mathematically that there was virtually no statistical relationship between students' test scores and their school performance, thus shattering the rationale for the anthropometric testing program. Nevertheless, the program was significant historically as it introduced mental testing to American psychology. Testing eventually would play a pivotal role in the development of psychology, and of professional psychology in particular.

In 1896 at the University of Pennsylvania, Lightner Witmer (1867–1956), a former student of both Cattell and Wundt, established what was arguably the first psychological clinic in the world (McReynolds, 1997). Soon after experiencing some success in treating children with learning and/or behavioral problems, Witmer became an advocate for psychology's practical utility, urging his colleagues at the 1896 APA annual convention to apply their science to "throw light upon the problems that confront humanity" (Witmer, 1897, p. 116). As his caseload grew, Witmer expanded his clinic staff. In 1907, Witmer founded the journal *Psychological Clinic*, which mostly published case reports of those treated in his clinic, evidencing the utility of psychological science. He named this newly defined field "clinical psychology," and used the journal as a vehicle to campaign for a specialized program of education and training that would enable psychologists to do this work (Baker, 1988).

Reflecting America's progressive era, with its characteristic emphasis on using new technologies to increase efficiency, Frank Parsons (1854–1908) opened the Vocational Bureau at the Civic Service House in Boston in 1908. Reasoning that a sound choice of one's vocation would lead to greater life satisfaction and work productivity, Parsons, met individually with young people, administering and interpreting tests in order gain insights into their talents, limitations, and interests, and then advising them accordingly. Although he died prematurely, his book, *Choosing a Vocation* (1909), which is considered his most important work, was published posthumously. He is regarded as the founder of the American guidance and counseling movement. Thus, at the turn of the century in America, there were psychologists and others, such as Frank Parsons, who purported to use psychological science—primarily in the form of mental tests—to address real-world problems. Unlike the highly specialized subfields of today, early professional psychologists did not differentiate themselves, and were commonly referred to as "consulting psychologists" or "clinical psychologists," though this latter term was not used in the sense in which it is meant today (Benjamin & Baker, 2004).

World War I (WWI) and the Advance of Applied Psychology

Psychologists' involvement in WWI affirmed the field's practical utility, and as a consequence applied psychology grew swiftly. Indeed, by the mid 1930s, one in every three APA members was employed in an applied setting (Capshew, 1999). Psychologists' primary role remained that of mental tester, as psychiatrists assumed dominance over diagnosis and treatment of psychopathology; however, in the late 1920s and 1930s psychologists would begin to push the boundaries of their field, assuming increasingly diverse responsibilities in clinical settings, and planting the seeds for interdisciplinary tensions (Cautin, 2009; Horn, 1989; Reisman, 1976).

Clinical Psychology and Mental Testing

Although Cattell's anthropometrics testing program ended abruptly, following Wissler's discovery, the endeavor to measure individual differences persisted, led by the development of intelligence tests by Alfred Binet (1857–1911). Binet's work was followed by the work of Henry Herbert Goddard (1866–1957), who translated Binet's test into English and re-standardized it for American use, and by Lewis Terman (1877–1956), who introduced the concept of the intelligence quotient (IQ), and revised the *Binet-Simon*, renaming it the *Stanford-Binet*.

With the country's involvement in World War I, Terman and Goddard, among others psychologists, were asked to develop intelligence tests that could be administered to groups, as opposed to individuals, which had been the norm. Robert Yerkes (1876–1956), who was the president of the American Psychological Association in 1917, headed this undertaking, and the resultant tests, referred to as *Army Alpha* and *Army Beta*, were administered to over 2 million military recruits (Camfield, 1973). Psychologists' involvement in WWI affirmed the utility of psychological testing, and enhanced psychology's popularity with the public. Indeed, during the 1920s Americans seemed elated over psychology's potential for improving their lives (Cautin, Freedheim, and DeLeon, 2013).

Assessment would expand into areas of aptitude and career interests, and later into the personality domain, first with the development of projective tests such as the Rorschach and the Thematic Apperception Test, and then objective tests such as the MMPI (Benjamin & Baker, 2004; Cautin, 2011). Psychologists' expertise in clinical assessment would continue to expand, due, in part, to the Child Guidance Movement, which provided psychologists with increasing opportunities to hone their assessment skills and to expand the breadth of their clinical activities and expertise (VandenBos, Cummings, & DeLeon, 1992; Cautin, 2011).

The Child Guidance Movement

The Child Guidance Movement was another outgrowth of Progressive reform in America. Derived from the mental hygiene movement (Grob, 1994; Horn, 1989), which advocated for prevention of psychopathology through early intervention, the Child Guidance Movement officially began in 1922 with the establishment of a series of demonstration clinics designed to address the problem of juvenile delinquency through prevention. Although juvenile delinquency inspired the earliest child guidance clinics, by the 1920s these clinics were serving a much more eclectic population of children, who presented with a broad range of educational, behavioral, and emotional problems (Cautin, 2011; Napoli, 1981).

The speedy growth in child guidance clinics after 1925 created an acute demand for trained professionals from psychiatry, clinical psychology, and social work to treat troubled children. In response to this need, the Commonwealth Fund launched an extensive training program, offering fellowship awards, and in effect setting the standards for training and practice in the field (Horn, 1989). Its major contribution to psychologists' training was its program at the Institute for Child Guidance, which trained 15 full-year fellows, the most significant of whom was Carl Rogers (1902–1987), one of the first to conduct systematic research on psychotherapy and who would be known for his nondirective form of counseling and psychotherapy—client-centered therapy (Rogers, 1942, 1951, 1957).

Psychologists' role at the child guidance center, although initially to administer and interpret psychological tests, progressively expanded to include the provision of psychotherapy, albeit always under the supervision of the psychiatrist. A clear hierarchy existed among the main child guidance professionals, but "practice at the clinics encouraged considerable collaboration and permitted a blurring of roles" (Horn, 1989, p. 99). This is not to say, however, that interdisciplinary relations were without tensions.

Early Organizational Efforts of Professional Psychologists

Due to the impact of WWI on the public's interest in psychology and to the growing number of employed psychologists in applied settings, professional psychology continued to grow throughout the early decades of the 20th century. Eager to apply their new science to real life problems, early applied psychologists were in competition with a cadre of pseudoscientific practitioners, who had hitherto provided psychological services to the public. In the interest of helping the public to identify bona fide psychologists, applied psychologists petitioned the APA in 1915 for the creation of a certification program. When the APA refused, several psychologists, including J. E. Wallace Wallin (1876–1969) and Leta S. Hollingworth (1886–1939), founded the American Association of Clinical Psychologists (AACP) in 1917. The leadership of AACP explored possibilities for credentialing and standardized specialized training, both of which were already customary in medicine and engineering (Benjamin & Baker, 2004). Contrary to some psychologists who argued that the master's degree was sufficient to earn the title, "Psychologist," Hollingworth (1918) warned "that it will hardly be possible for applied psychologists to succeed (in clinical practice at any rate), without the doctor's degree [... for] the doctor's degree has come to signify adequate skill in him who presumes to direct human welfare" (pp. 282–283). Moreover, Leta Hollingworth argued for "the 'invention' of a new degree, — Doctor of Psychology,— which would involve six years of training, including college, with an additional apprenticeship year (instead of research)." Hollingworth further argued that legal certification would be necessary, but that a standardized curriculum must precede it. With this in mind, she called on the APA to establish a standing committee that would "prepare a list of departments of psychology, where prescribed training has been made available" (p. 281). But for the majority of the APA membership, the concerns of applied psychologists were either considered of secondary importance or simply irrelevant to the mission of the organization; thus, Hollingworth's plea fell on deaf ears.

The activities of clinical psychologists also met resistance from the psychiatric community. In December 1916, the New York Psychiatrical Society appointed a committee "to inquire into the activities of psychologists and more particularly of those who have termed themselves 'clinical psychologists' in relation to the diagnosis and treatment of abnormal conditions" (Hollingworth, 1917, p. 224). Although acknowledging "the wide usefulness of the application of psychological knowledge and of the findings of certain psychological tests [largely in education and business]", the committee recommended "that the Society express its disapproval and urge upon thoughtful psychologists and the medical profession in general an expression of disapproval of the application of psychology to responsible clinical work except when made by or under the direct supervision of physicians qualified to deal with abnormal mental conditions" (p. 225). Moreover, the committee recommended that "the Society disapprove of psychologists...undertaking to pass judgment upon the mental condition of sick, defective or otherwise abnormal persons when such findings involve questions of diagnosis, or affect the future care and career of such persons" (p. 225).

Not surprisingly, psychologists responded swiftly to this report, arguing that psychologists were indeed the professionals most qualified to deal with mental abnormality. For example, with a sardonic tone, Franz (1917) wrote:

> It has not infrequently been assumed [by psychiatrists] that no training in normal psychology is needed for the understanding of abnormal mental conditions. On the contrary, for the appreciation of diseased bodily conditions it is considered necessary to study anatomy, physiology, pharmacology...Is this reasoning, we may ask, an indication of adherence to the doctrine of psychophysical parallelism or only an ordinary form of prejudice or bad logic. (Franz, 1917, p. 228)

Aside from the emerging interdisciplinary tensions that were ignited by the expanding role of psychologists in clinical settings, intradisciplinary tensions were palpable as well. Indeed, the very formation of the AACP induced a meeting of the APA, whose leadership was concerned about the negative effect another psychology organization might have on its own power (Cautin, 2009; Samelson, 1992). In 1919, following two years of difficult negotiations, the AACP agreed to dissolve as a separate organization and join APA as the Section on Clinical Psychology (Routh, 1994). As part of this compromise, however, the APA agreed to pursue a certification program for consulting psychologists. But, alas, this certificate program was abandoned after several years, when only about 25 psychologists had become certified (Routh, 1994; Samelson, 1992).

Many of the applied psychologists who had in vain appealed to the APA for professional help decided to establish their own organizations. In 1930, the Association of Consulting Psychologists (ACP) was formed from the New York State Association of Consulting Psychologists. Although it aspired to function as a national organization, New York psychologists dominated the ACP membership (Benjamin & Baker, 2004; Cautin, 2009). In 1937, many distinct professional psychology groups, including the ACP, merged to become the American Association for Applied Psychology (AAAP), and the Clinical Section of the APA

disbanded (Routh, 1994). The AAAP proved successful in meeting the needs of its membership, growing stronger with each year, but its existence would be cut short by the country's imminent involvement in World War II (WWII).

World War II (WWII): A Watershed in the History of Professional Psychology

During the first half of the 20th century, professional psychology had not yet secured its professional status, due, in part, to the APA's disinterest in professional issues. Not surprisingly, there were no standardized training guidelines in professional psychology; training was largely unsystematic and informal (Routh, 2000), reflecting the nature of the field as a whole (Cautin, 2006). Describing the state of training in the inchoate field of clinical psychology in the early 1940s, Miller (1946) wrote:

> All too commonly, training was an individually determined hodge-podge of poorly integrated university courses, clinical internships, private study of special techniques, and unsupervised practice. There was no agreement throughout the country on how curricula should weave together all the divergent strands into a properly designed education for clinical psychologists. (p. 182)

Although several splinter groups formed throughout the 1930s to advocate for standardized training curricula (Dewsbury & Bolles, 1995), their efforts ultimately had limited impact, perhaps since most psychologists at the time were employed in academic settings (Tryon, 1963). However, with the outbreak of WWII, the field of psychology would undergo a sea change. Intradisciplinary tensions that had previously characterized psychology abated, at least temporarily, as various institutional, environmental, and economic factors began to transform the field, affecting clinical psychology in particular.

World War II and the Growth of Professional Psychology

As the country braced for war, academic and practicing psychologists alike joined forces to serve their country. Motivated by their wartime collaboration, psychologists from within and outside the APA united in a newly re-constituted APA (Capshew & Hilgard, 1992). Although originally established in 1892 as an elite learned society, the new APA was dedicated to "the advancement of psychology as a science, as a practice, and as a means of promoting human welfare" (Wolfle, 1946, p. 3); no longer could the APA leadership dismiss professional issues as irrelevant to its mission. Importantly, the organizational structure of the reformulated APA afforded equal status to both academics and practitioners alike, and, as such, smoothed the way for the furtherance of the professional psychologists' agenda (see Crawford, 1992).

> The new APA embodied the lessons of World War II. The psychology community's wartime alliance with the military establishment signaled the start of a new social contract; psychologists sought to broaden their base of social support by marketing their expertise more widely. They had learned to submerge their narrow specialty interests in favor of a broad consensus on the great practical value of their discipline. (Capshew & Hilgard, 1992, p. 171)

WWII produced an unparalleled number of neuropsychiatric casualties (Farrell & Appel, 1944). It became clear early on in the war that there was an acute shortage of psychiatrists to meet the growing needs of returning military veterans. As a consequence, the federal government began to look elsewhere for additional suitable mental health practitioners. In 1942, the federal government mandated that the Veteran's Administration (VA) and the United States Public Health Service (USPHS) work systematically to expand the pool of mental health professionals.

The VA and the Training of Psychologists

The addition of 16 million more military veterans had "thrown upon the Government of the United States a great responsibility" (Miller, 1946, p. 181). Accepting this responsibility, the VA committed itself to providing cutting-edge psychiatric care, which included an "integral role for clinical psychology" (p. 182). During the war, psychologists contributed both to diagnosis, using standardized psychological tests, and to treatment, conducting psychotherapy in a limited number of cases, thus proving themselves an essential component of the psychiatric team. The VA's urgent request for more adequately trained clinical psychologists prompted organized psychology to begin to articulate training standards (Shakow et al., 1945) and to evaluate extant training programs and facilities (Sears, 1946, 1947). Initially, the APA identified 22 universities for the VA as providing adequate doctoral training for clinical psychologists (Sears, 1946). The VA, with the support of the U. S. Public Health Service, asked the APA to develop a formal accreditation program for doctoral training in clinical psychology,

which would aid all federal agencies involved in training (Baker & Pickren, 2007).

In Fall, 1946, under the leadership of James Grief Miller (1916–2002), who had recently taken charge of the clinical psychology section of the VA, the VA initiated a training program in conjunction with the relatively few educational institutions recognized by the APA as providing adequate training for the doctoral degree (Baker & Pickren, 2007; Cautin, 2011; Miller, 1946).

Under Miller's (1946) plan, clinical psychologists would perform diagnostic, therapeutic, and research functions, with diagnosis being the psychologists' primary task. Miller established the doctoral degree as the minimum requirement for aspiring psychologists in the VA setting. Since there was a dearth of practicing psychologists with doctoral training, the VA did hire aspirants with some psychology training, although only on a temporary basis. These individuals were ultimately given until 1951 to obtain their doctorates, after which they would no longer be eligible to be employed at the VA. As part of the VA training program, students were expected to work part-time, and were paid hourly wages commensurate with their years of training. The universities were responsible for academic preparation, which included the determination of the specific curriculum and the required number of training hours. Faculty from affiliated universities were to serve as part-time consultants, conducting their own research and supervising students in their clinical work and research (Baker & Pickren, 2007).

The VA training program grew rapidly in ensuing years. There were over 200 trainees in the program's first year, and by 1950, the number of trainees had surpassed 600. Moreover, a formal evaluation conducted in 1956 noted that most graduates of the program tended to take staff positions in the VA, despite the fact that this was not a stipulation of their training (Wolford, 1956). The VA training program was both beneficial for the VA, whose veterans received services hitherto lacking, and for the universities, who secured funding and increased professional opportunities. The profession of clinical psychology also benefited from the VA training program, as training issues in clinical psychology were put into sharp focus.

National Institute of Mental Health (NIMH) and the Training of Psychologists

In addition to basic and applied research, the passage of the National Mental Health Act (NMHA) of 1946 authorized funding for the training of mental health professionals. The Division of Mental Hygiene of the U. S. Public Health Service (USPHS) was initially responsible for the implementation of the NMHA initiatives, but was eliminated following the inauguration of the National Institute for Mental Health (NIMH) in 1949 (Pickren, 2005).

In January 1947, the USPHS established the Training and Standards Section, known as the *Committee on Training*, to develop an adequate corps of qualified mental health professionals. Robert Felix, public health psychiatrist who would become the first director of the NIMH, described the members of the Committee on Training as "Special Consultants most qualified by knowledge and skill to furnish advice as to scope of activities and policy determinations" ("Agenda, Committee on Training," 1947, p. 1, as cited in Baker & Benjamin, 2005). Felix called the entire Committee to Washington for the first time on January 22, 1947, and appointed psychiatrist Edward Strecker as chair. (See Table 2.1 for a list of groups of members, Baker & Benjamin, 2005).

The Committee on Training consisted of four groups: psychiatry, psychiatric social work, psychiatric nursing, and clinical psychology. Psychiatrists outnumbered psychologists and social workers by a ratio of 4:1; there was only 1 psychiatric nurse. Further evidencing psychiatry's authority, the National Advisory Mental Health Council—the final arbiter of funding allocations—ultimately apportioned 40% of the approximate $1 million in available funds to psychiatry, equally dividing the remaining resources among psychology, social work, and psychiatric nursing (Baker & Benjamin, 2005; Pickren, 2005). The Committee on Training was responsible for distributing training grants and stipends, which enabled institutions to hire clinical faculty and allowed individual graduate students in approved university-based training programs to subsidize their education, respectively (Baker & Benjamin, 2005).

Notwithstanding psychiatry's dominance, however, clinical psychology earned a prominent place on the committee, owing as much to the field's demonstrated utility in the treatment of psychopathology as to key individuals whose work helped to strengthen psychology's professional status by establishing training standards (Baker & Benjamin, 2005). David Shakow (1901–1981), who was appointed to the USPHS's Committee on Training and was elected chair of its clinical psychology subgroup, is noteworthy in this regard (Baker & Benjamin, 2005).

Table 2.1. Participants in the Conference on Graduate Education in Clinical Psychology, Boulder, Colorado, August–September, 1949

Donald K. Adams, Duke University
Thelma G. Alper, Clark University
Eston J. Asher, Purdue University
Delton C. Beier, Indiana University
Chester C. Bennett, Boston University
Arthur L. Benton, University of Iowa
Robert G. Bernreuter, Pennsylvania State College
Robert Blake, University of Texas
Joseph M. Bobbitt, National Institute of Mental Health
Edward S. Bordin, University of Michigan
Joseph E. Brewer, Wichita (KS) Guidance Center
Robert A. Brotemarkle, University of Pennsylvania
Marion E. Bunch, Washington University
Jerry W. Carter, Jr., National Institute of Mental Health
Robert C. Challman, Menninger Foundation, Topeka, KS
Rex M. Collier, University of Illinois
Wayne Dennis, University of Pittsburgh
Graham B. Dimmick, University of Kentucky
John C. Eberhart, National Institute of Mental Health
Robert H. Felix, National Institute of Mental Health
Charles S. Gersoni, U.S. Army
Virginia T. Graham, University of Cincinnati
William R. Grove, Phoenix (AZ) Elementary Schools
Robert E. Harris, University of California Medical School
Starke R. Hathaway, University of Minnesota
Karl F. Heiser, American Psychological Association
Harold M. Hildreth, Veterans Administration, Washington, DC
Jane Hildreth, American Psychological Association Staff (Guest)
Nicholas Hobbs, Columbia University
Howard F. Hunt, University of Chicago
William A. Hunt, Northwestern University
Paul E. Huston, University of Iowa

(continued)

Table 2.1. (continued)

Max L. Hutt, University of Michigan
Carlyle Jacobsen, University of Iowa
Marshall R. Jones, University of Nebraska
Bert Kaplan, Harvard University
E. Lowell Kelly, University of Michigan
Isabelle V. Kendig, St. Elizabeth's Hospital, Washington, DC
David B. Klein, University of Southern California
James W. Layman, University of North Carolina
Lyle H. Lanier, University of Illinois
George F. J. Lehner, University of California, Los Angeles
George E. Levinrew, American Association of Psychiatric Social Workers
Howard P. Longstaff, University of Minnesota
Bertha M. Luckey, Cleveland (OH) Public Schools
Jean W. McFarlane, University of California, Berkeley
Cecil W. Mann, Tulane University
Dorothea A. McCarthy, Fordham University
Dwight W. Miles, Western Reserve University
James G. Miller, University of Chicago
O. Hobart Mowrer, University of Illinois
Paul Henry Mussen, University of Wisconsin
C. Roger Myers, University of Toronto
T. Ernest Newland, University of Tennessee
John Gray Peatman, City College of New York
Albert I. Rabin, Michigan State University
Victor C. Raimy, University of Colorado
Dorothy Randall, University of Colorado (Conference Assistant)
Eliot H. Rodnick, Worcester (MA) State Hospital
Julian B. Rotter, Ohio State University
Seymour B. Sarason, Yale University
Martin Scheerer, University of Kansas
Mary Schmitt, National League of Nursing Education
Laurance F. Shaffer, Columbia University
David Shakow, University of Illinois Medical School, Chicago
John W. Stafford, Catholic University
Charles R. Strother, University of Washington

Earl E. Swarzlander, Veterans Administration Hospital, Long Island, NY
Ruth S. Tolman, Veterans Administration Hospital, Los Angeles, CA
Brian E. Tomlinson, New York University
George Richard Wendt, University of Rochester
Carroll A. Whitmer, University of Pittsburgh
Clarence L. Winder, Stanford University
Dael Wolfle, American Psychological Association
Helen M. Wolfle, American Psychological Association

Source: Baker & Benjamin, 2005

Shakow began to formulate his ideas regarding clinical psychology training during his tenure at Worcester State Hospital, where he served as Chief Psychologist and Director of Psychological Research from 1928 to 1946. He was an evangelist for professional development in the field:

> The science of psychology has responsibilities in the matter which cannot be evaded. The need for applied psychological work is great and unless psychology can provide adequately trained personnel, other disciplines, which recognize both the need and responsibilities, will take over the function of which are more properly the province of the psychologist (Shakow, 1942, 277–278).

As a member, if not chair, of various committees related to professional training in the field, Shakow made much progress toward the professionalization of training standards. As a member of the Committee on the Training of Clinical Psychologists (CTCP), appointed by the AAAP, Shakow drafted a four-year doctoral program that integrated systematic fundamental didactics with clinical experiences in assessment and psychotherapy (Shakow, 1942). Following the integration of the AAAP and the APA, Shakow chaired the Subcommittee on Graduate Internship Training, which met at the Vineland Training School in 1944 (Baker & Benjamin, 2000). The resultant committee report, or what became known as the "Shakow Report," identified three primary functions of the clinical psychologist—research, diagnosis, and therapy—and supported the doctoral standard for practice in the field (Shakow et al., 1945). Two years later, at the urging of the VA and the USPHS, the APA established the Committee on Training in Clinical Psychology (CTCP) to formulate a standard training program in clinical psychology, develop standards for institutions providing such training, and visit and write evaluative reports on each of these institutions (Baker & Benjamin, 2000). Then-APA President, Carl R. Rogers, asked Shakow to chair this committee. As chair of the CTCP, Shakow sent all members the "Shakow Report," soliciting their consideration and feedback. There was almost unanimous support of the document. In 1947, the APA officially endorsed the report (APA, 1947), which constituted "the most comprehensive statement of training for clinical psychology ever written, offering detailed recommendations on achieving competence in diagnosis, therapy, and research" (Baker & Benjamin, 2000, p. 244).

Shakow simultaneously chaired the clinical psychology subcommittee of the USPHS Committee on Training and APA's CTCP. But rather than constituting a conflict of interest, Shakow's dual appointments "represented Shakow's desire to serve and APA's ability to mobilize its members and resources to help support and promote the potential largesse resulting from the provisions of the National Mental Health Act of 1946" (Baker & Benjamin, 2005, p. 187). With Shakow as chair, the VA, USPHS, and the CTCP held a joint meeting in Washington, DC on September 5, 1948, where the federal agencies affirmed their desire to produce more qualified psychologists and their commitment to "stay out of the way of university departments and APA in the development of trainings standards for professional psychologists" (Baker & Benjamin, 2005, p. 187). By 1949, 43 doctoral training programs had been accredited, and 175 students had successfully completed doctoral training in clinical psychology (APA, 1948, 1949; Baker & Benjamin, 2005).

Defining Professional Psychology

Prompted by the acute need for mental health professionals, the VA and USPHS invested significantly in the development of professional psychology, providing training grants and stipends to grow this work force (Moore, 1992). Significant progress notwithstanding, the CTCP identified a number of concerns related to the nature of training, and the federal agencies were concerned with the lack of standardization in training programs nationwide. Indeed, there was no consensus in the field regarding "the principles and procedures" for training in clinical psychology (Baker & Benjamin, 2005, p. 244).

Clinical Psychology

Sponsored by the USPHS, now called the National Institute of Mental Health (NIMH), the APA organized the Boulder Conference on Graduate Education in Psychology, or what has come to be known as the "Boulder Conference" (Raimy, 1950). For two weeks in August–September of 1949, 73 individuals—mostly psychologists but also a few representatives from psychiatry, nursing, and social work—deliberated on essential and complex issues, such as private practice, core curriculum, master's level psychologists, and training for research, in the hopes of reaching consensus on a model of training for clinical psychologists (see Table 2.1 for a complete list of participants). The Boulder Conference was the first national conference held in the United States to consider clinical psychology training standards at the doctoral level, "despite the fact that psychology doctoral training programs in America had been around for more than 60 years by that time" (Benjamin & Baker, 2000, p. 233). In the end, 70 resolutions were passed and a common model of training—the "scientist-practitioner model," or "Boulder model"—was affirmed (see Raimy, 1950). The Boulder model designated core skills that the professional psychologist should have that were beyond the typical training of doctoral students in psychology. Practicum training was required, ideally in multiple settings, preparing students for a required one-year internship. Also essential for students of clinical psychology were research training and the preparation of a research dissertation.

Thus, according to the Boulder model of training, clinical psychologists were to be trained as researchers *and* as practitioners (Cautin, 2006; Farreras, 2005). Although some conference participants opposed the tenets of the Boulder model, particularly its psychiatric emphasis, for a variety of reasons, the scientist-practitioner model prevailed (Farreras, 2005), and is arguably the predominant training model today (Baker & Benjamin, 2000).

Counseling Psychology

It is important to note that few distinctions were made among the subspecialties of professional psychology, clinical and counseling and guidance, in particular, as Boulder participants called for an inclusive view of the field, which services "the frankly psychotic or mentally ill to the relatively normal clientele who need information, vocational counseling, and remedial work" (Raimy, 1950, pp. 112). In fact, Boulder participants embraced the recommendation that serious consideration be given to "the possibility of eventual amalgamation of these two fields" (p. 148). Such a proposal of integration notwithstanding, in the ensuing decade, stark boundary lines emerged among the specialties of clinical, counseling, and school psychology. As the Boulder conference was most closely aligned with clinical psychology per se, counseling psychologists were also eager to define the boundaries of their field as well as a distinct training model in order to benefit from the generous federal funding that was profiting the field of clinical psychology.

To this end, under the direction of University of Michigan faculty member and counseling center director, Edward Bordin, a conference entitled "The Training of Psychological Counselors" was held at Bordin's home institution in July 1948 and again in January 1949. Table 2.2 lists the Ann Arbor Conference participants. The purpose of this conference was to articulate proposals for a training model that would affirm the specific contributions that counseling and guidance could make to a national program of mental health (Baker & Joyce, 2013). The suggestions generated at the Michigan meetings were sent to APA's Division 17, which co-sponsored, with the APA, the Northwestern Conference in 1951. The participants of the Northwestern Conference upheld the primacy of the PhD degree and affirmed the Boulder concept of integrating

science and practice. Another outcome was the decision to change the division's name from Counseling and Guidance to Counseling Psychology, indicating its enthusiasm for aligning itself more closely with clinical psychology than with educational guidance. According to the Northwestern Conference report, the counseling psychologist

is to foster the psychological development of the individual. This includes all people on the adjustment continuum from those who function at tolerable levels of adequacy to those suffering from more severe psychological disturbances. Counseling psychologists will spend the bulk of their time with individuals within the normal range, but their training should qualify them to work in some degree with individuals at any level of psychological adjustment. (American Psychological Association, Division of Counseling and Guidance, 1952, p. 181)

The Northwestern Conference yielded important gains for the field of counseling psychology. Guidelines for a proposed curriculum were articulated, and consequently, the APA began accrediting counseling programs in 1953 [check date]. The VA created a job classification for counseling psychologists as well, further affirmation of the field's unique contribution to a national program of mental health.

Table 2.2. Participants at the Ann Arbor Conference

Joseph M. Bobbitt, Chief Psychologist, Office of Professional Services, National Institute of Mental Health, U.S. Public Health Service, Washington, DC

Edward S. Bordin, Chair and Editor of the Counseling Division of the Bureau of Psychological Services, Associate Professor of Psychology and Educational Psychology, University of Michigan

John A. Bromer, Assistant Personnel Director, Counseling Center, Prudential Insurance Co. of America

John M. Butler, Assistant Professor of Psychology, University of Chicago

Mitchell Dreese, Professor of Educational Psychology, Dean of the Summer Sessions, George Washington University

Clifford P. Froehlich, Specialist for Training Guidance Personnel, Occupational Information and Guidance Service; Office of Education, Federal Security Agency; Associate Professor of Education, Johns Hopkins University

Milton E. Hahn, Professor of Psychology, Dean of Students, University of California, Los Angeles

Nicholas Hobbs, Chair, Department of Psychology, Louisiana State University

Max L. Hutt, Associate Professor of Psychology, University of Michigan

E. Lowell Kelly, Director, Bureau of Psychological Services, Professor of Psychology, University of Michigan

Victor C. Raimy, Director of Clinical Training Program, Department of Psychology, University of Colorado

C. Gilbert Wrenn, Professor of Educational Psychology, University of Minnesota

Source: Baker & Joyce, in press

Nonetheless, the identify crisis for counseling psychologists persisted well into the 1960s. In 1959, the APA's Education and Training Board called for a systematic evaluation of the status of counseling psychology. Two committees appointed by Division 17 assessed the field. The first, which was never published, recommended that the field be dissolved into clinical psychology, citing the diffuse meaning of the term counseling and the relative lack of research emphasis in the field; the Division's leaders rejected this report (Baker & Joyce, in press). The second was a reaffirmation of the Northwestern Conference endorsement of counseling psychologists "as mental health service providers for a range of settings, clients, and disorders" (Benjamin, 2007, p. 172). Although the message of this committee was far more encouraging for the field than was the committee that had suggested that the Division dissolve, serious questions about the status and identity of counseling psychology endured. Consequently, Division 17 convened the Greyston Conference, a 3-day-long meeting held in January 1964, at which 32 recommendations were approved. Albert S. Thompson, an organizer and author of the conference report, commented that, "there was general agreement that counseling psychology had a special substance and emphasis in training, which were not necessarily included in current preparation" (Baker & Joyce, in press, p. 403). The Greyston Conference affirmed the tenets of the Northwestern Conference, defining the counseling psychologist in terms of three defining roles: the remedial/rehabilitative, the preventative, and the educational/developmental (Baker & Joyce, in press). The Greyston Conference served to consolidate and solidify all counseling psychologists in a common purpose.

School Psychology

By 1952, both clinical and counseling psychology, with financial support from the federal government, had established training programs in professional psychology. Comparatively, school psychology lagged behind; indeed, in 1953 there were only three doctoral training programs in school psychology: one at Pennsylvania State University (organized in the 1930s), New York University, and a newly organized program at the University of Illinois (Benjamin & Baker, 2004). However, arguing that there was a shortage of school psychologists to meet the needs of school children, school psychologists applied for NIMH funding through the APA's Education and Training (E & T) Board. The Board chair, E. Lowell Kelly, appointed a steering committee composed of five persons nominated by the board and five persons nominated by Division 16. After securing NIMH funding, the committee made preparations for 48 participants to convene at the Hotel Thayer in West Point, New York, from August 22 to August 31, 1954, just prior to the start of the annual meeting of the APA in New York City. Table 2.3 provides a listing of the Thayer conference participants, evidencing the wide range of professionals that assembled in the name of school psychology.

The work of the conference was documented in *School Psychologists at Mid-Century: A Report of the Thayer Conference on the Functions, Qualifications and Training of School Psychologists* (Cutts, 1955). Conference recommendations in many ways resembled those suggested for training for clinical and counseling psychologists. Training guidelines were published in the *American Psychologist* in 1963.

Key Issues and Controversies Regarding the Education and Training of Professional Psychologists
Beyond Boulder

The scientist-practitioner model of training, an explicit call for the integration of science and practice, was not without its critics, and, in the decades following the Boulder Conference, alternative training models developed. The first alternative to Boulder was the scholar-practitioner model, which was developed in the late 1960s and grew out of the concern that graduates of Boulder model were inadequately training to conduct clinical work; it was also accompanied by an alternative degree. The Doctor of Psychology (PsyD) and the scholar-practitioner model of training both were affirmed at the Vail Training Conference in Vail, Colorado in 1973 (Korman, 1976). These developments dovetailed with the rapid rise of the professional school movement (Stricker & Cummings, 1992), fostering the growth of the practice community and what was arguably a "golden age for practitioners" (Cautin, 2009, p. 217). The first freestanding professional school of psychology was established in California in 1970; such schools would proliferate rapidly over the ensuing decades. The number of doctorate granted by these programs would steadily increase, outpacing those granted from traditional programs by 1997 (Benjamin & Baker, 2004).

More recently, in the mid-1990s, the clinical scientist model was developed, along with the creation of the Academy of Psychological Clinical Science (APCS), both of which affirmed the prime

Table 2.3. Participants at the Thayer Conference

S. Spafford Ackerly, MD, Chair of the Department of Psychiatry and Mental Hygiene, and Director of Louisville Child Guidance Center Clinic, University of Louisville School of Medicine

Harry V. Bice, Consultant on Psychological Problems, New Jersey State Crippled Children's Commission, Trenton

Jack W. Birch, Director of Special Education, Board of Public Education, Pittsburgh, PA

Joseph M. Bobbitt (Guest), Chief, Professional Services Branch, National Institute of Mental Health, U.S. Public Health Service, Bethesda, MD

Edward S. Bordin, Associate Professor of Psychology, University of Michigan

Opal Boston, Supervisor, School Social Workers, Indianapolis (IN) Public Schools; President, National Association of School Social Workers

Esallee Burdette, Washington (GA) High School, representing the National Education Association Department of Classroom Teachers

Jerry W. Carter, Jr. (Guest), Chief Clinical Psychologist, Community Services Branch, National Institute of Mental Health, U.S. Public Health Service, Bethesda, MD

Walter W. Cook, Dean, College of Education, University of Minnesota

Ethel L. Cornell, Associate in Educational Research, State Education Department, Albany, NY

Norma E. Cutts, Professor of Psychology and Education, New Haven (CT) State Teachers College; Lecturer in Educational Psychology, Department of Education, Yale University

Gertrude P. Driscoll, Professor of Education, Teachers College, Columbia University

James M. Dunlap, School Psychologist, University City (MO) Public Schools

Merle H. Elliot, Director of Research, Oakland (CA) Public Schools

Mary D. Fite, Psychologist, Gilbert School, Multonomah County, OR

Robert Gates, Consultant, Education for Exceptional Children, State Department of Education, Tallahassee, FL

May Seagoe Gowan, Professor of Education, University of California, Los Angeles

Susan W. Gray, Associate Professor of Psychology, George Peabody College

Dale B. Harris, Professor and Director, Institute of Child Welfare, University of Minnesota

Nicholas Hobbs, Chair, Division of Human Development & Guidance, George Peabody College

Noble H. Kelley, Chair, Department of Psychology, Director of Psychological Services, Southern Illinois University

Samuel A. Kirk, Professor of Education and Director, Institute for Research on Exceptional Children, University of Illinois

Morris Krugman, Assistant Superintendent of Schools and Guidance, Board of Education, New York City

M. C. Langhorne, Chair, Department of Psychology, Emory University

Beatrice Lantz, Consultant, Division of Research and Guidance, Los Angeles County Schools

Max M. Levin (Guest), Psychologist, Training and Standards Branch, National Institute of Mental Health, U.S. Public Health Service, Bethesda, MD

Bertha M. Luckey, Supervisor, Psychological Service, Cleveland (OH) Board of Education

Boyd R. McCandless, Professor and Director, Iowa Child Welfare Research Station, State University of Iowa

Guy N. Magness, MD, Director, School Health Services of University City (MO) Public Schools

W. Mason Mathews, Chair, Laboratory Services (School Services), Merrill-Palmer School, Detroit, MI

Bruce V. Moore, Education and Training Board, American Psychological Association

(continued)

Table 2.3. (continued)

Frances A. Mullen, Assistant Superintendent of Schools in Charge of Special Education, Chicago Public Schools

C. Roger Myers, Professor of Psychology, University of Toronto, Department of Health

T. Ernest Newland, Professor of Education, University of Illinois

Ralph H. Ojeman, Professor of Psychology and Parent Education, Child Welfare Research Station, State University of Iowa

Willard C. Olson, Professor of Education and Psychology, and Dean, School of Education, University of Michigan

Harriet E. O'shea, Associate Professor of Psychology, Purdue University

Victor C. Raimy, Chair and Professor, Department of Psychology, University of Colorado

S. Oliver Roberts, Professor of Psychology and Education, Chair, Department of Psychology, Fisk University

Francis P. Robinson, Professor of Psychology, Ohio State University

Eliot H. Rodnick, Chair, Department of Psychology, Director of Clinical Training, Duke University

Milton A. Saffir, Director, Chicago Psychological Guidance Center; Principal of Marshall Elementary School, Chicago

Marie Skodak, Director, Division of Psychological Services, Dearborn (MI) Public Schools

Charles R. Strother, Professor Psychology, Professor of Clinical Psychology in Medicine, University of Washington

Simon H. Tulchin, Consulting Psychologist, New York City

William D. Wall, Department of Education, UNESCO, Paris

Emalyn R. Weiss, Supervisor of Special Education, Berks County Schools, Reading, PA

Albert T. Young Jr., School Psychologist, Falls Church (VA) Public Schools

Visitors at the conference:

Jack R. Ewalt, MD, Commissioner, Massachusetts Department of Mental Health, Professor of Psychiatry, Harvard Medical School

Palmer L. Ewing, Superintendent of Schools, Buffalo, NY

E. Lowell Kelly, Professor of Psychology, University of Michigan, President-Elect, American Psychological Association

Fillmore H. Sanford, Executive Secretary, American Psychological Association

Source: Cutts, 1955

importance of research. Concern over the variability across training programs, particularly with respect to "their relative emphasis on scientific research and clinical practice" (McFall, 2002, p. 664), led to the development of the clinical scientist model of training.

Nicholas Cummings, a pioneer in the professional school movement, has continued his long record of innovation in the training and delivery of mental health services with the establishment of a Doctor of Behavioral Health program at Arizona State University (School of Letters and Sciences, n.d.). The program prepares mental health providers who can provide integrated behavioral care in primary care and other medical settings.

Master's Level Practice

Another current issue in professional psychology stems from the growing number of master's-level mental health practitioners, which include psychologists, as well as social workers, licensed professional counselors, and marriage and family therapists (Cautin, Freedheim, & DeLeon, 2013).

The standard of the doctoral degree as the requirement for professional practice in psychology has been long-standing. It has served as the standard for training and for third-party reimbursement for psychotherapy. However that is being challenged on many fronts. Master's-level mental health professionals are trained in many different programs with many different forms of certification and licensure. The Council for Accreditation of Counseling and Related Educational Programs (CACREP) is a major accrediting body for master's level counselors. It accredits master's level programs with specialties in addiction counseling, career counseling, clinical mental health counseling, marriage, couple, and family counseling, school counseling, student affairs, and college counseling (CACREP, 2012).

Through a mix of market forces and advocacy, private insurers and government agencies increasingly recognize master's level practitioners as independent providers of counseling services. For example in 2012 the Department of Defense issued regulations allowing licensed counselors to practice independently within TRICARE, the health-care program for the Uniformed Services in America (American Counseling Association, 2012).

Conclusion

The history of education and training in professional psychology in America is about 100 years old. It is a history that is intertwined with the history of 20th century America, including the history of psychology. In many ways, psychology in America has been defined by its application to the issues of everyday life. The new science of psychology, which sought to understand human mind and behavior, offered a wide range of applications to the assessment of person-environment fit. Whether screening immigrants, placing schoolchildren, determining abilities for occupations, or classifying psychological problems, psychologists introduced a broad and ever-expanding set of skills that created a public demand and created a favorable public image for professional psychology. Public interest in psychology has been strong throughout the last century even though public understanding is limited. Within the first few decades of the 20th century, psychologists themselves recognized the need to define their practice and began to wrestle with the issues that define a profession, including issues of education, training, and licensure. These efforts were an attempt to establish a legitimate identity for professional psychology and to protect the public from those who would claim the title of psychologist without the proper training.

Applied psychologists in the early 20th century most often worked outside of the realm of academic psychology. As a new discipline in America, academic psychology faced its own set of issues and challenges as it attempted to claim a place among the more established disciplines and traditions of the academy. Then as now, those with an interest in professional practice found strength in numbers and organization.

At midcentury, professional psychology began a rapid ascent, which has continued unabated. World War II accelerated developments in professional psychology at lightning speed. The need for a national mental health workforce created tremendous synergies that brought together national organizations and government agencies, whose work remains with us today. To a large extent, social, political, and economic factors continue to influence the psychological profession: Armed conflict and war continue to inflict psychological casualties; increased social awareness of mental illness and societal tolerance mitigate impediments to individuals seeking mental health treatment; and effective lobbying for greater parity for psychologists' services in the health-care system all speak to the ongoing need and relevance of the psychological profession. Against this ever-changing landscape, education and training in professional psychology has followed suit. By examining and tuning its assumptions and practices, professional psychology has adapted to the demands of the environment.

References

American Counseling Association, (2012). Legislative Update.

American Psychological Association, Committee on Training in Clinical Psychology. (1947). Recommended graduate training program in clinical psychology. *American Psychologist, 2,* 539–558.

American Psychological Association, Committee on Training in Clinical Psychology. (1948). Training facilities: 1948. *American Psychologist, 3,* 317–318.

American Psychological Association, Committee on Training in Clinical Psychology. (1949). Doctoral training programs in clinical psychology: 1949. *American Psychologist, 4,* 331–341.

American Psychological Association, Division of Counseling and Guidance, Committee on Counselor Training. (1952). Recommended standards for training counselors at the doctoral level. *American Psychologist, 7,* 175–181.

Baker, D. B. (1988). The psychology of Lightner Witmer. *Professional School Psychology, 3,* 109–121.

Baker, D. B., & Benjamin, L. T., Jr. (2000). The affirmation of the scientist-practitioner: A look back at Boulder. *American Psychologist, 55,* 241–247.

Baker, D. B., & Benjamin, L. T. Jr. (2005). Creating a profession: The National Institute of Mental Health and the training of psychologists, 1946–1954. In W. E. Pickren and S. F. Schneider (Eds.), *Psychology and the National Institute of Mental Health: A historical analysis of science, practice, and policy* (pp. 181–207). Washington, DC: American Psychological Association.

Baker, D. B., & Joyce, N. R. (2013). Counseling Psychology. In D. K. Freedheim (ed.), *Handbook of psychology, Vol. 1: History of psychology* (pp. 397–406). Hoboken, NJ: Wiley.

Baker, R. R., Pickren, W. E. (2007). *Psychology and the Department of Veterans Affairs: A historical analysis of training, research, practice, and advocacy.* Washington, DC: American Psychological Association.

Balance, W. D., Evans, R. B (1975). Wilhelm Wundt 1832–1920): A brief biographical sketch. *Journal of the History of the Behavioral Sciences, 11,* 287–297.

Benjamin, L. T., Jr. (2007). *A brief history of modern psychology.* Malden, MA: Blackwell Publishing.

Benjamin, L. T., Jr., & Baker, D. B. (2000). Boulder at 50: Introduction to the section. *American Psychologist, 55,* 233–236.

Benjamin, L. T., Jr., & Baker, D. B. (2004). *From séance to science: A history of the profession of psychology in America*. Belmont, CA: Wadsworth/Thomson Learning.

CACREP, (2012). What is CACREP? Retrieved from http://www.cacrep.org/template/index.cfm

Camfield, (1973). The professionalization of American psychology, 1870–1917. *Journal of the History of the Behavioral Sciences, 9*, 66–75.

Capshew, J. (1999). *Psychologists on the march: Science, practice, and professional identity in America, 1929–1969*. New York, NY: Cambridge University Press.

Capshew, J., & Hilgard, E. R. (1992). The power of service: World War II and professional reform in the American Psychological Association. In R. B. Evans, V. S. Sexton, & T. C. Cadwallader (Eds.), *100 years: The American Psychological Association. A historical perspective* (pp. 149–175). Washington, DC: American Psychological Association.

Cattell, J. McK. (1890). Mental tests and measurements. *Mind, 15*, 373–381.

Cattell, J. McK. (1893). Tests of the senses and faculties. *Educational Review, 5*, 257–265.

Cautin, R. L. (2006). David Shakow: Architect of modern clinical psychology. In D. A. Dewsbury, L. T. Benjamin, Jr., & M. Wertheimer (Eds.), *Portraits of pioneers in psychology* (Vol. 6, pp. 207–221). Washington, DC: American Psychological Association, and Mahwah, NJ: Erlbaum.

Cautin, R. L. (2009). The founding of the Association for psychological science. Part 1. Dialectical tensions within organized psychology. *Perspectives on Psychological Science, 4*, 211–223.

Cautin, R. L. (2011). History of Psychotherapy, 1860–1960. In J. Norcross, G. Vanden Bos, and D. K. Freedheim (Eds.), *History of Psychotherapy* (2nd ed., pp. 3–38). Washington, DC: American Psychological Association.

Cautin, R. L., Freedheim, D. K., DeLeon, P. H. (2013). Psychology as a profession. In D. K. Freedheim (ed.), *Handbook of psychology, Vol. 1: History of psychology* (pp. 32–54). Hoboken, NJ: Wiley.

Crawford, M. P. (1992). Rapid growth and change at the American Psychological Association: 1945 to 1970. In R. B. Evans, V. S. Sexton, and T. C. Cadwallader (Eds.), *100 years: The American Psychological Association: A historical perspective* (pp. 177–232). Washington, DC: American Psychological Association.

Cutts, N. E. (1955). *School psychologists at mid-century*. Washington, DC: American Psychological Association.

Davidson, E. S., & Benjamin, L. T., Jr. (1987). A history of the child study movement in America. In J. A. Glover & R. Ronning (Eds.), *Historical foundations of educational psychology* (pp. 41–60). New York, NY: Plenum.

Dewsbury, D. A., & Bolles, R. C. (1995). The founding of the Psychonomic Society. *Psychonomic Bulletin & Review, 2*, 216–233.

Farrell, M. J., & Appel, J. W. (1944). Current trends in military neuropsychiatry. *The American Journal of Psychiatry, 101*, 12–19.

Farreras, I. G. (2005). The historical context for National Institute of Mental Health support of American Psychological Association training and accreditation efforts. In W. E. Pickren, & S. F. Schneider (Eds.), *Psychology and the National Institute of Mental Health: A historical analysis of science, practice, and policy* (pp. 153–179). Washington, DC: American Psychological Association.

Franz, S. I. (1917). Psychology and psychiatry. *Psychological Bulletin, 14*, 226–229.

Grob, G. N. (1994). *The mad among us: A history of the care of America's mentally ill*. Cambridge, MA: Harvard University Press.

Hall, G. S. (1883). The contents of children's minds. *Princeton Review, 2*, 249–272.

Hall, G. S. (1894). The new psychology as a basis of education. *Forum, 17*, 710–720.

Hollingworth, L. S. (1917). Activities of clinical psychologists. *Psychological Bulletin, 14*, 224–225.

Hollingworth, L. S. (1918). Tentative suggestions for the certification of practicing psychologists. *Journal of Applied Psychology, 2*, 280–284.

Horn, M. (1989). *Before it's too late: The child guidance movement in the United States, 1922–1945*. Philadelphia: Temple University Press.

Korman, M. (Ed.). (1976). *Levels and patterns of professional training in psychology: Conference proceedings, Vail, Colorado, July 25, 1973*. Washington, DC: American Psychological Association.

McFall, R. M. (2002). Training for prescriptions vs. prescriptions for training: Where are we now? Where should we be? How do we get there? *Journal of Clinical Psychology*, 58, 659–676.

McReynolds, P. (1997). *Lightner Witmer: His life and times*. Washington, DC: American Psychological Association.

Miller, J. G. (1946). Clinical psychology in the Veterans Administration. *American Psychologist, 1*, 181–189.

Moore, D. L. (1992). The Veterans Administration and its training program in psychology. In D. K. Freedheim (Ed.), *History of psychotherapy: A century of change* (pp. 776–800). Washington, DC: American Psychological Association.

Napoli, D. S. (1981). *Architects of Adjustment: A history of the psychological profession in the United States*. Port Washington, NY: Kennikat Press.

Parsons, F. (1909). *Choosing a vocation*. New York: Houghton Mifflin.

Pickren, W. E. (2005). Science, practice, and policy: An introduction to the history of psychology and the National Institute of Mental Health. In W. E. Pickren and S. F. Schneider (Eds.), *Psychology and the National Institute of Mental Health: A historical analysis of science, practice and policy* (pp. 3–15). Washington, DC: American Psychological Association.

Raimy, V. C. (Ed.) (1950). *Training in clinical psychology*. Englewood Cliffs, NJ: Prentice Hall.

Reisman, J. M. (1976). *A history of clinical psychology*. New York, NY: Halstead Press.

Rogers, C. R. (1942). *Counseling and Psychotherapy*. New York, NY: Houghton Mifflin.

Rogers, C. R. (1951). *Client-centered therapy: Its current practice, implications, and theory*. Boston, MA: Houghton Mifflin.

Rogers, C. R. (1957). The necessary and sufficient conditions of therapeutic personality change. *Journal of Consulting Psychology, 21*, 95–103.

Routh, D. K. (1994). *Clinical psychology since 1917: Science, practice, and organization*. New York, NY: Plenum.

Routh, D. K. (2000). Clinical psychology training: A history of ideas and practices prior to 1946. *American Psychologist, 55*, 236–241.

Samelson, F. (1992). The APA between the World Wars: 1918–1941. In R. B. Evans, V. S. Sexton, & T. C. Cadwallader (Eds.), *100 years: The American Psychological Association.*

A historical perspective (pp. 119–147). Washington, DC: American Psychological Association.

School of Letters and Sciences (n.d.). Behavioral Health (DBH). Retrieved from https://sls.asu.edu/graduate/proginfo/lsbevhedbh

Sears, R. R. (1946). Graduate training facilities. I. General information II. Clinical psychology. *American Psychologist, 1,* 135–150.

Sears, R. R. (1947). Clinical training facilities: 147. *American Psychologist, 2,* 199–205.

Shakow, D. (1942). The training of the clinical psychologist. *Journal of Consulting Psychology, 6,* 277–288.

Shakow, D., Brotemarkle, R. A., Doll, E. A., Kinder, E. F., Moore, B. V., & Smith, S. (1945). Graduate internship in psychology: Report by the Subcommittee on Graduate Internship Training to the Committee on Graduate and Professional Training of the American Psychological Association and the American Association for Applied Psychology. *Journal of Consulting Psychology, 9,* 243–266.

Stricker, G., & Cummings, N. A. (1992). The professional school movement. In D. K. Freedheim (Ed.), *History of psychotherapy: A century of change* (pp. 801–828). Washington, DC: American Psychological Association.

Tryon, R. C. (1963). Psychology in flux: The academic-professional bipolarity. *American Psychologist, 18,* 134–143.

VandenBos, G. R., Cummings, N. A., DeLeon, P. H. (1992), A century of psychotherapy: Economic and environmental influences. In D. K. Freedheim (ed.), *History of psychotherapy: A century of change* (pp. 65–102). Washington, DC: American Psychological Association.

Wissler, C. (1901). The correlation of mental and physical tests. *Psychological Review Monograph Supplements, 3*(6).

Witmer, L. (1897). The organization of practical work in psychology. *Psychological Review, 4,* 116–117.

Wolfle, D. (1946). The reorganized American Psychological Association. *American Psychologist, 1,* 3–6.

Wolford, R. A. (1956). A review of psychology in VA hospitals. *Journal of Counseling Psychology, 3,* 243–248.

Training Models in Professional Psychology Doctoral Programs

Debora J. Bell *and* Estee M. Hausman

Abstract

Since 1949, training models have defined doctoral training in professional psychology, serving to provide an identity for the field of professional psychology. This chapter reviews the development, central features (namely, emphases on science and practice), and implementation and evaluation of the scientist-practitioner model, scholar-practitioner model, and clinical-scientist models. The scientist-practitioner model is discussed as it integrates science and practice. The features of applied scholarship, practice, and science in the practitioner-scholar model are described, whereas the emphasis on evidence-based practice and training in scientific clinical psychology are characteristic of the clinical-scientist model. Training models provide an identity for graduate programs, but in some ways they have fractured the field of psychology with divisions by model. We suggest that professional psychology can continue to benefit from the advantages of models, but must also move beyond models as the primary basis for defining identity. We recommend that the profession work diligently toward integration to define itself to the public and address the profession's challenges, while remaining focused on training science-based, competent professional psychologists.

Key Words training models, scientist-practitioner, Boulder model, practitioner-scholar, scholar-practitioner, Vail model, clinical scientist, clinical-science model

Foundations for formal training models date back to the late 1800s when the profession of psychology—applying the science of psychology to assessment and interventions to improve individuals' lives—began to emerge (see Cautin & Baker, chapter 2, this volume, for a detailed review). Interestingly, the profession was defined first by the practice of clinical psychology and only later by training. In the last 100+ years, several training models have been developed to guide standards and practice of doctoral-level education in professional psychology. This chapter briefly describes the three predominant models in doctoral education—*scientist-practitioner*, *practitioner-scholar*, and *clinical-scientist models*; discusses the contributions and limitations of training models to professional psychology; and offers recommendations

for maximizing training models' contributions to advancing the science and practice of professional psychology. To set the stage for the aforementioned discussions, a brief overview of the historical context in which training standards emerged is provided.

Historical Context

The profession of psychology existed for approximately 50 years before its training was formally articulated and systematized. Witmer, generally credited with founding clinical psychology, began the first psychology clinic in 1896. Over the next several years a handful of other psychology clinics opened across the country (Edelstein & Brastead, 1983; McReynolds, 1996). The year after Witmer opened his clinic, he began to offer a summer course in The Psychological Clinic at the University of

Pennsylvania. However, it is not clear what, if any, training specific to clinical psychology was offered at other institutions (Routh, 2000). Over the next 50 years, eight institutions began to figure prominently in training individuals who became active in the profession of clinical psychology. However, this was no guarantee that the institutions offered a clinical psychology program. Rather, it is the graduates of these programs (e.g., Shakow, Raimy) who were instrumental in developing the first training standards for professional psychology (Routh, 2000). Similarly, although the first clinical internship began in 1908, the role of internship training as a formal part of doctoral education was not at all secure—few graduate programs required internship as part of the degree, and the largely unpaid internships tended to be a luxury that many students could not afford (Rogers, 1939).

The end of World War II in 1945 crystallized the need for training standards. With thousands of war veterans in need of psychological services, the demand for clinical psychologists clearly outstripped supply. To meet this demand, the Veteran's Administration (VA) and United States Public Health Service (and later the National Institute of Mental Health) asked the American Psychological Association (APA) to identify the training necessary for clinical psychologists and to provide a list of universities that offered such training (Donn, Routh, & Lunt, 2000). Thus, the APA established the Committee on Training in Clinical Psychology, headed by Shakow. The resulting report (titled "Recommended Graduate Training Program in Clinical Psychology," often dubbed "the Shakow Report"; APA Committee on Training in Clinical Psychology, 1947) described a recommended program of training in clinical psychology and served as the basis for evaluating training programs that later evolved into the profession's accreditation system. The report included many elements of present day professional psychology training, such as coursework in the science of psychology and professional application, and applied experiences through fieldwork and internship. Importantly, the report called for training in both research and practice, and suggested that well-balanced clinical psychologists would contribute to advancement of psychology through both activities (Edelstein & Brastead, 1983). The Shakow report laid the groundwork for the scientist-practitioner model that would emerge from the Boulder Conference a few years later. The report also considered suggestions to separate a professional degree for clinical psychologists from the research-oriented PhD, but rejected them in favor of the more integrative science-practice degree (Donn et al., 2000).

Scientist-Practitioner Model Development: Boulder and Gainesville Conferences

In 1949, 73 representatives of professional psychology gathered in Boulder, Colorado for a 2-week Conference on Graduate Education in Clinical Psychology (the "Boulder Conference"; Benjamin & Baker, 2000). This conference was tasked with examining the then current models of training in clinical psychology and the national needs for psychological services, and recommending a model for providing graduate education in clinical psychology that would allow standardization across the profession. The agenda was wide-ranging, including discussions of curriculum (e.g., in the science of psychology, professional practice topics, ethics), research training, applied training, sequence of training (e.g., undergraduate access to clinical courses, master's training, postdoctoral training, internship timing), specialization, student selection and support, faculty training, societal needs, relationship to other professions, and the role of the federal government in training (Benjamin & Baker, 2000; Raimy, 1950). By the end of the Boulder Conference, approximately 70 resolutions were adopted that established the framework for training in professional psychology. Several of these resolutions become the foundation for all of professional psychology (e.g., inclusion of both research and applied training, foundations in broader field of psychology, ethics training, attention to student qualifications and faculty involvement) and are still in place today as part of accreditation and licensure standards (Commission on Accreditation—CoA, 2007; Association of State and Provincial Psychology Boards, 2008). The resolution that is most uniquely associated with the Boulder conference is the integration of science and practice. Thus, the terms *scientist-practitioner model* and *Boulder Model* often are used synonymously.

Following the Boulder conference, this training model was used by most graduate programs in clinical, as well as counseling and school, psychology, yet it was not formally articulated or endorsed by the broad training community. The 1990 Gainesville conference (Belar & Perry, 1992) was convened to do just that. Co-sponsored by major education, training, and credentialing organizations in North American professional psychology, conference attendees created and affirmed a document that outlined the basic principles and components of scientist-practitioner training. Major themes of the conference included reaffirmation of the scientist-practitioner model as necessary to meet the needs of the ever-changing discipline of psychology, the notion that science and practice are not points on a continuum nor parallel activities or skills, but are to be integrated within the diverse roles and activities in which professional psychologists engage, and explicit expansion of the model's applicability to all defined practice areas (clinical, counseling, school) as well as newly emerging areas.

Central Characteristics

Didactic and experiential training in research and practice. A central feature of the scientist-practitioner model that has become integral to all professional psychology training is training in both research and practice. From the outset, the Boulder conference attendees identified two basic societal needs to be addressed by clinical psychologists: professional services and research contributions. Raimy (1950) reported that "the Conference made an important decision when it recommended that research be given a place of equal and coordinate importance with practice in the education of graduate students…" (p. 23), noting that despite considerable discussion about whether all graduate students could be trained in both areas, conference attendees agreed on the importance of research training in preparation of all professional psychologists. Two crucial points raised in the Boulder conference documents and echoed over the next 60 years support training in both research and practice for all professional psychologists (Raimy, 1950; Belar & Perry, 1992; Belar, 1998/2006; Jones & Mehr, 2007). The first point is that discovery of knowledge through systematic research and critical analysis of available data has traditionally been more distinctive of professional psychology than other professions. Thus, research contributions are an important and unique way in which professional psychology can meet societal needs. The second point is that research is not just the purview of academic psychologists in university settings, but is also a key role for psychologists in applied settings. In addition to needing sufficient research expertise to evaluate the evidence base for assessment and intervention procedures, psychologists in applied settings also often are called upon to conduct evaluation research and thus must be competent not just as consumers, but also producers of research.

As described in the scientist-practitioner model, training includes both didactic and experiential components to training in research and practice, with core faculty involved in both domains of training (Belar & Perry, 1992; Raimy, 1950). Specifically, training focuses on acquiring knowledge, skills, and attitudes (SKAs) (i.e., competence) related to scientific psychology; professional psychology (e.g., theories and scientific bases of assessment and intervention); evaluation of existing assessment and intervention methods/instruments and the designing new ones; critical thinking and hypothesis testing in both research and practice activities; designing, conducting, and interpreting research, including at least one predissertation project and the dissertation; and conceptualizing, assessing, and intervening with multiple problems and populations in multiple settings (Belar & Perry, 1992; Raimy, 1950). However, it is not so much the inclusion of both research and practice training, but their integration that is a hallmark of the science-practitioner model.

Science-practice integration. Although the importance of including both science and practice in professional psychology training is a point of general agreement across training models, the manner in which these two activities or skill sets coexist distinguishes training models from one another. The scientist-practitioner model emphasizes that *integration* of science and practice is critical to growth of the profession and meaningful contributions to society. Co-existence without integration (e.g., research and practice as two ends of a continuum of training emphasis or as parallel and separate activities) is not acceptable, because this model emphasizes that professional psychologists continually use both science and practice in mutually informing ways. The vision shared by proponents of the scientist-practitioner model is that integration leads to a product that is more than the sum of its parts—and thus leads to more meaningful advances in understanding human behavior and personality, assessing and intervening with maladaptive functioning, and promoting adaptive functioning, than either research or practice would alone (Belar, 2008; Jones & Mehr, 2007).

Implementation and Evaluation of the Model

Training the scientist-practitioner. Training the scientist-practitioner is not quite as simple as providing training in both research and practice; explicit and ongoing training in integration is an essential component of this training model. Participants in the Gainesville conference agreed that many programs that identified as scientist-practitioner did not meet the ideal of fully integrated science-practice training (Belar & Perry, 1992). Several possible explanations for suboptimal science-practice integration have been offered, including potential personality differences between students who are interested in research versus practice, seemingly disparate skills involved in the critical and questioning nature of research versus the confidence in one's knowledge that facilitates clinical work, or the challenges to academicians in "publish or perish" environments of being effective science-practitioner role models (e.g., Frank, 1984; Mittelstaedt & Tasca, 1988). Given the challenges involved in integrative training, one contribution of the Gainesville conference report was the explicit description of multiple ways in which integration could or should be accomplished in didactic and practice activities. For example, conference proceedings emphasized that didactic science training should include skills needed to evaluate and develop clinical tools and should generate ideas that can be tested in both applied and research contexts. The conference report also asserted that practicum experiences should involve systematic application of knowledge from science to practice and systematic collection and communication of information) (Belar & Perry, 1992). These sorts of explicit suggestions might seem obvious, but it is clear from writings in the late 1980s and 1990s, and continuing today, that integrating science and practice is not as straightforward as it sounds.

Scientist-practitioner professional roles. Boulder-model advocates tend to agree that professionals may not engage in research and practice equally nor be equally competent in both domains, and that scientist-practitioners may hold many different jobs (e.g., Belar, 1998/2006; Horn et al., 2007). Scientist-practitioners may include researchers in academic or applied settings, practitioners in private or community settings, or individuals who engage in both research and practice activities. What characterizes all these individuals is that they approach their varied professional activities from an integrative perspective. Their practice is informed by research, including both the existing evidence base and their own ongoing research (e.g., case-specific hypothesis testing, program-evaluation research in their setting). Their research is informed by practice, including addressing personal and social factors that contribute to human adjustment and maladjustment, and evaluating assessment and intervention techniques in both controlled and natural practice settings. Dissemination is also a crucial part of science-practice integration. Although critics of the scientist-practitioner model have often pointed to low publication rates of practitioners as evidence of the model's limitations (e.g., Frank, 1984; see also Horn et al., 2007), traditional scientific publication is but one outcome of science-practice integration. In addition, scientist-practitioners may engage in many other methods of dissemination such as developing evidence-based and practically applicable treatment manuals, disseminating easily digestible scientific information to the lay public, or consulting with other health care professionals about how to apply psychological science knowledge to patient care.

Evaluation of the scientist-practitioner model. In the 60 years since its introduction, the scientist-practitioner model has had several critics, but many more supporters. Critics of the model have tended to argue that the original model emphasized research and practice as equally important but separate activities (e.g., Shapiro, 1967), that the original model intended integration to reflect the application of scientific knowledge to practice versus requiring competence in actually doing research (e.g., Stricker & Trierweiler, 1995), or that the current notion of science-practice integration is not practical or feasible (e.g., Frank, 1984; Horn et al., 2007) and that training should focus on the activities students will engage in after graduation (Rothenberg & Matulef, 1969). As evidence, critics have cited surveys indicating that the majority of graduates of scientist-practitioner programs do not publish research after they graduate (Frank, 1984). However, advocates of the model cite multiple benefits of scientist-practitioner training beyond publication, such as the ability to scientifically evaluate client or program outcomes and to disseminate science-based knowledge and clinical services (e.g., Rickard & Clements, 1986).

Supporters of the scientist-practitioner model suggest that, even if ideal integration is still an aspirational goal for some programs, "the scientist-practitioner model with its interlocking skills in science and practice has been the source of growth for our clinical science and science-based practice" (Belar, 2008, p. 15) and that continued integration is critical to further advances in the profession. Supporters also suggest that this training model is ideal for those who wish to use scientific methods in professional practice (Belar, 1998/2006), an approach that is increasingly relevant as our profession, the health care community, and the public demand evidence-based services. Belar and others present evidence that the scientist-practitioner model does indeed "work" and that integration of science and practice may be better than it was 60 years ago. Unlike Shakow's era, in which graduate programs focused on coursework and research supervised by faculty with little applied involvement, the majority of clinical program faculty now are involved in applied work as part of their professional activity, and the majority of programs provide in-house practicum training supervised by core faculty (Belar, 1998/2006). Student surveys indicate that although many students plan to pursue clinical practice jobs, they consider research quite important, and most plan to adhere to a scientist-practitioner model and continue with some research involvement after graduation (Merlo, Collins, & Bernstein, 2008; Parker & Detterman, 1988).

Data also support the active role of both science and practice in Boulder-model training programs. For example, Cherry, Messenger, and Jacoby (2000) documented that scientist-practitioner-program students and faculty engage in more grant-supported research, publish more journal articles, and present more often at conferences than practitioner-scholar-model students (although they rank lower in grant supported research and journal authorships than clinical scientist program students and faculty). Further, scientist-practitioner students engage in comparable amounts of clinical service during training. Scientist-practitioner students also report that they spend substantial amounts of time engaged in research (37%), clinical service (29%), and integrative (17%) activities (Merlo et al., 2008). After graduation, scientist-practitioner students take jobs in a broad range of research and applied settings, and their weekly activities are characterized by an intermediate amount of research and applied involvement as compared to clinical-scientist and practitioner-scholar program graduates (Cherry et al., 2000). Scientist-practitioner-model students obtain internships at comparable rates (88–90%) and at generally comparable sites (e.g., VAs, medical centers, hospitals) as clinical-scientist students (Neimeyer, Rice, & Keilin., 2007; Sayette, Norcross, & Dimoff, 2011).

Practitioner-Scholar and Related Models
Development: Vail Conference

Alternatives to the scientist-practitioner model began to be formulated at the Vail (Colorado) Conference held in 1973. This conference resulted in the development of the PsyD degree and defined a philosophy for new doctoral training models that would focus primarily on professional practice training. The Vail Conference promoted an "ideological commitment to the tradition of empiricism and a clear affirmation of the fundamental importance of the scientific endeavor" (Korman, 1973, p. 19), while arguing for a predominant focus on preparing students for practice careers. Given the practice emphasis, ideal educators would be faculty and administrators who were actively pursuing professional practice in addition to their roles as educators (Korman, 1973). The Vail conference also emphasized flexibility in the location of training programs (e.g., in university departments or freestanding institutions) and a commitment to diversity among faculty and graduate students, as well as in opportunities for students to work with diverse clients and underserved populations. Interestingly, the Conference did not define a specific training model for the proposed PsyD degree (Korman, 1973). Instead, it paved the way for several related training models, including the practitioner-scholar, scholar-practitioner, practitioner, and local-clinical-scientist models. Although these training models share several core characteristics, they also vary somewhat in implementation emphasis.

Central Characteristics

Practice emphasis. Critics of the scientist-practitioner model argue that professional psychology graduates largely enter into practice careers and, thus, training should be geared toward these careers. Before establishment of the Vail model, proponents of practice-based education complained that professional training was insufficient to prepare students for practice careers, claiming that training delivered in university-based scientist-practitioner programs, may deprecate professional careers (Rothenberg & Matulef, 1969). Rothenberg and Matulef (1969) asserted that "the wrong people are training our professional oriented students!" (p. 33).

To address these issues, the Vail model aims to prepare students for "delivery of human services in a manner that is effective and responsive to individual needs, societal needs, and diversity" (McHolland, 1992, p. 159). A key feature of training is the comprehensive nature of clinical experiences, beginning early in graduate training. These models value diversity in clinical experiences obtained from a range of practica that are supported by formal coursework and supervised by professional role models. The Vail model also holds a broad view of clinical training that includes aspects of professional practice such as "administrative skills, program development and evaluation, and field research" (Korman, 1973, p. 103).

Role of science and research. In the Vail model, scientific training is provided in the context of clinical work and practica (Stoltenberg et al., 2000), and is tailored for the purpose of training students as consumers of research. However, participants in the Vail conference agreed that training in program evaluation and effectiveness research was important for professional psychologists (Korman, 1973). Consequently, science training focuses on translating research and theory into practice, evaluating the utility of intervention research, and considering the effectiveness of their own clinical practice (Marwit, 1982). Practitioner-scholar programs vary in their commitment to research training, with some suggesting that a research emphasis detracts from professional training (Rothenberg & Matulef, 1969). Importantly, proponents of these models argue that conducting research is not essential for being a consumer of research. Thus, the Vail conference called for more diverse definitions of dissertations that support students' roles as professional psychologists. Dissertations may include empirical research studies, special projects, single-case study designs, and scholarly writings on psychological theory (Peterson, Peterson, Abrams, Stricker, & Ducheny, 2009).

Implementation and Evaluation of the Model

Practitioner-scholar, scholar-practitioner, and practitioner models. The terms *practitioner-scholar* and *scholar-practitioner* are often used interchangeably to refer to the same professional training model (we use the term *practitioner-scholar* to refer to all these model variants) in which students receive professional training with the goal of becoming practicing psychologists. These programs value a range of clinical endeavors as well as "theoretical analyses, methodological innovations, or any other intellectually disciplined enterprise" (Peterson, 1976, p. 793). Thus, training reflects these values, with clinical training aimed to produce practitioners

and training in scholarly inquiry aimed to prepare students to apply psychological knowledge and theory. Of note, practitioner-scholar faculty members model professional identities as both scholars and practitioners; they publish scholarly works and continue their involvement in professional service delivery (Cherry et al., 2000), in addition to their roles as supervisors and educators.

Similar to the practitioner-scholar model in many ways, the practitioner model shares a commitment to the Vail tradition and to training practitioners, but differs in how it implements the Vail conference philosophy. The practitioner model centers almost solely on the identity of a practitioner. Scholarly work and scholarly inquiry is typically not a training goal beyond limited focus on the ways that science is relevant to practice. This model often is adopted in PsyD programs located at free-standing institutions where there is not the same emphasis on publishing research and scholarly works as in programs housed in more traditional university departments. As a result, faculty in practitioner programs serve as practitioner role models; they are most likely to engage in supervision and ongoing clinical work and typically do not publish (Peterson, 1985).

Local clinical-scientist model. This is the model embraced by the National Council of Schools and Programs of Professional Psychology (NCSPP). It represents an attempt to address the gap between science and practice for professional psychology students and involves training graduate students in the use of a particular critical-thinking process with which to conduct their professional work. The local clinical-scientist model might be thought of as a training philosophy that is overlaid on the practitioner-scholar or related training model, or a method of science-practice integration that is used with these training models. In fact, most NCSPP programs that subscribe to the local clinical-scientist model actually define themselves as a combination of local clinical scientist and practitioner-scholar model programs.

Training in the local-clinical-scientist model is described as "strongly naturalistic, empiricist, hypothesis-focused, logical, and pragmatic" (Trierweiler, Stricker, & Peterson, 2010, p. 126). Its defining characteristics are a commitment to disciplined inquiry and consideration of local factors in both science and practice. Disciplined inquiry refers to a critical-thinking process that can be applied in both clinical work and scientific endeavors. This stems from the idea that "epistemology and critical thinking become more central to professional training" (Peterson et al., 2009, p. 21), such that students must be trained in a way to understand and think through the information presented to them once they leave graduate school. One significant feature of disciplined inquiry is the consideration of local contextual factors that contribute to a client's presenting problem (for a case example, see Peterson et al., 2009). The local clinical scientist must integrate information from the scientific literature, the individual client's characteristics, local influences, and other factors in case conceptualization (Peterson et al., 2009). Disciplined inquiry is also emphasized when it comes to evaluating, conducting, and synthesizing scientific research. For example, Peterson et al. (2009) describe a situation in which the local clinical scientist might use disciplined inquiry to develop a parent training group and evaluate the program. The local clinical scientist would consider the current literature on parent training as well as "of the necessary information, what is not available and therefore must be collected in a disciplined, though inexpensive, way? What are the relevant outcome variables, and how can relevant data be collected?" (p. 16). Trierweiler, Stricker, & Peterson (2010) describe the task of the local clinical scientist as "the ongoing, localized identification of important empirical phenomena and their interpretation in terms of relevant scientific hypotheses" (p. 126).

Students in local-clinical-scientist programs often do engage in scientific endeavors, but this is not a primary training emphasis. Importantly, there is a great deal of variability in participation in scientific work among students of these programs. Some NCSPP programs require doctoral dissertations in which some students elect to conduct empirical research for their projects, whereas others choose to engage in more applied scholarly work (Peterson et al., 2009). More specifically, as described by Peterson et al.:

> Types of dissertations may include the following: (a) theoretical analyses; (b) surveys; (c) analyses of archival data; (d) outcome research, including program development and evaluation; (e) systematic qualitative investigations; (f) public policy and legislative analysis; (g) case studies; and (h) group-based nomothetic investigations. (2009, p. 17).

Evaluation of the practitioner-scholar and variant models. Research on outcomes of these training programs has not made fine-grained distinctions among practitioner-scholar, scholar-practitioner, practitioner, or local-clinical-scientist programs, instead investigators often combine them or use institutional affiliation or research-practice emphasis as rough indicators of model. Most of this research supports a relative emphasis on practice versus research. For example, empirical evidences suggests that students in practitioner-scholar programs engage in predominantly professional service activities, spend only a small portion of their time on research, and have fewer professional presentations and publications than students in scientist-practitioner or clinical-scientist programs. Interestingly however, these studies have demonstrated that practitioner-scholar students do not spend more time in service delivery training than students from more research-focused models (Cherry et al., 2000; Sayette et al., 2011). In contrast, practitioner-scholar graduates devote more time to professional service activity (approximately 60% of their week) than scientist-practitioner or clinical scientist graduates (Cherry et al., 2000). Practitioner-scholar and local clinical-scientist model graduates are often employed in a range of practice settings, such as medical centers and hospitals, private practice, community mental health centers, but also some academic settings (Cherry et al., 2000; Peterson et al., 2009). Several studies have indicated that students from practitioner-scholar and practice-focused programs obtain internships at lower rates than students from more research-focused or research-practice balanced programs (Neimeyer et al., 2007; Sayette et al., 2011). Likewise, graduates of practitioner-scholar and practice-focused programs score lower on the Examination for Professional Practice in Psychology (EPPP) licensing exam than their peers at equal emphasis or more research-oriented programs (Yu et al., 1997). Internship and job placements do reflect a strong practice focus, including a tendency for practitioner-scholar and practice-emphasis programs to be more likely than programs from other models to place their students at internships and jobs in university counseling centers, community mental health centers, and other contexts such as schools, family clinics, military internships, or forensics facilities (Cherry et al., 2000; Neimeyer, et al., 2007).

Clinical Scientist Model
Development: McFall Manifesto and Indiana and New York Conferences

The most recent alternative to the scientist-practitioner training model is the clinical-scientist model, which evolved from a series of papers and conferences in the early to mid-1990s. The critical pieces of what became the clinical-scientist model first were described in a paper dubbed the "McFall Manifesto" (McFall, 1991). In this paper, McFall proposed central principles to define the science of clinical psychology and discussed implications for clinical practice and training. His definition of psychological clinical science shared much with the ideals of the scientist-practitioner model. However, the specifics of the Manifesto resulted from what many clinical psychologists, particularly those with strong research orientations, saw as limitations in the way the scientist-practitioner model had evolved, as well as changing market conditions that supported cost-efficient service delivery by master's-level professionals. As such, McFall's paper made a strong call for greater emphasis on science and research in doctoral-level training and practice, and preparation for science-based careers.

Two conferences served to solidify the clinical-scientist model (McFall, 2006a). The first, Clinical Science in the 21st Century, was hosted in April, 1994 by Indiana University and aimed "to analyze the changing landscape in scientific clinical/health psychology and to chart a course for advancing the interests of clinical science" (Academy of Psychological Clinical Science, n.d.). Among issues discussed at the conference were the challenges to providing high quality clinical scientist training and services especially in light of the demands of current accreditation and licensing requirements, limited funding for research and education, and the rapidly changing scope and knowledge base of scientific psychology. One outcome of the conference was establishment of the Academy of Psychological Clinical Science (APCS), through which like-minded training programs could work together to facilitate advances in clinical-scientist training. The second conference was the inaugural meeting of the APCS held in New York City in July, 1995. At this conference, representatives from APCS member programs drafted a mission statement that defined clinical science, and discussed clinical-science goals relevant to training, research, application, knowledge dissemination, and resources and opportunities to support these activities (APS, 2006). Unlike the Boulder and Vail conferences, the conferences that developed the clinical-scientist model did not result in a single published conference proceedings document. Instead, the central characteristics of the clinical-scientist training model can be gleaned from a combination of APCS materials found on the

organization's website and the McFall Manifesto, which was endorsed as a supporting document.

Central Characteristics

Definition of clinical science. This model defines clinical science "as a psychological science directed at the promotion of adaptive functioning; at the assessment, understanding, amelioration, and prevention of human problems in behavior, affect, cognition or health; and at the application of knowledge in ways consistent with scientific evidence" (APCS, no date, "Mission," para. 1). The model's use of the term *clinical science* represents an attempt to address perceived weaknesses in prior training models, including deviations from the "scientific values that have served for a century as the keystone for doctoral training in all areas of psychology" (McFall, 2006a, p. 367).

Primacy of science in clinical psychology. The clinical-scientist model places scientific methods and evidence at the core and makes it very explicit that clinical psychology does not exist without science. The APCS mission statement underscores the importance of empirical approaches to all activities in which clinical psychologists engage, including development of scientifically valid assessment and intervention methods, application of these methods to address problems in human functioning, and dissemination of knowledge to consumers, health professionals, and policy makers (APCS, n.d.). Even more strongly, the McFall Manifesto states that "scientific clinical psychology is the only legitimate and acceptable form of clinical psychology" (p. 76) and challenges the profession to critically examine all its practices for scientific validity, to distinguish clearly between science and pseudoscience, and to "blow the whistle" on practices that fail to meet rigorous standards of scientific evidence (McFall, 1991). McFall further maintained that psychological services should not be administered, except under strict experimental control, without an explicit description of the exact nature of the service and of benefits that had been validated scientifically, as well as evidence that possible negative effects that might outweigh benefits had been ruled out empirically. This recommendation actually originated with Rotter (1971). However, McFall pointed out that the profession has been quite slow to adopt this level of quality assurance; although empirically supported treatments exist for some problems, many clinical services continue to be offered without such support. He challenged the profession to cease delivery of unvalidated services and devote resources and expertise to the science that would expand the arsenal of empirically based procedures.

Training for clinical scientist research careers. McFall's Manifesto (1991) argued that doctoral training must have as its principle objective the production of the most competent clinical scientists possible. Similar to the scientist-practitioner model (e.g., Belar & Perry, 1992), McFall maintained that clinical scientist training would prepare graduates for a variety of careers in research, applied, or administrative settings. What is central to a clinical-scientist focus, however, is that, in each setting, clinical scientists are fundamentally scientists; their professional activities, both research and applied, contribute to advancement of scientific knowledge and methods. Again, although science-practitioner model supporters have repeatedly called for science-practice integration in training and professional activities and identity (e.g., Belar, 2008), McFall argued that the clinical-scientist model is much less ambiguous regarding this goal.

APCS's training goals seem to go further in specifying the desired career trajectories of clinical-scientist program graduates, stating that clinical scientist programs should "foster the training of students for careers in clinical science research, who skillfully will produce and apply scientific knowledge" (APCS, n.d.). Although successful implementation of clinical science includes application and dissemination (APCS goals 4 and 5; APCS, n.d.), involvement in research is the primary training goal. The focus on training clinical science researchers is further articulated in the eligibility criteria for a newly emerging accreditation system, the Psychological Clinical Science Accreditation System (PCSAS, 2011). This accreditation is limited to doctoral programs with a primary mission to train students "for successful careers as *research scientists in clinical psychology*" (PCSAS, 2011, "Eligibility Standards." para.3) and a primary goal to "produce graduates who are competent and successful at (a) conducting research relevant to the assessment, prevention, treatment, and understanding of health and mental health disorders, and (b) using science methods and evidence to design, develop, select, evaluate, implement, deliver, supervise, and disseminate empirically based assessments, interventions, and prevention strategies" ("Eligibility Standards." para.5).

Flexible, individualized, integrative training. As with other aspects of this model, the clinical-scientist model's recommendations regarding the structure of graduate training emerged out of perceived limitations in the training prescribed by the Boulder model. As McFall (2006b) notes, the recommended training that emerged in the mid-20th century was necessarily influenced by the scientific, technological, societal, and political realities of that era, and it would be surprising if much of the recommended training was not outdated. However, because many of these training recommendations have been solidified in accreditation and licensure requirements, they have been resistant to much change despite the profession's efforts (e.g., Schilling & Packard, 2005). In addition, despite the stated significance of science in psychology, the field generally does not have evidence to support its training methods or program components (Bickman, 1999; McFall, 2006b). Rather, training often seems to be based on accreditation and licensure requirements and what has been done before, rather than a scientific database. Thus, in the context of current scientific knowledge and technology, societal needs, and market forces, and the absence of compelling evidence supporting the current structure and content of doctoral training, the clinical-scientist model advocates training that is scientific, integrative, individualized, and outcomes-oriented, but whose content is largely not prescribed. McFall (2006b) presented a blueprint for training in clinical scientist programs that outlines general principles and recommendations for training, and PCSAS further articulates what clinical scientist program accreditors look for in training programs.

McFall's (2006b) blueprint begins by articulating several guiding principles, including the view that scientific clinical psychology represents an applied science whose contributions and advancement depend on integration with other areas of psychology and other sciences, and the goal of doctoral training is to train research scientists rather than graduates whose primary function will be as mental health care providers. It then suggests that programs essentially start from scratch and design their curricula to meet their clinical scientist training goals and capitalize on the interests, expertise, and opportunities available to their faculty and students. With this approach, standardization of doctoral training would not be expected. However, evaluation data would clearly be essential to defining and refining high quality training. McFall's blueprint also lays out things that clinical scientist programs should avoid, including a vocational school-style focus on particular jobs and an overemphasis on practice training guided by accrual of hours or experiences rather than by the primary clinical-scientist mission to advance understanding and effective application of psychological science. Finally, the blueprint calls for a critical examination of doctoral training, identifying and evaluating differences among training models and programs so that we can better understand which differences matter and can develop a scientific knowledge base for training decisions.

PCSAS accreditation standards follow the general theme of the McFall blueprint, encouraging flexibility, individual tailoring, and innovative, integrated training that facilitates student competence in both research and practice. PCSAS materials (PCSAS, 2011) indicate that clinical science "is not restricted to one particular set of courses, training methods, or content areas,...[and] programs are encouraged to design curricula that promote integration, innovation, collaboration, and exploration across diverse areas of psychology and other sciences" (PCSAS, 2011, section D.2.b, Curriculum Design). Across the entire curriculum, programs are to provide evidence that supports their curriculum's effectiveness in producing competent and successful clinical-scientist graduates.

Implementation and Evaluation of the Model

The clinical-scientist model's place in professional psychology has yet to be defined fully. At present, it is restricted to programs in clinical psychology, but whether this is a function of its origin within clinical psychology or reflects some more fundamental philosophical distinctions between clinical and other areas of professional psychology remains to be seen. Full implementation of an individualized, innovative, and integrative clinical scientist curriculum as envisioned by McFall and others is still an aspirational goal for many programs. This is likely due, at least in part, to the constraints of accreditation standards that require specific content and breadth of training, sometimes at the expense of depth in evidence-based graduate training (Davila & Hajcak, 2012). Whether curricula move closer to the clinical-scientist ideal, either within the existing APA-affiliated accreditation system or the emerging PCSAS system, remains to be seen. Perhaps more intractable are the constraints of licensing laws and statutes that in many states are very specific about curriculum requirements for license-eligibility (e.g., requiring specific coursework or specific credit hours). Given the slow speed with which state legislation often changes, tension between training program priorities and licensure requirements is likely to remain an issue for clinical scientist programs who wish to produce license-eligible graduates.

Empirical evaluations of the clinical-scientist model suggest that the model has some identifiable distinctions from other training models that are consistent with the model's philosophy and training goals. For example, Cherry et al. (2000) compared clinical scientist, scientist-practitioner, and practitioner-scholar programs and demonstrated that clinical scientist program students outpaced both their scientist-practitioner and practitioner-scholar program peers in their involvement in grant-supported research, journal publications, postgraduation employment in academic settings, and postgraduation involvement in basic and applied research. Clinical scientist program students did not differ in the amount of service delivery training during graduate school, but did engage in less service delivery after graduation. Similarly, Sayette et al. (2011) examined accredited PhD programs in clinical psychology, comparing APCS-member programs to university-based non-APCS programs and programs housed in specialized institutions (i.e., not offering comprehensive education beyond psychology or counseling). They identified similar differences in research emphasis and grant support, with APCS programs reporting more than other program types. Internship match, an important indicator of training program success, also supports the success of clinical scientist programs. Sayette et al. (2011) found that APCS programs and non-APCS university-based programs had comparable high rates of placing students in accredited or APPIC member internships (93% and 91%, respectively), and both had higher placement rates than specialized institution programs (61.5%). Similarly, Neimeyer et al. (2007) compared science-oriented, science-practice balanced, and practice-oriented programs (after demonstrating that these divisions were comparable to model-based divisions) and demonstrated that science-oriented and balanced programs had higher internship placement rates. They also found that science-oriented and balanced programs were more likely to place students in VA-hospital and medical-center internships, and less likely to place them in community-mental-health-center internships. Given the research-active nature of many VAs and medical centers (and indeed, the 10 APCS-member internships are all affiliated with VAs or medical centers), this suggests that clinical-scientist-model students are finding model-appropriate internships.

Applicability of Models in Professional Psychology
Across Program Type

The training models in professional psychology largely extend across the substantive practice areas (e.g. clinical, counseling, and school). These models all emerged within clinical psychology, but as they have continued to develop, most have subsequently been adapted for training doctoral students in counseling and school psychology. This is mainly due to the commitment to training in both psychological science and practice at the doctoral level across defined practice areas in professional psychology.

The similarities between clinical and counseling psychology were noted at the Boulder Conference and the conferees believed that many aspects of training in clinical psychology could be translated to counseling psychology (Raimy, 1950). Subsequently, the Gainesville conference made the suitability of this training explicit (Belar & Perry, 1992). Counseling psychology has embraced the scientist-practitioner model (Cassin, Singer, Dobson, & Altmaier, 2007), but has been more hesitant in adopting other models (Stoltenberg et al., 2000). In fact, counseling psychology has an ongoing tradition of endorsing the scientist-practitioner model as central to the practice area at their training conferences (Meara et al., 1988; Fouad et al., 2004) and in published materials (e.g., Murdock, Alcorn, Heesacker, & Stoltenberg, 1998; Stoltenberg et al., 2000). Similar to clinical psychology, however, counseling psychology continues to debate the most effective way to train graduate students in integration of science and practice.

Because of the value of training in education and educational settings in school psychology, the Boulder Conference maintained that training in clinical psychology was not applicable to school psychology (and other related fields). However, similar to clinical and counseling psychology, the majority of school psychology doctoral programs are scientist-practitioner programs (Tharinger, Pryzwanksy, & Miller, 2008), with a few programs offering the more practice-focused PsyD degree. Across training models, school psychology training is characterized by additional competencies in education, learning, and children's school-based needs. For example, field work in most school-psychology programs, regardless of training model, typically involves working in a school or hospital setting. Thus, in school psychology, the scientist-practitioner and practitioner-scholar models are adapted for research and practice in educational and school settings.

For example, the Blueprint III training model supported by the National Association for School Psychologists (NASP) maintains a commitment to both science and practice. In this model, two of the foundational competencies are "a well-confirmed knowledge base in psychology and education, and the application of the scientific method to practical delivery of the knowledge base" (Ysseldyke et al., 2006, p. 12), mirroring the scientist-practitioner model in many ways. Many doctoral programs in school psychology emphasize the use of empirically based interventions (Shernoff, Kratochwill, & Stoiber, 2003).

As noted earlier, the clinical-scientist model has only been adopted by clinical psychology graduate programs to date. Similar to the scientist-practitioner and practitioner-scholar models, this seems to reflect, at least in part, that the model originated within clinical psychology. In theory, this model could certainly be used by counseling and school psychology programs that are committed to empirical research and empirically based practice. However, given the strong allegiance to the scientist-practitioner model demonstrated by counseling and school-psychology programs, even after the practitioner-scholar model emerged as an alternative(Neimeyer et al., 2007 Stoltenberg et al., 2000), it would not be surprising to see the clinical-scientist model grow slowly outside of clinical psychology.

Across Doctoral Degree Type

The PhD was established as the degree associated with the scientist-practitioner model at the Boulder Conference (Raimy, 1950) and more recently has also become the degree of the clinical-scientist model. In addition to establishing the PsyD degree, the Vail conference stipulated that professional training programs award the PsyD degree, whereas scientist and scientist-practitioner programs should award the PhD (Korman, 1973). Accordingly, most practitioner-scholar, scholar-practitioner, and practitioner programs grant the PsyD degree to graduates. However, there are practitioner-scholar programs that grant the PhD degree and scientist-practitioner that grant the PsyD degree. This often generates much confusion about the distinctions between the two degrees and the accompanying training models.

Confusion about degree and training model distinctions is complicated further by the many similarities shared by PhD and PsyD degree programs. Students of both degree programs receive some degree of research training, conduct clinical work, and complete a predoctoral internship. This is due, in part, to the fact that accreditation requirements apply to all professional psychology programs and are not specific to a particular degree. Programs granting both degrees also maintain a commitment to both science and practice in training students. Finally, research suggests that students of PhD and PsyD programs engage in equivalent amounts of professional-service delivery during their graduate training (Cherry et al., 2000).

The largest difference between PhD and PsyD programs lies in the amount of emphasis placed on science and practice, respectively. Typically, PhD programs place a greater emphasis on science-based education, with research-based dissertations and research assistantships, and more professional authorships, whereas PsyD programs emphasize practice-based education (Cherry et al., 2000). These relative training emphases in PhD and PsyD programs reflect students' career goals. In the survey by Cassin et al. (2007), PhD students indicated a greater interest in research and academic careers, whereas PsyD students reported a career focus on clinical work in clinics, hospital settings, or private practice.

For Master's Level Training

Historically, master's-level training has been omitted from consideration in professional psychology training. The Boulder conference maintained that the practicing degree in clinical psychology was the doctorate (Raimy, 1950). This was based on two important considerations: (1) who could claim the title "clinical psychologist" and (2) how much training was considered sufficient to develop the skills and knowledge necessary to effectively and safely conduct clinical practice. Importantly, the conferees determined that two years of master's training was insufficient to gain enough experience and skills to warrant the title of clinical psychologist. They noted a need for subdoctoral providers of professional services, but did not formulate plans for how to incorporate master's training into professional psychology.

Master's level training has continued to be a subject of great debate in professional psychology due to increasing demands for psychological services and greater costs for services delivered by doctoral level psychologists. Supporters of professional master's training have raised two important issues: (1) that master's-level clinicians *do* engage in professional service delivery and (2) that doctoral students who fail to complete their programs are often granted

master's degrees (Jones, 1979). These ideas were formally articulated at the Vail conference, which called for a deviation from the status quo by broadening professional psychology to include master's-level training (Korman, 1973). Several authors have proposed alternative conceptualizations of training at both the master's and doctoral level (e.g. Jones, 1979), and national organizations have evolved to address training standards and accreditation of master's in psychology programs (e.g., Council of Applied Master's Programs in Psychology; Masters in Psychology Accreditation Council). However, master's-levels training continues to remain largely outside the domain of professional psychology.

In addition to time required for degree completion, one major way in which master's- and doctoral-level training differs is the focus on science and practice. Whereas doctoral training frequently includes competence in both science and practice, master's programs typically emphasize either science or practice singularly. For example, many master's programs provide introductory training in psychological science or practice in preparation for attending a doctoral program in psychology. Students enrolled in research-based master's programs may become involved in faculty research, receive introductory training in statistical techniques, and complete an empirically based master's thesis. Alternatively, these programs may offer some field training, but this is often limited in scope and does not provide the training required by most states to become licensed following graduation. Thus, most students graduating from these programs often then apply to doctoral programs to continue their training.

There are also master's programs that provide practice degrees. These are mostly in fields outside of psychology (e.g. LPC, Ed.S.), but some states do grant licensure to master's level clinicians in psychology as well. These programs involve coursework and field work aimed to prepare students for clinical practice. These programs may incorporate scientific training into clinical training, but scientific training is not a major emphasis. Consistent with this practice emphasis, the practitioner-scholar models are most applicable to these master's programs.

For Internship Training

Although training models have been defined largely in the context of doctoral-program training, they are also relevant to the doctoral internship. First, as with doctoral programs, accredited internships must declare a training model that they use to guide their training (CoA, 2007). In contrast to doctoral programs, recent surveys of internships indicate that more than 50% self-identify as practitioner-scholar or related (e.g., practitioner, local clinical scientist) programs, with another 20% identifying as scientist-practitioner and fewer than 1% identifying as clinical-scientist programs (Rodolfa, Kaslow, Stewart, Keilin, & Baker, 2005). However, as Rodolfa et al. demonstrate, stated training model has questionable correspondence to the training that internships actually provide; training models were not consistently related to differences in how programs conceptualized or implemented their training (Rodolfa et al., 2005). Similarly, Stedman and colleagues found that regardless of training model, most internships' training activities seem consistent with a practitioner or practitioner-scholar model, and that practice-based theoretical orientations (e.g., cognitive-behavioral, psychodynamic, systems) may better communicate what sort of training internships offer (Stedman, Hatch, Schoenfeld, & Keilin, 2005; Stedman, Hatch, & Schoenfeld, 2007). Based on these data, alternatives to the current training-model system have been suggested, including using practice-oriented theoretical models or competency domains to describe and evaluate internship training (e.g., Rodolfa et al., 2005; Stedman et al., 2007). However, it seems that theoretical models and competency domains are at least somewhat orthogonal to training models—it is possible to train various competencies, and to train assessment and intervention from various theoretical orientations, within scientist-practitioner, practitioner-scholar, or clinical-scientist perspectives. The fact that most internships do so from a self-identified practitioner-scholar perspective does not mean that others do not or could not train from another training-model perspective. Indeed, with the (albeit limited) growth of the pool of APCS-member clinical-scientist internships since Rodolfa et al. (2005) collected data in 2003, it seems that traditionally identified training models may yet have a role to play in internship training. Thus, as Rodolfa et al. (2005) suggest, it seems wise for the profession to further develop our understanding of how internships use training models, including their approach to science-practice integration, their theoretical orientation, and their focus on specific competencies, to guide training.

A second way in which training models might be relevant to internship is the extent to which a prospective intern's doctoral training model influences internship placement. Most research on internship placement has not examined the issue by program model, but instead by program or degree type (e.g., clinical, counseling, school; PhD vs. PsyD) or research emphasis. As is clear from preceding sections, program type and research emphasis serve as only rough markers for model, but may nevertheless yield some useful information. Several studies have examined internship placement for programs defined by research-practice emphasis (e.g., Neimeyer et al., 2007), program type (e.g., Keilin et al., 2007), or some combination of these factors (Norcross et al., 2010; Sayette et al., 2011), and have drawn similar conclusions. In general, PhD-granting programs and research-oriented or research-practice balanced programs place students in APA or CPA accredited and APPIC-member internships at higher rates than do PsyD-granting programs or practice-emphasis programs. In addition, of the handful of programs that Parent and Williamson (2010) identified as unequal contributors to the APPIC internship match (having large numbers of applicants to the match but extremely low placement rates), virtually all were PsyD and practice-oriented programs. Given that most internships seem to align with a practitioner-scholar or practitioner model, this evidence for advantage to intern applicants from more research-emphasis or equal-emphasis programs is interesting and suggests that factors other than program-model match may be at play.

Surveys of factors that internship programs consider crucial in selecting interns support the idea that doctoral-training model is just one element influencing internship placement. Rodolfa et al. (1999) and later Ginkel, Davis, and Michael (2010) surveyed internship training directors about what they considered to the most influential factors in selecting interns. Across both studies, the factors considered most pertinent seemed to either reflect personal intern applicant characteristics (e.g., interview, professional demeanor) or to transcend training model (e.g., fit between applicant goals and internship opportunities, supervised clinical experience, coursework completion). Factors that may vary across training models, such as specific practice experiences or research productivity, fell into the lower or midrange portion of the importance rankings. However, it is essential to note that these data were collected from a broad range of internship directors; training model, via its implications for specific training experiences, may indeed influence the "fit" factor identified as most important.

Implications of Model for Doctoral Training: the Good, the Bad, and the Ugly

The Good: Contributions of Model to Quality Training

Almost since the inception of training in professional psychology, models have been an important part of programs' identity. Have they been helpful? In several respects, models do indeed seem to have made positive contributions to training. For example, by providing a framework of training goals and standards, models guide program development, implementation, and evaluation. Coursework, practicum experiences, and scientific endeavors are streamlined according to a basic program focus. Ideally, these experiences are tailored for the targeted outcomes of the program's training model. As described earlier, available data suggest that doctoral programs are generally successful at producing graduates who meet their training model's outcome goals, suggesting that programs are successfully preparing graduates for their intended career paths. Training models foster program evaluation by identifying the values, goals, and training outcomes that serve as the basic criteria for evaluation. For example, scientist-practitioner doctoral programs can evaluate whether they successfully integrate science and practice in their research and application training. Clinical scientist programs can evaluate the extent to which their graduates conduct research to advance the empirical base for intervention, whereas practitioner-scholar programs might focus on evaluating how successfully their graduates utilize the scientific literature to guide their practice.

Training models have also resulted in the grouping of like-minded programs (e.g. the development of APCS, NCSPP, and CUDCP: the Council of University Directors of Clinical Psychology). This is beneficial for several reasons. First, these like-minded programs serve as a training support group for each other. Second, members of these groups have historically made collaborative advances at conferences and other trainings. For example, with growing use among prospective students of the Internet for information about graduate programs, CUDCP passed a resolution to encourage all member programs to post "full disclosure" data on their websites, to inform the public about important program characteristics (e.g. statistics on applicant and admitted students, time to program completion, program costs, internship placements, licensure, attrition; Burgess, Keeley, & Blashfield, 2008). By 2006, a similar set of information became required public disclosure for all accredited programs (IR

C-20, initially adopted May, 2006; CoA, n.d.). These organizations also promote and encourage program evaluation through their culture of shared training goals and quality standards.

Finally, training models can facilitate communication with the public regarding a program's training philosophy, values, and training focus. For example, all accredited programs will share significant commonalities in training components, including curricular offerings and at least basic requirements for research and applied experiences. However, knowing a program's training model can help prospective students better understand the philosophy that the program will emphasize in training, the research or practicum training opportunities that will be available, and the careers for which graduates will be best prepared. Prospective students then have more accurate expectations of programs, which allows for more informed decision-making about what programs will best suit their interests and goals. In turn, when graduate programs receive applications from prospective students who are better fits for their program, this should contribute to a stronger graduate student body (for that program) and better program outcomes.

The Bad and Ugly: Limitations of Models for Quality Training

Despite the positive contributions of models to professional psychology training, they also come with limitations. For instance, it is not clear that training models as they have evolved are either necessary or sufficient to guide doctoral-level professional psychology training. Certainly, the profession has not considered a specific model to be necessary, instead taking a "thousand flowers" approach and encouraging diversity in professional psychology education (Benjamin, 2001). This creates an atmosphere in which models can guide training to meet different goals and needs, but can also spark continual and likely irreconcilable arguments about which model is best. As Belar notes, "discussions of educational philosophy are always value- and opinion-driven, as there is no clear scientific evidence to support one model of education and training over another in promoting public welfare" (Belar, 1998/2006, p. 77). To the extent that these arguments continue, they are much like "ethnic clashes" (Peterson, 2010, p. 59), occurring with no clear resolution and at the expense of profession-level advances.

Ironically, these arguments occur in the context of training that shares considerable overlap across identified training model. Repeatedly, the profession has identified principles that guide training regardless of model, such as grounding in the science of psychology including its content and methods; grounding in research, systematic, inquiry, and critical thinking; emphasis on delivery of effective services in a variety of settings and to a variety of consumers; and sensitivity to changes in science, technology, and the marketplace (e.g., Belar, 2008; Eby Chin, Rollock, Schwartz, & Worrell, 2011). However, the focus on differences versus commonalities has threatened to diminish the clear and unique identity of professional psychologists. In truth, psychologists are frequently seen as little different from other, and often less costly, mental health providers rather than professionals who are uniquely qualified to integrate research and practice in the development and delivery of effective health care (Belar, 2008; Bray, 2011; Eby et al., 2011).

Although models may be hotly debated in the training community, it is not clear that they are particularly meaningful outside academic training. The public does not know (or care) what training models exist; the treatment-seeking public wants to know that they can expect effective services and the degree-seeking public wants a meaningful and marketable education. As noted earlier, there is little correspondence between internships' stated models and their actual training activities or emphases, and doctoral programs from all model types demonstrate reasonable outcomes. In the authors' experiences, undergraduate students frequently do not know what the major training models are or what they imply for doctoral training. Rather, students want to know what activities they will participate in during graduate school and what careers they will prepare for. This may explain, in part, why studies of what factors students consider important in selecting graduate programs ask students about specific experiences like research and practicum opportunities, and general factors such as "fit with program," funding, or emotional climate (e.g., McIlvried, Wall, Kohout, Keys, & Goreczny, 2010; Walfish, Stenmark, Shealy, & Shealy, 1989). They do not ever ask students about training models.

Advancing Professional Psychology: Do Training Models Have a Role?

Given the ways in which training models both reflect and contribute to rifts within the field (Eby et al., 2011) as well as their questionable relevance outside it, do they have a role in promoting a stronger and more effective profession? We would argue that they do, for both philosophical and practical

reasons. The challenge is to identify a role that is realistic, attainable, and that facilitates rather than stalls progress.

To begin to identify this role, it is useful to consider the alternative of abandoning training models as anachronisms that have outlived their usefulness. This is likely both unrealistic and ill-advised, for a few reasons. First, it is simply unlikely to work. Humans love to characterize, define, and categorize. If we jettison current training models, it is probable that something else would take their place. Second, as noted earlier, current training models do serve useful purposes—they provide a framework for designing, implementing, and evaluating training programs, as well as describing them in terms of some of the most important issues in the profession (e.g., science and practice identities; Eby et al., 2011). Alternatively, should we settle on a common training model that reflects the core identity and standards of professional psychology? Again, it is probably not realistic to think that the profession as a whole will be able to settle on one philosophical and values-based training model; the existing models exist because they have strong proponents and a large support base, and presumably because they offer something worthwhile. Although the profession is moving toward increased accountability, attempting to identify a "winning" model (from the existing models or a new one) through outcomes evaluation is also unlikely to work well, given disagreements about what the most important outcome variables are, what evidence is considered sufficient, and so on. As in the treatment-evaluation literature, evaluation of training models is likely to be best accomplished with questions such as "what works best under what conditions, for what purposes, and for whom?" The complexity of this question suggests that consistent with the profession's thousand-flowers approach, there is no one-size-fits-all training model.

An approach that is gaining increasing traction in the profession is to focus beyond training models to the common values and issues in professional psychology. This involves bringing together individuals who represent diverse training models and interest groups in professional psychology for the purposes of wrestling with issues in the profession, identifying shared values, and pooling resources to address the issues and advance the profession. Examples of such collaborative efforts are seen in the formation and outcomes of the Council of Chairs of Training Councils (http://www.psychtrainingcouncils.org/), which has been instrumental in several tasks such as defining practicum, developing standards for evaluating students' practicum and professional competencies, and creating a toolkit for internship development. Another example of a collaborative effort is *Training and Education in Professional Psychology*, a journal devoted to the broad professional psychology training community, that is a product of the efforts of both the Association of Psychology Postdoctoral and Internship Centers (APPIC) and APA. These collaborative efforts are not simple, nor do they lead to quick solutions (e.g., see Eby et al.'s, 2011 description of their process of having authors from five different training councils collaborate on a paper on the future of professional psychology training), but they are an essential part of moving our profession forward so that it is less like "a thousand randomly blooming flowers, and more like the various sections of an orchestra, each with its own part to play in developing optimal psychological services to the public" (Eby et al., 2011, p. 66).

Having training models as harmonious sections of professional psychology's orchestra has potential benefits for the profession and the public. First, greater collaboration and cohesion across models may allow the profession to focus less on differences across models and more on presenting each model clearly. For example, CUDCP recently established a set of expectations for internship eligibility, to be shared with students and internship sites, based on goals of its scientist-practitioner and clinical scientist programs (CUDCP, 2011). Likewise, once the public understands who psychologists are as a whole and how they contribute uniquely to health care, it may be easier to describe model-based variations on the core identity in ways that matter to potential students, clients, and colleagues. Second, a culture of collaboration facilitates continued progress on critical issues in the profession. For instance, the current internship imbalance is affecting programs from all training models, and the solution will require involvement from all (Bieschke et al., 2011). In an era of increasing need for integrative, collaborative efforts across health care professions (Belar, 1998/2006), we must get better at collaborating within professional psychology.

Conclusions and Recommendations

Training models have a strong role in the development, implementation, and evaluation of doctoral-level professional psychology training. Although they are less clearly related to later stages of training (e.g., internship) and not always evident or meaningful to the public, training models have the potential to guide and inform these audiences as well. Our review indicates that the predominant training models—scientist-practitioner, practitioner-scholar, and clinical scientist—share several core values and principles, but also demonstrate important differences in how they envision and carry out education and training, most notably in the relative emphasis on research and practice in training focus and career goals. However, differences often devolve into "model wars" (Bieschke et al., 2011) that can seriously interfere with the profession's advancement. Based on the contributions and limitations of training models to professional psychology, we offer several suggestions for maximizing their positive impact.

First, we recommend that the profession continue to look beyond training models and focus on integrative, collaborative efforts to clearly define our profession and address issues facing us. As several have suggested, no one but professional psychologists really understand or care about our training models; members of the public merely care about well-trained professionals and quality health care. In a nutshell, they want competent providers and evidence-based, effective care. Providing these as part of the larger system of health-related scientists and health care providers requires that we become integrated and harmonious parts of the orchestra. In particular, two points of integration—our profession's longstanding commitment to science-based practice (e.g., Belar, 1998/2006) and our increasing focus on competencies (see Fouad & Grus's chapter 3, this volume)—are perhaps the most significant ways in which this can be achieved.

Second, we suggest that in the context of an integrated, collaborative identity, training models can be used effectively to supplement and sharpen our identities as professional psychologists. As the identity of the orchestra is cemented, the distinctive roles and contributions of various sections can become clearer. However, training models should always be consistent with the core identity of professional psychology. Third, we recommend that programs and the profession make greater efforts to describe training models more transparently and explicitly to the public, focusing on what the models provide and how they matter. Finally, echoing recommendations from throughout the training community, we strongly recommend ongoing and careful evaluation of how training models impact professional psychology education and training, with particular attention to outcomes that are relevant to advancing our science and practice. It is these program- and profession-level evaluations that will guide further development of training models in professional psychology.

References

Academy of Psychological Clinical Science (APCS). (n.d.). Origins and backgrounds. Retrieved May 30, 2012 from http://acadpsychclinicalscience.org/index.php?page=origins.

American Psychological Association Committee on Training in Clinical Psychology. (1947). Recommended graduate training program in clinical psychology. *American Psychologist, 2*, 539–558. doi: 10.1037/h0058236

Association for Psychological Science (APS). (2006). A new alliance of doctoral training program forms. Retrieved May 30, 2012 from http://www.psychologicalscience.org/index.php/publications/observer/1996/january-96/a-new-alliance-of-doctoral-training-programs-forms.html.

Association of State and Provincial Psychology Boards (ASPPB). (2008). ASPPB's guide for students and faculty: Entry requirements for the professional practice of psychology. Retrieved June 1, 2012 from http://www.asppb.net/files/public/09_Entry_Requirements.pdf/

Belar, C. D. (2006). Graduate education in clinical psychology: "We're not in Kansas anymore." *Training and Education in Professional Psychology*, (Suppl.), 69–79. (Reprinted from *American Psychologist*, 1998, *53*, 456–464). doi: 10.1037/1931-3918.S.69

Belar, C. D. (2008). Changing education needs of psychologists: Do we need more medical knowledge, basic science and more psychological science? *Journal of Clinical Psychology in Medical Settings, 15*, 12–17. doi: 10.1007/s10880-008-9097-8

Belar, C. D., & Perry, N. W. (1992). National Conference on Scientist-Practitioner Education and Training for the Professional Practice of Psychology. *American Psychologist, 47*, 71–75. doi: 10.1037/0003-066X.47.1.71

Benjamin, L. T. Jr., (2001). American psychology's struggle with its curriculum: Should a thousand flowers bloom? *American Psychologist, 56*, 735–742. doi: 10.1037/0003-066X.56.9.735

Benjamin, L. T. Jr., & Baker, D. B. (2000). Boulder at 50: Introduction to the section. *American Psychologist, 55*, 233–236. doi: 10.1037/h0087859

Bickman, L. (1999). Practice makes perfect and other myths about mental health services. *American Psychologist, 54*, 965–978. doi: 10.1037/h0088206

Bieschke, K. J., Bell, D., Davis, C. III, Hatcher, R., Peterson, R., & Rodolfa, E. R. (2011). Forests, grazing areas, water supplies, and the internship imbalance problem: Redefining the paradigm to implement effective change. *Training and Education in Professional Psychology, 5*, 123–125. doi: 10.1037/a0024902

Bray, J. H. (2011). Training for the future of psychological practice. *Teaching and Education in Professional Psychology, 5*, 69–72. doi: 10.1037/a0023713

Burgess, D., Keeley, J., & Blashfield, R. (2008). Full disclosure data on clinical psychology doctorate programs. *Training and Education in Professional Psychology, 2*, 117–122. doi: 10.1037/1931-3918.2.2.117

Cassin, S. E., Singer, A. R., Dobson, K. S., & Altmaier, E. M. (2007). Professional interests and career aspirations of graduate students in professional psychology: An exploratory survey. *Training and Education in Professional Psychology, 1*, 26–37. doi: 10.1037/1937-3918.1.1.26

Cherry, D. K., Messenger, L. C., & Jacoby, A. M. (2000). An examination of training model outcomes in clinical psychology programs. *Professional Psychology: Research and Practice. 31*, 562–568. doi: 10.1037/0735-7028.31.5.562

Commission on Accreditation (CoA). (2007). Guidelines and principles for accreditation of programs in professional psychology. Washington, DC: American Psychological Association.

Council of University Directors of Clinical Psychology (CUDCP). (2011). Expectations for internship eligibility. Retrieved June 1, 2012 from http://www.cudcp.us/files/Reports/CUDCP%20Internship%20Expectations%20(2011).pdf

Davila, J., & Hajcak, G. (2012). From fractionism to integration: Problems and possible alternatives for clinical science training. *The Behavior Therapist, 35*, 1–3.

Donn, J. E., Routh, D. K., & Lunt, I. (2000). From Leipzig to Luxembourg (via Boulder and Vail): A history of clinical psychology training in Europe and the United States. *Professional Psychology: Research and Practice, 31*, 423–428. doi: 10.1037/0735-7028.31.4.423

Eby, M. D., Chin, J. L., Rollock, D., Schwartz, J. P., & Worrell, F. C. (2011). Professional psychology training in the era of a thousand flowers: Dilemmas and challenges for the future. *Training and Education in Professional Psychology, 5*, 57–68. doi: 10.1037/a0023462

Edelstein, B. A., & Brastead, W. S. (1983). Clinical training. In M. Hersen, A. Kazdin, & A. Bellack (Eds.), *The clinical psychology handbook* (pp. 35–56). New York: Pergamon Press.

Fouad, N. A., McPherson, R. H., Gerstein, L., Bluestin, D., L., Elman, N., Helledy, K.,I., Metz, A. J. (2004). Houston, 2001: Context and legacy. *The Counseling Psychologist, 32*, 15–77. doi: 10.1177/0011000003259943

Frank, G. (1984). The Boulder model: History, rationale, and critique. *Professional Psychology: Research and Practice, 15*, 417–435. doi: 10.1037/0735-7028.15.3.417

Ginkel, R. W., Davis, S. E., & Michael, P. G. (2010). An examination of inclusion and exclusion criteria in the predoctoral internship selection process. *Training and Education in Professional Psychology, 4*, 213–218. doi: 10.1037/a0019453

Horn, R. A., Troyer, J. A., Hall, E. J., Mellott, R. N., Cote, L. S., & Marquis, J. D. (2007). The scientist-practitioner model: A rose by any other name is still a rose. *American Behavioral Scientist, 50*, 808–819. doi: 10.1177/0002764206296459

Jones, A. C. (1979). A model of psychological practice for PhD and MA professionals. *Professional Psychology, 10*, 189–194.

Jones, J. L., & Mehr, S. L. (2007). Foundations and assumptions of the scientist-practitioner model. *American Behavioral Scientist, 50*, 766–771. doi: 10.1177/0002764206296454

Keilin, W. G., Baker, J., McCutcheon, S., & Peranson, E. (2007). A growing bottleneck: The internship supply-demand imbalance in 2007 and its impact on psychology training. *Training and Education in Professional Psychology, 1*, 229–237. doi: 10.1037/1931-3918.1.4.229

Korman, M. (Ed.) 1973. *Levels and patterns of professional training in psychology*. Washington, DC: American Psychological Association.

Marwit, S. J. (1982). In support of university-affiliated schools of professional psychology. *Professional Psychology, 13*(2), 181–190. doi: 10.1037/0735-7028.13.2.181

McFall, R. M. (1991). Manifesto for a science of clinical psychology. *The Clinical Psychologist, 44*, 75–88.

McFall, R. M. (2006a). On psychological clinical science. In T. A. Treat, R. R. Bootzin, & T. B. Baker (Eds.), *Psychological clinical science: Papers in honor of Richard M. McFall* (pp. 363–396). New York: Psychology Press.

McFall, R. M. (2006b). Doctoral training in clinical psychology. *Annual Review of Clinical Psychology, 2*, 21–49. doi: 10.1146.annurev.clinpsy.2.022305.095245

McHolland, J. D. (1992). National Council of Schools of Professional Psychology core curriculum conference resolutions. In R. L. Peterson, J. McHolland, R. J. Bent, E. Davis-Russell, G. E. Edwall, K. Polite, D. L. Singer, & G. Stricker (Eds.), *The core curriculum in professional psychology* (pp. 155–166). Washington, DC: American Psychological Association. doi: 10.1037/10103-029

McIlvried, E. J., Wall, J. R., Kohout, J., Keys, S., & Goreczny, A. (2010). Graduate training in clinical psychology: Student perspectives on selecting a program. *Training and Education in Professional Psychology, 4*, 105–115. doi: 10.1037/a0016155

McReynolds, P. (1996). Lightner Witmer: A centennial tribute. *American Psychologist, 51*(3), 237–240. doi: 10.1037/0003-066X.51.3.237

Meara, N. M., Schmidt, L. D., Carrington, C. H., Davis, K. L., Dixon, D. N., Fretz, B. R.,…Suinn, R.M. 1988). Training and accreditation in counseling psychology. *The Counseling Psychologist, 16*, 366–384. doi: 10.1177/00110000088163005

Merlo, L. J., Collins, A. B., & Bernstein, J. (2008). CUDCP-affiliated clinical psychology student views of their science training. *Training and Education in Professional Psychology, 2*, 58–65. doi: 10.1037/1931-3918.2.1.58

Mittelstaedt, W. T., & Tasca, G. (1988). Contradictions in clinical psychology training: A trainees' perspective of the Boulder model. *Professional Psychology: Research and Practice, 19*, 353–355. doi: 10.1037/0735-7028.19.3.353

Murdock, N. L., Alcorn, J., Heesacker, M., & Stoltenberg, C. (1998). Model training program in counseling psychology. *The Counseling Psychologist, 26*, 658–672. doi: 10.1177/0011000098264008

Neimeyer, G. J., Rice, K. G., & Keilin, W. G. (2007). Does the model matter? The relationship between science-practice emphasis in clinical psychology programs and the internship match. *Training and Education in Professional Psychology, 1*, 153–162. doi: 10.1037/1931-3918.1.3.153

Norcross, J. C., Ellis, J. L., & Sayette, M. A. (2010). Getting in and getting money: A comparative analysis of admission standards, acceptance rates, and financial assistance across the research–practice continuum in clinical psychology programs. *Training and Education in Professional Psychology, 4*, 99–104. doi: 10.1037/a0014880

Parent, M. C., & Williamson, J. B. (2010). Program disparities in unmatched internship applicants. *Teaching and Education in Professional Psychology, 4*, 116–120. doi: 10.1037/a0018216

Parker, L. E., & Detterman, D. K. (1988). The balance between clinical and research interests among Boulder model graduate students. *Professional Psychology: Research and Practice, 19*, 342–344. doi: 10.1037/0735-7028.19.3.342

Peterson, D. R. (1976). Need for the doctor of psychology degree in professional psychology. *American Psychologist, 31*, 792– 798. doi: 10.1037/0003-066X.31.11.792

Peterson, D. R. (1985). Twenty years of practitioner training in psychology. *American Psychologist, 40*, 441–451. doi: 10.1037/0003-066X.40.4.441

Peterson, R. L. (2010). Threats to quality in professional education and training: The politics of models, obfuscation of the clinical, and corporatization. In M. B. Kenkel and R. L. Peterson (Eds.), *Competency-based education for professional psychology* (pp. 55–65). Washington, DC: American Psychological Association. doi: 10.1037/12068-003

Peterson, R. R., Peterson, D. L., Abrams, J., Stricker, G., & Ducheny, K. (2009). The National Council of Schools and Programs of Professional Psychology education model 2009. In M. B. Kenkel & R. L. Peterson (Eds.), *Competency-based education for professional psychology* (pp. 13–42). Washington, DC: American Psychological Association.

Psychological Clinical Science Accreditation System (2011). Accreditation review standards and criteria. Retrieved June 1, 2012 from http://www.pcsas.org/review.php.

Raimy, V. C. (Ed.). (1950). *Training in clinical psychology.* New York: Prentice Hall.

Rickard, H. C., & Clements, C. B. (1986). Compared to what? A frank discussion of the Boulder model. *Professional Psychology: Research and Practice, 17*, 472–473.

Rodolfa, E. R., Kaslow, N. J., Stewart, A. E., Keilin, W. G., & Baker, J. (2005). Internship training: Do models really matter? *Professional Psychology: Research and Practice, 36*, 25–31. doi: 10.1037/0735-7028.36.1.25

Rodolfa, E. R., Vieille, R., Russell, P., Nijjer, S., Nguyen, D. Q., Mendoza, M., & Perrin, L. (1999). Internship selection: Inclusion and exclusion criteria. *Professional Psychology: Research and Practice, 30*, 415–419. doi: 10.1037/0735-7028.30.4.415

Rogers, C. R. (1939). Needed emphases in the training of clinical psychologists. *Journal of Consulting Psychology, 2*, 1–6. doi: 10.1037/h0056807

Rothenberg, P. J., & Matulef, N. J. (1969). Toward professional training: A special report from the National Council on Graduate Education in Psychology. *Professional Psychology, 1*, 32–37. doi: 10.1037/h0028677

Rotter, J. B. (1971). On the evaluation of methods of intervening in other people's lives. *Clinical Psychology, 24*, 1–2.

Routh, D. K. (2000). Clinical psychology training: A history of ideas and practices prior to 1946. *American Psychologist, 55*(2), 236–241. doi: 10.1037/0003-066X.55.2.236

Sayette, M. A., Norcross, J., & Dimoff, J. D. (2011). The heterogeneity of clinical psychology Ph.D. programs and the distinctiveness of APCS programs. *Clinical Psychology: Science and Practice, 18*, 4–11. doi: 10.1111.j.1468-2850.2010.01227.x

Schilling, K., & Packard, R. (2005). The 2005 Inter-Organizational Summit on Structure of the Accrediting Body for Professional Psychology: Final proposal. Retrieved May 30, 2012 from http://www.psyaccreditationsummit.org.

Shapiro, M. B. (1967). Clinical psychology as an applied science. *British Journal of Psychiatry, 113*, 1039–1042. doi:10.1192.bjp.113.502.1039

Shernoff, E. S., Kratochwill, T. R., & Stoiber, K. C. (2003). Training in evidence-based interventions (EBIs): What are school psychology programs teaching? *Journal of School Psychology, 41*, 467–483. doi: 10.1016/j.jsp.2003.07.002

Stedman, J. M., Hatch, J. P., & Schoenfeld, L. S. (2007). Toward practice-oriented theoretical models for internship training.

Training and Education in Professional Psychology, 1, 89–94. doi: 10.1037/1931-3918.1.2.89

Stedman, J. M., Hatch, J. P., Schoenfeld, L. S., & Keilin, W. G. (2005). The structure of internship training: Current patterns and implications for the future of clinical and counseling psychologists. *Professional Psychology: Research and Practice, 36,* 3–8. doi: 10.1037/0735-7028.36.1.3

Stoltenberg, C. D., Pace, T. M., Kashubeck-West, S., Biever, J. L., Patterson, T., & Welch, D. I. (2000). Training models in counseling psychology: Scientist practitioner versus practitioner-scholar. *The Counseling Psychologist, 28,* 622– 640. doi: 10.1177/0011000000285002

Stricker, G., & Trierweiler, S. J. (1995). The local clinical scientist: A bridge between science and practice. *American Psychologist, 50,* 995–1002. doi: 10.1037/0003-066X.50. 12.995

Tharinger, D. J., Pryzwanksy, W. B., & Miller, J. A. (2008). School psychology: A specialty of professional psychology with distinct competencies and complexities. *Professional Psychology: Research and Practice, 39,* 529–536. doi: 10.1037/0735-7028.39.5.529

Trierweiler, S. J., Stricker, G. & Peterson, R. L. (2010). The research and evaluation competency: The local clinical scientist-review, current status, future directions. In M. Kenkel & R. L. Peterson (Eds.), *Competency-based education for professional psychology* (pp. 125–141). Washington, DC: American Psychological Association.

Walfish, S., Stenmark, D. E., Shealy, S., & Shealy, S. (1989). Reasons why applicants select clinical psychology graduate programs. *Professional Psychology: Research and Practice, 20,* 350–354. doi: 10.1037/0735-7028.20.5.350

Ysseldyke, J., Morrison, D., Burns, M., Ortiz, S., Dawson, P., Rosenfield, S.,...Telzrow, C. (2006). *School psychology: A blueprint for training and practice III.* Bethesda, MD: National Association for School Psychologists.

Yu, L. M., Rinaldi, S. A., Templer, D. I., Colbert, L. A., Siscoe, K., & Van Patten, K. (1997). Score on the Examination for Professional Practice in Psychology as a function of attributes of clinical psychology graduate programs. *Psychological Science, 8,* 347–350. doi: 10.1111/j.1467-9280.1997. tb00423.x

Rethinking the Core Curriculum for the Education of Professional Psychologists

Roger L. Peterson, Wendy L. Vincent, *and* Molly Fechter-Leggett

Abstract

This chapter argues for a core curriculum in the training of professional psychologists. There are four overlapping approaches to the discussion. First, there is the general argument for a core curriculum in education that goes back far beyond the beginning of professional psychology. Second, there are the arguments for "common" and "essential" elements of professional curricula, drawn from medicine and law (see Peterson, Vincent, & Fechter-Leggett, 2011). Third and fourth, within psychology there are two intellectual lines of development of the core curriculum. The third is the set of arguments for a core that has evolved into the competencies movement (e.g. Fouad et al. 2009; Peterson et al., 1992). The fourth, which like the third continues to this date, is referred to by psychology accreditation (by the Commission on Accreditation of the American Psychological Association) as broad and general education. This is followed by a review of key psychology licensure and accreditation issues. An argument that the core curriculum should provide a fundamental background for professional practice is developed. A detailed example is presented. Finally the importance of *context* as an addition to the core is put forward.

Key Words: core, curriculum, education, professional, psychology

In this chapter we argue for a core curriculum in the training of professional psychologists. There are four overlapping approaches to the discussion. First, there is the general argument for a core curriculum in education that goes back far beyond the beginning of professional psychology. Second, there are the arguments for "common" and "essential" elements of professional curricula, drawn from medicine and law (see Peterson, Vincent, & Fechter-Leggett, 2011). Third and fourth, within psychology there are two intellectual lines of development of the core curriculum. The third is the set of arguments for a core that has evolved into the competencies movement (e.g. Fouad et al. 2009; Peterson et al., 1992). The fourth, which like the third continues to this date, is referred to by psychology accreditation (by the Commission on Accreditation of the American Psychological Association [CoA]) as broad and general education. This is followed by a review of key psychology licensure and accreditation issues. An argument that the core curriculum should provide a fundamental background for professional practice is developed. A detailed example is presented. Finally the importance of *context* as an addition to the core is put forward.

General Argument for a Core Curriculum

Hundreds of arguments for an undergraduate and professional core curricula have appeared over the last century and a half. As an influential exemplar, we describe the *Harvard Red Book* (Harvard Committee, 1945) next. Most descriptions say that education should include components from the humanities, the social sciences, and the hard sciences. Some identify a specific canon; others propose selecting from a list of particular courses; still others support distribution requirements.

Though Harvard itself has moved on to other carefully constructed rationales for its current core curriculum (e.g., Harvard University Faculty of Arts and Sciences, 2006), the intellectual argument made in 1945 by the Harvard Committee is instructive in the current context. This classic document saw one of the goals of general education to be responsive to "common standards and common purposes" (p. 4). Though it seems quaint in some ways and was strongly influenced by World War II, the famous, extremely influential volume colloquially called the *Harvard Red Book* (Harvard Committee, 1945) sounds a chord still relevant to psychology some 70 years later: "The question has therefore become more and more insistent: what then is the right relationship between specialistic [sic] training on the one hand, aiming at any one of a thousand different destinies, and education in a common heritage and toward a common citizenship [in the discipline of psychology, we need to add] on the other?" (p. 5). Broad and general education "should not be confused with elementary education" (Harvard Committee, 1945, p. 198). As acknowledged in the *Red Book,* there is a difference between a course designed to advance the study of a specialist and one "designed to provide an understanding of an area such that it facilitates insight into general intellectual relationships and connections between ideas and bodies of learning within the discipline" (cf. Harvard Committee, 1945, pp. 56-57, p. 191). Such courses provide more than a soon-forgotten, trivial body of facts, and instead provide an attitude of mind and a way of effective thinking (cf. Harvard Committee, 1945, pp. 64-65). Courses that accomplish such purposes are what we hope to include in a core curriculum for professional psychologists.

"Common" and "Essential" Knowledge

The core-curriculum model for which we advocate in this chapter presents the necessary common knowledge approach to meaningful broad and general scientific education (as distinct from professional/clinical education) for professional psychologists. This approach argues that students ought to learn particular elements of scientific knowledge that professional psychologists need to know for their professional work ("necessary" and "essential") and guarantees that psychologists, quite reasonably, share some common knowledge ("common"). In addition, broad and general education of this sort is necessary to meet licensure and other regulatory requirements.

It would be extremely desirable to initiate a spirited national conversation among professional psychologists to identify the key areas of scientific information and particular pieces of scientific knowledge that are critical to their professional work. An examination of the "common" and "essential" from law and medicine are good first steps.

The idea of required, shared knowledge is seldom questioned in American legal and medical education. Our sister professions of law and medicine have such requirements. The disciplines of law and medicine recognize the need for students to be educated in specific core subjects in order to be able to practice in their respective fields.

In law, the American Bar Association (ABA), the governing body for law school education, expects that ABA-accredited law schools cover a fundamental educational curriculum comprised of the following: substantive law; legal analysis; legal writing; history, goals, structure, values, rules, and responsibilities of the profession; and necessary professional skills to practice effectively and responsibly (ABA Standards, 2008–2009). Further, the Multistate Bar Examination (MBE) covers the six core areas taught in ABA-accredited law schools: constitutional law, contracts, criminal law and procedure, evidence, real property and torts (National Conference of Bar Examiners, 2013). These areas are not viewed by law schools as trivial or something to be covered as an undergraduate; instead they are foundational components of graduate legal education.

In medicine, according to Bandaranayake (2000), the two terms applied most in relation to a core curriculum are *common* and *essential*. "The core should be looked upon as that which is common, rather than essential, and that which is essential should be determined within the core. It is mastery of the latter that must be insisted on for safe practice" (Bandaranayake, 2000, p. 560). In this context, the various governing bodies of the field of medicine (pre—and post-MD) acknowledge the importance of specific cores or domains of learning necessary to training medical doctors (Association of American Medical Colleges, 2005).. The United States' and Canada's nationally recognized accrediting body for medical education programs granting MD degrees is the Liaison Committee on Medical Education (LCME). They refer to *content areas* that include a curriculum of basic science, clinical, behavioral, and socioeconomic subjects. Content from courses in anatomy, biochemistry, genetics, physiology, microbiology and immunology, pathology, pharmacology and therapeutics, and preventative medicine must be covered, in addition to clinical instruction in all organ systems (LCME, 2008). The Accreditation Council for Graduate Medical Education (ACGME), which accredits graduate medical education programs in the United States, does not refer to the concept of a core curriculum in its requirements. Instead, this governing body refers to six general competencies: (1) patient care,(2) medical knowledge, (3) practice-based learning and improvement, (4) interpersonal and communication skills, (5) professionalism, (6) systems-based practice. Although they do not represent a curriculum, they are principles that institutions can use to develop a core curriculum of study at the graduate medical level (ACGME, 2007, p. 649).

It is not clear to us what would be different in the academic areas that make up psychology to suggest that our conceptual thinking should be different from those who train professionals in law and medicine. Instead, and this is speculation, maybe the difference is in the context in which much of psychology education occurs. In a large university in with a huge undergraduate psychology major, it is no surprise that the early courses, with their textbooks and multiple-choice orientation, are seen as watered-down. In contrast, in a law school or medical school, in which the students will graduate with advanced professional degrees and beginning graduate courses are large, faculty do not disparage the large beginning courses in professional education. This is another instance in which conclusions about key issues are influenced by context (Kagan, 2012).

Some History

There are a number of papers written about various aspects of the core curriculum. The most recent is by Zlotlow, Nelson, & Peterson (2011) and focuses on the "broad and general" requirements as seen through the window of APA accreditation. This is discussed in much more detail later. Earlier work by Peterson et al. (1992) included a variety of perspectives and was a transitional document in the movement from lists of courses toward the competency movement. The areas now called "broad and general" received comparatively little treatment as a professionally focused, competency-based core was put forward. Peterson (1992a) took on the larger issues from a social constructionist perspective. Weiss (1992) examined each of the training conferences to critically evaluate the professions hesitancy to move toward competencies.

Issues relevant to a core curriculum were apparent at the Boulder Conference (Raimy, 1950). From the beginning in 1947, the initial APA Committee on Training in Clinical Psychology chose for "breadth of training (generalism) as opposed to depth (specialization)" (quoted in Altmaier, 2003, p. 40). "A clinical psychologist must first and foremost be a psychologist in the sense that he [sic] can be expected to have a point of view and a core of knowledge an Id training which is common to all psychologists..." (quoted in Altmaier, 2003, p. 41). Altmaier also reported that, from the beginning in 1947, there was some tension about whether the Committee itself should set standards or if that was usurping a department's role. In 1960, there was a similar tension about whether the Committee should be advisory and consultative rather than evaluative. Similar issues remain today in the context of conversations about the degree of authority over curriculum that the CoA ought to have. Of course the Commission has evolved to become increasingly evaluative. The list of areas has evolved over time as is appropriate (Zlotlow et al., 2011).

The Competency Movement and Broad and General Education

The 1990 meeting of the National Council of Schools and Programs of Professional Psychology (NCSPP) led to the publication of *The Core Curriculum in Professional Psychology* (Peterson et al., 1992). Unlike the focus of the current chapter, that book put forward the six initial competencies *as* the core curriculum. Only one paper was on the academic-scientific core (Webbe, Farber, Edwall, & Edwards,1992) that foreshadowed the current material. There also were papers on women (Edwall & Newton, 1992) and on diversity (Davis-Russell, Forbes, Bascuas, & Duran, 1992) that, although short of proposing a diversity competency, gave the field a sense of what was on the horizon. A list that included but expands on what became the CoA broad and general list appeared only in the conference resolutions (p. 162). NCSPP's understanding at the time and throughout its later model papers was similar to that of Berenbaum and Shoham's (2011) that these areas were aspects of the knowledge that were to be integrated with the skills and attitudes fundamental to the competencies. Retrospectively, it is interesting to note that finding agreement on a list of six competencies may have been a much easier task than finding specific agreement on knowledge areas. We could agree on what most professional psychologists actually do as long as we did not have to agree on what they should read and know.

There are at least two versions of how broad and general education fits with the current competency movement. Both versions see each competency as an integration of knowledge, skills, and attitudes (KSAs) in applied areas. The first interpretation grew directly from the initial 1992 material (Peterson et al., 1992) and has continued through each statement of the NCSPP practitioner-scholar model (Peterson, Peterson, Abrams, & Stricker, 1997; Peterson, Peterson, Abrams, Stricker, & Ducheny, 2010). Other academic areas contribute to the knowledge element and are so labeled: "other required knowledge" (Peterson et al., 2010, pp. 31–32). Broad and general courses are elements of the knowledge aspect, but not competencies in themselves.

The second interpretation, from the Competencies Conference (Kaslow et al., 2004) and the Benchmarks work (Fouad et al., 2009), groups the broad and general courses with a competence in scientific knowledge. This line of thinking appears elsewhere in this volume. The scientific knowledge and methods competence is defined as the trainee's ability to

> Understand research, research methodology, techniques of data collection and analysis, biological bases of behavior, cognitive affective bases of behavior, and development across the lifespan, and evidences respect for scientifically derived knowledge. An essential component of scientific methods is scientific knowledge.(Fouad et.al., 2009, p. S8)

This view specifies that the content of broad and general courses is part of a foundational competency and undergirds an array of professional competencies. But this view de-emphasizes the content itself as relevant to particular professional competencies and instead emphasizes the foundational science aspect. Their positions are consistent with the view of core curriculum espoused in this chapter, which emphasizes the scientific preparation for practice.

Neither conceptualization is wrong, and the arguments advanced in this chapter could be put forward under either flag. The NCSPP model has the advantage of emphasizing applied practice areas, but its competencies in relationship and diversity are conceptually problematic and arguably more "foundational," rather than being on a par with intervention and assessment. The Benchmarks and the Cube Model that emerged from the Competencies Conference (Rodolfa et al., 2005) conceptually clarify the "functional competencies," but the results are a very complex model that may undervalue some of the material in the broad and general areas.

Broad and General Education

The *Guidelines and Principles* (American Psychological Association, 2009) of the CoA state that programs are to provide "broad and general preparation for practice at the entry level" (p. 4). Not only should that preparation "be based on the existing and evolving body of knowledge, skills, and competencies that define the declared substantive practice area(s)," but it should be "well integrated with the broad theoretical and scientific foundations of the discipline and field of psychology in general" (p. 4).Later, the *Guidelines and Principles* state that "the students shall be exposed to the current body of knowledge in at least the following areas: biological aspects of behavior; cognitive and affective aspects of behavior; social aspects of behavior; history and systems of psychology; psychological measurement; research methodology; and techniques of data analysis" (pp. 9–10).

The CoA's *Guidelines and Principles* are not clear about what else is to be required. Certainly, programs are to teach the:

> scientific, methodological, and theoretical foundations of practice in the substantive area(s) of professional psychology in which the program has its training emphasis. To achieve this end, the students shall be exposed to the current body of knowledge in at least the following areas: individual differences in behavior; human development; dysfunctional behavior or psychopathology; and professional standards and ethics. (pp. 9–10)

The CoA's current view of the broad and general requirements is found in implementing regulation IR C-16, "Evaluating Program Adherence to the *Principle of Broad and General Preparation* for Doctoral Programs." A revised version was developed in July of 2011, which provided detail on each of the areas, a description of what defined appropriate faculty competence to teach each of these areas, as well as a definition of graduate level assignments (APA, 2011). The July 2011 version appears in Figure 4.1.

No explicit, detailed rationale for broad and general education appears in the *Guidelines and Principles* (2009) or in the official communications of the CoA. However, Zlotlow and her colleagues (2011) described what is known of the history of broad and general education. It is not too much of an overstatement to say that the Boulder

The Guidelines and Principles for Accreditation of Programs in Professional Psychology (G&P) stipulate, in Section II, B.1, that preparation at the doctoral level should be broad and general. According to the G&P:

"This preparation should be based on the existing and evolving body of knowledge, skills, and competencies that define the declared substantive practice area(s) and should be well integrated with the broad theoretical and scientific foundations of the discipline and field of psychology in general."

The purpose of this broad and general training is preparation for entry level practice (Section II, B.1) consistent with local, state/provincial, regional, and national needs for psychological services (Section III, Doctoral Graduate Programs, Domain F.2(c)). Thus, the Commission on Accreditation (CoA) believes that all graduates from accredited doctoral programs, regardless of substantive practice area, should develop competence in the breadth of scientific psychology as part of this preparation for entry-level practice. The CoA evaluates a program's adherence to this provision in the context of the G&P, Domain B.3 (reprinted, in part, below) using the following guidelines:

"In achieving its objectives, the program has and implements a clear and coherent curriculum plan that provides the means whereby all students can acquire and demonstrate substantial understanding of and competence in the following areas:

(a) The breadth of scientific psychology, its history of thought and development, its research methods, and its applications. To achieve this end, the students shall be exposed to the current body of knowledge in at least the following areas: biological aspects of behavior; cognitive and affective aspects of behavior; social aspects of behavior; history and systems of psychology; psychological measurement; research methodology; and techniques of data analysis;

(b) ...individual differences in behavior; human development; dysfunctional behavior or psychopathology; and professional standards and ethics."

This Implementing Regulation refers specifically to all of the content areas specified in Domain B.3(a) (biological aspects of behavior; cognitive and affective aspects of behavior; social aspects of behavior; history and systems of psychology; psychological measurement; research methodology; and techniques of data analysis) and two of the content areas in Domain B.3(b) (individual differences and human development).

Accredited programs must ensure students' understanding and competence in these specified content areas, including the history of thought and development in those fields, the methods of inquiry and research, and the applications of the research in the context of the broader domain of doctoral training in the substantive area(s) in which they are accredited (e.g., clinical, counseling, or school psychology, or combinations thereof). Thus, the CoA looks toward the program's specific training model and goals to determine the breadth needed to provide quality training, and as such, acknowledges that programs may use a variety of methods to ensure students' understanding and competence and that there are multiple points in the curriculum sequence at which these experiences may be placed. Of note is that the term "curriculum" is used broadly and does not refer only to formal courses. However, the CoA also considers several aspects of training to be necessary to meet the provisions of these aspects of the G&P.

Broad theoretical and scientific foundations of the field of psychology in general. This requirement addresses breadth of training both across and within multiple areas in the field of psychology, as decribed below. Across: Breadth across areas of psychology is addressed via the provision that the curriculum plan include biological aspects of behavior; cognitive and affective aspects of behavior; social aspects of behavior; history and systems of psychology; psychological measurement; research methodology; and techniques of data analysis, and human development. The CoA understands that these content areas may be addressed in separate places in the curriculum or in an integrative manner within the curriculum.

Within: Within each specified content area, it is understood that the "current knowledge in the area" is continually changing; as such, breadth and depth are seen as involving coverage of current knowledge in the area, as well as history of thought and development in the area, its methods of inquiry and research, and the evolving nature of the area. A curriculum plan that includes coverage of one or a few aspects of a

Figure 4.1 C-16. Evaluating Program Adherence to the Principle of "Broad and General Preparation" for Doctoral Programs (APA, 2011)

content area must provide clear and convincing evidence that the specific topics are used as a vehicle by which students develop understanding and competence in the broader content area, including its history of thought, methods of inquiry, and current and evolving knowledge base.

The following definitions are provided to assist programs with understanding the CoA's interpretation of several areas of Domain B.3(a-b). The CoA acknowledges that these lists are not checklists that reflect comprehensive lists of required topics. Rather, they are examples of the sorts of topics included in each area, but are not exhaustive and are expected to be fluid, reflecting the evolution of the field.

• (B.3a) Biological aspects of behavior: The CoA understands this to include multiple biological underpinnings of behavior, and may include topics such as the neural, physiological, and genetic aspects of behavior. Although neuropsychological assessment and psychopharmacology can be included in this category, they do not by themselves fulfill this category.

• (B.3a) Cognitive aspects of behavior: The CoA understands that this area may include the study of topics such as learning, memory, thought processes, and decision-making. Cognitive testing and cognitive therapy do not by themselves fulfill this category.

• (B.3a) Affective aspects of behavior: The CoA understands that this area may include topics such as affect, mood, and emotion. Psychopathology and mood disorders do not by themselves fulfill this category.

• (B.3a) Social aspects of behavior: The CoA understands that this area may include topics such as group processes, attributions, discrimination, and attitudes. Individual and cultural diversity and group or family therapy by themselves do not fulfill this category.

• (B.3a) Psychological measurement: The CoA understands this to mean training in psychometric theory and application beyond applied assessment.

• (B.3b) Individual differences: The CoA understands that this may include topics such as personality, diversity, measurement issues, psychometrics, psychopathology, intelligence.

• (B.3b) Human development: The CoA understands this to include transitions, growth, and development across an individual's life. Curricula limited to one developmental period is not sufficient.

Although the G&P specifies that preparation in the substantive practice area(s) should be well-integrated with broad theoretical and scientific foundations, exposure to the specified content areas should not be presented solely within an applied context. Rather, they should be addressed as sub-disciplines in the field of psychology in their own right, as developed and understood by researchers and scholars within these areas. In other words, demonstrating that the program is consistent with the G&P in this regard would preclude coverage only of the application of these aspects of the content area to practice problems or settings (such as cognitive therapy, group therapy, multicultural counseling).

Faculty qualifications. Because coverage of the specified content areas is intended to provide exposure to specified sub-disciplines of psychology, the curriculum plan in these content areas should be developed, provided, and evaluated by faculty who are well qualified in the content area. Faculty may be considered qualified by degree (e.g., major or minor area of concentration) or other educational experience (e.g., respecialization, ongoing professional development or other systematic study, current research productivity in the area). It is the program's responsibility to specify clearly articulated procedures for ensuring appropriate faculty qualifications.

Graduate level understanding and competence. Accredited programs should clearly document how the curriculum plan ensures graduate-level understanding and competence. The CoA will look for certain pieces of evidence in evaluating graduate level, including students' exposure to a curriculum plan that utilizes primary source materials (including original empirical work that represents the current state of the area), emphasizes critical thinking and communication at an advanced level, and facilitates integration of knowledge in the breadth areas with the program's substantive area(s) of practice. For example, if the program uses a course to satisfy an aspect of Domain B.3 of the G&P, it may be appropriate in some instances to use textbooks that target undergraduate audiences as a minor part of the course (e.g., as foundational reading to introduce the subject area to students) if the majority of the course involves graduate level readings. Programs must also document that students have substantial opportunities to acquire and demonstrate graduate level understanding and competence, as defined above. If a program elects to use

Figure 4.1 C-16. (continued)

students' prior education or experiences to partially satisfy breadth requirements, the program must also document how each student demonstrates graduate-level understanding and competence in the relevant content areas.

Flexibility in curriculum plans to ensure student understanding and competence in specified content areas. As with all aspects of accreditation review, the CoA recognizes that programs may meet the provisions of the G&P using a variety of methods. For example, programs may provide courses or other educational experiences within their program, may allow students to use prior experiences to demonstrate exposure to the content areas, or may use students' performance on specified outcome measures to demonstrate understanding and competence. The curriculum plan should be documented in sufficient detail so that a reviewer or site visitor can readily understand how the relevant areas are included in the overall educational process in the program, what activities students must engage in to achieve competency and understanding in each area, and how the resulting understanding and competency are evaluated.

If the program chooses to supply courses directed to cover these areas within its required curricular offerings, then it must ensure that the courses provide all students with exposure to the current and evolving knowledge in the relevant area(s), are taught at the graduate level, and are delivered by qualified faculty (as specified above). Where elective courses can be used to satisfy the requirements, the program must clearly explain how it ensures that all students demonstrate substantial understanding of and competence in the required areas, regardless of what course the student chooses to take. Likewise, if the program chooses options other than courses to satisfy the requirements, the program must clearly explain how the experiences and activities allow all students to demonstrate substantial understanding of and competence in the required areas.

Doctoral programs that admit students who begin the program with demonstrated competence in the breadth of psychological science may satisfy these requirements by providing more focused coverage of these domains consistent with program goals and objectives. Programs that elect to meet the broad and general requirements through this more focused approach must explain how, for each student, the combination of prior coursework/experience and the graduate curriculum provided is consistent with the content areas provided in B.3(a), as well as individual differences, and human development [B.3(b)].

(Commission on Accreditation, November 2001; revised July 2011)

NOTE: Programs that elect to meet the broad and general requirements through a combination of prior educational experiences and more focused graduate instruction in those areas must still ensure that their curricula are appropriate in relation to local, state/provincial, regional, and national needs for psychological services, such as licensure, consistent with Domain F.2(b) of the G&P.

Figure 4.1 C-16. (continued)

Conference included a list of areas with some similarity to the current version and substantially more detail (Zlotlow et al., 2011, p. 2). Zlotlow et al.'s paper (2011) includes a number of other versions of this list that have emerged over the years.

The Current Situation, the CoA, and Implementing Regulation C-16

Based upon informal conversations among training directors and faculty, requiring knowledge of the areas of biological aspects of behavior, research methodology, techniques of data analysis, and psychological measurement is not controversial, even though what is included in each area probably is. Requiring knowledge of some or all of the following may elicit some differences of opinion (though we know of no survey of these issues): cognitive and affective aspects of behavior (including memory, emotion, learning, and social cognition), social

aspects of behavior (social psychology and social theory), diversity, evidence-based practice, and, trailing behind, history and systems of psychology. IR C-16 requires courses that have very explicit characteristics beyond a simple catalog of areas. The sorts of courses that are proposed in this chapter do not require much more specificity than already appears.

It seems likely that changes would be made when these passages are rewritten. As of January 2013, the *Guidelines and Principles* have been reopened in a process managed by the CoA. It should take at least a year and maybe two or more. One reasonable idea is that there should be two distinct areas: Those experiences meeting the broad and general requirements deserve scrutiny by the CoA, whereas those experiences providing education in the "substantive areas" should be left to the model and, therefore, to the program.

Meeting Licensure and Accreditation Requirements

On the most pragmatic level, the great majority of programs have determined that they must meet the most recent versions of the American Psychological Association (APA) Commission on Accreditation's (CoA) *Guidelines and Principles* (2009) and state licensing requirements, both of which require a broad and general psychology education. The issue of national accreditation standards and the broad and general requirements that are included arises because, like law and medicine, clinical, counseling, and school psychology are professional areas (within the CoA's scope of accreditation) which are committed to protect the public (Altmaier, 2003; Nelson & Messenger, 2003) through accredited professional education and ultimately through licensure. The curriculum required of all other doctoral level psychologists, except those in professional areas, is quite reasonably left to academic departments, as if they were art historians, sociologists, or anthropologists. The fact that programs participate in accreditation is de facto evidence that a program is to a substantial degree interested in licensure for its graduates. Graduates from programs with a research emphasis, in, for example, experimental psychopathology, for whom licensure is not relevant, have no need to participate in accreditation. Within the current regulatory structure (Zlotlow et al., 2011), programs that wish to retain full local control of their curriculum cannot necessarily assure their graduates of a curriculum that assures licensure. It is important to remember that it is not just the programs and the CoA that determine curriculum. Individual licensing boards across the United States and Canada have particular curricular requirements, typically based on courses, which are often quite detailed and demanding. For the most part these boards are not controlled by academics.

Broad and General Education 2011

In 2011, *Training and Education in Professional Psychology* published a special section on broad and general education. It included a piece on history by Zlotlow and colleagues (2011), one on the necessary common knowledge approach by Peterson and colleagues (2011), which this chapter modifies and extends; a scientist-practitioner perspective by Collins and Callahan (2011); and a clinical science perspective by Berenbaum and Shoham (2011). Those interested in a deeper immersion in this material should read them all.

All these authors concur that there ought to be required broad and general knowledge in professional psychology, but they fail to achieve consensus about what it should be. Both Collin and Callahan (2011) and Berenbaum and Shoham (2011) report small, informal faculty studies on this issue and found no agreement. Collins and Callahan note that the half-life of psychological knowledge is five years. Berenbaum and Shoham note that faculty should be bringing students cutting-edge information. Of course, faculty should not be teaching obsolete information. However, these perspectives subtly change the meaning of broad and general from foundational to current. We doubt that lawyers and physicians have this problem. Certainly it would be quite interesting to add to the curriculum list something like "critical key findings from the last five years."

There are other perhaps more parsimonious explanations for the failure to achieve consensus. Maybe the regulatory language has become a de facto political compromise that allows programs to have quite different courses and experiences meet the "same" requirements. Moreover, perhaps professional psychologists of the various camps have been educated differently. We all know and, therefore, ultimately value different things. All the authors whose broad and general positions were characterized in earlier paragraphs described different and often nonoverlapping curricula, all acceptable to the CoA. The EPPP does guarantee some common knowledge of general psychology but it is seldom scientific information directly relevant to professional practice like that in the examples that are presented later in this chapter. At this point, there is no clear specification of the array of such knowledge, no clear standard, and no check point. Therefore, being bright people, it may well be that those psychologists across the country get by quite well without knowing what we have indicated as common and essential material. They/we don't know there is material out there that it would be good to know. Like most of us, they/we may have taken limited core courses that did not get them to notice what is missing. As UlricNeisser said,

> The fact that some attributes go unnoticed does not make the object seem incomplete, of course. Properties we don't notice are like ideas we have not had. They leave no gap in the world; it takes information to specify gaps. (1976, p. 69)

In professional circumstances, in which the rewards are for increased professional specialization and narrowing, it is not surprising that psychologists would not pick up on unfamiliar material that puts their everyday professional information in some different interpretive context and specifies a gap. Good examples that will appear later are Schacter's (1996) presentation on memory, Kagan's (2007) on emotion, and Kagan's (2012) on context. Without more common knowledge, It is not surprising that psychologists so frequently disagree (e.g., scientist-practitioner versus practitioner-scholar; psychodynamic theory versus cognitive behavior therapy) and high-level conversations become difficult.

We do not mean to suggest that any one group has been more attentive to these questions or put our own groups forward as more successful in this area. Like that of other groups, all the NCSPP work (Peterson et al., 1992; Peterson et al., 1997; Peterson et al., 2010 shows the same lack of attentiveness to core curricular issues. Until recently, many professional program faculty were educated in traditional scientist-practitioner programs and should quite reasonably have similar attitudes.

It may be that psychologists are overly influenced by the narrowness of many big, art and sciences university psychology majors. Psychology is one of the most popular undergraduate majors. The basic courses are text oriented and multiple choice is the rule of the day. If we ask that undergraduates have what may turn out to be a watered-down pregraduate-psychology preparation, the risk of the Collins and Callahan (2011) proposal, the doctoral-level graduates may end up even narrower in their preparation and quite far from the cutting-edge that Berenbaum and Shoham (2011) root for.

Preferred Essential Courses/Experiences for Relevant Scientific Information

What is "essential" for professional psychology education? What scientific information is relevant to professional practice? Specifically, what do all professional psychologists need to know in a pragmatic, useful sense—to practice their profession? We submit that the areas described earlier in the APA *Guidelines and Principles* (2009) are a reasonable start (see Zlotlow et al., 2011). The second question is what "common" knowledge should we all have if we are to be psychologists and have collegial relationships grounded on that common knowledge. Again, the areas in the APA's *Guidelines and Principles* (2009) are a good start. Whatever our level of agreement now, the doors to this conversation and debate should be wide open and welcoming as the field develops. Even now, there are

further areas that deserve discussion, some of which are mentioned later. In this intellectual context, we wish to again acknowledge a long-standing bias toward the value of a core curriculum (Peterson et al., 1992; Peterson, 1992a, 1992b).

The kinds of courses and experiences we might hope for in a core psychology curriculum would be, "designed to provide an understanding of an area such that it facilitates insight into general intellectual relationships and connections between ideas and bodies of learning within the discipline" (Harvard Committee, 1945, pp. 56–57, p. 191). Some might see such courses as just another survey. In Collins and Callahan's (2011) mention of existing "in-depth" courses, in Berenbaum et al. (2011), as well as in the public feedback submitted to the Commission on Accreditation (American Psychological Association, Commission on Accreditation, 2010), it is implied that these survey courses would be like those offered to undergraduates at a sophomore level. In contrast, graduate courses are put forward as focused, challenging, and deep.

We suggest a different analogy. An "essential" professional psychology course with scientific information relevant to professional practice would be like examining the results of the elections across the country to identify national trends, directions, interpretations, practical significance, economic support, and the like. In the same way, a narrow course would be like studying the results from a single state or a single city. Either might be done in a challenging or deep way, on one hand, or a superficial way, on the other. It appears that a narrower course, deep or surface, might meet some portion of the course goals discussed here (e.g., even though it might contain only some subset of essential material).

The idea of using "existing" courses brings up pragmatic issues that were mentioned in Collins and Callahan (2011) and put forward directly as resource issues in the Council of Graduate Departments of Psychology feedback on IR C-16 submitted to the CoA (American Psychological Association, Commission on Accreditation, 2010). Many large graduate departments can easily offer "in-depth" courses from another area that might be a narrow and limited approach to that which is essential. These sorts of courses may not have been designed with any intention to meet a breadth requirement. Course selection is usually accomplished via a distributional approach, which allows students to select from a list in a particular broad and general category (e.g., the cognitive and affective list might include separate courses in intelligence, learning, emotion, social cognition, or memory). This sort of solution brings up perennial issues of breadth, of the quality of the course, of the quality of the teaching, of issues of department loads, and of program coherence, as the *Guidelines and Principles* (2009, p. 7) say, the curriculum should be "sequential, cumulative, and graded in complexity."

On the other hand, to specially create a quality "essential" course in these days of specialization may be difficult. In many institutions, few faculty have sufficiently deep, plus broad and general, scholarly education themselves to do such a course justice (even with special preparation of publication in the area). Such a course may well require additional department resources. The necessity of presenting high quality, challenging, and stimulating courses is important from both perspectives. If courses turn out to be weak, poorly taught, irrelevant, and not even close to essential, it is hard to see why they would be required for accreditation.

However, if excellent courses were developed and required across programs, then all professional psychologists would share elements of core psychology knowledge, which would provide a basis for communication with one another, as well as a framework for developing advanced competency (Fouad et al., 2009). It follows that a very fruitful conversation should occur about what we should include as essential in scientific preparation for practice in psychology a broad and general education in psychology, not whether we should have such a thing.

Cognitive and Affective Bases of Behavior: An Example

Let us provide an example drawing on Peterson's course on cognitive affective bases of behavior. It is included to show how a particular core area can be developed so as to include essential material in the scientific preparation for practice. There are a number of reasons to describe a course at this level of detail: (a) It may not be obvious what a course designed to provide scientific preparation for practice actually looks like. (b) It is important to show that the courses being proposed are more than lists of topics. (c) There is some implicit pedagogy in this sort of course. (d) It helps to differentiate this sort of course from many that are typically offered.

Perhaps we might begin to agree that a required course on cognitive and affective bases of behavior could include material on the following elements: (a) cognitive vision of psychology, what we call cognitive psychology as a metatheory (e.g., Barone, Maddox, & Snyder, 1997; Mahoney,

1991); (b) learning; (c) memory (e.g., Schacter, 1996); (d) social cognition and heuristics (e.g., Barone et al., 1997; Kunda, 1999); (e) emotion (e.g., Kagan, 2007; Lewis, Haviland-Jones, & Barret, 2008); (f) relevant epistemologies (e.g., Gergen, 2009; Mahoney, 1991; D. R. Peterson & R. L. Peterson, 1997); and (g) relevant issues of diversity (see Bruner 2002; Kagan, 2007; Kunda, 1999). Here is a point where we agree with Collins and Callahan's perspective (2011): The boundaries of the core areas are not firm, and they change as the discipline moves. Although it may be possible to identify at a point in time some aspects of knowledge that are in the center of an area, it would be a mistake to imagine that the boundaries will or should remain clear and firm over the years.

Being selective, let's start with memory. Daniel Schacter's *Searching for Memory: The Brain, the Mind, and the Past* (1996) is an exquisitely written book on many of the topics needed for broad and general education. Its downside is that all the other readings may seem to the students to be flat, dull, and poorly written in comparison. Schachter's book (1996) is 15 years old, but many of the central issues in memory remain uptodate. The quality of the readings are important, because quality in part will determine what students remember a year later, five years later, or a decade later.

The primary data of psychologists in the professional situation are memories. Though psychologists can observe his or her client's behavior in the consulting room, most attention goes to the client's *report* of his or her memories, whether they are about the week's events or things that happened earlier in life. Even if one argues that behavior or emotions are central, psychologists deal primarily with the clients' memories of behavior or emotion through self-report and the narratives presented in the consulting room. All the material described later comes from Schacter (1996). Certainly professional psychologists need to know about the differences between semantic, procedural, and episodic memory; something about the various kinds of amnesias; and state dependent, mood congruent, and associative retrieval. They need to know that the metaphorical universal library view of the brain popularized by neurosurgeon Wilder Penfield in the 1950s is wrong. All memories cannot be retrieved by touching some spot on the exposed brain with an electrode. Instead, graduates need to know that even high-level memories are reconstructions, that current expectations can be incorporated, and that one tends to re-remember the past in light of current attitudes. Further, they need to know about the potency of suggestibility, that hypnotic recall is unreliable, and that, according to Ceci and others (cited in Schacter, 1996), half the children remember suggested events as their own memories, even when they come from some other source. They need to know that although a few incidents of sexual abuse can be forgotten, there is little evidence of massive forgetting by those who have suffered years of abuse.

Turning to social cognitive psychology, a psychologist should know about heuristics (e.g., Kunda, 1999). Students should have already learned about base rates from a measurement course. They should know that people tend to give a brief interaction as much credence in making judgments as long-term acquaintance (Kunda, 1999), like a social psychological version of Paul Meehl's famous work. They should know about the availability heuristic, egocentric bias, and the fundamental attribution error. If they know all that, they should also know in the context of diversity that the fundamental attribution error is fundamentally Western, something not found in Japan. And whether it provides the groundwork for understanding depressogenic thinking or covert rehearsal, they should have absorbed the set of findings that suggest that frequent imagining increases the likelihood of an event.

Turning to emotion, Jerome Kagan's (2007) impressive recent book *What Is Emotion?* is dense both with data, conceptual material, and detailed attention to diversity. Much more difficult reading than Schacter, the book reads like a 271-page *Psychology Bulletin* article. It is hard to choose some representative ideas. Here are some key ones:

> The commensurability of brain activity, behaviors, and verbal reports for emotions is unknown. The utility of nominating a small select set of emotions as basic states (the atoms of human affect), to be contrasted with a much larger number deemed as less fundamental, is the second issue. (p. 190)

Later:

> The primary message of this book is a plea for accommodation to the rich complexity of this domain. It is an error to restrict the investigation of emotions to a small number of states that happen to have popular English names, certain facial expressions, behavioral consequences, or histories of rewarding or punishing experiences. (p. 215)

Certainly there are other approaches. For those drawn to a variety of different, sometimes conflicting, perspectives on emotion, Lewis et al. (2008) could be selected.

Similar paragraphs could have been written about all the other areas originally named: cognitive psychology as a metatheory (e.g., Mahoney, 1991), learning, relevant epistemologies (e.g., Gergen, 2009; Peterson & Peterson, 1997), and diversity. There is always more material emerging on the cutting edge; take, for example, the recent ideas of Jerome Bruner, one of the founders of cognitive psychology. He has put forward thoughtful and provocative ideas about the importance of narrative and of the narrative self (Bruner, 2002).

Implicit in this long-course example is the idea that all content that fits particular broad and general requirements should not be seen as equally desirable. We advocate content that meaningfully and explicitly supports and provides a scientific basis for professional practice. Just as in the current circumstances, we suspect that the CoA along with the licensing boards will be the arbiters of which courses and experiences meet these criteria. Course objectives and pedagogies should explicitly support this overarching scientific vision. What ultimately should be included should be open to discussion and debate both among involved faculty across the country and students and faculty in a particular program. Of course, there should be some variation. If we value training evidence-based practitioners, they *all* need to know the relevant evidence in each of the core areas and about other substantive areas of science that underlie practice. From what is known about broad and general curriculum requirements, many psychologists will not have been trained in this detail. As a result, it seems possible that errors are being made (e.g., if memories are accepted without question), and harm is being done (e.g., if the possibility of therapist suggestion of memories is not considered).

Of course, there is a need to balance rigor and depth of core, essential material with the practical demands of programs that are already overflowing with course requirements. Certainly we have all heard convincing arguments for enhanced attention to elective concentrations, to research methods, to assessment, to supervision and management, to evidence-based practice, and so on. It seems to us that these demands make it all the more important that time spent on the core is devoted to essential material.

Emphasizing Context as Part of the Core

We propose a new, systematic area of attention for the core curriculum—a focus on the *context* of professional psychology. Jerome Kagan, in his book *Psychology's Ghosts: The Crisis in the Profession and the Way Back* (2012) argues that much of what is wrong with psychology, both in the profession and the research that supports it, is the lack of attention to context. We suggest adoption of his "broad definition of context, which applies primarily but not exclusively to humans who interpret the symbolic meaning of a setting, include the person's sex, ethnicity, developmental stage, social class, and cultural background" (p. 22). He strongly emphasizes the "significance of the context in which individuals from different social classes and cultures try to cope with each day's responsibilities through their private interpretations of experiences in their distinctive contexts " (p. viii). Of course, Kagan (2012) is not the only scholar to argue for the importance of context. In fact Peterson (2005) made a much more limited and comparatively anemic argument that context was underemphasized in clinical psychology. Some of the same issues have emerged in the field's increasing emphasis on diversity and in the constructionist literature (e.g., Gergen, 2009). Kagan is arguing that material that some professional psychologists often see as part of diversity and, therefore, a bit off to the side is actually in the very intellectual center of the field of professional psychology.

Trierweiler and Stricker's work on the "local clinical scientist" as a model for professional psychology necessarily emphasizes context. Their metaphor of adopting Sherlock Holmes or Mrs. Marple as a model for scientific investigations inherently focuses on context (Stricker & Trierweiler, 1995; Trierwiler & Stricker, 1992; Trierweiler & Stricker, 1998; Trierweiler, Stricker, & Peterson, 2010. In a similar idea, Kagan quotes John Tukey, one of the world's most respected mathematical statisticians, as saying, "If psychological data are allowed to speak for themselves, they will typically lie to you" (quoted in Kagan, 2012, p. 45). Tukey advised psychologists to adopt the perspective of detectives looking for hidden clues rather than automatically using standard approved statistics to prove a favorite idea (Kagan, 2012, p. 45). Within professional psychology, Trierweiler and Stricker are among the very few that can be seen as systematically and scientifically responsive to the importance of context.

In their earlier paper on broad and general education in professional psychology, Peterson and colleagues (2011) described a variety of additions to the core that, at the time, seemed unrelated and idealistic. Now it is clearer that many of these proposed additions may be part of the missing context of psychology and together turn out to be much more coherent and crucial than it seemed before. They are (a) local cultures; (b) social class and economics; and (c) epistemology. None of these are part of the typical professional psychology curriculum, and all attend to some element of context.

Local cultures. To understand the importance of local settings and local cultures, psychologists should have some exposure to the discipline of anthropology (e.g., Geertz, 2000b) with its hesitance to seek universal conclusions, its respect for diversity and culture, and its valuing of thick description. Further, as Peterson has argued elsewhere, in both our professional work and our scientific work, we need to attend more to local cultures (Geertz, 2000a; Peterson & Peterson, 1997). Peterson and Peterson (1997), in the context of epistemology, developed a detailed and sophisticated argument about how an understanding of local culture is critical to an understanding of the phenomena of professional psychology. Using this same knowledge and intellectual approach, perhaps we could come to better understand the different factions in professional psychology as cultures (Peterson, 2010).

Social class and economics. Social class is a key underexamined element of psychological phenomena (Kagan, 2012).To understand social class, one must have a basic understanding of the influence of poverty, some economics, and the misuse of power from the sociological perspective (Rorty & Mednieta, 2005). This observation is consistent with the perennial critique that professional psychology is too much about individual, intrapsychic phenomena and too little about social phenomena (e.g., Sarason, 1981, 1982). It may be obvious that programs with a child emphasis cannot understand families with diverse backgrounds and schools in poor communities without this background. However, it is just as true of adult lives. Without some expertise in economics, business, and organizations, our graduates cannot understand, let alone create and manage, mental health care delivery systems. It may be that we select students who love to attend to the nuances of interpersonal behavior or the details of statistical analysis, which guarantees that others will run our businesses and end up dictating the kinds of treatments that are offered. We cannot expect psychologists to understand the underserved, the insurance companies, the climate of health care, and the concept of parity without understanding economics and systems at some reasonable level.

Epistemology. Peterson and Peterson, (1997) show a need for a professional psychology that is grounded in its own. The next step is taken in what has come to be known as critical psychology (e.g., Gergen, 2009). Such knowledge might result in us finding a way to be a little more open to a wider variety of research methods and a little less smug about our own preferences.

So could such a new *essential* core requirement be developed in the context of accreditation? We already have cognitive and affective bases of behavior, biological bases of behavior, social bases of behavior, and others. There could easily be one more area called contextual aspects of behavior, which included, among other things, local cultures with just a taste of anthropology, social class and economics, and epistemology. Just as with the other areas, there could be a particular course, or these areas could emerge across the curriculum.

This proposal and the entire chapter has been based on the implicit if not explicit assumption that an appropriate core curriculum could, at least mostly, be contained within the areas historically identified with psychology as broad and general education (Zlotlow et al., 2011). There would, no doubt, be a different intellectual outcome, maybe a number of different outcomes, if we were starting from a blank sheet of paper, even if we restricted ourselves to carefully argued, potentially essential and common areas. Certainly, programs are already too long and too expensive. Still, noting the absence of material on context, there are many curricular elements missing. It is our observation that even when there is a tiny window of curriculum space, professionally oriented programs add another course on treatment. Similarly, research programs add another research course. The elements of context should be candidates for that small new niche.

Beyond the Core

Even filled with all this knowledge, professional psychologists cannot ignore their own vital participation in the community life and immersion in the rhythm of our various local cultures. Psychologists need to be comfortable in the world of humanities as a manifestation of local cultures, at the very least, with attention to serious fiction about people and films to understand cultural narratives, all as windows into human experience, daily life, and culturally shared visions. It is a way of being in other people's minds. The same is true of current students' level of attentiveness to the digital-visual-audio-electronic world. It is a

necessary connection to culture. Faculty are invariably worried that our students will not read at all once they graduate, even inside psychology. It would be good if they could read broadly. Beyond the scope of this chapter, Harvard has recently (2006) prepared another general education report, which included culture, ethics, the United States, reason and faith, and science and technology as areas of study. Probably, the well-educated professional psychologists should know something about these areas, too.

Although we have articulated the strengths of the essential, common-knowledge approach along with the scientific bases of practice rationale for the core curriculum, there are some drawbacks and possible risks associated with this approach: (a) limiting time for students' specialized focus whether in professional training or research; (b) forcing students to take what could sometimes turn out to be mediocre courses and/or courses about which they are ambivalent; (c) forcing faculty to teach mediocre courses and/or courses about which they are ambivalent; (d) increasing cost of programs; (e) distracting faculty from their specialized research or areas of practice. We dutifully include these concerns, but we do not believe any of them need to be so problematic as to ignore these ideas.

Conclusion

Many of the wars in psychology (e.g., scientist-practitioner versus practitioner-scholar, psychodynamic versus CBT, academics versus practitioners) appear to have to do with a lack of appreciation for the knowledge and perspectives of others. It is not just psychology's wars that are produced. Errors reflecting these differences in professional practice may appear as well. We encourage vigorous debate and discussion about what areas of education are essential and ought to be held in common in a core curriculum. Perhaps we can avoid listing all the books and articles you ought to read to "be more like me"—a clear temptation. However, one of the advantages of the common knowledge approach is that psychologists will all overlap more and, through this, feel if not that they are on the same team, that at least they are playing the same game. Peterson (2010) has discussed the discouraging, divisive, and futile professional psychology culture wars that have emerged around whether programs should produce more or less research. Just as important, high-quality broad and general education as manifested in a core curriculum will enliven that research and make it more relevant, lasting, and productive as well as raise the standards of professional work. This is an essential thing to do to embrace our common mission as psychologists.

References

ACGME Board (2007, February, 13). *Common Program Requirements: General Competencies*. Retrieved September 23, 2008, from http://www.acgme.org/Outcome/comp/GeneralCompetenciesStandards21307.pdf.

Altmaier, E. M. (2003). The history of accreditation of doctoral program in psychology. In E. M. Altmaier (Ed.), *Settings standards in graduate education: Psychology's commitment to excellence in accreditation* (pp. 39–60). Washington, DC: American Psychological Association.

American Bar Association (2008–2009). *Standards and rules of procedure for approval of law schools*. Retrieved November 6, 2008, from http://www.abanet.org/legaled/standards/standards.html

American Psychological Association, Commission on Accreditation. (2009). *Guidelines and principles for accreditation of program in professional psychology*. Washington, DC: APA. Retrieved January 3, 2013, from: http://www.apa.org/ed/accreditation/about/policies/guiding-principles.pdf

American Psychological Association, Commission on Accreditation. (2010). Public Comment Solicitation Program. Changes to IR C-16: Evaluating adherence to broad and general preparation (doctoral programs). Retrieved November 10, 2010, from: http://apaoutside.apa.org/AccredSurvey/Public/ViewComments.asp?t=085024.

American Psychological Association, Commission on Accreditation. (2011). Implementing regulation IR C-16: Evaluating adherence to broad and general preparation (doctoral programs). Retrieved January 3, 2013, from: http://www.apa.org/ed/accreditation/about/policies/implementing-guidelines.pdf

Association of American Medical Colleges (2005). *The AAMC project on the clinical education of medical students*. Washington, DC: Association of American Medical Colleges.

Bandaranayake, R. (2000). The concept and practicability of a core curriculu in basic medical education. *Medical Teacher*, 22, 560–563. doi:10.1080/01421590050175523

Barone, D. F., Maddux, J. E., & Snyder, C. R. (1997). *Social cognitive psychology: History and current domains*. New York: Plenum.

Berenbaum, H., & Shoham, V. (2011). Broad and cutting-edge training in applied psychology: A clinical science perspective. *Training and Education in Professional Psychology*, 5, (1), 22–29. doi: 10.1037/a0022603

Bruner, J. (2002). *Making stories: Law, literature, life*. New York: Farrar, Straus and Giroux.

Collins, F. L., & Callahan, J. L. (2011). Alternatives to a core curriculum to accomplish broad and general training: A scientist-practitioner perspective. *Training and Education in Professional Psychology*, 5 (1), 15–21. doi: 10.1037/a0022528

Davis-Russell, E., Forbes, W. T., Bascuas, J., & Duran, E. (1992). Ethnic diversity and the core curriculum. In R. L. Peterson, J. McHolland, R. J. Bent, E. Davis-Russell, G. E. Edwall, E. Magidson, K. Polite, D. L. Singer, & G. Stricker (Eds.), *The core curriculum in professional psychology* (pp. 147–154). Washington, DC: American Psychological Association and National Council of Schools of Professional Psychology.

Edwall, G. E., & Newton, N. (1992). Women and the core curriculum. In R. L. Peterson, J. McHolland, R. J. Bent, E. Davis-Russell, G. E. Edwall, E. Magidson, K. Polite, D. L. Singer, & G. Stricker (Eds.), *The core curriculum in professional psychology* (pp. 141–146). Washington, DC: American Psychological Association and National Council of Schools of Professional Psychology.

Fouad, N. A., Grus, C. L., Hatcher, R. L., Kaslow, N. J., Hutchings, P. S., Madson, M. B., Collins, F. L., & Crossman, R. E. (2009). Competency benchmarks: A model for understanding and measuring competence in professional psychology across training levels. *Training and Education in Professional Psychology*, 3, S5–S26. doi: 10.1037/a0015832

Geertz, C. (2000a). *Local knowledge: Further essays in interpretive anthropology* (2nd ed.) New York: Basic Books.

Geertz, C. (2000b). *The interpretation of cultures*. New York: Basic Books.

Gergen, K. J. (2009). *An invitation to social construction.* (2nd ed.). London: Sage.

Harvard Committee.(1945). *General education in a free society*. Cambridge, MA: Harvard University.

Harvard University Faculty of Arts and Sciences (2006). *Preliminary report, Task force on general education*. Cambridge, MA: Harvard University.

Kagan, J. (2007). *What is emotion? History, measures, and meanings*. New Haven & London: Yale University Press.

Kagan, J. (2012). *Psychology's ghosts: The crisis in the profession and the way back*. New Haven & London: Yale University Press.

Kaslow, N. J., Borden, K. A., Collins, F. L. Jr., Forrest, L.,Illfelder-Kaye, J., Nelson, P. D.,...Willmuth, M. E. (2004). 2002 Competencies Conference: Future directions in education and credentialing in professional psychology. *Journal of Clinical Psychology*, 60,699–712. doi: 10.1002/jclp.20016

Kunda, Z. (1999). *Social cognition: Making sense of people*. Cambridge, MA: MIT Press.

Lewis, M., Haviland-Jones, J. M., & Barrett, L. F. (Eds.) (2008). *Handbook of emotions*. (2nded.). New York: Guilford.

Liaison Committee on Medical Education (2008, June). *Functions and structure of a medical school*. Washington, D.C.: Association of American Medical Colleges.

Mahoney, M. J. (1991). *Human change processes*. New York: Basic Books.

National Conference of Bar Examiners (2013). *Multistate tests*. Retrieved September 7, 2013, from http://www.ncbex.org/multistate-tests/mbe/mbe-faq/

Neisser, U. (1976). *Cognition and reality: Principles and implications of cognitive psychology*. San Francisco: Freeman.

Nelson, P. D., & Messenger, L. C. (2003).Accreditation in psychology and public accountability. In E. M. Altmaier (Ed.), *Setting standards in graduate education: Psychology's commitment to excellence in accreditation* (pp. 7–28). Washington, DC: American Psychological Association.

Peterson, D. R., & Peterson, R. L. (1997). Ways of knowing in a profession: Toward an epistemology for the education of professional psychologists. In D. R. Peterson, *Educating professional psychologists: History and guiding conception* (pp. 191–228). Washington, DC: APA Books.

Peterson, R. L. (1992a). Social construction of the core curriculum in professional psychology. In R.L. Peterson, J. McHolland, R. J. Bent, E. Davis-Russell, G. E. Edwall, E. Magidson, K. Polite, D. L. Singer, & G. Stricker (Eds.), *The core curriculum in professional psychology* (pp. 23–36). Washington, DC: American Psychological Association & National Council of Schools of Professional Psychology.

Peterson, R. L. (1992b). The social, relational, and intellectual context of the core curriculum and the San Antonio Conference. In R.L. Peterson, J. McHolland, R. J. Bent, E. Davis-Russell, G. E. Edwall, E. Magidson, K. Polite, D. L. Singer, & G. Stricker (Eds.), *The core curriculum in professional psychology* (pp. 3–12). Washington, DC: American Psychological Association & National Council of Schools of Professional Psychology.

Peterson, R. L. (2005). 21st century education: Toward greater emphasis on context—Social, economic, and educational. *Journal of Clinical Psychology, 61*, 1121–1126. doi: 10.1002/jclp.20149

Peterson, R. L. (2010). Threats to quality in professional education and training: The politics of models, obfuscation of the clinical, and corporatization. In M. B. Kenkel & R. L. Peterson (Eds.) *Competency-based education for professional psychology* (pp. 55–66). Washington, DC: American Psychological Association.

Peterson, R. L., McHolland, J., Bent, R. J., Davis-Russell, E., Edwall, G. E., Magidson, E., Polite, K., Singer, D. L., & Stricker, G. (Eds.) (1992). *The core curriculum in professional psychology.* Washington, DC: American Psychological Association & National Council of Schools of Professional Psychology.

Peterson, R. L., Peterson, D. R., Abrams, J. C., & Stricker, G. (1997). The National Council of Schools and Programs of Professional Psychology educational model. *Professional Psychology: Research and Practice, 28*, 373–386. doi: 10.1037/1931-3918.S.1.17

Peterson, R. L., Peterson, D. R., Abrams, J, Stricker, G., & Ducheny, K. (2010). The National Council of Schools and Programs of Professional Psychology education model 2009. In M. B.Kenkel & R. L.Peterson (Eds.) *Competency-based education for professional psychology* (pp. 13–42). Washington, DC: American Psychological Association.

Peterson, R. L., Vincent, W. L., Fechter-Leggett, M. (2011). The necessary common knowledge approach to broad and general education for professional psychologist. *Training and Education in Professional Psychology.* 5, 1, 9–14. doi: 10.1037/a0022524

Raimy, V. C. (Ed). (1950). *Training in clinical psychology.* Englewood Cliffs, NJ: Prentice-Hall.

Rodolfa, E. R., Bent, R. J., Eisman, E., Nelson, P. D., Rehm, L., & Ritchie, P. (2005). A Cube model for competency development: Implications for psychology educators and regulators. *Professional Psychology, Research and Practice, 36*, 347–354. doi: 10.1037/0735-7028.36.4.347

Rorty, R., & Mednieta, E. (Ed.)(2005). *Take care of freedom and truth will take care of itself: Interviews with Richard Rorty (Cultural memory in the present).* Palo Alto, CA: Stanford University Press.

Sarason, S. B. (1981). An asocial psychology and a misdirected clinical psychology. *American Psychologist, 36,* 827–836. *doi: 10.1037/0003-066X.36.8.827*

Sarason, S. B. (1982). Individual psychology: An obstacle to understanding adulthood. In S. B. Sarason, *Psychology and social action: Selected papers* (pp. 211–231). New York: Praeger.

Schacter, D. L. (1996). *Searching for memory: The brain, the mind, and the past.* New York: Basic Books.

Stricker, G., & Trierweiler, S. J. (1995). The local clinical scientist: A bridge between science and practice. *American Psychologist, 50,* 995–1002. doi: 10.1037/1931-3918.S.1.37

Trierweiler, S. J., & Stricker, G. (1992). Research and evaluation competency: Training the local clinical scientist. In R. L. Peterson, J. McHolland, R. J. Bent, E. Davis-Russell, G. E. Edwall, E. Magidson, K. Polite, D. L. Singer, & G. Stricker (Eds.), *The core curriculum in professional psychology* (pp. 103–113). Washington, DC: American Psychological Association and National Council of Schools of Professional Psychology.

Trierweiler, S. J., & Stricker, G. (1998). *The scientific practice of professional psychology.* New York: Plenum.

Trierweiler, S. J., Stricker, G., & Peterson, R. L. (2010). The research and evaluation competency: The local clinical scientist—Review, current status, and future directions. In M. B. Kenkel & R. L. Peterson (Eds.) *Competency-based education for professional professional psychology* (pp. 125–142). Washington, DC: American Psychological Association.

Webbe, F. M., Farber, P.D., Edwall, G. E., & Edwards, K.J. (1992). Academic-scientific core curriculum. In R. L. Peterson, J. McHolland, R. J. Bent, E. Davis-Russell, G. E. Edwall, E. Magidson, K. Polite, D. L. Singer, & G. Stricker (Eds.), *The core curriculum in professional psychology* (pp. 37–42). Washington, DC: American Psychological Association and National Council of Schools of Professional Psychology.

Weiss, B. J. (1992). Toward a competency-based core curriculum in professional psychology: A critical history. In R. L. Peterson, J. McHolland, R. J. Bent, E. Davis-Russell, G. E. Edwall, E. Magidson, K. Polite, D. L. Singer, & G. Stricker (Eds.), *The core curriculum in professional psychology* (pp. 13–21). Washington, DC: American Psychological Association and National Council of Schools of Professional Psychology.

Zlotlow, S. F., Nelson, P. D., & Peterson, R. L. (2011). The history of broad and general education in scientific psychology: The foundation for professional psychology education and training. *Training and Education in Professional Psychology, 5*(1), 1–8. doi: 10.1037/a0022529

Theoretical Orientation in the Education and Training of Psychologists

Eugene W. Farber

Abstract

Clinical theories have had a significant influence on professional psychology education and training, particularly in relation to psychotherapy. This chapter explores the contributions of four major theoretical orientations to psychology education and training: g the psychodynamic, cognitive-behavioral, humanistic-existential, and systemic traditions. The parameters specified by each theoretical system for the structure, focus, and processes of education and training are illustrated, along with their theoretically grounded perspectives on domains of professional competency. Next, attention is turned to examining emerging frameworks for psychology education and training that are grounded in models of psychotherapy integration. The chapter concludes with brief reflections on the potential for clinical theories to contribute to the articulation of emerging models of education and training in evidence-based psychology practice.

Key Words: psychology education, psychology training, theoretical orientation, personality theory, psychotherapy training

A theoretically informed clinical narrative for understanding psychological life ideally anchors and guides clinical intentions and actions in psychological practice. Psychological theories "are organizational schemes, ways of arranging and shaping facts, observations and descriptions" (Mitchell, 1988, p. 15). As such, theories are foundational to the conceptualization of psychological phenomena, and by inference, theoretical learning is fundamental to psychology education and training.

Freud's (1900) seminal opus in which he postulated that dreams were symbolic representations of compromises between unacceptable unconscious wishes and the censoring functions of the mind laid the groundwork for his initial psychoanalytic theory of psychopathology and psychotherapy, ushering in the era of clinical psychological theories and schools of psychotherapy. Over the century or so since Freud's contribution, a rich diversity of theories has evolved that not only fundamentally shapes psychology practice, but also provides key contributions to psychology education and training. Central among these theories are the psychodynamic, cognitive-behavioral, humanistic-existential, and systemic traditions.

The purpose of this chapter is to explore the influence of these major theoretical orientations on professional psychology education and training, with a particular focus on psychotherapy training. The chapter begins with a broad overview of the place of theory in psychology education. The chapter then details the contributions of the psychodynamic, cognitive-behavioral, humanistic-existential, and systemic theoretical orientations in shaping psychology education and training. This includes the influence of these respective systems on the structure, focus, and processes of psychotherapy training, as well as their potential for informing emerging competency-based education and training frameworks. Finally, the chapter explores integrative perspectives on psychotherapy education and training. The chapter concludes with brief reflections on theoretically informed education and training in evidence-based practice.

Theory in Psychology Education and Training

The Value of Theoretically Informed Training

The complexity of clinical work necessitates theoretical grounding. Simply put, clinicians must be proficient in using one or more theoretical models of psychological functioning in order to understand their clients, articulate a formulation of clinical symptoms and problems, comprehend psychotherapy processes, and apply technique (Binder, 2004; Wampold, 2010). As such, facilitating the development of theoretical knowledge is a key priority in professional psychology education and training.

Most trainees first are exposed to the major orientations and systems within personality psychology through course work. In describing an example curriculum, Lomranz (1986) suggests that learning is optimized by combining didactic and experiential pedagogy. In this model, didactic teaching focuses on metatheory (e.g., the philosophical grounding of theory, theory construction, the relationship of theory to scientific inquiry, cultural dimensions, the role of biology in psychological theory), theory (e.g., structural and process elements, developmental aspects, applications in conceptualizing psychopathology), and implications of theory for psychotherapy models and practice, change processes, and research. The curriculum also teaches critical evaluation of theoretical systems, including consideration of their cultural relevance and salient values, conceptual strengths and limitations, and potential pathways for contributing to theoretical integration.

In the experiential learning portion of the curriculum outlined by Lomranz (1986), students generate personal lifelines, using principles from personality theory to characterize ways in which their psychological development has been shaped by their experiences in living. Students also conduct biographical interviews, obtaining personal background and life history information from a person and applying theoretical learning to construct an interpretive psychobiography of that person's life. Exercises such as these facilitate early practice in applying theoretical concepts and systems in tangible ways, providing opportunity for what Binder

(2004) has characterized as a critical component of professional learning: the transfer of declarative (conceptual) knowledge to procedural (practical) knowledge in order to ensure that conceptual learning does not remain "inert."

In addition to the inherent value of learning about psychological theories, grounding in theory can facilitate the development of practice skills. For instance, it has been hypothesized that trainees who learn basic psychotherapeutic helping skills in the context of a theoretical framework may experience greater self-efficacy and psychotherapeutic effectiveness than those who are not guided by a theoretical frame of reference (Hill, Stahl, & Roffman, 2007). Also, a key generic component of learning clinical case formulation involves developing skills in elaborating an inferential explanatory framework for clinical problems that takes into account predisposing factors and precipitating events (Kendjelic & Eells, 2007). Therefore, theoretical knowledge can provide a critical conceptual foundation that the trainee can draw upon in learning these clinical inference skills in case formulation.

Although the significant value conferred by psychology education and training models grounded within specific theoretical orientations is clear, certain caveats must be kept in mind in applying these approaches. For example, key considerations in professional psychology education and training models include developmental processes in the professional evolution of students along with social role relationships between teachers/supervisors and their trainees (Bernard & Goodyear, 2009). Because these crucial aspects of education and training are not necessarily incorporated as an explicit focus within training models framed by theoretical orientation, a potential danger is that they might be underemphasized, not well articulated, or simply overlooked in these training approaches. Additionally, strict adherence to an artificially narrow focus in implementing a program of education and training within a particular theoretical framework may incur the risk of limiting the knowledge base of concepts, practice skills, and competencies that trainees develop and carry forth into their professional activities. Flexibility in the design and operation of theoretically grounded psychology education and training programs can help to mitigate these potential points of concern.

The Influence of Theoretical Orientation on the Training Approach

As might be expected, empirical demonstrations have shown that theoretical orientation influences the training styles and practices of clinical teachers. For example, in one study trainees perceived variations in supervisor roles and supervision foci based on the theoretical orientation of the clinical supervisor (Putney, Worthington, & McCullough, 1992). Similarly, experienced supervisors perceived theoretically consistent differences in supervisory emphasis and approach when asked to judge videotaped supervision sessions conducted by well-known psychotherapists representing varied theoretical orientations (Goodyear, Abadie, & Efros, 1984).

At a macro level, just as psychological theories provide conceptual roadmaps for explaining personality functioning, psychological health and dysfunction, and the processes and methods for facilitating psychological change (Morris, 2003; Wampold, 2010), they also offer substantive conceptual frameworks for psychology education, particularly in the area of psychotherapy training. Specifically, a given theoretical system or orientation stipulates its own unique set of parameters for organizing the structure, focus, and processes of professional training along with training outcomes. The *structure* refers to the component activities that comprise the training experience (e.g., didactic learning, clinical supervision). The *focus* encompasses the content areas that are salient within a given theoretical model. Finally, the *processes* refer to types and applications of pedagogical tools employed, particularly in the context of clinical supervision. The structure, focus, and processes of training cohere in accordance with the theoretical narrative within which they are framed, and synergistically contribute to training outcomes relative to key professional competencies that are specified in accordance with a particular theoretical framework (see Figure 5.1).

As will be shown, examining the training structure, focus, and processes specified by the psychodynamic, cognitive-behavioral, humanistic-existential, and systemic orientations illuminates the respective contributions of each to training and education in professional psychology. Additionally, given that each of these orientations specifies theoretically anchored training outcomes, including mastery of key competencies, they can inform currently evolving, competency-based professional psychology education and training models, along with frameworks for clinical supervision (e.g., Falender & Shafranske, 2010). A competency-based perspective specifies the acquisition of knowledge, skills, and attitudes across a spectrum of foundational and functional competency domains (Donovan & Ponce, 2009; Fouad et al., 2009; Kaslow et al., 2009; Rubin et al., 2007). Foundational competencies refer to fundamental professional knowledge structures and skills sets, and include reflective practice, professionalism, scientific knowledge, relationships, individual and cultural diversity, ethical and legal standards and policies, and interdisciplinary systems competency domains (Kaslow, Dunn, & Smith, 2008; Rodolfa et al., 2005). These foundational competencies provide the grounding for the acquisition and performance of functional competencies, including assessment, intervention, consultation, research and evaluation, teaching, supervision, administration, and advocacy (Kaslow, Dunn, & Smith, 2008; Rodolfa et al., 2005). As will be seen, each major theoretical orientation

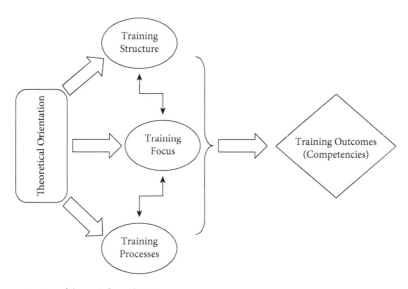

Figure 5.1. The organization of theory-informed training.

offers a particular vantage point from which to consider these foundational and functional competency domains in education and training.

Theoretically Grounded Systems of Education and Training

Of the myriad psychotherapy orientations that have appeared across the years, the psychodynamic, cognitive-behavioral, humanistic-existential, and systemic frameworks stand out as four of the most influential schools of psychotherapy theory and practice (e.g., Scaturo, 2012; Wampold, 2010). Their selection for systematic description herein reflects both their status as widely influential clinical theories, along with the substantive, longstanding, and richly textured contributions of these respective theoretical traditions and their variants to psychotherapy education and training (e.g., Bernard & Goodyear, 2009).

While the reach of these four orientations in psychology education and training is vast, they are by no means the only theoretical systems that students are apt to encounter in the course of their training. Examples of frameworks that are increasingly emphasized in psychology education and training include the biopsychosocial, neurobiological and neuropsychological, and cultural models (Calhoun & Craighead, 2006; Hernández, 2008; Larkin, 2009; Melchert, 2007). At present, however, the psychodynamic, cognitive-behavioral, humanistic-existential, and systemic theories retain the lion's share of influence in psychology education and training among theory-based models. Available survey data, while limited in breadth and scope, generally supports this view. For instance, one survey of American Psychological Association (APA)-accredited counseling psychology programs revealed that, as characterized by training directors, 43% of faculty subscribed to a cognitive or cognitive-behavioral orientation, 28% humanistic, 21% systemic, 19% psychodynamic, and 3% behavioral (Norcross, Evans, & Ellis, 2010). Additional survey research revealed that, among APA-accredited counseling psychology and predoctoral internship programs, respectively, 89% and 50% offered systemic training, 77% and 88% offered cognitive-behavioral training, 69% and 79% offered psychodynamic training, 69% and 43% offered humanistic-existential training, and 39% and 19% offered behavioral training (Lampropoulos & Dixon, 2007). Compellingly, this study revealed a favorable view of training in psychotherapy integration among the training programs surveyed.

This finding is consistent with survey data showing that 74% of internship directors of predoctoral psychology internship programs characterized their programs as eclectic, meaning that they incorporated varying configurations of the behavioral/cognitive-behavioral, psychodynamic, humanistic, and systemic orientations into their training curricula (Stedman, Hatch, & Schoenfeld, 2007).

Collectively, these survey findings illustrate that the psychodynamic, cognitive-behavioral, humanistic-existential, and systemic theoretical orientations are well represented in psychology education and training. What follows is a detailed illustration of their influence in the training arena. Each of these respective systems is defined by a conceptually rich theoretical tradition with a highly textured history and storied intellectual lineage. The nuance, complexity, and breadth of these approaches and their variants defy simple encapsulation. Yet, in order to provide a reference point for framing the discussion that follows, basic overarching concepts from each are summarized briefly in Table 5.1.

Psychodynamic Orientation

As conveyed in Table 5.1, psychodynamic inquiry concerns itself broadly with the influence of dynamically (motivationally) unconscious psychological phenomena on conscious life, the relationship between past and current experience (developmental framework), and the interplay between internal symbolic fantasy representations and engagements with the world of events and interpersonal relationships (for review, see Mitchell & Black, 1995). Across the diverse spectrum of psychodynamic ideas, a key issue involves the relationship of the intrapsychic world to actual encounters and events, including the degree to which theory and practice should be centered on the internal world of the individual or on the inter-relationships between intrapsychic life and the world of events and relationships (Mitchell, 2000; Mitchell & Black, 1995). The emphasis of contemporary relational and intersubjective psychodynamic models on understanding the inter-relationships of intrapsychic and interpersonal worlds has implications not only for the evolution of psychodynamically oriented practice, but also for the development of psychodynamically informed training (Yerushalmi, 1994). As such, as psychodynamic theory has developed and changed, so has its training emphasis.

Training structure. As the earliest of the major theoretical orientations, the psychodynamic tradition also was the first to articulate a formal training

Table 5.1. Basic Premises of Major Theoretical Orientations

Theory	Major Strands	Theory of Personality	Theory of Psychopathology	Theory of Change
Psychodynamic	Drive/ structure	Psychological life is organized by activities to modulate expression of unconscious impulses in accordance with both reality-oriented and socially proscribed requirements for adaptation	Symptoms reflect unresolved unconscious conflicts surrounding consciously unacceptable impulses, wishes, and motivations	Promote awareness and working through of unconscious conflicts
	Object relations/ relational	Personality functioning is organized by internalized cognitive-affective representations of relationships and interpersonal experience	Symptoms arise from maladaptive relational patterns and corresponding conflictual internalized representations of relationships	Use the psychotherapy relationship to promote internalization of more flexible representations of relationships and expand relational possibilities
Cognitive-behavioral	Cognitive	Psychological adaptation is shaped by cognitive templates through which environmental events are processed and understood	Symptoms reflect overly narrow, inflexible cognitive processing and interpretation of distressing events	Collaboratively challenge and encourage re-evaluation of inflexible beliefs and interpretations of distressing events
	Behavioral	Personality is shaped by environmental contingencies, including conditioning and reinforcement patterns	Symptoms arise and are sustained by patterns of conditioning and reinforcement	Alter environmental contingencies that sustain problematic behavior, including stimulus response patterns and reinforcers
Humanistic-existential	Humanistic	Psychological functioning is propelled by intentionality, values, and striving to actualize potentialities	Symptoms arise from perceived inconsistencies between the self-concept and experience and/or a thwarting of authentic self-expression	Use the psychotherapy relationship to heighten experiential awareness, promote authenticity of experiencing, and facilitate expression of potentialities
	Existential	Experience is organized by tension between basic psychological wishes and key existential realities	Symptoms spring from conflicts surrounding existential dilemmas in living	Engage a process of phenomenological self-reflection aimed at overcoming resistances to encountering existential conflicts
Systemic	Family systems	Individual functioning is embedded within a larger systemic context of reciprocal interaction patterns sustained by processes of circular causality	Symptoms emerge in the context of reciprocal relationship processes that characterize systemic functioning	Intervene at the systemic level to change reciprocal interaction patterns that sustain symptoms
	Social constructionist	Individual identity emerges from co-constructed shared narrative meaning systems elaborated in the context of social interchange	Symptoms become defined as such through the narrative context from which their meaning is co-constructed	Use therapeutic dialogue to explore jointly the meaning of symptoms and mutually develop alternative meaning systems

structure. While psychoanalytic training began in accordance with what was essentially a psychotherapy master and apprentice framework, over time the training structure was formalized within psychoanalytic institutes and included the triad of didactic learning focusing on both theory and clinical technique, personal psychotherapy (self-analysis or training analysis), and supervised clinical experience (Hyman, 2008). Although much of psychodynamically oriented psychotherapy training within professional psychology does not necessarily adhere to this formal institutional framework, the basic structure of training encompasses a combination of didactic learning, supervision, and encouragement to pursue personal psychotherapy as an experiential learning process (Strupp, Butler, & Rosser, 1988).

Training focus. Consistent with the structure of psychodynamic training, the training focus centers on three main strands of emphasis. One such strand involves the promotion of theoretical and clinical knowledge within a psychodynamic framework, which occurs mostly through formal didactic teaching and clinical supervision. A second major strand of training focuses on understanding psychodynamic processes in the context of the clinical encounter and is provided primarily in the context of clinical supervision. Engendering self-awareness and self-knowledge is a third major focus of psychodynamic training, reflected both in the clinical supervision process and in the credence given to personal psychotherapy/analysis as a component of training. In a broad sense, the emphasis on personal psychotherapy for the trainee reflects the theoretically informed value placed within the psychodynamic tradition on self-awareness and self-care as important ingredients of professional development (McWilliams, 2004). Personal psychotherapy provides both experiential learning about the psychodynamic psychotherapy process and opportunity for learning about the self. Inclusion of personal analysis as a part of traditional psychoanalytic training originated with the idea that the clinician was a psychotherapeutic instrument for whom self-awareness was essential to psychotherapeutic success. In the classical drive/structure framework, the personal analysis provided an arena within which the analyst in training could learn to reduce the impingements of countertransference on the psychoanalytic process. Adherents to contemporary relational psychodynamic perspectives regard personal psychotherapy as a training resource for learning to utilize self-knowledge to understand the meaning of countertransference reactions as they pertain to the qualities of the therapeutic relationship, as well as the client's psychological world.

Training processes. As noted earlier, the processes that comprise theoretically informed training are particularly evident in the clinical supervision approach of a given theoretical orientation. As such, key processes within psychodynamic training can be illuminated through consideration of its supervision framework. Clinical supervision, which has come to be regarded as the "signature pedagogy" for psychotherapy training (Goodyear, 2007; Watkins, 2011), has its origins as a training innovation in the psychodynamic tradition, with psychodynamic thought having a profound influence on both the conceptualization and practice of the supervisory process (Bernard & Goodyear, 2009; Hess, 2008; Watkins, 2011).

The processes of psychodynamic supervision aim to facilitate integration by the trainee of self, experience, and theoretical knowledge (Szecsödy, 2008). Therefore the supervisory process yields opportunities for the trainee to discuss theoretical concepts and experientially apply them in the context of learning to identify, understand, work with, and communicate about a client's unconscious psychological processes, the symbolic meaning of symptoms, defense mechanisms, relational representations, and the psychotherapy relationship (including transference/countertransference dynamics) (Hyman, 2008; Sarnat, 2012).

In addition to facilitating learning of the technical aspects of working with a client, the supervisory process involves examining the triadic inter-relationships between the psychological dynamics of the client, trainee, and supervisor, as well as the influences of the training setting (Bernard & Goodyear, 2009; Ekstein & Wallerstein, 1972; Frawley-O'Dea & Sarnat, 2001; Hyman, 2008; Sarnat, in press; Szecsödy, 2008). One well-known example is a focus on parallel process, in which patterns in the relationship between the trainee and client are mirrored in the supervisor-supervisee relationship. Psychodynamic psychotherapy supervisors view the occurrence of parallel process as a teachable moment that provides an opportunity for the trainee to integrate conceptual and experiential learning in working with the dynamic processes of the psychotherapy relationship (Bernard & Goodyear, 2009; Hyman, 2008; Sarnat, 2012). While the focus on triadic relationships in the supervisory process is an innovation of the psychodynamic tradition, this concept has been widely adopted across a range of supervision approaches and paradigms (Watkins, 2011).

In general, psychodynamic conceptualizations of the supervisor-trainee dyad have changed with the evolution of the theory. The assumptions of the classical psychoanalytic model informed a view of the supervisor as an expert teacher capable of objective oversight of the work of the trainee. In contrast, recent relational dynamic perspectives have contributed to the view that, while the supervisor retains clear responsibility for the teaching role and its attendant responsibilities, the supervisory relationship is characterized by the reciprocal intersubjective processes to which both the supervisor and supervisee contribute (Frawley-O'Dea & Sarnat, 2001; Sarnat, 2012). Within this relational dynamic framework, attending to the supervisory relationship is critical to the process of conducting clinical supervision.

Key competency domains emphasized. Just as the theoretical approach informs the structure, focus, and processes of training, it also influences the competency domains that are prioritized in education and training. In reflecting on what might constitute the criteria for evaluating psychodynamic competency, Tuckett and colleagues (Tuckett, 2005; Junkers, Tuckett, & Zachrisson, 2008) proposed three general interrelated "frames" through which clinical competence might be evaluated. The first of these is the participant-observational frame, which refers to the clinician's capacity simultaneously to remain engaged in the psychotherapy process while also sitting with and being curious about the client's experiential world in a reflective rather than reactive way. The second is the conceptual frame, which involves capacities for formulating credible and reasoned understandings of the unconscious meaning of clinical material expressed by the client and psychotherapy process in accordance with a psychodynamic framework for comprehending the clinical situation. Finally, the interventional frame refers to the capacity to formulate and implement psychotherapeutic strategies in a manner that maintains coherence with both the psychotherapist's position as a participant-observer and conceptual understanding of the client and clinical situation.

Guided by these competency "frames," Sarnat (2010) explored the contributions of psychodynamic training, particularly supervision, to cultivating foundational and functional competencies (e.g., Kaslow, Dunn, & Smith, 2008; Rodolfa et al., 2005). Sarnat (2010) proposes that the foundational competency domains of reflective practice and relationships are pertinent to the participant-observational frame, while the functional competencies of assessment and intervention are relevant to the conceptual and interventional frames.

Importantly, Sarnat (2010) illustrates the ways in which a psychodynamic framework can inform what it means to facilitate a process of competency-based training. For example, she points out that relationship competency within a relational psychodynamic perspective is not simply a set of skills for managing the relational exigencies of the psychodynamic psychotherapy situation, but rather is part and parcel of therapeutic action and change. Given the centrality of relationships in the model, a relational psychodynamic training approach provides a rich framework for cultivating competency in the use of the psychotherapy relationship within a participant observational frame as a principal vehicle of psychotherapeutic action. Similarly, facilitating reflective practice competency involves guiding the trainee in learning to "bear, observe, think about, and make psychotherapeutic use of one's own emotional, bodily, and fantasy experiences when in interaction with a client" (Sarnat, 2010, p. 23). Within a psychodynamic framework, training in assessment as a functional competency domain emphasizes the understanding of the multilayered contributions to problems and symptoms of conflictual conscious and unconscious psychological processes, internal working models of relationships, interpersonal life, and adaptive functions (defenses). Therapist use of experiential responses to the client also is a key element of training aimed at promoting assessment and case conceptualization competencies. Finally, the focus of psychodynamic training relative to the functional competency area of intervention involves both an emphasis on interpretive skills and on use of the relationship to engender psychotherapeutic change and healing (Sarnat, 2010).

Cognitive-Behavioral Orientation

The cognitive-behavioral orientation (see Table 5.1) emerged from efforts to combine human information-processing concepts with those from behavioral psychology, including the stimulus-response model of classical conditioning and the stimulus-response-consequence paradigm of operant conditioning, creating a stimulus-organism-response-consequence paradigm for conceptualizing psychotherapy (Goldfried, 2003). The evolution of ideas such as Bandura's (1986) social-cognitive theory further contributed to an emphasis on organismic cognitive mediational phenomena and the person-environment relationship, with a resulting integration of a cognitive information processing framework with behavioral concepts under the broad rubric of cognitive-behavioral psychotherapy (Goldfried, 2003; Steiman & Dobson, 2002). These approaches assume that psychopathology develops and is maintained by both characteristic thought patterns and behavioral responses to environmental events, though may vary in their relative emphasis on clinical intervention at the level of thought patterns and/or behavior (e.g., Beck, Rush, Shaw, & Emery, 1979; Steiman & Dobson, 2002). More recently, increasing attention has been given to inter-relationships between emotional processes and meaning systems within the cognitive-behavioral psychotherapy framework (Burum & Goldfried, 2007; Goldfried, 2003).

Training structure. The structure of cognitive-behavioral training can be conceived broadly as being comprised of didactic instruction, experiential learning activities, and supervised clinical practice experiences (Friedberg, Gorman, & Beidel, 2009; Rakovshik & McManus, 2010). Didactic instruction provides opportunities for theoretical learning, as well as developing skills in case formulation and clinical technique. This may include expert demonstrations of specific psychotherapeutic skill sets. Experiential learning is aimed at providing practice in the use of cognitive-behavioral principles, including the application of theory to the development of clinical case formulations and the use of cognitive-behavioral techniques. Experiential training may involve practice exercises, role play, and/or small group discussions. Clinical supervision is a critical component of training, providing opportunities for ongoing monitoring and feedback in the clinical applications of cognitive-behavioral theory and technique (Friedberg et al., 2009; Rakovshik & McManus, 2010).

Training focus. Broadly speaking, cognitive-behavioral psychotherapy training focuses on the development of declarative, procedural, and self-reflective capacities (Friedberg et al., 2009; Friedberg, Mahr, & Mahr, 2010). The declarative focus involves gaining knowledge of learning theory and cognitive information-processing models and their empirical underpinnings, as well as the principles of cognitive-behavioral psychotherapy that derive from these theoretical concepts. This is accomplished primarily through didactic instruction. The procedural focus involves the application of cognitive-behavioral concepts and principles to clinical case formulation and both the core and advanced skills that define cognitive-behavioral psychotherapy intervention (e.g., agenda setting, client self-monitoring, cognitive restructuring, managing homework, Socratic dialogue, behavioral practice). The procedural focus integrates declarative learning with experiential learning, with supervision providing a key modality for this aspect of training. The self-reflective focus emphasizes self-evaluation and self-monitoring skills in implementing the cognitive-behavioral model, including evaluating the effectiveness and impact of one's psychotherapeutic actions. Among the unique innovations of cognitive-behavioral training in this regard is its emphasis on systematic assessment and monitoring of trainee progress in learning the approach, including the use of performance evaluation measures to evaluate trainee adherence and fidelity to the model (Friedberg et al., 2009; Friedberg et al., 2010; Rosenbaum & Ronen, 1998; Sudak, Beck, & Wright, 2003).

Training processes. The process of cognitive-behavioral psychotherapy training mirrors that of the practice approach, with an overarching framework that tends to be systematic and linear. This is reflected particularly in the clinical supervision approach, which incorporates activities analogous to those that might characterize a typical session of cognitive-behavioral psychotherapy (Reiser & Milne, 2012; Rosenbaum & Ronen, 1998). For instance, in summarizing the literature in this area, Reiser and Milne (2012) note that a supervision meeting typically includes checking in and recapping topics covered in the previous meeting, outlining and systematically moving through an agenda for the current meeting, summarizing the activities of the supervision session, setting homework tasks, and receiving feedback.

In describing the supervisory process in detail, Rosenbaum and Ronen (1998) identify key parallels between cognitive-behavioral psychotherapy and the processes of supervision. For example, supervisory attention to cognitive constructions of the trainee parallels the focus in psychotherapy on the client's cognitions. Working in a supportive fashion, the supervisor uses Socratic questioning, which is a line of inquiry designed to focus the trainee on relevant clinical material and encourage systematic evaluation of evidence for clinical assumptions about the client. This strategy facilitates clinical reflection and guides trainee efforts in formulating and implementing a psychotherapeutic intervention strategy. Guided discovery is used to help trainees evaluate how they process information about their clients, providing opportunities to gain awareness of and reflect on their cognitive constructions of clients, including potential cognitive distortions that might compromise their understanding of client problems. Similar to the psychotherapy approach, cognitive-behavioral supervision also focuses on defining specific training goals along with plans and strategies for attaining them. Progress toward meeting these training goals is monitored continually in supervision. In addition, like in cognitive-behavioral psychotherapy, the supervisory process emphasizes trainee skills practice and experiential learning via role playing, behavioral rehearsal, and/or imagery exercises. Homework also is assigned, with the aim of continuing and reinforcing the learning process outside of supervision sessions. The supervisory process is collaborative, with the goals and focus agreed upon by both supervisor and trainee in accordance with the unique experiences and training needs of the supervisee. Collectively, these processes aim to facilitate the trainee's assimilation of a general cognitive-behavioral clinical frame, promote proficiency in the application of technique, and encourage clinical innovation and creativity while remaining firmly grounded within the theoretical and practical foundations of the cognitive-behavioral psychotherapy tradition (Rosenbaum & Ronen, 1998).

Key competency domains emphasized. In considering cognitive-behavioral psychotherapy training outcomes, Friedberg and colleagues (2010) have conceptualized three broad competency domains. The first involves the acquisition of declarative or factual knowledge of cognitive-behavioral theory, research, and technique. The second competency domain encompasses procedural knowledge required for effective practice. For instance, emphasis is placed on cultivating basic skills in cognitive-behavioral case formulation and the application of theory to practice, a capacity to cultivate a collaborative psychotherapy alliance, psychotherapeutic monitoring skills, an ability to promote client adherence to the model, and effectively using cognitive-behavioral techniques to maximize progress and change (Sudak et al., 2003). The final competency domain highlighted by Friedberg and colleagues (2010) is self-reflection, which refers to the capacity to effectively monitor, understand, and evaluate one's psychotherapeutic actions and their clinical impact.

In a recent account of the contributions of cognitive-behavioral psychotherapy supervision to competency-based professional psychology training, Newman (2010) has outlined several foundational competency domains that are particularly salient within the cognitive-behavioral training approach. First, relative to promoting competency in scientific knowledge, cognitive-behavioral training and supervision focus on the trainee's capacities to utilize and critically evaluate the scientific research as a part of informed practice. Relatedly, scientific hypothesis testing models are brought to bear to understand and evaluate clinical phenomena as they unfold in the course of psychotherapy. Cognitive-behavioral psychotherapy training and supervision also emphasize relationships competency via a focus on psychotherapist skills in fostering a productive and collaborative therapeutic alliance (Newman, 2010; Sudak et al., 2003). Additionally, the development of individual and cultural diversity competency in the application of cognitive-behavioral intervention with diverse populations increasingly is recognized as an important training priority (Friedberg et al., 2009; Newman, 2010). Finally, Newman (2010) explores the contributions of a cognitive-behavioral framework for promoting trainee competency in working within interdisciplinary systems, highlighting expanding opportunities for trainees to participate as members of interdisciplinary health care teams.

In discussing contributions of cognitive-behavioral training and supervision to the development of functional competencies, Newman (2010) characterizes specific intervention competencies cultivated in training, including proficiency in use of guided discovery, setting up opportunities to practice new behaviors, and conducting relaxation exercises. Training in intervention competency also focuses on psychotherapist self-monitoring processes and adopting a directive, yet collaborative stance within the psychotherapy relationships (Friedberg et al., 2010; Newman, 2010). Importantly, cognitive-behavioral psychotherapy training emphasizes an essential linkage of assessment and intervention competency to research/evaluation competency. Accordingly, Newman (2010) suggests that "[a]n overarching aspect of becoming an effective, competent CBT therapist is learning how to think like an empiricist" (p. 14).

Humanistic-Existential Orientation

As depicted in Table 5.1, the humanistic-existential orientation draws its theoretical framework from the cross-fertilization of the existential and humanistic psychology traditions (Burston, 2003; Cain, 2002; Schneider & Krug, 2010). The humanistic strands of the approach emphasize a motivational theory of human growth, including the psychological factors that facilitate or hinder intrinsic strivings toward fulfillment of individual potentialities. Existential theory focuses on elucidating the basic characteristics of the human condition and their impact on psychological experience, including key psychological dilemmas associated with specific givens of existence, such as the tension between the finiteness of life as an existential reality and the human wish to perpetuate existence. The humanistic and existential traditions share an individualized, contextual, and holistic approach to conceptualizing psychological life, and emphasize the role of personal agency, authenticity, and responsibility in living. A range of psychotherapies are represented under the humanistic-existential umbrella that share common emphases on experiential learning as the primary mechanism for psychological growth, and on the facilitative qualities of the psychotherapist's relational stance that are presumed to create the conditions for a client's experiential self-exploration and growth.

Training structure. Didactic instruction and clinical supervision anchor humanistic-existential psychotherapy training. A distinctive characteristic of the humanistic-existential training structure is that conceptual and technical learning activities, both in the classroom and in clinical supervision, typically incorporate an experiential learning component (Farber, 2010; Greenberg & Goldman, 1988). For example, experiential demonstration exercises frequently accompany didactic discussion of humanistic-existential principles to provide the trainee with a felt sense for a particular concept or technique. While psychotherapy is not a requirement of training per se, it is valued as a resource for cultivating trainee self-awareness and contributing to overall professional development.

Training focus. The training approach focuses broadly on the dual tasks of developing psychotherapeutic skills that promote experiential awareness and cultivating the relational facilitative conditions of psychotherapeutic change (Farber, 2010). At the core of the experiential focus of training is mastering the skill of illuminating what a client is experiencing in a present-oriented way. Applications of this training emphasis tend to vary across the range of humanistic-existential psychotherapies. For instance, within the Gestalt tradition, a classic experiential training exercise might combine a brief didactic overview of the awareness construct with an awareness "experiment" designed to connect didactic and experiential learning as well as enhance the trainee's self-awareness skills (e.g., Enright, 1970). In existential psychotherapy training, the supervisor tends to focus on systematic use of phenomenological concepts and methods in helping the trainee learn to facilitate the process of articulating

the client's experiential world (e.g., Adams, 2009). Informed by humanistic-existential assumptions regarding the role of the psychotherapy relationship in the change process, training also focuses on relational skills, including genuineness, respect, empathy, presence, and collaboration (Farber, 2012). In a parallel way, clinical supervision incorporates a focus on the supervisory relationship both to facilitate understanding of the client and to provide a supportive relational space within which trainee learning can unfold (Barnett, 2009; Farber, 2010; Pack, 2009). Attention also is given to the development of the person of the psychotherapist in both classroom training activities and clinical supervision of case material.

Training processes. In keeping with the ideographic and contextual emphases of the humanistic-existential tradition, training processes are individualized in accordance with the unique needs, experiences, and circumstances of the trainee. Trainees are encouraged to develop their psychotherapeutic styles to be congruent with their unique ways of being.

A fundamental assumption of the humanistic-existential framework is that experiencing informs understanding (Cooper, 2007; Pos & Greenberg, 2007; Schneider & Krug, 2010). A key training process that follows from this assumption involves attending to the experiential sphere. For instance, in focusing on conceptual and technical aspects of psychotherapy, the supervisor may combine informational instruction with exercises that help the trainee connect abstract ideas to experience. Similarly, in providing guidance in case formulation, the supervisor may encourage the trainee to attend to the experience of being with the client and promote attunement to the client's moment-to-moment here and now verbal and nonverbal expressions.

Relational processes in the context of supervision tend to mirror the humanistic-existential psychotherapy framework for working with clients. As such, the supervisor demonstrates a basic respect for the trainee, is collegial and collaborative, and models genuineness, acceptance, and presence in the supervisory relationship in order to create an environment that encourages professional growth and development (Farber, 2012; Pack, 2009; Patterson, 1983). Not only is this supervisory stance regarded as essential to facilitating the training process, in parallel fashion it also provides the trainee with an experiential referent to the ways in which the psychotherapy relationship can be facilitative of client growth.

A hallmark of the humanistic-existential training process is the high degree of emphasis given to the development of the person of the psychotherapist (Farber, 2010). This focus reflects the value placed on self-awareness and use of self as an instrument of change. Supervision encourages self-reflection and self-understanding as tools for seeing the client as clearly as possible and for ensuring that the trainee engages the psychotherapeutic process in a manner that is squarely in the service of the client. Self-knowledge and self-awareness also are presumed to undergird the capacities for authenticity and congruence in working with clients.

Key competency domains emphasized. A valuing and respectful attitude toward the client, skill in guiding a process of illuminating the client's experiential world, and the capacity to create relational conditions facilitative of the client's growth define good psychotherapy from a humanistic-existential psychotherapy perspective (Cooper, 2007). These three dimensions of good psychotherapy assume professional competence in specific foundational and functional competency domains that Farber (2010) identified as particularly salient in humanistic-existential education and training.

For example, consistent with its values-oriented theoretical foundations (Cooper, 2007), humanistic-existential training is anchored by an ethical sensibility, reflected by cultivating a commitment among trainees to a genuinely valuing and respectful stance in working with clients. Additionally, an emphasis on foundational ethical competency is a thread that informs the person of the psychotherapist training focus, which encourages honest self-appraisal in trainees, including evaluation of how their values and ethical responsibilities inform their clinical work and evolving professional identities (Farber, 2012).

Proficiency in facilitating experiential awareness with clients in the psychotherapy process presupposes reflective practice competency (Farber, 2010). As such, humanistic-existential psychotherapy training places a priority on cultivating trainee capacities for self-reflection, self-monitoring, and self-awareness, each of which is a component of reflective practice. These capacities are essential to the psychotherapist's efforts to grasp the client's experiential world, maintain awareness of potential biases and assumptions that might impede understanding of the client, and engage with the client's experience without losing sight of the experiential boundary between the self of the psychotherapist and the client.

Humanistic-existential training relative to the functional competency domains of assessment and intervention similarly emphasizes experiential inquiry skills (Farber, 2010). Specifically, assessment training focuses on developing skills in understanding a client's phenomenal experiential world and formulating a phenomenological description of that client's experiences within a whole person framework. With regard to intervention competency, the trainee learns to formulate decisions regarding how best to facilitate change in the client, drawing upon the conceptualization gleaned from the assessment process and applying specific skill sets aimed at engaging the client in experiential self-exploration. These intervention activities may include techniques to amplify awareness and explore salient psychological wishes and intentions, avoidance patterns, or experiential conflicts.

Finally, given the humanistic-existential emphasis on the psychotherapy relationship as facilitative of change, a focus on the foundational competency domain of relationships is a central activity of training. In particular, relational capacities such as authenticity, engaged presence, genuineness, and collaboration are highlighted, all of which are assumed to contribute to the facilitative conditions for psychotherapeutic change (Farber, 2010). The process-experiential focus of training also means that the supervisory relationship itself provides a vehicle for the trainee's development of relationships competency (Farber, 2012).

Systemic Orientation

The remarkable diversity of psychotherapies that fall under the rubric of the systemic orientation share a common emphasis on the elaboration of relational structures and processes that characterize the contextual organization of behavior within human systems, particularly family systems (for review, see Flaskas, 2010; 2011). Accordingly, as summarized in Table 5.1, linear cause-effect conceptualizations of individuals' behavior within a system give way to an appreciation for circular patterns of reciprocal interaction and mutual influence that constitute the emergent features of the system as a whole. As family systems theory has evolved, emphasis has shifted from a focus on discerning the behavior of the system, including its presumably distinctive structural and process dimensions, to an increasingly intersubjective framework for conceptualizing the system (Flaskas, 2011). According to this perspective, systemic functioning is understood in the context of socially constructed narrative meaning frameworks.

The psychotherapist's role is less one of entering the system in order to bring about change and more one of engaging in a collaborative dialogue with the family with the intent to co-construct an understanding of the problem along with alternative narratives for characterizing the system (Andersen, 1991; Anderson & Goolishian, 1992; Flaskas, 2011; Hoffman, 1992). Given the diversity of family therapy models, some of which have been informed by the psychodynamic, cognitive-behavioral, and humanistic-existential orientations, it is not possible to characterize the training structure, focus, and processes of these approaches in a uniform way. The description that follows, therefore, highlights general systemic principles in training and supervision.

Training structure. Like most theoretically informed training models, systemic training is comprised primarily of didactic instruction and clinical supervision. Supervision typically includes a combination of didactic and applied clinical activities (Habib, 2011; Styczynski & Greenberg, 2008). In addition to using videotaped recordings of trainee sessions, family therapy is well known for innovation in the use of live supervision, wherein the trainee meets with a family while the supervisor and trainee peers observe from behind a one-way mirror (Bernard & Goodyear, 2009). Within this arrangement, the supervisor provides real-time input by calling the trainee with suggestions or asking the trainee to leave the session briefly for consultation.

Training focus. The unique focus of systemic training is on learning to think conceptually about the system as the entity with which the psychotherapist engages, identify the emergent properties that define a family as a system, and intervene at the level of the system. These foci are particularly apparent in family therapy supervision (Styczynski & Greenberg, 2008). Training promotes several family therapy intervention proficiencies, including managing the moment-to-moment process of family sessions, developing tolerance and skill in working with family conflict, learning to animate interventions with an emotional tone that helps advance psychotherapeutic goals, and cultivating a broad intervention repertoire for intervening at the level of the family system. In some systemic models, trainees are encouraged to be curious about personal discovery regarding their families of origin (Bernard & Goodyear, 2009; Habib, 2011). Additionally, narrative processes relative to trainee-family interactions and trainee-supervisor interactions are a key focus in social constructionist supervision (Ungar, 2006). Finally, systemic training emphasizes

understanding culture and diversity in working with families (Fraenkel & Pinsof, 2001; Styczynski & Greenberg, 2008).

Training processes. Like each of the theory based training models described thus far, systemic training processes mirror the theory and practice aspects of family therapy and are illustrated most vividly in the supervision approach. Systemic supervisors tend to be active and directive, and in some instances even engage directly with families as a part of the training process. Some examples include supervisor consultation interviews with the family with the trainee present, appearances by the supervisor in the therapy room during live supervision, use of reflecting teams that discuss their impressions of the family while the family observes them, and supervisor-supervisee co-therapy with families (Celano, Smith, & Kaslow, 2010; Kaslow, Celano, & Stanton, 2005; Nutt & Stanton, 2008; Styczynski & Greenberg, 2008). It also is common for several trainees to observe and participate in discussions of either live or videotaped sessions. In these respects, the systemic training process unfolds in a relatively "public" way (Styczynski & Greenberg, 2008), requiring the supervisor to be especially tactful when giving potentially challenging feedback to trainees. Systemic supervisors consider the developmental level and clinical experience of their trainees in determining the training and supervisory parameters along a continuum ranging from basic conceptual and practice skills to advanced family formulation and intervention approaches (Styczynski & Greenberg, 2008).

Among the frequently highlighted dimensions of the systemic supervisory process is the attention given to inter-relationships among the family system, the family psychotherapist system, and the supervisory system (Bernard & Goodyear, 2009; Roberts, Winek, & Mulgrew, 1999). The concept of isomorphism, which has been conceptualized in varying ways in the family therapy training literature (White & Russell, 1997), may be utilized to illustrate parallel inter-relational patterns that may be observed across the family and supervisory systems. This use of the isomorphism concept is similar to the psychodynamic idea of parallel process.

Training informed by the social constructionist strands of the systemic orientation does not emphasize the directive stance that typifies traditional systemic training. Rather, the supervisor and trainee engage in a dialogue aimed at co-constructing an understanding of how best to conceptualize and address the concerns of the family in psychotherapy. The supervisory conversation also yields a co-construction of the trainee's developing narrative of self as a professional. As such, the supervisory relationship becomes a vehicle through which the trainee can construct a professional identity (Ungar, 2006).

Key competency domains emphasized. Articulating competencies in family psychology along with a competency-based framework for family psychology education and training is an important emerging priority (Celano et al., 2010; Kaslow et al., 2005; Nelson et al., 2007; Nutt & Stanton, 2008). In reflecting on a competency-based approach to systemic training, Celano and colleagues (2010) have outlined several essential components of systemic couple and family intervention that are a focus of the training process. First, the clinician must be able to apply a systemic epistemology to the formulation of clinical problems, which entails conceptualizing clinical phenomena in the context of a relational system. The clinician also must be skilled at forging systemic alliances with individuals within a family system, specific subsystems, and finally, the system as a whole. Knowledge of how current problematic systemic configurations might replicate relational patterns expressed across generations of the family of origin is a critical component of both systemic problem formulation and intervention. Interventions that reframe the family's view of the problem, increase family cohesion and communication, support the system's capacity to manage family conflict, and boost parenting skills are key components of a clinical repertoire for managing and enhancing interaction patterns within a family system. Finally, effective systemic practice requires both knowledge and skill in applying evidence-based principles in couple and family psychotherapy.

Reflective practice, ethical and legal standards, and individual/cultural diversity are the foundational competency domains that Celano and colleagues (2010) highlight as especially salient in the context of systemic training. For example, a supervisory focus with trainees on the use of reflective processes to guide clinical decision making in family work, evaluate co-therapy processes and roles, and cultivate attunement to possible influences of personal family-of-origin dynamics on clinical appraisals and intervention with families all emphasize reflective practice competency (Celano et al., 2010). In conducting systemic work, trainees must learn to navigate complex issues related to confidentiality boundaries, informed consent, privileged communication, the management of family secrets, the nature of psychotherapist alignments with each individual in a system, and such clinical challenges as family violence and divorce (Celano et al., 2010; Kaslow et al., 2005). As such, attention to ethical and legal standards is highly prioritized in systemic training. Systemic trainees also must gain proficiency in understanding the expression of cultural factors in family system functioning, family role definitions, and family perceptions of problems and potential solutions. Additionally, trainees need to learn how to assess the impact on family dynamics of differing attitudes and beliefs across generations within a family system regarding culture and diversity themes (Celano et al., 2010). For these reasons, systemic training invests heavily in the development of individual and cultural diversity competency (Celano et al., 2010; Kaslow et al., 2005; Nelson et al., 2007).

Assessment, intervention, and consultation competencies are cultivated using a systemic lens with regard to functional competency domains (Celano et al., 2010; Kaslow et al., 2005). For instance, assessment training highlights the importance of contextualizing the evaluation of clinical problems at multiple levels of family functioning, including individual, relational, and larger systemic levels. Development of intervention competency centers on the trainee's emerging capacity to intervene at the level of the system rather than relying solely on individual-level psychotherapy techniques. Finally, given the systemic view that family functioning is influenced by multiple systems, consultation and interprofessional collaboration also is a key functional competency domain emphasized in systemic training.

Integrative Trends in Education and Training

Even as the major theoretical systems described in this chapter evolved over the course of the 20th century as distinct frameworks for understanding psychological life, personality psychologists sought pathways for conceptual integration. Examples are seen in the work of Allport (1955) and Murray (1938). Contemporary theorists within personality psychology continue to advance this integrative tradition (e.g., Mayer, 2005). In psychotherapy circles, increasing recognition that no single theoretical system is sufficient for explaining the vast complexity and breadth of human psychological functioning yields a growing movement toward psychotherapy integration that reflects an emerging "... *zeitgeist* of informed pluralism" (Norcross, 2005, p. 4). Accordingly, recent years have witnessed a proliferation of psychotherapy approaches that integrate both conceptual and technical strands from across a range of theoretical orientations (e.g., Castonguay et al., 2004; Lebow, 2003, Schneider, 2008; Stricker & Gold, 2005).

From the multiple forms of psychotherapy integration that have been proposed, four broad pathways have emerged: *technical eclecticism, theoretical integration, elucidation of common factors*, and *assimilative integration* (for review, see Norcross & Goldfried, 2005). Technical eclecticism refers to approaches that draw systematically upon intervention options from across a range of theoretical schools in accordance with data-informed consideration of client characteristics and presenting clinical problems. Theoretical integration is defined by efforts to synthesize constructs from two or more theoretical systems into a supraordinate theoretical and practice framework that transcends the reach of the stand-alone theories from which it is derived. Common factors strategies focus on the integration of psychotherapy methods in accordance with commonalities across the spectrum of psychotherapy orientations relative to what is known about the elements and processes of change. Finally, assimilative integration involves the specification of a single theoretical system that serves as a primary roadmap to guide clinical conceptualization and intervention, while also selectively and flexibly drawing upon concepts and techniques from alternative psychotherapy systems in accordance with clinical needs and circumstances.

In addition to their impact on psychotherapy theory and practice, these respective innovations in psychotherapy integration have spawned an important dialogue on the trajectory and focus of contemporary psychology education and training regarding competency in integrative practice. A common thread that characterizes this dialogue involves articulating both educational opportunities and challenges in efforts to provide psychology trainees with the requisite didactic instruction and clinical experience needed for proficiency in the systematic application of psychotherapeutic pluralism (for review, see Norcross & Halgin, 2005).

Integrative Education and Training Approaches

Elaborating models for integrative psychotherapy education and training is a work in progress that tends to lag behind the proliferation of work on integrative psychotherapy practice (Castonguay, 2005; Consoli & Jester, 2005). As a result, unlike the training frameworks of the major theoretical orientations described in this chapter, elaboration of the structure, focus, and processes of integrative training is just beginning to unfold.

In general, proponents of integrative education and training advocate a combination of in-depth didactic course work on each of the major theoretical frameworks and systems of psychotherapy, course work in psychotherapy integration, and clinical experiences that provide opportunities for supervised application of integrative models (Castonguay, 2000; Consoli & Jester, 2005; Norcross & Halgin, 2005; Scaturo, 2012; Wolfe, 2000). Additionally, there is consensus that education and training cultivate in the trainee an integrative attitude characterized by openness to different points of view, a capacity to critically evaluate both conceptually and empirically the merits and limitations of a given psychotherapy system, and clinical flexibility in the psychotherapy process.

Illustrative of these general points is a six-step training model proposed by Norcross and Halgin (2005) as a consensus framework for integrative psychotherapy training. In the first step, trainees learn the core interpersonal skills that underlie good psychotherapeutic practice (e.g., empathy, respectfulness, active listening skills). In the second step, trainees receive didactic instruction on major theoretical frameworks of human psychology, followed in the third step by course work on systems of psychotherapy. This course work emphasizes applications of psychology theory to the behavioral change process and provides opportunities for trainees to explore points of comparison and conceptual integration across psychotherapy models. At this juncture in the training sequence, trainees are invited to select, at least provisionally, a preferred theoretical orientation that they perceive as congruent with their personal styles and approaches to clinical work. The fourth step involves the development of basic competency in at least two different systems of psychotherapy. Once trainees gain basic knowledge of different systems of psychotherapy, the fifth training step focuses on cultivating formal knowledge, skills, and attitudes in psychotherapy integration, including strategies for systematically integrating concepts and techniques from different theoretical frameworks consistent with the characteristics of a given client and clinical context. The final step in this training sequence involves gaining supervised clinical experience in the application of integrative principles with a range of clients, typically in the context of a clinical internship.

In addition to Norcross and Halgin's (2005) consensus model, integrative training approaches have begun to appear that are grounded within one or more of the major pathways to psychotherapy integration. For example, using a theoretical integration framework, Wolfe (2000) proposed a training model that emphasizes both cultivating trainee knowledge of diverse theoretical orientations and proficiency in conceptual integration of key constructs drawn from different theoretical systems. Anchored by a technical eclecticism framework, Beutler (1999) described an approach that centers on developing trainee skills in use of the evidence base both to ascertain client characteristics that are known to respond differentially to varying psychotherapy approaches and to implement systematically interventions from a range of psychotherapy systems in addressing client problems and concerns.

Using a developmental framework that also incorporates common factors principles, Castonguay and colleagues (Castonguay, 2000; Boswell & Castonguay, 2007) delineated a broad-based training model that assumes a sequence of developmental phases in learning how to work in an integrative way. The first phase is *preparation*, which focuses on basic mastery of assessment and interpersonal skills that are foundational to psychotherapeutic work. In this phase, trainees also are introduced to the major clinical theories (i.e., psychodynamic, cognitive-behavioral, humanistic-existential, systemic, and integrative orientations), basic principles of psychotherapeutic change, and key psychotherapy research findings. In the next training phase, *exploration*, trainees have opportunities to try out intervention protocols derived from each of the major theoretical orientations. The third training phase is *identification*, wherein trainees select one preferred psychotherapy orientation with which they feel most comfortable and focus on in-depth training in that particular approach. Next, in the *consolidation* phase of training, trainees deepen their technical and practical knowledge of their preferred psychotherapy approach and gain experience in applying their approach across a range of clinical settings, tasks, and psychotherapy modalities. The final phase of training, *integration*, typically occurs in the context of an internship and postdoctoral clinical training. In this phase, trainees learn to integrate ideas and strategies from varying psychotherapy orientations to accommodate psychotherapeutic principles and strategies not sufficiently articulated within their preferred theoretical framework. Within this developmental framework, emphasis also is placed on delineating core change principles that can be applied across the spectrum of psychotherapy orientations, providing both didactic and experiential learning opportunities, encouraging trainee self-reflection, and cultivating cultural competence (Boswell & Castonguay, 2007).

From a developmental perspective, there are differences in training approaches with respect to the timing of formal training in integrative principles. For instance, some models propose to introduce systematic integrative course work early on in training (Consoli & Jester, 2005). Conversely, some maintain that trainees must first gain foundational knowledge of the major psychotherapy systems as a prerequisite to learning integrative principles (Castonguay, 2000; Norcross & Halgin, 2005; Wolfe, 2000). Regardless of the differences across models regarding the developmental timing of in-depth integrative training, there is general agreement on the importance of encouraging in trainees an attitude of openness, theoretical pluralism, and critical thinking regarding the relative strengths and limitations of different theoretical orientations throughout the training process.

Key Competencies in Integrative Training

Learning integrative psychotherapy requires that trainees master fundamental interpersonal helping skills, gain both theoretical and empirical knowledge of the major theoretical orientations, understand the psychotherapy research literature relative to principles of change, and forge a conceptual and practical synthesis of psychotherapeutic principles and methods. As such, integrative training taps multiple competency domains. Yet, just as the articulation of integrative training models is in its early stages of development, so too is work on delineating an integrative framework for competency-based training.

Anchored by a combined assimilative integrationist and common factors training approach, Boswell, Nelson, Nordberg, McAleavey, and Castonguay (2010) characterized overarching integrative competency as springing from "a coherent understanding of the process of change within and between specific theoretical orientations and possession of a diverse clinical repertoire" (p. 4). Relative to this broad conceptualization of integrative psychotherapy competency, Boswell and colleagues (2010) identify several foundational competency domains that are especially salient in integrative training. One of these is reflective practice, which is required for maintaining awareness of and monitoring the ongoing psychotherapy process in the service of effective integrative clinical formulation, decision making, and intervention. Given that integrative training aims to facilitate mastery of multiple theoretical, clinical, and research knowledge domains, cultivating competency in scientific knowledge and methods also is a key area of focus. A training emphasis on integrative strategies for cultivating and managing the psychotherapy alliance taps relationships competency, including skill in identifying and managing alliance ruptures. A central feature of integrative psychotherapy involves combining knowledge of a range of psychotherapy systems and the evidence base to select and calibrate intervention strategies in accordance with a given client's unique characteristics and clinical needs. Relative to facilitating trainee proficiency in this area, competency in individual and cultural diversity is a crucial focus of the training process.

According to Boswell and colleagues (2010), trainee competency in the functional domain of intervention centers on learning to draw from multiple conceptual perspectives and synthesize a comprehensive understanding of the client and intervention approach. Additionally, integrative psychotherapy competency requires knowledge of empirical findings from the psychotherapy literature regarding psychotherapy process and outcome, change processes, and common factors. As such, the functional competency domain of research and evaluation also is a key focus of integrative training. Specifically, trainees must learn to be effective consumers of the evidence-based literature and be able to critically review, evaluate, and utilize research to inform integrative practice (Boswell et al., 2010).

Conclusion: Toward Theoretically Informed, Evidence-Based Education and Training

The main premise of this chapter has been that the major clinical theories in psychology—through their respective training structures, foci, and processes—have influenced significantly the shape and direction of professional training and education in psychology. Now, with an evidence-based framework emerging as the ascendant paradigm for 21st-century professional psychology practice, clinical theory is once again in a position to contribute to developing training approaches for evidence-based practice. The evidence-based model encourages clinicians to integrate research evidence,

clinical expertise, and client characteristics, preferences, and values in clinical decision making (Spring, 2007). To prepare trainees to practice within this framework, discussions are underway to articulate approaches to psychology education and training in evidence-based practice (e.g., Collins, Leffingwell, & Belar, 2007). For example, Collins and colleagues (2007) suggest that training programs teach methods for accessing and critically evaluating the evidence-based literature, encourage trainees to consult the evidence-based literature for answers to questions arising organically in the supervisory process, model science-practice integration, evaluate evidence-based practice competency in trainees across developmental levels of training, and cultivate an administrative infrastructure to support evidence-based training.

Along with these suggested training emphases, learning the concepts and applications of clinical theories also is a key part of preparation for effective evidence-based practice. After all, mastery of evidence-based principles is not simply a function of factual knowledge. It also requires skills in clinical inference, critical thinking, and synthetic processes that integrate clinical expertise, research evidence, and an understanding of client characteristics and circumstances to yield a coherent clinical formulation and intervention approach. Theory provides a supraordinate organizing structure that makes clinically meaningful integration of facts and processes possible within an evidence-based framework. As such, a training emphasis on cultivating theoretical knowledge informs the cultivation of clinical expertise in the trainee and undergirds the development of trainee proficiency in interpreting the clinical evidence base.

The underlying assumptions anchoring different theoretical systems are apt to result in a range of perspectives regarding the conceptualization and implementation of education and training in evidence-based practice. For example, reflecting its empiricist foundations, cognitive-behavioral training directly incorporates a focus on critical evaluation and the use of traditional quantitative research to guide practice and the use of empirical hypothesis-testing models to monitor and evaluate clinical work (e.g., Newman, 2010). An evidence-based training perspective within a humanistic-existential framework tends to highlight scientific pluralism, phenomenological and qualitative frameworks for understanding evidence, the synthesis of experiential and scientific knowledge, and both linear and nonlinear thinking in the clinical application of evidence-based principles (e.g., Farber, 2012; Mozdzierz, Peluso, & Lisiecki, 2011). Psychodynamic training may similarly emphasize nonlinear processes, including intuitive and improvisational capacities to integrate evidence-based principles in novel ways that match the unique requirements of a given clinical context (e.g., Binder, 2004; Sarnat, 2012). Systemic training provides a contextual framework for conceptualizing and applying evidence-based concepts with couples and families and learning about emerging evidence-based family intervention approaches (e.g., Celano et al., 2010), along with considering ways to think about evidence-based practice in the context of a postmodern perspective (e.g., Jacobs, Kissil, Scott, & Davey, 2010). Finally, the evolution of integrative training approaches provides theoretically pluralistic frameworks for exploring novel pathways for evidence-based education and training (e.g., Norcross & Halgin, 2005).

Just as the major theoretical systems described in the foregoing pages of this chapter have enriched the overall landscape of psychology education and training, they offer significant potential to contribute to the elucidation of training models for evidence-based psychology practice. Specifically, they provide conceptual models that guide the essential synthetic and integrative processes required for clinical decision making. Therefore clinical theories should receive the requisite attention by psychology educators, clinical supervisors, and researchers involved in the development and evaluation of evidence-based training approaches. The psychodynamic, cognitive-behavioral, humanistic-existential, and systemic orientations, along with the theoretical pluralism of integrative psychotherapy (e.g., Boswell & Castonguay, 2007; Boswell et al., 2010), share a longstanding legacy of contributions to psychology education and training. These traditions undoubtedly will continue to inform innovations in this domain, including evolving conceptualizations of training in evidence-based practice.

References

Adams, M. (2009). Phenomenology and Supervision. In E. van Deurzen & S. Young (Eds.), *Existential perspectives on supervision: Widening the horizon of psychotherapy and counseling* (pp. 43–55). Houndmills, Basingstoke, Hampshire, UK: Palgrave Macmillan.

Allport, G. W. (1955). *Becoming: Basic considerations for a psychology of personality*. New Haven: Yale University Press.

Andersen, T. (Ed.) (1991). *The reflecting team: Dialogues and dialogues about the dialogues*. New York: Norton.

Anderson, H., & Goolishian, H. (1992). The client is the expert: A not knowing approach to therapy. In S. McNamee & K. J. Gergen (Eds), *Therapy as social construction* (pp. 25–39). London: Sage.

Bandura, A. (1986). *Social foundations of thought and action: A social cognitive theory*. Englewood Cliffs, NJ: Prentice-Hall.

Barnett, L. (2009). The supervisory relationship. In E. van Deurzen & S. Young (Eds.), *Existential perspectives on supervision: Widening the horizon of psychotherapy and counseling* (pp. 56–67). Houndmills, Basingstoke, Hampshire, UK: Palgrave Macmillan.

Beck, A. T., Rush, A. J., Shaw, B. F., & Emery, G. (1979). *Cognitive therapy of depression*. New York: Guilford Press.

Bernard, J. M., & Goodyear, R. K. (2009). *Fundamentals of clinical supervision* (4th ed.). Upper Saddle River, NJ: Pearson.

Beutler, L. E. (1999). Manualizing flexibility: The training of eclectic therapists. *Journal of Clinical Psychology, 55,* 399– 404. doi: 10.1002/(SICI)1097-4679(199904)55:4<399::AID-JCLP4>3.0.CO;2-Z

Binder, J. L. (2004). *Key competencies in brief dynamic psychotherapy: Clinical practice beyond the manual*. New York: Guilford Press.

Boswell, J. F., & Castonguay, L. G. (2007). Psychotherapy training: Suggestions for core ingredients and future research. *Psychotherapy Theory, Research, Practice, Training, 44,* 378–383. doi: 10.1037/0033-3204.44.4.378

Boswell, J. F., Nelson, D. N., Nordberg, S. S., McAleavey, A. A., & Castonguay, L. G. (2010). Competency in integrative psychotherapy: Perspectives on training and supervision. *Psychotherapy Theory, Research, Practice, Training, 47,* 3–11. doi: 10.1037/a0018848

Burston, D. (2003). Existentialism, humanism, and psychotherapy. *Existential Analysis, 14,* 309–319. Retrieved from http://www.existentialanalysis.org.uk/journal/

Burum, B. A., & Goldfried, M. R. (2007). The centrality of emotion to psychological change. *Clinical Psychology: Science and Practice, 14,* 407–413. doi: 10.1111/j.1468-2850.2007.00100.x

Cain, D. J. (2002). Defining characteristics, history, and evolution of humanistic psychotherapies. In D. J. Cain & J. Seeman (Eds.), *Humanistic psychotherapies: Handbook of research and practice* (pp. 3–54). Washington, DC: American Psychological Association.

Calhoun, K. S., & Craighead, W. E. (2006). Clinical psychology in academic departments. *Clinical Psychology: Science and Practice, 13,* 278–281. doi: 10.1111/j.1468-2850.2006.00038.x

Castonguay, L. G. (2000). A common factors approach to psychotherapy training. *Journal of Psychotherapy Integration, 10,* 263–282. doi: 10.1023/A:1009496929012

Castonguay, L. G. (2005). Training issues in psychotherapy integration: A commentary. *Journal of Psychotherapy Integration, 15,* 384–391. doi: 10.1037/1053-0479.15.4.384

Castonguay, L. G., Schut, A. J., Aikins, D. E., Constantino, M. J., Laurenceau, J. P., Bologh, L., & Burns, D. D. (2004). Integrative cognitive therapy for depression: A preliminary investigation. *Journal of Psychotherapy Integration, 14,* 4–20. doi: 10.1037/1053-0479.14.1.4

Celano, M. P., Smith, C. O., & Kaslow, N. J. (2010). A competency-based approach to couple and family therapy supervision. *Psychotherapy Theory, Research, Practice, Training, 47,* 35–44. doi: 10.1037/a0018845

Collins, F. L., Leffingwell, T. R., & Belar, C. D. (2007). Teaching evidence-based practice: Implications for psychology. *Journal of Clinical Psychology, 63,* 657–670. doi: 10.1002/jclp.20378

Consoli, A. j., & Jester, C. M. (2005). A model for teaching psychotherapy theory through an integrative structure. *Journal of Psychotherapy Integration, 15*, 358–373. doi: 10.1037/1053-0479.15.4.358

Cooper, M. (2007). Humanizing psychotherapy. *Journal of Contemporary Psychotherapy, 37*, 11–16. doi: 10.1007/s10879-006-9029-6

Donovan, R. A., & Ponce, A. N. (2009). Identification and measurement of core competencies in professional psychology: Areas for consideration. *Training and Education in Professional Psychology, 3(Suppl.)*, S46–S49. doi: 10.1037/a0017302

Eckstein, R., & Wallerstein, R. S. (1972). *The teaching and learning of psychotherapy.* New York: International Universities Press.

Enright, J. B. (1970). Awareness training in the mental health professions. In J. Fagan & I. L. Shepherd (Eds.), *Gestalt therapy now: Theory, techniques, applications* (pp. 263–273). New York: Harper.

Falender, C. A., & Shafranske, E. P. (2010). Psychotherapy-based supervision models in an emerging competency-based era: A commentary. *Psychotherapy Theory, Research, Practice, Training, 47*, 45–50. doi: 10.1037/a0018873

Farber, E. W. (2010). Humanistic-existential psychotherapy competencies and the supervisory process. *Psychotherapy Theory, Research, Practice, Training, 47*, 28–34. doi: 10.1037/a0018847

Farber, E. W. (2012). Supervising humanistic-existential psychotherapy: Needs, possibilities. *Journal of Contemporary Psychotherapy, 42*, 173–182. doi 10.1007/s10879-011-9197-x

Flaskas, C. (2010). Frameworks for practice in the systemic field: Part 1—continuities and transitions in family therapy knowledge. *The Australian and New Zealand Journal of Family Therapy, 31*, 232–247. doi: 10.1375/anft.31.3.232

Flaskas, C. (2011). Frameworks for practice in the systemic field: Part 2—Contemporary frameworks in family therapy. *The Australian and New Zealand Journal of Family Therapy, 32*, 87–108. doi: 10.1375/anft.32.2.87

Fouad, N. A., Grus, C. L., Hatcher, R. L., Kaslow, N. J., Hutchings, P. S., Madson, M. B., Collins, F. L., Jr., Crossman, R. E. (2009). Competency benchmarks: A model for understanding and measuring competence in professional psychology across training levels. *Training and Education in Professional Psychology, 3(Suppl.)*, S5–S26. doi: 10.1037/a0015832

Fraenkel, P., & Pinsof, W. M. (2001). Teaching family therapy-centered integration: Assimilation and beyond. *Journal of Psychotherapy Integration, 11*, 59–85. doi: 10.1023/A:1026629024866

Frawley-O'Dea, M. G., & Sarnat, J. (2001). *The supervisory relationship: A contemporary psychodynamic approach.* New York: Guilford Press.

Freud, S. (1900). The interpretation of dreams. In *The standard edition of the complete psychological works of Sigmund Freud* (J. Strachey, Trans.), vols. 4 & 5. London: Hogarth, pp. 1–626.

Friedberg, R. D., Gorman, A. A., & Beidel, D. C. (2009). Training psychologists for cognitive-behavioral therapy in the raw world: A rubric for supervisors. *Behavior Modification, 33*, 104–123. doi: 10.1177/0145445508322609

Friedberg, R. D., Mahr, S., & Mahr, F. (2010). Training psychiatrists in cognitive behavioral psychotherapy: Current status and horizons. *Current Psychiatry Reviews, 6*, 159–170. doi: 10.2174/157340010791792563

Goldfried, M. R. (2003). Cognitive-behavior therapy: Reflections on the evolution of a therapeutic orientation. *Cognitive Therapy and Research, 27*, 53–69. doi: 10.1023/A:1022586629843

Goodyear, R. K. (2007). Toward an effective signature pedagogy for psychology: Comments supporting the case for competent supervisors. *Professional Psychology: Research and Practice, 38*, 273–274.

Goodyear, R. K., Abadie, P. D., & Efros, F. (1984). Supervisor theory into practice: Differential perception of supervision by Ekstein, Ellis, Polster, and Rogers. *Journal of Counseling Psychology, 31*, 228–237. doi: 10.1037/0022-0167.31.2.228

Greenberg, L. S., & Goldman, R. L. (1988). Training in experiential therapy. *Journal of Consulting and Clinical Psychology, 56*, 696–702. doi:10.1037/0022-006X.56.5.696

Habib, C. (2011). Integrating family therapy training in a clinical psychology course. *The Australian and New Zealand Journal of Family Therapy, 32*, 109–123. doi: 10.1375/anft.32.2.109

Hernández, P. (2008). The cultural context model in clinical supervision. *Training and Education in Professional Psychology, 2*, 10–17. doi: 10.1037/1931-3918.2.1.10

Hess, A. K. (2008). Psychotherapy supervision: A conceptual review. In A. K. Hess, K. D. Hess, & T. H. Hess (Eds.), *Psychotherapy supervision: Theory, research, and practice* (2nd ed.) (pp. 3–22). Hoboken, NJ: Wiley.

Hill, C. E., Stahl, J., & Roffman, M. (2007). Training novice psychotherapists: Helping skills and beyond. *Psychotherapy: Theory, Research, Practice, Training, 44*, 364–370. doi: 10.1037/0033-3204.44.4.364

Hoffman, L. (1992). A reflexive stance for family therapy. In S. McNamee & K. J. Gergen (Eds), *Therapy as social construction* (pp. 7–24). London: Sage.

Hyman, M. (2008). Psychoanalytic supervision. In A. K. Hess, K. D. Hess, & T. H. Hess (Eds.), *Psychotherapy supervision: Theory, research, and practice* (2nd ed.) (pp. 97–113). Hoboken, NJ: Wiley.

Jacobs, S., Kissil, K., Scott, D., & Davey, M. (2010). Creating synergy in practice: Promoting complementarity between evidence-based and postmodern approaches. *Journal of Marital and Family Therapy, 36*, 185–196. doi: 10.1111/j.1752-0606.2009.00171.x

Junkers, G., Tuckett, D., & Zachrisson, A. (2008). To be or not to be a psychoanalyst—How do we know a candidate is ready to qualify? Difficulties and controversies in evaluating psychoanalytic competence. *Psychoanalytic Inquiry, 28*, 288–308. doi: 10.1080/07351690801960871

Kaslow, N. J., Celano, M. P., & Stanton, M. (2005). Training in family psychology: A competencies-based approach. *Family Process, 44*, 337–353. doi: 10.1002/9781444310238.ch8

Kaslow, N. J., Dunn, S. E., & Smith, C. O. (2008). Competencies for psychologists in academic health centers (AHCs). *Journal of Clinical Psychology in Medical Settings, 15*, 18–27. doi: 10.1007/s10880-008-9094-y

Kaslow, N. J., Grus, C. L., Campbell, L. F., Fouad, N. A., Hatcher, R. L., Rodolfa, E. R. (2009). Competency assessment toolkit for professional psychology. *Training and Education in Professional Psychology, 3(Suppl.)*, S27–S45. doi: 10.1037/a0015833

Kendjelic, E. M., & Eells, T. D. (2007). Generic psychotherapy case formulation training improves formulation quality. *Psychotherapy: Theory, Research, Practice, Training, 44*, 66–77. doi: 10.1037/0033-3204.44.1.66

Lampropoulos, G. K., & Dixon, D. N. (2007). Psychotherapy integration in internships and counseling psychology doctoral programs. *Journal of Psychotherapy Integration, 17*, 185–208. doi: 10.1037/1053-0479.17.2.185

Larkin, K. T. (2009). Variations of doctoral training programs in clinical health psychology: Lessons learned at the box office. *Training and Education in Professional Psychology, 3*, 201–211. doi: 10.1037/a0016666

Lebow, J. L. (2003). Integrative approaches to couple and family therapy. In T. L. Sexton, G. R. Weeks, & M. S. Robbins (Eds.), *Handbook of family therapy: The science and practice of working with families and couples* (pp. 201–225). New York: Brunner-Routledge.

Lomranz, J. (1986). Personality theory: Position and derived teaching implications in clinical psychology. *Professional Psychology: Research and Practice, 17*, 551–559. doi: 10.1037/0735-7028.17.6.551

Mayer, J. D. (2005). A tale of two visions: Can a new view of personality help integrate psychology? *American Psychologist, 60*, 294–307. doi: 10.1037/0003-066X.60.4.294

McWilliams, N. (2004). *Psychoanalytic psychotherapy: A practitioner's guide*. New York: Guilford Press.

Melchert, T. P. (2007). Strengthening the scientific foundations of psychology: Time for the next steps. *Professional Psychology: Research and Practice, 38*, 34–43. doi: 10.1037/0735-7028.38.1.34

Mitchell, S. A. (1988). *Relational concepts in psychoanalysis: An integration*. Cambridge, Mass.: Harvard University Press.

Mitchell, S. A. (2000). *Relationality: From attachment to intersubjectivity*. Hillsdale, NJ: Analytic Press.

Mitchell, S. A., & Black, M. J. (1995). *Freud and beyond: A history of modern psychoanalytic thought*. New York: Basic Books.

Morris, S. J. (2003). A metamodel of theories of psychotherapy: A guide to their analysis, comparison, integration, and use. *Clinical Psychology and Psychotherapy, 10*, 1–18. doi: 10.1002/cpp.351

Mozdzierz, G. J., Peluso, P. R., & Lisiecki, J. (2011). Evidence-based psychological practices and therapist training: At the crossroads. *Journal of Humanistic Psychology, 51*, 439–464. doi: 10.1177/0022167810386959

Murray, H. A. (1938). *Explorations in personality*. New York: Oxford University Press.

Nelson, T. S., Chenail, R. J., Alexander, J. F., Crane D. R., Johnson, S. M., & Schwallie, L. (2007). The development of core competencies for the practice of marriage and family therapy. *Journal of Marital and Family Therapy, 33*, 417–438. doi:10.1111/j.1752-0606.2007.00042.x

Newman, C. F. (2010). Competency in conducting cognitive-behavioral therapy: Foundational, functional, and supervisory aspects. *Psychotherapy Theory, Research, Practice, Training, 47*, 12–19. doi: 10.1037/a0018849

Norcross, J. C. (2005). A primer on psychotherapy integration. In J. C. Norcross & M. R. Goldfried (Eds.), *Handbook of Psychotherapy Integration* (2nd ed.) (pp. 3–23). New York: Oxford University Press.

Norcross, J. C., Evans, K. L., & Ellis, J. (2010). The model does matter II: Admissions and training in APA-accredited counseling psychology programs. *The Counseling Psychologist, 38*, 257–268. doi: 10.1177/0011000009339342

Norcross, J. C., & Goldfried, M. R. (Eds.) (2005). *Handbook of Psychotherapy Integration* (2nd ed.). New York: Oxford University Press.

Norcross, J. C., & Halgin, R. P. (2005). Training in psychotherapy integration. In J. C. Norcross & M. R. Goldfried (Eds.), *Handbook of Psychotherapy Integration* (2nd ed.) (pp. 439– 458). New York: Oxford University Press.

Nutt, R. L., & Stanton, M. (2008). Family psychology specialty practice. *Professional Psychology: Research and Practice, 39*, 519–528. doi: 10.1037/0735-7028.39.5.519

Pack, M. (2009). Supervision as a liminal space: Towards a dialogic relationship. *Gestalt Journal of Australia and New Zealand, 5*, 60–78. Retrieved from http://www.ganz.org.au/ganz-journal.html

Patterson, C. H. (1983). A client-centered approach to supervision. *The Counseling Psychologist, 11*, 21–25. doi: 10.1177/0011000083111005

Pos, A. E., & Greenberg, L. S. (2007). Emotion-focused therapy: The transforming power of affect. *Journal of Contemporary Psychotherapy, 37*, 25–31. doi: 10.1007/s10879-006-9031-z

Putney, M. W., Worthington, E. L., & McCullough, M. E. (1992). Effects of supervisor and supervisee theoretical orientation and supervisor-supervisee matching on interns' perceptions of supervision. *Journal of Counseling Psychology, 39*, 258–265. doi: 10.1037/0022-0167.39.2.258

Rakovshik, S. G., & McManus, F. (2010). Establishing evidence-based training in cognitive behavioral therapy: A review of current empirical findings and theoretical guidance. *Clinical Psychology Review, 30*, 496–516. doi:10.1016/j.cpr.2010.03.004

Reiser, R. P., & Milne, D. (2012). Supervising cognitive-behavioral psychotherapy: Pressing needs, impressing possibilities. *Journal of Contemporary Psychotherapy, 42*, 161–171. doi: 10.1007/s10879-011-9200-6

Roberts, T. W., Winek, J., & Mulgrew, J. (1999). A systems/dialectical model of supervision: A symbolic process. *Contemporary Family Therapy, 21*, 291–302. doi: 10.1023/A:1021952013686

Rodolfa, E., Bent, R., Eisman E., Nelson, P., Rehm, L., & Ritchie, P. (2005). A cube model for competency development: Implications for psychology educators and regulators. *Professional Psychology: Research and Practice, 36*, 347–354. doi: 10.1037/0735-7028.36.4.347

Rosenbaum, M., & Ronen, T. (1998). Clinical supervision from the standpoint of cognitive-behavior therapy. *Psychotherapy Theory, Research, Practice, Training, 35*, 220–230. doi: 10.1037/h0087705

Rubin, N. J., Bebeau, M., Leigh, I. W., Lichtenberg, J. W., Nelson, P. D., Portnoy, S., Smith, I. L., & Kaslow, N. J. (2007). The competency movement within psychology: An historical perspective. *Professional Psychology: Research and Practice, 38*, 452–462. doi: 10.1037/0735-7028.38.5.452

Sarnat, J, (2010). Key competencies of the psychodynamic psychotherapist and how to teach them in supervision. *Psychotherapy Theory, Research, Practice, Training, 47*, 20–27. doi: 10.1037/a0018846

Sarnat, J. E. (2012). Supervising psychoanalytic psychotherapy: Present knowledge, pressing needs, future possibilities. *Journal of Contemporary Psychotherapy, 42*, 151–160. doi: 10.1007/s10879-011-9201-5

Scaturo, D. J. (2012). Supervising integrative psychotherapy in the 21st century: Pressing needs, impressing possibilities. *Journal of Contemporary Psychotherapy, 42*, 183–192. doi: 10.1007/s10879-011-9204-2

Schneider K. J. (Ed.). (2008). *Existential-integrative psychotherapy: Guideposts to the core of practice*. New York: Routledge.

Schneider, K. J., & Krug, O. T. (2010). *Existential-Humanistic therapy*. Washington, DC: American Psychological Association.

Spring, B. (2007). Evidence-based practice in clinical psychology: What it is, why it matters; what you need to know.

Journal of Clinical Psychology, 63, 611–631. doi: 10.1002/jclp.20373

Stedman, J. M., Hatch, J. P., & Schoenfeld, L. S. (2007). Toward practice-oriented theoretical models for internship training. *Training and Education in Professional Psychology, 1*, 89–94. doi: 10.1037/1931-3918.1.2.89

Steiman, M., & Dobson, K. S. (2002). Cognitive-behavioral approaches to depression. In F. W. Kaslow & T. Patterson (Eds.), *Comprehensive handbook of psychotherapy, volume 2, cognitive-behavioral approaches* (pp. 295–317). New York: John Wiley & Sons.

Stricker, G., & Gold J. (2005). Assimilative psychodynamic psychotherapy. In J. C. Norcross & M. R. Goldfried (Eds.), *Handbook of Psychotherapy Integration* (2nd ed.) (pp. 221–240). New York: Oxford University Press.

Strupp, H. H., Butler, S. F., & Rosser, C. L. (1988). Training in psychodynamic therapy. *Journal of Consulting and Clinical Psychology, 56*, 689–695. doi: 10.1037/0022-006X.56.5.689

Styczynski, L. E., & Greenberg, L. (2008). Supervision of couples and family therapy. In A. K. Hess, K. D. Hess, & T. H. Hess (Eds.), *Psychotherapy supervision: Theory, research, and practice* (2nd ed.) (pp. 179–199). Hoboken, NJ: Wiley.

Sudak, D. M., Beck, J. S., & Wright, J. (2003). Cognitive behavioral therapy: A blueprint for attaining and assessing psychiatry resident competency. *Academic Psychiatry, 27*, 154–159. doi: 10.1176/appi.ap.27.3.154

Szecsödy, I. (2008). Does anything go in psychoanalytic supervision? *Psychoanalytic Inquiry, 28*, 373–386. doi: 10.1080/07351690801962455

Tuckett, D. (2005). Does anything go? Towards a framework for the more transparent assessment of psychoanalytic competence. *International Journal of Psycho-Analysis, 86*, 31–49. doi: 10.1516/R2U5-XJ37-7DFJ-DD18

Ungar, M. (2006). Practicing as a postmodern supervisor. *Journal of Marital and Family Therapy, 32*, 59–71. doi: 10.1111/j.1752-0606.2006.tb01588.x

Wampold, B. E. (2010). *The basics of psychotherapy: An introduction to theory and practice*. Washington, DC: American Psychological Association.

Watkins, C. E. (2011). Psychotherapy supervision since 1909: Some friendly observations about its first century. *Journal of Contemporary Psychotherapy, 41*, 57–67. doi: 10.1007/s10879-010-9152-2

White, M. B., & Russell, C. S. (1997). Examining the multifaceted notion of isomorphism in marriage and family therapy supervision: A quest for conceptual clarity. *Journal of Marital and Family Therapy, 23*, 315–333. doi: 10.1111/j.1752-0606.1997.tb01040.x

Wolfe, B. E. (2000). Toward an integrative theoretical basis for training psychotherapists. *Journal of Psychotherapy Integration, 10*, 233–246. doi: 10.1023/A:1009492728103

Yerushalmi, H. (1994). A call for change of emphasis in psychodynamic supervision. *Psychotherapy Theory, Research, Practice, Training, 31*, 137–145. doi: 10.1037/0033-3204.31.1.137

Accreditation of Education and Training Programs

Elizabeth M. Altmaier

Abstract

Along with other professions, psychology engages in accreditation, a system of quality assurance to evaluate the various aspects of educating a professional psychologist. Accreditation builds on a program's ongoing strategies of self-study and change, with the addition of a formal review that includes an on-site evaluation of the program by faculty peers from other institutions. Both site visitors and the Commission on Accreditation judge the program's ongoing adherence to a set of standards regarding necessary content, processes, and policies. In psychology, accreditation is available for programs of study that result in the PhD and PsyD degree, for year-long internships that precede the granting of the doctoral degree, and for one or two year postdoctoral fellowships or residencies. This chapter describes the history of accreditation, outlines the current system, documents various external influences on accreditation, and considers several challenges to be met in the future.

Key Words: quality assurance, self-study, credentialing, profession

Introduction

For the readers of this chapter, hearing that accreditation has a 50-plus-year history may come as a surprise. Until the past two decades, both specialized and regional accreditation activities may have taken place somewhat "under the radar." those times are definitely now in the past since higher education has entered an era of significant controversy over accreditation policies. As an example, student loan debt has exceeded credit card debt in the United States, and much of the growth of student loan debt is for students' enrollment in nontraditional institutions. Should these institutions be regionally accredited if many or even most of their graduates fail to find employment after graduation? Within psychology, the imbalance between students seeking APA-accredited internships and the number of internship positions has grown to disturbing levels; in 2011, only 50% of students using the Association

of Psychology Postdoctoral and Internship Centers (APPIC) internship matching process were matched to accredited internships (APPIC, 2012). Should doctoral programs remain accredited when their students cannot obtain internships?

This chapter considers background, current models, and future issues related to accreditation in professional psychology. The first section traces the historical development of accreditation as an activity for both institutions and training programs that offer doctoral degrees in psychology. Current models of accreditation for psychology programs, internships, and postdoctoral fellowships are outlined in the second section, along with examples of accreditation criteria. National structures that govern psychology accreditation are described in the third section. The last section considers challenges and difficulties in accreditation, and possible solutions to these concerns.

History of Accreditation

The history of higher education in the United States dates to the founding of the early colleges: Harvard University in 1636, the College of William and Mary in 1693, Yale University in 1701, and Princeton University in 1746. These colleges were established to provide a liberal arts curriculum for the clergy. That mission changed in the mid 1800s, when legislators recognized that the growth in population in their states created a need for each state to establish educational institutions to provide its citizens with access to an education that prepared them for day to day living, including skills in literacy and mathematics. President Lincoln signed the Morrill Land-Grant Act in 1862, establishing "land grant" universities. By the end of the 1800s, the number of higher education institutions had grown to almost 500.

However, until the end of World War II, students attending these colleges and universities were primarily white, male, and upper class. This profile changed dramatically with two events. The first was the GI Bill, the provision of support for a college education to returning veterans after World War II. With tuition, books, and housing paid for, many veterans availed themselves of the opportunity to attend college: The number of college students grew from 1.5 million in the 1940s to 2.7 million in 1950. The second event was Civil Rights legislation in the 1960s, and the increase in applications by students previously denied access to higher education on the basis of their race. The original design of affirmative action was to give advantages to students who historically faced barriers in access to higher education.

Accreditation efforts first evolved in the late 1800s when groups of professionals began to judge educational standards and admission processes of institutions in their geographic region. This judgment was considered necessary to establish policies regarding student transferring credits between institutions and to articulate policies regarding best practices in higher education. The American Council on Education was established in 1918, and served as a coordinating body for the regional accreditors (e.g., Middle States Association of Colleges and Schools, New England Association of Schools and Colleges).

Specialized accreditation, the accreditation of programs of study rather than entire institutions, began in 1904, when the American Medical Association established the Council on Medical Education and Hospitals to accredit medical education programs. Accreditation within medicine was followed by the establishment of accreditation organizations for dentistry, law, engineering and pharmacy. In each of these cases, groups of professionals developed the standards for education in the profession, as well as means by which to classify preparation programs.

Psychology's involvement with specialized accreditation dates to the conclusion of World War II. As outlined by Nelson and Messenger (2003), in 1945 the Board of Directors of the American Psychological Association (APA) received a request from the Veterans Administration (VA) for a list of universities whose graduate departments of psychology provided adequate and appropriate training for clinical psychologists. This request came about as the VA considered how best to diagnose and treat large numbers of returning veterans who manifested psychological service needs. The APA responded by naming a Committee on Graduate and Professional Training, charged with developing criteria for departments to be judged as having appropriate faculties, facilities, curriculum, and resources for educating doctoral level psychologists.

Although some psychologists were at work developing the profession's first accreditation criteria, others were raising concerns about the negative potential of this "outside influence." Examples of these concerns were that an entire department would be known only by its clinical training, rather than by a broader departmental reputation. Another concern was that departments whose clinical programs were not initially approved would be restricted from later accreditation. Last was disagreement within the profession concerning the proper training resources and curriculum for graduate training in clinical psychology.

In response to these concerns, Raimy (1950) made a strong argument for the establishment of a system of accreditation in psychology. He noted that all professions must make statements concerning necessary components of quality training. Furthermore, in his view, accreditation was a process that lent itself to self-assessment of quality and to identification of means by which to improve based on peer evaluation. Last, he observed that the profession had an ethical obligation to students who were increasingly seeking clinical psychology training programs and needed assurance of their quality.

The 1950s and 1960s were also a time of definition within specialty education in psychology. Following the Boulder Conference in 1949 (Raimy, 1950) was the Thayer Conference on school psychology (Cutts, 1955), the Greyston Conference on counseling psychology (Thompson & Super, 1964), and other conferences on psychology in general (e.g., the Miami Conference: Roe, Gustad, Moore, Ross, & Skokak, 1959). These conferences produced reports and policy statements that increased expectations for graduate training and education in psychology, including the need for additional practical training in practicum and internship settings.

By the middle of the 1960s, it became clear that both the criteria for and the procedures of accreditation needed revision. As an example of the pressure on procedures, adding internships for accreditation review in addition to doctoral programs dramatically increased the number of necessary site visits, and the committee members were no longer able to make all of the site visits themselves. The Committee on Evaluation at that time convened ad hoc working groups to develop new accreditation criteria and these new criteria, along with changed procedures, were adopted in 1971. The new criteria incorporated several alterations. First among them was the notion of the program adoption of a training model. The various conferences had led to conversations about models of training, including the scientist-practitioner model. (These models are described in more detail later in the chapter.) A second change was the development of specific criteria for practicum and internship. At this time, the Committee also began to use site visitors, and to develop procedures for their training.

Shortly after the new criteria were adopted, the common practice of training professional psychologists by faculty comprised primarily of researchers came under scrutiny in two ways. First, the Vail conference in 1973 (Korman, 1976) suggested a method of training that focused solely on professional preparation. Such models were already in existence, with the establishment of the California School of Professional Psychology in 1970. Second, at this point in accreditation's history, there was growth in the numbers of psychologists becoming licensed practitioners in their states. Licensure and certification review put greater emphasis on all institutions using similar methods of training so that all students with doctoral degrees presenting for licensure had similar qualifications.

In 1976, a process of reforming accreditation criteria and procedures was put into place within the APA. This reform, resulting in a set of criteria adopted in 1979, was meant to balance prescription and flexibility in the criteria themselves. For example, the criteria specified a minimum number of practicum training hours (400) across all programs, but allowed flexibility in curriculum. Unfortunately, the attempt to balance prescription with flexibility meant that accreditation judgments by site visitors and the Committee were more difficult. Programs that were "typical" in their requirements were familiar, and thus more easily judged. Programs that were more creative in their faculty credentials, curriculum, professional training, and the like were more difficult to evaluate.

In the late 1980s, several waves of conversation about the necessary components of education for doctoral psychologists occurred. First were a series of conferences within the specialties and within psychology more broadly: A total of seven conferences took place between 1981 and 1990 (see Kanz, 2003). Second was the work of an ad hoc group, the Joint Council on Professional Education in Psychology (JCPEP), that considered necessary components of preparation for practice and issued a final report in 1990 (Stigall et al., 1990). Third was the increasing challenge to accreditation from the perspective of diversity. Faith-based schools were committed to maintaining statements of required beliefs and behavior that appeared inimical with training of doctoral psychologists committed to the full range of human diversity, particularly with regard to sexual orientation.

The APA responded to these pressures by holding a national conference on accreditation in 1991. Also at that time, a new Committee on Accreditation reconsidered all accreditation criteria and procedures with a view to revising the scope of accreditation (for example, should master's programs be accredited? Should postdoctoral training programs be accredited?) and the criteria for accreditation. After a lengthy process, involving several iterations and much public input, the now-current criteria and procedures were approved by the Committee on Accreditation and the APA in 1995 and implemented beginning in 1996. It should be noted that, since then, various changes, mostly of a minor nature, have been made; as an example, there is a current requirement that programs display outcome data on their graduates on their public website. This requirement was implemented in response to initiatives promulgated by the Department of Education and the Council on Higher Education Accreditation. However, these updates were not made by changes in the criteria themselves, but by promulgation of a series of Implementing Regulations.

The 1996 criteria contained several significant changes. First, the scope of accreditation was broadened to include doctoral training programs in clinical, counseling, and school psychology; combinations of the aforementioned; and "emerging substantive areas of psychology." Second, accreditation was made available to postdoctoral programs in specialized fields of psychological practice.

The third change asked programs to articulate their own model of training and its intended outcomes and to provide evidence that their students had demonstrated these intended outcomes. This criterion shifted the focus of the review to the program itself and its model of training. Therefore, in contrast to the previous criteria that focused on inputs—the physical resources of classrooms and laboratories, faculty credentials, student credentials, and curriculum—the review of the program would shift to an examination of demonstrated outcomes. For example, did all students achieve competency in the skills the program deemed essential for practice?

This change challenged programs accustomed to specifying inputs rather than outcomes. Taking assessment as an illustration, the earlier criteria could have been met by a program demonstrating to site visitors that a required course in assessment was offered, the faculty member teaching that course had experience in assessment, relevant assessment resources (e.g., tests, software) were available to students, and students indeed enrolled in the course and completed it. But the new criteria asked that program faculty consider assessment as a competency to be fostered and evaluated: How did the program ensure that all students were competent in assessment? Increasing numbers of programs adopted a portfolio approach to assuring competencies. Returning to assessment as an example, in a portfolio a student might present an assessment report, including interview data and test scores, and answer questions by faculty during an oral examination.

Four principles underlying accreditation remained unchanged. Doctoral education and training should be broad and general preparation focused on entry to practice. Advanced training, such as that contained in postdoctoral residencies, was to be focused and in depth. Both science and practice were to be included in doctoral training, although it was acknowledged that different models would place various emphases on these two domains. And last, programs owned the responsibility for articulating a clear set of goals for training, and plans for determining the evidence that students met these goals.

At the time of the promulgation of these standards, it was expected that these changes would resolve problems described by a variety of concerned publics. For example, the previous criteria placed such an emphasis on input that they had been mischaracterized as a "checklist" mentality. Site visitors had, in fact, been given a brief checklist which some resorted to using alone without completely reviewing the criteria. Using a checklist gave program faculty and students the impression that criteria could be met with merely a "present" or "absent" judgment. Also, the previous criteria had prioritized certain models of training, particularly the scientist-practitioner model, which no longer was the model of choice for some programs. Those programs believed their model was misunderstood or misevaluated.

It is also important to note that the number and composition of the group of professionals charged with making accreditation decisions have changed over time. As mentioned earlier in the chapter, at the time of the 1996 criteria implementation, the group was termed the Committee on Accreditation, and it was composed of 21 persons who represented 5 constituencies: academic programs, internship programs, professional practice, and the public (students and consumers). In 2005, the Snowbird Summit was held in Utah to discuss issues and concerns about the structure and composition of the Committee on Accreditation, and this meeting's members recommended that the committee be enlarged to 32 persons and renamed the Commission on Accreditation. The Summit also made other recommendations regarding an annual assembly, expanded panel review process within decision making, and changed review cycles. In 2008, these changes were implemented.

Current Criteria
Self-study

Perhaps the most important aspect of the current criteria is that they were meant to guide *self-study*. Self-study has a long history in higher education. As Kells (1995) noted, no external sets of standards or criteria can replace the ongoing commitment to quality assurance that takes place through self-study. Is the accreditation process an event? If so, at one point in time a training director furiously writes a "self-study," sends it to a site visit team, who come to campus and busily looks for problems, and then the program "passes" review—a process culminated by sighs all around and a return to normal functioning. Or is the accreditation process a slice in an ongoing, faculty and student-led, iterative process in which program quality is continuously assessed, problems identified, solutions developed and implemented, and outcome data monitored? The latter is the intent of self-study, and the new criteria were meant to encourage this approach among programs.

> Accreditation is a voluntary, nongovernmental process of self-study and external review intended to evaluate, enhance, and publicly recognize quality in institutions and in programs of higher education … The accreditation process involves judging the degree to which a program has achieved the goals and objectives of its stated training model. That is, an accreditation body should not explicitly prescribe a program's educational goals or the processes by which they should be reached; rather, it should judge the degree to which a program achieves outcomes and goals that are consistent with its stated training model and with the guiding principles contained in this document (APA, 2009, pp. 11–12).

Thus, self-study forms the basis for the document that forms the basis of the accreditation review. In this document, the program uses narrative, data, and artifacts to document its own self-study's findings regarding the implementation of its program model and the achievement of its training goals and student outcomes.

Program Model

As mentioned in the preceding section, doctoral education in psychology has occurred through several distinct training models. Historically, the scientist-practitioner model (Belar & Perry, 1992; Raimy, 1950) was the dominant model. Within a scientist-practitioner model, students learn to perform independent research as well as to conduct assessment and psychotherapy. Each activity is intended to supplement the other (Altmaier & Claiborn, 1987) during graduate education, and all of them are expected to be present during students' subsequent careers in psychology. Stricker (Stricker & Tricrweiler, 2006) developed the concept of the local clinical scientist, where the clinical setting is analogous to the research setting, and scholarly standards of verifiability are used by the clinician in gathering and evaluating clinical observations. Thus, the scientist-practitioner model is implemented within each clinician.

In contrast, the practitioner model (Korman, 1976) was developed to guide the education of students who intended to enter full-time practice as a career. In this model, a wider number of practitioner skills were emphasized during graduate study, and the research emphasis was altered

to skills that would enable students to become effective consumers of research. Variations of the practitioner model—termed scholar-practitioner, practitioner-scholar, or practitioner-scientist—focused on educating students in the research skills they would need to conduct research to immediately improve their own practice. As an example, students might learn program evaluation methods in lieu of advanced courses in statistical modeling techniques.

Last, the clinical-scientist model (McFall, 2006) promotes scientific values within doctoral programs, particularly with regard to the rigorous evaluation of methods of assessment and psychotherapy and traditional standards of empirical scholarship. The strength of commitment to this model among its programs has led to the formation of an alternate accreditation model, discussed later in this chapter.

Whatever model is specified by the program, there are five components in the self-study that describe the model and its implementation. The *philosophy*, described by values and principles, introduces the program's model and the reasons for its selection. *Goals and objectives* are defined in terms of expected outcomes. As an example, one goal might be that students are proficient in delivering cognitive-behavioral-therapy approaches to children. Goals are operationalized in the language of competencies that would be seen among students after training.

How the program proceeds to provide education and training are *processes*. These may be academic courses, extracurricular experiences, types of supervision, academic policies, and the like. *Resources* enable the program to complete its processes and include faculty/staff, the physical environment including access to training facilities, financial support for the program and students, equipment and supplies including technology, and the institutional setting.

The *evaluation* component of the self-study is the integration of internal and external evaluation: How well is the program achieving its objectives? For example, are the resources sufficient for students and faculty? Is there a means by which faculty can interact with students to judge their competencies in several areas? Are training and educational processes consistent, that is, do they apply to all students?

Criteria

Accreditation criteria are organized into six domains. Each is outlined briefly in the extracted paragraphs that follow, and one criterion is given as an illustration of the domain.

Eligibility. The program is eligible for accreditation when the purpose of the program is within the purview of psychological accreditation and the training occurs in an institution appropriate for doctoral education. An example is the criterion that the institution must be regionally accredited in order for its psychology program to be reviewed.

A. 2. The program is sponsored by an institution of higher education accredited by a nationally recognized regional accrediting body in the United States, or, in the case of Canadian programs, the institution is publicly recognized by the Association of Universities and Colleges of Canada as a member in good standing.

Program philosophy, objectives, and curriculum plan. Because of the flexibility of model, the program must begin its self-study by defining its choice of model, and then its objectives and accompanying curriculum plan.

B. 2. The program specifies education and training objectives in terms of the competencies expected of its graduates. Those competences must be consistent with: The program's philosophy and training model; The substantive areas of professional psychology for which the program prepares students at the entry level of practice.

Program resources. Resources include human resources (e.g., faculty who are full time or adjunct, practicum supervisors), student resources, physical facilities, and financial resources (e.g., for student support, faculty development).

C. 1. The program has an identifiable core faculty responsible for its leadership who function as an integral part of the academic unit of which the program is an element; are sufficient in number for their academic and professional responsibilities; have theoretical perspectives and academic and applied experiences appropriate to the program's goals and objectives; demonstrate substantial competence and have recognized credentials in those areas which are at the core of the program's objectives and goals; and are available to and function as appropriate role models for students in their learning and socialization into the discipline and profession.

Cultural and individual differences and diversity. Students and faculty function in a pluralistic and increasingly global culture, and the presence of faculty and students who have been underrepresented in academe is a necessary part of education for that culture. Therefore, within this criterion area, there are two emphases: first that faculty and students represent diversity broadly writ, and second that students must receive consistent training in multicultural competencies.

D. 2. The program has and implements a thoughtful and coherent plan to provide students with relevant knowledge and experiences about the role of cultural and individual diversity in psychological phenomena as it relates to the science and practice of psychology. The avenues by which these goals are achieved are to be developed by the program.

Student-faculty relations. The experience of students in their program, in terms of their working relationships with faculty, the policies that govern their academic work, and the means by which their difficulties are identified and remediated, are a critical aspect of program quality.

E. 4. At the time of admission, the program provides the students with written policies and procedures regarding program and institution requirements and expectations regarding students' performance and continuance in the program and procedures for the termination of students. Students receive, at least annually, written feedback on the extent to which they are meeting the program's requirements and performance expectations. Such feedback should include: timely, written notification of all problems that have been noted and the opportunity to discuss them; guidance regarding steps to remediate all problems (if remediable); and substantive, written feedback on the extent to which correct actions are or are not successful in addressing the issues of concern.

Program self-assessment and quality enhancement. As described earlier, the process of accreditation is fundamentally predicated on the program's internal processes for monitoring data and considering its success in meeting its stated goals and objectives. A key part of the new criteria was this domain, where the program explains the evaluation processes it uses and the data these processes have obtained.

F. 1. The program, with appropriate involvement from its students, engages in regular, ongoing self-studies that address: its effectiveness in achieving program goals and objectives in terms of outcome data (i.e., while students are in the program and after completion); how its goals and objectives are met through graduate education and professional training (i.e., its processes); and its procedures to maintain current achievements or to make program changes as necessary.

Public disclosure. In line with increasing calls for education accountability, the new criteria require that programs be transparent regarding goals and outcomes. (Although the criteria refer to written materials, there is increasing use of technology [i.e., websites] to communicate these data to the public, including prospective students.)

G. 1. The program is described accurately and completely in documents that are available to current students, prospective students, and other "publics." The descriptions of the program should include: its goals, objectives, and training model; its requirements for admission and graduation; curriculum; its faculty, students, facilities, and other resources; its administrative policies and procedures; the kinds of research and practicum experiences it provides, its educational and training outcomes; and its status with regard to accreditation, making available, as appropriate through its sponsor institution, such reports or other materials as pertain to the program's accreditation status.

Relationship with accrediting body. In line with ongoing self-study, the program is asked to notify the accrediting body of any substantive changes that might affect its compliance with the accreditation criteria. Rather than waiting for a scheduled review, this criterion contemplates more immediate interaction with the Commission on Accreditation in the event of significant program changes, such as loss of faculty resources.

H. 2. The program informs the accrediting body in a timely manner of changes in its environment, plans, resources, or operations that could alter the program's quality.

At the time of the implementation of these criteria, several challenges were evident. The first challenge was the building tension in higher education concerning external accountability. State legislatures and boards of trustees were concerned about rapidly increasing tuition, widespread criticism about undergraduate education was published (see Hacker & Dreifus, 2010, and Acrum & Roksa, 2011 for those arguments), and faculty roles in research versus teaching were discussed. A second crisis was funding: this crisis began in the late 1990s and has only become more severe today. Increasingly, public universities are public in name only: financial support for universities comes through student tuition and fees, grants, and fund raising, not public support through taxes.

A third challenge was that of changing technology. Technology is a challenge in two ways. First,

the interaction between faculty and students is altered by technology; students no longer need classrooms to "learn," and faculty are increasingly called upon to function in roles other than lecturing and apprenticing. Second, online course offerings have expanded to where they are present even in "bricks and mortar" institutions. Additionally, doctoral programs that are offered at a distance are challenging the concept of "residential" graduate education. Murphy, Levant, Hall and Glueckauf (2007) provide a summary of the findings of a task force on distance learning in psychology, among them a description of the difficulties meeting accreditation criteria when programs are completely or primarily delivered within a distance model.

The last challenge of these new criteria was the flexibility within them; the then-new criteria were meant to allow the proverbial "1000 flowers to bloom" (see Benjamin, 2006), a creative endeavor that would stretch the decision making of the Committee on Accreditation. Since the criteria were no longer input but output oriented, new types of judgments would need to be made, about an increasing diversity of program types and models, in new specialty areas beyond those traditionally accredited. At the time of the approval of the criteria and procedures, it was hoped that the benefits of this ambiguity would balance the inherent risks.

Organizational Structures Surrounding Accreditation

Many readers who are unfamiliar with accreditation in professional psychology might assume that decisions about criteria, scope, and procedures can be made solely within professional psychology. This assumption contributes to a significant misunderstanding; psychology's accreditation operates with three organizational contexts that exert substantial influence on the profession's activities. These three contexts—Department of Education, Council on Higher Education Accreditation, and Association of Specialized and Professional Accreditors—are discussed in this section.

United States Department of Education

Within the U. S. Department of Education (DoE), the Office of Postsecondary Education formulates policies and oversees programs intended to improve the quality of postsecondary education in the United States and to increase access to that education for all students. A specific function within that office "recognizes" accrediting agencies within categories of arts and humanities (e.g., National

Association of Schools of Dance, Commission on Accreditation), educational training (e.g., National Council for Accreditation of Teacher Education), legal education (e.g., American Bar Association), community and social services (e.g., Association for Clinical Pastoral Education, Inc., Accreditation Commission), personal care (e.g., American Board of Funeral Service Education, Committee on Accreditation), and health care (e.g., American Dental Association, Commission on Dental Accreditation). Psychology is recognized within the health care section. (See the DoE website for more information, www2ed.gov/admins/finaid/accred/index.html.)

Just as there are criteria for accreditation within psychology that programs must meet to be accredited, so there are criteria for the APA to meet in order for it, in turn, to accredit programs. These criteria have to do with processes and content. A process requirement, for example, is that there must be at least one member of a decision-making body who is a representative of the public (as an example, a former CoA member was the national leader of an organization for youth). Relevant to content, several criteria require that psychology's own accreditation criteria address recruiting and admissions practices, faculty, and student outcomes.

In a parallel fashion to programs being evaluated by the APA at certain intervals, the DoE requires accrediting agencies to submit for recognition renewal every five years. That submission must contain evidence that the agency is in compliance with all criteria for recognition. The Secretary reviews these renewal applications and invites public comment; once all information is received, a recognition decision is reached and publicized. It is important to note that the Department may ask to have representatives be included in a site visit, to sit in on decision making meetings, or to otherwise gain additional information about the agency's (in this case, the Commission on Accreditation) accreditation decision making.

DoE recognition is essential to the continued ability of APA to accredit programs in professional psychology;. APA cannot operate outside the context of the prevailing trends and concerns of higher education in general. An example of this influence is the development and application of a variety of implementing regulations (IRs) by the CoA that clarify or define expectations of training programs in interest areas of DoE. The April, 2010 communication from the CoA to programs (CoA, 2010) outlines IR D4-7, an IR pertinent to "thresholds for acceptable performance for accredited doctoral programs." That IR explains in detail the types of data that would trigger a determination by CoA that the program was operating below threshold: number of years to complete a program, percent of students leaving a program for any reason, percent of students accepted into an internship, and changes in student-faculty ratios. As an example, the CoA defines 7% of students leaving a program for any reason as a determination that the program operates below acceptable performance.

Council on Higher Education Accreditation

The Council on Higher Education Accreditation (CHEA) is a national association of over 3000 degree-granting colleges and universities that "recognizes" 60 accrediting organizations. CHEA is governed by a board that primarily contains college and university presidents; therefore, it is a prominent national presence on matters related to accreditation in federal legislation and policies. Importantly, CHEA is nongovernmental; this characteristic means that it operates outside the federal system and can serve a consultation and educative function as well as a regulatory function. CHEA maintains a website of information and resources at www.chea.org.

There are specified criteria that APA needs to meet in order to be recognized by CHEA as a national accreditation body (see CHEA, 2010). These criteria, as with DoE criteria, pertain less to content (for example, what courses should be in the curriculum) and more to processes. There are six criteria for recognition as follows: (1) the criteria and procedures adopted by the accrediting body advance academic quality, (2) the accrediting body demonstrates accountability, (3) planning for change and needed improvement occurs regularly, (4) decision-making procedures are transparent and fair, (5) ongoing review of accredited programs' practices occur, and (6) the accrediting body possesses sufficient resources to accomplish its activities.

CHEA promotes its own recognition as a means to accomplish several goals distinct from DoE. For example, CHEA intends to build on the accrediting organization's own capabilities to improve higher education through articulation and clarification of accreditation criteria and procedures. Additionally, CHEA attempts to promote academic quality by emphasizing standards regarding student achievement, expectations of faculty and students, and institutional missions. CHEA specifically focuses on the importance of each institution having an intentional mission and on the role of accreditation in helping institutions maintain their missions.

CHEA recognition is also periodic; however, in contrast to DoE, its recognition review occurs every 10 years. At the time this chapter was written, the APA was undergoing CHEA review. It is likely this process will result in feedback to the APA from CHEA regarding desirable future changes. Although having two "accreditors" of APA may seem unnecessary, most health-care organizations similar to APA have recognition from both DoE and CHEA: examples are the American Association for Marriage and Family Therapy, the American Occupational Therapy Association, and the American Speech-Language-Hearing Association.

Association of Specialized and Professional Accreditors

The third context for external influences on psychology accreditation is the Association of Specialized and Professional Accreditors (ASPA). This association of approximately 60 member associations serves as a voice for specialized accreditation within higher education and the federal and state governments. Member associations span human service (e.g., athletic training, funeral service), arts and humanities (e.g., music, dance), business (e.g., construction), engineering and information technologies (e.g., engineering, landscape architecture, industrial technology) and health care (e.g., nurse anesthesia, dentistry). Member institutions agree to meet a Code of Good Practice and are judged by the Board of Directors of ASPA to meet criteria for specialized accreditors (see www.aspa-use.org).

The Code of Good Practice (ASPA, 1995) is frequently referred to by specialized accreditors because it focuses on important issues. That Code contains six characteristics of accreditation as follows: (1) The accrediting body pursues its mission, goals and objectives and conducts operations in a trustworthy manner. (2) Accrediting procedures maximize service, productivity, and effectiveness. (3) There is a respect for institutional autonomy. (4) Accreditation reviews focus on the development of knowledge and competence. (5) The decision-making body exhibits integrity and professionalism. (6) The decision-making body has mechanisms in place to ensure that visiting teams, staff, and members are sufficiently trained and informed.

ASPA also takes positions on various issues in higher education. Among them is one of relevance to APA, that of professional doctorates such as the PsyD degree. In their position paper on professional doctorates, ASPA defined five desired characteristics of these degree programs. The reader will recognize that these characteristics have been considered in the professional programs of psychology, and indeed were identified by prior groups such as JCPEP (Stigall et al., 1990). First, the graduates of a professional degree program should demonstrate a level of professional practice appropriate to the stated purpose of the degree. Within psychology, that expectation translates to doctoral level competence. Second, advanced practice doctorates should be equipped to utilize current research related to the profession. Third, graduates should understand and support the work of other professionals and the contributions those professions make to society, ideally being able to function in multidisciplinary teams. Fourth, graduates should display advanced levels of communication skills and critical-thinking skills. And last, graduates should demonstrate the ability to identify critical population-based issues and form solutions that influence the health and welfare of society.

In summary, although accreditation as an activity within psychology operates independently, it also functions within a context of higher education that significantly influence criteria and procedures. These influences must be understood and acknowledged in order to maintain accreditation and to protect its future.

Current Issues and Future Trends

There are several pressing issues within accreditation, and others that are emerging. Four issues are considered in this section of the chapter: (1) the internship "imbalance," (2) online and distance education, (3) the potential of a competitive accreditation system within professional psychology, and (4) the planned revision of the accreditation criteria.

Internship Imbalance

The accreditation criteria currently require that a predoctoral internship be completed before the awarding of the doctoral degree (APA, 2009). There are two places where the internship is part of the accreditation criteria: in Domain A, Eligibility: "The program requires of each student a minimum of three full-time academic years of graduate study (or the equivalent) and completion of an internship prior to awarding the doctoral degree." The other location is Domain B, Program Philosophy, Objective and Curriculum Plan: "Describe and justify the sufficiency of practicum experiences required of students in preparation for an internship."

At the time of the development and approval of these criteria (mid 1990s), the number of students seeking an internship was roughly equivalent to the number of training slots available. Thus, programs were asked to consider, in their model of training, how much practicum was required for students prior to internship as a function of the program's overall objectives. It was less important for programs to document that all students were placed in an internship, since this was an outcome that was presumed to occur universally (see Keilin, 2000).

Although APA accredits internships, they are also members of an organization known as the Association of Psychology Postdoctoral and Internship Centers (APPIC). The criteria for membership in APPIC are distinct from APA accreditation requirements. Thus, there are APPIC member internships not accredited by APA for reasons of choice, financial burden, or developmental trajectory. APPIC (2012) membership criteria are as follows:

> An organized training program that, in contrast to supervised experience or on-the-job training, is designed to provide the intern with a planned, programmed sequence of training experiences; the presence of a doctoral level staff psychologist who is responsible for the integrity and quality of the training program, who is licensed in the jurisdiction where the program exists, and who is present at the facility a minimum of 20 hours a week; agency staff consists of a minimum of two full-time equivalent doctoral level staff who are licensed and who serve as primary supervisors of the interns; interns receive doctoral level supervision at least one hour a week for each 20 internship hours (e.g., two hours a week for a 40 hour internship); training in a range of assessment and intervention activities; 25% of an intern's time is spent in face to face delivery of services; the intern receives at least two hours a week of didactic training; internship is post-practicum and precedes the awarding of the doctoral degree; and the agency has at least two interns at any given time who are each at least half-time; there are clear descriptions of the internship and also policies regarding due process and intern evaluation; the interns are formally evaluated at least twice each year; and the internship has sufficient resources to achieve its goals and objectives (e.g., interns must be paid).

At the time of the writing of this chapter, APPIC listed 686 internship programs and 144 postdoctoral programs in its online directory. The APPIC website provides both historical statistical information and a list of resources at www.appic.org.

The situation that has been termed a "crisis" in the literature (see Stedman, Schoenfeld, Caroll & Allen, 2009 is that the number of applicants for internship has rapidly outgained the number of available positions. Although this differential was evident as far back as 1998, when APA and APPIC co-convened a conference on what was termed an "imbalance" (Keilin, Thorn, Rodolfa, Constantine, & Kaslow, 2000), the differential has been increasingly evident. In the 2007 match (the process by which intern applicants are matched to internship positions), statistics on the APPIC website indicate there were 949 unplaced applicants, 530 of whom found a position after the match process. However, these later positions often were unpaid, or created simply for the applicant's convenience. By 2012, the numbers were more alarming. During that match year, APPIC reports revealed that 4,435 students registered for the match but 368 withdrew prior to the process (likely because they did not receive any interest). Of the 4,067 students who participated in the match, 78% were matched but only 53% of the 4,067 were matched to an accredited internship. If the 368 who withdrew and the 915 who did not match, all continued their training another year and then reapplied, and the numbers of regular applicants the next year simply holds steady: in 2013 there will be approximately 5,700 applicants for 703 sites offering 3,200 positions.

Various solutions to this imbalance have been offered over time (see the *Special Issue* on the internship issue of *Training and Education in Professional Psychology*, 2007, volume 1, issue 4). These solutions have included increasing the number of internship positions, reducing the number of applicants, or changing the criteria for accreditation such that no internship is required for the doctoral degree.

Increasing the number of positions is an attractive solution put forward by many persons (i.e., Baker, McCutcheon, & Keilin, 2007). More recently, the APA has moved to provide financial assistance to internships to increase their capacity to become accredited. For example, the APA allocated up to $3 million dollars in 2012 (i.e., Internship Stimulus Package) to be spent over three years to award grants to unaccredited internships to cover the costs of accreditation application fees, intern stipends, and other financial barriers facing unaccredited programs. (These grants are limited to applicant internship programs operated by nonprofit entities.) The other change is that the CoA has approved a new accreditation status for internships and postdoctoral residencies, to become effective in 2013 if approved by the APA Board of Educational Affairs and Board of Directors. This change would provide for candidacy status and contingency status for programs that choose not to follow the current process of full accreditation. APPIC is supporting its member programs who meet the appropriate criteria to pursue both possibilities.

The second option, to reduce the number of applicants, is more controversial. Neimeyer, Rice, and Keilin (2007) provide data that reveal that programs with practice-oriented models had a lower match rate in the 2003 match (77%) than students from science-oriented and science-practice programs (88%). Similar data were found by Parent and Williamson (2010): their analysis of the 2000 through 2006 match data indicate that 15 programs, fewer than 4% of the total number of programs, contributed 30% of the unmatched applicants. Although it is intuitively attractive to ask these and other programs with more unmatched students to reduce their enrollment of students to decrease the number of students in the pipeline, it is not an option that many programs support. As discussed earlier in the chapter, most solutions to higher education problems come about through protracted discussions by a variety of organizations. There are also issues related to restraint of trade: Oehlert and Lopez (1998) note that any efforts by outside organizations to become involved in decisions made by individual students and institutions might leave the organizations exposed to litigation.

Stedman et al. (2009) proposed a new solution to the imbalance that would require programs to place at least 50% of their eligible students in internship or be placed on probation (an adverse accreditation decision). Programs placing fewer than 50% would then be required to reduce their entering class by 20% in order for students from those programs to participate in the APPIC match process in the next year. Over time, then, programs would achieve the 50% threshold or would reduce their entering class to a level whereby reliably 50% of the applicants were placed.

The fact that Stedman and colleagues' (2009) solution would require changes to the accreditation criteria has prevented its adoption to date. However, the CoA (CoA, 2012) proposed a new implementing regulation concerning a threshold of students accepted into internships. This regulation requires programs to provide the percentage of students accepted into internships in the annual program review process. Programs that place fewer than 50% of their students would be identified and asked to provide additional information concerning this problem to the CoA. This 50% threshold will likely go into effect after the CoA reviews the 2013 annual review data. However, the reality remains that the CoA will continue to need to make accreditation decisions predicated on a self-study and a site visit. Thus, there is not an immediate solution within the system of accreditation to the imbalance problem.

A third potential solution to the internship imbalance is to change the current accreditation criteria that require a predoctoral internship prior to the awarding of the doctoral degree. The internship was originally developed as a training component at a time when practicum placements were less extensive and resulted in students obtaining approximately 400 total hours of clinical work, of which 150 hours were direct contact. That phase is now outdated, given that most students apply for internship with approximately 1,200 to 1,500 hours of clinical work, of which 600 to 700 are in direct contact. Thus, many students now apply for internship with preparation equivalent to what students in previous decades had accumulated by the end of internship. Therefore, it could be argued the internship year is not necessary for the doctorate given the extensive clinical training in doctoral programs. In contrast to this characterization, Rodolfa, Owen, and Clark (2007) have questioned the veracity of practicum experiences that students claim to have.

The supply-demand crisis in professional psychology training is likely to persist. However, if prospective students become aware of the effect of the internship imbalance on their completion of graduate work, they may reconsider plans for graduate study in psychology, or they may select programs that are more successful in internship placement. Second, if the CoA implements the new regulation, these data regarding internship placement may figure into accreditation decision making. Third, as is outlined later in this chapter, it may be that the entire system is in need of reorganization, a process that will begin with revision of accreditation scope, criteria, and procedures.

Online and Distance Education

Distance education (see Moore and Kearsley, 2011) occurs when students receive part or all of their education via technological means such as online chat, wikis, and the like. Traditional terms include "web-facilitated," whereby a course uses Web-based technology to enhance a face-to—face course. A "blended/hybrid" model combines online with face-to-face delivery: examples are online discussions and online content delivery. Last, there is an "online" course whereby most or all content is delivered online and there are no face-to-face meetings. There are many institutions in which education is delivered online either primarily or in part, including bachelors, masters, and doctoral degree programs in psychology. In fact, psychology is among business and education as professional practice areas where there is "penetration," meaning the percent of programs delivered at a distance is a significant minority of the total number of programs, ranging from 20% to 30%.

The national state of distance learning in the United States was summarized by Allen and Seaman (2011). In their report, they assert several conclusions. First, 65% of chief academic officers (e.g., vice presidents of academic affairs) stated that online education was critical to their institutional long-term plans, and they would likely be increasing the number of courses offered through distance modalities. Second, 31% of all higher education students take at least one course online. Third, although 67% of academic officers believe their institution has evidence that learning outcomes achieved by distance education are equal to those achieved in traditional classroom formats, the other third of academic officers believe distance-related outcomes are inferior. Fourth, less than one-third of academic officers believe that their faculty accepts the legitimacy of distance education. Last, from the students' point of view, when student satisfaction is directly compared, the great majority of students find face-to-face and online courses to be about the same, with a small minority preferring face-to-face and an equally small minority preferring online.

In 2010 the CoA adopted implementing regulation C-27, which specified that "a doctoral program delivering education and training substantially or completely by distance education is not compatible with the Guidelines and Principles (the accreditation criteria) and could not be accredited." The APA (CoA, 2010) defined distance education as a formal process in which the majority of instruction occurs when students and faculty are not in the same place. Three aspects of distance education qualify as significant accreditation concerns and are noted in the CoA comment on IR C-27. First, is the lack of face-to-face interaction over a sustained time period between faculty and students. Historically, graduate programs required a year in "residence," a time when full-time enrollment increases student involvement with faculty both in and outside of formal classes.

Within psychology specifically, ongoing mentorship is thought to occur as faculty and students complete a variety of tasks—producing and publishing research, sustaining a clinical initiative, or completing a dissertation—over an extended time with many personal contacts. Although distance education models have residency requirements, these are typically completed in intense formats, such as over a long weekend or over a week.

A second concern is oversight of clinical training. When program faculty cannot directly supervise students clinically, they are reliant on the opinion of supervisors. In distance education programs, faculty may have never met these supervisors who work in clinical contexts that the faculty have never visited or viewed. This concern applies to a variety of clinical modalities, including assessment, intervention, supervision and consultation, and so on.

A third concern is that online programs typically have a higher attrition rate than traditional programs; whether this differential occurs because of lower admission requirements or unrealistic student expectations is not clear. A final concern is that most states' requirements for licensure as a psychologist require a year of residency at the degree-granting institution (see Association of State and Provincial Psychology Boards, [ASPPB]; http://www.asppb.net). Thus, students may complete a degree at an online institution but find they cannot be licensed in the state in which they desire to practice.

Alternate Means to Accreditation

As was detailed earlier in the chapter, the clinical scientist model of psychology graduate education focuses on science-centered education and training. Therefore, these programs emphasize the acquisition of a variety of scientific skills to design, evaluate, and disseminate empirically supported intervention and assessment modalities. Although graduates of programs adopting this model may enter practice, the majority of graduates are expected to develop career trajectories of contribution to science (e.g., research universities, medical schools, institutes of science). Baker, McFall, and Shoham (2009) outlined consequences to the health-care system when decision making regarding psychological treatments is guided by evidence that is nonscientific, or when interventions shown to be efficacious are not used by psychologists. Faculty working in clinical-scientist models assume these consequences, including a failure to impact clinical and public health, are due to the lack of adequate scientific training in graduate study in clinical psychology.

An independent, nonprofit organization was established in 2007 to promote a model of training that emphasized appropriate scientific training, and to establish a system of accrediting doctoral programs in this model as an alternative to APA accreditation. The Psychological Clinical Science Accreditation System (PCSAS) has functioned since its establishment to meet these goals. Currently, PCSAS has 14 accredited programs. The general criteria areas for accreditation include eligibility, general standards, science quality, quality improvement, and outcomes. For example, eligible programs: must grant PhD degrees in psychology and be housed in departments of psychology or their equivalent in accredited, research-intensive universities in the United States and Canada; must subscribe to an "empirical epistemology" and the scientific model; must state the primary mission of providing students with high-quality, science-centered education; and must have, as a main goal, the production of graduates with competence to conduct research relevant to health and mental health disorders.

As with any other accreditor, PCSAS operates within external systems of recognition described earlier in this chapter. Thus, PCSAS submitted a proposal to CHEA in 2011 to be recognized to accredit doctoral programs in psychology. The Board of Directors of CHEA determined that PCSAS was eligible to be reviewed by CHEA, and PCSAS then completed a self-evaluation. A CHEA observer was present at a decision-making meeting of PCSAS in late 2011, and the organization was placed on the CHEA agenda for 2012. The final decision was to recognize PCSAS, and this decision was made in September, 2012.

PCSAS accreditation is not incompatible with APA accreditation, and, in fact, APA also accredits most of the accredited programs in PCSAS. However, it is likely that institutions will fail to see a need for a program to participate over time in two parallel accreditation processes. It is unclear whether CHEA recognition of PCSAS will result in those programs declining accreditation by APA. A second issue is that PCSAS' operating budget is modest compared to the budgets of other agencies, and external fundraising targeted for a five year period that will end soon. Whether PCSAS can be financially sustained remains to be seen.

Revision of Accreditation Scope, Criteria and Procedures

It is not surprising that the CoA has determined to consider the development of a new set of accreditation standards. The current standards were implemented in 1996, and as is clear from this chapter, many changes have occurred in programs and institutions and within higher education. In order for APA to modify accreditation standards, requirements for its recognition by DoE and CHEA must be adhered to, in particular the requirements for input from all interested groups and organizations. Therefore, APA has proposed a roadmap of a 4-phase process as follows:

Phase 1. The CoA creates questions for input from relevant persons and organizations, and receives comments until October, 2012.

Phase 2. Based on their review of comments, the CoA will create additional questions for input, and will receive comments during 2013. During this phase, the CoA will also develop a strategy for creating new standards.

Phase 3. During 2013, the CoA will develop new standards and receive public comment.

Phase 4. During 2014, the CoA will revise the standards, receive public comment, and develop a final product for consideration by APA governance. Final action should occur during 2015.

Phase 1 is underway and CoA has promulgated questions for public response, clustered in specific domains. First, general questions pertained to the strengths and weaknesses of the current accreditation standards and perceived necessary changes in the next two decades. Second, questions about doctoral programs addressed perceptions of criteria related to faculty and students, necessary competencies, doctoral education generally, and the role of internship training. Third, questions regarding internship attended to the composition and organization of internship training, including necessary resources and intern evaluation. Fourth, postdoctoral residency questions were concerned with the necessary differentiation of postdoctoral training from doctoral training, including a focus on specialty training.

Given that the previous revision of the accreditation standards consumed about five years, it will be some time before the new standards are developed, approved, and implemented. With any change in standards comes a need to redefine the necessary members of the decision making body, to re-train site visitors, and to develop policy and procedure manuals. Therefore, complete implementation is a multiyear process.

Summary

It is instructive to compare current challenges within accreditation to those documented when accreditation was summarized about a decade ago. Beidel, Phillips, and Zlotlow (2003) outlined nine challenges to accreditation's future. Four of those challenges continue today: (1) using accreditation as quality assurance, (2) distance education, (3) governmental influence on accreditation, and (4) the components of adequate doctoral training.

One challenge noted in 2003 was the voluntary nature of accreditation. Accreditation was originally considered to be a voluntary, peer-driven system of quality assurance. However, increased external influence has created a context in which doctoral-program accreditation is required for licensure as a psychologist in several states and in which certain governmental monies can only be used for an accredited program or internship. It is likely that accreditation will be less voluntary and more essential in the future.

One challenge has been solved, albeit not in the way originally anticipated. Doctoral programs in Canada in the past could be jointly approved by the Canadian Psychological Association (CPA) and the APA, but that joint approval has been phased out. As of 2012, however, the two organizations signed the First Street Accord, attesting that both organizations view each other's accreditation guidelines and principles as equivalent. This mutual agreement applies to the accreditation activities each association undertakes in its own country. However, this agreement does not confer any accreditation status on a program in the other country.

Other challenges remain unsolved. First, the question of where to locate specialty education during training in professional psychology persists: Is it at the doctoral level, in the internship, or in the postdoctoral residency? Although specialties continue at the doctoral level (e.g., clinical, counseling, school), whether internship and postdoctoral training should be specialized versus general is still not clear. Second, the appropriate scope of accreditation—the programs to which accreditation is offered—remains unresolved. In 1996, it was anticipated that "emerging specialties" would be accredited, but that anticipation has not materialized. A third unresolved issue is how to understand and respond to influence exerted on accreditation activities by entities external to the CoA itself, both within APA and in the larger context of higher education and federal government.

It is obvious that a commitment to quality is very much evident in all the activities related to accreditation. Since that commitment has been present in the past 50 years of accreditation's history, it can be expected to continue. An optimistic view, therefore, considers the next several decades as a time for revision, renewal, and change within the larger context of the values of professional psychology.

References

Acrum, R., & Roksa, J. (2011). *Academically adrift: Limited learning on college campuses*. Chicago, IL: University of Chicago Press.

Allen, I. E., & Seaman, J. (2011). *Going the distance: Online education in the United States, 2011*. Babson Park, MA: Babson Survey Research Group. Retrieved September 26, 2012 from http://www.onlinelearningsurvey.com/reports/goingthedistance.pdf

Altmaier, E. M., & Claiborn, C. D. (1987). Some observations on research and science. *Journal of Counseling and Development, 66,* 51.

American Psychological Association, Commission on Accreditation. (2009). *Guidelines and principles for accreditation of programs in professional psychology*. Washington, DC: American Psychological Association.

Association of Psychology Postdoctoral and Internship Centers (2012). 2012 APPIC Match Statistics. Retrieved October 23, 20112 from http://www.appic.org/Match/MatchStatistics/MatchStatistics2012Combined.aspx

Association of Specialized and Professional Accreditors. (1995). *Member code of good practice*. Chicago, IL: Association of Specialized and Professional Accreditors. Retrieved September 19, 2012 from http://www.aspa-org.

Baker, J., McCutcheon, S., & Keilin, W. G. (2007). The internship supply-demand imbalance: The APPIC perspective. *Training and Education in Professional Psychology, 1,* 287–293.

Baker, T. B., McFall, R. M., & Shoham, V. (2009). Current status and future prospects of clinical psychology: Toward a scientifically principled approach to mental and behavioral health care. *Psychology of Science in the Public Interest, 9,* 67–103.

Beidel, D. C., Phillips, S. D., & Zlotlow, S. (2003). The future of accreditation. In E. M. Altmaier (Ed.), *Setting standards in graduate education: Psychology's commitment to excellence in accreditation* (pp. 134). Washington, DC: American Psychological Association.

Belar, C. D., & Perry, N. W. (1992). National conferences on scientist-practitioner education and training for the professional practice of psychology. *American Psychologist, 47,* 71–75.

Benjamin, L. T. (2006). American psychology's struggles with its curriculum: Should a thousand flowers bloom? *Training and Education in Professional Psychology, S*(1), 58–68.

Commission on Accreditation. (2010). *Policy and procedure update, April 2010*. Washington, DC: American Psychological Association. Retrieved September 19, 2012 from http://www.apa.org/ed/accreditation/about/policies/index.aspx

Commission on Accreditation. (2012). *Commission on Accreditation update, August 2012*. Washington, DC: American Psychological Association, Retrieved October 28, 2012 from http://www.apa.org/ed/accreditation/newsletter/2013/03/roadmap.aspx

Council for Higher Education Accreditation (2010). *Recognition of accrediting organizations*. Washington, DC: Council for Higher Education Accreditation.

Cutts, N. (1955). *School psychologists at midcentury: A report of the Thayer Conference on the functions, qualification, and training of school psychologists.* Washington, DC: American Psychological Association.

Hacker, A., & Dreifus, C. (2010). *Higher education? How colleges are wasting our money and failing our kids—and what can we do about it.* New York: Times Books.

Kanz, J. (2003). Introduction to the appendixes. In E. M. Altmaier (Ed.) *Setting standards in graduate education: Psychology's commitment to excellence in accreditation* (pp. 135–184). Washington, DC: American Psychological Association.

Keilin, W. G. (2000). Internship selection in 1999: Was the Association of Psychology Postdoctoral and Internship Centers match a success? *Professional Psychology: Research and Practice, 31,* 281–187.

Keilin, W. G., Thorn, B. E., Rodolfa, E. R., Constantine, M. G., & Kaslow, N. J. (2000). Examining the balance of internship supply and demand: 1999 Association of Psychology Postdoctoral and Internships Centers' match implications. *Professional Psychology: Research and Practice, 31,* 288–294.

Kells, H. R. (1995). *Self-study processes: A guide to self-evaluation in higher education* (4th ed.). Phoenix, AZ: Oryx Press.

Korman, M. (Ed.) (1976). *Levels and patterns of professional training in psychology.* Washington, DC: American Psychological Association.

McFall, R. (2006). Doctoral training in clinical psychology. *Annual Review of Clinical Psychology, 2,* 21–49.

Moore, M. G., & Kearsley, G. (2005). *Distance education: A systems view of online learning* (2nd ed.) Belmont, CA: Wadsworth Cengage Learning.

Murphy, M. J., Levant, R. F., Hall, J. E., & Glueckauf, R. L. (2007). Distance education in professional training in psychology. *Professional Psychology: Research and Practice, 38,* 97–103.

Neimeyer, G. J., Rice, K. G., & Keilin, W. G. (2007). Does the model matter? The relationship between science-practice emphasis in clinical psychology programs and the internship match. *Training and Education in Professional Psychology, 1,* 153–162.

Nelson, P. D., & Messenger, L. C. (2003). Accreditation in psychology and public accountability. In E. M. Altmaier (Ed.), *Setting standards in graduate education: Psychology's commitment to excellence in accreditation* (pp. 7–38). Washington, DC: American Psychological Association.

Oehlert, M. E., & Lopez, S. J. (1998). APA-accredited internships: An examination of the Supply and demand issue. *Professional Psychology: Research and Practice, 29,* 189–194.

Parent, M.C., & Williamson, J. B. (2010). Program disparities in unmatched internship applicants. *Training and Education in Professional Psychology, 4,* 116–120.

Raimy, V. C. (Ed.). (1950). *Training in clinical psychology.* New York: Prentice Hall.

Roe, A., Gustad, J. W., Moore, B. V., Ross, S., & Skokak, M. (Eds.) (1959). *Graduate education in psychology.* Washington, DC: American Psychological Association.

Rodolfa, E. R., Owen, J. J., & Clark, S. (2007). Practicum training hours: Fact and fantasy. *Training and Education in Professional Psychology, 1,* 64–73.

Stedman, J. M., Schoenfeld, L. S., Carroll, K., & Allen, T. F. (2009). The internship supply-demand crisis: Time for a solution is now. *Training and Education in Professional Psychology, 3,* 135–139.

Stigall, T. T., Bourg, E. F., Bricklin, P. M., Kovacs, A. L., Larsen, K. G., Lorion, R. P., et al. (Eds.) (1990). *Report of the Joint Council on Professional Education in Psychology.* Baton Rouge, LA: Land & Land.

Stricker, G., & Trierweiler, S. J. (2006). The local clinical scientist: A bridge between science and practice. *Training and Education in Professional Psychology, S*(1), 37–46.

Thompson, A. S., & Super, D. E. (Eds.). (1964). *The professional preparation of counseling psychologists: The report of the 1964 Greyston Conference.* New York: Columbia University Press.

PART 2

Competence and Competencies in Professional Psychology

Competency-Based Education and Training in Professional Psychology

Nadya A. Fouad *and* Catherine L. Grus

Abstract

Competency-based education and training in professional psychology focuses on ensuring that students develop specific competencies in their doctoral education, including practicum and internship. This has been termed moving to a "culture of competence" (Roberts, Borden, Christiansen, & Lopez, 2005), and actually has been comprised of several initiatives over the past decade. This article will discuss those various initiatives; the context for competency-based models in other professions and at other levels (e.g., undergraduate and master's programs) in psychology, and will present the most recent competency-based models in professional psychology. The article ends with recommendations and perspectives on future challenges.

Key Words: competency models, competency-based education, training in professional psychology, competency initiatives, doctoral education

Introduction

Competency-based training in professional psychology focuses on ensuring that students develop specific competencies in their doctoral education. Thus, the focus of training is on the student (or learner) and demonstrating how he or she has achieved competencies in various domains that have been deemed essential to be a psychologist, rather than on what the training program provides. This differs from previous models of training that emphasized a set number of hours of supervised experience needed, or completion of a set curriculum and coursework (Nelson, 2007). As may be expected, moving from traditional models of counting hours and coursework entails a fairly extensive shift in perspectives on training. Roberts, Borden, Christiansen, and Lopez (2005) called this a shift to a "culture of competence." In fact, the shift has consisted of a number of initiatives by various groups over several years. This chapter will examine the context for the shift to a competency-based model in psychology and other professions, and trace the history of the various initiatives. We will review the most recent iteration of competency-based models in professional psychology. Finally, we will provide recommendations and perspectives on future challenges.

The context for competency-based education and training stems from a convergence of three movements. The first is a general zeitgeist of accountability for professionals to benefit the public and not do harm (APA, 2010). A client/patient calling to make an appointment with a psychologist should trust that the psychologist is competent to practice. As a whole, the profession is accountable for that psychologist's competence, and has developed mechanisms to ensure that psychologists are competent. The mechanisms include giving jurisdictions the regulating authority to issue licenses to practice and for doctoral and internship training programs to be accredited when they meet standards of training. As we note in the next section, the link between competency-based outcomes and concern for client/patient care has been particularly apparent in the medical professions, with a general rise in the past two decades of accountability in health care.

A second factor in the development of competency-based training was a move toward outcome-based education and learner-based outcomes (Nelson, 2007). In other words, rather than focusing on what programs are teaching or the way they are teaching it, the emphasis in education is on what students are learning and how they are demonstrating it. The Council on Higher Education Accreditation (CHEA), which recognizes universities, colleges, and such accrediting bodies as the APA Commission on Accreditation has focused on learner outcomes since the mid 1990s (Ewell, 1998), deeming this as part of their accountability to the public for higher education. A focus on outcomes-based education led to changes in the 1996 Guidelines and Principles for Accreditation (APA, 1996). Programs were asked to indicate their goals and objectives for training, and to document the assessment of those outcomes. Without mandating a learner-based competency model, the 1996 shift in the Guidelines and Principles led to programs becoming more familiar with learner-based outcomes of training.

A third impetus for the current competency-based focus in professional training came from a concern about the cost of professional training in psychology. Recent psychology graduates were concerned that they were unable to find employment at a rate sufficient to allow them to begin to repay student loans because they could not seek licensure until at least a year after graduation. They also complained that, in comparison to medical residents, who became immediately licensed, they were treated with less respect in interdisciplinary settings. The APA Board of Directors recognized the need to mirror the level of professionalism held for professional graduates in medicine who are deemed ready to practice directly out of medical school. The result was a 2006 resolution by the APA Council of Representatives that recommended that entry to the profession be at the end of the doctorate. Specifically, the resolution recommended that applicants should be considered for admission to licensure upon completing a "sequential, organized, supervised professional experience equivalent to two years of full-time training that can be completed prior or subsequent to the granting of the doctoral degree" (APA, 2006). One of the two years is to be a pre-doctoral internship for those preparing for practice as health service providers.

Although the resolution was advisory, because APA does not itself license psychologists, the resolution nonetheless threw the professional training and regulatory communities into considerable turmoil. At that point, most states had three general requirements for licensure: a doctorate in applied psychology, a predoctoral internship (typically 1500–2000 hours) and a postdoctoral internship (also typically 1500–2000 hours). The resolution recommended eliminating the postdoctoral requirement. If this was to be adopted, students would have to be able to demonstrate competency to be a psychologist at the end of the doctorate. This meant that doctoral programs and predoctoral internship sites would have to jointly affirm the student was competent to practice, and licensing boards would have to essentially take their word that the student was competent. Thus, rather than assuming competence based on accrual of hours during the postdoctoral year, competence would be determined at the end of the doctorate. Mechanisms needed to be developed to ensure competence acquisition. Assessment tools needed to be created and curriculum needed to be in alignment with a competency-based model.

The recommendation also meant that licensing boards would have to develop policies on practicum training as well as internship training, since supervised training during the entire doctorate would now lead to licensure, rather than just the pre- and postdoctoral internships. The Association of State and Provincial Psychology Boards (ASPPB) has developed a set of guidelines for licensing boards to evaluate the predoctoral practicum experiences (ASPPB, 2009). As of this writing, about 20% of states do not have postdoctoral experiences required for licensure.

However, as the focus has turned to the outcomes of what students learn and to how the profession can be held accountable to demonstrate that the student is competent to practice psychology, several questions have emerged. What are the competencies that are central to becoming a psychologist? How can the competencies be flexible enough to accommodate the many different models of training in psychology? How can the competencies be assessed across various types of programs? Because training occurs across many years, how do the competencies develop over time? Are there specific benchmarks that are needed along the way to determine that competence is developing? Finally, and perhaps most critically, does a competency-based model make a difference in patient care? We address many of these questions in this article, although the last one is still open for investigation, especially within psychology. We turn next to the context for competency-based models in other professions.

National Context: Other Health Professions

The focus on accountability in higher education is broad in scope and has resulted in changes in the education and training in the health professions, with a specific emphasis on competency-based models. Such change is also driven by increased attention to accountability for patient care outcomes, reflecting an era in health care in which consumers increasingly expect health care providers to have the requisite competencies to deliver safe and effective services (Klass, 2007). Instrumental in moving this change process forward was a series of reports by the Institute of Medicine (IOM) that highlighted the need to improve safety in the delivery of health-care services through enhancing the preparation of health professionals (IOM, 2000; IOM, 2001; IOM, 2003). This growing emphasis on defining and measuring student learning outcomes via a competency-based approach subsequently has been reflected in both pedagogical shifts, some driven by discipline-specific accreditation mandates, and in the implementation of the recommendations of these reports.

Medicine, for example, through what started as the Medical School Objectives project in 1998, has not only developed six core competency domains (patient care, medical knowledge, practice-based learning and improvement, interpersonal and communication skills, professionalism, and systems-based practice) but as of 2002 began mandating that graduate medical education programs must demonstrate that students have attained these competencies as part of maintaining accreditation (AAMC, 1998; Carraccio, Wolfsthal, Englander, Ferentz & Martin, 2002; Green et al., 2009). The specific programmatic requirements have been phased in over time and at present programs also are being evaluated with respect to how they use aggregate data from their students' performance to enhance curriculum reform (Green et al., 2009). To assist in this process, specialty specific "milestones" or benchmarks of performance that are both developmental and observable are being formulated for use by programs in the assessment of competence (Green et al., 2009). Other health professions including nursing, dentistry, pharmacy are also emphasizing the assessment of competence as an important component of an education and training program (American Association of Colleges of Nursing, 2006; American Dental Education Association, 2008; American Association of Colleges of Pharmacy, 2004).

Major reports focused on competency-based education and training for health professionals also have been commissioned and their recommendations implemented. Perhaps most instrumental has been the Institute of Medicine's 2003 report on Health Professions Education: A Bridge to Quality (IOM, 2003). The report's authors noted that reform of education of health-care professions was necessary in order to promote quality health-care delivery. Five core competencies are articulated in the document and are meant for all health-care disciplines: (1) provide patient-centered care, (2) work in interdisciplinary teams, (3) employ evidence-based practice, (4) apply quality improvement, and (5) utilize informatics.

This link between quality patient care outcomes and the competencies acquired by health-care professionals also has shaped the focus of more recent competency-based education and training models (IOM, 2003). Specifically, the emphasis on competency-based education is intersecting with an increased attention on the provision of health-care services by health-care teams (IPEC, 2011). This will shift the focus from competencies for specific disciplines to competencies that are cross-cutting for health-service providers. Two types of models have emerged, those specific to interprofessional education and practice and those that articulate competencies that are applicable across multiple professions.

Two paradigms for interprofessional education and practice have been developed in North America. The Canadian Interprofessional Health Collaborative (2010) developed a competency model to articulate the competencies that would guide the education and training process for collaborative practitioners. The goal was that this paradigm would ultimately lead to better health outcomes for consumers. Six competency domains are posited in this model; interprofessional communication, patient/client/family/community-centered care, role clarification, team functioning, collaborative leadership, interprofessional conflict resolution. Interprofessional communication and patient/client/family/community-centered-care support are conceptualized to influence the other four domains in this model. In addition, the complexity of the patient care encounter, the context in which health-care services are being delivered, and quality improvement are all factors that impact the application of this framework.

A similar model was recently developed in the United States as a result of a collaboration between several health-care academic societies representing medicine, nursing, osteopathic medicine, pharmacy, dental, and public health (Interprofessional Education Collaborative Expert Panel, IPEC; 2011). An expert panel, known as the Interprofessional Education Collaborative was convened and developed a model for interprofessional collaborative practice that includes four competency domains: (1) values/ethics for interprofessional practice, (2) roles/responsibilities, (3) interprofessional communication, and (4) teams and teamwork. This document was developed in response to increased interest in the United States (U.S.) in interprofessional education and practice as well as health-care reform legislation enacted in 2011, again with the overarching belief that practitioners with interprofessional competencies will deliver improved health-care services.

A second type of competency model that is emerging in the health-care arena articulates competencies that are intended to be cross-cutting for multiple disciplines. For example, Multidisciplinary Competencies in the Care of Older Adults at the Completion of the Entry-level Health Professional Degree (Partnership for Health in Aging, 2010) is a model developed by a multidisciplinary work group to articulate the competencies needed to provide health-care services to older adults at entry-level to practice. The model was developed in recognition of the need to ensure a competent workforce to serve an aging U.S. population, but also in recognition of the many disciplines that are relevant to the health-care needs of older adults. A common framework, written in the language of expected competencies, not only provides a useful resource for interprofessional education, but also serves as a tool in advocacy efforts to seek resources to expand the health-care workforce prepared to serve older adults.

A second framework that articulates competencies that are meant to be applied to many disciplines is being developed by the Interprofessional Professionalism Collaborative (IPC) Behaviors (2012). This framework articulates competencies related to a concept termed interprofessional professionalism, defined by the IPC as:

> Consistent demonstration of core values evidenced by professionals working together, aspiring to and

wisely applying principles of altruism, excellence, caring, ethics, respect, communication, and accountability to achieve optimal health and wellness in individuals. (Holtman, Frost, Hammer, McGuinn & Nunez, 2011, p. 384)

Competency-based education and training is a major pedagogical emphasis at this time across the health professions. Although its widespread adoption can be linked to the patient safety movement (IOM, 2000; 2001; 2003), it also reflects the emphasis on accountability for learning outcomes that is widespread in higher education. What is noteworthy in this growing development and utilization of competency-based models in health-professions education is that these frameworks are adapting to changes in health-care-service delivery, evolving beyond the interests of single disciplines, to address such issues as competencies for working in interprofessional teams as well as competencies that cut across multiple disciplines. This suggests that competency-based education and training is more than a passing trend to meet federal or regulatory mandates but rather is proving a useful tool in preparing the next generation of health-care providers.

Nondoctoral Competency Models in Psychology

Although efforts to develop and implement competency-based education and training are well underway at the doctoral level in professional psychology, it also must be recognized that several national initiatives focus on competency-based education and training in psychology at the Master's, undergraduate and high school levels.

In response to a national tension between models of competencies that prepare master's level counselors, in 2011, the Society of Counseling Psychology and the Council of Counseling Psychology Training Programs appointed a group to develop a set of competencies that would guide training for counselors at the master's level. The working group's charge was to draft masters-level developmental competencies that would (a) capture the breadth of competency domains relevant to entry level practice as a professional counselor, (b) identify the core aspects of those domains and (c) identify the developmental trajectory for a master's in professional counseling. Their work was guided by the benchmarks competency model for doctoral level training that is described in the next section of the article, however, the group also assumed that professional counseling is distinct from professional doctoral-level psychology, and the professional socialization of counselors is also distinct. Similar to the doctoral-level benchmarks model, 16 competencies are organized into 6 clusters, with developmental progress noted for each of the two years of a master's program. At this point the competencies documents are being circulated for comment by members of the organization.

In 2006, the American Psychological Association (APA, 2007) approved as policy the Guidelines for the Undergraduate Psychology Major, a document that articulates a common set of outcomes for the undergraduate psychology major. These guidelines were developed to promote high-quality education in psychology at the undergraduate level. These guidelines were developed to serve as a resource, and are not mandated, to allow for flexibility in implementation given that undergraduate education in psychology occurs in diverse settings and contexts. Ten goals and learning outcomes for each are identified in these Guidelines and organized under two broad categories: knowledge, skills, and values consistent with the science and application of psychology; and knowledge, skills, and values consistent with liberal arts education that are further developed in psychology. Learning goals for this first category include: knowledge base in psychology, research methods in psychology, critical-thinking skills in psychology, application of psychology, values in psychology. In the second category, the learning goals consist of: information and technical literacy, communication skills, sociocultural and international awareness, personal development, and career planning and development. A companion document, the Assessment Cyberguide for Psychology (APA, 2009b) provides strategies and best practices for the assessment of student learning outcomes at the undergraduate level.

At the high-school level, the National Standards for High School Psychology Curricula (APA, 2011) articulates performance standards that the educational process should be designed to help students meet. Seven broad content areas are identified: scientific inquiry domain, biopsychology domain, development and learning, sociocultural context, cognition, individual variations, and the applications of psychological science. Diversity is to be infused throughout each of the standard areas. This document incorporates a hierarchical structure, each content domain has content standards that are more explicit, and these in turn have performance standards that are written in the form of measurable student learning outcomes.

Doctoral-Level Competency Initiatives in Psychology

As noted earlier, the 1996 changes to the Committee on Accreditation's Guidelines and Principles began a movement toward learner-based outcomes. Around the same time, the National Council of Schools and Programs of Professional Psychology (NCSPP) began to delineate the competencies required of their students in six competency areas: relationship, assessment, intervention, research and evaluation, consultation and education, and management and supervision (Kenkel & Peterson, 2010; Peterson, Peterson, Abrams, & Stricker, 1997; Peterson, Peterson, Abrams, Stricker & Ducheny, 2010). This model recently was updated to reflect developmental achievement levels that are specific knowledge, skills and attitudes to be attained within each of the competency domains (Peterson et al., 2010).

The NCSPP model preceded the 1996 Committee on Accreditation Guidelines and Principles change that asked programs to articulate their outcomes that aligned with their training model. This prompted various specialty programs to articulate their training models, including scientist-practitioner clinical psychology (Belar & Perry, 1992), counseling psychology (Murdock, Alcorn, Heesacker, & Stoltenberg, 1998) and clinical science (McFall, 1991).

Competencies Conference. In response to these various models and perspectives on training as well as the competencies movements in health care, a joint group decided to hold a national meeting with the purpose of helping to identify competencies in psychology training. The goals were to foster greater communication across training models, improve the competence of psychologists, and better serve the public (Kaslow, Borden, Collins, Forrest, Illfelder-Kaye, Nelson, et al, 2004). The conference was entitled "2002 Competencies Conference: Future Directions in Education and Credentialing." Organized principally by the Association of Psychology Postdoctoral and Internship Centers (APPIC) and the American Psychological Association's (APA) Education Directorate, the conference planning group consisted of 10 individuals representing various training constituencies who came together as a steering committee. They developed an online survey to identify the core competency areas in psychology training. Over 350 individuals responded from a variety of professional settings, including educators in doctoral programs and internship centers, psychologists in private practice and psychologists serving in regulatory capacities (e.g., licensing boards). Survey respondents were asked to indicate the core competencies needed for all professional psychologists, as well as any specific competencies needed for professional psychologists in various training models. Eight core competency areas were identified: scientific foundations, ethics, supervision, assessment, individual and cultural diversity, intervention, consultation, and professional development.

Invitations were issued to over 120 individuals from various training councils as well as members at large. Individuals were assigned to a workgroup focusing on one of the eight core competency areas. Two additional workgroups were formed, one on the assessment of competencies and a second focusing on specialties. Workgroups were asked to identify the various components of the competency and how they are acquired. Various activities were designed to provide members with opportunities to discuss how the competencies could be integrated. The conference ended with presentations from each group on the various subcomponents of their competency (Kaslow, et al. 2004). Workgroups were strongly encouraged to disseminate their findings and a number of articles based on this conference were published, including on scientific foundations (Bieschke, Fouad, Collins & Halonen, 2004); individual and cultural diversity (Daniel, Roysircar, Abeles & Boyd, 2004); ethics (de las Fuentes, Willmuth & Yarrow, 2005); professional development (Elman, Illfelder-Kaye & Robiner, 2005); assessment (Krishnamurthy et al., 2004);) intervention (Spruill et al., 2004) supervision (Falender et al., 2004); consultation (Arredondo, Shealy, Neale, & Winfrey, 2004 and assessing competence (Roberts et al., 2005).

The tenth group, which focused on specialties, developed a framework for competencies that has significantly influenced subsequent thinking about competencies (Rodolfa et al., 2005). The framework, called the Cube Model, is organized in three dimensions. The first dimension is termed foundational competencies, which are the competencies that underlie all the subsequent work that psychologists perform. The six foundational competencies included reflective practice/self-assessment, scientific knowledge and methods, relationships, ethics and legal standards/policy issues, individual and cultural diversity, and interdisciplinary systems. These six intersect with six functional competencies on a second axis.

Functional competencies comprise the domains in which psychologists work: assessment/diagnosis/conceptualization, interventions, consultations, research/evaluation, supervision/teaching and management/administration. Finally, the third axis of the Cube is developmental stage, from doctoral education to continuing specialty competency. For example, one cell of the cube might focus on the competencies needed to understand the ethics of assessment during doctoral education.

Practicum Competencies Outline. The 2002 Competencies Conference thus helped to identify and define the core competency areas in professional psychology. At the same time, the Association of Psychology Training Clinics (APTC) began to identify domains and levels of competence for practicum training. The Practicum Competencies Outline (Hatcher & Lassiter, 2007) identified the skills developed during practicum. Ten skills included relational/interpersonal, application of research, psychological assessment, intervention, consultation/interprofessional collaboration, individual and cultural diversity, ethics, leadership, supervisory skills, and professional development. An eleventh skill is termed meta-competencies, which is an evaluation of knowing the extent and limits of one's own knowledge. The skill is also termed skilled learning. The outline included a rating scale in which practicum supervisors were asked to rate students as novice, intermediate or advanced on each competency area.

Benchmarks Competencies Model. The Practicum Competencies Outline (Hatcher & Lassiter, 2007) was the first attempt to assess developmental level, the third dimension of the cube. Although the Outline was published in 2007, the practicum competencies were presented for discussion and review at the semi-annual meeting of the Council of Chairs of Training Councils (CCTC) in 2004 and 2005, prompting discussion of how to further delineate the developmental levels of the core competencies identified through the Competencies Conference and the Cube model.

A proposal was made to ask a workgroup to identify developmental stages for each of the competencies. A steering committee identified 36 individuals who had content area expertise in one or more areas of competencies and who worked at various stages of training (doctoral, internship, postdoctoral and specialty levels). The group came together in 2006 as the Benchmarks Workgroup for a two-day meeting. Four working groups were identified to determine the specific competency behaviors needed for students to be ready to progress to the next level of training. The four groups were: readiness to begin practicum training, readiness for internship, readiness for entry to practice, readiness to advanced practice and specialization.

Groups were asked to identify the subcomponents, termed essential components, of each competency area. They also were asked to identify the behavioral examples specific to their level. The latter was designed to operationalize the essential component. Participants were asked to consider behavior that, if observed, would provide evidence that the competency would have been met. Thus, for example, under the Individual and Cultural Diversity Competence, self-awareness was identified by all groups as an essential component. At the readiness for practicum group, this was operationalized as, *knowledge and awareness of one's own situation relative to dimensions of individual and cultural diversity*, demonstrated by articulating how ethnic group values influence who one is and how one relates to others. At the readiness for advanced practice and specialty level, this was operationalized as, *independently monitors and applies knowledge of self as a cultural being in assessment, treatment, and consultation with awareness/sensitivity to specific populations and problems*. This would be demonstrated by regularly and independently using knowledge of self to monitor and improve effectiveness as a professional. Overall, the developmental trajectory was defined by increasing levels of independence and accountability.

Each group completed this task for all 12 competency areas, then groups were re-formed to assess similarity in essential components for each competency area and to evaluate how the behavioral examples developmentally progressed. By the end of the two-day meeting, a complex document was developed that consisted of four columns (one for each developmental level), organized into 12 competency area, each with 2 or more essential components, and each with 2 or more behavior examples that operationalized the essential components. The 36 participants then were divided into 12 groups of 3; each group was asked to critically evaluate the developmental trajectory of one competency.

The final set of competencies by developmental stage was opened for comment and feedback by the training community. Concerns were voiced about the fourth level being too broad and encompassing more than one stage of development. Comments also focused on additional specific behavioral examples, and the need for additional competency areas.

The comments were reviewed by a small group of participants in the Benchmarks meeting. After considerable discussion, there was recognition that additional development was needed before dissemination of the fourth level (Readiness for Advanced Practice and Specialization) would be appropriate. The final publication only included the first three levels (Fouad, et al., 2009); further development on the fourth level is currently underway.

Three additional competencies were added to the first 12: Professionalism, Teaching, and Advocacy. The revised document was published in 2009 in a special issue of Training and Education in Professional Psychology (Fouad, et al, 2009), along with the Toolbox Assessment kit, discussed next. (Kaslow et al., 2009).

Benchmarks Revisions

The 2009 Benchmarks article reflected the culmination of a series of steps that involved many opportunities for feedback and comment about the content of the benchmarks. However, once they were published, it quickly became clear that the sheer length and complexity of the document itself was overwhelming to the point of interfering with practical implementation. Some of the scholars invited to comment on the benchmarks article confirmed this concern (e.g., DeMers, 2009). The Benchmarks Working Group charged with developing materials for implementation of the benchmarks also found resistance in using the benchmarks from supervisors and colleagues due to the length and comprehensiveness of the document. The group decided to hold a two day meeting in 2011 to address the concerns that the document was too difficult to use.

The decision was made to reframe the benchmarks into clusters of competencies. A nominal group technique (Murphy et al, 1998, Black et al, 1999) was used to achieve consensus on which competency went into which cluster. Six clusters were identified: professionalism, relational, science, applications, education, and systems. Professionalism included the competencies of professional values, ethics/legal standards, individual and cultural diversity, and reflective practice/self-care. Relational included the competency of relationships, and science included the competencies of scientific knowledge and methods and research/evaluation. These three clusters are considered foundational clusters. The three functional clusters are applications, education, and interdisciplinary systems. The application cluster included the competencies of assessment/diagnosis/conceptualization, intervention, consultation and evidence-based practice. The educational cluster included supervision and teaching competencies, and the interdisciplinary systems cluster included management/administration and advocacy competencies. Note that one additional competency, evidence-based practice, was included in the application cluster. This was included in recognition of the increasing importance of the competency (Wampold, Goodheart & Levant, 2007), as evidenced by specific inclusion as a Commission on Accreditation guideline (APA, 2009a).

In addition to grouping the competencies into clusters, the Benchmarks Working Group made three additional changes to the Benchmarks document. First, all of the behavioral examples were moved into an appendix. The second change was to add a rating scale associated with the benchmark competencies. Supervisors would be asked to evaluate how characteristic the competency description is of the student's behavior on a scale from 0 (not at all/slightly) to 4 (very). Third, rating forms for each level were made available as stand-alone documents. Individuals could download the rating form with all three levels (readiness for practicum, readiness for internship, and readiness for entry to practice), or just one level of interest to them. This removed a good deal of complexity from the document. The entire document, rating forms for each level, separately and combined, and the appendix are available on the APA Education Directorate website (http://www.apa.org/ed/graduate/benchmarks-evaluation-system.aspx).

A clear implication of these changes was the ability for programs to identify which clusters, competencies, and essential components would be critical for their particular program, and to identify the frequency that they expected to observe the competency. Thus, programs could make easier choices about which core competencies fit their training model, and the level to which they expected demonstration of that competency.

Specialty-Specific Competency Models. As general consensus has been reached with regard to what constitutes core competencies for professional psychology, various recognized specialties have also articulated specialty-specific competency models. Examples of models developed by specialty areas within professional psychology include clinical health (France, et al., 2008), professional geropsychology (Knight, Karel, Hinrichsen, Qualls & Duffy, 2009), clinical neuropsychology (Hannay et al., 1998), rehabilitation psychology (Stiers,

et al, in press), and school psychology (Daly, Doll, Schulte, & Fenning, 2011). Although these models understandably vary with respect to the content included, they also employ different frameworks, and their focus reflects the model for education and training specific to that specialty area.

Clinical health psychology has developed a competency model that reflects both the framework and much of the content included in the benchmarks model (France et al., 2008). Specifically, the core foundational competencies are included and supplemented by additional functional competencies specific to the practice of clinical health psychology. The functional competencies identified are specialty specific and are organized in terms of those that are knowledge-based and those that represent applied competencies; values and attitudes are assumed and not specifically articulated in this model. An additional similarity to the benchmarks is the guiding concept that the foundational competencies are integrated with the functional competencies.

Professional geropsychology, in response to the need to build a well-trained workforce to serve older adults, developed the Pikes Peak Model for training in professional geropsychology (Knight, et al, 2009). The Pikes Peak Model articulates the competencies that are necessary for competent practice with older adults with recognition that they may be acquired at different stages of professional development, including post-licensure. The Pikes Peak Model subsequently has been developed into a self-assessment tool that individuals and training programs can use to determine a professional development plan to develop any competencies that have not been acquired (Karel, Emery, Molinari and the CoPGTP Task Force on the Assessment of Geropsychology Competencies, 2010).

Another example of a specialty-specific competency model comes from clinical neuropsychology. The product of the Houston Conference for education and training in clinical neuropsychology articulated a developmental model for obtaining the requisite knowledge and skills in this specialty area. This model specifies at what levels in the education and training sequence they may be acquired (Hannay et al., 1998). More recently, the specialty of rehabilitation psychology has undergone a process to articulate core competencies specific to postdoctoral education and training (Stiers et al., in press). Six core areas have been identified (assessment, intervention, consultation, research and evaluation, supervision and teaching, management and administration). Within each of the core competency areas a series of activities, knowledge, skills, and abilities and corresponding behaviors could be observed.

Within the specialty of school psychology, attention has been focused on how competency models, such as the benchmarks, relate to other core documents, such as the competencies articulated in the accreditation standards put forth by the National Association of School Psychologists (NASP). Daly and colleagues (2011) note considerable overlap between these two models.

Assessment Toolkit. It has been noted (Kaslow, 2004) that adoption of a competency-based approach to education and training will require resources and understanding of the assessment of competence for full implementation of an education approach that is truly competency-based. Several key manuscripts were published in 2007 that provide a solid foundation for understanding considerations in the assessment of competence based on the work of a task force convened by the APA Board of Educational Affairs on the Assessment of Competence in Professional Psychology. A history of the assessment of competence is summarized by Rubin et al., (2007); models for the assessment of competence are presented by Leigh et al., (2007); challenges in the assessment of competence are addressed by Lichtenberg et al., (2007); and guiding principles for the assessment of competence are discussed by Kaslow, Rubin, Bebeau et al. (2007).

Building on this foundational literature in professional psychology, as well as resources that were developed for medical education (Andrews & Burruss, 2004; Bandiera, Sherbino & Frank, 2006), a work group was convened by APA's Board of Educational Affairs in 2007 and charged with developing a toolkit for the assessment of competence in professional psychology. The Competency Assessment Toolkit for Professional Psychology ("toolkit") provides a number of resources to assist in the implementation of a competency-based approach to education and training (Kaslow et al., 2009). One of the central components of the toolkit is what is termed assessment method fact sheets. The fact sheets briefly describe 15 different competency assessment methods deemed relevant to professional psychology education and training programs by the APA work group. The fact sheets address implementation, strengths, weaknesses, and associated psychometric properties for each method. Examples of the methods include competency evaluation rating forms, case presentations, record review, portfolios and standardized patients. The toolkit contains additional resources including grids that help to easily identify the best methods to assess specific competencies and for what level of education and training. The toolkit is intended to assist education and training programs in the measurement of student learning outcomes by providing information about a range of methods available to assess competencies, as well as specific information about how such methods are used and for the assessment of which competencies at which level. Consider, for example, a training program that wished to augment a focus on the competencies under the professionalism and relationship clusters of the benchmarks. The toolkit would identify the methods of 360 degree evaluation, and competence evaluation ratings forms or patient process and outcome data as useful, particularly at the levels of readiness for internship, entry level to practice, and advanced credentialing. Moreover, the toolkit encourages education and training programs to expand the methods used to assess their students' outcomes and thus engage in promising practices in the assessment of competence by employing a variety of methods or informants (Kaslow, Rubin, Bebeau et al, 2007).

Competency-based Education and Training, Licensure, and Continuing Professional Development

The press for accountability for student-learning outcomes certainly has been a factor driving the increased focus on competency models and the assessment of competence. However, within professional psychology the move toward increasingly adopting competency-based models for education and training also is garnering greater support as professional psychology struggles to address issues related to promoting quality. One key issue is the growing recognition of the reliance on accrued hours of supervised experience as a primary gatekeeping mechanism to determine trainees' competence at key transition points. The specific concern is the limited ability of such an approach to assure trainees are able to display the requisite competencies to move forward with their training (Kaslow & Keilin, 2006; McCutcheon, 2008). Reliance on accruing a set number of hours as a proxy for competence is a long-standing tradition in professional psychology that likely will be difficult to shift in light of issues such as the professional psychology internship imbalance. Rodolfa and colleagues reported on the steady and dramatic increases in the number of hours of supervised experience that trainees acquire prior to applying for internship, and many have concluded this is directly related to perceptions by trainees that the more hours they have accrued, the more likely they are to be perceived as competent by prospective internship sites (Rodolfa, Own & Clark, 2007; Kaslow & Keilin, 2006). This has caused many in the education and training community to question the implications of allowing hours of experience to serve as a proxy for competence for the promotion of quality (Kaslow, Pate & Thorn, 2005).

This increase in the number of hours that trainees acquire prior to internship was a major argument in support of the policy, noted earlier, that was approved by the APA in 2006 that states that eligibility for licensure should occur upon completion of the doctoral degree (APA, 2006). As such, hours of supervised experience completed during practicum training might be used toward meeting the required number of hours for licensure. This has resulted in considerable debate about what defines acceptable practicum experience (Schaffer & Rodolfa, 2011). Although to date this policy has yet to be adopted in the licensing laws of a majority of jurisdictions, it has been adopted in approximately nine, and despite attempts by the ASPPB to provide guidance about using practicum hours for licensure, there are inconsistencies across jurisdictions.

The rise in the number of hours of supervised experience that trainees acquire prior to internship, as well as the changes in requirements for licensure in some jurisdictions that allow these hours to count toward licensure, raise attention to the issues of the relationship between quantity and quality. Specifically, this highlights the fact that existing practices focus more on quantity of experience than the direct assessment of quality and provides a strong argument in support of using a competency-based approach to make such determinations, particularly with regard to "gatekeeping" determinations of readiness for independent practice (Kaslow & Keilin, 2006; McCutcheon, 2008; Rodolfa, Own, & Clark, 2007).

The development of competency models, such as the benchmarks, and their implementation by education and training programs offer an opportunity to enhance quality in education and training by the direct assessment of student learning outcomes. Nonetheless, professional psychology has yet to discontinue the practice of using hours of experience as a component of determining readiness for transitions such as independent practice. Such a change may be facilitated by efforts that are now focused on the maintenance of competence over one's professional lifespan.

ASPPB Practice Analysis

In 2010 ASPPB conducted a study of licensed psychologists as part of their periodic review of the test specifications for the Examination for Professional Practice in Psychology. Interestingly, this most recent practice analysis also sought to identify and validate competencies associated with professional practice (Greenberg, Caro, Smith, 2010). Over 5000 licensed psychologists responded to the survey developed for the practice analysis. Six competency clusters were identified: scientific knowledge, evidenced-based decision making/critical reasoning, interpersonal and multicultural competence, professionalism/ethics, assessment, and intervention/supervision/consultation. Although this represents a significant conceptual shift, at present no changes are being made to the EPPP to directly assess competence (DeMers, Van Horne & Rodolfa, 2008).

Continuing Professional Development and Competency

A challenge has been put forward to the health professions to extend accountability for learning outcomes to continuing professional development (IOM, 2010). Professional psychologists face both an ethical imperative to maintain their competence (APA, 2010) and, in many cases, a mandate from their licensing jurisdiction to engage in continuing-education activities, presumably also in service of promoting ongoing competence. However, little is understood about the relationship between continuing education, professional development, and ongoing competence. Data support a positive relationship between self-reported levels of professional competence and engagement in professional development (Taylor, Neimeyer Zemansky, Rothske, 2012). Lifelong learning also was related to scholarly and professional activities, as well as participation in continuing-education activities. Similarly, Neimeyer, Taylor, and Wear (2009) noted that a majority (81%) of licensed psychologists reported that there was a positive relationship between their continuing-education (CE) activities in the past year and their work-related effectiveness. Although these data provide some limited support for perceived relationships between continuing professional development, CE, and competence, one challenge in making more conclusive statements about these relationships lies in the myriad ways that learning can occur. Neimeyer, Taylor, and Cox (2012) define the differences between formal, informal, incidental and nonformal learning, noting that, of these, only formal learning is structured to meet the challenge of accountability. Specifically, formal learning includes independent verification that the learner participated, assessment of learning, evaluation of the experience, and organizational accountability.

Neimeyer, Taylor and Cox (2012) surveyed licensed psychologists about the range of continuing professional development activities in which they engaged and their self-perceived contributions to ongoing competence. The activities that were most strongly related to continuing professional competence, in order, were self-directed learning, peer consultation, and formal CE. Conducting outcomes assessments of services and serving on professional boards were rated as having the lowest relationship with competence. Although these results provide further evidence of the relationship between continuing professional development and competence, the finding that two of the top-rated learning activities (self-directed learning and peer consultation) are not considered formal learning opportunities poses a possible dilemma with respect to accountability for learning outcomes. Neimeyer, Taylor, and Cox (2012) suggest that the addition of mechanisms of verification and evaluation could help transform these activities into ones that meet the definition of formal learning.

Recommendations and Issues—Challenges and Vision for the Future

Embracing a culture of competence is an evolving process, and a number of issues must be addressed if the field is going to continue to move toward increased use of competency-based models for education and training. Key challenges include evaluating the extant competency models for their current and continued relevance and applying a competency-based focus to the remediation of trainees with problems of professional competence. It is also critical to continue to develop the culture of the assessment of competence. Additionally, training constituencies need to balance the necessary broad and general competencies for professional psychology with specialty specific competencies. It will be important to understand the interplay of the various competencies with one another and balance a focus on competency-based assessment with a broad perspective on the education and training process. It will also be critical to evaluate the impact

of adopting a competency-based approach to education and training on student learning outcomes. Finally, it is important to examine the similarities and differences of competency models focused specifically on preparation for practice and those focused on the practice of psychology.

The benchmarks model built on existing work to define competencies in professional psychology and underwent an extensive, multistep process of developing consensus of the components in the model. This would suggest that the benchmarks model is reflective of some consensus regarding the core competencies in professional psychology. Yet, the knowledge base in psychology is steadily increasing in volume and evolving rapidly (Neimeyer, Taylor & Rozensky, 2012). This raises the question: Are the necessary competencies for professional psychology included in models such as the benchmarks? Are some competency areas missing? Are some that are included unnecessary? A related challenge is determining the extent to which competency models such as the benchmarks reflect evolving areas of practice (e.g., in health-care settings) versus the extent that they reflect the current focus of our education and training programs.

A challenge with competency-based models is how to identify and remediate problems with competence (Kaslow, Rubin, Forrest, et al, 2007). This is particularly a challenge within the traditional cohort models in doctoral training. Cohort models of training focus on coursework that is developed for students in their first year, second year, and so on. But students may vary considerably in their acquisition of competence in various areas. When is the delay in acquisition of competence a problem that needs a remediation plan? How can programs allow for individual student development within their traditional course-delivery models, particularly in times of shrinking resources?

To the extent that there is growing consensus on the broad competency domains for professional psychology and the willingness to focus on measuring student learning outcomes, a challenge for the future is to continue to devote efforts to the assessment of competence. Recommended and promising practices both have been well documented in the literature (e.g., Kaslow, Rubin, Bebeau, et al., 2007). However, it remains less clear how broadly they are being adopted by education and training programs. Two key practices that warrant continued focus are the of use multimethod, multi-informant evaluations and the use of performance-based methods in which the evaluation resembles the actual behaviors that students will engage in (e.g., interviewing a standardized patient).

Belar (2009), in a commentary on the Benchmarks Model, offered a number of considerations that remain worthy of continued attention. Two, in particular, merit mention. The first, relates to the structure of the Benchmarks Model that focused on each core competency and defined developmental expectations for each separately. This discrete approach was preferred for reasons of feasibility, but it fails to reveal how the core competencies intersect with each other. Attention to this intersection should be addressed at some point in the future. A second caution raised by Belar is to avoid losing sight of issues of pedagogy by overly focusing on outcomes.

Another challenge is that the identification of competencies that cross many training models may have the consequence of preparing a generalist psychologist. This may have the unintended consequence of losing sight, over time, of the very real philosophical and disciplinary differences between disciplines within psychology. Thus, it is important that the training councils of counseling and clinical psychology follow the lead of school psychology to identify how their specialty demonstrates each competency.

Most of the competency models discussed in this article have been focused on training, rather than practice. However, we also identified the various competency initiatives occurring postlicensure, including the competencies identified in the ASPPB Practice Analysis. Both are significant initiatives, and of course, are linked together in that the competencies in which one is trained must lead to the competencies that are demonstrated in practice. However, the two models serve different purposes, in that the competencies for training are, of necessity, much broader than those for practice. It is important, thus, for both competency models to evolve in an integrated way, although they need not be identical.

The shift within professional psychology toward a competency-based approach to education and training highlights a shared core value: assuming responsibility for the quality of the education and training experience of each student. Assessing student learning outcomes through defined competencies offers a mechanism for ongoing quality assurance and improvement for both the individual student and for education and training programs. Further, as the field takes steps toward self-regulation it demonstrates our commitment to ensuring to the public that those who will engage in the practice of psychology have been prepared to do so in a competent manner.

Finally, as we noted at the beginning of this article, the ultimate evaluation of the shift to a culture of competence is whether it makes a difference in patient or client or patient care. It seems axiomatic that we are accountable to client or patients to ensure that psychologists are competent. But are some areas of competence more linked to increased mental health than others? Fundamentally, do these efforts in identifying and assessing competencies result in improved client or patient well-being? This is our biggest challenge as a field, and one we encourage psychologists to begin to address.

References

American Association of Colleges of Nursing (2006). The essentials of doctoral education for advanced nursing practice. Retrieved July 1, 2013 from: http://www.aacn.nche.edu/publications/position/DNPEssentials.pdf

American Association of Colleges of Pharmacy, (2004). Center for the advancement of pharmaceutical education educational outcomes. Retrieved July 1, 2103 from: http://www.aacp.org/resources/education/Documents/CAPE2004.pdf.

American Dental Education Association (2008). ADEA competencies for the new general dentist. Retrieved July 1, 2013 from: http://www.adea.org/about_adea/governance/Documents/ADEACompetenciesNewDentist.pdf

American Psychological Association (1996). Guidelines and principles for accreditation of programs in professional psychology. Washington, DC: American Psychological Association.

American Psychological Association (2006). Doctorate as minimum entry into the professional practice of psychology. Retrieved July 1, 2103 from: http://www.apa.org/about/policy/chapter-4b.aspx#doctorate-minimum.

American Psychological Association (2007). APA guidelines for the undergraduate psychology major. Washington, DC: Author. Retrieved July 1, 2103 from: http://www.apa.org/ed/precollege/about/psymajor-guidelines.pdf

American Psychological Association (2009a). Guidelines and principles for accreditation of programs in professional psychology. Retrieved July 1, 2103 from http://www.apa.org/ed/accreditation/about/policies/guiding-principles.pdf

American Psychological Association (2009b). The assessment cyberguide for learning goals and outcomes (2nd ed.). Retrieved July 1, 2013 from: http://www.apa.org/ed/governance/bea/assessment-cyberguide-v2.pdf

American Psychological Association (2010). Ethical principles of psychologists and code of conduct. Retrieved July 1, 2013 from: http://www.apa.org/ethics/code/index.aspx

American Psychological Association (2011). National standards for high school psychology curricula. Retrieved July 1, 2013 from: http://www.apa.org/education/k12/psychology-curricula.pdf

Andrews, L. B., & Burruss, J. W. (2004). Core competencies for psychiatric education: Defining, teaching, and assessing resident competence. Washington D.C.: American Psychiatric Publishing.

Arredondo, P., Shealy, C., Neale, M. C., & Winfrey, L. L. (2004). Consultation and interprofessional collaboration: Modeling for the future. *Journal of Clinical Psychology*, 80, 787–800. doi: 10.1002/jclp.20015

Association of American Medical Colleges (1998). Report 1. Learning objectives for medical student education guidelines for medical schools. Retrieved July 1, 2013 from: https://www.aamc.org/initiatives/msop/

Association of State and Provincial Psychology Boards (2009). Guidelines for practicum experience for licensure. Retrieved on February 20, 2012 from http://www.asppb.net/files/public/Final_Prac_Guidelines_1_31_09.pdf

Bandiera, G., Sherbino, J., & Frank, J. R. (Eds.). (2006). *The CanMEDS assessment tools handbook: An introductory guide to assessment methods for the CanMEDS competencies*. Ottawa, Ontario: The Royal College of Physicians and Surgeons of Canada.

Belar, C. D. (2009). Advancing the culture of competence. *Training and Education in Professional Psychology*, 3(4, Suppl), S63–S65. doi:10.1037/a0017541

Belar, C. D., & Perry, N. W. (1992). The National Conference on Scientist-Practitioner Education and Training for the Professional Practice of Psychology. *American Psychologist*, 47(1), 71–75. doi:10.1037/0003-066X.47.1.71

Bieschke, K. J., Fouad, N. A., Collins, F. L., & Halonen, J. S. (2004). The scientifically-minded psychologist: Science as a core competency. *Journal of Clinical Psychology*, 80, 713–724. doi: 10.1002/jclp.20012

Black, N. A., Murphy, M. K., Lamping, D. L., McKee, C. M., Sanderson, C. F. B., Askham, J., & Marteau, T. (1999). Consensus development methods: A review of best practice in creating clinical guidelines. *Journal of Health Services Research and Policy*, 4, 236–248.

Canadian Interprofessional Health Collaborative (2010). A national interprofessional competency framework. Retrieved July 1, 2013 from http://www.cihc.ca/files/CIHC_IP Competencies_Feb1210r.pdf.

Carraccio, C., Wolfsthal, S. D., Englander, R., Ferentz, K., & Martin, C. (2002). Shifting paradigms: From Flexner to Competencies. *Academic Medicine*, 77, 361–367. doi: 10.1 097/00001888-200205000-00003

Daly, E. J. III, Doll, B., Schulte, A. C. & Fenning, P. (2011). The competencies initiative in American professional psychology: implications for school psychology preparation. *Psychology in the Schools*, 48, 872–886. doi: 10.1002/pits.20603

Daniel, J. H., Roysircar, G., Abeles, N., & Boyd, C. (2004). Individual and cultural diversity competency: Focus on the therapist. *Journal of Clinical Psychology*, 80, 755–770. doi: 10.1002/jclp.20014

de las Fuentes, C., Willmuth, M. E., & Yarrow, C. (2005). Ethics education: The development of competence, past and present. *Professional Psychology: Research and Practice*, 36, 362–366. doi: 10.1037/0735-7028.36.4.362

DeMers, S. T. (2009). Real progress with significant challenges ahead: Advancing competency assessment in psychology. *Training and Education in Professional Psychology*, 3(4, Suppl), S66–S69. doi:10.1037/a0017534

DeMers, S. T., Van Horne, B. A., & Rodolfa, E. R. (2008). Changes in training and practice of psychologists: Current challenges for licensing boards. *Professional Psychology: Research and Practice*, 39(5), 473–479. doi:10.1037/0735-7028.39.5.473

Elman, N., Illfelder-Kaye, J. & Robiner, W. (2005). Professional development: A foundation for psychologist competence. *Professional Psychology: Research and Practice*, 36, 367–375. doi: 10.1037/0735-7028.36.4.367

Ewell, P. T (1998). Examining a brave new world: How accreditation might be different. National Center for Higher Education Management Systems (NCHEMS). Retrieved July 1, 2013 from: http://www.chea.org/Events/Usefulness/98May/98_05Ewell.asp.

Falender, C. A., Cornish, J. A. E., Goodyear, R., Hatcher, R., Kaslow, N. J., Leventhal, G.,...Grus, C. (2004). Defining competencies in psychology supervision: A consensus statement. *Journal of Clinical Psychology*, 80, 771–786. doi: 10.1002/jclp.20013

Fouad, N. A., Grus, C. L., Hatcher, R. L., Kaslow, N. J., Hutchings, P. S., Madson, M.,...Crossman, R. E. (2009). Competency benchmarks: A developmental model for understanding and measuring competence in professional psychology. *Training and Education in Professional Psychology*, 3(4, Suppl), November 2009, S5–S26. doi: 10.1037/a0015832

France, C. R., Mastes, K. S., Belar, C. D., Kerns, R. D., Klonoff, E. A., Larkin, K. T.,.... Thorn, B. E. (2008). Application of the competency model to clinical health psychology. *Professional Psychology: Research and Practice*, 39, 573–580. doi: 10.1037/0735-7028.39.6.573.

Green, M. L. Aagaard, E. M., Caverzagie, K. J., Chick, D. A., Homboe, E., Kane, G.,...Iobst, W. (2009). Charting the road to competence: Developmental milestones for internal medicine residency training. *Journal of Graduate Medical Education*, 1, 5–20. doi: 10.4300/01.01.0003

Greenberg, S., Caro, C. M. & Smith I.L. (2010). Executive summary study of the licensed psychologists in the United States and Canada. Retrieved July 1, 2013 from: http://www.asppb.net/files/PA_Executive_Summary_2010.pdf

Hannay, H. J., Bieliauskas, L., Crosson, B. A., Hammeke, T. A., Hamsher, K. deS. & Koffler, S. (1998). Proceedings of the Houston conference on specialty education and training in clinical neuropsychology. (Special issue). *Archives of Clinical Neuropsychology*, 13, 157–250.

Hatcher, R. L., & Lassiter, K. D. (2007). Initial training in professional psychology: The practicum competencies outline. *Training and Education in Professional Psychology*, 1, 49–63. doi: 10.1037/1931-3918.1.1.49

Holtman, M. S., Frost, J. S., Hammer, D. P., McGruinn, K & Nunez, L M. (2011). Interprofessional professionalism: Linking professionalism to interprofessional care. *Journal of Interprofessional Care*, 25, 383–385. doi: 0.3109/13561820.2011.588350

Institute of Medicine (2000). *To err is human: Building a safer health system*. Washington DC: National Academies Press.

Institute of Medicine (2001). *Crossing the quality chasm: A new health system for the 21st century*. Washington DC: National Academies Press.

Institute of Medicine (2003). *Health professions education: A bridge to quality*. A. C. Greiner, & E. Knebel (Eds.). Washington DC: National Academies Press.

Institute of Medicine (2010). *Redesigning continuing education in the health professions*. Washington, DC: National Academies Press.

Interprofessional Education Collaborative Expert Panel (2011). *Core competencies for interprofessional collaborative practice: Report of an expert panel*. Washington DC: Interprofessional Education Collaborative.

Interprofessional Professionalism Collaborative (2012) Behaviors. Retrieved May 31, 2012 from http://interprofessionalprofessionalism.weebly.com/index.html

Karel, M. J., Emery, E. E., Molinari, V. & CoPGTP Task Force on the Assessment of Geropsychology Competencies (2010). Development of a tool to evaluate geropsychology knowledge and skill competencies. *International Psychogeriatrics*, 22, 886–896. doi: 10.1017/S1041610209991736

Kaslow, N. J. (2004). Competencies in professional psychology. *American Psychologist*, 59, 774–781. doi: 10.1037/0003-066X.59.8.774

Kaslow, N. J., Borden, K. A., Collins, F. L., Jr., Forrest, L., Illfelder-Kaye, J., Nelson, P. & Rallo, J. S. (2004). Competencies Conference: Future Directions in Education and Credentialing in Professional Psychology. *Journal of Clinical Psychology*, 60, 699–712. doi: 10.1002/jclp.20016

Kaslow, N. J., Grus, C. L., Campbell, L. F., Fouad, N. A., Hatcher, R. L., & Rodolfa, E. R. (2009). Competency Assessment Toolkit for professional psychology. *Training and Education in Professional Psychology*, 3 (4, Suppl), S27–S45. doi:10.1037/a0015833

Kaslow, N. J. & Keilin, W. G. (2006). Internship training in clinical psychology: Looking into our crystal ball. *Clinical Psychology Science and Practice*, 13, 242–248. doi: 10.1111/j.1468-2850.2006.00031.x

Kaslow, N. J., Pate, W. E. III & Thorn, B. (2005). Academic and Internship Directors' Perspectives on Practicum Experiences: Implications. *Professional Psychology: Research and Practice*, 36(3), 307–317. doi:10.1037/0735-7028.36.3.307

Kaslow, N. J., Rubin, N. J., Bebeau, M., Leigh, I. W., Lichtenberg, J., Nelson, P. D.,...& Smith, I. L. (2007). Guiding principles and recommendations for the assessment of competence. *Professional Psychology: Research and Practice*, 38, 441–451. doi: 10.1037/0735-7028.38.5.441.

Kaslow, N. J., Rubin, N. J., Forrest, L., Elman, N. S., Van Horne, B. A., Jacobs, S. C.,...Thorn, B. E. (2007). Recognizing, assessing, and intervening with problems of professional competence. *Professional Psychology: Research and Practice*, 38(5), 479–492. doi:10.1037/0735-7028.38.5.479

Kenkel, M. B., & Peterson, R. L. (Eds.). (2010). Competency-based education for professional psychology. doi:10.1037/12068-000

Klass, D. (2007). A performance-based conception of competence is changing the regulation of physicians' professional behavior. *Academic Medicine*, 82, 529–535, doi: 10.1097/ACM.0b013e31805557ba

Knight, B. G., Karel, M. J., Hinrichsen, G. A., Qualls, S. H. & Duffy, M. (2009). Pikes Peak model for training in professional geropsychology. *American Psychologist*, 64, 205–214. Doi: 10.1037/a0015059.

Krishnamurthy, R., Vandecreek, L., Kaslow, N. J., Tazeau, Y. N., Milville, M. L., Kerns, R.,...Benton, S. A. (2004). Achieving competency in psychological assessment: Directions for education and training. *Journal of Clinical Psychology*, 80, 725–740. doi: 10.1002/jclp.20010

Leigh, I. W., Smith, I. L., Bebeau, M., Lichtenberg, J., Nelson, P. D., Portnoy, S.,...Kaslow, N. J. (2007). Competency assessment models. *Professional Psychology: Research and Practice*, 38, 463–473. doi: 10.1037/0735-7028.38.5.463

Lichtenberg, J., Portnoy, S., Bebeau, M., Leigh, I. W., Nelson, P. D., Rubin, N. J.,...Kaslow, N. J. (2007). Challenges to the assessment of competence and competencies. *Professional Psychology: Research and Practice*, 38, 474–478. doi: 10.1037/0735-7028.38.5.474

McCutcheon, S. M. (2008). Addressing problems of insufficient competence during the internship year. *Training and education in professional psychology*, 2, 210–214. doi: 10.1037/a0013535

McFall, R. M. (1991). Manifesto for a science of clinical psychology. *Clinical Psychology*, 44, 75–88.

Murdock, N. L., Alcorn, J., Heesacker, M., & Stoltenberg, C. (1998). Model training program in counseling psychology. *The Counseling Psychologist*, 26(4), 658–672. doi:10.1177/0011000098264008

Murphy, M. K., Black, N. A., Lamping, D. L., McKee, C. M., Sanderson, C. F. B., Askham, J., & Marteau, T. (1998). Consensus development methods, and their use in clinical guideline development. *Health Technology Assessment*, 2(3). Downloaded from http://www.hta.ac.uk/fullmono/mon203.pdf.

Neimeyer, G., Taylor, J. & Cox, D. (2012) On hope and possibility: Does continuing professional development contribute to ongoing professional competence? *Professional Psychology: Research and Practice*, 43(4), 476–486.

Neimeyer, G. J., Taylor, J. M. & Rozensky, R.H. (2012). The diminishing durability of knowledge in professional psychology: A Delphi Poll of specialties and proficiencies. *Professional Psychology: Research and Practice*, 43(4), 364–371.

Neimeyer, G. J., Taylor, J. M., & Wear, D. M. (2009). Continuing education in psychology: Outcomes, evaluations, and mandates. *Professional Psychology: Research and Practice*, 40(6), 617–624. doi:10.1037/a0016655

Nelson, P. D. (2007). Striving for competence in the assessment of competence: Psychology's professional education and credentialing journey of public accountability. *Training and Education in Professional Psychology*, 1(1), 3–12. doi:10.1037/1931-3918.1.1.3

Partnership for Health in Aging (2010) Multidisciplinary competencies in the care of older adults at the completion of the entry-level health professional degree. Retrieved July 1, 2013 from: http://www.americangeriatrics.org/files/documents/pha/PHAMultidiscComps.pdf.

Peterson, R. L., Peterson, D. R., Abrams, J. C., & Stricker, G. (1997). The National Council of Schools and Programs of Professional Psychology education model. *Professional Psychology: Research and Practice*, 28, 373–386. doi: 10.1037/0735-7028.28.4.373

Peterson, R. L., Peterson, D. R., Abrams, J. C., Stricker, G. & Ducheny, K. (2010). The National Council of Schools and Programs of Professional Psychology: Educational Model 2009. In. M. B. Kenkel and R. L. Peterson (Eds), *Competency-based education for professional psychology* (pp. 13–42). Washington, DC: American Psychological Association. doi: 10.1037/12068-001

Roberts, M. C., Borden, K. A., Christiansen, M. D., & Lopez, S. J. (2005). Fostering a culture shift: Assessment of competence in the education and careers of professional psychologists. *Professional Psychology: Research and Practice*, 36, 355–361. doi: 10.1037/0735-7028.36.4.355

Rodolfa, E. R., Bent, R. J., Eisman, E., Nelson, P. D., Rehm, L., & Ritchie, P. (2005). A Cube model for competency development: Implications for psychology educators and regulators. *Professional Psychology: Research and Practice*, 36, 347–354. doi: 10.1037/0735-7028.36.4.347

Rodolfa, E. R., Own, J. L. & Clark, S. (2007), Practicum training hours: Fact and fantasy. *Training and Education in Professional Psychology*, 1, 64–73. doi: 10.1037/1931

Rubin, N. J., Bebeau, M., Leigh, I. W., Lichtenberg, J., Smith, I. L., Nelson, P. D.,...Kaslow, N. J. (2007). The competency movement within psychology: An historical perspective. *Professional Psychology: Research and Practice, 38*, 452–462. doi: 10.1037/0735-7028.38.5.452

Schaffer, J. B. & Rodolfa, E. R. (2011). Intended and unintended consequences of state practicum licensure regulation. *Training and Education in Professional Psychology, 5*, 222–228. doi: 0.1037/a0024998

Spruill, J., Rozensky, R. H., Stigall, T. T., Vasquez, M., Binghman, R. P., & Olvey, C. D. V. (2004). Becoming a competent clinician: Basic competencies in intervention. *Journal of Clinical Psychology, 80*, 741–754. doi: 10.1002/jclp.20011

Stiers, W., Barisa, M., Stucky, K., Pawlowski, C., Tubbergn, M. V., Turner, A.,...Caplan, B. (in press). Guidelines for competency development and measurement in postdoctoral training in rehabilitation psychology. Manuscript submitted for publication.

Taylor, J. M., Neimeyer, G. J., Zemansky, M. & Rothske, S. (2012). Exploring the relationship between lifelong learning, continuing education, and professional competencies. In G. J. Neimeyer and J. M. Taylor (Eds.) *Continuing professional development and lifelong learning: Issues, impacts and outcomes* (pp 83–102). New York, NY: Nova Science Publishers.

Wampold, B. E., Goodheart, C. D., & Levant, R. F. (2007). Clarification and elaboration on evidence-based practice in psychology. *American Psychologist, 62*(6), 616–618. doi:10.1037/0003-066X62.6.616

The History and Importance of Specialization in Professional Psychology

Jeff Baker *and* David R. Cox

Abstract

Board certification of psychologists providing healthcare services to the public has a long history that continues to evolve. Most healthcare professions provide a peer-review process for the credentialing and board certification of individuals that provide healthcare services to the general public. Board certification within a specialty area has developed from within almost every respected healthcare profession. As psychology has progressed, the necessity of specialties, and recognition of those competent to practice in a specialty area, has become increasingly apparent. The explicit identification of very clear definitions and expectations for training and education within a specialty area facilitates this culture change. Some specialty areas (e.g., clinical neuropsychology) within psychology have more clearly embraced board certification, whereas others continue to work to establish board certification as a norm. Specialty board certification is not required, but is a voluntary process within the profession of psychology; certification is overseen by the American Board of Professional Psychology (ABPP). Board certification through ABPP is considered by most psychologists as recognition of advanced skills, knowledge, and attitudes. This chapter provides a history of the specialty credentialing process, discusses the issues regarding board certification, and how it is important to the profession of psychology.

Key Words: specialization, psychology, specialty, ABPP, professional, certification

The History and Importance of Specialization in Professional Psychology

Over the course of the last century, the practice of psychology has developed and matured. Psychologists have worked to differentiate psychology from early precursors, such as phrenology, hypnotherapy, spiritualism, and even psychoanalysis. Despite these efforts, popular perceptions of psychology often are shaped by inaccurate media presentation, such as those portrayed on television and in the print press (Benjamin, 2006). Innovations, such as the establishment of a core curriculum for training programs, licensing of psychologists, and board certification of psychologists in various specialty areas have helped establish, define, and refine the credibility of the profession and those who work within it. These developments also protect the public from those that do not meet the requirements expected of professional psychologists (Cox, 2010).

Psychologists have evoked varied reactions from the public as the profession has evolved over the decades (Murstein & Fontaine, 1993). An informed public expects that individuals engaged in providing psychological services are licensed; board certification is an attempt by the profession to identify for the public and the profession those providers that are qualified in a given psychological specialty. Board certification goes beyond licensure for the general practice of psychology, and provides certification of an individual's competence to practice in a specialty area, thereby serving a purpose of informing and protecting the public (Nezu, 2009).

Board certification in a specialty has not been as ubiquitous in psychology as it has been in medicine (CertiFACTS Online, 2012) although there is increasing momentum in the field as well as increased expectation that psychologists in healthcare settings become board certified (Kaslow, Graves, & Smith, 2012; Robiner, Dixon, Miner & Hong, 2012). Rozensky (2011) asserted that the coming reform in health care will result in a necessity for psychology to broadly employ board certification and that psychologists will want to become board certified to maintain a presence that establishes a taxonomy and certification process equivalent to other health care specialties.

Why Specialization Is Important

The history of specialization in any profession is related to the evolution of credentialing and the need for verification of expertise. If you go back 100 years there were very few specialists in the health professions; the vast majority of those involved in professional services were generalists and not specialists. With continued rapid advancements in technology and knowledge, no service provider can develop and retain all the competence (i.e., knowledge, skills, and attitudes) needed to treat everyone for every issue.

Psychology, like other disciplines, requires greater specialization as it evolves beyond "basic training." For instance, in the early 1950s and 1960s most automobile mechanics met competence criteria centering on basic mechanical skills with combustion engines. As the field of auto mechanics has expanded, it now takes someone with advanced practice skills to be able to diagnosis and repair today's automobile engine (Occupational Outlook Handbook, online bureau of statistics, http://www.bls.gov/ooh/Installation-Maintenance-and-Repair/Automotive-service-technicians-and-mechanics.htm).

Specialization in medicine is well recognized today. The general practitioner in medicine in the 1950s provided 90% of health care. As knowledge expanded and the use of advanced diagnostic equipment proceeded, medicine began developing specialists. Knowledge has pushed medicine into specialization and the same evolution may be true for psychology. The American Board of Medical Specialties (ABMS) is recognized as the gold standard in physician certification; it has 800,000 physicians that are certified by ABMS (Online publication of the American Board of Medical Specialties, 2011) (retrieved from http://www.certificationmatters.

org/about-abms.aspx). According to the ABMS, there are currently 24 approved medical specialties.

Psychology is no different in regard to a rapidly growing information base and the requisite necessity to keep up to date. Indeed, the "half-life" of knowledge in specialty areas suggests the need for continuous updating on the part of specialists (Neimeyer, Taylor, & Rozensky, 2012). Psychology specialization has emerged in response to the reality that general training models do not have the curricular space required to address the knowledge and training experience needed for specialization beyond the entry-level doctorate in psychology.

Medicine has demonstrated that recognition of specialty areas of practice and board certification in those specialties is one way that a profession can clearly define itself. Other health professions have seen a similar evolution. For example, physical therapy emerged out of medicine (Mock, Pemberton & Coulter, 1934) and has recently begun to aggressively develop internships/residencies for the graduates of their doctoral programs though currently this is not a requirement to practice physical therapy. According to the American Board of Physical Therapy Specialties (n.d.; retrieved from http://www.abpts.org/Certification/About/), the profession of physical therapy has developed specialist certification over the years in a variety of areas including, but not limited to, orthopedics, sports medicine, burn treatment, and pediatrics.

Dentistry developed specialization in domains requiring advanced competence (Moulton & Schifferes, 1960). The profession of dentistry also has generated a number of different specialties due to the rapid development of technology and knowledge needed for certain procedures in dentistry including endodontic, periodontics, and orthodontics to name a few (Occupational Outlook Handbook, online Bureau of Labor Statistics; retrieved from: http://www.bls.gov/ooh/Healthcare/Dentists.htm).

The American Psychological Association (APA) is moving forward with a taxonomy for the profession as psychologists work to clarify the concepts of specialty, sub-specialty, specialization, and specialists (Rozensky, 2012). Formal agreement on such constructs requires working through the various committees, review processes, and politics of large organizations and the profession; conceptualization and implementation of specialty training is likely to remain fluid over time. The distinctions of specialty (an area of practice in psychology), subspecialty (a focused area within a specialty), specialization (education and training), and specialist (an individual practicing within a specialty area) are relevant in the evolution of the taxonomy. Further, collaborative efforts on the part of major organizations in professional psychology are essential to successfully change the professional culture.

Education and Training

Education and training in psychology has evolved from laboratory science to applied clinical practice, eventually reaching a developmental stage in which more focused specialization within applied professional practice was deemed appropriate. Graduate study in psychology in the United States began in the 1880s. In 1897, in what may have been the earliest step in the evolution of psychological specialties, Witmer (1907) established a unique and specific curriculum for the area of psychology focused on training professionals that Witmer labeled *clinical psychologists* (Benjamin, 2006). This curriculum and his clinical team-based work with children, began the specialty areas of clinical psychology and school psychology, respectively (Rozensky, 2011).

Benjamin (2005) provided an overview of some of the historic developments in professional psychology, specifically clinical psychology, reporting on the creation of the American Association of Clinical Psychologists (AACP) in 1917 and the call for a specialty doctoral degree and certification for clinical psychologists in 1918. The APA initially viewed its role as limited to advocating for psychology as a science (as opposed to a clinical practice) and a debate ensued between the two organizations, ultimately resulting in the dissolution of the AACP as it became a clinical psychology section within APA in 1919. Various efforts over the subsequent years continued the push for clearer recognition of clinical psychologists as distinct from the larger profession of psychology. The American Association for Applied Psychology (AAAP) was formed, but then joined forces with APA within a decade. APA then established formal accreditation for clinical psychology. At one time in the early 1900s, clinical psychology was considered for inclusion as a subspecialty of medicine. This inclusion was considered by organized psychology but that movement did not go forward and psychology continued to pursue practice as an independent profession, whereas the profession of psychiatry evolved within medicine (Lloyd & Dewey, 1997; Witmer, 1907). Only in the last 20 years or so has psychology been recognized as a health profession by the federal government and

been added as a health provider through the Centers for Medicaid and Medicare Services (CMS).

It was in the early 1940s that the APA designated a committee to assist in determining a method to identify university departments that were capable of training doctoral level psychologists. The Committee on Training in Clinical Psychology of the APA (1947) reported its work in *Recommended Graduate Training Program in Clinical Psychology*, establishing a "broad and general" basis for such training. This development led other professional training councils in psychology to establish similar training standards in counseling psychology (APA, 1952) and, later, school psychology.

Despite these efforts, there remained a lack of consensus on the minimum essential curriculum for training in psychology, leading to what became known as the Boulder Conference in 1949 (Raimy, 1956). The Boulder Conference's Scientist-Practitioner Model became the foundation for many, if not most, of the training programs in clinical psychology in the latter half of the twentieth century (Benjamin, 2005). It was the Boulder Conference that defined much of what is considered the core curriculum in psychology. The areas of assessment, biological bases of behavior, social bases of behavior, research design and methods, and ethics were key components of the curriculum.

In general, graduate education in psychology has continued to be based on a concept of broad and general, as opposed to specialized, training. "Broad and general", however, may be defined differently by different entities. The APA journal *Training and Education in Professional Psychology* recently published a series of articles about this very issue (Berenbaum & Shoham, 2011; Collins & Callahan, 2011; Peterson, Vincent, & Fechter-Leggett, 2011; Zlotlow, Nelson, & Peterson, 2011). The history of efforts to delineate the broad and general model is presented, as is the notion that such a curriculum can be identified. Alternative models are presented suggesting that ready identification may not be so easy, and may be impacted by (for example) the half-life of knowledge, the expansion of knowledge, and use of competency-based (as opposed to curriculum-based) training.

The requirement for appropriate training in the foundational aspects of psychology is designed to protect the public by assuring that all psychologists have met *at least* these requirements. Practicing psychologists are bound by ethical guidelines not to practice in areas in which they have not acquired the expected knowledge, skills, and attitudes via a formal training program or postdoctoral/post graduate education referred to in the APA Ethics, Standard 2.01 Boundaries of Competence (APA, 2002; APA, 2010).

Psychology doctoral training programs that are accredited expect graduates to be generalists at the time of graduation. Many programs have a specialty option available depending on the expertise of the faculty and applied training available, but all students are expected to master the broad and general competencies. Medicine has instilled a culture wherein the expectation is that all graduates will continue to pursue graduate specialization training through a formal residency training program. In contrast, psychology has not historically required graduate specialization or developed a broad infrastructure for these formal postdoctoral experiences. There are only 140 APPIC member postdoctoral psychology training programs as of early 2013 (APPIC Directory On Line at www.appic.org) and many of these are not specialty focused. Whereas, medicine has available the Graduate Medical Education (GME) funds, which support the vast majority of their trainees in completing specialty training, psychology has very few resources for this type of training. The Graduate Psychology Education (GPE) fund was less than $5 million in 2013 and not clearly earmarked for specialty training; medicine receives more than 400 times that amount even though it was capped in 1997 with the Balanced Budget Act. There is now a push to remove that cap for medicine (Academic Medicine, AMEDnews.com, http://www.ama-assn.org/amednews/2012/08/27/prl20827.htm, August 27, 2012). Psychology needs to be part of that discussion in order to build an infrastructure that supports postdoctoral and specialty training.

Just as in medicine, a psychology trainee is expected to obtain competence in the essential areas of practice, yet there may be specific training institutions where advanced competence is also expected. Some programs have faculty with expertise that offer trainees preparation in certain focus or specialty areas, but these programs must still prepare students to meet the general core-curriculum guidelines. This broad and general expectation was established by the APA Commission on Accreditation (CoA) and is supported within the field that this exposure applies to all graduates with the doctoral degree from an accredited program. Many physicians will focus primarily on research and/or teaching and they may not engage in clinical practice; nonetheless, all are trained to practice clinical medicine by obtaining the necessary competence required by their accreditation standards.

Doctoral programs in psychology typically cannot provide training in all the specialty areas. Foundational training in psychology is required by the CoA and all programs must provide broad and general training in these foundational competencies. Students may be interested in specialization, but cannot focus on specialization while ignoring the history and systems in psychology that includes the biological, social, and cognitive-affective bases of behavior and individual differences. This foundation is essential for preparation that begins at the doctoral level and serves as a basis for advanced practice obtained through postdoctoral training.

Students may get some exposure and perhaps externships or rotations related to a specialty that provides some level of preparation and exposure to that specialty. The accredited doctoral training experience includes a one year internship in professional psychology. Internships, like doctoral training programs, may have more special interest areas or faculty with specialized competence, but they must also provide the broad and general training required of all professional psychologists. There are no specialty programs accredited at the internship level, but there are many that have a specific specialty focus or track in training areas such as neuropsychology, rehabilitation, clinical child and adolescent psychology, and so forth.

Specialty Differentiation

Although there has been development and evolution of several distinct training models, graduate education and training is not always, in and of itself, considered "specialty" training. Some consider specific types of doctoral education (e.g., clinical, counseling and school psychology) to be specialty oriented, whereas others consider such training general preparation for the post-doctoral training that leads to specialization. Ongoing inconsistency in the use of terms such as "specialization," "emphasis," "track," and similar terms in graduate training programs has, at least in part, been an impetus for clarification of the training model taxonomy within professional psychology (APA, 2012a).

Roberts (2006) described the "essential tension" between broad and general training in psychology on one hand and specialization on the other. Citing the historical roots of the APA's Commission for the Recognition of Specialties and Proficiencies in Professional Psychology (CRSPPP), he addressed the ongoing debate that some in the profession have regarding psychology as a singular or unitary field versus a field comprised of multiple specialty areas.

Specialization is an "inevitable and necessary product of developmental processes in a discipline and a profession" (Roberts, 2006, p. 863).

In 2010, a workgroup comprised of representative of the Council of Specialties (CoS), CoA, CRSPPP, and the American Board of Professional Psychology (ABPP) proposed a definition of "specialty" that would be acceptable to each of the groups. The APA (2011b, p. 2), through a document put forth by the CRSPPP, adopted that definition of specialty:

> A *specialty* is a defined area of professional psychology practice characterized by a distinctive configuration of competent services for specified problems and populations. Practice in a specialty requires advanced knowledge and skills acquired through an organized sequence of education and training in addition to the broad and general education and core scientific and professional foundations acquired through an APA or CPA accredited doctoral program.* Specialty training may be acquired either at the doctoral or postdoctoral level as defined by the specialty.
> * Except where APA or CPA program accreditation does not exist for that area of professional psychology.

Also described in that document, and distinct from specialty, is *proficiency*. Proficiency is defined as a circumscribed activity within psychology such as a specific procedure, technique or skill that may be used in practice. For example, biofeedback is a proficiency—a technique that might be used in the general practice of psychology and/or in a variety of specialty areas.

It is of note that CRSPPP recognition of a specialty addresses an area of *psychology*, as opposed to the specific training and experience of an individual *psychologist*. CRSPPP recognition may include a specialty area as having a method of designating that individuals are competent in that specialty, yet CRSPPP itself does not address the designation/recognition of individual psychologists. Applications for recognition of a specialty are expected to contain a description of a means, whereby the competence of individual practitioners in that specialty area may be evaluated (APA, 2011b), and that is often through board certification examination as conducted by the ABPP.

Emergence of Specialty Credentialing

At roughly the same time as some of the developments in training and education, there was again a call for some level of recognition of those psychologists that were adequately trained to provide clinical services to the public. This demand came on the heels of World War II, and an increased need for providers of mental health services. Noting that membership in a division of APA indicated *interest* in a certain aspect of psychology, *not specialization* in that area, the APA participated in establishing the American Board of Examiners in Professional Psychology (ABEPP) in 1947. The ABEPP was started via a loan from the APA and modeled itself after specialty board certification in medicine, initially identifying three specialty areas: clinical psychology, personnel-industrial (which later became industrial/organizational psychology), and personnel-educational (which later became counseling and guidance, and subsequently, counseling psychology). Despite requests from outside entities such as state boards to undertake certification at the "journeyman" level, the ABEPP aimed to identify *specialists* as practitioners at a higher level of competence than that "journeyman" level at which state certification was being granted (Bent, Packard, & Goldberg, 1999). Early on, a perception that ABEPP was elitist hindered the growth of board certification with professional psychology. A review and revamping of the process in the 1960s led to process changes as well as a name change to the current ABPP. Some of the changes included eliminating a written examination that had shown little discriminative power and increased focus on the content of the oral examination phase of the process (two specialty boards, forensic psychology and clinical neuropsychology, do currently have a written examination).

In the 1970s, the ABPP deferred recognition of new specialty areas to APA; however, APA moved at a pace much slower that the ABPP felt was appropriate and a recognition process for new specialty areas evolved within ABPP (Bent et al., 1999). That led to the eventual establishment of specialties in clinical neuropsychology, forensic psychology, family psychology, health psychology, behavioral psychology, psychoanalysis in psychology, group psychology, and rehabilitation psychology by the end of the 1990s. Most recently, police and public safety psychology has affiliated as a specialty board with ABPP. Currently, ABPP is comprised of 14 Specialty Boards (Table 8.1). CRSPPP recently recognized geropsychology as a specialty, and that group is in the process of applying to become an ABPP-affiliated specialty board. Some ABPP specialty boards are not CRSPPP recognized as specialties (e.g., group psychology, police & public safety psychology, rehabilitation psychology), whereas some CRSPPP recognized specialties

Table 8.1. Specialty Boards Affiliated with the American Board of Professional Psychology (as of 2012)

Specialty	Year of ABPP Affiliation	Year of CRSPPP Recognition
Clinical Psychology	1947	1998
Counseling Psychology	1947	1999
Industrial/Organizational Psychology	1948 (dissolved; reformed as Organizational & Business Consulting)	1996
School Psychology	1968	1998
Clinical Neuropsychology	1984	1996
Forensic Psychology	1985	2001
Couple and Family Psychology	1990	2002
Clinical Health Psychology	1991	1997
Cognitive & Behavioral Psychology	1992	2000
Psychoanalysis in Psychology	1996	1998
Rehabilitation Psychology	1997	In process
Group Psychology	1997	not recognized
Clinical Child & Adolescent Psychology	2003	1998
Organizational & Business Consulting Psychology	2003	1996 (as I/O)
Police & Public Safety Psychology	2011	Proficiency 2008 Spec. app. In process
Geropsychology	In process	2011

(e.g., geropsychology) are not ABPP affiliated specialty boards (however, geropsychology is in the process of formal affiliation with ABPP). There are several reasons for this lack of synchronization, some perhaps merely related to the timing in receipt and processing of applications. However, recognizing a mutual desire to have professional psychology "all on the same page," ABPP and CRSPPP continue to work to ascertain how the different organizations can work collaboratively so as to reach the goal of common recognition of specialties.

Appropriate Credentialing

Unfortunately, practitioners who are not properly prepared or credentialed may find themselves in difficult straits, and those that hired them may be astonished that they now have wasted time and money. Litigation continues to increase for those who were not properly prepared or trained. There is an argument that psychologists face enough hurdles when entering the profession and are hurting themselves by requiring more and more credentialing. However, professional guidance and principles are in place to protect both the professional and consumers. Professional standards attained through credentialing can take time and require expense. There are certain "vanity boards" that will require only a resume and a cashier's check to determine if applicants can be "board certified." The newly self-anointed vanity board, then, has a revenue stream with regular dues or fee payments each year in order to maintain this "board certification." Consumers may not know the difference when someone presents that they are "board certified" from one of these vanity boards; even new psychologists do not always know the differences between a vanity board and a legitimate board, such as ABPP.

New graduates might be taken advantage of and may worry that, if they do not submit their money now for the "grandfathering" period, they will be left behind without doing any substantiation of the organization that is providing specialty or "board certification." A credential stating "board certified" can be misleading to the public if there is no legitimate credentials verification and examination process involved in the board-certification process. Psychologists seeking board certification should evaluate the background and history of the organization to determine its legitimacy. Many psychologists in training rely on their mentors or supervisors to serve as their role models when making decisions regarding what qualifications are important or legitimate. Most focusing on getting through the curriculum, obtaining an internship, and completing the requirements for licensure before they even begin the road to specialization. Some specialties have begun to promulgate that model and graduate programs and mentors are now articulating the importance of obtaining qualifications to be appropriately identified as a specialist. The ABPP Early Entry program (described later) is another means of educating students in the psychology profession about specialization and board certification.

Identifying legitimate credentialing processes are a critical role for mentors and advisors in psychology. CRSPPP has recently been charged with recognizing board certification organizations for APA. In order to be recognized by CRSPPP, the organization or certifying body must, among other requirements, (a) be a nonprofit organization governed by an independent board of directors; (b) award certification based upon review of training, licensure, and ethical conduct status of the applicant; (c) use means of examination such as oral exam, written exam, and/or work samples, and such examination instruments must clearly delineate the relevant specialty practice areas to be assessed; (d) provide publicly available documents, such as candidate handbooks; (e) maintain a publicly available database of current status of certified individuals; (f) make publicly available information regarding the organization's standards and procedures; and (g) provide evidence of applying process improvement procedures (APA, 2012b; retrieved from: http://www.apa.org/ed/graduate/specialize/recognition-criteria.pdf).

The ABPP Board Certification Process in Brief

Since 1947, the ABPP has been certifying psychologists and has come to be recognized as the "gold standard" in board certification in psychology (Nezu, Finch, & Simon, 2009). A detailed description of the process of becoming board certified in psychology through the ABPP has been provided by Nezu et al. (2009), and the reader is referred there as well as to the ABPP website (www.abpp.org). However, a brief overview of the process is provided herein so as to provide at least a basic understanding of the steps involved.

Until relatively recently, one was not even eligible to *apply* for ABPP board certification until five years after receiving one's doctoral degree. With the increased focus on standardization and competency-based education and training, the foundation of professional psychology has been transmitted to trainees in a much more reliable fashion than in years past (Kaslow, 2004; Rodolfa et al., 2005). This has also led to earlier adoption of specialization of practice for many psychologists, including the evolution of specialty postdoctoral training programs. The natural progression after such specialized postdoctoral training is board certification. Such competency-based education and training has permeated the profession and with expectations about coming healthcare reform, there seems to be a real momentum growing with regard to competency-based education, training, and board certification (Kaslow et al., 2012; Rozensky, 2011). In many circles, there is recognition of a cultural change occurring in the profession. Establishing board certification as one of the goals of professional training, ABPP initiated a program in 2007 as an outreach to students and as an attempt to facilitate understanding and acceptance of board certification within psychology.

That program, the Early Entry Program (or Early Entry Option) has been very successful, as evidenced by the fact that it has been embraced by students and their faculty/trainers alike. In addition, many training institutions are encouraging, if not sponsoring, their students, interns, and postdoctoral residents to participate. Individuals who are in these early stages of the professional development process—as early as graduate school—are now welcome to start the application process, with necessary documentation of requirements filed with ABPP as they completed the requirements sequentially. This permits the individual to become familiar with the process and expectations of board certification early on, join electronic discussion groups, and perhaps associate with a mentor (Talley, 2009) and self-identify as "en route" to board certification as a part of one's professional identity. Essentially, the program permits students, interns, and postdoctoral residents to initiate filing credentials with ABPP earlier in their professional training. This program does not grant any exception to the credentials review or examination process. There is a discount to the application fee for those that start the process in this program, yet all requirements for successful attainment of ABPP board certification remain the same. In other words, the Early Entry Program does not provide for an "easier" route, except insofar as "easier" may arise out of greater familiarity with the process.

The ABPP board-certification process includes several phases: credentials review, submission of practice samples, and oral examination. These aspects of the process are similar for each ABPP specialty board. At the discretion of the specialty board, a written (e.g., multiple choice) examination may also be included in the process. Presently, only forensic psychology and clinical neuropsychology include such exams.

All ABPP specialty boards (See Table 8.1), have what are referred to as generic requirements, and they are the same for each specialty board, yet there are different specialty-specific requirements for each specialty. The generic requirements, as well as each board's specialty-specific criteria, are available online www.abpp.org. A doctorate in psychology from an APA-accredited program or one that is listed in the Association of State and Provincial Psychology Boards (ASPPB, 2010)/National Register Designation Program is a minimum requirement for application, with relatively few exceptions. More widespread adoption of APA accreditation occurred in the late 1970s/early 1980s. ABPP set 1983 as the "cut-off date" after which doctoral degree programs must be APA accredited or designated by the ASPPB/NR designation system in order to be eligible for ABPP. All applicants must hold an unrestricted license for the independent practice of psychology, and the license must be based on a doctoral degree (some jurisdictions do license based on a master's degree, but such a license would not meet the ABPP requirements).

If an application meets the requirements of the generic review, the application is moved to the specialty board for review of the specialty-specific requirements. Those requirements are *in addition* to the ABPP generic requirements. Meeting the generic requirements for ABPP is a for review at the specialty board level. Although the specific requirements for each specialty differ, most specialties require completion of postdoctoral training in the specialty area, and/or completion of coursework or training in

a particular are of practice that is essential to that specialty. Depending on the specialty board, either completion of a formal residency program and/or supervised experience may satisfy the requirement. The education, training, and experience expected of a candidate are defined by the specialty board. An excellent example of this is the adoption of The Houston Conference Guidelines by the American Board of Clinical Neuropsychology (ABCN) (see www.theabcn.org). Participants from clinical neuropsychology were invited to participate in a meeting in Houston, Texas and together they created a document that delineates the requirements for credentials as a clinical neuropsychologist. These were presented as "guidelines" when agreed upon in the 1990s, and they are now strongly considered as "essential" for those that are completing their training today. These guidelines explicitly delineate the education, training, and experience necessary for specialization in the field of neuropsychology and have been adopted by the ABCN as requirements for all applicants who graduated in 2005 or more recently.

Following acceptance and approval of credentials, the next step for most of the ABPP specialty boards is submission of practice samples. It should be noted here that there are two exceptions to this; the ABCN and the American Board of Forensic Psychology (ABFP) at this point require passing a written, multiple-choice examination prior to being permitted to submit practice samples. Specific details required in practice samples are beyond the scope of this chapter and should always be obtained from the most up-to-date examination manual as posted by each specialty board on the ABPP website (www.abpp.org). Although varying across specialty boards somewhat, two case presentations or other samples of professional work, along with a personal statement, are the most common types of practice samples. Some boards require that a submission include audio/video recording of one's practice, some accept written materials. There is generally a relatively broad range of what may be covered in the practice samples, as it is understood that different clinical settings or employment roles may impact the types of cases or materials one can present. Davidson (2009) provides a good overview of the practice sample submission process.

Some boards provide some flexibility in the type of materials suitable for practice samples by those that have been in the field for 15 or more years; this is referred to as the "senior option." The senior option is not in any way a "grandparenting" process, and is not intended to be otherwise "easier" nor more stringent. Most of the ABPP boards recognize that many psychologists well into their careers may have practice areas that extend beyond traditional clinical case work, such as program development, research, and administration. It is still essential that the clinical foundations be demonstrated through the board certification process (inclusive of practice sample and oral examination phases), even when the work samples reflect unique areas of practice such as program development or program evaluation.

It is very important that the specific guidelines described for submission of practice samples be followed. Upon submission of the practice sample, the material is reviewed by the specialty board and either accepted, returned for some revisions, or deemed unacceptable. In this sense, the process is not unlike that of submitting an article for publication. In other words, having a practice sample returned for some revision should not be perceived as a "failure," but rather as an indication that the candidate is generally on the path.

In her chapter on oral exam preparation, F. Kaslow (2009) also provides details relevant to the oral examination process. Each of the specialty boards require the oral examination, which is typically roughly three hours long. The intention of the process is to be collegial throughout; although sometimes anxiety provoking, it is common to hear feedback that the process was engaging, challenging yet friendly, and sometimes even "fun." Some boards (e.g., clinical psychology, clinical child and adolescent psychology, couple and family psychology) use a model wherein the examination is conducted with the examinee meeting with three examiners at once, whereas others (e.g., rehabilitation psychology, counseling psychology) use more of an "assessment-center" model in which the examinees spend part of their time with different examiners. In each model, the goal remains that same: to assess the competency of the candidates with reference to the various competency areas. As with the practice sample, the oral examination differs from specialty board to specialty board.

The oral examination typically focuses on material arising from the practice sample as well as other areas. All specialty boards include examination on legal and ethical issues. These are often by way of material that is within the context of the submitted practice sample and/or vignettes that are provided at the time of the examination. Some specialty boards use vignettes for clinical cases that the candidate must comment on. The oral examination is often viewed as an opportunity for the candidate to demonstrate "thinking on one's feet," ability to conceptualize a case and demonstrate diagnostic and/or treatment planning competence. The ABCN process, for example, includes "fact-finding," in which the candidate must query the examiner for information that would be useful in a hypothetical case. Regardless of the specialty board, the candidate should go into the examination prepared to discuss the practice samples in detail, provide appropriate basis for what was done with a case and how it was done, and be up to date with relevant literature (F. Kaslow, 2009).

Within the practice sample phase, as well as in the oral examination process, it is important that the psychologist provide evidence of competency in the foundational and functional competencies recognized in professional psychology. There has been an evolution within the profession of these competencies (N. Kaslow, 2004; N. Kaslow and Ingram, 2009; Fouad, et al, 2009; American Psychological Association, 2011a). For the past decade, the ABPP has focused on the foundational and functional competencies as described by N. Kaslow and Ingram (2009), and integration of the more recent revisions (APA, 2011a) into specialty-board requirements begins in 2014 as specialty boards undergo their routine internal quality assurance reviews. (see Tables 8.2 and 8.3).

Table 8.2. ABPP Competencies pre-2013

Foundational Competencies	Functional Competencies
Interpersonal Interactions	Assessment
Individual and Cultural Diversity	Intervention
Ethical and Legal Foundations	Consultation
Professional Identification	Science base and application
	Supervision, teaching, & management*

* may not be applicable to all practitioners

Table 8.3. ABPP Competencies as of 2013

Foundational Competencies	Functional Competencies
Professionalism	Assessment
Reflective Practice/Self-Assessment/Self-Care	Intervention
Scientific Knowledge and Methods	Consultation
Relationships	Research/Evaluation
Individual and Cultural Diversity	Supervision*
Ethical Legal Standards and Policy	Teaching*
Interdisciplinary systems	Management-Administration*
	Advocacy

* may not be applicable to all practitioners

Why Bother? Professional Development and Expectations versus Legal Requirements

It may not be against the law for physicians to practice in specialty areas without board certification, but it is generally a common expectation by the state boards that individuals should not practice in areas where they do not have expertise (requisite skills, knowledge, and attitudes). Expertise in medicine is typically defined as supervised training in the doctoral program plus additional specialized training experience (residency training program) under the supervision of a board certified specialist and/or work experience. Often, this may include further education via skills-training workshops provided by recognized training organizations wherein one can obtain skills and knowledge.

Conceptually, this is not dissimilar from psychology. However, psychology has not pushed for board certification at the same rate that medicine has. Most state boards of psychology examiners do expect psychologists to provide verification that they are qualified to provide clinical services through documentation of training and letters of verification and recommendation required by the state board. However, specialty areas of competence are rarely required by most jurisdictions unless the use of a specialty title is allowed by the jurisdiction. If a problem arises with the licensee, it is not unusual for the state board to request additional documentation about training and work experience that relates to the boundaries of specialty practice in psychology, such as working with children and adolescents, forensics, or neuropsychology. When the state board receives a complaint, they will request the licensed provider submit evidence of education, training, or work experience that qualifies them for providing specialty services in the practice of psychology. If the individual is claiming or presents himself or herself to the public as having this type of expertise, then evidence must be presented to the state board that supports the individual's background in training, education, or experience. Board certification is one indication—in the view of most state boards—that an individual is qualified to practice in that specialty.

Despite that expectation, state licensure boards, in general, are a long way away from the expectation that individuals have board certification to practice in specialty areas. The licensing agencies often do require documentation that is identified as acceptable attainment of skills, especially if a complaint or concern is raised by the public. The push for board certification by the profession of psychology also often has lacked support from academic teachers of psychology who do not hold board certification (and may not be licensed due to exemptions in state law). Only a small percentage of psychology practitioners hold board certification. As a younger profession, it is not entirely unexpected that this evolutionary process is not on a par with medicine or dentistry, where, in order to practice in certain areas of specialization, it is required, or at least widely expected, that one obtain board certification.

Since there is no *requirement* for board certification by most states for specialty practice, why is there a need for recognition of specialization within psychology? There are medical centers and hospitals that will not consider an individual for privileges within the hospital without board certification. This is true for both medicine and psychology. Board certification for both medicine and psychology came about in part due to the need for a mechanism to verify an individual's claim of expertise. Some medical schools now also require board certification by psychologists for medical staff privileges and promotion. Some medical schools now require it for appointment to any staff psychologist position or they may provide a time limit to obtain board certification in order to maintain an appointment on the clinical/medical staff. In addition to some medical schools requiring board certification, the Veteran's Administration Health Care System (VAs) and Department of Defense (DoD) military facilities now recognize board certification and in most cases offer a pay differential for those with board certification.

These are significant incentives for board certification (appointment and pay differential), but the primary reason behind board certification is the education of, and protection of, the public. If the profession itself does not offer this level of self-regulation, the public may be left unaware of the qualifications needed to practice psychology in a specialty area. The public may then turn to those less qualified, or worse, those that do not have appropriate qualifications for offering services beyond a title that is not protected (e.g., "psychotherapist" is not a protected title in most states).

Additional reasons to become board certified include:

- The exponential growth of psychological knowledge leaves no alternative but specialization.
- Our work environments impel us to specialize.
- Our professional context reinforces the need for specialization.
- The generic nature of psychology licensing in North America presumes additional professional self-regulation of specialty practice.
- Most important, protecting the public from charlatans and the ill-prepared requires personal and professional self-regulation.

Psychologists tend to be engaged, active learners, interested in self-reflection and professional growth (Baker, Hatcher, Hsu, McCutcheon, Rodolfa and Wise (2007). In addition to the opportunity to engage in another level of learning in preparation for the specialty certification examination, self-reflection is required during the process of becoming board certified through the ABPP. Licensed psychologists typically are serving others in providing patient care, and, thus, they are more externally focused. This self-reflection provides an opportunity to re-establish priorities and provides a time to focus on the individual. This self-reflection is an important competency expected by the profession. (Pope-Davis, Coleman, Liu and Toporek, 2003) The ABPP certification process requires extensive but manageable requirements. Preparation for the board certification process through ABPP includes:

- The chance to articulate your own views and perspectives in a more advanced and sophisticated way as part of the preparation and oral exam.
- A structure to facilitate self-assessment where the individual gets to set his or her own pace in developing their case study, which facilitates better self-understanding and case conceptualization.
- An important continuing professional education opportunity (fulfills, in some states, the CE requirements for the biennium in which board certification occurs; those who are successful receive CE credits from ABPP, an APA approved CE provider).
- More mobility opportunities as many state licensure boards recognize the ABPP and have a facilitated licensing process.
- Highest credential for a psychologist and denotes an advanced level of competence (knowledge, skills, attitudes).
- "Final examination" that gives legitimacy to the profession, along with public confidence one gets when being referred to as a board-certified specialist.
- Assurance to the public that you are a specialist who has successfully completed the educational, training, and experience requirements of the specialty, including an examination designed to assess the competencies required to provide quality services in that specialty.
- A credential that is understood by other professionals and the public.

The preceding points were taken from a presentation at the APPIC 2007 Conference in Baker, J. and Kaslow, N. (2007) "Board Certification for Internship Training Directors."

Concluding Remarks

Specialization in psychology is still in the early acceptance phase by psychologists. As the public becomes more aware of the need for expertise, they will look for this certification. Much like in medicine, where most individuals would not make an appointment with a neurosurgeon that was not board certified in that specialty, this will lead to the expectation of board certification within the profession of psychology.

It is essential to establish and demonstrate the competence to provide quality and effective psychological services to the public. Such competence is a reflection of attending an accredited doctoral and internship training program, participating in a programmatic postdoctoral residency, and completing other key milestones such as licensure and board certification.

Does everyone need to be a specialist and be credentialed? Perhaps not, but it is a standard that the public as well as other health professions recognize. The need for specialists has arisen due to the vast increase in technology and knowledge. The advent of the Affordable Care Act has led Rozensky (2012) to predict that psychology as a profession is nearing the point of *needing* specialization and that psychologists as individual professionals will *want* board certification in order to stay relevant in the coming health care environment.

References

Academic Medicine, AMEDnews.com, http://www.ama-assn.org/amednews/2012/08/27/prl20827.htm, August 27, 2012).

American Board of Medical Specialties (2011). Certification matters. Retrieved from: http://www.certificationmatters.org/about-abms.aspx

American Board of Physical Therapy Specialties. (n.d.) About specialist certification. Retrieved from: http://www.abpts.org/Certification/About/

American Psychological Association. (2002). Ethical principles of psychologists and code of conduct. *American Psychologist, 57, 1060–1073.* doi: 10.1037/0003-066X.57.12.1060

American Psychological Association. (2010). 2010 Amendments to the 2002 "Ethical principles of psychologists and code of conduct." *American Psychologist, 65,* 493. doi: 10.1037/a0020168

American Psychological Association (2011a). Revised competency benchmarks for professional psychology. Retrieved from: http://www.apa.org/ed/graduate/competency.aspx.

American Psychological Association. (2011b). Principles for the recognition of specialties in professional psychology. Retrieved from: http://www.apa.org/about/policy/principles-recognition.pdf

American Psychological Association. (2012a). Education and training guidelines—A taxonomy for education and training in professional psychology health service specialties. Retrieved from: http://www.apa.org/ed/graduate/specialize/taxonomy.pdf

American Psychological Association. (2012b). Recognition of organizations that provide certifications in specialties and proficiencies in professional psychology. Retrieved from: http://www.apa.org/ed/graduate/specialize/application-process.aspx

American Psychological Association, Division of Counseling and Guidance, Committee on Counselor Training. (1952). Recommended standards for training counseling psychologists at the doctorate level. *American Psychologist, 7,* 175–181. doi: 10.1037/h0056299.

Association of Psychology Postdoctoral and Internship Centers (APPIC) Directory on Line. (2013). http://www.appic.org

Association of State and Provincial Psychology Boards. (2010). ASPPB model act for licensure and registration of psychologists. http://www.asppb.net/files/Final_Approved_MLRA_November_2010.pdf

Baker, J., Hatcher, R., Hsu, J., McCutcheon, S., Rodolfa, E., and Wise, E. (2007). *Panel dialogue about the sequence of psychology training—practicum to practice.* Paper presented at Association of Psychology Postdoctoral and Internship Centers (APPIC) Membership Conference, San Diego, CA, April.

Baker, J. and Kaslow, N. (2007) *Board Certification for Internship Training Directors.* Paper presented at Association of Psychology Postdoctoral and Internship Centers (APPIC) Membership Conference, San Diego, CA, April.

Benjamin, L. T., Jr. (2005). A history of clinical psychology as a profession in America (and a glimpse at its future). *Annual Review of Clinical Psychology, 1,* 1–30. doi:10.1146/annurev.clinpsy.1.102803.143758

Benjamin, L. T., Jr. (2006). American psychology's struggles with its curriculum: Should a thousand flowers bloom? *Training and Education in Professional Psychology,* S(1), 58–68. doi: 10.1037/1931-3918.S.1.58

Bent, R. J., Packard, R. E., and Goldberg, R. W. (1999). The American Board of Professional Psychology, 1947 to 1997: A historical perspective. *Professional Psychology: Research and Practice, 30,* 65–73. doi: 10.1037/0735-7028.30.1.65

Berenbaum, H. and Shoham, V. (2011). Broad and general training in applied psychology: A clinical science perspective. *Training and Education in Professional Psychology, 5,* 22–29. doi: 10.1037/a0022603

CertiFACTS Online. (2012). Why is a particular physician not board certified? Retrieved from: http://www.certifacts.org/faq.html#14

Collins, F. L., Jr. and Callahan, J. L. (2011). Alternatives to a core curriculum to accomplish broad and general training: A scientist-practitioner perspective. *Training and Education in Professional Psychology, 5,* 15–21. doi: 10.1037/a0022528

Committee on Training in Clinical Psychology of the American Psychological Association. (1947). Recommended graduate training program in clinical psychology. *American Psychologist, 2,* 539–538. doi: 10.1037/h0058236

Cox, D. R. (2010). Board certification in professional psychology: Promoting competency and consumer protection. *The Clinical Neuropsychologist, 24,* 493–505. doi: 10.1080/13854040902802947

Davidson, C. S. (2009). Preparing the practice sample. In C. M. Nezu, A. J Finch, and N. P. Simon (Eds.) *Becoming board certified by the American Board of Professional Psychology* (pp. 83–96). New York: Oxford University Press.

Fouad, N. A., Grus, C. L., Hatcher, R. L., Kaslow, N. J., Hutchings, P. S., Madson, M., Collins, F. L., Jr., & Crossman, R. E. (2009). Competency benchmarks: A developmental model for understanding and measuring competence in professional psychology. *Training and Education in Professional Psychology, 3*(4, Suppl), S5–S26. doi: 10.1037/a0015832

Kaslow, F. W. (2009). How to prepare for the oral exam. In C. M. Nezu, A. J Finch, and N. P. Simon (Eds.) *Becoming board certified by the American Board of Professional Psychology* (pp. 103–113). New York: Oxford University Press.

Kaslow, N. J. (2004). Competencies in professional psychology. *American Psychologist, 59,* 774–781. doi: 10.1037/0003-066X.59.8.774

Kaslow, N. J. and Ingram, M. V. (2009). Board certification: A competency-based perspective. In C. M. Nezu, A. J Finch, and N. P. Simon (Eds.) *Becoming board certified by the American Board of Professional Psychology* (pp. 37–46). New York: Oxford University Press.

Kaslow, N. J., Graves, C. C., & Smith, C. O. (2012). Specialization in psychology and health care reform. *Journal of Clinical Psychology in Medical Settings, 19,* 12–21. doi: 10.1007/s10880-031-9273-0

Lloyd, M. A. and Dewey, R. A. (1997, August 28). Areas of specialization in psychology. [Online]. Available: http://www.psywww.com/careers/specialt.htm

Mock, H. E., Pemberton, R., & Coulter, J. S. (1934). Principles and practice of physical therapy. *The Journal of the American Medical Association,* 102(14), 1183–1183. doi:10.1001/jama.1934.02750140069035

Moulton, F. R. & Schifferes, J. J. (1960). *The Beginning of Modern Dentistry.* The Autobiography of Science. New York: Doubleday.

Neimeyer, G. J., Taylor, J. M., & Rozensky, R. H. (2012). The diminishing durability of knowledge in professional psychology: A delphi poll of specialties and proficiencies. *Professional Psychology: Research and Practice, 43,* 364–371. doi: 10.1037/a0028698

Nezu, C. M. (2009). Why seek board certification? In C. M. Nezu, A. J Finch, & N. P. Simon (Eds.), *Becoming board certified by the American Board of Professional Psychology* (pp. 27–36). New York: Oxford University Press.

Nezu, C. M., Finch, A. J., Jr., & Simon, N. P. (2009). *Becoming board certified by the American Board of Professional Psychology.* New York: Oxford University Press.

Occupational Outlook Handbook (online, 2012) Bureau of Labor Statistics: http://www.bls.gov/ooh/Healthcare/Dentists.htm).

Peterson, R. L., Vincent, W. L., and Fechter-Leggett, M. (2011). The necessary common knowledge approach to broad and general education for professional psychologists.

Training and Education in Professional Psychology, 5, 9–14. doi: 10.1037/a0022524

Pope-Davis, D., Coleman, H., Liu, W. and Toporek, R. (Eds.). (2003). In *handbook of multicultural counseling competencies in counseling & psychology* (p. 170). Thousand Oaks, CA: Sage.

Raimy, V. C. (1956). The problem with specialization in training. In C. R. Strother (Ed.), *Psychology and mental health* (pp. 41–52). Washington, DC: American Psychological Association.

Roberts, M. C. (2006). Essential tension: Specialization with broad and general training in psychology. *American Psychologist, 61,* 862–870. doi: 10.1037/0003-066X.61.8.862

Robiner, W. N., Dixon, K. E., Miner, J. L., & Hong, B. A. (2012). Board certification in psychology: Insights from medicine and hospital psychology. *Journal of Clinical Psychology in Medical Settings, 19,* 30–40. doi: 10.1007/s10880-031-9280-1

Rodolfa, E., Bent R. J., Eisman, E., Nelson, P. D., Rehm L. & Ritchie, P. (2005). A cube model for competency development: Implications for psychology educators and regulators. *Professional Psychology: Research and Practice, 36,* 347–354. doi: 10.1037/0735-7028.36.4.347

Rozensky, R. H. (2011). The institution of the institutional practice of psychology: Health care reform and psychology's future workforce. *American Psychologist, 66,* 797–808. doi: 10.1037/a0025074

Rozensky, R. H. (2012, August). *Impact of the New Education and Training Guidelines—A Taxonomy.* Symposium conducted at the Annual Meeting of the American Psychological Association, Orlando, FL.

Witmer, L. (1907). Clinical psychology. *The Psychological Clinic, 1,* 1–9.

Zlotlow, S. F., Nelson, P. D. & Peterson, R. L. (2011). The history of broad and general education in scientific psychology: The foundation for professional psychology education and training. *Training and Education in Professional Psychology,* 5, 1–8. doi: 10.1037/a0022529

Practicum Training in Professional Psychology

Robert L. Hatcher *and* Erica H. Wise

Abstract

The practicum is the first and longest phase in the sequence of applied training for doctoral students in professional psychology. Changes in the American Psychological Association (APA) Model Licensure Act, in regulatory guidelines, and in accreditation standards and regulations have brought increased attention to practicum training in recent years. Practicum training has a long history that can be traced to the very beginnings of professional psychology. Designed to prepare students for subsequent clinical training, the practicum is the responsibility of the graduate program. This chapter discusses the methods and policies that programs design to manage and optimize the quality of students' practicum experiences. Competency goals for practicum training have been an important focus for the developing competencies movement in professional psychology. These competencies are reviewed in this chapter, along with the practices and methods typically used in practicum settings to help students acquire them.

Key Words: practicum, competencies, Professional Psychology Graduate Program Administration, teaching methods

Introduction

The practicum is the first step in applied training for doctoral students in professional psychology (Hatcher & Lassiter, 2007). Although many students have had some previous experience working in professional settings, practicum is their introduction to practice in professional psychology. Practicum is the longest portion in the sequence of training for practice, generally involving two to three years' experience for at least 10 hours per week, and often longer (Hatcher, Grus, & Wise, 2011; Rodolfa, Owen, & Clark, 2007). As the first in a series of training experiences leading toward independent practice, practicum prepares the student for the internship that follows. After graduation, many undertake one or more years of postdoctoral training, as required for licensure by most licensing jurisdictions (Schaffer & Rodolfa, 2011).

The practicum experience is a key element in every doctoral program's overall plan for training in professional psychology, and is intended to complement the didactic and research/scholarly aspects of training. The importance of integrating practicum training with the overall training plan is increasingly emphasized in publications and accreditation standards (Hatcher et al., 2011; American Psychological Association Commission on Accreditation [CoA], 2012). Because practicum involves real-life professional practice, it engages the student in a full range of professional issues. Care for clients; ethics; professionalism; integration of science and practice; interprofessional relationships; openness to supervision and learning; indeed the full gamut of professional knowledge, skills, attitudes, and behaviors is engaged in the relatively controlled setting of practicum training. As a result, practicum offers the opportunity for substantial growth as a professional psychologist in training, and helps to develop the foundational competencies, including the elements of professionalism, expected of independent professionals. Practicum helps students gauge their own abilities and interests, and often helps students decide how they wish to direct their future training and careers.

As an integral aspect of the doctoral program's curriculum, organizing and managing the practicum experience is the obligation of the program. Practicum gives doctoral programs the opportunity to extend their training models beyond coursework and research/scholarship to include practical training. Faculty generally are involved in practicum training, as advisors, through a program-supervised training clinic, through serving as supervisors in external practicum sites, or through seminars designed to integrate practicum experience with program goals. For many doctoral programs, research programs based in the departmental training clinic or other clinical settings provide valuable integration of research and clinical activities and goals. As an essential part of the gatekeeping function of graduate training, the practicum allows programs to ensure that their students demonstrate the initial competencies required to be a professional psychologist, and to determine whether students are able to utilize supervised training to grow in the competency domains expected of a professional psychologist. As a part of the accreditation process, the nature and quality of the program's management of the practicum is reviewed by the APA Commission on Accreditation (2009, 2012).

In recent years, as a consequence of a resolution passed by the APA Council of Representatives, (CoR; 2006), some portions of practicum have been accepted as part of the professional experience required for licensure in a number of states (Schaffer & Rodolfa, 2011). This controversial move is expected to influence the nature of practicum training in the future.

Background
EARLY HISTORY

The requirement for a year of full-time internship training was established in the period following World War II, when training in professional psychology transitioned to its organized, modern form. As the internship requirement took shape, the need to prepare students to make good use of their internship experience was widely recognized (Morrow, 1946; Raimy, 1950; Shakow, 1956). From these early beginnings, the terminology evolved to describe the first step in pre-internship training as pre-practicum training or clerkships, which were generally focused on learning specific skills, often in a classroom setting (e.g., intelligence assessment). The practicum followed, which was generally broader in focus, and dealt with actual clients, in preparation for the internship that caps the doctoral training sequence. In addition, there was extensive and ongoing discussion of the need to integrate and coordinate the doctoral program and the training sites at both the practicum and internship levels (Raimy, 1950; Shakow, 1956).

LENGTH OF PRACTICUM

Programs generally report requiring three years of practicum training (Hatcher et al., 2011), with the goal of helping students develop the competence needed to benefit from internship training. However, a number of significant factors put pressure on this goal. Students have experienced increasing urgency over the years to gain ever-larger numbers of practicum hours so as to be competitive for the increasingly competitive internship match, and there is evidence of a substantial increase of reported hours since the mid-1990s (Rodolfa et al., 2007). However, there is no evidence that greater numbers of hours facilitate internship placement (Dixon & Thorn, 2000; Rodolfa et al., 2007). The belief that more practicum hours can help with placement success may give students a greater sense of control over the matching process, which overall tends to feel like a risky gamble.

PRACTICUM AND LICENSURE

The resolution passed by the APA Council of Representatives (CoR) in 2006, and subsequent revision to the Model Licensing Act (CoR, 2010) to eliminate the requirement for postdoctoral training for licensure is likely to be an increasingly important external influence on practicum training. These actions were taken for a variety of reasons including the widespread belief that the increased number of practicum hours, together with the internship year, provide sufficient practical training for competent independent practice, and thus for licensure. This move led to a strong reaction from the Association for State and Provincial Psychology Boards (ASPPB), the organization for psychology licensing boards in the United States and Canada. Concerned about the uneven nature and quality of practicum training, the ASPPB released its Guidelines on Practicum Training for Licensure in 2009, intended for use by states and provinces considering implementation of the CoR's recommended changes. The Guidelines detail extensive required characteristics of practicum training to qualify as counting toward licensure, which have been incorporated into new regulations adopted by a few states so far (Schaffer & Rodolfa,

2011). Although there is no requirement that all practicum training conform to these guidelines, the ASPPB anticipated that they would influence doctoral programs in the implementation of their practicum programs, and accrediting bodies in their program evaluations (ASPPB, 2009, p. 6). Although these guidelines may have a positive effect in ensuring the quality of practicum training, there is also the risk of restricting the range of training opportunities for students. For example, the requirement that at least 75% of supervision be by a licensed doctoral level psychologist may make obtaining practicum experience in rural settings or with special populations more difficult. Further, the Guidelines are not responsive to the expectation that students would take increasing responsibility for their work as their training progresses, such that early, intensive supervision is followed by less intensive supervision as the student matures in competence.

Goals of Practicum

Practicum is intended first and foremost to help students develop their identity and competencies as professional psychologists. The student and the doctoral program have many shared goals for practicum. These include:

• Developing core competencies in preparation for internship.
• Identifying areas of competency strengths and weaknesses.
• Testing out prior interests in practice (e.g., working with children with autism).
• Moving beyond prior interests to gain exposure to new, alternative experiences.
• Focusing on specialized areas after initial general practicum training.

In addition, the doctoral program has its own goals for a student's practicum experience, including:

• Actualizing the program's training model in practice settings (e.g., emphasis on empirically supported treatments).
• Identifying students not able to perform competently in practice and providing them with additional experience as needed—gatekeeping and remediation.
• Ensuring that students are prepared to compete for internships and to perform competently as an intern.
• Meeting accreditation standards that increasingly recognize the importance of the full sequence of applied training.

THE GOALS OF PRACTICUM: PRACTICUM COMPETENCIES

Special attention has been given in recent years to the competencies students are expected to demonstrate during training, including pre-practicum and practicum competencies (Fouad et al., 2009; Hatcher & Lassiter, 2007). Acceptance of competencies as a compelling framework for training has helped bring the focus back to the essential goals of practicum training. Student competencies are recognized as the most important goals for practicum. The competencies movement has helped to clarify and articulate the specific goals of the practicum experience. The Association of Directors of Psychology Training Clinics (now Association of Psychology Training Clinics, APTC) and the Council of Chairs of Training Councils (CCTC) jointly developed the Practicum Competencies Outline (Outline; Hatcher & Lassiter, 2006, 2007), which focuses on competencies expected before practicum begins, and those expected at the end of practicum. This work was largely incorporated into the Benchmarks Competencies (Benchmarks; Fouad et al., 2009), and these documents overlap substantially. Both documents are organized around three general principles: possession of necessary baseline attitudes, skills, and values; progression from dependence on close supervision to the growing capacity for independent practice; and increasing sophistication and depth of skills and knowledge.

Preparation for practicum

Prior to entering practicum training, students usually participate in a series of preparatory courses and pre-practicum training activities that serve both to ready them for the practicum, and to gauge whether they have the personal characteristics that are required to undertake professional activities such as client care. Hatcher and Lassiter (2006, 2007) describe the range of knowledge, skills, attitudes, and behaviors that should be expected of students entering practicum, calling them "baseline competencies." These encompass a range of personal characteristics as well as signs that the student is able to demonstrate satisfactory aptitude for more specific elements of clinical skills. This developmental stage was incorporated into the work of the Competencies Conference (Kaslow et al., 2004; Rodolfa et al., 2007). The Practicum Competencies Outline (Hatcher & Lassiter, 2006) notes that

> Before beginning practicum the student should possess and demonstrate a set of basic personal and

intellectual skills, attitudes and values, and a core of professional knowledge. This core knowledge and these skills, attitudes and values are baseline competencies of the professional psychologist. We argue that it is inappropriate to undertake formal clinical professional training with students who have not acquired these skills. The work of subsequent clinical training is to shape and refine these baseline skills into professional skills. (p.5)

In addition, students need theoretical and practical preparation for the practicum, which are provided by programs' curricula. Coursework directed to pre-practicum competencies often includes courses on personality and psychopathology, intervention, assessment, and ethics, and a seminar designed to acquaint students with the values and attitudes expected of professional psychologists. Some programs include courses that introduce students to specific intervention skills, including empathy, reflective listening, and other skills (Ivey, Ivey, Zalaquett, & Quirk, 2012; Hill, 2009)

Hatcher and Lassiter (2006, 2007) summarize these basic personal and intellectual skills, attitudes, and values, and core of professional knowledge. Under the overall heading of "personality characteristics, intellectual and personal skills," they include such qualities as openness to feedback, interest and respect for others and their unique experiences, and empathy. Also included are cognitive skills such as problem solving ability, organized, critical thinking, curiosity and flexibility, as well as affective skills such as affect tolerance, tolerance for uncertainty and for interpersonal conflict. Personal characteristics such as honesty and integrity, desire to help others, openness to new ideas, are noted, and the ability to communicate one's ideas verbally and nonverbally. Finally, under this overall category are included reflective skills, such as the ability to examine one's own motives, attitudes, and behaviors, and one's effect on others; and personal skills, comprising personal organization, personal hygiene, and appropriate dress. Outlining these personal characteristics is important in giving guidance to pre-practicum students, and in helping programs to identify and address issues that may become severe problems in actual practicum work and later internship experience (Hatcher & Lassiter, 2007).

Knowledge and skills from classroom experience is the second grouping of pre-practicum requirements, expected to be engaged and developed during practicum. "Prior to practicum training, students should have acquired basic theoretical and research knowledge related to diagnosis, assessment, and intervention; diversity; ethics; skills in seeking out and applying research knowledge in the clinical setting. Practicum students should possess sufficient mastery of basic information and skills to prepare them to make good use of the practicum experience. Some coursework may occur concurrently with practicum, but care must be taken to be sure that the practicum does not demand knowledge that the student does not yet possess. This may be a matter for negotiation between practicum sites and the doctoral program" (Hatcher & Lassiter, 2006, p. 5).

Specific areas that should be covered sufficiently to prepare for practicum are assessment and clinical interviewing, which, in addition to education in test construction and validity, includes "training in principles and practice of systematic administration, data-gathering and interpretation for assessment, including identifying problems, formulating diagnoses, goals and case conceptualizations; understanding the relationship between assessment and intervention, assessment of treatment progress and outcome" (Hatcher & Lassiter, 2006, p. 6). Students are also expected to receive classroom training in intervention (with associated practical experience such as role plays or brief, focused clerkships) that includes knowledge of the theoretical and empirical bases of intervention, training in basic clinical skills, such as empathic listening, framing problems, and so on, and in assessment of treatment progress and outcome.

Classes also should provide background in ethical and legal principles, including principles of ethical practice and decision making (APA, 2002a) and an introduction to legal knowledge related to the practice of psychology. Often these topics are covered in an introductory proseminar, which may also introduce students to issues of individual and cultural difference (ICD), although many programs have a separate or additional course specifically dedicated to ICD. Introduction to ICD includes knowledge and understanding of the principles and findings related to ICD as they apply to professional psychology, and training in understanding one's own ethnic/racial, socioeconomic, gender, sexual orientation as well as one's attitudes toward diverse others relative to the dimensions of ICD (e.g., class, race, physical disability, and so on. A major theme related to ICD is the need to consider ICD issues in all aspects of professional psychology work (e.g., assessment, treatment, research, relationships with colleagues; Hatcher & Lassiter, 2006, pp. 5–6).

As Hatcher and Lassiter (2007) point out, programs use this preparation period to assess the student's readiness for practicum training. The monitoring of these pre-practicum competencies is an early and important aspect of the gatekeeping function of clinical programs. Programs may decide that a student is simply unsuited for work with clients, may delay the start of practicum to see if remedial work is effective, or may decide to monitor identified competence problems during the practicum itself(Forrest, Shen-Miller, & Elman, 2007; Jacobs, et al., 2011).

Programs vary as to when their students begin practicum, some starting as early as the first semester of the program. For those that start early, classroom training in theory and practical skills may occur concurrently with practicum itself. This places a special burden on doctoral programs to ensure that practicum experience is conducted within the range of students' acquired skills and abilities, requires a higher level of careful monitoring of student performance to ensure that the baseline competencies are in evidence early in practicum training, and necessitates a particularly active screening and remediation program for students who show deficits in baseline competencies.

Pre-practicum and practicum competencies are the focus of two of the three developmental steps in the report on Benchmarks Competencies prepared by Fouad and colleagues (2009), the third being internship/readiness for practice. There are relatively few differences between the Practicum Competencies Outline and the Benchmarks document in terms of content, although the organization of the content differs to some degree. The differences are due primarily to the Benchmarks' broader focus on the early years of graduate training, encompassing the full range of professional competencies expected by graduation, whereas the Outline focuses on the practicum itself, and the prerequisites for entering practicum. The Benchmarks do detail some additional pre-practicum expectations directly related to practicum training, including some aspects of professionalism, such as "basic understanding of core professional values," "thinking like a psychologist," reliability, awareness and adherence to institutional policies, understanding of confidentiality and informed consent, self-care, and beginning knowledge of supervision (Fouad et al., 2009).

Competencies acquired during practicum

In addition to pre-practicum competencies, both the Outline (Hatcher & Lassiter, 2006,

2007) and the Benchmarks (Fouad et al., 2009) offer comprehensive descriptions of competencies expected as a result of practicum training itself. The Benchmarks document is more detailed, and includes behavioral anchors that illustrate how the competencies might be evident in the behavior of practicum students.

Consistent with the work of the Competencies Conference (Kaslow et al., 2004; Rodolfa et al., 2005), the Benchmarks document divides competencies into two groups: foundational competencies, which apply to all professional activities, such as ethics, and functional competencies, which encompass the specific activities of professional practice such as assessment. The foundational competencies include:

1. Professionalism, which is defined overall as "professional values and ethics as evidences in behavior and comportment that reflects the values and ethics of psychology, integrity, and responsibility." At the practicum level, professionalism includes integrity, professional deportment, accountability, concern for the welfare of others, and the emergence of professional identity as a psychologist.

2. Reflective practice/self-assessment/self-care, which at the practicum level includes intermediate levels of self-awareness and reflectiveness regarding professional practice, increasingly accurate self-assessment of competence, and developing self-care abilities.

3. Scientific knowledge and methods, which includes valuing and applying scientific methods in professional practice, knowledge of the scientific bases of behavior, and knowledge of and application of evidence-based practice. These are values and skills that practicum training is expected to help nurture.

4. Relationships. This critical competency is a key element of practicum experience, which typically gives considerable attention to learning how to develop and maintain professional relationships. This comprises forming productive relationships with all parties, including supervisors; the ability to negotiate differences and conflict, and to receive feedback nondefensively from supervisors and peers; and expressive skills, such as communicating effectively, and understanding professional language. Difficulties with this competency domain are often the focus of remediation during practicum (Jacobs, et al., 2011).

5. Individual and cultural diversity (ICD), including understanding and monitoring one's own cultural identities in work with others, use of knowledge of self to monitor professional behavior, initiating and receiving feedback from supervisors regarding ICD, and sensitive use of ICD knowledge in professional work.

6. Ethical, legal, and professional standards in professional activities, including beginning skills in identifying ethical issues, knowing to consult with supervisors about these issues, and integrating these standards into professional work; beginning use of ethical decision model in collaboration with the supervisor; and recognizing one's own moral principles and ethical values in discussions with supervisors.

7. Interdisciplinary systems is a foundational competence that is chiefly expected as a result of internship; however some basic knowledge, and demonstration of cooperation and consultation with other disciplines is expected at the practicum level. However, many advanced practicum sites involve extensive interdisciplinary interaction (e.g., those in hospital settings), which may yield considerable mastery of this competency.

The functional competencies include:

1. Assessment, including choosing appropriate assessment measures with the help of the supervisor; knowledge of the limitations of assessment methods; application of knowledge of normal and abnormal behavior, the role of ICD in assessment. Students on practicum are expected to be able to write a basic psychological report and to speak effectively about it.

2. Intervention is broadly defined as "interventions designed to alleviate suffering and to promote health and well-being of individuals, groups, and/or organizations" (Fouad et al., 2009, p.). Intervention includes knowledge components, comprising knowledge of interventions and explanations for their use; theory of change; and the basis for selecting treatments based on the presenting problems. It also includes action components, such as investigating treatment literature related to a presenting problem, writing case conceptualization reports and collaborative treatment plans; developing rapport with clients; applying specific evidence-based interventions; and consulting supervisors when appropriate. Intervention also includes assessing and documenting treatment progress and outcomes, and taking action on the basis of findings. These activities may be the heart of many practicum experiences.

3. Consultation, like interdisciplinary systems, is a competency for which there are limited expectations at the practicum level. Basic knowledge is expected regarding the roles of the consultant, the methods for selecting assessment tools for referral questions, and the approaches to intervention based on consultation findings. However, advanced practicum placements may offer more extensive experience in this area.

4. Research/evaluation covers both generating research that contributes to the professional knowledge base, and utilizing research in the conduct of professional practice. At the practicum level, the expectation is that the student will begin to apply research knowledge to practice, including the use of methods to assess client progress and outcome.

5. Supervision, as with consultation and interdisciplinary systems, involves primarily information-level competence at the practicum level according to Fouad et al. (2009). The knowledge that would come from a course on supervision, supplemented by engagement in the processes of their own work, are the emphasis here, although some sites offer advanced practicum students the opportunity to conduct supervision under the supervision of a faculty or staff member.

6. Teaching is a competence that is relevant primarily to other activities during the practicum years.

7. Management/administration is defined by Fouad et al. as management of the direct delivery of services, and/or the administration of organizations, programs, or agencies. Here the expectations are more for the ability to be responsive to managers and administrators, and the policies, regulations, and expectations of the practicum site, rather than to show developed abilities in these roles.

8. Advocacy at the practicum level involves working with clients to develop and promote self-advocacy plans, and recognition of the appropriate professional boundaries in advocating for clients.

A revision of the Benchmarks Competencies has been designed to make the Benchmarks more useable for doctoral programs, practicum sites, and internship programs (Hatcher et al., 2013). This revision includes evidence-based practice (EBP; Levant & Hasan, 2008) as an additional functional competency, and stresses its role in all functional competencies. The practicum offers initial practical training in the methods of finding and applying evidence-based approaches to assessment, intervention, and other functions of professional psychology.

Implementing Competencies-Based Practicum Training: How Competency-Based Practicum Training Is Operationalized by Doctoral Programs

THE DOCTORAL PROGRAM'S TRAINING PLAN

Doctoral programs set their own practicum competency goals as part of developing their overall training plan. Competency documents such as the Benchmarks (Fouad et al., 2009; see also Hatcher, Fouad, et al., 2012) can provide systematic guidance for developing these plans, which should reflect the program's particular approach to implementing the overall training goals articulated for professional psychology. Competency-based program training plans can help make clear how practicum training fits in with the other elements of the plan such as didactics, research, scholarship, and internship training.

ORGANIZING AND MANAGING PRACTICUM

The overall training plan lays the groundwork for the practicum program that is set up for achieving practicum competency goals. Doctoral programs set up the structure, the guiding policies and criteria, and the implementation of the practicum program. The CoA requires that programs take responsibility for planning and overseeing the practicum training their students receive (CoA, 2009, 2012). This oversight has tended to be done informally, with relatively little use of written practicum plans or formal contracts with practicum sites, although these and other policies and procedures are used by a number of programs (Hatcher et al., 2011). Programs are also required to integrate the practicum training experience into the academic program, which may be done through practicum seminars, faculty supervision on site, colloquia, and other means.

SETTINGS FOR PRACTICUM TRAINING

Practicum training occurs in two categories of settings. An estimated 65% of doctoral programs have in-house or closely affiliated clinics (Hatcher et al., 2011). The 35% of programs that do not have in-house clinics conduct all of their practicum training in outside agencies.

In-house training clinics

Programs with in-house clinics use them for initial practicum training, and more advanced and/or more specialized training often takes place in external practicum sites (frequently called externships). In-house clinics are operated by or closely affiliated with the doctoral program, and generally have practicum training as their primary goal. This allows them to focus their efforts on introducing students to clinical work less affected by the pressures of meeting service and income goals faced by most community and hospital agencies. In-house clinics provide very close faculty supervision, making extensive use of video and audio tapes, live supervision, sitting in, and group review of recorded sessions. Training at the in-house clinic may continue at a less intensive level after the first year of practicum training, when students are at externships (Hatcher et al., 2011). External practicum training occurs most frequently in medical settings (36%) and in community mental health centers and other social-service agencies (25%). University counseling centers (25%) and other settings, including schools, round out the picture (Hatcher, Wise, Grus, Mangioni, & Emmons, 2012).

External practicum sites (externships)

Programs without training clinics utilize outside sites for the entire practicum training sequence, and they work to ensure that students will be effectively introduced to clinical practice at a pace that matches their developing competence. Some of the advantages of an in-house clinic can be built into the pre-practicum curriculum so that the program does not have to rely on busy placements to help with developing the early stages of clinical competence. For example, an introductory practicum course can be developed that takes on many of the initial training tasks that would otherwise be assumed by the training clinic. These include developing interviewing and initial assessment skills, alliance-building skills, documentation obligations and methods, and understanding and using the supervisory process to build competence. These steps are important also because some of the teaching methods commonly used in training clinics, such as review of electronic recordings in supervision, are used infrequently in external practicum sites (by 16% of external sites; Hatcher, Wise et al., 2012). Issues of monitoring early competencies are increased when the practicum site is external to the program, because of the need for focused communication and shared values regarding early performance issues. All programs must evaluate the range of possible practicum placements to determine which are best suited to training beginning versus more advanced practicum students, and this task is even more important when the program relies on these sites to provide aspects of introductory training.

Advantages of in-house training clinics

In-house clinics are specifically designed to assist students in developing their initial skills as professional psychologists. Directors of in-house clinics are often either faculty members themselves or have significant affiliated faculty appointments (Hatcher et al., 2011). Supervisors are generally faculty members as well. This arrangement helps the doctoral program to ensure that the training students received reflects and embodies the program's training model and goals. In-house clinics can work closely with the doctoral program to monitor student progress and to identify students who are having competence problems so that remedial action can be taken or counseling out of the program can occur. These clinics are more likely to share the doctoral program's investment in effective assessment of student competence than is the case with heavily used community agencies. In contrast to outside agencies, in-house clinics may smooth (though not eliminate) many of the issues that are faced when communicating with the program regarding a student who is not able to perform up to the level of competence expected. For example, a program may be more likely to inform an in-house clinic about its concerns about a student's competence. Conversely, an in-house clinic faculty supervisor would likely experience lower barriers to informally sharing concerns about a student with the program than would an external supervisor in an external community agency setting.

Organizational support for training clinics

An active national organization of training clinics, the APTC, supports the work of campus-based clinics and their directors with an active listserv, document resources, guidelines for clinic administration and structure, joint research projects, and annual meetings (www.aptc.org). This organization has been active in promoting standards for practicum training.

DOCTORAL PROGRAM ADMINISTRATION OF PRACTICUM

Accreditation standards require that doctoral programs take responsibility for administering their students' practicum training (APA CoA, 2009). This requires setting up an administrative structure with policies and procedures, planning practicum experiences for students, and evaluating student progress in practicum.

Administration

Practicum programs are typically administered by the director of clinical training (DCT) or a faculty member appointed to the role, who is sometimes the director of the in-house training clinic. Other arrangements are also used, including a faculty committee, and in some smaller programs the faculty advisor manages the individual student's practicum experience (Hatcher et al., 2011).

Policies and procedures

Programs set up policies and procedures to manage the practicum. These may include establishing criteria for students' eligibility for practicum, which may include meeting appropriate pre-practicum competence criteria such as those outlined above. In other programs, practicum is simply expected as part of the training sequence, and only students who have shown serious deficits in academic performance are excluded from starting. Students are generally required to have two years of quarter- to half-time practicum experience. About half of programs begin practicum training in the first year, the remainder beginning in the second. Practicum placements, particularly those in outside agencies, vary in length from as little as 4–6 weeks to a calendar year.

Evaluations of student progress and competence are generally required at the middle and the end of the student's practicum experience. Programs typically have established ways to get feedback from practicum sites, which is particularly important if significant competence problems arise requiring remedial or other intervention by the program. Problems arising during practicum are often the first test of the program's procedures for remediation of competence problems. Doctoral programs generally develop administrative set ups to review the student's progress in practicum at established intervals, and, at least, at the end of the academic year. These reviews are shared with students at least yearly, and are a key part of planning for additional practicum experience. Many programs assist their students in keeping track of their practicum hours and activities, which is critical both for application for internship and in an increasing number of states for licensure (Hatcher et al., 2011).

Managing the relationship with external practicum sites is an essential administrative task. Programs have considerably less control over what and how the student is taught at external sites, and so must pick these sites carefully to ensure that the program's goals and standards are met by the training experience offered at the site. This can be a special challenge in geographical areas that are rich in training programs, where competitive matching programs have been established for practicum positions. It is advisable to gather detailed knowledge about the site and the training it offers, and to develop a contract that covers the agreed course of training that the student will receive. The contract should cover the kinds of experiences the student should expect, the hours involved, the duration of the practicum, the nature and frequency of supervision, the types and frequency of feedback regarding the student's performance, and a contact person at the site who will be the liaison to the doctoral program. Gathering student feedback about the site during and after the practicum is crucial to evaluating the quality of the program and adherence to the contract. Many programs conduct site visits at external agencies, and/or have a faculty supervisor affiliated with the site. The APA CoA now asks doctoral programs to demonstrate how they exert control over the training experiences students receive in external practicum sites (APA CoA, 2009).

As part of evaluating external sites (and planning for in-house clinics), programs decide on what sorts of experiences they will accept as legitimate practicum hours. These accepted experiences include a wide range of activities, a range that has increased in recent years as psychologists have found new ways and new settings in which to work. A consensus document developed by the Council of Chairs of Training Councils details a set of these accepted practicum training experiences (www.psychtrainingcouncils.org/document; see also Hatcher, Wise, et al., 2012).

Planning practicum experiences for students

Programs vary in the degree of individualized planning they offer for the practicum experience. Ideally, as a part of the student's overall graduate training plan, the elements of the practicum experience are tailored to match the specific training needs and goals of the student, and modified as these needs evolve during graduate training. The opportunity to consult with a faculty advisor and plan an optimal set of experiences is important, though this is not done uniformly across doctoral programs. Planning

for an individual student is ideally anchored in a good assessment of the student's current level of competence, organized by a competency framework such as the Benchmarks Competencies or the Practicum Competencies Outline. Particularly when the program does not have an in-house clinic, care should be taken to ensure that the student is placed first in a setting that will attend carefully to the student's needs as a beginning professional psychologist. In planning additional experiences, the student's specific interests should be balanced with the need to ensure that the practicum experiences will provide the broad training required by many internship sites.

Additional guidance on administration of practicum programs is available on the Council of Chairs of Training Councils' website (www.psychtrainingcouncils.org/document), the APTC website (www.aptc.org) and in Hatcher et al., 2011.

Evaluating student progress in practicum

Evaluation forms derived from the competency-based training plan can help track student progress and identify more and less developed areas of competence (Hatcher, Fouad, et al., 2012). The APA Education Directorate has an extensive section on its website that contains model forms as well as suggestions for how to implement evaluations of competence during training (http://www.apa.org/ed/graduate/benchmarks-evaluation-system.aspx). Students report finding these more or less detailed competency outlines and assessments to be very helpful and reassuring as they progress through their graduate training, because they clarify and delimit what can seem to be a daunting and expansive set of expectations, and they help them set understandable and achievable goals for each step during their training (Hatcher, Fouad, et al., 2012).

Quality Standards for Practicum Training

As the development of the ASPPB practicum guidelines (2009) indicates, quality standards for practicum training have become a salient issue following upon the APA decision to recommend practicum as fulfilling licensing requirements. The effort to bring standards into practicum training began prior to ASPPB's guidelines, however. The CoA has taken increasing notice of practicum training, partly in light of the proposed changes to the model licensing law, and partly due to efforts by the CCTC and APTC to develop more uniform standards for practicum training. The CoA's Guidelines and Principles (2009) set out overall requirements for practicum training. These requirements, articulated in Domain B.4, are as follows:

(a) Place students in settings that: are clearly committed to training; supervise students using an adequate number of appropriate professionals; and provide a wide range of training and educational experiences through applications of empirically supported intervention procedures.

(b) Integrate the practicum component of the students' education and training with the other elements of the program and provide adequate forums for the discussion of the practicum experience.

(c) Ensure that the sequencing, duration, nature, and content of these experiences are both appropriate for and consistent with the program's immediate and long-term training goals and objectives.

(d) Describe and justify the sufficiency of practicum experiences required of students in preparation for an internship.

> It is the program's responsibility to describe and document the manner by which students achieve knowledge and competence in these areas. Furthermore, given its stated goals and expected competencies, the program is expected to provide information regarding the minimal level of achievement it requires for students to satisfactorily progress through and graduate from the program, as well as evidence that it adheres to the minimum levels it has set (CoA, 2009, pp. 7–8).

The CoA (2012) later developed a set of implementing regulations, IR C-26, that spell out further requirements for practicum training programs. Among the important points in this IR are that the program's curriculum plan:

1. Include a clear statement of the goals and objectives for practicum training;
2. Document outcome measures on how practicum training meets these goals and objectives; and
3. Specify how practicum is clearly integrated with other elements of the program. This includes a description of how academic knowledge is integrated with practical experience through forums led by psychologists for the discussion of the practicum experience, and that practicum training is sequential, cumulative and graded in complexity, and designed to prepare students for further organized training (CoA, 2012, IR C-26).

Programs are also expected to have clearly articulated administrative policies and procedures governing the practicum program, including methods to ensure the quality of training at the practicum site, to evaluate and correct problems at the site, to ensure appropriate matches between students and sites, and to ensure that science and practice are appropriately integrated during the practicum experience. In addition, programs are to describe how they use feedback from site supervisors to evaluate student competence, to define their standards for acceptable performance, and to explain their policies for remediation or dismissal if students fail to meet these standards (CoA, 2012, IR-26).

Additional quality issues have been addressed, including determining what activities constitute practicum and can be counted as practicum experience for application to internship (Council of Chairs of Training Councils, 2007) and for licensure (ASPPB, 2009), and developing standards for the supervision of practicum experience. In addition, the APTC administrative and policy guidelines suggest standards for developing and maintaining quality practicum programs (2008).

WHAT CONSTITUTES A PRACTICUM HOUR?

For some years there was considerable discussion of what constitutes a practicum hour, fueled by concern over the increasing number of hours reported on the APPIC application for psychology internship (AAPI; Rodolfa, et al., 2007). In recent years the intensity of this discussion has diminished, due in part to implementation of APPIC's clearer definition of the categories of practicum activity on its application form. The ASPPB Guidelines also specify that only direct contact and supervision hours can count for licensure. From the point of view of graduate training, the focus on hours is of much less importance than the knowledge, skills, and attitudes that students gain from their practicum experiences—the varieties of competence they gain from practicum, needed to prepare for internship. Given the competency goals for practicum, the issue of what a practicum hour is broadens to the question of what sorts of activities are judged as contributing appropriately to gaining competence during practicum. This issue was examined in two studies that appeared in 2005 (Kaslow, Pate, & Thorn, 2005; Lewis, Hatcher, & Pate, 2005). The CCTC developed a consensus document detailing a set of activities acceptable as practicum experience (CCTC, 2007), which was endorsed by all of the major training councils in professional psychology. This document was the basis for two more recent studies (Hatcher et al., 2011; Hatcher, Wise et al., 2012) that demonstrate a widening range of activities judged as contributing to student competence, from the always highly endorsed direct client contact and supervision, to outcomes assessment, team administration, and outreach. Only a few domains remained controversial, including interaction with offsite professionals, consultation with parents or caregivers, and site administration.

How Foundational and Functional Competencies Are Taught in Practicum Training

Practicum training is expected to address both foundational and functional competencies, although the explicit focus at practicum training sites tends to be on the functional competencies such as assessment and intervention. The foundational competencies, such as professionalism, tend to be addressed as they arise in the course of engaging in the functional competencies. In this section, we will discuss how the foundational and functional competencies are taught in the practicum setting, with special emphasis on how the training goals of the doctoral program are realized. We begin with the foundational competencies, such as ethics, which infuse everything psychologists do. This discussion is followed by a review of how functional competencies are taught in practicum. We want to emphasize that we are providing intentionally broad examples of how these competencies might be incorporated into practicum training with the goal of examining the interface between theory and practice. These are not intended to be specific recommendations for how training might best occur in a specific program.

Integrating Foundational Competencies into Practicum Training

This section will consider strategies for incorporating foundational competencies into practicum training. Using the grouping of competencies proposed by Fouad et al. (2009) and further integrated by Hatcher, Fouad et al. (2012), this section considers the foundational competencies categorized as: (a) Professionalism (including Ethical Legal Standards & Policy, Professional Values & Attitudes, Individual and Cultural Diversity (ICD), Reflective Practice/Self-Assessment/Self-Care); (b) Relational (Relationships); and (c) Science (including Scientific Knowledge & Methods; Research/Evaluation).

PROFESSIONALISM
Ethical legal standards and policy: Ethical context and practice-based competencies.

Ethical and legal competencies provide critical underpinning to all training endeavors, and can be integrated into practicum training at two levels: first in the ethical and legal context for training and supervision, and second in the everyday use of ethics in practice, known as practice-based ethics.

Ethical and legal context

Practicum training occurs within an ethical and legal context. It is properly conducted in accord with ethical, legal, and professional principles and standards. Faculty and supervisors demonstrate ethical and legal competence in how they set up and operate the overall academic training program and in how they conduct practicum training. Modeling ethical and legal practice is extremely important for shaping students' approach to ethical practice. In medicine this has been called the "hidden" or "informal" curriculum (Hafferty, 1998; Hafferty & Castellani, 2010; Martin, 1976), referring to the ways that faculty and supervisors actually behave, which may differ from what is taught if it is taught at all. Further, in order to understand and apply ethical principles consistently, ethical practice needs to be articulated to graduate students.

Education and training are addressed in many states' Psychology Practice Acts. Programs should be alert to the fact that some states specify how clinically related education and training must occur, whereas others leave substantial oversight to the academic training programs. The APA Ethics Code (APA, 2002a) directly applies to all education and training and provides substantial guidance and standards regarding educational practice. The code is incorporated by reference into many practice acts. In addition to providing graduate students with an early foundation in this didactic material, education on these matters serves to inform them of their obligations and rights as trainees.

Competence and client welfare. Standard 2.01 (a) of the APA Ethics Code, Boundaries of Competence, is especially important. This standard states that "Psychologists provide services, teach, and conduct research with populations and in areas only within the boundaries of their competence, based on their education, training, supervised experience, consultation, study, or professional experience." (APA, 2002a, p. 1063). This standard provides the ethical basis for why supervisors provide supervision only in areas of established competence. This standard can be challenging, and ethical dilemmas commonly arise when graduate students gain exposure to contemporary evidence-based practices that may be unfamiliar to their supervisors. Faculty supervisors need to carefully and continuously monitor the limits of their own technical competence. For example, it is clear that a faculty supervisor without training in neuropsychology should not supervise neuropsychological assessments of patients suspected of traumatic brain injury. However, it may be less clear whether a faculty member with general cognitive-behavior-therapy training, and who has learned about dialectical behavior therapy (DBT) through reading and continuing education, is competent to supervise a graduate student who is providing DBT to an adult client participating in an adjunctive structured skills training group. There are many such examples in training programs, and it can be difficult to sort out the nuances in practice. Similarly, Biever, Gómez, Gonzáez, and Patrizio (2011) discuss the challenges in providing competent training and supervision in a multicultural linguistic context. It is not unusual for a training program to have several graduate students who are bilingual in English and Spanish, who may wish to provide services to Spanish speaking clients in the clinic. As with all ethical problemsolving, it is critical to identify the underlying dilemma. In this case the dilemma is likely to be the students' and faculty member's wish to provide training and service to the community versus the limits of the supervisor's competence to effectively oversee and train in these areas. The multiple roles and functions served by clinical supervision can add to the complexity of decisionmaking. Supervisors serve the training needs of the current students, the clinical needs of the current clients, and provide gatekeeping to protect the welfare of current and future clients (Bernard & Goodyear, 2009). Some of these factors might influence supervisors to step outside the bounds of their own competence, whereas considerations of client welfare and risk management might pull toward a more conservative stance. Open discussion of these issues among faculty supervisors and graduate students is an example of how ethical principles can be effectively taught in the context of practicum training.

Delegation of work to others. Standard 2.05, Delegation of Work to Others, is also central to practicum training: "Psychologists who delegate work to...supervisees...take reasonable steps to...authorize only those responsibilities that such persons can be expected to perform competently

on the basis of their education, training and experience...with the level of supervision being provided." (APA, 2002A, p. 1064). Faculty supervisors are ethically responsible for ensuring that students in training have sufficient preparation and oversight to ensure competent service to the client. It can be useful to help students understand that practicum training would not be needed if practicum students were already fully competent. A frank discussion of the learning edge (Fryer-Edwards et al., 2006) provides some helpful reassurance to students early in their training that they are not expected be fully competent from the start. Ongoing assessment and communication regarding the practicum student's learning edge is critical to ensure that the student is challenged but not overwhelmed. Both the student and the client may suffer if a reasonable balance is not maintained. Graduate students become very engaged in a discussion of how to find this balance, and can readily understand the benefits of a developmental approach to competencies. Dissemination and discussion of expected developmental competencies is a critical aspect of ensuring that students are informed about training expectations, and they demonstrate in action the ethical obligation of the program and the faculty supervisor to communicate these expectations.

Informed consent. The ethical standards related to Informed Consent (10.01) are the basis for requiring graduate students to inform clients about variety of matters related to treatment, including the fact that their work is being supervised. It may feel awkward to the beginning (or more experienced) graduate students to inform clients that they are being supervised and to provide the client with the name of the supervisor. It is important that graduate students fully understand that this is a clear ethical obligation when legal responsibility for the treatment resides with the supervisor. This issue can be discussed with the student along with other aspects of informed consent for treatment, including the rationale and importance of notifying clients of limits to confidentiality related to mandated child abuse reporting and other mandated or permissive exceptions in state or federal law, and the right to be informed about recordings of sessions and case discussions in the training seminar (Barnett, Wise, Johnson-Greene & Bucky, 2007).

Graduate student and program rights. Standard 7 (Education and Training) is directly relevant to the ethical competency and is especially useful to discuss thoroughly with graduate students at the outset of graduate and practicum training. Graduate students are likely to be reassured that it is the responsibility of accredited doctoral programs to ensure that graduate students who complete the training program will be eligible for licensure as stated in 7.01 (Design of Education and Training Programs). Standard 7.02 (Descriptions of Education and Training Programs) specifies that program content must be accurately described. This standard also requires that programs provide information on other parameters of graduate training that are likely to be of interest to graduate students including training goals and objectives, program requirements, and stipends. Standard 7.04 (Student Disclosure of Personal Information) is particularly relevant to practicum training, although it applies more broadly. This provides protection to students regarding the extent to which they will be required to disclose personal information. The two exceptions to this boundary for graduate students are when prior notice of disclosure requirements has been given or if there is the need to assess or assist graduate students experiencing personal problems that interfere with competency or that create risk to themselves or another. This standard provides for a delicate balance between the student's right to privacy and the program's right to train according to its explicated model, and to protect the student and the public if the student's personal problems cause risk. Standard 7.05 (Mandatory Individual or Group Therapy) essentially brings the issues discussed earlier into the realm of therapy for graduate students. It clarifies that evaluation and treatment functions will not be performed by the same individual.

Ethical standard 7.06 (Assessing Student and Supervisee Performance) makes it clear that doctoral programs and supervisors are responsible for ensuring that evaluations occur as specified in the ethics code and in accordance with the program's policies and procedures. A frank discussion of the obligation to evaluate graduate students "...on the basis of their actual performance..." (APA, 2002A, p. 1069) can provide an early, shared understanding of the balance that programs must find between supportive (formative) evaluations and the ethical obligation to provide summative competency-based evaluations. The competency outlines and the on-line APA resources described earlier can be integrated into the discussion, especially if they have been used to inform the program's practicum evaluation policies and procedures.

The Multiple Relationship standard (3.05) can pave the way for any needed discussion about potential conflicts in roles that could impair objectivity or judgment. It can be a difficult, but useful discussion

to ask graduate students to consider whether being asked to perform personal favors may constitute exploitation as defined 3.05. Similarly, graduate students also may need to consider how they would respond if a student in a class that they are teaching were to be inadvertently assigned to them in the clinic. Notions of power differentials—between students and their advisors or faculty supervisors, or between students and their own students and clients—can be hard for an anxious graduate student to fully appreciate, but it is helpful to introduce this perspective early in training. Such discussions also pave the way for graduate students to serve as ethical supervisors as they move into new roles later in their graduate training and in their future careers. Finally, Standard 7.07 (Sexual Relationships with Students and Supervisees) prohibits sexual relationships with students or supervisees over whom we have evaluative authority.

Practice-oriented ethical competencies

As graduate students move from readiness for practicum to readiness for internship, their knowledge of the ethical principles is expected to progress from basic to intermediate levels (Fouad et al., 2009). In addition, there is an expectation that the graduate student is able, with greater independence, to identify ethical issues as they arise in practice, supervision, and other settings. Furthermore, the internship-readiness level incorporates the expectation that graduate students are able to recognize their own values and the complex intersection of ethical values and moral principles. In terms of more specific teaching strategies, there are many examples of how practice-based vignettes can become the stimulus for incorporating ethical competencies. Responding to requests for records, child abuse reporting, and the handling of clinical emergencies all provide fodder for ethical discussions that have a high level of relevance when they involve an actual situation in which the student is involved. Similarly, discussing how to respond when a client asks a personal question of the graduate student therapist (a common concern for beginning therapists) or what to do if assigned a university student client who lives nearby in the graduate clinician's apartment complex and rides the same bus to campus, is dating or friends with a graduate student colleague, or is enrolled in a course for which the student serves as a teaching assistant, can all provide opportunities to consider ethical principles beyond agency or clinic guidelines. It has become increasingly common for adolescent or young adult clients to request to "friend" their therapist on Facebook. Beginning therapists may have special difficulty in setting limits with clients in such situations. Based on a de-identified examples, practicum students might be asked how they would respond if a client asked the therapist to be a Facebook friend, to turn off the video camera, or to not document something that was about to be shared in a session. These sorts of applied case-oriented ethical discussions tend to be very engaging for students and provide opportunities for learning that have significant meaning, relevance, and emotional impact. Incorporating vignettes from prior years in the clinic into seminars also tends to be very engaging for beginning students since they know that these situations really happen.

PROFESSIONAL VALUES AND ATTITUDES

Professionalism is defined as: "professional values and ethics as evidenced in behavior and comportment that reflects the values and ethics of psychology, integrity, and responsibility" (Fouad et al., 2009). Professionalism includes integrity, professional deportment, accountability, concern for the welfare of others, and the emergence of professional identity as a psychologist. This is a general and inclusive competency that intersects explicitly to some extent with the ethical competency (ethical behavior and knowledge is included in "integrity"). However, professionalism is conceptualized more broadly to include deportment (appropriate presentation of self in various contexts), responsibility, genuine caring and concern for others, and the emergence of professional identity. As a reminder, all the foundational competencies are by definition applicable to all areas of training. The question for this section is how can each of the foundational competencies under consideration best be taught in practicum?

As with the ethical competency, there is a critical role for faculty supervisors in teaching and modeling professionalism. How can this be done? At the broadest level, it is important to be honest and direct in interactions with graduate students and to expect the same from them. Let's start with a consideration of a particularly high stress occurrence in clinical training and the opportunities it provides. When there is a client emergency, faculty and supervisors model and teach professional values and behavior through compassionate care, taking the time needed to ensure safety, client advocacy, and the knowledge and application of ethics, among others. Even though training clinics and other practicum sites generally screen clients to match the competence levels of their student therapists, unanticipated situations arise that offer ample opportunities to learn both specific (functional) and foundational competencies. If a graduate student's client needs to be evaluated for inpatient admission at a local medical center, the supervisor would strongly encourage the graduate student to accompany the client through the process to the extent feasible in the setting. This is an opportunity to focus on enacting the ethical competency, Concern for the Welfare of Others. In addition to modeling and discussing the importance of spending the time needed to ensure careful assessment and compassionate care for the client, there can be frank discussion of the need to take action to ensure client safety even if it is against the client's wishes. In addition, attention to the emotions involved in enacting one's professional obligations provides an excellent opportunity to inculcate professional values. Along the way, discussion can focus on the importance of clear, assertive, and respectful communication with other providers and the need to advocate for the client's needs (see Deportment). A subsequent seminar meeting or supervision session can be spent reviewing the ethical standards (and the related functional competencies) related to client disclosures without consent, cooperation with other professionals (including law enforcement), assessing for risk, providing continuity of care, the importance of documentation and so forth. Understanding statutory definitions of "dangerousness to self or others," involuntary commitment statutes, and other legal issues is much more meaningful at an intellectual and emotional level in the context of a specific case.

While encouraging the valuing of client welfare, it is also necessary to teach the importance of boundaries. Thus, as indicated earlier, supervisors set clear expectations that client emergencies are handled with a willingness to take the time needed (even if other personal or professional obligations must be compromised), that calls are returned in a timely manner, and that reasonable accommodation is made for scheduling (or rescheduling) appointments. Conversely, graduate students are encouraged not to agree to schedule routine appointments at times that will genuinely create undue hardship for them. As another example, if the supervisor notices that the graduate student's sessions commonly run significantly over time, it is important to address this directly. Teaching how to structure a session by setting an agenda or identifying when the discussion has veered off-course is arguably an essential component of the intervention-implementation competency. Moreover, the ability to be assertive in a compassionate manner with clients is itself an essential component of the foundational relationships competency. As another example, if a supervisor notices that graduate student self-disclosures are not clinically appropriate, it would be helpful to discuss the value of establishing personal-professional boundaries and to clarify the difference between a personal and professional therapeutic relationship. If this continues to be a concern, despite direct discussion and feedback, the supervisor might consider whether the student may need remediation in this area.

Practicum sites benefit from having clearly understood policies and procedures that are enforced consistently. Since the advent of federal privacy laws, the potential risks associated with security breaches have significantly intensified. Although graduate students should not be paralyzed by fear, it is important for them to understand that security is a critical issue in practicum settings. Many clinics and supervisors can neglect to recognize that factors they take for granted as experienced psychologists are genuinely confusing or overwhelming to the beginning graduate student. In addition to ensuring that a practicum training site operates effectively, there are many teachable moments for graduate students that they will carry forward into their own future practice. As a common concern, when graduates fall behind in maintaining documentation, it is essential to note this and to help determine what is causing the problem. The practicum is also the ideal setting to focus on Professional Identity, which is broadly defined as "thinking like a psychologist." This can be accomplished via encouraging graduate students to join a professional association, to read applied journals, and by explicating the distinctions between psychologists and other professionals whose scope of practice overlaps to a greater or lesser extent with ours. Faculty supervisors can model with their own attendance at colloquia and their own lifelong learning practices and habits.

INDIVIDUAL AND CULTURAL DIVERSITY (ICD)

There are three sections to the ICD competency as currently conceptualized: self, other, and interaction of self and other (Fouad et al., 2009). Practicum training can be a powerful tool for ensuring that this foundational competency is addressed and that multicultural course work is integrated into clinical practice. There are many examples of how this competence can be taught in practicum with the goal of developing professionals who will be effective with an increasingly diverse population. Basic concepts may need to be taught if the graduate students begin practicum training prior to formal training in multiculturalism. Overall, individual supervision and directed readings are likely the best format for initial discussions of the graduate students' and clients' location on these dimensions. It can be very valuable to assign readings that are relevant and provocative early in practicum training. For example, since many training clinics offer reduced fees and serve clients who are of limited financial means, assigning a reading that addresses training in the context of poverty (e.g., Smith, 2009) and discussing it in class can be very helpful. More generally, assigning and discussing readings that focus on areas of diversity that are common in the setting can be very helpful. It is challenging to teach ICD competency if students have not been exposed to the very basic concepts and definitions—including power, privilege, oppression, prejudice, intersectionality (that we each embody multiple/intersecting identities), institutional racism, and microaggression. Creating an environment in which students do not feel embarrassed or shamed by what they do not know is particularly important. Programs vary in how explicitly they endorse ICD values in their public statements. Sensitivity is important in all cases, but especially in programs where these topics are not part of the daily discourse. It is, of course, common to discuss areas of diversity that are represented by faculty supervisors and the graduate students themselves in addition to their clients. This may require a level of process-oriented discussion that is unlikely to occur elsewhere.

The use of vignettes can be very useful in addressing diversity in the interaction and self and other. In particular, de-identified brief case summaries that reflect clients who have come to the clinic for treatment can be incorporated in various ways into class discussion. Familiarity with the basic diversity concepts and terms described earlier will lead to much richer discussion. The discussion of case vignettes can serve to illustrate how others are shaped by ICD and context. Our own reactions provide insight into our own location on these dimensions. Considerations of case conceptualization and treatment can elucidate the final dimension of the interaction of self and others.

Practicum training provides a very useful setting for familiarizing graduate students with the excellent APA Practice Guidelines. These guidelines are high quality systematic reviews of best practices with various groups that are developed by content experts and are carefully vetted before they are adopted by APA (APA, 2002b). Examples of current practice guidelines that are particularly relevant for teaching ICD competencies include (APA, n.d.):

• Guidelines for Psychological Practice with Girls and Women.
• Guidelines for Psychological Practice with Older Adults.
• Guidelines on Multicultural Education, Training, Research, Practice and Organizational Change for Psychologists.
• Guidelines for Psychological Practice with Lesbian, Gay and Bisexual Clients.
• Guidelines for Assessment of and Intervention with Persons with Disabilities.
• Guidelines for the Evaluation of Dementia and Cognitive Change.

The full set of current APA Practice Guidelines can be found at http://www.apa.org/practice/guidelines/index.aspx. These practice guidelines can be incorporated as required reading into practicum seminars. A possibly more effective approach is to ask graduate students to integrate ICD journal articles or chapters into their case conceptualizations and presentation of diverse clients. Based on a survey of professional psychologists, it was determined that psychologists are more likely to be able to identify best multicultural practices than they are to endorse actually *following* these practices (Hansen, et al., 2006). This is an example of the "hidden curriculum" mentioned earlier (Hafferty & Castellani, 2010). Considering the implications of this finding for training programs, Hansen and colleagues (2006) recommend that, in addition to typical multicultural training practices, supervisors might initiate "…a frank discussion about why clinicians do not always do what they believe to be important. Identifying and openly discussing these barriers may improve the ability of practitioners to follow through when doing psychotherapy with clients who differ racially/ethnically from themselves." (p. 73). Discussing barriers to the use of multicultural knowledge and skills might also be an important step in improving the multicultural competence of our profession in the future. Finally, ethical considerations can be brought into the discourse, allowing for additional integration of key foundational competencies.

REFLECTIVE PRACTICE, SELF-ASSESSMENT, AND SELF-CARE

The value of reflective practice and self-assessment is in many ways reflected in the attitudes that faculty supervisors bring to their work. To do effective clinical work, graduate students must be able to slow down a bit in order to attend to themselves and their clients, even though the ability to function effectively, even when anxious, uncertain, or fatigued, can serve well in many areas of their training. One study (Shapiro, Brown, & Biegel, 2007) found that mindfulness-based stress reduction in trainees was related to increased positive affect and self-compassion. In fact, Grepmair and colleagues (2007) found that patients in a psychosomatic hospital whose therapists were taught Zen meditation were more likely than patients of the non-Zen trained therapists to benefit in numerous ways, including self-reported reductions in somatization, obsessiveness, paranoia, anxiety, anger, and psychoticism, and social contact. Other authors (e.g., Christopher & Maris, 2010; Wise, Hersh & Gibson, 2011) have developed more specific strategies for incorporating these practices and values into graduate training. Practicum seminars can be ideal settings for discussing the research on mindfulness interventions for therapists and for practicing mindfulness or relaxation exercises that can also be used with clients as appropriate. Encouraging graduate students to experience mindfulness and presence in the moment can provide an extremely beneficial counterpoint to their busy and often multitasking lives. Informing them of the research related to the positive benefits for psychologists of incorporating mindfulness practices can introduce these notions at a critical point in their personal and professional development. More generally, encouraging graduate students to practice on themselves the psychological skills that they use with their clients can deepen learning and also serve as a reminder that we are not so different from our clients and share in many of the challenges that they experience.

Self-care for psychologists in training and in later practice is a burgeoning area (e.g., Barnett & Cooper, 2009; Wise, Hersh & Gibson, 2011; 2012). Practicum seminars and individual or small-group supervision can be particularly conducive to discussions of the stresses that are experienced and can encourage positive activities that serve to balance the challenges of clinical work and doctoral training. Naturally occurring life events can serve as opportunities to teach self-care in context. For example, graduate students can be encouraged to consider their readiness to see clients following a personal loss such as a death in the family. In particular, it can be useful to discuss the critical difference between returning to campus to take an exam versus conducting a client session in terms of the emotional energy that is involved. Integration of the foundational ethical and self-care competencies can occur in considering the meaning and application of Ethical Standard 2.06 (Personal Problems and Conflicts). Mindfulness-based practices and principles and positive psychology (e.g., gratitude practice) can be taught to graduate students as interventions that are especially applicable to the self (e.g., Wise, Hersh & Gibson, 2012). The recognition of harmful attitudes and cognitions such as excessive self-criticism, ruminative thinking, and perfectionism provides an additional opportunity for learning about psychological principles that can be effectively used with clients and with oneself. Several recent articles have explicitly included a consideration of self-care for graduate students (Myers, et al., 2012; Wise & Gibson, 2012). Also worthy of consideration is an approach based on a recent comprehensive systematic review of *therapeutic lifestyle changes* (resulting in the easy to remember acronym TLCs) that were proposed for psychologists to promote to their patients (Walsh, 2011). In addition to incorporating elements of mindfulness, spirituality, and positive psychology, this article also includes evidence-based recommendations for nutrition and exercise that are designed to promote physical health. Of potential interest to graduate students for themselves as well as their clients, the proposed TLCs incorporate an awareness of our evolutionary need to be in nature and the negative impact of overexposure to contexts of *hyper-reality* and *media immersion*. Graduate students might be encouraged to discuss the extent to which their studies and relaxation practices may promote unhealthy distancing from nature-based activities.

RELATIONAL

The relational realm includes Interpersonal Relationships, Affective Skills, and Expressive Skills. Clinical work and the clinic seminar provide ample opportunities for the integration of interpersonal skills. In addition to focusing on the therapeutic relationship in early clinical work, practicum training provides an excellent opportunity for observing affective skills in the interactions with the supervisor, other professionals, and graduate student peers. Clinical presentations in practicum provide the graduate student with an opportunity to develop case conceptualization skills and many opportunities to hone their ability to communicate effectively with peers. Conversely, providing effective feedback to their graduate-student peers is an early

supervision skill that can be built upon in subsequent training. Affective competencies can be developed in practicum training, but can best be understood as pre-practicum skills as defined by Hatcher and Lassiter (2007). Effective communication can be discussed and observed throughout therapy sessions and in clinic documentation or assessment reports. In the clinical work itself, sharing a case conceptualization with the client, providing the client with psycho-education, or giving feedback on an assessment report all provide opportunities to develop and assess relational competencies.

Although the concept of "parallel process" (McNeill & Worthen, 1989) may not be common to CBT or other evidence-based discourse, it is a robust psychological principle, and identifying it when it occurs can deepen relationship discussions. For example, we might note in a supervisory session that a graduate student seems more anxious about working with an anxious client and is seeking an unusual level of structure and specific strategies from the supervisor. As supervisors, we may note that we are beginning to feel a bit anxious ourselves and be concerned that we won't be able to assist the graduate-student's efforts to assist the client. Directly addressing the elements of parallel process in this situation can very effectively deepen the graduate-student's appreciation of the power of relationship dynamics. In settings in which graduate students present case conceptualizations, they might be encouraged to integrate consideration of parallel process into their presentation. Another common relationship dynamic occurs when an internal struggle the client is experiencing (i.e., whether to end a dysfunctional relationship) can become externalized into the therapeutic relationship such that therapists find themselves taking a side in the conflict.

Therapy training is also an ideal setting for graduate students to identify their own tendencies in relationships, such as to intellectualize, avoid emotions, or become distracted when clients avoid their own feelings. Such tendencies are best discussed in a normalized fashion—that we all have our own personalities, histories, and styles that we bring with us to the therapeutic endeavor. It is helpful if graduate students have begun to recognize their own tendencies or styles in a pre-practicum course that has included some videotaped role-play and feedback.

Scientific Knowledge And Methods

Scientific mindedness and an appreciation of the scientific foundations of psychology are directly relevant to practicum. Depending on the model endorsed by the program, research and the scientific method can be integrated throughout. Research on empirically supported relationships (e.g., Norcross, 2011) and therapeutic alliance are just a few examples of research that can be readily integrated into how we teach therapeutic process that is relevant across models of psychotherapy. Encouraging graduate students to apply what they have learned in their evidence-based-treatment courses to their work with specific clients is an ongoing focus of practicum training in many settings. When training clinics or other practicum sites integrate research (e.g., examining outcomes or conducting clinical trials), additional opportunities are provided for graduate students to bridge science and practice.

Functional Competencies

Foundational competencies are expressed in varying ways through the everyday, functional activities that a professional psychologist performs. As discussed earlier in the chapter, teaching the functional competencies, such as assessment and intervention, are the major activities in practicum training. This section considers some salient issues in teaching the functional competencies.

Evidence-Based Practice (EBP)

This critical functional competency is an expression of the foundational competence of scientific knowledge and methods in an applied setting. The core tenet of EBP (APA, 2005) is to find the most effective treatment for the client consistent with the individual client's values and preferences. Ideally, the basic principles of EBP have been taught in the doctoral program's therapy/intervention courses and will be further developed as graduate students begin to assess and treat clients. As a functional competency, evidence-based practice is embedded in the specific area of practice that is the focus of training in the practicum (e.g., assessment, consultation). Practicum can integrate the practice of EBP through teaching specific skills that include developing searchable questions and integration of the information obtained into treatment planning (see Thorn, 2007). A commonly taught method uses the mnemonic acronym PICO (also called the Pico format) in which a searchable, evidence-based question is developed as follows:

P = Patient: Who is your patient? What is your patient's primary complaint, sex, age, race/ethnicity and relevant history?

I = Intervention: What assessments or interventions are you considering for your patient? What treatments have been shown to be effective?

C = Comparison: Is there an alternative or comparison to what you are considering?

O = Outcome: What is the desired or expected outcome?

Searches can be demonstrated in practicum or supervision using this method and through exposure to resources that are designed to provide client-centered data. Graduate students are certainly familiar with Google and are generally experienced with accessing PsycINFO for research-based literature searches, but they may be unfamiliar with searching for evidence-based practice literature. For example, the Cochrane Library (www.thecochranelibrary.com/) provides access to top-quality vetted systematic reviews and the Turning Research Into Practice Database (TRIP; www.tripdatabase.com/) is a free online resource for answering applied research questions. Thus, EBP includes seeking systematic reviews or other resources related to the client population, to the presenting concern or diagnosis, to effective treatments, as well as the application of scientific findings to the specific situation(s) that are the focus of assessment or intervention. A common practice is for a supervisor to guide the student in the use of these resources with respect to a particular case the student has been assigned. Routinely incorporating an expectation of evidence-based searching can be an excellent strategy for integrating evidence-based practice into practicum training.

The use of broad transtheoretical client progress monitoring and outcome assessment in the practicum setting (e.g., Lambert, 2007) is a valuable part of EBP and provides additional opportunities to integrate science and practice. Training clinics are ideal settings for this activity. Data from client tracking can be used for process and outcome studies.

Assessment

Programs vary in the extent to which assessment training is integrated into practicum training. Most practicum sites have an assessment component, and some in-house training clinics are entirely assessment oriented. An introductory course that covers the basic theories of measurement, the broad types of assessment measures, and how to respond to referral questions and write reports provides the academic underpinnings of learning assessment in the practicum. Conducting assessments as a junior partner of a more advanced graduate student and starting with limited assessment questions are among the strategies for taking a developmental approach to assessment training. Practicum students also can be introduced to the practice of supervision in the context of assessments done by more junior students. Many training clinics offer outpatient assessment designed to answer questions about academic and personality functioning. More specialized neuropsychological assessment is more typically taught to advanced graduate students in specialized external practice settings.

Intervention

Many doctoral programs include an introduction to clinical skills in the first year followed by clinical practice in the second year. The preclinical course might include an overview of basic helping skills including paraphrasing and summarizing client statements, reflecting thoughts and feelings, and so on. There are many approaches to this training. Several are particularly comprehensive and include an evidence based and multicultural focus (e.g. Ivey et al., 2012). If there is a seminar associated with the introduction to clinical practice, opportunities to review the essentials of clinical interviewing and apply them to the specific setting tend to be very helpful to graduate students in early clinical training. A benefit to starting with the "essentials" approach outlined by Ivey and colleagues (2012) and others (or of a careful review if these materials were covered in a first year or preclinical course) is that it is not bound to a specific theoretical orientation. These essentials (e.g., active listening, verbal and nonverbal encourages, etc.) serve graduate students well throughout their training and practice. In addition, these models help students understand what therapy needs to look like (e.g., a beginning, a middle, and an end to each session) and provide some broad concepts such as "re-storying" or "reframing" the client's presenting concern. These factors can be applied across theoretical models. Early discussion of the need to balance validation and change, the role of self-disclosure and other meta- or transtheoretical concepts can be learned early in a preclinical course or at the outset of practicum training, and then integrated into practice as they arise. An additional and complementary approach to these discussions is to focus on common factors. Although these basic preclinical skills may be applied differently in different settings, they are as relevant to work in an integrated care setting as they are to traditional clinical treatment setting. Opportunities

to openly discuss their concerns and anxiety tend to be very reassuring to graduate students as they begin clinical practice. Reminders to resist the urge to engage in problem solving by offering premature suggestions before understanding complex client concerns are helpful. When this occurs in treatment, the beginning graduate student can be supportively engaged in noticing when this occurs. In training clinics, reviewing recordings of sessions by the supervisor and the graduate student, both separately and together, can provide critical early feedback on therapeutic style. As with other competencies, graduate students generally benefit from specific and concrete input early in training. More advanced graduate students benefit from a focus on conceptualization and personalized adaptations of interventions in a broad range of applied settings.

As graduate students develop more advanced clinical skills, they are exposed to additional training in hospital or community based settings. These external practicum placements tend to be less closely affiliated with the doctoral program and provide for additional training experiences and the development of professional identity. Specialized practicum placements will be discussed in more detail in a later section.

Consultation

Programs vary in the extent to which this competency is incorporated into training, although it is generally taught as a more advanced skill. Graduate students in School Psychology or in the child track of a clinical program will likely train in school-based settings where they may serve as a consultant to teachers or administrators. Similarly, placement in hospital settings may involve consultation to medical personnel or integrated health-care-treatment teams. In addition to school or integrated health settings, advanced practicum placements in prisons, businesses, court systems, or other settings in which the provision of traditional psychological services is not the primary function, are ideal settings for developing competency in consultation.

Supervision

A primary goal for supervision training at the practicum level is to provide graduate students with the academic foundation and skills that will allow them to effectively develop more advanced supervision skills on internship. Supervision competencies can be integrated into practicum training at the outset. As discussed earlier, the way in which we establish the ethical and legal context of training begins the process of training our graduate students to be ethical and competent supervisors. In addition to providing them with the essential knowledge related to ethical supervision, we have also modeled attention to roles, power differentials, rights, and obligations. Best-practice approaches to supervision training (e.g., Falender & Shafranske, 2004) generally recommend formal course work combined with an opportunity to apply the skills. Basic didactic material would include an understanding of basic models (e.g., social-role discrimination, theoretical and developmental models; see Bernard & Goodyear, 2009 for an in-depth review), methods (direct observation, process, etc.), paired with carefully graded and supervised experiences in providing supervision to a more junior graduate student. As they learn to serve as the front-line supervisor for a more junior colleague, graduate students can be beneficially introduced to the supervision of supervision model.

Interdisciplinary Systems

Early practicum training at in-house clinics tends to be less interdisciplinary than later stages of training in external sites. Over 50% of external sites are medical settings, community mental health, or other social-service agencies (Hatcher et al., 2012), which have interdisciplinary staff. Students at these sites have the opportunity to experience the shared and distinctive contributions of other professions first hand, and learn how to function in multi- and interdisciplinary contexts. The doctoral program practicum courses lay the groundwork for benefiting from these experiences, although this may be an area where more extensive and deliberate teaching could be fostered. Little is known about how supervisors at external sites introduce students to the concepts and issues of interdisciplinary systems. Graduate students can be encouraged to become familiar with the APA Guidelines for Psychological Practice in Health Care Delivery Systems (Masters, France & Thorn, 2009; APA, ND). These Guidelines address the expanded activities undertaken by psychologists in diverse health-care settings. The emphasis in this document is on retaining a clear role as a psychologist while working effectively in an interdisciplinary context.

Advocacy

The majority of doctoral programs (86%) believe that advocacy training should count toward practicum hours (Hatcher et al., 2011). Lewis (2010) has proposed a developmental model for incorporating

social justice competencies into practicum training. This model encourages the explicit discussion of social justice constructs and definitions early in doctoral training. Early clinical experiences include a careful consideration of differential privilege and a positive focus on client empowerment. More advanced practicum training might occur in community settings in which graduate students receive direct exposure to differential power and privilege. In addition, these advanced practica might offer opportunities for more direct political or systems interventions.

The Future of Practicum Training

Practicum training seems destined to play an increasingly important role in doctoral education in professional psychology. As part of the general development of accreditation standards, the CoA increasingly is attending to the quality of practicum training, expecting more oversight and planning by the doctoral program and more attention to students' competency outcomes. The standards proposed by ASPPB (2009) are likely to shape practicum training, posing significant challenges to doctoral programs that want to assist their students in streamlining the licensure process while maintaining diverse opportunities for practicum training. Research on the practicum demonstrates the ongoing challenge of ensuring that the approaches to professional work taken by practicum sites are consistent and supportive of the doctoral program's training model, especially in the areas of EBP and the use of effective observation methods for supervision.

As psychological practice continues to expand into integrated health-care settings, it will be critical to examine current training practices, which typically focus on more traditional skills. Current training models that allow for the development of nuanced clinical skills with individuals, couples, or families may need to be supplemented by more extensive training in interdisciplinary skills, consultation, and supervision in order to function effectively in integrated care settings.

We expect that students and doctoral programs will continue to feel pressure toward high numbers of practicum hours, but also to become more sophisticated in selecting practicum experiences that best match the interests of prospective internship sites.

The beginnings of professional psychology took shape in activities that would now be called practicum, when Lightner Witmer set up his clinic at the University of Pennsylvania in 1896 and began to train others (McReynolds, 1997). We believe that awareness of practicum as a vital part of training in professional psychology is a sign of the strength and vitality of our field.

References

American Psychological Association (2002a). Ethical principles of psychologists and code of conduct. *American Psychologist, 57*, 1060–1073.

American Psychological Association (2002b). Criteria for practice guidelines development and evaluation. *American Psychologist, 57*, 1048–1051.

American Psychological Association (August 2005). Policy Statement on Evidence-Based Practice in Psychology. Retrieved from www.apa.org/practice/resources/evidence/evidence-based-statement.pdf?

American Psychological Association (n.d.). APA Guidelines for Practitioners. Retrieved from http://www.apapracticecentral.org/ce/guidelines/index.aspx.

American Psychological Association Commission on Accreditation. (2009). Guidelines and principles for accreditation of programs in professional psychology. Retrieved from http://www.apa.org/ed/accreditation/about/policies/guiding-principles.pdf

American Psychological Association Commission on Accreditation. (2012). Implementing Regulations Section C: IRs Related to the Guidelines and Principles: IR-C-26: Practicum guidelines for doctoral programs. Retrieved from http://www.apa.org/ed/accreditation/about/policies/implementing-guidelines.pdf

American Psychological Association Council of Representatives. (2006). *Meeting minutes February 17–19, 2006.* Washington, DC: American Psychological Association.

American Psychological Association Council of Representatives (2010). Model Act for State Licensure of Psychologists. Retrieved from www.apa.org/about/policy/model-act-2010.pdf

Association of Psychology Training Clinics. (2008). Administrative guidelines for psychology training clinics. Retrieved from http://aptc.org/public_files/guidelines_02-12-08_rev_1.pdf

Association of State and Provincial Psychology Boards (2009). ASPPB guidelines on practicum experience for licensure. Retrieved from http://www.asppb.net/files/public/Final_Prac_Guidelines_1_31_09.pdf.

Barnett, J. E., & Cooper, N. (2009). Creating a culture of self-care. *Clinical Psychology: Science and Practice, 16*(1), 16–20. doi:10.1111/j.1468-2850.2009.01138.x

Barnett, J. E., Wise, E. H., Johnson-Greene, D., Bucky, S.F. (2007) Informed consent: Too much of a good thing or not enough? *Professional Psychology: Research and Practice, 38*, 179–186.

Bernard, J. M., & Goodyear, R. L. (2009). *Fundamentals of clinical supervision* (4th ed.). Needham Heights, MA: Allyn & Bacon.

Biever, J. L, Gómez, J. P., Gonzáez, C. G. & Patrizio, N. (2011). Psychological services to Spanish-speaking populations: A model curriculum for training competent professionals. *Training and Education in Professional Psychology, 5*, 81–87. doi: 10.1037/a0023535

Christopher, J. C. & Maris, J.A. (2010). Integrating mindfulness as self-care into counseling and psychotherapy training. *Counseling and Psychotherapy Research, 10*, 114–125. doi:10.1080/14733141003750285

Council of Chairs of Training Councils (2007). Recommendations for practicum policies. Retrieved from http://psychtrainingcouncils.org/pubs/Practicum%20Administrative%20Revision%20&%20Cover%20Note%20%206-27-07%20%20.pdf

Dixon, K. E., & Thorn, B. E. (2000). Does the internship shortage portend market saturation? 1998 Placement data across the four major national training councils. *Professional Psychology: Research and Practice, 31*, 276–280. doi: 10.1037/0735-7028.31.3.276

Falender, C. A., & Shafranske, E. P. (2004). *Clinical supervision: A competency-based approach.* Washington, D.C.: American Psychological Association.

Forrest, L., Shen-Miller, S., & Elman, N. S. (2007). Psychology trainees with competence problems: from individual to ecological conceptualizations. *Training and Education in Professional Psychology, 2*, 183–192. DOI: 10.1037/1931-3918.2.4.183

Fouad, N. A., Grus, C. L., Hatcher, R. L., Kaslow, N. J., Hutchings, P. S., Madson, M., …Crossman, R. E. (2009). Competency benchmarks: A developmental model for understanding and measuring competence in professional psychology. *Training and Education in Professional Psychology, 3*, S5–S26. doi: 10.1037/a0015832

Fryer-Edwards, K., Arnold, R. M., Baile, W., Tulsky, J. A., Petracca, F., & Back, A. (2006). Reflective teaching practices: An approach to teaching communication skills in a small-group setting. *Academic Medicine, 7*, 638–644. doi: 10.1097/01.ACM.0000232414.43142.45

Grepmair, L., Mitterlehner, F., Loew, T., Bachler, E., Rother, W., & Nickel, M. (2007) Promoting mindfulness in psychotherapists in training influences the treatment results of their patients: A randomized, double-blind, controlled study. *Psychotherapy and Psychosomatics, 76*, 332–338. doi:10.1159/000107560

Hafferty, F. W. (1998). Beyond curriculum reform: Confronting medicine's hidden curriculum. *Academic Medicine, 73*, 403–407.

Hafferty, F. W., & Castellani, B. (2010). The increasing complexities of professionalism. *Academic Medicine, 85*, 288–301. doi: 10.1097/ACM.0b013e3181c85b43

Hansen, N.D., Randazzo, K.V., Schwartz, A., Marshall, M., Kalis, D., Frazier, R., …Norvig, G. (2006). Do we practice what we preach? An exploratory survey of multicultural psychotherapy competencies. *Professional Psychology: Research and Practice, 37*, 66–74. doi: 10.1037/0735-7028.37.1.66

Hatcher, R. L., Fouad, N. A., Grus, C. L., McCutcheon, S. M., Campbell, L., & Leahy, K. L. (2013). Competency benchmarks: Practical steps toward a culture of competence. *Training and Education in Professional Psychology, 7*, 84–91

Hatcher, R. L., Grus, C. L., & Wise, E. H. (2011). Administering practicum training: A survey of graduate programs' policies and procedures. *Training and Education in Professional Psychology, 5*, 244–252. doi: 10.1037/a0025088

Hatcher, R. L., & Lassiter, K. D. (2006). The Practicum Competencies Outline: Report on practicum competencies. Retrieved from http://www.aptc.org/public_files/Practicum%20Competencies%20FINAL%20(Oct%20'06%20Version).pdf

Hatcher, R. L., & Lassiter, K. D. (2007). Initial training in professional psychology: The Practicum Competencies Outline. *Training and Education in Professional Psychology, 1*, 49–63. doi: 10.1037/1931-3918.1.1.49

Hatcher, R. L., Wise, E. H., Grus, C. L., Mangioni, L., & Emmons, L. (2012). Inside the practicum in professional psychology: A survey of practicum site coordinators. *Training and Education in Professional Psychology, 6*, 220–228.

Hill, C. E. (2009). *Helping skills: Facilitating exploration, insight, and action*. Washington, DC: American Psychological Association.

Ivey, A. E., Ivey, M. B., Zalaquett, C. P., and Quirk, K. (2012). *Essentials of intentional interviewing: Counseling in a multicultural world* (2nd ed.). Pacific Grove, CA: Brooks/Cole. doi: 10:0840034563

Jacobs, S. C., Huprich, S. K., Grus, C. L., Cage, E. A., Elman, N. S., Forrest, L., & Kaslow, N. J. (2011). Trainees with professional competency problems: Preparing trainers for difficult but necessary conversations. *Training and Education in Professional Psychology, 5*, 175–184. doi: 10.1037/a0024656

Kaslow, N. J., Borden, K. A., Collins, F. L., Jr., Forrest, L., Illfelder-Kaye, J., Nelson, P. & Rallo, J. S. (2004). Competencies conference: Future directions in education and credentialing in professional psychology. *Journal of Clinical Psychology, 60*, 699–712. doi:10.1002/jclp.20016

Kaslow, N. J., Pate, W. E., & Thorn, B. (2005). Academic and internship directors' perspective on practicum experiences: Implications for training. *Professional Psychology: Research and Practice, 36*, 307–317. doi:10.1037/0735-7028.36.3.307

Lambert, M. J. (2007). Presidential address: What we have learned from a decade of research aimed at improving psychotherapy outcome in routine care. *Psychotherapy Research, 17*, 1–14. doi: 10.1080/10503300601032506

Levant, R. F., & Hasan, N. T. (2008). Evidence-based practice in psychology. *Professional Psychology: Research and Practice, 39*, 658–662. doi: 10.1037/0735-7028.39.6.658

Lewis, B. (2010). Social justice in practicum training: Competencies and developmental implications. *Training and Education in Professional Psychology, 4*, 145–152. doi: 10.1037/a0017383

Lewis, B. L., Hatcher, R. L., & Pate, W. E. (2005). The practicum experience: A survey of practicum site coordinators. *Professional Psychology: Research and Practice, 36*, 291–298. doi:10.1037/0735-7028.36.3.291

Martin, J. R. (1976). What should we do with a hidden curriculum when we find one? *Curriculum Inquiry, 6*, 135–151.

Masters, K. S., France, C. R., & Thorn, B. E. (2009). Enhancing preparation among entry-level clinical health psychologists: Recommendations for "best practices" from the first meeting of the Council of Clinical Health Psychology Training Programs (CCHPTP). *Training and Education in Professional Psychology, 3*, 193–201.

McNeill, B. W., & Worthen, V. (1989). The parallel process in psychotherapy supervision. *Professional Psychology: Research and Practice, 20*, 329–333. doi: 10.1037/0735-7028.20.5.329

Morrow, W. R. (1946). The development of clinical psychology internship training. *Journal of Consulting Psychology, 10*, 165–183. doi: 10.1037/h0053807

McReynolds, P. (1997). *Lightner Witmer: His life and times*. Washington, D.C.: American Psychological Association. doi: 10.1037/10253-000

Myers, S.B., Sweeney, A.C., Popick, V., Wesley, K., Bordfeld, A., & Fingerhut, R. (2012). Self-care practices and perceived stress levels among psychology graduate students. *Training and Education in Professional Psychology, 6*, 55–66. doi: 10.1037/a0026534

Norcross, J.C. (2011). *Psychotherapy relationships that work: Evidence-based responsiveness*. New York: Oxford University Press.

Raimy, V. C. (Ed.). (1950). *Training in clinical psychology (the Boulder Conference)*. New York: Prentice Hall.

Rodolfa, E. R., Bent, R. J., Eisman, E., Nelson, P. D., Rehm, L., & Ritchie, P. (2005). A cube model for competency development: Implications for psychology educators and regulators. *Professional Psychology: Research and Practice, 36*, 347–354. doi:10.1037/0735-7028.36.4.347

Rodolfa, E. R., Owen, J. J., & Clark, S. (2007). Practicum training hours: Fact and fantasy. *Training and Education in Professional Psychology, 1*, 64–73. doi:10.1037/1931-3918.1.1.64

Schaffer, J. B., & Rodolfa, E. R. (2011). Intended and unintended consequences of state practicum licensure regulation. *Training and Education in Professional Psychology, 5*, 222–228. doi: 10.1037/a0026823

Shakow, D. (1956). The improvement of practicum training and facilities. In C. R. Strother (Ed.), *Psychology and mental health* (pp. 53–75). Washington, DC: APA.

Shapiro, S.L., Brown, K., & Biegel, G. (2007). Self-care for health care professionals: Effects of MBSR on mental well being of counseling psychology students. *Training and Education in Professional Psychology, 1*, 105–115. doi:10.1037/1931-3918.1.2.105

Smith, L. (2009). Enhancing training and practice in the context of poverty. *Training and Education in Professional Psychology, 3*, 84–93. doi: 10.1037/a0014459

Thorn, B.E. (2007). Evidence-based practice of psychology. *Journal of Clinical Psychology, 63*, 607–609. doi: 10.1002/jclp.20384

Walsh, R. (2011). Lifestyle and mental health. *American Psychologist, 66*, 579–592. doi:10.1037/a0021769

Wise, E. H., & Gibson, C.M. (2012). Continuing education, ethics and self-care: A professional life span perspective. In G. J. Neimeyer and J. M. Taylor (Eds.) *Continuing Professional Development and Lifelong Learning: Issues, Impacts and Outcomes* (pp. 199–222). New York: Nova Science Publishers, 199–222.

Wise, E. H., Hersh, M. A., & Gibson, C. M. (2011). Ethics and self-care: A developmental lifespan perspective. *Register Report, 37*, 20–29.

Wise, E. H., Hersh, M. A., & Gibson, C. M. (2012). Ethics, self-care and well-being for psychologists: Reenvisioning the stress-distress continuum. *Professional Psychology: Research and Practice, 43*, 487–494.

Internship Training

Stephen R. McCutcheon *and* W. Gregory Keilin

Abstract

Doctoral education of health service psychologists includes a year of clinical experience as a required element for conferral of the degree. This chapter reviews the historical development of the internship and describes common structural components, including governance structures, funding mechanisms, and issues related to timing in the sequence of training. Special attention is paid to current problems and controversies, including the supply/demand imbalance, stipend support, broad and general training, emerging markets, financial responsibilities of doctoral programs, and accreditation as a national standard.

Key Words: internship, internship imbalance, supply/demand imbalance, doctoral education of health service psychologists, sequence of training, accreditation

Internship Training

The internship has long been a critical element in the sequence of training leading to the doctoral degree in clinical, counseling, or school psychology. Indeed, the internship has variously been called the capstone, and more recently, the keystone experience for health service psychologists (HSP), reflecting its special importance (McCutcheon, 2011). As currently conceptualized, the internship is an immersion experience, constituted primarily of supervised, direct contact with the recipients of services (which may include individuals, families, communities/systems, or other providers). This supervised direct service is complemented by other structured learning activities (e.g., seminars, patient care rounds, case conferences). Thus, the internship is an educational experience that serves to extend and integrate prior learning, rather than being on-the-job training. It usually follows upon successful completion of all classroom requirements and practica experiences, which, in combination, provide students with a foundation of scientific knowledge, professional values and attitudes, and the rudiments of clinical practice.

Though occurring later in the sequence of training, the internship remains broad and general in emphasis (Zlotlow, Nelson & Peterson, 2011), and is intended to promote intermediate to advanced knowledge, skills, and attitudes in a wide array of HSP competencies (APA, 1996). Broad and general training, in the context of supervised clinical immersion, aims to solidify trainee competencies, to prepare new professionals in adapting to newly emerging practice opportunities and professional roles, and very importantly, to integrate knowledge of psychological science and practice at a qualitatively higher level of organization. Finally, the internship is intended as preparation for entry to practice and eventual licensure, or for entry to specialty training at the postdoctoral level.

Key Historical Developments

Wars have far-reaching impacts on societies, including how health care is organized and delivered. The calamity of World War II greatly impacted the health professions, and particularly altered the identity and role of health service psychologists in the United States. Concerned with meeting the burgeoning demand for mental health services, the Department of Veterans Affairs (VA) and the United States Public Health Service (PHS) hired large numbers of clinical and counseling psychologists. This initiative greatly expanded employment opportunities for psychologists in the nation's medical care system, and cemented the professional psychologist's identity as being a valuable front-line clinical provider. To accomplish this expansion, VA and PHS solicited the APA to develop mechanisms by which the quality of doctoral education could be evaluated. Beginning in 1946, with the appointment of a roundtable on internship training of Clinical Psychologists, APA launched a major initiative a year later when it created a Special Committee on Training in Clinical Psychology. The report of this committee included important standards for the development of internship training (Shakow, 1965).

Other developments and conferences that would come to form the bedrock of training for HSP, as well as the role and function of the internship, followed in quick succession. The 1949 Boulder Conference is widely recognized for articulating the scientist-practitioner model and for underscoring the central importance of science-practice integration in service delivery. Equally important, though less widely recognized, the Boulder Conference firmly established the internship as a required element of the doctoral degree (Raimy, 1950). Counseling Psychology followed suit in 1951 by likewise requiring completion of an internship, and a year later, while establishing practicum standards, reaffirmed the value of the internship as a culminating experience in the sequence of training (Kaslow & Webb, 2011). This bifurcated model of doctoral education in professional psychology was further institutionalized as a consequence of federal training dollars funneled to doctoral programs (e.g., National Institute of Mental Health training grants) and internships (e.g., VA internships). An underlying assumption prevalent during these times was that residency in the doctoral program primarily provided students with a knowledge base of scientific psychology, but that skillful application of this science required supervised experience in an applied setting, which was not necessarily or frequently available within the academic institution. In many doctoral programs, science and practice might frequently occur in different settings, and their integration (to the extent that it occurred) might take place sequentially and not necessarily

simultaneously. That is, science often occurred in the home doctoral program and clinical practice skills often were developed outside academic walls.

Following upon the VA's establishment of internship programs designed to fuel a much-needed workforce, the APA's Office of Accreditation invited internship programs to undergo external review beginning in 1956 (Belar & Kaslow, 2003). By the end of that year, 28 internship programs had achieved accredited status [as of 2013, that number has increased to 461, with an additional 26 programs accredited by the Canadian Psychological Association (CPA) and three programs with joint accreditation]. Early models of internship training were greatly influenced by the preponderance of VA programs (and their associated clinical needs), by newly emerging accreditation standards and conference reports, and by historical definitions of the psychologist's role. As a result, internship programs during this period emphasized training in personality and cognitive assessment, and individual psychotherapy and counseling (directed toward pathological and nonpathological conditions, respectively). The 1965 Chicago Conference on the Professional Preparation of Clinical Psychologists further confirmed the importance of the year-long, culminating clinical experience. It also highlighted the value of a greater breadth of experience that should include exposure to a range of clinical conditions, with a diverse population of clients, and employing an array of intervention approaches and modalities (i.e., not solely individual psychotherapy) (Hoch, Ross, & Winder, 1966).

Internship training certainly reached a maturational milestone with the appearance, in 1968, of the Association of Psychology Internship Centers (APIC). This organization began as an informal group of educators primarily concerned with developing a venue for the exchange of information and discussion of internship issues of common concern (Kaslow & Keilin, 2004). It fairly quickly evolved to become the highly organized force it is today, functioning as one of the most visible and influential training councils in professional psychology. Today, the Association of Psychology Postdoctoral and Internship Centers (or APPIC, having changed its name in 1992 in order to more accurately reflect its added focus on postdoctoral training) is a national organization representing internship and postdoctoral programs in North America. Its primary activity is administration of the computerized internship Match, which now annually involves nearly 4,500 students in Clinical, Counseling and

School Psychology programs, and more than 700 internship sites.

APPIC is a voluntary membership organization that requires applicant programs to meet sixteen criteria related to minimum standards for educational resources, processes, and structures (e.g., required hours of supervision, number of supervisors and interns, evaluation and due process procedures). These membership criteria are in accord with important APA/CPA accreditation criteria but are considerably less stringent. Furthermore, APPIC membership is granted on the basis of a paper review of a membership application, whereas APA/CPA accreditation involves a lengthy self-study (usually running several hundred pages) along with a site visit that provides observable verification. APPIC views membership as a critical step in a program's quality improvement but repeatedly reminds its membership that accreditation remains a desired goal. In this regard, it is important to note that roughly 30% of APPIC member programs are not accredited.

In addition to administering the Match, APPIC provides a menu of other services, including assistance in the creation and development of new programs, the dissemination of training resources, the publication (in partnership with APA) of a journal devoted to HSP education and training (*Training and Education in Professional Psychology*), and resources and leadership in a number of initiatives and conferences that have advanced internship training. Notable examples include the 1987 National Conference on Internship Training in Psychology (co-sponsored with the Department of Clinical and Health Psychology at the University of Florida, Gainesville), which produced a detailed policy statement on a host of issues that greatly influenced the conceptualization of the internship (Belar et al., 1989). Delegates at the Gainesville conference endorsed statements regarding which psychologists required an internship, when it should occur in the sequence of training, minimal expectations for entry to the internship, and the relationship between the internship and doctoral program. Regarding the latter, delegates asserted that internship "must be an extension of and consistent with prior graduate education and training" (Belar et al., 1989, p. 7). That is, the culminating year should not reflect a basic change in the student's direction or course of training, but should be an experience that builds upon, elaborates, and integrates that prior learning. No longer should the internship be viewed as something distinct and set

apart, or worse yet, considered as a necessary evil; it should be viewed as an integral element in a seamless sequence of training leading to conferral of the doctoral degree and eventually, entry to practice and licensure. Also noteworthy was the endorsement—made in 1987—that training should occur within *accredited* internship programs, as a means of ensuring minimum quality standards. This aspiration remains unfulfilled 25 years later. As previously mentioned, only 70% of APPIC member programs are accredited in 2013, and a recent APA Board of Educational Affairs (BEA) statement calling for accreditation as a standard in HSP education remains controversial (APA, 2011).

Reflecting its role as a major voice for the community of internship educators, APPIC co-sponsored other notable conferences and meetings, including the 1997 "Supply and Demand" conference (APA, 1998); the 2002 Competencies Conference (from which came the concept of foundational and functional competencies, as embodied in the Cube model, which, in turn, laid the groundwork for the Competency Benchmarks) (chapter 7, this volume) (Kaslow et al., 2004; Rodolfa et al., 2005); and the 2008 Imbalance meeting (colloquially dubbed the Courageous Conversation), which produced the Imbalance Grid that specifies eleven action items that the attendant training councils agreed upon in order to mitigate the imbalance between the number of students seeking an internship and the number of available positions (Grus, McCutcheon, & Berry, 2011).

Reminiscent of APPIC's founding, the Council of Chairs of Training Councils (CCTC) began in 1985 as an informal forum in which the Chairs or Presidents of seven doctoral and internship training councils could meet to exchange information and discuss issues of common concern, with the aim of improving and strengthening professional education and its teaching. Today, CCTC includes 17 member councils (across the entire sequence of training, including practicum and postdoctoral councils) and numerous other groups in observer status. CCTC is partially underwritten by APA but remains an independent group that works closely and collaboratively with its member councils, and with APA and its Boards and committees. CCTC might best be thought of as a "round table" at which competing values and interests are debated. It operates largely by consensus and is explicitly not a decision-making body, and thus its deliberations have no binding authority over its individual member councils. Nonetheless, CCTC has emerged as an important group in terms of drafting policies, launching initiatives, creating accountability, and bringing increased coordination to the sequence of HSP education and training. In particular, CCTC has been an instrumental partner in the development and implementation of competency initiatives, and in efforts to mitigate the internship imbalance. Because it can speak with a single voice for the interests of its disparate Training Council members, CCTC has become an influential advisor and advocate on issues related to internship training. In this capacity, CCTC joined with APA in 2012 to hold a follow-up to the 2008 Imbalance meeting (dubbed Courageous Conversation II), and participated in the interorganizational Health Service Psychology Education Collaborative (HSPEC). A proposed follow-up conference will, among other substantive topics, likely revisit the placement of the internship in the sequence of training.

Internship Structures and Mechanisms

Duration. The vast majority of internships are one-year, full-time placements in service-delivery settings. The profession recognizes an alternative model consisting of a half-time, two-year internship. Such positions are felt to better accommodate the needs of some students, especially nontraditional or older students, who have financial, health, or family needs that constrain them from a full-time commitment. Surveys conducted by APPIC have indicated that approximately 5% of students who participate in the APPIC Match preferred a two-year, half-time program. However, this arrangement is less cost-effective for a training site and can be difficult to implement. For example, a site must be very thoughtful to ensure that a part-time intern has experiences and responsibilities that are substantially advanced when compared to the similarly part-time practicum student, and must, likewise, be thoughtful about implementing training (e.g., seminars) that may include both first- and second-year cohorts. For such reasons, the number of half-time positions in the APPIC Match is negligible, and such positions are largely confined to California, where the California Psychology Internship Council (CAPIC) has promoted this as an alternative model.

In contrast, the model of full-time internship training confers many significant advantages. In particular, full-time training allows for a clinical immersion that promotes a qualitatively different learning experience when compared to prior practicum experiences. Working with clients and other providers on a daily basis to manage a succession of clinical challenges, the intern can achieve a more advanced level of competence across foundational and functional competency domains than could be achieved in practicum placements. In large part, these advanced competencies develop as a function of the responsibility or "ownership" that the full-time intern can achieve as a consequence of being present throughout the work week. Likewise, interprofessional skills (including consultation, nascent leadership, patient advocacy, and harmonious team functioning) are promoted precisely because the full-time intern can become a member of a team of providers. The practicum student or part-time intern is often more a "visitor" than an essential team member, and is less likely to assume full clinical responsibility simply as a consequence of their absence during large portions of the week.

A one-year internship most typically entails 1500–2000 hours, depending on how a site calculates personal leave, sick leave, professional leave, and holidays (Tracy, Bucchianeri, & Rodolfa, 2011). Nonetheless, despite this variability, this range of accumulated hours is in accord with accreditation and licensure standards, and is intended to ensure that interns have sufficient experience for conferral of the doctoral degree and to qualify for licensure.

Models of training. APA accreditation requires that an internship program identify its model of training (e.g., scientist-practitioner, scholar-practitioner) and articulate the linkages between that model and the program's goals, objectives and learning methods. However, there is evidence that, in most cases, the pragmatic nature of clinical work in an internship setting does not lend itself easily to formulating training strictly within the framework of these models (Rodolfa, Kaslow, Stewart, Keilin, & Baker, 2005). Although programs may differ in their broad orientation or viewpoint, and differ in the degree to which they support or promote research activities, the internship year remains fundamentally a clinical immersion experience that occurs within a service-delivery system. The practicalities of such work tend to promote an integrative and pragmatic approach to clinical work and training. Practices that achieve measurable positive outcomes in a particular setting are passed along; effective professional roles and functions in a particular workplace are modeled; training is driven more directly by what "works" in the specific, local circumstances and less by abstractions and theories.

Organizational structures. The basic organization of internship sites differs in some meaningful ways. These distinctions include the nature of the relationship between the doctoral and internship program, the timing of the internship relative to the completion of coursework, and the internship governance structure. As discussed in a later section, these issues of organizational structure have important implications for financial viability of the internship and, thus, for mitigation of the internship imbalance.

Historically, internship sites generally have been entirely independent of the doctoral program. Indeed, the APPIC Match allows students to locate internships anywhere in North America that best fit their background, learning needs, and career preferences. The implicit assumption is that the internship is an autonomous and self-contained experience. For precisely this reason, CCTC adopted recommendations for communication between doctoral and internship programs so that the two parties would share information regarding the student for whom they shared responsibility (CCTC, 2007). As previously mentioned, the continuity between doctoral and internship training was affirmed as an important value at the Gainesville Conference (Belar et al., 1989). In this context, three distinct models for program relationships have emerged:

Non-affiliated independent internships. Internship training most frequently occurs in agencies or institutions that are administratively and legally independent of doctoral programs. The internship site assumes responsibility for all aspects of training, including financial support of the program and trainees, supervision, and didactics. Training objectives, learning methods, and evaluation of learner outcomes conform to the internship program's mission and goals, rather than those of the doctoral program. In this arrangement, trainers must pay attention to several tasks, such as selecting students of differing educational backgrounds who will nonetheless provide a "good fit" with the internship site, providing a coordinated internship curriculum that meets the needs of students who necessarily vary in their learning backgrounds and needs, and maintaining communication with home doctoral programs that might vary substantially in their expectations for student outcomes.

This arrangement provides distinct advantages for both training sites and students. The autonomous internship can select students from a regional or national pool that includes students from a wide range of doctoral programs. Diversity of intern experiences and educational backgrounds is a highly valued quality among internship faculty. Such diversity

consistently brings fresh perspectives and new knowledge to the site's faculty, which is often cited as an important incentive to providing internship training. Such diversity greatly enriches the learning environment for all involved. Likewise, the opportunity to complete training in an institution other than the home doctoral program provides an enriching experience for students that broadens their professional horizons.

Exclusively-affiliated internships. This organizational structure sits at the opposite end of the continuum from the independent internship. An exclusively-affiliated internship (formerly known as a captive internship) is administratively connected to a doctoral program, and is often to be operated by the doctoral program for the benefit of its own students (CCTC, 2010). It serves, essentially, as an extension of the doctoral program's educational offerings, and is likely to provide some degree of financial underwriting. In such an arrangement, interns are selected entirely from the student body of the affiliated doctoral program. This structure represents the highest degree of responsibility that a doctoral program may demonstrate in providing access to internship for its students.

Partially-affiliated internships. This arrangement sits midway on the continuum of affiliation with a doctoral program. A partially-affiliated internship site has entered into an agreement with a local doctoral program to reserve a portion of its internship positions for students from that program. This can be accomplished by designating a "track" in the APPIC Match for students from a specified program, or by a less formal agreement to give preference to students from that program in constructing the rank-order list submitted to the Match. Although not as common, it is possible for an internship site to develop affiliations with more than one doctoral program. This partial affiliation has benefits for both parties to the arrangement: doctoral programs benefit by assurance that their students are advantaged in ranking by a particular internship site, and in exchange, that site typically receives financial or in-kind support from the affiliated doctoral program (e.g., faculty to conduct seminars).

Given the economic challenges experienced by some sites in maintaining an internship program, even modest tangible support from a doctoral program may allow for an otherwise financially marginal site to achieve sustainability. Additionally, both exclusively and partially affiliated programs have an administrative relationship with a doctoral program that makes continuity of educational goals and objectives more likely across the sequence of training. In large part, the affiliated internship exists in order to extend and fulfill the mission of the supporting doctoral program.

There are also a number of potential risks and disadvantages to affiliated (exclusively or partially) internships (Collins, Callahan, & Klonoff, 2007). First, affiliation with a doctoral program is no guarantee of quality. In fact, a doctoral program that has a poor track record of placing students via the Match can use an affiliated arrangement to conceal its deficiencies rather than solve them. Thus, as with all internship programs, affiliated arrangements should be subject to external review at the highest standard.

Another potential disadvantage of this type of arrangement is that students who attend an affiliated internship will often have similar clinical experiences, and even some of the same supervisors, as they did throughout their doctoral program, particularly when doctoral faculty play a key role in the affiliated internship program. This can result in less diversity of experiences, supervisors, and perspectives for the student and less diversity of interns for the internship program. These factors diminish many of the advantages of the internship experience that were described earlier.

Timing of internship in the sequence of training. The vast majority of doctoral students complete internship during their final year in the doctoral program, following completion of all required practicum and coursework. Completion of the internship and dissertation are final requirements for conferral of the doctoral degree, and are most commonly completed simultaneously. Thus, the internship has been described as a *capstone* experience, emphasizing its place as a culminating year (Lamb, Baker, Jennings, & Yarris, 1982), or as a *keystone* experience, emphasizing the significance of the year in the integration of competencies (McCutcheon, 2011). In the majority of states, provinces, and jurisdictions in North America, graduates are required to complete an additional year of postdoctoral supervised experience in order to qualify for licensure as an independent health services practitioner. A substantial minority of jurisdictions now allow licensure upon completion of the internship, in accordance with the APA policy on postdoctoral experience required for licensure. One outcome of this policy change is to give heightened importance to clinical experiences (especially practicum) that occur earlier in the sequence of training. Because capstone or keystone internships are most commonly independent of doctoral programs, and

because the internship year may lead directly to licensure for an increasing number of students, this model places an extra burden on sites to communicate and collaborate in the overall education of the intern, as well as imposes an increased responsibility on the internship for gatekeeping of students prior to entry to the profession (CCTC, 2007).

It is noteworthy that the capstone or keystone models are commonly found in affiliated internships. Although the burden of communication may be eased by the formal administrative relationship that spans the divide between doctoral and internship years, this type of arrangement can also present challenging ethical issues that should be carefully considered by the affiliated doctoral and internship programs. One such issue is that the "gatekeeping" role of the internship may conflict with the affiliated doctoral program's desire to move its students through the program to graduation (see APA ethical standard 3.06, Conflict of Interest; American Psychological Association [2010]). Similarly, financial or other incentives provided by the doctoral program to the internship site may conflict with the internship's ethical responsibility to provide accurate trainee evaluations (see APA ethical standard 7.06, Assessing Student and Supervisory Performance).

A variation on the capstone/keystone models is worth noting. In the integrated training structure model, internship is conducted half-time across two years, during which the student continues coursework at the affiliated doctoral program (CCTC, 2010). The intent is to maximize the integration of classroom knowledge and direct clinical experience. A major challenge is to distinguish such part-time clinical experience from earlier practicum training (which may have been completed in the same setting); to promote professional-level responsibility, clinical care continuity, and leadership within the constraints of part-time attendance; and to foster the development of professional identity in a person, who for major portions of time, remains in a student role. Perhaps due to such challenges and the fact that this structure can be at odds with some APPIC requirements, the integrated training structure is not a widely implemented alternative to the capstone model and is largely limited to professional school programs at this time.

Governance structures. As already mentioned, the governing relationship between internship and doctoral programs is a distinguishing feature with many implications for implementation of training. The autonomous, capstone internship is most likely to operate in an independent institution devoted to providing health, behavioral health and/or mental health services to a variety of recipients (e.g., patients, families, other health-care providers, teachers, systems). In such a setting, the internship program will be administratively embedded within the host institution (e.g., medical school internship), and the mission, goals, and policies of the internship will be consistent with, and promoting of, the larger institution's priorities. The independent internship will collaborate with interns' home doctoral programs for the benefit of the intern, but the doctoral program will have no actual managerial authority in the conduct of their students' final year of training.

In an *allied* governance structure, a partially- or exclusively-affiliated internship will be embedded within the administrative structure of the host institution, but will have additionally forged a formal administrative relationship with a "feeder" doctoral program. Without compromising the administrative integrity of either institution, such a formal relationship between school and site for purposes of operating the internship allows for greater shared responsibilities and exchange of resources. Of course, such an arrangement also introduces complexities that make management of the program more difficult. These complexities are exacerbated when the affiliated sites are themselves housed within independent institutions (e.g., a University-based doctoral program and a state-financed Community Mental Health Center). The complexities are eased when both doctoral and internship programs are housed within a larger, single institution (e.g., a University doctoral program and a University Student Counseling Center).

Consortia models are a final governance structure of great importance. In a consortium, independent entities that otherwise lack sufficient resources to offer internship training on their own create a formal contractual relationship to pool their training resources, and by doing so, have the means and ability to host an internship program that spans their individual sites. Consortia arrangements are a critical tool in building internship capacity; small or underfunded sites can combine to offer training that would otherwise not exist. Consortia sometimes are created with encouragement and financial support of a doctoral program, which, in an allied framework, brings together community-based clinic sites with which the doctoral program has previously worked, perhaps in providing practicum training. In this hub-and-spoke structure, the doctoral program provides a valuable organizational impetus

and expertise that can lead to an affiliated pool of internship positions. Alternatively, independent sites within a community or region may link together in a network of relative equal partners for the purpose of pooling training resources. The impetus in such a case is more likely to arise from the personnel or service needs of the involved internship sites and not the needs of a local doctoral program.

In forming a consortium, the training partners accrue many economies of scale as well as access to shared resources (including practical resources, such as assessment instruments, and less tangible resources, such as faculty diversity or professional esteem). At the same time, consortia require formal agreements that specify contractual obligations between the entities. These can be complicated to obtain and maintain, especially when they involve shared financial and staffing obligations, or when they occur across sites with differing service orientations or missions. Moreover, successful construction and implementation of a consortium requires careful consideration of a shared training model, policies and practices. Despite these hurdles, the consortium model continues to hold promise for growth and innovation in internship training.

Internship Supply and Demand Imbalance

Over the past 20 years, the profession has become increasingly concerned with the imbalance between the number of students seeking a predoctoral internship and the number of positions available through the APPIC Match (APPIC, 2007). More recently, the term "internship crisis" is almost routinely used in order to describe the severity of the imbalance, with more and more students seeking internships without a concomitant increase in available positions. The internship imbalance has generated personal hardship and distress, numerous professional meetings, scholarly activity, and various calls to action and proposed mitigations. This section will provide some recent data about the scope of the imbalance, discuss its impact on the quality of the experience, and review the activities of the profession to date in addressing these concerns.

Scope of the problem. Although long discussed and debated, the internship imbalance has become more acute in recent years. Between 2002 and 2012, the number of registered applicants grew from 3,073 to 4,435—an increase of 1,362 applicants or 44%. A substantial portion of this growth occurred just recently, with an increase of 545 applicants between 2010 and 2012.

Over this same 10-year period, the number of positions available for these applicants grew at a much slower pace, increasing by 438 positions (from 2,752 to 3,190, or 16%). Of these new positions, the majority (279 or 64%) were created in a two-year period, between 2006 and 2008. This period of growth ended with the onset of the economic downturn that occurred in the United States in 2008–2009. In fact, APPIC reported that initial registration figures for the 2009 Match predicted a very significant increase in positions, but that increase (nearly 250 positions) vanished as the economic situation became more serious and sites removed positions from the Match.

Thus, in 2012, the imbalance was the worst at any point in APPIC's history, with the number of registered applicants (4,435) exceeding the number of positions (3,190) by 1,245. Preliminary data from the 2013 APPIC Match, still in process at this writing, suggests a slight improvement in the imbalance, as the number of positions increased by 186 (as compared to the previous year), whereas the number of registered applicants increased by 46.

Internship quality. If one is to understand the true scope of the imbalance between applicants and internship positions, one must look beyond the numbers to the *quality* of the positions available. In the 2012 APPIC Match (APPIC, 2012), a total of 2,363 accredited positions were available, which means that an accredited position was available for only 53% of all registered applicants, a figure that can only be described as alarming. Not only does this lack of accredited positions threaten the quality of the internship experience for many students, it also raises questions about protection of the public and the credibility of the profession (McCutcheon, 2011).

Trainees who are not successful in the Match are left with several less-than-optimal options. They can choose to apply again the following year and hope for a better outcome, an option that delays the completion of their degree and increases their financial burden (e.g., an additional year of tuition, costs to apply and travel for interviews, more student loans). A second possibility is to contact training directors to see if an extra (usually unpaid) position can be created at an existing internship site. A small number of trainees are able to find such placements each year (Keilin, Baker, McCutcheon, & Peranson, 2007), even though APA and APPIC policies do not permit unfunded positions except in unusual and infrequent circumstances.

A third option is to try to create an "internship" experience at a facility that does not have an internship program, an approach that appears to be occurring with increasing frequency. Although such placements might have the advantage of allowing students to graduate, and helps to prevent these trainees from rolling over into the following year's Match. thus increasing the imbalance, it also means that these students are completing internships that have not been externally reviewed and are of unknown or questionable quality. It is also an approach that puts trainees at risk for having significant difficulties with future employment and/or licensure, depending upon their geographic and career aspirations.

Because the increasing imbalance forces more and more trainees to pursue nonaccredited, non-APPIC internships, and because it opens the door for such internships to be created to take advantage of the free labor that can be provided by these students, concern has been raised that we are inadvertently creating a "two-tiered" system of internship training (Baker, McCutcheon, & Keilin, 2007). Few barriers exist to the development and proliferation of such programs, as the laws and licensing board regulations in many jurisdictions do not set minimum requirements for an internship or even require one at all (Hatcher, 2011; DeMers, 2011). Thus, it is often the sole responsibility of doctoral programs to set and enforce standards for the internship experience, a responsibility that can conflict with the pressure of accreditation standards that value the successful placement of trainees into internship programs.

Potential solutions. Trainees who face an approximately one-in-four chance of not securing a position in the APPIC Match are understandably eager for information that improves their odds relative to other competitors. Such information aimed to improve one's personal odds of matching represents a *strategic* approach to the imbalance (i.e., what activities and accomplishments will make me more competitive when I apply for internship?). This strategic approach to the imbalance contrasts with the *structural* approach, which seeks to understand and explain the underlying structural factors in the education and workforce pipelines that result in a substantial mismatch between the number of students accepted into doctoral training, the number of available internship positions, and the number of positions predicted to become available in the professional workforce. More finely detailed analyses focus not only on the quantity of positions, but also on quality indicators of enrolled students, costs of training, quality assurance at the program level, and "right sizing" the education pipeline not solely in terms of numbers but also in regard to specific professional skills and practice specialties predicted to be needed in an evolving health care environment. Unfortunately, predictions about the future of health service psychology employment opportunities and wage stability in the face of increased trainee enrollment remain clouded in the absence of a professional psychology workforce analysis (Rozensky, Grus, Belar, Nelson, & Kohut, 2007).

The chronic nature of the imbalance demonstrates that it is not the result of short-term or transient misallocations in the educational pipeline; instead, it is the result of structural forces (e.g., economic) that advantage the enrollment of large numbers of students and the proliferation of doctoral programs, while disadvantaging a comparable growth in settings that traditionally house internship programs. For this reason, the 2008 Imbalance meeting produced this pivotal outcome: an agreement among the doctoral training councils responsible for educating HSP that their constituent doctoral program members would commit to altering the Match imbalance by either increasing the supply of quality-vetted internship positions or by reducing enrollment, proportional to a given program's success or difficulty in placing students in internships (Grus, McCutcheon, & Berry, 2011). For example, programs that consistently failed to place at least 75% of their students would either voluntarily reduce future enrollment (on the assumption that the low placement rate was de facto evidence that the program had saturated the internship "market" available to that particular program) or alternatively, would build internship capacity by providing financial or in-kind contributions to local entities for the benefit of their own students (i.e., create partially-affiliated internships). The central feature of this agreement is worth making explicit: doctoral programs should assume responsibility for access to all required elements of the doctoral degree, including the internship. In a system built largely of independent internship entities, essentially all doctoral programs will have a role to play in mitigating the imbalance by fine-tuning their class sizes and/or by contributing to internship capacity. Doctoral programs that have a substantial and persistent lack of success in placing their students will have a correspondingly greater duty to adjust enrollment or contribute to the creation of new internship positions. Given this obligation to build capacity, it is useful to review the advantages to a site in providing internship training, as well as the fundamentals of internship financing.

Benefits of providing an internship program. Education and training in many professions often is characterized by a relatively lengthy professional "adolescence" in which the developing professional learns the competencies, attitudes, ethics, and culture of the profession they are entering by direct instruction and complementary experience. The internship year serves just such a purpose (Kaslow & Rice, 1985), and as such, is often remembered later by many psychologists as having been a transformative or catalytic year. Because sharing in the responsibility to educate the next generation, through individual mentorship and apprenticeship, is another common feature of professions, many psychologists find reward and value in designing, building, and maintaining internship programs. These advantages include:

1. Creating a pipeline of potential employees by educating a new generation of likely candidates, especially in domains of special local need or capability (e.g., integrated primary care providers, multicultural providers).

2. Attracting a higher caliber pool of potential employees by training them at sites that might otherwise be overlooked in the workforce by virtue of location or reputation (e.g., rural or remote sites, state hospitals serving the seriously mentally ill).

3. Expanding access to services in marginalized communities or with underserved populations by utilizing lower-cost trainee providers.

4. Improving staff morale and professional growth through participation in training.

5. Enhancing the quality of service delivery by the necessity to emphasize best practices and newly emerging practices within the context of training.

6. Improving overall program quality by submitting oneself to review, whether the review is conducted informally by students who provide feedback simply in the course of being consumers or formally through external quality assurance mechanisms (e.g., accreditation).

Funding considerations. Establishing an internship program brings substantial advantages to a clinical service organization. Building internship capacity also entails incorporating the costs associated with training, including staffing (especially staff time devoted to program administration, supervision and training), office space, clerical and technical support, technology (including computers, telephones, and remote devices, such as secure messaging), and stipends (including benefits, leave, and liability coverage). Such internship costs are most frequently supported by agency operational budgets, which are justified on the grounds that the advantages of hosting a program (as outlined above) outweigh the direct and indirect costs. On the face of it, these costs can seem substantial, particularly to a service agency that might already be operating on the margin. At the same time, many agencies discover that the cost of internship training can be partially or fully offset by the increased service delivery functions provided by the interns.

As one product of the 2008 Imbalance meeting, CCTC created an internship toolkit that includes comprehensive and detailed instructions for conducting a cost-benefit analysis, as well as suggestions for securing external funding (CCTC, 2010). Among these suggested resources are contracts provided by local and state governments, federal grants (e.g., Graduate Psychology Education, or GPE), private foundation grants (e.g., Hogg Foundation), cost offsets (e.g., income-generating sponsorship of continuing education programs for psychologists in the community), and scholarships (e.g., Federal Work Study programs administered on University campuses). The CCTC toolkit makes special mention of fee-for-service reimbursement in underwriting internship training. Although some agencies have succeeded in billing for intern services, almost all third-party payers limit reimbursement to licensed, independent providers (LIPs). A relative few agencies have created work-arounds to this limitation: (a) out of pocket payment on a sliding-scale for services provided by interns relative to the full fee paid for LIP services in the same agency, or (b) third-party payment for interns who are registered, licensed, or credentialed by the state as a master's-level provider. This latter arrangement carries risk for the intern, in that some state licensing boards have been unwilling to accept such hours for purposes of establishing eligibility for licensure as a psychologist, on the grounds that the hours were accrued in the conduct of another profession (for which the intern was already licensed or registered) and not in the conduct of training to become a psychologist.

The various funding streams reviewed in the CCTC toolkit offer creative opportunities for securing moderate sources of funding, yet also underscore the essential need for internship training to be embedded in the operating budgets of host agencies or educational institutions. The central importance of internships in the education of HSP cannot depend primarily on the quixotic nature of external government funding or the generosity of sympathetic foundations. We will return to this point in our later discussion of the responsibility that doctoral programs bear for supporting the required elements of the doctoral degree.

Current Issues and Controversies

The internship imbalance and workforce analysis. When psychologists gather to talk about the internship, the imbalance is the engine that drives most discussions. The imbalance touches upon issues of equity, quality, opportunity, identity, social justice, and workforce. It causes us to ask where we have gone aground as a profession, and how we might reshape our future to ensure both quality of education and access to opportunity. Many agree that, as now constituted, the current situation is not sustainable.

As described earlier, the causes of the imbalance are complex. Depending on one's perspective, it is caused by: (a) insufficient capacity among internship sites, which is itself, due to the economics of internships that are financially divorced from doctoral programs, as well as the historical underfunding of mental and behavioral health programs; (b) excess trainee enrollment, which is fueled by economic incentives to increase class size and tuition payments; or (c) a combination of both forces.

As a consequence, efforts to mitigate the imbalance have tended to emphasize one or the other side of the equation (supply versus demand), though the complexity of the situation requires a coordinated series of incremental actions that address the multiple factors contributing to the imbalance (Grus, McCutcheon, & Berry, 2011). Although such a multipronged approach has gained widespread acceptance among the doctoral training councils, others advocate more radical changes to the internship structure in order to more quickly resolve the imbalance (Larkin, 2011). All of these approaches, whether incremental or more sweeping in scope, are seriously hampered by the lack of a workforce analysis for health service psychology. In the absence of quality data regarding the number of students in the educational pipeline, their internship placement outcomes, their job attainments, and workforce opportunities for psychologists (including geographic distribution, specialty needs, and reimbursement patterns), we are limited in devising a rational plan to mitigate the imbalance. Without a clear understanding of workforce needs and employment trends in the next five, 10, or 20 years, we are in the dark when arguing that enrollments should be lowered or that internship capacity should be increased to meet health care needs. Central to solving the internship imbalance is production of a workforce analysis for health service psychology.

Necessary steps to mitigate, let alone solve, the imbalance remain in dispute. Less in dispute is the increasing realization that successful mitigation will take many years, very substantial changes to the internship system, or both.

Broad and general training. Doctoral training in professional psychology requires broad and general training (Zlotlow, Nelson, & Peterson, 2011). Being both a science and a practice (grounded in the biological, psychological, and social sciences), psychology education requires the integrative experience provided by generalist training. At the same time, scientific advances, new employment opportunities, and the maturing of psychology as a discipline all provide countervailing weight in the direction of increased specialization earlier in the sequence of training.

It was not so many years ago that internship and postdoctoral training emphasized the elaboration and refinement of skills in diagnostic assessment and individual psychotherapy targeted primarily at mental health disorders rather than health conditions more broadly (Kaslow & Webb, 2011). However, coincident with the redefinition of professional psychology as a discipline and practice devoted to improving patient and community *health*, and with the consolidation and formal recognition of an increasing number of HSP specialties, the character of broad and general training, as well as the utility of our traditional models of training (e.g., scientist-practitioner, practitioner-scholar) during the internship year have been questioned (Berenbaum & Shoham, 2011).

Some argue that broad and general education is more appropriately offered at the undergraduate level, allowing for advanced and increasingly specialized training at the doctoral and internship levels (e.g., clinical health doctoral programs, child clinical internships). Although internship programs continue to demonstrate broad and general training through underlying programmatic structures (e.g., expected learning outcomes, student competency evaluations, cross-cutting seminars), the organization of clinics in many internships naturally lend themselves to learning experiences that are either highly focused or frankly specialized (e.g., traumatic brain injury evaluations, mood disorders clinics, rehabilitation care). Because systems of service delivery continue to become more highly articulated or "branded" for marketing purposes, it is likely that clinical training experiences will follow the same pattern. Internship programs likely will offer training in focused areas where the public expresses a need and a demand, and will grapple to identify the best methods of educating interns in the underlying and unifying science of psychology while still promoting experience in cutting edge practices.

Financial relationship between doctoral and internship programs. Historically, university-based doctoral programs had insufficient access to clinical care settings that would be necessary for the practice and attainment of students' clinical competencies. Thus, it was sensible for students to leave the academic environment of their doctoral program in order to immerse themselves in clinical care, for the purposes of integrating science and practice, of refining their knowledge in the real-world forge of health care settings, and of expanding their perspectives through interaction with a greater diversity of supervisors and mentors. However, this disjunction between doctoral and internship programs comes at a cost. The separation of training sites often requires students to move far from home for their final year of training, leaving friends and sometimes family behind. The advantage of greater diversity in supervision risks discontinuity in students' educational plans and trajectories. Perhaps most importantly, this bifurcated model of training creates a situation in which doctoral programs have financial incentive to increase enrollment, whereas internship programs face various limitations imposed by the economics of health care settings (McGrath, 2011). Inevitably, doctoral programs can accommodate a greater number of students than can internship programs, a structural imbalance that almost guarantees a bottleneck at the point of entry to internship.

To date, most efforts aimed at mitigating the imbalance have emphasized building internship capacity. This may be due to the belief that more HSP are needed to address unmet health needs. It may also result from the fact that discussions focusing on capacity building are easier and less conflictual than discussions focused on moderating enrollment. However, underlying these discussions is the question regarding the appropriate role of doctoral programs in ensuring student completion of the entire sequence of training leading to the doctoral degree. In particular, what should be the obligation of the doctoral program in financially supporting the internship requirement? This discussion has taken many directions. Some have questioned the need for an internship year, arguing that an increased focus on practicum training, or alternatively, an increased focus on clinical science in lieu of clinical practice and licensure, both obviate the need for an internship year. In contrast, conferees at the 2008 Imbalance meeting agreed on the principle that doctoral programs bore responsibility for internship placement, to the extent that they should either adjust enrollment or financially contribute to increasing capacity to a degree that is proportional to each program's success in placing students in internships.

Given that the internship is a required element of the doctoral degree, it is reasonable that doctoral programs should share responsibility for ensuring their students' access to such a required element. This acknowledgment serves to link enrollment decisions to internship placement rates, providing a necessary link between these two events that introduces a natural market force. Such acknowledgment of responsibility is most easily observed in doctoral programs that have initiated, developed and financially supported partial and wholly affiliated internship programs. These arrangements recognize that doctoral programs bear responsibility to provide students access to the entire array of required elements, and serve as a check and balance on enrollment and placement.

Intern stipends. The number of internship positions is limited by the costs incurred in supporting an internship program. Intern stipends and benefits are a major driver of these costs. From one perspective, the imbalance can be "solved" if programs are not required to pay stipends, thereby allowing internship programs to offer as many positions as can be accommodated by their other resources (e.g., number of supervisors, access to clients) rather than by their budget for intern stipends. It has been argued, particularly in financially strapped jurisdictions, that access to mental health services sometimes relies on care by unpaid interns, and that requirement of a stipend both limits intern opportunity as well as care for the underserved. Although this position has been argued with force, the preponderance of opinion is in favor of providing intern stipends. In part, there is concern that acquiescence to accepting unpaid services by interns in a harsh budget environment only undermines the profession's efforts to gain parity in healthcare. Why value something that is readily made available for free? Why pay professional staff if similar services can be provided by unpaid labor? More fundamentally, the payment

of a stipend in exchange for service is evidence of the profession's respect for its own students. This is the central feature of the APA Graduate Students' (APAGS) position on the necessity of intern stipends: "respectful internship sites pay emerging health services psychologists a reasonable stipend, provide benefits, and set manageable working hours for interns" (APAGS, 2012).

Competency-based education. Competency-based education has become firmly rooted in current conceptualizations of internship training (Kaslow et al., 2004). The Competency Benchmarks (and associated initiatives) articulate a range of knowledge, skills, and attitudes that characterize preparation for HSP at the prepracticum, practicum, and internship levels (Fouad et al., 2009). Aside from providing both students and educators with concrete examples of expected performance throughout the sequence of training, the Benchmark document very importantly provides operational definitions for the education of HSP. No longer limited to assessment and intervention, the health service psychologist is characterized by a great many competencies (the Benchmarks document identifies 16 such domains). Correspondingly, HSP internships invariably offer supervised experiences that promote many, if not most or all, of these competencies. Adopting a competency framework at the internship level provides an impetus for re-conceptualizing the training experience, for improving efficiency of training, and for describing expected student learning outcomes. At the least, a competency-based approach requires us to specify how various competencies are achieved through the variety of clinical experiences available at a given internship site, as well as how they are behaviorally defined and measured. In a competency-based approach, training inputs (e.g., length of time in training) become less the focus than training outputs (e.g., intern ability to produce treatment gains).

The timing of internship in the sequence of training. If the internship imbalance is viewed as a "bottleneck" due to insufficient positions at a critical point in the pipeline (rather than as a systemic imbalance between student enrollment and later employment opportunities), then it is reasonable to ask if the imbalance could be solved simply by granting the degree at the completion of the dissertation requirement and by making the clinical internship a postdoctoral experience. Those who argue for this change offer the following arguments: (a) expanded practicum hours fulfill the need for clinical training that was the original purpose of the pre-doctoral internship; (b) the internship creates a discontinuity in the sequence of training whereby doctoral programs are held accountable for intern training outcomes that are not in their control; (c) a clinical internship slows the pace of students who intend to pursue research careers and who do not intend to become licensed practitioners; (d) continued enrollment in the doctoral program during the internship year creates a financial burden for students who must pay at least nominal tuition; (e) entering the internship with a doctoral degree creates an approximate parity with medical residents, and increases the potential for billing of services that would be used to underwrite internship costs; and (f) the scarcity of internship positions creates an ethically precarious position for doctoral programs that are unable to guarantee access to an internship, even though they require it for conferral of the degree.

These arguments are countered with the following: (a) in the relatively less regulated and less controlled arena of practicum training, there is great variability in quantity and quality of experiences reported by students when applying for internship, calling into question whether practicum supplants the need for a clinical immersion experience (McCutcheon, 2009; Hatcher, Wise, Grus, Mangione, & Emmons, 2012); (b) changes to state licensing laws allowing entry to practice following completion of the internship have resulted in a proliferation of regulations related to practicum hours that has increased rather than reduced barriers to mobility (Schaffer & Rodolfa, 2011); (c) efforts to make the internship postdoctoral will require many state licensing boards to return to legislatures very soon after having made the argument that postdoctoral experience is not necessary for licensure. This position runs the risk of seeming contradictory and self-serving, and has the potential for unintended consequences from state legislatures that might think the profession is seeking to reduce protections for the public in exchange for benefit to the profession; (d) science-oriented students who hope to obtain faculty positions in clinical training programs, and thereby become the primary mentors for future clinical providers, have a correspondingly greater responsibility to develop their clinical competencies and promote their integration of science and practice by completing an internship year. Perhaps paradoxically, the students who are most interested in pursuing a research career in a degree-granting doctoral program are most likely to have teaching responsibilities for clinical topics that require their own clinical experience. Allowing such students to "opt out" of an internship threatens to weaken graduate training for future classes of students; (e) in most jurisdictions, billing for services is linked to licensure status rather than degree status, making it unlikely that doctoral-level interns (in the absence of independent licensure) will be able to bill third-party payers; (f) the number of students who elect not to attend an "optional" postdoctoral internship is likely to be negligible, given the many employment forces that exist that would make it a de facto necessity (e.g., federal employment). The net contribution to solving the imbalance would likewise be negligible but would incur both costs and risks, and (g) internship sites that currently fund nondoctoral level interns would be faced with the prospect of determining stipends for doctoral-level (though not independently licensed) providers. Likely, this would lead to inflation of stipends, which, in the absence of third-party payment, would result in potentially significant cuts to the number of positions, thereby making the imbalance dramatically worse rather than better.

Accreditation as a national standard. Although APA or CPA accreditation is widely accepted as the standard for doctoral programs in health service psychology, there has not been a similar consensus regarding accreditation at the internship level. Among the current 711 internship members of APPIC, only 490 (69%) of programs are APA/CPA accredited, whereas 221 (31%) are not accredited. These proportions have been relatively stable for a decade or more, despite APPIC's strong encouragement that its members pursue accredited status. Because internships are more likely to operate in the community, lack the institutional support of academic departments, and operate on the financial margins in the arena of underfunded mental health care, such training programs are more likely than doctoral programs to suffer financial limitations or instabilities (McGrath, 2011), which make direct and indirect costs associated with accreditation a perceived barrier (Berry, 2012). The consequence, however, is that an important element of doctoral education (the internship) is allowed to operate without the external quality vetting required for earlier portions of a student's education. If one agrees that doctoral training should occur in accredited programs, and that the clinical internship should be required for conferral of the degree, then arguably, it is inconsistent to argue that the internship should not also be completed in an accredited setting. How else can the accredited doctoral program ensure a minimal level of quality training for its students during their keystone year?

The question of accreditation as a standard for internships has resurfaced periodically, but was recently given new impetus by the confluence of key changes in health care as well as dialogues about the sequence of training leading to entry to practice. Foremost, the passage of the Affordable Care Act underscores the critical importance of psychology's inclusion in the health care marketplace. In order to assert a legitimate role for HSP in newly designed health care delivery, it is essential that the profession takes responsibility for self-regulation and accountability to the public. Accreditation is the system through which this is demonstrated (Nelson & Messenger, 2003). For psychology to successfully compete with other professions that also seek health care dollars, the profession must support a process of quality vetting that guarantees acceptable standards throughout the sequence of training. This is central to our profession's social contract with the public, and is a reasonable expectation in exchange for access to public dollars. Moreover, in an era of increasing federal oversight of education, it is in psychology's interest as an independent profession to sincerely and actively self-regulate. Better that we take charge of ensuring quality at the internship level than to leave this task for state or federal governmental agencies. Finally, as discussed earlier, proposals to mitigate the internship imbalance sometimes have included suggestions that would have the impact of degrading training quality in favor of increasing access. Because such an outcome would be especially detrimental to the profession's reputation in this time of health care transformation, the training councils responsible for educating HSP students affirmed at the 2008 Imbalance meeting (and repeatedly have reaffirmed at bi-annual meetings of CCTC) that any efforts to mitigate the imbalance must not have a deleterious impact on educational quality (Grus, McCutcheon & Berry, 2011). As more states adopt licensure laws that allow entry to practice following conferral of the degree, the clinical training obtained during internship takes on greater importance: for increasingly large numbers of our students, the internship year has become their final opportunity for clinically intensive practice under supervision. Given this reality, lowering standards in order to increase internship access is contrary to the public interest, and thereby, contrary to our profession's interest.

In response to these various currents, there has been a revitalized interest in making accreditation a standard for the internship. The APA Board of Educational Affairs (BEA), CCTC, and APAGS recently endorsed APA/CPA accreditation as the standard for graduate training in health service psychology. At its March 2011 meeting, CCTC endorsed a vision statement that called for APA/CPA accreditation as the standard for all levels of training (doctoral, internship, and fellowship), with the understanding that this would be phased in over a period of years in order to allow currently nonaccredited programs reasonable time to achieve this status, thereby protecting currently enrolled students (CCTC, 2011). This proposal moved forward to BEA, which supported the standard of accreditation at the doctoral and internship levels in a much-expanded "Statement on Accreditation" (Belar, 2011), which describes in greater detail the rationale and a process for implementation. Student support for this development, as one element of an overall strategy, is found in the APAGs statement on the imbalance (APAGS, 2012).

Although momentum seems to be building to establish accreditation as a standard for internships, there is recognition of many complex implications and potential consequences that must be addressed simultaneously. For example, adoption of this standard has limited impact if it is not eventually linked to licensure. Thus, attendance at nonaccredited doctoral and internship programs is not discouraged unless access to licensure is made more difficult or not possible as a consequence. Further, legitimate empirical questions exist regarding whether attendance at an accredited internship results in improved trainee competence when compared to attendance at a nonaccredited program. Given that the movement in favor of accreditation is substantially a response to legitimate political sensitivities about the positioning of HSP vis-a-vis other health care professionals, it is also true that a profession committed to evidence-based educational practices has a duty to empirically investigate this question. Finally, there is widespread recognition that an abrupt adoption of accreditation as a standard threatens to dramatically worsen the imbalance in the short term (CCTC, 2011). If the very substantial number of nonaccredited APPIC-member programs were denied participation in the APPIC Match due to their noncompliance with the accreditation standard, the already-critical imbalance could become so intolerable that it could undermine support for the very existence of internship training. In recognition of this scenario, implementation of the standard would occur over a period of years so as to allow both APPIC-member and non-member internship programs the time necessary to achieve accredited status.

Expanded roles and markets. Psychology practice has greatly benefited from newly developed professional roles and expanding markets. This is seen most dramatically in psychology's evolution from a discipline devoted primarily to mental health concerns to one that has expanded to embrace *health* conditions. New practice opportunities have been the result, and along with that, a need for new educational models and experiences. As U.S. health care is transformed in the wake of the Affordable Care Act, and as HSP continues to mature and further specialize, it is inevitable that internship training will advance to keep abreast of new opportunities (e.g., integrated primary care, interprofessional models of care delivery, and advances in neuroscience). Such changes will include new content areas and practice competencies, but may also include more substantial alterations in *how* training is delivered (e.g., remote technologies) and, perhaps, *when* it is delivered in the overall sequence of training leading to licensure.

References

American Psychological Association. (1996). *Guidelines and principles for accreditation of programs in professional psychology.* Adopted by the APA Council of Representatives, 1995.

American Psychological Association. (1998). *Proceedings from the National Working Conference on Supply and Demand: Training and employment opportunities in professional psychology.* Washington, DC: Author.

American Psychological Association. (2010). American Psychological Association ethical principles of psychologists and code of conduct. Retrieved March 17, 2013, from http://www.apa.org/ethics/code.

American Psychological Association Board of Educational Affairs. (2011). BEA statement on accreditation. November, 2011.

American Psychological Association of Graduate Students. (2012). Response to the internship crisis. Retrieved February 22, 2013 from http://www.apa.org/apags/issues/internship-crisis-response.aspx

Association of Psychology Postdoctoral and Internship Centers. (2007). *APPIC Clearinghouse Statistics 1986-1999.* Retrieved February 9, 2013, from http://www.appic.org/Match/Match-Statistics/Clearinghouse-Statistics

Association of Psychology Postdoctoral and Internship Centers. (2012). *2012 APPIC Match Statistics—Combined Results: Phase I and Phase II.* Retrieved February 9, 2013, from http://www.appic.org/Match/MatchStatistics/MatchStatistics2012Combined.aspx

Baker, J., McCutcheon, S., & Keilin, W. G. (2007). The internship supply-demand imbalance: The APPIC perspective. *Training and Education in Professional Psychology, 1,* 287–293. doi: 10.1037/1931-3918.1.4.287

Belar, C. (2011). A developmental milestone. *Monitor on Psychology, 42,* 49.

Belar, C. D., Bieliauskas, L. A., Larsen, K. G., Mensh, I. N, Poey, K., & Roehlke, H. J. (1989). The National Conference on Internship Training in Professional Psychology. *American Psychologist, 44,* 60-65. doi: 10.1037/0003-066X.44.1.60

Belar, C. D., & Kaslow, N. J. (2003). The history of accreditation of internship programs and postdoctoral residencies. In E. M. Altmaier (Ed), *Setting standards in graduate education: Psychology's commitment to excellence in accreditation* (pp. 61–89). Washington, DC: American Psychological Association.

Berenbaum, H., & Shoham, V. (2011). Broad and cutting-edge training in applied psychology: A Clinical Science perspective. *Training and Education in Professional Psychology, 5,* 22–29. doi: 10.1037/a0022603

Berry, S. (2012). *Helping non-accredited internships move toward accreditation.* Paper presented at the meeting of the Association of Psychology Postdoctoral and Internship Centers, April 26–28, 2012, Tempe, AZ.

Collins Jr., F. L., Callahan, J. L., & Klonoff, E. A. (2007). A scientist-practitioner perspective of the internship Match imbalance: The stairway to competence. *Training and Education in Professional Psychology, 1,* 267–275. doi: 10.1037/1931-3918.1.4.267

Council of Chairs of Training Councils. (2007). CCTC recommendations for communication. Retrieved February 22, 2013, from http://www.psychtrainingcouncils.org/documents.html

Council of Chairs of Training Councils. (2010). Internship toolkit. Retrieved February 22, 2013, from http://www.psychtrainingcouncils.org/documents.html

Council of Chairs of Training Councils. (2011). Minutes of CCTC meeting, March 24, 2011.

DeMers, S. T. (2011). An ASPPB perspective on Hatcher's "The internship supply as a Common-Pool Resource: A pathway to managing the imbalance problem." *Training and Education in Professional Psychology, 5,* 141–143. doi: 10.1037/a0024901

Fouad, N. A., Grus, C. L., Hatcher, R. L., Kaslow, N. J.,...Crossman, R. E. (2009). Competency benchmarks: A model for understanding and measuring competence in professional psychology across training levels. *Training and Education in Professional Psychology, 3,* S5–S26. doi: 10.1037/a0015832

Grus, C. L., McCutcheon, S. R., & Berry, S. L. (2011). Actions by professional psychology education and training groups to mitigate the internship imbalance. *Training and Education in Professional Psychology, 5,* 193–201. doi: 10.1037/a0026101

Hatcher, R. L. (2011). The internship supply as a common-pool resource: A pathway to managing the imbalance problem. *Training and Education in Professional Psychology, 5,* 126–140. doi: 10.1037/a0024658

Hatcher, R. L., Grus, C. L., & Wise, E. H. (2011). Administering practicum training: A survey of graduate programs' policies and procedures. *Training and Education in Professional Psychology, 5,* 244–252. doi: 10.1037/a0025088

Hatcher, R. L., Wise, E. H., Grus, C. L., Mangione, L., & Emmons, L. (2012). Inside the practicum in professional psychology: A survey of practicum site coordinators. *Training and Education in Professional Psychology, 6,* 220–228. doi:10.1037/a0029542

Hoch, E. L., Ross, A. O., & Winder, C. L. (1966). Conference on the professional preparation of clinical psychologists: A summary. American Psychologist, *21,* 42–51. doi: 10.1037/h0021107

Kaslow, N. J., Borden, K. A., Collins, F. L., Forrest, L., Illfelder-Kaye, J., Nelson, P. D....Willmuth, M. E. (2004). Competencies Conference: Future directions in education and credentialing in professional psychology. *Journal of Clinical Psychology, 60,* 699–712. doi: 10.1002/jclp.20016

Kaslow, N. J., & Keilin, W. G. (2004). Association of Psychology Postdoctoral and Internship Centers. In W. E. Craighead and C. B. Nemeroff (Eds.), *The concise Corsini encyclopedia of psychology and behavioral sciences* (3rd ed., pp. 963–967). New York: Wiley.

Kaslow, N. J., & Rice, D. G. (1985). Developmental stresses of psychology internship training: What training staff can do to help. *Professional Psychology: Research and Practice, 16,* 253–261. doi: 10.1037/0735-7028.

Kaslow, N. J., & Webb, C. (2011). Internship and postdoctoral residency. In J. C. Norcross, G. R. VandenBos, & D. K. Freedheim (Eds), *History of psychotherapy: Continuity and change* (2nd ed., pp. 640–650). Washington, DC, US: American Psychological Association.

Keilin, W. G., Baker, J., McCutcheon, S., & Peranson, E. (2007). A growing bottleneck: The internship supply-demand imbalance in 2007 and its impact on psychology training. *Training and Education in Professional Psychology, 1,* 229–237. doi: 10.1037/1931- 3918.1.4.229

Lamb, D. H., Baker, J., Jennings, M., & Yarris, E. (1982). Passages of an internship in professional psychology. *Professional Psychology: Research and Practice, 13,* 661–669. doi: 10.1037/0735-7028.13.5.661

Larkin, K. T. (2011). Behavioral contingencies involved in common pool resource management. *Training and Education in Professional Psychology, 5,* 213–216. doi: 10.1037/a0026282

McCutcheon, S. R. (2009). Competency benchmarks: Implications for internship training. *Training and Education in Professional Psychology, 3,* S50–S53. doi: 10.1037a0016066

McCutcheon, S. R. (2011). The internship crisis: An uncommon urgency to build a common solution. *Training and Education in Professional Psychology, 5,* 144–148. doi: 10.1037/a0024896

McGrath, R. E. (2011). Resolving the internship imbalance: Expanding the Commons or limiting the cattle? *Training and Education in Professional Psychology, 5,* 202–204. doi: 10.1037/a0026277

Nelson, P. D., & Messenger, L. C. (2003). Accreditation in psychology and public accountability. In E. M. Altmaier (Ed.), *Setting standards in graduate education: Psychology's commitment to excellence in education* (pp. 7–38). Washington, DC: American Psychological Association.

Raimy, V. C. (ed.). (1950). *Training in clinical psychology.* New York: Prentice-Hall.

Rodolfa, E., Bent, R., Eisman, E. Nelson, P., Rehm, L., & Ritchie, P. (2005). A cube model for competency development: Implications for psychology educators and regulators. Professional Psychology: *Research and Practice, 36,* 347–354. Doi: 10.1037/0735- 7028.36.4.347

Rodolfa, E. R., Kaslow, N. J., Stewart, A. E., Keilin, W. G., & Baker, J. (2005). Internship training: Do models really matter? *Professional Psychology: Research and Practice, 36,* 25–31. doi: 10.1037/0735-7028.36.1.25

Rozensky, R. H., Grus, C. L., Belar, C. D., Nelson, P. D., & Kohut, J. L. (2007). Using workforce analysis to answer questions related to the internship imbalance and career pipeline in professional psychology. *Training and Education in Professional Psychology, 1,* 238–248. doi: 10.1037/1931-3918.1.4.238

Schaffer, J. B., & Rodolfa, E. R. (2011). Intended and unintended consequences of state practicum licensure regulation. *Training and Education in Professional Psychology, 5,* 222–228. doi: 10.1037/a0024998

Shakow, D. (1965). Seventeen years later: Clinical psychology in light of the 1947 Committee on Training in Clinical Psychology Report. *American Psychologist, 20,* 353–362.

Tracy, E. N., Bucchianeri, M. M., & Rodolfa, E. R. (2011). Internship hours revisited: Further evidence for a national standard. *Training and Education in Professional Psychology, 5,* 97–101. doi: 10.1037/a0023294

Zlotlow, S. F., Nelson, P. D., & Peterson, R. L. (2011). The history of broad and general education in scientific psychology: The foundation for professional psychology education and training. *Training and Education in Professional Psychology, 5,* 1–8. doi: 10.1037/a0022529

Postdoctoral Training in Professional Psychology

Christina K. Wilson, Allison B. Hill, Dorian A. Lamis, *and* Nadine J. Kaslow

Abstract

This chapter reviews the history of postdoctoral training; the development of national standards and accrediting bodies such as the Association of Postdoctoral and Internship Training Centers (APPIC) and the APA Commission on Accreditation (CoA) (formerly the Committee on Accreditation); and the types of opportunities available, including those targeted toward specialty practice and informal postdoctoral training. This chapter concludes by highlighting advantages and challenges of postdoctoral experiences, the host of personal and professional factors that may guide one's decisions related to postdoctoral training, and recommendations for future directions.

Key Words: postdoctoral residency/training, specialties, accreditation, competencies

The supervised postdoctoral training experience marks the end of the formal educational and training sequence in professional psychology. The postdoctoral movement in professional psychology occurred in response to myriad factors, including but not limited to the explosion of practice competencies and the emergence of specialties (Kaslow & Webb, 2011). There is growing recognition of the value of supervised postdoctoral training with regard to professional identity development and solidification (Kaslow, McCarthy, Rogers, & Summerville, 1992). In addition, supervised postdoctoral training significantly increases people's job marketability (Kaslow & Echols, 2006; Kaslow et al., 1992; Logsdon-Conradsen et al., 2001; Sato, Simon, Jelalian, & Spirito, 2012; Stewart & Stewart, 1998; Stewart, Stewart, & Vogel, 2000).

In most, but not all jurisdictions, a supervised postdoctoral experience is a requirement for licensure. Indeed, there has been considerable controversy over the years with regard to the necessity of postdoctoral training for licensure, as well as competing perspectives regarding the value of formal

postdoctoral residency experiences. There is, however, general consensus, that such experience is invaluable for specialization (Eby, Chin, Rollock, Schwartz, & Worrell, 2011; Nezu, Finch, & Simon, 2009). Thus, not surprisingly, supervised postdoctoral experience typically is considered a necessary pre-requisite for board certification.

The first formal national conference on postdoctoral training in professional psychology, which was hosted by the Association of Psychology Postdoctoral and Internship Centers (APPIC), did not take place until 1992, and thus it was not until that time that standards for postdoctoral education and training were clearly delineated (Belar et al., 1993). It was not until 1997 that the American Psychological Association's (APA) Committee on Accreditation (CoA; now Commission on Accreditation) began accrediting postdoctoral training programs (Belar & Kaslow, 2003). In recent years there has been increasing attention to this phase of professional development.

This chapter considers the postdoctoral experience in professional psychology broadly. Most of our focus is on formal training experiences. Research postdoctoral training is not the focus of our discourse. After defining the postdoctoral training experience in professional psychology, including its origins, attention is paid to the settings in which postdoctoral training is most likely to occur and the content and funding of such training. Consideration is given to the advantages and disadvantages of formal versus informal postdoctoral training experiences. We conclude with a discussion of the challenges of postdoctoral training and recommendations and future directions for enhancing the postdoctoral experience.

Defining Postdoctoral Training in Professional Psychology

Postdoctoral training is typically the final phase of professional development prior to licensure and before people embark on a career as a psychologist (Kaslow & Echols, 2006). This stage of training facilitates the development of feelings of self-efficacy and confidence in independent practice, solidifies professional identity, and ensures that individuals early in their career are competent as clinicians and clinical researchers (Kaslow & Keilin, 2008; Kaslow et al., 1992). Postdoctoral training also has critical implications for professional practice opportunities. For example, it is seen as a key experience in the development of specialty competencies (Boake, Yeates, & Donders, 2002; Bowers, Rickers, Regan, Malina, & Boake, 2002). Furthermore, participation in postdoctoral training also can influence opportunities for licensure and affect the availability of professional and employment opportunities postlicensure. Increasingly, jurisdictions emphasize participation in postdoctoral training as part of the licensing process. In 1980, only 20 states required postdoctoral training (Stewart & Stewart, 1998). As of 2012, all but 13 states in the United States include postdoctoral training as a requisite component of the licensure process, which reflects the increasing value the profession places on these experiences (Association of State and Provincial Psychology Boards, 2012). This is despite the fact that in 2010, the American Psychological Association (APA) passed a Model Act for State Licensure of Psychologists in which a postdoctoral experience was no longer required (Retrieved December 14, 2012 from http://www.apa.org/about/policy/model-act-2010.pdf).

Origins of Postdoctoral Training

Over the past four decades (Belar, 1992a, 1992b; Belar & Kaslow, 2003; Wiens, 1993), efforts to develop and advance postdoctoral training have been undertaken by several organizations and interest groups. These efforts have emphasized education, training, and accreditation procedures. It is critical to understand historical underpinnings in order to provide a context for contemporary discourse on this important phase of professional development in the early careers of psychologists. Accreditation of programs is relatively new at the postdoctoral level; however, attention to the need for postdoctoral training in clinical psychology dates back to the Boulder Conference in 1949, which was the first national conference to define a training model for professional psychology (Belar & Kaslow, 2003; Raimy, 1950). At the time, the model of education and training articulated that a 1-year internship in the third year of graduate study would be required. Based on this model of education, the internship was to be the primary vehicle for intensive clinical training, after which students would return to the university to complete a clinically informed dissertation. To become proficient in psychotherapy, however, Boulder conference attendees stated that postdoctoral training would be required, and, delegates to the Boulder Conference asserted that psychotherapy training itself should be largely postdoctoral (Belar et al., 1993).

At the Stanford (1955) and Miami (1958) (Roe, Gustad, Moore, Ross, & Skodak, 1959) conferences the value of postdoctoral training was further affirmed, and the model of a 4-year academic program followed by a 2-year postdoctoral internship was proposed for clinical psychology (Belar & Kaslow, 2003). This model was referred to as the "4 plus 2" model (Belar et al., 1993). That model failed to gain majority support, although it still has proponents at the present time (Belar & Kaslow, 2003). As a result, although postdoctoral training was seen as highly valued, the one-year doctoral internship was reaffirmed.

At the 1965 Chicago Conference, participants came to the agreement that postdoctoral training should be regarded as an ethical responsibility for aspiring psychologists in order to obtain the status of "expert" (Hoch, Ross, & Winder, 1966). Delegates supported postdoctoral education and training as a way to obtain advanced and specialized skills, but warned it should not be construed as a method of remediation for deficiencies at the doctoral level (Belar & Kaslow, 2003). As such, themes such as advanced training and pursuit of excellence defined postdoctoral training, and it was seen as essential for those who desired to teach, supervise, or enter independent practice (Hoch et al., 1966).

The Menninger Clinic held the first conference to focus exclusively on postdoctoral education and training in 1972 (Weiner, 1973). Although delegates shared information and concerns, no specific guidelines for postdoctoral training were set forth. One concern raised by delegates was that postdoctoral programs functioned more as "trade schools" than centers for advanced training in the discipline of psychology (Belar, 1992a,1992b; Belar & Kaslow, 2003). In other words, delegates feared that postdoctoral programs focused on having residents be "workhorses" learning a trade rather than trainees being socialized into a profession. Yet, the perceived need for an organized postdoctoral training year remained. Shakow noted, "In all the conferences and reports I have referred to, it was either implicitly or explicitly recognized that a doctoral program with a one-year internship was insufficient to turn out a truly competent clinical psychologist" (Shakow, 1973, p.12).

Development of National Standards

Beginning in the late 1970s, guidelines for postdoctoral training were developed in various specialty areas, including but not limited to health, clinical neuropsychology, rehabilitation, clinical child and pediatric, primary care, family therapy, forensic, geropsychology, serious mental illness, and consulting and organizational psychology (American Psychological Association, 2007; Bersoff et al., 1997; Garcia-Shelton & Vogel, 2002; Hannay et al., 1998; Kaslow, Celano, & Stanton, 2005; Lowman et al., 2002; McDaniel, Belar, Schroeder, Hargrove, & Freeman, 2002; Moye & Brown, 1995; Patterson & Hanson, 1995; Pingitore, 1999; Roberts et al., 1998; Routh, 1977; Sheridan et al., 1988; Shullman, 2002; Spirito et al., 2003; Stewart, Horn, Becker, & Kline, 1993). A common theme across these areas of practice was the commitment to the scientist-practitioner model of education and training (Belar et al., 1993; Wegener, Hagglund, & Elliott, 1998), which is defined as a training model that integrates science and practice in psychology in which each consistently informs the other (Lane & Corrie, 2006). However, no general standards were in place for postdoctoral training in professional psychology. In August of 1990, the Joint Council on Professional Education in Psychology (JCPEP) recommended that specialization in professional psychology occur at the postdoctoral level and, furthermore, that there should be accreditation for the programs for such specialty training.

Although APPIC was the first body to develop standards for approval as early as the mid-1970s, no accreditation process of postdoctoral training programs existed until 20 years later. Moreover, various constituency groups expressed interest in developing standards for accreditation throughout the late 1980s and early 1990s. At the first National Conference on Internship Training in Psychology in 1987 (Gainesville Conference), concerns were raised about the lack of quality assurance in postdoctoral training, and delegates asserted the need for another national conference to articulate standards for the postdoctoral year (Belar et al., 1989). Some delegates cautioned that there was potential for exploitation of postdoctoral residents in terms of inadequate and unfair financial compensation. As such, there was a call for a subsequent national conference to articulate standards for postdoctoral training that could serve as the basis for accreditation processes.

To promote a collaborative and cohesive accreditation process for the postdoctoral field, the American Board for Professional Psychology (ABPP) hosted a meeting at the University of Minnesota in 1991. The outcome of this meeting was the creation of the Interorganizational Council for the Accreditation of Postdoctoral Training Programs (IOC) (Belar & Kaslow, 2003). This interorganizational council was comprised of key organizations associated with accrediting, licensing, and credentialing in professional psychology. The IOC was established in an effort to promote excellence in postdoctoral training. In existence from 1992 through 1997, the members of the IOC crafted accreditation guidelines for postdoctoral training programs in professional psychology. In the later years of their existence, IOC members worked collaboratively with members of the CoA to establish guidelines for accrediting postdoctoral training programs, create a self-study document template, devise mechanisms for accrediting postdoctoral residencies, and formulate an infrastructure for selecting site visitors and reviewers. The IOC was sunsetted when its members, representative of the relevant constituency groups, were confident that the standards and procedures devised by the CoA with regard to postdoctoral program accreditation were appropriate.

In response to concerns expressed at preceding national conferences regarding the lack of consistent standards for postdoctoral training, several organizations (e.g., APPIC, ABPP) co-sponsored the first National Conference on Postdoctoral Training in Professional Psychology in Ann Arbor, Michigan in 1992 (Belar et al., 1993). During this four-day conference, participants addressed issues related to the purposes of postdoctoral training; entrance and exit criteria; program content, structure, and organization; and evaluation processes. Its purpose was to clearly articulate criteria that will provide guidance to training programs, students, credentialing authorities, accreditation bodies, and consumers of psychological services (Belar et al., 1993). The outcome of this conference formalized current postdoctoral education and training practices, and conference participants produced a policy document that addressed the purposes of postdoctoral training, entrance requirements, program content, structure, and organization, faculty-staff, and evaluation mechanisms (Kaslow & Keilin, 2008). As a result, they developed principles and adopted a policy statement detailing recommendations for initiatives to foster excellence and innovation in training, which included guidelines for accrediting postdoctoral programs.

In 1994, the American Psychological Association (APA) held a National Conference on Postdoctoral Education in Psychology in Norman, Oklahoma in order to examine ways to enhance the competence needed for psychologists to contribute maximally to teaching, research, and practice. Specifically, the attendees provided models for postdoctoral and continuing education and training; established a taxonomy and terminology; proposed mechanisms for documenting program adequacy and training competence; identified and developed funding opportunities; and offered processes for trainee and program outcomes assessment (Kaslow & Keilin, 2008).

Accordingly, in 1996, the CoA adopted and implemented guidelines for postdoctoral education and training programs in professional psychology (Belar & Kaslow, 2003). Postdoctoral accreditation in professional psychology was initiated by APA in 1997. To become accredited, a program must submit a comprehensive self-study document that provides detailed information with regard to the program's training goals and objectives, policies/procedures, the competencies expected of the postdoctoral residents in the program, and outcome data demonstrating that residents achieve these competencies at the developmentally expected level. The self-study and other associated materials must include the program's public statement of a commitment to training individuals in a substantive traditional or specialty practice area. Accredited programs also must demonstrate that their residents are to attain an advanced level of competence in theories and effective methods of psychological assessment, diagnosis, and intervention, consultation, program evaluation, supervision, teaching, administration, professional conduct, strategies for scholarly inquiry, ethics and the law, and cultural and individual diversity. Moreover, postdoctoral residents are required to complete at least 1500 hours of total time, which can be done on a part-time or full-time basis. The postdoctoral training program must include a programmatic sequence of training experiences, an appropriately qualified licensed psychologist as training director, two or more qualified and licensed psychologists on staff or faculty, two hours or more a week of individual supervision, additional hours of learning activities, and a requirement that residents spend at least 25% of their time in professional psychological services (Kaslow & Keilin, 2008). Accredited programs are to be a minimum of 1 year in length; however, it is understood that certain specialty areas (e.g., clinical neuropsychology) may require up to three years. At the accreditation site visit and in the review of all the accreditation materials by the CoA, all of the previously-noted information is considered in making an accreditation decision.

Postdoctoral training often is specialty focused. Through the auspices of APA's Commission for the Recognition of Specialties and Proficiencies in Professional Psychology (CRSPPP), specialties within professional psychology have been determined. With regard to some specialty areas, the CoA has augmented general accreditation guidelines with specialty specific guidelines by request of organizations that are members of the Council of Specialties. The accreditation process for postdoctoral residencies involves professional judgment as to the degree to which a program has achieved the goals and objectives of its stated training model. A core principle is as follows:

> Postdoctoral residency education and training in professional psychology reflect the natural evolution and expansion of the knowledge base of the science and practice of psychology, and should be of sufficient breadth to ensure advanced competence as a professional psychologist and of sufficient depth and focus to ensure technical expertise and proficiency in the substantive traditional or specialty practice areas of professional psychology for which the residents are being prepared (American Psychological Association, 2000) (p.3).

Initially, accreditation was for programs that were broad and general in nature, but over time, accreditation became available for specialty programs.

APPIC does not accredit postdoctoral programs, however, it reviews programs and determines membership status for programs that meet a certain level of quality and training standards, such as being coordinated by a designated psychologist, having an organized sequence of training that is a minimum of one year in duration, providing appropriate supervised experiences under a minimum of two psychologists for at least four hours per week, requiring direct service experiences for at least 25% of the experience, and being guided by due process procedures. The APPIC Membership Directory offers a listing of their member programs and indicates their APA accreditation status. As of January 1, 2013, there are 145 postdoctoral members in APPIC. APPIC has offered an optional postdoctoral match in the past, but does not provide a matching service at the present time.

Another relevant group is The Association of Postdoctoral Programs in Clinical Neuropsychology (APPCN). APPCN's mission is to ensure the provision of high quality competency-based postdoctoral residency training in clinical neuropsychology. APPCN evaluates postdoctoral training programs for membership based on their commitment to the guidelines that emerged from the Houston Conference on Specialty Education and Training in Clinical Neuropsychology, the availability of appropriate training resources, and the offering of training experience that encourage APPCN member program graduates in pursuing board certification in clinical neuropsychology through ABPP.

As Kaslow and Keilin describe, despite efforts to develop national standards, most programs fall outside of the APPIC and APA systems, which results in insufficient quality control for many postdoctoral programs. Furthermore, because licensing boards do not expect applicants to have attended an accredited postdoctoral training program, there is little incentive for programs to seek APPIC membership or APA accreditation (Kaslow & Keilin, 2008).

Nonetheless, at present, there are 42 accredited postdoctoral training programs and 37 accredited specialty practice programs (including clinical neuropsychology, clinical health psychology, clinical child psychology, rehabilitation psychology, and forensic psychology) with some sites having more than one accredited program (American Psychological Association, 2012a, 2012b).

Settings

A review of APA accredited and APPIC member postdoctoral residency programs reveals that the primary settings in which formal postdoctoral training occurs are Veterans Affairs Medical Centers (VAMCs), academic health-sciences centers, free-standing hospitals (e.g., children's hospitals, private general hospitals, private psychiatric hospitals), and university counseling centers. However, positions also are available at Armed Forces Medical Centers, community mental health centers, consortium, correctional facilities (e.g., prisons), private outpatient clinics, psychology departments, school districts, and state/county/other public hospitals. Informal positions may occur in any of the aforementioned settings, but often occur in private practice contexts, either individual or group practices. In addition, some postdoctoral training experiences can be found in industry contexts and these often are more organizational and business consulting in nature. There are advantages and disadvantages to training received in each of these settings related to a number of factors including, but not limited to: availability of professional practice or applied training experiences that can be used to accumulate hours toward licensure, interdisciplinary and interprofessional training and collaboration, teaching and supervising opportunities, publication and grant writing experiences, and protected research time (Sato et al., 2012). In addition, there is variability across settings with regard to pay, benefits, and employment opportunities (Sato et al., 2012)

Postdoctoral Training Content

Content of postdoctoral training experiences can vary widely based on the program focus (i.e. generalist versus specialty training) and structure (i.e., formal, informal). In addition, some programs use particular theoretical orientations, such as cognitive behavioral, psychodynamic, or systemic, to inform the emphasis and process of training (Sanders & Steinberg, 2012). Moreover, often times, programs are specialty focused, given the strong emphasis placed on specialty training at the postdoctoral level (Drum & Blom, 2001).

Largely, the content of postdoctoral training is driven by national competency-based guidelines encompassing several foundational and functional domains of professional practice. Understandably, the majority of competency guidelines pertain to clinical practice, including theoretical knowledge and familiarity with interventions, ethics, and individual and cultural diversity. However, as the roles of professional psychologists are multifaceted, many of the requisite competencies of a psychologist are related to tasks taking place outside the therapy room. Psychologists are called on in several capacities: as researchers, scholars, supervisors, administrators, managers, consultants, teachers, and program evaluators. As such, the content of postdoctoral training programs must be broad enough to prepare graduates for the variety of work contexts of practicing psychologists while providing a profundity of clinical training that strengthens clinical expertise.

To aid in such efforts, the Council of Chairs of Training Programs (CCTC) approached the APA Board of Educational Affairs with a proposal to develop a document that identified guidelines for and measurable objectives of competence for various stages of psychology training, including readiness for professional practice (Fouad et al., 2009). The outcome of that proposal was the development of the Assessment of Competency Benchmarks Work Group (hereinafter referred to as "the Workgroup"), which was tasked with the creation of the Benchmarks document (Fouad et al., 2009). The Benchmarks document addressed specific levels of training and referenced the set of foundational and functional competencies of professional psychology outlined in the Cube Model developed at the 2002 Competencies Conference, with some modifications based on feedback from constituent and professional groups and committees (Kaslow, 2004; Kaslow et al., 2004; Rodolfa et al., 2005). In this model, foundational competencies refer to a set of skills, values, and knowledge that underlie the tasks performed by psychologists in work settings. Functional competencies are key job functions that rely on the successful application of foundational competencies for successful resolution.

The Benchmarks document outlines specific criteria that can be used to evaluate whether an individual is ready for independent practice. Although the document identifies core competencies across various levels of training, there are certain foundational and functional competencies that are particularly relevant for individuals in postdoctoral training. For example, knowledge regarding interdisciplinary systems, including familiarity with interdisciplinary contexts and the role of psychologists in interdisciplinary settings, is a key foundational competency for many practicing psychologists. The behavioral anchors associated with this competency domain include multisystemic perspectives on patient care and successful collaboration and communication with other professionals (Fouad et al., 2009).

In addition, there also are several functional competencies that are particularly salient at the postdoctoral level, such as supervision, administration/ management, and advocacy. Postdoctoral training is the first opportunity for many individuals to fully engage in these activities, and, therefore, marks a significant departure from predoctoral training experiences. Specific activities that indicate readiness to practice as a supervisor include the development of a supervision contract, ability to articulate the limits of one's own competencies and to address complex cultural, legal, and ethical issues (Falender et al., 2004; Falender & Shafranske, 2004; Falender & Shafranske, 2007, 2008). Furthermore, those entering professional practice are expected to have the necessary competence to supervise trainees with different levels of experience, including individuals in other professions and peers, as appropriate. In regard to administration and management, competencies following postdoctoral training include the ability to manage, evaluate, and improve delivery systems, including administrative, technological, financial, staffing, and organizational demands. Postdoctoral-level competency also is achieved when an individual has developed an advanced understanding of advocacy, including opportunities to empower patients/clients and utilize one's role as a psychologist to advance change on institutional, community, societal levels (Fouad et al., 2009).

The Benchmarks document marked a significant improvement in the development of postdoctoral training expectations and provides helpful guidelines that can be used to develop training objectives and evaluate trainee progress. However, the competencies outlined in the Benchmark document largely pertain to psychologists and trainees involved in health services practice, and may, therefore, differ from psychologists serving in other settings, such as academic or research settings. Furthermore, one important area not addressed by the Benchmark document is the specific training demands and requirements involved in specialty practice.

As previously noted, the primary objective of postdoctoral training is to gain advanced competencies related to professional practice in the broad and general sense, as well as to specialty practice. As such, specialty or emphasis areas (e.g., neuropsychology, forensics, geropsychology, and child and adolescent clinical/pediatric psychology) have developed postdoctoral training experiences guided by the specific practice demands in those areas. For the most part, the competency domains covered in the Benchmarks documents are relevant for postdoctoral training that is specialized in nature. However, postdoctoral residency programs that offer in-depth specialty training tend to emphasize opportunities for trainees to work in relevant professional contexts (e.g. interdisciplinary teams, legal settings), while simultaneously developing familiarity with and expertise in the theoretical, scientific, cultural, clinical, ethical, and professional standards of conduct for psychologists in those settings (Boake et al., 2002; Drotar, Palermo, & Ievers-Landis, 2003; Hinrichsen, Zeiss, Karel, & Molinari, 2010; Malesky & Proctor, 2012).

Funding and Salaries

There are multiple avenues of potential funding for formal postdoctoral training programs in professional psychology (Kaslow & Keilin, 2008). Specifically, funding sources may include hospital funding through patient care activities, research projects, National Institutes of Health's (NIH) Individual National Research Service Awards (NRSAs), and other federally funded programs (Drotar et al., 2003; Stucky, Buterakos, Crystal, & Hanks, 2008). Postdoctoral residents in professional psychology should recognize that some programs have multiple sources of funding with several tracks and need to understand how potential slots are funded and the implications for their training when applying to positions. The availability and stability of funds may influence the opportunity for planning and program development as well as the quality of the postdoctoral training (Drotar et al., 2003). In order for additional programs and positions to become available, the APA has made efforts toward passing legislation to support psychology postdoctoral training programs. However, more needs to be done to secure further funding streams to increase the number of available residency opportunities.

There is great variability in the salaries offered for full-time APA accredited and nonaccredited positions. Of the postdoctoral programs participating in the 2010–2011 APPIC Directory, the median salary was $38,000 (range: $28,000–78,000). The highest paid postdoctoral residents were employed in military settings (average salary: $68,500); whereas, the lowest paid postdoctoral trainees were in psychology department settings ($25,000) (Lese-Fowler, 2010). As of the 2010–2011 training year, the average salary for APA accredited programs was $44,700 (range: $29,500–78,500), whereas, the average salary for non-APA accredited program positions was $35,900 (range: $20,000–74,000).

Formal versus Informal Training Experiences

Postdoctoral training also can vary based on the structure of program. Formal programs provide an organized sequence of training that is well-supervised and includes appropriate didactic and experiential components. Typically, such programs are guided by a developmental framework with regard to training (Kaslow et al., 1992). There are many potential advantages of participating in a formal program (Sato et al., 2012). Such training programs provide a structured system in which to accumulate the requisite postdoctoral hours for licensure. More formal didactic experiences are provided, including seminars, plentiful supervision, and opportunities for clinical research. These programs not only offer specialty training, but also the opportunity to gain the relevant experience needed to fulfill requirements for specialty board certification through ABPP (Nezu et al., 2009). Supervisors and job mentors in these formalized programs typically facilitate job searches and networking, which, combined with the quality of training received in these programs, enhances job marketability. Individuals who complete formal programs typically are very satisfied with their training experience and find it to be helpful to both their personal and professional development (France & Wolf, 2000).

Although participation in formal postdoctoral training programs focused on advanced broad and general or specialty training is fairly common, some individuals choose more informal experiences, and may elect to accrue supervised hours and additional training by working under the supervision of licensed psychologists in a number of settings. There are distinct advantages to informal training. First, opportunities to establish informal postdoctoral experiences can address geographic, financial, or relationship factors influencing an individual's training choices (Kaslow et al., 1992). A survey of predoctoral interns found that personal factors, such as the proximity of programs to one's family, were key considerations in selecting postdoctoral training programs (Stewart et al., 2000). Furthermore, depending on program funding, it may be possible to receive higher pay in informal training settings that pay postdoctoral residents competitive salaries. Despite these advantages, there are also several potential downsides to participating in informal postdoctoral training. For example, in a survey on postdoctoral training, 68% of individuals completing formal postdoctoral training rated their experiences as "very valuable," whereas only 38% of those with informal postdoctoral training provided an equivalent rating. Additionally, 8% of respondents with informal postdoctoral training rated their experiences as "not valuable," a designation not selected by any of those with formal postdoctoral training experiences (France & Wolf, 2000). These outcomes are consistent with studies of specialized postdoctoral residency programs as well; psychologists who had completed geropsychology postdoctoral residencies reported high levels of professional competence and satisfaction with their training experiences (Karel, Molinari, Gallagher-Thompson, & Hillman, 1999). Furthermore, opportunities to obtain advanced training in assessment and treatment interventions has been cited as a primary reason for seeking formalized postdoctoral training by individuals at this training level (Logsdon-Conradsen et al., 2001).

Benefits of Postdoctoral Training

The decision about whether to pursue postdoctoral training, including formal training, is a personal one. In making such a decision, the benefits as well as pitfalls of such training must be considered. The following are some of the most salient and significant benefits of postdoctoral training (Sato et al., 2012).

The primary goal of postdoctoral training—from the perspective of trainers and program leaders—is the protection of the public and consumers through the development of rigorous standards of competence. Thus, the foremost benefit of postdoctoral training in professional psychology is that it offers one the opportunity to further hone and expand one's competence. This may entail the receipt of more specialty-focused training, but this does not necessarily have to be the case. With the continued explosion of knowledge, skills, and attitudes required for effective practice, many believe that individuals are not ready for independent practice upon the completion of the internship experience. Indeed in a survey of training directors of academic, predoctoral, and postdoctoral psychology programs in the United States, most directors of predoctoral and postdoctoral training programs felt that graduates were not ready for independent practice until they completed a supervised postdoctoral experience (Rodolfa, Ko, & Petersen, 2004). Interestingly, however, the majority of training directors of academic programs surveyed believed that students were competent to practice upon receipt of their degree and should not be required to engage in a postdoctoral experience prior to licensure, These discrepancies among training directors regarding when trainees meet minimum standards of competence point to the need for further clarification and agreement amongst the professional community regarding these distinctions.

Second, supervised postdoctoral training often helps one meet the criterion of licensure within their state or province. In a recent informal survey with current and former postdoctoral residents and postdoctoral mentors, accruing supervised hours for licensure was noted to be the most common reason that individuals engaged in postdoctoral training (Forand & Appelbaum, 2011). Details with regard to state and provincial psychology board licensure and certification requirements regarding the postdoctoral experience can be found in the Association of State and Provincial Psychology Boards (ASPPB) Handbook on Licensing and Certification Requirements, which is located on the ASPPB website (www.asppb.org).

Third, the postdoctoral year(s) often marks the transition from trainee to psychologist, and it is during this process that professional development as a psychologist often is solidified (Kaslow et al., 1992). The process of identity solidification in postdoctoral residents is associated with developing expertise in a focused area of interest, manifesting a deepening investment in the work, experiencing an enhanced sense of confidence and self-efficacy, having a greater appreciation of oneself as a psychologist, gaining respect from an interdisciplinary cadre of colleagues as a psychologist, and forging more collegial relationships with other psychologists.

Challenges to Postdoctoral Training

Although there are multiple personal and professional advantages to postdoctoral experiences, the growing movement among states, employers, and certification bodies to require this level of training is not without controversy. Efforts to protect consumers from harm through strict training and licensing requirements are warranted, and must be measured against the relative disadvantages of these efforts.

A number of personal and professional developmental pitfalls have been noted with regard to postdoctoral training. Potential personal drawbacks in this vein include continued financial sacrifice, potential need to relocate to secure postdoctoral training and then possibly again for employment and associated stresses, and the challenges of balancing career and personal/familial demands. In the professional developmental arena, potential drawbacks include prolonged status as a trainee, the relatively limited supply of quality postdoctoral experiences, the lack of parity with training requirements of other health professions, disagreement amongst professionals regarding the basic criteria that must be fulfilled for an individual to be deemed ready for professional practice, and the increasing breadth and depth of clinical training experiences occurring during graduate school and internship (Hogg & Olvey, 2007; Olvey, Hogg, & Counts, 2002; Patterson, 2000; Rodolfa et al., 2004; Sato et al., 2012).

One of the most contentious arguments against postdoctoral training is the concern regarding the limited number of available postdoctoral opportunities relative to the growing numbers of graduates seeking these positions. Though research regarding the supply of postdoctoral positions is sparse, the dearth of training programs has been commented upon across a number of papers on this topic (Hogg, Keen, Barton, & Yandell, 1999; Hogg & Olvey, 2007; Kaslow et al., 1992; Stewart & Stewart, 1998). With the exception of the Association of Postdoctoral Programs in Clinical Neuropsychology (APPCN), there are no formal matching programs for postdoctoral residencies. However, APPCN and other organizations, such as APA and APPIC, do provide information regarding available programs on their websites. To solve this problem, some graduates have taken nontraditional approaches and sought out supervisors or settings where they can accrue supervised hours in an informal manner. Other graduates have found themselves in what Clay describes as "the post-doc trap," a precarious position of either not being able to obtain a postdoctoral residency, or accepting positions that are outside of their desired specialty area as a means to complete the licensing process for their chosen state of practice (Clay, 2000). As a result of these difficulties, some states have reversed the trend toward requiring postdoctoral training. In 2008, several states, including Arizona, Maryland, and Connecticut, made regulatory or legislative changes to remove this prerequisite for licensure (Munsey, 2009).

Another source of contention regarding the current emphasis on postdoctoral training is the amount of training required of psychologists relative to other health professions. Across the health sciences, psychology is the only discipline that requires students to obtain 3,000 hours of supervised training experiences prior to receiving a degree (Patterson, 2000). Furthermore, in a study exploring time to licensure across 13 professions, including social work, law, and physical therapy, time to licensure was longest for psychologists (Olvey et al., 2002). Of note, although physicians can be licensed after their internship year, the completion of their training and their entry to independent practice entails a residency, which typically is a minimum of three years and in many specialties, including psychiatry, four or more years. Some have argued that easing training requirements for licensure would expand the types of opportunities available for psychologists, including reimbursements by managed care companies (Stewart & Stewart, 1998). However, physicians during their residency training cannot be reimbursed by insurance companies.

One factor that likely influences opinions regarding when graduates are ready for independent practice is the recent expansion of clinical training experiences that occur during graduate training. Partly driven by students' efforts to be marketable for the increasingly competitive internship application process, students are often entering predoctoral internships having amassed significant supervised clinical experience. According to APPIC, the mean number of practicum assessment and intervention hours reported by students in the application cycle for the 2011 internship match were 148 and 573, respectively (Association of Psychology Internship and Predoctoral Centers, 2012). The extensive amount of practicum training received by students has caused some to argue that the necessity of postdoctoral training has become obsolete, and that, therefore, practicum hours should be counted toward supervised professional practice hours required for licensure (Patterson, 2000). Critics of this argument, however, have raised important concerns regarding the lack of existing standards amongst practicum training. The creation of national standards may be challenging given the wide variability in the quality of training, supervision, and clinical experiences students receive across practicum sites (American Psychological Association, 2000). In addition, there is marked disagreement among training directors in different contexts (i.e., academic, intern, postdoctoral) regarding the numbers of hours of practicum training needed to advance to the next phases of training (Ko & Rodolfa, 2005).

Although the current discussion of the utility and appropriateness of postdoctoral training has focused on the experiences of graduates more broadly, there may be some variation in the necessity of postdoctoral experience based on scope and goals for practice. More specifically, many graduates focused on developing expertise in specialty areas use the postdoctoral training year as an opportunity to increase their competency in a very specific domain, which is imperative since many practicum and internship training programs are more generalist in scope. Understandably, guidelines for evaluating competency for generalists are broader than those required for practitioners in specialty areas, such as pediatrics or health psychology. The differences in scope of practice may necessitate the development of separate set standards for specialists, such as those required in board certification processes.

Future Directions and Recommendations

Postdoctoral training is an opportunity to develop advanced competency and expertise for the professional practice of psychology. As mentioned, it is a time to develop a professional identity in addition to honing research and clinical competencies. However, the area of postdoctoral training continues to evolve as national standards, accreditation procedures, and licensure requirements shift. Moving forward, it is important to note how postdoctoral training programs can respond to these changes while maximizing opportunities for psychology trainees to enter the workforce successfully. Additionally, we must acknowledge the changing landscape of our national health-care system and its influence on postdoctoral training and the field of psychology as a whole. Furthermore, as the limited availability of postdoctoral training programs has been cited as a key barrier for some individuals, identifying ways to expand these opportunities is essential. Finally, facilitating improved communication between programs can aid in the development of a more comprehensive and unified postdoctoral network.

Many postdoctoral candidates will have had practica and internship experience in various clinical and research settings; however, various aspects of professional development receive less attention at these phases of development. Individuals at the postdoctoral level of training may need guidance on specific aspects of career development including job acquisition and negotiation skills, business acumen, development of professional networks and career goals, and successful balancing of work-life demands in order to establish fulfilling and successful careers as psychologists. As such, postdoctoral residencies should encourage their residents to develop professional networks and participate in local, regional, and national organizations (Drotar et al., 2003). Supervisors and mentors in these programs also should provide trainees with adequate guidance concerning the critical next steps in their careers and support to complete the necessary professional tasks (e.g., exploration of career options, which may entail interviewing for academic positions or

clinical staff positions or writing a grant, completion of the licensure process) (Drotar et al., 2003). Important but often neglected, postdoctoral training mentors also can provide valuable modeling and professional socialization, as well as feedback on the value of integrating personal and professional responsibilities, how to schedule writing into the workday/workweek, and how to manage clinical care and research demands (Karel & Stead, 2011; Kaslow & Mascaro, 2007).

Failed job acquisition or licensure efforts can present a significant barrier to professional advancement even for those with extensive clinical and research expertise. As such, postdoctoral-level training should include discussions of how to prepare a curriculum vitae for employment purposes, opportunities to practice job talks, and guidance in engaging in job interviews and negotiations (Drotar et al., 2003). Another critical task for most residents is application for professional licensure. Residency programs need to recognize the vital nature of this endeavor and allow time and structure to obtain the necessary licensure hours and documentation and to review material and study as needed (Drotar et al., 2003). Incorporating these professional development components into residency programs will ensure that, in addition to adhering to established standards of education and training, such programs provide opportunities for innovative and creative models of professional practice.

The field of psychology is presently in a time of rapid change—thus, postdoctoral training programs must also prepare their trainees for dealing with current marketplace issues and future roles and functions. For example, it is now necessary to enable psychologists to practice in multiple jurisdictions, within a virtual environment, or across state and national borders (Eby et al., 2011). They also must be capable of adapting to the changes in the health-care climate (Kaslow, Graves, & Smith, 2012; Rozensky, 2012a, 2012b). As the field moves forward, some have argued that training requires the synthesis of all of the aspects represented in the directorates of APA—education, practice, public interest and science (Eby et al., 2011). Given the complexity of these demands, innovative strategies, such as the integration of career mentorship into postdoctoral level experiences, can serve to effectively bolster these training efforts (Kaslow & Mascaro, 2007). Furthermore, there has been a shift in the profession toward a "culture of competence," which emphasizes measuring student learning outcomes, articulated as competencies, as a primary focus of the education and training process (Fouad et al., 2009). The collective efforts to advance a competency-based approach to professional psychology education and training outcomes is also driven by the fact that there is a need for a better, competency based definition, or readiness for entry to practice (Fouad et al., 2009). As Kaslow and Webb state, "for psychotherapy training to move forward as a competency-based and evidence-based activity, it behooves us as a profession to foster a dialogue among educators at all training levels—but particularly the postdoctoral training level—regarding the essential components of psychotherapy competence" (Kaslow & Webb, 2011) (p. 647).

Changes in the health-care system also have implications for postdoctoral training programs. As a result, many postdoctoral sites are finding it difficult to fund their programs and to fund faculty/staff time to supervise, which limits the availability of postdoctoral training experiences (Belar & Kaslow, 2003; Spruill & Pruitt, 2000). Identifying innovative and economically viable ways to fund additional postdoctoral training programs can help address this challenge.

Strengthening networks and establishing more formalized communication standards among postdoctoral training programs is needed to address the current difficulties and opportunities facing trainees. Proposals to develop *centers of excellence* for postdoctoral education were advanced as early as 1990 to address these needs (Graham & Fox, 1991). Although never established, many of the challenges these centers were designed to address continue two decades later. With respect to communication among and between programs, it would be helpful to develop a cohesive directory of postdoctoral programs that list the program goals, content, and emphasis, and summarize feedback from the trainees. Furthermore, research-based efforts are needed to further our understanding of the professional realities of psychologists, including their current professional activities, perceptions regarding the impact of postdoctoral residency training on career development, perceived strengths and weaknesses of postdoctoral training, and recommendations for program improvements. Finally, it would be useful to disseminate information about the challenges and innovative methods of postdoctoral training at national and regional meetings. Psychologists have much to learn from one another about effective and ineffective methods of postdoctoral training—as such—interchange in strongly encouraged (Drotar et al., 2003).

References

American Psychological Association. (2000). *APA Commission on Education and Training Leading to Licensure in Psychology, Reston, VA*. Washington, DC: Author.

American Psychological Association. (2007). Guidelines for education and training at the doctoral and postdoctoral levels in consulting psychology/organizational consulting psychology. *American Psychologist, 62*, 980–992. doi: 10.1037/0003-066X.62.9.980

American Psychological Association. (2012a). Accredited specialty practice postdoctoral residency programs. Retrieved December 5, 2012 from http://www.apa.org/ed/accreditation/programs/specialty.aspx.

American Psychological Association. (2012b). Accredited traditional practice postdoctoral residency programs. Retrieved December 5, 2012 from http://www.apa.org/ed/accreditation/programs/traditional.aspx.

Association of Psychology Internship and Predoctoral Centers. (2012). 2011 APPIC Match: Survey of Internship Applicants Part 1: Summary of Survey Results. Retrieved December 5, 2012, from, http://www.appic.org/Match/MatchStatistics/ApplicantSurvey2011Part2011.aspx.

Association of State and Provincial Psychology Boards. (2012). *Handbook of licensure and certification requirements for psychologists in the US and Canada*. Montgomery, AL: Author.

Belar, C. (1992a). Conferences on internship and postdoctoral training. In A. E. Puente, J. Matthews, & C. Brewer (Eds.), *Teaching psychology in America: A history* (pp. 301–310). Washington DC: American Psychological Association.

Belar, C. D. (1992b). Education and training conferences in graduate education. In A. E. Puente, J. R. Mathews, & C. L. Brewer (Eds.), *Teaching psychology in American: A history* (pp. 285–299). Washington DC: American Psychological Association.

Belar, C. D., Bieliauskas, L. A., Klepac, R. K., Larsen, K. G., Stigall, T. T., & Zimet, C. N. (1993). National Conference on Postdoctoral Training in Professional Psychology. *American Psychologist, 48*, 1284–1289. doi: 10.1037/0003-066X.48.12.1284

Belar, C. D., Bieliauskas, L. A., Larsen, K. G., Mensh, I. N., Poey, K., & Roehlke, H. J. (1989). The National Conference on Internship Training in Professional Psychology. *American Psychologist, 44*, 60–65. doi: 10.1037/0003-066X.47.1.71

Belar, C. D., & Kaslow, N. J. (2003). The history of accreditation of internship programs and postdoctoral residencies. In E. M. Altmaier (Ed.), *Setting standards in graduate education: Psychology's commitment to excellence in accreditation* (pp. 61–89). Washington DC: American Psychological Association.

Bersoff, D. N., Goodman-Delahunty, J., Grisso, J. T., Hans, V. P., Poythress, N. G., & Roesch, R. G. (1997). Training in law and psychology: Models from the Villanova conference. *American Psychologist, 52*, 1301–1310. doi: 10.1037/0003-066X.52.12.1301

Boake, C., Yeates, K. O., & Donders, J. (2002). Association of Postdoctoral Programs in Clinical Neuropsychology: Update and new directions. *The Clinical Neuropsychologist, 16*, 1–6. doi: 10.1076/clin.16.1.1.8333

Bowers, D. A., Rickers, J. H., Regan, T. M., Malina, A. C., & Boake, C. (2002). National survey of clinical neuropsychology postdoctoral fellows. *The Clinical Neuropsychologist, 16*, 221–231. doi: 10.1076/clin.16.3.221.13847

Clay, R. A. (2000). The postdoc trap. *Monitor on Psychology, 31,* Retrieved November 3, 2012, from http://www.apa.org/monitor/may00/postdoc.aspx.

Drotar, D., Palermo, T., & Ievers-Landis, C. E. (2003). Commentary: Recommendations for the training of pediatric psychologists: Implications for postdoctoral training. *Pediatric Psychology, 28,* 109–113. doi: 10.1093/jpepsy/28.2.109

Drum, D. J., & Blom, B. E. (2001). The dynamics of specialization in professional psychology. *Professional Psychology: Research and Practice, 32,* 513–521. doi: 10.1037//0735-7028.32.5.513

Eby, M. D., Chin, J. L., Rollock, D., Schwartz, J. P., & Worrell, F. C. (2011). Professional psychology training in the era of a thousand flowers: Dilemmas and challenges for the future. *Training and Education in Professional Psychology, 5,* 57–68. doi: 10.1037/a0023462

Falender, C. A., Cornish, J. A. E., Goodyear, R., Hatcher, R., Kaslow, N. J., Leventhal, G.,...Grus, C. (2004). Defining competencies in psychology supervision: A consensus statement. *Journal of Clinical Psychology, 80,* 771–786. doi: 10.1002/jclp.20013

Falender, C. A., & Shafranske, E. (2004). *Clinical supervision: A competency-based approach.* Washington DC: American Psychological Association.

Falender, C. A., & Shafranske, E. P. (2007). Competence in competency-based supervision practice: Construct and application. *Professional Psychology: Research and Practice, 38,* 232–240. doi: 10.1037/0735-7028.38.3.232

Falender, C. A., & Shafranske, E. P. (2008). *Casebook for clinical supervision: A competency-based approach.* Washington DC: American Psychological Association.

Forand, N. R., & Appelbaum, A. J. (2011). Demystifying the postdoctoral experience: A guide for applicants. *The Behavior Therapist, 34,* 80–86. Retrieved from http://www.abct.org/Members/?m=mMembers&fa=JournalsPeriodicals#sec3

Fouad, N. A., Grus, C. L., Hatcher, R. L., Kaslow, N. J., Hutchings, P. S., Madson, M.,...Crossman, R. W. (2009). Competency benchmarks: A model for the understanding and measuring of competence in professional psychology across training levels. *Training and Education in Professional Psychology, 3,* S5–S26. doi: 10.1037/a0015832

France, C. M., & Wolf, E. M. (2000). Issues related to postdoctoral education and training in professional psychology: Results of an opinion survey. *Professional Psychology: Research and Practice, 31,* 429–434. doi: 10.103//0735-702831.4.429

Garcia-Shelton, L., & Vogel, M. E. (2002). Primary care health psychology training: A collaborative model with family practice. *Professional Psychology: Research and Practice, 33,* 546–556. doi: 10.1037/0735-7028.33.6.546

Graham, S., & Fox, R. E. (1991). Postdoctoral education for professional practice. *American Psychologist, 46,* 1033–1035. doi: 10.1037/0003-066X.46.10.1033

Hannay, H. J., Bieliauskas, L. A., Crosson, B. A., Hammeke, T. A., Hamsher, K., & Koffler, S. P. (1998). Proceedings from the Houston Conference on Specialty Education and Training in Clinical Neuropsychology. *Archives of Clinical Neuropsychology, 13,* 157–250. doi: Retrieved from http://acn.oxfordjournals.org/

Hinrichsen, G. A., Zeiss, A. M., Karel, M. J., & Molinari, V. A. (2010). Competency-based geropsychology training in doctoral internships and postdoctoral fellowships. *Training and Education in Professional Psychology, 4,* 91–98. doi: 10.1037/a0018149

Hoch, E. L., Ross, A. O., & Winder, C. L. (1966). Conference on the professional preparation of clinical psychologists: A summary. *American Psychologist, 21,* 42–51. doi: 10.1037/h0021107

Hogg, A., Keen, B., Barton, J., & Yandell, D. (1999). Between a rock...: Postdoctoral supervision in Arizona. *Arizona Psychologist, 19,* 4–9. Retrieved from http://www.azpa.org/

Hogg, A., & Olvey, C. D. V. (2007). State psychological association creates a postdoctoral residency and internship training program. *Professional Psychology: Research and Practice, 38,* 705–713. doi: 10.1037/0735-7028.38.6.705

Karel, M. J., Molinari, V., Gallagher-Thompson, D., & Hillman, S. L. (1999). Postdoctoral training in professional geropsychology: A survey of fellowship graduates. *Professional Psychology: Research and Practice, 30,* 617–622. doi: 10.1037/0735-7028.30.6.617

Karel, M. J., & Stead, C. D. (2011). Mentoring geropsychologists-in-training during internship and postdoctoral fellowship years. *Educational Gerontology, 37,* 388–408. doi: 10.1080/03601277.2011.553560

Kaslow, N. J. (2004). Competencies in professional psychology. *American Psychologist, 59,* 774–781. doi: 10.1037/0003-066X.59.8.774

Kaslow, N. J., Borden, K. A., Collins, F. L., Forrest, L., Illfelder-Kaye, J., Nelson, P. D., et al. (2004). Competencies Conference: Future directions in education and credentialing in professional psychology. *Journal of Clinical Psychology, 80,* 699–712. doi: 10.1002/jclp.20016

Kaslow, N. J., Celano, M. P., & Stanton, M. (2005). Training in family psychology: A competencies-based approach. *Family Process, 44,* 337–353. doi: 10.1111/j.1545-5300.2005.00063.x

Kaslow, N. J., & Echols, M. M. (2006). Postdoctoral training and requirements for licensure and certification. In T. J. Vaughn (Ed.), *Psychology licensure and certification: What students need to know* (pp. 85–95). Washington D.C.: American Psychological Association.

Kaslow, N. J., Graves, C. C., & Smith, C. O. (2012). Specialization in psychology and health care reform. *Journal of Clinical Psychology in Medical Settings, 19,* 12–21. doi: 10.10007/s10880-011-9273-0

Kaslow, N. J., & Keilin, W. G. (2008). Postdoctoral training. In F. T. L. Leong, E. M. Altmaier & B. D. Johnson (Eds.), *Encyclopedia of counseling: Changes and challenges for counseling in the 21st century* (pp. 337–341). Los Angeles: Sage.

Kaslow, N. J., & Mascaro, N. A. (2007). Mentoring interns and postdoctoral residents in academic health centers. *Journal of Clinical Psychology in Medical Settings, 14,* 191–196. doi: 10.1007/s10880-007-9070-y

Kaslow, N. J., McCarthy, S. M., Rogers, J. H., & Summerville, M. B. (1992). Psychology postdoctoral training: A developmental perspective. *Professional Psychology: Research and Practice, 23,* 369–375. doi: 10.1037/0735-7028.23.5.369

Kaslow, N. J., & Webb, C. (2011). Internship and postdoctoral residency. In J. C. Norcross, G. R. Vandebos & D. K. Friedheim (Eds.), *History of psychotherapy: Continuity and change* (2nd edition, pp. 640–650). Washington D.C.: American Psychological Association.

Ko, S. F., & Rodolfa, E. R. (2005). Psychology training directors' views of number of practicum hours necessary prior to internship application. *Professional Psychology: Research and Practice, 36,* 318–322. doi: 10.1037/0735-7028.36.3.318

Lane, D. A., & Corrie, S. (2006). *The modern scientist-practitioner: A guide to practice in psychology*. London, UK: Routledge.

Lese-Fowler, K. P. (Ed.). (2010). *Internship and postdoctoral programs in professional psychology (39th edition), 2010-2011.* Washington, D.C.: Association of Psychology Postdoctoral and Internship Centers.

Logsdon-Conradsen, S., Sirl, K. S., Battle, J., Stapel, J., Anderson, P. L., Ventura-Cook, E.,,...Kaslow, N. J. (2001). Formalized postdoctoral fellowships: A national survey of postdoctoral fellows. Professional Psychology: *Research and Practice, 32*, 312–318. doi: 10.1037/0735-7028.32.3.312

Lowman, R. L., Alderfer, C., Atella, M., Garman, A. N., Hellkamp, D., Kilburg, R.,,...O'Roark, A. (2002). Principles for education and training at the doctoral and postdoctoral level in consulting psychology/organizational. *Consulting Psychology Journal: Practice and Research, 54*, 213–222. doi: 10.1037/1061-4087.54.4.213

Malesky, L. A., & Proctor, S. L. (2012). Training experiences essential for obtaining a forensic psychology postdoctoral fellowship. *Journal of Forensic Psychology Practice, 12*, 163–172. doi: 10.1080/15228932.2012.650146

McDaniel, S. H., Belar, C. D., Schroeder, C. S., Hargrove, D. S., & Freeman, E. L. (2002). A training curriculum for professional psychologists in primary care. *Professional Psychology: Research and Practice, 33*, 65–72. doi: 10.1037/0735-7028.33.1.65

Moye, J., & Brown, E. (1995). Postdoctoral training in geropsychology: Guidelines for formal programs and continuing education. *Professional Psychology: Research and Practice, 26*, 591–597. doi: 10.1037/0735-7028.26.6.591

Munsey, C. (2009). More states forgo a postdoc requirement. *Monitor on Psychology, 40*, 10. Retrieved from http://www.apa.org/monitor/2009/12/postdoc.aspx

Nezu, C. M., Finch, A. J., Jr., & Simon, N. P. (Eds.). (2009). *Becoming board certified by the American Board of Professional Psychology*. New York: Oxford University Press.

Olvey, C. D. V., Hogg, A., & Counts, W. (2002). Licensure requirements: Have we raised the bar too far? *Professional Psychology: Research and Practice, 33*, 323–329. doi: 10.1037//0735-7028.33.3.323

Patterson, D. R., & Hanson, S. L. (1995). Joint Division 22 and ACRM guidelines for postdoctoral training in rehabilitation psychology. *Rehabilitation Psychology, 40*, 299–310. doi: 10.1037/0090-5550.40.4.299

Patterson, T. (2000). Why the internship should be postdoctoral. *Progress: Family Systems Research and Therapy, 9*, 9–12. Retrieved from: http://www.richardatkins.co.uk/atws/journal/133.html

Pingitore, D. P. (1999). Postdoctoral training in primary care health psychology: Duties, observations, and recommendations. *Profesional Psychology: Research and Practice, 30*, 283–290. doi: 10.1037/0735-7028.30.3.283

Raimy, V. C. (Ed.). (1950). *Training in clinical psychology*. New York: Prentice Hall.

Roberts, M. C., Carlson, C. I., Erickson, M. T., Friedman, R. M., LaGreca, A. M., Lemanek, K. L., et al. (1998). A model for training psychologists to provide services for children and adolescents. *Professional Psychology: Research and Practice, 29*, 293–299. doi: 10.1037/0735-7028.29.3.293

Rodolfa, E. R., Bent, R. J., Eisman, E., Nelson, P. D., Rehm, L., & Ritchie, P. (2005). A cube model for competency development: Implications for psychology educators and regulators. *Professional Psychology: Research and Practice, 36*, 347–354. doi: 10.1037/0735-7028.36.4.347

Rodolfa, E. R., Ko, S. F., & Petersen, L. (2004). Psychology training directors' views of trainees' readiness to practice independently. *Professional Psychology: Research and Practice, 35*, 397–404.

Roe, A., Gustad, J. W., Moore, B. V., Ross, S., & Skodak, M. (1959). *Graduate education in psychology*. Washington DC: American Psychological Association.

Routh, D. K. (1977). Postdoctoral training in pediatric psychology. *Professional Psychology: Research and Practice, 8*, 245–250. doi: 10.1037/0735-7028.8.2.245

Rozensky, R. H. (2012a). Health care reform: Preparing the psychology workforce. *Journal of Clinical Psychology in Medical Settings, 19*, 5–11. doi: 10.1007/s10880-011-9287-7

Rozensky, R. H. (2012b). Psychology in academic health centers: A true healthcare home. *Journal of Clinical Psycholgy in Medical Settings, 19*, 353–363. doi: 10.1007/s10880-012-9312-5

Sanders, K. A., & Steinberg, H. R. (2012). Supervision and mentoring of clinical psychology predoctoral interns and postdoctoral residents. *Journal of Cognitive Psychotherapy: An International Quarterly, 26*, 226–235. doi: 10.1891./0889-8391.26.3.226

Sato, A. M., Simon, V. A., Jelalian, E., & Spirito, A. (2012). Recommendations for a postdoctoral fellowship. In M. Prinstein (Ed.), *The portable mentor: Expert guide to a successful career in psychology* (2nd edition, pp. 303–318). New York: Springer.

Shakow, D. (1973). History and development of postdoctoral clinical training. In I. B. Weiner (Ed.), *Postdoctoral education in clinical psychology* (pp. 9–20). Topeka, KS: The Menninger Foundation.

Sheridan, E. P., Matarazzo, J. D., Boll, T. J., Perry, N. W., Weiss, S. M., & Belar, C. D. (1988). Postdoctoral education and training for clinical service providers in health psychology. *Health Psychology, 7*, 1–17. doi: 10.1037/0278-6133.7.1.1

Shullman, S. L. (2002). Reflections of a consulting counseling psychologist: Implications of the principles for education and training at the doctoral and postdoctoral level in consulting psychology for the practice of counseling psychology. *Consulting Psychology Journal: Practice and Research, 54*, 242–251. doi: 10.1037/1061-4087.54.4.242

Spirito, A., Brown, R. T., D'Angelo, E., Delamater, A., Rodrigue, J., & Siegel, L. J. (2003). Society of Pediatric Psychology Task Force Report: Recommendations for the Training of Pediatric Psychologists. *Journal of Pediatric Psychology, 28*, 85–98. doi: 10.1093/jpepsy/28.2.85

Spruill, J., & Pruitt, S. D. (2000). Preparing psychologists for managed care settings: Enhancing internship training programs. *Professional Psychology: Research and Practice, 31*, 305–309. doi: 10.1037/0735-7028.31.3.305

Stewart, A. C., & Stewart, E. A. (1998). Trends in postdoctoral education: Requirements for licensure and training opportunities. *Professional Psychology: Research and Practice, 29*, 273–283. doi: 10.1037//0735-7028.29.3.273

Stewart, A. C., Stewart, E. A., & Vogel, D. L. (2000). A survey of interns' preferences and plans for postdoctoral training. *Professional Psychology: Research and Practice, 31*, 435–441. doi: 10.1037/0735-7028.31.4.435

Stewart, J. A., Horn, D. L., Becker, J. M., & Kline, J. S. (1993). Postdoctoral training in severe mental illness: A model for trainee development. *Professional Psychology: Research and Practice, 24*, 286–292. doi: 10.1037/0735-7028.24.3.286

Stucky, K., Buterakos, J., Crystal, T., & Hanks, R. (2008). Acquiring CMS funding for an APA-accredited postdoctoral psychology fellowship program. *Training and Education in Professional Psychology*, 2, 165–175. doi: 10.1037/1931-3918.2.3.165

Wegener, S. T., Hagglund, K. J., & Elliott, T. R. (1998). On psychological identity and training: Boulder is better for rehabilitation psychology. *Rehabilitation Psychology*, 43, 17–29. doi: 10.1037/0090-5550.43.1.17

Weiner, I. B. (Ed.). (1973). *Postdoctoral education in clinical psychology*. Topeka, KS: Menninger Foundation.

Wiens, A. N. (1993). Postdoctoral education-training for specialty practice: Long anticipated, finally realized. *American Psychologist, 48*, 415–422. doi: 10.1037/0003-066X.48.4.415

Research Training in Professional Psychology

Jeffrey H. Kahn *and* Lewis Z. Schlosser

Abstract

Although graduate training models differ in their emphasis on research, research training in one form or another is a core component of the doctoral training in professional psychology programs in the United States. Research training typically is designed to produce three ultimate or distal outcomes: (a) consumption and application of research, (b) treatment of psychological practice as a scientific endeavor, and (c) production of original research. En route to meeting these goals, however, research training affects several intermediate or proximal outcomes-research competence, research self-efficacy, research interest and attitudes, and research outcome expectations. The authors review the state of the research on these proximal and distal outcomes of such training, including their measurement and their interrelationships. Then the authors explicate the specific elements of graduate training that lead to these outcomes, focusing specifically on the research training environment, required course work and research experiences, and mentoring and advising.

Key Words: research training, research consumption, research productivity, research competency, research interest, research self-efficacy, research outcome expectations, research training environment (RTE), mentoring, advising

Training students to be competent in research is central to the philosophy of most doctoral training models within professional psychology. Beginning with the Boulder Conference in 1949 and continuing into the 21st century, the integration of science and practice has been an indispensible element of applied psychology training (e.g., Bieschke, Fouad, Collins, & Halonen, 2004; Meier, 1999; Stricker & Trierweiler, 1995). Developing research competence has become particularly salient in recent years as a result of psychology's focus on evidence-based practice and empirically supported interventions (American Psychological Association [APA], 2006; Bauer, 2007; Waehler, Kalodner, Wampold, & Lichtenberg, 2000; Wampold, Lichtenberg, & Waehler, 2002). This movement highlights the need to train professional psychologists to be competent in both the consumption and production of research (Gelso & Fretz, 2001).

Consistent with these ideas, research training is a prime component of doctoral training in professional psychology (especially—but not exclusively—in Ph.D. programs), and the graduate program is the setting in which the bulk of research training typically and optimally occurs (Gelso, 1993). Most professional psychology programs emphasize both practitioner (e.g., didactic training in counseling theories and assessment, practicum experiences) and research (e.g., didactic training in research methods, a doctoral dissertation); however, research training has received considerably less attention in the professional training literature than has practitioner training. On one hand, this disparity is understandable given that graduate students in professional psychology historically have been more interested in a practice career than a research career (Cassin, Singer, Dobson, & Altmaier, 2007; Gelso, 1979, 1993). On the other hand, immersion in sound theories and rigorous methodologies bearing on empirical research are necessary to strengthen the training of all professional psychologists, regardless of career trajectory.

In the decade since Gelso and Lent's (2000) comprehensive chapter on research training in the *Handbook of Counseling Psychology*, scholarly attention on research training and related topics has increased. In this essay, we review the extant theory, research, and practice concerning research training in professional psychology. We start by describing how research training fits with typical graduate training models in professional psychology. We then articulate the tangible outcomes of research training that have been studied in research on research training, both in terms of proximal and distal outcomes. We then describe the specific elements of the research training environment (RTE), required training experiences, and characteristics of advisory and mentoring relationships that presumably lead to these outcomes. We conclude by presenting future directions for both sound practice and evaluation of research training in professional psychology.

Research Emphases Among Diverse Graduate Training Models

Doctoral programs in professional psychology vary in their training goals and emphases, including the nature of research training and the degree to which research training is integrated into the curriculum and training experiences. We briefly review the most common models of graduate training in professional psychology and describe how training in traditional academic research and science-practice integration occur within these models. We note that there is a substantial amount of variability across programs that adopt the same training model, so this review is necessarily general.

The *scientist-practitioner model*, perhaps the best known training model in professional psychology, has been in place since clinical psychology's Boulder Conference in 1949, counseling psychology's Northwestern Conference in 1951, and school psychology's Thayer Conference in 1954. The scientist-practitioner model has been reaffirmed throughout the years as the optimal approach to professional psychology training (Belar & Perry, 1992) and is now widespread: 73% of counseling psychology programs, 65% of clinical psychology programs, and 60% of school psychology programs refer to the scientist-practitioner model in their program description (Horn et al., 2007). The

overarching essence of the scientist-practitioner model is to tie research and practice together. The goal is not to train equal numbers of scientists and practitioners but rather to train people to *integrate* scientific methods with psychological practice (Belar & Perry, 1992).

But what does it mean to integrate science and practice? In other words, what is the operational definition of the scientist-practitioner? Gelso and Fretz (2001) proposed a three-level model of functioning within the scientist-practitioner model. First, the minimal level of functioning for psychologists involves being scientific via consumption and application of research findings. This would take the form, for example, of a practitioner keeping abreast of the research literature and engaging in evidence-based practice. The second level of functioning requires psychologists to be skeptical and think critically when practicing. This level also requires psychologists' dependence on a "scientific process" (p. 54) when assessing and treating clients. For example, a practitioner may generate hypotheses about the efficacy of a given intervention, deliver the intervention, and then assess whether the hypothesis was supported based on the client's response to the intervention. The third and most demanding level of functioning is to engage in empirical research by collecting original data and reporting those data to the field. This involves formulating research questions (that may or may not involve explicit hypotheses) and conducting original research to answer those questions. A psychologist here, for example, would design and implement an empirical study, analyze the data, and submit a manuscript describing that work for publication. Gelso and Fretz suggested that professional psychology will be strengthened to the degree that an individual engages in all three levels.

Subsequent training models share the core goal of integrating science with practice, but do so with different emphases. The 1973 Vail model (i.e., the *practitioner-scholar model*) gave rise to the development of professional schools of psychology and the PsyD degree; this model places less emphasis on academic research as compared to the scientist-practitioner model. Instead, this model emphasizes scientific inquiry at the client level. The practitioner-scholar model parallels the idea of the *local clinical scientist* (Stricker & Trierweiler, 1995) who integrates science and practice by adopting a scientific attitude throughout clinical work (e.g., recognizing evidence supporting or failing to support a clinical hypothesis). Science and practice are therefore integrated when the practitioner uses scientific thinking in a clinical setting, applies scientific findings to her or his clinical work, and treats the clinical interaction as a scientific interaction (Stricker & Trierweiler, 1995). For example, a clinician might use observations of a client as data to generate a theory of the client's presenting problem and then consult the research literature to determine the best course of treatment with that client, all the while considering alternative explanations for a client's interactions in therapy.

The *clinical-scientist model* (which, despite the similar name, differs from the concept of the *local clinical scientist*), proposed by the Academy of Psychological Clinical Science (2007), places an even greater emphasis on using science in clinical practice than either of the two previously described models. The goal of this model is to train *clinical scientists* who are committed to empirical approaches to testing hypotheses and advancing knowledge. This model may be viewed as similar to the scientist-practitioner model in theory yet with more of an emphasis on science. Proponents of this model believe that clinical practice should be fully grounded in science and that psychological practice should be conducted by scientists.

As of the turn of the century, most training programs (59%), at least among those in clinical psychology, followed the scientist-practitioner model, with approximately equal numbers espousing the practitioner-scholar model (20%) and clinical-scientist model (21%) (Cherry, Messenger, & Jacoby, 2000). These programs do not differ just in name; they differ in the type of training they provide as well as the outcomes expected of students (Cherry et al., 2000). For example, students in clinical-scientist programs spend more of their time doing research than students in scientist-practitioner programs; students in practitioner-scholar programs spend the least amount of time doing research. Moreover, graduates of clinical-scientist programs are most likely to gain employment in academic settings, whereas graduates of practitioner-scholar programs are most likely to gain employment in mental-health or counseling centers. Thus, although internships that endorse different training models largely do not differ from one another (Rodolfa, Kaslow, Stewart, Keilin, & Baker, 2005), academic training programs do differ as a function of their training model.

Another recent model of science-practice integration followed from the 2002 Competencies Conference: Future Directions in Education and Credentialing in Professional Psychology, sponsored by the Association of Psychology Postdoctoral and Internship Centers. Recognizing that a scientific approach to the practice of psychology is a critical core competency for practitioners, the conference's scientific-foundations work group developed a five-component model for practicing psychologists to be considered "scientifically-minded" (Bieschke, 2006; Bieschke et al., 2004). Similar to the model proposed by Gelso and Fretz (2001), Bieschke and colleagues' model includes (1) "appropriately and habitually" (Bieschke, 2006, p. 79) consuming and applying research findings, (2) critically thinking about practice and practice outcomes, and (3) conducting original inquiry. They also add two additional components to their model: (4) mindfulness of the impact that sociocultural variables may have on practicing psychologists, and (5) accountability of practices to individuals and groups who have a direct interest in and may be affected by the services provided by psychologists (e.g., agency, managed care organizations). Fouad and colleagues' (2009) Competency Benchmarks document builds on these ideas by delineating the essential components of scientific mindedness and integrating them into the wider set of core competencies in professional psychology. Specifically, essential components of scientific mindedness include, in order of trainee development, critical scientific thinking, valuing and applying scientific methods to professional practice, and independently applying scientific methods to practice (Fouad et al., 2009).

In summary, extant doctoral training models of science-practice integration suggest several levels or domains of functioning. Although the models differ in their emphases on the degree to which science is a part of practice, there is enough overlap in core areas to draw conclusions about how psychologists would optimally use science in their work. First, psychologists are encouraged to use research findings to guide their clinical work. This may take the form of drawing from the literature or applying empirically supported treatments. Second, psychologists are encouraged to function as local clinical scientists in their work with clients. This involves treating clinical activities as scientific endeavors. Third, in whatever form is most relevant, psychologists are encouraged to produce original research. This might involve traditional data collection, analysis, and dissemination, and/or local program evaluations.

Given these aspirations for professional psychologists, research training clearly is a necessary part of doctoral training. The dynamic interplay between science and practice is also a vital part of professional psychology's maturation process. For clinical, counseling, and school psychology to continue to evolve as disciplines, science ought to be relevant to practice, and practitioners ought to base their work on science. Specifically, as Jones and Mehr (2007) highlighted, practitioners who are competent in research will render more effective services, research will add to a database that informs practice, and involvement in practice will help researchers to take on studies with social value. Thus research and practice are functionally inseparable in applied psychology, and, as a result, effective research training is essential in professional psychology doctoral programs.

Outcomes of Research Training

Consistent with the role of research that is implicit in graduate training models, research training ultimately should affect three outcomes: (a) becoming a competent consumer of research, (b) treating psychological practice as a scientific endeavor, and (c) being involved in the production of original research. We refer to these as *distal* outcomes, not because they necessarily occur late in a student's training but because there are intermediate—or proximal—outcomes that are affected as part of the process of attaining the distal outcomes. These proximal outcomes include the acquisition of research knowledge and skills, self-efficacy with respect to doing research, interest in and valuing of research, and research outcome expectations. Because the distal outcomes are so closely connected to the philosophies of the graduate training models we just discussed, we will describe those outcomes first.

Distal Outcomes

Consumption of research findings. In an academic research setting, psychologists consume research findings as part of their daily work life. The research base is consulted to generate ideas for new research studies, build theories to explain psychological phenomena, and understand topical areas that are the subject of psychology courses that they teach.

However, most professional psychologists spend a majority of their time in practice rather than science, and the consumption of research findings has a different purpose for practice endeavors than it does for research endeavors. One place of intersection for scientists and practitioners is evidenced-based practice in psychology, defined as "the integration of the best available research with

clinical expertise in the context of patient characteristics, culture, and preferences" (APA Presidential Task Force, 2006, p. 273). One of the intentions behind evidence-based practice in psychology is the effective consumption of research. For example, a practitioner might consult the research literature to choose a specific treatment for a given client issue, or a practitioner may draw from the empirical literature to generate hypotheses about a given client's presenting problem.

Carter (2002), in fact, believes that all practitioners engage in evidence-based practice, but we know of only one empirical study that has addressed exactly what form this engagement takes. Wallis and colleagues (2008) conducted a consensual qualitative research study in which they interviewed 10 practicing psychologists about how they integrate science with practice. Among the seven domains that emerged from the data was one called "how participants consume research." Two typical activities among the psychologists were *reading the literature* (e.g., "receives journals and skims articles of interest") and *participating in workshops and conferences* (e.g., "attends conferences to hear about new research"). Variant (i.e., less common) activities included *interacting with trainees, holding membership in professional associations*, and *participating in professional discussions about research*. A second domain was called "how science contributes to practice," and this domain also captured ideas relevant to the consumption of research. A typical category within this domain was the attitude that *science guides interventions* (e.g., "research is important because it shows what treatments are amenable to different populations"). Variant categories were *research provides confidence in treatment* and *research aids assessment activities*. Wallis and colleagues provide us with a beginning understanding of the mechanisms by which practitioners incorporate science into their daily professional lives.

Treating practice as a scientific endeavor. There is an undeniable art to psychotherapeutic practice, yet there also is a science. With respect to that science, a practitioner who engages in evidence-based practice is continuously asking what works with which clients under what circumstances and why (Carter, 2002). In other words, an effective practitioner is a scientist who formulates theories and hypotheses, uses data to test those hypotheses, and revises them accordingly. For example, clients fare better when clinicians routinely track client outcome and approach therapy in a way that is consistent with client progress (Lambert et al., 2003).

The aforementioned Wallis study suggests that clinicians do indeed use client data. In a domain called "how participants gather and use client data," a typical category was *uncovering information through interviewing* (e.g., "uses clinical interviews and questioning to gather information about clients"), and a second was *using formal assessment methods to gather data* (e.g., "uses specific assessment devices"). However, Lambert and colleagues (e.g., Lambert & Vermeersch, 2008) suggest that gathering data is not enough; a competent practitioner ought to use those data to draw conclusions about whether to maintain or modify the course of treatment (e.g., considering whether a mid-treatment correction is necessary with a client who does not respond to initial treatment efforts).

In addition to seeing clinical activities as a scientific endeavor, there is increasing pressure on practicing psychologists to demonstrate the effectiveness of their work to stakeholders (Bieschke et al., 2004). For example, practitioners commonly are asked to document and provide data demonstrating client progress to insurance providers (Lambert & Hawkins, 2004). Thus, practitioners are wise to consider their work with each client as an $N = 1$ outcome study.

Involvement in and production of original research. Training programs that adopt the clinical-scientist model, as well as many that adopt the scientist-practitioner model, have the goal of training scientists—that is, graduates who go on to generate new research findings in the field. Thus, just as the implicit goal of clinical training is to produce practitioners who work effectively with clients, for many programs the goal of research training is to produce scientists who conduct traditional, academic research.

However, as mentioned, most students in professional psychology are more interested in psychological practice than psychological research, and traditional, academic research is challenging for many practitioners to initiate (Lampropoulos et al., 2002). Indeed, many of the initial studies of research training in professional psychology were predicated on the worrisome fact that most graduates of professional psychology programs do not produce any research after the dissertation and that many professional psychologists spent little time doing research (e.g., Watkins, Lopez, Campbell, & Himmell, 1986). Researchers interested in studying the process and outcomes of research training therefore have examined trends and predictors of research productivity both among current students as well as professionals.

A central methodological theme across this research is the variability of definitions and operationalizations of research productivity. Some studies have focused exclusively on publication counts (e.g., Brems, Johnson, & Gallucci, 1996; Kahn & Schlosser, 2010; Mallinckrodt & Gelso, 2002). For example, in Brems and colleagues' (1996) comparison of the research productivity of clinical versus counseling psychologists, they measured research productivity as counts of citations in the PsychLIT database, although they separated publications into different categories (e.g., books, journal publications); they found few differences in the publication records of clinical versus counseling psychologists. Other studies have used an expanded content domain of productivity. For example, Barrom, Shadish, and Montgomery (1988) examined publication counts as well as outcomes such as writing grants, being involved in data collection, writing a theoretical or practice-based article, writing a research presentation, and engaging in activities related to treatment evaluation. Whereas one might agree that the content domain of research productivity ought to account for more than just publications, a challenge with this expanded domain is what weight to place on various activities. For example, should one publication in a scholarly journal be weighted the same as one presentation at a local conference?

If one is satisfied with publications as the primary measure of scholarly productivity, then Duffy and colleagues (Duffy, Jadidian, Webster, & Sandell, 2011; Duffy, Martin, Bryan, & Raque-Bogdan, 2008) have presented a structured, objective index of research productivity that may have promise. Their Integrated Research Productivity Index (IRPI) considers the individual's weighted publication score (weighted by order of authorship and number of authors on a given publication), mean citation count across publications, and the length of the individual's publishing career. Thus, the IRPI considers the quantity of published research, the quality of published research, and the rate of publishing by accounting for career length. Duffy and colleagues (2008) found that the IRPI is correlated highly with publication counts and citations, but it represents a blend of that information, thus satisfying those who value quantity as an indicator of productivity well as those who value quality.

A method of assessing research productivity that construes productivity more broadly involves a self-report strategy. Kahn and Scott (1997) developed the Scholarly Activity Scale (SAS) as a way to measure involvement in and production of research in a gross but straightforward way. The nine-item SAS assesses both past scholarly accomplishments and current scholarly activity. Respondents indicate the number of publications, presentations, and so forth, but they also indicate whether they are currently collecting data or performing other scholarly work. Scores are dichotomized to produce a checklist, whereby the respondent receives a score of 1 for any item that she or he has productivity/ involvement in and a score of 0 otherwise. This scale has since been used in a handful of studies (e.g., Hollingsworth & Fassinger, 2002; Kahn, 2001; Kahn & Schlosser, 2010; Szymanski, Ozegovic, Phillips, & Briggs-Phillips, 2007). The advantage of self-report is that the respondent can describe involvement in research activities that would not show up in a database search (e.g., currently collecting data for a research project). The primary drawback is that obtaining self-reports requires the participation of the target individuals; thus it is not nearly as simple as providing an objective measure based on a database search.

These methodological issues aside, there is a strong belief that publishing original research is the *sine qua non* of research productivity. Although publications may be the currency of academic psychology, research involvement and productivity clearly take many forms. For example, psychologists who are involved in training might conduct surveys of training directors to discover helpful training ideas, even if there is no intention to publish the results. As another example, practitioners may lead workshops at local conferences describing a novel approach to therapy that has been developed at their agency, thus providing less-formal dissemination. The point is that a myopic focus on publications overlooks valuable scientific contributions, so we believe it is best if research training can affect many forms of scholarly productivity, including cumulative accomplishments as well as current involvement in research activities. A broader view also values many of the scholarly products of practitioners who, for example, may be less likely to publish in journals than present at conferences.

Proximal Outcomes

Research training activities provided by a doctoral program may not directly or immediately affect competence as a consumer of research, the treatment of psychological practice as a scientific endeavor, and being involved in the production of original research. Rather, these distal outcomes often are achieved incrementally through more intermediate or proximal outcomes or goals. These goals include research knowledge and skills, research self-efficacy, research interest (which includes value of doing research and motivation), and research outcome expectations. To a large extent, the definitions of these proximal outcomes and their relations with one another have been guided by social-cognitive career theory (SCCT; Lent, Brown, & Hackett, 1994). SCCT, which is based on Bandura's (1986) general social-cognitive theory and has been applied to myriad topics within vocational psychology, suggests that individual and contextual factors influence one's level of self-efficacy and outcome expectations with respect to performing a behavior. Self-efficacy and outcome expectations regarding the behavior, in turn, influence one's interest in engaging in that behavior, and then interest and self-efficacy predict performance. Thus, these proximal outcomes theoretically are dependent on one another.

Research knowledge and skills. Clearly the ability to consume research, think scientifically, and conduct original research requires some minimal level of knowledge and skills concerning research. Indeed, specific knowledge and skills are essential (but not the only) elements of competence with respect to a professional ability (Kaslow et al., 2004). Despite the obvious link between training goals and the acquisition of research knowledge and skills, surprisingly little published research has examined research competence as a training outcome. Indeed, Heppner, Kivlighan, and Wampold (2008) indicated that research competence was a "missing construct" (p. 44) in the research on research training.

Wampold (1986) and others suggest that research competence comprises many types of knowledge and skills. Knowledge would include understanding research design and methodological issues (e.g., when counterbalancing is necessary, what it means to manipulate or control variables), psychometrics (e.g., reliability and validity theory), and various forms of data analysis (e.g., hypothesis testing, understanding forms of quantitative and qualitative analysis). Skills include being able to work with the literature (e.g., selecting, comprehending, critically analyzing, and integrating the literature), conceptualizing research questions and hypotheses (e.g., wording hypotheses in testable ways), and working with data (e.g., skills with statistical software, coding qualitative interviews accurately). Another important skill that has relevance beyond mere research is writing (Heppner et al., 1999), specifically, writing logically, objectively, and parsimoniously.

There have been relatively few empirical investigations of research competence. Royalty and Reising

(1986) surveyed counseling psychologists to assess their self-perceptions of current skills in 23 areas. A factor analysis revealed four factors: (1) research design skills, (2) practical research skills, (3) quantitative and computer skills, and (4) writing skills. Participants' current research design skills, practical research skills, and quantitative and computer skills were significantly correlated with number of publications per year. The specific skills in which their sample of psychologists was most confident were, in order of competence, (a) writing, (b) asking questions amenable for investigation, (c) background preparation, (d) selecting a population, and (e) operationally defining variables. The skills to which they felt their training program best contributed were (a) background preparation, (b) asking questions amenable to investigation, (c) confidence about doing research, (d) statistical skills, (e) selecting a population, and (f) operationally defining variables.

One potential drawback of Royalty and Reising's (1986) study was that individuals may not be in the best position to judge their own research competence in an objective manner. Schlosser and Kahn (2007) therefore developed the Research Competence Scale, a 9-item advisor-rated measure of student research competence. The competencies were derived from several sources (e.g., Forester, Kahn, & Hesson-McInnis, 2004; Wampold, 1986), and they included competencies such as knowledge of research designs and design issues, knowledge of statistical analyses and statistical issues, ability to perform statistical analyses, writing skills, ability to integrate research with the literature, and ability to collect data effectively. Schlosser and Kahn found that the student's research competence (as rated by the advisor) was positively correlated with the student's own report of research self-efficacy, a proximal outcome addressed in the next section.

Research self-efficacy. Self-efficacy, as described by Bandura (1986), refers to one's expectations that a behavior can be achieved. With respect to research, one's research self-efficacy refers to one's confidence in being able to successfully complete various tasks related to the research process, such as conducting a literature review and analyzing data (Bieschke, 2006). Research self-efficacy is believed to be important because it provides motivation to persist in the face of obstacles; thus, students with higher levels of research self-efficacy are expected to be more productive than students with lower levels of research self-efficacy (Gelso, 1993).

Research self-efficacy is measured via student self-report. The most frequently used measure of research self-efficacy is Phillips and Russell's (1994) Self-Efficacy in Research Measure (SERM), as well as Kahn and Scott's (1997) short-form adaptation of the SERM. The 33-item, full-length SERM contains items assessing self-efficacy with respect to the four aspects of research skills identified by Royalty and Reising (1986): (a) research design skills (e.g., controlling threats to validity, formulating hypotheses), (b) practical research skills (e.g., collecting data, making time for research), (c) quantitative and computer skills (e.g., knowing which statistics to use, using statistical packages), and (d) writing skills (e.g., writing a presentation for a conference, writing a literature review). Respondents rate their level of confidence on a scale from 0 (*no confidence*) to 9 (*total confidence*). Kahn and Scott developed a 12-item short form of the SERM that is used and interpreted the same way as the longer SERM.

Other measures of research self-efficacy have been used, including the 51-item Research Self-Efficacy Scale (RSES; Bieschke, Bishop, & Garcia, 1996; Greeley et al., 1989), the unpublished 23-item Research Attitudes Measure (RAM; O'Brien, Malone, Schmidt, & Lucas, 1998), the 13-item Research Instruction Outcomes Tool (RIOT; Szymanski, Whitney-Thomas, Marshall, & Sayger, 1994), and Holden, Barker, Meenaghan, and Rosenberg's (1999) 9-item Research Self-Efficacy Scale (RSE) that was developed with social work students in mind. Forester et al. (2004) conducted a factor analysis of three of these measures (SERM, RSES, and RAM) and determined that the domain of research self-efficacy comprises confidence in data analysis, research integration, data collection, and technical writing.

In many respects, these measures of self-efficacy are interchangeable. Regardless of the specific measure of research self-efficacy used, research self-efficacy is associated with research involvement and productivity. Specifically, research self-efficacy is associated with greater research involvement and productivity among graduate students (Brown, Lent, Ryan, & McPartland, 1996; Kahn, 2001; Kahn & Scott, 1997; Phillips & Russell, 1994), university faculty (Landino & Owen, 1988; Vasil, 1992, 1993), and a sample of counseling psychologists (Royalty & Reising, 1986).

Research interest. Research interest, in the most general sense, refers to one's liking of research tasks. Research interest is believed to be a significant proximal outcome of research training, because students who are more interested in research would be more likely to engage in research tasks. However, research interest often is conceptualized in tandem with valuing engagement in research during one's career (Gelso, 1993) or research motivation (e.g., Deemer, Martens, & Podchaski, 2007). Thus, research interest is a multifaceted outcome.

Leong and Zachar (1991) developed the Scientist-Practitioner Inventory (SPI) as a tool to examine graduate students' interest in science and practice tasks. A factor analysis of the SPI revealed seven factors, four of which were associated with science tasks: (a) research activities, (b) statistics and design, (c) teach/guide/edit, and (d) academic ideas. Zachar and Leong (2000) found that scientist interests were stable at $r = .50$ over a 10-year period. Moreover, interest in science activities predicted the number of hours spent in research and writing activities as well as the number of empirical publications 10 years later. Also, as would be expected, clinical and counseling psychologists who worked in university psychology departments had significantly higher scientist interest than those who worked in other settings.

Another common measure of research interest is Bishop and Bieschke's (1998) Interest in Research Questionnaire (IRQ). This scale lists 16 research activities, such as "reading a research journal article" and "being a member of a research team," and respondents rate their degree of interest in that activity. Thus, the IRQ has conceptual overlap with the SPI, although it seems more focused on research per se versus broader scientific activities. Several studies with the IRQ have shown that research interest is highly correlated with research self-efficacy (e.g., Bishop & Bieschke, 1998; West, Kahn, & Nauta, 2007).

Two associated constructs have been discussed in the context of research interest. First, Gelso (1993) has described student "attitudes toward research" (p. 468) as being an important goal of research training. He defined research attitudes as (a) interest in doing research and (b) the value of research in students' future careers. Gelso and colleagues (Gelso, Mallinckrodt, & Judge, 1996; Royalty, Gelso, Mallinckrodt, & Garrett, 1986) developed and used the Attitudes Toward Research Measure in their work, a 4-item measure with items that assess current interest as well as value of research after graduation. Interest in and value of doing research items are highly correlated with one another, thus supporting their inclusion in the same measure.

Second, Deemer, Martens, and colleagues (Deemer, Martens, & Buboltz, 2010; Deemer, Martens, Haase, & Jome, 2009; Deemer et al., 2007)

examined student research motivation as being relevant to one's research interest. Specifically, mastery approach goals (i.e., demonstrating competence to self through achievement) in particular are predictive of research interest (Deemer et al., 2007, 2009). These findings led Deemer et al. (2010) to develop the Research Motivation Scale (RMS) to be used as a predictor of research attitudes, interest, and productivity. The RMS has three factors: (a) intrinsic reward (e.g., conducting research provides feelings of satisfaction), (b) failure avoidance (e.g., avoiding research because of fear of failure), and (c) extrinsic reward (e.g., wanting to earn respect by conducting research). Although Deemer and colleagues have established the relevance of research motivation to research interest, we also see conceptual overlap between this construct and research outcome expectations, which we discuss next.

Research outcome expectations. Like many of the other proximal outcomes, the concept of research outcome expectations stems from Bandura's (1986) social-cognitive theory. Outcome expectations refer to the expected consequences (either positive or negative) of engaging in a behavior. In terms of research, outcome expectations reflect the expected consequences of engaging in research (Bieschke, 2006). For example, will engaging in research help one's career, or will it lead to frustration? As posited by SCCT (Lent et al., 1994), research self-efficacy partly determines one's research outcome expectations, and research outcome expectations partly determine one's interest in research.

The only measure of research outcome expectations of which we are aware is the Research Outcome Expectations Questionnaire (ROEQ) (Bieschke, 2000; Bishop & Bieschke, 1998). The ROEQ comprises a series of potential outcomes associated with doing research that are rated by respondents. As would be predicted by SCCT, research outcome expectations are positively correlated with research self-efficacy and research interest (Bard, Bieschke, Herbert, & Eberz, 2000; Bishop & Bieschke, 1998; Kahn, 2001). In fact, the relation between research outcome expectations and research interest is typically found to be near $r = .70$, thus suggesting that students may have a hard time discriminating between their research interest and the expected outcomes of engaging in research.

How Research Training Leads to Proximal and Distal Outcomes

Now that the desired outcomes of research training have been delineated, we turn to a discussion of how best to attain these outcomes for students. The most comprehensive theory of research training offered in the professional psychology literature—Gelso's (1979, 1993) theory of the RTE—speaks to this very issue. Other forces are at play, however, including specific aspects of the curriculum, required research experiences, and the mentoring and advising relationships students have. Below we discuss each of these forces.

The Research Training Environment (RTE)

According to Gelso (Gelso 1979, 1993, 1997; Gelso, Baumann, Chui, & Savela, in press), the RTE represents all of the elements of the graduate training program that reflect attitudes toward research. These attitudes comprise those from faculty, students, and other members of the department or university, but faculty members likely have the greatest influence. The primary importance of the RTE is not its influence on students learning about research; rather, an effective RTE will lead students to be more interested in research, value research more, be more motivated about research, and have a greater sense of self-efficacy concerning research. In other words, an effective RTE promotes positive attitudes toward research (defined by Gelso as one's interest in research and valuing of research), and an effective RTE promotes students' self-efficacy with respect to doing research. Thus, similar to the SCCT perspective, Gelso believes that students must develop positive attitudes toward research as well as have confidence about their own research skills as prerequisites to producing research.

An effective RTE is many things. According to Gelso (1993), it comprises ten ingredients, although typically nine are measured in empirical studies, so we will discuss only those nine. Factor analyses suggest that five ingredients are delivered through instruction, whereas the remaining four are interpersonally based (Kahn & Gelso, 1997). The instructional ingredients of a positive RTE include (1) encouraging students to generate research ideas from their own interests when they are developmentally ready to do so (e.g., guiding advisees to look within themselves for personally meaningful research ideas), (2) teaching varied approaches to conducting research (e.g., teaching qualitative as well as quantitative approaches to research), (3) wedding science with clinical practice (e.g., helping an advisee draw upon clinical experiences to develop a testable research question), (4) emphasizing that all studies have flaws (e.g., reassuring

students that their own research will not be perfect), and (5) teaching statistics and research design in a relevant way (e.g., reassuring students that they do not have to be experts in statistics to be competent researchers). The four interpersonal ingredients of an effective RTE are (6) encouraging students to become involved in research in minimally threatening ways early in their training (e.g., joining a research team during the first year), (7) reinforcing students for their research efforts (e.g., providing funding for student travel, providing verbal reinforcement to students), (8) emphasizing the social elements of conducting research for those students with strong interpersonal needs (e.g., building a strong advisor-advisee working alliance, being a part of research teams), and (9) having faculty members who serve as role models of appropriate scientific behavior (e.g., faculty members sharing excitement about research as well as research failures).

In research-training studies the RTE is typically measured at the student level, that is, by having a given student rate her or his perceptions of the RTE. These perceptions are typically assessed by the 54-item Research Training Environment Scale-Revised (RTES-R) (Gelso et al., 1996). The RTES-R assesses the nine aforementioned ingredients of the RTE, with 6 items per ingredient; thus, scores for each ingredient can be obtained as well as a total score reflecting global perceptions of the RTE. An 18-item short form (RTES-R-S) (Kahn & Miller, 2000) has also been developed, with 2 items per ingredient, although only a total score should be used with this brief scale.

Empirical research on the RTE strongly supports Gelso's (1993) propositions (see Gelso et al., in press, for a complementary review). Students who perceive their RTE to be positive have greater interest in research (Bishop & Bieschke, 1998; Kahn, 2001; Kahn & Scott, 1997; Mallinckrodt, Gelso, & Royalty, 1990; Royalty et al., 1986) and greater research self-efficacy (Bishop & Bieschke, 1998; Gelso et al., 1996; Kahn, 2001; Kahn & Scott, 1997; Phillips & Russell, 1994) than students who perceive their RTE to be more deficient. Moreover, there is a positive relation between perceptions of the RTE and research productivity, both when measured concurrently (Krebs, Smither, & Hurley, 1991) and separately over a 15-year period (Mallinckrodt & Gelso, 2002). A series of structural equation models and path analyses suggests that this RTE-productivity relationship is mediated by many of the proximal outcomes described above, specifically, research interest, research self-efficacy, and research outcome expectations (Bishop & Bieschke, 1998; Kahn, 2001; Kahn & Scott, 1997).

Recently, Kahn and Schlosser (2010) noted that research on student perceptions of the RTE is somewhat inconsistent with the view of the RTE as a program-level, versus student-level, variable. They advocated for a multilevel perspective on research on the RTE. In accord with this view, they sampled students from 40 doctoral programs in clinical, counseling, and school psychology and examined aggregate program ratings of the RTE. These aggregate ratings were positively related to ratings of the RTE by the program faculty (based on a faculty version of the RTES-R developed for their study), faculty ratings of the quality of student-faculty relations in the program, the collective research self-efficacy of students in the program, and the quality of students' relationships with their advisors.

In addition to the research on global perceptions of the RTE, there has been research on its specific ingredients. All nine of the ingredients measured by the RTES-R are associated with research self-efficacy and research attitudes (again, interest in and value of doing research) among doctoral students (Gelso et al., 1996). However, Shivy, Worthington, Wallis, and Hogan (2003) found that graduate students tend to favor the interpersonal ingredients of the RTE more than the instructional ingredients in terms of their importance. Targeted research on specific ingredients of the RTE is rare, although Love, Bahner, Jones, and Nilsson (2007) examined whether or not early exposure to research was associated with self-efficacy. In their survey of doctoral students in counseling psychology, Love and colleagues found that it was not the amount of research experience that was related to research self-efficacy, but early involvement in team research experiences and student's satisfaction with research experiences that were associated to research self-efficacy.

In summary, Gelso's (1993) RTE theory provides training programs with a checklist of sorts representing desirable components of research training. Training directors and program faculty interested in improving the quality of research training are advised to self-assess how their program maps onto Gelso's descriptions of a positive RTE. Stark, Perfect, Simpson, Schnoebelen, and Glenn (2004) provide an excellent description of a positive RTE for a training program in school psychology. However, we note that there may be additional ingredients of an effective RTE. For example, Bieschke, Eberz, Bard, and Croteau (1998) have articulated the need to create affirmative lesbian, gay, and bisexual RTEs,

and Liu, Sheu, and Williams (2004) demonstrated the importance of a multicultural RTE to research training. Thus, attention to issues of diversity as it relates to research (e.g., support for conducting research with diverse samples, encouraging research strategies that are indigenous to the student's culture) may represent an additional valuable element of a positive RTE.

The internship RTE. Research training does not occur exclusively in the student's home doctoral program. Although most of the research on the RTE has focused on the student's academic graduate program, a pair of studies has examined the pre-doctoral internship RTE (Phillips, Szymanski, Ozegovic, & Briggs-Phillips, 2004; Szymanski et al., 2007) with the premise that effective research training involves exposure to clinicians who integrate research and science into their work. Moreover, from a practical perspective, a supportive internship RTE would facilitate interns completing their dissertations in a timely manner.

Thus, Phillips et al. (2004) developed the Internship Research Training Environment Scale (IRTES) to assess the adequacy of the internship RTE. Based on data from interns at university counseling centers (Phillips et al., 2004), as well as a follow-up analysis with early career professionals (Szymanski et al., 2007), four factors of the IRTES emerged: (a) discussing/mentoring (i.e., the internship program spent time discussing the interns' research), (b) resources (i.e., the internship program provided time and concrete resources to do research), (c) modeling (i.e., internship program staff were involved in and enjoyed research activities), and (d) recognition/encouragement (i.e., the internship program staff showed care and encouragement about the interns' research). We note that this factor structure did not map onto either Gelso's (1993) nine ingredients nor to the instructional/ interpersonal distinction found by Kahn and Gelso (1997). Thus, the internship RTE does not show the exact same organization as the academic RTE, but modeling and reinforcement did emerge as factors/ingredients in both.

In terms of training outcomes, Phillips et al. (2004) found that interns who perceived their internship RTE as being more positive reported more positive research outcome expectations as well as higher scholarly productivity, although the internship RTE was uncorrelated with research interest and research self-efficacy. With their sample of postdoctoral psychologists reflecting back on their internship RTE, Szymanski et al. (2007)

replicated earlier path analyses (e.g., Kahn, 2001) that focused on the academic RTE of current students. Specifically, research outcome expectations mediated the relationship between the internship RTE and research interest, and research self-efficacy mediated the relationship between the internship RTE and scholarly productivity.

Required Research Experiences

Gelso's (1993) RTE theory not only addresses the affective tone of a student's research training, but also the tangible training experiences a student receives. Clearly, programs vary widely in their training models, curricula, and so forth. However, some training experiences are likely to be fairly constant across programs, such as supervised research experiences (e.g., a dissertation) and course work stipulated by American Psychological Association (APA) accreditation guidelines and principles (e.g., training in research methodology and data analysis). It is these more common experiences that we now address.

Coursework. Courses in research methodology and statistics are common among doctoral training programs in professional psychology. Clinical and counseling psychology PhD programs typically require 1.5 years of statistics/measurement courses as well as course work in research methods (Aiken, West, & Millsap, 2008). Historically there has been some debate as to how large a role didactic statistics training ought to have in professional psychology (see Wampold, 1986), but given the complexity of statistical analyses used in even the most practitioner-friendly journals (let alone the journals primarily read by academic psychologists), we believe that didactic statistics training is necessary to train a students to be fully competent in research. As Wampold (1986) suggested (and what seems to be a common practice; Aiken et al., 2008), students should be exposed to coursework in statistics (beginning with univariate statistics and progressing to multivariate statistics), research design, and psychometrics. Moreover, because statistics and research design cannot be untied (Gelso, 1993), statistics courses should address methodology and vice-versa. These courses in statistics, methods, and measurement would be in addition to any course work in content areas that survey the research literature. For example, a graduate course on current theory and research in professional psychology would have strong scientific undercurrents, so students would gain additional research training in such content courses.

Supervised research experiences. Doctoral programs typically require a supervised research experience (Peluso, Carleton, & Asmundson, 2010), which usually consists of a dissertation and may also include a thesis or research competency project. There is no substitute for conducting an independent research study, as it provides numerous research skills articulated above (e.g., writing, data analysis, comprehension of the literature). Conducting one's own study also provides an opportunity to learn practical research skills, such as writing an Institutional Review Board (IRB) protocol and supervising research assistants. Finally, working on a research project with one's advisor and perhaps in a research team reinforces the notion of science as a partly social experience, thereby strengthening the RTE of a program.

But how should these research experiences be incorporated into a student's training? Thinking developmentally (see Wampold, 1986), the first research experience ought to be one in which the student serves as an apprentice to the advisor, simply observing the research process, as asking a first-year student to develop his or her own research project might evoke progress-inhibiting anxiety about the research process. A research practicum, in which all aspects of the research process are simulated, would be a valuable second step in research training. Then the supervised research experience could be offered, as the student should be well-prepared to tackle independent research at this time.

Mentoring and Advising

In addition to providing concrete, tangible training experiences, effective research training also includes vital interpersonal elements. Specifically, much of a student's research training is provided by an advisor or research mentor. We agree with Schlosser and Gelso (2001) that the advisor and mentor are not necessarily the same person and that while nearly all students have an advisor fewer are fortunate enough to have a mentor. As Schlosser, Knox, Moskovitz, and Hill (2003) explained, the advisor is often assigned to the student and has the most responsibility for guiding the student through the program. Moreover, the relationship with an advisor can be positive, negative, or anywhere in between. A mentor, on the other hand, by definition has a positive relationship with the student (Schlosser & Gelso, 2001). Referring to someone as a mentor, which is often done retrospectively as an honor (Weil, 2001), speaks to the quality and depth of relationship between mentor and protégé. Of course, people can be both an advisor and a mentor.

Despite these differences, advisors and mentors can both have a profound influence on research training. Outside of course work, which is provided by a collective of different instructors, the advisor or mentor is often the primary person responsible for providing direct supervision of the student's research experiences. Moreover, interpersonal ingredients of the RTE (e.g., having a faculty role model and reinforcement of student research endeavors) are typically communicated—both verbally and nonverbally—through the advisor or mentor. Thus, whereas effective advisors and mentors provide expert guidance and advice regarding specific research projects (thereby teaching research knowledge and skills), they also communicate excitement about research, provide support to the student, and aid the student's development as a researcher and psychologist.

Empirical research on the importance of mentoring in professional psychology was provided by Hollingsworth and Fassinger (2002). They operationalized mentoring as including psychosocial (focus on affective elements of research training) and career (aiding student acquisition of specific knowledge) components. They found that the mentoring experiences of counseling psychology doctoral students were strongly associated with both perceptions of the RTE and with their research involvement/productivity. Moreover, mentoring experiences were positively correlated with research self-efficacy and research attitudes (interest in and value of research). A study of male clinical psychologists suggested that those who had a research mentor were more likely to do research in their careers (Dohm & Cummings, 2003). Moreover, the best predictors of being involved in research were having opportunities to publish research articles and meet experts, two opportunities that mentors can provide to their students.

Some advising relationships, however, yield mixed effects on students' research outcomes. Two qualitative studies explored both positive and negative aspects of the advisor-advisee relationship. In a study of advisees, Schlosser et al. (2003) found that counseling psychology doctoral students who were satisfied with their advising relationship differed from those who were unsatisfied in terms of (among other things) the rapport they felt with their advisor, their comfort disclosing personal information to their advisor, the way the advisor processed conflict with the advisee, the frequency of meetings with the advisor, the advisor's focus on the advisee's career and professional development,

and the advisee's overall perceived costs and benefits associated with the advisory relationship. In the second study, Knox, Schlosser, Pruitt, and Hill (2006) conducted interviews with counseling psychology faculty members; these faculty members reported that a quality advisor-advisee relationship was characterized by such things as mutual respect, effective communication, and a similarity in career paths.

From this research, then, the relationship between the advisor and advisee emerges as central to graduate training; Hill (1997) even suggested that a relationship with a mentor is akin to the counselor-client working alliance in therapy. Consistent with this view, Schlosser and colleagues (Schlosser & Gelso, 2001, 2005; Schlosser & Kahn, 2007) have empirically examined the role of the advisor-advisee working alliance on research training outcomes. Schlosser and Gelso (2001) developed the Advisory Working Alliance Inventory-Student (AWAI-S), a measure of the working alliance between the advisor and advisee from the student's perspective. The advisory working alliance comprises three dimensions: (a) rapport (i.e., how well the advisor and advisee get along interpersonally), (b) apprenticeship (i.e., the degree to which the advisor aids the professional development of the advisee), and (c) identification-individuation (i.e., how much the advisee wants to be like the advisor). Schlosser and Gelso (2001) found that student ratings of a more positive advisory alliance were associated with greater research self-efficacy and more positive attitudes toward research. Schlosser and Gelso (2005) later developed an advisor-rated measure of the advisory alliance (the AWAI-A); advisor ratings of the advisory alliance were positively correlated with advisee interest in science and practice and perceptions of the advisee's research self-efficacy. Finally, in a study of advisor-advisee dyads (Schlosser & Kahn, 2007), advisors and advisees showed moderate ($r = .31$) agreement on their perceptions of the alliance. Moreover, the alliance was positively correlated with advisee research competence and research self-efficacy. Thus, a strong advisory alliance is a good thing.

More recently, Schlosser and colleagues (Schlosser, Lyons, Talleyrand, Kim, & Johnson, 2011a, 2011b; Schlosser, Talleyrand, Lyons, Kim, & Johnson, 2011) have articulated a multicultural theory of advising relationships. This emergent theory was constructed to understand how cultural variables (e.g., racial identity, acculturation) operated within and impacted advisor-advisee relationships. As applied psychology continues to embrace multiculturalism, in addition to welcoming a more culturally diverse workforce of students and professionals, this theory will have significant utility for understanding advising relationships in the 21st century. Given the established correlations between advising relationships and research related-outcomes (e.g., Schlosser & Gelso, 2001, 2005; Schlosser & Kahn, 2007), the theory can help us understand how to be effective research mentors and protégés in a world that continues to become more and more diverse.

Conclusion and Future Directions

Research training is a fundamental component of doctoral training in professional psychology. Relatedly, we assert that such training provides an essential scientific foundation for all professional psychologists, whether academically or clinically based. Research training in graduate school thus helps to develop scientists who conduct rigorous and relevant research and practitioners who adopt a scientific approach to their clinical work.

Although our literature review has addressed a variety of topics, it is also true that the majority of empirical investigation on research training over the past few decades has concentrated on only some of these topics, primarily, research self-efficacy and interest, the RTE, and advising relationships. Granted, these topics have been explored with substantial depth, but the scientific study of research training in professional psychology has not sufficiently addressed other issues. We therefore outline several profitable directions for future theory, research, and training efforts designed to enhance research training.

1. A good deal of empirical research has examined the scholarly productivity of doctoral students in professional psychology as well as the productivity of faculty in those programs. Almost no empirical work has been done on how psychologists, especially clinicians, consume research, nor on how they treat psychological practice as a scientific endeavor. There is a dire need for greater understanding of such phenomena, which may then lead to more informed theories about how these training outcomes are best attained and what form these outcomes take in practice.

2. A related need is to discern the optimal research-training strategy for students who intend to seek careers in psychological practice. Certainly students interested in practice might find a home in a practitioner-scholar program, but it is unreasonable to presume that practice-oriented students would not be able to receive adequate practitioner-relevant research training in a scientist-practitioner or clinical-scientist PhD program. Thus, we suggest working towards defining best research-training practices for practitioners. Of particular value for such students may be research training that focuses on integrating regular outcome assessment into therapy and conducting program evaluations.

3. A corresponding need is to examine person-by-environment interactions on training outcomes. A host of student factors are potentially relevant to the research training process, including vocational interests, cognitive style, gender, and cultural background (Gelso & Lent, 2000). Educators must avoid the trainee uniformity myth, whereby all trainees are to be trained using the same approach. Likewise, training efforts that are insensitive to a student's developmental level are unlikely to be successful. Thus, a complete conceptualization of best practices for research training needs to consider the characteristics of the trainee.

4. Ideas about effective components of the RTE have been discussed since Gelso's first article on the topic in 1979, yet in all of the years since then there have been no published experimental studies testing these propositions. Thus, a potentially fruitful direction for future research is to conduct intervention research to see whether changes to the RTE or required training experiences have the desired changes in training outcomes. Such research need not rise to the rigorous standards of a randomized control trial; it could simply involve pre-/post-test comparisons within a particular program. For example, does implementing a student research award in a doctoral program affect the research attitudes of students in the program? Addressing the question of causality will help to provide educators guidance for optimizing research training.

References

Academy of Psychological Clinical Science. (2007). APCS home page. Retrieved November 20, 2007 from the World Wide Web: http://psych.arizona.edu/apcs/index.php.

Aiken, L. S., West, S. G., & Millsap, R. E. (2008). Doctoral training in statistics, measurement, and methodology in psychology: Replication and extension of Aiken, West, Sechrest, and Reno's (1990) survey of PhD programs in North America. *American Psychologist*, 63, 32–50. doi: 10.1037/0003-066X.63.1.32

American Psychological Association Presidential Task Force on Evidence-Based Practice. (2006). Evidence-based practice in psychology. *American Psychologist, 61,* 271–285. doi: 10.1037/0003-066X.61.4.271

Bandura, A. (1986). *Social foundations of thought and action: A social cognitive theory.* Englewood Cliffs, NJ: Prentice-Hall.

Bard, C. C., Bieschke, K. J., Herbert, J. T., & Eberz, A. B. (2000). Predicting research interest among rehabilitation counseling students and faculty. *Rehabilitation Counseling Bulletin, 44,* 48–55. doi: 10.1177/003435520004400107

Barrom, C. P., Shadish, W. R., & Montgomery, L. M. (1988). PhDs, PsyDs, and real-world constraints on scholarly activity: Another look at the Boulder model. *Professional Psychology: Research and Practice, 19,* 93–101. doi: 10.1037/0735-7028.19.1.93

Bauer, R. M. (2007). Evidence-based practice in psychology: Implications for research and research training. *Journal of Clinical Psychology, 63,* 685–694. doi: 10.1002/jclp.20374

Belar, C. D., & Perry, N. W. (1992). National conference on scientist-practitioner education and training for the professional practice of psychology. *American Psychologist, 47,* 71–75. doi: 10.1037/0003-066X.47.1.71

Bieschke, K. J. (2000). Factor structure of the Research Outcome Expectations Scale. *Journal of Career Assessment, 8,* 303–313. doi: 10.1177/106907270000800307

Bieschke, K. J. (2006). Research self-efficacy beliefs and research outcome expectations: Implications for developing scientifically-minded psychologists. *Journal of Career Assessment, 14,* 77–91. doi: 10.1177/1069072705281366

Bieschke, K. J., Bishop, R. M., Garcia, V. L. (1996). The utility of the research self-efficacy scale. *Journal of Career Assessment, 4,* 59–75. doi: 10.1177/106907279600400104

Bieschke, K. J., Eberz, A. B., Bard, C. C., & Croteau, J. M. (1998). Using Social Cognitive Career Theory to create affirmative lesbian, gay, and bisexual research training environments. *The Counseling Psychologist, 26,* 735–753. doi: 10.1177/0011000098265003

Bieschke, K. J., Fouad, N. A., Collins, F. L., & Halonen, J. S. (2004). The scientifically-minded psychologist: Science as a core competency. *Journal of Clinical Psychology, 60,* 713–723. doi: 10.1002/jclp.20012

Bishop, R. M., & Bieschke, K. J. (1998). Applying social cognitive theory to interest in research among counseling psychology doctoral students: A path analysis. *Journal of Counseling Psychology, 45,* 182–188. doi: 10.1037/0022-0167.45.2.182

Brems, C., Johnson, M. E., & Gallucci, P. (1996). Publication productivity of clinical and counseling psychologists. *Journal of Clinical Psychology, 52,* 723–725. doi: 10.1002/(SICI)10 97-4679(199611)52:6<723::AID-JCLP15>3.0.CO;2-O

Brown, S. D., Lent, R. W., Ryan, N. E., & McPartland, E. B. (1996). Self-efficacy as an intervening mechanism between research training environments and scholarly productivity: A theoretical and methodological extension. *The Counseling Psychologist, 24,* 535–544. doi: 10.1177/0011000096243012

Carter, J. A. (2002). Integrating science and practice: Reclaiming the science in practice. *Journal of Clinical Psychology, 58,* 1285–1290. doi: 10.1002/jclp.10112

Cassin, S. E., Singer, A. R., Dobson, K. S., & Altmaier, E. M. (2007). Professional interests and career aspirations of graduate students in professional psychology: An exploratory survey. *Training and Education in Professional Psychology, 1,* 26–37. doi: 10.1037/1931-3918.1.1.26

Cherry, D. K., Messenger, L. C., & Jacoby, A. M. (2000). An examination of training model outcomes in clinical psychology programs. *Professional Psychology: Research and Practice, 31,* 562–568. doi: 10.1037/0735-7028.31.5.562

Deemer, E. D., Martens, M. P., & Buboltz, W. C. (2010). Toward a tripartite model of research motivation: Development and initial validation of the Research Motivation Scale. *Journal of Career Assessment, 18,* 292–309. doi: 10.1177/1069072710364794

Deemer, E. D., Martens, M. P., Haase, R. F., & Jome, L. M. (2009). Do mastery approach goals and research outcome expectations mediate the relationship between the research training environment and research interest? Test of a social cognitive model. *Training and Education in Professional Psychology, 3,* 250–260. doi: 10.1037/a0017384

Deemer, E. D., Martens, M. P., & Podchaski, E. J. (2007). Counseling psychology students' interest in research: Examining the contribution of achievement goals. *Training and Education in Professional Psychology, 1,* 193–203. doi: 10.1037/1931-3918.1.3.193

Dohm, F., & Cummings, W. (2003). Research mentoring and men in clinical psychology. *Psychology of Men & Masculinity, 4,* 149–153. doi: 10.1037/1524-9220.4.2.149

Duffy, R. D., Jadidian, A., Webster, G. D., & Sandell, K. J. (2011). The research productivity of academic psychologists: Assessment, trends, and best practice recommendations. *Scientometrics, 89,* 207–227. doi: 10.1007/s11192-011-0452-4

Duffy, R. D., Martin, H. M., Bryan, N. A., & Raque-Bogdan, T. L. (2008). Measuring individual research productivity: A review and Development of the Integrated Research Productivity Index. *Journal of Counseling Psychology, 55,* 518–527. doi: 10.1037/a0013618

Forester, M., Kahn, J. H., & Hesson-McInnis, M. (2004). Factor structures of three measures of research self-efficacy. *Journal of Career Assessment, 12,* 3–16. doi: 10.1177/1069072703257719

Fouad, N. A., Grus, C. L., Hatcher, R. L., Kaslow, N. J., Hutchings, P. S., Madson, M. B., Collins, F. L., & Crossman, R. E. (2009). Competency benchmarks: A model for understanding and measuring competence in professional psychology across training levels. *Training and Education in Professional Psychology, 3,* S5–S26. doi:10.1037/a0015832

Gelso, C. J. (1979). Research in counseling: Methodological and professional issues. *The Counseling Psychologist, 8*(3), 7–35. doi: /10.1177/001100007900800303

Gelso, C. J. (1993). On the making of a scientist-practitioner: A theory of research training in professional psychology. *Professional Psychology: Research and Practice, 24,* 468–476. doi: 10.1037/0735-7028.24.4.468

Gelso, C. J. (1997). The making of a scientist in applied psychology: An attribute by treatment conception. *The Counseling Psychologist, 25,* 307–320. doi: 10.1177/0011000097252013

Gelso, C. J., Baumann, E. C., Chui, H. T., & Savela, A. (in press). The making of a scientist-psychotherapist: The research training environment and the psychotherapist. *Psychotherapy.*

Gelso, C., & Fretz, B. (2001). *Counseling psychology* (2nd ed.). Belmont, CA: Wadsworth.

Gelso, C. J., & Lent, R. W. (2000). Scientific training and scholarly productivity: The person, the training environment, and their interaction. In S. D. Brown & R. W. Lent (Eds.), *Handbook of counseling psychology* (3rd ed.) (pp. 109–139). New York: Wiley.

Gelso, C. J., Mallinckrodt, B., & Judge, A. B. (1996). Research training environment, attitudes toward research, and research self-efficacy: The revised Research Training Environment Scale. *The Counseling Psychologist, 24,* 304–322. doi: 10.1177/0011000096242010

Greeley, A. T., Johnson, E., Seem, S., Braver, M., Dias, L., Evans, K., Kincade, E., & Pricken, P. (1989). *Research Self-Efficacy Scale*. Unpublished scale presented at the Conference of the Association for Women in Psychology, Bethesda, MD.

Heppner, P. P., Kivlighan, D. M., & Wampold, B. E. (2008). *Research design in counseling (3nd ed.)*. Belmont, CA: Thomson Higher Education.

Hill, C. E. (1997). The effects of my research training environment: Where are my students now? *The Counseling Psychologist, 25*, 74–81. doi: 10.1177/0011000097251007

Holden, G., Barker, K., Meenaghan, T., & Rosenberg, G. (1999). Research self-efficacy: A new possibility for educational outcomes assessment. *Journal of Social Work Education, 35*, 463–476.

Hollingsworth, M. A., & Fassinger, R. E. (2002). The role of faculty mentors in the research training of counseling psychology doctoral students. *Journal of Counseling Psychology, 49*, 324–330. doi: 10.1037/0022-0167.49.3.324

Horn, R. A., Troyer, J. A., Hall, E. J., Mellott, R. N., Coté, L. S., & Marquis, J. D. (2007). The scientist-practitioner model: A rose by any other name is still a rose. *American Behavioral Scientist, 50*, 808–819. doi: 10.1177/0002764206296459

Jones, J. L., & Mehr, S. L. (2007). Foundations and assumptions of the scientist-practitioner model. *American Behavioral Scientist, 50*, 766–771. doi: 10.1177/0002764206296454

Kahn, J. H. (2001). Predicting the scholarly activity of counseling psychology students: A refinement and extension. *Journal of Counseling Psychology, 48*, 344–354. doi: 10.1037/0022-0167.48.3.344

Kahn, J. H., & Gelso, C. J. (1997). Factor structure of the Research Training Environment Scale-Revised: Implications for research training in applied psychology. *The Counseling Psychologist, 25*, 22–37. doi: 10.1177/0011000097251004

Kahn, J. H., & Miller, S. A. (2000). Measuring global perceptions of the research training environment using a short form of the RTES-R. *Measurement and Evaluation in Counseling and Development, 33*, 103–119.

Kahn, J. H., & Scott, N. A. (1997). Predictors of research productivity and science-related career goals among counseling psychology graduate students. *The Counseling Psychologist, 25*, 38–67. doi: 10.1177/0011000097251005

Kahn, J. H., & Schlosser, L. Z. (2010). The graduate research training environment in professional psychology: A multilevel investigation. *Training and Education in Professional Psychology, 4*, 183–193. doi: 0.1037/a0018968

Kaslow, N. J., Borden, K. A., Collins, F. L., Forrest, L., Illfelder-Kaye, J., Nelson, P. D., & Rallo, J. S. (2004). Competencies Conference: Future Directions in Education and Credentialing in Professional Psychology. *Journal of Clinical Psychology, 60*, 699–712.

Knox, S., Schlosser, L. Z., Pruitt, N. T. & Hill, C. E. (2006). A qualitative examination of graduate advising relationships: The advisor perspective. *The Counseling Psychologist, 34*, 489–518. doi: 10.1177/0011000006290249

Krebs, P. J., Smither, J. W., & Hurley, R. B. (1991). Relationship of vocational personality and research training environment to the research productivity of counseling psychologists. *Professional Psychology: Research and Practice, 22*, 362–367. doi: /10.1037/0735-7028.22.5.362

Lambert, M. J., & Hawkins, E. J. (2004). Measuring outcome in professional practice: Considerations in selecting and using brief outcome instruments. *Professional Psychology: Research and Practice, 35*, 492–499. doi: 10.1037/0735-7028.35.5.492

Lambert, M. J., & Vermeersch, D. A. (2008). Measuring and improving psychotherapy outcome in routine practice. In. S. D. Brown & R. W. Lent (Eds.), *Handbook of counseling psychology* (4th ed.) (pp 233–248). Hoboken, NJ: Wiley.

Lambert, M. J., Whipple, J. L., Hawkins, E. J., Vermeersch, D. A., Nielsen, S. L., & Smart, D. W. (2003). Is it time for clinicians to routinely track patient outcome? A meta-analysis. *Clinical Psychology: Science and Practice, 10*, 288–301. doi: 10.1093/clipsy.bpg025

Lampropoulos, G. K., Goldfried, M. R., Castonguay, L. G., Lambert, M. J., Stiles, W. B., & Nestoros, J. N. (2002). What kind of research can we realistically expect from the practitioner? *Journal of Clinical Psychology, 58*, 1241–1264. doi: 10.1002/jclp.10109

Landino, R. A., & Owen, S. V. (1988). Self-efficacy in university faculty. *Journal of Vocational Behavior, 33*, 1–14. doi: 10.1016/0001-8791(88)90030-9

Lent, R. W., Brown, S. D., & Hackett, G. (1994). Toward a unifying social cognitive theory of career and academic interest, choice, and performance. *Journal of Vocational Behavior, 45*, 79–122. doi: 10.1006/jvbe.1994.1027

Leong, F. T. L., & Zachar, P. (1991). Development and validation of the Scientist-Practitioner Inventory for psychology. *Journal of Counseling Psychology, 38*, 331–341. doi: 10.1037/0022-0167.38.3.331

Liu, W. M., Sheu, H., & Williams, K. (2004). Multicultural competency in research: Examining the relationships among multicultural competencies, research training and self-efficacy, and the multicultural environment. *Cultural Diversity and Ethnic Minority Psychology, 10*, 324–339. doi: 10.1037/1099-9809.10.4.324

Love, K. M., Bahner, A. D., Jones, L. N., & Nilsson, J. E. (2007). An investigation of early research experience and research self-efficacy. *Professional Psychology: Research and Practice, 38*, 314–320. doi: 10.1037/0735-7028.38.3.314

Mallinckrodt, B. & Gelso, C. J. (2002). Impact of research training environment and Holland personality type: A 15-year follow-up of research productivity. *Journal of Counseling Psychology, 49*, 60–70. doi: 10.1037/0022-0167.49.1.60

Mallinckrodt, B., Gelso, C. J., & Royalty, G. M. (1990). Impact of research training environment and counseling psychology students' Holland personality types on interest in research. *Professional Psychology: Research and Practice, 21*, 26–32. doi:10.1037/0735-7028.21.1.26

Meier, S. T. (1999). Training the practitioner-scientist: Bridging case conceptualization, assessment, and intervention. *The Counseling Psychologist, 27*, 846–869. doi: 10.1177/0011000099276008

O'Brien, K. M., Malone, M. E., Schmidt, C. K., & Lucas, M. S. (1998, August). *Research self-efficacy: Improvements in instrumentation*. Poster session presented at the annual conference of the American Psychological Association, San Francisco, CA.

Peluso, D. L., Carleton, R. N., & Asmundson, G. J. G. (2010). Clinical psychology graduate students' perceptions of their scientific and practical training: A Canadian perspective. *Canadian Psychology, 51*, 133–139. doi: 10.1037/a0018236

Phillips, J. C., & Russell, R. K. (1994). Research self-efficacy, the research training environment, and research productivity among graduate students in counseling psychology. *The Counseling Psychologist, 22*, 628–641. doi: 10.1177/0011000094224008

Phillips, J. C., Szymanski, D. M., Ozegovic, J. J., Briggs-Phillips, M. (2004). Preliminary examination and measurement of the internship research training environment. *Journal of Counseling Psychology, 51*, 240–248. doi:10.1037/0022-0167.51.2.240

Rodolfa, E. R., Kaslow, N. J., Stewart, A. E., Keilin, W. G., & Baker, J. (2005). Internship training: Do models really matter? *Professional Psychology: Research and Practice, 36,* 25–31. doi:10.1037/0735-7028.36.1.25

Royalty, G. M., Gelso, C. J., Mallinckrodt, B., & Garrett, K. D. (1986). The environment and the student in counseling psychology: Does the research training environment influence graduate students' attitudes toward research? *The Counseling Psychologist, 14,* 9–30. doi: 10.1177/0011000086141002

Royalty, G. M., & Reising, G. N. (1986). The research training of counseling psychologists: What the professionals say. *The Counseling Psychologist, 14,* 49–60. doi: 10.1177/0011000086141005

Schlosser, L. Z. & Gelso, C. J. (2001). Measuring the working alliance in advisor-advisee relationships in graduate school. *Journal of Counseling Psychology, 48,* 157–167. doi: 10.1037/0022-0167.48.2.157

Schlosser, L. Z. & Gelso, C. J. (2005). The Advisory Working Alliance Inventory-Advisor Version: Scale development and validation. *Journal of Counseling Psychology, 52,* 650–654. doi: 10.1037/0022-0167.52.4.650

Schlosser, L. Z., & Kahn, J. H. (2007). Dyadic perspectives on advisor-advisee relationships in counseling psychology doctoral programs. *Journal of Counseling Psychology, 54,* 211–217. doi: 10.1037/0022-0167.54.2.211

Schlosser, L. Z., Knox, S., Moskovitz, A. R., & Hill, C.E. (2003). A qualitative study of the graduate advising relationship: The advisee perspective. *Journal of Counseling Psychology, 50,* 178–188. doi: 10.1037/0022-0167.50.2.178

Schlosser, L. Z., Lyons, H. Z., Talleyrand, R. M., Kim, B. S. K., & Johnson, W. B. (2011a). Advisor-advisee relationships in graduate training programs. *Journal of Career Development, 38,* 3–18. doi: 10.1177/0894845309358887

Schlosser, L. Z., Talleyrand, R. M., Lyons, H. Z., Kim, B. S. K., & Johnson, W. B. (2011). Multicultural issues in graduate advising relationships. *Journal of Career Development, 38,* 19–43. doi: 10.1177/0894845309359285

Schlosser, L. Z., Lyons, H. Z., Talleyrand, R. M., Kim, B. S. K., & Johnson, W. B. (2011b). A multiculturally-infused model of graduate advising relationships. *Journal of Career Development, 38,* 44–61. doi: 10.1177/0894845309359286

Shivy, V. A., Worthington, E. L., Wallis, A. B., & Hogan, C. (2003). Doctoral research training environments (RTEs): Implications for the teaching of psychology. *Teaching of Psychology, 30,* 297–302. doi: 10.1207/S15328023TOP3004_03

Stark, K. D., Perfect, M., Simpson, J., Schnoebelen, S., & Glenn, R. (2004). Encouraging academic careers: One of many desirable career options for doctoral school psychologists. *School Psychology Quarterly, 19,* 382–397. doi: 10.1521/scpq.19.4.382.53505

Stricker, S., & Trierweiler, S. J. (1995). The local clinical scientist: A bridge between science and practice. *American*

Psychologist, 50, 995–1002. doi: 10.1037/0003-066X.50.12.995

Szymanski, D. M., Ozegovic, J. J., Phillips, J. C., & Briggs-Phillips, M. (2007). Fostering scholarly productivity through academic and internship research training environments. *Training and Education in Professional Psychology, 1,* 135–146. doi:10.1037/1931-3918.1.2.135

Szymanski, E. M., Whitney-Thomas, J., Marshall, L., & Sayger, T. V. (1994). The effect of graduate instruction in research methodology on research self-efficacy and perceived research utility. *Rehabilitation Education, 8,* 319–331.

Vasil, L. (1992). Self-efficacy expectations and causal attributions for achievement among male and female university faculty. *Journal of Vocational Behavior, 41,* 259–269. doi: 10.1016/0001-8791(92)90028-X

Vasil, L. (1993). Gender differences in the academic career in New Zealand universities. *New Zealand Journal of Educational Studies, 28,* 143–153.

Waehler, C., A., Kalodner, C. R., Wampold, B. E., & Lichtenberg, J. W. (2000). Empirically supported treatments (ESTs) in perspective: Implications for counseling psychology training. *The Counseling Psychologist, 28,* 622–640. doi: 10.1177/0011000000285004

Wallis, J. M., Kahn, J. H., Curran, J. L., Delahunt, C. L., Dixon, S. R., & Knox, S. (2008, March). *How professional psychologists use science in practice.* Poster session presented at the 2008 International Counseling Psychology Conference, Chicago, IL.

Wampold, B. E. (1986). Toward quality research in counseling psychology: Curricular recommendations for design and analysis. *The Counseling Psychologist, 14,* 37–48. doi: 10.1177/0011000086141004

Wampold, B. E., Lichtenberg, J. W., & Waehler, C. A. (2002). Principles of empirically supported interventions in counseling psychology. *The Counseling Psychologist, 30,* 197–217. doi: 10.1177/0011000002302001

Watkins, C. E., Lopez, F. G., Campbell, V. L., & Himmell, C. D. (1986). Contemporary counseling psychology: Results of a national survey. *Journal of Counseling Psychology, 33,* 301–309. doi: 10.1037/0022-0167.33.3.301

Weil, V. (2001). Mentoring: Some ethical considerations. *Science and Engineering Ethics, 7,* 471–482. doi: 10.1007/s11948-001-0004-z

West, C. R., Kahn, J. H., & Nauta, M. M. (2007). Learning styles as predictors of self-efficacy and interest in research: Implications for graduate research training. *Training and Education in Professional Psychology, 1,* 174–183. doi: 10.1037/1931-3918.1.3.174

Zachar, P., & Leong, F. T. L. (2000). A 10-year longitudinal study of scientist and practitioner interests in psychology: Assessing the Boulder Model. *Professional Psychology: Research and Practice, 31,* 575–580. doi:10.1037/0735-7028.31.5.575

13 Psychology Licensure and Credentialing in the United States and Canada

Stephen T. DeMers, Carol Webb, *and* Jacqueline B. Horn

Abstract

The history of licensing and credentialing in psychology and its relationship to education and training are reviewed. The purposes, processes, and methods that licensing boards utilize are discussed in both the credentialing of entry-level licensees and in the responsibility to monitor and investigate complaints from the public. Finally, current challenges facing licensing boards, particularly the use of technology in the education of psychologists and in provision of psychological services and the inconsistency in licensure requirements across jurisdictions, are explored.

Key Words: psychology, licensing, regulation, credentialing, training and licensure

Psychology Licensure and Credentialing In the United States and Canada

This chapter seeks to increase awareness of both the historical development of regulatory mechanisms in psychology and the current status and future concerns related to licensing and credentialing of psychologists in the United States and Canada. Regardless of the profession under discussion, professional regulation is a process designed to limit entry into the profession to qualified practitioners and to monitor the professional conduct of these recognized practitioners.

According to *Merriam-Webster's Dictionary On-line* (2012), a profession is described as a "calling" or vocation involving specialized knowledge and long and intensive preparation. Numerous authors (e.g., Gross, 1978; Weissman, 1984) list the hallmarks of a profession that distinguish it from a trade or other commercial activity. These hallmarks include: (a) academic training programs that prepare individuals to practice the profession, (b) recognized societies or organizations composed of members of the profession that develop standards for training and promote the acquisition of

new knowledge, (c) a code of ethics or standards of professional conduct that represent the shared commitment to provide competent and ethical professional services, and (d) a process of professional regulation that restricts entry to the profession to those meeting the acceptable standards of training and that monitors the professional conduct of recognized members of the profession to ensure adherence to ethics codes and other recognized standards. Clearly, the link between psychology's licensing and credentialing community and its academic and training community is an important one; and this link is a shared responsibility for setting standards that is necessary for our profession to thrive. Psychology regulators use the standards created by professional organizations as a basis for the laws and rules governing entry to practice and professional conduct; concomitantly, educators and trainers must devise training programs that meet the specific criteria needed for entry to practice that regulators devise. A collaborative and mutually respectful relationship between regulators and educators/trainers is optimal, not only for entry into the profession of new generations of psychologists, but also for efforts aimed at maintaining the competence of already licensed psychologists.

In this chapter, we present the history and purpose of psychology licensure laws and the common standards and processes that licensing boards employ to control entry into the profession. Next, we describe the methods that licensing boards use to monitor and control the professional conduct of credentialed practitioners, including the relationship between codes of ethics and legally enforceable codes of professional conduct. Finally, we address some of the challenges limiting effective professional regulation in psychology. These challenges currently include an enduring inconsistency in licensure standards across jurisdictions, and inadequate provisions for the recognition of new modalities of psychology training and practice. Throughout this chapter, we tie the issues critical to regulation to the education and training of psychologists and highlight where there has been good collaboration, as well as where more consistency and communication are needed.

Historical Perspective on Psychology Licensure

In the United States and Canada, professional regulation began with the passage of medical practice acts in the late 1800s designed to protect the public from charlatans offering useless or harmful remedies. The U.S. Supreme Court issued an important decision in the case of *Dent v. West Virginia* (1889) that recognized the legitimate interests of states to monitor and control the behavior of physicians in order to protect the health and safety of their citizens (Schaffer, DeMers & Rodolfa, 2011). This decision by the highest court in the United States led to the passage of medical practice acts in almost every state legislature by 1912. These medical practice acts created regulatory boards that set minimum standards for academic training as a physician, issued licenses to those individuals who met those minimum standards, and made it illegal for others to claim to be physicians or to engage in any of the healing arts listed in the law as part of the scope of medical practice. These early medical practice acts were typically sweeping in their scope, essentially describing medical practice as providing for the health and well-being of all citizens (Schaffer, DeMers & Rodolfa, 2011).

Although medical licensing laws set the foundation for the psychology licensing acts that were to follow, they also impeded the passage of such laws. Often physicians and medical associations strongly opposed early attempts to pass psychology licensing acts in state legislatures. This opposition reflected their belief that mental health fell within the broad definition of the medical scope of practice and, therefore, physicians should provide or supervise all mental health services. Psychologists, however, believed that psychology had become sufficiently distinct from routine medical practice, and thus was an independent and autonomous profession worthy of a separate licensing act for psychology in order to adequately protect the public (DeMers and Schaffer, 2012).

Professional regulation in psychology is accomplished through an interplay between professional societies, like the American Psychological Association (APA) or the Canadian Psychological Association (CPA), and legislatively mandated or sanctioned regulatory bodies, such as psychology licensing boards or colleges. The APA was founded in the late 1800s as a scientific society focused on the study of human behavior. However, the development of psychological theories and measurement instruments that could be applied to the treatment or resolution of human problems led to early concerns about who was qualified to use such methods. In 1938, APA established the first Committee on Scientific and Professional Ethics to address these and other concerns about the application of psychological methods and tools to the real life problems of individuals (Ford, 2001). In the mid- to late-1940s the issues of standards and controls in professional psychology were explored directly by the Conference of State Psychology Associations (Carlson, 1978). It is likely that the emergence of medical practice acts, combined with the increased use of psychological methods and principles to evaluate developmental delays in children, screen military recruits, and treat patients in mental hospitals, led to the need for both a formal system of professional regulation in psychology and standardized training that would adequately prepare individuals for licensure. The first licensing act for psychology was passed in Connecticut in 1945 (DeMers, 1998; Reaves, 1996). Like most early psychology laws, the Connecticut law protected the title of "psychologist," but did not preclude others (particularly physicians) from using psychological methods. In 1960, Ontario passed the first licensing law for psychology in Canada. By 1977, all states had passed some form of psychology regulation, and in 1990, Prince Edward Island was the last Canadian province to enact a psychology licensing law. Currently there are 64 psychology regulatory boards throughout the U.S. and Canada, including the 50 states, 10 provinces, the District of Columbia, Guam, Puerto Rico, and the U.S. Virgin Islands (ASPPB, 2012a).

The purpose of all licensure laws is to protect the public from professionals who practice incompetently or unethically. According to the Association of State and Provincial Psychology Board's (ASPPB) website,

> … (licensing) laws are intended to protect the public by limiting licensure to persons who are qualified to practice psychology as defined by state or provincial law. The legal basis for licensure lies in the right of a jurisdiction to enact legislation to protect its citizens. The concept of *caveat emptor*, or buyer beware, is considered an unsound maxim when the consumer of services cannot be sufficiently informed to beware. Hence, jurisdictions have established regulatory boards to license qualified practitioners. (ASPPB, 2012b)

Like any profession, psychology requires specialized knowledge and skill, acquired through advanced and extensive training and practice. The average citizen is not equipped to judge whether the psychological services received are appropriate and meet the standard of care accepted within the profession. Consequently, state legislatures and other governing bodies agree to limit who may legally identify themselves as psychologists and who may provide services defined as psychological in exchange for the professional's agreement to operate in the best interests of the public by following recognized standards of care and professional conduct. Licensing boards and colleges enforce and regulate this contract between the profession and society.

One implication of this contract between society and the profession is that licensing boards and colleges have a statutorily defined purpose that differs from that of state/provincial and national psychological associations. Licensing boards focus on the protection of the public, while professional societies focus on promoting the profession and the welfare of their members. These purposes often overlap, however, because professional societies generally recognize that increasing public knowledge about the profession and adopting rigorous standards for education and professional conduct also result in better protection of the public. Typically, professional societies have established standards for education and training of students, in order to insure that those individuals have the competencies necessary for entry into the profession. Licensing boards view the standards and quality-control mechanisms developed by professional societies to promote and advance the profession (e.g., accreditation of

training programs) as important tools in their efforts to protect the public, and so these standard curricula typically form the basis for licensing boards to develop regulations regarding the training necessary for entry-level practice and licensure. As the ASPPB (2010b) website notes: "By ensuring high standards for those who practice, the board serves the best interests of both the public and the profession."

As more states developed separate psychology licensing boards, it became evident that there was a growing need, not only for a common standard of training, but also for a common examination to aid in the identification of competent psychological practitioners. This need for a common examination was the impetus for the creation of the American Association of State Psychology Boards (AASPB) in 1961 (Carlson, 1978). The organization's name was later changed to the ASPPB to accurately reflect the Canadian as well as U.S. participation in the organization from its inception. ASPPB started with representatives from 21 member jurisdictions from both the United States and Canada. (This chapter uses the term *jurisdiction* when referencing the governmental entity responsible for regulating professional practice, whether that entity is a state in the United States, a province in Canada, or a territory of either country. Similarly, this chapter uses the term *licensing board* to refer to the legally appointed, elected, or recognized agency within a jurisdiction with the authority to regulate the profession of psychology. Such regulatory bodies are called by different names in different jurisdictions, most typically, Board of Psychology in the United States, or College, Register, or Order of Psychologists in Canada.)

As noted earlier, ASPPB's early focus was on the development of a common examination. In 1964, the Association administered the first version of the Examination for Professional Practice in Psychology (EPPP) to one candidate in Virginia. By June 1968, multiple forms of the EPPP had been developed and the exam had been administered in 28 states and provinces to hundreds of applicants for a license in psychology (Reaves, 2004). For many years, the EPPP was administered as a proctored paper-and-pencil exam given only twice a year on a specified date in April and October. In 2001, the EPPP transitioned to computer delivery and it now is administered continuously through local computer-based testing centers to approximately 5,700 candidates annually in 64 member jurisdictions across the United States and Canada. It is currently offered in English, with a French version available because of legal requirements in Canada that examinations be offered in French. A Spanish exam currently is being prepared for use in Puerto Rico because of regulations in that country that require such a version.

The EPPP has always been a multiple-choice test with items written by a group of content experts across various specialties and research areas in psychology. Although the specific number of items contained on the EPPP has changed during its more than 50-year history, the structure and purpose of the EPPP as an assessment of essential foundational and practice specific knowledge has remained unchanged (DeMers, 2009). The EPPP assesses knowledge deemed essential for practice in psychology (DeMers, 2009). It has been validated through a series of practice analyses (Rosen, Reaves, & Hill, 1989; Rehm & Lipkins, 2006, the most recent of which was completed in 2010. These practice analyses have involved surveys or focus groups of practicing psychologists who are asked to rate specific knowledge statements within the field on their importance for entry-level practice and for protection of the public. These strategies follow the recommended procedures for validating a licensure examination (AERA, APA & NCME, 1999). The passing score on the EPPP is largely uniform across jurisdictions with almost all adopting the ASPPB recommended pass point.

ASPPB has expanded its mission over the years beyond the Examination Program to include the development and creation of model licensing laws and an *ASPPB Code of Conduct* (ASPPB, 2005); a disciplinary data system (DeMers & Schaffer, 2012; an ongoing educational program, including an annual convention and midwinter meeting; guidelines relevant to certain regulatory matters (e.g., practicum training leading to licensure) (ASPPB, 2009); publications and other training materials and programs for members of regulatory bodies; and a mobility program that promotes efforts to standardize psychological training throughout the United States and Canada, in part to help make it easier for psychologists to relocate to other jurisdictions (DeMers, Van Horne, & Rodolfa, 2008). Many of the various programs and publications available through ASPPB have been developed through collaborative efforts with other psychological associations and the training councils involved in the psychology education and training community.

Mission and Scope of Psychology Licensing Laws

As noted earlier, the main purpose of psychology licensing laws is to protect the public from unqualified, incompetent, impaired, or unethical individuals who seek to provide psychological services. Consumer groups and many psychologists themselves misperceive the mission of psychology regulatory boards as focused on protecting the profession. But the mission, and the activities pursued by boards to accomplish that mission, is clearly focused on protection of the public. Psychology licensing laws and the regulatory boards they create accomplish this mission through several main activities,,namely, defining the practice of psychology, issuing credentials to qualified and competent practitioners, and investigating complaints against practitioners who are already credentialed. Each of these main activities involves several aspects that are described in the sections that follow.

DEFINING THE NATURE AND SCOPE OF THE PRACTICE OF PSYCHOLOGY

Licensing laws define the practice of psychology and the scope of practice for psychologists. Such statutory language serves two purposes. First, it defines what constitutes psychological services, such as assessment and intervention, as recognized activities under the statute. Second, defining the scope of psychological practice stipulates that boards of psychology have jurisdiction over certain activities of licensed psychologists, so that if harm or potential harm to the public occurs, or if a psychologist acts in an unethical manner, disciplinary and remedial action can be taken (Retfalvi & Simon, 1996).

The recently revised APA Model Licensing Act states the following:

> Practice of psychology is defined as the observation, description, evaluation, interpretation, and modification of human behavior by the application of psychological principles, methods, and procedures, for the purposes of (a) preventing, eliminating, evaluating, assessing, or predicting symptomatic, maladaptive, or undesired behavior; (b) evaluating, assessing, and/or facilitating the enhancement of individual, group, and/or organizational effectiveness—including personal effectiveness, adaptive behavior, interpersonal relationships, work and life adjustment, health, and individual, group, and/or organizational performance, or (c) assisting in legal decision-making.
>
> The practice of psychology includes, but is not limited to, (a) psychological testing and the evaluation or assessment of personal characteristics, such as intelligence; personality; cognitive, physical, and/or emotional abilities; skills; interests; aptitudes;

and neuropsychological functioning; (b) counseling, psychoanalysis, psychotherapy, hypnosis, biofeedback, and behavior analysis and therapy; (c) diagnosis, treatment, and management of mental and emotional disorder or disability, substance use disorders, disorders of habit or conduct, as well as of the psychological aspects of physical illness, accident, injury, or disability; (d) psychoeducational evaluation, therapy, and remediation; (e) consultation with physicians, other health care professionals, and patients regarding all available treatment options, including medication, with respect to provision of care for a specific patient or client; (f) provision of direct services to individuals and/or groups for the purpose of enhancing individual and thereby organizational effectiveness, using psychological principles, methods, and/or procedures to assess and evaluate individuals on personal characteristics for individual development and/or behavior change or for making decisions about the individual, such as selection; and (g) the supervision of any of the above (APA, 2011, p. 215).

In over a dozen states, the psychology licensing law separates licensees into health service providers and general applied practice providers based on their training and experience. Only health service providers are legally allowed to offer health-related services including diagnosis, treatment, and intervention for health related disorders. General applied practice providers may provide psychological services in other areas such as industrial/organizational psychology or consultation. Most jurisdictions have laws that employ a generic model using the broad definition of the practice of psychology found in the APA Model Act and then require that practitioners follow their ethical responsibility to limit their activities to their demonstrated areas of training and competence.

Although the main purpose of defining psychological practice is to require licensure in psychology in order for individuals to lawfully engage in these activities, most laws also exempt from licensure certain other categories of individuals who may be trained in psychology. Individuals with advanced degrees in psychology who teach in institutions of higher education, or who work in settings like federal institutions (e.g., Veteran's hospitals, military installations, federal prisons) or some state agencies, are typically exempt from state licensure laws. Many federal agencies require such personnel to be licensed in at least one state or province, but not necessarily where they are assigned. Federal agencies have their own mechanisms for professional regulation. Many U.S. states have eliminated the previously common exemption for state employees based on the principle that professionals providing services in public agencies should meet the same standards as individuals practicing in nonpublic settings. Many states have also placed limits on exemptions for university teachers and researchers, requiring those university employees also be licensed who are involved in the delivery or supervision of services to the public through such venues as training clinics or research involving clinical trials of new techniques, since the potential for harm still exists. Thus, most psychologists involved in training and education in clinical or health services related programs must themselves be licensed in order to provide supervision for their students.

Finally, most psychology licensing laws in the United States exempt both school psychologists, who fall under the authority of a Department of Education, and licensed individuals from other regulated professions who provide services within their own legislatively recognized scope of practice. Thus, psychiatrists, psychiatric nurses, clinical social workers, and licensed professional counselors may all engage in some of the services that are part of the defined practice of psychology, but those services are also recognized as part of the legitimate scope of practice of those other groups.

Credentialing Qualified Practitioners

Psychology licensing acts are designed to protect the public by identifying and credentialing only those individuals who are qualified and competent to practice psychology safely and ethically. Psychology regulatory boards accomplish this goal by establishing strict standards for educational preparation and supervised experience and by administering examinations to measure the professional knowledge and skills of the applicant for licensure. Each jurisdiction establishes specific educational requirements for licensure as a psychologist, including degree level and type (e.g., PhD, EdD, PsyD, MS, MA, MEd), institutional accreditation (e.g., university must be regionally accredited in the U.S. or recognized by Royal Charter in Canada), and completion of an approved program of study. All jurisdictions require applicants to obtain their training as psychologists from a program that provides an organized sequence of study in the field of psychology. For jurisdictions requiring a doctoral degree in psychology for licensure, adequacy of the doctoral training program is demonstrated by accreditation of the program by the APA or CPA or by designation as a psychology doctoral program by the ASPPB/National Register Joint Designation System (for psychology doctoral programs that fall outside the scope of APA or CPA accreditation).

Two states, West Virginia and Vermont, allow the independent practice of psychology based on receipt of an acceptable master's degree in psychology. Another 12 states have statutes that permit practice at the master's degree level provided the individual is supervised by a licensed doctoral psychologist, either permanently or for an initial period of some years, after which they may be granted the ability to practice autonomously. In those states authorizing supervised practice with a master's degree in psychology, such practitioners typically are not referred to as "psychologists" but are allowed to use a variety of titles, including "psychological associate" or "psychological examiner."

In Canada, four provinces require the doctoral degree in psychology for independent practice (British Columbia, Manitoba, Ontario, and Quebec), whereas two other provinces (Nova Scotia and New Brunswick) are amending their regulations to require the doctoral degree. Four provinces (Alberta, Newfoundland and Labrador, Prince Edward Island and Saskatchewan) and one territory (Northwest Territories) allow independent practice with either the master's or doctoral degree in psychology. In Canada, all psychology degree granting programs must reside in a provincially approved and recognized institution of higher education.

In addition to setting degree requirements and assessing adequacy of the training program, each jurisdiction through its psychology licensing law adopts specific requirements for supervised professional experiences necessary for licensure eligibility. Most jurisdictions require two years of full-time supervised experience, one year of which must be postdoctoral (ASPPB, 2012a). Recently, about a dozen U.S. states have amended their laws to require the two years of supervised experience, but allow more flexibility regarding whether there must be a postdoctoral year of experience. The *APA Model Act for Licensure of Psychologists* (2011) embraces this flexibility in an attempt to lower student debt and recognize practicum training that occurs during the doctoral program. However, removing the postdoctoral requirement may have had the unintended consequence of limiting professional mobility by making those licensed without a postdoctoral year of supervised experience ineligible for licensure

in states that still require such a year (Schaffer & Rodolfa, 2011).

Finally, each jurisdiction also adopts one or more examinations that applicants for licensure must pass at specified levels. All psychology regulatory boards in the United States and most in Canada (Quebec is the single exception) require passing the EPPP. Some jurisdictions also give oral or written examinations focused on their mental health laws, ethics, practice competence or some combination of these. These "complementary" or "supplementary" exams typically are locally developed, normed or standardized, and scored.

Currently, the profession of psychology (including professional societies, councils of academic faculty, groups representing field supervisors, and groups involved with regulation, accreditation and credentialing) is exploring the feasibility of moving toward the assessment of competence to evaluate outcomes of training or readiness for entry to practice (Fouad et al., 2009; Kaslow et al., 2009; Roberts, Borden, Christiansen, & Lopez, 2005). Roberts et al. (2005) have framed these efforts to consider assessment of competence as a shift away from the traditional practice of educators and regulators who viewed competence as merely the accumulation of graduate credits or hours of supervised experience. Kaslow, et al. (2009) provide a comprehensive review of a range of competency assessment methods for professional psychology, including using standardized patients, portfolios, structured rating systems, consumer satisfaction surveys, and other tools. They also discuss the methodological strengths and weaknesses of each method for assessing the practice competence of professional psychologists. Rodolfa, Schaffer, and Webb (2010) argue that the "culture of competence must be paired with the culture of competence assessment" (p. 296). DeMers & Schaffer (2012) suggest that if some reliable and valid methods to assess practitioner competence can be developed and adopted across the training sequence leading to licensure, then regulatory bodies may be able to incorporate these new strategies of assessment in determining eligibility for licensure. (Wise, 2010). In addition, adoption of a defensible system of competency assessment by licensing boards could then create an environment in which the EPPP may be given earlier in the sequence of training (e.g., at completion of coursework) followed by administration of these new competency assessment examinations upon completion of all required supervised experience (DeMers, 2009). Wise (2010) has also suggested that assessment of competency could bolster efforts to improve ongoing assessment of continuing professional competence at the time of licensure renewal.

The increased interest in developing new methods to assess competence should not mislead one to assume that there are no means of assessing professional competence currently in place. At present, most academic training programs and licensing boards rely on ratings of trainees completed by practicum, internship, and postdoctoral residency supervisors (ASPPB, 2012a; DeMers, 2009). It is appropriate that supervisor ratings serve as one important measure of competence, because supervisors often directly observe the behaviors of students in the practice setting.

However, there are also problems with relying on supervisors' evaluations. Both supervisors and faculty are in dual roles with students that can be problematic for the objectivity of the evaluation (Johnson et al., 2008). Faculty and supervisors have a vested interest in the success of their students, because outcomes, such as licensure rates and the attainment of employment, reflect on the training the student received. As a result, graduate programs and supervisors may have incentives to evaluate students positively, even if they exhibit inadequate competence (Johnson et al, 2008). Clearly then, more objective and valid measures of competence are needed (Fouad et al, 2009; Kaslow et al, 2009). Likewise it would be useful for regulators to understand the process of supervisor evaluation, including whatever training supervisors have received to insure that the evaluations are both reliable and valid. It may be that the education and training community will need to develop methods for supervisor training that promote reliability and validity so that regulators can rely more consistently on the supervisor evaluations they receive.

The upshot is, then, that there is no consistently applied standard of education, supervised experience or examination that is uniform across the United States or Canada. Although the major professional associations like APA, CPA and ASPPB certainly exert considerable influence over members of the profession who serve on licensing boards, the ultimate decisions about setting the educational, supervised experience or examination standards often rest with the legislative body (e.g. state or provincial government) that created and oversees the psychology regulatory board (DeMers & Schaffer, 2012; Retfalvi & Simon, 1996; Wand, 1993). Regulatory boards have the authority and duty to

suggest changes in the standards they use, but any party can seek to amend the standards. The final decision about changes to these standards is typically made by a political entity, such as a state legislature or provincial ministry, and is subject to the political forces at work in any locality.

For example, the Canadian government adopted an Agreement on Internal Trade in 1995 that required all trades and professions with certified or licensed practitioners to remove any "unjustified" barriers to labor mobility within Canada. Given the diversity of education requirements for psychology, licensure across the provinces, psychology regulatory boards, or colleges as they are commonly known, worked together to develop a mutual recognition agreement based on attainment of a set of prescribed competencies rather than academic degrees. However, the issue of who may use the title "psychologist" in provinces that formerly restricted that title to individuals with doctoral degrees has remained controversial. In 2009, the provincial ministers in Canada amended the 1995 Agreement in a way that has the potential to require all provinces to award the title "psychologist" to any individual so credentialed in another province regardless of academic degree.

Such diverse and fluctuating requirements for entry into the profession of psychology, both within and across jurisdictions, have resulted in great hardship for licensed psychologists who seek to relocate. They may find that differences in licensing laws across jurisdictions make them suddenly unacceptable for licensure in a new jurisdiction (DeMers, Van Horne & Rodolfa, 2008). This same patchwork quilt of licensure standards in psychology has seemed to confuse the public about the training that psychologists receive prior to being credentialed to practice, or indeed, who or what psychologists are (DeMers & Schaffer, 2012). As previously mentioned, one of the long-standing missions of ASPPB has been to bring greater uniformity across jurisdictions in the standards for licensure so that the public is less confused, and so that practitioners can move more freely across jurisdictions without fear of being denied a license in the new jurisdiction simply because of idiosyncrasies in jurisdictions' licensing laws (DeMers, Van Horne, & Rodolfa, 2008).

Investigating Complaints

Another major activity undertaken by psychology regulatory boards to fulfill their mission is investigating complaints of incompetent or unethical practice made against currently licensed practitioners. Each psychology licensing act specifies the grounds for which someone licensed as a psychologist may be disciplined, and the process by which such a charge is to be investigated and adjudicated (DeMers & Schaffer, 2011; Reaves, 1996).

Because a license to practice one's profession is clearly a property right of some value and consequence, a governmentally sanctioned process to deny, restrict, or rescind such a license must be conducted with adequate attention to the individual's rights of due process and appeal (DeMers & Schaffer, 2012). In the United States, most psychology licensing boards operate within the legal realm of administrative law and the process must comply with the Administrative Procedures Act that governs such action by the state (Stromberg et al., 1988). In Canada, the regulatory bodies operate according to a set of rules or governing bylaws that are typically submitted to the provincial government for approval.

According to Stromberg et al. (1988), most state and provincial laws provide some form of the following due process rights: adequate notice of the charges, right to a fair and impartial hearing, an opportunity to present evidence and confront witnesses, a decision based solely on the evidence, a record of the proceedings, and a process for appealing the decision. Similar legal protections and processes exist in federal and provincial law in Canada (Reaves, 1996).

Although some complaints are dismissed and others are settled through a negotiated agreement of stipulated conditions of remedy (e.g., mandatory supervision, additional training in ethics), complaints involving charges of significant misconduct or those charges that are contested are resolved through a hearing process. Before a hearing is scheduled, most jurisdictions in the United States and Canada require that the psychology board must have received a signed, written complaint, conducted an initial investigation of the merits of the charges, notified the psychologist of the specific charges, identified witnesses and subpoenaed documents, and taken any necessary depositions. The hearing itself is conducted in a variety of formats across jurisdictions depending on local law and the resources available to the regulatory board. In some jurisdictions the hearing is conducted before the regulatory board with the board serving as a panel of inquiry and a decision-making body. In other situations, regulatory boards are assisted in this process by hearing officers, who rule on motions and arbitrate disputes. In still other arrangements, a hearing officer alone hears cases, and recommendations

and transcripts of the proceedings are made available to the board, which later renders its decision. Following an adverse decision, a psychologist may appeal to a separate legal tribunal (e.g., a circuit court in a state) if he or she believes there had not been a fair and impartial hearing of the complaint.

As a result of the hearing, the regulatory board issues its findings of fact and conclusions of law; that is, its findings of what it believes happened and whether such facts constitute a violation of the licensing law. Where a violation is found, the regulatory board may impose an appropriate sanction ranging from a reprimand to a permanent revocation of one's license to practice. Other common sanctions imposed, either alone or in combination, include suspension of the license for a certain time, restriction in the type of clients or problem areas addressed, a return to supervised practice, additional training or education, therapy, restitution of assets, reimbursement of fees, and administrative fines (Reaves, 1996).

Despite the common misperception among licensed psychologists that complaints are rampant (Williams, 2001), a survey of all licensing boards conducted by Van Horne (2004) found that the number of complaints filed against psychologists was relatively low. Van Horne reported that the number of complaints reported to ASPPB equaled only 2% of the number of all licensees in each year from 1996 to 2001 when these numbers were averaged across all jurisdictions reporting. Van Horne cautions that this should not be interpreted as 2% of all licensed psychologists receive complaints each year, since some individuals receive multiple complaints, some individuals hold licenses in multiple jurisdictions, and one complaint can be acted upon by more than one jurisdiction.

Since 1983, ASPPB has maintained a Disciplinary Data System (DDS) that collects and disseminates summaries of disciplinary actions from its member psychology regulatory boards throughout the United States and Canada. Until 1996, the summary reports of disciplinary actions were disseminated in printed form, first annually and then quarterly, as the number of reports grew. Beginning in 1996, the ASPPB Disciplinary Data System was placed online whereby jurisdictions could report and retrieve information about disciplinary actions against a specific individual via a secure searchable database, giving regulatory boards immediate and timely access to all disciplinary actions contained in the system.

The consequences of being found in violation of a psychology licensing act are not limited to the sanctions imposed by the regulatory board. Reports from the DDS are routinely distributed to other relevant psychology credentialing or professional associations, as well as to all regulatory boards (DeMers & Schaffer, 2012). The current distribution list of the ASPPB Disciplinary Data System includes the ethics committees of the APA and the CPA, the American Board of Professional Psychology (ABPP), the National and Canadian Registers of Health Service Providers in Psychology, and the U.S. Department of Health and Human Services National Practitioner Data Bank. Given recent government initiatives, media attention and consumer activism, it is quite possible that information from the DDS soon may be made available to the general public through the ASPPB website as a means for helping boards to discharge their responsibility to protect the public using modern methods of information dissemination.

As a result of such broad distribution, individuals sanctioned by their home jurisdiction may find sanctions imposed by other regulatory boards where they hold additional licenses, by professional association ethics committees, by other credentialing bodies like ABPP, or even by insurance companies and managed health-care providers.

Since psychology regulatory boards are composed of psychologist as well as public members, many psychologists notified of charges lodged against them expect or hope to receive "friendly" treatment from their psychologist peers on the board. However, psychologists serving on regulatory boards learn and understand that the role entrusted to them by the legislative act creating the board of psychology requires them to protect the public and not show blind allegiance to the profession. Furthermore, the rules established to protect the rights of psychologists who are accused of violations necessitates a formal and complete investigation of all complaints, making informal resolution unlikely. However, since boards of psychology typically decide the issues raised in a complaint, a psychologist unjustly accused can be assured that the panel of individuals who will decide the merits of the complaint is likely composed of other psychologists who will understand the conduct of the professional probably better than the average citizen who serves on a civil or criminal jury panel.

Current and Future Issues

Like any profession, psychology is constantly progressing in its science and practice. Although such innovations demonstrate that psychology is an evolving discipline, such professional evolution often presents a number of challenges to psychology regulatory mechanisms that were established at an earlier stage in the development of the profession. Although there are many regulatory challenges, we will focus on two topics of particular relevance to the education and training community, namely, the lack of consistency across jurisdictions in the educational and training standards required to call oneself a psychologist and to practice independently, and the need to develop effective methods to regulate new models of service delivery.

Education and Training Standards for Independent Practice

Since the Boulder Conference in 1949 (Raimy, 1950), organized psychology in the United States has espoused the doctoral degree as the entry level for independent practice in psychology. Most licensing laws for psychology passed in the United States and Canada have required this standard since Connecticut first law adopted it as the required level of training for independent practice (Retfalvi & Simon, 1996). As noted earlier, a handful of states and provinces adopted a master's degree standard rather than the doctorate, sometimes due to the lack of availability of doctoral level psychologists to fill positions; sometimes due to political forces at work; and sometimes due to concerns about cost, access to care in rural areas or other factors. Many colleges and universities continued to prepare individuals at the master's degree level and many early licensing laws contained exemptions from the doctoral standard for state and local government, allowing publicly funded mental health agencies to employ individuals who did not meet the educational requirements for independent practice in that jurisdiction. Also, departments of education in the United States began credentialing school psychologists for practice in the nation's public schools, and most of these state departments of education adopted a nondoctoral educational standard for independent practice as school psychologists (Fagan & Wise, 2007). All these factors created a situation in which controversy was likely to emerge over the standard for independent practice in psychology.

Such controversy has emerged in several different ways. Exemption from licensure requirements for publicly employed psychologists has been challenged by patient advocates and by professional associations resulting in the virtual elimination of such exemptions. Individuals with master's degrees credentialed as psychological associates and working under mandatory supervision in jurisdictions allowing for such practice are now seeking to extricate themselves from the supervision requirement by changing psychology licensing laws to allow independent practice with a master's degree or by seeking licensure in another mental health profession that does not require the doctorate for independent practice. In a few U.S. states, school psychologists with nondoctoral credentials from state departments of education have sought and obtained the right to practice independently outside the purview of the public school system. In Canada, although some provinces have replaced a previous master's degree standard for independent practice with a new doctoral standard, the federal initiative to promote labor mobility has resulted in provinces with a doctoral standard being required to allow some form of independent practice for individuals trained to the master's degree level.

Consequently, unlike medicine and law, the profession of psychology in the United States and Canada has never successfully advanced a universally accepted standard of educational preparation for its practitioners. The APA and CPA have promulgated standards of accreditation of training programs that adhere to the doctoral standard (APA, 2009). For many years, APA and ASPPB have disseminated model licensure acts for psychology in an attempt to promote greater consistency in licensing laws across the country. Despite these efforts, inconsistencies in standards remain. Recently, several emerging sources of divergence appear to further compromise professional coherence and mobility.

The increased use of online delivery of graduate education courses, and even entire degree programs, has raised the question of whether physical presence within a training environment is a necessary condition for professional preparation in psychology. The rapid expansion of online or distance education training programs requires educators to redefine quality assurance measures and requires regulators to determine the appropriate use of online instruction in professional preparation (DeMers et al., 2008). Recognizing the diversity of web-based instruction and its constant evolution, regulations specifying educational requirements for psychology licensure in terms of distance education seem challenging at best (Murphy, Levant, Hall, & Glueckauf, 2007).

This movement away from reliance on a physical campus to a virtual campus where students are linked via the Internet with professors, other students, and the resources necessary for learning, presents huge benefits in terms of greater access to instruction; but this instructional approach also leads to questions about on-campus residency requirements. The *APA Accreditation Guidelines and Principles* (Section A.4.) requires of each student "a minimum of 3 full-time academic years of graduate study—at least 2 of which must be at the institution from which the doctoral degree is granted and at least 1 year of which must be in full-time residence or the equivalent thereof" (APA, 2012). One of the stated purposes of the one-year, full-time minimum residence requirement is to permit faculty, training staff, supervisors, and administrators to assess student competence. Given growing concerns about lack of communication between practicum supervisors, internship sites and graduate programs, offering greater flexibility in meeting residency requirements could call into question the integrity of doctoral training (Johnson, et al, 2008). Another challenge for accreditation panels as well as regulators is the likelihood that transcripts do not necessarily accurately or completely reflect either the manner or quality of instruction, thus making review of credentials more difficult.

Most psychology licensing laws never anticipated completion of a doctoral degree in psychology without regular direct physical contact for a sustained period of time with program faculty and a training cohort. Consequently some states are revising their licensure laws to define residency requirements in such a way as to require some minimal period of time (typically at least one year) of physical presence on the regionally accredited campus awarding the doctoral degree. The *ASPPB Model Act for Licensure and Registration of Psychologists* (ASPPB, 2010) includes such a requirement and a definition of residency. The APA Commission on Accreditation has issued an implementing regulation (APA, 2012) that also describes the goal and desired outcomes that come from physical presence on campus. This accreditation regulation also states that programs that are predominately or substantially delivered online are not in compliance with its residency standard.

Telepractice

Today, many licensed psychologists and other providers of mental health services are either providing or are considering providing psychological services across jurisdictional boundaries due to client mobility, their own mobility, or innovative practice opportunities. Such practice across jurisdictional boundaries involving use of the Internet or other electronic communication methods presents unique challenges as yet unaddressed by most psychology licensing laws (APAPO, 2010). Most current psychology licensing laws presume that psychological services are delivered in a particular jurisdiction by an individual who is licensed to practice in that jurisdiction. What happens to professional regulation when psychological services are delivered to clients via the Web or other telecommunications systems across state, provincial, or even national boundaries? If a client feels harmed, to whom do they complain: the board of psychology where they reside, which may have no jurisdiction over an out-of-jurisdiction provider, or the jurisdiction where the provider resides, which may feel the activity did not occur in that jurisdiction?

Beyond the significant complexities and legalities of filing complaints, the use of technology to deliver psychological services raises new questions about the limits of what constitutes acceptable practice in this medium (Reed, McLaughlin, & Milholland, 2000). Although one can easily think of examples of national or international experts who could and should be available for consultation about rare or specialized cases or topics (Glueckauf, Pickett, Ketterman, Loomis & Rozensky, 2003), should more routine psychotherapy be conducted using online messaging platforms or Web-based communications vehicles for the convenience or benefit of the practitioner or the client? In the absence of any system of national or international licensing, the regulation of psychological services delivered via electronic means is tenuous at best, and perhaps nonexistent (DeMers & Schaffer, 2012).

Nevertheless, the use of telecommunications and information technology to provide access to health assessment, diagnosis, intervention, and information across distance is a reality (Maheu & Gordon, 2000). Whether called telepractice or telepsychology, such use of innovative service delivery methods generally does not refer to occasional phone conversations or emergency phone contacts with an ongoing client with whom one has regular meetings. Instead, the controversy focuses on using telepractice as the primary or even sole means of delivering services, or the issue of frequently using electronically based media such as the Internet for clinical communications with clients or patients.

The reality of telepractice is that a psychologist can provide services without physically entering another jurisdiction and possibly without knowing the actual location of the consumer receiving services (Reed, McLaughlin, & Milholland, 2000). Such innovations in service provision challenge traditional regulatory mechanisms and thus require creative approaches to consumer protection (APAPO, 2010).

Although this rapidly evolving method of professional practice raises significant risks to consumers from misconduct, security breaches or the inability to deal effectively with emergency situations, it also allows for significant improvements in access to care when delivered competently and appropriately. Licensing boards have no desire to impede the delivery of effective services, but the board does have a legal responsibility to ensure that these innovative service delivery methods are performed in a manner that protects the public from harm. In this developing area of practice, psychologists will need to be aware not only of their ethical, regulatory and legal obligations, but also about newly emerging standards of care for such practice (APAPO, 2010; Glueckauf et al., 2003).

A recent article from the APA Practice Organization (2010) raises a number of persistent questions, as yet mostly unanswered, with regard to the complexities of telepsychology practice. What part of the practice of psychology can be competently and ethically delivered via largely electronic means? Should the jurisdictional board where the psychologist is practicing, or the jurisdictional board where the client receives services, or both, regulate the practice? What records are kept, by whom, and for how long? How is accurate and secure identification of the client and the professional established? How will an emergency be handled? What are the limits of confidentiality? Will professional liability insurance cover practice across jurisdictional lines?

The questions are many for the education and training community, the practicing psychologist, and the licensing entity. The challenges of effectively regulating such electronic practice seem to be almost insurmountable without requiring licensure in every jurisdiction where services are being provided. However, requiring full licensure in every jurisdiction where a psychologist may have a temporary contact with a client seems unlikely to be an effective regulatory approach. New structures or systems that offer a means to better regulate temporary, electronic practice by a provider licensed in another jurisdiction seems like a more fruitful path to pursue. The profession, including the educators, trainers, accreditors, and the regulators will need to develop and then embrace these new structures, as well as consistent regulations for telepractice services, if practitioners can be reasonably expected to comply (DeMers et al., 2008).

In 2011, APA, ASPPB and the APA Insurance Trust (APAIT) created a joint task force to develop guidelines for the practice of telepsychology. These guidelines have now been completed and approved by the three organizations supporting this task force. The guidelines address both the types of psychological services that can be ethically and competently delivered using these innovative technologies, and the regulatory issues created by providing services across jurisdictional boundaries. Now that these guidelines have been approved, training programs may need to offer specific instruction on "best practices" in using telepsychology approaches, and licensing laws will need to be changed to recognize any new rules or structures that offer better regulation of such service delivery models.

Conclusions

Credentialing and regulation of individuals to practice psychology in the United States and Canada is a complex and multifaceted process. It involves the interplay of professional associations, educators, and trainers, legislatively created regulatory bodies, state and provincial governments, and the public. The sole purpose for the passage and continuation of psychology licensing laws is to protect the public from incompetent or unethical practitioners. When the public (or at least their elected public representatives) loses confidence in the ability of the profession to regulate itself, then psychology licensing laws are either modified or rescinded. Although it may be tempting for the profession to feel that it knows best how to regulate the practice of psychology, the profession must be mindful to educate the public about the reasons underlying its preferred standards and policies or risk having them rejected by those representing the public's interests. It is imperative that the education and training and the regulatory communities routinely collaborate with each other in order to develop consistent standards for training psychologists and to put forth a unified view of what training and educational experiences are necessary to produce competent entry-level psychologists. That understanding can then be used by legislative bodies as they consider and hopefully adopt those standards endorsed by both the training and regulatory communities. Such consistency in standards not only promotes the licensure of competent and ethical practitioners and promotes easier professional mobility across jurisdictions; it also reinforces the public's view of psychology as a credible and unified profession.

As modern society changes through technological advances, marketplace forces, and government initiatives, it may be necessary to modify the standards and processes that have been created to both educate and regulate the profession of psychology to date. The United States and Canada have been world leaders in the development of education and credentialing mechanisms and fair and impartial disciplinary proceedings for psychologists. Despite the challenges outlined earlier, hopefully that leadership can continue for the benefit of the consumers of psychological services and the profession itself.

References

American Educational Research Association (AERA), American Psychological Association (APA) and National Council on Measurement in Education (NCME). (1999). *Standards for educational and psychological testing.* Washington, DC: American Psychological Association.

American Psychological Association. (2009). *Guidelines and principles for accreditation of programs in professional psychology.* Washington, DC: APA. Retrieved from http://www.apa.org/ed/accreditation/about on 1/18/10.

American Psychological Association. (2011). Model act of state licensure of psychologists. *American Psychologist, 66,* 214– 226. doi: 10.1037/a0022655

American Psychological Association. (2012). Implementing Regulation C–27. Retrieved from http://search.apa.org/search?query=residency on October 13, 2012.

American Psychological Association Practice Organization. (Summer, 2010). Telehealth: Legal basics for psychologists. Good Practice. Washington, DC: APAPO. 2–7.

Association of State and Provincial Psychology Boards. (2005). *ASPPB code of conduct.* Retrieved from http://www.asppb.net/i4a/pages/index.cfm?pageid=3353 on October 22, 2012.

Association of State and Provincial Psychology Boards. (2009). *ASPPB Guidelines for Practicum Training Leading to Licensure.* Retrieved from http://www.asppb.net/i4a/pages/index.cfm?pageid=3473 on September 15, 2012.

Association of State and Provincial Psychology Boards. (2010). *ASPPB Model Act for Licensure and Registration of Psychologists.* Retrieved from http://www.asppb.net/i4a/pages/index.cfm?pageid=3352 on September 15, 2012.

Association of State and Provincial Psychology Boards. (2012a). *Handbook of licensure and certification requirements in the United States and Canada.* Retrieved from http://www.asppb.org/HandbookPublic/before on October 3, 2012.

Association of State and Provincial Psychology Boards. (2012b). *The purpose of licensure and certification.* Retrieved from http://www.asppb.net/i4a/pages/index.cfm?pageid=3390, on October 23, 2012.

Carlson, H. (1978). The ASPPB story: The beginnings and first 16 Years of the American Association of State Psychology Boards, 1961–1977. *American Psychologist, 33,* 486–495. doi: 10.1037/0003–066X.33.5.486

DeMers, S. T. (1998). Credentialing issues: Current and future in the U.S. and Canada. In A.S. Bellack & M. Hersen (Eds.) *Comprehensive Clinical Psychology.* New York: Pergamon. doi: 10.1016/B0080–4270(73)00273–X

DeMers, S. T. (2009). Understanding the purpose, strengths, and limitations of the EPPP: A response to Sharpless and Barber. *Professional Psychology: Research and Practice, 40,* 348–353. doi:10.1037/a0015750

DeMers, S. T. & Schaffer, J. (2012). The regulation of psychologists. *In* S. Knapp, M. Gottlieb, M. Handelsman, and L. VandeCreek (*Eds*) APA Handbook of Ethics in Psychology. Washington, *DC*: American Psychological Association Books.

Dent v. West Virginia, 129 U.S. 114, 9 St. Ct. 231 (1889).

DeMers, S. T., Van Horne, B. V., & Rodolfa, E. R. (2008). Changes in training and practice of psychologists: Current challenges for licensing boards. *Professional Psychology: Research and Practice*, *39*, 473–479. doi: 10.1037/0735–7028.39.5.47

Fagan, T. K. & Wise, P. S. (2007). *School psychology: Past, present and future* (3rd ed.). Bethesda, MD: NASP.

Ford, G. G. (2001). *Ethical reasoning in the mental health professions*. Boca Raton, FL: CRC Press.

Fouad, N. A., Grus, C. L., Hatcher, R. L., Kaslow, N. J., Hutchings, P. S., Madson, M. B.,…Crossman, R. E. (2009). Competency benchmarks: A model for understanding and measuring competence in professional psychology across training levels. *Training and Education in Professional Psychology*, *3*, S5–S26. doi: 10.1037/a0015832

Glueckauf, R. L., Pickett, T. C., Ketterson, T. U., Loomis, J. S., & Rozezensky, R. H. (2003). Preparation for the delivery of telehealth services: A self–study framework for expansion of practice. *Professional Psychology: Research and Practice*, *34*, 159–163. doi: 10.1037/0735–7028.34.2.159

Gross, S. J. (1978). The myth of professional licensing. *American Psychologist*, *11*, 1009–1016. doi: 10.1037/0003–066X.33.11.1009

Johnson, W. B., Elman, N. S., Forrest, L., Robiner, W. N., Rodolfa, E., & Schaffer, J. B. (2008). Addressing professional competence problems in trainees: Some ethical considerations. *Professional Psychology: Research and Practice*, *39*, 589–599. doi: 10.1037/a0014264

Kaslow, N. J., Grus, C. L., Campbell, L. F., Fouad, N. A., Hatcher, R. L., & Rodolfa, E. R. (2009). Competency assessment toolkit for professional psychology. *Training and Education in Professional Psychology*, *3*, S27–S45. doi: 10.1037/a0015833

Maheu, M. & Gordon, B. (2000). Counseling and therapy on the internet. *Professional Psychology: Research & Practice*, *31*, 484–489. doi: 10.1037/0735–7028.31.5.484

Merriam–Webster Dictionary On–Line (2012). *Definition of "profession"*. Retrieved from http://www.merriam-webster.com/dictionary/profession on September 6, 2012.

Murphy, M., Levant, R., Hall, J. & Glueckauf, R. (2007) Distance education in professional training in psychology. *Professional Psychology: Research & Practice*, *38*, 97–103. doi: 10.1037/0735–7028.38.1.97

Raimy, V. C. (1950). *Training in clinical psychology*. New York: Prentice Hall.

Reaves, R. P. (1996) Enforcement of codes of conduct by regulatory boards and professional associations. In L. J. Bass, S. T. DeMers, J. R. P. Ogloff, C. Peterson, J. Pettifor. R. P. Reaves, T. Retfalvi, N. P. Simon, C. Sinclair, & R. Tipton, *Professional conduct and discipline in psychology*. Washington, DC: American Psychological Association.

Reaves, R. (2004). *The history of licensure of psychologists in the United States and Canada*. Invited address presented at the Third International Congress on Licensure, Certification and Credentialing of Psychologists. Montreal, Canada. April, 2004.

Reed, G., McLaughlin, C., & Milholland, K. (2000). Ten interdisciplinary principles for professional practice in telehealth: Implications for psychology. *Professional Psychology: Research & Practice*, *31*, 170–178. doi: 10.1037/0735–7028.31.2.170

Rehm, L. P., & Lipkins, R. H. (2006). The Examination for Professional Practice in Psychology. In T. J. Vaughn (Ed.), *Psychology licensure and certification: What students need to know* (pp. 39–53). Washington, DC: American Psychological Association. doi: 10.1037/11477–004

Retfalvi, T. & Simon, N. P. (1996). Licensing, certification, registration, chartering and credentialing. In L. J. Bass, S. T. DeMers, J. R. P. Ogloff, C. Peterson, J. Pettifor. R. P. Reaves, T Retfalvi, N. P. Simon, C. Sinclair, & R. Tipton, *Professional conduct and discipline in psychology*. Washington, DC: American Psychological Association.

Roberts, M. C., Borden, K. A., Christiansen, M. D., & Lopez, S. J. (2005). Fostering a culture shift: Assessment of competence in the education and careers of professional psychologists. *Professional Psychology: Research and Practice*, *36*, 355–361. doi: 10.1037/0735–7028.36.4.355

Rodolfa, E., Schaffer, J., & Webb, C. (2010). Continuing education: The path to life–long competency? *Professional Psychology: Research and Practice*, *41*, 295–297.

Rosen, G. A., Reaves, R. P., & Hill, D. S. (1989). Reliability and validity of psychology licensing exams: Multiple roles and redundant steps in development and screening. *Professional Psychology: Research and Practice*, *20*, 272–274. doi: 10.1037/0735–7028.20.4.272

Schaffer, J., DeMers, S. T., & Rodolfa, E. (2011). Licensing and Credentialing. In J. Norcross, G. Vandenbos & D. Freedheim (Eds), *History of psychotherapy: Continuity and change* (2nd Ed.). Washington, DC: American Psychological Association. doi: 10.1037/12353–042

Schaffer, J. and Rodolfa, E. (2011). Intended and unintended consequences of state practicum licensure regulation. *Training and Education in Professional Psychology*, 5 (4), 222–228.

Sinclair, C., Simon, N. P. & Pettifor, J. (1996). History of ethical codes and licensure. In L. J. Bass, S. T. DeMers, J. R. P. Ogloff, C. Peterson, J. Pettifor. R. P. Reaves, T Retfalvi, N. P. Simon, C. Sinclair, & R. Tipton, *Professional conduct and discipline in psychology*. Washington, DC: American Psychological Association.

Stromberg, C., Haggarty, D., Mishkin, B., Leibenluft, R., Rubin, B., McMillian, M., & Trlling, H., (1988). *The psychologist's legal desk reference*. Washington, DC: National Register of health Service Providers in Psychology.

Van Horne, B. A. (2004). Psychology licensing board disciplinary actions: The realities. *Professional Psychology: Research and Practice*, *35*, 170–178.

Wand, B. (1993). The nature of regulation and entrance criteria. In K. Dobson & D. Dobson (Eds.), *Professional psychology in Canada*. Toronto, ON: Hoegrefe & Huber. doi: 10.1037/0735–7028.35.2.170

Weissman, H. N. (1984). Professional standards from the perspective of the sociology of professions. *Professional Psychology: Research and Practice*, *15*(4), 471–472. doi: 10.1037/0735–7028.15.4.471

Williams, M. H. (2001). The question of psychologists' maltreatment by state licensing boards: Overcoming denial and seeking remedies. *Professional Psychology: Research and Practice*, *32*, 341–344. *doi:* 10.1037/0735–7028.32.4.341

Wise, E. (2010). Maintaining and enhancing competence in professional psychology: Obsolescence, life long learning and continuing education. *Professional Psychology: Research and Practice*, *41*, 289–292.

Ten Trends in Lifelong Learning and Continuing Professional Development

Greg J. Neimeyer *and* Jennifer M. Taylor

Abstract

The contemporary commitment to competence in professional psychology occurs even as the field itself confronts considerable challenge and change. This chapter addresses key elements of those challenges and changes as they articulate with related developments in the field of continuing education and lifelong learning. Conceptual and empirical developments are forcing significant reconsideration and reformulation of the mechanisms of continuing professional development within and beyond professional psychology, and these are joined by renewed forces of accountability, increased specialization, and the profusion of new knowledge and emerging technologies. These and other developments are discussed in relation to 10 critical trends that currently confront the field of continuing professional development, each of which poses potential problems as well as prospects for the broader field of professional psychology and the probable future it faces.

Key Words: professional development, continuing education, lifelong learning

The field of professional psychology is experiencing seismic shifts in its foundations, with rumblings coming from all quarters. Renewed demands for professional accountability have registered an impact, as has the need for evidence-based practices, the rise of interprofessional training and collaborative care, the increase in specialization, and the rapid profusion of new knowledge and technologies, to say nothing of broader heath care reform. Each of these, and many other forces, has contributed to a continuously reconfigured landscape shaped by powerful forces both within and beyond the profession itself. While the reverberations can be traced to no single epicenter, a significant percentage of them converge upon the field's renewed commitment to professional competence. Ongoing professional competence requires a continuing commitment to lifelong learning and to the processes and practices that maximize it. This article addresses 10 contemporary trends in lifelong learning and continuing professional development that serve as visible outcroppings of the forces at work

within the field. These trends are neither mutually exclusive nor exhaustive of the full range of developments unfolding at this time. Nonetheless, they represent a set of critical forces in the reconfiguration of the field of professional psychology and the probable future that it faces.

1. Designating Continuing Education Activities

Although the principle purposes of continuing professional development (CPD) are commonly agreed upon (i.e., the maintenance of competence, the improvement of services, and the protection of the public; Wise et al., 2010), the mechanisms for accomplishing these objectives are not. The remarkably diverse and widely variable activities qualifying as CPD in different jurisdictions (Daniels & Walter, 2002; Webb & Horn, 2012) stand testament to the conceptual disconnect between the focused objectives of CPD on the one hand and the strikingly diffuse and poorly articulated activities that support those objectives on the other. Even a partial list provides a kaleidoscopic spectrum of activities, all ostensibly in the service of a common set of objectives. These CPD activities include publishing or presenting books or papers; listening to professional tapes or CDs; consulting with peers; sitting on professional boards; preparing or taking classes; developing or participating in professional workshops; attending talks, grand rounds, or conferences; conducting manuscript or book reviews; watching webcasts; completing self-assessments; undergoing advanced credentialing (e.g., board certification through the American Board of Professional Psychology [ABPP]); and completing formal continuing education (CE) programs, each of which is recognized by one or more boards as a creditable activity in support of license renewal.

On the face of it, this loosely federated cavalcade of diverse activities would seem to have little in common with one another and would seem to vary widely in relation to how much they might contribute either to ongoing professional competence or to public confidence. Surprisingly little work, either at conceptual or empirical levels, has been directed at this disconnect, leaving unexamined the assumption that these activities are equally effective and largely interchangeable mechanisms for maintaining professional competence. Recent work, however, has begun to focus attention on the extent to which the activities that comprise CPD contribute to, or fulfill, their stipulated objectives. This work has had conceptual as well as empirical expressions, both of which remain tentative and provisional.

At conceptual levels, Neimeyer, Taylor, and Cox (in press) have drawn attention to critical distinctions among various forms of CPD activities, arguing that not all CPD activities are equivalent and that some are likely to be superior to others in satisfying the stipulated objectives of CPD. Borrowing from Lichtenberg and Goodyear (2012), Neimeyer and colleagues (in press) distinguish among *formal* learning, *informal* learning, and *incidental learning* (see also Neimeyer, Taylor, Wear, & Linder-Crow, 2012). *Formal learning* provides a structured educational context with predetermined objectives against which the nature and extent of learning can be measured. The individual is placed in the express role of "student" with the declared objective of learning some stipulated material or skills. Formal learning is closely monitored or supervised and includes assessments of learning. And it is itself evaluated by the learners who provide feedback regarding the nature of their learning experience.

Formal learning occurs within a recognized institutional or organizational context that remains accountable for the integrity of the experience. The completion of a graduate course would be one example of this type of formal learning, as would the completion of a formal CE program or formal credentialing process.

The second form of CPD consists *of informal learning* activities. Informal learning also positions the learner in the role of "student," but the nature of the experience is more self-directed. Lacking formal learning objectives, informal learning is neither assessed nor supervised, but rather conducted independently by the learner who nonetheless participates in the activity for the purpose of learning. Informal learning ordinarily does not require the learner to reflect on or evaluate the nature of the learning experience. Informal learning lacks an institutional or organizational context to serve as an accountable agent to ensure the integrity of the learning experience. Listening to professional CDs or reading journal articles or professional books are examples of informal learning.

The third form of learning *is incidental learning*. Incidental learning consists of learning that occurs as an indirect byproduct of engaging in some professional activity. The primary purpose of the activity is not that learning, per se, so individuals participating in incidental learning are not positioning themselves in the role of a student. On the contrary, they are often the expert, as in the case of conducting manuscript reviews, sitting on boards, teaching courses, or presenting professional workshops. In each of these instances, the individual may accrue considerable new knowledge, but that is not the primary, or even an intended, outcome. In other words, the learning that occurs is incidental to the primary purpose of the activity. For that reason, incidental learning does not ordinarily involve supervision, does not include learning objectives or invite assessments of any sort, and does not invite reflection upon, or evaluation of, the learning experience. Nor does it occur within an accountable organization or institution tasked with monitoring or measuring any learning that occurs.

In addition to formal, informal, and incidental learning, Neimeyer and colleagues (in press) outline a fourth type of learning that is a more common component of education in European nations. This involves *non-formal* learning. Non-formal learning places the individual in the express role of a student, but the learning occurs outside of a recognized or accredited institutional or organizational context. It is similar to formal learning insofar as it is structured and organized, which distinguishes it from informal or incidental learning. But it lacks the institutional oversight or formal organization to verify, authorize, or credential the activity. Attending grand rounds, going to a professional conference, or participating in a departmental colloquium all serve as examples of non-formal learning.

Neimeyer and colleagues (in press) argue that the distinctions between formal, informal, incidental, and non-formal learning carry critical implications for the field of CPD in professional psychology precisely because they contribute differentially to fulfilling its objectives (see also Lichtenberg & Goodyear, 2012). In the current era of accountability and competence, they argue that formal forms of learning might offer distinctive advantages over the other three forms of learning and might better align the field of CPD with related competency and evidence-based movements on the contemporary landscape of professional psychology. Neimeyer and colleagues (in press) argue that four features of formal learning nominate themselves for particular distinction in this regard. These features include (1) the use of independent verification regarding the completion of the activity, (2) an independent assessment of learning, (3) the evaluation of the learning experience by the participant, and (4) organizational accountability for lapses in relation to the implementation, monitoring, or evaluation of the learning experience, according to some predetermined and publically accessible guidelines that govern that nature of the learning experience.

By limiting creditable CPD activities to instances of formal learning, Neimeyer and colleagues (in press) argue that the field of professional psychology would accrue three significant advantages. First, it would maximize the likelihood that CPD activities would contribute to the maintenance of competence because formal learning both targets and measures precisely such a goal. Formal CE workshops, accredited graduate classes, or competency-based credentialing processes (i.e., ABPP) are more likely to generate and document relevant learning and mastery than, say, the self-directed reading of journal articles (informal learning), sitting on psychology boards (incidental learning), or attending departmental job colloquia (non-formal learning).

Second, formal learning activities would be more likely to contribute to the public trust in the profession because they are the only form of learning that involve independent verification of the completion of those activities or organizational accountability in relation to them. Recent evidence to this effect can be found in Taylor and Neimeyer (2012b), where a survey of public perceptions regarding the value of a range of CPD activities found that the most highly valued CE activities in the eyes of the public were formal learning activities (e.g., becoming board certified and completing formal CE). In contrast, self-reported colloquium attendance, journal reading, conference attendance, and board participation were not viewed favorably and for that reason may not articulate ideally in an evidence-based world where verification and documentation may better fulfill the expectations for public accountability.

Third, Neimeyer and colleagues (in press) point out that only those formal types of learning offer the possibility for systematic improvement over time because only formal types of learning measure the learning that occurs and solicit feedback from participants that is designed to improve future educational efforts. There are no mechanisms in place in self-directed reading, departmental colloquium attendance, or board participation to measure the learning that has occurred or to reflect upon, critique, and subsequently improve, the educational processes associated with them. Therefore, Neimeyer and colleagues argue that only formal types of learning are likely to be able to support the future weight of the field's evidence-based aspirations and the public's renewed call for professional accountability.

Provisional work has begun to explore the extent to which different types of learning and CPD activities fulfill the stipulated objectives of CPD. In a survey of more than 1,600 licensed psychologists, Neimeyer and colleagues (in press) assessed the extent to which a variety of formal, informal, incidental, and non-formal forms of CPD were perceived as contributing to ongoing professional competence. Tellingly, across the range of 11 different CPD activities that they examined, the activities ranged widely in relation to the extent that they were perceived as contributing to ongoing professional competence. Overall, self-directed learning, peer consultation, and formal CE programs were viewed as the CPD activities that contributed most to continuing professional competence, whereas completing a graduate course, conducting outcome assessments with clients, and serving on professional boards were viewed as contributing the least. It is noteworthy that two of the top three CPD activities reflected informal types of learning (self-directed learning and peer consultation), underscoring Neimeyer and colleagues' observation that all forms of CPD activities (formal, informal, incidental, and non-formal) can result in significant new learning. Given this, in an evidence-based world, efforts should be made to convert these informal forms of learning into formal approaches. Self-directed learning can be converted into a formal learning experience, for example, by turning it into an independent study CE program, replete with learning objectives and an examination, and an evaluation of the learning experience. Likewise, peer consultation could become a regularly scheduled professional experience that could conform to the guidelines of formal CE, subjecting it to the forces of accountability without jeopardizing its educational value or its contributions to enhanced competency. The central point, however, is that in the absence of measurement and feedback, informal, incidental, and non-formal types of learning lack systematic mechanisms for improvement. As a result, they cannot profit from this recursive feedback process or demonstrate progressive improvement across time. To the extent that an evidence-based culture demands a continuing quest for excellence predicated on empirical data that inform and document this movement, only formal learning would seem to satisfy these criteria. As Neimeyer, Taylor, Wear, and colleagues (2012) note, as the field of professional psychology enters an evidence-based age of accountability, it may invite peril to assume that the outcomes associated with formal types of learning would necessarily extend to informal, incidental or non-formal types of CPD activities. On the contrary, the impact of self-directed reading (informal learning), sitting on professional boards (incidental learning), or attending departmental colloquia (non-formal learning) on improving clinical outcomes or protecting the public may lack not only empirical, but perhaps even conceptual, warrant. Formal types of learning may better provide stronger warrants in this regard. Only future research, however, will be able to determine the precise forms and types of CPD activities that might best fulfill their stipulated objectives. The continuing call for standardization of CPD activities, both within the field of professional psychology (Fagan, Ax, Liss, Resnick, & Moody, 2007) and beyond it (Institute on Medicine [IOM], 2010), assures that the nature of CPD activities is likely to continue to receive ongoing conceptual and empirical attention in the years ahead.

2. Mandating Continuing Education

While the activities that comprise CPD continue to receive attention, so too does the issue of mandating CE. In fact, in the past 40 years, formal CE for practicing psychotherapists has become an increasingly common requirement for license renewal (Neimeyer & Taylor, 2010). In 1975, only three states required CE, but by 1990, 19 states had adopted CE mandates. By 2003, 41 states had CE mandates, and currently 45 of the 51 United States (U.S.) licensing jurisdictions require CE for re-licensure, with others considering similar mandates of one form or another (Neimeyer & Taylor, 2010; Neimeyer et al., in press). However, states vary widely in the amount of CE that is mandated, the CE topics that are required in each state, and the types of professional development that count towards mandatory CE (See section 1 of this chapter, Designating Continuing Education Activities). Even policies on recordkeeping and enforcement of CE vary across states (see Adams & Sharkin, 2012).

While there are many variations with regard to state mandates for CE, there are also many reasons mandates were enacted. One of the earliest impetuses for mandatory CE was the public call for accountability and the demand for professionals to engage and document their ongoing lifelong learning (Hellkamp et al., 1989). While the relatively recent and rapid rise in mandated CE stands testament to the field's commitment to accountability, this commitment has done little to stem the debate that has raged for years regarding whether CE *should* be mandated. Indeed, the pros and cons of mandated CE have been one of the longest-standing and most conspicuous features of the landscape of professional psychology (see Adams & Sharkin, 2012; Sharkin & Plageman, 2003; Zemansky, 2012).

While research reporting resistance to mandatory CE dates back to the 1960s (see Ellsworth, 1968), mandatory CE is rising in popularity in many states (see Neimeyer & Taylor, 2010). Proponents of mandated CE point to research suggesting that, in the absence of mandates, a substantial minority of psychologists may engage in little or no formal CE activity (see Neimeyer, Taylor, & Wear, 2009; Neimeyer, Taylor, & Philip, 2010). Thus mandatory CE may encourage those who may otherwise become "CE minimalists" to participate in lifelong learning (Phillips, 1987), although some research presents conflicting findings (see Brown et al., 1982; Sharkin & Plageman, 2003).

Two studies have examined what changes occur after CE mandates are enacted. Brown and colleagues (1982) found that requiring CE increased participation in formal CE activity without decreasing participation in informal forms of CPD (e.g., colloquia, talks, reading). In addition, following the enactment of CE mandates, an increasing number of opportunities were available for CPD. Recent work by Neimeyer, Taylor, Zemansky, and Rothke (2012) examined participation patterns in CE among psychologist before and during the process of enacting CE mandates in Illinois. Neimeyer and colleagues found that awareness of the upcoming CE mandates was linked with greater participation in formal, but not informal, CE. Those who were aware of the impending mandates completed one third more CE credits, a finding that further supports the earlier findings of Neimeyer and colleagues (2009) and Neimeyer, Taylor, & Philip (2010).

While many states have moved towards mandated CE, several have experienced resistance. For example, although legislation for mandated CE in the state of New York was first proposed 40 years ago (Lewinsohn & Pearlman, 1972), psychologists in New York still do not have any requirements for CE participation. One reason for resistance to mandatory CE stems from the skepticism some experience over whether the benefits outweigh the potential burdens of mandatory CE. Those who oppose mandatory CE point to the cost and inconvenience of obtaining CE credits, question the quality and availability of relevant CE programs, and express concerns over the lack of clear, objective evidence that the knowledge gained from CE programs successfully translates into practice and improved client outcomes (see Melnyk et al., 2001; Zemansky, 2012).

Additionally, some psychologists oppose mandatory CE because they do not desire to engage in regulated lifelong learning activities and question whether a legal mandate is essential, in addition to the ethical mandates that already stipulate the importance of maintaining competence. Furthermore, an estimated 36% of psychologists report concerns about exposing their lack of knowledge and their apathy towards learning novel ideas (Allen, Nelson, & Sheckley, 1987; Zemansky, 2012), and these concerns may also contribute to a reluctance to embrace mandated CE.

Indeed, Neimeyer and colleagues (2009) and Neimeyer, Taylor, and Philip (2010) found evidence that the opponents of mandatory CE may be those who, in general, complete the lowest amount of CE voluntarily. In their study of 1,146 psychologists, those in the bottom quartile of CE completion demonstrated significantly higher opposition to CE mandates compared with their colleagues who participated in CE more regularly.

While the debate over the necessity of mandatory CE rages on, the vast majority of psychologists (75%–85%) support the idea of mandated CE (Fagan et al., 2007; Neimeyer et al., 2009; Sharkin & Plageman, 2003). This is true even within non-mandated jurisdictions (Neimeyer, Taylor, & Philip, 2010). And, although growing evidence clearly indicates the impact of CE mandates on levels of CE participation, only future efforts to document the impact of CE on new learning, professional competence, and improved service delivery will likely quell continuing concerns regarding mandating CE.

3. Measuring CE Outcomes

A comparison of the literatures on outcomes in psychotherapy and those in CE is instructive. The former field provides substantial, sustained, and sophisticated inquiry into a wide range of meaningful processes and outcomes that are central to the objectives of the practice. More than 40 years of meta-analytic psychotherapy research, for example, tease apart the relative contributions of a whole range of therapist and client characteristics, behaviors, and processes in relation to the reduction in distress, the restoration of function, and the maintenance of treatment gains across time (Norcross et al., 2010). The literature shows the kind of theoretical and methodological progression, and corresponding advances in knowledge that would be expected to follow from the enduring, collective efforts of multiple programs of research converging on issues that are central to their discipline.

By contrast, empirical studies in CE are scant rather than substantial, periodic rather than sustained, and elemental rather than sophisticated, both in their conceptual and methodological rigor (Neimeyer et al., 2009). Although the earliest empirical efforts in this field can be traced back nearly 40 years, the field reflects little theoretical or methodological progression, continuing to measure only the most trivial of its potential outcomes, such as descriptive accounts of participation rates. Research on CE in psychology offers no meta-analyses of outcomes nor, indeed, even any experimental studies (Daniels & Walter, 2002). If the field of psychotherapy research were reduced to the current level of knowledge and practices in the field of CE research, we would know little more than how many people participated in therapy and how satisfied they were with it. There would be no independent measures of effectiveness, no "hard" outcomes, and no attention whatsoever to the differential effectiveness of different therapists, clients, or treatments in relation to any designated outcome. In short, the field of psychotherapy research would be a sporadic, pre-experimental patchwork of survey research lacking in theoretical sophistication and methodological rigor.

Many factors account for the developmental arrest that has been experienced within the field of research in CE. The substantial misalignment of its measured outcomes in relation to its stipulated objectives looms large as one such factor. While formal CE is designed to maintain and enhance professional competence, to improve professional service delivery and outcomes, and to protect the public, these are not the outcomes most frequently assessed in research in this area. By contrast, the most frequently assessed outcomes typically include only the documentation of attendance at CE programs and ratings of participant satisfaction, with measures of perceived learning representing a more recent inclusion. Objective measures of learning are strikingly scarce in the literature, as are any efforts to trace the translation of new learning into practice or the outcomes that follow from this translation. In short, the overall balance of available outcome data continues to support the conclusion that there is "an inverse relationship between the strength of the outcomes utilized in the field of CE and the frequency with which these outcomes are utilized" (Neimeyer et al., 2009, p. 622). In other words, the weakest forms are the most common (e.g., attendance and satisfaction), while the strongest are the scarcest (e.g., objective learning or improved service delivery).

Notwithstanding the infancy of work in this area, its provisional results are encouraging. Psychologists complete an average of more than 22 formal CE credits per year, for example (Neimeyer, Taylor, & Philip, 2010; Wise et al., 2010), and substantial numbers complete significantly more than that (Neimeyer et al., 2009). To this is added all of the informal types of CPD, which amounts to scores (Neimeyer et al., in press) or even hundreds (Brown, Leichtman, Blass, & Fleisher, 1982) of additional hours each year. Recent work by Neimeyer and colleagues (in press), for example, found that the licensed psychologists in their nationwide sample reported completing an average of more than 23 hours of formal CE and an additional 135 hours of informal CE. The question that arises, though, concerns the outcomes that are associated with this participation. If *participation* in CE is robust, are its *outcomes* likewise robust?

The answer remains largely unknown because, surprisingly, the relevant questions have rarely been asked, and more rarely still, actually answered. Apart from participation in CE, per se, the most frequently studied outcome of CE in psychology is participant satisfaction (Neimeyer et al., 2009). A longstanding literature attests to participants' consistently favorable appraisals of their formal CE experiences (Neimeyer et al., 2009; Sharkin & Plageman, 2003). Neimeyer and colleagues (2009), for example, reported that approximately 80% of their respondents characterized the CE programs that they had completed as being good to excellent. It is noteworthy, however, that participant satisfaction reflects an evaluation of the CE program, and not of the participant, and for that reason does little to enhance consumer confidence and less still to document any learning outcomes (VandeCreek, Knapp, & Brace, 1990).

More useful assessments of CE outcomes can be found on the higher steps of a "hierarchy of CE outcomes" (Mazmanian et al., 2012; Neimeyer et al., in press). If participant attendance and satisfaction represent the lowest rungs on the ladder, then higher steps might measure actual levels of learning, the translation of that learning into practice, and the impact of that translation on actual service delivery and outcomes. Neimeyer and colleagues (2009) reported that nearly two thirds (64%) of their sample of psychologists reported high or very high levels of learning from their CE experiences, findings that are broadly consistent with the earlier findings of Sharkin and Plageman (2003). These findings are supported by the recent results of a randomized controlled trial of a CE program delivered online (Webber et al., 2012). This study assessed the levels of new learning associated with three different methods of online CE delivery, noting the significant knowledge gains associated with each condition based on objective posttest assessments.

Additionally, the translation of new knowledge into actual practice has been the subject of some attention, as measured through self-report and objective measures. In their survey of over 1,000 psychologists, for example, Neimeyer, Taylor, and Philip (2010) found that a substantial percent of them (63%) reported that their formal CE experiences frequently translated into their practices. These findings are consistent with the results of objective assessments of knowledge translation that have occurred within a broader group of professionals across the allied health fields (Young & Willie, 1984). In addition, it is increasingly clear that certain kinds of instructional methods can facilitate this translation (IOM, 2010). The inclusion of multiple media, multiple exposures, and the opportunity for practice and rehearsal with supervised feedback commonly enhance the translation of new learning into actual practice (IOM, 2010; see section 4 of this chapter, Best Practices in Continuing Education).

Although the translation of these behaviors into enhanced competence or service delivery outcomes is a highly desirable goal (Mazmanian et al., 2012), the field of professional psychology is just now beginning to approximate these objectives. In their survey of more than 6,000 licensed psychologists, Neimeyer and colleagues (2009) found that 81% of their respondents stated that their CE experiences over the previous year facilitated their clinical effectiveness. Very recent work has extended these findings by trying to identify the particular types of CPD activities that contribute most to ongoing professional competence. In their work on this topic, Neimeyer and colleagues (in press) found that the top three forms of CPD associated with self-reported perceptions of continuing competence were self-directed learning, peer consultation, and formal CE. Still, the correspondence between self-report data concerning the perceived effects of CE and the actual effects as demonstrated through independent, objective assessments remain largely unknown. Emerging work within the field of professional psychology is just now turning to address these questions by providing measures of objective assessment (Webber et al., 2012) and by encouraging the efforts to maximize the translation of this learning into actual practice contexts. Only by continuing to trace this process of translation and its impact of service delivery and outcomes will the field begin to complete the highest steps in the hierarchy of outcomes outlined by Mazmanian et al. (2012) and Neimeyer and colleagues (in press). And only when these efforts are situated within contexts of controlled experimental research will the field begin to gain ground in relation to other evidence-based research within the field of professional psychology.

4. Best Practices in Continuing Education

The measurement of outcomes in CPD serves to inform the field's understanding of best practices. The overall effectiveness of CE has been the subject of enduring debate. Historically, the methodological weakness of much published work in the area has limited the conclusions that could be drawn from it (Bertram & Brooks-Bertram, 1977). The absence of

reliable and valid outcome measures, inconsistency in relation to the nature of the outcomes assessed, and the absence of replication attempts all qualify the interpretability of available data in this area (Davis et al., 1999). More recent work, however, has begun to redress some of the methodological limitations of earlier work, adding rigor to this area of research. A close inspection of this work begins to shed light on the apparently contradictory conclusions that CE does not work in some contexts (e.g., Sibley et al., 1982) but does in others (Davis et al., 1995; Neimeyer et al., 2009).

In what represents one of the broadest systematic reviews of research in this area, the IOM (2010) published its recent *Redesigning Continuing Education in the Health Professions*, reviewing more than 18,000 articles related to CE, adult learning, and knowledge translation in the process. From this review, the institute identified a subset of relevant and rigorous research to include in its more detailed critical analysis. These included 62 studies and 20 systematic reviews and meta-analyses across a variety of health professions (IOM, 2010). Among these were 29 randomized controlled trials that assessed changes in clinical practice or practice-related outcomes. The review concluded by noting that, "Although CE research is fragmented and may focus too heavily on learning outside of clinical settings, there is evidence that CE works, in some cases, to improve clinical practice and patient outcomes" (p. 39).

Efforts to explore those cases in which CE does seem to work have helped to sculpt an image of "best practices" within the field. Although this image is provisional and still emerging, a convergence of findings has identified a variety of methods that are more "predisposed toward success" than others (Slotnick & Shershneva, 2002). These include interactive techniques, simulations, and e-learning opportunities, particularly when these learning activities include multiple exposures and utilize multiple different forms of instruction (Davis et al., 1995).

Interactive techniques, including methods such as audit/feedback and academic detailing, where third-party experts bring tailored treatment of relevant topics onsite to train providers, generally have demonstrated their effectiveness. And the same is true for interactive workshops that include elements of demonstration, discussion, skills rehearsal, and feedback (O'Brien et al., 2001). Simulations have been found to be effective, as well, at least in some instances (IOM, 2010). The evaluation of simulations is made more difficult by their intrinsic diversity, ranging from low-fidelity simulations (e.g., case discussions) to high-fidelity simulations (e.g., standardized patients). Simulations are designed to assist in the transfer of knowledge to clinical practice, moving beyond declarative knowledge to actual performance.

E-learning offers a range of learning experiences that can include many elements that contribute to effective learning comprehension and knowledge transfer and application (IOM, 2010). This includes increasing interactivity and feedback, providing the opportunity to extend the number of exposures to the material, and the utilization of multiple media.

An illustration of this can be found in the work of Webber and colleagues (2012; cited in Neimeyer, Taylor, Wear, et al., 2012). In their randomized controlled trial of Web-based CE, objective assessments revealed that participants in audio-visual, audio-only, and text-only learning conditions all demonstrated significant, but not equivalent, learning. Those in the audio-only condition showed substantially lower levels of learning while the highest levels of learning were associated with the audio-visual condition, again underscoring the potential value of utilizing multiple media.

In concluding their assessment of the broader field of CE, the IOM (2010) identifies five factors associated with more effective CE activities. These include programs that (1) incorporate needs assessments to ensure the relevance of the material to the needs of the learners, (2) include interactivity (e.g., group reflection, rehearsal opportunities), (3) employ feedback to engage participants in the learning process, (4) use multiple methods of instruction and allow adequate time to process the content, and (5) simulate the actual clinical setting.

In contrast to these "best practices," didactic presentations consistently have been shown to be relatively ineffective in relation to knowledge retention and transfer (O'Brien et al., 2001), if not in knowledge acquisition (Dunning et al., 2004), as has the use of print media such as brochures or self-study posters. Didactic methods of instruction, however, predominate within psychology (Shern, 2010; Wise et al., 2010), as they do in other allied health fields, where as much as 90% of the creditable CE programs are provided in didactic formats (IOM, 2010). Shern (2010) wryly depicted these didactic presentations as representing a "Spray and Pray" technique, where the presenter "sprays" out information to a legion of listeners and "prays" that some of it sticks. As Dunning and colleagues

(2004) note, however, such mass learning has long been associated with rapid knowledge losses, as well as gains, compared with more distributed forms of learning that facilitate better retention and knowledge transfer. In order to conform to best practices in relation to adult learning, continuing professional education needs to orchestrate the use of a range of different methods that converge on common elements of adult learning, such as experiential learning, reflection, and problem-based learning strategies. As the IOM (2010) concludes, there is evidence that "health professionals often need multiple learning opportunities and multiple methods of education, such as practicing self-reflection in the workplace, reading journal articles that report new clinical evidence, and participating in formal CE lectures, if they are to most effectively change their performance and, in turn, improve patient outcomes" (p. 47).

5. Conceptualizing and Assessing Competence

While multiple methods of learning provide opportunities to enhance professional competence, it is equally important to both understand and evaluate what it means to be professionally competent. The call to address and define competencies in the field of psychology dates back more than 70 years and has continued as a recurrent theme in the development of the professional across time. As early as 1941, Hunter wrote an article in the *Psychological Review* urging the psychological community to examine competence as a crucial component of the selection of graduate students and the field's professional responsibility. Later, in 1947, a proposal was published for a code of ethics for professional psychologists. In that proposal, the first responsibility of professional psychologists focused on the importance of providing the public with a high level of competence in professional services (see *American Psychologist*, 1947). When the APA Code of Ethics was formally recognized in 1959, its second principle emphasized the psychologist's responsibility both to the public and to the profession to practice with competence. Since that time, the "call to competence" has gained progressively greater attention, with substantial gains occurring in relation to defining, conceptualizing, and operationalizing aspects of competence (Fouad et al., 2009; Kaslow et al., 2004; Rodolfa, Schaffer, & Webb, 2010).

A significant step toward defining professional competencies occurred in 1986. The National Council of Schools and Programs in Professional

Psychology (NCSPP) identified six core professional competency areas (relationship, assessment, intervention, research and evaluation, consultation, and management or supervision competencies). The NCSPP noted that each competency includes knowledge, skills, and attitudes that are required for professional practice.

Building on this model, the American Psychological Association's Committee on Accreditation (CoA) used this model when it modified its Guidelines and Principles for Accreditation in 1996. A few years later, at the 2002 Competencies Conference: Future Directions in Education and Credentialing, more than 130 psychologists with diverse perspectives and occupations in the field expanded on the NCSPP's core competencies (Kaslow et al., 2004). This led to the development of a model that distinguished between foundational and functional competencies and that identified the level of competency that should be attained by the time a psychologist reached three critical junctures: during practicum training, during the pre-doctoral internship, and at the point of licensure for independent practice. This model was termed the "Cube Model" (see Rodolfa et al., 2005). Foundational competencies are described as the knowledge, skills, and attitudes critical to the field of professional psychology that create the basis for professional functioning (e.g., scientific-mindedness, relationship skills competency). Functional competencies are described as the capabilities to carry out the functions and roles of a professional psychologist (e.g., assessment, intervention competency).

In order to further clarify and define professional competencies at each phase of professional development, the Council of Chairs of Training Councils and the APA Board of Educational Affairs convened at the 2007 Tempe Summit and developed several competency benchmarks (e.g., behavioral markers) that are fundamental for each competency domain. The Competency Benchmarks Work Group then built upon the Cube Model, further defining the twelve competencies in greater detail and stipulating three additional competencies (professionalism, advocacy, and teaching) (Fouad et al., 2009). Those competencies were subsequently subjected to further conceptual (E. Rodolfa, personal communication, July 17, 2012) and empirical scrutiny (Taylor & Neimeyer, 2012a), resulting in a revision, reclustering, and reduction in the number of competencies that nonetheless preserved the distinction between foundational and functional competencies. Exploratory and confirmatory factor analytic work

has introduced a third distinction, as well, identified as "continuing competencies" that address aspects of lifelong learning (Taylor & Neimeyer, 2012a).

Even as the field converges upon a common conceptualization of professional competence, it lacks widely accepted, psychometrically sound, and easily accessible methods of measuring it. Currently, professional competencies are not routinely assessed throughout the professional career, as the public generally assumes (see Wise et al., 2010). Instead, competencies are demonstrated only indirectly and periodically though the absence of complaints being lodged against a psychologist, through self-reflection, and through ethical stipulations that psychologists should practice only in areas in which they are competent (Rubin et al., 2007). In addition, psychologists may elect to undergo board certification in one or more areas of identified specialization. The American Board of Professional Psychology recognizes 14 areas of specialization, each with its own mechanisms for competency-based examination and review prior to awarding board certification in that area. Approximately 4% of professional psychologists are board certified in one or more areas at this time (Neimeyer, Taylor, Wear, et al., 2012). Beyond that, the only requirements to demonstrate ongoing professional development follow from legal mandates to participate in CE as a precondition of license renewal (Rodolfa et al., 2010). The requirements for CE, however, are not competency based and are currently neither uniform nor universal across various licensing jurisdictions in the United States (see section 2 of this chapter, Mandating Continuing Education).

As the conceptualization of foundational and functional competencies continues to take shape, so has the expressed need within the field to identify or develop adequate forms of assessment to accompany these conceptual advances (see Kaslow et al., 2009). As Rodolfa and colleagues (2010) note, "It seems to us that in the current 'culture of competence'(Roberts, Borden, Christiansen, & Lopez, 2005) providing a means of assessing ongoing competence ranks in importance with providing a means for maintaining competence. Thus, the culture of competence must be paired with the 'culture of competence assessment'" (p. 296).

Building on this need, Taylor and Neimeyer (2012a) developed the Professional Competencies Scale (PCS), an assessment that follows a conceptual framework that recognizes foundational, functional, and continuing competencies. In creating the PCS, Taylor and Neimeyer translated the benchmarks for each professional competency outlined in Fouad and colleagues (2009) into items to form the scale, preserving the distinction between foundational and functional competencies and adding a third domain of continuing competencies to reflect the need for ongoing professional lifelong learning. These competencies include a broad range of dimensions, from personal (e.g., self-care) to systemic considerations (e.g., interdisciplinary systems). The results of a series of exploratory and confirmatory factor analyses resulted in a revised and shortened version of the PCS (PCS-R) that demonstrated excellent fit with the three competency domains (foundational, functional, and continuing competencies), each with strong reliabilities and moderate-to-strong indicators of concurrent and predictive validity. Instruments such as this may bring a measure of rigor and relevance to the assessment of professional competency in a way that is useful for gauging the development, maintenance, and enhancement of competence across the professional lifespan. As professional psychology embraces the "culture of competence" (Roberts et al., 2005), the field is likely to continue to embrace and demand a variety of assessment tools that can provide valid and accessible measures of competence in a way that articulates with prevailing conceptualizations of the construct. The availability of such instruments would contribute importantly to the efforts to document and develop continuing professional competencies in the in the years ahead.

6. Understanding the Intersection Between Personal and Professional Life

In understanding and assessing competence, it is crucial to also understand how a professional's personal life may affect his or her professional competence. Self-care is critical to ethical practice and professional competence (Wise et al., 2010). There is a growing realization that engagement in self-care and stress management, or lack of such, can affect clinical effectiveness. In fact, some research suggests that self-care may be even more important on average for psychologists than for the public because psychologists have been noted in research to suffer the highest rates of suicide among a wide range of other professions (Ukens, 1995).

Other studies support the fact that psychologists are susceptible to distress (Taylor & Neimeyer, 2012a; Wise et al., 2010). Many psychologists have experienced childhood trauma, including physical and sexual abuse (see Pope & Tabachnick, 1994). In addition, more than half of psychologists report

feeling overworked or burnt out, nearly half report experiencing relationship issues and depression, 10% report suicide ideation or attempts, and 7% report issues of substance abuse, levels that routinely exceed those of their professional colleagues in other areas (Brodie & Robinson, 1991; see also Rupert, Stevanovic & Hunley, 2009; Wood et al., 1985). In fact, substance abuse has been reported as common enough to merit action by nearly every licensing board, and professional impairment has been reported among 5% to 15% of psychologists (Laliotis & Grayson, 1985; see also Good, Thoreson, & Shaughnessy, 1995 and Smith, Moss, & Burton, 2009).

Research demonstrates that psychological distress can affect professional competence. In fact, several researchers have conceptualized professional development and competence as including a range of personal qualities, including interpersonal relationship skills, positive personality traits and attitudes, self-care, and self-awareness (e.g., Wise, 2008).

In addition, psychologists are prone to what researchers call "compassion fatigue," or the result of burnout due to the constant "caring cycle," which occurs through the repeated stages of empathy, client attachment, and the end of the therapeutic relationship (Figley, 1995). This process can leave psychologists feeling depleted. Work-family conflict has also been found to be related to greater levels of emotional exhaustion, negative feelings toward clients, and fewer feelings of achievement (Rupert et al., 2009).

Although there can be many causes of psychological distress, the causes can at times lead to the same result: problems of professional competence and ethical violations. Because research suggests that distress is linked with diminished competence, Smith et al. (2009) note that the field of professional psychology needs to give greater attention to issues of psychologist distress, depression, substance abuse, and burnout. Consistent with this observation, Taylor, Neimeyer, and Wear (2012) discovered several significant relationships between personal and professional domains of psychologists. For example, stress levels were significantly and inversely related to life satisfaction and adjustment, self-care, and perceived professional competence.

In fact, other health professions (e.g., medicine, nursing) have long recognized that impairment and distress exists among professionals and have created programs to address these issues, beginning in the 1970s (Laliotis & Grayson, 1985). Although it was not until the 1980s that psychologists began to recognize the potential impact of significant personal distress on professional functioning, the trend towards recognizing and researching how distress can affect clinical effectiveness has continued to grow since that time. By 1986, the Advisory Committee on the Impaired Psychologist (ACIP), now called the Advisory Committee on Colleague Assistance, was created to address issues of professional incompetence due to psychological impairment. However, to this day, there remain no comprehensive methods to address psychologists' problems of professional competence (see Smith et al., 2009).

However, some suggestions have been proposed to support psychologists who are in distress and at risk for incompetence. One suggestion has been to mandate therapy for psychologists or ethics offenders. Studies suggest that many psychologists (34%) support mandatory therapy for all professionals (Wood, Klein, Cross, Lammers, & Elliott, 1985), and other studies even suggest that upwards of 87% of psychologists favor allowing licensing boards to mandate therapy for maintenance of licensure.

Research also suggests that most psychologists report that therapy has been beneficial for them. In a study of psychologists, Pope and Tabachnick (1994) found that 84% of psychologists in their study had received therapy, with an average of four years spent in therapy, but most had not been in therapy within the past 15 years. The majority of those who received therapy (85.7%) of them reported that their therapy experiences were exceptionally or very helpful. However, although many who have been in therapy report that it was helpful for them, many in this sample also noted that they are unsure if *mandated* therapy would be effective.

Other researchers suggest that psychologists who commit ethics violations that may stem from psychological distress should complete a mandatory ethics course (e.g., Wood et al., 1985). However, these courses may not truly accomplish the purpose that they are designed to accomplish. While some researchers have found that the majority of psychologists believe that CE courses have improved the ethics of their practice (Neimeyer et al., 2009), other researchers have found little support for the impact of ethical courses on increase awareness of ethical issues (Welfel & Lipsitz, 1983). Additionally, other researchers suggest that the topics in ethics courses are not focused enough on specific ethical problems that certain psychologists face (Vasquez, 1988). Furthermore, sanctions are sometimes used when psychologists commit ethics violations. However, as Layman and McNamara (1997) note, there is little research that suggests that such punishments decrease future violations.

A final suggestion for responding to psychologists who are in emotional distress was posed by the ACIP. ACIP wrote a manual as a guide for state psychological associations to create programs to prevent and remediate burnout and impairment (see Schwebel et al., 1994). Many states have produced programs designed to support psychologists who are under distress. However, studies regarding the effectiveness of colleague support programs need further attention (Layman & McNamara, 1997). Overall, future research needs to be devoted to exploring ways to support psychologists who are facing emotional distress in support of the clients whom they serve, the psychologists themselves, and the integrity of the profession as a whole.

7. Self-Assessment, Reflection, and Evaluation

Effective self-assessment, self-directed lifelong learning, and continuing professional competence have long been linked in the field of professional psychology. Accurate self-assessment has been regarded as a pre-condition to effective self-directed learning (Morris, 2012), effective self-directed learning has been regarded as a key to the ongoing maintenance of competence (Candy, 1991), and ongoing competence has been linked closely to the effectiveness of service delivery and outcomes (Beutler, Crago, & Arizendi, 1986). Therefore, in the calculus that leads to continuing competence and enhanced outcomes effective self-assessment figures as a critical factor in the equation.

Unfortunately, self-assessment is as flawed as it is prominent among individuals in the health care professions. Davis and colleagues (2006) performed a systematic literature review regarding the accuracy of physician self-assessments and discovered some significant concerns. In their review of 725 articles in this area, Davis and colleagues reserved for closer inspection only those 17 studies with the greatest conceptual relevance and methodological rigor. Within those 17 studies a total of 20 comparisons were made between self-assessments of competence and observed measures of competence based on some external or objective assessments. Six of these studies focused on predictive self-assessment, or the ability of the physician to predict his/her performance on a future competency-based measure. Nine of the comparisons were retrospective self-assessments where participants were asked to rate their performance, which was then judged against external indicators. And two studies contained concurrent self-assessments, asking physicians to identify current learning needs.

Out of the 20 total comparisons between self-assessments and external assessments, 13 demonstrated little, no, or inverse relationships between self-assessments and external indicators. Seven of the comparisons showed a positive relationship between self- and external assessments. As an example, one study showed an association between physician's self-rated sensitivity to emotional and psychological issues in patients and the diagnosis of these concerns as reflected in a chart audit.

However, even in the context of the minority of those potentially promising findings, significant concerns loomed large. For example, across a number of studies, it appears that those who perform least well by external indicators also self-assess the least accurately, meaning that their self-assessments cannot be relied upon to inform corrective action or skills remediation. For example, Parker, Alford, and Passmore (2004) found that residents scoring in the lowest quartile of a knowledge-based family practice examination recognized their learning needs the least accurately. Dunning and colleagues (2004, p. 73) refer to this as the "plight of the incompetent" who are not in the position to recognize just how poor their performance is. As Dunning and colleagues (2004) note, "Their deficits cause them to make errors and also prevent them from gaining insight in to their errors" (p. 73).

As noted elsewhere (Neimeyer et al., 2009; Wise et al., 2010), the empirical study of competence in professional psychology is a generation behind that of medicine. But as Dunning and colleagues (2004) make clear, there is little reason to expect psychologists to be different from physicians in this regard because the processes that contribute to flawed self-assessment are common to being human. "When one looks at the accuracy of self-assessment in the workplace, from the office cubicle to the executive boardroom," note Dunning and colleagues, "one sees that people tend to hold overly inflated self-views that are modestly related to actual performance" (p. 90).

The reasons for this inaccuracy are legion, including a variety of contextual, psychological, and cognitive factors. One of these factors follows from the recognition that people believe themselves to be above average on traits that are ill-defined more than on ones that are better defined and constrained, and many self-assessments are of this kind. Self-assessed competence is a case in point since the concept of "competence" is often quite broad and poorly defined. Only recently has the field of professional psychology begun to develop benchmarks for professional competence and to specify those benchmarks in behavioral terms (Fouad et al., 2009), which may increase the accuracy with which competence can be assessed (see section 5 of this chapter, Conceptualizing and Assessing Competence).

In the absence of a clear-cut operationalization of competence, the process of self-assessment is especially vulnerable to two substantial sources of error: the unavailability of corrective information on the one hand and the neglect of it on the other (Dunning et al., 2004). In the first case, self-assessments are erroneous because people often lack all of the information they need to make accurate assessments. And on the second count, they often neglect to attend to relevant information that they do have at hand (Dunning et al., 2004).

Knowing these sources of error allows for developing mechanisms for countering them, and considerable literature has addressed these mechanisms. Four examples illustrate some of the options in this regard. They include *reviewing past performance, benchmarking, peer assessment, and cultivating mindfulness.*

Reviewing past performance has been shown to result in more accurate self-appraisal. Watching videotapes of their prior performance, for example, can increase the accuracy of residents' assessment of their interviewing skills (Ward et al., 2003), and conducting this review with their faculty enhances the accuracy still further (Lane & Gottlieb, 2004). This review does not need to be a videotape review. As Cochran and Spears (1980) have demonstrated, having students periodically rate their own performance and then meet with a faculty member who provided an independent assessment of their performance resulted in the students' appraisals converging with their supervisors' assessments over time.

Benchmarking consists of anchoring a self-appraisal in relation to the performance of others. In one study, family-practice residents completed an exercise in which they interviewed a mother who might have physically abused her child and then rated how well they viewed themselves as having done. They then watched their own videotaped interview along with four benchmark interviews that ranged widely in the competence of the interview skills (Martin, Regehr, Hodges, & Mcnaughton, 1998) and were asked evaluate their own performance in relation to those benchmarks. The correlation between self-ratings and supervisor ratings of the residents' interviews were significantly higher after students had viewed the benchmark interviews because the videos provided a comparative basis to help anchor the assessment of their own performance.

Peer assessment may prove particularly valuable in contexts in which supervisor appraisal is not available. Peer assessment calls attention to weaknesses or deficits that individuals may not be aware of, providing an opportunity for addressing or remediating them. Peer assessments are generally reliable and correlated highly with teachers' evaluations (Falchikov & Goldfinch, 2000). There are also other collateral advantages to peer assessment, including better overall performance as a function of peer review and more positive attitudes toward the learning experience following peer assessments (Topping, 1998).

Beyond improving students' flawed evaluations of their own work, peer assessment creates more "time on task," provides learners with an opportunity to practice their skills, and prompts them to be more reflective while encouraging greater accountability and responsibility (Topping, 1998). Greater accuracy in self-assessment, improved overall performance, and increased social skills are all commonly reported outcomes associated with the use of peer assessment (Marcoulides & Simkin, 1991).

Cultivating an attitude of mindfulness involves the development of a non-judgmental attunement to one's physical and mental processes during everyday tasks in order allow a greater awareness and to prevent an individual from falling prey to customary practices, prejudices, expectations, or projections (Epstein, 1999). Deviation from best practices often can result from personal, emotional, and cognitive processes that are the express target of mindful practices that encourage instead an awareness of, and attunement to, these processes. A desire to be appreciated, respected, or valued; feelings of potential embarrassment; or mounting feelings of being overwhelmed can all invite actions that depart from best practices, for example, as can attempts at resolution such as avoidance, rationalization, externalization, or denial. Mindfulness is an attitude that is simultaneously disciplined and permissive. It operates as an ongoing curiosity to create an attunement to experience, to invite novelty, and to encourage the explicit awareness of a wide range of contextual, emotional, and relational features that may otherwise remain in implicit awareness (Polanyi, 1974) and, as a result, may be unavailable in the course of decision making or service delivery.

Express attention to processes of self-assessment is likely to continue to attract attention within the field of professional psychology in the years ahead. The reliance of the field on accurate self-appraisal in support of identifying and remediating professional needs ensures that continued work is likely to be dedicated to enhancing the availability, reliability, and validity of professional self-assessments.

8. Technology Trends in Continuing Education

Technology innovations provide increasingly convenient and cost-effective ways to support lifelong learning, and emerging technologies occupy progressively more important roles in ongoing educational efforts. This is not surprising given the meteoric rise in Internet access and Web-based applications. In 2000, 360,985,492 people worldwide had access to the Internet. Just eight years later this number skyrocketed to 1,463,632,361 people, a usage growth of 305.5% (Nielsen/Net Ratings, 2008). The impact of Internet-based training has been palpable within the field of professional psychology where a premium has been placed both on accessibility and convenience.

Convenience has been demonstrated to be a significant factor in CE selection (see Fagan et al., 2007; Neimeyer, Taylor, & Wear, 2010). Internet CE courses offer the convenience of learning wherever and whenever the learner is ready. Indeed, although CE topics are considered an important factor in deciding which CE course to choose, research suggests that the *accessibility* of continuing education boosts CE activity (Brown et al., 1982; Neimeyer, Taylor, & Philip, 2010; Neimeyer et al., 2009), and online CE programs offer easy accessibility to learning.

Online CE has the potential to address many of the common shortcomings of traditional, on-site CE. Accessibility has been a widely regarded impediment to traditional (e.g., classroom) CE courses, for example, and online CE expands accessibility considerably. In addition, several studies pinpoint other common impediments to participation in CE. These include time commitments, family commitments, and the price of CE courses (Allen et al., 1987; Sharkin & Plageman, 2003). Because accessibility, convenience, and costs are considered so crucial, online CE programs may offer advantages. Online courses are cost-effective because they aid in autonomous learning (Brandys, Polak, Mendyk, & Polak, 2006) and do not require the travel and registration expenses that traditional CE courses may require.

And because they can be completed in the home or the office, they may be less disruptive and better integrated into professional and family functioning.

While online CE courses are advantageous in several regards, research suggests that psychotherapists most commonly continue to complete formal CE through on-site programs (Neimeyer, Taylor, & Philip, 2010) and tend to prefer these on-site to online or home study CE programs (Fagan et al., 2007). It appears, as Daniels and Walter (2002) note, that, "Web-based distance-learning programs have emerged in behavioral health, but have not replaced live, didactic continuing education as the norm" (p.361).

Even so, technology-based CE is a growing trend in the field, and there is some evidence that Web-based CE can facilitate the development and enhancement of professional skills. Sholomskas and colleagues (2005) explored the role of technology in lifelong learning and examined three types of training programs in their study of clinical psychologists. One learning program featured a manual as the only means of learning, another program included a manual and Web-based training, and the final program featured a manual in addition to a training seminar and supervision. Results demonstrated that the seminar/supervision program improved the participants' skills and adherence with the program the most, followed by the website program and finally the manual program. In addition, after a follow-up, participant skills in the seminar/supervision group and the Web site group were maintained or enhanced, whereas skills in the manual group tended to remain the same or decrease.

Another more recent randomized controlled trial of online CE was conducted by Webber and colleagues (2012; cited in Neimeyer, Taylor, Wear, et al., 2012). In their study, researchers examined the effectiveness of three online CE modalities (audio-visual, audio-only, and text-only learning conditions) on the participants' knowledge improvement. While participants in each condition *perceived* similar improvements in learning from their CE programs, the *objective* assessments of the participants' pre- and post-test scores suggested that participants in the audio-only condition demonstrated significantly lower levels of learning than participants in the audio-visual and text-only conditions. This finding provides some preliminary evidence that online CE programs can be effective, though some forms of online delivery may be more effective than others (see also Daniels & Walter, 2002).

However, the professional community has met CE technology with mixed feelings. Although the Internet has quickly become a widely used tool for learning, online CE carries with it some potential weaknesses. Internet programs can create a felt distance between the learner and the teacher, which may diminish learning and lead some learners to discontinue them prematurely. In addition, Web-based courses may not be particularly user-friendly and responsive to a learner's needs (Brandys et al., 2006), and they may minimize collegial interaction and affiliation, characteristics of ongoing professionalization that have been linked to the maintenance of competencies and the reduction in disciplinary actions (Knapp & VandeCreek, 2012). Continued efforts are needed to enhance the user interface, as well as user interaction, in relation to online training programs.

Nonetheless, some online interactive CE programs have been well received, and research suggests that the gender gap between those who feel comfortable and positively about computers is narrowing (Mitra, Joshi, Kemper, Woods, & Gobble, 2006). While the use of advanced technology in education is gaining greater acceptance and accessibility, it is still a relatively novel (Neimeyer, Taylor & Philip, 2010) and rapidly evolving (Daniels & Walter, 2002) field, particularly within the health professions (IOM, 2010). Indeed, while other disciplines have long embraced the role of innovative, interactive technologies in learning, psychology has suffered from a significant developmental delay in this regard. For example, war simulation games have long been used to train soldiers, flight simulators have been used to refine pilot skills, and businesses have long used strategy games as a tool to foster learning and measure competency. Professional psychology, by comparison, has been a relative latecomer in the endorsement and utilization of emerging technologies in ongoing professional training.

Within the broader health professions, CE technology plays a progressively more critical role. The use of point-of-service decision tools, online simulations, pop-up cases, sensitive dialogue boxes, and smart phone-based videos and social networking tools are common components of medical communities (IOM, 2010). As Daniels and Walter (2002) point out, "Continuing education will rely on the Internet and other developing mediums to support distance learning, interactive videoconferences, Web-based distribution of information and curriculum resources, interactive learning, and simulation techniques" (p. 371-372). Thus technology is beginning to transform the way that CE is delivered and promises to continue to offer tools that will support the efficiency and effectiveness of ongoing professional development (see also Mitra et al., 2000).

9. Diminishing Durability of Professional Knowledge

Technological advancements in CPD are designed to enhance the dissemination of knowledge. Nonetheless, attention continues to be dedicated to the deterioration of knowledge, as well, given the threat it poses to the ongoing maintenance of professional competence. Indeed, the growing concern about potential knowledge obsolescence was an original animus for CE. Early research conceptualized obsolescence as a function of the passage of time or the reduction in the efficiency of performance over time (Mahler, 1965). Some of the earliest research on professional obsolescence occurred in the fields of engineering and business, work that continues to this day (National Academy of Engineering, 2005). Zelikoff (1969), for example, studied the changes in the core curricula of engineering programs over time, noting the discontinuation of old courses and the development of new ones across a 30-year period. Based on an analysis of the change in program requirements, he developed engineering erosion curves for knowledge obsolescence as a function of the time since graduation. Results indicated that, in the absence of continued learning, engineers who had graduated 30 years earlier would have only about 5% of the current knowledge customarily required, while those who had graduated 10 years earlier would have about 55% of the requisite knowledge. Likewise, in the field of medicine, Rosenow (1971) found that physicians faced a significant drop in their competence over time when tested on 700 items regarding their contemporary medical knowledge.

While the passage of time is one key indicator of potential obsolescence, researchers have emphasized other elements, as well. Among them are the incongruity between professional skills and job demands (Burack & Pati, 1970) and the relative amount of information that a given individual possesses in relation to the total knowledge available in the field (Mali, 1969).

Knowledge atrophy appears to be the subject of ongoing consideration and concern throughout many disciplines (Cohen & Dubin, 1970), although the precise relationship to this knowledge atrophy and performance capability remains to be determined. Nonetheless, a chorus of scholars and practitioners has given voice to the key role of CE and ongoing professional development as critical antidotes to the otherwise entropic process of knowledge loss over time (Adams & Sharkin, 2012; Neimeyer et al., 2009; Webb & Horn, 2012; Wise et al., 2010; Zemansky, 2012).

In conceptualizing this knowledge loss, Dubin (1972) introduced the concept of the "half-life" of professional knowledge, borrowing the concept from of nuclear physics and taking it to mean "the time after completion of professional training when, because of new developments, practicing professionals have become roughly half as competent as they were upon graduation to meet the demands of their profession" (p. 487). Studying the increasing rapidity of new knowledge in the field of psychology over a 20-year period, Dubin (1972) estimated the half-life of knowledge in the field of psychology to be approximately 10-12 years at the time of his writing. Given the conclusion that the half-life of knowledge decreases as the rate of new knowledge production increases, it seems probable that "the current half-life of the professional psychology doctoral degree is likely to be significantly shorter" today (Wise et al., 2010, p. 289).

Recent data appear to support this assessment. Two studies have estimated the current half-life of professional knowledge within the field of professional psychology to be seven to nine years (Neimeyer, Taylor, Wear, et al., 2012; Neimeyer, Taylor, & Rozensky, 2012). This means that even early career psychologists, typically regarded as those who have graduated within the last seven years, could already begin experiencing substantial, perhaps even disconcerting, levels of knowledge obsolescence. Given the ongoing profusion of knowledge within the field, these concerns are redoubled when looking towards the future of the field and the ever-accelerating pace of knowledge obsolescence.

The accelerating rate of new knowledge was underscored in a Delphi poll of the future of professional psychology. Using the best-available prognostic methodology, Neimeyer, Taylor, and Rozensky (2012) explored the anticipated half-life of knowledge in 14 specialties recognized by the Commission on the Recognition of Specialties and Proficiencies in Psychology (e.g., clinical neuropsychology, clinical health psychology, school psychology, counseling psychology, industrial and organizational psychology, etc.) and seven recognized proficiencies in the field (e.g., biofeedback, psychopharmacology, sport psychology). Results of their work demonstrated two primary findings.

First, there was significant variability in the anticipated half-lives across the various areas, from a high of 17.07 years (in psychoanalytic psychology) to a low of 3.64 years (in psychopharmacology), with an overall half-life of 7.07 for professional psychology in general.

In addition to this substantial variability, however, virtually every specialty and proficiency showed a probable decline in the half-life of knowledge within its area, with some areas such as psychopharmacology, clinical neuropsychology, and clinical health psychology showing declines of 20% or more in their predicted half-lives of knowledge over the course of the next 10 years.

Such findings underscore the importance of having mechanisms in place for the rapid dissemination of new knowledge to keep pace with the accelerating pace of the generation of new knowledge. Fortunately, the rapid proliferation of emerging technologies (see section 8 of this chapter, Technology Trends in Continuing Education) represents a major boon in this regard, although it also introduces additional challenges associated with availability of such a profusion of information. Central to these challenges is the need to sort through the available information and appraise it critically since all available information is not equally reliable or valid (Norcross, Hogan, & Koocher, 2008). Moving forward, the tandem trends concerning the diminishing durability and the rapid availability of knowledge in professional psychology are likely to continue in the foreseeable future. Because the forces of obsolescence are not borne evenly across the various areas of professional psychology, mechanisms for identifying the areas marked by the fastest rate of knowledge obsolescence will need to be created in order to develop CE programs in a timely way that address the areas of greatest growth and need across time.

10. Developing a Continuing Education Infrastructure

The increasingly rapid obsolescence of knowledge creates a further impetus for examining the overall infrastructure for CE. The earliest accounts of CE in professional psychology show concerted attention to the adequacy of the infrastructure for providing ongoing training and documenting the effects of that training. In his "National Agenda for Continuing Education in Psychology," Webster (1971) underscored the critical need to identify and train competent instructors, to stipulate key topics of central importance, to provide widespread access to advanced training in designated areas of need in order to maintain professional competencies, and to document the effectiveness of this training to the profession and its multiple constituents.

Neimeyer and Taylor (2010) have likened the years following Webster's clarion call to the construction of a house. The early years were marked by laying the foundation of a CE system, the middle years by framing the mandates that would support the structure of CE, and the subsequent years in building out the systems for providing that education through developments at local, regional, or national levels, including the construction of the APA's CE Sponsor Approval System. The most recent years have been likened to a building inspection, with the field turning back to assess the product of its labor and to determine whether what it has built warrants a certificate of occupancy.

Different inspectors see different things, of course, but the collective appraisal is one that is marked by a balance of promise and pitfalls. Although appraisal of the infrastructure continues, the convergence of opinion currently suggests that if the present structure of CE in professional psychology provides shelter, it is best regarded as temporary shelter because it does not fully conform to the highest building standards available at this time. A range of concerns contributes to this collective appraisal, but three sets of issues are particularly prominent.

The first has to do with the state- and province-based regulation of CE in relation to license renewal and the kaleidoscopic inclusion of a substantial range of widely variable activities as creditable CE activities in varying jurisdictions (see section 1 of this chapter, Designating Continuing Education Activities), but few with any empirical warrants for their inclusion (Neimeyer et al., in press). In the absence of any federating influences, the requirements for license renewal range from mandating as many as 30 CE credits per year to as few as zero (Adams & Sharkin, 2012), and there is strikingly little commonality in relation to what counts as creditable activity from one licensing jurisdiction to another (Webb & Horn, 2012). In the absence of standardization, it is difficult to gain the public trust by stipulating a commonly agreed-upon set of requirements that fulfill the principal objectives of CE, which include maintaining professional competence, enhancing service delivery and outcomes, and protecting the public.

A second, more troubling concern follows from one of the principle reasons for this lack of standardization. This lack of standardization exists, in part, because the field does not yet know what activities or experiences would fulfill the stipulated objectives of CE. This, in turn, is a product of the longstanding inattention to the empirical study of the processes, procedures, and outcomes associated with CE in psychology. The rallying cry issued by Webster (1971) more than 40 years ago for more research in this regard has largely gone unanswered, leaving Neimeyer and colleagues (2009) to characterize the current state of research as a pre-experimental patchwork of largely survey research conducted on samples of convenience. In consequence, the field has not benefited from the systematic knowledge gains, nor has it experienced the growth and maturation that would ordinarily accompany sustained programs of research focused on key issues within the field. What is required is an alignment with the increasingly predominant, evidence-based approaches evident elsewhere in the allied health fields. Evidence-based continuing education can be regarded as professional education that has an ongoing commitment to evaluating educational practices and assessing educational outcomes in support of understanding, promoting, and demonstrating the effectiveness of CE in psychology (Neimeyer et al., 2009). A renewed commitment to evidence-based CE may best situate the field of professional psychology to determine the extent to which it is capable of fulfilling its principal objectives in relation to CE, and to identify and remediate any shortfalls it may encounter (Neimeyer et al., in press).

A third concern regarding the current structure of CE in psychology is that the field itself is changing rapidly, challenging the processes and procedures of CE to keep pace. Some of these changes can be viewed as internal to the field while others can be seen as external. Internal changes include the increasingly rapid profusion of knowledge within the discipline and the corresponding movement towards specialization (see section 9 of this chapter, Diminishing Durability of Professional Knowledge). This in turn calls for the systems of CE both to provide more advanced levels of training to support these higher levels of specialization and to develop and utilize mechanisms for more rapid dissemination of new knowledge.

Even while forces of specialization and knowledge profusion are working their effects on the field, professional psychology is also caught in the crosscurrents of broader tidal influences that cut across the health professions. The movement towards interprofessional and collaborative care is central in this regard, creating the need for whole new fields of learning in relation to providing coordinated, patient-centered care (APA, 1998).

In response to this collection of concerns, as well as others, the IOM (2010) recently has advocated a radical reconfiguration of the entire CE system in what has been dubbed wryly as "Redesigning Continuing Education: Extreme Makeover Edition" (Neimeyer & Taylor, 2011). In particular, the IOM has recommended the development of a new national-private institute to coordinate and guide the development, implementation, and study of CPD across the full range of health professions. The principle functions of the institute would be to (1) identify, develop, and disseminate necessary content and knowledge among the health professions; (2) coordinate regulation across jurisdictional boundaries; (3) finance CPD for the purpose of improving professional performance and outcomes; and (4) develop a scientific basis for the practice of CPD.

The vision of the institute is holistic and interprofessional, providing learning opportunities that range from the classroom to the point of care. The system is envisioned as being based on educational methods, with theories and findings drawn from a variety of fields, and embracing information technologies to provide professionals with greater opportunities to learn effectively and to document the nature of their learning and their knowledge transfer.

Summary

CE and lifelong learning represent enduring commitments within the field of professional psychology. They stretch backwards from the earliest moments of training and professionalization and outwards toward the furthest reaches of professional practice. The 10 trends discussed in this article reflect corridors that cut across the contemporary landscape of professional psychology, conveying traffic as they extend themselves further along the courses of their continuing development. At points they run parallel and at others they intersect, as when emerging technologies merge into the already fast-flowing profusion of new knowledge within the field, further fueling both the diminishing durability of knowledge in the field and the forces of specialization. Movements towards evidence-based practices, mandated CE, outcome measurement, and best practices carry the field in similar directions, toward greater accountability and possibility—accountability in relation to the field itself and to its public, and possibility in relation to better understanding and improving the processes and procedures that support the field's ongoing quest for increased competency.

The 10 trends reviewed here are neither mutually exclusive nor exhaustive of the relevant developments that continue to make inroads into the current landscape of professional psychology. They are joined by many other continuing developments—interprofessional training and collaborative care, multiculturalism and internationalism, and advanced credentialing and (re)certification, to name a few—that collectively crisscross the field's current territory and direct it towards its future. Assuredly these and other trends will take further twists and turns, merging and yielding, dividing and multiplying, and jointly forming a growing network of roadways that will require ongoing orchestration and attention. Taken together, these roadways will help to form the field's ongoing commitment to CPD and to sustain the principal objectives associated with that commitment: to enhance professional competence, to improve service delivery, and to protect the public it serves.

References

Adams, A., & Sharkin, B. S. (2012). Should continuing education be mandatory for re-licensure? Arguments for and against. In G. J. Neimeyer, & J. M. Taylor (Eds.), *Continuing professional development and lifelong learning: Issues, impacts and outcomes* (pp. 157–178). Hauppauge, NY: Nova Science Publishers.

Allen, G. J., Nelson, W. J., & Sheckley, B. G. (1987). Brief reports: Continuing education activities of Connecticut psychologists. *Professional Psychology: Research and Practice, 18,* 78–80. doi: 10.1037/0735-7028.18.1.78

American Psychological Association. (1998). *Interprofessional health care services in primary care settings: Implications for the education and training of psychologists.* Retrieved from http://www.apa.org/ed/resources/samhsa.pdf

Bertram, D.A., & Brooks-Bertram, P. A. (1977). The evaluation of continuing medical education: A literature review. *Health Education Monographs,* 5, 330–362.

Beutler, L. E., Crago, M., & Arizendi, T. G. (1986). Research on therapist variables in psychotherapy. In S. L. Garfield, & A. E. Bergin (Eds.), *Handbook of psychotherapy and behavior change* (pp. 257–310). New York: Wiley.

Brandys, J., Polak, S., Mendyk, A., & Polak, M. (2006). An e-learning system for pharmacist continuing education in Poland. *Pharmacy Education, 6,* 65–70. doi: 10.1080/15602210600568013

Brodie, J., & Robinson, B. (1991). MPA distress/impaired psychologists survey: Overview and results. *Minnesota Psychologist, 27,* 627–686.

Brown, R. A., Leichtman, S. R., Blass, T., & Fleisher, E. (1982). Mandated continuing education: Impact on Maryland psychologists. *Professional Psychology, 13,* 404–411. doi: 10.1037/0735-7028.13.3.404

Burack, E. H., & Pati, G. C. (1970). Technology and managerial obsolescence. *Michigan State University Business Topics, 18,* 49–56.

Candy, P. C. (1991). *Self-direction for life-long learning: A comprehensive guide to theory and practice.* San Francisco, CA: Jossey-Bass.

Cochran, S. B., & Spears, M. (1980). Student self-assessment and instructors' ratings: A comparison. *Journal of the American Dietetic Association, 76,* 253–257.

Cohen, D. M., & Dubin, S. S. (1970). *Measuring professional updating in mathematical competence.* University Park: Department of Planning Studies, Continuing Education, Pennsylvania State University.

Daniels, A. S., & Walter, D. A. (2002). Current issues in continuing education for contemporary behavioral health practice. *Administration and Policy in Mental Health, 29,* 359–376. doi: 10.1023/A:1019653123285

Davis, D. A., Mazmanian, P. E., Fordis, M., Van Harrison, R., Thorpe, K. E., & Perrier, L. (2006). Accuracy of physician self-assessment compared with observed measures of competence a systematic review. *JAMA, 296,* 1094–1102. doi: 10.1001/jama.296.9.1094

Davis, D., Thomson O'Brien, M. A., Freemantle, N., Wolf, F. M., Mazmanian, P., & Taylor-Vaisey, A. (1999). Impact of formal continuing medical education: Do conferences, workshops, rounds, and other traditional continuing education activities change physician behavior or health care outcomes? *JAMA, 282,* 867–874. doi: 10.1001/jama.282.9.867

Davis, D.A., Thomson, M.A., Oxman, A.D., & Haynes, R. B. (1995). Changing physician performance: A systematic review of the effect of continuing medical education strategies. *JAMA, 274,* 700–705. doi: 10.1001/jama.274.9.700

Dubin, S. S. (1972). Obsolescence or lifelong education: A choice for the professional. *American Psychologist, 27,* 486–498. doi: 10.1037/h0033050

Dunning, D., Heath, C., & Suls, J. (2004). Flawed self-assessment: Implications for health, education, and the workplace. *Psychological Science in the Public Interest, 5,* 69–106. doi: 10.1111/j.1529-1006.2004.00018.x

Ellsworth, R. B. (1968). *Survey of Oregon certified psychologists.* Unpublished manuscript.

Epstein, R. M. (1999). Mindful practice. *JAMA, 282,* 833–839. doi: 10.1001/jama.282.9.833

Fagan, T. J., Ax, R. K., Liss, M., Resnick, R. J., & Moody, S. (2007). Professional education and training: How satisfied are we? An exploratory study. *Training and Education in Professional Psychology, 1,* 13–25. doi: 10.1037/1931-3918.1.1.13

Falchikov, N., & Goldfinch, J. (2000). Student peer assessment in higher education: A meta-analysis comparing peer and teacher marks. *Review of Educational Research, 70,* 287–322. doi: 10.2307/1170785

Figley, C. R. (1995). Compassion fatigue as secondary traumatic stress disorder: An overview. In C. R. Figley (Ed.), *Compassion fatigue: Coping with secondary traumatic stress disorder in those who treat the traumatized* (pp. 1–20). New York, NY: Brunner/Mazel.

Fouad, N. A., Grus, C. L., Hatcher, R. L., Kaslow, N. J., Hutchings, P. S., Madson, M. B., et al. (2009). Competency benchmarks: A model for understanding and measuring competence in professional psychology across training levels. *Training and Education in Professional Psychology, 3,* S5–S26. doi: 10.1037/a0015832

Good, G. E., Thoreson, P., & Shaughnessy, P. (1995). Substance use, confrontation of impaired colleagues, and psychological functioning among counseling psychologists: A national survey. *The Counseling Psychologist, 23,* 703–721.

Hellkamp, D., Imm, P., and Moll, D. (1989). Mandatory continuing education (MCE): Desirable or undesirable? A survey of executive officers of state psychological associations. *The Journal of Training and Practice in Professional Psychology*, 3, 33–46.

Hunter, W. S. (1941). On the professional training of psychologists. *Psychological Review*, 48, 498–523. doi: 10.1037/h0053967

Institute of Medicine. (2010). *Redesigning continuing education in the health professions*. Washington, DC: The National Academies Press.

Kaslow, N. J., Borden, K. A., Collins, F. L. Jr., Forrest, L., Illfelder-Kaye, J., Nelson, P., & Rallo, J. S. (2004). Competencies conference: Future directions in education and credentialing in professional psychology. *Journal of Clinical Psychology*, 60, 699–712.

Kaslow, N. J., Grus, C. L., Campbell, L. F., Fouad, N. A., Hatcher, R. L., & Rodolfa, E. R. (2009). Competency assessment toolkit for professional psychology. *Training and Education in Professional Psychology*, 3, S27–S45.

Knapp, S., & Vandecreek, L. (2012). Disciplinary actions by a state board of psychology: Do gender and association membership matter? An update. In G. J. Neimeyer, & J. M. Taylor (Eds.), *Continuing professional development and lifelong learning: Issues, impacts and outcomes* (pp. 151–154). Hauppauge, NY: Nova Science Publishers.

Laliotis, D. A., & Grayson, J. H. (1985). Psychologist heal thyself: What is available for the impaired psychologist? *American Psychologist*, 40, 84–96. doi: 10.1037/0003-066X.40.1.84

Lane, J. L., & Gottlieb, P. P. (2004). Improving the interviewing and self-assessment skills of medical students: Is it time to readopt videotaping as an educational tool? *Ambulatory Pediatrics*, 4, 244–248. doi: 10.1367/A03-122R1.1

Layman, M. J., & McNamara, J. R. (1997). Remediation for ethics violations: Focus on psychotherapists' sexual contact with clients. *Professional Psychology: Research and Practice*, 28, 281–292. doi: 10.1037/0735-7028.28.3.281

Lewinsohn, P. M., & Pearlman, S. (1972). Continuing education for psychologists. *Professional Psychology*, 3, 48–52. doi: 10.1037/h0021495

Lichtenberg, J.W., & Goodyear, R. K. (2012). Informal learning, incidental learning, and deliberate continuing education: Preparing psychologists to be effective lifelong learners. In G. J. Neimeyer, & J. M. Taylor (Eds.), *Continuing professional development and lifelong learning: Issues, impacts and outcomes* (pp. 73–81). Hauppauge, NY: Nova Science Publishers.

Mahler, W. R. (1965). Every company's problem: Managerial obsolescence. *Personnel*, 42, 8–16.

Mali, P. (1969). Measurement of obsolescence in engineering practitioners. *Manage*, 21, 48–52.

Marcoulides, G.A., & Simkin, M.G. (1991). Evaluating student papers; the case for peer review. *Journal of Education for Business*, 67, 80–84. doi: 10.1080/08832323.1991.10117521

Martin, D., Regehr, G., Hodges, B., & Mcnaughton, N. (1998). Using videotaped benchmarks to improve the self-assessment ability of family practice residents. *Academic Medicine*, 73, 1201–1206. doi: 10.1097/00001888-199811000-00020

Mazmanian, P. E., Berens, T. E., Wetzel, A. P., Feldman, M., & Dow, A. W. (2012). Planning for change in psychology: Education, outcomes, and continuing professional development. In G. J. Neimeyer, & J. M. Taylor (Eds.), *Continuing professional development and life-long*

learning: Issues, impacts and outcomes (pp. 311–335). Hauppauge, NY: Nova Science Publishers.

Melnyk, W. T., Allen, M. F., Nutt, R. L., O'Connor, T., Robiner, B., Linder-Crow, J., et al. (2001). ASPPB guidelines for continuing professional education. *Association of State and Provincial Psychology Boards*. Retrieved from http://www.asppb.org/publications/guidelines/cpe.aspx

Mitra, A., Lenzmeier, S., Steffensmeier, T., Avon, R., Qu, N., & Hazen, M. (2000). Gender and computer use in an academic institution: Report from a longitudinal study. *Journal of Educational Computing Research*, 23, 67–84. doi: 10.2190/FC2G-TCUV-XKW8-W32G

Mitra, A., Joshi, S., Kemper, K. J., Woods, C., & Gobble, J. (2006). Demographic differences and attitudes toward computers among healthcare professionals earning continuing education credits online. *Journal of Educational Computing Research*, 35, 31–43. doi: 10.2190/8123-3KU2-648J-7593

National Academy of Engineering (2005). *Educating the engineer of 2020: Adapting engineering education to the new century*. Washington, D.C.: The National Academies Press.

Morris, R. (2012). Self-assessment guide and professional development plan: facilitating individualized continuing professional development. In G. J. Neimeyer, & J. M. Taylor (Eds.), *Continuing professional development and lifelong learning: Issues, impacts and outcomes* (pp. 103–130). Hauppauge, NY: Nova Science Publishers.

Neimeyer, G. J., & Taylor, J. M. (2010). Continuing education in psychology. In J. C. Norcross, G. R. VandenBos, & D. K. Freedheim (Eds.), *History of psychotherapy: Continuity and change* (pp. 663–671). Washington, DC: American Psychological Association.

Neimeyer, G. J., & Taylor, J. M. (2011). Redesigning continuing education: Extreme makeover edition. [Review of the book *Redesigning continuing education in the health professions*, by Committee on Planning a Continuing Health Care Professional Institute, Institute of Medicine]. *PsycCRITIQUES*, 56(27). doi: 10.1037/a0024099

Neimeyer, G. J., Taylor, J. M., & Cox, D. (2012). On hope and possibility: Does continuing professional development contribute to ongoing professional competence? *Professional Psychology: Research and Practice*, 43, 476–486.

Neimeyer, G. J., Taylor, J. M., & Philip, D. (2010). Continuing education in psychology: Patterns of participation and perceived outcomes among mandated and nonmandated psychologists. *Professional Psychology: Research and Practice*, 41, 435–441. doi: 10.1037/a0021120

Neimeyer, G. J., Taylor, J. M., & Rozensky, R. (2012). The diminishing durability of knowledge in professional psychology: A Delphi poll of specialties and proficiencies. *Professional Psychology: Research and Practice*, 43, 364–371.

Neimeyer, G. J., Taylor, J. M., & Wear, D. M. (2009). Continuing education in psychology: Outcomes, evaluations and mandates. *Professional Psychology: Research and Practice*, 40, 617–624. doi: 10.1037/a0016655

Neimeyer, G. J., Taylor, J. M., & Wear, D. (2010). Continuing education in psychology: Patterns of participation and aspects of selection. *Professional Psychology: Research and Practice*, 41, 281–287. doi: 10.1037/a0019811

Neimeyer, G. J., Taylor, J. M., Wear, D., & Linder-Crow, J. (2012). Anticipating the future of CE in psychology: A Delphi poll. In G. J. Neimeyer, & J. M. Taylor (Eds.), *Continuing professional development and life-long* learning: Issues, impacts and outcomes (pp. 377–394). Hauppauge, NY: Nova Science Publishers.

Neimeyer, G. J., Taylor, J. M., Zemansky, M., & Rothke, S. E. (2012). Do CE mandates matter? The effects of CE mandates on CE participation. In G. J. Neimeyer, & J. M. Taylor (Eds.), Continuing professional development and lifelong learning: Issues, impacts and outcomes (pp. 187–195). Hauppauge, NY: Nova Science Publishers.

Nielsen/Net Ratings (2008). Internet usage statistics: The internet big picture. Retrieved from http://www.internetworldstats.com/stats.htm

Norcross, J. C., Hogan, T. P., & Koocher, G. P. (2008). Clinician's guide to evidence-based practices: Mental health and the addictions. New York: Oxford University Press.

Norcross, J.C., Vandenbos, G. R., & Freedheim, D. K. (Eds.). (2010). History of psychotherapy: Continuity and change. Washington, DC: American Psychological Association.

O'Brien, M.A., Freemantle, N., Oxman, A.D., Wolf, F., Davis, D. A., & Herrin, J. (2001). Continuing education meetings and workshops: Effects on professional practice and health care outcomes. Cochrane Database System Reviews, 2, CD003030. doi: 10.1002/14651858.CD003030.pub2

Parker, R. W., Alford, C., & Passmore, C. (2004). Can family medicine residents predict their performance on the in-training examination? Family Medicine, 36, 705–709.

Phillips, L. E. (1987). Is mandatory continuing education working? Mobius, 7, 57–64. doi: 10.1002/chp.4760070110

Polanyi, M. (1974). Personal knowledge: Towards a post-critical philosophy. Chicago, IL: University of Chicago Press.

Pope, K. S., & Tabachnick, B. G. (1994). Therapists as patients: A national survey of psychologists' experiences, problems, and beliefs. Professional Psychology: Research and Practice, 25, 247–258. doi: 10.1037/0735-7028.25.3.247

Roberts, M. C., Borden, K. A., Christiansen, M. D., & Lopez, S. J. (2005). Fostering a culture shift: Assessment of competence in the education and careers of professional psychologists. Professional Psychology: Research and Practice, 36, 355–361. doi: 10.1037/0735-7028.36.4.355

Rodolfa, E., Bent, R., Eisman, E., Nelson, P., Rehm, L., & Ritchie, P. (2005). A cube model for competency development: Implications for psychology educators and regulators. Professional Psychology: Research and Practice, 36, 347–354.

Rodolfa, E., Schaffer, J. B., & Webb, C. (2010). Continuing education: The path to life-long competence? Professional Psychology: Research and Practice, 41, 295–297. doi: 10.1037/a0020424

Rosenow, E. C., Jr. (1971, April). Medical knowledge self-assessment programs. Paper presented at 173rd Annual Meeting of the Medical and Chirurgical Faculty of State of Maryland, Baltimore, MD.

Rubin, N. J., Bebeau, M., Leigh, I W., Lichtenberg, J. W., Nelson, P. D., Portnoy, S., et al. (2007). The competency movement within psychology: An historical perspective. Professional Psychology: Research and Practice, 38, 452–462. doi: 10.1037/0735-7028.38.5.452

Rupert, P. A., Stevanovic, P., & Hunley, H. A. (2009). Work-family conflict and burnout among practicing psychologists. Professional Psychology: Research and Practice, 40, 54–61. doi: 10.1037/a0012538

Schwebel, M., Skorina, J. K., & Schoener, G. (1994). Assisting impaired psychologists: Program development for state psychological associations (Rev. ed.). Washington, DC: American Psychological Association.

Sharkin, B. S., & Plageman, P. M. (2003). What do psychologists think about mandatory continuing education? A survey of Pennsylvania psychologists. Professional Psychology: Research and Practice, 34, 318–323. doi: 10.1037/0735-7028.34.3.318

Shern, D. (2010, February). Health care reform, chronic disease and the emerging role for psychologists. Presentation to the Council of Chairs of Training Councils Joint Conference of Training Councils in Psychology: Assuring competence in the next generation of psychologists. Orlando, FL.

Sholomskas, D. E., Syracuse-Siewert, G., Rounsaville, B. J., Ball, S. A., Nuro, K. F., & Carroll, K. M. (2005). We don't train in vain: A dissemination trail of three strategies of training clinicians in cognitive-behavioral therapy. Journal of Consulting and Clinical Psychology, 73, 106–115. doi: 10.1037/0022-006X.73.1.106

Sibley, J. C., Sackett, D. L., Neufeld, V., Gerrard, B., Rudnick, K. V., & Fraser, W. (1982). A randomized trial of continuing medical education. New England Journal of Medicine, 306, 511–515. doi: 10.1056/NEJM198203043060904

Slotnick, H. B., & Shershneva, M. B. (2002). Use of theory to interpret elements of change. Journal of Continuing Education in the Health Professions, 22, 197–204. doi: 10.1002/chp.1340220403

Smith, P. L., Moss, S. B., & Burton, S. (2009). Psychologist impairment: What is it, how can it be prevented, and what can be done to address it? Clinical Psychology: Science and Practice, 16, 1–5. doi: 10.1111/j.1468-2850.2009.01137.x

Taylor, J. M., & Neimeyer, G. J. (2012a). The development of the Professional Competencies Scale: An assessment of foundational, functional, and continuing competencies for psychologist. (Unpublished doctoral dissertation). University of Florida, Gainesville, FL.

Taylor, J. M., & Neimeyer, G. J. (2012b). To protect and serve: Public perceptions of continuing professional development activities in psychology. Manuscript submitted for publication.

Taylor, J. M., Neimeyer, G. J., & Wear, D. (2012). Professional competency and personal experience: An exploratory study. In G. J. Neimeyer, & J. M. Taylor (Eds.), Continuing professional development and life-long learning: Issues, impacts and outcomes (pp. 249–261). Hauppauge, NY: Nova Science Publishers.

Topping, K. (1998). Peer assessment between students in colleges and universities. Review of Educational Research, 68, 249–276. doi: 10.2307/1170598

Ukens, C. (1995). The tragic truth. Drug Topics, 139, 66.

Vandecreek, L., Knapp, S., & Brace, K. (1990). Mandatory continuing education for licensed psychologists: Its rationale and current implementation. Professional Psychology: Research and Practice, 21, 135–140. doi: 10.1037/0735-7028.21.2.135

Vasquez, M. J. T. (1988). Counselor-client sexual contact: Implications for ethics training. Journal of Counseling and Development, 67, 238–241. doi: 10.1002/j.1556-6676.1988.tb02590.x

Ward, M., MacRae, H., Schlachta, C., Mamazz, J., Poulin, E., Reznick, R., & Regehr, G. (2003). Resident self-assessment of operative performance. American Journal of Surgery, 185, 521–524. doi: 10.1016/S0002-9610(03)00069-2

Webb, C., & Horn, J. B. (2012). Continuing professional development: A regulatory perspective. In G. J. Neimeyer, & J. M. Taylor (Eds.), Continuing professional development and life-long learning: Issues, impacts and outcomes (pp. 131–149). Hauppauge, NY: Nova Science Publishers.

Webber, E., Taylor, J. M., & Neimeyer, G. J. (2012). *Continuing education in psychology: A comparison of measured levels of learning resulting from home study methods of continuing education*. Unpublished manuscript, University of Florida, Gainesville, FL.

Webster, T. G. (1971). National priorities for the continuing education of psychologists. *American Psychologist, 26*, 1016–1019. doi: 10.1037/h0032256

Welfel, E. R., & Lipsitz, N. E. (1983). Wanted: A comprehensive approach to ethics research and education. *Counselor Education and Supervision, 22*, 320–332. doi: 10.1002/j.1556-6978.1983.tb01769.x

Wise, E. H. (2008). Competence and scope of practice: Ethics and professional development. *Journal of Clinical Psychology: In Session, 64*, 626–637. doi: 10.1002/jclp.20479

Wise, E. H., Sturm, C. A., Nutt, R. L., Rodolfa, E., Schaffer, J. B., & Webb, C. (2010). Life-long learning for psychologists: Current status and a vision for the future. *Professional Psychology: Research and Practice, 41*, 288–297. doi: 10.1037/a0020424

Wood, B. J., Klein, S., Cross, H. J., Lammers, C. J., & Elliott, J. K. (1985). Impaired practitioners: Psychologists' opinions about prevalence, and proposals for intervention. *Professional Psychology: Research and Practice, 16*, 843–850. doi: 10.1037/0735-7028.16.6.843

Young, L., & Willie, R. (1984). Effectiveness of Continuing Education for Health Professionals: A Literature Review. *Journal of Allied Health, 13*, 112–123.

Zelikoff, S. B. (1969). On the obsolescence and retraining of engineering personnel. *Training and Development Journal, 23*, 3–15.

Zemansky, M. (2012). A review of concerns in regard to the implementation of the CE mandate in Illinois. In G. J. Neimeyer, & J. M. Taylor (Eds.), *Continuing professional development and lifelong learning: Issues, impacts and outcomes* (pp. 179–185). Hauppauge, NY: Nova Science Publishers.

Trainee Selection, Development, and Evaluation

PART 3

Trainee Selection,
Development, and
Evaluation

Selecting Graduate Students: Doctoral Program and Internship Admissions

Jesse Owen, Kelley Quirk, *and* Emil Rodolfa

Abstract

Selecting students for psychology doctoral programs and doctoral internships is a challenging process because the costs for doctoral students, academic and internship programs, the profession, and the public can be high. This chapter reviews the literature examining predictors of doctoral student selection by academic and doctoral internship programs. Although there is limited research specifically examining counseling/clinical academic program selection factors, there is some support indicating that GRE scores are predictive of academic performance but not of clinical performance. Structured interview procedures as compared to less structured interviews are better at differentiating between doctoral students. Other methods of assessment, such as letters of recommendation, have little value in the prediction of doctoral student performance. New methods for selection of doctoral students are also discussed.

Key Words: doctoral students, training, education, doctoral internship, counseling psychology, clinical psychology

Selecting students for doctoral academic programs and doctoral internships can be an arduous and challenging process, with many factors influencing the ultimate decision. Although programs differ in their training philosophies, clinical foci, and resources, many commonalities still remain in the admission process. The focus of this chapter is to examine the literature on student selection for doctoral programs in clinical/counseling psychology, as well as for doctoral internships. Our ultimate goal is to provide implications and recommendations for the selection of students and trainees.

Student Selection in Doctoral Programs

From the vantage point of faculty in doctoral programs, the doctoral-student-selection process generally entails two phases: (1) review of applicants' admission material (e.g., graduate records examination (GRE) scores, grade point average (GPA)/transcripts, letter of intent, personal essay,

vita, and letters of recommendation) and (2) interview of applicants who have passed the initial screening phase. Although all this information, to varying degrees, weighs into the final decision (King et al., 1986), it is unclear how useful any of these criteria are in the selection of doctoral students. The answer to this question likely rests with the ultimate training goals for any given program. Doctoral programs vary in their training philosophy (e.g., clinical-scientist vs. scientist-practitioner vs. practitioner-scholar) and within these training philosophies the relative emphasis on research and practice varies considerably. Nonetheless, there are two overarching themes in doctoral training: (1) the functional aspects of being a psychologist, essentially the clinical work, accented by the requirement of the doctoral internship, and (2) the engagement/appreciation for the empirical basis of foundational psychological and clinical research. These aspects of doctoral training have been described in several ways over the years and most recently they have been categorized within functional and foundational competencies (see Fouad et al., 2009; Kaslow et al., 2004; Rodolfa et al., 2005 for comprehensive review of competencies within counseling/clinical psychology).

Prior to discussing the common selection factors typically examined in research, we believe that the issue of 'fit' between the applicant and program, the financial needs of universities as well as universities' accreditation requirements (e.g., the need to graduate X number of doctoral students per year) merits attention. The issue of fit is difficult to fully operationalize, but at the core is the degree to which the applicant's goals for training/professional pursuits are compatible with the program's training goals (and vice versa). For instance, an applicant that would like to have a profession as a faculty at a research intensive university would likely have a better fit with programs that have a strong emphasis on the production of research. Alternatively, a doctoral program might select an applicant whose research interests are a closer match with faculty as compared to an applicant who scored higher on the GRE or had a higher GPA. It is likely that fit shapes both applicants' and programs' selection process (Norcross, Evans, & Ellis, 2010).

There are also financial and university requirement issues when it comes to selecting doctoral students. For instance, for-profit universities depend heavily on student enrollment for maintaining budgetary operations. Thus, the degree to which programs might be more or less liberal with acceptance criteria can vary as a function of need. For instance, PsyD programs typically accept more students with lower GRE scores as compared to PhD programs (Norcross, Ellis, & Sayette, 2010). Alternatively, programs can face pressure to graduate a number of doctoral students to assist with requirements for maintaining Carnegie status (e.g., research intensive). These practical issues in doctoral-student selection are seldom discussed in public forums, but merit more conversation. As universities make decisions to act more like a business than a pillar of academic excellence, the fields of counseling and clinical psychology may ultimately feel the impact.

Beyond relative fit and the pragmatic issues discussed earlier, the larger issue in doctoral-student selection rests with this relatively simple question: How will faculty in clinical and counseling psychology doctoral programs know whether the selection criteria are indeed useful? Or do faculty, aided by various criteria, rely on their intuition

when making selection decisions (Highhouse, 2008). The selection process for entry into doctoral programs, described earlier with some variants, is an established practice with decades of precedent. Thus, we will examine some of the pros and cons of these selection criteria.

Graduate Records Examination (GRE)

The GRE is one of the most commonly utilized selection criteria, and for many programs it is weighted heavily in the decision-making process (Chernyshenko & Ones, 1999; Norcross, Kohout, & Wicherski, 2005). For instance, many programs use the GRE as a screening tool and have cutoff scores that students must exceed before faculty consider other forms of information, such as interviews or personal statements (see Rem, Oren, & Childrey, 1987).

The utility of the GRE in predicting graduate grades and comprehensive exams has been called into question. Chernyshenko and Ones (1999) statistically corrected for the restriction of range in GRE scores and found that GRE scores accounted for approximately 13% to 49% of the variance in graduate comprehensive exams and graduate GPA. Kuncel et al. (2010) conducted a meta-analysis of approximately 100 studies and found that GRE scores (both verbal and quantitative) accounted for approximately 7% to 8% of the variance in the GPAs of doctoral students. Further, GRE scores accounted for approximately 9% to 10% of the variance in faculty ratings of doctoral student performance. These findings are consistent with prior meta-analyses (see Goldberg & Alliger, 1992; Morrison & Morrison, 1995). The degree to which these findings are promising or problematic likely rests within programs and how they utilize the GRE in their selection process.

Although there have been statistical attempts to help correct for the restriction of range in GRE scores, these issues cannot be fully reconciled (e.g., graduate GPAs are also restricted). Also, we only know about the predictive validity of the GRE for students *who were admitted into graduate programs*. Thus, the logic of utilizing such empirical support for the GRE is flawed. Simply, we do not know whether GRE scores for those who did not get admitted would predict their graduate GPAs. Second, academic or clinically based outcomes in most research-student selection studies lack any meaningful indicators of validity (and at times reliability). For instance, we do not know of any studies that have examined the association between student selection criteria and actual clinical outcomes (e.g., pre-/postchanges of clients' psychological distress). Rather, most academic and clinical outcomes are based on professors' ratings of students' performance or GPAs. GPAs are generally restricted in range—as many doctoral programs use a grading system ranging from A to C, with a C indicating a failing grade. Professors' ratings of students' abilities have intuitive appeal, but they are generally not supported with any measure of reliability or validity to other outcomes.

For clinical and counseling programs, the question about whether the GRE will predict clinical abilities is paramount. The empirical literature on the predictive ability of student selection criteria to clinical abilities and/or research acumen is significantly limited and with mixed results (e.g., Allred & Briggs, 1988; Market & Monke, 1990). For example, King et al. (1986) found that doctoral students' GRE verbal scores were *negatively* related to their GPAs for clinically based courses. They also found no significant association between GRE quantitative scores and GPAs for quantitative courses. Piercy et al. (1995) found no significant associations between GRE scores and academic, clinical, and research ratings from professors. Consistently, previous research has found little association between GRE scores and clinical abilities (Hines, 1986). Consequently, GRE scores may be useful, in part, to understand how graduate students will perform overall in graduate education, but appears to provide limited information regarding the how students will be able to learn and, in turn, practice the profession of psychology.

Letters of Recommendation

Letters of recommendation are another source of information commonly utilized in doctoralstudent selection, and they have been rated as important by selection committees and training directors (e.g., Lopez, Oehlert, & Moberly, 1996; Rodolfa et al., 1999). Letters of Recommendation are intended to give a sense of an applicant's experience, character, and conscientiousness. However, studies have found they may not provide the intended information. Written by supervisors, faculty, advisers, and others who can attest to the applicant's character and performance, often these letters contain an abundance of praise with limited indications of any weaknesses or shortcomings (Stedman, Hatch, & Schoenfeld, 2009; Grote, Robiner, Haut, 2001). There is a recognition that letters of recommendation should be balanced in their comments of the student; however,

in the high-stakes system that is currently extremely competitive, could one bad letter (or one that mentions applicant limitations) have deleterious effects for an applicant? Simply, as Stedman et al. (2009) pointed out, letters of recommendation do not successfully differentiate applicants. However, they may play a different role in the selection process. For instance, Puplampu, Lewis, and Hogan (2003) found that letters of recommendation are used as a way to verify other applicant information.

In reality, admission committees typically encounter many dilemmas when examining letters of recommendation. For instance, how can committee members understand the value of any given letter? At this point, it is common knowledge that nearly all applicants are in the "top 10%" (Miller & Van Rybroek, 1988). Additionally, many letters of recommendation include statements, such as "in the past [X] years of being a professor [name of student] is one of the very best I have mentored." Letter statements like these are so commonplace, it is unclear what meaning they have for selection committees. More confusion arises from other aspects of letters of recommendation. For instance, there are often variations in the length of letters and depth of the description of the applicant. Typically letters from academic programs faculty are significantly longer than letters from practitioners, and letters from psychologists are longer than letters from professionals from other specialties. Are differences in letter length and depth reflective of the applicant or the writer or both? Is the omission of certain information truly telling?

All applicants have weaknesses and shortcomings. However, the competitive and high-stakes nature of the process seems to have suppressed the willingness of letter writers to suggest any constructive criticism. As a result, many letters sing sterilized praises of each applicant, forcing interviewers to make assumptions about nuances in word choices. Ironically, it may be the most beneficial thing for interviewers to know about the limitations of letters of recommendation as they make the important decision of who will be a good fit for their program.

Although the request to change how letters of recommendation are written and pleas to limit the positive bias are present in the literature (Stedman et al., 2009), no change appears on the horizon. Due to the limited utility of letters of recommendation, programs may consider eliminating this requirement, which would certainly free up countless hours for taxed, overworked faculty and other professionals in writing these letters. However, the likelihood of eliminating letters of recommendation is minimal, and, as a result, programs may wish to consider using letters with caution or, even better, might consider requiring a structure to the letters of recommendations that includes both positive and growth areas of the applicant. This would provide the program important information that they can explore during an applicant's interview.

Interviews

Interviews are a frequently utilized method to select doctoral students. Although interviews of potential doctoral students vary in structure and content, the utility of these methods have been called into question. Highly structured interviews have more support for their utility than unstructured interviews (Conway, Jako, & Goodman, 1995). For example, structured interviews across various disciplines accounted for 6% of the variance in training success over cognitive abilities (Ziegler, MacCann, & Roberts, 2011). However, Berry et al. (2007) found that the association between interview ratings and cognitive abilities was higher when the interviewer had awareness of the cognitive abilities of the interviewee—a situation that is common in the selection of doctoral students (e.g., awareness of GRE scores). Yet, highly structured interviews resulted in a lower association between interview ratings and cognitive abilities. Thus, while doctoral interviews might be confounded with the applicant's cognitive abilities, providing a highly structured interview format may be helpful to buffer these effects.

The degree to which findings in other disciplines will translate to clinical and counseling psychology is unknown. For example, King et al. (1986) found a positive relationship between more favorable ratings during the interview and the number of incomplete courses. Moreover, interview ratings of applicants were not significantly related to professors' ratings of their academic abilities during the program or their GPA in courses. Nonetheless, one lesson can be gleaned from the work examining interviews—highly structured interviews are advantageous.

Faculty and applicants are both looking for a match between personal goals and interests—a professional fit. Beyond assessing the fit of the professional goals and interests of applicants, faculty/interviewers commonly describe a "feeling" they get for an applicant, swaying them toward a desire to make an offer to a specific applicant. During interviews, the degree of fit can be influenced by personality characteristics, professional demeanor,

and interview disposition. These personality expressions are significant because they suggest how one might carry themselves in professional settings and within clinical roles. For example, garnering a sense that a person is too abrasive, arrogant, or lacks self-awareness might suggest to an interviewer that these characteristics would manifest within the therapy room and within professional relationships as well.

However, faculty also must be aware of their own biases during interviews and within their ratings of applicants (see Huffcutt, Van Iddekinge, & Roth, 2011). For instance, individuals have been known to make relatively quick judgments, based on limited information and subsequently search for information to confirm these initial judgments (Dawes, 1994; Gambrill, 2005; Owen, 2008). Common tendencies to identify easily identifiable information, or the availability heuristic (Faust, 1986; Gambrill, 2005), may be particularly salient in the interview process because there is limited time to gather information. Indeed, psychologists are not immune to forming quick impressions based on limited information—within three minutes (cf. Sandifer, Hordern, & Green, 1970; also see Ambady, Bernieri, & Richeson, 2000; Ambady & Rosenthal, 1992 for reviews). Making quick judgments, based on unbalanced information, may not be problematic when they are accurate; however, this is not typically the case. These initial impressions can and likely do guide future interactions and evaluations—even in the face of disconfirmatory information (Chapman & Johnson, 2002; Owen, 2008). For example, Parmley (2007) found that therapists did not adjust their judgments of clients, even when they were given direct evidence to disconfirm their beliefs. It is important to recognize that these initial impressions formed primarily on limited cursory information may capture students' narratives about their relational or cultural history. Although these biases will likely not be fully overwritten, it is important to have structures in place to mitigate their influence, especially, as interviews generally are weighted more than the other information in the selection process (King et al., 1986). Consequently, when it comes to interviews, it is crucial to recognize biases, actively work to gain balanced information, and be humble to accept other sources of information.

Notwithstanding these biases that can occur in the interview process, in-person interviews may be well suited to identify students' relative ability to form and engage in relationships that are genuine, collaborative, and empathic. When students and faculty engage with an applicant, many develop a kind of *feeling* about the candidate, encoding and interpreting the way the person carries him or herself and interacts with others. Although it is often difficult to articulate this feeling, it is often one of the most critical factors in forming an opinion about accepting or rejecting the student. This feeling or gut-reaction needs to be better elucidated and articulated. It is more than a feeling—it is the synthesis of perceived behaviors, nonverbals, interpersonal dynamics, and personality expressions. It makes sense that many professions wish to discard or diminish this feeling because it does not seem grounded in fair and concrete standards and criteria. We propose that these reactions need to be better understood, defined, and linked to key professional roles and outcomes. However, we caution about utilizing a gut reaction without checking biases and identifying (operationalizing) the sources of these feelings, because there could be inherent biases that might plague the process (e.g., stereotyping, discrimination, etc). The biases just described may be experienced or described within the guise of gut reactions or intuition but may be nothing more than a series of confirmatory biases that have been reinforced over the years (also see Ambady et al., 2000 and Gladwell, 2005 for value of intuition). Therapists necessarily bring who they are into the therapy office and into the therapy relationship. Paying attention to, and better understanding, the applicant as a person is wise. Interactions between applicants and current students in the program, faculty, and staff serve as rich illustrations of who the candidate might become as a student, colleague, researcher, and therapist.

Case Example

The following case example illustrates how multiple small expressions of personality can form a general *feeling* about a candidate—rooted in specific behaviors—as well as what that feeling might suggest about professional dynamics.

Following the review of applications, the faculty of a counseling psychology doctoral program invites a group of students to an in-person interview. All students are invited to attend a student-hosted welcome dinner the night before the interview. Applicants Jessica and Rebecca both agree to attend, arrive on time, appropriately dressed, and engage with current graduate students while eating dinner. However, at the end of the night, students report notable differences in their experiences and perceptions of each applicant. Students recalled Jessica excitedly asking questions about the program, admitted to being nervous about the process, and inquired about surrounding area/city. With Jessica, students said they really got a feel for who she was, and could easily perceive her excitement about the prospect of entering the program. Her questions about the city and her acknowledgement of being nervous felt real and students were able to relate to her. At dinner, she made efforts to find commonality between herself and those around her, and the conversation flowed easily. When asked about her experiences in school, she, of course, talked about her strengths and positive experiences, but also acknowledged the truth of how hard it can be to master scientific writing and to keep up with classes.

Descriptions of interactions with Rebecca were a bit different; students described difficulty in keeping up a conversation with her, and found it hard to really get a sense of who she was. Rebecca chatted some about her hometown and her recent vacation, while apparently not making much of an effort to really connect with others. Students were struck by her lack of questions about the program and her seeming disengagement, and were even more surprised when she reported not being nervous at all about the process. The seemingly stoic front that Rebecca exhibited made it hard for others to really gauge her interest, personality, and desires or fears. They felt shut out, and perceived no effort on Rebecca's part to bridge that gap.

Interestingly, the faculty had similar reactions about Jessica and Rebecca through the structured interview process. However, they did not fully recognize some of the interpersonal issues that the students identified. Thus, the student feedback was valuable to make selection decisions.

These case examples have real and meaningful connections to professional dynamics. The behaviors of each applicant can be thought to represent their own relational style and say a bit about their personality. Jessica sought to form connections, found commonalities between herself and others, and allowed herself to be real about her own struggles and fears. It is easy to imagine how this might be exhibited in the therapy office, with Jessica potentially having an easier time forming an alliance and a real relationship with a client. Her readily expressed excitement for the program also seemed to suggest that she possessed the motivation and drive to succeed in a demanding program. She was able to effectively use herself to form connections with others in a real way, beyond a cookie-cutter interviewee performance, which made others trust they were seeing who she really was.

On the other hand, Rebecca seemingly struggled to form connections, for whatever reason. Perhaps she was too anxious about the process, perhaps too preoccupied with finding the right questions and answers, or unwilling or unable to let down her guard to be able to allow others to get to know her. These potential obstacles could easily be expressed in therapy or within other professional relationships. To learn and grow in a training program, one must be able to admit fears and weaknesses to be able to work on them. In therapy, one must be able to be real with a client, use appropriate self-disclosure, and express real reactions or empathic feelings when fitting. A therapist must be able to recognize when mistakes have been made and should be willing to address them to repair any potential rupture that has occurred. Beyond working from a manualized intervention, therapists must be able to form a real and productive relationship with clients, as well as with colleagues and supervisors.

Doctoral Internship

The ratio between number of positions available for internship and number of students applying is admittedly discrepant and has been a source of concern for decades (Baker, McCutcheon, & Keilin, 2007; Hatcher, 2011). One outcome of this inequality is an ever-increasing level of competitiveness involved in attaining an internship placement. This can be seen as a positive aspect as it motivates students to strive to be better, more competent and prepared, and to seek out ways to bolster their abilities. Unfortunately, this inequity also increases students' anxiety and hypervigilance about their prospects of finding an internship.

Students currently applying for internship have increasingly high numbers of clinical hours, publications, and research experience (Rodolfa, Owen, & Clark, 2007). However, this competitiveness also muddies the waters of what these increases really mean and obscures the differences between enhancements in professional competencies and mere inflation of numbers. At the end of the day, training directors' selection processes seek to identify students who will effectively utilize training experiences to become competent clinicians and/or academics in the field. Yet, there is currently no reliable and consistent way this is accomplished, with the closest approximation being the APPIC Application for Psychology Internship essays, letters of recommendation, grades, scores, hours, and the in-person interview.

Over the past 20 years, empirical studies have begun to disentangle factors involved in the application process, seeking to identify salient and superfluous factors. These studies have found mixed results. For example, Rodolfa and colleagues (1999) surveyed 249 accredited internship training directors, who indicated what criteria is most and least important in selecting students to fill internship slots. Overall, there was strong agreement on important inclusion criteria such as career goal fit, clinical experience, interview, letters of recommendation, and personal insight. In addition, these authors also found some agreement on exclusion criteria such as lack of APA standing of the applicant's program of study, incomplete coursework and/or comprehensive exams, and low numbers of supervised practicum hours. Although the consistency between sites is an interesting and important finding, questions arise about the implications of these criteria. For example, even though certain criteria were endorsed by most training directors as important, there were numerous other factors also identified as vital. Using a 7-point likert-scale, training directors rated 18 inclusion criteria with a mean score above 5.

Building on these results, a similar study was conducted about 10 years later, again asking training directors for their perspective on what is and what is not important in identifying qualified applicants (Ginkel, Davis, & Michael, 2010). These authors found the same prioritization of fit between student and site as well as number of supervised hours and experience. However, they identified a greater emphasis placed on personality characteristics. In comparison, Rodolfa et al. (1999) found the top three criteria reported by training directors to be applicant fit, clinical experience, and completion of coursework. In the more recent study by Ginkel et al. (2010), the top three criteria were reported to be fit, the interview, and professional demeanor of the applicant. The contrast between these studies suggests a shift in the thinking of training directors in how they evaluate candidates, exerting greater focus on personal attributes that may say more about how an individual will function as a student and professional. This finding is interesting, given the dearth of evidence supporting the reliability and validity of personal attribute assessments. Clearly, more research is needed to provide training directors and selection committees an empirically supported way forward in the selection process. Beyond agreeing on the relevant criteria, it is crucial to have a clear understanding of what these criteria actually reflect in a reliable and valid way.

What does it mean to intern-selection committees that applicants have 1500 clinical hours versus 1000 and does it matter during the selection process or more importantly does it impact the students' competence as well as desire to learn? Hours give little insight about the types of experiences they are associated with and the degree to which a student mastered skills or internalized feedback. In addition, the interview has been repeatedly cited by studies as extremely important in determining fit between applicants and programs (e.g. Stedman, 2007). Is a well-executed interview merely a reflection of a student's ability to engage in a way they have been told is appropriate or is it an accurate reflection of the interpersonal style of the applicant? Furthermore, as the competition for internship placement continues to increase, and the process becomes more standardized, it becomes even more difficult to determine if the "fit" between student and site is a product of actual fit or a student's attempt to increase the chances of attaining a placement by putting and keeping a best foot forward.

But how are these attributes assessed? Are the same criteria used for each applicant? Do different raters and different programs/sites assess these things differently? When it comes down to deciding between three or four great applicants, how does "fit" play a role? At the end of the day, internship directors seek to admit a developmentally competent student who will contribute to the goals of their respective programs and institutions. Through the use of interviews, grades, letters of recommendation, and other criteria, directors attempt to answer this question: Will this student be a good fit for our site? The gap between these criteria and the answer to this question is difficult to answer.

Student Selection: A New View

Although there is never going to be a perfect system for selecting doctoral students or doctoral interns, we propose two factors that might serve as a useful heuristic to guide doctoral student selection that are rooted in psychotherapy research and student development: Facilitative Interpersonal Skills and Cognitive Complexity.

Facilitative Interpersonal Skills

Facilitative interpersonal skills (FIS; Anderson, Ogles, Patterson, Lambert, & Vermeersch, 2009) refers to an individual's ability to effectively and accurately communicate and interpret messages as well as the ability to persuade others in helpful ways. This domain proves to be particularly important within the field of psychology due to students' work with clients, supervisors, and colleagues. Training directors are in search of students who exhibit appropriate and effective interpersonal skills, yet assessment of this domain is difficult. The current model proposes two distinct factors of FIS that can be useful to assess during the selection process.

The first aspect of FIS is the *quality* of the relationships one is able to build, including the relationship with supervisors, with peers, and the therapeutic relationship a student must build with clients. Within the therapeutic relationship, it is important that students are able to be genuine, are able to form a strong alliance, and are self-aware. These ideas are supported as critical relational facets in psychotherapy literature with studies highlighting the importance of empirically supported relationships as they relate to therapy outcomes (see Norcross & Wampold, 2011).

The empirical literature has identified several aspects of the therapeutic relationship that are thought to be important and influential with therapy outcomes. In many ways, the relationship between client and therapist is the vehicle through which therapists express empathy, unconditional support, and acceptance. Grounded in this relationship, therapist and client work together (ideally) to collaborate on the aims and course of therapy. The alliance is thought to be one of the most crucial components of the therapeutic relationship, and is conceptualized as the agreement between client and therapist on the tasks and goals for therapy, couched within a strong relational bond. Empirical studies continue to identify strong associations between outcome and alliance, with recent studies finding the alliance to account for approximately 8% of outcome (Horvath, Del Re, Flückiger, & Symonds, 2011). Several other relational factors have been identified as important, and contribute to positive therapeutic outcomes. Accurate expressions of empathy can be a crucial factor in therapy, and has been found to account for approximately 9% of variance in outcome (Elliott, Bohart, Watson, & Greenberg, 2011). However, not all empathy is created equal, nor are the effects. Empathy must be accurate—meaning, therapist empathy must be congruent with the client's perception of the issue (Ickes, 2003). This is recognized by clients in the accuracy of the therapist's conception of the big picture and the nuance of their struggle, as well as by the judgment of the congruence and authenticity of the therapist's expression. All these components contribute to the "real relationship," which is thought to be a genuine connection between client and therapist, free (mostly) from transference and countertransference or any feigned or forced inter-actions (Gelso, 2009). At the heart of this concept is the aspiration that both client and therapist will be able to make contact with each other, without the influence of roles or power or defenses, allowing each to form realistic perceptions of the other.

From an intern-selection process, trainers may want to assess these therapeutic relational abilities via video submissions, role plays, or direct therapeu-tic reports (e.g., average of client ratings on mea-sures of alliance or supervisor ratings of trainees' alliance ability). This approach is a logical exten-sion of current practices wherein students are com-monly asked to reflect on their own way of being in "personal essays" or during the interview pro-cess through questions about their "interpersonal strengths and weaknesses." Yet, instead of assessing students' reflective abilities, these techniques offer a more direct assessment of students' relational acu-men. In doing so, there will be a more clear connec-tion between the student-selection process and the activities that they will be asked to do during their graduate training years.

The second element of FIS is the effectiveness of professional relationships. It is one thing to be able to exhibit the aforementioned aspects of a quality relationship, such as empathy and self-awareness, but these skills are merely a foundation for effec-tive relationships. One must be flexible and respon-sive within professional relationships to make them effective. For example, in working with clients, therapists/students must modify their approach to best suit the individual needs and dynamics of each client and their unique concerns. Operating only from an empathic or real relationship approach is devoid of the necessary flexibility to maintain an effective therapeutic relationship. One must also be self-aware within these relationships, accurately per-ceiving when a path must be altered, and then must be willing to change course. This dynamic helps generate and maintain more effective relationships across many professional domains.

Identification of an applicant's level of FIS is relevant for training directors in making decisions about who will be best suited for clinical practice. Asking applicants to respond to complex clinical situations in the interview is one way to structure the interview and examine applicants' abilities to engage in FIS. Here are some example dilemmas that might be useful during the interview process.

Dilemma I

A client that you have been working with for several weeks arrives for her regularly scheduled 4:00 p.m. appointment at your office. The woman presented for therapy due to the recent loss of a sig-nificant relationship and was initially very distressed. However, she has been doing markedly better in the last few sessions, expressing renewed feelings of hope and stability. Today, she walks through your office, sits down, and announces that she went out to lunch and had a few drinks and is now feeling moderately drunk. You express to the client that this is not acceptable, that your agency has a policy against seeing clients who are intoxicated, and that she will need to reschedule. Angrily, the client tries to persuade you to change your mind, and when this fails, she picks up her keys to leave, dropping them on the floor on her way out.

What are you initial concerns for the client?

Would you see the client or follow the agency policy? Why or why not?

When the client attempts to leave, would you attempt to take her keys from her?

What concerns do you have regarding your relationship and the trajectory of therapy at that point?

Dilemma II

You and a client have been working together for several sessions. During one session, you pose an interpretation/challenge that the client is not happy about. In fact, it offends and angers the client quite a bit. Although you attempt to calm the client down and explain your vantage point, the client stands to leave, hoping to storm out of your office.

Do you stand, attempting to stop the client from leaving?

Do you stay seated, letting the client leave if they wish?

If they do leave, what are you immediate concerns?

What concerns do you have about your work at this point?

What aspects of the therapeutic relationship may now be in flux?

Dilemma III

As a practicum student, you have recently been placed at a new training site and have been working with your clients and supervisor for a few weeks. Your supervisor has suggested that you regularly assess your clients for depression, anxiety, and self-harm. In addition to these routine evaluations, your supervisor also has suggested that you assess *all* clients for a new personality disorder that she has recently become fascinated by. In fact, she believes a large proportion of the population may in fact experience some degree of this disorder, and as such, she would like you to screen all your clients for it. The disorder and assessment tool are not well validated, and you are skeptical of the diagnosis. However, your supervisor is asking you to administer the measure to all of your clients.

What are your initial tendencies to respond?
What are the issues at stake for your clients?
How might you handle the situation with your supervisor?

Within these three dilemmas, there is arguably no "right" answer or outcome. Ultimately, these questions seek to understand the ways in which trainees process and make decisions about difficult situations. Ideally, responses would reflect consideration of multiple viewpoints, different potential pathways of action, and possible consequences and benefits of choices. It is hoped that answers to these dilemmas include perspective taking of the client, supervisor, or colleagues, and is sensitive to the intersection of multiple dynamics embedded in one scenario. Responses that exhibit an overreliance on dogmatic or rigid perspectives may suggest that the trainee has difficulty making autonomous choices or does not engage in a self-reflective process. For example, answers that rely on textbook "solutions" or overdependency on "what my supervisor tells me to do" may exhibit a lack of independent thinking or evaluation of risks and benefits of interpersonal situations. Those who are able to bring themselves into the process, evaluating their reactions and how their personality and culture may evoke certain responses, show a willingness to examine internal processes during difficult situations.

Cognitive Complexity

With regard to doctoral student or doctoral intern selection, it would behoove programs to select students who have high cognitive complexity (Holloway & Wampold, 1986). Cognitive complexity guides how students interact with their professors, supervisors, empirical articles, and their clients (Owen & Lindley, 2010; Spengler, Strohmer, Dixon, & Shivy, 1995). Cognitive complexity generally applies to many of the competencies desired for psychologists, such as how to make ethical decisions or the selection of treatments based on empirical evidence and clinical expertise.

There are various forms of cognitive complexity, such as daily thoughts or session thoughts, which reflect basic knowledge, such as GRE scores or knowledge about specific psychological concepts (Owen & Lindley, 2010; Spengler et al., 1995). Additionally, meta-cognitions involve the ability to reflect on thought processes (King & Kitchener, 1994). This ability is consistent with competencies that involve self-reflective processes and conceptualization abilities of the therapy process (Owen & Lindley, 2010). However, the heart of the cognitive complexity rests with how individuals understand the nature of knowledge and the acquisition of knowledge or epistemic cognitions.

Epistemic models generally describe the developmental nature of thought process moving from a dualistic, relativistic, to constructivist belief system. More specifically, epistemic models describe the ways individuals view the certainty of knowledge, the acquisition of knowledge, and the process of making decisions (cf. King & Kitchener, 1994). Generally, higher levels of cognitive complexity are denoted by an appreciation of relative instability of knowledge and yet still being able to form a decision based on available information (Owen & Lindley, 2010). Moreover, knowledge acquisition is done through a thoughtful analysis of various sources of information (e.g., experts, data, and personal experiences) and not resting on simple heuristics or authorities for answers.

For most issues in counseling and clinical psychology there are multiple, potentially equal answers. For instance, therapists constantly are challenged to answer this fundamental question: What therapy approach should be utilized for client X who also experiences diagnosis Z at this time? Decisions like these lead to no clear-cut solutions, and warrant critical examination. Thus, we want therapists who can evaluate evidence in a critical way to make informed clinical decisions. These decisions are not easy and should not be relegated to conventional wisdom or reliance on authorities.

To assist in the assessment of cognitive complexity, we provide some example questions that illustrate ill-defined problems in counseling and clinical psychology. We recognize that the difficulty of these questions will need to vary based on the setting (e.g., doctoral-student interviews versus doctoral-intern interviews). However, we hope that these examples will provide a basis for the development of other questions.

Cognitive Complexity Question I

Studies comparing theory-based models of psychotherapy (empirically supported treatments) have shown that bona-fide therapies are effective and they are similarly effective (i.e., the dodo bird verdict; Wampold et al., 1997). This has led to several conclusions. On the one hand, bonafide therapies are effective, but they work in different ways to assist clients. That is, there are multiple equally valid ways (e.g., techniques/approaches) to assist clients' change. On the other hand, bona-fide therapies are effective, but the specific techniques in these therapies are not directly responsible for change. Rather, there may be common factors that are responsible for change (e.g., therapist effects, client factors, alliance, empathy, congruence).

What is your perspective on this issue?

Provide support for your position.

Describe how your perspective on this issue is reflected in your theory of psychotherapy.

Cognitive Complexity Question II

Some psychologists believe that most integrative forms of therapy are not empirically supported. Among other critiques, psychologists on this side of the debate typically claim that integrative therapists seldom have randomized clinical trials to support their efficacy, the therapies are less theoretically cohesive, and what support they do have rests within common therapeutic factors (e.g., alliance, empathy) versus specific theoretically consistent factors. Other psychologists claim that some integrative forms of therapy are empirically supported. They claim that there is empirical support for integrative therapies via a range of methodological approaches, the use of nontheoretically specific interventions in randomized clinical trials (e.g., the use of CBT techniques within psychodynamic therapy) have been shown to predict therapy outcomes, and the theoretical model is more important than the specific techniques.

What is your position on this debate?

Provide a cogent rationale for your position and a counterargument for oppositional position(s).

Are there cases in which your position may be more (or less) valid?

Cognitive Complexity Question III

You are a research assistant in a lab that works with psychotherapy clients in a clinical trial comparing two interventions. Specifically, some clients are assigned to a treatment therapy group that contains what is thought to be the most helpful and impactful aspect of therapy, whereas other clients are assigned to a group that does not contain this

aspect (primarily just support and venting). It seems that the intervention is helping the participants in the treatment group, as reported by the clients and as observed in their overall symptom reduction. However, those in the other group are not receiving the valuable intervention, and although no members seem to be deteriorating, they are not improving at all either. You feel concerned about the well-being of those in the nonintervention group and feel frustrated about the fairness of one group receiving a treatment that is reducing distressing symptoms while the other participants are continuing to experience significant distress.

What are your initial concerns here?

What actions, if any, might you take? Why?

What are the critical issues to consider?

These tough questions pose an opportunity for trainees to exhibit engagement in complex thinking, to evaluate multiple and conflicting pieces of information, and to take a stand on an issue. Trainees who respond in an overtly black-and-white manner may possess a deficit in being able to see a diversity of positions that are still grounded in sound support and logic. These answers may take the form of an over-reliance on personal experience or a single-minded orientation that misses the richness of the "grey" in tough situations. On the other hand, those responses that avoid clear and definitive positions may be reluctant to assert their voice or to be "wrong," and they may lack critical risk taking that will ultimately foster professional growth. Ideally, responses should reflect multiple sources of knowledge, flexibility in thinking, evaluation of competing ideas, and commitment to a well-reasoned answer. In this way, trainees exhibit an ability to be reflexive, independent, and able to take a stand in critical areas.

Conclusions

This paper has reviewed relevant literature describing the selection of psychology doctoral students and interns. Based on this review, traditional methods of selecting students in doctoral programs should be reexamined and this examination will result in the development of new procedures to select doctoral students and interns.

One possible way to examine the selection process is to create training-research networks, which are similar to the practice-research networks, wherein multiple training programs collect the same information and pool the data for greater impact and generalizability. At this point, most research about student selection for counseling/clinical programs and for doctoral internship is incomplete. Although this is problematic in and of itself, there is very little scholarship in this area as it relates to clinical/counseling programs. The applied or industrial/organizational psychology literature is a useful source of broad-based understanding of selection processes (Berry, Sackett, & Landers, 2007); however, it may lack the needed domain specificity for counseling/clinical programs (e.g., doctoral students in chemistry likely differ from doctoral students in a counseling psychology program).

Based on current research, the GRE is beneficial; although, it may not help explain much of the variance in the clinical/counseling skills that students are being most directly trained in and will be essential for their careers as psychologists. The GRE, however, appears to help explain other facets of students' performance—for example, ability in nonclinical/counseling courses—that are also essential for graduation and foundational to the practice of psychology. Simply put, the GRE is a standard well-accepted assessment of prospective students, which has acceptable levels of data to support its use and sufficient data to refute its use as well. Thus, the use of the GRE is a complex decision that is based on the preferences of the faculty, idiosyncratic experiences with students (e.g., one student with a high or low GRE score who did poorly/well/created significant problems), and pressures from outside sources to admit students with high GRE scores. At the end of the day, faculty will need to consider their ethical responsibilities for ensuring that their decisions are guided and supported by well-standardized tests.

Although the GRE has been used to assess potential readiness for graduate education, there currently is no examination to provide information about the readiness of students to proceed to internship training. As the profession of psychology continues to emphasize the "culture of competence" (Roberts, Borden, Christiansen, & Lopez, 2005) there have been increasing calls for a tool to assess readiness for internship. Specifically there have been discussions about the utility of requiring a passing score for entry to internship training on the current national licensing examination, the Examination for Professional Practice in Psychology (EPPP). However, the EPPP or the GRE do not fully assess students' readiness for internship because they do not capture students' skills or attitudes only their knowledge base. It will be helpful for the profession to continue to explore mechanisms to effectively assess readiness for internship for both academic directors of training as well as internship training directors.

There is limited support for letters of recommendation. It is likely that these letters make decision makers feel better about the decisions they make, as they find confirmatory evidence to support or deny acceptance into a program within vaguely written positive letters. There have been calls for more balanced letters (e.g., continue to include positive comments, but also include some areas of growth) that will provide more useful information to internship training directors. Responding to these calls for more balanced letters will be difficult. Academic Directors of Training and faculty are focused on helping their students find internships and as Rodolfa et al. (1999) found, one letter of recommendation that indicates problems or concerns has the power to eliminate an applicant from the internship pool. If there were to be a change in how letters are written, it is clear that there would have to be broad-based support and agreement by all members of the academic training councils. Given the low likelihood of a significant change in how letters are written, it may be useful to have the training councils review the current literature and come to a decision about future use of the letters of reference in the internship-selection process.

As Ginkel et al. (2010) found, interviews were highly rated by internship-training directors. However, level of structure will enhance its utility, as highly structured interviews appear to be more useful than unstructured interviews. It is also necessary to have multiple sources of input (multiple raters, blinded to each other's ratings as well as other sources of data [e.g., personal statement]) as these additional sources of data will provide a helpful context to the interview. When conducting the interview, faculty/staff will find it useful to remain aware of their biases, which may influence their views and evaluations of applicants.

The fit or match between student and program (be it doctoral program or internship site) is a prevailing theme in student-selection decisions. Although some work has been done attempting to define fit, additional research on defining "fit" and how it is explicated during the student selection process would be helpful to applicants and faculty alike. Specifically, it is very likely that match may mean different things to different students and faculty. Many questions could be examined that would benefit the profession and the process of selection. For examples: (a) Does the emphasis on match encourage students to search for programs and internship sites in a manner that is positive and career advancing? (b) Does the focus on match prompt students to better navigate the interview process? (c) Does match influence the agreement on expectations between student and program? (d) Is there a hierarchy of selection criteria (e.g., funding trumps research match) that influences match decisions?

In addition to enhancing the profession's understanding of the critical concept of match, it will be beneficial to increase the attention paid to aspects that impact therapeutic and academic environments, which are difficult to accurately assess. For instance, empathy, genuineness, and being real in therapy are associated with better therapeutic outcomes. The interview process, however, is a stressful event, in which being "real" or genuine is desired but may not occur. Thus, assessing for applicants' facilitative interpersonal skills will be a challenge, but one that may be better able to predict therapeutic skills when compared for instance, to the GRE. Similarly, faculty seek to accept doctoral students/interns who are more cognitively complex and not just vehicles of knowledge who reiterate what is taught to them. The ability to reason and make thoughtful complex decisions is at the heart of clinical/counseling psychology, and it will be beneficial to take cognitive complexity into consideration in the selection process.

Based on our review we recommend the following for consideration by both programs and the profession:

1. The GRE does not help provide a very clear picture of students' clinical abilities. Thus, the use of the GRE in student selection should be accompanied by other sources of information. Using a GRE Score as a cut factor in selection without taking into account other sources of information may result in eliminating students with abilities not evaluated by the GRE.

2. Programs should develop structured interview procedures. The current literature strongly supports the use of structured interviews over less-structured interviews. The use of alternative forms of information within the interviews or in combination with interviews may be helpful, such as role plays, client/supervisor reports of therapeutic processes based on clinical measures, video recorded sessions, or mock sessions. Interviews should also be structured to provide applicants a chance to display their relationship-building skills as well as their ability to think in depth regarding issues they may potentially encounter during their training.

3 Letters of recommendation, although a standard process in the selection process, have many flaws, and the profession may wish to critically review their current use. Hours of faculty time go into writing letters, but if the letters are not taken seriously, then their use and utility in the selection process should be examined. Perhaps the training councils can agree to better structure the process of writing letters or it may be useful for the training councils to consider abandoning the use of letters of reference in the selection of internships.

4. Selecting students into doctoral programs is a critical process that will influence not only the future of the program, but the future of the profession. As the profession continues to take steps toward a culture of competence, the selection processes should reflect these changes and should incorporate an assessment of the students' competencies as established by the profession.

As the selection process is improved, there will be increased confidence in the decisions made and training programs, as well as the profession, and, in turn, the public will benefit.

References

Allred, G., & Briggs, K. (1988). Selecting marriage and family therapy program applicants: One approach. *American Journal of Family Therapy, 16,* 328–336.

Ambady, N., Bernieri, F. J., & Richeson, J. A. (2000). Toward a histology of social behavior: Judgmental accuracy from thin slices of the behavioral stream. In M. P. Zanna (Ed.), *Advances in experimental social psychology* (pp. 201–271). San Diego, CA: Academic Press.

Ambady, N., & Rosenthal, R. (1992). Thin slices of expressive behavior as predictors of interpersonal consequences: A meta-analysis. *Psychological Bulletin, 111,* 256–274.

Anderson, T., Ogles, B. M., Patterson, C. L., Lambert, M. J., & Vermeersch, D. A. (2009). Therapist effects: Facilitative interpersonal skills as a predictor of therapist success. *Journal of Clinical Psychology, 65,* 755–768.

Baker, J., McCutcheon, S., & Keilin, W. G. (2007). The internship supply–demand imbalance: The APPIC perspective. *Training & Education in Professional Psychology, 1,* 287–293.

Berry, C. M., Sackett, P. R., & Landers, R. N. (2007). Revisiting interview-cognitive ability relationships: Attending to specific range restriction mechanisms in meta-analysis. *Personnel Psychology, 60,* 837–874.

Chapman, G. B., & Johnson, E. J. (2002). Incorporating the irrelevant: Anchors in judgments of belief and value. In T. Gilovich, D. Griffin, & D. Kahneman (Eds.), *Heuristics and biases: The psychology of intuitive judgment* (pp. 120–138). New York: Cambridge University Press.

Chernyshenko, O. S., & Ones, D. S. (1999). How selective are psychology graduate programs? The effects of the selection ratio on GRE score validity. *Educational and Psychological Measurement, 59*, 951–961.

Conway, J. M., Jako, R. A., & Goodman, D. F. (1995). A meta-analysis of inter-rater and internal consistency reliability of selection interviews. *Journal of Applied Psychology, 80*, 565–579.

Dawes, R. M. (1994). *House of cards: Psychology and psychotherapy built on myth*. New York: Free Press.

Elliott, R., Bohart, A. C., Watson, J. C., & Greenberg, L. S. (2011). Empathy. *Psychotherapy, 48*, 43–49.

Faust, D. (1986). Research on human judgment and its application to clinical practice. *Professional Psychology: Research and Practice, 17*(5), 420–430.

Fouad, N. A., Grus, C. L., Hatcher, R. L., Kaslow, N. L., Hutchings, P. S., Madson, M.,...Crossman, R. E. (2009). Competency benchmarks: A model for understanding and measuring competence in professional psychology across training levels. *Training and Education in Professional Psychology, 3*(4 Supp), S5–S26.

Gambrill, E. (2005). *Critical thinking in clinical practice: Improving the quality of judgments and decisions* (2nd ed). Hoboken, NJ: Wiley.

Gelso C., J. (2009). The real relationship in a postmodern world: Theoretical and empirical explorations. *Psychotherapy Research, 19*, 253–264.

Ginkel, R. W., Davis, S. E., & Michael, P. (2010). An examination of inclusion and exclusion criteria in the predoctoral internship selection process. *Training and Education in Professional Psychology, 4*, 213–218.

Gladwell, M. (2005). *Blink*. New York: Little, Brown, and Company.

Goldberg, E. L., & Alliger, G. M. (1992). Assessing the validity of the GRE for students in psychology: A validity generalization approach. *Educational and Psychological Measurement, 52*, 1019–1027.

Grote, C. L., Robiner, W. N., Haut, A. (2001). Disclosure of negative information in letters of recommendation: Writers' intentions and readers' experiences. *Professional Psychology, 32*, 655–661.

Hatcher, R. L. (2011). The internship supply as a common-pool resource: A pathway to managing the imbalance problem. *Training and Education in Professional Psychology, 5*, 126–140.

Highhouse, S. (2008). Stubborn reliance on intuition and subjectivity in employee selection. *Industrial and Organizational Psychology: Perspectives on Science and Practice, 1*, 333–342.

Hines, D. (1986). Admissions criteria for ranking master's level applicants to clinical doctoral programs. *Teaching of Psychology, 13*, 64–67.

Holloway, E. L., & Wampold, B. E. (1986). Relation between conceptual level and counselingrelated tasks: A meta-analysis. *Journal of Counseling Psychology, 33*, 310–319.

Horvath, A. O., Del Re, A., Flückiger, C., & Symonds, D. (2011). Alliance in individual psychotherapy. *Psychotherapy, 48*, 9–16.

Huffcutt, A. I., Van Iddekinge, C. H. & Roth, P. L. (2011). Understanding applicant behavior in employment interviews: A theoretical model of interviewee performance. *Human Resource Management Review, 21*, 353–367.

Ickes W. *Everyday mind reading*. Understanding what other people think and feel. New York: Prometheus Books; 2003.

Kaslow, N. J., Border, K. A., Collins, Jr., F. L., Forrest, L., Illfelder-Kaye, J., Nelson, P. D., Rallo, J. S. (2004). Competencies conference: Future directions in education and credentialing in psychology. *Journal of Clinical Psychology, 60*, 699–712.

King, D. W., Beehr, T. A., & King, L. A. (1986). Doctoral student selection in one professional psychology program. *Journal of Clinical Psychology, 42*, 399–407.

King, P. M., & Kitchener, K. S. (1994). *Developing reflective judgment: Understanding and promoting intellectual growth and critical thinking in adolescents and adult*. San Francisco: Jossey-Bass.

Kuncel, N. R., Wee, S., Serafin, L., & Hezlett, S. A. (2010). The validity of the Graduate Record Examination for master's and doctoral programs: A meta-analytic investigation. *Educational and Psychological Measurement, 70*, 340–352.

Lopez, S. J., Oehlert, M. E., & Moberly, R. L. (1996). Selection criteria for American Psychological Association-accredited internship programs: A survey of training directors. *Professional Psychology: Research and Practice, 27*, 518–520.

Market, L. F., & Monke, R. H. (1990). Changes in counselor education admissions criteria. *Counselor Education & Supervision, 30*, 48–58.

Miller, R. K., & Van Rybroek, G. J. (1988). Internship letters of recommendation: Where are the other 90%? *Professional Psychology: Research and Practice, 19*, 115–117.

Morrison, T., & Morrison, M. (1995). A meta-analytic assessment of the predictive validity of the Quantitative and Verbal components of the Graduate Record Examination with graduate grade point average representing the criterion of graduate success. *Educational and Psychological Measurement, 55*, 309–316.

Norcross, J. C., Ellis, J. L., & Sayette, M. A. (2010). Getting in and getting money: A comparative analysis of admission standards, acceptance rates, and financial assistance across the research/practice continuum in clinical psychology programs. *Training and Education in Professional Psychology, 4*, 99–104.

Norcross, J. C., Evans, K. L., & Ellis, J. L. (2010). The model does matter II: Admissions and training in APA-accredited counseling psychology programs. *The Counseling Psychologist, 38*, 257–268.

Norcross, J. C., Kohout, J. L., & Wicherski, M. (2005). Graduate study in psychology: 1971 2004. *American Psychologist, 60*, 959–975.

Norcross, J. C., & Wampold, B. E. (2011). Evidence-based therapy relationships: Research conclusions and clinical practice. *Psychotherapy, 48*, 98–102.

Owen, J. (2008). The nature of confirmatory strategies in the initial assessment process. *Journal of Mental Health Counseling, 30*, 362–374.

Owen, J., & Lindley, L. D. (2010). Therapists' cognitive complexity: review of theoretical models and development of an integrated approach for training. *Training and Education in Professional Psychology, 4*, 128–137.

Parmley, M. C. (2007). The effects of the confirmation bias on diagnostic decision making. *Dissertation Abstracts International: Section B, 67*(8-B), 4719.

Piercy, F. P., Dickey, M., Case, B., Sprenkle, D., Beer, J., Nelson, T., & McCollum, E. (1995). Admissions criteria as predictors of performance in a family therapy doctoral program. *The American Journal of Family Therapy, 23*(3), 251–259.

Puplampu, B. B., Lewis, C., & Hogan, D. (2003). Reference taking in employee selection: Predication or verification? *IFE Psychologist: An International Journal, 11*, 1–11.

Rem, R. J., Oren, E. M., Childrey, G. (1987). Selection of graduate students in psychology: Use of cutoff scores and interviews. *Professional Psychology: Research and Practice, 18,* 485–488.

Roberts, M. C., Borden, K. A., & Christiansen, M. D., Lopez, S. J. (2005). Fostering a culture shift: Assessment of competence in the education and careers of professional psychologists. *Professional Psychology: Research and Practice, 36,* 355–361.

Rodolfa, E., Bent, R., Eisman, E., Nelson, P., Rehm, L., & Ritchie, P. (2005). A cube model for competency development: Implications for psychology educators and regulators. *Professional Psychology: Research and Practice, 36,* 47–354.

Rodolfa, E., Owen, J. & Clark, S. (2007). Practicum training hours: Fact & fiction. *Training and Education in Professional Psychology, 1*(1), 64–73.

Rodolfa, E. R., Vieille, R., Russell, P., Nijjer, S., Nguyen, D. Q., Mendoza, M., & Perrin, M. (1999). Internship selection: Inclusion and exclusion criteria. *Professional Psychology: Research and Practice, 30,* 415–419.

Sandifer, M. G., Hordern, A., & Green, L. M. (1970). The psychiatric interview: The impact of the first three minutes. *American Journal of Psychiatry, 126,* 968–973.

Spengler, P. M., Strohmer, D. C., Dixon, D. N., & Shivy, V. A. (1995). A scientist-practitioner model of psychological assessment: Implications for training, practice and research. *Counseling Psychologist, 23,* 506–534.

Stedman, J. M. (2007). What we know about predoctoral internship training: A 10-year update. *Training and Education in Professional Psychology, 1,* 74–88.

Stedman, J. M., Hatch, J. P., & Schoenfeld, L. S. (2009). Letters of recommendation for the predoctoral internship in medical schools and other settings: Do they enhance decision making in the selection process? *Journal of Clinical Psychology in Medical Settings, 16,* 339–345.

Wampold, B. E., Mondin, G. W., Moody, M., Stich, F., Benson, K., & Ahn, H. (1997). A metaanalysis of outcome studies comparing bona fide psychotherapies: Empirically, "all must have prizes." *Psychological Bulletin, 122,* 203–225.

Ziegler, M., MacCann, C., & Roberts, R. D. (2011). Faking: knowns, unknowns, and points of contention. In M. Ziegler, C. MacCann, & R. D. Roberts (Eds.), *New perspectives on faking in personality assessment* (pp. 3–16). New York: Oxford University Press.

Trainee Evaluation in Professional Psychology

David S. Shen-Miller

Abstract

Trainee evaluation occurs throughout professional psychology training, from the application process through graduation and beyond. Evaluation occurs across the training system, from term-to-term through program milestones and capstone events. Through this process, trainers fulfill their social contract with accrediting bodies and the public, socialize future psychologists, enhance trainees' professional functioning, and gatekeep the profession to produce the best-prepared and highest-functioning graduates possible (Bernard & Goodyear, 2004; Bourg, 1986; Kenkel, 2009; Kennedy & Lingard, 2007). This chapter provides a historical overview of trainee evaluation, information about formative and summative assessments, measurement considerations, potential biases, challenges and implications, and ethical and legal aspects of evaluation. The responsible, thoughtful, reflective use of evaluation is emphasized as a means to promote best practices in evaluation, increase accountability in training, assess the extent to which training programs meet their goals, and enhance the use of evaluation to advance trainee performance. The chapter is set within a contextual focus, as evaluation involves stakeholders across the training ecology in proximal and distal contexts (e.g., training programs, accrediting bodies, mental health practitioners, clients) and is inextricable from the systems in which trainees develop (Forrest, Elman, & Miller, 2008). Implications and future directions for practice and research are discussed.

Key Words: psychology training, trainee evaluation, competency benchmarks, functional and foundational competencies, toolkit

"Psychology…remains an amorphous, inexact, and even mysterious discipline. Possession of a graduate degree in psychology does not signify the absorption of a body of knowledge as does the medical, engineering, or law degree…legislatures…draw on the brave assumption that whatever is taught in the varied graduate curricula of university psychology departments will make one a competent psychologist" (Wellner, 1978, p. 6, cited in Nelson, 2007).

Trainee evaluation occurs throughout professional psychology training, from the moment of entry (or consideration for entry) through internship, graduation, and beyond. Evaluation forms the basis for predictable, reliable, quality performance by graduates of professional psychology programs, and is part of a social contract between psychology trainers, accrediting bodies, and the public (Bourg, 1986). In addition, it serves a number of concurrent aims, including enhancing professional functioning, socializing future psychologists, and gatekeeping the profession (Bernard & Goodyear, 2004; Kaslow et al., 2009; Kennedy & Lingard, 2007). Through evaluation, trainers fulfill their gatekeeping, educational, and ethical responsibilities to prospective students, employers, regulators, and the public to produce the highest functioning graduates possible (Kenkel, 2009; Kitchener, 1992; McCutcheon, 2009; Schulte & Daly, 2009; Younes, 1998). In the process, trainers improve their own training mechanisms, identify areas for improvement, and develop support and remediation plans for trainees and programs (Belar, 2009; McCutcheon, 2009; Schulte & Daly, 2009). Trainee evaluation occurs across the training system, from midterm and final evaluations, to program milestones and capstone events (e.g., dissertation, internship). Although some aspects of training may more obviously include evaluation (e.g., clinical work, research, coursework), others (e.g., interpersonal interactions) may be less directly or formally evaluated.

Below, a historical overview of trainee evaluation is provided, leading up to and including the competency benchmarks movement. Formative and summative assessments, measurement considerations, potential biases, challenges and implications of evaluation, and ethical and legal aspects of evaluation are addressed. Because of the prominence of the competency benchmarks movement within psychology, much of the discussion on trainee evaluation focuses on competency evaluation. This discussion occurs within a contextual focus, based on the reality that as an essential and foundational part of psychology training, evaluation involves stakeholders across the training ecology in proximal and distal contexts (e.g., training programs, accrediting bodies, mental health practitioners, clients), and is inextricable from the systems in which trainees develop (Falender et al., 2004; Forrest, Elman, & Shen Miller, 2008).

History of Evaluation

Evaluation in psychology training began with attention to educational processes and outcomes, focusing on individual trainees and graduates (through credentialing, licensure, certification) and programs and institutions (through accreditation; Matarazzo, 1977). Initially, trainees were assessed relative to their mastery of curriculum and content knowledge (DeMers, 2009; Kaslow et al., 2009; McCutcheon, 2009; Nelson, 2007). Over time, through zeitgeist and political shifts, programs experienced internal and external pressures to emphasize learning outcomes consistent with the actual practice of psychology. One major change occurred in 1973 with the Vail conference, in response to concerns that training programs' and licensing and credentialing bodies' focus on content knowledge (rather than the skills necessary for competent psychological practice) led to inadequate protection for the public (Koocher, 1979; Korman, 1973; Nelson, 2007; Peterson, 1997). Following this conference, programs began to shift toward evaluating the extent to which trainees achieved skills necessary for competent practice, moving from an "output"-based approach (what graduates knew and how much they produced in terms of research productivity and laboratory resources) to an "input"-based approach (how graduates incorporate what they have learned into their professional performance; Donova & Ponce, 2009; McCutcheon, 2009).

These changes continued in 1976 and 1977 as the American Psychological Association (APA)'s Board of Professional Affairs, APA's Education and Training Board, the Council of Graduate Departments of Psychology, state psychology licensure boards, and the National Register of Health Service Providers in Psychology held education and credentialing meetings to establish a required knowledge base for graduate programs in psychology that could serve as a competence guide for psychologists in training (Nelson, 2007). At around the same time, the National Council of Schools and Programs of Professional Psychology (NCSPP) shifted toward specific learning outcomes and competencies, which was reinforced in the final report of the Joint Council of Professional Education in Psychology in 1990 (Nelson, 2007).

Around this time, the United States (U.S.) Department of Education was calling for increased attention to learning outcomes, and across the nation individuals were concerned about psychology's ability to affect people's lives. The 1980s and 1990s saw increased calls for accountability in education across universities and in psychology programs from the U.S. Secretary of Education, state higher education authorities, and practitioners and licensing authorities, which led to major changes in accreditation standards. These changes included heightened focus on assessment, establishment of competence domains, matching training models with expected outcomes, and identifying specifically *how* trainees demonstrated competence in the areas of knowledge and skills outlined by their programs (Nelson, 2007).

The Competencies Movement

In the context of these changes in accreditation, education and training, multiple health-care training programs turned to competencies as a desired way to conceptualize and evaluate education and training outcomes (Kaslow et al., 2009). The NCSPP developed the first model of competence for education and training in professional psychology in 1997 (Kaslow et al., 2009; Peterson, Peterson, Abrams, & Stricker, 1997), followed by the Practicum Competencies initiative (led by the Council of Chairs of Training Councils and the Association of Directors of Psychology Training Clinics) in 2001 (Hatcher & Lassiter, 2007). In 2002, at the Competencies Conference: Future Directions in Education and Credentialing, representatives from training, credentialing and regulation, research, practice, public interest, and education worked toward consensus on core foundational and functional competencies necessary for professional psychology practice, and for methods to infuse and assess competencies in education and training (Kaslow, 2004; Kaslow et al., 2004, 2007). The most well-known outcomes were the "cube" model of competency assessment (Rodolfa et al., 2005), which provided a developmental model for assessing foundational and functional competencies (Fouad et al., 2009) similar to the NCSPP's Developmental Achievement Levels (Kenkel, 2009), and a set of guiding principles for the assessment of competence (Kaslow et al., 2007). Principles for the assessment of competence include: (a) major culture shift within programs; (b) conceptualizing competencies as generic, holistic, and developmental abilities; (c) the use of a developmental perspective in assessment; (d) integration of formative and summative evaluations; (e) collaboration across constituency groups; (f) reflection of fidelity to practice, and use of valid and reliable methodologies; (g) incorporation of generic and specialty foundational and functional competencies; (h) use of a multitrait, multimethod, and multi-informant process; (i) use of self-reflection and self-assessment; (j) focus on interpersonal functioning and professional development; (k) inclusion of and sensitivity to individual and cultural diversity; (l) specific focus on ethics as a cross-cutting competency; (m) attention to *capability* (i.e., skill adaptability, ability to generate knowledge, ongoing improvement) in addition to competence; (n) inclusion of strategies to address competence problems once identified; and (o) training evaluators in effective evaluation methodologies (Kaslow et al., 2007).

The APA's Board of Educational Affairs' Task Force on Assessment of Competence in Professional Psychology later refined Rodolfa et al.'s model, producing guidelines and principles for assessing competence and operationalizing the essential components and behaviors of all benchmark outcome competencies (functional and foundational) across all levels of education and training consistent with these guiding principles (Fouad et al., 2009). In this revision (Fouad et al., 2009), behavioral criteria were associated with each domain of functional and foundational competence, including essential components for each competency along with examples of behavioral anchors at each of the three major stages of transition within doctoral-level training: readiness for practicum, readiness for internship, and readiness for entry into practice (Kaslow et al., 2009). Also in 2009, the Assessment of Competency Benchmarks Workgroup produced a "toolkit" to help trainers select and implement assessment methods to identify "learning outcomes of greatest relevance to effective professional functioning" for trainees planning to provide health services and seek credentialing (Kaslow et al., 2009, p. S28). This toolkit also built on the guiding principles and recommendations for the assessment of competence (Kaslow et al., 2007).

These shifts also affected accreditation, licensure, and credentialing (McCutcheon, 2009). Accreditation standards began to stipulate that programs specify education and training objectives in terms of expected competencies of graduates (McCutcheon, 2009). In keeping with the competencies movement, the Mutual Recognition Agreement of the Regulatory Bodies for Professional Psychologists in Canada provided competency-based recommendations for evaluating those seeking entry into the profession; this agreement led to changes in accreditation, as well as the training and evaluation of trainees in professional psychology programs (Hadjistavropoulos, Kehler, Peluson, Loutzenhiser, & Hadjistavropoulos, 2010; Hunsley & Barker, 2011).

Competence Defined

The competency movement marked a "cultural shift" within professional psychology (Roberts, Borden, Christiansen, & Lopez, 2005); competence across multiple domains often forms the basis of trainee evaluation. In their frequently cited definition, Epstein and Hundert (2002) defined competence as a developmental, context-dependent, and impermanent skill set that includes the

> habitual and judicious use of communication, knowledge, technical skills, clinical reasoning, emotions, values, and reflection in daily practice for the benefit of the individual and community being served … competence depends on habits of mind, including attentiveness, critical curiosity, self-awareness, and presence. (pp. 227–228)

This definition meshes with that of the workgroups at the 2002 Competencies Conference;

those groups identified both functional and foundational competence domains of "(a) scientific foundations and research; (b) ethical, legal, public policy/advocacy, and professional issues; (c) supervision; (d) psychological assessment; (e) individual and cultural diversity; (f) intervention; (g) consultation; and (h) professional development" (Roberts et al., 2005, p. 359). Roberts and colleagues pointed out that although some domains (e.g., ethics, diversity) are necessary for all tasks related to psychological practice, others (e.g., assessment, supervision) are specific to certain roles or tasks and are therefore functional in nature. Roberts and colleagues noted that the workgroups identified two additional areas of competence including "personal suitability or fitness for the profession...[and] information management and evaluation of the nature and quality of information" (p. 359) related to the use and application of research and scholarship, (e.g., hypothesis generation, testing, and self-assessment) along with other aspects of professional functioning that may be more inherent to individuals (e.g., empathy).

Competence exists along cognitive, relational, affective, moral, behavioral, and integrative dimensions. It is typically divided into foundational (i.e., knowledge, skills, attitudes and values that form the base from which psychologists perform their specific duties and functions) and functional competencies (i.e., daily functions that psychologists perform), and is typically measured or evaluated through performance (Kaslow et al., 2009). Foundational competencies include scientific knowledge and acumen; professionalism; performance in interpersonal relationships; respect for and integration of ethics, legal standards, and individual and cultural diversity; and ability to assess, evaluate, and function in interdisciplinary systems (Kaslow et al., 2009). Functional competencies include assessment, intervention, consultation, research, evaluation, supervision, teaching, administration, management, and advocacy (Fouad et al., 2009; Kaslow, Falender, & Grus, 2012; Rodolfa et al., 2005).

Reactions to the Competencies Movement

A number of authors have identified the benefits of competency benchmarks, including increased protection of the public, flexibility in training around trainee needs and progress, heightened connection between graduate training and necessary skills for professional psychological practice, and keeping pace with other health-care professions (e.g., Belar, 2009; DeMers, 2009; Donova & Ponce, 2009; Fouad et al., 2009; Kenkel, 2009; Schulte & Daly, 2009). The shift to competency-based approaches has transformed the ecologies in which psychologists are trained, including changes at the accreditation, regulation, credentialing and program levels (Kaslow et al., 2012), and has moved evaluation from a normative to a criterion basis, holding all trainees to a common standard rather than ranking them in relation to one another (Falender et al., 2004; Peterson, 2004). The competency model conveys the functional and foundational knowledge, skills, and attitudes required of a professional psychologist to trainers, trainees, other health professionals, and the public (Kenkel, 2009; Schulte & Daly, 2009), and its focus on reflection, self-care, establishment of professional identity, and effective interpersonal skills includes emerging as well as existing skills (Donova & Ponce, 2009). By providing concrete, essential components of core competencies, behavioral anchors, and specific levels of training and outcomes for evaluation (e.g., readiness for practicum, internship, entry to practice), the benchmarks may resolve concerns that programs with different training models are producing graduates who share the label of "professional psychologist" despite possessing highly variable skills and/or competencies (DeMers, 2009). Donova and Ponce also noted that the clarity of the benchmarks may help trainers confront and/or develop remediation plans with trainees having difficulty developing or maintaining competence, commenting that students who do well in an easily defined area (e.g., academics), may perform less well in less clearly defined domains (e.g. interpersonal sensitivity, professionalism). Operationalization of competencies also provides a clearer paper trail if remediation or dismissal is needed (Gilfoyle, 2008).

Competency benchmarks have been incorporated into training (e.g., Falender & Shafranske, 2004; Falender et al., 2004; France et al., 2008; Kaslow et al., 2012; Kerns, Berry, Frantsve, & Linton, 2009), applicant screenings for doctoral programs (Kenkel, 2009; McCutcheon, 2009) and post-licensure decisions related to readiness and/or fitness to practice (Kerns et al, 2009). The benchmarks also have affected training philosophies and approaches to training across psychology, and different specializations have adapted and refined them (e.g., France et al., 2008; Masters, France, & Thorn, 2009). Researchers have also focused on applying the diversity aspects of the benchmark competencies to training in supervision (e.g., Kune & Rodolfa, 2013; Wong, Wong, & Ishiyama, 2013).

Nevertheless, the competencies have not been universally accepted without critique. For example, some authors (e.g., DeMers, 2009; McCutcheon, 2009; Roberts et al., 2005) have raised administrative and organizational concerns about how to classify competencies, and questions about validation and evaluation of the benchmarks. These authors questioned whether all areas of competency (e.g., advocacy) are measurable, and the advisability of universal application of the benchmarks, given differences among training models in perceptions of competence and the acquisition of competence. Others (e.g., McCutcheon, 2009; Schulte & Daly, 2009) raised concerns about unintended consequences (e.g., competency benchmarks becoming a uniform standard for professional psychology and for comparisons across programs). Some authors (e.g., McCutcheon, 2009; Roberts et al., 2005) have indicated the need to (a) identify which competencies are critical and which are preferred (e.g., competence in management and administrative versus intervention and conceptualization), (b) determine whether equal levels of competence are required across all areas; and (c) consider the extent to which competencies are aspirational or reflective of real-world practice.

In addition, some authors have critiqued an isolated notion of competency, observing that, in actual practice, significant overlap exists among competencies. Schulte and Daly (2009) noted that measuring competence is difficult, given the contextualized and overlapping nature of some competencies. Belar (2009) agreed, emphasizing the need to recognize how competencies interrelate and interact, and stressing that competency evaluation should include "real-life" (vs. analog) assessment and target complex competencies (e.g., clinical decision making) that transcend whether trainees simply "get it right." Kreiter and Bergus (2009) similarly emphasized the difference between evaluating observable attributes (assumed to generalize to similar skills) and underlying constructs (e.g., clinical reasoning), assumed to consist of foundational skills.

At the same time, just as the national zeitgeist moved psychology toward a utilization focus on competencies, other movements within the larger profession of psychology (and beyond) continue to affect trainee evaluation at local and national levels. For example, McCutcheon (2009) noted that APA Council of Representatives' suggestion to eliminate the postdoctoral year of training may heighten the need for standardization of practicum hours and evaluation due to concerns about client care post

graduation. He emphasized that the potential to grant licensure after successful completion of internship "makes vivid for internship faculty their increased responsibility as gatekeepers for the profession" (p. S51).

Systemic Considerations

In addition to the critiques already noted, some authors have noted that (a) trainee development is embedded within the training system, and (b) systemic dynamics influence trainee evaluation (e.g., Forrest, Elman, & Shen Miller, 2008; Lichtenberg et al., 2007; Shen-Miller, Forrest, & Elman, 2009; Shen-Miller, Forrest, & Burt, 2012; Schulte & Daly, 2009). Consequently, those authors have advocated that trainee evaluation and competency evaluation include a systemic focus. Schulte and Daly pointed out that trainers often assume that competence is an individual trainee trait, rather than contextually situated, arguing that an exclusive focus on individual competence misses larger contextual concerns (e.g., agency setting, regulatory environment, complexity of the case, trainee caseload, trainer misbehavior) that may affect development or performance. Other authors have noted that conflict among trainers and/or systemic dysfunction can affect trainee performance as well as evaluation (Jacobs et al., 2011; Shen-Miller et al., 2012), as can a lack of institutional support (Lichtenberg et al., 2007). In addition, Peterson (2004) noted that faculty members hold various attitudes (i.e., *romantic, modernist,* and *postmodern*) toward training that also can affect the process of trainee evaluation. *Romantic* attitudes emphasize interpersonal, intuitive, soulful, deeply committed relational and creative qualities (viewed as "soft," "female," qualities, associated with humanist and object relations approaches), whereas *modernist* approaches are rooted in enlightenment ideology, emphasizing rationality, knowledge, and solvable problems (viewed as "hard," "male," and scholarly, associated with knowledge, creation, and acquisition, as well as behavioral, cognitive, and systems approaches). *Postmodernist* approaches include multiple views on reality, and emphasize context, constructionism, reflexivity, emic, multiculturalism, and narrative approaches. Peterson asserted that these different attitudes toward training permeate program cultures around evaluation; for example, modernist approaches tend to value knowledge production and evaluation over interpersonal skill development, which affects program goals (e.g., focused on production of knowledge), everyday classroom activities (organized in seminar format), and student evaluation formats (competition versus criterion based).

Accordingly, assessments should involve trainers and other stakeholders from across the training system (including other trainees), and they should be multidimensional and multimethod (e.g., including grades, practicum and internship evaluations, and other program benchmarks such as comprehensive examinations; Kaslow et al., 2007; Petti, 2008). Kaslow et al. (2009) agreed, recommending a comprehensive approach to evaluation including multiple methods and informants, and cross-sectional and longitudinal data, noting that some competencies develop and are best evaluated over the long term. Trainers should also examine personal and program training philosophies, as well as consistency among evaluation tools, goals, and philosophies.

A sustained, systemic approach to evaluation can address such concerns and improve the overall quality of training, feedback, and development. A number of authors (e.g., Gonsalvez & Freestone, 2007; McCutcheon, 2009) have highlighted the value of collaboration between training programs and practicum and internship sites on the use of, training in, and agreement about evaluation tools. For example, Kenkel (2009) emphasized the importance of trainer endorsement of the use of competency benchmarks across the education and training ecology (i.e., doctoral programs, internships, postdoctoral programs, licensing boards). Systemic agreement on the use of benchmarks may heighten chances that trainers across sites and at each level of training will evaluate trainees according to similar standards. Simultaneously, such agreements may highlight accountability across the training system, clarifying which trainers are responsible for providing training in competencies that are appropriate to their agency's mission, and decreasing chances that trainers will avoid intervening with trainees having difficulty with competence problems (Forrest et al., 2008; Johnson et al., 2008).

Calls for trainers to give honest, accurate feedback could also benefit from a systemic approach to evaluation. Emphasizing consistency in feedback and networks of support for students across the training ecology may strengthen trainers' resolve in delivering honest, accurate feedback, as may bolstering trainers' comfort and knowledge about the importance of maintaining good working relationships while giving honest feedback (Schulte & Daly, 2009). Choosing evaluation tools that encourage honest, accurate, systemically based feedback can

also promote these results, because no one trainer will be singled out for providing difficult feedback (Baldo, Softas-Nall, & Shaw, 1997; Jacobs et al., 2011; Jordan, 2002; Schulte & Daly, 2009).

The Role of Program Culture in Evaluation

Program faculty can move toward consistent, systemic evaluation through crafting individual program cultures to shape trainees' (and trainers') attitudes about evaluation (Peterson, 2004) and their willingness to engage in it. Program factors such as trainers': (a) interactions among themselves and with students; (b) modeling roles and professional behavior; (c) understanding differences between client and student roles; and (d) theoretical positions on evaluation all affect program-wide attitudes about evaluation and can be targeted to enhance investment in the process (Peterson, 2004). Other factors (e.g., student evaluation of trainers, the extent to which the environment is competitive versus collaborative, implications of evaluation, fears about risk taking, and the perceived safety of the environment) similarly affect attitudes about evaluation and can be similarly and strategically addressed (Peterson, 2004). Developing program cultures in which feedback and ongoing evaluation are integrated into daily life and students are trained to give and receive feedback and engage in self-assessment can instill beliefs that such assessments continue across the professional lifespan rather than winding down following graduation and licensure (Kenkel, 2009; Roberts et al., 2005). Roberts et al. pointed to Belar et al.'s (2001) series of self-directed questions about requisite knowledge and skills as an excellent source for teaching self-assessment of competence among trainees.

As another way to build trainee confidence in evaluation, Peterson (2004) advocated for faculty openness to being evaluated, noting, "the willingness to be observed and evaluated increases one's legitimacy as an assessor of the professional functioning of others. Faculty members should not expect to create a culture in which students are willing to be observed and evaluated without modeling it themselves" (p. 424). Peterson suggested that faculty members who actively seek and model receptiveness to feedback create a program culture in which evaluation and feedback are considered necessary and desirable parts of graduate training. On a related noted, Donova and Ponce (2009) commented that using a set of required skills assumes that trainers are competent to impart such skills and that programs are equipped to deliver training in all competency areas to trainees; those authors suggested that trainers may need to demonstrate their ability to teach the competencies needed for trainees to reach the benchmarks.

Evaluating Trainees

Best practices in trainee evaluation start with definitions and clear communication about what is to be evaluated and careful consideration in choosing measures and timing, followed by detailed, specific feedback, from multiple raters, which identifies (a) areas for growth and self-improvement, (b) a timeline for change and improvement, and (c) specific ways to improve performance (Kenkel, 2009; Kress & Protivnak, 2009; London, 2003). Similar to Peterson's (2004) observations (noted earlier), Cowburn, Nelson, and Williams (2000) recommended that evaluation measures be consistent with programs' philosophies about training. Formal evaluation of skills also conveys their importance to trainees (Brooks, Mintz & Dobson, 2004). Nelson (2007) suggested that evaluations should help trainees advance their thinking beyond individual domains of competencies (e.g., assessments, interventions) to more complex and integrative competencies (e.g., differential diagnosis, case conceptualization, reflective thinking), and commented that trainers use these criteria to evaluate the effectiveness of their evaluations. Trainee evaluation also provides opportunities to reexamine the clarity of training goals and objectives, the effectiveness of the training program and teaching methods (e.g., pedagogical approaches with multiple learner characteristics and learning styles; Belar, 2009; Kreiter & Bergus, 2009; McCutcheon, 2009; Norcross, Stevenson, & Nash,1986), and the impact of services on the community (Roberts et al., 2005). For example, McCutcheon (2009) recommended that trainers ask a mix of program-directed questions to complement evaluation:

> What are the goals of our program? What are the competencies that we consider important in our graduates? What level of attainment is minimally necessary for successful completion of the internship? What elements of our program facilitate intern development in these competencies?…What faculty characteristics, with which students, under what circumstances, make successful training more likely? How do we know when our training has been successful? (p S51)

Trainee evaluation occurs in summative and formative formats (Black & William, 1998). Formative evaluations provide ongoing assessments with the purpose of providing corrective, developmentally oriented feedback to facilitate growth and development, whereas summative evaluations occur at predetermined developmental endpoints for the purposes of assessing progress, readiness to enter a new stage of training, and gatekeeping. Although most evaluation is formative, the endpoints involving summative evaluation may have higher stakes due to their gatekeeping functions (Roberts et al., 2005).

In terms of competency-based assessment, the competencies should always first be identified, as should the methods by which they will be evaluated and the behavioral indicators to be employed (Kaslow et al., 2009). The training setting and level should dictate the types of evaluations used and the level of competency expected, as different domains and expectations of competence emerge at different points in training (Fouad et al., 2009; Kaslow et al, 2009; Roberts et al., 2005). Such a developmental focus to evaluation is consistent with the Guidelines and Principles for Accreditation (American Psychological Association, 2002), which mandate sequential, cumulative, and increasingly complex training for practice based on developmental level (Roberts et al., 2005). Skills, values, and attitudes are typically assessed through behaviors, and many have suggested that skill assessment be done using an integrative approach rather than looking at analog or isolated evaluations of competencies (e.g., Belar, 2009). Because of the interlinked nature of the competency benchmarks, evaluation can be both compensatory (higher scores in some domains of competency are allowed to compensate for a lower score in another domain to influence the total evaluation score) and noncompensatory (overall minimum scores are required in each domain and as an overall minimum total score; failure to meet a minimum score in one area means failure to achieve overall competence; Roberts et al., 2005).

Choosing Evaluation Measures

Choosing evaluation measures involves considerations of cost, efficiency, practicality, time commitment, ease of administration, and acceptance by administrators, other trainers, trainees, and any people (e.g., clients, peers) participating in the evaluation procedures (Kaslow et al., 2009; Roberts et al., 2005; Veloski, Fields, Boex, & Blank, 2005). In addition, evaluators should consider (a) the competencies to be measured, (b) who will serve as evaluators, (c) the contexts in which assessments will be given and evaluated; (d) the instruments' psychometric properties (e.g., reliability, validity, fidelity), feasibility of use, and strengths and weaknesses; and (e) particulars (including standardization) of coding, scoring and interpreting (Epstein & Hundert, 2002; Kaslow et al., 2009). Schulte and Daly (2009) cautioned that evaluation methods must be empirically supported, including attention to the "consequential validity" (p. S57) of assessments in terms of the implications of their outcomes on trainees, clients, the profession, and the public. This includes attending to the types of questions being answered with an instrument, particularly when competence problems or suitability for the profession are a concern; trainers should reflect on and evaluate their decisions made on the basis of such measurements (Schulte & Daly, 2009). Noting that evaluation requires varying levels of time and energy, DeMers (2009) suggested that trainers select more informative and time intensive measures earlier in training, and less time-consuming (and less informative) measures later in training or after training is completed.

A highly detailed and helpful resource in selecting evaluation measures comes from Kaslow and colleagues (2009), who presented a competency assessment toolkit grounded in competency initiatives in professional psychology and informed by competency evaluation measures in other health-care disciplines. The authors described the toolkit as an "armamentarium for professional psychology," detailing tools that trainers could use to design comprehensive, multimodal, multi-method trainee evaluations. In this paper, Kaslow and colleagues (2009) presented detailed information about a number of evaluation measures, including recommended developmental levels, psychometric properties, strengths, challenges, implementation and applications to competency domains, and utility in formative and summative evaluations. The toolkit also provides insight into matching evaluation methods with specific competencies, program resources and training levels, and is aligned with the competency benchmarks for professional psychology identified by the Assessment of Competency Benchmarks Workgroup. The authors also noted the importance of considering contextual factors such as program resources, training level, and formative/summative evaluation when choosing evaluation measures.

Specific tools in the toolkit include: (a) 360-degree evaluations (retrospective, concurrent, and individual evaluations); (b) annual or end-of-rotation performance reviews; (c) case presentation reviews (targeting understanding of client system, application of theory and evidence base, treatment approach and implementation, and personal reactions to the case including countertransference); (d) client/patient process and outcome data (e.g., working alliance, symptom checklists pre- and post, ratings from trainees and/or outside evaluators, client satisfaction survey, diagnostic interviewing); (e) Competency Evaluation Rating Forms (numerical behavioral markers for foundational and functional competencies); (f) consumer surveys (service delivery satisfaction, as opposed to clinical process and outcome); (g) performance ratings of direct observation; (h) Objective Structured Clinical Examinations (multiple, standardized clinical encounters or role plays with actors portraying clients with psychological symptoms); (i) portfolios (i.e., written documents, video/audio recordings of sessions or other information); (j) reviews of records (for quality and accuracy of essential elements of client/patient cases); (k) self-assessment; (l) other simulations and/or role plays of actual clinical scenarios; (m) observable, standardized client/patient interviews, assessments, or interventions with mock clients; (n) structured oral examinations (which can include vignettes, analysis of live or recorded performances, role playing); and (o) written examinations (e.g., multiple choice, essay, matching, fill in the blank, integrative problem solving, demonstration of critical thinking and judgment).

Timing of Evaluation

Evaluation occurs across the training spectrum and timeline, both formally and informally, and is a dynamic, ongoing, and ever-evolving process (Cowburn et al., 2000). Kennedy and Lingard (2007) noted the need for near-constant assessment of trainee competence to ensure quality of care and patient safety. Although summative evaluation is assessed at formal endpoints of training, trainers typically are also thinking about trainees' readiness to move to the next level of practice or training when engaging in formative evaluation. Some authors have pointed out that evaluation actually begins with reviewing applicants for graduate study (e.g., Kenkel, 2009), whereas others (e.g., Elman, Illfelder-Kaye, & Robiner, 2005; Kaslow et al., 2009) urged regulatory and credentialing communities to focus on evaluation through the end of training and into licensure. The process of trainee evaluation begins with tight, clear regulation of standards for trainers and trainees, regulated and structured by accrediting bodies and trainer oversight from the beginning of training through internship, gradually loosening over time through postdoctoral training and ending at licensure. However, some (e.g., Kaslow et al., 2007; Kenkel, 2009; Kerns et al., 2009; McCutcheon, 2009) have argued that competencies be assessed across the professional lifespan through postdoctoral residency and postlicensure and ending with retirement. Within psychology there is growing emphasis on maintaining competence for both generic licensure and specialty board certification.

To some extent, the type of evaluation determines its timing. For example, Kaslow et al. (2009) suggested that written examinations potentially are the most useful in assessing readiness to practice, from the practicum to entry into practice domain. Those authors argued that this type of evaluation also has utility in advanced credentialing situations. Hadjistavropoulos et al. (2010) noted the importance of giving students time to develop and apply the feedback they are given in formative evaluations, prior to summative evaluation. Participants in LaFrance, Gray, & Herbert's (2004) study also discussed the importance of the timing of training, noting that students are socialized early in social work education to the role of social justice and activism (related to suitability for the profession), which can affect their trajectories of development of this competency. Craig, Gordon, Clarke, & Oldmeadow (2009) observed that some faculty members argued that conducting summative (gatekeeping) evaluations earlier in their program would increase student motivation, performance, and gatekeeping, noting, "inevitably, students (take) summative assessments more seriously" (p. 539). Those authors noted that summative or gatekeeping evaluations that happen too soon may disadvantage trainees who may need additional time to catch up due to "nontraditional backgrounds" (i.e., non-science academic backgrounds entering medicine). They assessed formative and summative evaluations for four cohorts of students over a four-year period, finding that early administration of some types of summative evaluation disadvantaged students who had the capacity to meet program requirements, but needed extra time due to a lack of preparation prior to entering the program.

Other authors have found that the timing of ratings is important, as evaluations conducted early in training are not sound predictors of later performance (e.g., Gonsalvez & Freestone, 2007; Lazar & Mosek, 1993). Commenting on this lack of predictability in their study of fieldwork supervisors' evaluations of trainees over time, Gonsalvez and Freestone offered several possible reasons for changes in trainee performance, including placement differences (e.g., clinical populations, problem behaviors, clinical settings), varying rates of trainee growth and skill development, and differences in supervisor theoretical orientations. On the other hand, those authors also found that the skill set being measured may influence predictability; although field instructors' early ratings on trainees' interpersonal and professional skills had little predictive value early in training, these demonstrated increased predictive power when assessed later in the training process.

Consequently, the format of evaluations should be considered in conjunction with timing. Craig et al. (2009) found that students with nonscience or alternative backgrounds tended to perform worse on fact-based assessments and somewhat better on critical thinking assessments earlier in their training, and they level out and match peers with science backgrounds later in training. Thus, trainers should consider the *format* and *type* of evaluation when considering its timing, especially when considering the needs of specific students and their policies on admissions.

Finally, questions persist regarding the maintenance of competence among already licensed psychologists, and whether evaluation should continue after licensure. After doctoral study, evaluation is typically limited to the Examination for Professional Practice in Psychology (EPPP) and evaluation by a postdoctoral supervisor (although most states and provinces provide an ethics and jurisprudence exam). Kerns et al. (2009) noted that after licensure,

> despite the aspirational statements about lifelong learning...for most psychologists the required review and feedback from their years of training and supervision suddenly vanish for the rest of their careers...licensing boards never again objectively assess the psychologist's competence, even when renewing the license. (p. 216)

Diversity and Trainee Evaluation

Consideration of the standards against which trainees are measured is an essential part of trainee evaluation. Donova and Ponce (2009) noted that authors of the competency benchmarks did not discuss the sociocultural factors that went into selecting, defining, and operationalizing the benchmarks, leaving the possibility that cultural biases informed both the process and final product. Those authors called for attention to the cultural competence of the tools identified in Kaslow et al.'s (2009) toolkit, particularly as the majority of tools require input from others in the training system. Lack of attention to cultural competence and/or potential biases among raters could seriously affect the outcomes of trainee evaluation through over- or underidentification of competence problems (Elman, Forrest, Vacha-Haase, & Gizara, 1999; Forrest, Elman, Gizara, & Vacha-Haase, 1999; Forrest et al., 2008; Gizara & Forrest, 2004; Shen-Miller et al., 2012; Shen-Miller, Forrest, & Elman, 2009). Roberts et al. (2005) similarly noted the importance of evaluating the cultural relevance of assessment measures, although they did not provide any particular suggestions for doing so.

Previous mental health researchers have evaluated intersections of diversity with evaluation, particularly in the area of supervision. For example, Bernard (1994) noted discrepancies between how supervisors treat race, class and gender issues during supervision sessions and during trainee evaluation, commenting that it is "far too probable that, within supervision, culture is honored in the relationship and dismissed in evaluation" (p. 169). Cook (1994) agreed, noting that unspoken assumptions about race and culture affect every aspect of supervision, including how the supervisory relationship is established, expectations are set, clients are assigned, treatments are planned, clients are conceptualized, and supervisees are evaluated. Writing from a social psychology perspective, Harber (1998) summarized underlying dynamics that affect cross-cultural trainee evaluation, often leading to overly positive bias from Euro-Americans toward People of Color. Those dynamics included: (a) wishes to display egalitarian values to self and others, (b) norms of kindness, (c) sympathy based on history of stigmatization, (d) general awkwardness or ambivalence around issues of race/ethnicity, and (e) holding lower standards for People of Color due to negative stereotypes. Similarly, McNeill, Hom, & Perez (1995) described the likelihood of White professors providing "excessive praise and avoidance of criticism" (p. 250) to trainees of color. Turning to other areas of diversity, a number of authors have suggested that biases and dynamics related to gender and/or sexual identity (e.g., Burkard, Knox, Hess, & Schultz, 2009; Chung, Marshall, & Gordon, 2001; Falender & Shafranske, 2004; Granello, 2003; Wester &Vogel, 2002) that affect psychotherapy also exist in supervision.

Empirical evidence supports these assertions. For example, Forrest et al. (under review) found that when thinking about how culture and language issues might complicate clarity about competence assessments when working with international students, Directors of Training (DTs) expressed concerns about inadvertent racism (not addressing a competence problem due to fear of misunderstanding or being perceived as disrespectful of cultural differences) and accusations of cultural insensitivity being used by a trainee to avoid acknowledging competence problems. This finding is consistent with other examinations of DTs and faculty members' concerns when working at intersections of diversity with trainee competence problems (Shen-Miller et al., 2009, in press). Helms (1982, discussed in Cook & Helms, 1988) found that White supervisors differentially and unfavorably compared "multicultural" to White trainees in areas of receiving feedback, reflexivity, and logistical aspects of supervision (e.g., keeping appointments). Others have uncovered evidence of overly positive biases. Harber (1998) found that majority undergraduate students' evaluations of a hypothetically Black peer's essay was more positively evaluated in terms of subjective (i.e., content) but not objective (i.e., structure) aspects. In addition, in their analog study, Chung et al. (2001) asked supervisors for feedback on a hypothetical trainee case conceptualization and found male supervisors gave significantly lower evaluations and less positive feedback when the supervisee was depicted as female. However, those authors found no significant evidence of bias in supervisors' evaluations based on the putative race of the trainee.

Researchers in occupations other than psychology have reported equivocal results with regard to the influence of diversity on evaluation. Doerner, Spier, and Wright (1989) investigated whether sex or ethnicity influenced performance evaluations of trainees in postacademy law-enforcement training, and found not only that female and Black trainees tended to have lower scores than White and male trainees during early stages of field training, but also that rater characteristics (i.e., race, sex) proved to be statistically significant when evaluating trainee performance during these early stages. In a meta-analysis focused on general occupations, Kraiger and Ford (1985) found that ratee evaluations varied by race, with same-race ratings significantly higher than cross-race ratings. Those authors noted that group composition and research setting moderated effect sizes such that the size of results increased as number of Black ratees decreased, and field studies had larger effect sizes than analog studies. However, Sackett and DuBois (1991) compared Kraiger and Ford's (1985) data with data from a large-scale military study and a large-scale civilian study, and challenged conclusions that raters typically evaluate same-race ratees more highly. Sackett and DuBois (1991) found that Black participants consistently received lower ratings than White participants from both Black and White raters, though ratings from White raters were substantially lower. In contrast, White ratees received virtually identical ratings from both Black and White raters. Sackett and DuBois (1991) noted that the military study and roughly half the studies included in Kraiger and Ford's meta-analysis involved peer ratings, and in subsequent analyses noted that Black peers provided higher ratings for Black ratees, pointing out potential bias in rater training (supervisors are more likely than peers to have rater training).

In contrast, Waldman and Avolio (1991) pointed out that although researchers have identified differences in race-based performance evaluation bias (with cross-race typically less positive than same-race evaluations for Black ratees), differences tend to disappear in nonanalog studies when controlling for other performance characteristics (e.g., experience, ability, education). Conducting a large-scale study of U.S. Department of Labor data, Waldman and Avolio (1991) examined same- and cross-race (Black-White only) supervisory ratings from a broad cross-section of occupations, and considered aptitude, education, and job experience. The authors found that although ratee race accounted for 3% of the variance in performance evaluations, when controlling for ability and experience, the effects diminished to 0.3% of the variance. The authors pointed out that their findings did not include other job-related criteria or dynamics (e.g., job assignments, compensation, networking, information sharing), noting wide variance in evaluations across occupations, speculating that the "perceived fit of the individual to the job may also affect performance evaluations" (p. 899).

Challenges to Evaluation

Challenges exist with regard to trainee evaluation, including relationship bias, trainer and peer difficulty giving honest, direct feedback, problems of instrumentation and definition (including measuring unintended skills), trainee anxiety, time limitations, unexamined power and philosophical differences, evaluating trainees with competence

problems, and assessing some areas of competency (e.g., multicultural competence, interpersonal functioning) (Lichtenberg et al., 2007). In addition, Lichtenberg et al. (2007) pointed out that these and other challenges exist within the context of a lack of consensus among trainers about the importance of implementing competency evaluation across the professional lifespan.

Relationship Bias

Trainers may experience tensions regarding dual functions as educators and gatekeepers (Belar, 2009; Elman & Forrest, 2004; Gizara & Forrest, 2004; Jacobs et al., 2011; Johnson, 2008; Roberts et al., 2005). Most psychology educators feel more comfortable in the nurturer than the evaluator or gatekeeper role (Goodyear & Sinett, 1984; Jordan, 2002), which may explain Scott, Ingram, Vitanza, & Smith's (2000) finding that supervisors often neglect formative and summative evaluation in supervision. Gonsalvez and Freestone (2007) hypothesized:

> It is possible that the supportive and nurturing role supervisors are called to play in their own therapy with clients, and the formative role they play in building up skills and confidence in an often anxious and sometimes vulnerable trainee, conspire against objective and critical supervisory judgments. (p. 28)

Johnson (2007, 2008) agreed, noting that as trainer-trainee relationships involve increasing levels of mutuality, support, loyalty, and advocacy, trainers find that the process of conducting honest, clear evaluation of trainees and fulfilling their gatekeeping roles becomes more complicated. Across studies, mentors have reported and/or demonstrated difficulty being objective and honest when evaluating mentees, particularly when engaging in advocacy roles as well as when trainees are demonstrating problems with professional competencies (Johnson, 2008).

As part of the feelings that arise in these close relationships, trainers may view students with the same lenses used to view clients (particularly in supervisory relationships; Peterson, 2004). Trainers may not want to give negative ratings because of concerns about how those will influence the relationship or a trainee's future, and they may inappropriately frame trainee difficulties (and lack of challenging evaluation) in terms of developmental level (Schulte & Daly, 2009). Donova and Ponce (2009) noted that awareness that doctoral-level graduates owe an average of between $57,791 and

$102,196 (APA, 2008) may also affect the veracity of ratings. Conversely, trainers may experience negative transference or countertransference toward a trainee, and be unsure about how to manage those feelings to engage in fair, balanced evaluation (Jacobs et al., 2011). Peterson (2004) noted that faculty members' beliefs about relationships between faculty and students, evaluation, and loyalty to one's own theoretical orientation can create a program culture that affects pedagogical interactions and evaluations, which can make competency evaluation feel like an "evaluation of personhood" (p. 424) rather than of one's competencies.

Program structures also may contribute to relationship bias due to potential overreliance of training programs on the evaluation of one clinical supervisor (Gonsalvez and Freestone, 2007) or faculty member (Baldo et al., 1997). To combat these difficulties, several authors (Belar, 2009; Gonsalvez & Freestone, 2007) suggested that programs elicit reviews from trainers who are not as connected to the trainee or who are from other departments (similar to an outside dissertation committee member). Roberts et al. (2005) suggested that raters should be free from "demand characteristics" and avoid the personal and program "politics" of evaluations to provide solid, honest feedback (p. 358). In addition, pressure on faculty members not to dismiss or counsel students out of programs for financial reasons may present a fundamental conflict-of-interest with regard to evaluation. Such pressures and conflicts likely exist also during program admissions decisions, due to pressure to enroll a predetermined minimum number of new students (Brear & Dorrian, 2010; Peterson, 2003; Owens, Quirk, & Rodolfa's chapter 18, this volume).

Few researchers have studied the validity and reliability of supervisor evaluations, although those who have done so uncovered phenonema to support concerns regarding relationship bias in evaluation. For example, Lazar and Mosek (1993) compared relevant course grades with supervisor ratings of the performance of 70 students in social work and concluded that the influence of the relationship between supervisor and supervisee (e.g., issues of likeability, familiarity, similarity) on supervisor ratings was sufficient to invalidate and "contaminate" (p. 117) trainee evaluation, noting that criteria that affected the grade from one fieldwork supervisor (i.e., empathy, positive regard, congruence) had no relation to the grade assigned by a previous supervisor. Similarly, Robiner, Saltzman, Hoberman, and Schirvar (1997) found that most supervisors

(59%) acknowledged that their own ratings and other supervisors' assessments were biased, with only a small percentage (11%) believing otherwise. The most common biases identified by participants included leniency (39%) and central tendency (43%), more than doubling the percentage identifying strictness as a bias (16%). Such biases may have been present among participants in Ginsburg, Regehr, and Mylopoulos's (2009) study of medical school faculty members, who identified difficulty giving low marks to students, even when their responses clearly warranted doing so. And in a study of 12 years of supervisor ratings and evaluations of masters and doctoral students, Gonsalvez and Freestone (2007) found evidence of leniency bias and halo bias, noting high intercorrelations among 11 performance ratings despite the fact that early ratings of most skills (particularly clinical skills) did not consistently predict later ratings of the same skills. This poor predictive validity of supervisors' ratings is troubling, particularly considering early identification and intervention with trainees who may benefit from remediation.

Feedback Among Peers

Similar difficulties in honest or direct feedback/evaluation have been identified when asking peers to evaluate each other. Peer ratings may be overly focused in one aspect of evaluation or another, and trainees may be reluctant to identify problems in their peers for fear of affecting their progress, despite perceiving high rates of their peers as having competence problems (e.g., Oliver, Bernstein, Anderson, Blashfield, & Roberts, 2004; Rosenberg Getzelman,Arcinue, & Oren, 2005; Shen-Miller et al., 2011; Veilleux et al., 2012). Some researchers have found that peers avoid identifying problems in their peers for fear of negatively affecting their relationships with peers and/or trainers, as well as how they are perceived in their programs (Shen-Miller et al., 2011). To avoid these dilemmas, Kenkel (2009) suggested that peer feedback and evaluation be incorporated into formative feedback only, rather than summative feedback.

Operational Definition, Instrumentation, and Standardization

Researchers have also raised significant concerns regarding empirical support for evaluation instruments and definitions of competence, including the competency benchmarks (e.g., DeMers, 2009; Kenkel, 2009; Lichtenberg et al., 2007). Kaslow (2004) observed that "psychologists do a reasonable job of evaluating knowledge, but assessment methodologies with regard to skills and attitudes are less well-developed and utilized" (p. 778); most strategies used to assess competence come from other health professions than psychology (Kaslow et al., 2009). Petti (2008) agreed that "a standardized method of evaluating clinical competencies remains an essential but elusive task" within psychology (p. 147). Part of the difficulty stems from a dearth of research in core issues (Robiner et al., 1997) and psychometric aspects of evaluation; many evaluation forms and processes (e.g., supervisor ratings) have not been psychometrically evaluated and are likely plagued by halo effects (Dienst & Armstrong, 1988), including significant inflation of recommendation letters and supervisor evaluations (Robiner et al., 1998; Miller & van Rybroek, 1988). Consequently, Kaslow et al. (2009) recommended psychologists develop standardized assessment tools, protocols, and procedures to measure relevant functional and foundational competencies, to be used across training programs and credentialing bodies.

Standard psychometric concerns (e.g., general instrument reliability, validity, and practicality) also affect instruments and pose challenges to evaluation (Lichtenberg et al., 2007; Veloski et al., 2005). Veloski and colleagues (2005) reviewed 134 medical-training studies that assessed professionalism for discussion of instrument validity and reliability, and found that, in many cases, authors did not report concurrent or predictive validity of measures, reported low (or no) levels of content validity of instruments, and rarely discussed instrument practicality. In their review, the authors rated measures used in only 15 of the 134 studies as having "high" or "very high" validity, and noted that, in most studies, content validity was based "solely on the judgment of convenience samples of local experts, with limited attention to construct, concurrent, or predictive validity" (p. 369). Similarly, in their Competency Assessment Toolkit, Kaslow et al. (2009) provided psychometric information on multiple evaluation methods, noting that many commonly used evaluation tools have only limited psychometric information and/or support.

This problem may be compounded by the reality that trainers continue to use evaluation instruments despite lack of evidential support. For example, although some researchers (e.g., Borders & Fong, 1994; Dienst & Armstrong, 1988) uncovered weak interrater reliability when comparing supervisor's ratings of trainees with ratings by other observers,

trainers continue to assign significant weight to supervisor evaluations in trainee evaluation, due to beliefs that directly observing clinical work leads to more accurate assessment (Norcross et al., 1986). Another example involves evaluation instruments for multicultural counseling skills; Constantine and Ladany (2000) found that not one subscale out of four self-report multicultural-counseling- competence measures significantly correlated with actual multicultural-case-conceptualization ability. In addition, subscales on three out of the four instruments reviewed had significant and positive relationships with a measure of social desirability (Constantine & Ladany, 2000). Similarly, in a study of counseling trainees, Ladany, Inman, Constantine, & Hofheinz (1997) found no significant relation between self-reported multicultural counseling competence and actual multicultural case conceptualization. Despite these findings, self-report instruments for evaluation of multicultural competence continue to be in regular use. And in another example, Kreiter and Bergus (2009) noted that despite low cross-case correlations, low reliability, and little empirical evidence that performance-based assessments are more valid than written tests, beliefs persist among medical trainers that clinical problem solving provides accurate assessment of clinical reasoning. Kreiter and Bergus argued that specific problem-solving approaches that involve construct-centered rather than task-centered problems may cause trainers to evaluate factual knowledge (e.g., a trainee's basic knowledge for solving parts of the examination) rather than clinical reasoning. Craig et al. (2009) observed that even when support (or disconfirming evidence) for an evaluation tool does emerge, those findings are not always transformed to practice, pointing out, "evidence-based education…is just as hard to promote as evidence-based clinical practice." (p. 550).

Other challenges include lack of consensus on measures and conflicting definitions and values among raters, including differences in how raters construc situations (Lichtenberg et al., 2007; Ginsberg, Regehr, & Lingard, 2004; Ginsburg et al., 2009). Lack of operational definitions or conflicting values can lead trainers to overemphasize the role of trainee characteristics and underemphasize the role of context (i.e., fundamental attribution error) when evaluating performance, and have difficulty distinguishing between intentions and actions (including complex interplay among multiple motivations and contextual realities that underlie behavior) (Ginsburg et al., 2009). Ginsburg et al.

(2009) examined medical faculty members' ratings of students' written responses to professionally challenging situations. Although they emphasized looking beyond behaviors and focusing on trainees' reasoning and motivation, the authors found that evaluators varied in their beliefs about the relative importance of the rationale for behavior versus actual behavior, leading to low interrater reliability.

These differences in values and beliefs are exacerbated when combined with lack of clarity about what is actually being evaluated. Roberts et al. (2005) pointed out trainers at each level of training (i.e., graduate programs, internship, postdoctoral training, licensure and regulatory bodies, certification programs) hold different definitions of competence and use different measures and procedures. They suggested that,

> Faculty in doctoral training programs and psychologists involved in continuing education need to refine and operationalize what professional knowledge, skills, and attitudes they value... members of the practice community need to document the self-assessment practices and competence-building activities that help them develop and maintain competency. (p. 360)

Measuring Complex Skills and/or Unintended Skills

Kaslow et al. (2009) pointed out that some tools measure other, unintended skills. For example, Kennedy and Lingard (2007) pointed out that trainers using case presentations to evaluate clinical decision making may be measuring trainees' recall, written, and/or oral communication skills, rather than decision-making processes. Hadjistavropoulos et al. (2010) agreed, noting that in case presentations, a student's difficulty with expressive skills may give the false impression that she/he is struggling in core clinical competencies. Other researchers have noted problems with analog evaluations. For example, written exams on professionalism or moral reasoning may be better at assessing medical students' *knowledge* of what they should do, rather than what they would actually *do* in a situation (Ginsburg, Regehr, & Mylopoulos, 2007; Rethans et al., 2002). These findings are similar to those of graduate students in psychology; in a landmark study (Bernard & Jara, 1986), participants were provided with ethical dilemmas and asked (a) what they *should* do, followed by (b) what they *would* do in a given situation. The authors found that more than half of participants admitted that they would not adhere

to their own interpretations of what was required of them by the Ethical Principles, raising additional questions regarding measurement accuracy.

Other researchers (e.g., Belar, 2009; Schulte & Daly, 2009) have identified problems with evaluation due to the complexity of certain skills and competencies. Other difficulties in this area include difficulty assessing skill integration, ever-developing professional judgment, and the limited generalizability of competence across contexts (Belar, 2009; Schulte & Daly, 2009). Petti (2008) stated that evaluation for practice (e.g., EPPP) is most often knowledge-rather than practice-based, and that there are no widely used measures for evaluating readiness to practice based on actual skill performance. Those authors offered a model (i.e., the Clinical Proficiency Progress Review) for evaluating students' clinical competencies, and included normative outcome data. Hadjistavropoulos et al. (2010) noted that, despite the reality that many skills incorporate multiple competencies concurrently (e.g., clinical skills, case conceptualization, interpersonal skills, research competence, ability to utilize scientific evidence, ethical and professional skills, skills related to supervision), most skills are evaluated individually. Although some skills are evaluated easily, methods for evaluating others (e.g., foundational competencies such as professionalism) may be less clear (Elman et al., 2005; Ginsburg et al., 2009; Lichtenberg et al., 2007).

Measures that could provide complex, multivaried assessment of intersecting competencies are often underused. For example, although case presentations are good tools for evaluating readiness for internship (Kaslow et al., 2009; Petti, 2008) and can serve to evaluate multiple competencies, very few programs use formal guidelines for developing or evaluating case presentations (Hadjistavropoulos et al., 2010). Hadjistavropoulos and colleagues (2010) suggested using case presentations in combination with other tools (e.g., consumer surveys, live or recorded observations, performance ratings, written exams) to explore such complexities.

Trainee Anxiety

DeMers (2009) identified additional evaluation challenges related to trainee anxiety, suggesting that trainees may avoid challenging cases and choose settings, clients, or diagnoses that will allow the best chance at successful outcomes. He suggested that raters include the severity and complexity of situations along with competencies being measured. Peterson (2004) agreed, noting that "safe" environments (often necessary for growth) are often equated with "evaluation-free" environments. Peterson noted that, ironically, evaluation-free or low-evaluation environments tend to create higher levels of trainee anxiety, fostering imposter syndrome and high levels of competitiveness, as well as desires for "riskless risks" in which people wish for trial-and-error learning with no penalties. Peterson argued that evaluation-free environments are not feasible, given training and gatekeeping responsibilities, and recommended "evaluation-rich" environments based on an ongoing flow of evaluative information and feedback (p. 422).

Time Limitations

Other challenges to evaluation include limited time to evaluate skills and provide meaningful feedback. Good, solid trainee evaluation requires significant investment of trainer time and energy. Craig and colleagues (2009) noted program and individual pressures bearing on aspects of trainee evaluation (i.e., grading, organizing, and arranging of assessments), and observed that these and other pragmatics often affect the timing, frequency, content, and structure of assessments. Gardner, McCutcheon, and Fedoruk (2010) examined mental health nursing supervision and found that many nurses resolve immediate clinical difficulties in informal conversations with peers and colleagues, later eschewing discussion of the event in formal supervision despite opportunities in that setting to deepen their work through thoughtful, reflective interactions. Those authors pointed out that pressures to gain information and solve problems quickly amid the often rushed, overworked, harried environment of a clinical setting may make nurses more likely to seek immediate, informal supervision rather than wait for formally scheduled supervision. Gardner and colleagues noted that this can have the unintended consequence of interfering with skill development for attending to details such as narrative, body language, clinical depth, and subtle nuances of the interpersonal clinical relationship.

Inattention to Power and Philosophical Assumptions

Cowburn et al. (2000) observed that assessment involves epistemological assumptions about the role of objectivity and evaluator positionality, commenting that trainee evaluation often includes assumptions that trainers are neutral, "objective" observers, with scant attention to how trainers' identities affect their perceptions of competencies, skills, and interactions with trainees. These authors noted that such positivist approaches tend to perpetuate power and privilege and to devalue culturally specific ways of knowing, and although positivist approaches may be modified in practice, when trainees struggle, trainers tend to return to perceiving themselves as the accurate, objective assessor of competency. In addition to using multiple raters, Cowburn et al. (2000) recommended a reflexive approach in which evaluators consider how their identities may affect trainer-trainee interactions (in practice settings), perceptions of competencies and skills, and the dynamic nature of assessment and evaluation. Cowburn and colleagues (2000) noted that these types of changes in evaluation in social work (vis-à -vis the competencies movement) were driven by principles of fairness, justice, equality, and included heightened attention to power in the trainer-trainee relationship, deconstruction of gender- and ethnicity-based privilege and oppression, and transparency in evaluation.

Evaluating Trainees with Competence Problems

Trainee evaluation also plays a significant role in work with trainees with competence problems, especially with those on remediation plans or in danger of dismissal. In these instances, additional considerations may arise, including trainee vulnerability and anxiety, heightened consequences for negative evaluations, and the potential for difficult conversations and feedback to trainees (Jacobs et al., 2011; Elman & Forrest's chapter 19, this volume). Often trainers have not received training in working with trainee-competence problems prior to an incident, which can make evaluation more difficult. Rapisarda and Britton (2007) conducted a focus-group study with faculty members and practicing professionals to evaluate the effectiveness of supervision as remediation for professional counselors. Although participants were working with professionals and not trainees, some of the findings likely apply. Participants raised concerns about their own competence and responsibility to evaluate professionals with competence problems, including: (a) the effect of sanctioned counselor attitudes on supervision process and outcome; (b) protection and liability for the supervisor, particularly if the sanctioned counselor re-offended or did not cease problematic behavior; (c) multiple role concerns about who the client is; (d) lack of training in this type of supervision; (e) lack of information about the difficulty; and (f) lack of clear, objective criteria for evaluating the relative success of the supervision. Petti (2008) noted a similar problem in terms of a dearth of research identifying when a trainee is unsuitable for the profession, despite trainers' responsibility to act as gatekeepers for the profession.

Philosophical differences among trainers about one's roles and responsibilities in trainee evaluation, particularly when a trainee is struggling with professional competence problems, may affect decisions about how to proceed with evaluation. LaFrance et al. (2004) noted differences between field instructors (willing to work with students to resolve personal life difficulties interfering with clinical work) and faculty (typically distancing themselves from students' personal lives and focusing on students' academic work).

Forrest et al. (2013) also found evidence of the influence of program dynamics on evaluation of trainees with competence problems. In their study, directors of training (DTs), participants who believed their programs were effective in addressing trainees with problems of professional competence (TPPC) noted the importance of shared decisions, responsibilities, and actions, as well as the involvement of multiple individuals from across the training ecology (e.g., adjunct faculty, field supervisors, other trainers). Participants also mentioned the value of mentoring junior faculty in difficult conversations and increasing awareness and commitment to intervening with TPPC in their departments and programs. The authors found that DTs described cultures of avoidance and individualistic attitudes in program cultures that were less effective in working with TPPCs, including denying that problems existed, stalling, avoiding taking action, taking action in a way that located the problem in the student, or hoping the problem would resolve on its own or without faculty involvement (e.g., mandating therapy and waiting for the student to complete it). Participants noted reasons for avoidance including "lack of an organized system for handling TPPC...junior faculty afraid of becoming embroiled in conflict with other faculty prior to tenure decisions, general apprehension about giving negative feedback to students, fear of damaging the advisor-advisee working relationship, and general diffusion of responsibility" (p. 14). Other obstacles included faculty members seeing students as extensions of themselves, and faculty members who lacked (a) insight into how their own interpersonal processes affected students, and (b) awareness about the role of diversity in student behavior (Forrest et al., under review). Such findings are similar to those of other researchers in this area, who have found that the existence of previous conflicts and existing tensions around diversity issues impair trainers' abilities to raise concerns and have conversations about trainees when diversity intersects with competence problems (Gizara & Forrest, 2004; Shen-Miller et al., 2009; Shen-Miller et al., 2012).

Training Evaluators

Ethical, competent trainee evaluation involves ensuring that evaluators are trained in the administration, scoring, and psychometric properties of assessments (APA, 2002; Kaslow et al., 2007, 2009). Yet the number of trainers with formal training in trainee evaluation is unclear (Kaslow et al., 2007). As a corollary, although a number of professional organizations and task forces have recognized the importance of supervision in psychology training and practice, a majority of clinicians and trainers have not received formal training in supervision (Falender et al., 2004). This observation is consistent with findings that trainees often have more training than their trainers in multicultural counseling (Bernard & Goodyear, 2004; Constantine, 1997; Gatmon et al., 2001) and that many trainers (and graduate students) have not received explicit training in intervening with TPPC (Forrest et al., under review; Jacobs et al., 2011; Shen-Miller et al., 2011). Lack of training and/or differences among trainers in their level of training in evaluation may lead to difficulty evaluating trainees at individual and program levels, including problems giving negative feedback or engaging in difficult conversations (Jacobs et al., 2011). To ameliorate these concerns, trainers can ensure that their training systems are clear about the importance of competencies and on how these will be imparted to trainees and later assessed (Kaslow et al., 2012; Kenkel, 2009). Key elements to consider include training the evaluators—program leaders must ensure that trainers are knowledgeable regarding the clinical issues and skills being assessed—and standardization of all measures, scoring, and any participants (e.g., mock clients). Trainers should be sure to have familiarity with methods of evaluation, and should explore the ease of administration. Avoiding having evaluation decisions fall to one faculty member or trainer can facilitate a stronger, more cohesive training team, and talking with raters across systems can strengthen inter-rater reliability and overcome potential influences on ratings via contextual elements or different emphases or concerns at different sites.

Ethical and Legal Aspects of Trainee Evaluation

Ethical issues related to trainee evaluation include informed consent regarding the types of assessments used, ensuring that trainers are teaching the skills on which trainees will be evaluated, and the types of measures to be used. APA's Committee on Accreditation similarly requires that accredited programs and internships demonstrate how trainers assess students' clinical competencies, and APA's (2002) *Ethical Principles of Psychologists and Code of Conduct* requires that trainees receive information about the extent to which personal information may need to be disclosed during training. Accordingly, trainers should inform trainees of the definitions of the competencies and values to be assessed prior to (or at the beginning of) training, along with the methods that trainers will use to observe and assess those values and competencies (Roberts et al., 2005). Hadjistavropoulos et al. (2010) also emphasized the need to give trainees clear guidelines for developing and presenting expected outcomes (e.g., case presentations), as well as ensuring that they receive sufficient practice opportunities with the formats used to present their learning (and that trainers use to assess learning outcomes).

One major ethical consideration involves confidentiality and client care. Although a number of authors have emphasized assessments that target "real" versus artificial situations, some assessment scenarios (e.g., live clinical observation) provide excellent opportunities to evaluate trainees in action while posing ethical risks (e.g., endangering clients). In contrast, other approaches (e.g., role plays) provide a more limited and perhaps artificial look at the skills used in practice, yet do not risk client confidentiality (Kaslow et al., 2009). This tension between trying to assess as closely as possible a trainee's actual professional performance while honoring client confidentiality is one that pervades not only evaluation but also analog versus in-vivo training considerations. Related concerns include boundary issues, as students may feel pressure to share their interactions with clients, content of supervision sessions, or personal reflections with trainers during evaluation (Hadjistavropoulos et al., 2010).

Doing evaluation ethically and fairly requires attending to such issues, as well as to power in the evaluative relationship. Justice in trainee evaluation requires attention to interpersonal processes underlying assessments, and to assessment structures and procedures, along with evaluative criteria (Cowburn et al., 2000). Evaluation and the timing of evaluation should be congruent with program philosophies for admission (Craig et al., 2009); for example, programs that allow students with non-psychology or counseling degrees to enter should allow those

students time to catch up on material prior to administering gatekeeping exams.

In addition, it is critical to ensure that trainers teach the skills to be assessed and be knowledgeable in terms of best practices in trainee evaluation (Belar, 2009). Moreover, greater attention needs to be paid to the ethics of improving measures' ecological validity and using the appropriate measures to assess competencies needed for professional practice (Belar, 2009). Programs need formal evaluation guidelines and should consider evaluation committees. In addition, programs should establish predetermined passing scores on evaluation measures prior to using with trainees (Carracio & Englander, 2004). On the level of systemic ethics, Nelson (2007) argued for links between (a) professional education and training constructs and (b) training content and licensure and credentialing examinations.

Finally (and as noted earlier), it is ethically incumbent on trainers to provide honest and direct feedback, and to address situations in which trainee evaluation uncovers or verifies competence problems in training (Johnson, 2008; Kitchener, 1992). Given the high likelihood that a mentoring or advising role may compromise trainee evaluation, trainers must engage actively in thinking through the balance of gatekeeper and educator roles in all their iterations (Gizara & Forrest, 2004; Jacobs et al., 2011; Johnson, 2008).

Implications: The Future of Trainee Evaluation

In terms of the future of trainee evaluation, many of the challenges detailed earlier provide inspiration for future directions. The competency benchmarks movement has provided concrete, behavioral anchors for achievement that can inspire new methods of evaluation, and Kaslow et al.'s (2009) compendium of tools presents a number of existing options as well as inspiration for the future. For example, trainers could enhance existing evaluation measures through incorporating emerging technologies (e.g., e-portfolios, use of virtual clients/patients) with relevant theories and research to develop new assessment techniques (Kaslow et al., 2009). Programs can continue working to set the stage for career-long evaluation, and emphasizing self-evaluation across the lifespan. Through modeling and changing program cultures, trainers can make evaluation less adversarial, more collaborative, and linked clearly to optimal professional functioning (Kenkel, 2009; Roberts et al., 2005; Schulte & Daly, 2009).

Potential and actual changes within the profession raise significant questions that will need to be answered as well. For example, how will the possible elimination of the postdoctoral year change the salience of trainee evaluation, particularly in light of evidence that some trainees are deemed "unsuitable" yet are passed on to subsequent training levels (Johnson et al. 2008)? Trainers might think systemically about the fact that evaluating multiple competencies across multiple areas of training present significant opportunities to streamline the evaluation process, and look for opportunities to collaborate and share training tasks while building networks of support for trainees at all levels of functioning.

Certainly, more research is needed in all areas of trainee evaluation discussed earlier, particularly with regard to psychometric support and methods for training in trainee evaluation. As a final suggestion, scholars might examine whether expertise in the practice of (and research on) trainee evaluation is distributed equally across all areas of clinical training. For example, do trainers in some areas of the training system (or in some disciplines) receive more support or training in evaluation than others? Are trainees evaluated more intensely during earlier stages of training? Are trainers more likely to grant advanced trainees a "social pass" because of their extended time in a program? Other ethical questions persist; for example, Peterson (2003) noted that unqualified students are sometimes accepted into doctoral programs, which is reminiscent of Gaubatz and Vera's (2002) notion of *gateslipping*, albeit from an entry versus exit perspective. This reality raises questions about trainers' ethical obligations to those students and, more broadly, continues the question about our roles as trainers, educators, and evaluators for future generations of professional psychologists.

References

American Psychological Association. (2002). Ethical principles of psychologists and code of conduct. *American Psychologist, 57,* 1060–1073.

American Psychological Association. (2008). 2007 APA early career psychologist survey. Retrieved July 15, 2013, from http://www.apa.org/earlycareer/pdf/2007_Early_Career_Psychologists_Survey_Report.pdf

Baldo, T. D., Softas-Nall, B. C. & Shaw, S. F. (1997). Student review and retention in counselor education: An alternative to Frame and Stevens-Smith. *Counselor Education and Supervision, 36,* 245–25.

Belar, C. D. (2009). Advancing the culture of competence. *Training and Education in Professional Psychology, 3*(4S), S63–65. doi:10.1037/a0017541

Belar, C. D., Brown, R. A., Hersch, L. E., Hornyak, L. M., Rozensky, R. H., Sheridan, E. P.,...Reed, G. W. (2001). Self-assessment in clinical health psychology: A model for ethical expansion of practice. *Professional Psychology: Research and Practice, 32,* 135–141.

Bernard, J. M. (1994). Multicultural supervision: A reaction to Leong and Wagner, Cook, Priest and Fukuyama. *Counselor Education and Supervision, 34,* 159–172. doi:10.1002/J.1556-6978.1994.tb00323.x

Bernard, J. M., & Goodyear, R. K. (2004). *Fundamentals of clinical supervision* (3rd ed.). Boston: Allyn & Bacon.

Bernard, J. L., & Jara, C. S. (1986). The failure of clinical psychology graduate students to apply understood ethical principles. *Professional Psychology: Research and Practice, 17*(4), 313–315.

Black, P., & William, D. (1998). Assessment and classroom learning. *Assessment in Education, 5,* 7–75. doi:10.1080/0969595980050102

Borders, L. D., & Fong, M. L. (1994). Cognitions of supervisors-in-training: An exploratory study. *Counselor Education and Supervision, 33*(4), 280–293. Doi: 10.1002/j.1556-6978.1994.tb00294.x

Bourg, E. F. (1986). Evaluation of student competence. In J. E. Callan, D. R. Peterson, & G. Stricker (Eds.), *Quality in professional training* (pp. 83–96). Norman, OK: Transcript Press, National Council on Schools of Professional Psychology.

Brear, P., & Dorrian, J. (2010). Gatekeeping or gate slippage? A national survey of counseling educators in Australian undergraduate and postgraduate academic training programs. *Training and Education in Professional Psychology, 4*(4), 264–273. doi: 10.1037/a0020714

Brooks, B. L., Mintz, A. R., & Dobson, K. S. (2004). Diversity training in Canadian predoctoral clinical psychology internships: A survey of directors of internship training. *Canadian Psychology, 45*(4) 308–312.

Burkard, A. W., Knox, S., Hess, S. A., & Schultz, J. (2009). Lesbian, gay, and bisexual supervisees' experiences of LGB-affirmative and nonaffirmative supervision. *Journal of Counseling Psychology, 56*(1), 176–188. doi: 1 0.1037/0022-0167.56.1.176

Carraccio, C., & Englander, R. (2004). Evaluating competence using a portfolio: A literature review and web-based application to the ACGME competencies. *Teaching and Learning in Medicine, 16,* 381–387.

Chung, Y. B., Marshall, J. A., & Gordon, L. L. (2001). Racial and gender biases in supervisory evaluation and feedback. *Clinical Supervisor, 20,* 99–111.

Constantine, M. G. (1997). Facilitating multicultural competency in counseling supervision: Operationalizing a practical framework. In D. B. Pope-Davis & H. L. K. Coleman (Eds.), *Multicultural counseling competencies: Assessment, education and training, and supervision* (pp. 310–324). Thousand Oaks, CA: Sage.

Constantine, M. G., & Ladany, N. (2000). Self-report multicultural counseling competence scales: Their relation to social desirability attitudes and multicultural case conceptualization ability. *Journal of Counseling Psychology, 47*(2), 155–164. doi: 10.1037//0022-0167.47.2.155

Cook, D. A. (1994). Racial identity in supervision. *Counselor Education and Supervision, 34,* 132–141.

Cook, D. A., & Helms, J. E. (1988). Visible racial/ethnic group supervisees' satisfaction with cross-cultural supervision as predicted by relationship characteristics. *Journal of Counseling Psychology, 35,* 268–274.

student attitudes toward "impaired" peers in clinical psychology training programs. *Professional Psychology: Research and Practice, 35,* 141–147. doi:10.1037/0735-7028.35.2.141

Peterson, D. R. (1997). *Educating professional psychologists: History and guiding conception.* Washington, DC: American Psychological Association. Francisco: Jossey-Bass.

Peterson, D. R. (2003). Unintended consequences: Ventures and misadventures in the education of professional psychologists. *American Psychologist, 58,* 791–800.

Peterson, R. L. (2004). Evaluation and the cultures of professional psychology education programs. *Professional Psychology, Research and Practice, 35*(4), 420–426.

Peterson, R. L., Peterson, D. R., Abrams, J. C., & Stricker, G. (1997). The National Council of Schools and Programs of Professional Psychology educational model. *Professional Psychology: Research and Practice, 28,* 373–386.

Petti, P. V. (2008). The use of a structured case presentation examination to evaluate clinical competencies of psychology doctoral students. *Training and Education in Professional Psychology, 2*(3), 145–150. doi: 10.1037/1931-3918.2.3.145

Rapisarda, C. A., & Britton, P. J. (2007). Sanctioned supervision: Voices from the experts. *Journal of Mental Health Counseling, 29*(1), 81–92.

Rethans J., Norcini J. J., Baron-Maldonado M, et al. (2002). The relationship between competence and performance: implications for assessing practice performance. *Medical Education, 36,* 901–909.

Roberts, M. C., Borden, K. A., Christiansen, M. D., & Lopez, S. J. (2005). Fostering a culture shift: Assessment of competence in the education and careers of professional psychologists. *Professional Psychology: Research and Practice, 36*(4), 355–361. doi: 10.1037/0735-7028.36.4.355

Robiner, W. N., Saltzman, S. R., Hoberman, H. M., & Schirvar, J. A. (1997). Psychology supervisors' training, experiences, supervisory evaluation and self-rated competence. *The Clinical Supervisor, 16*(1) 117–144. doi: 10.1300/J001v16n01_07

Robiner, W. N., Saltzman, S. R., Hoberman, H. M., Semrud-Clikeman, M., & Schirvar, J. A. (1998). Psychology supervisors' bias in evaluations and letters of recommendation. *Clinical Supervisor, 16*(2), 49–72.

Rodolfa, E., Bent, R., Eisman, E., Nelson, P., Rehm, L., & Ritchie, P. (2005). A cube model for competency development: Implications for psychology educators and regulators. *Professional Psychology: Research and Practice, 36,* 347–354.

Rosenberg, J. I., Getzelman, M. A., Arcinue, F., & Oren, C. Z. (2005). An exploratory look at students' experiences of problematic peers in academic professional psychology programs. *Professional Psychology: Research and Practice, 36,* 665–673. doi:10.1037/0735-7028.36.6.665

Sackett, P. R., & DuBois, C. L. Z. (1991). Rater-ratee race effects on performance evaluations: Challenging meta-analytic conclusions. *Journal of Applied Psychology, 76*(6), 873–877.

Schulte, A. C., & Daly, III, E. J. (2009). Operationalizing and evaluating professional competencies in psychology: Out with the old, in with the new? *Training and Education in Professional Psychology, 3*(4S), S54–58.

Scott, K. J., Ingram, K. M., Vitanza, S. A., & Smith, N. G. (2000). Training in supervision: A survey of current practices. *The Counseling Psychologist, 28,* 403–422.

Shen-Miller, D. S., Forrest, L., & Burt, M. (2012). Contextual influences on faculty diversity conceptualizations when working with trainee competence problems. *The Counseling Psychologist, 40*(8), 1181–1219. doi: 10.1177/0011000011431832

Shen-Miller, D. S., Forrest, L., & Elman, N. (2009). Training directors' conceptualizations of the intersections of diversity and trainee competence problems: A preliminary analysis. *The Counseling Psychologist, 37,* 483–518. doi:10.1177/0011000008316656

Shen-Miller, D. S., Grus, C., Van Sickle, K., Schwartz-Mette, R., Cage, E., Elman, N. S.,...Kaslow, N. J. (2011). Trainees experiences with peers having competence problems: A national survey. *Training and Education in Professional Psychology, 5*(2), 112–121.

Veilleux, J. C., January, A. M., VanderVeen, J. W., Reddy, L.F., & Klonoff, E. A. (2012). Differentiating amongst characteristics associated with problems of professional competence: Perceptions of graduate student peers. *Training and Education in Professional Psychology, 6*(2), 113–121. doi: 10.1037/a0028337

Veloski, J. J., Fields, S. K., Boex, J. R., & Blank, L. L. (2005). Measuring professionalism: A review of studies with instruments reported in the literature between 1982 and 2002. *Academic Medicine, 80*(4), 366–370.

Waldman, D. A., & Avolio, B. J., (1991). Race effects in performance evaluations: Controlling for ability, education, and experience. *Journal of Applied Psychology, 76*(6), 897–901.

Wester, S. R., & Vogel, D. L. (2002). Working with the masculine mystique: Male gender role conflict, counseling self-efficacy, and the training of male psychologists. *Professional Psychology: Research and Practice, 33,* 370–376.

Wong, L. C. J., Wong, P. T. P., & Ishiyama, F. I. (2013). What helps and what hinders in cross-cultural clinical supervision: A critical incident study. *The Counseling Psychologist, 41*(1), 66–85. doi: 10.1177/0011000012442652

Younes, M. (1998). The gatekeeping dilemma in undergraduate social work programs: Collision of ideal and reality. *International Social Work, 41,* 145–153.

Mentoring in Psychology Education and Training: A Mentoring Relationship Continuum Model

W. Brad Johnson

Abstract

In the past two decades, intentional mentoring of trainees has garnered rapidly increasing attention in professional psychology training settings. Effective mentoring portends numerous benefits for trainees. Yet, the psychology profession continues to struggle with differentiating mentorship from other training roles, and it is clear that many advising and supervising relationships do not evolve into mentoring relationships. This chapter distills the literature on mentoring in psychology training environments, including the competencies required for effective mentoring. A mentoring relationship continuum model is offered to clarify that mentoring describes the quality and character of a developmental relationship, not a discrete category of relationship. Next, the author summarizes the virtues of a constellation framework for mentoring, one that encourages trainees to develop a wide consortium of developmental mentors. Finally, several recommendations are directed to professional psychology program leaders.

Key Words: advising, mentoring, training, psychology, professional

Training psychologists increasingly are called to become intentional and deliberate mentors for graduate students, interns, and postdoctoral residents (Ellis, 1992; Johnson, 2002; Kaslow & Mascaro, 2007; Kitchener, 1992). Formal study of mentorship was triggered by Daniel Levinson's developmental theory of the *life structure* and the observation that, "the mentor relationship is one of the most complex, and developmentally important a [person] can have in early adulthood" (Levinson, Darrow, Klein, Levinson, & McKee, 1978, p. 97). Literature reviews of mentoring research across diverse professions and organizations have produced bold assertions such as, "the benefits to the protégé can be so valuable that identification with a mentor should be considered a major developmental task of the early career" (Russell & Adams, 1997, p. 3), and at least one educator has suggested that graduate departments have a "moral responsibility" to ensure that students are mentored by faculty (Weil, 2001, p. 471). Research

targeting both psychology trainees and psychologists lends support to the value of mentoring; a satisfying mentorship is a strong predictor of satisfaction with graduate education (Clark, Harden, & Johnson, 2000; Cronan-Hillix, Davidson, Cronan-Hillix, & Gensheimer, 1986; Johnson, Koch, Fallow, & Huwe, 2000). As a result, researchers have promoted mentoring as a distinct area of professional competence (Johnson, 2002; 2003) and as an essential ingredient in the future success of psychology as a profession (Forehand, 2008). The Council of Graduate Schools (2008) now lists mentoring as one of six key factors leading to PhD completion, and a growing number of formal mentoring programs are now offered by state psychological associations and the American Psychological Association (APA) (Burney, et al., 2009). Finally, psychology graduate students often are implored to deliberately seek and nurture mentorships with training faculty (Johnson & Huwe, 2003; Kuther, 2008).

This chapter will review the construct of mentorship, including definitional issues, demonstrated benefits, prevalence, and lingering methodological and theoretical problems in the mentoring research literature. The competencies required for effective mentoring then are described. The author then provides a mentoring relationship continuum model in which the term *mentoring* is used to describe the quality and character of a developmental relationship versus a relationship category. The virtues of mentoring constellations are presented as a framework for facilitating professional development and competence enhancement. The chapter concludes with several recommendations for professional psychology training program leaders.

Definitions of Advising and Mentoring in Graduate, Internship, and Postdoctoral Training

A persistent problem in both the theoretical and empirical literature on mentoring is a tendency for authors to label nearly any supportive or developmentally oriented relationship as mentoring (Mertz, 2004). Terms such as sponsor, advisor, guide, role-model, and mentor often are used interchangeably and without thoughtful operational definition (Friday, Friday, & Green, 2004; Johnson, Rose, & Schlosser, 2007). The terms *advising* and *mentoring* are often the most difficult to conceptually distinguish in training environments.

Advising

Schlosser, Knox, Moskovitz, and Hill (2003) defined the academic advisor as, "the faculty member who has the greatest responsibility for helping guide the advisee through the graduate program" (p. 179). Advising is a formal assigned role in nearly every graduate program. The advisor serves as the student's primary contact point with the larger faculty (Weil, 2001) and advisors are generally expected to perform specific technical functions such as providing information on programs and degree requirements, engaging students in research activities, and monitoring advisee progress (Brown, Daly, & Leong, 2009; Gelso, 1993; Johnson, 2007a; Schlosser, Lyons, Talleyrand, Kim, & Johnson, 2011b). Schlosser and Gelso (2001) found that doctoral programs in psychology use several different terms to identify the person who performs the roles and functions of an advisor (e.g., mentor, major professor, committee chair, and dissertation chair). Most agree that an advisor does not a mentor make: "Advising and mentoring are not synonymous. One can be an advisor without being a mentor and certainly one can be a mentor to someone without being that person's advisor. It appears that far more students have advisors than mentors" (Schlosser & Gelso, 2001, p. 158). Advising relationships may be positive, negative, or insignificant, and they may or may not evolve into the closer, emotionally connected, and reciprocal relationships that characterize mentoring (Johnson, 2007a; Schlosser et al., 2003).

In internship and postdoctoral training settings, the foregoing discussion remains relevant, although the term *supervision* would replace *advising*. In postdoctoral fellowships, internships, and even practicum settings, assigned supervision relationships may remain hierarchical, transactional, and defined by stark differences between the trainer and trainee roles; conversely, they may become rich developmental relationships that some authors have described as transformational in nature and which take on the characteristics of mentorships (Johnson, 2007c; Kaslow, Falender, & Grus, 2012).

Mentoring

The first operational definition of mentoring was offered by Kram (1985) who proposed that mentoring relationships facilitate an individual's professional development through two categories of "mentoring functions." *Career functions* included sponsorship, exposure, and visibility, coaching, protection, and provision of challenging assignments. *Psychosocial functions* included role modeling, acceptance, and confirmation, counseling, and friendship. A significant volume of empirical work has consistently confirmed these general function categories (Higgins & Thomas, 2001; Turban & Dougherty, 1994). In academic and clinical training settings, mentoring has generally been defined as a dynamic, reciprocal, personal relationship in which a more experienced trainer (mentor) acts as a guide, role model, teacher, and sponsor of a less experienced trainee (protégé) (Johnson, 2002; Johnson & Ridley, 2008). Johnson reflected that,

> As intimate and long-term alliances, graduate school mentorships often begin informally and involve some degree of attraction based on common interests (mutual interests of an enduring and intellectual nature), mutual validation (mutual expressions of positive regard and admiration), reciprocity (sharing of one's experience), increasing trust, and successful collaboration. (2003, p. 129)

Emphasizing the salience of the role-model function of mentoring for psychology trainees, O'Neil and Wrightsman (2001) asserted that, "A mentor is much more than an academic advisor. The mentor's values represent idealized norms that can have considerable influence on how mentees see themselves and the profession" (p. 112). Describing exceptionally competent mentors, Johnson and Ridley (2008) suggested that, "Outstanding mentors are intentional about the mentor role. They select protégés carefully, invest significant time and energy in getting to know their protégés, and deliberately offer the career and support functions most useful for their protégés" (p. xi). In sum, mentorships in psychology training environments have been distinguished by these characteristics: (a) positive emotional valence, (b) increasing mutuality, (c) a range of career and psychosocial functions, (d) an intentional focus on the development of the protégé's career and professional identity, and (e) a generative interest on the part of the mentor in passing along a professional legacy (Johnson et al., 2007; Schlosser, Lyons, Talleyrand, Kim, & Johnson, 2011b).

The Benefits of Mentoring Relationships

In a recent study of college students seeking employment, participants reported significantly greater attraction to an organization when it was depicted as having a formal mentoring program (Allen & O'Brien, 2006). A review of the voluminous mentoring outcome research in organizations seems to affirm the perception among employment-seekers that mentoring matters. Integrating hundreds of rigorous studies, meta-analyses and other quantitative reviews make it clear that those who report being mentored accrue substantial career and personal benefits over those who are not mentored (Allen & Eby, 2003; Chao, 2009; Eby, Allen, Evans, Ng, & DuBois, 2008; Kammeyer-Mueller & Judge, 2009; Ragins, Cotton, & Miller, 2000; Underhill, 2005). Across professional disciplines and varieties of organizations, mentoring is consistently correlated with enhanced work satisfaction and performance, higher retention, better physical health and self-esteem, positive work relationships, stronger organizational commitment, career motivation, professional competence, and career recognition and success (cf., Eby et al., 2008).

Informal Versus Formal Mentoring

Among the most consistent findings from research on mentorships in organizations is the conclusion that protégés in *informal relationships* (the term *informal* here does not suggest undue familiarity or informality in the relationship, but merely the manner in which the relationship is initiated) report more and stronger outcomes than those in formally assigned mentorships (Chao, 2009; Chao, Walz, & Gardner, 1992; Egan & Song, 2008; Ragins & Cotton, 1990; Ragins et al., 2000; Russell & Adams, 1997). Informal mentorships emerge through mutual initiation and ongoing interaction, free of external intervention or planning. In psychology training settings, both trainees and trainers appear to seek out mentorship matches based on similarities, shared interests, and frequent positive interactions (Johnson, 2007a). Ragins and Cotton (1990) nicely described the sometimes unconscious process at work in faculty/supervisors as they gravitate toward providing mentoring to specific trainees: "Informal mentoring relationships develop on the basis of mutual identification and the fulfillment of career needs. Mentors select protégés who are viewed as younger versions of themselves, and the relationship provides mentors with a sense of generativity or contribution to future generations" (p. 530).

In light of the well-documented success of informal mentoring in the business world, many organizations have moved to formalize the mentoring process: "Rather than leaving mentoring to happenstance, formal programs have given organizations control over who is mentored, when they are mentored, and even how they are mentored" (Chao, 2009). Formal mentoring relationships are instigated by organizations and involve some process of assigning or matching dyads and some level of subsequent oversight and evaluation (Chao et al., 1992; Egan & Song, 2008; Ragins et al., 2000). Chao (2009) observed that formal and informal mentorships vary on four specific dimensions. These include: (a) *Intensity*—Informal mentorships are more emotionally intense because both members of the dyad are committed naturally and intrinsically; (b) *Visibility*—Informal relationships are typically less visible, operating without formal recognition, endorsement, or even awareness by the organization; (c) *Focus*—Informal mentorships tend to have a more generalized focus on the development and wellbeing of the protégé versus a prescribed focus or organizationally-specified goals; (d) *Duration*—In contrast to the clear parameters common of formal programs, informal mentorships are unconstrained in terms of variable such as frequency of meetings, relationship time-frame, and expectations about termination.

In terms of outcomes, formal mentoring programs produce far fewer benefits for protégés and are far less effective than naturally-occurring informal mentorships (Ragins, 2012; Ragins & Cotton, 1990; Underhill, 2005). Because formally assigned mentoring dyads have no initial basis for mutual attraction, less frequent similarity in interests and characteristics, and no opportunity to assess each other's potential for success as mentor or protégé, it may come as little surprise that formally assigned dyads report less commitment to the relationship (Haggard & Turban, 2012; Underhill, 2005). In her review of formal mentoring programs, Chao (2009) concluded that, "finding a true mentor in a formal program may be like trying to find true love on a blind date—it can happen, but the odds are against it" (p. 315). No research to date has explored formal versus informal mentorship in graduate education.

Mentoring Outcomes in Psychology Training Settings

Shortly following Levinson's seminal study of mentoring in adult development (Levinson et al., 1978), Merriam (1983) discovered very little attention to mentorship in academe. Subsequent efforts have resulted in a slowly evolving outcome literature related to effects of mentoring relationships on the experience and success of graduate students. It is a noteworthy concern that the extent of mentoring-outcome literature in psychology comes exclusively from graduate school settings. With the exception of some descriptive literature (e.g., Karel & Stead, 2011; Kaslow & Mascaro, 2007; Sanders & Steinberg, 2012), there is currently no data on the prevalence or nature of mentoring in internship and postdoctoral settings.

Mentoring functions received. A number of studies have evaluated the relative frequency of Kram's (1985) *career* versus *psychosocial* functions in trainer-trainee relationships. In several studies, doctoral students rate each of Kram's functions as descriptive of their primary mentor's behavior (Atkinson, Neville, & Casas, 1991; Clark et al., 2000; Fallow & Johnson, 2000; Johnson et al., 2000). In the largest study of this type employing doctorates in professional psychology, Clark and colleagues (2000) reported that the most common functions received by trainees included direct training and instruction, acceptance, support and encouragement, role modeling, sponsorship for desirable positions, and opportunities to engage in research. Strong mentorships in academe seem to require some time to develop (Johnson et al., 2007; Schlosser & Gelso, 2001), and it appears that relationship duration is related to the nature

of the functions provided by a mentor; career functions are most evident early on, whereas psychosocial functions evolve more slowly (Erdem & Ozen, 2003). Further, as psychosocial functions become more prevalent in a relationship, satisfaction with the relationship increases (Tenenbaum, Crosby, & Gliner, 2001).

There is also increasing evidence that different components of mentoring relate to different outcomes (Forehand, 2008). A recent study of 477 doctoral students from two research-intensive universities revealed that, although career mentoring was most predictive of publications, presentations, and degree milestones, psychosocial mentoring was a much stronger predictor of satisfaction with the advisor and the mentoring relationship (Lunsford, 2012). Lunsford's findings confirm earlier conclusions that career functions are essential for markers of achievement and progress in the graduate program and beyond, whereas psychosocial functions are critical to professional identity, confidence, and well-being (Erdem & Ozen, 2003; Johnson, 2007a; Kram, 1985; Swerdlik & Bardon, 1988; Tenenbaum et al., 2001). Finally, male and female psychology doctoral students report receiving equivalent levels of various mentoring functions from graduate school mentors (Harden, Clark, Johnson, & Larson, 2009). The lone exception was that female students with male mentors reported higher levels of mentor encouragement, support, and acceptance.

Academic productivity. Mentoring relationships during graduate school appear to facilitate both degree completion and subsequent scholarly productivity. Graduate students that report a strong mentoring relationship are more likely to complete their degrees in a timely fashion (Ferrer de Valero, 2005; Tenenbaum et al., 2001), and one study revealed that female "early finishers" were more likely to have a very supportive doctoral program mentor (Maher, Ford, & Thompson, 2004). Further, mentored graduate students are significantly more likely to publish articles and present at conferences than those who report no mentor relationship (Cameron & Blackburn, 1981; Cronan-Hillix et al., 1986; Paglis, Green, & Bauer, 2006). This mentoring effect on productivity is sustained long after graduation. For instance, Hollingsworth and Fassinger (2002) found that the strength and valence of the research mentoring relationship in graduate school had a significant positive effect on research productivity following graduation. The correlation between graduate program research mentoring and scholarly output following graduation has been replicated in samples of both male and female graduate students (Dohm & Cummings, 2002; 2003). It is interesting that this mentoring-productivity effect may even predict career eminence. Zuckerman (1977) discovered that American Nobel Prize laureates had often been mentored by previous prize winners at some point during their training. In psychology, eminent psychologists—those with obituaries published in the *American Psychologist*—were not only mentored by famous psychologists during their graduate training, but were often described as prolific mentors themselves (Kinnier, Metha, Buki, & Rawa, 1994).

Networking and initial employment. Mentored trainees often report being more "tied in" or connected to important players, committees, and sources of information and power than nonmentored trainees, both within their local institution and in the profession at large (Atkinson et al., 1991; Clark et al., 2000; Johnson, 2007a; 2007b). Mentored trainees are more likely to gain the inside track on access to organizational power-holders, eminent scholars in the mentor's constellation of colleagues, and allocation of resources (e.g., stipends, grants, fellowships), not to mention invitations for co-authorship (Johnson & Huwe, 2003; Kuther, 2008). Likewise, studying with a well-cited mentor is a strong predictor of postdoctoral employment (Cameron & Blackburn, 1981; Sanders & Wong, 1985).

Professional competence and confidence. In psychology, trainees frequently describe enhancement of professional skill as a salient outcome of their primary mentorship (Schlosser et al., 2003). Those who report being mentored, report greater attention to professional values and enhanced development of clinical competence (Atkinson et al., 1991; Johnson, 2007b; Ward, Johnson, & Campbell, 2005). Just as important, mentored trainees are more likely to report a stronger sense of professional confidence or *sense-of-self* in the profession than nonmentored trainees (Russell & Adams, 1997; Schlosser et al., 2003). In his pioneering research, Levinson reported that one of the most important benefits to protégés was his or her journey to, "realization of the dream" (Levinson et al., 1978, p. 98), by which he referred to a mentor's effort to first help a protégé articulate an ideal professional dream and subsequently, create a developmental environment in which that dream might be realized. In psychology- training environments, excellent mentors work to help trainees adopt what Packard (2003) referred to as *possible-selves* or images of what they can ultimately

become in life and in the profession of psychology. Trainees that receive strong psychosocial mentoring (e.g., acceptance, affirmation, emotional support) are most likely to report a strong sense of professional confidence (Atkinson et al., 1991; Clark et al., 2000).

Satisfaction with the training program. A final mentoring benefit for trainees—and arguably for training programs themselves—is the degree to which one is ultimately satisfied with one's training experience. A small number of survey studies in psychology have scrutinized the association between having an identifiable mentor in graduate school and subsequent satisfaction with the degree program and institution writ large (Clark et al., 2000; Cronan-Hillix et al., 1986; Fallow & Johnson, 2000; Johnson et al., 2000; Lunsford, 2012; Tenenbaum et al., 2001). Although few, these studies reveal a consistent finding that satisfaction with one's primary mentor correlates positively with satisfaction with the degree program. The positive valence of a mentorship becomes associated with the training experience overall; it appears that many program shortcomings can be tolerated as long as trainees feel personally engaged with an individual faculty member/supervisor (Johnson, 2007a).

The Prevalence of Mentorship in Psychology Training Environments

Recent reviews of literature on mentorship in psychology graduate training are reasonably consistent in reporting that, on the whole, between one-half and two-thirds of all doctoral students in psychology report having a graduate program mentor (Johnson, 2007b; Schlosser et al., 2011b). Research with psychology doctoral students spanning four decades (Atkinson, Casas, & Neville, 1994; Clark et al., 2000; Cronan-Hillix et al., 1986; Johnson et al., 2000; Kirchner, 1969; Mintz, Bartels, & Rideout, 1995; Swerklik & Bardon, 1988) is consistent with a large recent study of nearly 500 doctoral students from numerous disciplines at research universities indicating that 57% agreed that their advisor had become a mentor (Lunsford, 2012). Clinical psychology trainees are less likely (53%) than nonclinical (e.g., experimental) doctoral students (69%) to report mentoring (Johnson et al., 2000), and within clinical psychology, PsyD students (56%) are less likely to report a mentor than PhD students (73%: Clark et al., 2000). In spite of some rich description of mentoring at the postdoctoral level (Karel & Stead, 2011), there remains no data regarding the prevalence of mentoring in internships and postdoctoral fellowships.

When race is included as a salient variable in mentoring prevalence surveys, results indicate that racial minority trainees are mentored at rates that equal (Clark et al., 2000; Johnson et al., 2000; Smith & Davidson, 1992) or exceed (Atkinson et al., 1994; Atkinson et al., 1991) those of majority group trainees. Although there is no evidence that within psychology training environments, racial differences between trainer or trainee create disparities in mentoring prevalence or outcomes (Johnson, 2007b), there is interesting evidence from organizational research that when cross-race mentors and protégés differ with respect to preferred method for addressing racial differences (direct engagement versus avoidance), the potential for disconnection or conflict increases (Thomas, 1993).

Finally, there is no consistent evidence of any gender difference with respect to prevalence of mentoring, method of mentorship initiation, relationship duration, mentoring functions received, or the career or psychosocial benefits derived by the trainee (Clark et al, 2000; Dohm & Cummings, 2002; 2003; Green & Bauer, 1995; Harden et al., 2009; Tenenbaum et al., 2001). This is true, even in training programs in which nearly all the faculty are male (Green & Bauer, 1995). If anything, female trainees report greater benefits from mentorships with both male and female faculty than their male counterparts (Harden et al., 2009).

Lingering Conceptual and Methodological Problems

Mentoring theory and research in education generally and psychology training environments specifically remains preliminary. There are several persistent conceptual difficulties and several methodological weaknesses in the current mentoring literature (Johnson et al., 2007). Definitional dysfunction persists in this literature. The term "mentoring" is often used indiscriminately in reference to a wide array of relationship forms and activities depending on the organization, the profession, and the individuals involved (Johnson, 2007a). Mentorship studies in higher education often fail to operationally define mentoring or differentiate mentoring from other relationship forms on questionnaires and surveys. Of particular concern is the likelihood that the extant research on advising and mentoring lacks validity because participants are rarely presented with clear definitions of advising, mentoring, and other trainer-trainee relationships

in order to render responses that clearly reflect experiences specific to mentorship. Additionally, Lunsford (2012) recently observed that in spite of considerable evidence for differentiation between career and psychosocial functions within mentoring relationships (Kram, 1985), mentoring is often assessed using dichotomous (yes/no) questions that fail to take distinct mentoring functions into account. Lunsford further recommended that researchers should think more broadly about mentoring; "most doctoral students are embedded in a network of mentors" (Lunsford, 2012, p. 266). Because most trainees report multiple mentors as well as support from peers and persons external to their training program, future research should address mentoring networks as well as individual mentors (Johnson, 2007a). Mentoring research in psychology has heretofore consisted almost exclusively of retrospective surveys of psychologists' experiences during graduate school. We know very little about the prevalence or nature of mentoring during internship or postdoctoral fellowship training (Johnson et al., 2007). The self-report questionnaires employed in existing studies have unknown reliability and validity and the response rates are often poor (Crosby, 1999; Merriam, 1983). Existing mentoring studies lack much sophistication and there is not a single longitudinal study of mentoring in psychology (Forehand, 2008). Finally, it is concerning that mentoring in professional psychology has been examined exclusively from the perspective of trainees. There is a significant need for research on developmental training relationships from the perspective of training psychologists (e.g., Lunsford, Baker, Griffin, & Johnson, in-press).

Toward an Integrated Model of Mentoring in Professional Psychology

Perhaps the most glaring obstacle to studying and practicing mentorship in professional psychology education and training is the pervasive conceptual confusion surrounding the nature of mentoring, including the contours between mentoring and various trainer-trainee roles. In contrast to academic advising and clinical supervision—assigned and formalized training roles—a mentoring relationship often lacks a clear starting and ending date. Quite often, mentoring is an honorific term applied to a developmental relationship only in retrospect, long after the active phase of the relationship has ended (Weil, 2001). Further, advising and supervising relationships may be positive, negative, or marginal in valence and value, while mentoring nearly always implies a positive, connected, and valuable interpersonal relationship (Johnson, 2003; 2007c; Ragins et al., 2000; Schlosser et al., 2003; Schlosser et al., 2011b). In the best circumstances, assigned advisors and supervisors may develop rich supportive connections with trainees. But when an assigned relationship is dissatisfying or even harmful to a trainee, it is unlikely to manifest many of the qualities of mentorship (Johnson et al., 2007).

Previous authors, noting the definitional confusion often associated with mentoring, have recommended various taxonomies of developmental relationships (D'Abate, Eddy, & Tannenbaum, 2003; Johnson et al., 2007; Mertz, 2004; Ragins et al., 2000), often observing that distinct trainer roles might exist on a continuum defined by the degree of intent to develop or shape a trainee. For instance, Mertz (2004) speculated that: "One might place these roles on a continuum defined by the degree of involvement, relational reciprocity, level of emotional connection, or the extent to which the faculty member is deliberate in delivering specific functions" (p. 58). Although the notion of a developmental continuum in trainer-trainee relationships is useful, it is problematic to continue to speak in terms of categories of relationships—particularly when it comes to mentoring. As an alternative, a continuum model that construes mentoring as a quality versus a category of relationship will be presented following an integration of the mentoring literature with the prevailing structure for conceptualizing competence in psychology.

Mentoring Competencies

In his treatise on the need for more effective mentoring in the profession, Forehand (2008) noted that psychologists who mentor should have in their repertoire the competencies required to tailor the relationship to benefit the trainee. Competencies are the elements or components of competence—in this case, competence to mentor; competencies consist of discrete knowledge, skills, and attitudes and their integration (Fouad et al., 2009; Kaslow et al., 2004).

Johnson (2003) offered the Triangular Model of Mentor Competence, which held that excellent mentorship requires the presence of foundational character virtues (integrity, caring, prudence), salient abilities (cognitive, emotional, relational), and numerous skill-based competencies (e.g., structuring relationships, mentor functions, respect for autonomy). According to Johnson, none of these elements is adequate in isolation, but rather, "it is

the integration of these components in relationships with students that characterizes competence [to mentor]" (Johnson, 2007a, p. 73). The Triangular Model posited that genuine competence in the mentor role was a deep and integrated structure requiring the mentor to skillfully manage and integrate various virtues, abilities, and focal skills—all in the service of developing a trainee.

More recently, the competency movement in professional psychology has provided a broad framework for conceptualizing the various domains of competency in psychology. For instance, the Cube Model of Competence (Rodolfa et al., 2005) argued that competence as a psychologist—including competence to mentor psychology trainees—may consist of both foundational and functional competencies. *Foundational competencies* are, "the building blocks of what psychologists do," whereas the *functional competencies*, "describe the knowledge, skills, and values necessary to perform the work of a psychologist" (Rodolfa et al., 2005, pp. 350–351). In order to consider mentoring competence from the perspective of the competency benchmarks in professional psychology, I now offer a preliminary sample of both foundational and functional competencies with relevance to mentoring.

Foundational competencies

The following list of foundational mentoring competencies dovetail with several benchmark foundational competencies for psychologists including reflective practice, self-assessment, relationships, and individual-cultural diversity (Fouad et al., 2009). Each competency might be construed as a fundamental or supporting competency for specific functional mentoring competencies (Johnson, 2003; 2007a).

• *Relationship formation*: Various strands of research on mentorship reveal that a mentor's interpersonal—and specifically communication—skills are a powerful predictor of attraction to the mentor and the relationship (Rose, 2003; Schlosser et al., 2011a). A strong working alliance often hinges on the mentor's ability to thoughtfully form and structure the trainer-trainee relationship to maximize both the benefits of the relationship for the trainee and the efficacy of the dyad's communication (Huber, Sauer, Mrdjenovich, & Gugiu, 2010).

• *Helping orientation and empathy*: It is difficult to mentor without genuine concern for and interest in the life experience, professional development, and well-being of one's trainees. Evidence suggests that mentors with prosocial personality traits (other-oriented empathy, helpfulness) were more likely to offer psychosocial mentoring functions (in addition to career assistance) to trainees (Allen, 2003). Empathy for trainees is often expressed through active, deliberate listening and accurate reflection of the trainee's anxieties and concerns.

• *Interpersonal warmth*: Given the choice, most trainees prefer to work with a trainer who exudes emotional warmth and caring (Johnson, 2007a; Rose, 2003). When trainers are emotionally approachable, engaging, and concerned, an assigned advising or supervising relationship is more likely to evolve into a mentoring relationship.

• *Personal health and self-awareness*: Psychologists who mentor should demonstrate self-care, self-awareness, tolerance of fallibility, and transparency (Barnett, Baker, Elman & Shoener, 2007; Johnson, 2002; Wise, Hersh & Gibson, 2012). An effective mentor demonstrates an appreciation for his or her relative strengths and weaknesses and models professional boundaries in relationships and balance between work and leisure/family.

• *Humility*: Effective mentors are likely to be humble regarding talents and achievements, generous with trainees, and comfortable acknowledging relative shortcomings (Johnson, 2007a). In one fascinating study, Godshalk and Sosik (2000) found that mentors who underestimated their success as leaders were paradoxically given the highest ratings by mentees. The authors concluded: "Mentors who behave as transformational leaders may be generally humble, modest individuals who are conservative in their self-assessments and who think less of self-centered outcomes associated with their behaviors and more of their protégés" (p. 308).

• *Sensitivity to matters of culture and stigma*: Effective mentoring requires competency in multicultural knowledge, skills and attitudes. Matters of gender, race, ethnicity, and sexual orientation, among many other diversity variables, are likely to factor prominently or subtly in many trainer-trainee mentoring relationships (Alvarez, Blume, Cervantes, & Thomas, 2009; Atkinson et al., 1991; Schlosser et al., 2011a; Thomas, 1990; 1993). Awareness of the principles underlying stigma and the more common experiences and concerns of trainees with LGBT identities are especially important (Russell & Horne, 2009).

• *Capacity for professional intimacy*: Professional intimacy describes the, "closeness, affection, trust, and commitment that allow and promote risk-taking and self-disclosure" (*Rogers & Holloway, 1993*, p. 297). A foundational mentoring competency, professional intimacy allows the trainer to create a mentoring relationship characterized by mutual validation, reciprocity, trust, and some measure of collaborative flexibility.

Functional competencies

Complimenting these foundational mentoring competencies are several functional competencies—specific knowledge, skills, and attitudes necessary for the execution of effective mentoring relationships (Eby et al., 2008; Johnson, 2003; Johnson & Ridley, 2008; Kram, 1985; O'Neil & Wrightsman, 2001; Wright & Wright, 1987). The following list of competencies may have the greatest overlap with the benchmark functional competencies of consultation, supervision, and teaching (Fouad et al., 2009; Kaslow et al., 2004). This is an abbreviated list, meant to capture the more salient functional competencies of mentoring.

• *Accessibility and engagement*: Effective mentors create space for trainees, both physically in the form of office hours and presence around the program and emotionally in the form of genuine interest and concern (Forehand, 2008; Kaslow & Mascaro, 2007). The mentoring role requires a willingness to seek out trainees for "check-ins," an attitude of invitation and interest that encourages trainee contact, and implementation of structures such as routinely scheduled meetings that create opportunity for relationship development.

• *Provision of encouragement and support*: Provision of strong emotional support is consistently ranked by mentees as one of the most important mentor functions (Clark et al., 2000). Supportive mentors help trainees manage the pressures of professional training, often highlighting the trainee's talents and capacity for success. Yet the effective mentor balances support with appropriate challenge, often encouraging trainees to take on new and unfamiliar roles (Schlosser et al., 2011a).

• *Tailoring mentoring to the developmental needs of trainees*: Astute mentors are cognizant of trainee developmental level and work to apply developmentally appropriate mentor functions in the relationship (Brown et al., 2009; Kram, 1985). For instance, more junior trainees may suffer a sense of being an "imposter" in the training program, necessitating more mentor psychosocial support, whereas many advanced trainees may seek collegiality in mentoring relationships as a way of feeling validated or endorsed for entry into the profession (Johnson, 2007a).

• *Intentional modeling*: Effective mentoring trainers accept the fact that trainees need to watch them perform the critical tasks of the discipline (Johnson, 2002; Russell & Adams, 1997). As a consequence they are deliberate about modeling professional and ethical practice and invitational in encouraging trainees to watch them perform important tasks in the profession (e.g., teaching, clinical work, research, supervision).

• *Sponsorship*: As any training relationship takes on more mentoring qualities, mentors become more attentive to opportunities to nominate, endorse, and promote trainees for opportunities both within and beyond the program. When a trainer endorses, nominates, or includes a trainee in a co-authored work product, the trainer accords the trainee *reflective power*—power of the mentor by extension.

• *Appropriate self-disclosure*: As a mentoring competency, timely self-disclosure can effectively bolster trainee confidence, alleviate anxiety, and model professional problem-solving and balance (Johnson, 2007a). Through judicious self-disclosure tailored to the present needs of a trainee, a mentor may offer salient life lessons, provide examples to steer by, and reduce the trainee's chances of making similar mistakes.

Of course, self-disclosure heightens intimacy and mutuality and must, therefore, be used thoughtfully by a mentor.

• *Balancing advocacy with gatekeeping*: Particularly as any training relationship transitions to the more relational-collegial end of the mentoring relationship continuum, effective mentors are naturally inclined to engage in greater advocacy, protection, and collegial friendship with trainees. But this inclination must be skillfully balanced with the trainer's professional obligation to evaluate trainees' objectively and serve a gatekeeper role on behalf of the profession (Johnson, 2002; 2008).

The Mentoring Relationship Continuum Model

In the years since Levinson's landmark study of mentoring in adult development (Levinson et al., 1978), legions of writers and researchers have attempted to define the mentor relationship and distinguish it from other relationship forms. Yet, from the beginning, Levinson and colleagues recognized that mentoring was less a category than a quality of relationship: "Mentoring is defined not in terms of formal roles, but in terms of the character of the relationship and the functions it serves" (p. 98). I now offer a Mentoring Relationship Continuum (MRC) Model for application to all developmental relationships in psychology education and training.

The MRC is captured in Figure 17.1. The mentoring continuum depicts the assigned trainer-trainee roles of academic advisor and clinical

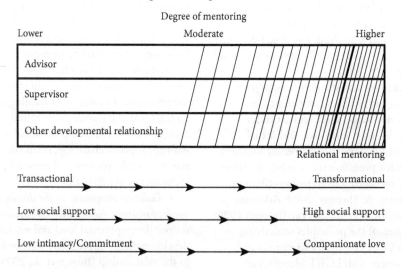

Figure 17.1. The Mentoring Relationship Continuum.

supervisor. It also includes other informal developmental relationships between trainees and various professors, research supervisors, or other professionals. The illustrative figure accounts for the fact that these other developmental relationships may follow a similar mentoring trajectory at times. The model applies equally to developmental relationships that are formally assigned or established by the dyad members themselves, perhaps on the bases of positive interactions, shared interests, or mutual liking. All the developmental relationships depicted on the continuum include career/competence development, support in navigating program requirements, and various forms of support and encouragement (Thomas, 1990). As a developmental relationship evolves along the mentoring continuum from left to right, it may be characterized more and more by the qualities of mentoring. Johnson (2007c) described the transition this way:

> As an advising or supervising relationship evolves into a more active and reciprocal relationship, when the supervisor [or advisor] begins to offer a range of both career and emotional or psychosocial functions, and as the supervisor [or advisor] becomes more intentional about bolstering the [trainee's] professional development and success, the supervisory [or advising] assignment evolves to take on more of the characteristics of mentorship. (p. 261)

As a training relationship progresses, it will ideally become characterized by many of the distinctive elements of mentoring relationships (Johnson, 2007a; Kram, 1985; Wright & Wright, 1987). These include:

- Reciprocity, collegiality, authenticity, and mutuality.
- Provision of both career and psychosocial mentoring functions.
- Intentional role-modeling.
- A safe harbor for self-exploration.
- Transformation in the trainee's professional identity.
- A connection that endures beyond the formal role assignment.

As indicated in Figure 17.1, routine advising and supervising relationships are appropriately described as *transactional* in nature at the outset, with both members of the dyad gravitating to the structure and formality of hierarchical trainee-trainer relationship styles (Johnson, 2007c; Kaslow, Falender, & Grus, 2012). Transactional trainers render a focused service (e.g., academic advice, clinical supervision, knowledge transfer, feedback, oversight, evaluation) in exchange for salary or assistance. The assigned trainer role assumes nothing about the level of bonding or genuine collaboration between trainee and trainer. Although a useful starting point for assigned developmental relationships, an exclusively transactional relationship may soon be outgrown by trainees as they become more skilled, more confident, and more inclined to prefer collaboration and collegiality with advisors and supervisors (Johnson, 2007c; Kaslow, Falender, & Grus, 2012).

As a developmental relationship moves to the right of the mentoring continuum, it will ideally become more *transformational* in nature (Bass, 1985). Transformational mentors seek to inspire and transform their trainees through sincere and well-timed guidance, encouragement, modeling, and visioning. Sternberg (2002) reflected that a transformational mentor, "inspires one, reveals new ways of understanding professional and personal matters, and motivates one to transcend who one is to become a different kind of professional and perhaps, person" (p. 68). The transformational mentor becomes deliberately familiar with and committed to the personal and career success of the trainee, and tailors functions to further the trainee's short- and long-range goals as these are identified (Johnson, 2007a). It is important that the mentoring trainer maintain an accurate perception of his or her role vis-à-vis the trainee, including the extent to which the relationship is evolving toward a transformative connection (Schlosser et al., 2011a).

Figure 17.1 also indicates that as any developmental relationship takes on mentoring elements the trainee is likely to experience an increasing degree of social support. Strong developmental relationships are likely to involve the provision of one or more of the following facets of support: (a) *emotional support*, such as reassurance of self-worth and concern; (b) *appraisal support*, such as feedback and appraisal of competence; (c) *informational support*, such as consultation and advice; and (d) *instrumental support*, such as tangible assistance in the form of time and resources (Higgins & Thomas, 2001). To the extent that a trainee can count on an advisor or supervisor for a growing level of social support, empowerment, empathy, and authenticity, the quality of the relationship and the working alliance within the dyad will also grow and result in substantial personal and professional benefits for the trainee (Liang, Tracy, Taylor, & Williams, 2002; Schlosser & Gelso, 2001; Schlosser et al., 2011a).

As a developmental relationship takes on mentoring aspects over time, trainer and trainee develop implicit psychological mentoring contracts. *Psychological contracts* are beliefs regarding the terms and conditions of a reciprocal exchange agreement between two parties (Rousseau & Tijoriwala, 1998). Because mentoring relationships are voluntary exchange relationships in which participants expect to receive future benefit from the relationship, it is reasonable to expect psychological contracts to evolve within these relationships (Haggard & Turban, 2012). Psychological contract theory implies that mentoring trainers should attend to growing psychological obligations to trainees and how these implicit obligations impact appropriate execution of the assigned role.

Another feature of evolving mentoring relationships is a gradual increase in *intimacy* (feelings of closeness and connection that give rise to the experience of warmth and a genuine desire to promote the wellbeing of the other) and *commitment*. In the context of Sternberg's triangular theory of love (Sternberg, 1986), a relationship defined by commitment and intimacy is labeled *companionate love*. Sternberg described companionate love this way: "This kind of love evolves from a combination of intimacy and decision/commitment components of love. It is essentially a long-term, committed friendship, the kind that frequently occurs in marriages in which the physical attraction has died down" (1986, p. 124).

A final element of the MRC model is the densely shaded—*relational mentoring*—area on the far right of the continuum. A few mentoring relationships in graduate training environments develop into closely bonded, highly mutual collegial relationships that Ragins and colleagues have described as relational mentorships (Fletcher & Ragins, 2007; Ragins, 2012). When a developmental relationship reaches the relational mentoring end of the mentoring continuum, it may be defined by several salient features (Johnson, Barnett, Elman, Forrest, & Kaslow, 2012; Kram, 1985; Ragins, 2012):

• *Fundamentally reciprocal*—Relational mentorships involve mutual influence, growth, and learning. Mutuality may take the form of reciprocal assistance, mutual understanding, and shared interests.

• *Fluid expertise and complementarity*—Trainer and trainee develop the ability to easily and authentically switch between learner and expert roles as appropriate. As colleagues, members of

the dyad are comfortable recognizing that each may have complimentary knowledge, skills, and attitudes that emerge in their relationship as offsetting strengths and weaknesses (McManus & Russell, 2007). Their varying competencies allow them to mutually address each other's developmental needs.

• *Increasing vulnerability*—Effective relational mentoring requires the ability to reveal one's shortcomings and developmental needs and to have those needs recognized and addressed in a nonjudgmental and supportive way. Mutuality takes the form of empathy and recognizing one's own experiences in the other.

• *Extended range of intended outcomes*— Successful relational mentoring may bolster not only career success but it is just as likely to stimulate a stronger sense of professional identity, enhanced competencies, resilience in the face of personal or medical challenges, or more effective work-family balance.

• *Holistic approach*—Relational mentoring acknowledges the interaction between work and nonwork domains and recognizes that high-quality collegial relationships can influence the quality of life generally (Ragins, 2012). So, competent relational mentoring may bolster specific professional competencies while simultaneously building self-efficacy, compassion, emotional intelligence, and work-recreational balance.

It is critical to recognize that not all advising or supervising relationships take on mentoring qualities. Mentoring prevalence rates clearly suggest otherwise (e.g., Clark et al., 2000). Moreover, only a few training relationships eventually develop the qualities of a collegial/relational mentorship. When mentoring does occur, the transition from assigned roles to a relationship defined by mentoring elements is often subtle, occurs gradually, and must always be defined from the perspective of the trainer-trainee dyad. The threshold between a formal developmental relationship assignment and a genuine mentoring relationship is not bright or dichotomous, but it is nearly always unidirectional in that a strong mentoring relationship is unlikely to devolve into a more transactional, hierarchical, and unsupportive relationship. The MRC model depicts this gradual transition with increasing frequency of vertical lines, indicating the steady increase in mentoring qualities. The degree to which any single advisor's or supervisor's relationships are defined by mentoring—theoretically depicted in the MRC model by a terminus point somewhere on the continuum—will be determined by a host of factors including context (some training program milieus are more conducive to mentorship), the number of trainees the trainer is assigned, personal traits and interpersonal skills of both members of the dyad, frequency of interaction, motivation, competence, and both the personal qualities and degree of "match" with the trainees to which one is assigned (Johnson, 2003; 2007a). Although it may not be essential to label good developmental relationships as "mentoring relationships," it is useful for trainers to remain aware of this gradual mentoring relationship transition and the associated implications for trainer role behaviors, trainee expectations, professional boundaries, and implied obligations to the trainee (Johnson, 2007a). Finally, although the MRC model construes mentoring as a quality or character of a training relationship, it is appropriate—even desirable—for program faculty and leaders to promote mentoring as an aspirational ideal.

Developmental Networks in Professional Psychology: The Mentoring Constellation

Although this chapter has focused nearly exclusively on the qualities and character of individual trainer-trainee mentoring relationships, many authors have recently called for attention to broader conceptions of mentoring in the lives of graduate students and other early professionals, including interns and postdoctoral fellows. Termed developmental networks or mentoring constellations, these network perspectives call for attention to the variety of developmental relationships in the lives of professional trainees (Higgins & Kram, 2001; Higgins & Thomas, 2001). A developmental network has been described as, "the set of relationships an individual has with people who take an active interest in and action to advance the individual's career by assisting with his or her personal and professional development" (Higgins & Thomas, 2001, p. 224). Increasingly, mentoring researchers are interested in more than the number of developers in the life of a junior professional, but also in the quality of an individual's entire set of developmental relationships (Higgins & Thomas, 2001). Moreover, evidence suggests that although the quality of the primary mentoring relationship affects short-term career outcomes, it is the composition and quality of a trainee's entire constellation of developmental relationships that account for long-run trainee career outcomes (Higgins & Thomas, 2001).

Because it is unlikely that any single mentoring faculty member or supervisor can adequately deliver every mentoring function or operate in every critical role with a trainee, trainers should promote a rich constellation of primary mentorships, role models, peers, extra-organizational career helpers, and other sources of mentoring in the life of trainees (Johnson et al., 2007). In professional psychology training programs, sources of developmental support may include active peer mentoring structures, vertical team mentoring, and computer-mediated or E-mentoring programs. Peer mentoring may occur informally or through formally assigned peer-sponsor or supervisor structures (McManus & Russell, 2007). There is evidence that peer mentorships offer important psychosocial functions (e.g., emotional support, personal feedback, friendship) for trainees (Kram & Isabella, 1985; Mullen, 2005). Peer mentoring can offer trainees a comparatively safe environment in which to express personal and professional dilemmas, anxieties, and vulnerabilities (Higgins & Kram, 2001; McManus & Russell, 2007).

One promising strategy for bolstering trainees' mentoring networks, while easing the burden on trainers with significant numbers of advisees or supervisees, is the implementation of mentoring teams (Johnson, 2007b). Hughes and colleagues (1993) proposed the Research Vertical Team (RVT) model of dissertation supervision designed to increase timely degree completion, productivity, and appreciation of the value of collaboration. In the RVT system, each faculty advisor leads biweekly research team meetings comprised of students from each year in the graduate program (first year through dissertation completion). An unexpected byproduct of the RVT system was a significant increase in peer mentoring (Hughes et al., 1993). RVTs offered a consistent source of emotional and professional support among student peers, increased student engagement in collaborative or "team" research products, and enhanced the formulation of individual mentorships both between team leader and trainees, and among trainees.

Ward and colleagues (2005) extended the RVT model to practitioner-oriented professional psychology programs. Termed the Practitioner Research Vertical Team (PRVT), this team mentoring model uses a similar integrated vertical structure with a broader focus on preparation of competent clinical practitioners and facilitation of mentoring bonds among team members (Ward, et al., 2005). Whether research or practice oriented, team models allow reductions in redundancy in individual meetings with advisees while boosting support, collaboration, and peer mentoring among trainees.

An additional element of some mentoring constellations is E-mentoring or computer-mediated developmental relationships between a trainee and peers, faculty members or supervisors, special-interest groups, or even a "famous" psychologist in the trainee's area of scholarly or practice interest (Bierema & Merriam, 2002). Although electronic relationships are unlikely to take the place of in vivo developmental relationships, they do offer several benefits as adjunctive sources of mentoring including easy access, fewer demands for scheduling meetings, and the opportunity for more egalitarian and less formal interactions.

The Mentoring Constellation illustrated in Figure 17.2 is an extension of the competence constellation recently developed by Johnson and colleagues (2012), a similar developmental relationship model for psychologists in practice. The mentoring constellation is centered around the trainee and encompasses all relational sources of personal and professional development. The first level of developmental relationship, the primary mentors, includes key training faculty (e.g., advisor, supervisors) and closest peers in the program. Primary mentors include a trainee's most intimate, committed, supportive, and influential developmental mentors. Secondary mentors represent a somewhat broader level of collegial and developmental support, characteristically including less intimate and committed though supportive and helpful professors, supervisors, and program peers. The

mentoring exosphere is the third structural dimension of the mentoring constellation. It incorporates more tertiary developmental connections between a trainee and various role models, friends, research or supervision team members, and training faculty/supervisors with whom the trainee has sparse but nonetheless developmentally meaningful contact. Relationships at this level in the constellation tend to be more formal, defined by less emotional support and reciprocity, and perhaps limited to discrete episodes of guidance or assistance (Johnson et al., 2012). The final layer of the mentoring constellation is the training program culture. This macrodimension influences the development and functioning of the other constellation levels. To the extent that a professional psychology training program authentically values and promotes mentoring of trainees, and to the degree that program trainers are empowered, equipped, and rewarded for excellent mentoring, mentoring relationships may be abundant or infrequent.

As in the case of a competence constellation for practicing psychologists (Johnson et al., 2012), it is essential to note that the boundaries between layers of the mentoring constellation are permeable; over time, the unique consortium of personal and professional developers in the life of any trainee is likely to evolve and change (Johnson et al., 2012). Moreover, there are at least three variables that likely contribute to the overall value of a mentoring constellation (Higgins, Chandler & Kram, 2007; Higgins & Kram, 2001; Higgins & Thomas, 2001; Ragins, 2012). First, the greater the *diversity* of a

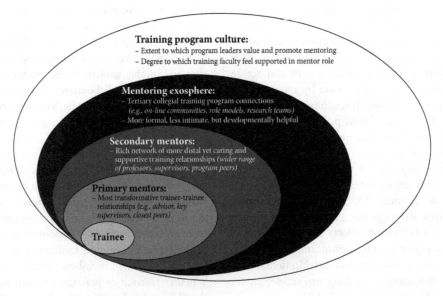

Figure 17.2. The Mentoring Constellation.

constellation—defined as the range of sources from which the trainee receives ongoing mentoring—the more likely it is to be positively linked to career and personal development. Second, the *strength of ties* or degree of commitment on the part of a trainee's mentors will often determine the level of social support, reciprocity, and emotional support available to the trainee. Finally, the degree to which the trainee is intentional about initiating mentoring connections with trainers, peers, and others will have significant bearing on both the number and intensity of mentoring functions received (Kram, 1985; Higgins et al., 2007).

Conclusion and Recommendations for Program Leaders

Research evidence offers resounding support for the conclusion that early career professionals who experience mentoring accrue substantial career and personal benefits. Career mentoring functions are linked with essential markers of achievement and progress through a training program, whereas psychosocial functions are critical to professional identity development, confidence, and well-being. Mentoring relationships with trainers have been reliably linked with specific outcomes including scholarly productivity, networking, initial employment, professional competence, and satisfaction with the training program.

The mentoring relationship continuum model offers a means of integrating disparate theoretical perspectives on mentoring in graduate and professional training. Although advising and supervising relationships are assigned roles leading to relationships that may be positive, negative, or insignificant to the trainee, mentoring implies a positive, connected, valuable interpersonal relationship. Professional psychology trainer-trainee relationships will ideally become characterized by many of the distinctive elements that define mentoring. Moving from left to right across the mentoring continuum, training relationships are hypothesized to manifest greater levels of mutuality/reciprocity, career and psychosocial mentoring functions, social support, perceived obligation to the other member of the dyad, and companionate love (intimacy + commitment). Although not all training relationships will take on the qualities of a collegial mentorship, it is crucial that trainers aspire to create the necessary and sufficient conditions for mentoring to occur.

I conclude this chapter with several recommendations for psychologist trainers and program leaders in professional psychology graduate programs, internships, and postdoctoral fellowships. Each recommendation is intended to enhance the frequency and efficacy of trainer-trainee mentoring relationships.

Consider Potential for Competent Mentoring in Faculty/Supervisor Hiring

Although potential for success in the mentoring role can most elegantly be evaluated at the hiring stage (Johnson, 2007a), it is clear that most psychology training programs do not emphasize mentoring competency as a job requirement. Johnson and Zlotnik (2005) found that among 636 academic job ads in the *Monitor on Psychology*, only 7.5% mentioned advising and 3.9% mentioned mentoring. Only one of these ads requested evidence of efficacy in the advising or mentoring role. Discussions of salient mentoring competencies (e.g., Johnson, 2003) have not translated into consistent scrutiny of training program faculty/supervisors with respect to foundational mentoring competencies (e.g., relationship formation, helping orientation, empathy, interpersonal warmth, self-awareness, humility, cultural sensitivity, capacity for professional intimacy) (Fouad et al., 2009; Kaslow et al., 2009). It is evident that not all trainers are equally suited to the mentor role and that some training program faculty/supervisors may create relationships with trainees defined by ineffectiveness, conflict, neglect, or even harm (Allen & Eby, 2003; Johnson & Huwe, 2003). Training program leaders are encouraged to carefully assess job candidates' mentoring track record, possibly through behaviorally based interviewing and contact with a sample of the candidate's former trainees.

Deliberately Prepare Trainers for the Mentoring Role

Just as it is unreasonable to assume that all training program faculty/supervisors have the foundational competence necessary for mentoring, it is also unreasonable to assume that trainers will be prepared for their role as mentoring advisors and supervisors without appropriate training and supervised experience. Johnson (2002; 2003) recommended training for the mentoring role that included trainee development, mentoring functions, relationship structuring and management, strategies for responding to conflict or misunderstanding, and mentoring the culturally different trainee. New trainers should be evaluated for functional mentoring competencies (e.g., accessibility, engagement, encouragement, role modeling, sponsorship, appropriate self-disclosure, balancing advocacy with gatekeeping) discussed earlier in this chapter. Effective training modalities might include some combination of new trainer orientation, mentoring workshops, supervision during the first year of training work with trainees, and ongoing peer consultation groups for trainers.

Explicitly Assess and Reinforce Mentoring

Karon (1995) reflected that very often, the activities most likely to lead to promotion and tenure for training faculty were unrelated, or worse, negatively correlated with devoting time to trainees: "...helping a student to do interesting, important, or creative research, or enhancing the student's intellectual development or clinical skills, has nothing to do with getting the faculty member's grant research done (the activity on which the faculty member's salary and advancement may depend)" (p. 212). There are a number of valid and reliable measures of mentor functions present in training relationships (for a review, see Johnson, 2007a). If program leaders evaluate the quality of trainer-trainee relationships with the same intensity that they evaluate trainer efficacy as a teacher, supervisor, and researcher, it is likely that training psychologists will begin to devote more attention to mentoring relationships with trainees. It is equally important to consistently reinforce excellence in the mentor role. Such rewards might include annual mentoring awards, weight in promotion and tenure decisions, credit in course load allocations, and various salary increments (Johnson, 2002).

Teach Psychology Trainees to Value Mentoring Relationships

Ragins (2012) described mentoring schemas as, "fluid cognitive maps derived from past experiences and relationships that guide...perceptions, expectations, and behaviors in mentoring relationships" (p. 523). In essence, trainees learn through their own developmental relationships with professors and clinical supervisors how to both value and conduct mentoring relationships. At their core, mentoring schemas are knowledge and emotion structures of what mentoring relationships look like (Ragins & Verbos, 2007). In order for professional psychology trainers to help trainees develop the necessary mental maps or schemas of quality mentoring, they must expose trainees to collaborative, reciprocal, supportive, and safe relationships with trainers. Creating such relational schemas is likely to bolster the probability that trainees will subsequently construct constellations of colleagues to support their ongoing competence as psychologists (Johnson et al, 2012).

Balance Informal and Formal Approaches to Mentoring

In light of the demonstrated value of high-quality mentoring in professional training relationships, how far should program leaders go when it comes to formally matching trainers and trainees, and later, governing or monitoring developing mentorships? Studies reviewed in this chapter suggest that informal mentorships offer more benefits and greater satisfaction than formally assigned relationships (Chao, 2009; Egan & Song, 2008). Nonetheless, most professional psychology training relationships begin with formally assigned advising or supervising roles.

Research on mentoring efficacy in formal programs offers several guidelines for program leaders as they consider fostering a mentoring culture within assigned training roles. First, when both participants in the dyad perceive some choice in the decision to enter a relationship—often based on matching factors such as mutual liking, shared interests, and positive experiences—mentorships are likely to be more successful and satisfying (Allen, Eby, & Lentz, 2006). This perception of choice may be less important for trainees, but considerably relevant from the perspective of mentors (Allen & O'Brien 2006; Parise & Forret, 2008). Second, program leaders must balance strong support for mentoring and accountability requirements for trainers with trainer autonomy in structuring and managing training relationships. Organizational research suggests that many good mentors may be "turned off" by excessive monitoring and accountability/assessment of mentoring relationships (Eby, Lockwood, & Butts, 2006). In other words, perceived intrusiveness or meddling on the part of program administration may undermine trainer willingness to mentor. Finally, program leaders should find avenues for facilitating trainer-trainee interaction and meeting frequency during the first several months of any assigned training role. Evidence from both organizational settings and doctoral program advising relationships confirms that frequency of interaction in the first months of any mentorship is among the strongest predictors of eventual mentor relationship efficacy (Huber et al., 2010; Underhill, 2005).

References

Allen, T. D. (2003). Mentoring others: A dispositional and motivational approach. *Journal of Vocational Behavior, 62*, 134–154. doi: 10.1016/S0001-8791(02)00046-5

Allen, T. D., & Eby, L. T. (2003). Relationship effectiveness for mentors: Factors associated with learning and quality. *Journal of Management, 29*, 469–486. doi: 10.1016/S0149-2063(03)00021-7

Allen, T. D., Eby, L. T., & Lentz, E. (2006). The relationship between formal mentoring program characteristics and perceived program effectiveness. *Personnel Psychology, 59*, 125–153. doi:10.1111/j.1744-6570.2006.00747.x

Allen, T. D., & O'Brien, K. E. (2006). Formal mentoring programs and organizational attraction. *Human Resources Development Quarterly, 17*, 43–58. doi: 10.1002/hrdq.1160

Alvarez, A. N., Blume, A. W., Cervantes, J. M., Thomas, L. Rey. (2009). Tapping the wisdom tradition: Essential elements to mentoring students of color. *Professional Psychology: Research and Practice, 40*, 181–188. doi: 10.1037/a0012256

Atkinson, D. R., Casas, A., & Neville, H. (1994). Ethnic minority psychologists: Whom they mentor and benefits they derive from the process. *Journal of Multicultural Counseling and Development, 22*, 37–48. doi:10.1002/j.2161-1912.1994.tb00241.x

Atkinson, D. R., Neville, H. & Casas, A. (1991). The mentorship of ethnic minorities in professional psychology. Professional Psychology: *Research and Practice, 22*, 336–338. doi: 10.1037/0735-7028.22.4.336

Barnett, J. E.; Baker, E. K.; Elman, N. S.; Schoener, G. R. (2007). In pursuit of wellness: The self-care imperative. *Professional Psychology: Research and Practice, 38*, 603–612. doi: 10.1037/0735-7028.38.6.603

Bass, B. M. (1985). *Leadership and Performance*. New York: Free Press.

Bierema, L. L., & Merriam, S. B. (2002). E-mentoring: Using computer mediated communication to enhance the mentoring process. *Innovative Higher Education, 26*, 211–227.

Brown, R. T., Daly, B. P., & Leong, F. T. L. (2009). Mentoring in research: A developmental approach. *Professional Psychology: Research and Practice, 40*, 306–313. doi:10.1037/a0011996

Burney, J. P., Celeste, B. L., Johnson, J. D., Klein, N. C., Nordal, K. C., & Portnoy, S. M. (2009). Mentoring professional psychologists: Programs for career development, advocacy, and diversity. *Professional Psychology: Research and Practice, 40*, 292–298. doi:10.1037/a0015029

Cameron, S. W., Blackburn, R. T. (1981). Sponsorship and academic career success. *Journal of Higher Education, 52*, 369–377.

Chao, G. T. (2009). Formal mentoring: Lessons learned from past practice. *Professional Psychology: Research and Practice, 40*, 314–320. doi:10.1037/a0012658

Chao, G. T., Walz, P. M., & Gardner, P. D. (1992). Formal and informal mentorships: A comparison on mentoring functions and contrast with nonmentored counterparts. *Personnel Psychology, 45*, 619–636. doi:10.1111/j.1744-6570.1992.tb00863.x

Clark, R. A., Harden, S. L., & Johnson, W. B. (2000). Mentor relationships in clinical psychology doctoral training: Results of a national survey. *Teaching of Psychology, 27*, 262–268. doi:10.1207/S15328023TOP2704_04

Council of Graduate Schools (2008). *PhD completion project*. Retrieved from http://www.phdcompletion.org/

Cronan-Hillix, T., Davidson, W. S., Cronan-Hillix, W. A., & Gensheimer, L. K. (1986). Student's views of mentors in psychology graduate training. *Teaching of Psychology, 13*, 123–127.

Crosby, F. J. (1999). The developing literature on developmental relationships. In A. J. Murrell, F. J. Crosby, & R. J. Ely (Eds.), *Mentoring dilemmas: Developmental relationships within multicultural organizations* (pp. 3–20). Mahwah, NJ: Erlbaum.

D'Abate, C. P., Eddy, E. R., & Tannenbaum, S. I. (2003). What's in a name? A literature-based approach to understanding mentoring, coaching, and other constructs that describe developmental interactions. *Human Resource Development Review, 2*, 360–384.

Dohm, F. A., & Cummings, W. (2002). Research mentoring and women in clinical psychology. *Psychology of Women Quarterly, 26*, 163–167. doi: 10.1111/1471-6402.00055

Dohm, F. A., & Cummings, W. (2003). Research mentoring and men in clinical psychology. *Psychology of Men and Masculinity, 4*, 149–153. doi: 10.1037/1524-9220.4.2.149

Eby, L. T., Allen, T. D., Evans, S. C., Ng, T., & DuBois, D. L. (2008). Does mentoring matter? A multidisciplinary meta-analysis comparing mentored and non-mentored individuals. *Journal of Vocational Behavior, 72*, 254–267. doi: 10.1016/j.jvb.2007.04.005

Eby, L. T., Lockwood, A. L., & Butts, M. (2006). Perceived support for mentoring: A multiple perspectives approach. *Journal of Vocational Behavior, 68*, 267–291. doi: 10.1016/j.jvb.2005.07.003

Egan, T. M., & Song, Z. (2008). Are facilitated mentoring programs beneficial? A randomized experimental field study. *Journal of Vocational Behavior, 72*, 351–362. doi: 10.1016/j.jvb.2007.10.009

Ellis, H. C. (1992). Graduate education in psychology: Past, present, and future. *American Psychologist, 47*, 570–576. doi: 10.1037/0003-066X.47.4.570

Erdem, F., & Ozen, J. (2003). The perceptions of protégés in academic organizations in regard to the functions of mentoring. *Higher Education in Europe, 28*, 569–575.

Fallow, G. O., & Johnson, W. B. (2000). Mentor relationships in secular and religious professional psychology programs. *Journal of Psychology and Christianity, 19*, 363–376.

Ferrer de Valero, Y. (2005). Departmental factors affecting time-to-degree and completion rates of doctoral students at one land-grant research institution. *The Journal of Higher Education, 72*, 341–367.

Fletcher, J. K., & Ragins, B. R. (2007). Stone center relational cultural theory. In B. R. Ragins & K. E. Kram (Eds.), *The handbook of mentoring at work: Theory, research, and practice* (pp. 373–399). Thousand Oaks, CA: Sage.

Forehand, R. L. (2008). The art and science of mentoring in psychology: A necessary practice to ensure our future. *American Psychologist, 63*, 744–755. doi: 10.1037/0003-066X.63.8.744

Fouad, N. A., Grus, C. L., Hatcher, R. L., Kaslow, N. J., Hutchings, P. S., Madison, M. B.,...Crossman, R. E. (2009). Competency benchmarks: A model for understanding and measuring competence in professional psychology across training levels. *Training and Education in Professional Psychology, 3*, S5–S26. doi: 10.1037/a0015832

Friday, E., Friday, S. S., & Green, A. L. (2004). A reconceptualization of mentoring and sponsoring. *Management Decision, 42*, 628–644.

Gelso, C. J. (1993). The making of a scientist-practitioner: A theory of research training in professional psychology.

Professional Psychology: Research and Practice, 24, 468–476. doi: 10.1037/1931-3918.S.1.3

Godshalk, V. M., & Sosik, J. J. (2000). Does mentor-protégé agreement on mentor leadership behavior influence the quality of a mentoring relationship? *Group and Organizational Management, 25*, 291–317. doi: 10.1177/ 1059601100253005

Green, S. G., & Bauer, T. N. (1995). Supervisory mentoring by advisers: Relationships with doctoral student potential, productivity, and commitment. *Personnel Psychology, 48*, 537–561. doi: 10.1111/j.1744-6570.1995.tb01769.x

Haggard, D. L., & Turban, D. B. (2012). The mentoring relationship as a context for psychological contract development. *Journal of Applied Social Psychology, 42*, 1904–1931. doi: 10. 1111/j.1559-1816.2012.00924.x.

Harden, S. L., Clark, R. A., Johnson, W. B., & Larson, J. (2009). Cross-gender mentorship in clinical psychology doctoral programs: An exploratory study. *Mentoring and Tutoring: Partnership in Learning, 17*, 277–290. doi: 10.1080/13511260903050239

Higgins, M. C., Chandler, D. E., & Kram, K. E. (2007). Developmental initiation and developmental networks. In B. R. Ragins & K. E. Kram (Eds.), *The handbook of mentoring at work: Theory, research, and practice* (pp. 349–372). Thousand Oaks, CA: Sage.

Higgins, M. C., & Kram, K. E. (2001). Reconceptualizing mentoring at work: A developmental network perspective. *Academy of Management Review, 26*, 264–288.

Higgins, M. C., & Thomas, D. A. (2001). Constellations and careers: Toward understanding the effects of multiple developmental relationships. *Journal of Organizational Behavior, 22*, 223–247. doi: 10.1002/job.66

Hollingsworth, M. A., & Fassinger, R. E. (2002). The role of faculty mentors in the research training of counseling psychology doctoral students. *Journal of Counseling Psychology, 49*, 324–330. doi: 10.1037/0022-0167.49.3.324

Huber, D. M., Sauer, E. M., Mrdjenovich, A. J., & Gugiu, P. C. (2010). Contributions to advisory working alliance: Advisee attachment orientation and pairing methods. *Training and Education in Professional Psychology, 4*, 244–253. doi: 10.1037/a0019213

Hughes, H. M., Hinson, R. C., Eardley, J. L., Farrell, S. M., Goldberg, M. A., Hattrich, L. G., Sigward, T. M., & Becker, L. S. (1993). Research vertical team: A model for scientist-practitioner training. *The Clinical Psychologist, 46*, 14–18.

Johnson, W. B. (2002). The intentional mentor: Strategies and guidelines for the practice of mentoring. *Professional Psychology: Research and Practice, 33*, 88–96. doi: 10.1037/0735-7028.33.1.88

Johnson, W. B. (2003). A framework for conceptualizing competence to mentor. *Ethics and Behavior, 13*, 127–151. doi: 10.1207/S15327019EB1302_02

Johnson, W. B. (2007a). *On being a mentor: A guide for higher education faculty*. Mahwah, NJ: Erlbaum.

Johnson, W. B. (2007b). The benefits of student-faculty mentoring relationships. In T. D. Allen & L. T. Eby (Eds.), *The Blackwell handbook of mentoring: A multiple perspectives approach*. Malden, MA: Blackwell.

Johnson, W. B. (2007c). Transformational supervision: When supervisors mentor. *Professional Psychology: Research and Practice, 38*, 259–267. doi: 10.1037/0735-7028.38.3.259.

Johnson, W. B. (2008). Are advocacy, mutuality, and evaluation incompatible mentoring functions? *Mentoring and Tutoring: Partnership in Learning, 16*, 31–44. doi: 10.1080/13611260701800942

Johnson, W. B., Barnett, J. E., Elman, N. S., Forrest, L., & Kaslow, N. J. (in press). The competence constellation: A developmental network model for psychologists. *Professional Psychology: Research and Practice*.

Johnson, W. B., & Huwe, J. M. (2003). *Getting mentored in graduate school*. Washington, DC: American Psychological Association.

Johnson, W. B., Koch, C., Fallow, G. O., & Huwe, J. M. (2000). Prevalence of mentoring in clinical versus experimental doctoral programs: Survey findings, implications and recommendations. *Psychotherapy, 37*, 325–334. doi: 10.1037/0 033-3204.37.4.325.

Johnson, W. B., & Ridley, C. R. (2008). *The elements of mentoring (revised edition)*. New York: Palgrave Macmillan.

Johnson, W. B., Rose, G., & Schlosser, L. Z. (2007). Student-faculty mentoring: Theoretical and methodological issues. In T. D. Allen & L. T. Eby (Eds.), *The Blackwell handbook of mentoring: A multiple perspectives approach* (pp. 49–70). Malden, MA: Blackwell.

Johnson, W. B., & Zlotnik, S. (2005). The frequency of advising and mentoring as salient work roles in academic job advertisements. *Mentoring and Tutoring: Partnership in Learning, 13*, 95–107.

Kammeyer-Mueller, J. D., & Judge, T. A. (2009). A quantitative review of mentoring research: A test of a model. *Journal of Vocational Behavior, 72*, 269–283. doi: 10.1016/j. jvb.2007.09.006

Karel, M. J., & Stead, C. D. (2011). Mentoring geropsychologists-in-training during internship and postdoctoral fellowship years. *Educational Gerontology, 37*, 388–408. doi: 10.1080/03601277.2011.553560

Karon, B. P. (1995). Becoming a first-rate professional psychologist despite graduate education. *Professional Psychology: Research and Practice, 26*, 211–217. doi: 10.1037/ 0735-7028.26.2.211

Kaslow, N. J., Borden, K. A., Collins, F. L., Forrest, L., Illfelder-Kaye, J., Nelson, P. D., & Rallo, J. S. (2004). Competencies conference: Future directions in education and credentialing in professional psychology. *Journal of Clinical Psychology, 60*, 699–712. doi: 10.1002/jclp.20016

Kaslow, N. J., Falender, C. A., & Grus, C. (2012). Valuing and practicing competency-based supervision: A transformational leadership perspective. *Training and Education in Professional Psychology, 6*, 47–54. doi: 10.1037/ a0026704

Kaslow, N. J., Grus, C. L., Campbell, L. F., Fouad, N. A., Hatcher, R. L., & Rodolfa, E. R. (2009). Competency assessment toolkit for professional psychology. *Training and Education in Professional Psychology, 3*, S27–S45. doi: 10.1037/a0015833

Kaslow, N. J., & Mascaro, N. A. (2007). Mentoring interns and postdoctoral residents in academic health sciences center. *Journal of Clinical Psychology in Medical Settings, 14*, 191–196. doi: 10.1007/s10880-007-9070-y

Kinnier, R. T., Metha, A. T., Buki, L. P., & Rawa, P. M. (1994). Manifest values of eminent psychologists: A content analysis of their obituaries. *Contemporary Psychology, 13*, 88–94. doi: 10.1007/BF02686860

Kirchner, E. P. (1969). Graduate education in psychology: Retrospective views of advanced degree recipients. *Journal of Clinical Psychology, 25*, 207–213. doi: 10.1002/

1097-4679(196904)25:2<207::AID-JCLP2270250232>3. 0.CO;2-B

Kitchener, K. S. (1992). Psychologist as teacher and mentor: Affirming ethical values throughout the curriculum. *Professional Psychology: Research and Practice, 23*, 190–195. doi: 10.1037/0735-7028.23.3.190

Kram, K. E. (1985). *Mentoring at work: Developmental relationships in organizational life*. Glenview, IL: Scott Foresman.

Kram, K. E., & Isabella, L. A. (1985). Mentoring alternatives: The role of peer relationships in career development. *Academy of Management Journal, 28*, 110–132. doi: 10.2307/256064

Kuther, T. L. (2008). *Surviving graduate school in psychology: A pocket mentor*. Washington, DC: APA.

Levinson, D. J., Darrow, C. N., Klein, E. B., Levinson, M. H., & McKee, B. (1978). *The seasons of a man's life*. New York: Ballentine.

Liang, B., Tracy, A. J., Taylor, C. A., & Williams, I. M. (2002). Mentoring college-age women: A relational approach. *American Journal of Community Psychology, 30*, 271–288. doi: 10.1023/A:1014637112531

Lunsford, L. (2012). Doctoral advising or mentoring? Effects on student outcomes. *Mentoring and Tutoring: Partnership in Learning, 20*, 251–270.

Lunsford, L., Baker, V., Griffin, K., & Johnson, W. B. (in press). Mentoring: A typology of costs for higher education faculty. *Mentoring and Tutoring: Partnership in Learning.*

Maher, M. A., Ford, M. E., & Thompson, C. M. (2004). Degree progress of women doctoral students: Factors that constrain, facilitate, and differentiate. *Review of Higher Education, 27*, 385–408. doi: 10.1353/rhe.2004.0003

McManus, S. E., & Russell, J. E. A. (2007). Peer mentoring relationships. In B. R. Ragins & K. E. Kram (Eds.), *The handbook of mentoring at work: Theory, research, and practice* (pp. 273–297). Thousand Oaks, CA: Sage.

Merriam, S. B. (1983). Mentors and protégés: A critical review of the literature. *Adult Education Quarterly, 33*, 161–173.

Mertz, N. T. (2004). What's a mentor anyway? *Educational Administration Quarterly, 40*, 541–560.

Mintz, L. B., Bartels, K. M., & Rideout, C. A. (1995). Training in counseling ethnic minorities and race-based availability of graduate school resources. *Professional Psychology: Research and Practice, 26*, 316–321. doi: 10.1037/0735-7028.26.3.316

Mullen, C. R. (2005). *Mentorship primer*. New York: Peter Lang.

O'Neil, J. M., & Wrightsman, L. S. (2001). The mentoring relationship in psychology training programs. In S. Walfish & A. K. Hess (Eds.), *Succeeding in graduate school: The career guide for psychology students* (pp. 113–129). Mahwah, NJ: Erlbaum.

Packard, B. W. L. (2003). Student training promotes mentoring awareness and action. *Career Development Quarterly, 51*, 335–345.

Paglis, L. L., Green, S. G., & Bauer, T. N. (2006). Does advisor mentoring add value? A longitudinal study of mentoring and doctoral student outcomes. *Research in Higher Education, 47*, 451–476.

Parise, M. R., & Forret, M. L. (2008). Formal mentoring programs: The relationship of program design and support to mentor's perceptions of benefits and costs. *Journal of Vocational Behavior, 72*, 225–240.

Ragins, B. R. (2012). Relational mentoring: A positive approach to mentoring at work. In K. S. Cameron & G. M. Spreitzer (Eds.), *The oxford handbook of positive organizational scholarship* (pp. 519–536). New York: Oxford University Press.

Ragins, B. R., & Cotton, J. L. (1990). Mentoring functions and outcomes: A comparison of men and women in formal and informal mentoring relationships. *Journal of Applied Psychology, 84*, 529–550.

Ragins, B. R., Cotton, J. L., & Miller, J. S. (2000). Marginal mentoring: The effects of type of mentor, quality of relationship, and program design on work and career attitudes. *Academy of Management Journal, 43*, 1177–1194. doi: 10.2307/1556344

Ragins, B. R., & Verbos, A. K. (2007). Positive relationships in action: Relational mentoring and mentoring schemas in the workplace. In J. E. Dutton & B. R. Ragins (Eds.), *Exploring positive relationships at work: Building a theoretical and research foundation* (pp. 91–116). Mahwah, NJ: Erlbaum.

Rodolfa, E., Bent, R., Eisman, E., Nelson, P., Rehm, L., & Ritchie, P. (2005). A cube model for competency development: Implications for psychology educators and regulators. *Professional Psychology: Research and Practice, 36*, 347–354. doi: 10.1037/0735-7028.36.4.347

Rogers, J. C., & Holloway, R. L. (1993). Professional intimacy: Somewhere between collegiality and personal intimacy? *Family Systems Medicine, 11*, 263–270.

Rose, G. L. (2003). Enhancement of mentor selection using the ideal mentor scale. *Research in Higher Education, 44*, 473–494.

Rousseau, D. M., & Tijoriwala, S. A. (1998). Assessing psychological contracts: Issues, alternatives, and measures. *Journal of Organizational Behavior, 19*, 679–695. doi: 10.1002/(SICI)1099-1379(1998)19:1+<679::AID-JOB971>3.0.CO;2-N

Russell, G. M., & Horne, S. G. (2009). Finding equilibrium: Mentoring, sexual orientation, and gender identity. *Professional Psychology: Research and Practice, 40*, 194–200. doi: 10.1037/a0011860

Russell, J. E. A., & Adams, D. M. (1997). The changing nature of mentoring in organizations: An introduction to the special issues on mentoring and organizations. *Journal of Vocational Behavior, 51*, 1–14.

Sanders, J. M., & Wong, H. Y. (1985). Graduate training and initial job placement. *Sociological Inquiry, 55*, 154–169.

Sanders, K. A., & Steinberg, H. R. (2012). Supervision and mentoring of clinical psychology predoctoral interns and postdoctoral residents. *Journal of Cognitive Psychotherapy: An International Quarterly, 26*, 226–235. doi:10.1891/0889-8391.26.3,226

Schlosser, L. Z. & Gelso, C. J. (2001). Measuring the working alliance in advisor-advisee relationships in graduate school. *Journal of Counseling Psychology, 48*, 157–167. doi: 10.1037/0022-0167.48.2.157

Schlosser, L. Z., Knox, S., Moskovitz, A. R., & Hill, C. E. (2003). A qualitative study of the graduate advising relationship: The advisee perspective. *Journal of Counseling Psychology, 50*, 178–188. doi: 10.1037/0022-0167.50.2.178

Schlosser, L. Z., Lyons, H. Z., Talleyrand, R. M., Kim, B. S. K., & Johnson, W. B. (2011a). A multiculturally infused model of graduate advising relationships. *Journal of Career Development, 38*, 44–61. doi: 10.1177/0894845309359286

Schlosser, L. Z., Lyons, H. Z., Talleyrand, R. M., Kim, B. S. K., & Johnson, W. B. (2011b). Advisor-advisee relationships in graduate training programs. *Journal of Career Development, 38*, 3–18. doi: 10.1177/0894845309358887

Smith, E. P., & Davidson, W. S. (1992). Mentoring and the development of African-American graduate students. *Journal of College Student Development, 33*, 531–539.

Sternberg, R. J. (1986). A triangular theory of love. *Psychological Review, 93*, 119–135. doi: 10.1037/0033-295X.93.2.119

Sternberg, R. J. (2002). The teachers we never forget. *Monitor on Psychology, 33*, 68.

Swerdlik, M. E., & Bardon, J. I. (1988). A survey of mentoring experiences in school psychology. *Journal of School Psychology, 26*, 213–224. doi: 10.1016/0022-4405(88)90001-5.

Tenenbaum, H. R., Crosby, F. J., & Gliner, M. D. (2001). Mentoring relationships in graduate school. *Journal of Vocational Behavior, 59*, 326–341. doi: 10.1006/jvbe.2001.1804

Thomas, D. A. (1990). The impact of race on managers' experiences of developmental relationships (mentoring and sponsorship): An intra-organizational study. *Journal of Organizational Behavior, 11*, 479–492. doi: 10.1002/job.4030110608

Thomas, D. A. (1993). Racial dynamics in cross-race developmental relationships. *Administrative Science Quarterly, 38*, 169–194. doi: 10.2307/2393410

Turban, D. B., & Dougherty, T. W. (1994). Role of protégé personality in receipt of mentoring and career success. *Academy of Management Journal, 37*, 688–702. doi: 10.2307/256706

Underhill, C. M. (2005). The effectiveness of mentoring programs in corporate settings: A meta-analytical review of the literature. *Journal of Vocational Behavior, 68*, 292–307. doi: 10.1016/j.jvb.2005.05.003.

Ward, Y. L., Johnson, W. B., & Campbell, C. D. (2005). Practitioner research vertical teams: A model for mentoring in practitioner focused doctoral programs. *The Clinical Supervisor, 23*, 179–190. doi: 10.1300/J001v23n01_11

Weil, V. (2001). Mentoring: Some ethical considerations. *Science and Engineering Ethics, 7*, 471–482.

Wise, E. H.; Hersh, M. A.; Gibson, C. M. (2012). Ethics, self-care and well-being for psychologists: Reenvisioning the stress-distress continuum. *Professional Psychology: Research and Practice, 43*, 487–494. doi: 10.1037/a0029446

Wright, C. A., & Wright, C. D. (1987). The role of mentors in the career development of young professionals. Family Relations, *36*, 204–208. doi: 10.2307/583955

Zuckerman, H. (1977). *Scientific elite: Nobel laureates in the United States.* New York: The Free Press.

Clinical Supervision and the Era of Competence

Carol A. Falender *and* Edward P. Shafranske

Abstract

Clinical supervision provides the primary means by which the applied practice of psychology is transmitted to future generations of psychologist practitioners. It is a core professional competency that provides the foundation for the development and maintenance of clinical competence of the psychologist while safeguarding the welfare of clients and protecting the public and the profession. Efforts to enhance accountability in the preparation of psychologists led to a call to establish a "culture of competence" in clinical training and throughout the profession. Competency-based clinical supervision is an approach in clinical training that responds to that call, and it places emphasis on the identification of knowledge, skills, and attitudes/values that are assembled to form specific clinical competencies. It systematically describes supervision processes to develop, assess, and provide feedback leading to professional competence. Continuing efforts are required to evaluate the effectiveness of clinical supervision processes, impacts on supervisee development, and clinical outcomes.

Key Words: clinical supervision, competency-based supervision, competent supervision, supervisor competence

Clinical supervision is a core competency of psychological practice, providing the foundation for development and maintenance of clinical competence of the psychologist. For the graduate student, intern, postdoctoral resident, and even postlicensure psychologist, clinical supervision provides the primary means by which a student of psychology gradually transitions and develops into a professional practitioner who values lifelong learning. This is no small task; supervision involves teaching how to apply science-informed knowledge to solve clinical problems, providing ongoing socialization to the profession, inculcating and strengthening values and ethics, enhancing respect and appreciation for all persons, and establishing habits of self-reflection and metacompetence. Building on a foundation of academic studies and research activities, trainees (i.e., graduate students, interns, postdoctoral residents as well as psychologists obtaining advanced specialization training) engage in supervised professional experience leading to the development of specific clinical competencies. The many impacts of this applied training, particularly the relationships and experiences gained within clinical supervision, are long-lasting and serve as major influences on the development of trainees and practitioners (Orlinsky, Botermans, & Rønnestad, 2001). In addition to the immediate impact on clinical competence in the applied setting, supervision promotes attitudes and skills in self-assessment and encourages commitment to continuous, lifelong learning and enhancement of expertise (Falender & Shafranske, 2012b).

Although we emphasize its role in transmitting the profession to future generations of practitioners, clinical supervision has—as its highest duty—to ensure the protection of the public as consumers of psychological services. Simply put, the welfare of the client supersedes all other obligations. Supervision, specifically when focused on the assessment of and development of clinical competence, simultaneously safeguards the client while facilitating the professional development of the supervisee. In addition to enhancing training and ensuring client welfare, the increasing emphasis on competencies informs processes of accreditation and credentialing (DeMers, Van Horne, & Rodolfa, 2008; Falender & Shafranske, 2012b; Nelson, 2007), which serve as the essential mechanisms to protect the public from incompetent or unethical practice (DeMers & Schaffer, 2012). In this chapter, we present a framework for competency-based clinical supervision, identify its core components, and highlight features of effective supervision. We conclude the chapter with a discussion of emerging issues in contemporary supervisory practice and identify contemporary challenges and future directions.

Competence as the Organizing Framework in Clinical Supervision

Although it is likely that most supervisors would claim that supervision is (and always has been) about developing competence, we believe supervision practices that are explicitly *competency-based* provide the best opportunity for development of clinical competence. The competency framework orients supervision to the practical task of training supervisees to integrate the knowledge, skills, and attitudes or values required to perform specific clinical tasks. In addition, such an approach fosters close alignment between training objectives, assessment procedures, and learning strategies by clearly articulating the aforementioned components involved in each competency. Further, this orientation is in step with contemporary trends in clinical training and professional development. When Roberts, Borden, Christiansen, and Lopez (2005) called for a "culture of competency" they heralded a change in approach to clinical training and supervision consistent with the general sea change in psychology. The movement is broad-based, is occurring in many professions (e.g., dentistry, medicine, and nursing) (McMahon & Tallia, 2010; Spielman, Fulmer, Eisenberg, & Alfano, 2005), and signals a new era in professional training in which the emphasis changes from the acquisition of knowledge to the performance and assessment of competencies (Nelson, 2007). Similarly, the competencies movement shifts the focus from input (e.g., number of faculty, supervisors, course units, psychodiagnostic assessments)

to output (e.g., demonstration of specific competencies at junctures of training) when evaluating training programs and granting accreditation (Roe, 2002; Nelson, 2007). This fundamental reorientation to competence has resulted in enhanced accountability of psychological training and greater attention to client and supervision outcomes, and is in lockstep with advances in evidence-based practice (Falender, Burnes, & Ellis, 2012; Falender & Shafranske, 2012b). Competency-based clinical supervision presents a conceptual and pragmatic approach to establish a culture of competence in training; however, such paradigmatic change is not readily or universally accepted, or easily accomplished. Understanding some of the inherent challenges in implementing a competency-based framework provides a useful context for discussion of contemporary approaches to clinical supervision.

Graduate Education and Clinical Training

The orientation to competence best occurs when there is a close correspondence in learning objectives in academic preparation and clinical training. However, disconnects exist across disciplines between curricula, the pedagogy employed in most graduate schools, the clinical training provided, the agencies and clinical settings where practices are implemented, as well as in commitment to competency-based training (Falender & Shafranske, 2010; Manuel, Mullen, Fang, Bellamy, & Bledsoe, 2009). For example, a graduate student can obtain stellar grades in his or her understanding of a particular evidence-based treatment or knowledge of its clinical efficacy without ever demonstrating competence in the use of the treatment. This is due in part to circumstances in which pedagogy is oriented primarily (if not exclusively) on the acquisition of knowledge, which sets narrow learning objectives and may unwittingly minimize or ignore the development of clinical competence as the endpoint of doctoral education. Beyond the observed differences in educational goals and philosophy, a lack of coordination often exists between academic training institutions and clinical practice settings, such as practicums and internships (Kaslow, Pate, & Thorn, 2005). Moreover, the linkage between graduate education, training, and licensure may be poorly articulated (Schaffer & Rodolfa, 2011). When such disconnects occur, graduates may not be adequately prepared to demonstrate the clinical competencies required for professional practice in psychology. Such a disconnect has been demonstrated for both marriage and family therapy master's programs (Nelson & Graves, 2011) and psychiatry training (Boyce, Spratt, Davies, & McEvoy, 2011) by comparing the expected competency frameworks with actual competencies of entry-level professionals. When graduate programs fail to emphasize competence development, responsibility for its assessment and development falls on supervisors at internship and postdoctoral training sites. This results in training focused on "catching up" just at the point that a consolidation of competence and preparation for entry into the profession is expected. In this emergent culture of competence, traditional practices of academic and practicum structure, learning, and supervision are coming under scrutiny. To ensure that graduate education leads to the acquisition of specific competencies and accountability, problem-based learning and teaching approaches based on specific competency structures need to replace existing, traditional models of pedagogy (Baillie, et al., 2011).

Clinical Supervision

Challenges and barriers also exist to the implementation of competency-based clinical supervision (Kaslow, Falender, & Grus, 2012). The shift in supervision practice from an apprentice or osmosis transmission approach to one explicitly based on competency development places greater focus on the supervisor's assessment of the supervisee's competence to complete particular clinical tasks (Dijksterhuis et al., 2009). Such a shift in approach requires supervisors to upgrade and transform their supervision and assessment skills. For example, rather than assume that a supervisee is prepared to perform a specific clinical service based on his or her standing in the academic institution or year in training, the supervisor must assess the supervisee's actual performance of the competencies required to perform a clinical service. The assessment of a supervisee's competence requires a specific supervisor skill set as well as adequate time and resources to perform the competency-based assessment. It is on the basis of this assessment as well as consideration of the level of independence viewed acceptable that *entrustability* in the supervisee is established (Dijksterhuis et al., 2009; Falender & Shafranske, 2004).

The corresponding transformation in clinical supervision involves multiple levels: (a) identifying, practicing, transmitting, and ensuring implementation of the skills, knowledge, and attitudes for the practice of effective clinical supervision and effective assessment and monitoring of the

supervisee; (b) instilling motivation for the change to competency-based practice in individuals and settings; and (c) providing specialized training for supervisors in clinical supervision to foster the change from supervision through osmosis to one guided by formalized practice. Due to the complexity of the supervisor responsibilities to clients, supervisees, training institutions, and so on, tensions may arise from the multiple functions performed in supervision. Supervisors must facilitate and maintain effective supervisory relationships, create with supervisees training goals and the means to attain their goals tailored to their training needs (and the clinical requirements of their clients), often while managing job performance and conducting evaluations. In addition, supervisors ensure compliance of staff and supervisees with agency regulations while promoting everyone's professional development (Tebes et al., 2011). These multiple roles may create tensions between supportive interactions and evaluation or gatekeeping (i.e., supervisor judgment of supervisee suitability) functions. Clinical supervision as practiced in this emergent culture of competencies bears a number of responsibilities to clients, the public-at-large, the supervisee, the profession, and associated academic and training institutions. This requires careful consideration of supervision as a distinct professional competency and examination of its features and best practices.

Clinical Supervision: A Distinct Professional Competency

Whether its origin can be traced back to the psychotherapy-based supervision approaches of Freud (Frawley-O'Dea & Sarnat, 2001), even though he never explicitly defined supervision, or to Witmer, a student of Wundt and a founder of psychology (Hess, 2011), supervision is today defined as a distinct professional competency. Generally, definitions of supervision are distinguished by inclusion (or exclusion) of the following component elements: a priority on ensuring client safety and welfare, hierarchical and/or collaborative supervisory relationship, existence of the power differential, performance monitoring and an evaluative component, transparency of supervisor appraisal of the supervisee, enhancing the development and/or competence of the supervisee, attention to personal factors and unusual emotional reactivity on the part of the supervisee, and developmental complexity increasing over time. Supervision may have been previously viewed as the simple transmission of clinical skills from the supervisor to the supervisee;

however, contemporary definitions of supervision are increasingly more complex, emphasizing the collaborative and interpersonal nature of the learning process, examining effective supervisory techniques and considering the context of the power differential resulting from the supervisor's evaluative and gatekeeping functions. From the counseling psychology perspective, Bernard and Goodyear (2009) defined supervision as,

> An intervention provided by a more senior member of a profession to a more junior member or members of that same profession. This relationship is evaluative and hierarchical, extends over time, and has the simultaneous purposes of enhancing the professional functioning of the more junior person(s); monitoring the quality of professional services offered to the clients that she, he or they see; and serving as a gatekeeper for those who are to enter the particular profession. (p. 7)

Milne (2009) who studies cognitive behavioral therapy supervision criticized Bernard and Goodyear's definition for not being easily operationalized to provide empirical support. He proposed that supervision is,

> The formal provision by approved supervisors of a relationship-based education and training that is work-focused and which manages, supports, develops, and evaluates the work of colleague/s. It, therefore, differs from related activities such as mentoring and therapy, by incorporating an evaluative component and by being obligatory. The main methods that supervisors use are corrective feedback on the supervisee's performance, teaching, and collaborative goal setting. (p. 15)

However, this definition does not directly address the major supervision functions of protection of the public and gatekeeping for the profession.

In a competency-based frame, Falender and Shafranske (2004) defined clinical supervision as,

> A distinct professional activity in which education and training aimed at developing science-informed practice are facilitated through a collaborative interpersonal process. It involves observation, evaluation, feedback, facilitation of supervisee self-assessment, and acquisition of knowledge and skills by instruction, modeling, and mutual problem-solving. Building on the recognition of the strengths and talents of the supervisee, supervision encourages self-efficacy. Supervision ensures that clinical (supervision) is conducted in a competent manner in which ethical standards, legal prescriptions, and professional practices are used to promote and protect the welfare of the client, the profession, and society at large. (p. 3)

Falender and Shafranske also identified four superordinate values (Integrity-in-Relationship; Ethical, Values-based Practice; Appreciation of Diversity; and Science-informed, Evidence-based Practice) and supervision pillars (Supervisory Relationship, Inquiry, and Educational Praxis) as integral in their competency-based approach to clinical supervision.

Competency-Based Clinical Supervision

Competency-based clinical supervision is "an approach that explicitly identifies the knowledge, skills and values that are assembled to form a clinical competency and provides the means to develop learning strategies and evaluation procedures to meet criterion-referenced competence standards in keeping with evidence-based practices and the requirements of the local clinical setting" (Falender & Shafranske, 2007, p. 233). Implementation of competency-based clinical supervision (Falender & Shafranske, 2004; 2007; see also Scott-Tilley, 2008) is achieved through a series of steps following the clear identification of competencies and their associated components (i.e., knowledge, skills, and attitudes/values) (see Benchmarks, Fouad et al., 2009) as an example of clearly defined competencies). Table 18.1 presents supervisor responsibilities in performing competency-based clinical supervision.

In addition to performing the responsibilities listed in Table 18.1, adoption and commitment to the competency model throughout the training process (close coordination between academic and training institutions, e.g., practica and internship sites, regarding training goals, objectives and performance expectations; recruitment and selection of supervisees; conduct of supervision and training, including didactic training and modes of supervision, e.g., individual, group, live supervision; evaluation; and learning outcomes, etc.) are necessary to fully implement the approach. The clarity and transparency of the transformation to competency-based supervision are essential components because the process may be difficult and require specific competencies and strategies (Kaslow et al., 2012).

Supervisee Competencies

The assessment of supervisee competencies is of major importance throughout the course of training and orients all learning activities. Substantial

Table 18.1. Supervisor Responsibilities in Competency-Based Clinical Supervision

1. The supervisor examines his or her own clinical and supervision expertise and competency.
2. The supervisor continuously monitors the quality of care provided to the client, directs supervisee activities, and intervenes as appropriate to ensure client welfare.
3. The supervisor engages with the supervisee to facilitate development of a viable supervisory relationship, leading to the emergence of a working alliance.
4. The supervisor delineates supervisory expectations, including standards, rules, and general practice.
5. The supervisor identifies setting-specific competencies the supervisee must attain for successful completion of the supervised training experience.
6. The supervisor collaborates with the supervisee in developing a supervisory agreement or contract for informed consent, ensuring clear communication in establishing competencies and goals, tasks to achieve them, evaluation procedures, and logistics.
7. The supervisor models and engages the supervisee in self-assessment and development of metacompetence (i.e., self-awareness of competencies) from the onset of supervision and throughout.
8. The supervisor collaborates with the supervisee in developing approaches to evaluation and feedback and provides ongoing feedback, verbal and written, to the supervisee and the academic institution (as appropriate), actively monitors the effectiveness of supervision, and encourages and accepts feedback from supervisee.
9. The supervisor collaborates with the supervisee in identifying and implementing processes of learning, assessing the effectiveness of supervisor interventions in facilitating supervisee development, and tailoring supervision and training activities to the learning style of the supervisee.
10. The supervisor maintains communication and responsibility for assessing and remediating supervisee performance problems and observing and addressing strains in the supervisory relationship.

Based on Falender & Shafranske, 2004, 2007, 2008, 2012

attention has been devoted to supervisee competencies (Fouad et al., 2009; Greenberg, Caro, & Smith, 2010; Hatcher & Lassiter, 2007; Kamen, Veilleux, Bangen, VanderVeen & Klonoff, 2010) as one facet of metacompetence for the entry level (licensed) psychology practitioner. Assessment of competence of the supervisee is facilitated by use of Benchmarks and other competence frames (e.g., National Council of Schools and Programs of Professional Psychology [NCSPP], 2007). Assessment provides the foundation for development of the supervisory alliance through a collaborative process of supervisor and supervisee identifying areas of relative weakness and tasks to achieve greater competence, with ongoing supervisor feedback to reflect on evolving supervisee competence. Accountability is enhanced through formalization of the assessment and development processes (Falender & Shafranske, 2012b). Development of competency trajectories (e.g., Benchmarks) has contributed to the advancement of a competency-based supervision model as supervisors assist supervisees in collaborative identification of targeted areas for growth and the development of a plan to implement these identified competencies (Falender et al., 2012). Additional benefits of

a competencies approach are the opportunities for supervisees to increase accuracy of self-monitoring and for supervisors and supervisees to collaboratively assesses the adequacy and refine the set of competencies being rated as has been done in health administration (Bradley et al., 2008).

Empirical research to determine validity and reliability of proposed competencies is in its infancy. In the lead article of a special issue of *The Counseling Psychologist*, Falender et al. (2012) described the necessity for empirical study of the Benchmarks competencies to determine the validity of the developmental progression and the integrity of the stated competencies as comprehensive and meaningful in the developmental training trajectory. Significant efforts are underway to determine the most efficient and effective assessment procedures (Kaslow et al., 2009) of supervisee competencies.

Supervisor Competencies and Training

Although consensus exists regarding the critical importance of clinical supervisor competence (Falender et al., 2004; Hoge et al., 2009), a requisite for effective supervision, a lack of training in clinical supervision persists among licensed practitioners and even among supervisees in the training pipeline (e.g., in Canada, Hadjistavropoulos, Kehler, & Hadjistavropoulos, 2010; in the United States, Crook-Lyon, Presnell, Silva, Suyama, & Stickney, 2011; Lyon, Heppler, Leavitt, & Fisher, 2008; in Australia, Kavanagh et al., 2008), thereby compromising transmission of enhanced supervisor competencies (Kaslow et al., 2012). In Canada, with over 70% of programs responding (n = 20), Hadjistavropoulos et al. (2010) reported that although approximately 50% of programs required some coursework in clinical supervision, the amount and content were highly variable, with, for example, only 46% addressing liability. Twenty-five percent required a practicum with peer supervision, and an additional 40% offered an elective with some opportunity for supervision experience. Surveys in the United States have had lower response rates (52% for Lyon et al., 2008; 32% with predominantly counseling respondents for Crook-Lyon et al., 2011). Lyon et al. (2008) reported that among interns, 39% completed a course in clinical supervision (26% clinical; 73% counseling); 61% reported no coursework on clinical supervision. Forty-four percent of interns reported experience supervising a trainee—generally at counseling centers; the median time supervising was 40 hours; over half offered no supervision training. Counseling-psychology trainees received more supervision training than clinical-psychology trainees, but generally, the major influence on supervision practice was judged by trainees to be the personal experience of having been supervised (Crook-Lyon et al., 2011).

Falender et al. (2004) described a structure of knowledge, skills, and values or attitudes as a preliminary model of entry-level supervisor competence, and subsequently, Rings, Genuchi, Hall, Angelo, and Cornish (2009) provided support from training directors' ratings of the scope and structure of the components of supervisor competence. Ironically, beyond these entry-level competencies, minimal attention has been directed to the identification, assessment, and attainment of the competencies of supervisors. Inattention to the assessment of supervisor competence seems to have fostered a degree of complacency in the training environment in attitudes toward the necessity for supervisor training or requirements to meet standards of supervisory competence. Rings and colleagues (2009) found that supervisors generally undervalued supervisor training, both the necessity for training and the value of training itself. Consequences of the supervisor training vacuum may be ineffective (Magnuson,

Wilcoxon, & Norem, 2000) or even harmful supervision (Ellis et al., 2010), which compromises both the quality of training and client care.

To assess supervisor competence we suggest the following questions (cf. Falender et al., 2004):

• Has the supervisor completed a course/training in clinical supervision?
• Has the supervisor received supervision of supervision and has he or she been verified as ready to supervise?
• Has the supervisor used video or live supervision (or audio) in supervision practice?
• Does the supervisor's supervision reflect diversity infused in practice?
• Does the supervisor give supervisee(s) ongoing developmental and corrective feedback?
• Does the supervisor engage in and model self-assessment, reflection, and demonstrate self-awareness and openness to consultation as needed?
• Does the supervisor require client outcome assessment?

Godley, Garner, Smith, Meyers, and Godley (2011) proposed supervision certification to ensure uniform skills for implementation and ongoing supervision. Internationally, Australia mandates a two-year supervision training sequence and certification. Sweden established state-sponsored supervision in 1974 with a two-year psychotherapy supervisor-training program as a prerequisite for performing supervision (Sundin, Ogren, & Boethius, 2008), and the United Kingdom (U.K.) maintains a voluntary register of accredited clinical supervisors (Gonsalvez & Milne, 2010).

Competency-Based Clinical Supervision: Psychotherapy-Based Supervision Models

With the advent of the competencies movement (Kaslow et al., 2004; Kenkel & Peterson, 2010) and the shift in conceptualization of treatment interventions with a goal of integrating competency-based training and supervision, each theoretical psychotherapy model has identified paradigmatic competencies. Part of the task is to develop a framework for transmission of competence to future generations of practitioners—and to systematically assess, provide feedback, and support the development of the supervisee. Supervisors employing humanistic (Farber, 2010), psychodynamic (Frawley-O'Dea & Sarnat, 2001), cognitive-behavioral (Newman, 2010), integrative (Boswell, Nelson, Nordberg,

Mcaleavey, & Castonguay (2010), couples, and family (Celano, Smith, & Kaslow, 2010) models each have identified foundational and functional supervisor competencies. Psychotherapy-based approaches to supervision are uniquely suited to provide training that is theoretically consistent, since the supervisee is immersed in the specific orientation's understanding of processes of change and growth when conducting treatment and learning in supervision (Beck, Sarnat, & Barenstein, 2008). For example, the structure of supervision in cognitive therapy parallels a clinical session in its formal use of check-in, agenda setting, homework, and so on (Beck et al.). Similarly, psychodynamic supervision reflects an emphasis on the relational dimension in both clinical and supervisory settings (Sarnat, 2010). Although the use of psychotherapy-based approaches makes inherent sense, further study is required to assess their effectiveness in facilitating supervisee competence.

Effective Practices and Competency-Based Clinical Supervision

Increasingly, research is addressing effective supervision. Much of the resultant research is process oriented, looking at relationship, personal factors or transference-countertransference, and other interactional components. Although increasing attention is on the parameters of supervision, conclusions about what constitutes effective supervision have risen out of prelicensure supervisee and supervisor self-report rather than associations with client outcomes or supervisory outcomes (Wheeler & Richards, 2007). The abundance of evidence regarding effective practices comes from qualitative research with very small sample sizes; analysis of consensual qualitative data and critical analysis predominate.

Components of effective supervision (Falender & Shafranske, 2004) include:

• Demonstrating respect for the supervisee and client(s).
• Collaboratively assessing supervisee competence (with supervisee self-assessment and supervisor feedback) and developing goals and tasks.
• Forming a supervisory alliance.
• Identifying strains to the supervisory relationship and working to repair them.
• Clarifying supervisee roles and supervisor expectations.
• Reflecting on and enhancing supervisor competence in supervision and clinical practice.

• Infusing diversity among client, supervisee, and supervisor.
• Reflecting on worldviews, attitudes for treatment planning, conceptualization assessment, and intervention.
• Enhancing the supervisee's reflection on clinical work and the process of supervision and clinical practice.
• Engaging the supervisee in skill development using interactive methods.
• Attending to personal factors, unusual emotional reactivity, and countertransference.
• Giving ongoing accurate, positive, and corrective feedback.
• Observing directly—live or video.
• Monitoring and being a gatekeeper.

Skills Associated with Effective Clinical Supervision

Although essential to the implementation of supervision, educationally and contextually sound *skills* have received substantially less focus in supervision literature. Although some attention has been focused on countertransference management, multicultural practice, reflection, group supervision, and self-disclosure (Ladany, Friedlander, & Nelson, 2005; Walker, 2010), the lack of a skill-based pedagogy for supervisor training or supervisor competency standards has resulted in supervision not receiving the strong scrutiny of empirical analysis. Although model-specific or manualized supervision is often more skill-based (Palmer-Olsen, Gold, & Wooley, 2011), its research base remains inadequate.

A comprehensive approach to skills development was elaborated in Falender and Shafranske (2012a) as a guide for supervisors; however, further empirical study is needed to establish effectiveness. Although not intended to be exhaustive in scope, the following discussion presents the major components in competency-based clinical supervision.

Alliance

Alliance is a key factor associated with positive therapeutic and self-reported supervision outcomes. Whereas particular attention has been devoted to factors that influence the development of the therapeutic alliance, increasing focus is now being directed to the role of the supervisor in facilitating alliance in supervision (e.g., Bambling, 2009; Falender & Shafranske, 2012b). Although a large amount of research has focused on supervisory alliance, its relationship to positive supervision outcomes, supervisee development, and its metatheoretical nature (Crook Lyon & Potkar, 2010), relatively little is known about the impact of specific supervisory practices on development of the supervisory alliance. The majority of empirical studies concern the role of certain background characteristics on alliance. For example, attachment style (Dickson, Moberly, Marshall, & Reilly, 2011) and the personal characteristics of the supervisor such as warmth, empathy, respect, trust, genuineness, flexibility, and competence appear to be associated with the development of alliance.

Bordin (1983) described the supervisory working alliance derived from the therapeutic working alliance of mutual agreements with clarity and mutuality, tasks resting on the clear mutual understanding about tasks that shared goals impose, and bonds associated with carrying out the mutually agreed upon enterprise. From this perspective, supervisory alliance first emerges out of a collaborative process regarding goals and the means to achieve the goals (summarized in Falender & Shafranske, 2004). These goals include "mastering specific skills, enlarging understanding of clients and the therapeutic process, increasing awareness of self and impact on process, overcoming personal and intellectual obstacles towards learning and mastery, deepening one's understanding of concepts and theory, and maintaining standards of service" (Bordin, 1983, p. 37–38).

Much of the research on supervisory alliance is an outgrowth of this framework. A strong supervisory relationship has been identified as a sine qua non of positive supervision outcomes (Crook Lyon & Potkar, 2010), although outcome assessment of supervision is generally based on supervisee self-report, a factor limited by metacompetence, or not knowing what one does not know. Therefore, supervisors are advised to carefully attend to its formation and to employ alliance strength assessment (Bahrick, 1989) to provide the supervisor and supervisee with insight into the alliance. It is useful to conceptualize the tensions that emerge in supervision as products of naturally occurring negotiations between the subjectivities of the supervisor and supervisee. Each individual experiences the supervisory interactions uniquely and misunderstanding and strains result at times from those differences. Working to resolve strains and ruptures may strengthen the relationship and enhance the supervisory process (Falender & Shafranske, 2012; Safran, Muran, Stevens, & Rothman, 2008).

Although Bordin's approach highlights many of the crucial elements affecting supervision alliance, in our view it does not fully capture the complexity of the supervision process. For example, Bordin's conceptualization did not include the impact of supervisor evaluation and gatekeeping, specific functions that shift the balance of mutuality in relationships and likely affect alliance. Further, feminist supervisors (Porter, 1995; Vargas, Porter, & Falender, 2008) have suggested supervisory transparency and communication to bridge the potential tensions resulting from the supervisory power differential; however, there has been only minimal research in this area (Green & Dekkers, 2010). Although further empirical investigation is required, it seems logical to propose that supervisory alliance synergistically emerges out of the complex interaction of common factors (personal characteristics of supervisor and supervisee), supervision processes (e.g., collaboration) and contextual factors (clinical environment and challenges).

Diversity

Integral to client care (as well as to the development of the supervisory alliance) is respect and awareness of individual differences and appreciation of multicultural diversity. Although the importance of culture and individual differences is widely acknowledged and conveyed in clinical guidelines (e.g., APA, 2000) as well as required by APA's policy on evidence-based practice (2006), a gap exists between beliefs about salience and actual clinical performance. Generally, psychologists assess themselves as being more culturally competent than their specific behavioral responses indicate (Hansen et al., 2006) and they endorse more multicultural strategies than they would actually use in practice (Sehgal et al., 2011). The same appears to be the case in clinical supervision. For example, supervisors self-report that they frequently introduce the subject of diversity, yet their supervisees fail to support this assertion (Duan & Roehlke, 2001; Green & Dekkers, 2010). Further, supervisees claim that if the subject was raised, it was usually the supervisee who initiated a discussion. These findings are not entirely surprising given evidence that the importance of supervisor self-knowledge of diversity (i.e., values, prejudices, and biases) has been underaddressed in the supervision literature (Falender, Shafranske, & Falicov, 2014; Schroeder, Andrews, & Hindes, 2009).

Why is diversity an important consideration in supervision? Supervision as an interpersonal process brings into interaction the multicultural identities of supervisor and supervisee with respect to the client. It is in supervision that one can learn not just to appreciate individual differences and context but to use that awareness to better tailor interventions and form effective, culturally sensitive therapeutic relationships. Further, diversity is both a moral and ethical imperative in supervision (Salter & Salter, 2012), as moral judgments are based on life philosophy and guided by religious, personal, and diversity-guided values. The beliefs and values that influence a client's practical decisions about "how to live life" affect treatment, which has led some to characterize psychotherapy as an ethical or moral enterprise (Smith, 2009; see also Richardson, Fowers, & Guignon, 1999). Ethics is how decisions are made to achieve moral outcomes and distinguish right from wrong. In supervision, this integrated approach to morality and ethics has been little addressed, aside from feminist supervision.

The importance of cultural competence and sensitivity cannot be overstated, because supervision is attenuated by the power differential inherent in the relationship and can have profoundly negative effects. Power, privilege, and diversity are essential factors in clinical supervision but are often misunderstood, minimized, or neglected. Strains in the supervisory alliance can be exacerbated by inattention to the worldview of the supervisee or client, or framing the supervisory or clinical relationships and the conduct of treatment and supervision without consideration of context and individual differences. Such situations pose significant lapses and have the potential for strain and rupture in both supervisory and therapeutic relationships (Jernigan, Green, Helms, Perez-Gualdron, & Henze, 2010; Singh & Chun, 2010). In addition, bias can be expressed implicitly or explicitly, in microaggressions (Sue et al., 2007), in minimization (Helms & Richardson, 1997), or in preconceptions, with the result of mistrust and miscommunication (Dovidio, Gaertner, Kawakami. & Hodson, 2002). What can be done to bring multicultural diversity into supervision?

The first step a supervisor can make is to engage in a self-appraisal of his or her commitment and experience in integrating a multicultural lens in supervision. The exercise of metacompetence, specifically asking what one does not know, as well as adopting a stance of cultural humility can safeguard against errantly assuming expertise in facilitating culturally responsive supervision. Such reflection can naturally lead to identification of areas for further professional development as well as learning from the supervisee, clients, and others. Essential components that precede discussions of diversity include a respectful and strong supervisory relationship, and a skill-initiating discussion of the impact of behavior or attitudes on the client and on the supervisory relationship as it, in turn, impacts the client. Fortunately, supervision models have been developed to address specific diversity categories (e.g., Latina: Field, Chavez-Korell, & Rodríguez,, 2010; queer people of color: Singh & Chun, 2010; oppression and privilege, Hernandez & McDowell, 2010), as well as texts focusing on diversity in supervision, training, and treatment (Falender et al., in press; Gallardo, Yeh, Trimble, & Parham, 2011). Most models consider multiple identities of client(s), supervisee-therapist, and supervisor, varying worldviews, the impact of these on client treatment and supervision process and effective practices.

Awareness of Personal Factors and Management of Countertransference

One of the principle functions of clinical supervision is to facilitate awareness of the role of personal factors in the conduct of psychotherapy. Consistent with appreciation for multicultural diversity, we suggest that clinical understanding is always a matter of perspective and the therapeutic process is always impacted by the inescapable influences of the clinician's (and supervisor's) life experiences and relationships, personal interests, commitments, and cultures out of which he or she constructs meaning (cf. Falender & Shafranske, 2004, p. 83). The *person* of the therapist is always in the therapy room. In considering personal factors, we make distinctions between the therapist's emotional responsiveness (which is necessary for empathic engagement and clinical understanding) and emotional reactivity (which involves heightened emotional arousal and consequently suspends empathic engagement with the client). The supervisor assists the supervisee in identifying the subtle or dramatic "distinctly different, unusual or idiosyncratic acts or patterns of therapist experience and/or actions toward a client [that constitute] deviations from baselines in the therapist's usual practice" (Kiesler, 2001, pp. 1061–1062), which constitute therapist reactivity, commonly referred to as countertransference. The supervisory aim is to enhance awareness, to encourage the supervisee to be mindful of his or her reactions, and to use such awareness in service of the treatment as well as to better manage reactivity (see Falender and Shafranske, 2012a, and Shafranske and Falender, 2008, for further illustration of the processes involved in managing therapist reactivity).

Legal and Ethical Considerations

Supervisor competence in legal and ethical arenas is usually presumed and includes a broad spectrum of knowledge, skills, and values/attitudes regarding clients *and* supervisees. Maintaining competence in legal and ethical matters may be challenging, as practitioners are not always as competent as they believe. For instance, Pabian, Welfel, and Beebe (2009) found that three-quarters of respondents to their survey were misinformed about state laws regarding legal duty to warn but nevertheless expressed confidence in their knowledge and competence. Further, psychologists may know the ethical standard but not practice it (Bernard, Murphy, & Little, 1987), and rational models do not consider inherent bias in thinking and practice (Tjeltveit & Gottlieb, 2010 Tversky & Kahneman, 1974). Evidence suggests that supervisor ethical lapses and supervisee lack of understanding of supervisory ethics impact clients and supervisees. Negative consequences include confusion about legal requirements and ethical standards, poor modeling of professionalism, loss of trust, respect and authority, and challenges to the integrity of the supervisor (Cikanek, Veach, & Braun, 2004; Lapid Moutier, Dunn, Hammond, & Roberts, 2009). Far from rare occurrences, Ladany, Lehrman-Waterman, Molinaro, and Wolgast (1999) indicated that supervisees reported that over half of their supervisors had committed ethical infractions (see also Wall, 2009). These ethical lapses included behaviors or omissions that directly impacted the quality of the supervision. The most frequently cited infractions were failure to adhere to ethical guidelines regarding performance evaluation and monitoring of supervisee activities, violating areas of confidentiality with respect to supervision, and working with alternative theoretical perspectives. It is important to note that the infraction of confidentiality represented not a breach of privilege, but rather the supervisor's failure to define the parameters of confidentiality in the supervisory relationship; of course, much supervisory information is *not* confidential and supervisors must—at times—share supervisee information with training colleagues and teams, the degree-granting university, and state and provincial licensing boards. Supervisors should be mindful that, in addition to providing direct guidance or instruction when addressing legal and ethical issues in supervision, their own conduct will perhaps have the greatest impact in transmitting professionalism and ethical conduct to their supervisees.

Supervision Contract

A supervision contract is generally accepted as a component of effective supervision (Falender & Shafranske, 2004; Fouad et al., 2009; Thomas, 2007; 2010). The supervision contract provides informed consent by identifying processes and goals of supervision, defining clarity of expectations generally and for supervisee self-assessment and how that is bolstered by frequent supervisor feedback. The contract defines the components and expectations for successful completion of training, as well as procedures should competencies not be met. Supervision contracts are essential tools in establishing clarity that translates to a strengthened supervisory alliance (Falender & Shafranske, 2004) and clarifies setting and supervisor expectations. Additional contract components include formats and procedures of supervision, requirements (e.g., video, live observation, homework), mutual expectations, evaluation criteria, limits of confidentiality regarding supervisee disclosures to the supervisor, what constitutes emergencies in the setting and appropriate actions, supervisor contact, and setting specific procedures including those that might be contained in a personnel manual.

Adherence to the Ethical Principles of Psychologists and Code of Conduct (APA, 2010), and frequent reference to the code in supervision strengthens and assists in the integration of ethical practice. Most supervisees have had one course in ethics, and it may have focused on avoidance of risk (Tjeltveit & Gottlieb, 2009). Supervisees may not have elaborate understanding of ethical application or supervisor ethical responsibilities (Cikanek, Veach, & Braun, 2004; Lee & Cashwell, 2001). The supervisor is responsible for maintaining competence in ethics and legal standards, providing supervision that meets legal and ethical standards, ensuring the supervisee identifies and manages ethical issues as they arise, modeling ethical behavior and ethical decision making in all aspects of supervision and practice, and identifying and dealing with ethical breaches.

The supervisor's role is complicated by multiple potentially overlapping roles and expectations of supervisees, settings, and administration. For instance, supervisors may be expected to form strong supervisory alliances, and to mentor, support, and advocate for supervisees while also evaluating, monitoring, providing corrective and evaluative feedback to multiple entities (e.g., academic institutions, training committees, licensing boards, future employment sites). Of course, supervisors also must practice gatekeeping to ensure the protection of the clients and the profession, while maintaining good training success statistics to report to accrediting bodies. It is no wonder that tensions result when fulfilling the complex responsibilities of clinical supervision (Johnson, 2008). The use of an interactional process in formulating the contract promotes clear understanding of responsibilities and expectations, and reinforces supervision as a collaborative and transparent process. Further, the contract provides the backbone of competency-based clinical supervision by articulating the competencies and the means by which they will be developed and evaluated.

Reflective Practice: Inquiry, Self-Assessment, and Metacompetence

One of the most important competencies developed in supervision is the ability to accurately assess one's clinical competence, yet, little is known about the precise means by which this skill is developed. Schön (1983, 1987) persuasively articulated the importance of reflection-on-action, which contributes to the ability for reflection-in-action. However, there is a paucity of empirical research examining the effectiveness of specific supervision practices that constitute reflective practice and result in metacompetence, that is, the ability to assess what one knows and what one does not know.

Accurate self-assessment is generally viewed as an essential component of professional growth and development. However, accuracy of individuals' self-assessment across disciplines has been generally disappointing (Davis et al., 2006; Dunning, Heath, & Suls, 2004). Lafferty, Beutler, and Crago (1989) reported that less effective therapists showed poorer self-evaluation skills, rating their patients as more involved in therapy, and as making more progress in treatment, than did an observer. Although a correlation was reported between self-assessment and expert ratings of competence in a study of cognitive behavioral therapists in the U.K., less competent therapists over-rated their own competence more than therapists who met competence criteria (Brosan, Reynolds, & Moore, 2008). Curran et al. (2012) reported that family-practice residents' self-reported confidence in their ability to do particular skill tasks was not associated with observed performance on those tasks. All this should not be surprising given that self-knowledge and self-appraisal barely plays a role in education (Wilson, 2009).

Reflective practice is initiated in clinical supervision by the supervisor's use of inquiry. By inquiry we mean any intervention that encourages supervisees to self-reflect on their behavior and to derive understanding of an aspect of the clinical process and their contributions to it. Further, reflective practice involves developing awareness of the means and assumptions by which supervisees arrived at that understanding and the processes that informed clinical decision making and led to specific therapist actions. Also, developing self-knowledge goes beyond enhancing awareness of cognitive assumptions and appraisals and includes developing increasing facility in recognizing emotional states, including awareness of emotional reactivity, memories of past emotional responses as related to clinical interactions, as well as prediction of future emotional states (Falender & Shafranske, 2012a; Wilson, 2009).

Self-reflective practice evolves out of the processes of reflection that have been performed in supervision. The ways in which the supervisor engages in inquiry (the nature of questions that are asked, the focus of inquiry, or the processes of self-assessment) provides models that will be internalized and used to encourage self-reflection. One example of a process of inquiry and self-reflection was described by Safran and colleagues (2008). In their approach they begin group supervision with a mindfulness induction exercise that "can help supervisees to develop an awareness of an openness to their own experience rather than focus on their intellectual understanding" (p. 144), which sets the stage for self-reflective practice among the group members. Such processes used over the course of a training rotation likely influence skill development in self-awareness. Although a comprehensive discussion of reflective practices is beyond the scope of the chapter, it is important for supervisors to be familiar with practices that may contribute to developing skills in self-assessment and metacompetence and to collaboratively explore with the supervisee approaches that lead to heightened self-awareness. Methods of evaluation and feedback, described in the following sections, contribute to the supervisee's skill in self-assessment and are foundational in focusing learning and enhancing competence.

Evaluation

Evaluation plays a central role in competency-based clinical supervision. Emphasis is placed on the assessment of the supervisee's ability to assemble knowledge, skills, and attitudes/values to perform a specific clinical competency. This requires both the identification of the various aspects that are required to perform the competency and the development of methods to observe and evaluate these areas. With the various competency documents (e.g., Benchmarks: Fouad et al, 2009) available, the structure of supervision can be conducted with specific attention to evaluating the foundational and functional competencies. However, caution is indicated because supervisor ratings using the Benchmarks model are untested. Although such a process is intensive, it yields evaluative data on which specific learning strategies can be targeted. This is an ambitious undertaking, particularly in light of the present state of evaluation practices.

Methods of supervision assessment are variable, and direct observation has been the exception rather than the standard of practice. Supervisors commonly rely on supervisee self-reports of clinical processes, which pose significant limitations in obtaining accurate data. As supervisee recall is impacted by memory, inattention to nonverbal behavior, therapist bias (Haggerty & Hilsenroth, 2011) and metacompetence, supervision that solely relies on self-reports is necessarily limited in terms of actual supervisee behavior and its effects on the clinical process. The supervisor's direct access to the clinical session by live observation or review of session recordings provides the direct line to competence assessment. Observing actual behavior, supplemented by supervisee self-report and reflection, is the route to more accurate assessment of the development of supervisee skills, knowledge, and attitudes. Reasons why live or video observation is either not or only minimally used include time constraints, concerns about inducing anxiety in the supervisee, confidentiality (Haggerty & Hilsenroth, 2011), and restrictions due regarding the legal standing of the client (e.g., prohibitions in forensic settings).

Direct observation is a sine qua non in medical training and ongoing competency assessment in psychology (Holmboe et al., 2011), and it has been found to be associated with enhanced supervisee and client outcomes (Haggerty & Hilsenroth, 2011). In medicine, observation of general competencies has been less than reliable, suggesting the need for larger samples of observations and attention to reliability across raters and competencies (McGill, van der Vleuten, & Clarke, 2011). This research highlights the value of live observation that incorporates an adequate number of sample behaviors relating to the competency and multiple raters, not simply the supervisee's self-assessment.

In addition to evaluating supervisee competence, the competency-based approach to supervision requires that the same efforts be applied to assess the adequacy of supervision and its impact. Approaches include evaluating supervisor competence, supervisee competence, processes of supervision, supervision outcomes, and treatment outcomes. Although the preponderance of research finds that supervision is helpful, more precise measurement of its effects and effectiveness is required. The use of goal-setting and feedback practices appear to be of value not only in the evaluation of supervision effectiveness but they also contribute to stronger supervisory working alliances, enhanced supervisee self-efficacy, and increased supervisee satisfaction with supervision (Lehrman-Waterman & Ladany, 2001). Recent research efforts have shown promise in the evaluation of the effects of specific supervisor behaviors (Milne, 2010); however, much more is needed to be done to establish efficacy of evidence-based supervision practice. Milne (Milne, 2008, 2009) provides an exemplar. Milne and his colleagues developed an observational instrument, "Process Evaluation of Training and Supervision," for cognitive behavioral supervision, which allows coding of supervisor behaviors and association to specific supervisee learning modes such as experiencing, reflecting, conceptualizing, and experimenting. Another example is found in work conducted by Zarbock, Drews, Bodansky, and Dahme (2009) in which supervisor and supervisee questionnaires were developed to assess dimensions of relationship, problem solving, and clarifying. They reported that although there was agreement on satisfaction with the process of supervision, supervisor and supervisee perceptions of the supervision session were not correlated.

Given the complexity of supervision, and the lack of assessment devices for supervisor competence or supervision efficacy, evaluation will need to be multifaceted to include satisfaction, process variables, client outcomes, and supervision outcomes. Promising techniques include the excellent compendium of competency assessment tools (Kaslow et al., 2009) published in the issue of *Training and Education in Professional Psychology* in which the Competencies Benchmarks also appear as well as the Rochester Objective Structured Clinical Evaluation (ROSCE), a format for live observation of trainees modified from the medical model Objective Structured Clinical Exam (OSCE) (Le Roux, Podgorski, Rosenberg, Watson, & McDaniel, 2011).

Feedback

Feedback is a normative part of the supervisory process in which the supervisor provides monitoring and information about developing competencies of the supervisee. Through feedback, the supervisor ensures ongoing attention to clinical competence with clients, specific clinical competencies, professionalism, and use of supervision feedback. Feedback is a type of formative evaluation, or ongoing progress monitoring. Despite its importance to the training process, provision of meaningful ongoing formative feedback has not been a consistent or even frequent practice of supervisors in psychology (Hoffman, Hill, Holmes, & Freitas, 2005) or in medicine (Daelmans, Hoogenboom, Scherpbier, Stehouwer, & van der Vleuten, 2005). Surprisingly, many supervisors actually withhold feedback on counseling performance and the supervision itself (Ladany & Melincoff, 1999). Provision of difficult feedback appears to be perceived as so problematic for supervisors that it simply may not occur, especially if it relates to foundational competencies such as professionalism (Hoffman et al., 2005). This current state is particularly disappointing given the fact that the provision of accurate feedback is a core component of supervision and is associated with supervisee perceptions of successful supervision (Henderson, Cawyer, & Watkins, 1999). Competency-based clinical supervision necessarily involves the provision of continuous formative feedback specific to targeted competencies in addition to cumulative evaluations. We present a series of recommendations about giving feedback in Table 18.2.

Learning Strategies

Clinical supervision at its core aims at developing clinical competence and professionalism. Effective learning strategies ensure that clients are provided high-quality professional care and supervisees receive training leading to the development of competence. Historically, learning has been facilitated through the encouragement of self-reflection and exchange of verbal information, including evaluative comments, transmission of knowledge, advice, support, and directives. For example, Milne (2009) scrutinized 24 empirical studies of supervision and found that teaching and instruction was the most frequent learning strategy employed by supervisors (in 75% of the studies) and feedback was second, reported in 63% of the studies (p. 54). Milne (2008, 2009) has called into question the manner in which supervision is generally performed and has proposed the adoption of an experiential theory of supervision. Although verbal methods are retained in gathering information, thereby heightening awareness, and clarifying supervisee understanding, greater emphasis is placed on promoting experiential learning by the supervisee when conducting treatment as well as within supervision itself. Role plays, live supervision, reflection on recorded sessions, use of active learning tasks, directed imagery, mindfulness procedures, and review of objective feedback measures, expand the means by which learning may be facilitated. An evidence-based approach is required

Table 18.2. Recommendations for Providing Feedback

1. Invite supervisee self-reflection and self-assessment and reinforce skills in metacompetence.
2. Provide a framework for the feedback you will give that communicates the importance of the competence issue to be addressed and identifies the developmental context, (e.g., "normative" developmental challenge, doesn't meet performance expectations, exceeds expectations).
3. Feedback given should be formative and continuous, which will contribute to the summative evaluation.
The most effective feedback is:
4. Specific (behaviorally anchored) and ideally close in time to the behavior or the review.
5. Delineates the knowledge, skills, attitudes/values that require attention.
6. Identifies existing strengths on which competence will be enhanced.
7. Frames competence with a developmental orientation.
8. Invites reflection and articulation of the specific area of competence targeted for development.
9. Leads to discussion of learning outcomes and strategies, including ways to enhance learning during supervision.
10. Describes next steps in developing competence and suggests self-assessment strategies and describes the form of assessment to be performed by supervisor.
11. Engages supervisee commitment and sets expectations.
12. Invites feedback regarding the process.

to better assess and identify learning strategies that may be provided to facilitate clinical competence.

Outcomes

Although client improvement is ostensibly the raison d'etre of supervision, only a handful of studies have explored the impact of supervision on client outcomes (Bambling, King, Raue, Schweitzer, & Lambert, 2006; Callahan, Almstrom, Swift, Borja, & Heath, 2009; Proctor, 2010; Unsworth, Cowie, & Green, 2012) with some results supporting the impact of supervision on supervisee morale and client satisfaction and outcome (Knudsen, Ducharme, & Roman, 2008). Research has often combined results from supervision of trainees in the pipeline toward licensure with that of licensed practitioners of multiple disciplines and orientations (e.g., specific to cognitive behavior from the learning disability field (Milne & James, 2002). These studies also represent very different methodologies and trajectories (Watkins, 2011) and may be methodologically challenged (Ellis, D'Iuso, & Ladany, 2008). Regular tracking of client response to treatment is associated with enhanced treatment outcomes (Lambert, 2010; Reese et al., 2009; Worthen & Lambert, 2007) and should be systematically incorporated in supervision practice. Given the importance of supervision, increased attention to systematically investigating the impacts of specific supervision practices and factors on treatment outcome and in the development of clinical competence is warranted.

Addressing Supervisees with Problematic Performance and Gatekeeping

Supervisors face particular challenges when encountering supervisees who are not meeting performance expectations (Forrest, Miller, & Elman, 2008; Kaslow et al., 2007). Although the obligation to ensure client welfare supersedes other responsibilities, supervisors are inevitably drawn into role conflicts when managing situations in which entrustability of the supervisee is in question. Careful assessment of competence is required when assessing whether a trainee is ready and capable to perform clinical responsibilities as well as to continue in clinical training. A deliberative process is required in which the supervisor must carefully differentiate between performance difficulties (which are developmentally normative), performance problems (indicated by an inability to achieve an acceptable level of *competence* after sufficient training and supervision and/or lapses in *capability*, i.e., the exercise of competence), and professional competence

problems such as significant lapses in professional judgment and failure to adhere to professional, ethical, and legal standards (Falender, Collins, & Shafranske, 2009). Use of a competency-based model of supervision provides the infrastructure that supports the identification of clinical competencies, formative evaluation and continuous assessment of performance and approaches to learning essential to all training; however, its utility becomes even more apparent when evaluating and addressing performance difficulties. Assessment of supervisee performance should focus exclusively on professional performance, and observations should be recorded using behavioral anchors and descriptions consistent with the knowledge, skills, and attitudes/values associated with clinical competencies and standards of professionalism, ethics, and legal mandates. Clinical supervisors should be particularly mindful to operate within their professional role and responsibilities and care should be taken to not engage in clinical assessment nor use diagnostic language, either of which is a role violation and a legal breach (Falender et al., 2009). Similarly, the casual use of the term *impairment* to describe performance difficulties is inappropriate and may trigger a host of unexpected consequences based on the Amendment to the Americans with Disabilities Act (Collins, Falender, & Shafranske, 2011; Falender et al., 2009). Remediation plans can be readily developed and processes of evaluation can be implemented to support the supervisee's efforts for improvement. Such deliberations should not be conducted in isolation but, rather, the supervisor of record, academic Director of Training, and others bearing professional accountability should obtain appropriate administrative, legal, and professional consultation to reach an outcome that safeguards the public and the profession when performing gatekeeping responsibilities (Bodner, 2012; Vacha-Haase, Davenport, & Kerewsky, 2004).

Self-Care: A Clinical Competency

Among the competencies affecting clinical competence, self-care is rarely mentioned, yet it contributes significantly to psychologists' ability to offer the best level of care to their clients and to meet other professional obligations. As self-care is an ethical imperative (Norcross & Guy, 2007), it also extends to avoiding ethical mediocrity or practicing with mindless, rote compliance. Self-care might best be seen professionally as enhancing movement toward excellence (Tjeltveit & Gottlieb, 2010). It is a value and a competence that requires attention in clinical training and supervision; although, given the demands and pressures encountered by most clinical educators, it may engender cognitive dissonance. Supervisor responsibility for teaching and modeling self-care to supervisees has been neglected and may even create tension or represent a multiple supervisory role. Administrative responsibilities of supervisors may require heightened productivity at the expense of supervisee attention to self-care. Consideration of self-care is essential during clinical training, since it is during training that lifestyle decisions and habits shape the emerging balance between professional responsibilities and involvement and personal commitments and values. Supervisors may introduce supervisees to the emerging literature on self-care and protective factors (e.g., adequate sleep and social support: Myers et al., 2012). On a related topic, supervisors should be mindful of the strains that supervisees experience in conducting clinical work, particularly because supervisees generally are vulnerable to vicarious traumatization by virtue of their clinical inexperience and the severity of client presentation (Osofsky, 2004; West, 2010).

Supervision in Context

The need for enhanced attention to supervision as a unique competency arises from a confluence of influences, including developments in the context in which clinicians provide community-based mental health care. This shift is defined by greater individual therapist autonomy, financial pressures resulting in increased caseloads, increasing complexity of diagnoses and co-occurring disorders, implementation of evidence-based practice, collaboration across systems of care, and shared client-therapist decision making in the recovery model (Hoge, Migdole, Farkas, Ponce, & Hunnicutt, 2011). Highlighting the importance of competency-based approaches, the Annapolis Coalition (Hoge, Tondura, & Marralli, 2005; O'Connell, Morris, & Hoge, 2004) convened to address training issues for preparing the health-care workforce in the 21st century. They concluded that rather than using metrics such as minimum levels of time at clinical sites or graduating with the knowledge required to pass a written certification examination (i.e., the "input" model), preparation should focus on achieving and measuring particular articulated competencies specific to the professions (i.e., the output model). In addition, development of supervision skills was defined as a high priority for effective leadership development, especially in light of the increasing erosion of clinical supervision in implementation of systems of care

(Hoge et al., 2009). The coalition also addressed concerns that training occurs in professional "silos" with students not learning interdisciplinary collaboration (Hoge, Jacobs, Belitsky, & Migdole, 2002), a core component of healthcare competency and a foundational competency in Benchmarks (Fouad et al., 2009).

Further impetus for an approach with greater accountability came from the Institute of Medicine (National Research Council, 2006) that identified large discrepancies in availability of culturally syntonic, respectful services and in appropriate, evidence-supported treatments. Contextually based supervision would enhance competence and provide support and oversight in cultural competence as well as enhance fidelity in the implementation of evidence-based clinical practices (see, for example, Aarons, Sommerfeld, Hecht, Silovsky, and Chaffin, 2009).

Current Challenges and Future Directions

We begin this concluding section with the question: Is attention to the *attainment* of competence the end point in this emerging culture of competence? We suggest not. Let us explain. Unfortunately the word *competence* may be construed by some to mean a finite point to be achieved at the end of a training experience or at licensure, rather than as one point on the trajectory of professional development. In our view the profession is at a critical junction when it comes to operationalizing definitions of competence since the view of competence as an end state obscures the day-to-day reality that clinicians must continuously enhance their skills to respond to the clinical needs of their clients. A natural tension exists between movement toward a more formulaic and "end point" view of competence and a nuanced vision of competence, which does not identify a firm endpoint, but rather establishes a threshold of competence on which continuous professional development ensues. Such is the case specifically in clinical supervision. Is completion of a graduate course in supervision or having a brief period of supervision of supervision sufficient to achieve competence? In our view, a more comprehensive and dynamic approach to defining clinical competence and advancing supervision practice will include: (a) facilitating efforts to arrive at true consensus on what constitutes supervisor competence and the role of training to achieve it, (b) identifying processes demonstrated to enhance supervision effectiveness, (c) identifying processes that enhance outcomes of supervision, and (d) incorporating client outcomes as a standard of practice not as a measure of supervision outcome per se, but as a tool to enhance supervision practice. Attention to reliable measurement of the clinical competence of the supervisee will expand supervisor competence through the development of valid and reliable means of monitoring clinical performance, and will enhance accountability of the clinical process and supervision. At the same time, supervision cannot be reduced to a template or set of rules, but must encompass the affective, reflective, and wisdom-expertise aspects of communication and performance. In addition to this ambitious, expansive agenda, there are areas that are emergent and require focused attention in the near term. This is particularly the case in the role of clinical supervision in implementing evidence-based practice and in the dissemination of empirically supported treatments.

Evidence-Based Clinical Supervision

Given the American Psychological Association ([APA], 2006) policy of evidence-based practice (EBP), it is necessary that supervision incorporate the principles set forth in that document. Evidence-based approaches to clinical supervision include specific manualized supervision of an EBP (e.g., Henggeler & Schoenwald, 1998), supervision practices relating to particular EBP models, and evidence-support for particular models or practices including process, content, and outcomes of supervision. In the first category, manualized supervision, few models exist but there is momentum from the U.K. where cognitive behavioral supervision competencies have been developed (Roth & Pilling, 2008). In the second category, evidence-based practice rollouts, recognition of the importance of supervision is increasing. Evidence supports clinical supervision as an essential component in evidence-based practice trials. Schoenwald, Sheidow, and Chapman (2009) found supervisor focus on adherence to treatment principles predicted greater therapist adherence that, along with the process of supervision, predicted changes in client outcomes. In actual practice, supervision may lack precision on the practice elements associated with specific client presenting problems (Accurso, Taylor, & Garland, 2011); however, focus on clinical interventions is a central part of the evidence-based protocol and should be for supervision as well. To illustrate, Schoenwald and colleagues (2009) found that supervisor focus on adherence to treatment principles predicted therapist adherence as well as supervisee adherence to the

structure and process of supervision was associated with change in client (youth) behavior. However, higher supervisor focus on supervisee development was associated with weaker improvements in youth functioning. The authors concluded that different aspects of supervision affect client outcomes and merit future study, and they speculated that less technically competent supervisors may have prioritized developmental focus on the supervisee over adherence and attention to outcomes, indicating the need for formal supervision training (Schoenwald et al., 2009). Particular supervisor behaviors were associated with more successful implementation of EBPs: facilitating team meetings and quality improvement activities, building supervisee skills, and monitoring and using outcomes (Carlson, Rapp, & Eichler, 2012).

Although its importance is established, specific attention to effective supervision practices is a neglected aspect of implementation of many evidence-based practices (Roth, Pilling, & Turner, 2010); in general, randomized trials do not describe training, ongoing monitoring, or supervision provided. Often, very experienced therapists are enlisted and provide a high quality of supervision, but omission of such detail compromises replication. Roth and colleagues (2010) suggested creation of a minimum standard of describing supervision arrangements (number of sessions, frequency, duration), supervisor qualifications and experience, and supervision format and location as a minimum for reports on randomized trials. Omission of these data highlights the low valence attached to clinical supervision and may handicap community implementation of EBPs. Further, confusion exists between consultation and supervision with the terms used interchangeably, thereby not respecting the power, evaluative, and formal aspects of supervision and the distinctions between supervision and consultation.

As evidence-based protocols roll out, program leaders are discovering that introducing research results or evidence support to practitioners may not be sufficient to change clinical practice. Suspicion regarding evidence-based practice, insufficient knowledge or skills, limited ongoing supervision/monitoring at all levels of the training system (i.e., individual, organizational and systemic), and limitations in the necessary resources of time, access, and funding necessary pose significant barriers to implementation of evidence-based treatments (Manuel et al., 2009). In addition, many of the psychotherapy-based and EBP supervision protocols focus on fidelity to the model or theory, but do not systematically or comprehensively address the plethora of supervision dimensions such as unusual emotional reactivity, alliance management, diversity, or legal and ethical aspects all of which affect the effectiveness of supervision (Falender & Shafranske, 2010).

Although there is agreement that clinical supervision needs to be empirically supported to ensure efficacy for clients and supervisees (Gonsalvez & McLeod, 2008; Hunsley & Barker, 2011; White & Winstanley, 2010), little systematic evidence has been compiled. Some of the questions posed (and yet to be answered) are how to: (a) identify mechanisms that promote change and development in supervisees and change and enhanced outcomes in clients; (b) measure process and outcomes of the supervision process and client outcome; and (c) transform training settings to enhance accountability and attention to achieving specific supervisee competencies (Kaslow et al., 2012). Even when supervision accompanies EBPs, there is no framework for maximizing effective supervision or evidence of impact of practices on outcomes (e.g., Accurso et al., 2011). Part of the complexity is the potential inversion of the typical power hierarchy: Supervisees may know more about evidence-based practices than their supervisors, and supervisors have the ethical imperative to gain advanced training and competence (Owen, Tao, & Rodolfa, 2005). Even with established criteria for supervisee competencies, gaps exist in training protocols (e.g., Daly, Doll, Schulte, & Fenning, 2011; Ponniah et al., 2011) and in formal assessment of competency outcomes. Certainly challenges lie ahead in the ongoing development of clinical supervision as a unique professional competence. However, principles derived from evidence-based practice, the accumulation of sound theory, and emergent approaches to empirical investigation provide a hopeful future.

Developing expertise in evidence-based practice does not result in rote performance of empirically supported interventions, rather clinical judgment, attention to client values and other contextual factors, sensitivity and attention to the therapeutic relationship shape the nature and conduct of treatment. Therefore, advances in training in EBP go well beyond the narrow prescriptions presented in many treatment protocols. In our view, development of skills in evidence-based practice builds on a host of clinical competencies that are addressed in clinical supervision. Many of these clinical competencies have already been discussed in this chapter; however, there are two additional clinical competencies that we wish to highlight that are often absent from discussion: clinical wisdom and virtuous behavior. We suggest that these qualities anchor the ethical practice of professional psychology. Baum-Baicker and Sisti (2012) defined clinical wisdom to be "a multifaceted concept that involves the capacity to accept a set of seemingly contradictory or dialectical realities: logic and paradox, pragmatism and idealism, and rule setting and bending" (p. 325). Many clinicians (and supervisors) we expect will appreciate the nuance of this perspective. On reflection, they may discover that much of their effectiveness derives, not only from their application of knowledge and established practices, but also involves creativity and sensitivity to the dynamic processes unfolding in treatment. Virtuous behavior reflects our belief that professional practice is always values based and requires incorporation of the highest ethical standards. Competency-based clinical supervision draws upon the best of psychology (its principles and practices) and aims to clearly articulate the knowledge, skills and attitudes/values that contribute to effective practice. While pursuing competencies, attention must remain on the complexity and artfulness of clinical supervision as well as integration of the multiple ethical, cultural, diversity, legal, conceptual, and theoretical underpinnings. Competence cannot be reduced to a set of instructions but must be evolving and related to wisdom and ongoing development of expertise.

References

Aarons, G. A., Sommerfeld, D. H., Hecht, D. B., Silovsky, J. F., & Chaffin, M. J. (2009). The impact of evidence-based practice implementation and fidelity monitoring on staff turnover: Evidence for a protective effect. *Journal of Consulting and Clinical Psychology, 77*, 270–280. doi:10.1037/a0013223

Accurso, E. C., Taylor, R. M., & Garland, A. F. (2011). Evidence-based practices addressed in community-based children's mental health clinical supervision. *Training and Education in Professional Psychology, 5*, 88–96. doi:10.1037/a0023537

American Psychological Association. (2000). *Guidelines for multicultural education, training, research, practice and organizational change.* Washington, DC: Author.

American Psychological Association. (2010). *Ethical principles of psychologists and code of conduct.* Retrieved on July 30, 2013 from http://www.apa.org/ethics/code/index.aspx

American Psychological Association, Presidential Task Force on Evidence-Based Practice. (2006). Evidence-based practice in psychology. *American Psychologist, 61*(4), 271–285. doi:10.1037/0003-066X.61.4.271

Bahrick, A. S. (1989). Role induction for counselor trainees: Effects on the supervisory alliance. *Dissertation Abstracts International, 51*(03), 1484. (UMI No. 9014392).

Baillie, A. J., Proudfoot, H., Knight, R., Peters, L., Sweller, J., Schwartz, S., & Pachana, N. A. (2011). Teaching methods to complement competencies in reducing the "junkyard" curriculum in clinical psychology. *Australian Psychologist, 46,* 90–100. doi:10.1111/j.1742-9544.2011.00036.x

Bambling, M. (2009). Alliance supervision to enhance client outcomes. In N. Pelling, J. Barletta, & P. Armstrong (Eds.), *The practice of clinical supervision* (pp. 121–137). Brisbane, Australia: Australian Academic Press.

Bambling, M., King, R., Raue, P., Schweitzer, R., & Lambert, W. (2006). Clinical supervision: Its influence on client-rated working alliance and client symptom reduction in the brief treatment of major depression. *Psychotherapy Research, 16*(3), 317–331. doi:10.1080/10503300500268524

Baum-Baicker, C., & Sisti, D. (2012). Clinical wisdom in psychoanalysis and psychodynamic psychotherapy: A philosophical and qualitative analysis. *Journal of Clinical Ethics, 23,* 13–27. Retrieved on July 30, 2013 from http://www.clinicalethics.com/

Beck, J. S., Sarnat, J. E., & Barenstein, V. (2008). Psychotherapy-based approaches to supervision. In C. A. Falender & E. P. Shafranske (Eds.), *Casebook for clinical supervision: A competency-based approach* (pp. 57–96). Washington, DC: American Psychological Association. doi:10.1037/11792-004

Bernard, J. L., Murphy, M., & Little, M. (1987). The failure of clinical psychologists to apply understood ethical principles. *Professional Psychology: Research and Practice, 18,* 489–491. doi:10.1037//0735-7028.18.5.489

Bernard, J. M., & Goodyear, R. K. (2009). *Fundamentals of clinical supervision* (4th ed.). Upper Saddle River, NJ: Pearson.

Bodner, K. (2012). Ethical principles and standards that inform educational gatekeeping practices in psychology. *Ethics & Behavior, 22*(1), 60–74. doi:10.1080/10508422.2012.638827

Bordin, E. S. (1983). Supervision in counseling: II. Contemporary models of supervision: A working alliance based model of supervision. *The Counseling Psychologist, 11,* 35–42. doi:10.1177/0011000083111007

Boswell, J. F., Nelson, D. L., Nordberg, S. S., Mcaleavey, A. A., & Castonguay, L. G. (2010). Competency in integrative psychotherapy: Perspectives on training and supervision. *Psychotherapy: Theory, Research, Practice, Training, 47,* 3–11. doi:10.1037/a0018848

Boyce, P., Spratt, C., Davies, M., & McEvoy, P. (2011). Using entrustable professional activities to guide curriculum development in psychiatry training. *BMC Medical Education, 11,* 96–101. Retrieved on July 30, 2013 from: http://www.ncbi.nlm.nih.gov/pubmed/22112295

Bradley, E. H., Cherlin, E., Busch, S. H., Epstein, A., Helfand, B., & White, W. D. (2008). Adopting a competency-based model: Mapping curricula and assessing student progress. *Journal of Health Administration Education, 25,* 37–51. Retrieved on July 23, 2013 from http://www.aupha.org/i4a/pages/index.cfm?pageid=3321

Brosan, L., Reynolds, S., & Moore, R. G. (2008). Self-evaluation of cognitive behavioral therapy performance: Do therapists know how competent they are? *Behavioural and Cognitive Psychotherapy, 36,* 581–587. doi:10.1017/S1352465808004438

Callahan, J. L., Almstrom, C. M., Swift, J. K., Borja, S. E., & Heath, C. J. (2009). Exploring the contribution of supervisors to intervention outcomes. *Training and Education in Professional Psychology, 3*(2), 72–77. doi:10.1037/a0014294

Carlson, L., Rapp, C. A., & Eichler, M. S. (2012). The experts rate: Supervisory behaviors that impact the implementation of evidence-based practices. *Community Mental Health, 48,* 179–186. doi:10.1007/s10597-010-9367-4

Celano, M. P., Smith, C. O. & Kaslow, N. (2010). A competency-based approach to couple and family therapy supervision. *Psychotherapy: Theory, Research, Practice, Training, 47,* 35–44. doi:10.1037/a0018845

Cikanek, K., Veach, P. M., and Braun, C. (2004). Advanced doctoral students' knowledge and understanding of clinical supervisor ethical responsibilities. *The Clinical Supervisor, 23,* 191–196. doi:10.1300/J001v23n01_12

Collins, C., Falender, C., & Shafranske, E. (2011). Commentary on Rebecca Schwartz-Mette's 2009 article, "Challenges in addressing graduate student impairment in academic professional psychology programs." *Ethics & Behavior, 21*(5), 428–430. doi:10.1080/10508422.2011.604547

Crook Lyon, R. E., & Potkar, K. A. (2010). The supervisory relationship. In N. Ladany & L. J. Bradley (Eds.), *Counselor supervision: Principles, processes, and practice* (4th ed., pp. 15–52). New York: Routledge.

Crook-Lyon, R. E., Presnell, J., Silva, L., Suyama, M., & Stickney, J. (2011). Emergent supervisors: Comparing counseling center and non-counseling center interns' supervisory training experiences. *Journal of College Counseling, 14,* 34–49. doi:10.1002/j.2161-1882.2011.tb00062.x

Curran, V. R., Butler, R., Duke, P., Eaton, W. H., Moffatt, S. M., Sherman, G. P., & Pottle, M. (2012). Effectiveness of a simulated clinical examination in the assessment of the clinical competencies of entry-level trainees in a family medicine residency programme. *Assessment and Evaluation in Higher Education, 37,* 99–112. doi:10.1080/02602938.2010.515009

Daelmans, H. M., Hoogenboom, R. I., Scherpbier, A. A., Stehouwer, C. A., & van der Vleuten, C. M. (2005). Effects of an in-training assessment programme on supervision of and feedback on competencies in an undergraduate internal medicine clerkship. *Medical Teacher, 27*(2), 158–163. doi:10.1080/01421590400019534

Daly, E. J., Doll, B., Schulte, A. C., & Fenning, P. (2011). The competencies initiative in professional psychology: Implications for school psychology preparation. *Psychology in the Schools, 48,* 872–886. doi:10.1002/pits.20603

Davis, D. A., Mazmanian, P. E., Fordis, M., Van Harrison, R., Thorpe, K. E., & Perrier, L. (2006). Accuracy of physician self-assessment compared with observed measures of competence: A systematic review. *Journal of the American Medical Association, 296,* 1094–1102. doi:10.1001/jama.296.9.1094

DeMers, S. T., & Schaffer, J. B. (2012). The regulation of professional psychology. In S. J. Knapp, M. C. Gottlieb, M. M. Handelsman, & L. D. VandeCreek (Eds.), *APA handbook of ethics in psychology, Vol 1: Moral foundations and common themes* (pp. 453–482). Washington, DC: American Psychological Association. doi:10.1037/13271-018

DeMers, S. T., Van Horne, B. A., & Rodolfa, E. R. (2008). Changes in training and practice of psychologists: Current challenges for licensing boards. *Professional Psychology: Research and Practice, 39,* 473–479. doi:10.1037/0735-7028.39.5.473

Dickson, G. L., Moberly, M. J., Marshall, Y., & Reilly, J. (2011). Attachment style and its relationship to working alliance in the supervision of British clinical psychology trainees. *Clinical Psychology and Psychotherapy, 18,* 322–330. doi:10.1002/cpp.715

Dijksterhuis, M. G., K., Voorhuis, M., Teunissen, P. W., Schuwirth, L. W. T., ten Cate, O. T. J., Braat, D. D. M., & Scheele, F. (2009). Assessment of competence and progressive independence in postgraduate clinical training. *Medical Education, 43*, 1156–1165. doi:10.1111/j.1365-2923.2009.03509.x

Dovidio, J. F., Gaertner, S. L., Kawakami, K., & Hodson, G. (2002). Why can't we just get along? Interpersonal biases and interracial distrust. *Cultural Diversity and Ethnic Minority Psychology, 8*, 88–102. doi:10.1037//1099-9809.8.2.88

Duan, C., & Roehlke, H. (2001). A descriptive "snapshot" of cross-racial supervision in university counseling center internships. *Journal of Multicultural Counseling and Development, 29*(2), 131–146. doi:10.1002/j.2161-1912.2001.tb00510.x

Dunning, D., Heath, C., & Suls, J. M. (2004). Flawed self-assessment: Implications for health, education, and the workplace. *Psychological Science in the Public Interest, 5*(3), 69–106. doi:10.1111/j.1529-1006.2004.00018.x

Ellis, M. V., Berger, L. R., Ring, E., Swords, B., Hanus, A., Siembor, M., & Wallis, A. (2010, August). *Construct validity of harmful and inadequate clinical supervision*. Paper presented at the 118th Annual Convention of the American Psychological Association, San Diego, CA.

Ellis, M. V., D'Iuso, N., & Ladany, N. (2008). State of the art in the assessment, measurement, and evaluation of clinical supervision. In A. K. Hess, K. D. Hess, & T. H. Hess (Eds.), *Psychotherapy supervision: Theory, research, and practice* (2nd ed., pp. 473–499). Hoboken, NJ: Wiley.

Falender, C. A., Burnes, T., & Ellis, M. (2012). Multicultural clinical supervision and benchmarks: Empirical support informing practice and supervisor training. *The Counseling Psychologist. Advance online publication*. doi:10.1177/0011000012438417

Falender, C. A., Collins, C. J., & Shafranske, E. P. (2009). "Impairment" and performance issues in clinical supervision: After the 2008 ADA Amendments Act. *Training and Education In Professional Psychology, 3*(4), 240–249. doi:10.1037/a0017153

Falender, C. A., Cornish, J. A. E., Goodyear, R., Hatcher, R., Kaslow, N. J., Leventhal, G., & Sigmon, S. T. (2004). Defining competencies in psychology supervision: A consensus statement. *Journal of Clinical Psychology, 60*(7), 771–785. doi:10.1002/jclp.20013

Falender, C. A., & Shafranske, E. P. (2004). *Clinical supervision: A competency-based approach*. Washington, DC: American Psychological Association.

Falender, C. A., & Shafranske, E. P. (2007). Competence in competency-based supervision practice: Construct and application. *Professional Psychology: Research and Practice, 38*, 232–240. doi:10.1037/0735-7028.38.3.232

Falender, C. A., & Shafranske, E. P. (Eds.) (2008). *Casebook for clinical supervision: A competency-based approach*. Washington, DC: American Psychological Association.

Falender, C. A., & Shafranske, E. P. (2010). Psychotherapy-based supervision models in an emerging competency-based era: A commentary. *Psychotherapy: Theory, Research, Practice, Training, 47*, 45–50. doi:10.1037/a0018873

Falender, C. A., & Shafranske, E. P. (2012a). *Getting the most out of clinical supervision: A practical guide for practicum students and interns*. Washington, DC: American Psychological Association.

Falender, C. A., ... Shafranske, E. P. (2012b). The importance of competency-based clinical supervision and training in the twenty-first century: Why bother? *Journal of Contemporary Psychology, 42*(3), 129–137. doi:10.1007/s10879-022-9198-9

Falender, C. A., Shafranske, E. P., & Falicov, C. (Eds.) (2014). *Diversity and multiculturalism in clinical supervision: A Competency-Based Approach*. Washington, DC: American Psychological Association.

Farber, E. W. (2010). Humanist-existential psychotherapy competencies and the supervisory process. *Psychotherapy: Theory, Research, Practice, Training, 47*, 28–34. doi:10.1037/a0018847

Field, L. D., Chavez-Korell, S., & Rodríguez,, M. M. D. (2010). No hay rosas sin espinas: Conceptualizing Latina-Latina supervision from a multicultural developmental supervisory model. *Training and Education in Professional Psychology, 4*, 47–54. doi:10.1037/a0018521

Forrest, L., Miller, D. S. S., ... Elman, N. S. (2008). Psychology trainees with competence problems: From individual to ecological conceptualizations. *Training and Education in Professional Psychology, 2*, 183–192.

Fouad, N. A., Grus, C. L., Hatcher, R. L., Kaslow, N. J., Hutchings, P. S., Madson, M. B., & Crossman, R. E. (2009). Competency benchmarks: A model for understanding and measuring competence in professional psychology across training levels. *Training and Education in Professional Psychology, 3*(4 Suppl), S5–S26. doi:10.1037/a0015832

Frawley-O'Dea, M. G., & Sarnat, J. E. (2001). *The supervisory relationship: A contemporary psychodynamic approach*. New York: Guilford Press.

Gallardo, M. E., Yeh, C., Trimble, J., & Parham, T. A. (2011). *Culturally adaptive counseling skills: Demonstrations of evidence-based practices*. Thousand Oaks, CA: Sage Publications.

Godley, S. H., Garner, B. R., Smith, J. E., Meyers, R. J., & Godley, M. D (2011). A large scale dissemination and implementation model for evidence-based treatment and continuing care. *Clinical Psychology: Science and Practice, 18*, 67–83. doi:10.1111/j.1468-2850.2011.01236.x

Gonsalvez, C. J., & McLeod, H. J. (2008). Toward the science-informed practice of clinical supervision: The Australian context. *Australian Psychologist, 43*, 79–87. doi:10.1080/00050060802054869

Gonsalvez, C. J., & Milne, D. L. (2010). Clinical supervisor training in Australia: A review of current problems and possible solutions. *Australian Psychologist, 45*(4), 233–242. doi:10.1080/00050067.2010.512612

Green, M. S., & Dekkers, T. D. (2010) Attending to power and diversity in supervision: An exploration of supervisee learning outcomes and satisfaction with supervision. *Journal of Feminist Family Therapy, 22*, 293–312. doi:10.1080/08952833.2010.528703

Greenberg, S., Caro, C. M., & Smith, I. L. (2010). *Study of the practice of licensed psychologists in the United States and Canada*. Montgomery, AL: Association of State and Provincial Psychology Boards.

Hadjistavropoulos, H., Kehler, M., & Hadjistavropoulos, T. (2010). Training graduate students to be clinical supervisors: A survey of Canadian professional psychology programmes. *Canadian Psychology, 51*, 206–212. doi:10.1037/a0020197

Haggerty, G., & Hilsenroth, M. J. (2011). The use of video in psychotherapy supervision. *British Journal of Psychotherapy, 27*, 193–210. doi:10.1111/j.1752-0118.2011.01232.x

Hansen, N. D., Randazzo, K. V., Schwartz, A., Marshall, M., Kalis, D., Frazier, R., ... Norvig, G. (2006). Do we practice what we preach? An exploratory survey of multicultural psychotherapy competencies. *Professional Psychology: Research and Practice, 37*(1), 66–74. doi:10.1037/0735-7028.37.1.66

Hatcher, R. L., & Lassiter, K. D. (2007). Initial training in professional psychology: The practicum competencies outline. *Training and Education in Professional Psychology, 1*(1), 49–63. doi:10.1037/1931-3918.1.1.49

Helms, J. E., & Richardson, T. Q. (1997). How "multiculturalism" obscures race and culture as differential aspects of counseling competency. In D. B. Pope-Davis, & H. K. Coleman (Eds.), *Multicultural counseling competencies: Assessment, education and training, and supervision* (pp. 60–79). Thousand Oaks, CA: Sage Publications.

Henderson, C. E., Cawyer, C. S., & Watkins, C. E., Jr. (1999). A comparison of student and supervisor perceptions of effective practicum supervision. *The Clinical Supervisor, 18*, 47–74. doi:10.1300/J001v18n01_04

Henggeler, S. W., & Schoenwald, S. K. (1998). *The MST supervisory manual: Promoting quality assurance at the clinical level.* Charleston, SC: MST Institute.

Hernandez, P., & McDowell, T. (2010). Intersectionality, power, and relational safety in context: Key concepts in clinical supervision. *Training and Education in Professional Psychology, 4*, 29–35. doi:10.1037/a0017064

Hess, A. K. (2011). Psychotherapy supervision. In J. C. Norcross, G. R. Vandenbos, & D. K. Freedheim (Eds.). *History of psychotherapy: Continuity and change* (2nd ed., pp. 703–722). Washington, DC: American Psychological Association.

Hoffman, M. A., Hill, C. E., Holmes, S. E., & Freitas, G. F. (2005). Supervisor perspective on the process and outcome of giving easy, difficult, or no feedback to supervisees. *Journal of Counseling Psychology, 52*(1), 3–13. doi:10.1037/0022-0167.52.1.3

Hoge, M. A, Jacobs, S., Belitsky, R., & Migdole, S. (2002). Graduate education and training for contemporary behavioral health practice. *Administration and Policy in Mental Health, 29*, 335–357. doi:10.1023/A:1019601106447

Hoge, M. A., Migdole, S., Farkas, M. S., Ponce, A. N., & Hunnicutt, C. (2011). Supervision in public sector public health: A review. *The Clinical Supervisor, 30*, 183–203. doi:1 0.1080/07325223.2011.604276

Hoge, M. A., Morris, J. A., Stuart, G. W., Huey, L. Y., Bergeson, S., Flaherty, M. T.,...Madenwald, K. (2009). A national action plan for workforce development in behavioral health. *Psychiatric Services, 60*, 883–887. doi:10.1176/appi. ps.60.7.883

Hoge, M. A., Tondura, J., & Marralli, A. F. (2005). The fundamentals of workforce competency: Implications for behavioral health. *Administration and Policy in Mental Health, 32*, 509–531. doi:10.1007/s10488-005-3263-1

Holmboe, E. S., Ward, D. S., Reznick, R. K., Katsufrakis, P. J., Leslie, K. M., Patel, V. L....Nelson, E. A. (2011). Faculty development in assessment: The missing link in competency-based education. *Academic Medicine, 86*, 460–467. doi:10.1097/ACM.0b013e31820cb2a7

Hunsley, J., & Barker, K. K. (2011). Training for competency in professional psychology: A Canadian perspective. *Australian Psychologist, 46*, 142–145. doi:10.1111/j.1742-9544.2011.00027.x

Jernigan, M. M., Green, C. E., Helms, J. E., Perez-Gualdron, L., & Henze, K. (2010). An examination of people of color supervision dyads: Racial identity matters as much as race. *Training and Education in Professional Psychology, 4*, 62–73. doi:10.1037/a0018110

Johnson, W. B. (2008). Are advocacy, mutuality, and evaluation incompatible mentoring functions? *Mentoring & Tutoring: Partnership in Learning, 16*, 31–44. doi:10.1080/13611260701800942.

Kamen, C., Veilleux, J. C., Bangen, K. J., VanderVeen, J. W., & Klonoff, E. A. (2010). Climbing the stairway to competency: Trainee perspectives on competency development. *Training and Education in Professional Psychology, 4*, 227–234. doi:10:1037/a0021092

Kaslow, N. J., Borden, K. A., Collins, F. L., Forrest, L., Illfelder-Kaye, J., Nelson, P. D.,...Willmuth, M. E. (2004). Competencies conference: Future directions in education and credentialing in professional psychology. *Journal of Clinical Psychology, 60*, 699–712. doi:10.1002/jclp.20016

Kaslow, N. J., Falender, C. A., & Grus, C. (2012). Valuing and practicing competency-based supervision: A transformational leadership perspective. *Training and Education in Professional Psychology, 6*, 47–54. doi:10.1037/a0026704

Kaslow, N. J., Grus, C. L., Campbell, L. F., Fouad, N. A., Hatcher, R. L., & Rodolfa, E. R. (2009). Competency assessment toolkit for professional psychology. *Training and Education in Professional Psychology, 3*(4, Suppl), S27–S45. doi:10.1037/a0015833

Kaslow, N. J., Pate, W. E., & Thorn, B. (2005). Academic and internship directors' perspectives on practicum experiences: Implications. *Professional Psychology: Research and Practice, 36*, 307–317. doi:10.1037/0735-7028.36.3.307

Kaslow, N. J., Rubin, N. J., Forrest, L., Elman, N. S., Van Horne, B. A., Jacobs, S. C., & Thorn, B. E. (2007). Recognizing, assessing, and intervening with problems of professional competence. *Professional Psychology: Research and Practice, 38*(5), 479–492. doi:10.1037/0735-7028.38.5.479

Kavanagh, D. J., Spence, S., Sturk, H., Strong, J., Wilson, J., Worrall, L.,...Skerrett, R. (2008). Outcomes of training in supervision: Randomised controlled trial. *Australian Psychologist, 43*(2), 96–104. doi: 10.1080/0005006080205056534

Kenkel, M. B., & Peterson, R. L. (Eds.). (2010). *Competency-based education for professional psychology.* Washington, DC: American Psychological Association.

Kiesler, D. J. (2001). Therapist countertransference: In search of common themes and empirical referents. *Journal of Clinical Psychology, 57*(8), 1053–1063. doi:10.1002/jclp.1073

Knudsen, H. K., Ducharme, L. J., & Roman, P. M. (2008). Clinical supervision, emotional exhaustion, and turnover intention: A study of substance abuse treatment counselors in the clinical trials network of the National Institute on Drug Abuse. *Journal of Substance Abuse Treatment, 35*, 387–395. doi:10.1016/j.jsat.2008.02.003

Ladany, N., Friedlander, M. L., & Nelson, M. L. (2005). *Critical events in psychotherapy supervision: An interpersonal approach.* Washington, DC: American Psychological Association.

Ladany, N., Lehrman-Waterman, D., Molinaro, M., & Wolgast, B. (1999). Psychotherapy supervisor ethical practices: Adherence to guidelines, the supervisory working alliance, and supervisee satisfaction. *The Counseling Psychologist, 27*(3), 443–475. doi:10.1177/0011000099273008

Ladany, N., & Melincoff, D. S. (1999). The nature of counselor supervisor nondisclosure. *Counselor Education and Supervision, 38*, 161–176. doi:10.1002/j.1556-6978.1999. tb00568.x

Lafferty, P., Beutler, L. E., & Crago, M. (1989). Differences between more and less effective psychotherapists: a study of

Unsworth, G., Cowie, H., & Green, A. (2012). Therapists' and clients' perceptions of routine outcome measurement in the NHS: A qualitative study. *Counselling and Psychotherapy Research: Linking Research with Practice, 12*(1), 71–80. doi: 10.1080/14733145.2011.565125

Vargas, L. A., Porter, N., & Falender, C. A. (2008). Supervision, culture, and context. In C. A. Falender & E. P. Shafranske (Eds.). *Casebook for clinical supervision: A competency-based approach* (pp. 121–136). Washington, DC: American Psychological Association.

Vacha-Haase, T., Davenport, D. S., & Kerewsky, S. D. (2004). Problematic students: Gatekeeping practices of academic professional psychology programs. *Professional Psychology: Research and Practice, 35*, 115–122.

Walker, J. A. (2010). Supervision techniques. In N. Ladany & L. J. Bradley (Eds.), *Counselor Supervision* (4th ed., pp. 97–122). New York: Routledge.

Wall, A. (2009). Psychology interns' perceptions of supervisor ethical behavior. (Doctoral dissertation) Retrieved from Proquest. (3359934)

Watkins, C. E. (2011). Does psychotherapy supervision contribute to patient outcomes? Considering thirty years of research. *The Clinical Supervisor, 30*, 235–256. doi:10.1080/07325223.2011.619417

West, A. (2010). Supervising counselors and therapists who work with trauma: A Delphi study. *British Journal of Guidance and Counseling, 38*, 409–430. doi:10.1080/03069885.2010.503696

Wheeler, S., & Richards, K. (2007). The impact of clinical supervision on counsellors and therapists, their practice and their clients: A systematic review of the literature. *Counselling and Psychotherapy Research, 7*, 54–65. doi:10.1080/14733140601185274

White, E., & Winstanley, J. (2010). A randomised controlled trial of clinical supervision: Selected findings from a novel Australian attempt to establish the evidence base for causal relationships with quality of care and patient outcomes, as an informed contribution to mental health nursing practice development. *Journal of Research in Nursing, 15*, 151–167. doi:10.1177/1744987109357816

Wilson, T. D. (2009). Know thyself. *Perspectives on Psychological Science, 4*, 384–389. doi:10.1111/j.1745-6924.2009.01143.x

Worthen, V. E., & Lambert, M. J. (2007). Outcome oriented supervision: Advantages of adding systematic client tracking to supportive consultations. *Counselling & Psychotherapy Research, 7*(1), 48–53. doi:10.1080/14733140601140873

Zarbock, G., Drews, M., Bodansky, A., & Dahme, B. (2009). The evaluation of supervision: Construction of brief questionnaires for the supervisor and the supervisee. *Psychotherapy Research, 19*, 194–204. doi:10.1080/10503300802688478

Trainees with Problems of Professional Competence

Linda Forrest *and* Nancy S. Elman

Abstract

Addressing trainees with problems of professional competence (PPC) has long been a challenge for those responsible for education and training in professional psychology. Although few in numbers, trainers regularly report occurrences of trainees with PPC, and have often acknowledged failure to adequately remediate or dismiss them. Over the past 15 years or so, great progress has been made in addressing PPC, and there is a growing conceptual and empirical literature including contributions from other professions (e.g., counseling, social work and medicine). This chapter addresses the developments, current knowledge, and resources to assist trainers in professional psychology in the identification, remediation, and/or dismissal of trainees with PPC. It describes two major areas of progress: (a) understanding PPC within the evolving culture of competency, and (b) conceptualizing the individual trainee with PPC as located within a larger training ecology/system. Next it shifts our focus to improvements in remediation and then the boundaries between what is personal and what is professional. It identifies four areas in which trainers are not in agreement about the uses of personal information in decisions during identification, remediation, or dismissal, paying particular attention to the challenges of remediation. It ends with recommendations to improve the management of trainees with PPC, the training environment, and professional psychology education and training at the national level.

Key Words: professional competence problems, professional competence, education and training, impairment

Introduction

Educators and trainers in professional psychology are responsible for screening, selecting, regularly evaluating trainees across the training experience, advancing those who meet professional competency standards established for each stage in the training process and remediating and/or dismissing those who do not. These critical responsibilities must be enacted in a thoughtful and careful manner to guarantee the well-being of the trainee, protection of the public, and the reputation of the profession. Although the actual number of trainees dismissed from programs due to PPC is small, many more require intervention, and, in some cases, formal remediation, to eventually be successful in

developing the professional competence to become a psychologist.

Faculty and trainers regularly report occurrences of trainees with PPC, and have often acknowledged failure to adequately remediate or dismiss them. Professional competence problems exist across the spectrum of training and "consume inordinate administrative and supervisory time and energy" (Kaslow et al., 2007b, p. 480).

In this chapter we address the significant developments, current knowledge, and resources to assist trainers in professional psychology in the identification, remediation, and/or dismissal of trainees with PPC. First, we describe the influence of the competency movement on the work of PPC including

---

Note: The authors have published together for over a decade, jointly sharing the workload and responsibilities with a long history of alternating first authorship. For this chapter we used a new system to determine first authorship—a coin toss.

(a) delineation of core competencies necessary for professional psychology, (b) development of a typology of assessment strategies for each of the competencies, and (c) an important terminology shift from "impairment" to problems of professional competence. Although many improvements have occurred in the management of PPC due to the evolving competency framework, we identified three areas that require further attention: continued efforts to retire the *impairment* term, the need for a typology of common competence problems, and the application of the competency framework to other levels of the training ecosystem.

Second, we present the current state of knowledge about PPC as understood within a systemic, ecological model of doctoral education and training. Conceptual and empirical work from the perspectives of trainees' peers and faculty/other trainers is reviewed and assessed. Understandings about the institutions within which programs operate and applicable ethical and legal challenges are examined. We end this section with a brief description of cultural influences (e.g., race, gender) on PPC.

Next, we identify increased understanding and improvements in what makes a good remediation. Then, utilizing the personal and professional boundaries framework (Pipes, Holstein, & Aguirre, 2005), we identify four areas in which trainers differ in their position and approaches to what constitutes the appropriate boundary between what is personal and professional when working with PPC. The chapter concludes with suggestions for future directions that we believe will enhance PPC interventions and improve training systems.

A Note on Terminology

Throughout this chapter we have chosen to use the term *trainee* to describe all those who are engaged in the process of becoming a psychologist across the full spectrum of education and training including academic programs, internships, and postdoctoral residencies. We prefer *trainer*, as the inclusive term to capture educators, faculty, supervisors and others involved in the training of psychologists. Both terms describe the diversity of those involved with greater parsimony, consistency, and utility.

A Competence Framework for PPC
Advances and Accomplishments

The shift to a culture of competency (Roberts, Borden, Christiansen, & Lopez, 2005) in professional psychology has created important momentum and resulted in numerous benefits for educators and trainers in their identification and remediation of trainees with competence problems.

Competency developments create conceptual foundation. Core competencies for professional psychology were identified and agreed on at the 2002 Competency Conference (Kaslow et al., 2004) creating a consistent national framework that could be communicated to the public and across programs, faculty, and trainees. The establishment of the Benchmark Work Group in 2006 led to the delineation of a developmental trajectory for each competency (Fouad et al., 2009). Educational milestones were identified at specific points along the training continuum (e.g., readiness for practicum, for internship, and for entry into practice). Competence benchmarks provided trainers with yardsticks to evaluate trainees within and across programs and to better identify trainees who had not yet reached developmental benchmarks and thus required more time and attention (e.g., remediation plan) to progress to the next level of training. Similarly the benchmarks facilitated clearer communications with trainees about core competencies and expected levels of performance at each stage of development, thus giving trainees advance notice about professional expectations. With the publication of the benchmark documents, essential components and behavioral markers were established for 15 professional competencies (Fouad et al., 2009) providing additional guidance for trainers managing PPC.

According to Forrest and Campbell (2012), the competency efforts made an "important contribution toward addressing the complexities present in evaluating clinical skills especially when problems develop." (p. 129). Faculty, supervisors and peer trainees have long reported that the most common and troubling issues were problems with behavior, attitude, and judgment that most frequently occurred in practice settings and were often refractory to supervision (e.g., defensiveness, lack of self-reflection and/or empathy for others). By including professionalism and interpersonal relationships as core competencies, the benchmarks provided a way to focus on the most challenging PCC dilemmas, the preponderance of difficulties in the intrapersonal and interpersonal sphere (Brear, Dorrian & Luscri, 2008; Kaslow et al., 2007b). Prior to the delineation of the competency benchmarks, trainers were often vague or ambiguous (or avoided altogether) communications with trainees about standards related to personal behaviors, professional demeanor and interpersonal relationships.

Articulating the essential elements of professionalism (Elman, Illfelder-Kaye & Robiner, 2005) and interpersonal relations competencies (Fouad et al., 2009) helped to address concern about the influence of personal and interpersonal traits and characteristics on the development of competence.

Assessment of competency. The focus on a competency culture also resulted in greater attention being paid to the assessment of competence. The establishment of the Taskforce on Assessment of Competence in 2003 (Kaslow et al., 2007a; Lichtenberg et al., 2007; Rubin et al., 2007) later led to a comprehensive assessment typology (Kaslow et al., 2009). Multiple assessment strategies were identified with recommendations about appropriate assessment tools for measuring specific competencies. This, in turn, has helped in the identification of trainees with PPC, and improved the methods available for evaluating changes in competencies over time and determining whether progress is being made during remediation.

Terminology improvements. A third advancement has been increased clarity about the difficulties associated with using the term *impairment* to address trainees with problems. Historically, *impairment* has been the most common term used to describe both trainees and professionals whose behavior or performance does not meet professional and ethical standards. Numerous difficulties with the term have been identified especially when used in training environments (Collins, Falender, & Shafranske, 2011; Elman & Forrest, 2007; Falender, Collins, & Shafranske, 2005, 2009; Forrest, Elman, Gizara, & Vacha-Haase, 1999; Gizara & Forrest, 2004). APA's Advisory Committee on Colleague Assistance (APA, 2006) acknowledged variations in definitions of impairment, noted the lack of consensus, and stated, "A universal definition of distress and impairment in professional functioning has not yet been created" (p. 6).

The cultural shift within professional psychology toward a competence framework provided the foundation for new terminology grounded in competency language. Elman and Forrest (2007) recommended terms like *problems of professional competence* (PPC) or *professional competence problems* that linked the critical concepts of professionalism, competence, and problems together. They also identified eight benefits that resulted from "situating the recommended terminology within the competence framework" (Elman & Forrest, p. 506). Competence terminology contributes to a more open and transparent dialogue with trainees

about professional standards and when they are or are not being met. Also, the new terminology keeps the focus on professional behaviors, skills, and performance, requires trainers to accurately describe behaviors that do and do not meet competency standards, and facilitates modeling for trainees the professional skills involved in identifying and responding to individuals who are exhibiting PPC. Further, competence terminology facilitates inculcating in trainees a commitment to open and transparent communication with colleagues about competence concerns, leaving them "more prepared to address these challenging responsibilities as professional psychologists" (Elman & Forrest, p. 507). Using terminology grounded in competence also means that remediation plans can be better tied to specific benchmarks and increases the likelihood that interventions and assessment strategies will match desired outcomes.

The terminology shift also solved perennial problems associated with the term, *impairment*. Targeting the evaluation of performance and professional behaviors (Elman & Forrest, 2007) helped clarify that trainers should not be determining the etiology of personal problems and should avoid the dual role of being both an educator and diagnostician (Schoener, 1999). Falender and her colleagues (2009) articulated a clear boundary for the use of diagnostic nomenclature in evaluating professional performance stating:

> Use of any form of diagnostic nomenclature inappropriately transforms the supervisory relationship into a clinical one. Thus, if the supervisor begins to think of the supervisee as "borderline," "disturbed," or "suffering from major depressive disorder, " the supervisor is diagnosing the supervisee and modeling inappropriate behavior. No supervisor can or should conduct a comprehensive diagnostic evaluation, nor should he or she obtain the requisite historical, medical, familial, and contextual data necessary for an accurate diagnosis. Furthermore, mere diagnostic labeling transforms the supervisor's perspective and would be minimally considered a boundary crossing, if not a violation (p. 244).

Also the use of diagnostic labels to describe a trainee may violate Ethical Standard 9.01 that states(a) "psychologists base the opinions contained in their…. diagnostic or evaluative statements…. on information and techniques sufficient to substantiate their findings" and (b) "…psychologists provide opinions of the psychological characteristics of individuals only after they have conducted an examination of the individual adequate to support their statements or conclusions." (American Psychological Association, 2010, p. 12).

Finally, an important benefit of "competence problem" terminology in describing substandard performance is that it does not overlap with the impairment language used in the ADA (1990, 2008) and removes the potential for confusion about the legal meaning of impairment in the ADA. In reviewing the ADA Amendments Act of 2008, Falender and her colleagues (2009) asserted that the amendments create even greater risk of legal liability than they originally thought (Falender et al., 2005) and concluded that the ADA guidelines "can no longer prudently be ignored or minimized" (Falender et al., 2009, p. 242). Using PPC rather than impairment language reaffirms that trainees with disabilities may receive accommodations, but will still be held accountable to meet the professional standards that constitute the essential functions of becoming a psychologist.

Perusal of the literature suggests that professional competence problems terminology is progressively gaining acceptance. Since the 2007 recommendations, most authors have cited the impairment terminology risks and embraced newer competency terminology (Behnke, 2008; Jacobs et al., 2011; Johnson, Barnett, Elman, Forrest, & Kaslow, 2012 Kaslow et al., 2007b; McCutcheon, 2008; Shen-Miller, Forrest & Elman, 2009, Shen-Miller et al., 2011, Shen-Miller, Forrest, & Burt, 2012; Veilleux, January, VanderVeen, Reddy, & Klonoff, 2012; Wester, Christianson, Fouad, & Santiago-Rivera, 2008).

Areas That Need Further Attention

Although much progress has been made in understanding and managing problems in professional functioning during training, we have identified three gaps in the scholarship and current practices in education and training that need further attention: (a) the impairment term is still being used in inappropriate ways, (b) the lack of a typology delineating common categories of competence problems, and (c) the competency framework has not been applied to the larger training ecology (e.g., trainers, administrators, lawyers).

Continued use of *impairment*. Although concerns with impairment terminology have been well articulated and its restriction to the case of a disability has been identified (Collins et al., 2011; Elman & Forrest, 2007; Falender et al., 2005, 2009; Forrest et al., 1999; Kaslow et al., 2007b), *impairment* is still used to describe inadequate professional competence, particularly in articles (Barnett & Cooper, 2009; Smith & Moss, 2009) focused on professional practice. This creates a disjuncture between terminology used in training and professional practice and also raises concerns about the potential for similar legal risk in practice settings.

Lack of typology of competence problems. We have yet to agree upon a common typology that delineates competence problems. In 1999, Forrest and her colleagues summarized concerns with the typology of trainee competence problems including: (a) no common terminology for categories exists, (b) categories were not mutually exclusive and exhaustive, and (c) categories mixed descriptions of inadequate competence with potential explanations or causes for substandard performance. Since 1999, several efforts have been made to develop a conceptual typology of PPC during training. Schwartz-Mette (2011) proposed two metalevel categories: (a) legally defined disabilities and (b) nondisability problems. The nondisability problems were further divided into four subcategories of underlying explanations including: (a) behavior problems, (b) psychological problems (e.g., maladaptive personality traits), (c) situational problems (e.g., death in the family, divorce), and (d) developmental problems (e.g., educational deficiencies). Schwartz-Mette acknowledged that problems could involve either competence achieved and then lost, or competence never achieved.

In their study of peers' perceptions of fellow trainees, Veilleux and colleagues (2012) utilized similar categories: (a) diminished functioning and (b) inability to reach competence and thus unsuitable for the profession. They assessed three types of causes for the competence problems: (a) trait characteristics, (b) general distress, and (c) chronic externalizing pathology. Similarly, Falender et al. (2009) proposed two categories for understanding substandard performance: (a) normative developmental challenges; and (b) problematic performance, using breach of entrustability and risk to clients to distinguish the two categories. Falender and her colleagues avoided any emphasis on the etiology or root causes of the competence problems.

Finally, Kaslow and her colleagues (2007b) differentiated several reasons or origins of competence problems: (a) situational, (b) developmental, and (c) personality and interpersonal dynamics. They also offered an exhaustive list that merged categories, levels, and causes of problems including (a) lack of adequate training, (b) inability to acquire an acceptable level of competency, (c) inability or unwillingness to acquire professional standards, (d) failure to respond to feedback, (e) lack of continuously growing or making progress, (f) lack of self-awareness with regard to weaknesses, (g) problems with professionalism and/or interpersonal interactions, (h) exhibition of prejudicial attitudes, (i) lack high levels of integrity, (j) personal problems, emotional reactions or distress that cannot be controlled and that affect professional functioning. These authors' rubrics illustrate the problems of creating a mutually exclusive, exhaustive, useable, parsimonious typology of competence problems during training. Whereas all share descriptive categories in common, differences in the foci (performance versus cause) and level and degree of specificity and complexity of categories suggest that we are far from having a useful and reliable typology of competence problems to guide educators and trainers.

Brear and colleagues (2008) reviewed 14 descriptive studies conducted between 1983 and 2006 that assessed categories of "unsuitability" for the profession. They found little uniformity in wording, substantial overlap and variations in the descriptive categories, and little effort to operationalize terms. Intrapersonal problems were the most common category of problem reported, followed by interpersonal problems, deficiencies in clinical skills, and ethical violations. Types of problems included in the intrapersonal category (e.g., adjustment disorders, depressive disorders, maturity/integrity, emotional problems, personality disorders, psychopathology, substance abuse, suicide attempts) reaffirm our concern about the lack of a consistent and useful typology of PPC. This work also confirms that trainers may be confusing consequences with causes, diagnosing without adequate psychological assessment or necessary informed consent, and creating legal and ethical jeopardy for programs. We caution trainers to be vigilant about distinguishing between addressing professional performance consequences and determining underlying causes, noting that we are on much firmer ground in addressing remediation and dismissal if the focus is on observable professional-competence outcomes.

Competency framework not applied to training ecology. A third gap we identified is that the competency framework has been applied to individual trainees, but it has not yet been applied to other participants in the training ecology. There is substantial focus on the identification and remediation of trainee competence problems, yet there is little to no writing on the PPC of others in the training system or how to improve their competence. Mention is occasionally made that faculty incompetence or unethical behavior is a factor in whether the behavior of a trainee with PPC can be addressed (e.g., if a supervisor or faculty member has crossed appropriate boundaries with that same trainee). As well, there is some concern that not all trainers understand the policies and practices needed to adequately address PPC and, therefore, either do not or cannot accomplish necessary interventions and may be creating legal risks for the program. We believe the competence framework offers the same potential to improve how we address and assess the competence of other members (e.g., trainers, administrators, attorneys) of the training environment and the training system as a whole.

Systemic Understandings of Trainee Competence Problems

The gradual evolution toward addressing trainee performance within a competencies framework has been accompanied by an equally gradual trend from understanding the problematic behavior of a single trainee to a broader systemic or ecological framework. In 1999, Elman, Forrest, Vacha-Haase, and Gizara suggested that impairment or incompetence (now termed PPC), and intervention to address it, is incomplete if considered only from the perspective of the individual trainee. They recommended viewing PPC in the context of complex systemic factors and articulated a need for:

> …a developmental, contextual, systemic understanding of impairment that places trainees, trainers, training programs and practicing psychologists in the larger contexts of client care, the structure of psychological practice, and the structure and responsibility of professional organizations as well as historical, cultural and societal forces (Forrest et al., p. 713).

Over the past dozen years, the increasing focus on aspects of the training system has included trainees' peers, program training directors, faculty and supervisors (the mesosystem), the larger training exosystem of program and institutional policies, ethical standards, legal requirements of fairness and due process (Gilfoyle, 2008), and broad cultural and diversity influences (macrosystem). Taken together, these efforts have led to recognition of the importance of prevention and *early* intervention with trainees and trainers who are following well-understood institutional policies and themselves feel competent and empowered to act ethically and legally. The sections that follow describe a systemic or ecological perspective and the challenge of PPC at each level of the training ecology.

Systemic Conceptual Models

Three recent papers have proposed conceptual models of competence that are nested in systemic perspectives. Forrest, Elman, and Shen-Miller (2008) adapted Bronfenbrenner's ecological model (1979) as a framework for understanding the development and maintenance of trainee problems, suggesting a broad and multifaceted basis for both prevention of and intervention with PPC. Tailoring the Bronfenbrenner ecosystemic model of the developing individual situated in the microsystem, mesosystem, ecosystem, and macrosystem, Forrest and her colleagues provided a description of multiple and reciprocally interacting aspects of the psychology training system that influence PPC.

Advancing the notion of an ecological model that transcends training and practice, Johnson and his colleagues (Johnson et al., 2012) elaborated a communitarian model of a shared obligation of the community of professionals to one another. The communitarian model supports training in preparation for intervening with colleagues as an ethic of care and social justice, evolving from an assumption of interdependence rather than individualism. They suggested:

> Perhaps most important, trainees must be explicitly prepared for the role of colleague in competence consultations (Johnson et al., 2008). New psychologists should demonstrate competence in providing peer review; in constructively engaging troubled colleagues in what may be difficult conversations about their competence; and in demonstrating care for colleagues, those they serve, and the profession (Biaggio et al., 1998; Forrest et al., 2008; Jacobs et al., 2011; O'Connor, 2001). Graduating psychologists with these values and skills will help create the shift from an individual to a communitarian approach to competence. (p. 565).

These papers share an aspirational focus on the reciprocal relationship of the individual trainee or practitioner with peers, trainers, policy makers, and the broader laws and ethics of our culture.

Finally, Hatcher (2011), in a paper addressing the internship match imbalance, provided a model of overarching systemic relationships using an economic construct, common pool resources (CPR). In articulating the research on CPRs, Hatcher suggested that successful governance, on behalf of all, requires recognition of a shared problem, and sufficient trust and goodwill to engage and relinquish some individual freedom of choice to achieve a common good. Although not the problem for which Hatcher employs the CPR construct, this model, like others that emphasize the training ecosystem, may be useful for identifying and determining appropriate intervention with PPC. Peers, faculty, supervisors (local and in other institutions), administrators and the field as a whole share a common goal of training competent professional psychologists and providing quality care to those we serve. Participation in effective "governance" of the problem, although requiring some loss of independence (e.g., trainers cannot operate totally independently in relationship to a trainee), may facilitate addressing problems earlier and more effectively. Although not specifically mentioned in Hatcher's exploration of the match imbalance, given the increasing competition for internships (Baker, McCutcheon & Keilin, 2007), programs eager to attain desirable placement rates may be more likely to neglect to intervene or require remediation that would become part of the trainee's record, an action that might limit success in the internship match, and reflect poorly on the training program and its faculty/supervisors.

In sum, numerous models have emphasized the importance of variables that impact the development and functioning of an individual trainee, suggesting that an ecological or systemic view is far more useful for explaining behavior and implementing change. We have organized the remainder of this section utilizing this ecological perspective to capture the complexity of the psychology training system and enhance success in addressing PPC.

The Training Ecosystem

In this section we elaborate the movement toward a more broadly systemic view of the identification, assessment, and intervention with PPC. Progress has been made on preparing the whole system to be able to respond effectively through expanded national attention by trainers to PPC. Empirical and conceptual publications have fostered knowledge and capacity building for the field, enriched by changes in accreditation, increased clarity regarding legal mandates, revised ethical standards, and a burgeoning understanding of the impact of cultural mores and diversity on addressing PPC.

Efforts to disseminate information that expands training programs' ability to address PPC has included presentations to national training conferences, such as the 2010 Joint Mid-Year Meeting of Training Councils in Psychology (Elman, 2010), Association of Psychology Postdoctoral and Internship Centers

(APPIC, Behnke, 2009; Kaslow, Forrest, Elman, Grus & Baker, 2010), Commission on Accreditation (CoA) Assemblies (Baker, 2008; Elman, Springer, & Baker, 2009), Association of State and Provincial Psychology Boards (ASPPB, Elman, 2003; Forrest, 2005), and training council conferences: Council of University Directors of Clinical Psychology (CUDCUP, Veilleux et al., 2010), Council of Counseling Psychology Training Programs (CCPTP, Forrest & Elman, 2009, 2010), National Council of Schools of Professional Psychology (NCSPP, Elman, 2001), and Association of Directors of Psychology Training Clinics (ADPTC, Elman, 2002; Forrest, 2001). These have focused on competence of trainers to create policies and procedures that are preventive, effective, and minimize risk for the programs as well as for trainees.

The sections that follow demonstrate the growth in the last decade in attending to: (a) trainees and their peers (mesosystem), (b) faculty and supervisors (mesosystem), (c) the institutional, legal, and ethical influences (exosystem) and (d) the role of diversity and broad cultural factors influencing the profession and the educational enterprise (macrosystem).

Trainees (mesosystem). Since 2000 a number of studies on trainee perspectives on PPC have been published (Dodds, 2002; Oliver, Bernstein, Anderson, Blashfield & Roberts, 2004; Rosenberg, Getzelman, Arcinue, & Oren, 2005; Shen-Miller et al., 2011; Swann, 2003; Veilleux et al., 2012). This continues a trend of a number of dissertations from the 1990s (Burgess, 1994; Gizara, 1997; Vacha-Haase, 1995). Also, two student papers (Bodner, 2012; Schwartz-Mette, 2009) that focused on ethical challenges in addressing PPC received the Annual Student Ethics Prize awarded by the APA Ethics Committee. Many of the studies that addressed trainee perspectives or experiences with PPC have been conducted *by* trainees either independently (often as dissertation studies) or in collaboration with faculty researchers. The Working Group on Problems of Professional Competence, which has been active since the 2002 Competencies Conference, has had trainee members and early career professionals from its onset. Trainees' interest often arises from experiences with peers in their own doctoral program and awareness of a lack of clarity and guidance from faculty about how to respond to PPC. Engagement in the question of addressing PPC is likely a good unobtrusive measure of trainees' concern and commitment to understand PPC and its implications for training and the reputation of the profession they are entering.

Consistent themes emerge from trainee-driven or -focused research on PPC. Trainees report almost universal awareness of one or more peers with PPC and typically in numbers substantially higher than faculty report (e.g., Gaubatz & Vera, 2006; Mearns & Allen, 1991; Oliver et al., 2004; Rosenberg et al., 2005; Shen-Miller et al., 2011). Study participants reported having limited options for responding to their peers with common responses likely adding to the difficulties (e.g., avoiding their peer, gossiping with others about their peer). Trainees typically did not address concerns about a peer with faculty members partly because both the trainees and the faculty are uncertain about confidentiality (see discussion later in the chapter about this issue). They also reported that they were uncertain about what if any actions their trainers were taking to address their peer's problems. When trainees perceived that trainers did not adequately address PPC (e.g., trainee was passed on to internship or graduated with no apparent intervention or record of problems), trainees expressed great concern for the quality of their own training and the future of the profession (Rosenberg et al., 2005). A few studies (Swann, 2003; Veilleux et al., 2012) reported the extent to which trainees feel knowledgeable about program policies and procedures. Veilleux and colleagues (2012) found that 62.9% of doctoral trainees in their survey did not know of the existence of policies for identifying PPC, and overall attitude toward program climate was significantly correlated with trainees' belief in faculty effectiveness.

Knowledge of program policies for identification, remediation, and dismissal of trainees with PPC appears to be increasing in the past few years, partly in connection with CoA requirements (Domain E, Faculty-Student Relations). The extent to which trainers have addressed these policies with trainees as notice for due process appears to have increased. Some programs are providing training in how to respond when confronted with a peer with PPC. At the time of program orientation, some programs are requiring written acknowledgment of understanding and accepting program policies that include expectations related to PPC. Yet additional program attention to PPC policies and procedures, training students to understand and develop skills to use them, and modeling competence to address complex challenges is needed to improve trainee competence in addressing PPC.

Faculty and other trainers (mesosystem). Although empirical research has been limited, anecdotal evidence of concerns about trainers' behaviors when PPC arises has long been present: in trainees' perceptions of faculty and supervisors, noted earlier, in conversations and seminars at professional meetings of psychology trainers, and in requests for consultations and assistance brought to both authors of this chapter and others (Kaslow, personal communication). We found no published research on the often-mentioned issue of trainers who themselves demonstrate PPC (e.g., boundary violating behavior with trainees, poor performance in teaching/supervising, personal problems) suggesting a need for examining this important challenge.

A number of papers in counseling and psychology have addressed the gatekeeping role of trainers when remediation or dismissal is the issue (Bodner, 2012; Brear & Dorrian, 2010; Brusseri, Tyler, & King, 2005; Elman & Forrest, 2004; Forrest et al., 2013; Huprich & Rudd, 2004; Lamb, Cochran, & Jackson, 1991; Lamb, Presser, Pfost, Baum, Jackson & Jarvis, 1987; McAdams, Foster & Ward, 2007; Vacha-Haase, Davenport, & Kerewsky, 2004). Two studies (Gaubatz & Vera, 2006; Mearns & Allen, 1991) reported that trainers recognize fewer incidents of PPC than trainee's peers, confirming the perception of trainees reported earlier.

Elman et al. (1999) suggested that one factor in trainers' failure to address PPC is the tendency toward "social loafing," (p. 716), assuming that others in the group will act if I do not. Gaubatz and Vera (2002) and others described the challenges of gatekeeping and its alternative, "gateslipping," in which trainees are allowed to progress or graduate with substandard competence. In their survey, faculty in programs with more formalized procedures were significantly more likely to address trainee deficiencies than those without or with less formal procedures. Brear and Dorrian's (2010) survey of Australian counselor educators found that hindrances to gatekeeping for PPC included: lack of clear evidence of problems (67%), bias toward leniency in evaluation (53%), and fear of reprisal/litigation from the student (33%). The highest ranked factors that enabled good gatekeeping were a sense of professional responsibility (96%) and support from colleagues (90%).

The conceptual papers, descriptive research, and anecdotal reports on trainer behavior further confirm that addressing PPC is both challenging and stressful. Trainers who often are confused about whether a trainee's behavior rises to the level that requires formal attention (e.g., remediation plan) are apt to blame themselves and/or feel sad about not having identified or repaired the issue with

trainees with whom they have had a close working relationship, and they express fear of reprisal in negative teaching evaluations or the threat of litigation (Gaubatz & Vera, 2002). In addition, trainers often struggle with the discrepancy between the highly valued nurturing growth-facilitating roles acquired in their own training to be psychotherapists (Jacobs et al., 2011), and concern that negative feedback will be perceived as shaming in an evaluative, judgmental role that emphasizes the hierarchical positional power of faculty (Vasquez, 1999). Also, trainers sometimes reported not communicating concerns with other trainers, expecting that they would not be responsive, particularly noting gaps in communication between training faculty and field-based supervisors (Lamb, 1999), each assuming that they had no structure or authority for communicating concerns until PPC reached critical proportions. Gizara and Forrest (2004) noted how little preparation for dealing with PPC the supervisors in their study reported and that identifying trainee problems felt isolating and raised fears of trainee PPC being seen as a reflection of their own supervisory incompetence. Brusseri and colleagues (2005) concluded: "Other identified challenges included faculty resistance to, and lack of experience in, evaluating some domains, differences in standards among faculty, and concerns regarding the reliability and validity of suitability-related evaluations" (p. 442).

In interviews with directors of training (DTs), Elman & Forrest (2004) described variations in how programs address remediation with either a more "hands on" or more "hand off" approach to directly addressing PPC (e.g., leaving the remediation up to the trainee rather than structuring the plan and formally assessing outcomes). Forrest et al. (2013) also described faculty behaviors that are helpful and harmful in addressing PPC. Of note in this study is the finding that trainer response to PPC appears to be a function of program-level functioning. Programs in which trainers' behaviors were more helpful were organized to be more intentional and acted early to address PPC as a program faculty, with the understanding that (a) decisions about a trainee are the responsibility of the group as a whole, (b) faculty are not expected to act alone, and (c) planful involvement of field-based supervisors and adjunct faculty is expected (Forrest et al., 2013). These programs also accepted the responsibility to have difficult conversations rather than avoid them. DTs saw it as a program responsibility to educate and support senior faculty and to mentor and support junior faculty (who have reported that they do not feel empowered to address PPC, especially when it involves challenging the view of a more senior faculty member). Two other studies surveying DTs' conceptualizations of diversity and its relationship to addressing PPC (Shen-Miller et al., 2009; Shen-Miller et al., 2012) will be discussed in the upcoming macrosystem section.

Several conceptual papers offer promising new directions for trainers' behavior and focus on decision-making strategies utilizing an information-processing model (Wester et al., 2008), difficult conversations about competence (Jacobs et al., 2011), actions that avoid legal challenges (Gilfoyle. 2008), and recommendations for improved management of the process (Kaslow et al., 2007b). Despite the barriers to addressing PPC, Jacobs et al. (2011) proposed that having difficult conversations with trainees about PPC is an ethical responsibility, as well as a trainer competence. Jacobs and colleagues (2011) recommended deliberately enhancing trainers' competence in difficult conversations and skills for better handling of PPC, as well as providing curricula for trainees to develop skills for having difficult conversations with peers who exhibit PPC.

Despite limited empirical research on trainers' behavior, it is increasingly clear that program structures (policies, strategies to address competencies, time constraints) and trainers' personal (attitudes toward nurturing or evaluating, level of skill for having difficult conversations, etc.) and interpersonal (sense of colleague support) factors are important in effectively addressing PPC. Thus, the knowledge, skills, and attitude to work with PPC can be viewed as a competence itself. An ecological view of psychology training suggests that attention to fostering and developing this competence in trainers is an important quality-enhancement function for programs and institutions. We turn now to the exosystem of programs, institutions, national policy, and the legal and ethical challenges of dealing with PPC.

Institutional, ethical and legal challenges (exosystem). In part, the challenges of addressing PPC in psychology training programs has been a function of the larger exosystem within which a particular training program and its faculty and students reside. These include institutional and national professional policies as well as the impact of ethical and legal determinants of action. Program faculty frequently report that inaction with trainees results from either not having policies in place for remediation or dismissal when necessary, or not having

adequately prepared the institution to understand and support the policies so that faculty can act in a timely and effective way. Cases have been reported anecdotally in which trainers have followed their policies, but when they moved to dismiss, the administration balked in resistance to potential conflict, uncertain costs, or fear of legal repercussions, even when the case is legally defensible.

Greater attention has been paid to components of the broader training context and has improved how programs and institutions create and utilize policies, standards, and laws. These include legal requirements for due process and fairness, questions about trainee privacy, the impact of the ADA, as well as considerable work done within professional psychology over the last decade including increased guidance from the 2002 revision of the APA Code of Ethics, CoA Guidelines and Principles, APPIC, and ACCA.

The complex intersection of ethical and legal aspects of the training exosystem impacts how programs address PPC. A basic legal premise in addressing PPC is the concept of due process, including notice of expectations and fairness in how educational programs treat trainees. As Behnke (2008) noted, notice is central to both legal and ethical responsibilities. Ethical standard 7.02 states, "programs take reasonable steps to ensure that there is a current and accurate description of the program...including requirements that must be met for satisfactory completion of the program" (APA, 2010, p. 9). Fairness means that trainers follow program policies and procedures consistently and congruently so that different standards are not used for different trainees (Gilfoyle, 2008).

Changes to Standard 7 in the 2002 Code of Ethics provided additional clarity for assessing and intervening with PPC. Standard 7.04 provides guidance on the conditions under which students may be required to disclose personal information: "if (1) the program or training facility has clearly identified this requirement in its admissions and program materials or (2) the information is necessary to evaluate or obtain assistance for students whose personal problems could reasonably be judged to be preventing them from performing their training or professionally related activities in a competent manner or posing a threat to the students or others" (APA, 2010, p. 9). Standard 7.05 provides important ethical guidance about the circumstances limiting mandated individual or group psychotherapy, providing trainees the option to select a practitioner unaffiliated with the program, and enjoining trainers who could be involved in evaluating trainees' performance from providing the therapy.

In addition to the ethical, due process, and fairness considerations, two other laws focused on privacy are important for trainers to consider when responding to PPC: Family Educational Rights and Privacy Act (FERPA) and the Health Insurance Portability and Accountability Act (HIPAA). FERPA prevents an educational institution from having a policy or practice of disclosing the education records of students (current or former), or personally identifiable information contained in education records, without the written consent of the student (Gilfoyle, 2008). Note that this protection is for records and not for observations or oral discussions by trainers of trainee behaviors. Although trainers are often concerned that HIPAA will prevent sharing trainee information in the same way that it protects client information, HIPAA applies primarily to health records, and, in general, does not cover academic programs or apply to educational records (Elman et al., 2009). HIPAA will not be discussed further in this paper but, as with all policies for PPC, program faculty and supervisors are encouraged to seek local review by attorneys and institutional administrators.

Although FERPA protections may appear intimidating to trainers in determining what information is acceptable to share when PPC issues arise, recently there has been further clarity about when such disclosure might be acceptable, with or without student consent. In the wake of the 2008 shootings by a student at Virginia Polytechnic Institute and State University (Virginia Tech), the United States (U.S.) Department of Education approved modifications to the legislation permitting such disclosure when "considering the totality of the circumstances, there must be *an articulable and significant threat* [emphasis added] to the health or safety of a student or other individuals," and that the disclosure be to any person whose knowledge of the information is necessary to protect against the threat. As one APA attorney noted, there has never been a dismissal case lost because of a violation of FERPA (Elman et al., 2009), and another stated "FERPA is rarely an impediment to a good faith, reasonable disclosure to others in an educational institution with a need to know" (Behnke, 2009).

The most important response to the protections afforded to trainees by FERPA is to ensure that consent to disclose relevant information is obtained in advance from all trainees. Programs that provide trainees with notice and obtain their written acknowledgment of what information may be shared, with whom and for what purpose, should expect to be able to share relevant information when it is in the service of attending to questions of professional competence. Behnke, Perlin, and Bernstein (2003) suggested a framework for determining what and when information is shared by proposing two principles: (a) the principle of "no surprises," meaning that people are informed in advance of what will be shared and with whom, and (b) the "parsimony principle," meaning that what is shared is limited to what is required to achieve the purposes of the disclosure.

As well, considerations of the ADA (1990), and its 2008 Amendments (discussed earlier in the terminology improvement section) require programs to ensure their policies and practices are in compliance with the law. In addition to avoiding the language of impairment, the ADA requires programs to avoid treating a trainee as though she/he had an impairment when the trainee has not brought forward a documented disability and a request for appropriate accommodations. A thorough review of implications of the ADA for training programs is not possible in this chapter, but can be found in these articles (Collins et al., 2011; Falender et al., 2005, 2009).

Space in this chapter does not permit a complete review of legal challenges brought by trainees against programs. In general when challenged in courts, program decisions have been upheld if the program has fairly followed its own policies and procedures. Others who have reviewed legal challenges brought by trainees against training programs have recommended review of PPC policies with institutional administrators and attorneys to be certain that policies are in compliance with due process, FERPA, and ADA standards, as well as state and local laws (Baldo, Softas-Nall, Shaw, 1997; Elman & Forrest, 2007; Forrest et al., 1999; Gilfoyle, 2008; McAdams & Foster, 2007; McAdams et al., 2007).

Within APA, increased attention to PPC has contributed to better understanding and guidance for action. The Working Group on Trainees with Competence Problems was established by the Council of Chairs of Training Councils (CCTC) shortly after the 2002 Competencies Conference and now receives staff support from the APA Education Directorate. This group has been responsible for creating useful information and resources to address PPC in a timely and corrective manner. A link to resources developed by this group and its members is available at http://www.apa.org/ed/graduate/competency-resources.aspx

A challenge addressed early by the Working Group was the lack of action and communication about PPC across training environments (e.g., between program trainers and supervisors in practica or internship), despite evidence that failure to share information about trainees impeded effective action (Lamb, 1999; Miller & Van Rybroek, 1988). In 2004, the Working Group developed and posted online recommendations for regular communications about trainees to reduce the gap between doctoral programs and internships (http://www.psychtrainingcouncils.org/CCTC%20 Recommendations%20for%20Communication. pdf). Points of communication when a problem develops are identified and a model statement provides notice about such interactions.

Concerns about the lack of communication between training programs and internships have also been addressed by APPIC. The internship application used for the internship match, now requires completion of an Application Certification (http://www.appic.org/Portals/0/downloads/AAPI_Sample_PDF.pdf) stating that the applicant has the responsibility of "producing adequate information for proper evaluation of my professional competence, character, ethics, and other qualifications and for resolving any doubts about such qualifications," (p. 12) and requiring the applicant to provide consent for the training program and the internship to release evaluative information to each other.

The Guidelines and Principles of the CoA have also influenced the way PPC is addressed in accredited training programs. Domain E, Student Faculty Relations (APA, 2009) addresses identification and remediation of problems in two important ways. First it requires that programs make their policies and procedures known to all trainees at the time of admission so that appropriate notice is provided. Second, it requires that trainees receive written notice of problems, guidance toward their remediation, and "substantive written feedback" (p. 11) on the extent to which corrective action has addressed the concern. As well, Domain B includes attention to the relationship between program faculty and field-based supervisors in requiring that programs "integrate the practicum component of the students' education and training with the other elements of the program" (APA, 2009, p. 8), thus ensuring a systemic interaction across the two components of the training system.

Taken as a whole, the guidance and actions of the Working Group, the Ethics Code, CoA, and APPIC provide movement toward a more systematic approach to intervening with trainees with PPC earlier and more effectively than was historically the case. Yet CCTC and individual training councils can go further in assisting training programs to adequately address PPC. How training programs address PPC has direct implications for the profession. ACCA along with the State, Provincial, and Territorial Psychological Associations (SPTAs) play a critical role in supporting competence of professional psychologists. We believe that attention to PPC at the training level is part of a life-long professional continuum (APA, 2006), and that successfully addressing competence challenges across the training system will make it easier for professionals to intervene early and adequately to prevent or ameliorate problems for colleagues and the profession.

Culture and diversity (macrosystem). In the past few years "greater attention has been paid to macrolevel ecological factors, such as how culture and diversity may impinge on faculty actions with trainees with competence problems" (Forrest & Campbell, 2012, p. 132). Macrolevel influences may cause trainers to both over-and underidentify problems of professional competence for nonmainstream trainees (Forrest et al., 1999; Forrest et al., 2008). For example, underidentification may occur because majority trainers fear appearing racist or sexist, and/or fear litigation brought by a nonmajority trainee asserting discriminatory practices. As well, "faculty of color may believe that their colleagues will not validate, support, or act on their concerns about a majority student and thus avoid identifying students as having competence problems" (Shen-Miller et al., 2012, p. 1183). Similarly, junior or untenured faculty may be cautious in identifying trainees with PPC if it creates conflicts with senior faculty who later may vote on their tenure decisions (Forrest et al., 2013). Overidentification might occur because trainers hold conscious or unconscious assumptions about diversity issues that may cause some trainers to see trainees from marginalized groups as less competent (Forrest et al., 2008; Vasquez, 1999).

Trainee diversity variables may influence trainees' ability to develop competence. Forrest and her colleagues (1999) speculated that some trainee behaviors that do not meet professional standards might be rooted in their cultural backgrounds and life experiences (e.g., learned hostilities to groups different from their own; collectivist orientation versus individual focus). Given that macrolevel dominant culture values, including discriminatory and prejudicial attitudes, are often insidious and are absorbed without conscious awareness of their harmful effects, trainers' attention to macrolevel cultural influences on the training environment is important. As Kaslow and her colleagues (2007) stated: "when assessing competence problems, consider the impact of beliefs, values, and attitudes about individual and cultural differences on decisions regarding problem identification, assessment, and intervention" (p. 484).

Research investigating cultural impact on addressing PPC has been sparse. Supervisors in Gizara and Forrest's study (2004) reported that differences in diversity demographics among trainers and between trainers and trainees complicated trainers' decision-making and hindered their effectiveness. Similarly Vacha-Haase, Davenport, and Kerewsky (2004) found that 11% of their sample of training directors reported that differences in race and ethnicity made dealing with trainees who were struggling more difficult. Shen-Miller and colleagues (Shen-Miller et al., 2009; Shen-Miller et al., 2012), reporting on how faculty conceptualize diversity and its influence on their actions with trainees with PPC, stated: "Training directors also (a) demonstrated less definitional clarity and conceptual sophistication when discussing the influences of race than those of gender and (b) described strong emotional reactions associated with race but not gender" (Shen-Miller et al., 2012, p. 1184). Shen-Miller and co-workers (2012) found that faculty differed in their evaluative stances with some who declared the importance of consistent professional standards for all trainees (color-blind evaluations), whereas other trainers affirmed their commitment to multicultural competence and the inclusion of trainees' cultural backgrounds and contexts as a significant component of their evaluations (culturally attentive evaluations). These differences, whether explicit or not, were described as a source of conflict among trainers when making decisions about trainees with PPC. The findings from this study also revealed helpful strategies (commitment to conversations about diversity, consultations, and examination of biases as a faculty group) and harmful strategies (historic conflicts reactivated during decisions about trainees with PPC, differential levels of multicultural expertise and competence, and assumptions about diversity-related conflicts) that influence how trainers respond to PPC.

Macrolevel cultural and diversity influences on education and training are most apparent in several recent court cases and legislative actions. Two recent court cases involved students dismissed from master's-level counseling programs because the client's sexual orientation was in conflict with the trainee's religious beliefs as well as their refusal to participate in the program's remediations (*Keeton v. Anderson-Wiley*,2011; *Ward v. Wilbank.*, 2010). Lawyers from the Alliance Defense Fund (ADF), a coalition of Christian lawyers representing the students, argued that the students' First Amendment rights were being violated because they were being forced to comply with remediation that required them to change their religious beliefs. The university attorneys argued that ethical codes and professional standards require counselors to provide services to categories of clients in a nondiscriminatory manner and educators have the right to determine the training necessary to develop these professional competencies, including remedial requirements. In both cases, the judges' rulings reinforced previous decisions that academic programs have the right to establish and enforce academic and professional standards required to successfully complete educational programs.

These court decisions provide some guidance for trainers responsible for professional psychology training programs about how to negotiate trainee value conflicts that impinge on the development of professional competencies. The right of trainers to establish and enforce educational and professional standards was affirmed. Critically, in both cases, the program provided notice in handbooks and curricular information about academic requirements that included upholding the ethical standards of the profession especially the nondiscrimination standard. The opportunity for trainees to freely express their religious beliefs in the classroom was upheld, yet the rulings supported faculty rights to determine professional standards including that students' must manage their personal beliefs in a manner that does no harm to clients. The court rulings reinforce the importance of keeping the focus NOT on trainees' beliefs, but on their professional behaviors and performance with clients. In the Ward case, there has also been an appeals-court ruling (*Ward v. Polite,* 2012) that provides additional guidance for faculty decisions and actions mostly focused on the fair and nondiscriminatory execution of the training program's referral policies (Behnke, 2012).

More recently, bills have been introduced in state legislatures that focus on protecting students' religious rights and by doing so limit faculty and program options. The University Students' Religious Liberty Act was introduced and passed by the Arizona House (Center for Arizona Policy,

2011; State of Arizona, 2011). The Act stated that "A university or community college shall not discipline or discriminate against a student...because the student refuses to counsel a client about goals that conflict with the student's sincerely held religious belief or conviction." Prior to passage, the final version of the bill was amended to include "if the student consults with the supervising instructor or professor to determine the proper course of action to avoid harm to the client." Similar religious freedom related to training or professional practice legislation has been introduced in Michigan (and passed by their House), Missouri, Nebraska and Tennessee. These recent developments in both court cases and state legislation have major implications for training programs. Bieschke and Mintz (2012) "argue that professional psychology is in danger of losing its professional autonomy in regard to setting standards for the profession and the academic freedom to determine the appropriate training for our students" (p. 196).

Two current efforts to address this danger have been initiated by the APA Board of Educational Affairs (BEA) and the journal, *Training and Education in Professional Psychology (TEPP)*. In late 2011, BEA established a Working Group on Restriction Affecting Diversity Training in Graduate Education to monitor judicial and legislative actions, as well as to develop proactive efforts that bring forth psychological knowledge to help shape this cultural dialogue. The charge to the Working Group's included preparing informative materials for education and training program administrators, faculty, and prospective and current students, as well as for state psychological associations and the general public, addressing the potential impact of legislative provisions or court rulings on diversity training in graduate education.

The second effort involves the publication of a special section of *TEPP* focused on educators and trainers' responsibilities when trainees personal beliefs conflict with the development of professional competence(Behnke, 2012; Bieschke & Mintz, 2012; Forrest, 2012). The first article in the special section (Behnke, 2012) summarizes the district and appeals court rulings (*Keeton v. Anderson-Wiley*, 2011; *Ward v. Polite*, 2012; *Ward v. Wilbanks*, 2010) and provides insights into the conflicts between students' First Amendment rights that protect their religious freedoms, and educators' rights to determine professional standards and their responsibility to evaluate whether students' are meeting those standards. Although the rulings

from the court cases point in a direction that solve some problems, the appeals-court ruling raises an important question about whether the program's referral policy existed and, if so, whether it was applied in a fair and nondiscriminatory manner (there is some evidence in the court record that referrals were allowed in some instances, but not others) and did not single out a student because of her religious beliefs. In the second article, Bieschke and Mintz (2012) provide a strong rationale for why trainees must be able to deliver competent care to clients who challenge their belief systems. They are also concerned about the potential for discriminatory referrals, yet their focus is on the trainee and whether the trainee is engaging in discrimination against a category or group of clients. In their article, Bieschke and Mintz (2012) also review current ethical standards (APA, 2010) on competence, discrimination, and termination (including referral), providing a pointed analysis about the contradictions among the standards that leaves trainers and trainees without clear guidance about what types of referrals are ethical. They conclude with a call for clarification about conflicting ethical mandates, and for development and adoption of a uniform training statement that applies to the breadth of training in professional psychology.

Whereas the court rulings are clarifying the macrosystemic influences as well as trainer and trainee rights, the legislative actions have simplified complex macrosystemic issues in a manner that overreaches and creates a sense of urgency for those responsible for professional training in psychology. Both the BEA Working Group and the *TEPP* special section make it clear that trainers must stay abreast of the recent developments in court cases and state legislation so that trainers are overseeing their programs consistent with the legal rulings, and psychologists are ready to advocate with their state representatives if these laws are introduced in their state legislatures.

These research studies, conceptual articles, anecdotal reports, court cases, and legislative action, all suggest that cultural and group differences as well as diversity conflicts increase the discomfort, confusion and stress associated with the identification, remediation, and/or dismissal of trainees with PPC. The limited research base, the potential intrusion by state laws and court rulings into education policy, the lack of frameworks for understanding the intersection of diversity and PPC, and limited professional guidance for handling diversity conflicts during training leave trainers vulnerable to enacting decisions that may not be based in a well-informed, educated, and legally defensible diversity framework. Much more work is needed to understand fully the complex influence of macro-level cultural assumptions about diversity that are in all likelihood embedded in both trainers and trainees' conceptualizations of professional competence and appropriate professional behavior (Donovan & Ponce, 2009).

Remediation

Until the recent emphasis on competencies, by far the most typical remediation recommended during training was that the trainee obtains personal psychotherapy (Forrest et al., 1999; Elman & Forrest, 2004). Over the past few years, cautions were raised about the use of personal psychotherapy as a common method for remediation (Behnke, 2008, 2009; Elman & Forrest, 2004; Gilfoyle, 2008), although its value for the developing psychologists remains significant. Progress has been made in identifying the potential limitations of personal therapy as a remediation, including the lack of evidence of (a) a formal remediation plan, (b) whether the student complied and attended therapy sessions, (c) whether the therapy addressed the areas of competence that caused the referral, and (d) whether therapy was successful. Also, most often, personal therapy remediation resulted in no feedback to the program being required from either the trainee or the treating therapist, largely due to an assumption that the trainee's confidentiality would be violated (Elman & Forrest, 2004).

Also, there have been improvements in addressing remediation of PPC in a timely and corrective way. One aspect of this is the need to provide a trainee with both notice and an opportunity to address the problems of competence as a part of due process and fairness. Early assessment and notification to the trainee about competence problems are imperative, thus giving the trainee full opportunity to address the deficiencies. In response to a federal lawsuit brought by a dismissed trainee, McAdams, Foster, and Ward (2007)offered many excellent program policy recommendations. A second article described a model for remediation to "both safeguard students' legal rights or justify dismissal if remediation is unsuccessful" (McAdams & Foster, 2007, p. 2).

McAdams and Foster's (2007) model for just and fair remediation includes both substantive and procedural due process. Substantive due process means that remediation should be relevant and comparable (neither overinclusive nor underinclusive) to the identified problem, and corrective in intent rather than punitive. Procedural due process includes clarity of expectations (advance notice), clearly identified supervision and support, regular progress evaluation, and documentation of the process to assure transparency. A remediation must be related to the competence in question, be capable of being effectively supervised and assessed by trainers, specify a timetable by which goals must be attained, and explicate the consequences of success or failure to attain the competence.

In general, remediation policies need to be clear but avoid excessive detail, because they are viewed as a legal contract between training programs and trainees. They must also accommodate unexpected problems, and must be doable for both the trainee and the faculty (Gilfoyle, 2008). Common remediations include: decreased client load, increased supervision, leave of absence and/or an additional practicum or second internship or residency, and extra coursework (Elman & Forrest, 2004; Kaslow et al., 2007b). When personal psychotherapy is required, programs should be clear that trainers (a) do not diagnose the trainee; (b) understand the distinction between personal and professional behavior; (c) handle confidentiality so that the program receives adequate knowledge from the therapist about progress toward identified goals; and (d) allow the student to select a personal therapist with expertise in working with PPC and one who is not a faculty member or supervisor, thus avoiding a dual relationship. Utilizing the competency benchmarks and assessment strategies, programs can more readily develop remediation plans targeted to respond to identified competence problems and achieve desired outcomes

As one strategy to assist programs in creating effective remediation for psychology trainees, the Ad Hoc Working Group on Trainees with Competence Problems created a template (http://www.apa.org/ed/graduate/competency.aspx), specifically structured as a contract to address ethical and due-process concerns, and document the remediation process over time. Importantly, it requires the explicit consent of the trainee and the program to participate in ways that give the trainee appropriate opportunity and guidance to attain the desired competencies. Steps taken by both the trainee and all involved trainers, expected outcomes, and summative evaluations are documented chronologically. The template can be modified to each program's policies and practices.

The Boundary Between Personal and Professional

When working with PPC, we discovered no standard of practice for addressing the boundary between personal and professional behavior. Across four areas, trainers and programs vary in how they understand and/or use: (a) diagnostic labels to describe competence problem, (b) trainers' psychological assessment skills to determine the nature of competence problems, (c) personal therapy as a focus of remediation plans, and (d) trainee privacy and confidentiality in the training culture. We will describe in more detail how each of these four issues creates uncertainty (and sometimes disagreement) among trainers, results in confusing messages to trainees, and sometimes, inconsistent programmatic actions.

In examining personal/professional distinctions in psychology, Pipes and colleagues(2005) commented that "we are committed to honoring a separate personal life, yet in our hearts, we really believe that the personal and the professional are often inseparable" (p. 330), suggesting that the confusion is not just an issue for trainers dealing with trainees with PPC, but is more broadly pandemic to the profession. Pipes and colleagues (2005) also asserted that there are "difficulties inherent in drawing distinctions between the personal and the professional" (p. 325), and provided a model for resolving the "fuzzy" boundary between the two by evaluating whether a personal behavior impacts professional behavior.

Personal Problems as a Major Category of Competence Problems

Using surveys of DTs, researchers have found that personal problems are identified as the most common reason that trainees' professional competence gets derailed (Brear et al., 2008). Once a trainee has been identified as struggling, especially in a practicum or other clinically focused component of training, personal problems become more salient and may become the focus of attention. Thus, for some trainers, the boundary between what is personal and what is professional shifts when competence problems are identified. Other trainers articulate a clear focus on professional performance and behavior when competence problems arise avoiding a focus on underlying personal issues that may be causing the problems in professional functioning (Falender et al., 2009).

Trainer Involvement in Psychological Assessment and Diagnosis

Similarly, the reasons given by some trainers for placing a trainee on remediation, or considering dismissal include diagnostic labels (e.g., personality disorders, anxiety disorders, adjustment disorders) suggesting another place where boundaries blur between professional and personal behaviors. Yet, other trainers (Falender et al., 2009; Kaslow et al., 2007b; Schoener, 1999) have recommended that trainers avoid any role associated with assessment and diagnosis of trainees, because it (a) creates an untenable dual role, (b) does not meet the spirit of assessment standards in the APA Ethics Code, and (c) risks diagnosis of an impairment that triggers actions required by the ADA (described earlier).

The Role of Personal Therapy in Remediation

As noted elsewhere, until recently, personal psychotherapy has been the most common form of remediation to improve professional functioning (Forrest et al., 1999). Part of the dilemma of using personal therapy as a remediation lies in the assumption that the trainee's personal qualities of moral character and psychological fitness (Johnson, Porter, Campbell & Kupko, 2005) prevent the trainee from performing competently. For many trainers, personal therapy has been viewed as the best place to address personal problems that interfere with professional functioning (Elman & Forrest, 2004). Yet, other trainers diligently work to avoid personal therapy as a component of remediation or see it as solely voluntary on the trainee's part because of the deeply personal nature of therapy, requiring great privacy and confidentiality. Even trainers who see personal therapy as an important component of remediation differ on what information if any should be shared or negotiated between the trainee and training program including the goals, the selection and expertise of the treating therapist, verification of attendance, and the content and outcomes of the therapy that influence professional performance (Elman & Forrest, 2004).

Boundaries of Trainee Confidentiality

Similar questions about the boundary between personal and professional arise around the extent of trainee confidentiality and its relationship to what trainers need to know to be able to address competence problems. Trainers vary on beliefs about the boundaries for trainee confidentiality (Elman & Forrest, 2004; Forrest & Elman, 2005). Some trainers go to great lengths to protect trainees' personal issues from other trainers because they feel strongly that addressing personal problems that affect professional functioning requires great sensitivity to the trainee's privacy and confidentiality. Other trainers believe that the person of the therapist is key to the therapeutic process. These trainers often establish transparent training climates in which they model open discussion among trainers and trainees about personal problems that interfere with good professional practice.

The meaning of trainee confidentiality is inherently different from client confidentiality, yet some trainers apply models of client confidentiality to interventions with trainees with PPC (Kaslow et al., 2007b). Assumptions that the core values of client–therapist models of confidentiality apply to trainees with competence problems are too simplistic, may inadvertently support privacy that leans toward secrecy about professional behavior and whether it meets professional standards, deny trainees models of trainers having difficult dialogues about competence concerns in preparation for future professional responsibilities, and limit trainers' options for communicating clearly to other trainees about standards of professional competence (Forrest & Elman, 2005). Challenges to privacy and confidentiality from the evolving use of the Internet and social media provide additional challenges to training programs that address the balance between the personal and the professional, but they are beyond the scope of this chapter.

A clear understanding of FERPA and how it applies to professional psychology trainees provides some guidance about what is private and can only be shared with the trainee's permission. Attention to *up front* agreements with trainees is essential including (a) what may be shared and with whom, and (b) the need for transparent communication about PPC among trainers and with other trainees (Gilfoyle, 2008). Also, provisions about what and how personal information may be shared during training has been established in Standard 7 of the Ethics Code described earlier in this chapter (APA, 2010).

Signs of Progress

Although many trainers believe that personal qualities are foundational to professional functioning, professional psychology has yet to arrive at clarity about the personal as it affects professional behavioral and competencies. In the aforementioned circumstances, trainers may make critical decisions without having well-thought-out models for exploring these questions: What is the appropriate boundary between what is personal and private and what is professional? What aspects of the personal so affect professional behaviors that they need

to be a part of the training process? What aspects of trainees' personal background and psychological struggles should be accessible to trainers, especially when PPC have been identified? These questions have not been adequately addressed in the general scholarship on education and training or the PPC literature. Limited guidance exists for trainers about when personal information should be accessible or how to talk with trainees about personal/professional boundaries when PPC are identified.

Some help in distinguishing the boundary between personal and professional can be found within the competency framework (Fouad et al., 2009). Within the professionalism and interpersonal relations competencies, personal behaviors that influence professional competence have been identified and benchmarked at three stages in the professional development process during training (Fouad et al., 2009). Applying the competency framework clarifies that the focus is on personal behaviors only when they have direct impact on professional behavior. A guidebook to the application of the Competency Benchmarks with further application for addressing and evaluating professionalism and remediation was published recently, may assist programs in these efforts, and is available at http://www.apa.org/ed/graduate/benchmarks-guide.aspx.

Similarly, meeting the spirit of the ADA provides another route to understanding personal/professional boundaries. Behaviors that are the result of a disability or impairment are considered private, and the ADA makes clear that it is the right of individuals to bring or not bring their disabilities to the attention of trainers so they can receive appropriate accommodations to meet the essential functions of becoming a psychologist. If educators believe that a disability affects a trainee's ability to perform the essential functions of being a psychologist, the requirements of ADA law are in effect for helping the trainer understand the boundaries between personal and professional.

To date, beside these two efforts (e.g., competency benchmarks and ADA legal requirements), no framework or guiding principles have been developed to assist trainers in determining what aspects of a trainee's personal problems might be considered when professional competence issues have been identified. We note that the focus on professionalism captures many of the personal behaviors at issue in PPC, yet there remains a deep-seated emotional response to trainees when personal problems interfere with the capacity to attain competence, and we urge further exploration of this challenging nexus.

Conclusions

During the past decade professional psychology has made significant progress in addressing trainees with PPC. These improvements have been accomplished in tandem with an evolution toward a competency-based approach to education and training in professional psychology. We note as well, progress in understanding that PPC is not solely a function of the individual trainee, but nested in larger interactive system. Conceptualizing the training environment as an ecological system has enhanced our understanding of the interacting roles of peers of the trainee, faculty and supervisors, and programmatic and institutional functioning, as well as the impact of broader ethical, accreditation, legal, and cultural factors. We have a clearer model and strategies for (a) the identification, remediation and dismissal of trainees who cannot attain desired competencies; and (b) gatekeeping responsibilities as a profession, although the application of those strategies remains fraught with continuing challenges of time and emotional costs.

Future Directions

Our review of progress to date points to important next steps to further improve the profession's ability to address PPC. Next, we describe recommendations for educational practices and future research to assure that improvements are grounded in empirical evidence as well as training goals that protect the profession and the public.

1. A few typologies of competence problems have emerged, yet the efforts to date have not provided useful guidance to educators. According to Collins and colleagues (Collins et al., 2011), "precision is crucial in classifying, describing and addressing the root causes of patterns of substandard performance in the clinical training setting" (p. 429). The best current hope for a useful and precise typology of competence problems during training may be the use of competency benchmarks as a framework, thus aligning the typology of competence problems with existing work on the functional and foundational competencies. We recommend that the typology address the challenges we identified: confusion created by mixing consequences with causes among the categories and the ethical and legal risk associated with the inclusion of categories focused on diagnoses of personal problems. Efforts across the training spectrum (perhaps through the vehicle of the Council of Chairs of Training Councils) to agree upon the language and establish categories that are mutually exclusive and behaviorally anchored would (a) create a common language for educators to communicate with trainees and across programs, (b) facilitate policy development, (c) decrease legal risk, (d) help research efforts, and (e) contribute to further refining best practices in remediation of competence challenges.

2. We recommend the explicit preparation of trainees to understand PPC policies and practices including (a) early exposure to program policies and the development of a communitarian sense of responsibility for colleagues' competence (Johnson et al., 2012), and (b) training in the skills for having difficult dialogues about competence problems (Jacobs et al., 2011). Creating skills during training for addressing peers with PPC will serve an important preventive role for the profession, enabling trainees once they complete training to act on their responsibility to peers who exhibit PPC in professional practice.

3. The competence of individual faculty and supervisors to manage PPC has not yet been adequately addressed. Trainers themselves sometimes demonstrate their own professional competence problems, and programs struggle to address trainer competence problems in the same way that they may avoid addressing trainee PPC. This avoidance further contributes to a failure to act (i.e., gateslipping) when trainees require intervention and models a hands-off approach to PPC for trainees. A second issue is whether trainers have the knowledge, skills, and attitudes and whether the program has the policies and strategies, grounded in understanding of the legal and ethical and cultural factors, to address PPC effectively. Preliminary research (Forrest et al., 2031) has suggested that more effective intervention takes place when programs are intentional about addressing PPC as a goal, when they prepare for action where it is needed, and when trainers act as a unit. More research is needed, particularly qualitative and case-study research to determine factors that enhance trainers' competence, as well as research that articulates the competence of the training ecology or system: how and which policies make a difference, what types of relationships with administrators and attorneys improve outcomes, and what aspects of multisystemic relationships are critical for success?

4. Variations among trainers about the boundaries between what is personal and private, and what is personal and professional, and thus

critical to good training, require greater attention from the training community. Because personal behaviors have ramifications for professional behavior, we recommend the development of a conceptual framework to guide educators and trainers about what and when aspects of trainee personal behavior should be accessible to trainers. Such a framework would be helpful as trainers (a) develop a system for categorizing types of PPC, (b) clarify their involvement in assessment or diagnosis, (c) structure remediation and clarify the program's relationship to personal therapy when it is part of a remediation plan, and (d) provide informed consent to trainees about the boundaries of their confidentiality during training. We recommend a national dialogue among trainers with the goal of producing a consistent and shared conceptual framework for addressing the current confusion about the boundary between personal and professional.

5 Furthermore, new models need to be developed that clearly identify the limits to confidentiality when applied to trainees with PPC. To adequately address issues of trainee confidentiality, the system must be prepared in advance with policies that clarify requirements when trainees need to allow access to personal factors. Informing trainees in advance of these requirements addresses the "law of no surprises" and "law of parsimony," which limit disclosures to what is required to achieve the purposes of the disclosure (Behnke et al., 2003). Trainees deserve to know the bottom line: Trainees' confidentiality is limited by the demands of meeting competence standards. There are limits to their confidentiality because they are training for a profession that must protect the public and client welfare is the priority. Consequently, professional competence standards must be met, and those in the training system must be able to talk freely about competence issues.

6. Despite the increased attention and progress made in addressing PPC, professional psychology has yet to provide any empirical evidence for long-term effectiveness of standard interventions with trainees with PPC. The scholarship to date is almost exclusively anecdotal, descriptive, and retrospective, and lacks evidence that intervention with trainees is related to competence later in professional practice. Nor do we have any knowledge of whether trainees who are better trained and knowledgeable about strategies for intervention with a peer with PPC are better able to address concerns about colleagues' competence later during professional

practice. Researchers in medicine (Papadakis et al., 2004, 2005) have made initial efforts to track medical students into practice and report that licensed board-disciplined physicians were more likely than nondisciplined physicians to have had problems of professionalism documented during medical school. Previously we recommended that the ASPPB's disciplinary database, which includes disciplinary data from state licensing boards, be used in conjunction with doctoral-program information as a feedback loop for training programs about those trainees who later have competence problems serious enough to come to the attention of licensing boards (Elman& Forrest, 2007). If it is an obligation of the professional training community to determine effective strategies for addressing competence problems to protect the public, it is imperative that preparation for this begins at the training level and that the effectiveness of intervention for both trainers and trainees is assessed empirically through prospective research.

7. Addressing PPC is not a problem for psychology alone. Improvements for professional psychology will be best accomplished in collaboration with other professions, particularly as psychology becomes more committed to being a health-care profession (APA, n.d.) and preparing professionals for interprofessional collaborative practice (Interprofessional Education Collaborative Expert Panel, 2011). Considerable work to address PPC in training has been reported in social work, counseling, nursing, and medicine. Education and training in professional psychology would be strengthened by increased collaboration with groups from these professions sharing challenges, innovations, and perhaps even research. We recommend using the resources of APA to build meaningful collaborations with these professional organizations to further the development of professional psychology's response to PPC.

References

American Psychological Association Advisory Committee on Colleague Assistance. (2006). *Advancing colleague assistance in professional psychology*. Washington, DC: American Psychological Association. Retrieved on July 21, 2013 from http://www.apa.org/practice/resources/assistance/monograph.pdf

American Psychological Association Commission on Accreditation. (2009). Guidelines and principles for accreditation of programs in professional psychology. Retrieved on July 23, 2013 from http://www.apa.org/ed/accreditation/about/policies/guiding-principles.pdf

American Psychological Association. (2010). Ethical principles of psychologists and code of conduct (2002, Amended June

1, 2010). Retrieved on July 21, 2013 from http://www.apa.org/ethics/code/index.aspx

American Psychological Association (n.d.). Psychology is a behavioral and mental health profession. Retrieved on July 21, 2013 from http://www.apa.org/about/gr/issues/health-care/profession.aspx

Americans with Disabilities Act of 1990, 42 U.S.C.A.§12101 et seq.

ADA Amendments Act of 2008, Pub. L. 110–325 (September 25, 2008).

Baker, J. (2008). *Implementing action plans for remediation within HIPAA and FERPA guidelines.* Symposium presented at the Commission on Accreditation Assembly, Minneapolis, MN.

Baker, J., McCutcheon, S., &Keilin, W. G. (2007). The internship supply-demand imbalance: The APPIC perspective. *Training and Education in Professional Psychology, 1,* 287–293. doi: 10.1037/1931-3918.1.4.287

Baldo, T. D., Softas-Nall, B. C., &Shaw, S. F. (1997). Student review and retention in counselor education: An alternative to Frame and Stevens-Smith. *Counselor Education and Supervision, 36,* 245–253.

Barnett, J. E., &Cooper, N. (2009). Creating a culture of self-care. *Clinical Psychology: Research and Practice, 16,* 16–20. doi: 10.1111/j.1468-2850.2009.01138.x

Behnke, S. H. (2008). Discussion: Toward elaborating and implementing a conceptualization of healthy, safe training environments. *Training and Education in Professional Psychology, 2,* 215–218. doi: 10.1037/a0014008

Behnke, S. H. (2009, April). *Legal and ethical issues with problematic trainees.* Invited address presented at the American Association of Psychology Postdoctoral and Internship Centers (APPIC). Portland, OR.

Behnke, S. H. (2012). Constitutional claims in the context of mental health training: Religion, sexual orientation, and tensions between the First Amendment and professional ethics. *Training and Education in Professional Psychology, 6,* 189–195. doi: 10.1037/a0030809

Behnke, S. H., Perlin, M., &Bernstein, M. (2003). *The essentials of New York mental health law: A straightforward guide for all disciplines.* New York: Norton.

Bieschke, K. J., &Mintz, L. B. (2012). Counseling psychology model training values statement addressing diversity: History, current use, and future directions. *Training and Education in Professional Psychology, 6,* 196–203.doi: 10.1037/a0030810

Bodner, K. E. (2012). Ethical principles and standards that inform educational gatekeeping practices in psychology. *Ethics and Behavior, 21,* 60–74. doi: 10.1080/10508422.2012.638827

Brear, P., &Dorrian, J. (2010). Gatekeeping or gate slippage? A national survey of counseling educators in Australian undergraduate and postgraduate academic training programs. *Training and Education in Professional Psychology, 4,* 264–273. doi: 10.1037/a0020714

Brear, P., Dorrian, J., &Luscri, G.(2008). Preparing our future counselling professionals: Gatekeeping and the implications for research. *Counselling & Psychotherapy Research, 8,* 93–101. doi: 10.1080/14733140802007855

Bronfenbrenner, U. (1979). *The ecology of human development: Experiments by nature and design.* Cambridge, MA: Harvard University Press.

Brusseri, M., Tyler, J., &King, A. (2005). An exploratory examination of student dismissals and prompted resignations from clinical PhD training programs: Does clinical competency matter? *Professional Psychology: Research and Practice, 36,* 441–445. doi: 10.1037/0735-7028.36.4.441

Burgess, S. L. (1994). The impaired clinical and counseling psychology doctoral student (Unpublished doctoral dissertation). California School of Professional Psychology, Berkeley/Alameda, CA.

Center for Arizona Policy. (2011). Family issues fact sheet (No. 2011–11). Retrieved on July 21, 2013 from www.azleg.gov/legtext/50leg/1r/bills/hb2565h.pdf

Collins, C., Falender, C. A., &Shafranske, E. P. (2011). Commentary on Rebecca Schwartz-Mette's 2009 article, "Challenges in addressing graduate student impairment in academic professional psychology programs". *Ethics and Behavior, 21,* 428–430. doi: 10.1080/10508422.2011.604547

Dodds, J. (2002). *Issues affecting graduate students' willingness to intervene with impaired peers. (Unpublished doctoral dissertation).* Texas A&M University, College Station, Texas.

Donovan, R. A., &Ponce, A. N. (2009). Identification and measurement of core competencies in professional psychology: Areas for consideration. *Training and Education in Professional Psychology, 3,* S46–S49. doi:10.1037/a0017302

Elman, N. S. (2001). *Dealing with problem students.* Invited address presented at the midwinter meeting of the National Council of Schools of Professional Psychology, Freeport, Grand Bahamas.

Elman, N. S. (2002). Trainees in trouble: Continuing the dialogue. Invited address at the annual meeting of the Association of Directors of Psychology Training Clinics, San Francisco, CA.

Elman, N. S. (2003). *Dialogue with ACCA.* Invited address at the annual meeting of the Association of State and Provincial Psychology Boards Annual Meeting, Scottsdale, AZ.

Elman, N. S. (2010). Leadership in dealing with trainees with competence problems: Administrative and interpersonal aspects. In J. Chin (Chair). Leadership. Plenary session at Joint Mid-Year Meeting of the Training Councils of Psychology, Orlando, FL.

Elman, N. S., &Forrest, L. (2004). Psychotherapy in the remediation of psychology trainees: Exploratory interviews with training directors. *Professional Psychology: Research and Practice, 35,* 123–130. doi: 10.1037/0735-7028.35.2.123

Elman, N. S., &Forrest, L. (2007). From trainee impairment to professional competence problems: Seeking new terminology that facilitates effective action. *Professional Psychology: Research and Practice, 38,* 501–509. doi: 10.1037/0735-7028.38.5.501

Elman, N. S., Forrest, L., Vacha-Haase, T., &Gizara, S. (1999). A systems perspective on trainee impairment: Continuing the dialogue. *Counseling Psychologist, 27,* 712–721. doi:10.1177/0011000099275005

Elman, N. S., Illfelder-Kaye, J., &Robiner, W. N. (2005). Professional development: Training for professionalism as a foundation for competent practice in psychology. *Professional Psychology: Research and Practice, 36,* 367–375. doi:10.1037/0735-7028.36.4.367

Elman, N., Springer, A., & Baker, J. (2009). *The impact of FERPA/HIPAA regulations on addressing trainees with problems of professional competence.* Symposium presented at the APA Commission on Accreditation Assembly, San Diego, CA.

Falender, C. A., Collins, C. J., &Shafranske, E. P. (2005). Use of the term "impairment" in psychology supervision. *California Psychologist, 38,* 21–22.

Falender, C. A., Collins, C. J., &Shafranske, E. P. (2009). "Impairment" and performance issues in clinical supervision: After the 2008 ADA Amendments Act. *Training* and Education in Professional Psychology, 3, 240–249. doi:10.1037/a0017153

Forrest, L. (2001). Trainees in trouble: Clinic directors' dilemmas. Invited address presented at the annual meeting of the Association of Directors of Psychology Training Clinics, Dallas, TX.

Forrest, L. (2005). Addressing competency problems during professional training. Invited address at the annual meeting of the Association of State and Provincial Psychology Boards. Portland, OR.

Forrest, L. (2012). Special section: Educators' and trainers' responsibilities when trainees' personal beliefs collide with competent care. *Training and Education in Professional Psychology, 6*, 187–188. doi: 10.1037/a0030799

Forrest, L., &Campbell, L. F. (2012). Emerging trends in counseling psychology education and training. In N. Fouad, J. Carter, & L. Subich [Eds.]. *APA handbook of counseling psychology: Theories, research and methods* (Vol. I, pp. 119–154). Washington, DC: APA Press.

Forrest, L., & Elman, N. S. (2005). Psychotherapy for poorly performing trainees: Are there limits to confidentiality? *Psychotherapy Bulletin, 40*, 29–37.

Forrest, L., & Elman, N. S. (2009). *Intervening with trainees not attaining professional competency*. Invited presentation at the Council of Counseling Psychology Training Programs Midwinter Meeting, Savannah, GA.

Forrest, L., &Elman, N. S. (2010). *Trainees with competence problems: Developing practical skills for unavoidable difficult conversations*. Invited presentation at the Council of Counseling Psychology Training Programs Midwinter Meeting, Orlando, FL

Forrest, L., Elman, N., Gizara, S., &Vacha-Haase, T. (1999). Trainee impairment: A review of identification, remediation, dismissal, and legal issues. *The Counseling Psychologist, 27*, 627–686. doi: 10.1177/0011000099275001

Forrest, L., Elman, N. S., Huprich, S. K., Veilleux, J. C., Jacobs, S., &Kaslow, N. J. (2013). Training directors' perceptions of faculty behaviors when dealing with trainee competence problems: A mixed method pilot study. *Training and Education in Professional Psychology, 7*, 23–32. doi: 10.1037/a0032068

Forrest, L., Elman, N. S., &Shen-Miller, D. S. (2008). Psychology trainees with competence problems: From individual to ecological conceptualizations. *Training and Education in Professional Psychology, 2*, 183–192. doi:10.1037/1931-3918.2.4.183

Foster, V., &McAdams, C. (2009). A framework for creating a climate of transparency for professional performance assessment: Fostering student investment in gatekeeping. *Counselor Education and Supervision, 48*, 271–284.

Fouad, N. A., Grus, C. L., Hatcher, R. L., Kaslow, N. J., Hutchings, P. S., Madson, M., & Crossman, R. E. (2009). Competency benchmarks: A model for the understanding and measuring of competence in professional psychology across training levels. *Training and Education in Professional Psychology,3*,S5–S26. doi:10.1037/a0015832

Gaubatz, M. D., &Vera, E. M. (2002). Do formalized gatekeeping procedures increase programs' follow up with deficient trainees? Counselor Education and Supervision, *41*, 294–305. doi: 10.1002/j.1556-6978.2002.tb01292.x

Gaubatz, M. D., Vera, E. M. (2006). Trainee competence in masters-level counseling programs: A comparison of counselor educators' and students' views. *Counselor Education and Supervision, 46*, 32–43. doi: 10.1002/j.1556-6978.2006.tb00010.x

Gilfoyle, N. (2008). The legal exosystem: Risk management in addressing student competence problems in professional psychology training. *Training and Education in Professional Psychology, 2*, 202–209. doi: 10.1037/1931-3918.2.4.202

Gizara, S., &Forrest, L. (2004). Supervisors' experience of trainee impairment and incompetence at APA-accredited internship sites. *Professional Psychology: Research and Practice, 35*, 131–140. doi: 10.1037/0735-7028.35.2.131

Gizara, S. S. (1997). *Supervisors' construction of intern impairment at APA-accredited internship sites*. Unpublished doctoral dissertation, Michigan State University, East Lansing.

Hatcher, R. L. (2011). The internship supply as a common-pool resource: A pathway to managing the imbalance problem. *Training and Education in Professional Psychology, 5*, 126–140. doi: 10.1037/a0024658

Huprich, S. K., & Rudd, M. D. (2004). A national survey of trainee impairment in clinical, counseling, and school psychology doctoral programs and internships. *Journal of Clinical Psychology, 60*, 43–52. doi:10.1002/jclp.10233

Interprofessional Education Collaborative Expert Panel. (2011). *Core competencies for interprofessional collaborative practice: Report of an expert panel*. Washington., D.C.: Interprofessional Education Collaborative.

Jacobs, S. C., Huprich, S. K., Cage, E., Elman, N. S., Forrest, L. Grus, C. L.,...Kaslow, N. J. (2011). Trainees with competence problems: Preparing trainers for difficult but necessary conversations. *Training and Education in Professional Psychology, 5*, 175–184. doi: 10.1037/a0024656

Johnson, W. B., Barnett, J. E., Elman, N. S., Forrest, L., &Kaslow, N. J. (2012). The competent community: Toward a vital reformulation of professional ethics. *American Psychologist, 67*, 557–569. doi: 10.1037/a0027206

Johnson, W. B., Elman, N. S., Forrest, L., Robiner, W. N., Rodolfa, E., &Schaffer, J. B. (2008). Addressing professional competence problems in trainees: Some ethical considerations. *Professional Psychology: Research and Practice, 39*, 589–599. doi:10.1037/a00114264

Johnson, W. B., Porter, K., Campbell, C. D., & Kupko, E. N. (2005). Character and fitness requirements for professional psychologists: An examination of state licensing application forms. *Professional Psychology: Research and Practice, 36*, 654–662. doi: 10.1037/0735-7028.36.6.654

Kaslow, N. J., Borden, K. A., Collins, F. L., Forrest, L., Illfelder-Kaye, J., Nelson, P. D.,...Willmuth, M. E. (2004). Competencies Conference: Future directions in education and credentialing in professional psychology. *Journal of Clinical Psychology, 80*, 669–712. doi: 10.1002/jclp.20016

Kaslow, N. J., Forrest, L., Elman, N., Grus, C., &Baker, J. (2010). *State of the art in recognizing, assessing, and intervening with students with competence problems*. Symposium presented at the annual meeting of the Association of Psychology Postdoctoral and Internship Centers, Orlando, FL.

Kaslow, N. J., Grus, C. L., Campbell, L. F., Fouad, N. A., Hatcher, R. L., &Rodolfa, E. (2009). Competency assessment toolkit for professional psychology. *Training and Education in Professional Psychology,3*,S27–S45. doi: 10.1037/a0015833

Kaslow, N. J., Rubin, N. J., Bebeau, M. J., Leigh, I. W., Lichtenberg, J. W., Nelson, P. D.,...Smith, I. L. (2007a). Guiding principles and recommendations for the assessment of competence. *Professional Psychology: Research and Practice, 38*, 441–451. doi: 10.1037/0735-7028.38.5.441

Kaslow, N. J., Rubin, N. J., Forrest, L., Elman, N. S., Van Horne, B. A., Jacobs, S. C.,...Thorn, B. E. (2007b). Recognizing, assessing, and intervening with problems of professional competence. *Professional Psychology: Research and Practice, 38*, 479–492. doi:10.1037/0735-7028.38.5.479

Keeton v. Anderson-Wiley, 664 F.3d 865 (11th Cir. 2011).

Lamb, D. H. (1999). Addressing impairment and its relationship to professional boundary issues; A response to Forrest, Elman, Gizara, and Vacha-Haase. *The Counseling Psychologist, 27*, 702–711. doi: 10.1177/0011000099275004

Lamb, D. H., Cochran, D. J., &Jackson, V. R. (1991). Training in organizational issues associated with identifying and responding to intern impairment. *Professional Psychology: Research and Practice, 22*, 291–296. doi: 10.1037/0735-7028.22.4.291

Lamb, D. H., Presser, N. R., Pfost, K. S., Baum, M. C., Jackson, V. R., &Jarvis, P. A. (1987). Confronting professional impairment during the internship: Identification, due process, and remediation. *Professional Psychology: Research and Practice, 18*, 597–603. doi: 10.1037/0735-7028.18.6.597

Lichtenberg, J., Portnoy, S., Bebeau, M., Leigh, I. W., Nelson, P. D., Rubin, N. J.,…Kaslow, N. J. (2007). Challenges to the assessment of competence and competencies. *Professional Psychology: Research and Practice, 38*, 474–478. doi: 10.1037/0735-7028.38.5.474

McAdams, C., & Foster, V. (2007). A guide to just and fair remediation of counseling students with professional performance deficiencies. *Counselor Education and Supervision, 46*, 2–13. doi: 10.1002/j.1556-6978.2007.tb00034.x

McAdams, C., Foster, V., &Ward, T. (2007). Remediation and dismissal policies in counselor education: Lessons learned from a challenge in federal court. *Counselor Education and Supervision, 46*, 212–229. doi: 10.1002/j.1556-6978.2007.tb00026.x

McCutcheon, S. (2008). Addressing problems of insufficient competence during the internship year. *Training and Education in Professional Psychology, 2*, 210–214. doi: 10.1037/a0013535

Mearns, J., &Allen, G. J. (1991). Graduate students' experiences in dealing with impaired peers, compared with faculty predictions: An exploratory study. *Ethics and Behavior, 1*, 191–202. doi:10.1207/s15327019eb0103_3

Miller, R., &Van Rybroek, G. (1988): Internship letters of recommendation: Where are the other 90%? *Professional Psychology: Research and Practice, 19*, 115–117. doi: 10.1037/0735-7028.19.1.115

Oliver, M. N. I., Bernstein, J. H., Anderson, K. G., Blashfield, R. K., &Roberts, M. C. (2004). An exploratory examination of student attitudes toward "impaired" peers in clinical psychology training programs. *Professional Psychology: Research and Practice, 35*, 141–147. doi:10.1037/0735-7028.35.2.141

Papadakis, M. A., Hodgson, C. S., Teherani, A., &Kohatsu, N. D. (2004). Unprofessional behavior in medical school is associated with subsequent disciplinary action by a state medical board. *Academic Medicine, 79*, 244–249. doi: 10.1097/00001888-200403000-00011

Papadakis, M. A., Teherani, A., Banach, M. A., Knettler, T. R., Rattner, S. L., Stern, D. T., & Hodgson, C. S. (2005). Disciplinary action by medical boards and prior behavior in medical school. *New England Journal of Medicine, 353*, 2673–2682. doi: 10.1056/NEJMsa052596

Pipes, R., Holstein, J., &Aguirre, M. (2005). Examining the personal-professional distinction: Ethics codes and the difficulty of drawing a boundary. *American Psychologist, 60*, 325–334. doi: 10.1037/0003-066N.60.4.325

Roberts, M. C., Borden, K. A., Christiansen, M. D., &Lopez, S. J. (2005). Fostering a culture shift: Assessment of competence in the education and careers of professional psychologists. *Professional Psychology: Research and Practice, 36*, 355–361. doi: 10.1037/0735-7028.36.4.355

Rosenberg, J. I., Getzelman, M. A., Arcinue, F., &Oren, C. Z. (2005). An exploratory look at students' experiences of problematic peers in academic professional psychology programs. *Professional Psychology: Research and Practice, 36*, 665–673. doi: 10.1037/0735-7028.36.6.665

Rubin, N. J., Bebeau, M., Leigh, I. W., Lichtenberg, J. W., Nelson, P. D., Portnoy, S.,…Kaslow, N., J. (2007). The competency movement within psychology: A historical perspective. *Professional Psychology: Research and Practice, 38*, 452–462. doi: 10.1037/0735-7028.38.5.452

Schoener, G. R.(1999). Practicing what we preach. *Counseling Psychologist, 27*, 693–701. doi: 10.1177/0011000099275003

Schwartz-Mette, R. A. (2009). Challenges in addressing graduate student impairment in academic professional psychology programs. *Ethics and Behavior, 19*, 91–102. doi:10.1080/10508420902768973

Schwartz-Mette, R. A. (2011). Out with impairment, in with professional competence problems: Response to commentary by Collins, Falender, and Shafranske. *Ethics and Behavior, 21*, 431–434. doi:10.1080/10508422.2011.604551

Shen-Miller, D., Forrest, L., &Burt, M. (2012). Contextual influences on faculty diversity conceptualizations when working with trainee competence problems. *Counseling Psychologist, 40*, 1181–1219. doi: 10.1177/0011000011431832

Shen-Miller, D. S., Forrest, L., &Elman, N. S. (2009). Training directors' conceptualizations of the intersection of diversity and trainee competence problems: A preliminary analysis. *Counseling Psychologist, 37*, 482–518. doi: 10.1177/0011000008316656

Shen-Miller, D. S., Grus, C. L., Van Sickle, K., Schwartz-Mette, R., Cage, E., Elman, N. S.,…Kaslow, N. J. (2011). Trainees' experiences with peers having competence problems: A national survey. *Training and Education in Professional Psychology, 5*, 112–121 doi: 10.1037/a0023824.

Smith, P. L., &Moss, S. B. (2009). Psychologist impairment: What is it, how can it be prevented, and what can be done to address it? *Clinical Psychology: Science and Practice, 16*, 1–15. doi: 10.1111/j.1468-2850.2009.01137.x

State of Arizona. (2011). House Bill 2565. Retrieved on July 21, 2013 fromwww.azleg.gov/legtext/50leg/1r/bills/hb2565h.pdf

Swann, C. (2003). *Students' perceptions of due process policies, procedures and Trainee problematic functioning.*(Unpublished doctoral dissertation). University of Pittsburgh, Pittsburgh, PA.

Vacha-Haase, T. (1995). *Impaired graduate students in APA-accredited clinical, counseling, and school psychology programs.*(Unpublished doctoral dissertation). Texas A & M University, College Station, Texas.

Vacha-Haase, T., Davenport, D. S., &Kerewsky, S. D. (2004). Problematic students: Gatekeeping practices of academic professional psychology programs. *Professional Psychology: Research and Practice, 35*, 115–122. doi: 10.1037/0735-7028.35.2.115

Vasquez, M. (1999). Trainee impairment: A response from a feminist/multicultural retired trainer. *The Counseling Psychologist, 27*, 687–692. doi:10.1177/0011000099275002

Veilleux, J. C., January, A. M., VanderVeen, J. W., Reddy, L. F., &Klonoff, E. A. (2012). Differentiating amongst characteristics associated with problems of professional compctence: Perceptions of graduate student peers. *Training and Education in Professional Psychology, 6,* 113–121. doi: 10.1037/a0028337

Veilleux, J. C., VanderVeen, J. W., Reddy, L. F., &January, A. M. (2010). Student perspectives on scientist-practitioner training and peers with problems in professional functioning: A CUDCP student report survey. Symposium presented at the annual meeting of the Council of University Directors of Clinical Psychology, Orlando, FL.

Ward v. Polite. (2012). 667 F. 3d 727.

Ward v. Wilbanks. (2010). No. 09-CV-112 37, 2010 U.S. Dist. WL 3026428 (E. D. Michigan, July 26, 2010).

Wester, S. R., Christianson, H. F., Fouad, N. A., &Santiago-Rivera, A. L. (2008). Information processing as problem solving: A collaborative approach to dealing with students exhibiting insufficient competence. *Training and Education in Professional Psychology, 2,* 193–201. doi: 10.1037/1931-3918.2.4.193

Ethics Issues in Training Students and Supervisees

Jeffrey E. Barnett *and* Ian D. Goncher

Abstract

Faculty members and clinical supervisors (trainers) play an important role in the professional development of their students and supervisees (trainees). In addition to offering education and clinical training to promote competent practice in their trainees, trainers have the opportunity to influence and guide the development of trainees into ethical professionals. This chapter addresses ways trainers should interact with trainees and how a focus on ethical practice is integrated into all training experiences through didactic instruction, informal discussions, and the modeling of ethical conduct in their relationships. Important issues addressed include creating a culture of ethics; promoting ethics acculturation; emphasizing and modeling a focus on self-care, balance, and wellness; the role of informed consent; how boundaries and multiple relationships may effectively be navigated; promoting integrity in research and publishing; establishing and maintaining clinical competence; and how to effectively work through ethical dilemmas and challenges. Recommendations for trainers are provided in each of these areas as they pertain to clinical practice, education, research, and supervision, and are addressed across the developmental continuum for trainees from graduate students to externs, to interns, to post-doctoral fellows.

Key Words: training, ethics, ethical practice, teaching, supervision, research

Those who train future psychologists have a significant responsibility to help trainees develop into ethical professionals. In doing so, there are many issues they must address through formal coursework and other didactic presentations, in clinical supervision, through discussions such as in mentoring relationships, and through the modeling of ethical behavior both in relationships with trainees and in all other relationships trainees may observe.

This chapter reviews psychology trainers' ethical obligations under the American Psychological Association's (APA) Ethical Principles of Psychologists and Code of Conduct (APA Ethics Code; APA, 2010a) and offers strategies for applying the Ethics Code to the process and context of training. Developing a culture of ethics for trainees is emphasized and includes a focus on ethics

acculturation and the use of a decision-making process or model when faced with ethical dilemmas and challenges. Methods for promoting ethical decision making, conduct, and practice for graduate students, externs, interns, and post-doctoral fellows is described, with particular attention devoted to the different training needs of these future psychologists at each stage of their professional growth and development.

In addressing a preventive approach to ethical conduct, the roles of self-care, psychological wellness, balance within and between one's professional and personal lives, and the roles of consultation, supervision, and personal psychotherapy are addressed. These issues are of vital importance since many of the habits and practices that will last throughout their careers will be established in trainees during these critical training periods. Further, the potential impact of failure to adequately address these issues on both trainees and on those to whom they provide professional services accentuates the importance of developing these vital habits early in trainees' professional development.

A number of additional issues are then discussed that emphasize how ethical challenges and dilemmas may be effectively addressed in the many roles and settings in which psychologists and trainees function. These include the academic setting, clinical settings, clinical supervision, research, and others. The authors provide recommendations regarding how to address crucial issues such as informed consent, competence, boundaries and multiple relationships, and academic and scientific integrity.

Trainers, Training, and Ethics

Those who train graduate students, faculty members, and clinical supervisors (hereafter referred to as *trainers*) play a significant role in the development of future professional psychologists. Although trainers play key roles in the formal education and clinical preparation of students and supervisees (hereafter referred to as *trainees*), their roles go far beyond sharing didactic information. Of paramount importance to their more formal or "official" roles as trainers, they also serve as role models, demonstrating in their day-to-day interactions with trainees, as well as with others, what it means to be a professional psychologist. Trainers play major roles in guiding trainees' acculturation into the profession of psychology, helping each to form a professional identity as a psychologist. In their day-to-day interactions with trainees, trainers display how professional psychologists conduct themselves, interact with others, provide professional services, approach and respond to challenging situations, and work through ethical dilemmas.

These interactions take place in the classroom and in clinical supervision sessions, in advising sessions, through informal mentoring, and in many other informal encounters. Although students may not idolize their trainers, they often hold them up as role models who they respect and emulate. Thus it is essential that trainers become cognizant of these less formal but equally important roles; hopefully, trainers will approach each role in a thoughtful and premeditated manner, making the most of opportunities to positively influence their trainees' professional development.

Examples of these opportunities are addressed in detail in this chapter along with salient avenues for creating a culture of ethical and caring professionalism. Some of these avenues include demonstrating respect for others in all their interactions, honoring diversity in these interactions, demonstrating an awareness of the areas and limits of their competence, displaying a commitment to and passion for ongoing professional development and lifelong learning, managing and negotiating boundary issues and multiple relationships, demonstrating respect for confidentiality, working to promote each trainee's autonomous professional functioning, and demonstrating a commitment to their own self-care and psychological wellness.

The General Principles of the APA Ethics Code (APA, 2010a) provide excellent guidance that may be incorporated into developing a strong foundation of ethical conduct and practice by academic faculty and clinical supervisors. As many authors have emphasized (e.g., Beauchamp & Childress, 2009; Kitchener, 2000; Knapp & VandeCreek, 2006), these underlying values of the profession of psychology, while not enforceable standards, provide psychologists with ethical goals to aspire to in all their professional roles and interactions with others. Thus professional psychologists will endeavor, in all their actions and interactions, to promote the best interests of those with whom they interact and to take steps to minimize all risks of exploitation and harm (Principle A: Beneficence and Nonmaleficence); to fulfill all obligations they have to others and to work to promote the ethical compliance of their colleagues (Principle B: Fidelity and Responsibility); to conduct themselves with honesty and integrity in all their professional interactions (Principle C: Integrity); to treat others fairly, act competently, and minimize the effects of bias in their interactions with others (Principle D: Justice); and to demonstrate respect for and a valuing of individual differences and diversity in all its forms (Principle E: Respect for People's Rights and Dignity).

The APA Ethics Code (APA, 2010a) also emphasizes that it "provides a common set of principles and standards upon which psychologists build their professional and scientific work" (p. 1) and that the Ethics Code applies to all roles in which psychologists function and in all settings in which they serve. Of particular relevance to faculty members and clinical supervisors is the Ethics Code's statement that it "requires a personal commitment and lifelong effort to act ethically; to encourage ethical behavior by students, [and] supervisees..." (p. 1).

Training in Ethics and Training to Be Ethical

All graduate programs in professional psychology include a focus on training in ethics as an essential component of each graduate student's curriculum (APA, 2009). Additionally, attention to ethics is integrated into a wide range of classes where ethics issues and dilemmas are found to be relevant. Examples include courses in psychological assessment, psychotherapy, diversity, and research. Ethical issues also should be integrated into the content and process of clinical supervision. Further, a focus on ethical practice is integrated into the training of interns and post-doctoral fellows. Indeed, at each stage of training and professional development, training in ethics is essential.

Beyond this didactic attention to ethics issues in the profession and practice of psychology, trainers have the opportunity to communicate to trainees the fundamental nature of ethics for psychologists in varied roles and settings by integrating a focus on ethics into all aspects of training and by actively seeking opportunities for teachable moments in interactions with trainees. In doing so, it is hoped that trainers will demonstrate, through their actions as well as words, how to be ethical in all they do.

These efforts will be based on the underlying ethical principles addressed earlier and will hopefully promote the development of what Kitchener (2000) describes as *virtuous character*, instilling moral virtues in each student's and trainee's being. This goal is consistent with Jordan and Meara's (1990) *virtue ethics* approach that emphasizes the consideration of the question *Who shall I be?* rather than a more rule-based approach to ethics that instead emphasizes the answer to the question *What shall I do?* Further, this approach to inculcating an ethically virtuous approach in trainees is consistent with what Handelsman, Knapp, and Gottlieb (2009) describe as *positive*, or *active*, ethics. This approach seeks not merely to meet minimal expectations, but rather to aspire to the highest ethical ideals of the profession; what Beauchamp and Childress (2009) refer to as *moral excellence*. Positive, or active, ethics sets a direction to work toward, with an emphasis on working to achieve the highest ideals of the profession, while encouraging the integration of personal values and ideals into professional roles and activities (Knapp & VandeCreek, 2006). Trainers hopefully will display this approach in all they do, and strongly promote and encourage this approach in their trainees.

Of additional relevance to this approach is Handelsman, Gottlieb, and Knapp's (2005) concept of *ethics acculturation*. These authors emphasize the importance of integrating one's personal values and ethics with the values and ethics of the profession. Those who rely solely on their own personal values and ethics may—in spite of good intentions and genuine compassion—end up harming clients due to violations of professional ethics standards. For example, a trainee who is very caring and compassionate toward others may begin a friendship with an isolated and depressed client that eventually results in boundary violations that are harmful to the client and that violate ethical standards. Alternatively, those who rely solely on the ethics of the profession in the absence of personal values and an attitude of caring may be at risk of following ethical standards mechanistically, meeting "the letter of the law," yet possibly overlooking the larger context of ethical practice. For example, a trainee who is singularly focused on strict compliance with the APA Ethics Code (APA, 2010a) may assiduously avoid all boundary crossings, such as never engaging in any touch or self-disclosure with clients, resulting in a potentially sterile clinical relationship and even inadvertent harm to a grieving client.

Ethics acculturation seeks an integration of personal and professional ethics and values. Trainers are positioned uniquely to play key roles in the process of guiding, assisting, and supporting trainees in the process of ethics acculturation. As Jordan and Meara (1990) so clearly state:

> People socialize one another into a professional culture that they continually construct and shape and from which they seek inspiration and support. As time passes, certain shared assumptions and values are "taken for granted" and form the character of the profession and are part of the individual characters of the professionals. (p. 110)

Ethical Decision Making

Psychology professionals and professionals-in-training may find it relatively straightforward to know what course of action to take in situations that present clearly ethical and unethical alternatives. Yet quite often psychologists and psychologists-in-training are confronted with ethical dilemmas—situations in which there appears to be no clearly appropriate or inappropriate course of action. At these times, reliance solely on the APA Ethics Code (APA, 2010a) for answers may prove insufficient and a process of ethical decision making will often be needed (Barnett & Johnson, 2008). The APA Ethics Code (APA, 2010a) makes it clear in its Introduction and Applicability section that the code cannot provide answers, or even specific guidance, for every situation a psychologist or trainee may face. Instead, the Ethics Code is described as one resource to be utilized as part of each individual's process of ethical decision making. In addition to seeking guidance from the Ethics Code when confronted with an ethical dilemma, psychologists and trainees should also consider laws and regulations germane to the situation, relevant practice guidelines, and applicable site-specific policies, along with seeking professional consultation, while applying a decision-making process. Additionally, consistent with ethics acculturation, the Ethics Code emphasizes that this decision-making process is applied by each individual in a manner that that also incorporates consideration of "the dictates of their own conscience" (p. 1).

A number of formal ethical decision-making models are available for use by psychologists and by those they educate and train. Barnett and Johnson (2008) provide a 10-step process that may be helpful for navigating a wide range of ethical dilemmas. These steps include: define the situation clearly; determine who will be impacted; refer to the ethical principles and standards; refer to relevant laws, regulations, and professional guidelines; reflect honestly on personal feelings and competence; consult with trusted colleagues; formulate alternative courses of action; consider possible outcomes for all parties involved; consult with colleagues and ethics committees; and make a decision, monitor the outcome, and modify your plan as needed. Other decision-making models have been developed for use in specific situations such as Younggren and Gottlieb's (2004) decision-making model for addressing multiple relationship dilemmas. Their model includes a number of factors to consider when faced with these dilemmas. It also poses a number of questions individuals should ask themselves when considering entering a multiple relationship. Regardless of the particular model used, we recommend that trainers actively include the use of an ethical decision-making process with their trainees whenever either of them is confronted by ethical challenges or dilemmas.

It is imperative that trainers not take on the role of ethics expert—that is, one who provides the definitive answer when an ethically ambiguous or challenging situation arises. Rather, it is hoped that trainers will provide guidance and support, actively engaging their trainees in a collaborative and thoughtful process of ethical decision making.

This approach is consistent with the goal of promoting each trainee's autonomous functioning as ethical professionals over time. Assisting trainees to develop such an approach to ethics also is consistent with the ethics acculturation approach that is so important to professional growth and development.

Creating a Culture of Ethics and Ethical Practice

In addition to providing expert instruction in ethics and ethical practice, educators and clinical supervisors have the opportunity to create a culture of ethical practice within their training programs. Doing so will model for trainees how to apply—in their day-to-day activities—what they learn in the classroom and in supervision sessions. Further, it is hoped by "walking the walk," trainers will have the greatest possible impact on their trainees' ethics acculturation and professional development.

Unfortunately, research suggests that there is much work to be done in terms of professional psychologists' modeling ethical behavior. As Kitchener (1992) stated "silence best characterizes the discussion of the ethical responsibilities of faculty members toward students in higher education in general and psychology education in particular" (p. 190). This observation is alarming because substandard ethical practices of faculty members and clinical supervisors may lead to the development of problems with professional competence in trainees. Rest (1994) argued that individuals choose to act morally because others have modeled moral action. Therefore, it is possible for the reverse of this to be true. de las Fuentes, Willmuth, and Yarrow (2005) emphasize this point and suggest that information gleaned from didactic instruction may be contradicted by trainer behavior modeled outside the classroom. Thus there are many informal teaching moments outside the classroom and supervision session that can impact trainees' development for better or worse. Knapp and VandeCreek (2006) refer to these informal training experiences as "implicit" or "underground" curricula that "refer to the institutional atmosphere within the program" (p. 216). To provide truly comprehensive training in the practice and application of ethical concepts, the training environment in which it occurs or "hidden curriculum" must actively and positively impact and influence trainees' ethical decision making. de las Fuentes and colleagues (2005) suggest that beyond classroom instruction a comprehensive ethics training program should include:

A living self-reflective application of ethical principles in the training environment demonstrated and modeled for trainees in order for it to become an enduring part of their professional identity...and training that focuses not only on the therapeutic environment but also on the social and cultural contexts within which training occurs. (p. 363)

The requirement of formal training in ethics in clinical psychology training (APA, 1979) highlights its importance. Yet classroom training is insufficient to achieve its goals. As training programs work to provide the most comprehensive education regarding ethical practice to the next generation of professional psychologists, it is imperative that the promotion of ethical conduct move beyond the classroom and that trainers promote a culture of ethics through the active modeling of ethical conduct representative of the highest ethical ideals of our profession.

Modeling Self-Care and Wellness

The tenets of social learning theory (Bandura, 1977) provide a rationale for professional psychologists to model ethical behavior. Social learning theory describes the modeling process that takes place as individuals vicariously learn through senior members of an organization (Manz & Sims, 1981). Mentors serve as the veteran models of behavior for their trainees and provide trainees with the rules and strategies that govern effective behavior in the organization (Dreher & Ash, 1990; Zagumny, 1993). Mentoring can be an essential part of graduate education in that it cultivates professional development and socialization to one's profession (Zhao, Golde, & McCormick, 2007). There is little doubt that the majority of professional psychologists endeavor to conduct themselves in a manner congruent with a moral and virtuous character. These professional psychologists provide an excellent model of striving to move beyond the minimal requirements of ethical practice and join explicit instruction on ethics with the implicit obligation to provide ethics training through personal example. However, research has identified several areas where improvement among trainers is needed. One such problematic area is interference in professional functioning. Lamb and colleagues (1987) asserted that interference in one's professional functioning can be manifested through:

(a) an inability and/or unwillingness to acquire and integrate professional standards into one's repertoire of professional behavior; (b) an inability to acquire

professional skills to reach an acceptable level of competency; (c) an inability to control personal stress, psychological dysfunction and/or excessive emotional reactions that interfere with professional functioning. (p. 598)

Interference in professional functioning can manifest for many professional and personal reasons. Many times the nature of their work predisposes psychologists to levels of stress that, if left unchecked, can have deleterious consequences on their ability to ethically perform their professional obligations (Baker, 2003). Psychologists can work long hours, feel isolated from colleagues, regularly deal with crises and emergencies, have many difficult clients with chronic conditions, and/or have clients that display suicidal or homicidal behavior. Psychologists can develop compassion fatigue and/or burnout due to routine work with very difficult populations that often demonstrate little progress. Further, psychologists can be affected by managed care constraints, increased red tape and paperwork, and poor reimbursements for services (e.g., Pope, Sonne, & Greene, 2006).

Additionally, psychologists are impacted by their personal lives. Personal stressors can include relationship difficulties, death in the family, divorce, physical illness or legal problems for self or family members, and financial problems (DeAngelis, 2002). Each of these factors may impact psychologists, both in their own right and through interactions with the many professional challenges and stressors faced by psychologists. In a national study of psychologists, Guy, Poelstra, and Stark (1989) found nearly 75% of the psychologists surveyed reported experiencing significant distress over the previous three years. More than one third of this group further reported an awareness of a reduction in quality of client care as a result and 5% reported that the treatment they provided was "inadequate" as a result of their distress. Studies suggest that psychologists experience significant problems with depression, relationship difficulties, alcohol abuse problems, and suicide (Deutsch, 1985; Gilroy, Carroll, & Murra, 2002; Good, Thoreson, & Shaughnessy, 1995; Pope & Tabachnick, 1994). Pope and Vasquez (2007) stated that psychologists experiencing interference in professional functioning may begin "disrespecting clients; disrespecting work; making more mistakes; lacking energy; using work to block out happiness, pain, and discontent; and losing interest" (p. 50). Henceforth, professional psychologists that experience significant distress and subsequent interference in professional functioning may fail to provide exemplary models of both clinical competence and ethical conduct. Coster and Schwebel (1997) discuss the goal of "well-functioning," which refers to continuing excellence in one's functioning over time as a professional, including when faced with job-related and personal stress.

Given the alarming rate at which psychologists experience professional and personal difficulties, trainers have an ethical obligation not only to provide didactic instruction but more importantly to model appropriate strategies that facilitate well-functioning and create a culture of ethical conduct within training programs. Over the past 30 years, there has been a considerable increase in programmatic requirements of formal ethics training (Wilson & Ranft, 1993) and requirements for continuing education in ethics training (APA, 2003a). Vasquez (1988) stated that training programs have a responsibility to provide a safe and positive environment for psychology trainees to explore themselves and the ethical issues inherent in the profession.

In addition to these didactic requirements, several models have emerged that emphasize the necessity of integrating an ethics acculturation component within graduate training. Within their ethics acculturation model, Handelsman, Gottlieb, and Knapp (2005) assert that psychology "represents a discrete culture with its own traditions, values, and methods of implementing its ethical principles" (p. 59). As such, they emphasize experiential learning within this cultural context as an integral component of ethics training. Handelsman and colleagues (2005) include an experiential learning component that involves a total immersion into the culture of psychology to adequately learn its traditions, values, and language. This concept is important in that it underscores the importance for trainers to serve as ethical role models. When students enter training programs, faculty and supervisors must be aware that they are setting the example of how professional psychologists should conduct themselves in the classroom, in clinical practice, and in the community. Kitchener (1992) provides specific responsibilities and recommendations for trainers in providing comprehensive ethics instruction. These suggestions emphasize modeling as a primary instructional tool to create a positive ethical environment for graduate trainees. As Kitchener (1992) states:

If they [psychology faculty members] expect students to exhibit a caring attitude toward those with whom

they work, then one of the attitudes that faculty need to model in teaching and mentoring is that of caring, which includes caring about the students. (p. 193)

In addition to the above suggestions, trainers should incorporate and actively model self-care. While the first five virtues that form the foundation of the General Principles of the APA Ethics Code focus on behavior by mental health professionals toward those they serve, the sixth virtue, Self-Care, focuses on the behavior of mental health professionals toward themselves. Principle A of the APA Ethics Code, Beneficence and Nonmaleficence (APA, 2010a), states: "Psychologists strive to be aware of the possible effect of their own physical and mental health on their ability to help those with whom they work" (p. 3). Further, Standard 2.06, Personal Problems and Conflicts, states:

(a) Psychologists refrain from initiating an activity when they know or should know that there is a substantial likelihood that their personal problems will prevent them from performing their work-related activities in a competent manner.

(b) When psychologists become aware of personal problems that may interfere with their performing work-related duties adequately, they take appropriate measures, such as obtaining professional consultation or assistance, and determine whether they should limit, suspend, or terminate their work-related duties. (p. 5)

All professional psychologists should model an active engagement in a continuous program of self-care (APA, 2010c; Baker, 2003; Barnett, Johnston, & Hillard, 2006; Barnett & Cooper, 2009; Norcross & Guy, 2007; Smith & Moss, 2009). Psychologists must demonstrate to trainees that self-care is not an indulgence, but an essential component in the prevention of distress and diminished professional functioning (Gizara & Forrest, 2004). Without adequate attention to self-care, all clinicians and eventually their trainees and clients will be negatively affected.

Psychologists can model self-care by engaging in positive, career-sustaining behaviors, seeking professional assistance, and balancing their professional and personal lives. They may provide implicit instruction by taking regular breaks during the workday; scheduling a variety of clients; participating in peer consultation or support groups; taking vacations; getting adequate exercise, diet, and rest; scheduling time for personal activities and time with family and friends; practicing meditation and other types of relaxation techniques; journaling; participating in hobbies; being involved in civic or professional organizations; and attending to their religious or spiritual side (Barnett, Eiblum, & Blair, 2003). Further, in a survey of 595 psychologists, Rupert and Kent (2007) found that maintaining a sense of humor, maintaining self-awareness/self-monitoring, maintaining a balance between one's personal and professional lives, maintaining one's professional identity/values, engaging in hobbies, and spending time with one's spouse, partner, or family were identified as the most important self-care strategies utilized by respondents.

Establishing strong mentoring relationships and professional role modeling is considered fundamental to achieving a culture of ethical training and self-care within the profession of psychology; these relationships play an essential role in the career development of professional psychologists (Mintz, Bartels, & Rideout, 1995). As Barnett and Cooper (2009) state, this is an endeavor that largely "falls on the shoulders of...training programs, clinical supervisors, and mentors" (p. 18), and it must be an active effort, not something left to chance.

Personal Psychotherapy

The programmatic requirement of personal psychotherapy during training requires special consideration due to its controversial nature within the profession. Although personal psychotherapy has been shown to provide personal and professional benefits for psychologists, including improvements in self-esteem, work functioning, social life, emotional expression, characterologic conflicts, and symptom severity (Orlinsky & Rønnestad, 2005), many graduate training programs do not actively encourage the use of personal psychotherapy by their students (Schwebel & Coster, 1998). Often programs recommend personal psychotherapy strictly for the purpose of performance remediation (Huprich & Rudd, 2004; Vacha-Haase, Davenport, & Kerewsky, 2004). When trainees lack faculty role models that encourage personal psychotherapy, they may minimize the potential value of psychotherapy for practitioners. Poor role modeling in this area also may foster the impression that personal psychotherapy is reserved solely for the remediation of serious psychopathology and not to promote wellness. Dearing, Maddux, and Tangney (2005) suggest that trainees are more likely to seek personal psychotherapy when faculty model positive attitudes toward the utilization of personal therapy as an appropriate

self-care strategy rather than merely as a remediation for problematic behavior.

The requirement of personal psychotherapy can be fraught with ethical concerns, and trainers should therefore give special attention to their ethical responsibilities in this area. The APA Ethics Committee (1987) provided six guidelines to assist programs and educators in addressing this issue. These guidelines include using appropriate informed consent procedures at the outset of treatment, avoidance of inappropriate multiple relationships, providing choice of psychotherapist for the trainee that recognizes cultural diversity, the use of only qualified providers, clarifying the limits of confidentiality with respect to the program, and making certain that there are financially feasible alternatives so that psychotherapy does not create undue economic hardships for trainees. Ethical concerns regarding trainee use of personal psychotherapy have been addressed in the APA Ethics Code (APA, 2010a) in Standards 7.04 (Student Disclosure of Personal Information) and 7.05 (Mandatory Individual or Group Therapy). Standard 7.04 states:

> Psychologists do not require students or supervisees to disclose personal information...except (1) if the program...has clearly identified this requirement in its admissions and program materials or (2) the information is necessary to evaluate or obtain assistance for students whose personal problems could reasonably be judged to be preventing them from performing their training or professionally related activities in a competent manner or posing a threat to the students or others. (p. 10)

Additionally, Standard 7.05 states that when psychotherapy is a mandated aspect of training students have "the option of selecting such therapy from practitioners unaffiliated with the program" and that "faculty who are likely to be responsible for evaluating students' academic performance do not themselves provide that therapy" (p. 10). These standards serve to minimize the potentially negative effects on trainees participating in personal therapy and maximize the benefits of said therapy in reaction to or prevention of personal distress and interference in professional functioning.

Is Personal Therapy an Ethical Imperative?

Regardless of whether personal psychotherapy is a mandated program requirement, the use of personal psychotherapy has been considered a potential ethical imperative for professional psychologists and trainees (Barnett & Goncher, 2008). The APA Ethics Code (APA, 2010a) requires psychologists to "undertake ongoing efforts to develop and maintain their competence" (p. 5) and to "take reasonable steps to avoid harming their clients/patients...and to minimize harm where it is foreseeable" (p. 6). Further, as has been highlighted, Standard 2.06, Personal Problems and Conflicts, requires that psychologists take appropriate measures, to include seeking assistance, when personal issues may impact their competence or effectiveness.

Therefore, it may follow that participation in personal psychotherapy may serve as one useful means for promoting ongoing competence and clinical effectiveness in addition to other stress management and self-care activities. The APA Ethics Code requires that each psychologist work toward the highest ideals of competence in their professional roles and activities. As Norcross (2005) recommends, training programs should recommend personal psychotherapy for their students, integrate its role into training, and develop low-cost resources for their students to increase the availability of accessible personal psychotherapy. It is also recommended that, as trainers create a culture of ethical awareness and ethical practice, they will demonstrate to students that personal psychotherapy is an invaluable aspect of each psychologist's lifelong professional development process.

Informed Consent in Education and Training

When psychologists begin any type of professional relationship, be it research, treatment, assessment, supervision, consultation, teaching, and/or other professional roles, they are both ethically and legally obligated to initiate the process of informed consent at the outset of each professional encounter (APA, 2010a Knapp & VandeCreek, 2006). According to Barnett, Wise, Johnson-Greene, and Bucky (2007) informed consent:

> is a shared decision-making process in which the professional communicates sufficient information to the other individual so that she or he may make an informed decision about participation in the professional relationship. (p. 179)

Within this definition is the fundamental concept that to respect the autonomy of the individual, psychologists must provide each individual all information necessary to allow for an adequate estimation of the risks and benefits that may potentially affect them during the course of the relationship. Although rooted in the ethical principle of Autonomy, informed consent incorporates all the ethical principles. For example, the principles of Fidelity and Beneficence and Non-Malfeasance are implicit in the informed consent process as to be adequately informed requires that all information be accurate to avoid the possibility of damaging the professional relationship and risking detriment to participant's functioning and future interactions with mental health providers. Kitchener (2000) states that informed consent:

> 1) allows individuals to make critical decisions about their own lives and ensures participation is voluntary 2) helps to protect consumers from harm by allowing them to evaluate the potential for a treatment, research procedure, or educational experience to affect them in negative ways, thus helping psychologists to avoid situations in which they might harm the consumer 3) can help build the trust and respect between the consumer and the professional. (p. 58)

Informed Consent in Teaching and Supervision

The informed consent process brings with it many important ethical considerations regarding providing instruction and supervision within the graduate training environment. Consistent with the ethical standards regarding informed consent in psychotherapy, research, and assessment, the APA Ethics Code (APA, 2010a) stipulates that educators also should provide accurate information to ensure that trainees are able to make informed decisions regarding participation in training programs, specific classes, and supervision (through course catalogs, syllabi, verbal discussions, and supervision contracts). Specifically, Standard 7.01, Design of Education and Training Programs, states that educational programs must take reasonable steps to ensure that they provide experiences that are deemed essential to obtain the credentials advertised by the programs. Additionally, graduate programs (Standard 7.02, Descriptions of Education and Training) and individual classes, (Standard 7.03, Accuracy in Teaching), must be described accurately. Further, Standard 7.05a, Mandatory Individual or Group Therapy, states that students should be informed beforehand if there are specific requirements for mandatory participation in personal or group psychotherapy. It is also important to keep in mind that these Ethics Code standards are applicable at all levels of training and in all settings. This includes the classroom and clinical settings, from graduate school and internship through post-doctoral fellowships. Although professional psychologists are ethically mandated to provide accurate information regarding program specifics, this process has only recently been described as informed consent (Remley & Herlihy, 2007). Trainers must remain sensitive to the fact that, as trainees make decisions about entering training programs, courses, and clinical rotations, they encounter myriad risks, expectations, and power differences with trainers. Much like clients and research participants, trainees should participate in ongoing informed consent to minimize harm and maximize educational benefits (Kitchener, 2000).

As with teaching, it is the ethical responsibility of each supervisor to ensure that appropriate informed consent occurs at the outset of the supervisory relationship to provide information that affords each supervisee the ability to make an informed decision about whether to participate in the relationship (Bernard & Goodyear, 2004). During the informed consent process, supervisors should provide information on the specifics of supervision to include the responsibilities of each party, available resources, pay or fee schedules, and emergency procedures. Further, informed consent should cover the importance of confidentiality, limits of confidentiality, the process of handling disagreements, termination procedures, evaluation criteria and timing, goal development, the role of theoretical orientation in the supervisory process, and rescheduling procedures (Barnett, Wise, Johnson-Greene, & Bucky, 2007). Informed consent should be ongoing throughout the supervisory process to facilitate the development of the supervisory relationship and to prevent areas of ambiguity that could potentially lead to harm for both the supervisee and the clients she or he serves. Additionally, it is important that trainers openly address the informed consent process with trainees, working to ensure that it is a collaborative process. In addition to respecting the needs and rights of the trainee, trainers should be thoughtful about what they model and its potential impact on how these future psychologists will handle informed consent with those to whom they provide professional services throughout their careers.

Further, professional psychologists should be mindful of using the Internet or social media to gather information about the individuals to whom they provide services. The exception to this recommendation is in instances in which gathering online information could prevent potential harm to the person or someone else, and therefore trumps informed consent policy (Kaslow, Patterson, & Gottlieb, 2011). For example, Kaslow and colleagues stated that in situations where patient information may need to be acquired quickly (i.e., psychiatric emergency room, inpatient unit) electronic information could be searched to prevent potential harm to the client, staff, or other patients on the unit. Although it is not illegal or considered a direct ethics violation, undisclosed Internet searches do not promote the autonomy of the client, student, and supervisee; each individual should have the expectation that they alone will determine what information to divulge in the context of a professional relationship (Kaslow et al., 2011). Kaslow and colleagues (2011) suggest that "policies regarding Internet searches of clients, trainees, students, and employees should be made clear at the outset through written contracts, informed consent forms, agency policies, and verbal statements and/or documents" (p. 110).

The process of informed consent sets the tone for each professional relationship; it helps ensure that ethical behavior frames each professional interaction. In addition to the aforementioned examples, the use of appropriate informed consent procedures assist professional psychologists in promoting and modeling professional integrity, ensuring appropriate boundaries and relationships, effectively evaluating trainee competence, and guiding the process of gate keeping in professional psychology.

Promoting Academic Integrity

As role models and in their day-to-day activities, trainers have a significant impact on the creation of an environment of academic integrity. Additionally, institutional and departmental policies on academic integrity will be important in creating an environment in which each faculty member's actions occur. Many graduate programs have a student honor code that each student is required to agree to at the outset of the educational experience. Such codes establish basic expectations for honesty, responsibility, and integrity. Relevant issues addressed include creating one's own work products without outside assistance unless specifically authorized to do so, to give appropriate credit to others for their work and to not claim others' work as one's own, to treat others with dignity and respect, to take responsibility for one's own actions, and others.

Faculty members play a vital role in the promotion of an environment of academic integrity by exhibiting these behaviors themselves and by having open discussions with students about their expectations for academic integrity in which they stress its importance. Further, faculty members must take personal responsibility for helping to promote academic integrity, contributing to a culture of ethics in the academic setting rather simply relying on existing rules and policies (Keller, Murray, & Hargrove, 2012). For example, in addition to teaching students how to avoid plagiarism, when reading students' written work, faculty members must take adequate time and give sufficient attention to identifying signs of plagiarism.

These responsibilities place trainers in the challenging position of needing to confront trainees about apparent unethical behavior and perhaps take punitive actions. While perhaps uncomfortable, ignoring unethical behavior likely will prove to be a pernicious form of role modeling inconsistent with faculty members' ethical obligations. For example, Principle C of the APA Ethics Code, Integrity (APA, 2010a), states that "Psychologists seek to promote accuracy, honesty, and truthfulness in the science, teaching, and practice of psychology" (p. 3).

Publication Credit

Supervising trainees' research endeavors and offering them opportunities to work together on research and writing projects are critical professional development opportunities that may be offered by mentors. In addition to being valuable learning experiences for trainees, they may also provide busy trainers with great assistance in meeting obligations for research productivity that may impact the senior person's career advancement and stature within the profession. There may therefore be an inherent conflict of interest in these situations that should be managed with great care and thoughtfulness.

Standard 8.12 of the APA Ethics Code, Publication Credit (APA, 2010a), makes it clear that authorship credit and order should be assigned based on each participant's relative contributions to the project and should not be based solely on seniority. Trainers will need to ensure that authorship credit issues are openly discussed at the initiation of a project and addressed as an informed consent issue with each participant's agreed upon roles and responsibilities specified, and the order of authorship clarified in advance (Fine & Kurdek, 1993). But merely receiving a trainee's agreement regarding work responsibilities and authorship order does not necessarily guarantee ethical practice. Trainees may be vulnerable to the trainers' influence, they may agree to inappropriate arrangements in order to be listed

as an author on a publication, and they may not know their rights in these situations. Trainers are responsible to ensure that each trainee collaborator's rights and best interests are safeguarded and that no exploitative outcomes occur.

Fine and Kurdek (1993) suggest that all authorship agreements be made based on each participant's substantive contributions to the project. The relative value of each type of contribution should be clarified and agreed to in advance so that each individual has realistic expectations about the role and value of their intended contributions. While such discussions and agreements are of great importance, some flexibility will be needed because at times certain participants may do more or less than was originally agreed. In these situations, the authorship order may need to be modified accordingly.

The APA Ethics Code's Standard 8.12, Publication Credit (APA, 2010a), also makes it clear that "except under exceptional circumstances, a student is listed as principal author on any multiple-authored article that is substantially based on the student's doctoral dissertation" (p. 11). Further, consistent with the guidance provided above, this standard requires that "faculty advisors discuss publication credit with students as early as feasible and throughout the research and publication process as appropriate" (p. 11). This standard highlights both the need to ensure that trainee research collaborators receive credit appropriate to their level of contributions to the project and to ensure that publication credit and authorship order be discussed openly from the outset and throughout the project based on changing circumstances.

Plagiarism

Standard 8.11 of the APA Ethics Code, Plagiarism (APA, 2010a) states, quite clearly and succinctly that all those bound by the APA Ethics Code "do not present portions of another's work or data as their own, even if the other work or data source is cited occasionally" (p. 11). This is an essential element of academic integrity, and trainers must play a key role in promoting this integrity through instruction of trainees about plagiarism and how to avoid it as well as through effective role modeling. Educational efforts, role modeling, and effective oversight will likely be helpful in reducing intentional plagiarism.

Yet the prevention of plagiarism should not be seen solely as an academic integrity issue as those committed to ethics and integrity will naturally not intentionally engage in plagiarism. Additional efforts may be needed to help prevent unintentional plagiarism, which may be unconscious (Perfect & Stark, 2008) or inadvertent (McCabe, Smith, & Parks, 2007). Trainees should be instructed on the nuances of plagiarism and guided in how to prevent it. Each trainee should become familiar with the standards included in the *Publication Manual of the American Psychological Association* (APA, 2010b), and its elements should be integrated into ongoing coursework.

Role modeling by trainers also plays a key role in the prevention of plagiarism by avoiding self-plagiarism. Even if it is one's own work that is being used in a publication, if it has been previously published, it must be appropriately cited, giving credit to the original publication. Trainers also may provide trainees with active oversight of their written work, perhaps using online technologies such as Turnitin (turnitin.com) among others. But, ultimately, it will be the active ongoing efforts of trainers to educate and sensitize trainees to these issues while providing sufficient oversight of trainee's scholarly work that will be crucial for decreasing the incidence of plagiarism and facilitating what Keller, Murray, and Hargrove (2012) describe as an ethical academic culture.

Boundary Issues and Multiple Relationships in Education and Training

Faculty members and clinical supervisors are each provided with opportunities to educate, train, and model for trainees what it means to be a professional psychologist. Essential to how psychologists conduct themselves in their professional roles is an understanding of boundaries and multiple relationships. These issues are most frequently addressed didactically in graduate course work on professional ethics. Trainers should additionally integrate these topics into assessment and psychotherapy. For interns and post-doctoral fellows who are functioning with ever-increasing independence and autonomy, it is essential that boundary issues and multiple relationships be discussed openly in clinical supervision and addressed in seminars and other didactic presentations throughout training. For example, McIlwraith and colleagues (2005) stress the importance of including "boundary issues/sexual dilemmas, ethics and professional issues,...in weekly professional issues seminars" held throughout the internship and fellowship year (p. 167). Further, as trainees progress toward independent practice, trainers should help them develop increasing sophistication in understanding and addressing these issues both through these seminars and clinical supervision experiences (Castonguay, 2000).

Ethics instruction that focuses on boundary issues and multiple relationships should not present these topics dogmatically or from a rules-based approach. Trainers should highlight the many nuances in professional relationships and encourage the use of a decision-making process when considering boundaries and multiple relationships (e.g., Younggren & Gottlieb, 2004). Rather than merely lectures and having students read articles on the topic, training should include an experiential component through which students will have the opportunity to apply decision-making models to a broad range of challenging situations and dilemmas. Knowing that trainees learn from both what they are taught and what they observe and experience, it is essential that trainers model the appropriate and thoughtful application of boundaries and multiple relationships in their day-to-day interactions with all those with whom they interact in the training environment. Supervisors can openly discuss how boundaries can change in real time with their trainees, yet simultaneously model appropriate boundary management as trainees move closer to being colleagues in their progression from graduate extern to intern to post-doctoral fellow.

Boundaries in the Academic Setting and in Clinical Supervision

Boundaries are described as the ground rules of the professional relationship that provide it with needed structure and which communicate acceptable and unacceptable roles and behaviors to all parties involved (Gutheil & Gabbard, 1993: Smith & Fitzpatrick, 1995). Boundaries in professional relationships include touch, self-disclosure, personal space, location, time, fees, gifts, and other elements. Boundaries may be rigidly observed (e.g., never sharing anything about oneself with others), they may be crossed (e.g., disclosing information about the trainer's personal background with a trainee), and they may be violated (e.g., confiding in a supervisee, sharing intimate information about conflicts in one's personal relationships).

As is often highlighted in the professional literature (e.g., Barnett, Lazarus, Vasquez, Moorehead-Slaughter, & Johnson, 2007), a *boundary crossing* may be ethically appropriate, consistent with professional roles, and not likely to result in exploitation or harm. In contrast, a *boundary violation*, by definition, is unethical, unacceptable, inconsistent with professional roles, and likely to result in exploitation and harm. Yet, simply avoiding all boundaries will not be a viable approach as they are ever-present in professional relationships and at times, to avoid crossing a boundary may result in harm (Lazarus & Zur, 2002). Trainers will have numerous opportunities to educate trainees by openly discussing their decision-making process when considering transgressing boundaries. This thoughtful approach will be important to trainees who will face many boundary dilemmas throughout their careers.

Through didactic presentations in academic coursework, discussions in advising and supervision sessions, and the modeling that occurs in academic and clinical settings, trainees learn about appropriate boundary crossings and inappropriate boundary violations. These discussions and exemplars of the appropriate navigation of boundaries will have a significant impact on how individuals manage and address boundaries throughout their careers.

Similarly, clinical supervisors are in a unique position to sensitize trainees to boundary issues, both between trainer and trainee and between trainee and clients. Clinical supervisors can take the initiative to actively promote discussions of boundary issues with their supervisees. Supervisors can model appropriate boundary crossings in the supervision session such as with appropriate and relevant self-disclosure, followed by open discussion with the supervisee about the crossing, the thought process that preceded it, factors considered, and its impact on the supervisee. Additionally, supervisors and can provide supervisees with guidance on how to navigate boundaries with their clients. Examples of boundaries that trainees will need to successfully navigate include:

• How much personal information to share with clients and how to respond to client requests for information about the trainee;
• How and when touch may appropriately be used with clients and when it is contraindicated;
• When meeting with clients outside the treatment room may be appropriate and how to do this appropriately; and
• When it is appropriate to extend the time spent with clients.

Supervisors will assist their trainees most by promoting a thoughtful decision-making process in each of these situations rather than providing trainees with specific recommended courses of action whenever trainees are faced with these situations. Relevant factors that can be considered by the trainee and discussed in supervision sessions prior to crossing such boundaries will include the trainee's motivations for crossing these boundaries, the client's mental health history and treatment needs,

how individual differences and client diversity factors may impact how the trainee's actions may be interpreted by the client, options and alternatives available to the trainee psychotherapist and their relative risks and benefits, how the client may be impacted by the boundary crossing as well as by not crossing the boundary, how the trainee's theoretical orientation may impact the decision, and the trainee's comfort with the anticipated actions. Supervisors can also ensure the open discussion of these factors during supervision sessions when processing potential boundary crossings by the supervisor with the supervisee, again modeling a thoughtful approach to considering boundaries.

Pope, Sonne, and Greene (2006) provide an excellent illustrative example of how clinical supervisors can cultivate a supervisory environment in which trainees are actively encouraged to self-disclose feelings such as attraction to clients that, if not openly discussed and addressed in supervision, might possibly result in the trainee engaging in boundary violations to include inappropriate and harmful multiple relationships. The creation of a safe and trusting environment in supervision that encourages and supports such disclosures and discussions, normalizing such feelings and assisting the trainee to work through any confusion, shame, or impulses experienced, will likely prove helpful for the client in question and potentially for many of the trainee's future clients as well (Barnett, Erickson Cornish, Goodyear, & Lichtenberg, 2007; Worthen & McNeill, 1996).

An additional challenge frequently faced in clinical supervision is the boundary between the clinical supervision relationship and a psychotherapy relationship (Bernard & Goodyear, 2004). Depending on one's theoretical orientation, it may be quite common for a supervisee's countertransference reactions to clients to become one focus of supervision sessions. This exploration may at times bring to light issues and conflicts experienced by the trainee. As trainees become more aware of their conflicts and develop more insight into their reactions to clients, they are likely to become more effective psychotherapists. Yet supervisors must guard against providing psychotherapy to supervisees. Role awareness is essential in these situations and when indicated, recommendations and referrals for individual psychotherapy for the trainee should be made.

Multiple Relationships in the Academic Setting and in Clinical Supervision

Multiple relationships occur when faculty members and clinical supervisors enter into a secondary relationship with a student or supervisee beyond the primary educator-student or supervisor-supervisee relationship or when they enter into an educational or supervisory relationship with an individual with whom they have a previous relationship. Due to the imbalance of power in these relationships secondary to the trainer's evaluative authority over the trainee, great care must be taken to ensure that the trainee's dependency and trust are not exploited. Yet, as is stated in Standard 3.05 of the APA Ethics Code, Multiple Relationships (APA, 2010a), not all multiple relationships are inappropriate. Only those multiple relationships that hold a reasonable likelihood of leading to exploitation of, or harm to, the trainee through impairment of "the psychologist's objectivity, competence, or effectiveness in performing his or her functions" (p. 6) need to be avoided.

Modeling appropriate multiple relationships and promoting open discussions about multiple relationships are important roles for trainers in promoting trainee professional development. Doctoral, internship, and postdoctoral training in professional psychology frequently involves trainers and trainees working closely for long hours over extended periods of time. The emotional closeness and intensity possible in these circumstances provide the opportunity for trainers to model appropriate boundary management and the avoidance of entering into inappropriate multiple relationships.

Most training programs have policies in place that emphasize that intimate relationships between faculty members/supervisors and students/supervisees over whom they have evaluative authority are inappropriate. Additionally, Standard 7.07 of the APA Ethics Code, Sexual Relationships With Students and Supervisees (APA, 2010a), states that "Psychologists do not engage in sexual relationships with students or supervisees who are in their department, agency, or training center or over whom psychologists have or are likely to have evaluative authority" (p. 10). Additionally, Standards 3.05 (Multiple Relationships), 3.08 (Exploitative Relationships), 3.06 (Conflicts of Interest), and 3.04 (Avoiding Harm) remain relevant to considerations of other types of multiple relationships with students and supervisees to include social, business, or other relationships that might impact the faculty member's or supervisor's objectivity or judgment and which may lead to exploitation or harm to the student or supervisee.

More broadly, the potential impact of such multiple relationships on other trainees, and on the training environment in general, should not be overlooked when considering multiple relationships with students and supervisees. Trainers are advised to consider Ethical Principle D: Justice, which advises psychologists to provide others with "equal access to and benefit from" psychologists and the services they provide (APA, 2010a, p. 3). Providing selected trainees with differential or "special" treatment can jeopardize achieving the goals of justice within the academic environment. Additionally, when trainers' objectivity and judgment become impaired, they risk violating the obligations they have been entrusted with to promote the professional growth and development of all their students and supervisees (Jorgenson, Hirsch, & Wahl, 1997).

Faculty Roles and Relationships with Students

Graduate training in professional psychology, by its very nature, must include experiences outside the classroom. If faculty members interacted only with students in the classroom, this would likely create a very sterile environment, one that is not conducive to students' professional development and growth. In addition to being instructors of academic courses, faculty members may serve in the roles of academic advisor, dissertation committee chair and research mentor, supervisor of a graduate research assistant and a graduate teaching assistant, and members of the same university or department committee. Additionally, faculty members may provide students with opportunities to collaborate on research and writing projects and to present their work together at professional conferences, to serve as reviewers of journal article submissions, and to serve on professional association committees and task forces together. Further, faculty members may serve as mentors to their students in general, providing guidance on issues such as career planning and how to balance personal life with professional responsibilities (Johnson, 2006; 2007).

The above examples illustrate the many possible multiple roles possible in the faculty-student relationship. As Barnett and Yutrzenka (1995) emphasize, multiple roles within a primary relationship are not "multiple relationships." These multiple roles provide students with essential opportunities for training and professional development that are each compatible with the primary faculty-student relationship when implemented ethically and appropriately. While boundaries need to be appropriately managed within these multiple roles they need not constitute multiple relationships.

Graduate Assistants, Multiple Roles, and Multiple Relationships

In many academic settings, graduate students may serve in the important roles of graduate teaching and research assistants. Graduate students serving in these roles often provide assistance to faculty members while simultaneously receiving valuable experience relevant to their professional development. Yet adding the additional role of teaching assistant or research assistant to the primary role of graduate student brings with it a range of challenges and dilemmas. For example, the graduate assistant may be working in the lab of a faculty member who is also that student's instructor in a course. Further, the graduate assistant may supervise peers enrolled in classes with him or her, and may work together on class projects or engage in social activities with these peers. These multiple roles and multiple relationships may prove to be quite challenging for graduate assistants as well as for the faculty who supervise them.

Branstetter and Handelsman (2000) have found that graduate assistants frequently receive little to no training to prepare them for the complexities and challenges of these roles and, when in these roles, they often receive little if any direct supervision. Graduate students need to receive sufficient training to competently carry out their graduate assistant roles, learning such relevant skills as how to effectively convey coursework to students, how to evaluate students, and how to manage interactions and relationships with students. In fact, graduate students and the faculty members who supervise them need a thorough understanding of the nature of the multiple roles and relationships present and how to effectively navigate the challenges that often arise.

As Johnson and Nelson (1999) have highlighted, appropriate multiple relationships between educators and graduate students, such as having a student also function as a graduate teaching or research assistant, may serve several significant functions for students and provide them with valuable experiences and opportunities not otherwise available. These appropriate multiple relationships may be highly enriching for students and offer them opportunities for professional development and growth, for the development of leadership, teaching, research, and supervision skills, as well as the opportunity for mentoring and interactions outside of typical classroom experiences.

These additional interactions have the potential to be highly enriching for students and faculty members alike, yet they bring with them significant challenges. While they function more as colleagues in these roles, an imbalance of power still exists, and the graduate student is still reliant on the faculty member's evaluation of his or her performance and functioning. Despite the often collegial nature of these relationships and the intimacy and time often spent working collaboratively, it is essential that faculty members maintain appropriate professional boundaries and not take advantage of the graduate student's dependency and trust. Faculty members must keep in mind that they are serving as professional role models and that how they conduct themselves with graduate students is an important aspect of the training students receive on how professional psychologists conduct themselves. Further, should these relationships be managed inappropriately such that a sexual relationship develops between faculty member and student, these relationships are typically found by students to be "coercive, ethically problematic and a hindrance to the working relationship" (Hammel et al., 1996, p. 93). Further, they invariably result in harm to the student (Lamb & Catanzaro, 1998), they may have a highly deleterious effect on the academic environment in general (Lamb, Catanzaro, & Moorman, 2003), and they often correlate with similar behavior on the part of these students when later in roles of power and authority (Biaggio, Paget, & Chenoweth, 1997).

Similarly, graduate students are placed in positions of power, authority, and trust when serving as graduate teaching and research assistants. In these roles, graduate students teach courses, write exam questions, grade exams and assignments, and either influence or assign course grades (Branstetter & Handelsman, 2000). While serving in the role of "faculty," graduate students are nonetheless still students. As students, they may lack the sophistication and experience needed to fully understand their new role. They also may be ill equipped to manage the many multiple relationship situations they are placed in such as teaching and grading a classmate or friend. How graduate assistants manage these relationships is important for all parties involved. Clearly, graduate assistants need education about the role of graduate assistant prior to entering this role and they need ongoing supervision and oversight by faculty members. Institutional and departmental policies are needed to provide faculty and graduate assistants with guidance on appropriate and inappropriate roles and behaviors. But, beyond lists of rules, instruction in ethical decision making is essential to assist faculty members and graduate assistants in navigating the many challenging situations and dilemmas they are likely to face in these roles (Oberlander & Barnett, 2005).

Interns and Post-Doctoral Fellows

Interns and post-doctoral fellows are truly professionals-in-training. As such, they are provided with ever-increasing autonomy and independence. They often provide clinical supervision to trainees at lower levels of education and training (Nyman, Nafziger, & Smith, 2010). For example, it is quite common for post-doctoral fellows to provide clinical supervision to interns and for both fellows and interns to provide clinical supervision to graduate student externs. It is thus quite important that trainers adequately prepare interns and post-doctoral fellows for their supervisory roles and stress to them their role-modeling function for junior colleagues. Since many of those they supervise may be their contemporaries, interns and post-doctoral fellows will need clear guidance on boundaries and multiple relationships, learning how to appropriately balance the supervisory role with collegiality (Burian & Slimp, 2000).

Interns and post-doctoral fellows will find themselves in a unique position. While they are still in a training setting and still in the student role, they also function as trainers of their junior colleagues. Interns and post-doctoral fellows who provide clinical supervision to junior colleagues should receive supervision of the supervision they provide. Trainers must provide important feedback on how fellows and interns are managing boundaries in their supervisory relationships.

Competence Issues

One of the ultimate objectives of education and training is the development of each student's professional competence. Competence is described by Epstein and Hundert (2002) as "the habitual and judicious use of communication, knowledge, technical skills, clinical reasoning, emotions, values, and reflection in daily practice for the benefit of the individual and the community served" (p. 226). This definition highlights the role of ethics acculturation and a focus on ethical decision making in addition to the importance of developing the necessary knowledge and skills needed to effectively provide services to others. Consistent with Standard 7.01 of the APA Ethics Code, Design of Education and Training Programs (APA, 2010a), educators must ensure that training programs provide students with the knowledge and skills necessary for competent and effective functioning as professional

psychologists. Thus training programs are obligated to develop educational and training experiences to prepare students for ethical and competent practice and to prepare them for licensure as psychologists.

Additionally, faculty members must ensure that they present information to students accurately, something that requires competence on the part of educators. Decisions about which courses faculty members should teach should not be taken lightly. In addition to possessing the needed competence in teaching methodology and pedagogy, each instructor should be competent in the relevant content area. Training programs may at times experience difficulties finding appropriately trained faculty to teach scheduled courses. The demands placed on training programs from faculty sabbaticals and other absences, staff turnover, and unanticipated increases in student enrollment may challenge programs to find appropriately trained faculty to teach courses. Despite these pressures, psychologists should approach the decision to teach a course outside of one's main areas of competence with great caution. Standard 2.01 of the APA Ethics Code, Boundaries of Competence, (APA, 2010a), clarifies this need, emphasizing the importance of only teaching courses "in areas only within the boundaries of their competence, based on their education, training, supervised experience, consultation, study, or professional experience" (p. 5). Similarly, clinical supervisors must possess competence in the clinical areas to be supervised as well as in the practice of clinical supervision. In doing so, faculty members and clinical supervisors help to ensure that students and trainees are provided with the knowledge and skills needed for competent practice. Additionally, they are modeling for the next generation of educators, supervisors, clinicians, and researchers the importance of only providing services within their areas of competence.

Clinical supervisors are entrusted with decision making about which tasks supervisees may perform, which clients they are able to treat, and how much and what type of supervision is needed to ensure that clients' best interests are met. Initially, supervisors should assess each supervisee's competence prior to the supervisee providing clinical services. This initial assessment can be used to create an individualized program of training or any needed remediation, and for determining the type and intensity of clinical supervision indicated (Barnett, Erickson Cornish, Goodyear, & Lichtenberg, 2007). Standard 2.05 of the APA Ethics Code, Delegation of Work to Others (APA, 2010a), is of relevance to this responsibility, stating that supervisors delegate only those tasks that supervisees "can be expected to perform competently on the basis of their education, training, or experience…with the level of supervision provided" (p. 5) and that supervisors ensure that they provide the needed supervision to ensure that services are competently provided. Supervisors also must provide ongoing evaluation of and feedback to supervisees and based on ongoing assessment of each supervisee's training needs. Similarly, faculty members working with graduate assistants must delegate to their graduate assistants only those tasks they are competent to perform.

To be truly competent, psychologists must attend to issues of diversity and multiculturalism in every professional role. Principles D and F of the APA Ethics Code (APA, 2010a) assert that psychologists must acquire knowledge of differences in the beliefs and practices of individuals of diverse backgrounds and incorporate how those beliefs and practices will potentially affect the provision of professional services. Psychologists must be cognizant that they are uniquely situated to promote equality and social justice by gaining an understanding the impact of each individual's ethnic and racial heritage, gender, age, sexual orientation, disability, religion/spiritual orientation, educational attainment/experiences, and socioeconomic status (Comas-Díaz, 2000). Therefore it is ethically imperative that psychologists engage in ongoing education and training in issues of diversity and multiculturalism to enhance the quality of their education, training, practice, and research activities. The *APA Guidelines on Multicultural Education, Training, Research, Practice, and Organizational Change for Psychologists* provides excellent information regarding the knowledge and skills needed to adequately address issues of multiculturalism in the professional practice of psychology (APA, 2003b) and should be a part of every student's education and training.

Evaluation of Competence

Each faculty member and clinical supervisor has an obligation to provide timely and relevant feedback to trainees. Standard 7.06 of the APA Ethics Code, Assessing Student and Supervisee Performance (APA, 2010a), requires that trainers "establish a timely and specific process for providing feedback to students and supervisees" (p. 10) and that relevant information about these processes be shared as part of the initial informed consent process and in the course syllabus. Each psychologist serving in a training role should provide a meaningful

evaluation process. This includes ensuring that trainees are evaluated "on the basis of their actual performance on relevant and established program requirements" (APA, 2010a, p. 10), that trainees are provided with constructive feedback, that they are given sufficient time to respond to the feedback provided (i.e., not providing feedback solely on the last day of a training experience), and that trainees receive the support and assistance needed to pursue remediation when indicated.

Because diminished emotional functioning, events in one's personal life, and related issues may impact trainees' competence, trainers may need to inquire about such issues when competence concerns arise. Consistent with Standard 7.04 of the APA Ethics Code, Student Disclosures of Personal Information (APA, 2010a), students and trainees may be required to share personal information when concerns exist about their competence and when "the information is necessary to evaluate or obtain assistance for students whose personal problems could reasonably be judged to be preventing them from performing…in a competent manner" (p. 10).

Gate Keepers of the Profession

In addition to working to assist and support students and trainees in their ongoing professional growth and development, educators and clinical supervisors serve the important function as gatekeepers of the profession, determining who possesses the needed competencies and attributes to function as a professional psychologist. As Kitchener (1992) states, "There is a specific ethical obligation not to graduate those who because of their incompetence or lack of ethical sensitivity would inflict harm on the consumers whom they have agreed to help" (p. 190). Thus while it is necessary to provide each trainee with the best possible training and supervision, sharing feedback and offering opportunities for remediation when needed, there are times when a trainee is not suitable for entrance into the profession.

Some trainees may not be able to develop the knowledge, skills, and attitudes (i.e., competence) needed for ethical and effective practice. Others may demonstrate over time that they do not possess the needed values, temperament, personality, or interpersonal attributes to function effectively in the profession. As Johnson and colleagues (2008) emphasize, "evidence of competence problems cannot ethically be ignored or avoided" (p. 590). These issues must be attended to regardless of the discomfort one may feel in addressing such issues with trainees and regardless of any pressure trainers may feel such as the need to achieve certain graduation/completion rates, maintain a certain level of enrollment, or to otherwise demonstrate the success of their training program.

Johnson and colleagues (2008) also emphasize the importance of understanding that the gatekeeping function of trainers is consistent with Standard 3.04 of the APA Ethics Code, Avoiding Harm (APA, 2010a), and that to fulfill this obligation each faculty member and clinical supervisor needs to be sensitized to this obligation. Further, faculty members and supervisors must be "competent to detect problems with competence in trainees and to deliver appropriate and useful feedback; provide training in the art of delivering difficult corrective feedback" (p. 591). Also, it is essential that administrators provide trainers with the needed support to ensure that they are able to effectively fulfill these obligations.

These issues will also be relevant when trainers are asked by students to write letters of recommendation on their behalf. It is important to understand that these letters may be a key element of the trainer's gatekeeper function. Trainers are often sensitive to the competitive nature of internships, post-doctoral fellowships, and other positions and they may therefore be inclined to assist trainees in obtaining these positions by writing the strongest letters possible. Yet it is important that trainers be honest when writing such letters. Failure to include negative information and concerns about a trainee in a letter of recommendation may represent a failure on the letter writer's part to meet his or her ethical responsibilities.

Several options potential letter writers can consider include discussing concerns with the student in advance of writing the letter, sharing a draft of the letter with the student and offering the student the opportunity to use the letter or not, or declining to write a letter for a student when concerns exist. Trainers should always consider their overarching obligations to the profession and to those to be served by the profession in the future. Ultimately, we encourage trainers to consider these obligations to the profession and to society, to provide the trainee with constructive feedback, and to write accurate letters that emphasizes both strengths and areas in need of growth. When significant concerns about the trainee's suitability for entrance into the profession exist, they should be clearly stated in the letter.

Concluding Remarks

Throughout this chapter, we have emphasized the essential qualities and skills required of professional psychologists to adequately address ethics issues within graduate training in professional psychology. We hope the information provided will serve to guide both the individual psychologist and training programs to create an ethical culture regarding professional practice, research, education, training, and supervision. More research is needed to continue to clarify the many potential applications of ethical decision making and implications of developing a culture of ethics. However, we believe that through open discussion with trainees, active training, and appropriate modeling of ethical conduct, trainers can do much to promote sound ethical decision making and ethical practice in their trainees. This preparation should form the basis of trainees' professional identity and conduct for years to come.

References

American Psychological Association (1979). *Criteria for accreditation of doctoral training programs and internships in professional psychology.* Washington, DC: Author.

American Psychological Association. (1987). *1986 report of the Ethics Committee.* Washington, DC: Author.

American Psychological Association (2003a). *Results of State Provincial Mandatory Continuing Education in Psychology (MCEP) Requirements Survey Results.* Available at: http://www.apa.org/ce/mcesurvey03.html

American Psychological Association. (2003b). Guidelines on multicultural education, training, research, practice, and organizational change for psychologists. *American Psychologist, 58,* 377–402.

American Psychological Association. (2009). *Guiding principles for accreditation of programs in professional psychology.* Available at: http://www.apa.org/ed/accreditation/about/policies/guiding-principles.pdf

American Psychological Association. (2010a). *Ethical principles of psychologists and code of conduct.* Available at: http://www.apa.org/ethics

American Psychological Association. (2010b). *Publication Manual of the American Psychological Association* (6th ed.). Washington, DC: American Psychological Association.

American Psychological Association. (2010c). *Survey findings emphasize the importance of self-care for psychologists.* Available at: http://www.apapracticecentral.org/update/2010/08-31/survey.aspx

Baker, E. K. (2003). *Caring for ourselves: A therapist's guide to personal and professional well-being.* Washington, DC: American Psychological Association.

Bandura, A. L. (1977). *Social learning theory.* Englewood Cliffs, NJ: Prentice Hall.

Barnett, J. E., & Cooper, N. (2009). Creating a culture of self-care. *Clinical Psychology: Science and Practice, 16,* 16–20. doi: 10.1111/j.1468-2850.2009.01138.x

Barnett, J. E., Eiblum, A., & Blair, A. (2003). Got self-care? *The Maryland Psychologist, 48*(4), 9, 11.

Barnett, J. E., Erickson Cornish, J. A., Goodyear, R. K., & Lichtenberg, J. W. (2007). Commentaries on the ethical and effective practice of clinical supervision. *Professional Psychology: Research and Practice*, 38, 268–275. doi: 10.1037/0735-7028.38.3.268

Barnett, J. E., & Goncher, I. (2008). Psychotherapy for the psychotherapist: Optional activity or ethical imperative? *Psychotherapy Bulletin*, 43, 36–40.

Barnett, J. E., & Johnson, W. B. (2008). *Ethics desk reference for psychologists*. Washington, DC: American Psychological Association.

Barnett, J. E., Johnston, L. C., & Hillard, D. (2006). Psychotherapist wellness as an ethical imperative. In L. VandeCreek & J. B. Allen (Eds.), *Innovations in clinical practice: Focus on health and wellness* (pp. 257–271). Sarasota, FL: Professional Resources Press.

Barnett, J. E., Lazarus, A. A., Vasquez, M. T., Moorehead-Slaughter, O., & Johnson, W. (2007). Boundary issues and multiple relationships: Fantasy and reality. *Professional Psychology: Research and Practice*, 38(4), 401–410. doi: 10.1037/0735-7028.38.4.401

Barnett, J. E., Wise, E. H., Johnson-Greene, D., Bucky, S. F. (2007). Informed consent: Too much of a good thing or not enough? *Professional Psychotherapy Research and Practice*, 38, 179–186. doi: 10.1037/0735-7028.38.2.179

Barnett, J. E., & Yutrzenka, B. A. (1995). Nonsexual dual relationships in professional practice, with special applications to rural and military communities. *The Independent Practitioner*, 14, 243–248.

Beauchamp, T. L., & Childress, J. F. (2009). *Principles of biomedical ethics* (6th ed.). New York: Oxford University Press.

Bernard, J. M., & Goodyear, R. K. (2004). *Fundamentals of clinical supervision* (3rd ed.). Boston, MA: Allyn & Bacon.

Biaggio, M., Paget, T. L., & Chenoweth, M. S. (1997). A model for ethical management of faculty-student dual relationships. *Professional Psychology: Research and Practice*, 28, 184–189. doi: 10.1037//0735-7028.28.2.184

Branstetter, S. A., & Handelsman, M. M. (2000). Graduate teaching assistants: Ethical training, beliefs, and practices. *Ethics & Behavior*, 10, 27–50. doi: 10.1207/S15327019EB1001_3

Burian, B. K., & Slimp, A. O. (2000). Social dual-role relationships during internship: A decision-making model. *Professional Psychology: Research and Practice*, 31, 332–338. doi: 10.1037//0735-7028.31.3.332

Castonguay, L. G. (2000). A common factors approach to psychotherapy training. *Journal of Psychotherapy Integration*, 10, 263–282. doi: 10.1023/A:1009496929012

Comas-Díaz, L. (2000). An ethnopolitical approach to working with People of Color. *American Psychologist*, 55, 1319–1325. doi: 10.1037//0003-066X.55.11.1319

Coster, J. S., & Schwebel, M. (1997). Well-functioning in professional psychologists. *Professional Psychology: Research and Practice*, 28, 5–13. doi: 10.1037/0735-7028.28.1.5

DeAngelis, T. (2002). *Normalizing practitioners' stress*. Available at: http://www.apa.org/monitor/julaug02/normalizing

Dearing, R. L., Maddux, J. E., & Tangney, J. P. (2005). Predictors of psychological help seeking in clinical and counseling psychology graduate students. *Professional Psychology: Research and Practice*, 36, 323–329.

de las Fuentes, C., Willmuth, M. E., & Yarrow, C. (2005). Competency training in ethics education and practice. *Professional Psychology: Research and Practice*, 36, 362–366. doi: 10.1037/0735-7028.36.4.362

Deutsch, C. J. (1985). A survey of therapists' personal problems and treatment. *Professional Psychology: Research and Practice*, 16, 305–315. doi: 10.1037//0735-7028.16.2.305

Dreher, G. F., & Ash, R. A. (1990). A comparative study of mentoring among men and women in managerial, professional, and technical positions. *Journal of Applied Psychology*, 75, 539–546. doi: 10.1037//0021-9010.75.5.539

Epstein, R. M., & Hundert, E. M. (2002). Defining and assessing professional competence. *Journal of the American Medical Association*, 287, 226–235. doi: 10.1001/jama.287.2.226

Fine, M. A., & Kurdek, L. A. (1993). Reflections on determining authorship credit and authorship order on faculty-student collaborations. *American Psychologist*, 48, 1141–1147. doi: 10.1037/0003-066X.48.11.1141

Gilroy, P. J., Carroll, L., & Murra, J. (2002). A preliminary survey of counseling psychologists' personal experiences with depression and treatment. *Professional Psychology: Research and Practice*, 33, 402–407. doi: 10.1037//0735-7028.33.4.402

Gizara, S. S., & Forrest, L. (2004). Supervisors' experiences of trainee impairment and incompetence at APA-accredited internship sites. *Professional Psychology: Research and Practice*, 35, 131–140. doi: 10.1037/0735-7028.35.2.131

Good, G. E., Thoreson, R. W., & Shaughnessy, P. (1995). Substance use, confrontation of impaired colleagues, and psychological functioning among counseling psychologists: A national survey. *The Counseling Psychologist*, 23, 703–721. doi: 10.1177/0011000095234010

Gutheil T. G., & Gabbard G. O. (1993). The concept of boundaries in clinical practice: theoretical and risk management dimension. *American Journal of Psychiatry*, 150, 188–196.

Guy, J. D., Poelstra, P. L., & Stark, M. J. (1989). Professional distress and therapeutic effectiveness: National survey of psychologists practicing psychotherapy. *Professional Psychology: Research and Practice*, 20, 48–50. doi: 10.1037//0735-7028.20.1.48

Hammel, G. A., Olkin, R., & Taube, D. A. (1996). Student-educator sex in clinical and counseling psychology doctoral training. *Professional Psychology: Research and Practice*, 27, 93–97. doi: 10.1037//0735-7028.27.1.93

Handelsman, M. M., Gottlieb, M. C., & Knapp, S. (2005). Training ethical psychologists: An acculturation model. *Professional Psychology: Research and Practice*, 36, 59–65. doi: 10.1037/0735-7028.36.1.59

Handelsman, M. M., Knapp, S., & Gottlieb, M. C. (2009). Positive ethics: Themes and variations. In C. R. Snyder & S. J. Lopez (Eds.), *Oxford handbook of positive psychology* (2nd ed., pp. 105–113). New York: Oxford University Press.

Huprich, S. K., & Rudd, M. D. (2004). A national survey of trainee impairment in clinical, counseling, and school psychology doctoral programs and internships. *Journal of Clinical Psychology*, 60, 43–52. doi: 10.1002/jclp.10233

Johnson, W. B. (2006). *On being a mentor: A guide for higher education faculty*. Mahwah, NJ: Erlbaum.

Johnson, W. B. (2007). Transformational supervision: When supervisors mentor. *Professional Psychology: Research and Practice*, 38, 259–267. doi: 10.1037/0735-7028.38.3.259

Johnson, W. B., Elman, N. S., Forrest, L., Robiner, W. N., Rodolfa, E., & Schaffer, J. B. (2008). Addressing professional competence problems in trainees: Some ethical considerations. *Professional Psychology: Research and Practice*, 39, 589–599. doi: 10.1037/a0014264

Johnson, W. B., & Nelson, N. (1999). Mentor-protégé relationships in graduate training: Some ethical concerns. *Ethics & Behavior*, 9, 189–210. doi: 10.1207/s15327019eb0903_1

Jordan, A. E., & Meara, N. M. (1990). Ethics and the professional practice of psychologists: The role of virtues and principles. *Professional Psychology: Research and Practice*, 21, 107–114. doi: 10.1037//0735-7028.21.2.107

Jorgenson, L. M., Hirsch, A. B., & Wahl, K. M. (1997). Fiduciary duty and boundaries: Acting in the client's best interest. *Behavioral Sciences and the Law*, 15, 49–62. doi: 10.1002/(SICI)1099-0798(199724)15:1<49::AID-BSL253> 3.0.CO;2-X

Kaslow, F.W., Patterson, T., & Gottlieb, M. (2011). Ethical dilemmas in psychologists accessing internet data: Is it justified? *Professional Psychology, Research & Practice*, 42, 105–112. doi: 10.1037/a0022002

Keller, P. A., Murray, J. D., & Hargrove, D. S. (2012). Creating ethical academic cultures within psychology programs. In S. J. Knapp, M. C. Gottlieb, M. M. Handelsman, & L. D. VandeCreek (Eds.), *APA handbook of ethics in psychology, Volume 2: Practice, teaching, and research* (pp. 219–260). Washington, DC: American Psychological Association.

Kitchener, K. S. (2000). *Foundations of ethical practice, research, and teaching in psychology*. Mahwah, NJ: Lawrence Erlbaum Associates.

Kitchener, K. S. (1992). Psychologist as teacher and mentor: Affirming ethical values throughout the curriculum. *Professional Psychology: Research and Practice*, 23, 190–195. doi: 10.1037//0735-7028.23.3.190

Knapp, S. J., & VandeCreek, L. D. (2006). *Practical ethics for psychologists: A positive approach*. Washington, DC: American Psychological Association.

Lamb, D. H., & Catanzaro, S. J. (1998). Sexual and nonsexual boundary violations involving psychologists, clients, supervisees, and students: Implications for professional practice. *Professional Psychology: Research and Practice*, 29, 498–503. doi: 10.1037//0735-7028.29.5.498

Lamb, D. H., Catanzaro, S. J., & Moorman, A. S. (2003). Psychologists reflect on their sexual relationships with clients, supervisees, and students: Occurrence, impact, rationales, and collegial intervention. *Professional Psychology: Research and Practice*, 34, 102–107. doi: 10.1037//0735-7028.34.1.102

Lamb, D. H., Presser, N. R., Pfost, K. S., Baum, M. C., Jackson, V. R., & Jarvis, P. A. (1987). Confronting professional impairment during the internship: Identification, due process, and remediation. *Professional Psychology: Research and Practice*, 18, 597–603.

Lazarus, A. A., & Zur, O. (Eds.), (2002). *Dual relationships and psychotherapy*. New York: Springer.

Manz, C., & Sims, H. P., Jr. (1981). Vicarious learning: The influences of modeling on organizational behavior. *Academy of Management Review*, 6, 105–113. doi: 10.2307/257144

McCabe, D. P., Smith, A. D., & Parks, C. M. (2007). Inadvertent plagiarism in younger and older adults: the role of working memory capacity in reducing memory errors. *Memory and Cognition*, 35, 231–241. doi: 10.3758/BF03193444

McIlwraith, R. D., Dyck, K. G., Holms, V. L., Carlson, T. E., & Prober, N. G. (2005). Manitoba's rural and northern community-based training program for psychology interns and residents. *Professional Psychology: Research and Practice*, 36, 164–172. doi: 10.1037/0735-7028.36.2.164

Mintz, L. B., Bartels, K. M., & Rideout, C. A. (1995). Training in counseling ethnic minorities and race-based availability of graduate school resources. *Professional Psychology: Research and Practice*, 26, 316–321. doi: 10.1037//0735-7028.26.3.316

Nyman, S. J., Nafziger, M. A., & Smith, T. B. (2010). Client outcomes across counselor training level within a multitiered supervision model. *Journal of Counseling & Development*, 88, 204–209. doi: 10.1002/j.1556-6678.2010.tb00010.x

Norcross, J. C., & Guy, J. D., Jr. (2007). *Leaving it at the office: A guide to psychotherapist self-care*. New York, NY: Guilford Press.

Norcross, J. C. (2005). The psychotherapist's own psychotherapy: Educating and developing psychologists. *American Psychologist*, 60, 840–850. doi: 10.1037/0003-066X.60.8.840

Oberlander, S. E., & Barnett, J. E. (2005). Multiple relationships between graduate assistants and students: Ethical and practical considerations. *Ethics & Behavior*, 15, 49–63. doi: 10.1207/s15327019eb1501_4

Orlinsky, D. E., & Rønnestad, M. H. (2005). *How psychotherapists develop: A study of therapeutic work and professional growth*. Washington, DC: American Psychological Association.

Perfect, T. J., & Stark, L. J. (2008). Why do I always have the best ideas? The role of idea quality in unconscious plagiarism. *Memory (Hove, England)*, 16, 386–394. doi: 10.1080/09658210801946501

Pope, K. S., Sonne, J. L., & Greene, B. (2006). *What therapists don't talk about and why: Understanding taboos that hurt us and our clients*. Washington, DC: American Psychological Association.

Pope, K. S., & Tabachnick, B. G. (1994). Therapists as patients: A national survey of psychologists' experiences, problems, and beliefs. *Professional Psychology: Research and Practice*, 25, 247–258. doi: 10.1037//0735-7028.25.3.247

Pope, K.S., & Vasquez, M.J.T (2007). *Ethics in psychotherapy and counseling: A practical guide* (3rd ed.). San Francisco, CA: Jossey-Bass.

Remley, T. P., & Herlihy, B. (2007). *Ethical, legal, and professional issues in counseling* (2nd ed.). Upper Saddle River, NJ: Prentice Hall.

Rest, J. R. (1994). Background: Theory and research. In J. R. Rest & D. Narvaez (Eds.), *Moral development in the professions: Psychology and applied ethics* (pp. 1–26). Hillsdale, NJ: Erlbaum.

Rupert, P. A., & Kent, J. S. (2007). Gender and work setting differences in career-sustaining behaviors and burnout among professional psychologists. *Professional Psychology: Research and Practice*, 38, 88–96. doi: 10.1037/0735-7028.38.1.88

Schwebel, M., & Coster, J. (1998) Well-functioning in professional psychologists: As program heads see it. *Professional Psychology: Research and Practice*, 29, 284–292. doi: 10.1037//0735-7028.29.3.284

Smith, D., & Fitzpatrick, M. (1995). Patient-therapist boundary issues: An integrative review of theory and research. *Professional Psychology: Research and Practice*, 26, 499–506. doi: 10.1037//0735-7028.26.5.499

Smith, P. L., & Moss, S. B. (2009). Psychologist impairment: What is it, how can it be prevented, and what can be done to address it? *Clinical Psychology: Science and Practice*, 16, 1–15. doi: 10.1111/j.1468-2850.2009.01137.x

Vacha-Haase, T., Davenport, D. S., & Kerewsky, S. D. (2004). Problematic students: Gatekeeping practices of academic professional psychology programs. *Professional Psychology:*

Research and Practice, 35, 115–122. doi: 10.1037/ 0735-7028. 35.2.115

Vasquez, M. (1988). Counselor-client sexual contact: Implications for ethics training. *Journal of Counseling and Development, 67*, 238–241. doi: 10.1002/j.1556-6676.1988.tb02590.x

Wilson, L. S., & Ranft, V. A. (1993). The state of ethical training for counseling psychology doctoral students. *The Counseling Psychologist, 21*, 445–456. doi: 10.1177/ 0011000093213009

Worthen, V., & McNeill, B. W. (1996). A phenomenological investigation of "good" supervision events. *Journal of Counseling Psychology, 43*, 25–34. doi: 10.1037//0022-0167.43.1.25

Younggren, J. N., & Gottlieb, M. C. (2004). Managing risk when contemplating multiple relationships. *Professional Psychology: Research and Practice, 35*, 255–260. doi: 10.1037/ 0735-7028.35.3.255

Zagumny, M. J. (1993). Mentoring as a tool for change: A social learning perspective. *Organizational Development Journal, 11*, 43–48.

Zhao, C-M., Golde, C. M., & McCormick, A. C. (2007). More than a signature: How advisor choice and advisor behavior affect doctoral student satisfaction. *Journal of Further and Higher Education, 31*, 263–281. doi: 10.1080/ 03098770701424983

Remedial and Disciplinary Interventions in Graduate Psychology Training Programs: 25 Essential Questions for Faculty and Supervisors

Stephen H. Behnke

Abstract

This chapter provides responses to 25 commonly asked questions regarding disciplinary and remedial interventions in graduate psychology training programs. The questions are designed to provide a framework and a process for programs responding to a trainee who is not fulfilling program expectations. The chapter distinguishes between interventions that are intended to terminate a trainee from the program and interventions that are designed to remediate a problem in competence. The chapter identifies ways to intervene that may both help programs minimize their exposure to legal liability and simultaneously respect and protect the interests of the trainees involved. The chapter begins with an overview of confidentiality in the context of psychology training as a prelude to discussions regarding liability. The chapter also addresses how FERPA, HIPAA, and the ADA apply in remedial and disciplinary processes.

Key Words: ADA, ethics, discipline, HIPAA, FERPA, law, liability, remediation, supervision, termination, training

Initiating a formal process to intervene in the progress of a trainee[1] through a graduate psychology training program, internship, or postdoctoral residency can be stressful for the individuals directly involved and for the training program as a whole. At times, the purpose of an intervention may be to address a specific area of competence in which a trainee is falling short; the intervention is designed to assist the trainee in enhancing his or her competence and moving toward successfully completing the program. At other times, the purpose of the intervention may be to terminate the trainee from the program without an attempt at remediation.

In this chapter, I refer to interventions designed to assist a trainee to enhance competence and move toward graduation as *remedial*, whereas interventions designed to terminate a trainee are referred to as *disciplinary*. Although there is some overlap between remedial and disciplinary proceedings defined in this way, there is an important distinction between interventions that are intended to assist a trainee through the program and interventions that are intended to end a trainee's participation in the program. In the chapter, I examine legal and ethical aspects of remedial and disciplinary interventions in graduate psychology training programs,[2] as well as topics that closely relate to these interventions about which training faculty and supervisors should be aware.

The 25 questions in the chapter arise from concerns that faculty and supervisors have raised in seeking legal and ethical consultations. The responses are designed to highlight general principles. The goal of the chapter is thus not to answer each question in detail, but rather to provide a framework that will help faculty and supervisors meet their goals when they initiate a formal process of intervention or encounter an issue that raises the possibility of an intervention. It is my hope that after reading this chapter, faculty and supervisors in graduate psychology training programs, internships, and postdoctoral residencies will have a grasp of how to approach remedial and disciplinary interventions, as well as a sense of when it is important or worthwhile to consult an attorney or human resources department during these challenging processes.

A basic framework of how confidentiality applies in training settings is a helpful beginning context for these 25 questions. Every clinical, counseling, and school psychologist is trained in the contours of psychotherapist-patient confidentiality. Faculty-student and supervisor-supervisee relationships are not bound by this same confidentiality. Confidentiality is nonetheless present in training relationships and settings in a variety of ways. First, patient-related information must always be treated as confidential. The foundation for confidentiality in treatment relationships stems from a plethora of legal, ethical, and regulatory sources, and training faculty and supervisors accordingly are bound by confidentiality when they handle patient-related information. Second, information related to remedial and disciplinary processes may be confidential by virtue of program and institutional rules. Confidentiality that stems from program and institutional policies is binding, and disclosures of information that violate such policies can expose the program, the institution, and individual faculty and supervisors to legal liability. Third, the confidentiality of written educational records is protected by certain laws. For this reason, psychologists in training programs need to be aware that when they disclose written educational records they must do so consistent with the relevant laws. Finally, many trainee-trainer interactions and communications are not bound by confidentiality laws, regulations, or policies. The principles that govern much of the communication that takes place regarding trainees arise from professionalism, discretion, prudence, and educational theory. As faculty and supervisors in training programs approach the challenging topics in this chapter, they may consider which of these four categories their communications relate to: patient information, remedial and disciplinary proceedings, written educational records, and the many informal communications that take place on a daily basis in all training programs. This general division of information will provide a starting point for psychologists to consider what rules of confidentiality govern the particular communication at issue.

Organization of Questions

Exposure to Legal Liability in Disciplinary and Remediation Processes

1. At what point in a disciplinary or remedial process should the head of a psychology program consult an attorney?

Psychology faculty and supervisors sometimes think of attorneys as similar to first responders: A person calls 911 when a thief has broken into the house, when the fire alarm goes off, or when someone needs emergent medical care. This first-responder model generally does not serve psychology training programs well. The reason is that, by the time a situation has gotten to the point at which the involvement of an attorney is necessary, the foundation for how the matter will turn out may already have been set. An alternative model is to think of the relationship with an attorney as much in proactive as in reactive terms; calling the fire department is a good thing to do when there is a fire, but installing a sprinkler system in the building may substantially minimize the damage should a fire break out.

Disciplinary and remedial interventions are governed by a set of legal, institutional, and programmatic rules. The program's policies and procedures will have a central role in virtually any intervention. It is therefore to a program's considerable advantage to have worked with an attorney to draft or review the relevant policies and procedures.

A working relationship with an attorney who is familiar with the program's policies and procedures has multiple advantages. Collaborating with an attorney in a prophylactic manner will help ensure that the policies and procedures are legally sound. In addition, the key players will know one another and be familiar with the texts that have a primary role in governing the intervention. The attorney will have a sense of the program and its goals. The ideal time to consult with an attorney is therefore well before a specific situation requiring intervention has arisen. It can be helpful to meet with the program's attorney on a regular, preventative basis, perhaps at the beginning of the academic or training year, to review relevant documents and to discuss any potentially problematic situations. The go-to attorney should always be the program's legal counsel, or the general counsel for the institution (often it will be an academic institution) in which the training program is situated. When a program does not have an attorney, it is worthwhile to retain one. Although such meetings may entail an expense, the value of having a well-considered plan for when the necessity of an intervention arises is almost certain to outweigh the initial expenditure. Regular contact will also give trainers a measure of confidence in addressing situations that arise in their programs.

It should be noted that there is often an in-house person who is responsible for personnel actions. This person may be situated in the human resources department. When an institution such as a mental health center or an academic medical center has a person who is responsible for addressing personnel matters, that individual can be very helpful and serve functions that complement those of the attorney.

2. What are the key documents, policies, guidelines, and rules relevant to disciplinary and remedial processes? How much legal knowledge do these documents presuppose?

There are several key texts relevant to disciplinary and remedial interventions with which program faculty and supervisors should be familiar. First and foremost, trainers[3] should be knowledgeable about their institution's policies and procedures. Additional valuable texts include the *Guidelines and Principles for Accreditation of Programs in Professional Psychology* (American Psychological Association [APA], Commission on Accreditation, 2007; hereinafter referred to as the Accreditation Guidelines), the APA Ethical Principles of Psychologists and Code of Conduct (APA, 2010; hereinafter referred to as the Ethics Code), the Americans with Disabilities Act of 1990 (ADA, 1990), the Family Educational Rights and Privacy Act of 1974 (FERPA, 1974), and the Health Insurance Portability and Accountability Act of 1996 (HIPAA, 1996). The jurisdiction's statutes and regulations governing the practice of psychology are also useful and are relevant to a range of situations that may arise. Several points may be helpful to keep in mind.

First, it is important to emphasize that trainers in psychology programs need *not* be attorneys.

Although a thorough familiarity with the Ethics Code and the Accreditation Guidelines—documents written by and for psychologists—should be considered essential for all trainers, a general understanding of the legal texts will virtually always suffice because there are very few legal emergencies. There is almost always time to contact an attorney and seek legal guidance regarding how HIPAA, FERPA, or the ADA applies to a specific situation. What is essential is that members of the program faculty/supervisory team have a good sense of *when* to contact an attorney rather than *what* an attorney will direct them to do. If the program has an ongoing relationship with an attorney, the attorney—or the person identified by the institution to fulfill this role—can help the program gain a sense of when contact is appropriate or necessary.

Second, there are principles that govern these documents. Examples include the importance of giving trainees notice of what is expected of them to complete the program and informing trainees of what process they are afforded should they encounter a problem that impedes their progress in the course of their academic or clinical work. Confidentiality is likewise a critical principle. It may be most helpful for trainers to think in terms of principles that govern these texts rather than getting mired in the details of the texts, which is the work of the attorneys.

Third, contrary to what program trainers may sometimes think, there is virtually never an impediment to disclosing information when a serious threat to health or safety has arisen. Although there may be some exceptions to this general rule—for example, disclosing HIV status raises serious legal and ethical concerns regarding stigma—the law almost always favors safety over confidentiality. Moreover, if given the choice, defending a breach of confidentiality lawsuit is preferable to defending a wrongful death lawsuit. For this reason, when trainers make a reasonable determination that an individual's health or safety is in serious danger, the time has passed to debate the intricacies of HIPAA or FERPA. Trainers should act to protect safety and analyze the law after. (See also questions 16 and 20.)

3. What are some of the central principles of the texts that govern remedial and disciplinary interventions that will help protect a program from incurring liability?

Although there is no rule or principle that unequivocally protects a training program from incurring liability, it is helpful to begin with the maxim that the law generally defers to educational institutions in determining the most effective ways to educate (Behnke, 2012). By virtue of this deference, courts give educational and training institutions wide latitude in determining the substance and structure of curricula based on educational principles. Courts are loath to second-guess educators on what they teach and how they organize their teaching plans. Likewise, courts will very likely defer to educators on what competencies are required to complete a particular course of study, determinations regarding which trainees do and do not have the requisite competencies, and remedial plans to ensure that a trainee who lacks a specific competence learns the appropriate knowledge, skills, or attitudes to complete a program successfully. In short, courts view educators—not courts—as being in the best position to make substantive decisions about the ingredients of a successful education.

A shift occurs when the focus moves from the substance of educational curricula and decisions regarding the skills and needs of particular trainees to the *processes* a program uses to address a trainees's progress in a training program. Although courts are not likely to take issue with a program's determination that a trainee is falling short or with the program's plan to assist the trainee through the program or even to remove the trainee from the program, courts are *very* likely to scrutinize how these decisions are made and implemented. Put another way, courts are as inclined to defer to programs on substance as they are *dis*inclined to defer to programs on process. The reason is that although courts view competence to make decisions about education as in the purview of educators, courts view themselves as having competence regarding procedural matters because therein lies the law's expertise: process. As a consequence, when legal problems arise for training programs in the context of remedial and disciplinary interventions, it is far more likely that the problem will arise by virtue of *how* a decision was made or implemented rather than by virtue of the decision itself.

A central feature to the law's way of looking at remedial and disciplinary interventions is *due process*. At the heart of due process is fairness. Due process says that an individual is entitled to *notice* of what is expected of him or her and a measure of *process* before a burden is imposed on the individual when those expectations are not met. Put simply, due process means that individuals must be informed of what is expected of them and be given a process through which to respond and comply before they are penalized when it appears those expectations may not have been fulfilled.

The question arises: What process is due? The answer to this question will depend on the circumstances. There is no set "amount" of due process that applies to every situation. Consider, for example, that an individual is entitled to more process when a trial may result in prison time than when a person is fined in traffic court for not paying a parking ticket. The reason is that the greater deprivation warrants more process—in this case, liberty versus a relatively small amount of money. Depriving people of their liberty requires more process than depriving people of their money. The question in a specific case is therefore not so much *what is due process* but rather *what process is due*, because the amount of process depends on what is at stake.

4. If a training program determines that a trainee requires additional work or that a trainee should be terminated from a program, what process does the program owe the trainee before implementing this decision?

The answer to this question is determined in large part—although not entirely—by the training program itself. The reason is that the program will—or should—have a handbook that sets forth the policies and procedures that govern remedial and disciplinary interventions. This handbook identifies the process that is due when the training program either imposes an added burden on a trainee's programmatic responsibilities in the form of a plan of remediation or removes the trainee from the program and thus deprives the trainee of the benefits of the time and financial resources the trainee has already put into the program.

There is no set formula for what a program's handbook must provide. The program has substantial discretion to structure its own policies and procedures. What is critical for programs to understand is that its handbook represents the program's communication to the trainee: These pages set forth the process due to you if this program determines that you are falling short in your progress or that you should no longer be in the program. Because courts view the processes that govern these decisions rather than the substance of the decisions as squarely within their expertise, courts are likely to scrutinize closely whether a program has followed its processes exactly when it imposes an added burden on the trainee in the form of a remediation plan or when the program terminates the trainee, should the trainee decide to challenge the program's action in court.

The take-home message is that program faculty and supervisors should review their program handbook with their attorney or the institution's designated person and should be familiar with what the handbook says, because the handbook will establish what process is due. The handbook sets forth what the program owes the trainee. When a trainee successfully challenges what a program has done, it is far more likely that the successful challenge has arisen from the program's failure to follow its own processes than what the program has decided needs to happen. For this reason, a good working relationship with the program's attorney can be very helpful.

5. How do program faculty and supervisors know what the program handbook should say about remedial and disciplinary proceedings?

Consulting with an attorney is the best way to ensure that the processes in the program handbook are legally sound and defensible. Program faculty and supervisors are certainly not expected to know what level of process is needed to pass legal muster—that is the attorney's job. Worthy of note, however, is that programs do not need to think in terms of what occurs in a court, where defendants are generally given much more process than what is required in an educational setting and where there are many more formal rules than are required for a training program to follow.

The law—and accrediting bodies—will require a minimum baseline of process. This minimum baseline is like a floor insofar as a program will have to offer at least that much process. It will be important that trainees are informed in writing of the basis for any decision made, have an opportunity to be heard by the decision makers (either orally or in writing), are allowed to respond to information that is part of the decision-making process, are told of the decision, and have a chance to appeal. Not a great deal more process is required by the law. Programs should not only think in terms of this minimum legal baseline, however, given that the program handbook will set forth the minimum requirements *for the particular program* that may be more than what the law would require. That is, a program may offer more—never less—process than what the law necessitates. The program will be bound by what its handbook contains, even if it goes above and beyond what the law requires.

6. The legal concept of due process requires that individuals be given notice of what is expected of them and afforded a process before being burdened or penalized when it appears those expectations have not been met. Are the concepts of notice and process found in psychology texts, such as the Ethics Code and Accreditation Guidelines?

Yes. Certain fundamental principles undergird many of the texts that structure and govern psychology training. A fundamental principle is fairness, which is the heart of due process. Due process is especially important for trainees, who are generally in a vulnerable position and may not able to assert their rights effectively. Both the Ethics Code and the Accreditation Guidelines emphasize notice and process. The Accreditation Guidelines (APA, Commission on Accreditation, 2007) state in Domain E: Student-Faculty Relations:

> At the time of admission, the program provides the students with written policies and procedures regarding program and institution requirements and expectations regarding students' performance and continuance in the program and procedures for the termination of students. Students receive, at least annually, written feedback on the extent to which they are meeting the program's requirements and performance expectations.

This concept is echoed in Standard 7.02 of the Ethics Code (APA, 2010), Descriptions of Education and Training Programs:

> Psychologists responsible for education and training programs take reasonable steps to ensure that there is a current and accurate description of the program content (including participation in required course—or program-related counseling, psychotherapy, experiential groups, consulting projects or community service), training goals and objectives, stipends and benefits and requirements that must be met for satisfactory completion of the program. This information must be made readily available to all interested parties.

The importance of these concepts becomes apparent insofar as both the Accreditation Guidelines and the Ethics Code have additional sections that directly address notice and process. The Accreditation Guidelines (APA, Commission on Accreditation, 2007) state in Domain A: Eligibility:

> The program adheres to and makes available to all interested parties formal written policies and procedures that govern: academic admissions and degree requirements; administrative and financial

assistance; student performance evaluation, feedback, advisement, retention and termination decisions; and due process and grievance procedures for students and faculty. It has policies and procedures that are consistent with those of its sponsor institution that pertain to faculty and student rights, responsibilities, and personal development.

Standard 7.06 in the Ethics Code, Assessing Student and Supervisee Performance (APA, 2010), states:

(a) In academic and supervisory relationships, psychologists establish a timely and specific process for providing feedback to students and supervisees. Information regarding the process is provided to the student at the beginning of supervision.

(b) Psychologists evaluate students and supervisees on the basis of their actual performance on relevant and established program requirements.

These sections of the Accreditation Guidelines and the Ethics Code capture central tenets of due process. Trainees are informed about program requirements, about the quality of their work in the program in "a timely and specific manner," about policies and procedures that govern their progress through the training program, and about problems in their work that may require or merit program intervention or termination and the procedures that govern such interventions. Due process protects fundamental fairness to trainees by providing notice of what the program expects and describing what will happen if those expectations are not met. It may be helpful to think of how the ethics, accreditation, and legal texts converge in terms of what kinds of information trainees should be provided. This convergence indicates that these texts are all addressing how to ensure that trainees are treated in a respectful, fair manner.

7. Often there is a significant gap in time between when academic or training faculty/supervisors perceive problems in a trainee and when a formal process of intervention is initiated. From the legal and ethical perspectives, when does a remedial or disciplinary process actually begin?

This question relates to what may be called the "rubber band" approach to remedial and disciplinary interventions. In the rubber band approach, a program is increasingly flexible with a trainee until a situation becomes intolerable. Only then does the program initiate a disciplinary or remedial process. The rubber band approach is consistent with the culture of a helping profession insofar as the benefit of every doubt is given until the situation becomes untenable and the trainers decide something must be done immediately.

The problem with the rubber band approach is that, when the breaking point is reached, the trainers have reached the limits of their tolerance and expect a speedy resolution. The relevant legal and ethical processes, however, have *just begun*. That is to say, when trainers allow a problematic situation to develop without addressing its problematic aspects, which include informing the trainee that there is a problem, there is no documentation and hence no history that form the foundation for a remedial or disciplinary intervention. Often, the relevant training standards have also been stretched in an effort either to accommodate the trainee, and/or to avoid confronting a difficult situation. For precisely this reason, Ethics Code Standard 7.06, Assessing Student and Supervisee Performance, calls for a "timely and specific" process for providing feedback to students so that situations are addressed long before the rubber band has snapped. In this manner, everyone involved, trainer and trainee alike, are aware when there are problems that may interfere with the trainee's successful completion of the program. This notice provides the program and the trainee the opportunity to work together to remedy the problem.

The concept of fairness is again relevant. When faculty and supervisors perceive that a trainee is having problems meeting program expectations, fairness calls for the trainee to be informed, that is, to be put on notice.

An artifact of the rubber band approach is that trainers may be frustrated on learning when the rubber band snaps that they are at square one in terms of laying a foundation for the program to intervene. This frustration may understandably be directed at the trainee. The Accreditation Guidelines and Ethics Code, however, will have been pointing toward a continuous process that would have been fairer to everyone involved. A way of thinking about the problems of the rubber band approach is that the law does not like surprises (Springer, Baker, & Elman, 2009). From the perspective of the law, it is preferable that parties are aware of a deteriorating situation as the situation deteriorates so that they may work to remedy the problem. When a situation "snaps" and a party involved claims not to have known how bad things had become, the law will examine who was responsible for ensuring that the relevant people were informed, and may explore how and why the responsible persons fell short. In graduate psychology training, this responsibility rests with faculty and supervisors.

8. Are there certain common mistakes that training programs make in implementing disciplinary or remedial interventions that make it more likely they will be successfully challenged in court? There is a case from Michigan that involved a trainee who did not want to affirm a homosexual lifestyle and who consequently did not accept a referral to treat a homosexual client for relationship issues. This trainee was terminated from the program and then filed a lawsuit, which the school settled. How does this court case fit into this analysis?

The most common mistakes that training programs make in implementing disciplinary or remedial interventions is that either they do not follow their own processes, or those processes are flawed in some important way. Courts are far more likely to find fault with process rather than with substance. It is therefore worthwhile for a program to consult with an attorney or some knowledgeable and appropriate person at the institution in drafting its process and in applying its process in a particular case.

The Michigan case involved a practicum trainee in a graduate counseling program. The trainee was referred a client suffering from depression. In reviewing the file prior to seeing the client, the trainee learned that the client was homosexual. The trainee, who described her religious beliefs as "orthodox Christian," told her supervisor that she would address any issue in treatment with the client other than his homosexual relationship, should relationship issues arise during the therapy. The client was referred to another therapist. The program then terminated the trainee from the program based on her refusal to affirm the client's homosexual relationship were the relationship to become an issue the therapy. The program based its decision, in part, on a program policy that prohibited referrals during the practicum stage of training and the discipline's ethics code which prohibited discrimination on the basis of sexual orientation.

Two federal courts heard this case: a district court (*Ward v. Wilbanks*, 2010) and an appeals court (*Ward v. Polite*, 2012). The district court found that that the policy in question—disallowing referrals during the practicum stage of training—was applied in a neutral fashion that served a legitimate purpose in upholding the American Counseling Association's *Code of Ethics* (American Counseling Association, 2005) and did not discriminate on the basis of religion. Based on this reasoning, the district court upheld the program's position. Had the case

ended there, the program would have prevailed. But the trainee appealed the decision.

The appeals court viewed the matter very differently than did the district court. The appeals court pointed out that the program's policy disallowing practicum trainees from referring cases was not in any of the program's policies—there was no such written policy—and the program had, in fact, allowed practicum students to make referrals in a variety of instances, such as when a trainee who had recently suffered a significant loss was allowed to refer a grieving client. The appeals court held that a jury could conclude the program had used the policy as a pretext to discriminate against the practicum student's religious beliefs. As a consequence, the appeals court reversed the district court's decision. The parties subsequently settled the matter so there were no further legal proceedings following the appeals court decision. The trainee received a sum of money from the university without the case ever having reached a jury.

The Michigan case illustrates the importance of process from the legal perspective. Neither the district nor the appeals court took issue with the program having a policy against discrimination on the basis of sexual orientation. Neither court had an issue with a policy against practicum students making referrals. The problem was rather with a policy disallowing practicum students from making referrals that were (a) not written down in any of the program's policies and procedures and (b) fraught with exceptions and not applied in a consistent manner. The combination of these two factors lead the appeals court to conclude that a reasonable jury could find that the program had used the unwritten, exception-ridden policy as a pretext for discriminating against the trainee based on her religious beliefs. The problem was not with the substance of a policy prohibiting discrimination on the basis of sexual orientation or a policy disallowing practicum students from making referrals. The problem was with how these policies were applied in the specific instance.

9. In a termination process, what is the relationship between an internship site's policies and procedures and the policies and procedures of the overall institution in which the internship is situated? Sometimes the institution's human resources department says that its policies and procedures must be followed before the trainee is terminated.

A trainee is entitled to due process before being terminated from an academic program or a clinical placement. What process is due is determined by the minimum baseline set by the law—the legal due process floor, one might say—whatever process the relevant accrediting bodies require, and whatever process the internship site provides over and above the legal due process floor. When the internship site is placed within a larger context such as a hospital, an academic medical center, a university, or a mental health center, there may be policies and procedures that provide additional process. The termination process must follow the policies and procedures of the institution in which the training program is situated. Adding to the complexity, in certain situations, interns are considered employees, a status that may bring additional legal protections.

A helpful way to think about the situation is that the internship is part of a team. Terminating an intern from a clinical training program is one of the most serious decisions the team can make, so it is essential that everyone on the team be aware of and involved with the process as it unfolds. The question then becomes who is part of the team when an intern may be terminated. Once the team members are identified, the faculty and supervisors most directly responsible for the intern's training can initiate a discussion about what role each member of the team will have as the process unfolds. Although approaching a difficult intern situation in this manner feels cumbersome, it both assures that the appropriate processes will be followed and apportions responsibility for the decision among a larger group of people. Fortunately, terminating an intern is a rare occurrence. The human resources department may bring to bear a significant amount of helpful experience, so there are considerable benefits, in addition to the burdens, of including human resources in a termination process.

Implementing Remediation Plans

10. When a program determines that a trainee is in need of remediation, how does the program know what to include in a remediation plan?

Approaching a remediation is a bit like lining up ducks. First, one should start with the program requirements: What competencies does the program state are requisites for graduation? Second, assess what expectations the trainee is not meeting: Where is the trainee falling short in acquiring the relevant competence or competencies? Third, identify steps the trainee must take in order to meet the program's expectations, and fourth, consider what amount of time and additional assessment is appropriate for

the trainee to move forward in a manner acceptable to the program. These four steps will anchor a remediation plan. Each step should be tied to the previous steps. What amount of time is appropriate for a trainee to address a problem in competence is linked to an assessment that indicates the trainee is not making adequate progress toward some specific program goal.

The APA has resources available to faculty and supervisors for these purposes. The Competency Benchmarks Project (see *A Practical Guidebook for the Competency Benchmarks*, http://www.apa.org/ed/graduate/benchmarks-guide.aspx) provides guidance on how to establish and assess competencies in graduate psychology training. This site has a tool kit designed to facilitate the practical application of competency benchmarks and a Competency Remediation Plan Template (http://www.apa.org/ed/graduate/competency.aspx). The value of these freely available materials is that they help organize and structure a competency-based program for graduate training in psychology.

A competency-based program is well suited to the legal, ethical, and accreditation requirements of notice and process for several reasons. First, a competency-based program identifies what competencies are required for successfully completing the program. Second, trainees' progress toward specific competencies can be measured. Third, deficits in competencies can be assessed and remedial plans formulated to move the trainee toward the relevant competencies. As a consequence, a well-designed and well-implemented competency-based program can be helpful in minimizing a program's exposure to liability when disciplinary or remedial interventions occur because the rationale for the intervention is built into the very structure and organization of the program.

11. Although the remediation template is helpful, the question remains: How much leeway does a court give a training faculty and supervisory team to write a remedial plan that the *training program* —rather than a court—thinks appropriate?

A court is not likely to second guess the central substantive features of a remediation plan. These include assessing that a particular trainee is in need of remediation, determining what remedial activities are appropriate to move the trainee toward the relevant competency or competencies, identifying specific supervisors or consultants to assist the trainee in successfully completing the remediation plan, and establishing a reasonable amount of time in which the remediation may occur. A court will likely view these components of a remediation plan as well within the training program's purview. A training program's position may be strengthened if the remediation plan has been a collaborative effort between the program and the trainee. Collaboration will help demonstrate that the training program has acted in good faith with the trainee's interests in mind and that the final plan is viewed as reasonable by the parties involved.

A court is not likely to defer to the program in one of several circumstances. First and foremost, a court will examine whether the training program adhered to its own policies and procedures in implementing the plan. In short, was the trainee given the notice and process set forth in the training program's policies and procedures? If not, a court may intervene to give the trainee some remedy. In addition, a court may scrutinize a trainee's claim that the plan was *unreasonable*. Such a claim might be that the trainee could not reasonably be expected to complete the plan in the time the training program had allotted or that the plan's requirements were unduly burdensome. If a remediation plan is unreasonable, it could suggest to a court that the training program was not acting in good faith and that the plan was a pretext for some other purpose such as to terminate the trainee from the program or to punish or penalize the trainee for some reason. A third claim that will get a court's attention is that the training program administers remediation plans in a manner that discriminates on an impermissible basis such as gender or race. An example of such a claim would be that the training programs treats one gender more harshly than the other when it writes its remediation plans. These three examples—the program has not followed its own policies and procedures, has imposed unreasonable and hence unrealistic remediation requirements, or has discriminated on an impermissible basis—are circumstances in which a court may *not* defer to a program's plan without carefully reviewing the plan.

12. How much remediation is a trainee entitled to before a program may terminate a trainee? Is failure to complete the first remediation plan a sufficient reason to terminate a trainee from the program, or must a trainee be given a second... or third... or even fourth chance?

This question is as important for its tone as for its substance. It is understandable that trainers

become frustrated by a perception that the process of remediation may be endless. The reality is much different. Terminating an individual from an academic program or an internship is a rare occurrence. An artifact of rare occurrences is that people are not well practiced at them. For this reason, when it begins to become clear that an intern is experiencing serious difficulty, it is to a program's advantage to consult with others—an attorney or someone from the institution's human resources department—who does have the relevant practice in addressing difficult situations. The stakes are high for all involved in a termination process.

A program's policies and procedures will set forth what process is due in a remedial intervention, provided the policies and procedures meet the minimum legal baseline for what is required and any accreditation requirements. The program will follow its policies and procedures in fashioning a remedial plan, ideally in collaboration with the trainee. The plan will give behavioral indicators for progress in the plan and a method of assessment to determine whether the plan has been successfully completed, as the remediation template provides (http://www.apa.org/ed/graduate/competency.aspx).

If a trainee does not successfully complete a remediation plan, the program is then in the position of determining whether further attempts at remediation are appropriate or whether the trainee should be terminated from the program. The program will again look to its policies and procedures as it makes this determination. The program is not required to go through an endless series of failed remediation plans, as the question implies. Provided that the program makes its determination in a reasonable, nondiscriminatory manner in accordance with its policies and procedures, the program has discretion in what it decides, including a decision to terminate a trainee. The relevant question is thus not how many remediation plans a program must offer but rather whether the program has made a reasonable, nondiscriminatory determination in a manner consistent with its policies and procedures. Again, having established clear policies and procedures early can be very helpful.

It is helpful for programs to be mindful that each remediation plan becomes part of the program's history. If a trainee challenges a remediation plan as discriminatory, a court may wish to compare how the specific plan compares to other remediation plans. Differences among remediation plans are acceptable, provided they are based on the unique circumstances of individual cases and sound educational reasons. When it appears to a court that similar cases are being treated differently, however, a program may then be in the position of explaining how the plan under scrutiny fits with the program's usual way of writing remediation plans. For this reason, programs should be mindful that every trainee's situation is unique but also that every remediation plan is part of a larger context.

13. Is it permissible to have therapy as part of a remediation plan?

Yes. It is helpful, however, not to confuse what is permissible with what is wise. It is worthwhile for programs to think carefully before making therapy a required part of a remediation plan for several reasons. First, it is useful to identify what specific competence therapy is intended to address. The program will want to articulate why it believes therapy will move the trainee toward the specific competence and to elaborate what particular therapy is appropriate for this purpose. Second, the program will need to determine whether it will require feedback from the therapist as part of the remediation plan requirements. As examples, the program may want to know simply whether the trainee attends sessions, or the program may want to know something about what goes on in the therapy such as whether the therapist views the trainee as committed to moving toward the identified competence and sees progress toward that goal. Reporting requirements affect the nature of therapy, which may be an important consideration in deciding whether to incorporate therapy into the remediation plan. Third, the program will need to consider how to assess and document whether the therapy has met its intended goal, and whether it will seek behavioral indicators other than feedback from the therapist to determine whether the remediation plan requirements have been met. Finally, Standard 7.06 in the Ethics Code, Mandatory Individual or Group Therapy (APA, 2010), places conditions on who may provide the therapy:

> 7.05 Mandatory Individual or Group Therapy
>
> (a) When individual or group therapy is a program or course requirement, psychologists responsible for that program allow students in undergraduate and graduate programs the option of selecting such therapy from practitioners unaffiliated with the program. (See also Standard 7.02, Descriptions of Education and Training Programs.)
>
> (b) Faculty who are or are likely to be responsible for evaluating students' academic performance do not themselves provide that therapy. (See also Standard 3.05, Multiple Relationships.)

These several considerations suggest that although they may do so, programs should think carefully about including therapy as part of a remediation plan. That therapy would be a positive step for a trainee and even helpful to the trainee advancing through the program does not necessarily mean that including therapy in a remediation plan is a good idea.

14. It is sometimes said that faculty and supervisors should speak with one voice when it comes to trainees under scrutiny. How should the faculty and supervisors who are not involved with the process interact with a trainee during the course of a remedial or disciplinary process? What are the limits about what can and cannot be said to trainers who are not involved in the process?

This question may be answered in two ways, first from a legal/ethical perspective and second from a policy perspective. From a legal/ethical perspective, program policies and procedures generally make remedial and disciplinary proceedings confidential. Confidentiality makes good sense insofar as a successful proceeding may depend on the disclosure of sensitive information. It may be difficult to conduct full and frank discussions if people are concerned that information will be disseminated among the trainers and trainees. For this reason, and to protect the trainee's privacy, the proceedings are confidential.

A good rule of thumb is that information is shared with faculty and supervisors on a need-to-know basis. For the faculty and supervisors generally, the need to know may consist of being informed that a problematic situation is being addressed in the appropriate venue. For faculty and supervisors involved in the proceeding, the need to know will likely consist of having all information relevant to the matter at hand to make the necessary decisions. For other trainers, perhaps those who are part of a remediation plan, the need to know may consist of information necessary for the trainer to work with the trainee as the plan envisions. The relevant question is what the faculty or supervisor needs to know.

Disclosing information above and beyond the need to know risks violating the trainee's confidentiality. Remedial and disciplinary proceedings are inevitably a source of stress within a training program. Inappropriate disclosures of confidential information generally serve only to make an already difficult situation more stressful and possibly more difficult to resolve. Such disclosures also can leave the trainee feeling as though he or she has not been treated respectfully. In addition, inappropriate disclosure of health or other program-related information may violate privacy laws.

Second, from a policy perspective, there are compelling reasons for faculty and supervisors to speak with one voice during the course of a remedial or disciplinary proceeding. During the proceeding, there will be identified individuals who will interact with the trainee. These trainers will be best informed about the relevant issues and the process. When other trainers who may not have all the relevant facts begin to engage the trainee about the matter, the risk of the trainee being provided incomplete or inaccurate information rises, and in worst-case scenarios, faculty members and supervisors can be at cross purposes.

Receiving misinformation and inconsistent communications from faculty or supervisors can be harmful to the trainee. Inconsistent or inaccurate information provided to the trainee can also increase the program's exposure in a subsequent lawsuit. It is in both the trainee's and the program's best interest to have clear, consistent, accurate information communicated. It is perfectly appropriate and may be helpful for a faculty member or supervisor to lend a sympathetic ear to a trainee in the midst of a remedial or disciplinary matter, but the role most helpful to the trainee will be as a listener rather than as a quasi-participant in the proceedings.

Privacy, Confidentiality, and Disclosures

15. There are a host of documents that govern privacy and confidentiality. Among these are the Ethics Code, HIPAA, FERPA, program policies, and licensing board regulations. Are program faculty and supervisors expected to be familiar with the requirements and exceptions to confidentiality in all of these documents? Are there principles that govern the disclosure of confidential information?

A person could easily spend an entire career analyzing how these texts interact with one another and are applied in practice. No psychologist will ever be expected to reach that level of mastery. Three principles, coupled with legal consultation, will provide helpful background for many decisions program faculty will need to make regarding disclosures of confidential information.

First, Standard 4.05, Disclosures (APA, 2010), provides a framework for disclosing confidential information:

4.05 Disclosures

(a) Psychologists may disclose confidential information with the appropriate consent of the organizational client, the individual client/patient or another legally authorized person on behalf of the client/patient unless prohibited by law.

(b) Psychologists disclose confidential information without the consent of the individual only as mandated by law, or where permitted by law for a valid purpose such as to (1) provide needed professional services; (2) obtain appropriate professional consultations; (3) protect the client/patient, psychologist, or others from harm; or (4) obtain payment for services from a client/patient, in which instance disclosure is limited to the minimum that is necessary to achieve the purpose. (See also Standard 6.04e, Fees and Financial Arrangements.)

The first principle derives from 4(a): "Confidential information may be disclosed with the consent of the client." This principle is the most straightforward, the simplest, and hence the most often overlooked feature of disclosure. Under the Ethics Code, HIPAA, and FERPA, trainees and clients may consent to the disclosure of confidential information. It is striking the number of times program faculty, supervisors, and administrators will have heated debates about whether they may disclose some information without ever having contemplated asking the trainee for his or her consent to do so. It is helpful for programs to be mindful that a trainee's consent is built into the process of psychology training. For example, the Association of Psychology Postdoctoral and Internship Centers' (APPIC) application for internship includes the following language:

> I hereby agree that personally identifiable information about me, including but not limited to my academic and professional qualifications performance, and character, in whatever form maintained, may be provided by my academic program to any internship training site to which I have applied and/or will match. I further agree that, following any internship match, similar information may be provided by the internship site to my graduate program and by my graduate program to the internship site. I understand that such exchange of information shall be limited to my graduate program, any internship site, and/or representatives of APPIC, and such information may not be provided to other parties without my consent. This authorization, which may be revoked at any

time, supersedes any prior authorization involving the same subject matter. (APPIC, n.d.)

It is worthwhile for the internship site and the graduate program to know that a trainee has signed this form and thereby provided consent to disclose information as part of the internship application process.

Whenever the possibility or necessity of disclosing information about a trainee arises, it is generally more helpful to begin with the question, "What does the trainee have to say about the disclosure?" rather than the question, "Is the disclosure allowed?" Although the second question may have to be asked, beginning with the first question may save the program a lot of time and energy. When asking for consent, it is important to remember that consent must be voluntary, and that, given the power differential between faculty, supervisors, and trainees, the program should be careful to avoid coercion in obtaining consent. With those caveats, a program should consider engaging a trainee in a discussion regarding consent to disclose information. However unlikely the prospect may seem to program faculty and supervisors, trainers should not assume that a trainee will refuse consent if asked in a respectful and sensitive manner.

Second, when disclosing information, faculty and supervisors should ask three questions: *why* the disclosure is being made, *what* information is needed to meet that purpose, and *to whom* the disclosure will be made given the *why* and *what*. This three-pronged principle is found in both the Ethics Code and HIPAA. Although HIPAA has relatively few direct applications to remedial and disciplinary interventions, the principle at issue is worthwhile in any instance in which a disclosure of information is made. The Ethics Code (APA, 2010) states:

> 4.04 Minimizing Intrusions on Privacy
>
> (a) Psychologists include in written and oral reports and consultations, only information germane to the purpose for which the communication is made.
>
> (b) Psychologists discuss confidential information obtained in their work only for appropriate scientific or professional purposes and only with persons clearly concerned with such matters.

Likewise, HIPAA (1996) has a "minimum necessary rule":

> (b) Standard: Minimum necessary
>
> (1) Minimum necessary applies. When using or disclosing protected health information or when requesting protected health information from another covered entity, a covered entity

must make reasonable efforts to limit protected health information to the minimum necessary to accomplish the intended purpose of the use, disclosure, or request.

This principle both protects trainees and helps minimize a program's exposure to a claim that it has improperly disclosed information.

Third, the *Tarasoff v. Regents of the University of California et al.* (1976) case held that safety trumps confidentiality. Although not every state has adopted the specific *Tarasoff* rule, this principle is near universal: When a reasonable person would judge that there is a serious threat to an individual's safety—either from self-harm or harm to someone else—it is legitimate, and perhaps mandated, to disclose the information necessary to avert the threat. This principle is built on some critical assumptions, for example that the harm to an individual's safety is serious and the threat is credible. When these assumptions are met, disclosing information to protect an individual's safety will virtually always be viewed by an adjudicatory body such as a court as a defensible disclosure.

These three principles, in the form of questions, form a good starting point for approaching a potential disclosure of information: First, has the trainee been asked to consent to the disclosure? Second, has the program considered why the disclosure is necessary, what information needs to be disclosed, and to whom the disclosure will be made? Third, is someone's safety at issue? Once the program has answered these questions, it will be well positioned to move toward determining how to handle the disclosure.

16. In a nutshell, what is the difference between HIPAA and FERPA?

Both HIPAA and FERPA are federal laws that are accompanied by an extensive set of regulations. Broadly speaking, HIPAA is designed to protect the privacy of healthcare information when that information is maintained by certain entities—called "covered entities"—and transmitted by certain electronic means. The website of the U.S. Department of Health and Human Services (2008) provides a substantial amount of information about HIPAA (http://www.hhs.gov/ocr/privacy/) including the HIPAA regulations (http://www.hhs.gov/ocr/privacy/hipaa/administrative/privacyrule/adminsimpregtext.pdf) and a detailed section on frequently asked questions.

According to the definition section in the HIPAA regulations (Section 160.103), a covered entity is: (1) A health plan. (2) A health care clearinghouse.

(3) A healthcare provider who transmits any health information in electronic form in connection with a transaction covered by this subchapter (http://www.hhs.gov/ocr/privacy/hipaa/administrative/privacyrule/adminsimpregtext.pdf) (HIPPA, 1996). Most academic institutions will, therefore, not be covered entities. The situation is somewhat more complex because HIPAA provides for a "hybrid entity" (HIPPA, 1996, Section 160.103), which are entities that provide *both* education/training *and* health care. Examples of hybrid entities could be academic medical centers, counseling centers, and student health centers (Springer, 2009). These entities are potentially bound by HIPAA rules.

HIPAA is of limited relevance to remedial and disciplinary proceedings in graduate psychology training because most of the records at issue in such proceedings will be records from the student's educational activities and so will be covered by FERPA rather than HIPAA. HIPAA is nonetheless important. Whenever a treatment record becomes part of a proceeding, faculty in charge of the proceeding should know who generated the record, who was the recipient of the services, how the record was transmitted, and who is responsible for ensuring that the record is maintained properly. Knowing whether the record is covered by HIPAA or FERPA will be relevant to answering these questions.

FERPA protects the privacy of educational records by governing their disclosure and dissemination. According to the U.S. Department of Education, "The Family Educational Rights and Privacy Act (FERPA) (20 U.S.C..,§ 1232g; 34 CFR Part 99) is a federal law that protects the privacy of student education records. The law applies to all schools that receive funds under an applicable program of the U.S. Department of Education" (http://www2.ed.gov/policy/gen/guid/fpco/ferpa/index.html). Thus, "An educational agency or institution subject to *FERPA* may not have a policy or practice of disclosing the education records of students, or personally identifiable information from education records, without a parent or eligible student's written consent" (U.S. Department of Health and Human Services & U.S. Department of Education, 2008).

As the U.S. Department of Health and Human Services does for HIPAA, the U.S. Department of Education provides extensive information about the application of FERPA in higher education settings on its website (http://www2.ed.gov/policy/higher-ed/guid/edpicks.jhtml?src=ln).

Several things about FERPA may be helpful for programs determining how the law applies in a disciplinary or remedial process. First, because virtually all institutions of higher education receive some funding from the U.S. government, a program should assume that FERPA applies until it is demonstrated otherwise. Second, FERPA governs *records in a written format*. Behavioral observations about a student do not constitute records under FERPA. The point is that FERPA does not govern all communications; FERPA governs policies and practices related to the disclosure of written materials in a student's record or material taken from that record. Every communication about a student is not a FERPA communication. Third, returning to a familiar theme, FERPA records may be released with the student's consent. Fourth, FERPA provides a number of exceptions that allow for the disclosure of records even in the absence of student consent. According to FERPA, educational records may be released without the student's consent to school officials with legitimate educational interest, to specified officials for audit or evaluation purposes, to comply with a judicial order or lawfully issued subpoena, and to appropriate officials in cases of health and safety emergencies (http://www2.ed.gov/policy/gen/guid/fpco/ferpa/index.html; this list of exceptions is not exhaustive).

The exception for "school officials with legitimate educational interest" gives substantial latitude in disclosing without the student's consent insofar as "legitimate educational interest" can be read broadly. Also, the emergency exception includes both "health and safety" and so extends beyond threats to physical harm. Information may also be disclosed if an illness seriously threatens a student's health. Even with these exceptions, it is still worthwhile to seek a student's consent for disclosure whenever feasible, and when disclosing, it is vital to follow the process set forth in Question 12 by disclosing the minimum information necessary for the purpose at hand. (The U.S. Department of Health and Human Services has a frequently-asked-questions website that addresses the application and interaction of HIPAA and FERPA in educational settings [http://www.hhs.gov/ocr/privacy/hipaa/faq/ferpa_and_hipaa/].)

17. I am head of the clinical area in a university-based department of psychology. Our program is small with a collegial atmosphere and we get to know our trainees well. By virtue of the quality of the trainees and our program's reputation, our trainees have generally done extremely well in the internship match. There are times when

I would like to share information with a clinical internship site about a trainee because I believe the site having this information will be helpful for the trainee to have a productive internship experience, and on certain occasions internship directors have wanted to speak with me when an intern was having difficulty. What constraints does FERPA have on my ability share such information?

FERPA protects confidentiality by limiting the disclosure of written educational records and material taken directly from those records. It is entirely possible that the exchanges at issue in the question do not involve information protected by FERPA. If, for example, the exchanges involve behavioral observations about the intern, FERPA is not a consideration because behavioral observations are not a written educational record.

It is always worthwhile to think in terms of process whenever disclosing information. One should begin with consent. If the intern has signed the APPIC authorization, the intern has consented to individuals from the internship site and the academic program sharing information. Also, it is useful to consider approaching the intern and raising the possibility of the discussion. If the intern is experiencing some distress from a problematic situation, the idea that the academic program and the internship are in touch may be experienced as helpful and/or supportive. There may even be times when including the intern in the discussion is appropriate. The decision about whether to inform the student of the communication or even to include the student in the discussion will involve training and sometimes clinical considerations.

If the intern does not consent to the discussion and revokes consent under the APPIC authorization, the conversation may still be possible provided there is nothing that binds the individuals from the student's future internship site and academic program to confidentiality. Moreover, Standard 4.06, Consultations, in the Ethics Code (APA, 2010) provides that information may be disclosed if it is necessary to accomplish the purpose of a consultation:

> 4.06 Consultations
> When consulting with colleagues,
> (1) psychologists do not disclose confidential information that reasonably could lead to the identification of a client/patient, research participant or other person or organization with whom they have a confidential relationship unless they have obtained the prior consent of the person or organization or the

disclosure cannot be avoided, and (2) they disclose information only to the extent necessary to achieve the purposes of the consultation. (See also Standard 4.01, Maintaining Confidentiality.)

There are multiple ways to explain why the head of the clinical program and the director of the internship site may exchange behavioral observations about a student. This discussion may be appropriate from the legal and ethical perspectives. Questions *from the training and clinical perspectives* remain: What do these individuals hope to accomplish in speaking, and what are the implications should the student become aware of the conversation? Put another way, simply because the conversation *can* take place does not necessarily mean that the conversation *should* take place. The wisdom of having the conversation rests with the professional judgment of the training faculty involved. The Association of Psychology Postdoctoral and Internship Centers may be a helpful consultative resource in determining what communications are appropriate. (http://www.appic.org/Problem-Consultation)

18. I am a clinical supervisor. Recently I became concerned about a supervisee's performance—a potential boundary violation was at issue—when the supervisee "reminded" me that the supervision is confidential and said I could not share anything we discussed. What are the limits to confidentiality in the supervisory relationship?

There are aspects of the supervisory relationship that are confidential. A licensed clinical supervisor has legal and ethical responsibility for a supervisee's clients because the unlicensed supervisee is practicing by virtue of the supervisor's license. For this reason, the supervisor should consider the clients as if they are his or her own because, from the legal and ethical perspective, they are. The supervisor should, therefore, consider all information related to the clients as confidential in the same manner as the information is confidential for the supervisor's own treatment clients. In an internship setting, there are often multiple people involved in a client's treatment. Sharing treatment-related information with others involved in a client's treatment is perfectly acceptable under HIPAA. The information should be limited to what is needed for treatment purposes. (See question 15.)

Information related to the supervisee's performance is *not* treatment-related information. A supervisor can—and should—discuss the supervisee's performance with other trainers who are responsible for the supervisee's training in venues where it is appropriate to do so. Although certain aspects of the supervisee's performance may relate to specific patients, a discussion can take place that conveys the quality of the supervisee's work and does not provide any information that identifies the client. If the information at issue could be educational records under FERPA, FERPA's exception is relevant: Information may be disclosed without a trainee's consent to school officials with a legitimate educational interest. To the extent that the supervisory relationship is confidential—or treated as confidential by virtue of professional, educational reasons rather than law, ethics or institutional policy—there are multiple avenues available to discuss the supervisee's performance with other individuals in the educational and training program who need to have the information in order to fulfill their program responsibilities.

19. At times, training programs must deal with remedial or disciplinary situations that cause significant distress among the trainees. The challenge is that the other trainees know something has occurred but often do not have all the facts, and rumors become rampant. What may be shared about a disciplinary or remedial process for the purpose of providing information to trainees in the program? May a program tell the trainees that the program is responding to concerns without giving details? (These questions generate significant disagreement in training programs, with risk management and group dynamic considerations often viewed as incompatible.)

A remedial or disciplinary intervention inevitably affects the program to some degree. At times, the effects can be relatively benign. A trainee is struggling in some area and the faculty or supervisors are well aware of the difficulty and work with the trainee to design a remedial program that will help the trainee move forward. Such an intervention can be experienced as providing helpful extra attention and may cause few if any negative ripples throughout the trainee's cohort. Often the trainee's peers are well aware of the situation and may tacitly or otherwise support the faculty or supervisors in providing additional help. In a case of this type, there may not be anyone who asks for—or is particularly interested in obtaining—additional information about what is going on.

At the other end of the spectrum are situations that can cause upheaval in a program. Faculty and supervisors may be faced with rumors and innuendo about what has happened or is likely to happen to the trainee in question. Trainees—and even faculty and supervisors—may split into factions. Faculty and supervisors who are believed to have a role in the intervention may be subject to unwarranted and uninformed criticism. Sexual involvements between trainers and students may especially lend themselves to these dynamics.

Faculty and supervisors responsible for the intervention—which in sexual involvements may entail termination of the trainer, not the trainee—must negotiate between the strictures of confidentiality and the group dynamics. The processes surrounding the intervention will likely be confidential. The challenge is that a lot of information may be circulating that is not accurate. If this information is about the specifics of the case, faculty and supervisors may simply not be able to provide accurate, correcting information. If, on the other hand, the information relates to how cases are handled generally or is about the rules or policies that govern a particular matter, faculty and supervisors may be able to disseminate correct information.

Faculty and supervisors thus need to consider how to interact with trainees from legal, ethical, and training perspectives. Information that relates to what happened in a specific matter that is the subject of a hearing will very likely be confidential and cannot be shared. There may be other information, however, that is entirely appropriate to share and may be helpful in addressing concerns and anxieties. Examples include the following: "Everyone involved in a disciplinary matter has an opportunity to present his or her side of the situation." "If anyone is not satisfied with the outcome of a proceeding, there is another chance to be heard." "The program handbook gives a lot of information about what happens when something in the program needs to be addressed. Everyone involved—including faculty, supervisors, and the program administration—is bound to follow the handbook."

Faculty and supervisors will have to determine what venue is most appropriate to provide information to concerned members of the program. There may be a special need to provide correcting information when rumors are circulating. In such an instance, faculty and supervisors may decide to use the usual manner of disseminating information throughout the program, or they may deem it appropriate to have a special meeting in which members of the program can ask questions and/or voice concerns. These decisions are made on what the faculty and supervisors believe is in the best interests of the training program. Distinguishing what information is permissible to disclose and what information is confidential and so may not be disclosed, as well as determining what forum is most appropriate to address questions and concerns, is best done in collaboration with the program's attorney or institution's human resources representative.

20. If a trainee makes threats against another individual, for example a faculty member or another trainee in the program, how do FERPA and obligations under *Tarasoff* (duty to protect) interact?

Like codes of ethics, the law is based on a set of values. One should consider that behind every rule—ethical or legal—there is a reason based upon a value. To the extent that one can think in terms of the values that lie behind the rules, decision making will be a correspondingly more straightforward, clear, and user-friendly process.

In general, with rare exceptions, the law places safety over confidentiality. *Tarasoff v. Regents of the University of California et al.* (1976) stands for the proposition that when safety and confidentiality come into conflict, confidentiality yields to safety. Both FERPA and HIPAA strike this same balance of values. Thus, although FERPA is designed to protect the confidentiality of school records, the law contains an exception that allows confidential information to be disclosed in order to project safety (http://www2.ed.gov/policy/gen/guid/fpco/ferpa/index.html).

HIPAA likewise has a safety exception. This exception was highlighted when, following the tragic shootings in Aurora, Colorado, and Newton, Connecticut, the Director of the Office of Civil Rights in the U.S. Department of Health and Human Services issued a letter to the nation's health care providers. The letter, issued on January 15, 2013, directly addressed the relationship between confidentiality and safety under HIPAA. The letter stated, in part:

> In light of recent tragic and horrific events in our nation, including the mass shootings in Newtown, CT, and Aurora, CO, I wanted to take this opportunity to ensure that you are aware that the Health Insurance Portability and Accountability Act (HIPAA) Privacy Rule does not prevent your ability to disclose necessary information about a patient to law enforcement, family members of the patient, or

other persons, when you believe the patient presents a serious danger to himself or other people.

The HIPAA Privacy Rule protects the privacy of patients' health information but is balanced to ensure that appropriate uses and disclosures of the information still may be made when necessary to treat a patient, to protect the nation's public health, and for other critical purposes, such as when a provider seeks to warn or report that persons may be at risk of harm because of a patient. When a healthcare provider believes in good faith that such a warning is necessary to prevent or lessen a serious and imminent threat to the health or safety of the patient or others, the Privacy Rule allows the provider, consistent with applicable law and standards of ethical conduct, to alert those persons whom the provider believes are reasonably able to prevent or lessen the threat. Further, the provider is presumed to have had a good faith belief when his or her belief is based upon the provider's actual knowledge (i.e., based on the provider's own interaction with the patient) or in reliance on a credible representation by a person with apparent knowledge or authority (i.e., based on a credible report from a family member of the patient or other person). These provisions may be found in the Privacy Rule at 45 CFR § 164.512(j).

Under these provisions, a healthcare provider may disclose patient information, including information from mental health records, if necessary, to law enforcement, family members of the patient, or any other persons who may reasonably be able to prevent or lessen the risk of harm. For example, if a mental health professional has a patient who has made a credible threat to inflict serious and imminent bodily harm on one or more persons, HIPAA permits the mental health professional to alert the police, a parent or other family member, school administrators or campus police, and others who may be able to intervene to avert harm from the threat (http://www.hhs.gov/ocr/office/lettertonationhcp.pdf).

Finally, Standard 4.05(b), Disclosures, in the Ethics Code (APA, 2010), allows for disclosures of confidential information in order to protect safety even in the absence of client consent:

> 4.05 Disclosures
>   (b) Psychologists disclose confidential information without the consent of the individual only as mandated by law, or where permitted by law for a valid purpose such as to (1) provide needed professional services; (2) obtain appropriate professional consultations; (3) protect the client/patient, psychologist, or others from harm; or

(4) obtain payment for services from a client/patient, in which instance disclosure is limited to the minimum that is necessary to achieve the purpose.

The *Tarasoff* case, HIPAA, FERPA, and the APA Ethics Code all lead to the same conclusion: If, relying on their professional judgment, trainers determine that it is necessary to disclose confidential information for the purpose of protecting an individual's safety, it is prudent and consistent with the law and professional ethics to do so. From the perspective of risk management, most attorneys would prefer to defend a client in a breach of confidentiality than in a wrongful death lawsuit.

Americans with Disabilities Act

21. If a faculty member or supervisor suspects that a trainee is struggling with a disability that is interfering with the trainee's progress through the program, does the ADA affect whether the faculty member or supervisor may bring that issue up with the trainee?

The ADA is intended to provide equal opportunity to individuals with disabilities in all areas of society. Under the ADA, equal opportunity entails equal access. The ADA is different from other civil rights laws insofar as the ADA recognizes that to provide equal opportunity and equal access, it may be necessary to treat people with disabilities differently. Who gets treated differently and what the differential treatment involves are questions that the ADA addresses. The ADA applies to trainees both when they are considered employees of an institution and when they are not.

Nothing in the ADA prohibits or even discourages a faculty member or supervisor from asking a trainee whether accommodation or special assistance is needed. To the contrary, such a discussion can be viewed as entirely consistent with the ADA and it is certainly consistent with good training. There are some considerations that may be helpful to have in mind before initiating such a discussion, however. First, the goal of raising the question about whether accommodation or special assistance is necessary is to invite a conversation, not to diagnose or prescribe a plan of action. Asking, rather than telling, should be the conversation's tone. Second, it is appropriate to ask whether a trainee needs special help, but it is the trainee's decision whether to accept the help. In this way, an accommodation under the ADA differs from a remediation plan; failure to engage in a remediation plan may result in a trainee being terminated from a program. Failure to accept an ADA

accommodation may never result in termination. The important point is that a program cannot require a trainee to accept an accommodation under the ADA. Finally, because raising the issue of a disability implicates legal requirements, it may be advisable and helpful to consult with the institution's attorney or human resources department before initiating the discussion. The reason is that once a trainee claims a disability and requests an accommodation, the program may then be under a legal obligation to offer the trainee accommodations. (See question 22.)

22. How far must a training program extend itself in accommodating a trainee's disability? Although psychology is a helping profession, there is also a limit to resources. Is accommodating a trainee's disability under the ADA considered a remedial plan?

Under the ADA, a trainee is responsible for informing the program that he or she has a disability and needs an accommodation. Once the trainee has done so—and only when the trainee has done so—the program is under a legal obligation to consider what the ADA terms "reasonable accommodations." The question then becomes what accommodations are considered reasonable under the law. By using the concept of reasonable accommodation, the ADA seeks to strike a balance: The goal of the law is to provide persons with disabilities equal access to opportunities in a manner that does not unduly disrupt the ability of institutions to engage in their usual activities. It is important to distinguish a reasonable accommodation under the ADA from a remedial plan. The purpose of the ADA is to ensure equal opportunity through equal access. The purpose of a remedial plan is to address a problem in a trainee's progress toward competence.

The law offers two ways of thinking about the question of what accommodations are reasonable. The law first approaches this question by saying that the accommodation should not cause the program "undue hardship." Financial resources may be considered in determining whether an accommodation would impose an undue hardship on a program. Under the ADA, there is no set amount for when a hardship becomes undue; this determination is specific to the setting. As an example, what would be an undue hardship for a psychologist in solo practice might not be an undue hardship for an educational institution. The context is a determining factor in what constitutes an undue hardship. Programs should also keep in mind that an accommodation, regardless of how reasonable from the program's perspective, yet which does not address the trainee's specific needs, may not meet the requirements of the ADA.

The law's second approach to the question of what accommodations are reasonable is to say that an accommodation need not "fundamentally alter" the program. Put simply, a program need not offer an accommodation that will turn the program into something other than what it is. Consider, for example, a psychology training program that identifies home-based visits as an area of core competency required of all graduates. Exempting a trainee from making home visits might be considered a fundamental alteration of the program and so would not be considered a reasonable accommodation if the trainee were to have a disability that prevented him or her from traveling to clients' homes. The important point for programs to keep in mind is that the concepts of undue hardship and fundamental alteration are ways that one determines whether an accommodation is reasonable under the ADA. The concepts, therefore, set the outer bounds of what accommodations are reasonable.

Within these outer bounds is a broad area in which the program and the trainee may explore together what accommodations will assist the trainee with a disability to meet the program's requirements and thus to benefit from the educational experience in a manner commensurate with other trainees. The ideal relationship between the trainee and program is a collegial, collaborative interaction that identifies what accommodations work for all the parties involved. The starting point for the conversation may be the trainee saying, "This accommodation is what I need" and the program responding "This accommodation is what we are able to offer." The program and the trainee then begin a negotiation whose goal is to meet everyone's needs in a reasonable manner. There is an important similarity between finding a reasonable accommodation under the ADA and drafting a remedial plan: Each should be the product of an interaction between the program and the trainee.

Professional Issues

23. Must a clinical training program notify a licensing board if a trainee is disciplined, especially if the behavior comes to light after the trainee submits his/her application materials to the licensing board, or after the trainee has already graduated from a training program?

The primary responsibility of the training program is to be truthful. Truthfulness means not providing a licensing board inaccurate or misleading information, usually on a form that the trainee must submit to get licensed. If the form asks whether a trainee has been the subject of a disciplinary or remedial action, the answer will usually be straightforward. The response can be more complex if the question asks if a supervisor has "concerns" about whether a trainee will be able to practice ethically, because the answer calls for a subjective response. It may be, for example, that a supervisor did have such a concern at one point but subsequently the concern was allayed. In such a case, the supervisor will use professional judgment in the answer.

If the information comes to light after the trainee has submitted application materials to the licensing board or has completed the program or even after becoming licensed, the program will have to determine what is the most appropriate response. Three considerations may be useful. First, the program can contact the Association of State and Provincial Psychology Boards (http://asppb.org) and ask for a consultation that will address the facts and circumstances of the specific case. Second, the program can contact the relevant licensing board. Usually such an inquiry may be made anonymously, but it is always possible that the call itself will indicate to the board which applicant is under scrutiny. Third, depending on the nature of the behavior at issue, the program may contact the trainee (or former trainee) and encourage the individual to self-report to the board. Self-reporting is generally preferable for a variety of reasons; from a risk management perspective, it protects the program from a defamation claim. Although a defamation claim is not likely to succeed if the report is made in good faith—public policy favors providing information to government agencies charged with protecting the public—nonetheless, if the trainee refuses to self-report, it is advisable for the program to consult with its attorney before informing the board. Often, if the trainee (or former trainee) understands that the program is serious about reporting, the individual will prefer to move forward on his or her own initiative because, in that case, the individual will have more control over how the situation is presented to the board.

24. Is it the responsibility of the psychology training program to address behavior that is unprofessional but that occurs outside the classroom or training site? Is it appropriate to do so?

The Ethics Code gives the APA Ethics Committee jurisdiction over behavior that is part of a psychologist's professional life. According to the Preamble of the Ethics Code (APA, 2010), professional behavior is distinct from "purely private" behavior:

> This Ethics Code applies only to psychologists' activities that are part of their scientific, educational, or professional roles as psychologists. Areas covered include but are not limited to the clinical, counseling, and school practice of psychology; research; teaching; supervision of trainees; public service; policy development; social intervention; development of assessment instruments; conducting assessments; educational counseling; organizational consulting; forensic activities; program design and evaluation; and administration…These activities shall be distinguished from the purely private conduct of psychologists, which is not within the purview of the Ethics Code.

Alongside this professional/purely private distinction, however, the Ethics Code also has the concept that there may be a connection between what goes on in a psychologist's private and professional lives.

Standard 2.06 in the Ethics Code (APA, 2010) explicitly draws a link between a psychologist's personal and professional lives:

> 2.06 Personal Problems and Conflicts
>
> (a) Psychologists refrain from initiating an activity when they know or should know that there is a substantial likelihood that their personal problems will prevent them from performing their work-related activities in a competent manner.
>
> (b) When psychologists become aware of personal problems that may interfere with their performing work-related duties adequately, they take appropriate measures, such as obtaining professional consultation or assistance and determine whether they should limit, suspend or terminate their work-related duties. (See also Standard 10.10, Terminating Therapy.)

Standard 2.06 says that psychologists have an ethical responsibility to consider the relationship between their personal life and their professional life. As the point of entry into the field, psychology training programs are in the position of assisting trainees to draw this connection as part of the trainees' professional development.

In determining when it is appropriate to address behavior that occurs outside the professional setting, trainers may find it helpful to keep three principles in mind. First, there are certain behaviors that, in and of themselves, raise serious questions about a trainee's judgment or current capacity to care for clients. Behavior constituting a felony, for example, would fall into this category. The Rules and Procedures that govern the APA Ethics Committee (APA, Ethics Committee, 2002) permit the Committee to take action when a psychologist has committed a felony. Behavior of this type is well within a program's discretion to address. Second, it is important to be mindful about the risks of making moral judgments. Not altogether that many years ago, homosexual behavior was considered illicit and an indication of psychological imbalance. It is far easier to mask moral judgments in the guise of professional and ethical judgments than many in the field of psychology would like to admit. Finally, there is a large grey area in which faculty will have various opinions about how to react. Driving while under the influence of alcohol and a shoplifting charge for a minor item are examples on which there may be no consensus. In these instances, engaging the trainee in a discussion may be the most productive course of action. If a trainee becomes recalcitrant and refuses the program's offer to meet and understand what may have happened, there may be other issues that the program needs to address with the particular trainee.

25. Does a trainer who has been asked to give a recommendation need to worry that a trainee might sue if the faculty member/supervisor says something negative about the trainee in a letter? What may the trainer say if the trainee has required a remedial intervention during the program?

The key to this question is that the faculty member or supervisor has been asked to give a recommendation. The trainee has thus given consent to disclose information to some other individual or program. In this case, a reasonable letter written in good faith, even though it may contain information that does not reflect well on the trainee, is highly unlikely to result in a successful legal action. There are faculty and supervisors who nonetheless request signed consent forms as part of the recommendation process.

There are other ways to minimize exposure. One way is to respond to the trainee in writing (perhaps by e-mail) and indicate what the faculty member or supervisor would need to address:

> Dear trainee, I am happy to write a strong letter on your behalf. I will need to mention the difficulty you

had in getting reports completed in a timely fashion, but I will also indicate that this problem was fully resolved by the end of your placement and that you took our discussions seriously and addressed my concerns.

A second way is to show the trainee the letter before sending and invite edits. Once the faculty member or supervisor has informed the trainee what the final draft will say and the trainee has agreed to use the letter, it will be extremely difficult for the trainee to claim at a later date that the letter was not written in good faith or that it was defamatory, libelous, or intentionally interfered with the trainee's professional prospects.

Letters of recommendation may be a more straightforward case than information communicated under the APPIC consent form for trainees in the match or in an application to a licensing board. The reason is that trainees often have more choices regarding whom they will ask to write a letter of recommendation, and they tend to choose a faculty member or supervisor with whom they have a good relationship. Trainees' degrees of freedom may be constrained when they must choose a clinical supervisor who can speak to their having accumulated a certain number of hours or when a program director is asked or invited to provide information and a trainee has signed a form consenting to the disclosure because the form is required by the APPIC process.

In these cases in which the trainee's range of choice regarding who will write a letter of recommendation may be more limited, it is helpful to keep three points in mind. First, truth is an absolute defense to defamation. If the information conveyed is accurate, behaviorally based, and avoids conclusory language or characterizations, it is very likely—indeed, almost certain—to withstand legal scrutiny. For example, it is preferable to write: "Mr. X had 15 reports due over the course of the semester. All but one report were submitted more than three days late," rather than, "Mr. X cannot get his work done on time." Second, an important question is whether the information is given in good faith. Put another way, is the communication done for the purpose of providing information that an individual or entity needs to do a professional task related to the trainee, or does the information appear more intended to harm or deprive the trainee of a professional opportunity? Third, a consultation from a trusted colleague can be very helpful, especially when the faculty member or supervisor has strong feelings about the trainee and questions—or should question—his or her own objectivity in writing an evaluative letter. Obtaining a consultation will demonstrate that the trainer acted in good faith,

Trainees raise challenges to recommendations and faculty-to-faculty communications in an exceedingly small percentage of cases. Courts will be deferential to trainers whose communications are done in good faith and are intended to further an educational purpose. Keeping these points in mind will help protect trainers against almost all challenges to the legitimacy of their recommendations and evaluations.

Final Comments

This chapter has provided an overview of remedial and disciplinary proceedings in graduate psychology training programs. The purpose of the chapter has been to provide a conceptual framework and a process for training programs that will help minimize their exposure to liability and simultaneously respect and protect the interests of the trainees involved. These twin goals—minimizing the program's exposure to liability and protecting the trainees' interests in a respectful manner—are the touchstone of a successful intervention. If this chapter has helped programs move toward these goals, it has achieved its purpose.

It is nonetheless important for programs to keep separate the concepts of a remedial plan and a reasonable accommodation under the ADA. The two concepts may interact when a trainee asks for a reasonable accommodation to complete a remediation plan. A trainee may be entitled to a reasonable accommodation in such a circumstance under the conditions described previously, that is, that the accommodation does not fundamentally alter a remediation plan that is based on the program's core competencies.

Notes

1 *Trainee* refers to an individual at any point in a formal training program and thus includes students who have just begun academic coursework in a graduate program and post-doctoral trainees who are accruing hours for licensure.
2 "Graduate Psychology Training Programs" includes both pre- and postdoctoral training programs.
3 *Trainers* refers to faculty, supervisors, and any other individuals who have direct responsibility for and oversight regarding an individual's progress through a psychology training program.

References

American Counseling Association. (2005). *ACA code of ethics.* Retrieved from http://www.counseling.org/Resources/aca-code-of-ethics.pdf

American Psychological Association. (2010). *Ethical principles of psychologists and code of conduct (2002, Amended June 1, 2010)*. Retrieved from http://www.apa.org/ethics/code/index.aspx

American Psychological Association, Commission on Accreditation. (2007). *Guidelines and principles for accreditation of programs in professional psychology*. Retrieved from http://www.apa.org/ed/accreditation/about/policies/guiding-principles.pdf

American Psychological Association, Ethics Committee. (2002). Rules and procedures. *American Psychologist, 57*, 626–645.

Americans With Disabilities Act of 1990, 42 U.S.C.A. § 12101 *et seq.* (West 1993).

Association of Psychology Postdoctoral and Internship Centers. (n.d.) *APPIC application*. Retrieved from http://www.appic.org/Portals/0/downloads/AAPI_Sample_PDF.pdf

Behnke, S. H. (2012). Constitutional claims in the context of mental health training: Religion, sexual orientation, and tensions between the first amendment and professional ethics. *Training and Education in Professional Psychology, 6*, 189-195.

Family Education Rights and Privacy Act of 1974, 20 U.S.C. § 1232g, 34 C.F.R. pt. 99.

Health Insurance Portability and Accountability Act of 1996, Pub. L. No. 104-191 Stat. 1936 (1996).

Springer, A. (2009, May). *HIPAA and FERPA: Privacy alphabet soup*. Paper presented at the American Psychological Association Commission on Accreditation, Accreditation Assembly, San Diego, California.

Springer, A., Baker, J. & Elman, N. (2009, May). *The Impact of FERPA/HIPAA regulations on addressing trainees with problems of professional competence*. Paper presented at the American Psychological Association, Committee on Accreditation, Accreditation Assembly, San Diego, CA.

Tarasoff v. Regents of the University of California et al., 551 P. 2d 334 (Cal. S. Ct. 1976).

U.S. Department of Health and Human Services & U.S. Department of Education. (2008). *Joint guidance on the application of the Family Educational Rights and Privacy Act (FERPA) and the Health Insurance Portability and Accountability Act of 1996 (HIPAA) to student health records*. Retrieved from http://www.hhs.gov/ocr/privacy/hipaa/understanding/coveredentities/hipaaferpajointguide.pdf

Ward v. Polite. (2012). 667 F. 3d 727.

Ward v. Wilbanks. (2010). No. 09-CV-112 37, 2010 U.S. Dist. WL 3026428 (E. D. Michigan, July 26, 2010).

When Training Goes Awry

Nadine J. Kaslow, W. Brad Johnson, *and* Ann C. Schwartz

Abstract

This chapter focuses on the myriad ways in which training may go awry. It first focuses upon trainees with problems of professional competence (TPPC), with consideration given to problems in core competency domains, psychosocial stress, psychological difficulties, and interpersonal challenges. It then addresses problems related to trainers (faculty members or supervisors), with a focus on challenges in training/supervisory technique; psychological and medical difficulties; and interpersonal, cultural, and ethical challenges. Subsequent sections address three additional categories: trainee-trainer matches, peers with problems of professional competence, and contextual factors. Following this, the paper provides recommendations with regard to strategies for reducing the likelihood that training will go awry related to each of the aforementioned categories and for addressing difficulties in each category when they do arise.

Key Words: problems of professional competence, trainee-trainer matches, peers

Fortunately, most trainees (graduate/practicum students, predoctoral interns, residents) make appropriate developmental progress and reach competency benchmarks in a timely fashion (Forrest, Elman, Gizara, & Vacha-Haase, 1999; Gaubutz & Vera, 2006; Oliver, Bernstein, Anderson, Blashfield, & Roberts, 2004; Shen-Miller et al., 2011). The bulk of trainers (faculty members, supervisors) are competent to teach and supervise and there is growing agreement on supervision competencies (Falender et al., 2004; Rings, Genuchi, Hall, Angelo, & Cornish, 2009). The large majority of trainee-trainer relationships are productive and positive. Most academic and clinical environments are generally conducive to effective education, training, and learning. However, when there are difficulties with trainees, trainers, trainee-trainer relationships, peers in the training environment, and/or the training context itself, training can go awry.

For example, there are disturbing data that reveal that many trainers offer inadequate supervision that is harmful to their trainees and to the trainees' patients (Ellis, 2010; Gray, Ladany, Walker, & Ancis, 2001). In addition, it has been asserted that one-third of supervisees view their supervision to be problematic in some fashion (West, 2003). This article addresses the myriad ways in which trainees, trainers, trainee-trainer matches, peers, and training contexts may contribute to difficulties in the training and learning process. We offer recommendations for effectively addressing and managing these various potential contributors to a maladaptive training process.

Trainees with Problems of Professional Competence (TPPC)

Survey data reveal that 4–10% of students each year exhibit competence problems (Forrest et al.,

1999; Huprich & Rudd, 2004). Historically, the term *impaired trainee* has been used to portray trainees who fail to meet minimal standards for advancement. However, the term *impairment* has been deemed problematic and potentially legally risky due to its overlap with definitions of disability and impairment under the Americans with Disabilities Act (Elman & Forrest, 2007; Falendar, Collins, & Shafranske, 2009). Thus, in recent years, there has been a growing consensus that the most appropriate terminology for students who fail to meet expected benchmarks within each competency domain is trainees with *problems of professional competence* (TPPC) (Elman & Forrest, 2007; Kaslow et al., 2007). That is, these individuals do not demonstrate the knowledge, skills, attitudes/values, and the integration of the aforementioned three concepts that would be linked with developmentally appropriate performance. There are a multitude of ways problems of professional competence may be manifested in trainees and cause training to go awry.

Problems in Core Competency Domains

TPPCs may demonstrate problems with professional competence in various competency domains (Fouad et al., 2009; Kaslow, 2004; Kaslow et al., 2004; Rodolfa et al., 2005). The generally agreed upon benchmark clusters include professionalism, relational, science, application, education, and systems. The following are the core competencies within each benchmark cluster.

- Professionalism—individual and cultural diversity; ethical, legal standards and policy; reflective practice/self-assessment/self-care.
- Relational—relationships (capacity to relate effectively and meaningfully with individuals, groups, and/or communities).
- Science—scientific knowledge and methods, research/evaluation.
- Application—evidence-based practice, assessment, intervention, consultation.
- Education—teaching, supervision.
- Systems—interdisciplinary systems/management/administration, advocacy.

Competency problems are evident when a trainee fails to demonstrate the essential components of one or more core competencies as indicated by a series of behavioral anchors (i.e., competency benchmarks) for each competency as expected at their level of professional development (Fouad et al., 2009). Indeed, the most frequently cited reason for students to be terminated from a program

is inadequate performance in the functional (i.e., what psychologists do) competency domains (i.e., (Vacha-Haase, Davenport, & Kerewsky, 2004). This is interesting, given that the majority of trainer distress relates to trainee competence problems in the foundational domains (i.e., knowledge, skills, and attitudes that are core to all of the functions of psychology).

Psychosocial Stress

Another group of TPPCs are those struggling with the psychosocial stress associated with training or various phase-of-life changes or conflicts. Sources of distress may include trainee age/life phase challenges (e.g., envisioning and solidifying a first adult life structure, including a career dream), perceived discrimination, problems with work/school-life balance, having a second career, geographic relocation, managing personal and/or familial real-life transitions and challenges, changes in one's support system, financial stress, academic responsibilities, cognitive challenges (Arnett, 2000; Levinson, Darrow, Klein, Levinson, & McKee, 1978; Sheehy, 2006). Handling such psychosocial stress may be particularly challenging for neophyte trainees, who are wrestling with concerns and anxieties about adequacy and competency as they work to assimilate a professional identity. In response to psychosocial stress, trainees often experience emotional disturbances, insomnia, isolation, role ambiguity, a sense of professional vulnerability and feelings commonly associated with the impostor syndrome (Bruss & Kopala, 1993; Clance, 1986; Johnson, 2007a; Mallinckrodt, Leong, & Kralj, 1989). The acuity/chronicity, severity, and nature of these issues combined with the trainee's own stage of personal and professional development, strengths, and level of social support will inform the extent to which the trainee actually manifests difficulties in competence.

Often, trainees encountering high levels of psychosocial stress have difficulties availing themselves of wellness activities, such as social support, regular exercise, hobbies, spirituality, and personal psychotherapy (El-Ghoroury, Galper, Sawaqdeh, & Bufka, 2012). Commonly reported barriers to doing so include insufficient time and money (El-Ghoroury et al., 2012).

Psychological Difficulties

An additional group of TPPCs exhibit psychological difficulties that may interfere with training in a variety of ways. Psychological problems may include limited self-awareness, as well as poor self-esteem and shame and a subsequent fear of criticism that require trainers to walk on eggs when delivering critical feedback (Barnes, 2004). Often, trainees who struggle with psychopathology (ranging from mood and anxiety disorders to more severe forms of mental illness) and substance-use difficulties have interference with their learning, consistent performance, and professional development (Enyedy et al., 2003). Although rates of mental health and substance-use problems have not been clearly documented among trainees, the relatively high levels in practicing professionals as well as the rates in graduate students more broadly are suggestive that mood, anxiety, and substance-use disorders are not uncommon and that suicidal behavior also occurs (Drum, Brownson, Denmark, & Smith, 2009; O'Connor, 2001; Silverman, Meyer, Sloane, Raffel, & Pratt, 1997).

Other trainees may manifest personality or character pathology in the form of narcissism or defensiveness that interfere with supervision and the receipt of constructive feedback (Forrest et al., 1999; Gill, 1999). Alternatively, trainees may demonstrate excessive competiveness and compulsivity or extreme perfectionistic strivings that lead to distress and interpretation of feedback as criticism. It is not uncommon for these trainees to have problems with affect regulation or relationship problems outside the training environment. Of particular concern are those individuals who have problems with integrity that may present as lying or dishonesty. Problems suggestive of personality difficulties are some of the most frequently noted concerns in TPPC (Forrest et al., 1999). However, it is likely that, similar to their licensed colleagues, trainees with personality problems are reluctant to seek appropriate mental health services when they are psychologically distressed (O'Connor, 2001).

Interpersonal Challenges

Sometimes related to the aforementioned psychological difficulties are trainee interpersonal difficulties. Problems in the foundational competency domain of interpersonal relationships that appear in the trainer-trainee relationship are some of the most problematic in the training process (Forrest et al., 1999). Interpersonal difficulties in the work setting may be a reflection of psychological problems, maladaptive interpersonal skills, trauma history, and/or history of professionally injuring experiences, etc. The rubric of interpersonal challenges includes, but is not limited to, problems with attachment, limitations with regard to level of emotional intelligence,

inadequate empathy and compassion, dependency/autonomy issues, lack of appropriate levels of self-disclosure (too much or too little), authority issues, problematic power dynamics, conflicts with peers and other colleagues, boundary problems, and cultural insensitivity (Nelson, Barnes, Evans, & Triggiano, 2008; Yourman, 2003; Yourman & Farber, 1996).

TPPCs do not seem to know how to maximally utilize supervisory or educational relationships, have expectations of their trainers or training relationships that are unarticulated and/or unrealistic, and ignore and/or appear unaware of the trainers' (or program's) expectations for their performance. Sometimes TPPCs overuse trainers in an effort to address unmet developmental needs (Mehlman & Glickhauf-Hughes, 1994). Here TPPCs may idealize their trainers as perfect parents in hopes of creating a corrective interpersonal experience. At other times trainees minimize their interactions with their trainers (as if they have nothing to learn). Some trainees complain or gossip about trainers behind their back without addressing the concerns directly with the trainers. More recently, the use of social media (e.g., Facebook) to complain about trainers has become commonplace.

Trainers: Faculty Members or Supervisors

Psychologists who train graduate students, interns, and postdoctoral residents enter into relationships in which they accept the trust and confidence of trainees to act in their best interests (Plaut, 1993). Training psychologists accept an ethical responsibility to benefit and not harm trainees, respect trainees' autonomy, demonstrate fairness, avoid insensitivity or bias, and model integrity in their relationships with trainees (American Psychological Association, 2010; Kitchener, 1992). Although many faculty members and supervisors are consistently astute ethically, skilled clinically, and competent in the art of training, this is not always the case.

When training goes awry, trainers' shortcomings may be implicated. These difficulties may be classified as inadequate or harmful, depending on how negative the impact is upon trainees (Ellis, 2010). Data from one study revealed that at least one-half to three-quarters of the trainees sampled reported receiving harmful or inadequate supervision at some point in their careers (Ellis, 2010). Evidence suggests that graduate school faculty and clinical supervisors sometimes cause or at least contribute to dysfunctional training relationships (Clark,

Harden, & Johnson, 2000; Johnson & Huwe, 2002; Nelson et al., 2008; Nelson & Friedlander, 2001). For example, trainees may feel less comfortable self-disclosing in these problematic training contexts, which in turn worsens the training relationship (Hess et al., 2008). Even productive and successful training relationships are vulnerable to misunderstanding, conflict, and ultimately, negative outcomes for trainees (Johnson, 2007a; Simon & Eby, 2003). In this section, we highlight some characteristics and behaviors of trainers that contribute to dysfunctional training relationships and may result in negative outcomes for trainees.

Challenges in Training/Supervisory Technique

There is mounting evidence that although some individuals may be naturally inclined to be gifted trainers, in general, training is required for someone to be competent as a trainer (Milne & James, 2002). Deficits in knowledge, skills, and attitudes may be related to inadequate training and preparation and exacerbated by inexperience (Eby, McManus, Simon, & Russell, 2000). It is not unusual for new assistant professors or begining supervisors to come directly from an internship or postdoctoral residency. One step removed from trainee status themselves, these neophyte trainers may lack competence with a range of clinical problems, treatment modalities, research designs, and statistical techniques, let alone mastery of the discipline. Those who are new to their role as trainers and associated authority, clout, and privilege may be most vulnerable to abusing their power (Ellis, 2010).

Some trainers themselves lack critical competencies making them ineffective as teachers and supervisors (Falender & Shafranske, 2004; Falender & Shafranske, 2007, 2008). Moreover, trainers may demonstrate deficits in specific competencies related to training (e.g., teaching, supervising). For example, trainers sometimes manifest challenges in their supervisory technique via unrealistic or irrational beliefs and expectations related to the trainee and the training relationship. In a related vein, their expectations may be inconsistent, sometimes shifting without notice to trainees. As another example, trainers may demonstrate difficulties in balancing the demands of the workplace and possibly their own personal lives with the trainee needs of their trainees. This lack of critical and/or specific competencies appears to be associated with less positive patient outcomes (Callahan, Almstrom, Swift, Borja, & Heath, 2009).

Because very few training programs afford trainees comprehensive training and supervised experience in these domains, trainers' problems with technical competence are not atypical (Hadjistavropoulos, Kehler, & Hadjistavropoulos, 2010; Johnson, 2007a). Of course, problems with technical competence may be intensified by trainers' own insecurity and anxiety about these deficits. Trainees may be particularly resentful of teachers and supervisors who attempt to hide their relative weaknesses in knowledge, skills, attitudes, and experience and react defensively when these are revealed (Clark et al., 2000). In addition, they may find the learning environments created by such trainers to not be conducive to optimal learning and professional growth.

One manifestation of problems in supervisory technique relates to a lack of sensitivty to trainees' developmental level and needs (Aten, Strain, & Gillespie, 2008; Kaslow, McCarthy, Rogers, & Summerville, 1992; Kaslow & Rice, 1985; Stoltenberg, 2005; Stoltenberg & McNeill, 2010). These trainers often have a difficult time engaging their trainees in collaborative and interpersonally connected alliances that become increasingly reciprocal as the trainee advances professionally (Johnson, 2007b). Moreover, they may not be attuned to trainees' development as mature junior colleagues (Barett & Barber, 2005). In addition, trainers may not develop appropriately as supervisors, which will challenge their capacity to effectively supervise trainees, particularly those with problems of professional competence (Aten et al., 2008).

One specific way in which trainers may lack technical competence is in addressing competence problems in trainees and in serving in the gatekeepr role (Ellis, 2010). They may offer inadequate formative feedback/evaluation such that trainees do not have sufficient opportunities to change the behaviors or correct shortcomings prior to the summative evaluation (Benson & Holloway, 2005). They often feel uncomfortable reporting trainees whose performance is below expected benchmarks because of an unwillingness to commit the time and effort necessary to do so. This may be reflected in a lack of adequate written documentation, in part due to a lack of familiarity with what information to record and how; limited awareness of potential remediation options; and fears of retaliation by the trainee, including appeals and legal processes (Dudek, Marks, & Regehr, 2005). In addition, they may exhibit an imbalance in their roles as gatekeeper versus advocate, such that they overlook problems of competence or fail to provide adequate support and direction.

Psychological and Medical Difficulties

Just as trainees may manifest psychological difficulties (e.g., mental health symptoms/diagnoses, substance-use problems) that impede training, so, too, may trainers. There are similiarities between the two. Of note, despite the research on mental health problems in practicing psychologists, no studies could be located specific to trainers. Yet it is reasonable to hypothesize that just as many psychologists with significant psychological difficulties continue to offer psychological services, despite being too distressed to do so competently (Guy, Poelstra, & Stark, 1989; Pope, Tabachnick, & Keith-Spiegel, 1987), many trainers may continue to train even when their psychological difficulties impair their capacity to do so effectively.

Although no literature specifically looks at the role of personality disorders in trainers and their impact on the training process, some relevant information suggests that maladpative personality traits may result in training going awry. For example, trainers may present with maladaptive personality traits such as narcissism, rigidity, or compulsivity that interfere with productive training relationships (Scandura, 1998). In a related vein, they may struggle an inordinate amount with issues of responsibility, authority, and power (Ellis, 2010). Common misuses of power by supervisors include favoritism, imposition of style/orientation, violations of confidentiality, and inappropriately using supervision to meet their own needs (Murphy & Wright, 2005). Trainees may experience these trainers as egotistical, bullying, critical, or perfectionistic; the effort required to maintain the relationship may be overwhelming for the trainee. When such power dynamics are dominant in the relationship, appropriate self-disclosure on trainee's parts often is inhibited (Hess et al., 2008). One additional example suggestive of a problem with boundaries that may be indicative of personality pathology is supervisors who self-disclose too much (Knox, Edwards, Hess, & Hill, 2011). Self-disclosure on the supervisors' parts may facilitate supervisory processes and outcomes, particularly when supervisors self-disclose to normalize trainees' experiences, build supervisory relationships, and/or make instructional points (Knox et al., 2011; Ladany & Walker, 2003). However, when self-disclosure is frequent and/or inappropriate in nature, it may have a deleterious effect on trainees (Knox et al., 2011).

One often acute manifestation of trainers' psychological difficulties appears in the form of burnout (Johnson & Barnett, 2011; Pope & Vasquez, 2010; Shapiro, Brown, & Biegel, 2007). Burnout refers to emotional exhaustion accompanied by distress, depersonalization, decreased motivation, and reduced effectiveness and personal accomplishment that occurs in the context of high stress and/or chronic emotional strain. There is evidence of relatively high levels of burnout and its correlates among licensed psychologists (Ackerley, Burnell, Holder, & Kurdek, 1988). In a related vein, trainers may experience vicarious traumatization (stress reactions in response to hearing the narratives of their traumatized patients) and compassion fatigue associated with the emotional challenges associated with their work (Shapiro et al., 2007). When these phenomena are not adequately addressed, they can negatively impact the training process.

Trainers (and trainees) may experience serious medical problems and their nature and/or treatment may negatively impact their level of professional competence (Johnson & Barnett, 2011). In addition, the attendant negative affect may make appropriate self-assessments challenging. If trainers are unable to recognize when their medical difficulties due to their emotional distress, denial, fear, and countertransferential reactions, and/or associated stressors make it impossible to train effectively, their continued attempts to educate their trainees are likely to negatively impact the training relationship and process (Johnson & Barnett, 2011).

Self-reflection is another core competency within professional psychology, and trainers have an ethical responsibility to continually self-assess, especially in the context of psychological or medical problems (Johnson & Barnett, 2011; Orchowski, Evangelista, & Probst, 2010). Developing reflectivity is a challenge to some extent for all trainees, but there are a significant group of trainees who experience myriad barriers to being self-reflective in a developmentally relevant fashion (Orchowski et al., 2010). Trainers who manifest a limited capacity for self-awareness often are engaged in supervisory relationships that are problematic. Unfortunately, problems in accurate self-assessment are rampant and likely are compounded in magnitude when trainers are struggling with their own emotional and/or physical well-being.

Interpersonal Challenges

As noted earlier, relationships constitute a core competency within professional psychology and problems in this competency domain on the part of a trainer often are a central reason for training to go awry (Westefeld, 2009). Even when trainers are technically competent and well-intended, they may lack the requisite interpersonal dexterity (e.g., emotional intelligence, affect regulation, capacity for attachment and appropriate separation, communication skill) necessary for efficacy in the trainer role (Batten & Santanello, 2009; Eby et al., 2000; Johnson & Huwe, 2002; Simon & Eby, 2003). In addition, they may fail to have the interpersonal sensitivity needed to ascertain trainees' levels of professional development and to provide the developmentally informed training and supervision that is the sine quo non of effective teaching (Westefeld, 2009). Counterproductive events have been found to occur in supervisions when trainees experience their supervisors as dismissive of their thoughts and feelings (Gray et al., 2001; Ladany, Friedlander, & Nelson, 2005).

One interpersonal behavior on the part of trainers that can be particularly problematic is that of interpersonal disengagement. When trainees are asked to report the source of dissatisfaction with their primary faculty mentor, complaints about unavailability, neglect, and other distancing behaviors top the list (Clark et al., 2000; Cronan-Hillix, Davidson, Cronan-Hillix, & Gensheimer, 1986). Inadequate oversight and engagement with trainees for whom one bears responsibility is likely to result in at least two negative training outcomes. First, unfulfilled obligations for quality teaching and supervision contribute to competency deficits in trainees. Second, neglected trainees, in an effort to interpret their trainers' disengagement, may erroneously attribute the neglect to their own inadequacy or failure in the eyes of the trainers. This outcome may have long-term consequences for the neophyte psychologists' professional self-esteem and confidence.

Another interpersonal behavior that can be problematic on the part of trainers is that of rigidity. This may take the form of rigid adherence to a particular theoretical framework, such that other views on the trainees' part are criticized or not even explored or respected. Although the teaching of a single model may allow for a greater coherence of conceptualization and associated interventions, when trainers teach theoretical purity rather than creative eclecticism or integration, there may be a failure to help trainees develop a thorough understanding of people's suffering and how it can most effectively be alleviated (Gabbard, 2005). On another note,

rigidity also may appear as a lack of willingness to acknowledge one's own mistakes and to share such errors, in part as a form of role modeling.

Finally, some trainers are so overly interpersonally sensitive to their trainees that they fail to remember their duty to protect the public (Forrest et al., 1999; Westefeld, 2009). Although trainers have the ethical responsibility to assure that their trainees are not harming others, some are so empathic about their trainees' personal struggles that they lose sight of the impact of these difficulties on the public. These trainers often are caught in the middle between their desire to be supportive and their responsibility to the public.

Cultural Challenges

Individual and cultural diversity is another core competency. Thus, for training and supervision to be effective, trainers must manifest a high degree of cultural competence. There is evidence to support the contention that a trainer's level of multicultural competence influences both the supervisory process and the outcome (Inman, 2006).

For training to be multiculturally responsive, gender sensitive, and lesbian-gay-bisexual-transgender-queer (LGBTQ) affirming, trainers must provide safe environments in which trainees are encouraged to examine gender, cultural issues pertaining to race/ethnicity, and topics related to sexual orientation in a fashion that positively impacts trainees, training relationships, and the clinical work (Burkard et al., 2006; Burkard, Knox, Hess, & Schultz, 2009; Dressel, Consoli, Kim, & Atkinson, 2007; MacKinnon, Bhatia, Sunderani, Affleck, & Smith, 2011; Pfohl, 2004; Porter, 2010). They facilitate cultural discussions and collaborative discourse that enable trainees to formulate and share their own culturally informed identity, develop multicultural self-efficacy, be cognizant of their own areas for growth in this arena, and continuously strive to be more culturally sensitive in all professional endeavors (Butler-Boyd, 2010; Constantine, 2001; Mori, Inman, & Caskie, 2009; Ober, Granello, & Henfield, 2009). Such a process is associated with higher levels of satisfaction with the supervision process (Mori et al., 2009). In addition, they demonstrate their own multicultural self-awareness, which serves as a model for cultural identity development and sensitivity to cultural intersectionalities in their trainees (Dressel et al., 2007). And, they are attuned to power dynamics in a fashion that supports trainees in having their voices heard (Hernandez & McDowell, 2010). They openly examine their own experiences of being both the sender and the recipient of microaggressions (Murphy-Shigematsu, 2010). High levels of trainer multicultural competence is associated with a productive and satisfying training relationships (Inman, 2006).

Conversely, trainers who are culturally unresponsive, ignore, actively discount, or dismiss cultural issues (Dressel et al., 2007). They manifest myriad microaggressions as well (Butler-Boyd, 2010). Similarly, those who are LGBTQ-nonaffirming are perceived by trainees to be biased or oppressive (Burkard et al., 2009). Multicultural conflicts between trainers and trainees, inappropriate application of multicultural approaches, and the lack of attention to diversity considerations can negatively affect the trainee, the training relationship, the trainee's clinical work, and associated patient outcomes (Burkard et al., 2006; Burkard et al., 2009; Kaduvettoor et al., 2009).

Ethical Challenges

Supervision dilemmas account for approximately 2% of the ethical dilemmas encountered by psychologists (Pope & Vetter, 1992), a number that may reflect an underestimation, given that the sample doing the reporting consisted of psychologists rather than trainees. In addition, there is empirical evidence that a significant percentage of trainees (51%) believe that their supervisors do not adhere to at least on ethical guideline. Common ethical violations relate to competence (discussed above), confidentiality, boundary problems, multicultural insensitivity, and multiple/dual roles/relationships (including inappropriate sexual/romantic relationships) (Ladany, Lehrman-Waterman, Molinaro, & Wolgast, 1999; West, 2003; Westefeld, 2009). Moreover, failure to properly carry out supervision is one of the most cited reasons that psychologists are sued (Pope & Vasquez, 2010).

Problems with the maintenance of boundaries on the part of trainers are a particular ethical challenge that can negatively impact the training process (Heru, Strong, Price, & Recupero, 2004). If learning to discern and honor the boundaries between one's personal and professional roles is an essential component of the ethical and legal standards competence for psychology trainees (Fouad et al., 2009), then it is essential that trainers model appropriate boundaries in their relationships with trainees (Barnett, 2008; Blevins-Knabe, 1992). At times, healthy and engaged trainer-trainee relationships will include social activities, travel to conferences, frequent advisory or supervisory interaction,

and a range of opportunities to glimpse each other's personal lives, which often are very nurturing and professionally supportive, yet sometimes fall within the context of boundary crossings (Barnett, 2008; Plaut, 1993). Of course, these multiple trainer roles can easily heighten the risk of boundary violations and exploitation of trainees. Trainers must maintain a clear-headed balance between the mentoring benefits of slowly developing mutuality and collegiality between trainer and trainee and the danger of harmful intrusions into one another's personal lives (Plaut, 1993).

The most transparent and egregious boundary violations and dual roles involve sexual contact between trainers and trainees (Hammel, Olkin, & Taube, 1996; Slimp & Burian, 1994). Such relationships clearly are unethical, frequently involve exploitation on the part of trainers, and nearly always are emotionally devastating for trainees and harmful to training relationships (American Psychological Association, 2010; Bartell & Rubin, 1990; Johnson & Huwe, 2002; Koenig & Spano, 2003). Yet, boundary violations and exploitation occur in many other ways, and may involve credit for academic work, emotional caretaking, or financial benefit.

Another form of exploitation, that also is an ethical violation, relates to cloning and theoretical abuse. Respect for the dignity and autonomy of trainees is an essential component of trainer ethical responsibility (American Psychological Association, 2010; Kitchener, 1992). Yet training relationships occasionally go awry when trainees, always occupying a power-down position in relation to trainers, feel coerced, either subtly or overtly, to please or comply with the trainer in one of two ways. First, evidence suggests that most trainers are vulnerable to attempting to "clone" trainees in their own image. For instance, when asked to name their "most successful" trainees, graduate school professors often list those trainees whose career paths most closely resembles their own (Blackburn, Chapman, & Cameron, 1981). Trainers may seek validation of their own career decisions by pressuring trainees to pursue similar trajectories and make similiar commitments to research and clinical foci. Theoretical abuse constitutes a second way in which trainers might compromise trainee autonmy. Theoretical abuse occurs when trainers use their position of power to dismiss trainees' perspectives and force or convince trainees to adopt the trainer's own theoretical position or construction of reality (O'Neill & Sankowsky, 2001). For instance, trainees may feel compelled to publicaly endorse and personally adopt their trainers' theoretical orientation to psychotherapy or preferred research paradigm. Cloning and theoretical abuse may provoke feelings of helplessness or resentment on the part of trainees (Clark et al., 2000).

Trainee-Trainer Matches

Trainee-trainer matches are optimal if a strong positive working alliance develops between the two individuals (Overholser, 2004). When both parties make such a commitment, the relationship tends to feel safe and respectful.

A number of factors contribute to positive matches. Both parties prioritize time for shared feedback. They encourage honest evaluation and engage in nondefensive sharing of personal contributions to counterproductive events and errors. Good working relationships also tend to occur if there is a good fit between the developmental level of the trainee and that phase of professional development most comfortable for the supervisor and similarities in conceptual/theoretical perspective (Ramos-Sanchez et al., 2002). Such a bond is associated with more effectively meeting the tasks of the supervisory process (Riggs & Bretz, 2006). In addition, a positive match is correlated with higher levels of appropriate trainee self-disclosure and lower levels of nondisclosure (Mehr, Ladany, & Caskie, 2010).

Training may go awry when there are dysfunctional trainer-trainee matches, often characterized by differences in expectations, a lack of mutual empathy and empowerment, conflict, or multiple roles (Walsh, Gillespie, Greer, & Eanes, 2003). In addition this occurs when negative supervisory events occur. It is not uncommon for such events to center around tensions related to supervision role and tasks; differing interpersonal styles and associated relational conflicts; issues of attraction; and conflicts related to ethical, legal, and multicultural issues.

These negative training encounters have a destructive impact on trainees' development, on trainers, and on the training/supervision process. The impact depends on trainees' developmental level and the strength of the working alliances. However, typically, they are associated with weaker supervisory alliances and lower levels of satisfaction with the training process and relationship (Eby, Durley, Evans, & Ragins, 2008; Ramos-Sanchez et al., 2002). Common reactions to such match problems on the part of one or both parties include paralysis, distancing, provocation, and/or sabotage.

Peers with Problems of Professional Competence

There is mounting evidence that trainees are aware of peers with problems of professional competence (Shen-Miller et al., 2011; Veilleux, January, VanderVeen, Reddy, & Klonoff, 2012). Indeed, more than 40% of trainees indicate having a peer who exhibits problems of professional competence (Mearns & Allen, 1991; Rosenberg, Getzelman, Arcinue, & Oren, 2005; Shen-Miller et al., 2011). The most frequently reported problems that peers report about members of their trainee cohort fall under the professionalism and relational competency clusters (Mearns & Allen, 1991; Oliver et al., 2004; Rosenberg et al., 2005; Shen-Miller et al., 2011). Peers perceive trainees with competence problems in a more sympathetic light when they are viewed as having difficulties that could be remediated versus those who are viewed as unable to attain competence and thus as unfit for a career in psychology (Veilleux et al., 2012).

Peers have significant concerns about colleagues with such difficulties (Oliver et al., 2004) and frequently become aware of maladaptive peer behaviors before their trainers do (Forrest et al., 1999; Huprich & Rudd, 2004). Trainees also report little confidence either that members of their cohort or their trainers will take the requisite action for addressing peer competence difficulties. In other words, they have concerns about *gateslipping*, that is the process of TPPCs being advanced through their training program without sufficient attention or remediation (Gaubutz & Vera, 2006). Trainees want trainers to effectively address their peers with problems of professional competence and either assist them with remediation efforts or help them to exit the program and potentially the profession.

Having a peer with a professional competence problem can negatively impact one's own learning and the training context and culture (Gaubutz & Vera, 2006; Mearns & Allen, 1991; Oliver et al., 2004; Rosenberg et al., 2005; Shen-Miller et al., 2011; Veilleux et al., 2012). This may be particularly true when the peer's difficulties are manifested in the form of peer-to-peer conflict. These challenges often are evident in the context of group supervision or group work teams. Often, trainees respond to peers with problems of professional competence by gossiping and withdrawing, and, as a result, they are less likely themselves to engage in behavior marked by professionalism.

Training Contexts

Any conceptualization of a training process gone awry must consider the broader context. For example, TPPCs do not exist in a vacuum, and, thus, in addition to considering the various individual manifestations of competency difficulties, it is essential to consider the ecological context in which these trainees are embedded (Forrest, Shen-Miller, & Elman, 2008). Specifically, it is useful to consider the trainee within five nested systems as described by Bronfenbrenner: microsystem, mesosystem, exosystem, macrosystem, and chronosystem (Bronfenbrenner, 1979). TPPCs often manifest difficulties in their microsystems, that is in their direct interactions with their trainers and peers. The mesosystem consists of interactions among colleagues, peers, and trainers. The exosystem pertains to such professional processes as competency benchmarks, remediation and dismissal policies, gatekeeping requirements, licensure, accreditation, and professional association policies. Cultural beliefs about being a psychologist, training practices to become a psychologist, and beliefs about various aspects of diversity are the constructs that fall within the macrosystem rubric. Finally, the chronosystem is a construct that incorporates such diverse notions as the developmental progression from novice to expert, capacity to function increasingly independently across the sequence of training, changes in specificity of professional competencies, the culture of competency assessment and accountability, and the supply/demand imbalance at each transition point.

Another aspect of the context that needs to be taken into account relates to context in which trainers are embedded. The following are examples to be considered in this regard. Often, there is a failure to carefully select and adequately prepare trainers for their roles. Frequently, there is a failure to communicate expectations/competencies for trainers and trainees. Moreover, trainers are often caught between institutional pressure and educational/supervisory demands. For example, they may be required to see high volumes of patients themselves in order to cover their own salaries, which may limit the time and resources that they have available to offer the depth and breadth of supervision required. Further, the extent to which a trainer is central to a training program may influence the training process. Although there are advantages to including outside faculty/supervisors (e.g., trusted trainers outside of the system, different perspectives offered), there can be many challenges as well (Ungar & Costanzo, 2007). Their lack of awareness of the institutional system may lead them to guide and advise trainees in a fashion that causes the trainees difficulty in managing their roles and responsibilities. In addition, such trainers may not have access to information about the trainee that would enable them to most effectively address competence difficulties exhibited by a trainee. As another example, there is evidence that it is not uncommon for people in positions of power to be aware of ethical violations on the part of the trainer and yet to do nothing about such problematic behavior (Ladany et al., 1999). A context that fails to address such violations is colluding in the failure of the training relationship and process.

The training program itself is another part of the context to be considered when understanding factors that lead to training going awry. Some programs provide limited support for trainers. It is not uncommon for trainers to have multiple competing demands placed upon them by their programs. Not uncommonly trainers are caught between institutional pressures and educational/supervisory demands. Sometimes trainers are forced to teach/supervise when they are not invested in doing so. Some programs have few core faculty/supervisors or the core trainers have little consistent interaction with the trainees and thus most of the training is provided by adjunct faculty or external supervisors. Such a setup often is associated with diffusion of responsibility for training (Johnson & Nelson, 1999). In addition, frequently, programs pay inadequate attention to matching trainers and trainees in a fashion that would increase the likelihood of maximum effectiveness of the relationship. Finally, often there are inadequate or the absence of policies and procedures governing the training enterprise (e.g., competencies required for successful program completion, procedures for responding to trainee-trainer conflict).

Recommendations

This section offers recommendations for minimizing the factors that can keep training from going awry.

Trainees

An extensive discussion of recommendations for effectively addressing TPPC when it appears to be the individual trainee that is the primary reason that training has gone awry is beyond the scope of this chapter. However, the following are some key recommendations related to training considerations vis-a-vis trainees that should be heeded in an effort to keep training on track.

In selecting trainees, trainers should strive to ascertain whether trainees possess the requisite levels of ethical engagement and psychological fitness to function productively within the profession (Johnson & Campbell, 2004). This is facilitated by the incorporation of a multi-informant evaluation of prospective trainees, with particular attention to foundational competencies (e.g., professionalism), not just intellectual prowess and potential for adequate performance in the functional competency domains.

To reduce the likelihood of exhibiting problems of professional competence, trainees should be encouraged to read the competency-based literature and to remain open to seeking out and benefitting from closer supervision, consultation, training, and mentoring related to the core competency domains. Trainees should be supported to engage in appropriate self-care activities as well. To this end, it is recommended that, from the outset, training programs focus on highlighting the importance of self-care and wellness activities and that such participation is modeled by the trainers (Baker, 2003; El-Ghoroury et al., 2012; Norcross & Guy, 2007).

More comprehensive training in self-assessment would be beneficial not just for TPPC, but for all trainees. A variety of pedagogies are available for facilitating the process of self-reflection (Guiffrida, 2005) and for doing so in a developmentally sensitive fashion (Orchowski et al., 2010). For example, directed self-reflection protocols can facilitate junior trainees' preparation for engaging in clinical work in new settings (Moffett, 2009). The supervisory relationship can serve as a context for encouraging here-and-now reflective conversations (Osborn, Paez, & Carrabine, 2007). In addition, there are some models for honing one's self-assessment of competence, such as those related to cultural self-awareness assessment (Roysircar, 2004). Moreover, there are models for reflective supervision that target helping trainees manage the strong affect and stress that may emerge in response to certain types of intense clinical work (Bernstein & Edwards, 2012). Of course, educational and training efforts related to self-assessment must underscore the challenges that individuals historically have had with regard to accurate self-reflection and thoughtful present strategies for improving such processes (Johnson, Barnett, Elman, Forrest, & Kaslow, 2012).

It is helpful with TPPC to encourage them to focus in more detail on developing and utilizing coping strategies to assist them in more effectively modulating their emotions, such as examining the ways in which they are impacted by their clinical endeavors and how this information informs them about patient issues (de Oliveira & Vandenberghe, 2009). With these trainees, supervisors can use a combination of modeling, facilitating, and exploring different perspective to teach them more skills in critical thinking, which, in turn, can improve their interpersonal capacities including empathy (Deal, 2003). Often it is advisable to recommend personal psychotherapy as part of a remediation process, particularly for TPPC whose psychological difficulties negatively impact their performance (Elman & Forrest, 2004). Trainees are most likely to avail themselves of personal therapy when they are in a training context in which personal therapy is valued (Dearing, Maddux, & Tangney, 2005).

In general, when dealing with TPPC, the following steps should be taken (Forrest et al., 1999; Forrest et al., 2008; Kaslow et al., 2007; Lamb, Cochran, & Jackson, 1991; Lamb et al., 1987; Wilkerson, 2006). First, the trainee's role in the difficulties should be identified and documented, followed by an opportunity for the trainee to reply and correct the problematic behaviors. All relevant parties (e.g., trainee, all key trainers, pertinent administrators) should be included in this and subsequent processes. Discussing professional competence problems with trainees often is a challenging process, and these discussions are likely to be most productive if trainers follow recent guidance with regard to having these difficult but necessary conversations (Jacobs et al., 2011). Second, if the problems persist, a competency-based remediation plan should be implemented, with specific expectations noted (Wilkerson, 2006). Finally, if there is a failure of this remediation plan, more serious consequences should be considered and enacted (e.g., probation, termination).

Trainers

Training programs should be more thoughtful about the trainers they select. They need to make a committed effort to select trainers based on their capacity to be effective trainers. For example, given that prosocial personality variables, such as other-oriented empathy and helpfulness, predict a commitment to training and mentoring (Allen, 2003), relationship competence should be a preeminent criterion when selecting faculty members or supervisors.

Being competent to train is an ethical responsibility for those that occupy training roles (Falender & Shafranske, 2007). Thus, professional psychology will benefit from a culture in which trainers receive adequate training and supervision in performing all their roles and responsibilities, are open to both self-assessment and input from others, and engage in ongoing professional development activities to hone their competence as trainers (Westefeld, 2009). In keeping with the growing culture of competence (Roberts, Borden, Christiansen, & Lopez, 2005), training and supervision should be competency-based (Kaslow, Falendar, & Grus, 2012; Tebes et al., 2011). When trainers receive supervision on their teaching/supervision, a critical-events perspective might be beneficial. This framework can assist trainers in forging productive working alliances with trainees and interacting with trainees in a sensitive fashion that strengthens the learning environment and is mindful of the trainees' level of professional development, cultural background, and emotional experiences (Ladany & Bradley, 2010; Ladany et al., 2005). Training and consultations focused on becoming effective trainers should address the ethical and professional obligations associated with balancing the roles of teacher/supervisor/mentor/guide with that of evaluator and gatekeeper (Johnson et al., 2008).

For trainers who are confronted with psychological and/or medical difficulties, the following strategies are recommended. First, health-challenged trainers should take part in a range of self-care activities, such as engaging in nurturing interpersonal relationships, focusing on physical health and well-being (e.g., exercise, food intake, sleep, substance use), setting boundaries, participating in personal psychotherapy, being involved in creative endeavors, and so on (Baker, 2003; Barnett, Baker, Elman, & Schoener, 2007; Norcross & Guy, 2007; Smith & Moss, 2009). In addition, it is imperative that they be mindful of their work-life balance and modify either their work or their personal situation to ensure as optimal an integration of the two as possible (Halpern & Murphy, 2009).

Just as ongoing self-assessment/self-reflection is critical for trainees, it is essential for trainers as well (Belar et al., 2001). Such self-examination can enable trainers to become increasingly cognizant of the ways in which their actions negatively impact their relationships with trainers and others in the training environment. They, too, need to be open to engaging in personal psychotherapy in order to improve their interpersonal interactions.

It is not uncommon for trainers to struggle to integrate diversity issues into their work with trainees and there are several barriers to their doing so. They should participate in continuing professional development activities related to cultural responsiveness vis-à-vis a diverse array of factors in the educational and supervisory process. They must be well versed in multicultural competencies and the implementation of such competencies and model them for their trainees (Westefeld, 2009). It behooves them to utilize mediated learning experiences for themselves and their trainees to ensure that a collaborative and facilitative learning environment related to issues of diversity is created for both parties (Yabusaki, 2010). Further, trainers need to not only work within the trainee's zone of proximal development (i.e., difference between what a trainee can do without help and what he/she can do with help) to ensure that such topics are infused into the training experience, but they also need to be mindful of their own zone of proximal development related to this topic (Yabusaki, 2010).

Trainers must engage in lifelong learning activities associated with honing their capacity for complex ethical decision making (Pope & Keith-Spiegel, 2008). They also must be informed about the complicated nature of the multiple relationships that are associated with supervision, become sophisticated and culturally informed in their thinking about boundary crossings and boundary violations, and be current in their understanding of strategies for preventing boundary violations (Barnett, Lazarus, Vasquez, Moorehead-Slaughter, & Johnson, 2007; Gottlieb, Robinson, & Younggren, 2007; Gutheil & Brodsky, 2011; Pope & Keith-Spiegel, 2008). As noted earlier, probably the most egregious boundary violation is sexual in nature, and some authors provide guiding principles and associated strategies for helping trainers manage their sexual feelings, rather than act on them (Gutheil & Brodsky, 2011). This, in turn, is associated with more productive supervisory relationships and the trainee's increased capacity to manage their patients' sexual issues (Koenig & Spano, 2003). For trainers who are vulnerable to engaging in boundary violations, ongoing supervision and consultation may be needed (Gabbard & Lester, 2002; Gottlieb et al., 2007).

Trainer-Trainee Matches

A number of steps can be taken to increase the likelihood that the match between trainer and trainee is positive. Both parties need to appreciate the importance of prioritizing relationship development. It is helpful if they tend to differences in theoretical and interpersonal styles and acknowledge these openly. It is recommended that they contextualize any dyadic conflicts in light of developmental and environmental factors. Addressing power imbalances can be critical, particularly as they process conflicts and negative interactional events directly and thoughtfully (Nelson et al., 2006). Both parties must be open to seeking consultation if direct communication is not effective. There are a variety of administrative steps that can increase the likelihood that a match is successful. For example, it is valuable to foster a culture that values the training dyad, monitors trainer-trainee relationships, assists in addressing problematic trainer-trainees relationships, and makes adjustments to such relationships when indicated. It also is helpful to have a supervisory contract (Falender & Shafranske, 2007) and to utilize tools to evaluate the supervisory process.

Peers

The burgeoning literature suggests a number of strategies that can be undertaken to minimize the effects of peers with competence problems on the training process (Oliver et al., 2004; Rosenberg et al., 2005; Shen-Miller et al., 2011). It is important that programs establish and implement a preventative curriculum and training experiences focused on the necessity of addressing peers with problems of professional competence and both trainee and trainer roles. Programs also should develop clearly outlined processes and procedures for trainees to follow when they observe peers with problems of professional competence.

Trainers must develop the capacity to adequately handle this sensitive issue. They must address the bidirectional impact on peers of trainees with problems of professional competence. It is essential that trainers consider effective ways for balancing the ethical and legal issues regarding confidentiality with the problems associated with secrecy and the value of transparency (American Psychological Association, 2010). It is most effective if trainers can find ways to be transparent, without being specific in a way that violates privacy. In all their efforts to address peers with problems of professional competence, trainers must be attuned to the legal exosystem and utilize a risk management approach in order to minimize legal risk, while promoting fairness and the integrity of the program (Gilfoyle, 2008).

Training Contexts

Training programs can take a number of steps to reduce the likelihood that training will go awry. It is essential that they have effective gatekeeping policies and procedures in place and that these practices be tied to competency expectations (Busseri, Tyler, & King, 2005; Wilkerson, 2006). These should pertain to informed-consent procedures, consistent evaluations, notification and documentation of concerns, graded and systemic approaches to intervention and follow-up for trainees and trainers alike (Vacha-Haase et al., 2004; Wilkerson, 2006). Consideration also should be given to the rights and responsibilities of all parties.

Training programs should ensure that trainees receive adequate and developmentally appropriate training in the provision of supervision (Falender & Shafranske, 2007, 2008). This will likely require increased training and supervision in this competency domain. However, it is likely to result in more effective trainers, who are less likely to be the reason that training is compromised. Parallel to this, trainers need to develop a training/supervisory model that guides their teaching efforts (Falender & Shafranske, 2007, 2008). They also need training and experience in addressing competence problems in trainees (Jacobs et al., 2011). Hopefully, such training will enable training contexts to ensure that TPPCs are addressed most appropriately. We need a culture in which being an effective trainer is viewed as a lifelong and high-priority professional developmental process.

Training is embedded in a litigious society and, thus, it is critical that trainers be mindful of the potential for lawsuits. As such, supervisors need to be certain that they adequately document their supervisory endeavors and follow the American Psychological Association's Ethical Principles of Psychologists and Code of Conduct (Westefeld, 2009).

Finally, to ensure that training is not compromised, it is imperative that there be transformational leaders in every training context that foster and facilitate a competency-based education and training culture (Kaslow et al., 2012). This would ensure that training environments are collegial and collaborative, respectful, empowering, highly professional, sensitive to diversity, and supportive of personal and professional growth (Nelson et al., 2008). Requisite policies and procedures must be in place to ensure the fairness and ethicality of the training environment and they must address difficulties in all members of the community in all competency domains. Such environments are likely to be associated with high levels of relational safety, trusting interaction, transparent and candid communication, creativity, and a sense of connection among all parties (Kaslow et al., 2012). In addition, such contexts value everyone taking seriously and addressing competence problems in any member (trainees or trainers) of the community (Johnson et al., 2012).

Concluding Comments

This chapter reviews the multiplicity of factors that may contribute to training going awry. It is important to remember that often, when training is problematic, there are multiple factors, not just one, that are relevant and need to be tended to. For example, if there is a TPPC coupled with a trainer with competence problems, training is more likely to be problematic and negative than if only one party has difficulties. This requires a thorough assessment of a problematic training context and acute situational awareness on the part of trainers in order to ensure that all relevant factors are identified and targeted for intervention,

Training is most likely to be positive and productive when there is a training context and culture that supports the competence of all of its members, trainees and trainers alike. In such an environment, all members prioritize their own personal and professional competency-related development, as well as the competence of other members of their community.

References

Ackerley, G. D., Burnell, J., Holder, D., & Kurdek, L. A. (1988). Burnout among licensed psychologists. *Professional Psychology: Research and Practice, 19,* 624–631. doi: 10.1037/0735-7028.19.6.624

Allen, T. D. (2003). Mentoring others: A dispositional and motivational approach. *Journal of Vocational Behavior, 62,* 134–154. doi: 10.1016/S0001-8791(02)00046-5

American Psychological Association. (2010). Ethical principles of psychologists and code of conduct. Retrieved from www.apa.org/ethics.

Arnett, J. J. (2000). Emerging adulthood: A theory of development from the late teens through the twenties. *American Psychologist, 55,* 469–480. doi: 10.1037//0003-066X.55.5.469

Aten, J. D., Strain, J. D., & Gillespie, R. E. (2008). A transtheoretical model of clinical supervision. *Training and Education in Professional Psychology, 2,* 1–9. doi: 10.1037/1931-3918.2.1.1

Baker, E. K. (2003). *Caring for ourselves: A therapist's guide to personal and professional well-being.* Washington DC: American Psychological Association.

Barett, M. S., & Barber, J. P. (2005). A developmental approach to the supervision of therapists in training. *Journal of Contemporary Psychotherapy, 35,* 169–183. doi: 10.1007/s10879-005-2698-8

Barnes, K. L. (2004). Applying self-efficacy theory to counselor training and supervision: A comparison of two approaches. *Counselor Education and Supervision, 44,* 56–69. doi: 10.1002/j.1556-6978.2004.tb01860.x

Barnett, J. E. (2008). Mentoring, boundaries, and multiple relationships: Opportunities and challenges. *Mentoring and Tutoring: Partnership in Learning, 16,* 3–16. doi: 10.1080/13611260701800900

Barnett, J. E., Baker, E. K., Elman, N. S., & Schoener, G. R. (2007). In pursuit of wellness: The self-care imperative. *Professional Psychology: Research and Practice, 38,* 603–612. doi: 10.1037/0735-7028.38.6.603

Barnett, J. E., Lazarus, A. A., Vasquez, M. J. T., Moorehead-Slaughter, O., & Johnson, W. B. (2007). Boundary issues and multiple relationships: Fantasy and reality. *Professional Psychology: Research and Practice, 38,* 401–410. doi: 10.1037/0735-7028.38.4.401

Bartell, P. A., & Rubin, L. J. (1990). Dangerous liaisons: Sexual intimacies in supervision. *Professional Psychology: Research and Practice, 21,* 442–450. doi: 10.1037/0735-7028.21.6.442

Batten, S. V., & Santanello, A. P. (2009). A contextual behavioral approach to the role of emotion in psychotherapy supervision. *Training and Education in Professional Psychology, 3,* 148–156. doi: 10.1037/1931-3918.a0014801

Belar, C. D., Brown, R. A., Hersch, L. E., Hornyak, L. M., Rozensky, R. H., Sheridan, E. P.,... Reed, G. W. 2001). Self-assessment in clinical health psychology: A model for ethical expansion of practice. *Professional Psychology: Research and Practice, 32,* 135–141. doi: 10.1037/1522-3736.6.1.625a

Benson, K. P., & Holloway, E. L. (2005). Achieving influence: A grounded theory of how clinical supervisors evaluate trainees. *Qualitative Research in Psychology, 2,* 117–140. doi: 10.1191/1478088705qp033oa

Bernstein, V. J., & Edwards, R. C. (2012). Supporting early childhood practitioners through relationship-based, reflective supervision. *NHSA Dialog: A Research-to-Practice Journal for the Early Childhood Field, 15,* 286–301. doi: 10.1080/15240754.2012.694495

Blackburn, R. T., Chapman, D. W., & Cameron, S. M. (1981). "Cloning" in academe: Mentorship and academic careers. *Research in Higher Education, 15,* 315–327. doi: 10.1007/BF00973512

Blevins-Knabe, B. (1992). The ethics of dual relationships in higher education. *Ethics and Behavior, 2,* 151–163. doi: 10.1207/s15327019eb0203_2

Bronfenbrenner, U. (1979). *The ecology of human development.* Cambridge, MA: Harvard University Press.

Bruss, K. V., & Kopala, M. (1993). Graduate school training in psychology: Its impact upon the development of professional identity. *Psychotherapy: Theory, Research, and Practice, 30,* 685–691. doi: 10.1037/0033-3204.30.4.685

Burkard, A. W., Johnson, A. J., Madson, M. B., Pruitt, N. T., Contreras-Tadych, D. A., Kozlowski, J. M., Hess, S.A.,... Knox, S. (2006). Supervisor cultural responsiveness and unresponsiveness in cross-cultural supervision. *Journal of Counseling Psychology, 53,* 288–301. doi: 10.1037/0022-0167.53.3.288

Burkard, A. W., Knox, S., Hess, S. A., & Schultz, J. (2009). Lesbian, gay, and bisexual supervisees' experiences of LGB-affirmative and nonaffirmative supervision. *Journal of Counseling Psychology, 56,* 176–188. doi: 10.1037/0022-0167.56.1.176

Busseri, M. A., Tyler, J. D., & King, A. R. (2005). An exploratory examination of student dismissals and prompted resignations from clinical psychology Ph.D. training. *Professional Psychology: Research and Practice, 36,* 441–445. doi: 10.1037/0735-7028.36.4.441

Butler-Boyd, N. M. (2010). An African American supervisor's reflections on multicultural supervision. *Training and Education in Professional Psychology, 4,* 11–15. doi: 10.1037/a0018351

Callahan, J. L., Almstrom, C. M., Swift, J. K., Borja, S. E., & Heath, C. J. (2009). Exploring the contribution of supervisors to intervention outcomes. *Training and Education in Professional Psychology*, 3, 72–77. doi: 10.1037/a0014294

Clance, P. R. (1986). *The impostor phenomenon*. New York: Bantam Books.

Clark, R. A., Harden, S. L., & Johnson, W. B. (2000). Mentor relationships in clinical psychology doctoral training: Results of a national survey. *Teaching of Psychology*, 27, 262–268. doi: 10.1207/S15328023TOP2704_04

Constantine, M. G. (2001). Multiculturally-focused counseling supervision: Its relationship to trainees' multicultural counseling self-efficacy. *Clinical Supervisor*, 20, 87–96. doi: 10.1300/J001v20n01_07

Cronan-Hillix, T., Davidson, W. S. I., Cronan-Hillix, W. A., & Gensheimer, L. K. (1986). Students' views of mentors in psychology graduate training. *Teaching of Psychology*, 13, 123–127. doi: 10.1207/s15328023top1303_5

de Oliveira, J. A., & Vandenberghe, L. (2009). Upsetting experiences for the therapist in-session: How they can be dealt with and what they are good for. *Journal of Psychotherapy Integration*, 19, 231–245. doi: 10.1037/a0017070

Deal, K. H. (2003). The relationship between critical thinking and interpersonal skills: Guidelines for clinical supervision. *The Clinical Supervisor*, 22, 3–19. doi: 10.1300/J001v22n02_02

Dearing, R., Maddux, J., & Tangney, J. (2005). Predictors of psychological help seeking in clinical and counseling psychology graduate students. *Professional Psychology: Research and Practice*, 36, 323–329. doi: 10.1037/0735-7028.36.3.323

Dressel, J. L., Consoli, A. J., Kim, B. S. K., & Atkinson, D. R. (2007). Successful and unsuccessful multicultural supervisory behaviors: A Delphi poll. *Journal of Multicultural Counseling and Development*, 35, 51–64. doi: 10.1002/j.2161-1912.2007.tb00049.x

Drum, D. J., Brownson, C., Denmark, A. B., & Smith, S. E. (2009). New data on the nature of suicidal crises in college students: Shifting the paradigm. *Professional Psychology: Research and Practice*, 40, 213–222. doi: 10.1037/a0014465

Dudek, N. L., Marks, M. B., & Regehr, G. (2005). Failure to fail: The perspectives of clinical supervisors. *Academic Medicine*, 80, S84–S87. doi: 10.1097/00001888-200510001-00023

Eby, L. T., Durley, J. R., Evans, S. C., & Ragins, B. R. (2008). Mentors' perceptions of negative mentoring experiences: Scale development and nomological validation. *Journal of Applied Psychology*, 93, 358–373. doi: 10.1037/0021-9010.93.2.358

Eby, L. T., McManus, S. E., Simon, S. A., & Russell, J. E. A. (2000). The protege's perspective regarding negative mentoring experiences: The development of a taxonomy. *Journal of Vocational Behavior*, 57, 1–21. doi: 10.1006/jvbe.1999.1726

El-Ghoroury, N. H., Galper, D. I., Sawaqdeh, A., & Bufka, L. F. (2012). Stress, coping, and barriers to wellness among psychology graduate students. *Training and Education in Professional Psychology*, 6, 122–124. doi: 10.1037/a0028768

Ellis, M. V. (2010). Bridging the science and practice of clinical supervision: Some discoveries, some misconceptions. *The Clinical Supervisor*, 29, 95–116. doi: 10.1080/07325221003741910

Elman, N., & Forrest, L. (2004). Psychotherapy in the remediation of psychology trainees: Exploratory interviews with training directors. *Professional Psychology: Research and Practice*, 35, 123–130. doi: 10.1037/0735-7028.35.2.123

Elman, N. S., & Forrest, L. (2007). From trainee impairment to professional competence problems: Seeking new terminology that facilitate effective action. *Professional Psychology: Research and Practice*, 38, 501–509. doi: 10.1037/0735-7028.38.5.501

Enyedy, K. C., Arcinue, F., Puri, N. N., Carter, J. W., Goodyear, R. K., & Getzelman, M. A. (2003). Hindering phenomena in group supervision: Implications for practice. *Professional Psychology: Research and Practice*, 34, 312–317. doi: 10.1037/0735-7028.34.3.312

Falendar, C. A., Collins, C. J., & Shafranske, E. P. (2009). "Impairment" and performance issues in clinical supervision: After the 2008 ADA Amendments Act. *Training and Education in Professional Psychology*, 3, 240–249. doi: 10.1037/a0017153

Falender, C. A., Cornish, J. A. E., Goodyear, R., Hatcher, R., Kaslow, N. J., Leventhal, G., Shafranske, E.,...Sigmon, S.T. (2004). Defining competencies in psychology supervision: A consensus statement. *Journal of Clinical Psychology*, 80, 771–786. doi: 10.1002/jclp.20013

Falender, C. A., & Shafranske, E. P. (2004). *Clinical supervision: A competency-based approach*. Washington DC: American Psychological Association.

Falender, C. A., & Shafranske, E. P. (2007). Competence in competency-based supervision practice: Construct and application. *Professional Psychology: Research and Practice*, 38, 232–240. doi: 10.1037/0735-7028.38.3.232

Falender, C. A., & Shafranske, E. P. (2008). *Casebook for clinical supervision: A competency-based approach*. Washington DC: American Psychological Association.

Forrest, L., Elman, N., Gizara, S., & Vacha-Haase, T. (1999). Trainee impairment: Identifying, remediating, and terminating impaired trainees in psychology. *The Counseling Psychologist*, 27, 627–686. doi: 10.1177/0011000099275001

Forrest, L., Shen-Miller, D. S., & Elman, N. (2008). Psychology trainees with competence problems: From individual to ecological conceptualizations. *Training and Education in Professional Psychology*, 2, 183–192. doi: 10.1037/1931-3918.2.4.183

Fouad, N. A., Grus, C. L., Hatcher, R. L., Kaslow, N. J., Hutchings, P. S., Madson, M., Collins, F.L.,...Crossman, R.E. (2009). Competency benchmarks: A model for the understanding and measuring of competence in professional psychology across training levels. *Training and Education in Professional Psychology*, 3, S5–S26. doi: 10.1037/a0015832

Gabbard, G. O. (2005). How not to teach psychotherapy. *Academic Psychiatry*, 29, 332–338. doi: 10.1176/appi.ap.29.4.332

Gabbard, G. O., & Lester, E. P. (2002). *Boundaries and boundary violations in psychoanalysis*. Washington DC: American Psychiatric Publishing, Inc.

Gaubatz, M. D., & Vera, E. M. (2006). Trainee competence in masters-level counseling programs: A comparison of counselor educators' and students's views. *Counselor Education and Supervision*, 46, 32–43. doi: Retrieved from http://www.unco.edu/ces/

Gilfoyle, N. (2008). The legal exosystem: Risk management in addressing student competence problems in professional psychology training. *Training and Education in Professional Psychology*, 2, 202–209. doi: 10.1037/1931-3918.2.4.202

Gill, S. (1999). Narcissistic vulnerability in psychoanalytic psychotherapy supervisees: Ego ideals, self-exposure and narcissistic character defenses. *International Forum for Psychoanalysis*, 8, 227–233. doi: 10.1080/080370699300056257

Gottlieb, M. C., Robinson, K., & Younggren, J. N. (2007). Multiple relations in supervision: Guidance for administrators, supervisors, and students. *Professional Psychology: Research and Practice, 38*, 241–247. doi: 10.1037/0735-7028.38.3.241

Gray, L. A., Ladany, N., Walker, J. A., & Ancis, J. R. (2001). Psychotherapy trainees' experience of counterproductive events in supervision. *Journal of Counseling Psychology, 28*, 371–383. doi: 101.1037//0022-0167.48.4.371

Guiffrida, D. A. (2005). The emergence model: An alternative pedagogy for facilitating self-reflection and theoretical fit in counseling students. *Counselor Education and Supervision, 44*, 201–213. doi: 10.1002/j.1556-6978.2005.tb01747.x

Guthcil, T. G., & Brodsky, A. (2011). *Preventing boundary violations in clinical practice.* New York: Guilford.

Guy, J. D., Poelstra, P., & Stark, M. (1989). Personal distress and therapeutic effectiveness: National survey of psychologists practicing psychotherapy. *Professional Psychology: Research and Practice, 20*, 48–50. doi: 10.1037/0735-7028.20.1.48

Hadjistavropoulos, H., Kehler, M., & Hadjistavropoulos, T. (2010). Training graduate students to be clinical supervisors: A survey of Canadian professional psychology programmes. *Canadian Psychology, 51*, 206–212. doi: 10.1037/a0020197

Halpern, D. F., & Murphy, S. E. (Eds.). (2009). *From work-family balance to work-family interaction: Changing the metaphor.* Mahwah, New Jersey: Erlbaum.

Hammel, G. A., Olkin, & Taube, D. O. (1996). Student-educator sex in clinical and counseling psychology doctoral training. *Professional Psychology: Research and Practice, 27*, 93–97. doi: 10.1037/0735-7028.27.1.93

Hernandez, P., & McDowell, T. (2010). Intersectionality, power, and relational safety in context: Key concepts in clinical supervision. *Training and Education in Professional Psychology, 4*, 29–35. doi: 10.1037/a0017064

Heru, A. M., Strong, D. R., Price, M., & Recupero, P. R. (2004). Boundaries in psychotherapy supervision. *American Journal of Psychotherapy*
, *58*, 76-89. doi: Retrieved from www.ajp.org

Hess, S. A., Knox, S., Schultz, J. M., Hill, C. E., Sloan, L., Brandt, S., Kelley, F.,...Hoffman, M.A. (2008). Predoctoral interns' nondisclosure in supervision. *Psychotherapy Research, 18*, 400–411. doi: 10.1080/10503300701697505

Huprich, S. K., & Rudd, M. D. (2004). A national survey of trainee impairment in clinical, counseling, and school psychology doctoral programs and internships. *Journal of Clinical Psychology, 60*, 43–52. doi: 10.1002/jclp.10233

Inman, A. G. (2006). Supervisor multicultural competence and its relation to supervisory process and outcome. *Journal of Marital and Family Therapy, 32*, 73–85. doi: 10.1111/j.1752-0606.2006.tb01589.x

Jacobs, S. C., Huprich, S. K., Grus, C. L., Cage, E. A., Elman, N. S., Forrest, L., et al. (2011). Trainees with professional competency problems: Preparing trainers for difficult but necessary conversations. *Training and Education in Professional Psychology, 5*, 175–184. doi: 10.1037/a0024656

Johnson, W. B. (2007a). *On being a mentor: A guide for higher education faculty.* Mahwah, NJ: Erlbaum.

Johnson, W. B. (2007b). Transformational supervision: When supervisors mentor. *Professional Psychology: Research and Practice, 38*, 259–267. doi: 10.1037/0735-7028.38.3.259

Johnson, W. B., & Barnett, J. E. (2011). Preventing problems of professional competence in the face of life-threatening illness. *Professional Psychology: Research and Practice, 42*, 285–293. doi: 10.1037/a0024433

Johnson, W. B., Barnett, J. E., Elman, N. S., Forrest, L., & Kaslow, N. J. (2012). The competent community: Toward a vital reformulation of professional ethics. *American Psychologist, 67*, 557–569. doi: 10.1037/a0027206

Johnson, W. B., & Campbell, C. D. (2004). Character and fitness requirements for professional psychologists: Training directors' perspectives. *Professional Psychology: Research and Practice, 35*, 405–411. doi: 10.1037/0735-7028.35.4.405

Johnson, W. B., Elman, N. S., Forrest, L., Robiner, W. N., Rodolfa, E. R., & Schaffer, J. B. (2008). Addressing professional competence problems in trainees: Some ethical considerations. *Profesional Psychology: Research and Practice, 39*, 589–599. doi: 10.1037/a0014264

Johnson, W. B., & Huwe, J. M. (2002). Toward a typology of mentorship dysfunction in graduate school. *Psychotherapy: Theory, Research, and Practice, 39*, 44–55. doi: 10.1037//0033-3204.39.1.44

Johnson, W. B., & Nelson, N. (1999). Mentor-protege relationships in graduate training: Some ethical concerns. *Ethics and Behavior, 9*, 189–210. doi: 10.1207/s15327019eb0903_1

Kaduvettoor, A., O'Shaughnessy, T., Mori, Y., Beverly, C., III., Weatherford, R. D., & Ladany, N. (2009). Helpful and hindering multicultural events in group supervision: Climate and multicultural competence. *The Counseling Psychologist, 37*, 786–820. doi: 10.1177/0011000009333984

Kaslow, N. J. (2004). Competencies in professional psychology. *American Psychologist, 59*, 774–781. doi: 10.1037/0003-066X.59.8.774

Kaslow, N. J., Borden, K. A., Collins, F. L., Forrest, L., Illfelder-Kaye, J., Nelson, P. D., Rallo, J.S. (2004). Competencies Conference: Future directions in education and credentialing in professional psychology. *Journal of Clinical Psychology, 80*, 699–712. doi: 10.1002/jclp.20016

Kaslow, N. J., Falendar, C. A., & Grus, C. L. (2012). Valuing and practicing competency-based supervision: A transformational leadership perspective. *Training and Education in Professional Psychology, 6*, 47–54. doi: 10.1037/a0026704

Kaslow, N. J., McCarthy, S. M., Rogers, J. H., & Summerville, M. B. (1992). Psychology postdoctoral training: A developmental perspective. *Professional Psychology: Research and Practice, 23*, 369–375. doi: 10.1037/0735-7028.23.5.369

Kaslow, N. J., & Rice, D. (1985). Developmental stresses of psychology internship training: What a training staff can do to help. *Professional Psychology: Research and Practice, 16*, 253–261. doi: 10.1037/0735-7028.16.2.253

Kaslow, N. J., Rubin, N. J., Forrest, L., Elman, N. S., Van Horne, B. A., Jacobs, S. C.,...Thorn, B. E. (2007). Recognizing, assessing, and intervening with problems of professional competence. *Professional Psychology: Research and Practice, 38*, 479–492. doi: 10.1037/0735-7028.38.5.479

Kitchener, K. S. (1992). Psychologist as teacher and mentor: Affirming ethical values throughout the curriculum. *Professional Psychology: Research and Practice, 23*, 190–195. doi: 10.1037/0735-7028.23.3.190

Knox, S., Edwards, L. M., Hess, S. A., & Hill, C. E. (2011). Supervisor self-disclosure: Supervisees' experiences and perspectives. *Psychotherapy, 48*, 336–341. doi: 10.1037/a0022067

Koenig, T. L., & Spano, R. N. (2003). Sex, supervision, and boundary violations: Pressing challenges and possible solutions. *Clinical Supervisor, 22*(3-19). doi: 10.1300/J001v22n01_02

Ladany, N., & Bradley, L. J. (Eds.). (2010). *Counselor supervision* (4th ed). New York: Routledge.

Ladany, N., Friedlander, M. L., & Nelson, M. L. (2005). *Critical incidents in psychotherapy supervision: An interpersonal approach*. Washington DC: American Psychological Association.

Ladany, N., Lehrman-Waterman, D. E., Molinaro, M., & Wolgast, B. (1999). Psychotherapy supervisor ethical practices: Adherence to guidelines, the supervisory working alliance and supervisee satisfaction. *Counseling Psychologist, 27*, 443–475. doi: 10.1177/0011000099273008

Ladany, N., & Walker, J. A. (2003). Supervisor self-disclosure: Balancing the uncontrollable narcissist with the indomitable altruist. *Journal of Clinical Psychology: In Session, 59*, 611–621. doi: 10.1002/jclp.10164

Lamb, D. H., Cochran, D. J., & Jackson, V. R. (1991). Training in organizational issues associated with identifying and responding to intern impairment. *Professional Psychology: Research and Practice, 22*, 291–296. doi: 10.1037/0735-7028.22.4.291

Lamb, D. H., Presser, N. R., Pfost, K. S., Baum, M. C., Jackson, V. R., & Jarvis, P. A. (1987). Confronting professional impairment during the internship: Identification, due process, and remediation. *Professional Psychology: Research and Practice, 18*, 597–603. doi: 10.1037/0735-7028.18.6.597

Levinson, D. J., Darrow, C. N., Klein, E. B., Levinson, M. H., & McKee, B. (1978). *The seasons of a man's life*. New York: Balletine.

MacKinnon, C. J., Bhatia, M., Sunderani, S., Affleck, W., & Smith, N. G. (2011). Opening the dialogue: Implications of feminist supervision theory with male supervisees. *Professional Psychology: Research and Practice, 42*, 130–136. doi: 10.1037/a0022232

Mallinckrodt, B., Leong, F. T. L., & Kralj, M. M. (1989). Graduate student stressful life events and stress symptoms. *Journal of College Student Development, 30*, 332–337. doi: Retrieved from http://www.jcsdonline.org/

Mearns, J., & Allen, G. J. (1991). Graduate students' experiences in dealing with impaired peers, compared with faculty predictions: An exploratory study. *Ethics and Behavior, 1*, 191–202. doi: 10.1207/s15327019eb0103_3

Mehlman, E., & Glickhauf-Hughes, C. (1994). Understanding developmental needs of college students in mentoring relationships with professors. *Journal of College Student Psychotherapy, 8*, 39–53. doi: 10.1300/J035v08n04_06

Mehr, K. E., Ladany, N., & Caskie, G. I. L. (2010). Trainee nondisclosure in supervision: What are they not telling you? *Counselling and Psychotherapy Journal, 10*, 103–113. doi: 10.1080/14733141003712301

Milne, D. L., & James, I. A. (2002). The observed impact of training on competence in clinical supervision. *British Journal of Clinical Psychology, 41*, 55–72. doi: 10.1348/014466502163796

Moffett, L. A. (2009). Directed self-reflection protocols in supervision. *Training and Education in Professional Psychology, 3*, 78–83. doi: 10.1037/a0014384

Mori, Y., Inman, A. G., & Caskie, G. I. L. (2009). Supervising international students: Relationship between acculturation, supervisor multicultural competence, cultural discussions, and supervision satisfaction. *Training and Education in Professional Psychology, 3*, 10–18. doi: 10.1037/a0013072

Murphy-Shigematsu, S. (2010). Microaggressions by supervisors of color. *Training and Education in Professional Psychology, 4*, 16–18. doi: 10.1037/a0017472

Murphy, M. J., & Wright, D. W. (2005). Supervisees' perspectives of power use in supervision. *Journal of Marital and Family Therapy, 31*, 283–295. doi: 10.1111/j.1752-0606.2005.tb01569.x

Nelson, M. L., Barnes, K. L., Evans, A. L., & Triggiano, P. J. (2008). Working with conflict in clinical supervision: Wise supervisors' perspectives. *Journal of Counseling Psychology, 55*, 172–184. doi: 10.1037/0022-0167.55.2.172

Nelson, M. L., & Friedlander, M. L. (2001). A close look at conflictual supervisory relationships: The trainee's perspective. *Journal of Counseling Psychology, 48*, 384–395. doi: 10.1037/0022-0167.48.4.384

Nelson, M. L., Gizara, S., Hope, A. C., Phelps, R., Steward, R., & Weitzman, L. (2006). A feminist multicultural perspective on supervision. *Journal of Multicultural Counseling and Development, 34*, 105–115. doi: 10.1002/j.2161-1912.2006.tb00031.x

Norcross, J. C., & Guy, J. D., Jr. (2007). *Leaving it at the office: A guide to psychotherapist self-care*. New York: Guilford.

O'Connor, M. F. (2001). On the etiology and effective management of professional distress and impairment among psychologists. *Professional Psychology: Research and Practice, 32*, 345–350. doi: 10.1037//0735-7028.32.4.345

O'Neill, R. M., & Sankowsky, D. (2001). The Caligula phenomenon: Mentoring relationships and theoretical abuse. *Journal of Management Inquiry, 10*, 206–216. doi: Retrieved from http://jmi.sagepub.com/

Ober, A. M., Granello, D. H., & Henfield, M. S. (2009). A synergestic model to enhance multicultural competence in supervision. *Counselor Education and Supervision, 48*, 204–221. doi: 10.1002/j.1556-6978.2009.tb00075.x

Oliver, M. N. I., Bernstein, J. H., Anderson, K. G., Blashfield, R. K., & Roberts, M. C. (2004). An exploratory examination of student attitudes toward "impaired" peers in clinical psychology training programs. *Professional Psychology: Research and Practice, 35*, 141–147. doi: 10.1037/0735-7028.35.2.141

Orchowski, L., Evangelista, N. M., & Probst, D. R. (2010). Enhancing supervisee reflectivity in clinical supervision: A case study illustration. *Psychotherapy Theory, Research, Practice, Training, 47*, 51067. doi: 10.1037/a0018844

Osborn, C. J., Paez, S. B., & Carrabine, C. L. (2007). Reflections on shared practices in a supervisory lineage. *Clinical Supervisor, 26*, 119–139. doi: 10.1300/J001v26n01_09

Overholser, J. C. (2004). The four pillars of psychotherapy supervision. *The Clinical Supervisor, 23*, 1–13. doi: 10.1300/J001v23n01_01

Pfohl, A. H. (2004). The intersection of personal and professional identity: The heterosexual supervisor's role in fostering the development of sexual minority supervisees. *Clinical Supervisor, 23*, 139–164. doi: 10.1300/J001v23n01_09

Plaut, S. M. (1993). Boundary issues in teacher-student relationships. *Journal of Sex and Marital Therapy*, *19*, 210–219. doi: Retrieved from http://www.tandf.co.uk/journals/titles/0092623X.asp

Pope, K. S., & Keith-Spiegel, P. (2008). A practical approach to boundaries in psychotherapy: Making decision, bypassing blunders, and mending fences. *Journal of Clinical Psychology, 64*, 639–652. doi: 10.1002/jclp.20477

Pope, K. S., Tabachnick, B. G., & Keith-Spiegel, P. (1987). Ethics of practice: The beliefs and behaviors of psychologists as therapists. *American Psychologist, 42*, 993–1006. doi: 10.1037/0003-066X.42.11.993

Pope, K. S., & Vasquez, M. J. T. (2010). *Ethics in psychotherapy and counseling* (4th ed.). New York: Wiley.

Pope, K. S., & Vetter, V. A. (1992). Ethical dilemmas encountered by members of the American Psychological Association: A national survey. *American Psychologist, 47,* 397–411. doi: 10.1037/0003-066X.47.3.397

Porter, N. (2010). Feminist and multicultural underpinnings to supervision: An overview. *Women & Therapy, 33,* 1–6. doi: 10.1080/02703140903404622

Ramos-Sanchez, L., Esnil, E., Goodwin, A., Riggs, S., Touster, L. O., Wright, L. K., Ratanasiripong, P.,...Rodolfa, E. (2002). Negative supervisory events: Effects on supervision satisfaction and supervisory alliance. *Professional Psychology: Research and Practice, 33,* 197–202. doi: 10.1037/0735-7028.33.2.197

Riggs, S. A., & Bretz, K. M. (2006). Attachment processes in the supervisory relationship: An exploratory investigation. *Professional Psychology: Research and Practice, 37,* 558–566. doi: 10.1037/0735-7028.37.5.558

Rings, J. A., Genuchi, M. C., Hall, M. D., Angelo, M.-A., & Cornish, J. A. E. (2009). Is there consensus among predoctoral internship training directors regarding clinical supervision competencies? A descriptive analysis. *Training and Education in Professional Psychology, 3,* 140–147. doi: 10.1037/a0015054

Roberts, M. C., Borden, K. A., Christiansen, M. D., & Lopez, S. J. (2005). Fostering a culture shift: Assessment of competence in the education and careers of professional psychologists. *Professional Psychology: Research and Practice, 36,* 355–361. doi: 10.1037/0735-7028.36.4.355

Rodolfa, E. R., Bent, R. J., Eisman, E., Nelson, P. D., Rehm, L., & Ritchie, P. (2005). A cube model for competency development: Implications for psychology educators and regulators. *Professional Psychology: Research and Practice, 36,* 347–354. doi: 10.1037/0735-7028.36.4.347

Rosenberg, J. I., Getzelman, M. A., Arcinue, F., & Oren, C. Z. (2005). An exploratory look at students' experiences of problematic peers in academic professional psychology programs. *Professional Psychology: Research and Practice, 36,* 665–673. doi: 10.1037/0735-7028.36.6.665

Roysircar, G. (2004). Cultural self-awareness assessment: Practice examples from psychology training. *Professional Psychology: Research and Practice, 35,* 658–666. doi: 10.1037/0735-7028.35.6.658

Scandura, T. A. (1998). Dysfunctional mentoring relationships and outcomes. *Journal of Management, 24,* 449–467. doi: 10.1177/014920639802400307

Shapiro, S. L., Brown, K. W., & Biegel, G. M. (2007). Teaching self-care to caregivers: Effects of a mindfulness-based stress reduction on the mental health of therapists in training. *Training and Education in Professional Psychology, 1,* 105–115. doi: 10.1037/1931-3918.1.2.105

Sheehy, G. (2006). *Passages: Predictable crises of adult life.* New York: Ballantine.

Shen-Miller, D. S., Grus, C. L., Van Sickle, K. S., Schwartz-Mette, R., Cage, E. A., Elman, N. S., Jacobs, S.C.,...Kaslow, N.J. (2011). Trainees' experiences with peers having competence problems: A national survey. *Training and Education in Professional Psychology, 5,* 112–121. doi: 10.1037/a0023824

Silverman, M. M., Meyer, P. M., Sloane, F., Raffel, M., & Pratt, D. M. (1997). The Big Ten Student Suicide Study: A 10-year study of suicides on midwestern university campuses. *Suicide and Life-Threatening Behavior, 27,* 285–303. doi: Retrieved from http://search.proquest.com/docview/224891519?accountid=

Simon, A. S., & Eby, L. T. (2003). A typology of negative mentoring experiences: A multidimensional scaling study. *Human Relations, 56,* 1083–1106. doi: 10.1177/0018726703569003

Slimp, P. A. O., & Burian, B. K. (1994). Multiple role relationships during internship: Consequences and recommendations. *Professional Psychology: Research and Practice, 25,* 39–45. doi: 10.1037//0735-7028.25.1.39

Smith, P. L., & Moss, S. B. (2009). Psychologist impairment: What is it, how can it be prevented, and what can be done to address it? *Clinical Psychology: Science and Practice, 16,* 1–15. doi: 10.1111/j.1468-2850.2009.01137.x

Stoltenberg, C. D. (2005). Enhancing professional competence through developmental approaches to supervision. *American Psychologist, 60,* 857–864. doi: 10.1037/0003-066X.60.8.85

Stoltenberg, C. D., & McNeill, B. W. (2010). *IDM supervision: An integrative developmental model for supervising counselors and therapists* (3rd ed.). New York: Routledge Taylor & Francis Group.

Tebes, J. K., Matlin, S. L., Migdole, S. J., Farkas, M. S., Money, R. W., Shulman, L., Hoge M.A. (2011). Providing competency training to clinical supervisors through an interactional supervision approach. *Research on Social Work Practice, 21,* 190–199. doi: 10.1177/1049731510385827

Ungar, M., & Costanzo, L. (2007). Supervision challenges when supervisors are outside supervisees' agencies. *Journal of Systemic Therapies, 26,* 68–83. doi: 10.1521/jsyt.2007.26.2.68

Vacha-Haase, T., Davenport, D. S., & Kerewsky, S. D. (2004). Problematic students: Gatekeeping practices of academic professional psychology programs. *Professional Psychology: Research and Practice, 35,* 115–122. doi: 10.1037/0735-7028.35.2.115

Veilleux, J. C., January, A. M., VanderVeen, J. W., Reddy, L. F., & Klonoff, E. A. (2012). Differentiating amongst characteristics associated with problems of professional competence: Perceptions of graduate student peers. *Training and Education in Professional Psychology, 6,* 113–121. doi: 10.1037/a0028337

Walsh, B. B., Gillespie, C. K., Greer, J. M., & Eanes, B. E. (2003). Influence of dyadic mutuality on counselor trainee willingness to self-disclose clinical mistakes to supervisors. *The Clinical Supervisor, 21,* 83–89. doi: 10.1300/J001v21n02_06

West, W. (2003). The culture of psychotherapy supervision. *Counselling and Psychotherapy Research, 3,* 12127. doi: 10.1080/14733140312331384492

Westefeld, J. S. (2009). Supervision of psychotherapy: Models, issues, and recommendations. *The Counseling Psychologist, 37,* 296–316. doi: 10.1177/0011000008316657

Wilkerson, K. (2006). Impaired students: Applying the therapeutic process model to graduate training programs. *Counselor Education and Supervision, 45,* 207–217. doi: 10.1002/j.1556-6978.2006.tb00143.x

Yabusaki, A. S. (2010). Clinical supervision: Dialogues on diversity. *Training and Education in Professional Psychology, 4,* 55–61. doi: 10.1037/a0017378

Yourman, D. B. (2003). Trainees disclosure in psychotherapy supervision: The impact of shame. *Journal of Clinical Psychology: In Session, 59,* 601–609. doi: 10.1002/jclp.10162

Yourman, D. B., & Farber, B. A. (1996). Nondisclosure and distortion in psychotherapy supervision. *Psychotherapy, 33,* 567–575. doi: 10.1037/0033-3204.33.4.567

PART 4

Culture and Context in Education and Training

A Contextual Perspective on Professional Training

Lynett Henderson Metzger, Jennifer A. Erickson Cornish, *and* Lavita I. Nadkarni

Abstract

A Contextual Perspective on Professional Training is a broad introductory chapter on culture and diversity bearing on education and training in psychology. The chapter begins by defining culture and context within psychology; reviews the history of multicultural education and training in psychology; introduces two continua on which to describe target and oppression statuses; briefly describes privilege and oppression; and discusses intersections of identity that should be considered by psychology trainees using an example of a supervisor, trainee, and client. The chapter concludes with suggested future directions, including a continued focus on understanding complex identities (especially among and between supervisors, supervisees, and clients), expanding the Individual and Cultural Diversity competency training sequence and integrating it with the other benchmark competencies, recommending research into evidence-based practice related to individual and cultural diversity, and highlighting the importance of including social justice and advocacy efforts in education and training.

Key Words: culture, context, diversity, multicultural, psychology, education, training, privilege, oppression

Introduction

Because all people exist within historical, social, economic, and political frameworks, psychologists must understand the influence of these perspectives on individual and group behavior. With the population of the United States becoming progressively diverse (U.S. Census Bureau, 2010), and an increased focus within the mental health field on globalization (e.g., Nelson, 2007), education and training related to culture and context has become increasingly important.

Culture can be defined in myriad ways; indeed, entire books have been written on the spectrum of meaning in different contexts (e.g., Faulkner, Baldwin, Lindsley, & Hecht, 2006).[1] In its broadest possible sense, "culture" encompasses shared understandings of self and other, a fundamental worldview transmitted interpersonally and intergenerationally and including "the norms, values, [and] standards by which people act" as well as the "ways distinctive in each society of ordering the world and rendering it intelligible" (Murphy, 1986, p. 14). Culture is thus simultaneously "a set of mechanisms for survival" and a blueprint for a collective "definition of reality" (Murphy, 1986, p. 14).

Although human cultural constructs presumably have existed in some form as long as the species itself, recognition of the integral nature of these aspects of identity-in-context to mental health functioning has evolved comparatively recently within psychology as a field. In the United States, dawning awareness of culture and context as rich sources of clinical meaning making grew out of the equality and empowerment movements of the 1960s and 1970s, and, in reality, only the current generation of researchers has come of age under a theoretical framework that validates and values diversity as a legitimate area of inquiry per se. Early feminist and person-of-color frameworks (see, e.g., Cross, Parham, & Helms, 1991; Helms, 1990; McIntosh, 2007; Sue, D. & Sue, D. M., 2007; Sue, D. W., & Sue D., 1990) laid the foundation for today's increasingly nuanced and inclusive understandings of identity formation. Modern trends in diversity education are rooted in rendering explicit this tacit understanding of *identity*—selfhood, or the distinct constellation of characteristics that define you as uniquely you and, critically, *not someone else* (see Identity, 2013). Identity is neither unidimensional nor static. Like sheets of transparency film stacked, one on top of another, to form a complex image, identity is multilayered, additive, and interactive. Multiple roles or statuses converge to form intersectional identities (see, e.g., Seaton, Caldwell, Sellers, Jackson, 2010), and are themselves the products of both internal and interpersonal dynamics that evolve over time.

Underlying the training protocols described in this chapter, then, is the fundamental recognition that difference matters. The specifics *of* difference, the variable impacts with which these dynamics play out, and the clinical implications of this lived experience constitute the bulk of the work done to date in the arena of multicultural awareness and form the basic outline for the discussion that follows.

Although it is impossible to adequately cover the area of culture and context within professional psychology education and training in one chapter, we have focused on three major areas of importance: the history of multicultural education and training in psychology, privilege and oppression, and intersections of identity.

History of Multicultural Education and Training in Psychology

Culture and context in psychology, sometimes expressed as Individual and Cultural Diversity (ICD) is considered a foundational competency (Fouad et al., 2009), necessary for effective and ethical psychological practice. Indeed, diversity is included in the American Psychological Association (APA) *Ethical Principles of Psychologists and Code of Conduct* (2010), both in terms of a general principle (respect for people's rights and dignity) and standards (unfair discrimination). The *Guidelines and Principles for Accreditation of Programs in Professional Psychology* (APA, 2009) incorporate cultural diversity and individual differences (Domain D) as a necessary accreditation domain across all developmental aspects of doctoral psychology education and training, including academic programs, internships, and postdoctoral fellowships. Recently, counseling

psychology developed a "values statement" related to "operationalizing, instilling, and assessing" diversity into academic training (Winterowd, Adams, Miville, & Mintz, 2009).

Recent surveys of students indicate their perceptions that, although diversity education is included in their academic programs, an increase in scope and emphasis may be needed. Clinical psychology students described their training as focusing primarily on ethnicity, race, and culture (Green, Callands, Radcliffe, Luebbe, & Klonoff, 2009). A similar national survey of counseling students revealed that these students desired increased training in social justice (Beer, Spanierman, Green, & Todd, 2012). Clearly, although progress has been made, much remains to be done to broaden psychology students' awareness of the importance of identity and context.

Competencies

As education and training in professional psychology has taken on the "culture of competence" (Roberts, Borden, Christiansen, & Lopez, 2005; also see Fouad and Grus, chapter 3, this volume), these concepts have been refined with increasing sophistication. The National Council of Schools and Programs of Professional Psychology (NCSPP), one of the leaders in the professional psychology competency movement, added diversity as a seventh competency area in 2002 (see Kenkel & Peterson, 2010). Individual and Cultural Diversity was one of the competency areas in the 2002 Competencies Conference (Daniel, Roysircar, Abeles, & Boyd, 2004). The Competency Benchmarks (Fouad et al., 2009) further refined ICD into four essential components: self as shaped by ICD, others as shaped by ICD, interaction of self and others as shaped by ICD, and applications based on individual and cultural context. Behavioral anchors for these essential components were described along a developmental continuum from readiness for practicum to readiness for internship to readiness for entry to practice. Ideas for assessing the ICD competence were provided by Kaslow et al. (2009) and included such methods as 360° evaluations (i.e., an attempt to collect a "full circle" of input from multiple raters in different types of professional relationships with the person being evaluated, such as supervisors, peers, and supervisees) to be used to assess readiness for internship, entry level to practice, and advanced credentialing.

The current revision of the Benchmarks continues to define ICD as "awareness, sensitivity, and skills in working professionally with diverse individuals, groups, and communities who represent various cultural and personal background and characteristics defined broadly and consistently with APA policy" (APA, 2011b). The revision has streamlined the original version, retaining the four subcategories outlined earlier and the developmental trajectory, and condensing the essential components and behavioral anchors.

American Psychological Association Guidelines

The APA has developed several relevant practice guidelines for professional psychology education and training related to culture and context, including:

- Guidelines on Multicultural Education, Training, Research, Practice, and Organizational Change for Psychologists (APA, 2002)
- Guidelines for Psychological Practice with Older Adults (APA, 2004a)
- Guidelines for Psychological Practice with Girls and Women (APA, 2007b)
- Guidelines for the Evaluation of Dementia and Cognitive Change (APA, 2012c)
- Guidelines for Psychological Practice with Lesbian, Gay, and Bisexual Clients (APA, 2012b)

Table 23.1. Revised Competency Benchmarks in Professional Psychology (June, 2011b) American Psychological Association: http://www.apa.org/ed/graduate/revised-competency-benchmarks.aspx

1. **Individual and Cultural Diversity**: Awareness, sensitivity and skills in working professionally with diverse individuals, groups and communities who represent various cultural and personal background and characteristics defined broadly and consistent with APA policy.

READINESS FOR PRACTICUM	READINESS FOR INTERNSHIP	READINESS FOR ENTRY TO PRACTICE
2A. Self as Shaped by Individual and Cultural Diversity (e.g.,cultural, individual, and role differences, including those based on age, gender, gender identity, race, ethnicity, culture, national origin, religion, sexual orientation, disability, language, and socioeconomic status)**and Context**		
Demonstrates knowledge, awareness, and understanding of one's own dimensions of diversity and attitudes towards diverse others	Monitors and applies knowledge of self as a cultural being in assessment, treatment, and consultation	Independently monitors and applies knowledge of self as a cultural being in assessment, treatment, and consultation
2B. Others as Shaped by Individual and Cultural Diversity and Context		
Demonstrates knowledge, awareness, and understanding of other individuals as cultural beings	Applies knowledge of others as cultural beings in assessment, treatment, and consultation	Independently monitors and applies knowledge of others as cultural beings in assessment, treatment, and consultation
2C. Interaction of Self and Others as Shaped by Individual and Cultural Diversity and Context		
Demonstrates knowledge, awareness, and understanding of interactions between self and diverse others	Applies knowledge of the role of culture in interactions in assessment, treatment, and consultation of diverse others	Independently monitors and applies knowledge of diversity in others as cultural beings in assessment, treatment, and consultation
2D. Applications based on Individual and Cultural Context		
Demonstrates basic knowledge of and sensitivity to the scientific, theoretical, and contextual issues related to ICD (as defined by APA policy) as they apply to professional psychology. Understands the need to consider ICD issues in all aspects of professional psychology work (e.g., assessment, treatment, research, relationships with colleagues)	Applies knowledge, sensitivity, and understanding regarding ICD issues to work effectively with diverse others in assessment, treatment, and consultation	Applies knowledge, skills, and attitudes regarding dimensions of diversity to professional work

• Guidelines for Assessment of and Intervention with Persons with Disabilities (APA, 2012a).

The APA also has developed many pertinent policy statements and resolutions (e.g., the Policy Statement on Sexual Orientation, Parents, and Children, APA, 2004b). Although these do not include all aspects of culture and context, they do represent a snapshot of the evolution of the field in recent years.

Sequence of Training

This chapter focuses on graduate education and training in professional psychology, but the sequence of training may be conceptualized on a developmental continuum from high school to advanced practice, including specialization and continuing competency. The *APA National Standards for High School Psychology Curricula* (APA, 2011a) suggest the infusion of diversity and awareness of individual differences throughout introductory psychology coursework in such a way as to encompass social and cultural diversity as well as diversity among individuals. High school students are expected to study stereotypes, prejudice, and discrimination, and to read research related to race and ethnicity, social-economic status, gender identity, sexual orientation, and cognitive and physical ability status.

Similarly, the *APA Guidelines for the Undergraduate Psychology Major* (APA, 2007a) "reflect the importance of diversity and cross-cultural issues in the discipline, as well as the growing internationalization of psychology" (p. 3). The guidelines include goals related to sociocultural and international awareness coupled with learning outcomes such as being able to "interact effectively and sensitively with people of diverse abilities, backgrounds, and cultural perspectives" and "understand how privilege, power, and oppression may affect prejudice, discrimination, and inequity" (p. 20), among others.

With regard to doctoral training, Rodolfa and colleagues (2005) proposed a competency cube model that covered doctoral, internship/residency, postdoctoral supervision, and continuing competency. The APA Competency Benchmarks (2006) initially included entry to practicum, entry to internship, entry to professional practice, and advanced practice and specialization; the current version (APA, 2011b, see Table 23.3) covers readiness for practicum, readiness for internship, and readiness for entry to practice. For instance, in the area of self as shaped by ICD, the psychology student who is ready for practicum will demonstrate "knowledge, awareness, and understanding of one's own dimensions of diversity and attitudes towards diverse others" (APA, 2011a). The student who is ready for internship "monitors and applies knowledge of self as a cultural being in assessment, treatment, and consultation," whereas the graduate who is ready for entry to practice "independently monitors and applies knowledge of self as a cultural being in assessment, treatment, and consultation" (APA, 2011a).

Although recent literature informs primarily doctoral education and training from practicum through entry to practice, Daniel et al. (2004) have outlined valuable suggestions for psychologists in all stages of practice related to racism, homophobia, and ageism. In addition, some ideas have been articulated for psychologists seeking competency in advanced practice and specialization working with specific population groups (Erickson Cornish, Schreier, Nadkarni, Henderson Metzger, & Rodolfa, 2010). Before expanding ICD to various populations, however, it is important to focus on the overarching ideas of privilege and oppression.

Privilege and Oppression

Crucial for psychology trainees in understanding the importance of ICD in clinical work and training is the recognition that differences do not occur in a vacuum. *Context* in this sense might be most easily conceptualized as milieu, the existing circumstances in which any given event occurs (see Context, 2013). For the purposes of this discussion, context refers to ambient reality—with the critical caveat that "reality" itself is largely socially constructed, and one's definition of it is informed to a significant degree by identity status.

Identity Status

Competencies-based diversity education must acknowledge the intertwined concepts of privilege and identity. Students, trainees, and professionals may all struggle with recognizing gaps and biases in their own perceptions. "I don't know who first discovered water," John Culkin is famously quoted as saying in *They Became What They Beheld* (Carpenter, 1970, p. 12), "but I'm certain it wasn't a fish." Philosophically, why would this be so? At the risk of anthropomorphizing, a fish presumably does not recognize itself as swimming *in* anything. Having never been confronted with any other way of being, the fish does not see its context as context; this is just how the world is. To put it another way: Why doesn't a fish "get" that it is swimming in water? *Because it doesn't have to.*

Those ways in which we have the ability to swim in the water without acknowledging it as such constitute our areas of *privilege*—aspects of identity our context accommodates without our having to consciously think about or work for. Decades ago, for example, Peggy McIntosh (2007) "unpacked" her now axiomatic definition of White privilege as "an invisible weightless knapsack of special provisions, maps, passports, codebooks, visas, clothes, tools, and blank checks" (p. 178). This concept has been expanded to include numerous other categories, and clinical training programs may benefit from incorporating experiential exercises focused on increasing awareness of specific privileges, such as those outlined next (adapted from Henderson Metzger, Nadkarni, Erickson Cornish, 2010, pp. 15–16):

• As a White student, my image is not routinely used on marketing materials, in photos, and so on, as evidence of the organization's diverse enrollment or hiring practices.
• As a person of an accepted faith-based denomination, I can rest assured that my religion will not be associated with terrorism.
• As a person who is traditionally abled, I can assume I will be able to attend a traditional college course (find suitable transportation; be able to gain access to the building; find a comfortable seat; and participate fully in the activities of the semester) without undue hardship.
• As a high school student, I can expect that not being able to recall a memory does not reflect anything about my age.
• As a person with a culturally validated body shape, I do not have to fear that people will roll their eyes, groan, complain, or ask to move when I am assigned a seat next to them on an airplane.
• As a native speaker of the language most commonly spoken where I live, I can question a sales assistant, service provider, or government official about a confusing or unclear item, bill, or policy without it being assumed that I do not understand enough to have a valid concern.
• As a cisgender (or nontransgender) individual, I am addressed by others using titles and pronouns that fit my concept of my own identity. I am never referred to by derogatory terms such as "S/he" or "It."

In these examples, the speaker is describing ways in which the existing cultural "water" accommodates a specific identity status. In each case, the holder of the privilege benefits from the identified area of difference. These narratives reflect areas of nontarget identity status, meaning privileged status in a given area. As is probably immediately apparent, however, there is more to the story. Change the identity status of the speaker, and the privilege goes away. For someone who is *not* White, *not* traditionally abled, *not* a native language speaker, and so on, life in the dominant social context feels far from an effortless glide through a sea of cultural givens in which one's place can be taken for granted. *Target identity status* refers to those aspects of self in which a person is *not* privileged—the ways in which one differs from the "mythical norm" with which the "trappings of power reside," as so eloquently described by Audre Lorde (2007, p. 116) in *Sister Outsider*.

Clients, supervisors, and supervisees may each hold different or overlapping areas of target status. This target status may be thought of as falling along a continuum, as outlined in Table 23.2, which allows for the framing of multiple identities in terms of saliency to the specific individual. It should be noted that this conceptualization is, by design, neither categorical (dividing identity descriptors into discrete, binary groupings) nor hierarchical (assigning value to identity characteristics and "ranking" them according to a priori assumptions of importance).

Reading from left to right and top to bottom, any given identification, characteristic, trait, group affiliation, or so on may be charted as representing some point along a trajectory from developmental to lifelong; universal to particular; mutable to immutable; and from invisible to visible. The last line on Table 23.2, incidental versus critical to identity, focuses on a holistic understanding of how salient the particular characteristic is to the person's core sense of self.

The target status of each intersectional identity outlined in this chapter can be framed within these

Table 23.2. Continuum of Target Status

Developmental ---------------------- Lifelong

Universal ---------------------------- Particular

Mutable ----------------------------- Immutable

Invisible ----------------------------- Visible

Incidental to identity-------------- Critical to identity

conceptual anchors. In terms of the first dimension, characteristics that represent a phase, stage, or moment in time (such as adolescence) would fall on the more developmental side of the continuum. A status that develops during the lifespan (such as illness or changes in ability status associated with aging) might fall somewhere toward the middle, whereas an identity present at birth that will remain static for the duration of the person's life (mental retardation in most cases, for example) would fall along the lifelong end of the spectrum.

A similar rubric can be applied for universal to particular, with the former referring to events or ways of being everyone or almost everyone experiences (like childhood) versus something comparatively individualistic or statistically rare (like losing one's legs in an automobile accident at age seven or being conjoined with a twin at birth).

Mutable characteristics are those considered subject to change over time, often involving some element of choice on the part of the individual (socioeconomic status is, at least theoretically, a mutable characteristic; in modern American culture, religion, political affiliation, and relationship status are generally thought of as mutable, as well). A status that is unchangeable, permanent, and not reflective of any degree of choice on the part of the holder of that status is considered immutable. Physical characteristics, such as skin color, often are cited as "immutable" (although that understanding may be too simplistic to adequately address all permutations of experience, as will be explored in more detail next).

Invisible characteristics are those not readily apparent or knowable by others, unless disclosed by the individual. Characteristics that are obvious and cannot be hidden or disguised are more visible. HIV status would likely fall somewhere along this continuum toward the invisible side, as would a racial identity for someone who could "pass" as White. Utilizing a wheelchair as one's only means of locomotion would fall more toward the visible side.

Taken together, these dimensions paint, in broad strokes, a picture of how incidental or critical to identity each characteristic is within the target status holder's context. With no intention to trivialize, the distinction might be illustrated by thinking of the relative saliency of a bad haircut versus transgender status. Although upsetting in its own way, even the most unfortunate hairstyle malfunction does not generally come close to touching on the social, emotional, cognitive, interpersonal, physiological, and related implications of fundamental

gender identification.[2] To what degree a target status is salient, how that salience is (or is not) manifested, and what meaning the individual makes of the status is a deeply personal (and often subconscious) algorithm, as unique as fingerprints—but with the added potential for change and variation across time and context. For psychology graduate students, particularly early training, the process of understanding these distinctions may be equal parts unsettling and crucial.

Exercise of privilege

As the interplay between target and nontarget identity statuses becomes increasingly clear, the focus shifts to the impact of the existence of privilege on both those who hold it in a particular area, and those who do not. If we conceptualize privilege as the unearned and largely unrecognized collection of entitlements, favorable presumptions, and cultural "benefits of the doubt" afforded to individuals in their areas of nontarget status, *oppression* might be thought of as the witting and unwitting exercise of that privilege.

Oppression is a slippery concept; few trainees (or, for that matter, professionals) want to think of themselves as oppressing others, and the word "oppressor" connotes, for many, white-sheeted Ku Klux Klan members burning crosses or SS officers beating prostrate concentration camp victims. *That isn't me*, a student or supervisor may exclaim, relief mingled with a certain degree of self-righteousness. Certainly the horrific extremes just cited fit the dictionary definition of oppression—"the exercise of authority or power in a burdensome, cruel, or unjust manner" (Oppression, 2013)—but the realities of 21st Century "—isms" (racism, sexism, heterosexism, ableism, ageism, etc.) require a more sophisticated analysis.

Contemporary racism (see Smith, Constantine, Graham, & Dize, 2008) and its variants bear, in form, only a passing resemblance to the inequities in law and fact of the early to mid-1900s. Today's oppression (at least in the United States) is more likely to be well intentioned, shrouded in political correctness, and stemming from ignorance or naiveté rather than overt maliciousness. Even the field itself is not immune. In her thought-provoking qualitative analysis, "Racism in Our Midst: Listening to Psychologists of Color," Tinsley-Jones (2001) asked eight psychologists of color to describe the impact of race/ethnicity on their professional lives. "No incidences of overt racial/ethnic discrimination were noted by participants to have occurred professionally" (p. 577); however, of the 20 total responses provided, 15 were negative.

This quality of being perceived (and perceiving one's self) as consistently "the other" in majoritarian society has enormous implications for clinical training and practice, and has given rise to concepts such as *microaggressions* ("brief, everyday exchanges that send denigrating messages to certain individuals because of their group membership"), *microinsults* ("subtle snubs," often unintended by the perpetrator, that convey demeaning messages about identity status), and *microinvalidations*(cues or communications that "exclude, negate, or nullify" the experience of certain groups) (Sue, 2010, pp. 24, 31, 37). These and other forms of oppression may be understood, once again, as falling at various points along a continuum.

Here, circumstantial oppression might refer to a specific "bubble" in which a person who typically has privilege does not, as when a member of an otherwise dominant group (such as an established religion) experiences discrimination in a microcosm environment (like a progressive academic institution). At the other end of the spectrum would be systemic discrimination representing the norm and default at every level of society. The far right side of the continuum constitutes the territory of institutionalized oppression, where laws, regulations, and the essential framework of society are set up to disenfranchise specific groups ("Jim Crow" laws in the United States and South Africa under Apartheid are clear examples of this). For some categories of difference, individuals may have the freedom to choose whether to place themselves in certain circumstances (e.g., a heterosexual who feels uncomfortable when patronizing establishments that market overtly to gay, lesbian, and bisexual patrons); with systemic oppression, there is no practical way to "opt out."

If the oppression at issue is a "moment in time" phenomenon, a fleeting unpleasantness that might occur once or twice over a person's lifetime because of a relatively unusual set of circumstances, it may be considered transient. Permanent oppression refers to the day-in, day-out, year-after-year lack of privilege that represents an ongoing fixture in the person's experience. These concepts are closely related to the circumstantial/systemic dimension, but imply a more temporal component. On the left side of the continuum, the individual impacted may have no choice about setting—a member of the military who is berated as a "stupid, lazy, rich American" while stationed briefly overseas, for example—but the occurrence represents a comparatively insignificant portion of the person's life experience. An immigrant to the United States in contrast, who faces daily, almost constant, scrutiny based on appearance, religious practice, accent, English as a Second Language (ESL) status, and so forth, is experiencing what would likely be considered permanent oppression, particularly if the target group membership is impossible or unlikely to change.

Isolated acts of oppression are those perpetrated by, basically, a single individual or relatively small group (such as extremists who picket funerals carrying signs with virulently heterosexist slogans). Pervasive acts of oppression are endemic in society and carried out at virtually all levels by virtually everyone not a member of the target group. Individuals whose appearance does not fall within culturally validated norms, for example, may find that they are routinely looked down upon by a wide cross-section of those whom they encounter.

When discussing acts of oppression, we most often envision discrimination that is perceived by the victim as coming wholly from outside sources—externalized oppression. This type of oppression is considered ego dystonic; it does not fit with the person's own self-assessment. There is another, more insidious form of oppression, as well, in which the subject of the oppression begins to believe the negative messages about identity status. As the "—ism" in question (be it racism, sexism, heterosexism, or any other form of bias) becomes increasingly ego *syntonic*, or in keeping with the individual's understanding of self, the victim becomes, in essence, one of the "oppressors." For example, in his book, *Who's*

Table 23.3. Continuum of Oppression

Circumstantial -----------------------	Systemic
Transient ----------------------------	Permanent
Isolated -----------------------------	Pervasive
Externalized ----------------------	Internalized
Related to a peripheral characteristic -----------	Related to the core sense of Self

Afraid of Post-Blackness, Touré (2011) describes the phenomenon of internalized racism:

> You're in Target. Is the security guard following you? You're not sure. You think he is but you can't be certain. Maybe he is, maybe he's not—maybe he's actually following another Black person you can't see. But he's probably following you. Or is he? They were following you in the last store and you couldn't see it but you could feel it. Maybe the guard is Black, so if you tried to explain it to a white friend they might not understand it as racist, but the guard's boss isn't Black. Or maybe he is. Maybe they're watching all the Blacks in the store more closely. Maybe the guard himself feels badly about the directive but has to follow it because they're watching him, too. Maybe what you're feeling are his ashamed vibes as if he's sending you a silent signal of apology for following you. Or maybe... now you're looking for Tylenol for migraines when all you needed was toothpaste. (pp. 117–118)

Touré goes on to quote a colleague describing the "sort of existential angst that Black people experience every day" (p. 118), even while noting the rejection of stereotypes by people of color. To the degree that a person with target status "buys into" society's negative messages about that status, the person has internalized the "—ism."

As with target status, the key concept regarding oppression is its saliency for the individual impacted by it, including those in training, service providers, and utilizers of mental health services. In asking to what degree the lack of privilege relates to a *peripheral characteristic* versus *core sense of self*, we are looking at whether the characteristic around which the person is being oppressed is incidental to identity—or the foundation of it, recalling our earlier definition of identity. Intuitively, the more systemic, permanent, pervasive, and internalized the oppression is, the more damaging it is likely to be to our core selves, those very characteristics that make us distinctly and uniquely who we are.

Although these tools are helpful as starting points for thoughtful reflection and discussion, they do not touch on every possible permutation of difference, nor do they exhaustively address any. These issues are nuanced and complex; the stakes are high for our clients, students, trainees, and supervisees, not to mention ourselves, and the questions are subtle ones. To take a single clinical example, Naumburg (2007), a Licensed Clinical Social Worker (LCSW), discusses the field of social work's traditional antipathy toward religious practice, and the implications for the "hidden diversity" of Judaism (p. 80). Noting that "Judaism is at once a religion, an ethnicity, and a culture," but that Jewish clients are often treated as "generic white Americans" (p. 80), he observes:

> That view can be quite problematic, especially for non-Jewish therapists whose cultural (and perhaps religious) default assumptions are, necessarily, based on the majority culture, which in the United States is Christian.... Assimilated Jews, who have grown up straddling the line between majority and minority culture, and who often "pass" as Protestant-Americans, can speak the majority language and, to varying degrees, even feel comfortable in American culture. If the client's Jewish identity isn't addressed, however, s/he may feel unheard and misunderstood, even if s/he isn't quite sure why. (p. 80)

Being Jewish, Naumburg continues,

> is about ambivalence, shame, pride, self-hatred, strong community, and fierce fights for the preservation and continuity of the Jewish people. It is about intense family bonds, and families split apart by war, by oceans, and by different beliefs. Being Jewish is not about any one thing, but for many Jews, it is the most important thing in their lives. For many others, however, it has only minimal significance. Given these complexities, clinicians should take mindful responsibility for addressing Judaism in their clinical work. (pp. 80–81)

Naumburg's words stand as good reminders of being thoughtful, in our clinical practices and daily lives, of recognizing and creating a space for more ways of being diverse than may "meet the eye" initially, while, of course, honoring the unique impact of visible difference. Indeed, the rich complexities of all of our clients should be greeted and welcomed, as reflected in the ethical principles of the mental health field.

Understanding these principles is a critical step toward clinical competence in the arena of social justice. These and related dynamics play out continually in psychological practice and training, be it in terms of supervisor/supervisee power differentials (see Dressel, Kerr, & Stevens, 2010), microaggressions in clinical practice (see Sue et al., 2007), or in terms of practitioners' own experiences with marginalization and tokenization (see Tinsley-Jones, 2001). For these reasons, much attention has been placed on the need for and application of diversity-focused curricula in the mental health field. We will now trace the evolution of education and training models to date, before shifting our attention to specific intersections of identity.

Intersections of Identity

Thus far, we have focused largely on theoretical constructs, such as privilege and oppression, as well as the philosophical principles that guide existing models of education and training. The point at which these concepts meet, of course, is the daily reality of clients, students, professors, supervisors, and clinicians from every mental health discipline and background. To each training opportunity (indeed, to every human interaction throughout our lives) we bring our many selves, including our areas of target and nontarget status. These multiple and interactive roles create enormous richness in our thoughts, feelings, reactions, and interpretations. They also make it all but impossible to evaluate one area of difference, one status, as being singularly salient at both the nomothetic and ideographic levels. Teasing out one aspect of identity becomes something of the process of evaluating which set of stripes defines "plaid"—some stitches may stand out more under particular circumstances, certainly, but remove any, and the pattern fails.

We have, therefore, chosen to look at *intersections of identity* rather than specific (and ostensibly discrete) population groups (individuals from an Iroquois cultural heritage, for example, or men). This approach ties in with the overarching theme of person in context. For many, the question, "Who Am I?" remains an unfinished interrogative in the absence of situational cues: To a large degree, identity cannot exist in the abstract. This is particularly true of the complex relationships between and among supervisors, trainees, and clients. Consider, for example, the following scenario:

> Dr. Henrietta Reinhardt is a 55-year-old upper middle-class, Jewish, heterosexual female who is currently supervising Mr. Leonard Barrera, a 28 year old second- year doctoral psychology student who identifies as a Mexican-American bisexual, bilingual, spiritually agnostic man from a low SES background, in his treatment of Ms. Carlotta Pereira, a petite, 75-year-old, biracial, Catholic, widowed, woman with type II diabetes who emigrated to Brooklyn, New York, from India when she was 2 years old.

Even this brief cross-section of target and nontarget statuses represents an amalgam of characteristics that fall at various points along both continua (see Tables 23.2 and 23.3). To what extent any of the aforementioned characteristics are particularly salient to the treatment of Ms. Pereira, and the supervision of Mr. Barrera, is largely a matter of context. It is critical to recognize the ways in which each of the identity statuses of supervisor, trainee, and client interact with their other statuses. It is with an understanding of these intersection identities that psychology students must meet the changes of an ever-changing therapeutic landscape.

Certainly, every mental health professional cannot be expected to be thoroughly knowledgeable, skilled, and possess all the necessary attitudes and values to work with each aspect of diversity and the intersections inherent in each constantly changing context. In considering diversity broadly, however, we can work toward helping our students to see all clients as culturally diverse, in different and important ways. We must assist students in avoiding the erroneous assumption that if they perceive themselves as sharing one identity status (such as apparent racial group affiliation) with a client, supervisor, or supervisee, culture must not be an issue in the therapy, training, or supervision—and the corollary error that, if they do *not*, culture must be the primary or exclusive focus of the work. We can guide our students through examples of how to talk about issues of difference as well as attune to what will work with a particular client. Such an approach will hopefully result in a more sophisticated understanding of the ambiguity and complexities of professional psychology practice, as opposed to focusing on assumed generic similarities and differences among groups of people.

Application to Clinical Training and Education

Developmentally, then, the process of acquiring ICD-specific training and using it effectively in the practice of psychology might be thought of as analogous to taking pictures with a camera with a variety of accessories. Clinical work, like photography, is at once an art and a science. There are technical as well as aesthetic aspects to each and both require a good "eye" for both literal and metaphorical content. Just as the photographer must choose the lens through which to best view the subject—and just as not every lens works equally effectively for every purpose—the therapist must carefully consider what aspects of identity (and *whose*) to bring into sharper focus, and when and how to do so. The culturally competent practitioner needs to be ever mindful of the "filters" through which presenting issues, interpretations, and interventions are framed, and select "lighting" appropriate for the task—perhaps to emphasize issues of particular importance from time to time, raise questions around identity that may not have previously come to the client's conscious awareness, or even engage in selective, well-boundaried, and clinically warranted self-disclosure (Farber, 2006)—all the while recognizing the risk inherent in over-utilizing "flash."

To apply these principles to our example, how might the sequence of ICD competency training (see Table 23.1) relate to Ms. Pereira's treatment by Mr. Barrera, under the supervision of Dr. Reinhardt? Dr. Reinhardt, an advanced practitioner, can (presumably) help Mr. Barrera (a student relatively early in training) progress through the Readiness for Practicum stage. In doing so, Mr. Barrera would "demonstrate knowledge, awareness, and understanding of [his] own dimensions of diversity and attitudes toward diverse others" by discussing his own identity in supervision, along with his attitudes toward his client (and possibly supervisor). In addition, he would demonstrate knowledge, awareness, and understanding of his client as a cultural being, and use that to better understand the interactions between himself and Ms. Pereira. Finally, he would "demonstrate basic knowledge of and sensitivity to the scientific, theoretical, and context issues related to ICD (as defined by APA policy) as they apply to professional psychology" and would understand the importance of considering ICD issues in all aspects of his work, including his assessment and treatment of Ms. Pereira. Guiding Mr. Barrera through this developmental process would require Dr. Reinhardt to exercise considerable patience and demonstrate strong supervisory skills, including recognition of the power differential inherent in the relationship.

What lenses, filters, and lighting get brought into Ms. Pereira's treatment (explicitly or implicitly) will be the product, in part, of the individual and shared understandings of self and other of everyone in the clinical snapshot. To concretize these concepts, we now examine a selection of diversity statuses (presented alphabetically next) as distinct and, at the same time, interconnecting in the client-trainee-supervisor triad.

Ability Differences

Nearly 20% of the U.S. population aged 5 years and older is living with one or more disabilities (United States Census Bureau, 2010). Disability may be considered an evolving concept including "physical, mental, intellectual or sensory impairments that, in the face of various negative attitudes or physical obstacles, may prevent those persons from participating fully in society" (United Nations Enable, 2006, Defining Disability section, para. 1). Of the general American public, 9.3 million people have a sensory disability, 21.2 million people have a condition limiting basic physical activities, and 12.4 million people have a physical or mental condition causing difficulty in learning, remembering, or concentrating (National Center for Health Statistics, 2007; U.S. Census Bureau, 2003). Additionally, over 26% of Americans ages 18 and older meet the diagnostic criteria for mental illness each year (Kessler, Chiu, Demler & Walters, 2005). To frame this area of difference in terms of the continua of target status and oppression presented earlier, disability status may be developmental, is eventually universal (albeit to substantially varying degrees), generally immutable, may be visible or invisible, and is often critical to identity. Persons with disabilities often are subject to systemic, permanent, pervasive, and internalized oppression that is usually related to the core sense of self (see Tables 23.2 and 23.3).

Although it could be considered a linguistic diversity, individuals who are deaf or hard of hearing often are included under ability status differences. American Sign Language (ASL), the primary language of culturally Deaf people, is a language distinct from English and complete with its own rules of grammar and syntax (Stokoe, Casterline, & Croneberg, 1976). The scarcity of mental health professionals who sign competently and specialize in working with Deaf people means that most Deaf people receive mental health care through the provision of sign language interpreters (Leigh & Pollard, 2003); thus training in this area is a vital, although often neglected part of psychology education.

What impact might ability status have on Ms. Pereira's treatment? Suppose she has one known medical diagnosis, Type II diabetes, for which she takes daily prescription medication. Most directly, Ms. Pereira's medical status will likely be incorporated diagnostically, listed with her mental health conditions for record-keeping and billing purposes. Other implications might include issues of basic access (e.g., can each member of the treatment team physically utilize the facilities without undue hardship?) and mental health status, with the latter being tacitly implicated in virtually every psychotherapy encounter. Less subject to scrutiny may be ability-status issues, including mental health considerations, on the part of Mr. Barrera or Dr. Reinhardt. These could vary from theoretically "invisible" learning differences that become more impactful as our bilingual student progresses through increasingly challenging graduate material, to early onset Alzheimer's disease as a supervisor approaches middle age, to a lifelong struggle with mood or body image—or an infinite number of other permutations of mental or physical difference. The question for training, education, and supervision becomes, "Are any challenges in this area (for the client, therapist, or supervisor) being recognized and adequately addressed?" As we again shift perspective, it is also worth considering how ability status might intersect with other variables—for example, age and gender.

Age

The population of the United States is aging as well as becoming increasingly diverse. The Centers for Disease Control and Prevention (CDC) National Center for Health Statistics (2007) reports that life expectancies have increased across racial and gender categories, and the average baby born in the United States in 2010 is projected to have a life expectancy of 78.3 years, which is. in turn. expected to increase to 78.9 by 2015 and 79.5 by 2020 (http://www.census.gov/compendia/statab/2011/tables/11s0103.pdf). Older adults experience unique challenges that are developmental, psychological, spiritual, physical and social. Age may be considered developmental, universal, immutable, visible, and eventually critical to identity (see Table 23.2). In considering the target status that age often holds in the United States, it is also necessary to examine and recognize the level of disempowerment potentially experienced by adults as they grow older. Smith (2007) notes, for example, that "mental health issues relevant to older individuals continue to be underrepresented in psychology, medical, and other health care programs" (p. 277). For many individuals, this oppression may be viewed as systemic, permanent, pervasive, internalized, and related to the core sense of self (see Table 23.2).

It would be misleading, however, to present the data on aging as exclusively negative; a recent issue of the *APA Monitor* bore the encouraging cover, "Good news about middle age," and discussed new research on strengths and resiliencies in older adults (Phillips, 2011). Understanding the complexity of these challenges, while appreciating the lifetime of experiences the older adult client may bring into the therapy room, is necessary for psychologists to competently treat this population. Thus, it is vital that all mental health providers receive adequate education on adult development and aging, and specifically aging/gerontology issues with specific minority/cultural groups. Included in this discussion could be the differences that exist between cultural groups with regard to attitudes toward the elderly.

Ms. Pereira may be variably conscious of her age as a target identity depending on the situation (participating in recreational activities at her residence, a retirement community geared toward active, single adults, for example, versus walking through lower Manhattan to attend a medical appointment). Similarly, in the context of her treatment, the roughly 20-year age increments separating her therapist, her therapist's supervisor, and Ms. Pereira herself may be clinically meaningful when one considers that each may have differing attitudes and values regarding aging. When considered in light of other identity statuses, for example, what did it mean to Ms. Pereira to come of age in midcentury America as a young, Catholic woman of blended racial ancestry? For that matter, how did growing up as a nonheterosexual male of Mexican ancestry in the United States in the 1980s and 1990s impact Mr. Barrera? What was the zeitgeist for Dr. Reinhardt's developmental trajectory, and how might all these dynamics influence the lenses and filters through which this case is viewed? Finally, age cannot be considered a freestanding variable; it must be considered contextually in light of other identity statuses. By way of illustration, we began this section by discussing mean life expectancies in the United States. These data belie a chilling reminder of ongoing racial disparities. For instance, a White female born in the United States in 2007 has an actuarial life expectancy of 80.8 years; an African American male born at the same time—70.0 years, a difference of more than a decade (http://www.census.gov/compendia/statab/2011/tables/11s0103.pdf).

Appearance and Size

According to the Centers for Disease Control and Prevention (2008), 33.9% of the U.S. population over age 20 may be considered obese. "Sizeism" is a relatively new concept in the diversity literature, yet may represent an unrecognized prejudice even among psychologists who treat clients presenting with problems related to size, weight, and body image (Abakoui & Simmons, 2010). Developing competencies in assessment, case conceptualization, and intervention related to appearance and size is important for psychologists in training, yet relatively little has been written on the subject. Weight, for example, may be considered developmental or lifelong, particular, mutable, visible, and incidental or critical to identity (see Table 23.3), yet oppression toward people who are perceived as obese may be systemic, permanent, pervasive both externalized and internalized, and related to a core sense of self (see Table 23.3). This issue may be particularly impactful in light of the changing dynamics of the American health care system and the American Medical Association's 2013 resolution recognizing obesity as a "disease state" (see Hensley, 2013). Unearned privilege for particularly attractive individuals and oppression against unattractive individuals is not generally included in current psychology education and training, yet may be an area of future direction.

In therapy and supervision, these issues might play out clinically with regard to specific presenting issues (around body image and/or eating disordered behavior, for example), or in more subtle, in-the-room dynamics (for example, conscious or subconscious attraction or negativity, unfounded expectations around intelligence, personality characteristics, or behavior based on assumptions rooted in physical appearance). In a situation like this, supervisors and supervisees might be encouraged to open the shutter for a moment and consider their own reactions and projections. In his iconic work *Love's Executioner*, Irvin Yalom (2000) describes his reaction to an obese client in the essay "Fat Lady" (p. 94): "I have always been repelled by fat women. I find them disgusting: their absurd sidewise waddle, their absence of body contour—breasts, laps, buttocks, shoulders, jawlines, cheekbones, *everything*, everything I like to see in a woman, obscured in an avalanche of flesh." Questions to explore might include: What does it mean to be "sexy" at 77, say, or "morbidly obese" in your late 20s? Does the meaning or saliency seem to change as a function of any other factor—sexual orientation, religion, educational status? Can only those who are viewed as *less* attractive than societal expectations be "targeted" for their appearance? Would perceptions differ if the trainee were *Ms.* Barrera, or if the client and/or supervisor were male?

Ethnicity

Ethnicity, often erroneously used interchangeably with race, can be defined as the commonalities and shared experiences among groups based on cultural values and patterns (e.g., collectivism, filial piety, familialism) that are transmitted over time to create a common history (Juby & Concepcion, 2005). According to Chang & Kwan (2009), "an ethnic group can form the basis for an ethnic identity when individuals begin the process of deciding that they belong to that ethnic group and use their ethnic group membership to establish a sense of who they are" (p. 115). Thus, ethnicity may be developmental or lifelong, universal or particular, mutable rather than immutable (as with race in most cases), invisible, and either incidental or critical to identity (e.g., highlighted within certain contexts such as within the family) (see Table 23.2). Prejudice toward ethnic groups may be circumstantial or systemic, transient or permanent, isolated or pervasive, externalized or internalized, and related to either peripheral characteristics or to the core sense of self (see Table 23.3).

It is critical that psychology trainees understand the complex nature of ethnic identity and the role it might play in their own identities, as well as those of their colleagues, supervisors, and clients. In the earlier example, each participant brings a potential awareness *of* ethnic identity (itself not a given); how each understands his or her ethnicity is more nuanced. Within the triad, for example, Dr. Reinhardt's identification of herself as "Jewish" may or may not include a religious component, may encompass a wide range of potential cultural variables, and is framed within a broader geographic, historical, and political context.

Gender

Gender has been defined as a "set of power relations in which—absent other cues and definitions—maleness signals authority, status, competence, social power, and influence, and femaleness signals lack of authority, low status, incompetence, and little power and influence" (Stewart & McDermott, 2004, p. 521). Gender identity influences all aspects of psychology (e.g., Stevens & Englar-Carlson, 2010; Smart, 2010), from differential rates of diagnosis for certain mental health disorders (see Skodol & Bender, 2003, noting men are diagnosed with Borderline Personality Disorder at about one-third the rate of women) to differential availability of services for certain types of presenting issues (see Monk-Turner & Light, 2010, describing the limited treatment options available for male victims of sexual assault). Gender dynamics can impact the therapeutic process itself; for example, men who are brought to psychotherapy by their female partners may feel insecure about the process of therapy and unsure about their role, which may result in critical and even condescending remarks toward the therapist or alternately may result in silence (Stevens & Englar-Carlson, 2010). Since many current psychology students are female, such relationships may be difficult to negotiate.

Although most psychology education and training currently focuses on "male" and female" aspects of gender, as Singh, Boyd, and Whitman (2010) note, awareness in the areas of *transgender* ("an umbrella term that refers to individuals whose gender identity transgresses traditional definitions of 'male' and 'female,'" p. 417), *intersex* ("a range of anatomical conditions in which an individual's anatomy or chromosomes are some combination of male and female," p. 420), and other gender identity statuses is becoming increasingly essential to competent practice. Discrimination is a reality of life for many individuals with these identifications, along with concomitant mental health concerns (see, e.g., Kirk & Belovics, 2008). Psychotherapy often is necessary in order for *noncisgender* (or transgender) individuals to receive appropriate treatments (e.g., hormones, surgery), so specific competencies are necessary for psychologists seeking to work with these populations. The "gatekeeper" function that mental health professionals serve in determining access to reassignment services can, understandably, have a deleterious effect on the therapeutic alliance (Bockting, Knudson, Goldberg, 2006, p. 19), and care should be taken to recognize the unique challenges faced by individuals undergoing these processes.

When considered broadly, including male, female, transgender, and intersex, gender may be seen as developmental or lifelong, universal or particular, mutable or immutable, invisible or visible, and incidental or critical to identity (see Table 23.1). Men, women, transgender, and intersex individuals may experience the entire continuum of oppression (see Table 23.2). Meaning-making around issues of self-esteem and self-efficacy, identity, appearance, sexuality, gender expression, and gender roles, along with a myriad of others, may vary among and between dyads in this treatment. Assumptions and expectations, power differentials, variances in communication styles, and different models of problem solving and collaboration have all been identified as potentially impactful in mixed-gender client/therapist and therapist/supervisor relationships (Doughty & Leddick, 2007). Interestingly, one seemingly intuitive recommendation involves actually *talking about* gender issues in the context of supervision, an apparently (comparatively) rare occurrence. Doughty and Leddick (2007) note that it has become increasingly "commonplace for counseling students to address their own personal bias regarding race and ethnicity, but not as common to explore a bias that is gender-related" (p. 26), despite evidence from a study of 289 psychology predoctoral interns suggesting higher levels of satisfaction with supervision when gender differences and similarities were discussed (pp. 26–27). Thus, it could be recommended that Dr. Reinhardt open a dialogue with Mr. Barrera, exploring the relationship between his gender identity, hers, and that of Ms. Pereira.

Immigration

The United States has seen many waves of immigration throughout its history. Immigration status is a key consideration for psychologists working with nonnative populations (Inman & Tummala-Nara, 2010). In the last decade, the number of individuals naturalized in the United States has steadily increased, with the majority of immigrants coming from Asia (36.6%), Mexico and Latin America (27.2%), and Europe (15.3%) (United States Department of Homeland Security, 2008). Each group has its own separate and distinct immigration pattern, based on the characteristics of the group, entry of the group, class, racism, and sociopolitical issues. Stressors encountered before, during, and after migration (including the reasons for the relocation, such as war or famine; trauma encountered during the journey; and generally lower economic status, limited access to resources, and experiences with discrimination upon arrival) can lead to mental health problems in adults and children (Pumariega, Rothe, & Pumariega, 2005).

Education and training in this area must include helping students understand their own perceptions of immigrants, relevant concepts such as acculturation and accommodation, and both pre- and postmigration factors. Although immigrants may have come from cultures with fairly consistent and functional values and practices, transitioning into a new cultural environment requires a reevaluation of cultural practices, within the context of a lack of a social structure that supports their cultural priorities and needs (Inman, Howard, Beaumont & Walker, 2007). Thus, individual, sociocultural, and structural/institutional barriers may influence the help-seeking attitudes and behaviors of immigrant communities (Fong, 2004). Similar to ethnicity, immigration status may be considered developmental or lifelong, universal or particular, mutable or immutable, generally invisible, and either incidental or critical to identity (see Table 23.2). The contexts within which the immigrant lives, works, and plays may help frame the saliency of the target status. Finally, students need to understand the historical racism regarding immigrant groups, because some are generally welcomed whereas others are viewed in more negative terms (see Pumariega, Rothe, & Pumariega, 2005, noting that discrimination can come, not just from mainstream American culture, but also from members of other immigrant groups).

Thus, prejudice toward such populations may cover the entire continuum of oppression (see Table 23.2). In the training case, it may be worthwhile for Mr. Barrera to explore Ms. Pereira's feelings of inclusion or exclusion as a young child, and the implication of those perceptions on her sense of self today. Likewise, it may behoove Dr. Reinhardt to facilitate discussions with Mr. Barrera regarding any perceived transference issues or countertransference issues surrounding personal or familial immigration status, acculturation, and related concepts.

Language

According to the U.S. census (2010), nearly 20% of the U.S. population spoke a language other than or in addition to English. Language and culture are necessarily interconnected such that culture has a profound influence on communication and personal language biases. So, similar to culture, language may be viewed as developmental, universal, mutable, generally visible, and either incidental or critical to identity (see Table 23.2).

Education and training programs in professional psychology need to prepare English-speaking mental health providers, in particular, to work with the innumerable dialects and languages that are used within various communities around the nation. It is also useful to explore the assumptions mental health providers may make about persons with accents, and the relative perception of some accents as exotic and intelligent, and others as threatening or uneducated.

Problems with language can result in misdiagnoses and treatment in both mental health and health-care centers. In particular, caution should be used when attempting to apply assessments or interventions cross-culturally, with population groups for which they have not been normed or validated. In a classic example cited by Greenfield (1997, p. 1116), researchers asked Kpelle participants from Liberia to complete a cognitive object-sorting task that involved (from the researchers' perspectives) dividing 20 items into linguistic groups such as food, implements, and clothing. Instead, the native participants paired the items *functionally*—the knife with the potato, because one is used to cut the other,

and so forth. In this example, simple translation—however accurate the literal words may be—did not address the divide inherent in measuring ability across cultural settings.

The use of "interpreters" in psychotherapy may be similarly crucial and problematic. When clients are interviewed and diagnosed in their non-native tongues, they may be more apt to receive a wrong or unwarranted diagnosis in comparison to when they are appropriately and sensitively interviewed in their primary languages. Additionally, the psychosocial differences and ways emotions may be experienced differently when clients speak in their native language is critical to consider. Thus, the continuum of oppression related to language may be circumstantial or systemic, transient or permanent, isolated or pervasive, externalized or internalized, but is generally related to the core sense of self (see Table 23.3).

In the training case, Mr. Barrera, speaks both English and Spanish fluently, and may work with other clients who are primarily Spanish speaking and whose group identity may be Latino/a—assuming his proficiency in that language rises to the level of *clinical* fluency, a higher bar than that demanded from general conversational skills. From a supervisory perspective, ethical and practical considerations make it difficult to supervise clinical services provided in a language one does not personally speak; if Dr. Reinhardt does not, herself, speak Spanish, it would be advisable for her to transfer supervision of any case that involved a substantial amount of content in a language other than English.

Political

Salient characteristics of our intersecting identities also carry with them politically and socially charged historical relations that often continue to have an impact on individual lives in the form of inequality and social stigma (Cole, 2009). The larger political context is very relevant, and political views may underscore hidden target and nontarget statuses. More importantly, subtle prejudices, particularly on the part of the supervisor and supervisee toward the client, may play out in expressions that appear political in nature on the surface. Clearly, political identities may be developmental or lifelong, universal or particular, and incidental or critical to identity, but are usually mutable, invisible (see Table 23.2).

According to Redding (2001), despite psychology's move toward embracing and encouraging the exploration of difference in our students, there appears to be a lack of sociopolitical diversity in education and training, with conservative views underrepresented. This "lack of political diversity biases research on social policy issues, damages psychology's credibility with policymakers and the public, impedes serving conservative clients, results in de facto discrimination against conservative students and scholars, and has a chilling effect on liberal education" (p. 205). Magnusson (2011) agrees that researchers tend to examine their body of work based in part on their social and political allegiances. Thus, political views may be subject to the entire continuum of oppression (see Table 23.3).

It is valuable to contextualize treatment and supervision in terms of the broader national, regional, and local political climate. Consider the following weblog quotation from a 1992 *New York Times* article describing reactions following the passage of Colorado's constitutional "Amendment 2," which barred municipalities within the state from enacting legislation designed to prevent discrimination based on sexual orientation:

> They sat around a cafe table two days after the election, but nobody felt much like eating. It seemed like they had just been on trial. And the verdict was not pleasant.
>
> "I feel like I've been kicked in the stomach," said Lawrence Pacheco, a 23-year-old gay man. "Do they really hate us that much?" (Herek, 2008)

The author goes on to describe anti-equal-rights initiatives in other states, as well as research conducted in the wake of such measures showing a variety of negative mental health correlates for gay, lesbian, and bisexual residents. The current legal and social climate, including a 2013 United States Supreme Court decision striking down part of the federal Defense of Marriage Act (see Schwartz, 2013), keeps sexual orientation at the forefront of an evolving public dialogue. Focusing for a moment on Mr. Barrera, it is difficult to imagine how living, attending a graduate training program, working, dating, and seeing clients in an atmosphere of such charged political tension could fail to impact his clinical practice and supervision. To provide adequate and holistic supervision, it will be necessary for Dr. Reinhardt to take into account the triggers Mr. Barrera and/or Ms. Pereira may be experiencing around this ostensibly "political" issue—as well as her own.

Race

Although defined in many ways, race is often based on the biology/genetics of a person (i.e., one's skin color, physical features, and hair texture).

It also has been defined as a social construction used to make psychological and cultural inferences about ascribed membership in a designated group (Sanchez & Davis, 2010). The following racial groups are officially recognized by the U.S. Census Bureau (2010): Asian (4.8%), Native Hawaiian/Pacific Islander (0.2%), Black/African American (12.6%), American Indian/Alaskan Native (0.9%), White (72.4%), Latino/Hispanic (16.3%), and Multiracial (2.9%).

Race almost always is considered at the far end of the continuum of target status described in Table 23.1 (i.e., lifelong, universal, immutable, visible, and critical to identity) and again at the far end of the continuum of oppression described in Table 23.3 (i.e., systemic, permanent, pervasive, internalized, and related to the core sense of self). In addition, race must be understood in the context of historical and institutionalized oppression and racism in its overt and subtle forms. For example, Ms. Pereira's Visual Racial Ethnic Group (often shortened to VREG) may be ambiguous. She may not present to most observers (especially those who do not share her racial/ethnic background) as being a person of color and thus, if she chooses, "pass" as White. In a racially diverse urban setting, Ms. Pereira's blended identity may be conceptualized as falling toward the invisible side of the spectrum; in another context, or for someone with a different complexion or combination of physical features, this might not be the case. Meaning making around race and its impact may also play out differently for someone of African descent, a recent immigrant from Sweden, a Palestinian asylum-seeker, and so on. Regardless, as Carter (1995) states, "race is not always apparent, but is always present because it is part of each person's personality and it is part of our institutional and social structures" (p. 227).

Because of the general saliency and complexity of race, it is essential that psychology students understand how racial identity influences everyone and the stimulus value that it may have for themselves, their colleagues, their supervisors, and their clients. There are several models in the literature regarding racial identity (see Training of Professional Ridley and Jeffrey, chapter 14, this volume).

The term *multiracial* refers to individuals whose racial heritage is comprised of multiple racial groups and "whose parents are of different socially designated racial groups" (Root, 1996, p. ix). An individual's self-definition may vary based on familiarity with terms and familial, social, political, and cultural contexts. These social contexts have a strong hand in shaping racial identity. Contexts can differ in their racial composition, thus influencing how a person understands identity or the extent to which he or she feels "White" or "Asian" (Harris & Sim, 2002). For example, when visiting the country of origin of one parent, a multiracial child might identify more closely with that racial identity than with the racial identity of the other parent. This "situational ethnicity" represents a "natural strategy in response to the social demands" of a dominant culture that asks for categorical self-definition in ways that leave persons of nuanced heritage feeling "fragmented and fractionalized" (Root, 2000, pp. 124, 120).

Situations can arise in clinical training in which one participant in treatment identifies race as a salient sociocultural characteristic, whereas another may not. This may result in widely differing worldviews, attributions of motivation, understandings of meaning, and so forth. Toporek, Ortega-Villalobos, and Pope-Davis (2004) relate the following "critical incident" in multicultural supervision, described by a supervisor in a mixed-race supervision dyad:

> My male supervisee who is White never took notes during our 45-minute supervisions. When I asked him why he never wrote anything down, he replied that he had a good memory and wanted to see the "big picture." He rarely asked questions which could be addressed beyond yes or no. My initial reaction was to think that this was his way of telling (showing) me that whatever I had to say to him was of neutral consequence. (p. 77)

From the supervisee's perspective, race may *not* have been consciously perceived as the motivating factor for his behavior in supervision. From the supervisor's perspective—and viewed through the lens of a lifetime of seeing racial identity as more than simply "water"—the trainee's behavior felt disrespectful and dismissive in a particularly racially salient way. In this case, the onus would clearly be on the supervisor to assist the student in developing effective clinical knowledge, skills, and values, which would likely include an exploration of the student's own racial identity and perspectives around race. However, the situation could be easily reversed, involving a supervisee—Mr. Barrera, for instance—or a client for whom race is a critical aspect of identity, and a supervisor for whom it is not, or any combination thereof. Because of the power differential between supervisee/supervisor and client/therapist, concerns around issues of racial identity may be especially challenging to voice and address.

Religion and Spirituality

Religion (an organized system of faith/worship/ traditions/rituals) and spirituality (a more general attunement with the universe) often are difficult to incorporate into mental health practice, yet are important for ethical and multiculturally sensitive treatment (Savage & Armstrong, 2010). Although it is impossible for psychology students to be educated and trained in all aspects of spirituality and religion that are likely to be pertinent to their clients, it may be useful to at least expose them to the six major world religions expressed in the United States (Islam, Buddhism, Hinduism, Christianity, Judaism, and Native American Spirituality), including the view of deity, beliefs, and tenets of the religion, view of life after death, religious practices, and views of marriage, divorce, roles in the family, and sexuality (see Table 13.5, Savage & Armstrong, 2010, pp. 408–409).

Religion and spirituality are generally seen as lifelong, universal, and invisible, but may be either mutable or immutable, and either incidental or critical to identity (see Table 23.2). Target status may vary depending on culture and context (see Table 23.3). Again, allusions to the religious identification (or lack thereof) for each of the participants in this therapeutic triad have been made earlier. Questions for consideration from a supervisory standpoint would include the following: To what extent would issues of spirituality get brought explicitly into the therapy and/or supervision room? For example, does Dr. Reinhardt identify as spiritually Jewish? Does she disclose her identity in direct or indirect ways, such as wearing a Star of David or canceling supervision to attend Yom Kippur services? What implications might these behaviors (or nonbehaviors) have on the therapeutic and supervisory alliances? Suppose Ms. Pereira considers herself to be a "devout Catholic," and describes deeply held spiritual convictions. From the distinct perspective of each member of the team, to what degree is that identity salient for treatment, and under what circumstances? Would the analysis change, for example, if Ms. Pereira were presenting for grief counseling following the death of her best friend of 50 years versus treatment for social anxiety? In either case, would Mr. Barrera draw upon any solace or meaning Ms. Pereira might find in her religious doctrine? Would he "challenge" her "irrational beliefs," or interpret them as denial mechanisms? How would he maintain the integrity of *his* beliefs without invalidating hers? Concretely, Dr. Reinhardt could encourage Mr. Barrera to educate himself regarding the general tenets of

Ms. Pereira's religious identification (as he likely would regarding other categories of difference), while recognizing that religious conviction is a deeply personal and idiosyncratic matter. She also could assist him in thinking through his own reactions and how he might respond effectively, ethically, and appropriately to faith-based content raised in session—if Ms. Pereira were to ask him about his own beliefs, for example, or if she were to request that he pray with her. Finally, it is worth considering what issues might arise if Mr. Barrera *himself* identified strongly with Ms. Pereira's faith. In what ways might the therapeutic alliance be enhanced, and at what risk?

Sexual Orientation/Sexual Identity

Worthington (2004) posited that sexual orientation and sexual identity were related but distinct constructs. Sexual orientation is innate and predispositional (lifelong, universal, immutable, invisible and either incidental or critical to identity in Table 23.2), whereas sexual identity may be considered to be an identification with one's sexual orientation (developmental, universal, mutable, invisible, and either incidental or critical to identity in Table 23.2). Crucial to the education and training for psychology students is an awareness of the literature surrounding the development of sexual identity and orientation, and an exploration of their own beliefs around Lesbian/Gay/Bisexual (LGB) issues that may influence their approach to treatment. Some additional discussion of social stigmas and obstacles, identity development, and counselor advocacy may be needed to provide a context for the synthesis of multiple levels of information. Psychology education and training must include an honest look at the systematic nature of prejudice against LGB populations. Such prejudice may be transient or permanent, but is usually pervasive, internalized, and related to the core sense of self (see Table 23.3). Recent polling suggests that perceptions of stigma may be changing: A Pew Research Center (2013) survey conducted in April of 2013 found that 92% of self-identified gay, lesbian, bisexual, and transgender respondents described society as having become more accepting over the past decade and expected this acceptance to increase over the decade to come. The report went on to catalog, however, a myriad of ways in which respondents reported having been targeted because of their sexual orientation or gender identity, ranging from being treated unfairly by an employer (21%) to being threatened or physically attacked (30%) to being subject to slurs or jokes (58%).

In clinical situations, heterosexual providers and supervisors need to educate themselves about these realities. As noted by Kirk and Belovics (2008), for example, LGB clients often bifurcate home and work life in an effort to insulate themselves from discrimination, and may make employment decisions based, in part, on whether a given employer's health plan covers domestic partners or same-sex spouses. For Mr. Barrera, obviously, sexual orientation represents a specific target status that may have particular salience in different contexts (geographically, politically, etc.) and at different developmental points, personally and professionally. His own experiences with acceptance or rejection around sexual identity, his "coming out" story, and the degree to which he has been exposed to external homophobia, as well as the degree to which he has internalized pro- and anti-LGB messages, may all play into his experience as a bisexual male in a clinical training setting. Certainly the field of psychology itself has not always been affirming of same-sex partnerships (listen to National Public Radio's 2002 broadcast, "81 Words" for a poignant reminder of the history of "Homosexuality" as a *DSM* disorder). In addition, as a bisexual individual, Mr. Barrera may find that he is not fully accepted by either the gay/lesbian community or the heterosexual community. These issues can play out therapeutically in a variety of ways. Again, part of the task of supervision is to recognize potential barriers to full and effective communication at each level of intervention (avoiding phrasing questions on phone screens and in intakes in such a way as to imply a heterosexist worldview—e.g., "Are you married?"; preferencing neutral terms such as "partner" and "Ms." over "husband" or "Mrs."; and recognizing the myriad of unspoken privileges enjoyed by heterosexual partners every day, such as the "right" to wear a wedding ring if they choose, hold hands in public, display photos of loved ones, refer to their partners by gender etc.).

Socioeconomic Status (SES)

Constructs such as social class and SES have been adopted from sociology, and include such indicators as income, occupational status, and educational level (Grusky, 2001). According to Liu, Corkery, and Thome (2010), social class contributes to a particular worldview and identity. For many psychology students, differences in social class with clients are difficult to overcome, and many tend to verbalize extreme feelings of discomfort in discussing issues relating to social class. Discussion of social class violates the myth of a classless society (Liu et al., 2010), such that the idea that social class is a mutable "target" status may be discredited. There continues to be an assumption that social mobility is possible and that those who are unable to obtain upward mobility have deficits that are more related to internal versus external, societal, or cultural factors. Thus, SES may be viewed as developmental or lifelong, universal, mutable or immutable, often visible, and generally critical to identity (see Table 23.2). With regard to the continuum of oppression (Table 23.3), prejudice based on SES may be systemic, permanent, pervasive, internalized, and related to the core sense of self.

Clearly, SES would be an interesting area of exploration for our training triad. Each of the three participants comes from a different background; they may share filters in some ways, and may have "blind spots" with regard to one another's perspective around key issues. Low SES has been found to correlate with a variety of physical and mental health issues, low self-esteem, and increased relational strain (Pope & Arthur, 2009). In addition, psychologists may often harbor unspoken discomfort or even hostility toward individuals from lower SES, having perhaps internalized society's messages that economic status is mutable, and if anyone stays poor it is because he or she is characterologically flawed in some way (Pope & Arthur, 2009). "In light of the personal accountability for one's SES, it is very difficult to develop and maintain a positive low-SES identity," note Pope and Arthur (2009, p. 57). "Consequently, psychologists may need to intentionally devote time for reflective practice and supervision to address internalised stereotypes, perceptions of SES group differences, and social stigma that may form barriers between themselves and their clients" (pp. 56–57). In contrast, Mr. Barrera may become aware of feelings of resentment or simply a lack of a shared "frame" as he processes clinical material with Dr. Reinhardt. It is incumbent upon Dr. Reinhardt to keep these issues in mind as potential sources of awareness and discussion in supervision.

Conclusions and Future Directions

Although education and training on issues of culture and diversity has increased in psychology (see Guthrie, 2004), clearly much remains to be done. Certainly, a continued focus on understanding complex identities (especially among and between supervisors, supervisees, and clients) must include areas not considered earlier. Geographic

location, for example, represents an underexplored aspect of cultural context. The world's population is becoming increasingly geographically mobile, with the result that different aspects of identities may intersect in new ways. According to the U.S. Census Bureau (n.d.), 19.3% of the population resided in rural areas as recently as 2010. Access to and quality of health and mental health services can vary, with rural residents often facing barriers to receiving needed care (National Healthcare Disparities Report, 2004). Of course, geography is only one of many areas of possible inclusion to be considered in developing curricula that fully explore the continua of target status and oppression. Considerable work is still needed to understand the implications of these dynamics on education, training, supervision, and clinical assessment and intervention.

With regard to developing the ICD competency area, a future innovation may include expanding the sequence of training to begin with psychology education in high school, continue through postdoctoral fellowship, and persist into advanced training and specialization. Operationalizing the ICD competency and exploring empirically validated ways to assess it are further issues in need of exploration. In addition, relating the ICD competency more explicitly to the other benchmark competencies (APA, 2011b) is an area of future need.

There is also a crucial need for evidence-based multicultural therapies (e.g., Berg-Cross & So, 2011). Scientific knowledge and methods, evidence-based practice, and research/evaluation are other critical benchmark competencies that clearly intersect with culture and context in psychology.

Finally, the field is moving from simple awareness of the potential impact of demographic factors on clinical concerns to the burgeoning recognition of the need for psychologists to become involved in advocacy and social justice endeavors. In fact, advocacy ("Actions targeting the impact of social, political, economic or cultural factors to promote change at the individual (client), institutional, and/or systems level") is a separate benchmark competency (APA, 2011b). Clearly, integrating ICD and advocacy is an important future direction for the field.

Notes

1. Note that culture in this chapter will be examined as potentially inclusive of, but distinct from, the conceptually related constructs of race (historically used to denote shared traits, including physical characteristics, assumed to be biologically derived but in fact functioning as largely socially constructed hierarchies among and between particular individuals and groups) and ethnicity (involving intra- and intergroup connections

formed based on shared geography, history, religious understandings, and so forth) (see Sanchez & Davis, 2010).

2. It is worth pointing out, however, that even an example this ostensibly straightforward is not perspective-neutral. Hair—with all its attendant variables of color, style, length, texture, quantity, or absence—remains a highly personal and (in many cases) visible marker of identity status. A "bad hair day" may connote very different things to a person who identifies as Euro-American, for example, versus a descendent of runaway African slaves for whom the quest for "visual conformity" might have been literally a matter of life and death. "Everything I know about American history I learned from looking at Black people's hair," quote Byrd and Tharps in their 2001 book, *Hair Story: Untangling the Roots of Black Hair in America*. "It's the perfect metaphor for the African experiment here: the toll of slavery and the costs of remaining. It's all in the hair" (p. 164).

References

Abakoui, R., & Simmons, R. E. (2010). Sizeism: An unrecognized prejudice. In J. A. Erickson Cornish, B. A. Schreier, L. I. Nadkarni, L. Henderson Metzger, & E. R. Rodolfa. (Eds). *Handbook of multicultural counseling competencies* (pp. 317– 350). Hoboken, NJ: Wiley.

American Psychological Association (2002). *Guidelines on multicultural education, training, research, practice, and organizational change for psychologists*. Washington DC: Author. Accessed 10 July 2013. Retrieved from http://www.apa.org/pi/oema/resources/policy/multicultural-guidelines.aspx doi: 10.1037/0003-066X.58.5.377.

American Psychological Association (2004a). Guidelines for psychological practice with older adults. *American Psychologist*, *59*(4), 236–260. doi:10.1037/0003-066X.59.4.236.

American Psychological Association (2004b). *Policy statement on sexual orientation, parents, and children*. Washington, DC: Author. Accessed 10 July 2013. Retrieved from http://www.apa.org/about/governance/council/policy/parenting.aspx

American Psychological Association (October 2006). *Final report of the APA Task Force on the Assessment of Competence in Professional Psychology*. Accessed 15 July 2013. Retrieved from:

American Psychological Association (October 2006). Final report of the APA Task Force on the Assessment of Competence in Professional Psychology. Accessed 15 July 2013. Retrieved from: www.apa.org/ed/resources/competency-revised.pdf

American Psychological Association. (2007a). *APA guidelines for the undergraduate psychology major*. Washington, DC: Author. Accessed 10 July 2013. Retrieved from http://www.apa.org/ed/precollege/about/psymajor-guidelines.pdf

American Psychological Association (2007b). *Guidelines for Psychological Practice With Girls and Women. A Joint Task Force of APA Divisions 17 and 35*. Accessed 10 July 2013. Washington, DC: Author. Retrieved from http://www.apa.org/practice/guidelines/index.aspx

American Psychological Association, Commission on Accreditation, Office of Program Consultation and Accreditation, Education Directorate. (2009). *Guidelines and principles for accreditation of programs in professional psychology*. Washington, DC: Author. Accessed 10 July 2013. Retrieved from http://www.apa.org/ed/accreditation/about/policies/guiding-principles.pdf

American Psychological Association. (2010). *Ethical principles of psychologists and code of conduct (2002, Amended June 1, 2010)*. Washington, DC: Author. Accessed 10 July 2013.

Retrieved from http://www.apa.org/ethics/code/index.aspx doi:10.1037/a0024003.

American Psychological Association (2011a). *National standards for high school psychology curricula*. Washington, DC: Author. Accessed 10 July 2013. Retrieved from: http://www.apa.org/education/k12/psychology-curricula.pdf

American Psychological Association. (June, 2011b). *Revised competency benchmarks in professional psychology*. Washington, DC: Author. Accessed 10 July 2013. Retrieved from http://www.apa.org/ed/graduate/benchmarks-evaluation-system.aspx

American Psychological Association (2012a). Guidelines for assessment of and intervention with persons with disabilities. *American Psychologist, 67*(1), 43–62. doi:10.1037/a0025892.

American Psychological Association (2012b). Guidelines for psychological practice with lesbian, gay, and bisexual clients. *American Psychologist, 67*(1), 10–42. doi: 10.1037/a0024659.

American Psychological Association (2012c). Guidelines for the evaluation of dementia and age-related cognitive change. *American Psychologist, 67*(1), 1–9. doi: 10.1037/a0024643

Beer, A. M., Spanierman, L. B., Green, J. C., & Todd, N. R. (2012). Advancing social justice: Enlisting student voices. *Journal of Counseling Psychology, 59*(1), 120–133.

Berg-Cross, L., & So, D. (2011). The start of a new era: Evidence-based multicultural therapies. *The National Register of Health Service Providers in Psychology. The Register Report* (37), 8–15.

Bockting, W., Knudson, G., & Goldberg, J. M. (2006). Counselling and mental health care of transgender adults and loved ones. Accessed 10 July 2013. Retrieved from http://transhealth.vch.ca/resources/library/tcpdocs/guidelines-mentalhealth.pdf

Byrd, A., & Tharps, L. (2001). *Hair story: Untangling the roots of Black hair in America*. New York, NY: St. Martin's. doi:10.1300/J485v09n03_03.

Carpenter, E.S. (1970). *They became what they beheld*. New York, NY: Outerbridge & Dienstfrey; distributed by E. P. Dutton.

Carter, R. T. (1995). *The influence of race and racial identity in psychotherapy: Toward a racially inclusive model*. New York, NY: Wiley.

Centers for Disease Control and Prevention (2008). FastStats: Obesity and Overweight. Accessed 10 July 2013. Retrieved from http://www.cdc.gov/nchs/fastats/overwt.htm

Chang, T., & Kwan, K. K. (2009). Asian American racial and ethnic identity. In N. Tewari & A. N. Alvarez (Eds.). *Asian American psychology: Current perspectives* (pp. 113–134). New York, NY: Psychology Press.

Cole, E. (2009). Intersectionality and research in psychology. *American Psychologist, 64*, 170–180. doi:10.1037/a0014564.

Context. (2013). From *Dictionary.com*. Accessed 10 July 2013. Retrieved from http://dictionary.reference.com/browse/context

Cross, W., Parham, T., & Helms, J. (1991). The stages of black identity development. Nigrescence models. In R. Jones (Ed.), *Black Psychology* (3rd ed., pp. 319–338). Berkeley, CA: Cobb & Henry.

Daniel, J. H., Roysircar, G., Abeles, N., & Boyd, C. (2004). Individual and cultural diversity competency: Focus on the therapist. *Journal of Clinical Psychology, 60*(7), 755–770. doi:10.1002/jclp.20014.

Doughty, E. A., & Leddick, G. R. (2007). Gender differences in the supervisory relationship. *Journal of Professional Counseling, Practice, Theory, & Research, 35*(2), 17–30.

Dressel, J. L., Kerr, S., & Stevens, H. B. (2010). White identity and privilege. In J. A. Erickson Cornish, B. Schreier,

L. I. Nadkarni, L. Henderson Metzger, & E. R. Rodolfa (Eds). *The handbook of multicultural counseling competencies* (pp. 443–474). Hoboken, NJ: Wiley.

Erickson Cornish, J. A., Schreier, B. A., Nadkarni, L. I., Henderson Metzger, L., & Rodolfa, E. R. (2010). *Handbook of multicultural counseling competencies*. Hoboken, NJ: Wiley.

Farber, B. (2006). *Self-disclosure in psychotherapy*. New York, NY: Guilford.

Faulkner, S. L., Baldwin, J. R., Lindsley, S. L., & Hecht, M. L. (2006). Layers of meaning: An analysis of definitions of culture. In J. R. Baldwin, S. L. Faulkner, M. L. Hecht, & S. L. Lindsley (Eds.). *Redefining culture: Perspectives across the disciplines*. Mahwah, NJ,: Erlbaum.

Fong, R. (2004). *Culturally competent practice with immigrants and refugee children and families*. New York: Guilford.

Fouad, N. A., Grus, C. L., Hatcher, R., L., Kaslow, N. J., Smith Hutchings, P., Madson, M. M.,... Crossman, R. E. (2009). Competency benchmarks: A model for understanding and measuring competence in professional psychology across training levels. *Training and Education in Professional Psychology*, *3*(4, Suppl), S5–S26. doi:10.1037/a0015832.

Green, D., Callands, T. A., Radcliffe, A. M., Luebbe, A. M., & Klonoff, E. A. (2009). Clinical psychology students' perceptions of diversity training: A study of exposure and satisfaction. *Journal of Clinical Psychology*, *65*(10), 1056–1070. doi:10.1002/jclp.20605.

Greenfield, P. (1997). You can't take it with you: Why ability assessments don't cross cultures. *American Psychologist*, *52*,1115–1124. doi: 10.1037/0003-066X.52.10.1115.

Grusky, D. B. (Ed.). (2001). *Social stratification: Class, race, and gender in sociological perspective* (2nd ed.). Boulder, CO: Westview Press.

Guthrie, R. V. (2004). *Even the rat was white: A historical view of psychology* (2nd ed). Upper Saddle River, NJ: Pearson.

Harris, D. R., & Sim, J. J. (2002). Who is multiracial? Assessing the complexity of lived race. *American Sociological Review*, *67*, 614–267. doi:10.2307/3088948.

Helms, J. (1990). *Black and white racial identity: Theory, research, and practice*. Westport, CT: Praeger.

Henderson Metzger, L., Nadkarni, L. I., & Erickson Cornish, J. A. (2010). An overview of multicultural counseling competencies. In J. A. Erickson Cornish, B. A. Schreier, L. I. Nadkarni, L. Henderson Metzger, & E. R. Rodolfa (Eds) *The handbook of multicultural counseling competencies*. Hoboken, NJ: Wiley.

Hensley, S. (2013, June 19). AMA says it's time to call obesity a disease. [Blog post]. Accessed 15 July 2013. Retrieved from http://www.npr.org/blogs/health/2013/06/19/193440570/ama-says-its-time-to-call-obesity-a-disease

Herek, G. (2008). Beyond homophobia: The psychological harm of anti-gay ballot campaigns. Accessed 10 July 2013. Retrieved from http://www.beyondhomophobia.com/blog/2008/11/25/anti-gay-ballot-campaigns-cause-psychological-harm/

Identity. (2013). From *Dictionary.com*. Accessed 10 July 2013. Retrieved from http://dictionary.reference.com/browse/identity

Inman, A. G., Howard, E. E., Beaumont, R. L., & Walker, J. A. (2007). Cultural transmissions: Influence of contextual factors in Asian Indian immigrant parents' experiences. *Journal of Counseling Psychology*, *54*, 93–100. doi:10.1037/0022-0167.54.1.93.

Inman, A. G., & Tummala-Nara, P. T. (2010). Clinical competencies in working with immigrant communities. In J. A. Erickson Cornish, B. A. Schreier, L. I. Nadkarni, L. Henderson Metzger, & E. R. Rodolfa (Eds). *Handbook of multicultural counseling competencies*. Hoboken, NJ: Wiley.

Juby, H. L., & Concepcion, W. R. (2005). Ethnicity: The term and its meaning. In Carter, R. T. (Ed.), *Handbook of racial-cultural psychology and counseling*, Vol. 1 (pp. 26–40). Hoboken, NJ: Wiley.

Kaslow, N. J., Grus, C. L., Campbell, L. F., Fouad, N. A., Hatcher, R. L., & Rodolfa, E. R. (2009). Competency assessment toolkit for professional psychology. *Training and Education in Professional Psychology*, *3* (4 Suppl), S27–S45. doi:10.1037/a0015833.

Kenkel, M. B., & Peterson, R. L. (Eds). (2010). *Competency-based education for professional psychology*. Washington, DC: American Psychological Association.

Kessler, R. C., Chiu, W. T., Demler, O., & Walters, E. E. (2005). Prevalence, severity and comorbidity of 12-month *DSM-IV* disorders in the national comorbidity survey replication. *Archives of General Psychiatry*, *62*(6), 617–627. doi:10.1001/archpsyc.62.6.617

Kirk, J., & Belovics, R. (2008). Understanding and counseling transgender clients. *Journal of Employment Counseling*, *45*, 29–43. doi:10.1002/j.2161-1920.2008.tb00042.x.

Leigh, I. W., & Pollard, R. Q. (2003). Mental health and deaf adults. In M. Marschark & P. E. Spencer (Eds.), *Oxford handbook of deaf studies, language and education* (pp. 203–215). New York, NY: Oxford University Press.

Liu, W.M., Corkery, J., & Thome, J. (2010). Developing competency with social class and classism in counseling and psychotherapy. In J. A. Erickson Cornish, B. A. Schreier, L. I. Nadkarni, L. Henderson Metzger, E. R. & Rodolfa. (Eds.), *Handbook of multicultural counseling competencies* (pp. 351–378). Hoboken, NJ: Wiley.

Lorde, A. (2007). Age, race, class, and sex: Women redefining difference. In N.K. Boreano (Ed.), *Sister Outsider: Essays and speeches by Audre Lorde* (pp. 114–123). Berkley, CA: Crossing Press.

Magnusson, E. (2011). Women, men, and all other categories: Psychologies for theorizing human diversity. *Nordic Psychology*, *63*(2), 88–114. doi:10.1027/1901-2276/a000034.

McIntosh, P. (2007). White privilege: Unpacking the invisible knapsack. In Paula S. Rothenberg (Ed.), *Race, Class, and Gender in the United States: An Integrated Study* (7th ed., pp. 177–182). New York, NY: Worth.

Monk-Turner, E., & Light, D. (2010). Male sexual assault and rape: Who seeks counseling? *Sex Abuse*, *22*, 255–265. doi:10.1177/1079063210366271.

Murphy, R. (1986). *Culture and social anthropology: An overture* (2nd ed). Englewood Cliffs, NJ: Prentice Hall.

National Center for Health Statistics. (2007). *Summary health statistics for the U.S. population: National health interview survey, 2005* (DHHS Publication No. PHS 2007–1561). Washington, DC: U.S. Government Printing Office.

National Healthcare Disparities Report (2004). Accessed 10 July 2013. Retrieved from http://archive.ahrq.gov/qual/nhdr04/nhdr04.htm

National Public Radio. (January 18, 2002). 81 words. [Radio Broadcast]. Accessed 10 July 2013. Retrieved from http://www.thisamericanlife.org/radio-archives/episode/204 /81-words

Naumburg, C. G. (2007). Judaism: A hidden diversity. *Smith College Studies in Social Work, 77*, 77–99. doi:10.1300/J497v77n02_06.

Nelson, P. D. (2007). The globalization of psychology: What does it mean? In M. Boenau & J. Tyson (Eds.), *The Educator: Newsletter of the Education Directorate, 5,* 1; pp. 3–5.Washington, D.C.: American Psychological Association.

Oppression. (2013). From *Dictionary.com.* Accessed 10 July 2013. http://dictionary.reference.com/browse/oppression

Pew Research Center. (2013). A survey of LGBT Americans. Accessed 15 July 2013. Retrieved from http://www.pewsocial-trends.org/files/2013/06/SDT_LGBT-Americans_06-2013.pdf

Phillips, M. (2011). The mind at midlife. *APA Monitor, 4,* 39–41.

Pope, J. F., & Arthur, N. (2009). Socioeconomic status and class: A challenge for the practice of psychology in Canada. *Canadian Psychology, 50,* 55–65.

Pumariega, A. J., Rothe, E. R., & Pumariega, J. B. (2005). Mental health of immigrants and refugees. *Community Mental Health Journal, 41,* 581–597. doi: 10.1007/s10597-005-6363-1.

Redding, R. E. (2001). Sociopolitical diversity in psychology: The case for pluralism. *American Psychologist, 56*(3), 205–215.

Roberts, M. C., Borden, K. A., Christiansen, M. D., & Lopez, S. J. (2005). Fostering a culture shift: Assessment of competence in the education and careers of professional psychologists. *Professional Psychology: Research and Practice, 36,* 347–354.

Rodolfa, E. R., Bent, R. J., Eisman, E., Nelson, P. D., Rehm, L., & Ritchie, P. (2005). A cube model for competency development: Implication for psychology educators and regulators. *Professional Psychology: Research and Practice, 36,* 347–354. doi:10.1037/0735-7028.36. 4.347.

Root, M. P. P. (1996). *The multiracial experience: Racial borders as the new frontier.* Thousand Oaks, CA: Sage.

Root, M. P. P. (2000). A Bill of Rights for racially mixed people. In M. Adams, W. Blemenfeld, C. R. Castañeda & H. W. Hackman (Eds.), *Readings for Diversity and Social Justice* (pp. 120–126). New York, NY: Routledge.

Sanchez, D., & Davis III, C. (2010). Becoming a racially competent therapist. In J. A. Erickson Cornish, B. A. Schreier, L. I. Nadkarni, L. Henderson Metzger, & E. R. Rodolfa (Eds.). *The handbook of multicultural counseling competencies* (pp. 271–272). Hoboken, NJ: Wiley.

Savage, J., & Armstrong, S. (2010). Developing competency in spiritual and religious aspects of counseling. In J. A. Erickson Cornish, B. A. Schreier, L. I. Nadkarni, L. Henderson Metzger, & E. R. Rodolfa, (Eds). *Handbook of multicultural counseling competencies* (pp. 379–414). Hoboken, NJ: Wiley.

Seaton, E. K., Caldwell, C. H., Sellers, R. M., Jackson, J. S. (2010). An intersectional approach for understanding perceived discrimination and psychological well-being among African American and Caribbean Black youth. *Developmental Psychology, 46,* 1372–1379. doi:10.1037/a0019869.

Singh, A. A., Boyd, C. J., & Whitman, J. S. (2010). Counseling competency with transgender and intersex persons. In J. A. Erickson Cornish, B. A. Schreier, L. I. Nadkarni, L. Henderson Metzger, & E. R. Rodolfa (Eds). *Handbook of multicultural counseling competencies* (pp. 415–442). Hoboken, NJ: Wiley.

Skodol, A. E. & Bender, D. S. (2003). Why are women diagnosed borderline more than men? *Psychiatric Quarterly, 74*(4), 349–360. doi: 10.1023/A:1026087410516. PMID 14686459.

Smart, R. (2010). Counseling competencies with women: Understanding gender in the context of multiple dimensions of identity. In J. A. Erickson Cornish, B. A. Schreier, L. I. Nadkarni, L. Henderson Metzger, & E. R. Rodolfa (Eds). *Handbook of multicultural counseling competencies* (pp. 475– 512). Hoboken, NJ: Wiley.

Smith, H. (2007). Psychological services needs of older women. *Psychological Services, 4,* 277–286. doi:10.1037/1541-1559.4.4.277.

Smith, L., Constantine, M., Graham, S. & Dize, C. (2008). The territory ahead for multicultural Competence: The "spinning" of racism. *Professional Psychology: Research and Practice, 39,* 337–345. doi:10.1037/0735-7028.39.3.337.

Stevens, M. A. & Englar-Carlson, M. (2010). Psychotherapy with men: Building practice competencies. In J. A. Erickson Cornish, B. A. Schreier, L. I. Nadkarni, L. Henderson Metzger, & E. R. Rodolfa (Eds) *Handbook of Multicultural Counseling Competencies* (pp. 195–230). Hoboken, New Jersey: John Wiley & Sons

Stewart, A. J., & McDermott, C. (2004). Gender in psychology. *Annual Review of Psychology, 55,* 519–544. doi:10.1146/annurev.psych.55.090902.141537.

Stokoe, W. C., Casterline, D. C., & Croneberg, C. G. (1976). *A dictionary of American Sign Language on linguistic principles* (rev. ed.). Silver Spring, MD: Linstok Press.

Sue, D., & Sue, D. M. (2007). *Foundation of counseling and psychotherapy: Evidence-based practices for a diverse society.* Hoboken, NJ: Wiley.

Sue, D. W. (2010). *Microaggressions in everyday life: Race, gender and sexual orientation.* Hoboken, NJ: Wiley.

Sue, D. W., Capodilupo, C., Torino, G., Bucceri, J., Holder, A., Nadal, K., & Esquilin, M. (2007). Racial microaggressions in everyday life: Implications for clinical practice. *American Psychologist, 62,* 271–286. doi:10.1037/0003-066X.62.4.271.

Sue, D. W., & Sue, D. (1990). *Counseling the culturally different.* Theory and practice. New York: Wiley.

Schwartz, J. (2013, June 26). *United States v. Windsor:* Between the lines of the Defense of Marriage Act opinion. *The New York Times.* Accessed 15 July 2013. Retrieved from http://www.nytimes.com/interactive/2013/06/26/us/annotated- supreme-court-decision-on-doma.html

Tinsley-Jones, H. A. (2001). Racism in our midst: Listening to psychologists of color. *Professional Psychology: Research and Practice 32*(6), 573–580. doi: 10.1037//0735-7028.32.6.573.

Toporek, R. L., Ortega-Villalobos, L., & Pope-Davis, D. B. (2004). Critical incidents in multicultural supervision: Exploring supervisees' and supervisors' experiences. *Journal of Multicultural Counseling and Development, 32*(2), 66–83. doi:10.1002/j.2161-1912.2004.tb00362.x.

Touré. (2011). *Who's afraid of post-Blackness?* New York, NY: Free Press.

United Nations Enable. (December 13, 2006). Convention on the rights of persons with disabilities. Accessed 10 July 2013. Retrieved from http://www.un.org/disabilities/default.asp?id=223.

United States Census Bureau. (n.d.). Urban, Urbanized Area, Urban Cluster, and Rural Population, 2010 and 2000: United States. *2010 Census Urban and Rural Classification and Urban Area Criteria.* Accessed 10 July 2013. Retrieved from http://www.census.gov/geo/reference/ua/urban-rural- 2010.html

United States Census Bureau. (2003). Disability status: 2000. Accessed 10 July 2013. Retrieved from http://www.census.gov/prod/2003pubs/c2kbr-17.pdf.

United States Census Bureau, People and Households. (2010). *People and Households–Data by Subject.* Accessed 10 July 2013. Retrieved from http://www.census.gov/people/

United States Department of Homeland Security. (2008). Yearbook of immigration statistics. Washington, D.C. U.S. Department of Homeland Security, Office of Immigration Statistics.

Winterowd, C. L., Adams, E. M., Miville, M. M., & Mintz, L. B. (2009). Operationalizing instilling, and assessing counseling psychology training values related to diversity in academic training. *The Counseling Psychologist, 37*(5), 676–704. doi:10.1177/0011000009331936.

Worthington, R. L. (2004). Sexual identity, sexual orientation, religious identity, and change: Is it possible to depolarize the debate? *The Counseling Psychologist, 32*(5), 741–749. doi: 10.1177/0011000004267566.

Yalom, I. D. (2000). Fat Lady. In *Love's Executioner* (rev. ed.) (pp. 93–125). New York, NY: Perennial.

Sex and Gender in Professional Psychology Education and Training

Nicholas Ladany *and* Myrna L. Friedlander

Abstract

The purpose of this chapter is to provide a framework for understanding how psychology educators and trainers can enhance gender competencies. The constructs of sex and gender are discussed, with a recognition that the literature has used these constructs in a confounding manner. Consistent with the multicultural literature, gender competence is defined based on its three components: gender knowledge, gender self-awareness, and gender skills. The theoretical and empirical literature is reviewed and gender competence is discussed in relation to education, or the direct, educative aspect of training, and psychotherapy supervision, the apprenticeship aspect of training. Case examples are provided as illustrations of the concepts considered.

Key Words: psychotherapy training, psychotherapy education, gender, sex

The importance of multicultural education and training is evidenced by the increased attention that multicultural variables have received in the literature (Inman & Ladany, 2014). In particular, gender, which has most typically been defined as, or linked to, biological sex, is recognized as a critical multicultural variable for psychologists and other mental health professionals in training. The overall purpose of this chapter is to provide a framework for understanding what we have learned about enhancing gender competencies of psychologists in professional education and training.

Broadly speaking, the purpose of education and training in applied psychology is to facilitate the development of professional competencies. Whereas education generally occurs in the classroom via didactic and experiential work, clinical training typically falls within the purview of supervision and supervised practice. Both activities are key to the development of competent delivery of psychological services to male and female clients and to clients whose gender identity differs from their biological sex.

Definitional clarity is critical to the understanding of gender in relation to professional education and training. Historically, the terms *sex* and *gender* have been used interchangeably in the literature and have, at times, been defined in contradictory ways, or not at all (e.g., Garfield & Bergin, 1986; Brown & Lent, 1984). Fassinger (2000) provided a compelling set of definitions for these terms, and also clarified the distinction between them. She defined sex as "a biological entity based on physiological, hormonal, reproductive, and genetic factors," whereas gender is "a socially constructed set of ideas, beliefs, and values based on historical, economic, sociopolitical, and cultural factors" (p. 347). If biological sex and gender were easily dichotomized (i.e., women and men; female and male), then using the terms interchangeably would be less problematic. However, neither sex nor gender is easily dichotomized, and, in fact, both are more accurately defined along continua. Moreover, sex and gender are influenced by a host of interactive biological and cultural factors that presently are poorly understood (Fassinger, 2000). As such, this chapter treads lightly in use of the terms *sex* and *gender*. To that end, in our discussion of the literature, we attempt to indicate whether we are referring to the traditional, discrete use of the term *sex* or to the broader construct of *gender*. In fact, in most of the literature, even when authors use the term *gender*, they actually are referring to biological sex. For these reasons, we primarily focus on the conventional dichotomization of sex and gender and attend primarily to theory and research related to heterosexual female and male factors, broadly including sex and gender. The reader is invited to refer to chapter 20 (Fassinger & Miles, this volume) for a discussion of sexual and gender orientation supervision.

Multicultural therapist[1] competence consists of three subconstructs: knowledge, self-awareness, and skills (Ladany & Inman, 2012; Rodolfa et al., 2005). A subtype or subvariable within multicultural competence is gender competence (Ancis & Ladany, 2010; Ancis, Szymanski, & Ladany, 2008), which has three subconstructs—gender knowledge, gender self-awareness, and gender skills—all of which may be related and interact with other multicultural factors.

Gender knowledge can be further broken down into general and specific knowledge. General knowledge refers to understanding biological, psychological, and social issues in relation to gender, whereas specific knowledge refers to understanding how gender can influence process and outcome in psychotherapy and how gender role socialization is internalized by *an individual client or by oneself, as the therapist (or supervisor). Gender self-awareness* is defined as a trainee's ability to reflect on and understand her or his own gender identity and how this identity can interact with a client's gender identity so as to lead to bias or misunderstanding. *Gender skills* refers to adeptness in performing therapy skills that are sensitive to gender dynamics; these include the ability to discuss gender similarities and differences in therapy and to develop a gender-sensitive working alliance, as well as self-efficacy in performing these skills. Gender competencies are relevant to both the psychotherapy context as well as the supervisory context.

In this chapter, we begin with a framework of how therapists-in-training develop gender competence. In doing so, we synthesize the theoretical and empirical literature and offer next steps in terms of empirical work that is needed. The chapter is divided into two sections, each of which attends differentially to the development of gender competence: (1) education, or the direct, educative aspect of training; and (2) psychotherapy supervision, the apprenticeship aspect of training. Throughout the chapter we offer case examples to illustrate the concepts discussed.

Didactic Education
Knowledge

Scholarship on the process of the teaching and learning of psychotherapy practice is highly limited; however, the content of what should be taught and learned recently has garnered attention. Based on several sources, including the American Psychological Association's *Guidelines and Principles for the Accreditation of Programs in Professional Psychology* (Committee on Accreditation, 2007), the Competencies Conference in professional psychology (Kaslow et al., 2004) and Rodolfa et al.'s (2005) model of competency development that emerged from this conference, Ladany and Inman's (2012) scientifically based knowledge domains, and the available literature on gender-related competence, we delineated seven knowledge domains for the knowledge aspect of gender competence. These include (1) the history of professional psychology; (2) research methods; (3) assessment, diagnosis, and case conceptualization; (4) psychotherapy approaches; (5) ethics; (6) multicultural diversity; and (7) psychotherapy supervision. Traditionally, aside from psychotherapy supervision, in graduate training these domains are addressed through coursework; however, students also acquire knowledge via other avenues, including personal experiences.

The history of professional psychology is an important academic area that influences how students understand gender. Indeed, with few exceptions, all the "founding fathers" of the profession (Freud, Jung, Rogers, Skinner, etc.) were men. Hence, their perspectives as men in the early 20th century arguably influenced the development of their theoretical approaches. However, women scholars also played a significant role in the development of the field (Milar, 2000; Russo & O'Connell, 1992), so that exclusion of women theorists in any history of professional psychology coursework is negligent, as well as academically imprudent.

Research methodology covers a variety of content areas, including quantitative and qualitative research approaches, as well as statistics. Integration of sex or gender as a variable in research investigations should be recognized. Moreover, there should be an understanding of how gender plays a role in the definitions of the primary constructs of scientific investigations, as well as the extent to which measurement scales are normed and validated across gender groups.

One of the most substantial areas of scholarship in relation to gender is related to assessment, diagnosis, and case conceptualization. As far back as Broverman, Broverman, Clarkson, Rosenkrantz, and Vogel's (1970) seminal work on perceptions of psychological health linked to the male norm, scholars have recognized that gender bias is a critical limiting factor in determining the adequacy of assessment, diagnosis, and case conceptualization. Recently, in a study of 29 therapists in training using a Q-sort methodology, Trepal, Wester, and Shuler (2008) found that participants adhered to traditional views of gender, which raised the concern that therapists may have a propensity to bring gender biases into the therapy room. This study highlights the concern that gender bias may be alive and well in the present day thinking of psychotherapists. To be sure, more investigations are warranted.

With regard to assessment, diagnosis, and case conceptualization, the *Diagnostic and Statistical Manual* (American Psychiatric Association [DSM-IV-TR], 2000) repeatedly has been criticized for gender bias in diagnostic categories (e.g., Ali, Caplan, & Fagnant, 2010; Landrine, 1989). For example, men are less likely to be diagnosed as having histrionic or borderline personality disorders than women who display the same symptomatology (Becker & Lamb, 1994; Ford & Widiger, 1989; Hamilton, Rothbart, & Dawes, 1986). More recently, concerns have been raised about the upcoming revision of the *DSM* in relation to gender issues associated with specific disorders, such as *paraphilic coercive disorder* and *premenstrual dysphoric disorder*, both of which are listed as mental disorders with limited scholarly backing or understanding of the sociopolitical ramifications of creating such disorders (Counselors for Social Justice, 2011). Finally, the prevalence and challenges of assessing, diagnosing, and conceptualizing alexithymia, or the challenge that many men have in expressing emotion as a consequence of their socialization, offers implications of understanding gender in relation to men (Levant et al., 2003). All these content areas are important to understand in relation to the teaching and learning of assessment, diagnosis, and case conceptualization.

It is fair to say that theoretical approaches to psychotherapy have received the most theoretical attention when it comes to differing perspectives on gender. In general, authors either have integrated gender as a primary component in their understanding of the human condition, such as feminist theoretical approaches (Brown, 2010; Enns, 1993, 2004; Silverstein & Goodrich, 2003), or offer a critique of what is lacking in relation to gender in the context of the major theoretical approaches (Gilligan, 1977). Feminist therapeutic approaches, which stem back to the 1960s, provided a significant paradigm shift to the dominant psychotherapy movements prior to that time. Feminist authors offered unique and valuable therapeutic concepts and techniques (e.g., the personal is political, the importance of collaboration and self-disclosure) that readily can be applied to the practice of psychotherapy from other theoretical perspectives. Moreover, feminist thought played a significant role in examining the inadequacy of traditional models of psychotherapy (e.g., Proctor, 2008; Stoppard, 1989; Wolter-Gustafson, 2008; Young-Bruehl, 1996). Although, the inclusion of the aforementioned content areas into didactic and experiential coursework would likely best meet graduate students' needs in relation to developing their knowledge base of gender in psychotherapy, this doesn't seem to be the case. Rather, a cursory review of some of the most popular texts on theories of psychotherapy reveals that feminist therapy often is relegated to the end of the book and a gender critique is neither provided nor integrated throughout the text.

Professional ethics is another content area that warrants attention in relation to gender. The bulk of scholarship in this area pertains to ethics in relation to psychotherapy with girls and women. Due to a variety of factors, including the awareness of professional gender bias, an American Psychological Association task force published guidelines aimed at addressing ethical considerations in the treatment of girls and women (APA, 2007). To date, no such guidelines have been written for men and boys; however, there has been the development of a literature base focused on men and masculinity (i.e., APA's journal *Psychology of Men & Masculinity*) and some emerging scholarship on ethical issues in relation to working with male clients (e.g., Vasquez, 2012) The guidelines for girls and women offer a rich source of content from which ethics education in relation to gender could be discussed. Eleven guidelines were provided that provide a rich source of content in relation to the professional ethics and include (APA, 2007, p. 960):

1. Psychologists strive to be aware of the effects of socialization, stereotyping, and unique life

events on the development of girls and women across diverse cultural groups.

2. Psychologists are encouraged to recognize and utilize information about oppression, privilege, and identity development as they may affect girls and women.

3. Psychologists strive to understand the impact of bias and discrimination on the physical and mental health of those with whom they work.

4. Psychologists strive to use gender sensitive and culturally sensitive, affirming practices in providing services to girls and women.

5. Psychologists are encouraged to recognize how their socialization, attitudes, and knowledge about gender may affect their practice with girls and women.

6. Psychologists are encouraged to use interventions and approaches that have been found to be effective in the treatment of issues of concern to girls and women.

7. Psychologists strive to foster therapeutic relationships and practices that promote initiative, empowerment, and expanded alternatives and choices for girls and women.

8. Psychologists strive to provide appropriate, unbiased assessments and diagnoses in their work with girls and women.

9. Psychologists strive to consider the problems of girls and women in their sociopolitical context.

10. Psychologists strive to acquaint themselves with and utilize relevant mental health, education, and community resources for girls and women.

11. Psychologists are encouraged to understand and work to change institutional and systemic bias that may impact girls and women.

Multicultural diversity includes gender issues that cut across many content areas, as well as how gender intersects with other multicultural factors (e.g., race, sexual orientation, etc.). An example of the former is the concept of *microaggressions* against women. Gender microaggressions are generally defined as brief, common, and hostile verbal and nonverbal behaviors directed at women (Capodilupo et al., 2010). Owen, Tao, and Rodolfa (2010) recently applied this concept to the therapeutic setting and developed a scale, the Microaggressions Against Women Scale (MAWS), which consists of items that ask female clients about microaggressions experienced in treatment. Results from Owen et al.'s study indicated that increased experiences of microaggressions predicted decreases in the working alliance and therapy outcome.

Other examples of multicultural diversity content in relation to gender include sexual objectification theory, in which psychological health is hypothesized to be compromised via the sociocultural and interpersonal objectification of women (Szymanski, Moffitt, & Carr, 2011); violence against women in terms of sexual assault and war (APA, 2007); women and the media, including the images used to portray women in advertising (Kilbourne, 1999); and contraceptive and reproductive rights for women (Centers for Reproductive Rights, n.d.). In addition there has been the emergence of scholarship on men and masculinity, such as the implications of gender role strain and the related concerns of alexithymia in relation to men's development (Levant, 2011).

Finally, along with content specifically focused on gender, there is scholarship related to the intersection of gender and cultural factors like race and ethnicity (Nadal, 2010), sexual orientation (Fassinger & Arseneau, 2007), social class (Lui, Stinson, Hernandez, Shepard, & Haag, 2009); and disability status (APA, 2007). To be sure, the complexities of addressing content in this area grow exponentially with the number of multicultural variables at play.

The final content area is psychotherapy supervision. Although the efficacy of teaching and learning didactic *content* areas has limited empirical support, this is not the case for psychotherapy supervision. Rather, supervision has been an active area of empirical scholarship, perhaps in large part because it is the primary means of directly imparting clinical knowledge to trainees. If the goal of training in psychotherapy is to integrate gender-related topics throughout the academic curriculum, then it presumably behooves educators to determine the extent to which gender has indeed been integrated.

To that end, there has been a series of investigations that provide some understanding related to this question. In a sample of clinical psychology students, for example, Johnson, Russell, Searight, Handal, and Gibbons (1993) found that gender issues were as neglected in supervised practice as in academic class work. However, students who received more gender-related instruction evidenced more positive attitudes about women in therapy. To be sure, a significant limitation of this study is that the data were obtained between 1987 and 1988, so that it is not known whether these results would be similar presently. In a more recent study, Kannan and Levitt (2009) interviewed clinical and counseling psychology graduate students who self-identified as feminist. Results indicated that participants integrated their feminist approaches in part or in whole with their therapeutic work. In addition, the experience of discrimination fueled participants' advocacy in this area, specifically by reaching out to mentors for assistance.

Four investigations related to curricular assessment and gender were conducted in relation to couple- and family-therapy training. Using syllabi as a source for content analysis, as well as interviews with faculty members, Winston and Piercy (2010) attempted to determine if curricula that infused gender were seen as different from curricula that had gender-specific courses. In general, the authors found no differences, in that both types of curricula attended to gender with a strong level of commitment. Using a similar approach, Leslie and Clossick (1996) found that gender training did not influence clinical decision making; however, gender training from a feminist perspective resulted in lower levels of sexism among participants who responded to clinical vignettes. An additional investigation compared gender coursework only with gender integration throughout the curriculum (Filkowski, Storm, York, & Brandon, 2001). The authors found that both approaches worked well to facilitate students' learning about gender and therapy. In a fairly comprehensive investigation, Coleman, Avis, and Turin (1990) ascertained the types of gender content that were integrated in couple- and family-therapy programs, as well as the obstacles to gender integration (e.g., trainee resistance and faculty awareness). Given the time period in which this study was undertaken, it is unknown whether similar results would be found today. In sum, the investigations about the inclusion of gender in graduate curricula suggest that students learn more when they are exposed to more gender-related content. Clearly, though, exploration of diverse professional training samples in contemporary programs is warranted.

Self-Awareness

Self-awareness as a component of gender competence consists of three aspects: (1) self-reflective practice, (2) gender identity, and (3) gender-based countertransference. Self-reflective practice is a critical component of developing and maintaining competence for students and professionals alike (Boswell & Castonguay, 2007; Committee on Accreditation, 2002). Self-reflective practice involves systematic self-assessments as a means to gaining more complex understandings of therapeutic models and techniques. It is seen as a process that can be conducted as part of didactic coursework, as well as practice-based training. In relation to gender, learning to self-reflect on one's own gender roles in family and work systems is one example of how students can gain a complex understanding of the influences of gender on everyday life. Journaling and mapping genograms with attention to gender are other examples of practice in self-reflection. Another means of facilitating self-reflective practice is through the use of experiential exercises. Werner-Wilson (2001), for example, illustrated the concepts of gender and power through experiential role-plays that introduced graduate students to feminist themes, which included some aspect of gender, power, and family diversity.

A second major factor in relation to developing self-awareness is the development of one's personal gender identity. With the past few decades has come the recognition that biological sex, considered in isolation, is not predictive of outcome in therapy. Specifically, reviews of multiple investigations found that matching the sex of client and therapist, or supervisee and supervisor, resulted in equivocal findings (Beutler, Crago, & Arizmendi, 1986; Haverkamp, 2012; Jordan, 2006). As a result, scholars began to look for more explanatory models, such as gender identity (e.g., Downing & Roush, 1985; McNamara & Rickard, 1989; Ossana, Helms, & Leonard, 1992).

A common feature of all these models is the notion that people move through stages or phases of identity development. Based on the commonalities of these models, and in order to provide a heuristic device for therapists and supervisors to assess identity development across multicultural variables, Ancis and Ladany (2001, 2010) developed the Heuristic Model of Nonoppressive Interpersonal Development (HMNID). The model begins with the premise that in the United States (and elsewhere) men belong to a socially privileged group, whereas women belong to a socially oppressed group. A second premise is that both men and women progress through stages of *means of interpersonal functioning*, which are thoughts, feelings, and behaviors that are a function of phase of gender identity. Whereas the labels of the phases are identical for men and women (i.e., adaptation, incongruence, exploration, integration), the means of interpersonal functioning differ for men and women. Examples of means of interpersonal functioning for men at each stage include adaptation (e.g., the belief that men and women have equal opportunities for employment advancement), incongruence (e.g., the use of rationalization as a defense for salary discrepancies between men and women), exploration (e.g., feelings of guilt when one's privilege is acknowledged), and integration (e.g., advocacy for gender equality). By contrast, examples of means of interpersonal functioning for women include adaptation (e.g., denial is a defense against disparities between men and women), incongruence (e.g., dissonance when learning that women psychologists' income is 80 cents to the male psychologist dollar), exploration (e.g., recognizing feelings of anger when oppression is recognized), and integration (e.g., advocacy for gender equality). In sum, in relation to gender identity, the HMNID can be used as a means of self-reflection, as a method for therapists to assess clients, and as a way for supervisors to assess clients and trainees.

The third type of self-awareness is gender-based countertransference, which is a form of multicultural countertransference (Inman & Ladany, 2014) and is arguably the opposite of a type of multicultural empathy (Comas-Dí, 2006). Refining the definition of multicultural countertransference, Inman and Ladany defined gender-based countertransference as unrealistic or biased thoughts, feelings, and behaviors, conscious or unconscious, that are based on gender dynamics that occur at the individual or environmental level (e.g., client, therapist, supervisor, training setting, family, community, nation). Walker (2010) offered a five-step model for managing countertransference that can be applied to gender-based countertransference: (1) become familiar with personal issues and triggers (e.g., gender roles in family of origin); (2) identify emotional, cognitive, or behavioral reactions to clients (e.g., frustration with a male client with traditional values); (3) consider the interference that a particular issues has on current or potential therapy work (e.g., distancing tendency when gender topics arise); (4) work through personal issues in therapy; and (5) develop management strategies in supervision.

Countertransference does not have to originate in the context of therapy, but also can occur in academic settings, such as during the teaching of helping skills in pre-practicum. Consider the following case example:

Case 1: Pre-practicum Group

In her small pre-practicum group, Liz Pena had become increasingly quiet. This group was composed of four beginners like her, who were practicing interviewing and basic relational skills using extended role plays. The instructor was an advanced PhD student, John Chen, who had a fair amount of clinical experience and was learning to supervise. The three other members of the group were two men and one woman, all novice first year graduate students like Liz.

Liz had been doing fairly well in this pre-practicum, although she was highly self-critical and ruminated for hours after each role-play about what she should have done differently and better as the counselor. Liz had entered the field of mental health counseling because she was the "go-to person" among her friends, and she'd been told many times by peers and family members that she was a "sympathetic listener." For this reason, even having had no actual clinical experience, Liz was confident about her ability to empathize with clients, to create a strong emotional bond, and to understand what a client was feeling at a deep level.

Now, at the midpoint of the semester, Liz was in a quiet crisis. The week prior she had role-played an adolescent who was the victim of date rape. The counselor was played by Allan Aldrich, one of Liz's male classmates. As the client, Liz found Allan to be "cold" in his approach to her. As the role-play continued, she also began to feel as if the client she was depicting was actually herself. This was "crazy," she thought, because in her life she'd never been molested, not even hit or slapped by anyone.

During the role-play, Liz began to cry, feeling both misunderstood and patronized by Allan. But what was even more devastating was the commentary afterward by her instructor and her peers. First, her peers gave Allan lots of positive feedback on his performance as the counselor. Then the group members began discussing "the client" as an object, not as a person. Even the instructor, John, commented how Liz was a "great borderline," a comment that led to laughter by others in the group. They did not recognize Allan's patronizing attitude, and they called Liz's tears "manipulative." At first, listening to the others, Liz was silently angry. She was astonished when the one woman in the group also praised Allan's performance.

Then, to her later shame, Liz found herself actually joining in on the attack, saying that she had "played it up for sympathy."

Highly uncomfortable with what had occurred in the pre-practicum, and feeling silenced by what had taken place during and after this role-play, Liz blamed herself and began to pull back from her peers. She began to view her tears during the role-play as a sign that she would be unable to handle deep emotional problems as a counselor. As the week progressed, Liz had serious thoughts of quitting the master's program and finding another profession where she would feel less vulnerable.

This case example illustrates aspects of all three components of self-awareness. First, self-reflective practice in place, but it went awry. That is, Liz was reflecting on the most negative aspects of the experience, but her internal process went from self-reflection to negative rumination. Second, Liz may have been in the exploration stage of gender identity, as evidenced by her sense of empowerment as a woman and the recognition that she was "silenced." Third, it is likely that some sort of gender-based countertransference reaction had occurred for Liz. That is, her strong emotions likely had a sensitive reference point, something that was worthy of self-exploration. Without support and guidance, however, Liz might well follow her inclination to leave her graduate program, never having understood the source of her discomfort.

Countertransference can be seen as a therapist issue, as indicated in this example, or as an issue for the supervisor, that is, as supervisor countertransference (Ladany, Constantine, Miller, Erickson, & Muse-Burke, 2000). Sometimes the supervisor must first look internally before engaging effectively with a supervisee. The following case illustrates this idea.

Case 2: Supervisor, Heal Thyself

Joel's supervisor, Alicia Stevens, found herself feeling exceptionally tired before each of her sessions with Joel. Reflecting on her own emotional state, she first attributed her lack of engagement to burnout. When a colleague pointed out that Alicia seemed to have a great deal of energy for her other clinical responsibilities, she realized that each week she dreaded her supervision session with Joel. Examining her own extreme disinclination aroused her curiosity about the interactions she had had with Joel over the first few weeks of his practicum under her supervision.

By taking a participant-observer position in their next session, Alicia realized—with some measure of surprise—that she was feeling somewhat intimidated by Joel. Talking it over with the same colleague, she found herself describing Joel's presentation as "arrogant." Each week he came into supervision prepared to discuss his cases, but these discussions were highly intellectualized. Although he raised some fascinating—and intellectually perplexing—questions about his clients' personalities and diagnoses, Joel showed little emotional engagement with the material. Moreover, he responded to Alicia's comments in an affable fashion, even at times a charming wit that belied a measure of contempt.

To this point in supervision, Joel had presented several audiotaped excerpts from his therapy sessions that were focused uniquely on eliciting the clients' background information and symptoms. Realizing that she had been drawn into Joel's intellectualizations, Alicia asked him to give her a few tapes to listen to in entirety. After some excuses that were seemingly legitimate, Joel did hand her two audiotapes of his work.

Listening to each session, Alicia was astonished at Joel's lack of emotional connection with either client. Berating herself for having missed this important piece, she acknowledged to herself that she was intimidated by Joel's highly confident presentation and that, unaware of her response to him, had been diminishing her own authoritative power in their relationship.

In their next session, Alicia began focusing on Joel's apparent lack of emotional engagement in his relationships with clients. Joel's initial response was more arrogant than usual, as he defended his work by citing research evidence for the interventions he had made in session. When asked directly about how he felt toward one of his clients, Joel responded with a long-winded answer about what the client needed from him.

It became clear to Alicia that Joel had no idea what she was communicating. Indeed, he had no actual understanding of how to demonstrate caring or compassion. Although he said that he "worried" about his client's welfare and "felt motivated to help," Joel could not articulate a single emotional reaction to any of his clients.

The next phase of supervision was focused almost uniquely on developing Joel's capacity for emotional relatedness. There was considerable resistance at first, but Alicia persisted in a firm yet empathic manner. This difficult work was—unfortunately—helped along when all of Joel's female clients dropped out of therapy precipitously. In fact, two female clients asked the clinic director to be re-assigned to a different therapist. By the middle of the semester, Joel had far fewer clients than his peers, and this comparison actually sent him into a depressive state.

Eventually, Alicia was highly effective in her work with Joel. She remained caring, supportive, and concerned as he spiraled from confusion, to an anxious crisis, to an overwhelming sense of defeat. Her relationship with Joel deepened as she focused him on what was going on between them and how he felt when she made empathic comments. She normalized his self-doubts by helping him to see the restrictive role that gender norms had played in his life, leading him to fear being emotionally vulnerable with anyone. Alicia provided Joel with required readings on gender role socialization and on building empathic therapeutic relationships. These readings gave Joel an intellectual perspective that helped him face his sense of failure without overpersonalizing his experience.

In supervision, Joel began to talk, with a depth of feeling, about some painful adolescent memories that had led him to shut down emotionally. He reflected on his traditional family upbringing, his highly masculine father and uncles, and the failure of several romantic relationships. He disclosed that every partner had accused him of being "emotionally distant" or "unfeeling" and that he had no idea what these words meant.

Alicia was careful to always bring back Joel's personal exploration—what he was disclosing about himself in supervision—to the implications for his clinical work, specifically his emotional bond with clients. She strongly urged Joel to go into therapy himself, "to see what it feels like from the other chair." Alicia gave him the names of several local therapists with whom she thought he would work well. Importantly, she waited to make this recommendation until Joel was able to articulate some distress about what was happening to him both professionally and personally. When she did so, Joel was eager to continue the personal journey he'd begun in supervision with his own therapist.

The crisis passed when Joel began using some of his supervisor's specific recommendations about how to make emotionally involving interventions with clients. Actually, he had great success in doing so. The supervision relationship matured in parallel fashion. What could have been the end of a promising career for a traditionally highly masculine supervisee was transformed through the supervisor's self-reflections, patience and compassion. As this case illustrates, the supervisor had to first work on her own countertransference before she was effectively able to engage with the supervisee.

Skills

When it comes to skills, it is essential to recognize that they exist on a continuum from lesser to greater adeptness, rather than as a simple dichotomy (Ladany & Inman, 2012). Using Inman and Ladany's (2014) model of multicultural skills, which is based on general therapist skills (Hill & Williams, 2000; Ladany & Inman, 2012), we focus on gender-specific skills. In particular, therapy skills can be categorized in four ways: (1) nonverbal skills, (2) helping skills, (3) skills in working with covert processes, and (4) skills related to therapeutic strategies and techniques.

To be gender skilled at the nonverbal level, therapists should be able to assess the meaning of a client's nonverbal cues. For example, and in the case of the intersection of multicultural skills of gender and race, therapists may consider avoidance of eye contact as a culturally consistent behavior with some minority group clients, rather than deem this avoidance as evidence of psychopathology (e.g., anxiety or paranoia). At the helping skills level, adeptness with gender empathy, a form of cultural empathy (Comas-Díaz, 2006), is critical in developing an alliance with a client. For example, it is helpful for a therapist to demonstrate empathy around issues of the suppression of affect for male clients who have been socialized to avoid feelings. In terms of covert processes, therapists should be able to assess their own and their clients' gender identities and consider how these identities may surface in a therapeutic setting. Finally, feminist therapeutic strategies and techniques like self-disclosure, bibliotherapy, and assertiveness training are important to possess when working with some women clients.

Although the literature offers a variety of theoretical avenues for understanding gender in psychotherapy, there have been limited attempts to develop measures to assess the multiple factors that make up gender competence. Rather, the available instruments assess specific or related factors, such as attitudes (Fassinger, 1994), identity development (Downing & Roush, 1985), and feminist identification (Chaney & Piercy, 1988). That said, one scale that seems to show promise is the Counseling Women Competencies Scale (Ancis, Szymanski, & Ladany, 2008), which assesses knowledge, self-awareness, and skills in relation to working therapeutically with women. The importance of gender knowledge, self-awareness, and skills is illustrated in the following case example.

Case 3: The Multiple Factors of Gender Competence

George Santoro, an intern at an urban community mental health center, was fairly confident about his clinical skills. After all, he had received superb evaluations from his three previous supervisors and was looking forward to graduating within the year. Being self-confident, he was surprised and dismayed when a client with whom he had been working for a few sessions, Amelia Janes, dropped out of treatment without having disclosed any negative sentiments about the way the therapy had been unfolding and without returning George's phone calls. Amelia was a 20-year-old transgendered woman who was undergoing testosterone treatment. Her presenting concern was depression over her family's harsh rejection of her identity transition.

George's supervisor, Frank Hendrix, began their weekly supervision session by informing George that Amelia had contacted the center director to request a change of therapist. George was blindsided by this news, having believed that his work with this client was going well. For his part, Frank was confused about what had transpired between her supervisee and this client, as—until this point—she had had little concern over George's work with any clients. In Frank's experience as a supervisor, it was rare for a client to request a transfer from an advanced intern who was as skilled as George Santoro seemed to be.

In this agency, there was no videorecording equipment, and interns typically did not audio record their sessions. Supervision with advanced interns like George was more consultative and collegial than directive or prescriptive. Thus, not having observed any of George's therapy sessions, when George became defensive on learning about Amelia's call to the center director, Frank wondered whether he had seriously misjudged this intern's skills.

A supportive inquiry about George's apparently strong feelings toward Amelia startled Frank. In a not so subtle way, George blamed Amelia for the failed treatment. Further exploration indicated that George had taken it upon himself to point out to Amelia the many ways that her transgendered identity was problematic. Also, in referring to Amelia, George slipped into using male pronouns. Inquiring further, Frank discovered that George believed that Amelia's identity needed to be challenged "for his own good." As George continued to explain his viewpoint, Frank understood clearly why Amelia had requested another therapist. It also became clear that George had felt personally threatened by a biologically male client who was in the process of becoming female.

This case illustrates a number of issues that have been identified. First, George's knowledge of transgender culture limited his ability to demonstrate a variety of gender skills such as empathy and using the correct pronouns. Second, George was unable to self-reflect on his own gender identity as well as the clients. Third, it is likely that the training environment (including the supervisor) failed to adequately cover the issues at hand, which, in turn, left George unprepared. In the end, unilateral termination was the therapy outcome.

Psychotherapy Supervision

In this section we provide an overview of supervision research on gender and offer a theoretical model that specifically addresses gender as a primary component. Throughout, we illustrate the ideas presented with case material.

Review of Literature

The empirical work on supervision and gender can be categorized into two themes. First, two investigations specifically attended to aspects of feminist supervision. Second, a series of investigations has been conducted on in-session behaviors and events related to gender.

FEMINIST SUPERVISION

As with supervision models in general, feminist models of supervision derive many constructs and ideas from feminist approaches to psychotherapy (Porter & Vasquez, 1997). Szymanski (2003), for example, provided a compelling model for integrating feminist models of therapy with feminist approaches to teaching; she created a scale that assesses the extent to which feminist practices are applied in supervision. The Feminist Supervision Scale is based on the theoretical literature on feminist supervision (Porter, 1995) and expands on this literature to include current feminist perspectives on the importance of the oppression of individuals based on race/ethnicity, sexual orientation, and social class. Results of a validation study provided evidence of the scale's psychometric properties. Four factors were identified: (1) collaborative relationships, (2) power analysis (i.e., addressing roles and boundaries and avoiding abuses of power), (3) diversity and social context (i.e., integrating multiple forms of diversity into supervisory work), and (4) feminist advocacy and activism.

In a follow-up study, Szymanski (2005) found that feminist supervision practices were related to feminist identity. In particular, these practices were inversely associated with passive acceptance of traditional male and female gender roles, and positively associated with feelings of anger about sexism and guilt for condoning sexist practices in the past, connectedness with women, commitment social advocacy for women, and feminist philosophical beliefs. In all, the theoretical and empirical work offered a strong foundation for continued work in integrating gender, specifically feminist constructs, in psychotherapy supervision.

IN-SESSION BEHAVIORS AND EVENTS

The broadest set of research endeavors in relation to gender in education, training, and supervision pertains to what happens in the supervisory context, specifically, behaviors between supervisee and supervisor. As indicated next, investigations on this topic use variety of methods, including content analysis of verbal behaviors, quantitative approaches, qualitative approaches, and a broader look at critical supervisory events.

The concept of power in supervisory relationships was examined in some early investigations. In one of the first investigations, Nelson and Holloway (1990) used a content analysis approach to examine how power and involvement messages occurred in 15-minute segments of supervision sessions. The authors found that female and male supervisors responded to high-power messages by female trainees with low power and encouraging messages less often than they did with male trainees. In addition, when a supervisor offered a low-power, encouraging message, female trainees were less likely than male trainees to respond with a high-power message. Second, in a qualitative investigation of power and gender, Hicks and Cornille (1999) found that female supervisees and supervisors were more likely than male supervisees and supervisors to perceive gender bias in supervision. Although somewhat dated, both of these studies suggest that power dynamics related to gender tend to be at play in supervisory dyads.

Three other studies used either discourse or content analysis to explore supervisees' and supervisors' behaviors. First, Friedlander, Siegel, and Brenock (1989) used a case-study methodology to examine parallel processes when all members of the supervision and therapy triad were women. Among the findings included the supervisor's use of an attractive and interpersonally sensitive approach over a task-oriented approach, which paralleled the most effective elements of the therapy relationship. Second, Granello, Beamish, and Davis (1997) used a content analysis to evaluate the audio recordings of 20 supervision sessions. The authors found that both female and male supervisors asked for opinions of therapy sessions more often from male supervisees. In addition, female supervisees were told what to do more often than their male counterparts. Third, Sells, Goodyear, Lichtenberg, and Polkinghorne (1997) examined supervisory dyads and their use of task focused versus relationship focused verbal statements. These researchers found that male supervisor—male supervisee dyads used significantly more task focused and less relationship focused verbal interactions than did the other dyadic constellations. Observations were based on

15-minute recorded segments of a single supervision session. No other distinctions were found among the other dyadic types. Fourth, studying matched and unmatched supervisory dyads, McHale and Carr (1998) used a discourse analysis of videotaped supervision sessions. There were two primary findings: (1) unexpectedly, female supervisors were more likely than male supervisors to use a directive supervisor style with a resistant trainee; and (2) supervisors in same-sex dyads displayed a more cooperative style than did supervisors in mixed dyads. In sum, the content analysis studies point to potential differences in the way gender matched and mismatched dyads interact, with biases toward gender roles.

More recently, Walker, Ladany, and Pate-Carolan (2007) investigated female supervisees' experiences of positive and negative gender-related events. The authors identified categories of positive gender-related events that included supervisor interventions, such as providing helpful conceptualizations of clients, processing feelings about a gender-related event, supporting the supervisee's professional development issues, and demonstrating empathic understanding of a client's assault history. Conversely, categories of negative gender-related events included supervisor interventions such as using gender stereotypes about the trainee or client, dismissing the gender-related issue when broached by the trainee, and initiating inappropriate behaviors toward the trainee. Positive gender-related events were positively related to the supervisory alliance and trainee self-disclosure.

Two other investigations examined the intersection of gender with other multicultural factors. First, in a large-scale study of supervisory multicultural discussions, Gatmon et al. (2001) found that discussion of gender similarities and differences in supervision was predictive of greater supervisee satisfaction. Miller and Ivey (2006) examined supervisor style and the intersection of spirituality and gender; this was one of the few investigations that incorporated gender with another multicultural variable. Unfortunately, inconsistent findings made interpretation of these findings difficult.

Finally, in an examination of self-disclosure in supervision, Heru, Strong, Price, and Recupero (2006) found that female and male supervisors differed in relation to setting boundaries with trainees. Specifically, male supervisors were more comfortable than female supervisors in meeting their supervisees outside of supervision, publishing aspects of their supervision work, and self-disclosing prior struggles with substance abuse.

Throughout these in-session behaviors and critical-events investigations, researchers consistently operationalized gender based on biological sex, which may account for the inconsistent findings across areas of investigation (i.e., artificially dichotomizing the variable). These findings seem to be consistent with the latest theoretical models that postulate a more complex understanding of gender. Moreover, most of these investigations were published more than a decade ago, thereby limiting our understanding of their relation to present day supervision practice.

Theoretical Models of Supervision and Gender

Initially, psychotherapy-supervision models emerged from psychotherapy models (Farber & Kaslow, 2010). Often, the psychotherapy-based supervision models did little to address some fundamental differences between psychotherapy and supervision, such as the fact that supervision is primarily educative, evaluative, and involuntary (Ladany & Inman, 2012).

Over the past two decades, authors have recognized that supervision is distinct from psychotherapy, albeit they have similar processes of change. The newer supervision models specifically attend to the uniqueness of psychotherapy supervision. In addition, these models tend to be pantheoretical and address aspects or techniques of supervision such as Socratic supervision (Overholser, 2004), interpersonal process recall (Kagan, 1984), supervisor self-disclosure (Ladany & Walker, 2003), and supervisor competencies (Falender & Shafranske, 2004). Although many of these techniques have little empirical support, Westefeld (2009) identified three models of supervision that were comprehensive and based, at least in part, on empirical research. These models include the Integrated Development Model (IDM; Stoltenberg, & McNeill, 2010), the Systems Approach to Supervision (SAS; Holloway, 1995), and the Critical Events in Supervision model (CES; Ladany, Friedlander, & Nelson, 2005), an interpersonal approach to supervision. Of these three models, only one, the CES model, included gender as a primary aspect (i.e., a primary critical event). Hence, we review the CES model as an approach that attends to gender issues in supervision.

The CES model is based on the premise that supervision consists of meaningful critical events that can occur within and/or between supervision sessions. In the model, 11 critical events were identified that the authors view as representing the major critical events that tend to occur in psychotherapy supervision: remediating skill difficulties and deficits, heightening multicultural awareness, negotiating role conflicts, working through countertransference, managing sexual attraction, repairing gender-related misunderstandings and missed understandings, addressing problematic supervisee emotions and behaviors, facilitating supervisee insight, facilitating supervisee corrective relational experiences, and working through therapist shame. Notably, three of these critical events have a gender tie (i.e., heightening multicultural awareness, managing sexual attraction, and repairing gender-related misunderstandings and missed understandings). For purposes of this review, we will focus on the latter as an illustrative example.

Four components have been identified as the primary aspects of any critical events. The first component is the supervisory working alliance, which is based on Bordin's (1983) tripartite model and consists of three components: a mutual agreement between supervisee and supervisor on the goals of supervision (e.g., outcomes of supervision like increased ability to conceptualize cases from a theoretical perspective), a mutual agreement between supervisee and supervisor on the tasks of supervision (e.g., manner of reviewing recordings, extent of countertransference focus), and an emotional bond between the supervisee and supervisor (i.e., mutual caring, liking, and trusting). There is a substantive literature to indicate that the supervisory alliance is related to supervision outcome (Ladany & Inman, 2012). In the task-analytic model of a critical event, the first component is the *marker*, which is an indication on the part of the supervisee that initiates the event, signaling to the supervisor that some specific intervention is required. Markers can be explicit, such as the supervisee asking to learn a specific technique, or implicit, such as the supervisee chronically forgetting to discuss his or her work with a specific a client or the supervisor noticing an

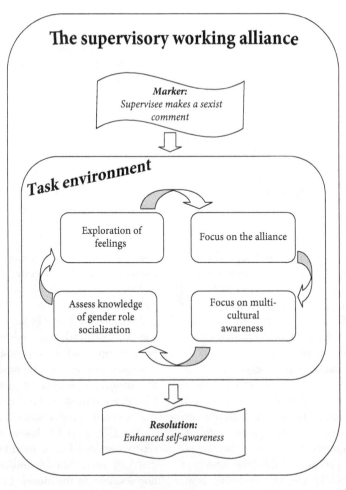

Figure 24.1. Repairing a Gender-Related Misunderstanding Critical Event.

unproductive behavior when reviewing a tape of the supervisee's therapy session.

The marker initiates the next phase, which is called the *task environment*. The task environment consists of various supervisor techniques, which Ladany and colleagues (2005) called *interaction sequences*, which are useful to resolve the critical event at play. Although there are unlimited techniques, Ladany and co-workers (2005) identified 11 such sequences, most of which are interpersonal in nature. These include (1) focus on the supervisory alliance, (2) focus on the therapeutic process, (3) exploration of feelings, (4) focus on countertransference, (5) attention to parallel process, (6) focus on self-efficacy, (7) normalization of the supervisee's experience, (8) focus on skill, (9) assessment of knowledge, (10) focus on multicultural awareness, and (11) focus on evaluation.

The final step in the critical event is the *resolution*, or outcome of the critical event. Positively resolved events occur when there is a positive change in the supervisee, whereas unresolved events are those that do not do so (Ladany et al., 2005). Four types of resolutions include enhancing self-awareness, knowledge, skills, and/or repairing a rupture in the supervisory working alliance.

To illustrate the model in relation to a gender event, we use the template in Ladany et al. (2005) to describe a critical event that involves repairing gender-related misunderstandings or a missed opportunity for understanding. In this case, the supervisor is a woman and the supervisee is a man. Let's assume that the supervisee makes a sexist comment that suggests an attempt to disempower the supervisor. The sexist comment becomes the marker of this critical event.

Recognizing the marker, the supervisor conceptualizes the critical event as a gender-based event. As the task environment begins, the supervisor likely engages in the following interaction sequences: exploration of feelings; focus on the supervisory alliance; assessment of the supervisee's knowledge of gender role socialization, which, at the same time, increased the supervisee's awareness; and focus on multicultural awareness. If the resolution is successful, the supervisee gains an awareness of how his comments were received by the supervisor and begins to consider how his behavior affects not only his clients but others in his personal and professional life. This example is illustrated in Figure 24.1. Conversely, an unsuccessful resolution of this gender-related event would involve no change on the supervisee's part, perhaps with defensive denial or extensive rationalization.

The following case illustrates the concepts identified in the CES model, with a slight variation on the interaction sequences in the template above.

Case 4: A Gender-Related Critical Event

Adrian Cardona was quite pleased with his ongoing supervision of Janyce Stillman, a first-year graduate student in practicum at Adrian's community agency. The two were like-minded theoretically, and Adrian found Janyce to be open and nondefensive. Moreover, she clearly had talent—she was one of those rare students who "have it in their bones," so to speak. That is, she was perceptive, intuitive, and engaging. These qualities were so apparent that their supervision sessions could focus on deepening Janyce's knowledge of client conceptualization, diagnosis, and treatment implementation rather than on the basic rapport and empathy skills that most novices need to learn in their first practicum.

Viewing Janyce as exceptionally competent for a novice, Adrian was nonplussed when Janyce's presentation in supervision one day was somewhat distracted, taciturn, and withdrawn. This out-of-character behavior on Janyce's part was a marker for a critical event. At first, Adrian had no idea where the discussion would lead them. It took some tactful probing before Janyce revealed the source of her discomfort. Apparently a young male client, named Todd, had been increasingly flirtatious with her in session over the past two weeks. Embarrassed and unsure about how to talk with Adrian about her unease with this client, Janyce had remained fairly silent.

Yesterday, however, Janyce's session had been a "disaster." Todd, had told her that she was "beautiful," that he wanted "to be" with her, and then—to her dismay—had crossed the room, knelt down and laid his head in her lap. Shocked, Janyce had stood up abruptly, saying, "You can't do that! Get up," whereupon Todd began yelling at her, calling her a "tease" and insisting that she'd been "leading him on" with her "flashing eyes" and her "sexy clothes." Completely distraught, Janyce ended the session abruptly and spent the next half hour in the restroom trying to compose herself.

Adrian was at first startled by Janyce's story. Then he became acutely uncomfortable, realizing that he, too, had found Janyce to be alluring. He could see how her highly masculine young client had misinterpreted Janyce's care and concern for him.

The task environment of this gender event focused, first, on an *exploration of Janyce's feelings* about what had taken place with Todd, feelings that included anger, shame, and tremendous worry about her ability to learn to be a therapist. Adrian elicited and then *normalized Janyce's feelings* (e.g., "Any therapist, no matter how experienced, would be shocked and upset about a client acting out like that in session"). The next phase of the event focused on trying to understand the client's behavior in light of what they knew of his personality and history. Engaging in this cognitive activity was a strategic move on Adrian's part, his objective being to help Janyce feel less vulnerable with him in supervision, that is, *focus on her conceptual skills and enhance her self-efficacy.*

Calmer now that she had disclosed the event and felt supported by Adrian, Janyce was able to demonstrate a conceptual understanding of Todd's behavior. Then she found the courage to ask Adrian what, if anything, she had done that Todd might have construed as "teasing." Although Janyce's question was quite uncomfortable for them both, Adrian was able to tell her that although he was certain that Janyce had done nothing overtly seductive with Todd, there were potentially behaviors that could have been misinterpreted by a male client with traditional values. These behaviors included her occasional pats on his back when he was leaving as well as how what she wore could be misinterpreted by the client. Adrian fumbled a bit before mentioning that perhaps she could "dress in an alternative professional style in the future." He further tried to explain that at times he had thought that her outfit was more suited for "going out" than for practicum. Adrian acknowledged his discomfort with these comments, then apologized for having had this impression before about her appearance but had been reluctant to mention it out of concern for how Janyce might interpret his remarks.

Janyce expressed appreciation for Adrian's candor, as well as his suggestions about how to present herself more professionally. She explained that she had never before had a professional job and was not sure how to dress, but that now she could see that "looking good" in her personal life should be different from "looking good" as a professional. Adrian then said, "your being a woman and me being a man" had interfered with his obligation to supervise her appropriately, that he was sorry for that lapse. The two then discussed their relationship frankly, and Janyce realized that she felt more shame telling Adrian about what had occurred with Todd than if she had had a female supervisor.

Adrian again *normalized Janyce's feelings*, checking in to see if she had any lingering embarrassment about their discussion of her appearance. When Janyce assured Adrian that she was appreciative and felt comfortable about their interaction, they agreed to continue speaking frankly about gender issues as they came up in discussions of clients or in their relationship in supervision. They concluded the supervision hour by discussing alternatives for how Janyce could speak with Todd about what had occurred in therapy the previous week. This conclusion of the supervision session signals a successful resolution of the gender-based critical event.

Another way to look at this case is to consider gender as a *figure-ground factor* in the therapeutic relationship that needs to be addressed in supervision (Ladany et al., 2005). For example, gender initially is the *figure* in the therapy relationship with Janyce and Todd, and is in the *ground* in the supervisory relationship with Adrian and Janyce. Later, when gender is brought into the supervisory relationship it becomes the *figure* and once worked through, moves back to the *ground* in both the supervisory and therapy relationships. Hence, the interpersonal events in therapy are mirrored in the interpersonal events in supervision.

Implications for Education, Training, and Supervision Theory and Research

In this chapter we reviewed the theoretical and empirical literature on sex and gender in relation to education, training, and supervision. It seems evident that inroads have been made in understanding and conceptualizing gender, both theoretically and empirically. However, these inroads are at best minor, particularly empirically. Thus, we offer this set of potential theoretical and empirical directions that we believe warrant continued attention.

• The integration of gender issues in psychotherapy training programs is important for the development of emerging professionals. Thus, to verify the extent to which gender issues are adequately taught in graduate curricula need to be assessed and evaluated.

• There are many gender-related constructs that are theoretically sound, but have no empirical methods or measures. Hence, there is a continued need for scale development to assist researchers, educators, and trainers in understanding the complexities of gender work.

• Assessing gender-related skills in psychotherapy work, and their link to psychotherapy outcome warrants attention.

• We need to continue to develop measures that attend to the complexities of the construct of gender rather than solely relying on a dichotomous understanding of the construct.

• The study of men and masculinity recently has emerged as an area of study, yet little has been postulated in the education, training, and supervision literature. To that end, we recommend that future researchers include men and masculinity in empirical study of supervision.

• The ideas linked to feminist supervision need expansion, and we encourage the development of a comprehensive model of feminist supervision that, in turn, could be tested empirically.

• Supervision approaches like the Critical Events in Supervision model (Ladany et al., 2005) need continued theoretical work to ensure adequate coverage of gender-related constructs.

• Significant work is needed to understand the most effective approaches to the teaching and learning of gender issues by novice psychotherapists.

• As technology enhances researchers' ability to discover patterns of gender-related discourse, a variety of lessons can be derived from in-session observations of clients, therapists, and supervisors.

Conclusion

The integration of gender issues into education, training, and supervision has existed since the 1970s. However, the initial interest has waxed and waned in the literature, and continued and significant attention is warranted. As the concepts of sex and gender have evolved and become more complex, so, too, has come the recognition that these concepts are not mutually exclusive and are related to additional constructs such as transgender and sexual orientation. The separation of these concepts is perhaps necessary in the early development of a

broader understanding, even though the distinctions are largely artificial. Indeed, there are two chapters in this current book that perpetuate the artificial multichotomization of these constructs. It is our hope that one day, our two chapters will be integrated into one comprehensive chapter containing a rich set of empirically based theoretical ideas on sex, gender, and sexual orientation, along with other related constructs that are equally compelling and meaningful.

Notes

[1] For the purposes of our chapter we use the terms *therapy* and *therapist* to include all activities of applied psychological principles such as counseling, counselor, psychotherapy, and psychotherapist.

[2] The authors would like to thank Marla Jensen, Alexander Polk, and Patrice Wakeley for their superb literature assistance for this chapter.

References

Ali, A., Caplan, P. J., & Fagnant, R. (2010). Gender stereotypes in diagnostic criteria. In J. C. Chrisler, D. R. McCreary, J. C. Chrisler, D. R. McCreary (Eds.), *Handbook of gender research in psychology, Vol. 2: Gender research in social and applied psychology* (pp. 91–109). New York: Springer. doi: 10.1007/978-1-4419-1467-5_5

American Psychiatric Association. (2000). *Diagnostic and statistical manual of mental disorders* (4th ed., text rev.). Washington, DC: Author

Ancis, J., & Ladany, N. (2001). Multicultural Supervision. In L. J. Bradley and N. Ladany (Eds.), *Counselor Supervision: Principles, Process, & Practice (3rd Edition).* (pp. 63–90). Philadelphia: Brunner-Routledge.

Ancis, J., & Ladany, N. (2010). A multicultural framework for counselor supervision: Knowledge and skills. In N. Ladany & L. Bradley (Eds.), *Counselor supervision* (4th ed., pp. 53–95). New York: Routledge.

Ancis, J. R., Szymanski, D. M., & Ladany, N. (2008). Development and psychometric evaluation of the counseling women competencies scale (CWCS). *The Counseling Psychologist, 36,* 719–744. doi: 10.1177/0011000008316325

APA. (2007). Guidelines for psychological practice with girls and women. *American Psychologist, 62,* 949–979.

Becker, D., & Lamb, S. (1994). Sex bias in the diagnosis of borderline personality disorder and posttraumatic stress disorder. *Professional Psychology: Research And Practice, 25*(1), 55–61. doi:10.1037/0735–7028.25.1.55

Beutler, L. E., Crago, M., & Arizmendi, T. G. (1986). Therapist variables in psychotherapy process and outcome. In S. L. Garfield and A. E. Bergin (Eds.), *Handbook of psychotherapy and behavior change* (3rd ed.). New York: Wiley.

Bordin, E. S. (1983). Supervision in counseling: II. Contemporary models of supervision: A working alliance based model of supervision. *The Counseling Psychologist, 11*(1), 35–42. doi:10.1177/0011000083111007

Boswell, J. F., & Castonguay, L. G. (2007). Psychotherapy training: Suggestions for core ingredients and future research. *Psychotherapy: Theory, Research, Practice, Training, 44*(4), 378–383. doi:10.1037/0033-3204.44.4.378

Brown, L. S. (2010). *Feminist therapy.* Washington, DC US: American Psychological Association.

Brown, S. D., & Lent, R. (1984). *Handbook of counseling psychology*. Oxford England: John Wiley & Sons.

Broverman, I. K., Broverman, D. M., Clarkson, F. E., Rosenkrantz, P. S., & Vogel, S. R. (1970). Sex-role stereotypes and clinical judgments of mental health. *Journal of Consulting and Clinical Psychology, 34*(1), 1–7. doi:10.1037/h0028797

Capodilupo, C. M., Nadal, K. L., Corman, L., Hamit, S., Lyons, O. B., & Weinberg, A. (2010). The manifestation of gender microaggressions. In D. Sue (Ed.), *Microaggressions and marginality: Manifestation, dynamics, and impact* (pp. 193–216). Hoboken, NJ: Wiley.

Centers for Reproductive Rights (n.d.). Time to get emergency contraception right. Retrieved on 23 July 2013 from http://reproductiverights.org/en/feature/time-to-get-emergency-contraception-right

Chaney, S. E., & Piercy, F. P. (1988). A feminist family therapist behavior checklist. *American Journal of Family Therapy, 16*(4), 305–318. doi:10.1080/01926188808250736.

Coleman, S. B., Avis, J. M., & Turin, M. (1990). A study of the role of gender in family therapy training. *Family Process, 29*, 365–374. doi: 10.1111/j.1545–5300.1990.00365.x

Comas-Díaz, L. (2006). Cultural Variation in the Therapeutic Relationship. In C. D. Goodheart, A. E. Kazdin, R. J. Sternberg (Eds.), *Evidence-based psychotherapy: Where practice and research meet* (pp. 81–105). Washington, DC: American Psychological Association. doi:10.1037/11423-004

Committee on Accreditation. (2007). *Guidelines and principles for accreditation of programs in professional psychologys*. Washington DC: APA. Retrieved from www.apa.org/ed/accreditation/about/policies/guiding-principles.pdf

Counselors for Social Justice (2011, August 26). Counselors for social justice position statement on the development of the diagnostic and statistical manual of mental disorders-5th ed. (DSM-5) and proposed draft revisions to DSM disorders and criteria. Retrieved from http://counselorsforsocialjustice.com/PDF/PositionStatementDSM5.pdf

Downing, N. E., & Roush, K. L. (1985). From passive acceptance to active commitment: A model of feminist identity development for women. *The Counseling Psychologist, 13*(4), 695–709. doi:10.1177/0011000085134013

Enns, C. Z. (1993). Twenty years of feminist counseling and therapy: From naming biases to implementing multifaceted practice. *The Counseling Psychologist, 21(1)*, 3–87. doi:10.1177/0011000093211001

Enns, C. (2004). *Feminist theories and feminist psychotherapies: Origins, themes, and diversity* (2nd ed.). New York: Haworth Press.

Falender, C. A., & Shafranske, E. P. (2004). *Clinical supervision: A competency-based approach*. Washington, DC: American Psychological Association. doi:10.1037/10806-000

Farber, E. W., & Kaslow, N. J. (2010). Introduction to the special section: The role of supervision in ensuring the development of psychotherapy competencies across diverse theoretical perspectives. *Psychotherapy: Theory, Research, Practice, Training, 47*(1), 1–2.

Fassinger, R. E. (1994). Development and testing of the Attitudes Toward Feminism and the Women's Movement (FWM) Scale. *Psychology of Women Quarterly, 18*(3), 389–402. doi:10.1111/j.1471-6402.1994.tb00462.x

Fassinger, R. E. (2000). Gender and sexuality in human development: Implications for prevention and advocacy in counseling psychology. In S. D. Brown, R. W. Lent (Eds.), *Handbook of counseling psychology* (3rd ed., pp. 346–378). Hoboken, NJ: Wiley.

Fassinger, R. E., & Arseneau, J. R. (2007). "I'd rather get wet than be under that umbrella": Differentiating the experiences and identities of lesbian, gay, bisexual, and transgender people. In K. J. Bieschke, R. M. Perez, K. A. DeBord (Eds.), *Handbook of counseling and psychotherapy with lesbian, gay, bisexual, and transgender clients* (2nd ed., pp. 19–49). Washington, DC: American Psychological Association.

Filkowski, M. B., Storm, C. L., York, C. D., & Brandon, A. D. (2001). Approaches to the study of gender in marriage and family therapy curricula. *Journal of Marital and Family Therapy, 27*, 117–122.

Ford, M. R., & Widiger, T. A. (1989). Sex bias in the diagnosis of histrionic and antisocial personality disorders. *Journal of Consulting and Clinical Psychology, 57*(2), 301–305. doi:10.1037/0022-006X.57.2.301

Friedlander, M. L., Siegel, S. M., & Brenock, K. (1989). Parallel processes in counseling and supervision: A case study. *Journal of Counseling Psychology, 36*(2), 149–157. doi:10.1037/0022-0167.36.2.149

Garfield, S. L., & Bergin, A. E. (Eds.). (1986) *Handbook of psychotherapy and behavior change* (3rd ed.). New York: Wiley.

Gatmon, D., Jackson, D., Koshkarian, L., Maros-Perry, N., Molina, A., Patel, N., & Rodolfa, E. (2001). Exploring ethnic, gender, and sexual orientation variables in supervision: Do they really matter? *Journal of Multicultural Counseling & Development, Special Issue, 29*, 102–113.

Gilligan, C. (1977). In a different voice: Women's conceptions of self and of morality. *Harvard Educational Review, 47*(4), 481–517.

Granello, D. H., Beamish, P. M., & Davis, T. (1997). Supervisee empowerment: Does gender make a difference? *Counselor Education & Supervision, 36*, 305–317.

Hamilton, S., Rothbart, M., & Dawes, R. M. (1986). Sex bias, diagnosis, and DSM-III. *Sex Roles, 15*(5–6), 269–274. doi:10.1007/BF00288316

Haverkamp, B. E. (2012). The counseling relationship. In E. M. Altmaier, J. C. Hansen (Eds.), *The Oxford handbook of counseling psychology* (pp. 32–70). New York, NY US: Oxford University Press.

Heru, A. M., Strong, D., Price, M., & Recupero, P. R. (2006). Self-disclosure in psychotherapy supervisors: gender differences. *American Journal of Psychotherapy, 60*, 323–334.

Hicks, M. W., & Cornille, T. A. (1999). Gender, power, and relationship ethics in family therapy education. *Contemporary Family Therapy: An International Journal, 21*(1), 45–56. doi:10.1023/A:1021910620587

Hill, C. E., & Williams, E. N. The process of individual therapy. In S. D. Brown, R. W. Lent (Eds.), *Handbook of counseling psychology* (3rd ed., pp. 670–710). Hoboken, NJ: Wiley.

Holloway, E. L. (1995). *Clinical supervision: A systems approach*. Thousand Oaks, CA: Sage.

Inman, A. G., & Ladany, N. (2014). Multicultural competencies in psychotherapy supervision. In F. T. L. Leong (Ed.-in-Chief), L. Comas-Diaz, V. C. McLoyd, G. C. N. Hall, & J. E. Trimble (Assoc. Eds.), APA handbooks in psychology: APA handbook of multicultural psychology: Vol. 2. Applications and training. (pp. 643–658). Washington, DC: American Psychological Association.

Johnson, M. K., Russell Searight, H. R., Handal, P. J., & Gibbons, J. L. (1993). Survey of clinical psychology graduate students' gender attitudes and knowledge: toward gender-sensitive psychotherapy training. *Journal of Contemporary Psychotherapy, 23*, 233–249.

Jordan, K. (2006). Beginning supervisees' identity. *The Clinical Supervisor, 25*, 43–51. doi: 10.1300/J001v25n01_04

Kagan, N. (1984). Interpersonal process recall: Basic methods and recent research. In D. Larson (Ed.), *Teaching psychological skills: Models for giving psychology away* (pp. 229–244). Monterey, CA: Brooks/Cole.

Kannan, D. & Levitt, H.M. (2009). Challenges facing the developing feminist psychotherapist in training. *Women & Therapy, 32*, 406–422. doi: 10.1080/02703140903153377

Kaslow, N. J., Borden, K. A., Collins, F. R., Forrest, L., Illfelder-Kaye, J., Nelson, P. D., &...Willmuth, M. E. (2004). Competencies Conference: Future directions in education and credentialing in professional psychology. *Journal of Clinical Psychology, 60*(7), 699–712. doi:10.1002/jclp.20016

Kilbourne, J. (1999). Deadly persuasion: *Why women and girls must fight the addictive power of advertising*. New York, NY: Free Press.

Ladany, N., Constantine, M. G., Miller, K., Erickson, C., & Muse-Burke, J. (2000). Supervisor countertransference: A qualitative investigation into its identification and description. *Journal of Counseling Psychology, 47*, 102–115. doi: 10.1037/0022-0167.47.1.102

Ladany, N., Friedlander, M. L., & Nelson, M. (2005). *Critical events in psychotherapy supervision: An interpersonal approach.* Washington, DC: American Psychological Association. doi:10.1037/10958-000

Ladany, N., & Inman, A. G. (2012). Training and supervision. In E. M. Altmaier and Hansen, J. C. (Eds.), *The Oxford handbook of counseling psychology* (pp. 179–207). New York: Oxford University Press

Ladany, N., & Walker, J. A. (2003). Supervision self-disclosure: Balancing the uncontrollable narcissist with the indomitable altruist. *Journal of Clinical Psychology, 59*(5), 611–621. doi:10.1002/jclp.10164

Landrine, H. (1989). The politics of personality disorder. *Psychology of Women Quarterly, 13*, 325–339. doi: 10.1111/j.1471-6402.1989.tb01005.x

Leslie, L. A. & Clossick, M. (1996). Sexism in family therapy: does training in gender make a difference? *Journal of Marital and Family Therapy, 22*, 253–269. doi: 10.1111/j.1752-0606.1996.tb00202.x

Levant, R. F. (2011). Research in the psychology of men and masculinity using the gender role strain paradigm as a framework. *American Psychologist, 66*(8), 765–776. doi:10.1037/a0025034

Levant, R. F., Richmond, K., Majors, R. G., Inclan, J. E., Rossello, J. M., Heesacker, M., &...Sellers, A. (2003). A multicultural investigation of masculinity ideology and alexithymia. *Psychology of Men & Masculinity, 4*(2), 91–99. doi:10.1037/1524-9220.4.2.91

Lui, W. M., Stinson, R., Hernandez, J., Shepard, S., & Haag, S. (2009). A qualitative examination of masculinity, homelessness, and social class among men in a transitional shelter. *Psychology of Men & Masculinity, 10*, 131–148. doi: 10.1037/a0014999

McHale, E., & Carr, A. (1998). The effect of supervisor and trainee therapist gender on supervision discourse. *Journal of Family Therapy, 20*, 395–411.

McNamara, K., & Rickard, K. M. (1989). Feminist identity development: Implications for feminist therapy with women. *Journal of Counseling & Development, 68*(2), 184–189. doi:10.1002/j.1556-6676.1989.tb01354.x

Milar, K. S. (2000). The first generation of women psychologists and the psychology of women. *American Psychologist, 55*(6), 616–619. doi:10.1037/0003-066X.55.6.616

Miller, M., & Ivey, D. C. (2006). Spirituality, gender, and supervisory style in supervision. *Contemporary Family Therapy: An International Journal, 28*(3), 323–337. doi:10.1007/s10591-006-9012-0

Nelson, M. L., & Holloway, E. L. (1990). Relation of gender to power and involvement in supervision. *Journal of Counseling Psychology, 37*, 473–481. doi: 10.1037/ 0022-0167.37.4.473

Ossana, S. M., Helms, J. E., & Leonard, M. M. (1992). Do "womanist" identity attitudes influence college women's self-esteem and perceptions of environmental bias?. *Journal of Counseling & Development, 70*(3), 402–408. doi:10.1002/j.1556-6676.1992.tb01624.x

Overholser, J. C. (2004). The four pillars of psychotherapy supervision. *The Clinical Supervisor, 23*(1), 1–13. doi:10.1300/J001v23n01_01

Owen, J., Tao, K., & Rodolfa, E. (2010). Microaggressions and women in short-term psychotherapy: Initial evidence. *The Counseling Psychologist, 38*(7), 923–946. doi:10.1177/0011000010376093

Porter, N. (1995). Supervision of psychotherapists: Integrating anti-racist, feminist, and multicultural perspectives. In H. Landrine (Ed.), *Bringing cultural diversity to feminist psychology: Theory, research, and practice* (pp. 163–175). Washington, DC: American Psychological Association. doi:10.1037/10501-008

Porter, N., & Vasquez, M. (1997). Covision: Feminist supervision, process, and collaboration. In J. Worell, N. G. Johnson (Eds.), *Shaping the future of feminist psychology: Education, research, and practice* (pp. 155–171). Washington, DC: American Psychological Association. doi:10.1037/10245-007

Proctor, G. (2008). Gender dynamics in person-centered therapy: Does gender matter?. *Person-Centered and Experiential Psychotherapies, 7*, 82–94. doi: 10.1080/14779757.2008.9688455

Rodolfa, E., Bent, R., Eisman, E., Nelson, P., Rehm, L., & Ritchie, P. (2005). A cube model for competency development: Implications for psychology educators and regulators. *Professional Psychology: Research and Practice, 36*(4), 347–354. doi:10.1037/0735-7028.36.4.347

Russo, N., & O'Connell, A. N. (1992). Women in psychotherapy: Selected contributions. In D. K. Freedheim, H. J. Freudenberger, J. W. Kessler, S. B. Messer, D. R. Peterson, H. H. Strupp, P. L. Wachtel (Eds.), *History of psychotherapy: A century of change* (pp. 493–527). Washington, DC: American Psychological Association. doi:10.1037/10110-013

Sells, J. N., Goodyear, R. K., Lichtenberg, J. W., & Polkinghorne, D.E. (1997). Relationship of supervisor and trainee gender to in-session verbal behavior and ratings of trainee skills. *Journal of Counseling Psychology, 44*, 406–412. doi: 10.1037/0022-0167.44.4.406

Silverstein, L. B., & Goodrich, T. J. (2003). *Feminist family therapy: Empowerment in social context.* Washington, DC: American Psychological Association.

Stoltenberg, C.D., & McNeill, B. (2010). *IDM supervision: An integrated developmental model for supervising counselors and therapists* (3rd ed.). San Francisco, CA: Jossey-Bass.

Stoppard, J. M. (1989). An evaluation of the adequacy of cognitive/behavioural theories for understanding depression in women. *Canadian Psychology/Psychologie Canadienne, 30*, 39–47. doi: 10.1037/h0079789

Szymanski, D. (2003). The feminist supervision scale: A rational/theoretical approach. *Psychology of Women Quarterly, 27,* 221–232.

Szymanski, D. (2005). Feminist identity and theories as correlates of feminist supervision practices. *The Counseling Psychologist, 33,* 729–747.

Szymanski, D. M., Moffitt, L. B., & Carr, E. R. (2011). Sexual objectification of women: Clinical implications and training considerations. *The Counseling Psychologist, 39*(1), 107–126. doi:10.1177/0011000010378450

Trepal, H. C., Wester, K. L., & Shuler, M. (2008). Counselors'-in-training perceptions of gendered behavior. *The Family Journal: Counseling and Therapy for Couples and Families, 16,* 147–154. doi: 10.1177/1066480708314256

Vasquez, M. T. (2012). Ethical considerations in working with men. In H. Sweet (Ed.), *Gender in the therapy hour: Voices of female clinicians working with men* (pp. 67–87). New York: Routledge/Taylor & Francis Group.

Walker, J. A. (2010). Supervisor techniques. In N. Ladany & L. Bradley (Eds.), *Counselor supervision* (4th ed., pp. 97–124). New York: Routledge.

Walker, J. A., Ladany, N. & Pate-Carolan, L. M. (2007). Gender-related events in psychotherapy supervision: female trainee perspectives. *Counselling and Psychotherapy Research, 7,* 12–18.

Werner-Wilson, R. J. (2001). Experiential exercises in MFT training: gender, power, and diversity. *Contemporary Family Therapy, 2,* 221–229.

Westefeld, J. S. (2009). Supervision of psychotherapy: Models, issues, and recommendations. *The Counseling Psychologist, 37*(2), 296–316. doi:10.1177/0011000008316657

Winston, E. J., & Piercy, F. P. (2010). Gender and diversity topics taught in commission on accreditation for marriage and family therapy education programs. *Journal of Marital and Family Therapy, 36,* 446–471.

Wolter-Gustafson, C. (2008). Casting a wider empathic net: A case for reconsidering gender, dualistic thinking and person-centered theory and practice. *Person-Centered and Experiential Psychotherapies 7(2),* 95–109. doi: 10.1080/14779757.2008.9688456

Young-Bruehl, E. (1996). Gender and psychoanalysis. *Gender and Psychoanalysis, 1,* 7–18.

Race and Ethnicity in the Education and Training of Professional Psychologists

Charles R. Ridley *and* Christina E. Jeffrey

Abstract

This chapter provides an explanation of the influence of race and ethnicity in education and training in professional psychology. The linkage between this diversity and power in the trainer-trainee relationship serves as the superordinate theme. The authors organize the chapter around nonabusive and abusive uses of power, interlaced with specific dynamics and examples related to the aforementioned diversity dynamics. Methods for developing culturally competent trainer-trainee relationships are discussed, as well as the difficulties a trainer might encounter with power dynamics when working with a trainee with problems of professional competence. The importance of a healthy trainer-trainee relationship is stressed in regards to a positive trainee outcome, both within and beyond a graduate program in professional psychology.

Key Words: race, ethnicity, professional development

Introduction

Power is an inextricable aspect of all human relationships (Castelfranchi, 2003). It is inescapable, at times threatening, typically misunderstood, but overall, integral to the interactions people have with each other. Because of this premise, power also is a dynamic central to the interactions of trainers and trainees during graduate and/or professional training.[1] Furthermore, manifestations of power in trainer-trainee relationships can be exuded through racial, ethnic, and cultural concomitants.

In this chapter, we consider race, ethnicity, and culture in the education and training of professional psychologists. Our thesis is that racial, ethnic, and cultural issues in trainer-trainee relationships are best understood within the context of the power differential that exists between the two parties. Along similar lines, research on cross-race relationships in mentoring indicates important dynamics in training process and outcome (Atkinson, Neville, & Casas, 1991; Ragins, 1997; Thomas, 1990; Thomas, 1993). The challenge in writing this chapter is daunting due to the

extensive literature and complex nature of the topic. A multitude of nuances and complexities could not be adequately covered in a single chapter. Therefore, to provide a focused discussion, we set forth as the superordinate theme: race, ethnicity, and culture in trainer power. Ragins (1997) similarly made a case that a power perspective is useful in examining the linkage between diversity and mentorship.

To achieve our objective, we organize the chapter into four major sections: (a) perspective on power and race, (b) nonabusive trainers, (c) abusive trainers, and (d) becoming a culturally competent trainer. Throughout the chapter we interject how the nuances of race, ethnicity, and culture manifest themselves in the power dynamics. We also discuss trainee responses to and interactions with trainer power.

Perspective on Power and Race

There are a variety of perspectives on power, and they emanate from various disciplines. One widely accepted point of view is that power is related to a power-agent's goal and action (Castelfranchi,

2003). The agent must be capable of achieving and motivated to achieve the goal. Thus, power may be increased if the agent is capable and motivated but diminished if the agent does not have either the motivation or the capability of achieving the goal. In his power-dependency model, Emerson (1962) framed power as the power agent's ability to control access to (facilitate or hinder) goals in which the power recipient has a motivational investment. Accordingly, what transacts in the relationship is a mutual dependency in which one party advantageously uses the dependency for goal attainment:

> The dependence of the actor A upon actor B is (1) directly proportional to A's *motivational investment* in goals mediated by B and (2) inversely proportional to the *availability* of those goals to A outside the A-B relationship. (Emerson, 1962, p. 32)

In many respects, trainers are in a one-up position over trainees in that they mediate numerous goals in which trainees have a motivational investment. Trainees, for instance, are invested in grades, recognition, affirmation, earning a degree, emotional support, letters of recommendation, financial assistance, access to professional networks, jobs on completion of training, opportunities to collaborate on research and scholarly activities. For all these goals, to some extent, trainers can control access. Given that power is an entity of social relationships, trainees are not powerless in the relationship, for they control access to goals in which trainers have a motivational investment. For example, trainees can exercise control over fulfilling trainers' emotional needs for respect, approval, and favorable course evaluations. Clearly, however, the balance of power highly favors trainers over trainees, making trainees more vulnerable to trainers who abuse their power.

In graduate education and training, diversity plays a critical role in the power dynamics of trainers and trainees. For one thing, diversity is on the rise. Although White trainers and trainees continue to outnumber minority trainers and trainees, the gap is gradually shrinking (APA, 2008; Hoffer et al., 2007). Therefore, diversity is worthy of examination, especially as it pertains to how trainers exercise their power. Trainers can be nonabusive or abusive. See Figure 25.1. Typically, trainees are open and responsive to nonabusive advisors, whereas they are appeasing or defiant to abusive trainers. Of course, there are exceptions and variations in trainee reactions.

Non abusive Trainers

Trainers who are nonabusive can potentially serve as a wellspring for healthy psychological behaviors and high quality productivity with trainees. This wellspring has the potential to flourish into a rushing river of creativity and strength as the goals and working alliance of the trainer-trainee relationship develop. In order to reach such rapid currents, however, trainers should demonstrate numerous characteristics that are both congruent and incongruent with holding a strict power position.

The realization that the relationship between trainer and trainee is hierarchical and reciprocal, not purely egalitarian or autocratic, is vital to facilitating the developing current associated with scientific and clinical contribution and trainer-trainee well-being. Literature has stressed that a trainer may be viewed as a teacher, competent clinician, and/or leader who mimics a vertical relationship of a parent-to-child figure, as well as a horizontal relationship of a peer-to-peer relationship (Creighton, Parks, & Creighton, 2008; Foo-Kune & Rodolfa, 2013; Keller & Pryce, 2010). This relationship can be strengthened through a trainer's demonstration of several sensitive characteristics, including the provision of safety, self-disclosure, vulnerability, feedback, and acknowledgment of cultural competencies.

At the most basic of all levels, nonabusive trainers should provide feelings of safety and academic support to their trainees, especially during the trainees' early transition from being an applicant to matriculating into the training program (Boyle & Boice, 1998; Creighton et al., 2008). This nascent stage is crucial for positive trainer interventions, as the months prior to entry into any distinguished program are frequently delineated by fierce competition through program interviews, standardized exam scores, impressive curriculum vitas, work experiences and successful academic careers (Cynkar, 2007; Davids & Brenner, 1971). Although competition can persist across the training program, safety can be established easily by trainers' fostering of collegiality amongst new trainees (Davids & Brenner, 1971; Boyle & Boice, 1998; Creighton et al., 2008). This can help quell discord, perceptions of needed competition, and ultimately help the trainees "flow" down the river in harmony. Communicating the training program structure is critical as well, as fully understanding the stresses and demands that trainees will inevitably face provides them with needed stability both within and outside of the training program (Boyle & Boice, 1998; Creighton et al., 2008).

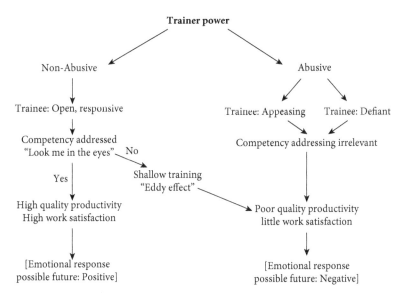

Figure 25.1. Trainer Power and Competency.

Feelings of safety and stability in the trainee are frequently enhanced by healthy amounts of self-disclosure and positive use of self from the nonabusive trainer as well (Foo-Kune & Rodolfa, 2013). Although this goes against the hierarchical or sometimes even paternalistic impulses of the trainer in the power position, exposing a level vulnerability can normalize some trainees' concerns, questions or self-conscious attitudes (Manathunga, 2007). As a wise trainer once said, "it's okay to be human." To be allowed to disclose and confide in a trainer and be met with an appropriate level of understanding validates the reciprocal nature of a healthy trainer-trainee relationship and can promote the development and exploration of professional identity (Noonan, Ballinger, & Black, 2007; Burnes, Wood, Inman, & Welikson, 2013; Foo-Kune & Rodolfa, 2013).

After a trainer has managed to communicate these feelings of safety and authenticity to the trainee, providing formative and summative feedback is crucial to the developing relationship and the current. Positive and challenging feedback has been reported to be invaluable to trainee psychological growth and stability, and feedback also strengthens collaborative styles of communication (Foo-Kune & Rodolfa, 2013; Burnes et al., 2013). Trainee attachment styles have even been considered in the desire for and receptivity of trainer feedback, and studies have found that the frequency of trainer feedback, regardless of quality, resulted in increased trainee productivity (Allen, Schockley, & Poteat, 2010). Not only can feedback align with a

trainer's self-disclosure, it can help built confidence in both new and established trainees.

If a trainer is able to provide these emotional and psychological experiences to a trainee while using his or her power responsibly, the two parties are more likely to travel toward the promising and exciting rapids of high-quality productivity and work satisfaction. Some argue that these provisions align with a person-centered mentoring approach, which stresses the valued interpersonal traits of empathy, congruence, safety, and unconditional positive regard (Wong, Wong, & Ishiyama, 2013).

However, an additional criterion must be met on the part of the trainer to ensure that the trainer-trainee relationship "flows" in the right direction. This criterion is cultural competency, which also aligns with the freedom to express cultural background and beliefs seen in the person-centered mentoring approach (Wong et al., 2013). Even when racial, ethnic, and cultural differences exist between a trainer and trainee, strong alliances can still form through the acknowledgment of multiculturalism and diversity. To address these differences constructively is arguably the highest holistic approach to the establishment of a healthy professional relationship.

Cultural Competency: "Look me in the Eyes"

Commitment to multiculturalism is a requirement for any accredited psychology training program (APA, 2007). After considerable time, research, and multiple American Psychological Association (APA) Task Force efforts devoted to the question of essential competencies for the practice of psychology, it is now clear that addressing cultural differences in professional relationships is an expectation for competent training, assessment and intervention (APA, 2002; APA, 2005; Fouad et al., 2009; Kaslow et al., 2004). Although the therapist-client relationship differs from the trainer-trainee relationship, the importance of cultural competency also is benchmarked as a key area of focus in clinical supervision (Wong et al., 2013). However, the method for addressing this area in supervision is arguably subjective as the interactions of trainer-trainee dyads differ across and within training programs.

Training relationships also are complex, even in homogeneous relationships. It can become more complicated in heterogeneous trainer-trainee relationships, and compounded by the fact that systemic guidelines for interacting in diverse training relationships are typically under-researched, unstandardized, and/or are incomplete (Gonzáez, 2006). Yet, diversified trainer-trainee relationships are unique in that "...distinct power functions of the mentoring component of the relationship, and...differences in power brought to the relationship by virtue of group membership" co-exist (Ragins, 1997, p. 494). From the trainee's perspective, a nonabusive trainer's willingness to acknowledge cultural differences has the potential of heightening the trainee's feelings of intimacy, safety, and congruence. Cultural competence can allow for a deeper recognition and appreciation of the trainee's identity by the trainer. Acknowledgment of the trainee's full identity, deemed the "look me in the eyes" phenomenon in this argument, can hold long-term benefits for the training relationship, even though it demands trainers to become emotionally vulnerable. Following are several proposed "problems" commonly experienced by trainees in regards to cultural competency, power, and the nonabusive trainer.

Problem 1: Avoiding Racial Differences

A temptation to seek out homogeneous training relationships may exist with both trainers and trainees. In terms of the trainer's experience, it is arguable that the power dynamic typically remains unthreatened or unaltered in racially matched relationships, as the vulnerability of discussing something as personal as racial differences is often perceived as unnecessary. In terms of the trainee's subjective experiences, some studies report that matched racial dyads can "...produce significant benefits" and provide heightened levels of interpersonal comfort (Gonzáez, 2006, p. 33; Allen, Day, & Lentz, 2005; Ragins, 1997). In addition, no additional vulnerability is required from either the trainer or the trainee in regards to addressing cultural competency.

Numerous studies on multiculturalism in training environments have shown the consistent preference of trainers and trainees for homogeneous relationships. Some trainees have reported higher ratings of interactions for trainers of similar ethnicities, whereas research on trainer-to-trainer relationships has revealed that "...racial and ethnic minority faculty and newly trained psychologists prefer to be [trained] by someone from their own race or ethnicity" (Brown, Daly, & Leong, 2009, p. 309). Such trends toward homogeneous relationships should not be surprising, as in a same-race dyad, the frequency of within-group racism and microaggressions can be minimized (Sue & Sue, 2012).

In terms of the training alliance, some trainees may find it easier to trust and receive guidance from someone of their own ethnic in-group due to perceptions of shared experiences (Blake-Beard, Bayne, Crosby, & Muller, 2011). Research has also linked group power and social identity, thus arguing that avoidance of heterogeneous relationships may be psychologically preferable as power conflicts are minimized in same-race groups (Deschamps, 1982; Tajfel & Turner, 1985; Ragins, 1997). Ultimately, it is of interest that members of similar groups are more likely to identify with each other than with members of different groups.

However, the assumption that homogeneous trainer-trainee relationships are the highest quality, most productive, and secure is not substantiated by the research (Atkinson et al., 1991). There is no prominent evidence that same-race dyads are impervious to common trainer-trainee relationship problems, such as trainer technical incompetence, neglect, relationship incompatibility, boundary violations, exploitation, abandonment, and unethical practices (Johnson & Huwe, 2002). These potential interpersonal problems stress that sharing the same ethnic group does not guarantee that both members will have relatable backgrounds, compatible interpersonal styles, and shared life experiences that can strengthen the training alliance. Ultimately, ethnic matching between trainer and trainee has not been shown to directly affect academic outcomes, increase trainee intrapersonal benefits, or ensure trainer-trainee compatibility (Blake-Beard et al., 2011; Atkinson et al., 1991).

Although having a willingness to discuss racial differences can be beneficial, trainers in heterogeneous relationships can become vulnerable through the disclosure of personal struggles. This type of disclosure is still not as intimidating to some as acknowledging racial differences. Seeking a homogeneous trainer-trainee relationship, whether as a conscious or unconscious effort, may provide the trainer with fewer feelings of vulnerability, yet is still incongruent with the notable shift toward competency-based training (Falender, Burnes, & Ellis, 2013). Seeking out only homogeneous training relationships is the ultimate in avoiding eye contact altogether.

Problem 2: Stereotypes and Attributions

Stereotypes are simplified, generalized labels applied to groups of people. They are distinguished from racial prejudice, which is a special case of stereotyping. Individuals who stereotype are not necessarily prejudiced, as stereotyping is an inevitable coping mechanism to avoid cognitive overload (Brown, 1965). An important consequence of stereotypes is misperception. Individuals within groups are perceived as homogeneous, whereas individuals between groups are perceived as heterogeneous (Hamilton & Trolier, 1986). The point here is that trainers, while respecting group differences, treat each trainee in cross-race trainer-trainee relationships as individuals and not assume their commonality with trainees in same trainer-trainee relationships.

Stereotyping is related to the exercise of power. It entails a self-perpetuating process wherein asymmetrical relationships are reinforced by stereotypes (Fiske, 1993; Ragins, 1995). Because minority group stereotypes are antithetical to power, they result in the perpetuation of the stereotypes of dominant groups to define power (Ragins, 1997).

Stereotypes and attributions of majority-group members often result in perceptions of diminished competency in minority-group members. From a trainer-trainee perspective, research suggests that trainees of all races may view minority trainers as having less power and less ability to provide for their trainees than majority trainers (Ragins, 1997). Even the success of a minority-group member is more frequently attributed to external ability and/or majority-member competence (Greenhaus & Parasuraman, 1993; Pettigrew & Martin, 1987; Ragins, 1997). If such poor attributions and stereotypes are internalized by either minority-trainers or trainees, they may begin to doubt their own competency and consequently inadvertently encourage attenuation of their organizational power (Ragins, 1997).

Advising or supervising styles in multicultural relationships have occasionally promoted stereotypical patterns of interaction as well. Helms (1984) challenged the frequent stereotype of how White, dominant-member groups should interact with minority-member groups in multicultural counseling. She explains that several deficiencies exist in cross-racial counseling models, including:

(a) an overemphasis on minority clients as the service recipients and majority professionals as the service providers, (b) a view of minority clients as so deviant that the counselor must possess the wisdom of Solomon and the patience of Job if he or she is ever to establish a cross-racial relationship, and (c) a lack of mechanisms by which to account for the interactions between two (or more) cultural perspectives…implicit in counseling relationships. (Helms, 1984, p. 153)

Similar applications of her theory can be applied to the trainer-trainee cross-race training relationship, especially when the professor is a member of the (typically White) majority-group.

Aligned with Helms' (1984) argument, it is frequently assumed that the minority-group trainee's cultural difference is the problem to be solved by White trainers. They solve the problem either by avoiding or adapting to the cultural differences. Such a focus on the minority-group trainee as the sole recipient of cultural competency, rather than an equal contributor, deviates from the previously established reciprocal nature of a healthy training relationship. In addition, viewing the White trainer as the wise, patient, and noble provider gives additional power and dominance to their already-powerful, dominant position. This stereotypical relationship pattern can not only lead to poor training, but can increase feelings of disenfranchisement in the minority-group trainee and promote racial inequalities seen outside of the training environment.

Problem 3: Dysconsciousness

A former colleague of the first author describes himself as a recovering racist. Earlier in his career, he was unaware of his uncritical stance toward racial inequity. Later in his career, he arrived at a painful point where he began a process of personal transformation. Although he would not claim complete recovery, he since has demonstrated considerable effectiveness in teaching, supervising, and mentoring trainees of color. King (1991) uses the term *dysconsciousness* to describe Whites who take their privileged position in society for granted. Dysconsciousness is an uncritical mind-set, one that leads individuals to justify racial inequity without questioning their underlying beliefs. King (1991) puts this phenomenon into perspective:

> Dysconsciousness is a form of racism that tacitly accepts dominant White norms and privileges. It is not the *absence* of consciousness (that is, not consciousness), but an *impaired* consciousness or distorted way of thinking about race as compared to, for example, critical consciousness. Uncritical ways of thinking about racial inequity accept certain culturally sanctioned assumptions, myths, and beliefs that justify the social and economic advantages White people have as a result of subordinating diverse others (Wellman, 1977). Any serious challenge to the status quo that calls this racial privilege into question inevitably challenges the self-identity of White people who have internalized these ideological justifications. (p. 137)

The tacit and uncritical acceptance of the status quo is the essential feature of dysconscious racism. King (1991) indicates that many Whites do not attribute racial inequity to structural racism in American society. Consequently, they find it easy to defend their status, although they would never describe it as White privilege.

To further elaborate on this concept, the terminology of being a member of a "White" race is sometimes shunted aside by Whites in exchange for social identifications that are not as saliently associated with racial inequality and prejudices (Helms, 1984). A dearth of literature exists on how Whites identify themselves in terms of racial beings, with evidence of Whites frequently opting for racial identification with culture-specific groups, such as Irish, Italian, or Jewish (Helms, 1984; Katz & Ivey, 1977). This denial of both White privilege and a lack of identity with a race that is associated with the dissemination of a racist system support the argument that poor racial consciousness can exist within majority-group members (Helms, 1984; Katz & Ivey, 1977).

When such attitudes are combined with the already complex power dynamic of the trainer-trainee relationship, devastating microaggressions and covert racism can occur between dysconscious, majority-group trainers and minority-group trainees. For example, a White, majority-group trainer who exhibits dysconsciousness might inaccurately prescribe training expectations that are more accommodating of White trainees. If a minority-group trainee struggles to meet such expectations, the dysconscious trainer may view the trainee as inadequate or a "weak-link" in the training program. However, the training method endorsed by such a trainer is ultimately operating in a way that maintains White privilege, furthers racial inequality, and increases unequal power dynamics for minority-group trainees. Perhaps most disturbing is that, while minority-group trainees more likely to experience consequences of dysconsciousness, they are less likely than majority-group members to report problematic racial issues (Helms, 1984; Webster, Sedlacek, & Miyares, 1979).

Problem 4: Cultural Incompetence

Addressing racial differences is not always necessary for the strengthening of the trainer-trainee alliance (Johnson & Huwe, 2002). Instead, some heterogeneous training relationships have benefited from a mutual agreement between the trainer and trainee in determining whether to discuss racial differences (Johnson & Huwe, 2002; Thomas, 1993). It has been found that the acknowledgment of racial differences does not necessarily facilitate the training relationship, but the agreement between trainer and trainee to discuss it that aided the trainer-trainee alliance (Thomas, 1993).

There is a danger, however, in not acknowledging racial differences, even in the case of a mutual agreement of avoidance. Cultural incompetency can emerge from the trainer without verbal warning to the trainee. Previous research has firmly established that cultural incompetence in trainers is harmful to trainees of color (Foo-Kune & Rodolfa, 2013). Culturally incompetent, yet aware trainers can raise their cultural competency through several methods. Brown et al. (2009) encourage several techniques outlined by Johnson (2002), who recommends that cross-cultural mentors should:

> Have appropriate attitudes and competencies …include[ing] (a) genuine concern for the experiences and welfare of minority group students, (b) diligent pursuit of cultural sensitivity—including investment of time learning about the unique cultural heritage of their protégés, and (c) appreciation of each mentee's uniqueness within his or her culture. (Johnson, 2002, p. 94)

Indeed, it is not all hopeless for culturally inept, nonabusive trainers if they are willing to be open to exposure, interaction, and providing support to trainees of different backgrounds. Ridley, Mendoza and Kanitz (1994) described multiple techniques for therapists to develop heightened multicultural competency, including methods of increasing cultural empathy, reading assignments, observational learning, introspection, and technology assisted training. Such methods are applicable to the trainer-trainee dyad as well as the counselor-client dyad.

However, the nonabusive trainer who continues to deny or ignore racial differences can permanently alter the trajectory of the initially promising trainer-trainee relationship. This leads to our last concern regarding cultural competence and the nonabusive trainer-trainee relationship: denial of the importance and impact of racial differences.

Problem 5: Downright Denial

Drastic consequences between trainer and trainee can still occur if significant cultural issues are blatantly denied, regardless of the positivity of the trainer-trainee relationship. According to Brown et al. (2009):

Cross-cultural differences have been identified as a barrier in the effective mentoring of racial and ethnic minority [trainees] in psychology. These cultural barriers arise from differences in attitudes, values, and beliefs when the [trainer] and [trainee] are from different cultural backgrounds. These differences may often lead to cultural miscommunication...[and] conflicts. (p. 309)

Such conflicts can include trainee feelings of powerlessness, self-doubt, inadequate supervision due to cultural or background barriers, negative interpersonal interactions, stereotyping, overt or covert racism and discrimination (Wong et al., 2013; Falender et al., 2013). Re-emphasizing that trainees are already in a "power-down" position, trainers who unintentionally exploit race-power differentials by denying it can increase the feelings of anxiety and depression in the minority-group trainee.

Our concept of "downright denial" can be aligned with the predominant problem of colorblindness. Colorblindness is the conception that racial considerations are no longer relevant in our current society, creating the illusion that we are all the same, regardless of race (Constantine, Smith, Redington, & Owens, 2008). Such attitudes can result in devastating microaggressions, in which the majority-group member harm people of color without understanding or realizing that they are (Constantine et al., 2008; Sue, Bucceri, Lin, Nadal, & Torina, 2007).

Davidson and Foster-Johnson (2001) wisely note that scientists are biased by their cultural backgrounds and values. Therefore, they are not impervious to the omission of culturally sensitive questions and interactions. In terms of research productivity, they note, "the questions we ask will dictate the results that we may—or may not—discover," and that promoting constructive conversations and questions about racial or ethnic differences is a trademark of a healthy training environment (Davidson & Foster-Johnson, 2001, p. 554). This omission also can be applied to the relationship between a trainer and trainee, as the types of questions both parties ask define whether the nature of the relationship is culturally competent. As Davidson and Foster-Johnson (2001) point out:

A culturally mature organization has the general clarity on race and ethnic issues that is indicated by a refusal to rely on stereotypes and by the use of valid character and skills assessments in the determination of assignments...There is an openness or readiness to share information and knowledge. (p, 565)

Indeed, acknowledging rather than denying multicultural differences can allow for the opportunity to address potential problems, discuss latent emotions, promote honesty, and enrich the training relationship.

This leads to our subargument regarding cultural competency in the trainer-trainee relationship. Deemed the "eddy effect," we describe the shift in the trainer-trainee relationship when cultural competency is shunted aside, regardless of the positive psychological and academic provisions of a nonabusive trainer. Through this "shunting," trainer-trainee well-being and work outcomes can be significantly diminished when compared to those seen in the culturally competent, non abusive trainer and trainee interactions.

Cultural Competency: The "Eddy Effect"

To return to the metaphor of a river current, the progression of the relationship between the trainer and trainee can become trapped in an eddy, or whirlpool, if competency issues are dismissed or ignored. The duo is still capable of making ripples across the river, thus changing and contributing to the motion of the waves that help define the earth that the river shapes. However, neither is able to reach the same thrill and reward of the racing rapids of a productive, harmonious, and strengthened relationship as trainers and trainees who address their cultural competencies. Instead, trainers' failure to provide the safety and intimacy of the acknowledgment of cultural diversities can cause their relationship current to turn back on itself and swirl in place.

At such a stage where an "eddy" has formed in a trainer-trainee relationship, work productivity can still be accomplished as the pair has already agreed to "flow" downstream together. However, the alliance may be damaged severely, and the opportunity for microaggressions, colorblindness, and incompetence remains. The scenario can result in poor work satisfaction, as trainers who deny the presence of microaggressions and the significance of race-power dynamics can deplete trainees' psychic energy, confidence, and affect their overall ability to learn (Shen-Miller, Forrest, & Burt, 2012; Boysen, Vogel, Cope, & Hubbard, 2009). Indeed, at its worst, silence on such a salient topic as multiculturalism can lead trainees to the same outcome of low quality productivity and dissatisfaction as trainees trapped with an abusive trainer. Refer to figure 01.

Abusive Trainers

Trainers who are abusive undermine the potential for healthy relationships with trainees and interfere with their productivity, development of confidence, and competency as a practitioner. Abuse is analogous to a dam that slows down, redirects, or outright obstructs the constructive flow of creativity, intellectual energy, and trust. In order to reach such negativity, trainers demonstrate characteristics that exploit their one-up positions with trainees. These can include dishonesty, hidden agendas, and cultural incompetence, and these may occur more frequently than expected. In one doctoral program, a disturbing 17% of psychology doctoral students experienced significant negative interactions with their primary mentors (Clark, Harden, & Johnson, 2000; Johnson & Huwe, 2002). Ultimately, trainers are responsible for preventing abusive relationships. In much the same way that therapists are accountable for their ethical behavior with clients, trainers are obligated to an implicit relational and educational contract with trainees.

Trainer abuse of power may be described in several ways, with each abuse capable of co-existing along with others. These abuses are wide-ranging and include exorbitant task demands, harsh or underserved criticism, public humiliation, neglect, professional sabotage, and boundary violations (Johnson & Huwe, 2002). Trainers who discount the power differential in the relationship and the trainee's need for constructive feedback, safety, and support easily can become abusive. A purely hierarchical relationship is fundamentally uncharacteristic of a healthy training relationship, as trainers and trainees both operate on a similar cost-benefit structure (Johnson

& Huwe, 2002). Therefore, although trainers can mediate access to a variety of goals in which trainees have a motivational investment, abuse will almost certainly occur if trainers cannot or will not meet basic trainee needs.

In abusive trainer-trainee relationships, trainees typically respond by taking either of two courses of action. They are appeasing or defiant (Kalbfleisch, 1997). *Appeasing* trainees are plagued with fear and anxiety. Their fears, which are real, concern such things as receiving poor grades, clinical evaluations, reputation among other trainers, negative letters of recommendations, increased workplace tension, and the potential loss of job opportunities. The last thing these trainees want to do is to jeopardize their status within their training program.

Defiant trainees take an opposite course of action. They set aside their fears, opting to challenge the abuse. Sometimes the defiance is self-destructive and results in a relational impasse. In other instances, the defiance is assertive whereby the trainee seeks to protect his or her rights without interfering with the rights of the trainer. However, in taking this stance, trainees nevertheless may encounter a backlash from the abusive trainer that fuels further conflict.

In relationships characterized saliently by abuse, there is often little point in addressing cultural competency, for abuse precludes the possibility of competence. Trainers who employ any of the aforementioned methods are arguably incapable of later connecting with their trainees through cultural competence. Even though a trainer may be culturally astute, the essential foundation of trust and support in the relationship does not exist. In the absence of such competence, we should all but expect low productivity, poor-quality work, and little work satisfaction. The ultimate outcomes are trainees who are disgruntled, have negative attitudes about their training program, and pass on their negative sentiments to prospective trainees. The following problems detail salient issues regarding power, race, and the abusive trainers.

Problem 1: Blaming the Victim

Not taking responsibility is as old as the human race. Blaming the victim takes shifting responsibility to another level. Here perpetrators shift the blame for their actions or the actions of others to the victims of those actions. In essence, they hold victims responsible for outcomes in their lives that are beyond their control. Ryan (1971) stated that blaming the victim "...so distorts and disorients the thinking of the average concerned citizen that it becomes a primary barrier to effective social change" (p. xv).

Blaming the victim can infiltrate trainer-trainee relationships. An example is the misattribution of academic or clinical inadequacies of trainees. In actuality, this may be a reflection of the inadequacies of the trainer or the training environment. Consider the trainer who has a deep-seated fear of being perceived as a racist. The last thing the trainer wants is to feel guilty about making a misstep with a minority trainee, let alone face a confrontation from colleagues about the behavior. This would be the ultimate in failed social consciousness. Yet the fear-driven behavior of the trainer may create a strain in the relationship, making it difficult for the minority trainee to function successfully in the relationship. Because of the trainer's position of power, the minority trainee can be labeled as problematic.

Blaming the victim is not limited to training relationships in which trainers are from majority groups and trainees from minority groups. Minority-group trainers can impose unfair attributions on White trainees. The trainees serve as convenient scapegoats for their feelings of inadequacy, which are sometimes rooted in their unresolved issues of being a victim of racism and sometimes being a victim of abuse unrelated to race. Furthermore, minority-group trainees can blame minority trainees for similar reasons they blame majority-group trainees. Their blaming sometimes can be more severe than the blame coming from a White trainer or their blaming of a White trainee.

Problem 2: False Generosity

Not every offer of assistance or support is genuine. Friere (2000) used the phrase *false generosity* to indicate so-called generous activities that actually are ingenious and strengthen the power differential between the oppressor and the oppressed:

> Any attempt to "soften" the power of the oppressor in deference to the weakness of the oppressed almost always manifests itself in the form of false generosity; indeed, the attempt never goes beyond this. In order to have the continued opportunity to express their "generosity," the oppressors must perpetuate injustice as well. (p.44)

Sometimes trainers co-opt trainees into academic endeavors that on the surface appear to be altruistic. In reality, the endeavors reflect more of the trainer's self-interest than the interest of the trainee. In this era of health disparities, for instance, the first author

has observed instances in which minority students have been used as a front for researchers to engage minority communities for the sole purpose of conducting studies in those communities. Although trainees are accorded the opportunity to participate in research, the benefits to the trainees nowhere approximate benefits to the trainers who stand to gain large extramural grants, accolades from peers, publications, and presentations at professional meetings. As an aside, the benefits accrued to the community frequently are questionable.

Unaware of the possibility of trainers having dubious motivations, trainees often are more than eager to work with trainers on research projects. Let's be clear, however; not every offer by a trainer carries inherent exploitation. Given the challenges trainers can face in accessing minority communities, it may be advantageous to have trainees who can assist as a conduit to the community. Trainers must maintain vigilance in understanding their motives, always recognizing they are at risk for co-opting minorities into self-serving and bias agendas (Sue & Sue, 2012).

Problem 3: Sense of Entitlement

People from dominant groups not only are the beneficiaries of privilege, they may believe they deserve the privilege and, therefore, expect certain types of treatment and opportunities to come their way (Goodman, 2001). This attitude is rooted in a false assumption that their privilege is a right, not something that must be earned. This attitude is something other than self-respect. It is arrogance, and it is accentuated by the expectation that their needs as entitled people should be met, and their needs supersede the needs of others.

There is a reliable indicator of an attitude of entitlement (Goodman, 2001). It becomes evident when individuals from the dominant group encounter a person from a disadvantaged group who is in authority over them or who has specialized expertise. In particular, they are suspicious of the competence, knowledge, or right of people from oppressed groups to have such status. Minority trainers may encounter trainees who have a sense of entitlement. When the trainer sets high expectations, the trainees may balk, sometimes forcefully challenging the trainer's right to be so demanding. If the trainer holds his or her ground, the trainee may complain to someone higher in authority, usually someone from the majority group. This puts the trainer in the position of defending his or his standards, while maintaining support for the trainee.

Problem 4: Microaggressions

According to Sue et al. (2007), microaggressions are "brief and commonplace daily verbal, behavioral, or environmental indignities, whether intentional or unintentional, that communicate hostile, derogatory, or negative racial slights and insults toward people of color" (p. 271). Perpetrators automatically enact these biases without conscious awareness (Dovidio & Gaertner, 2000). Although there are many kinds of microaggressions, three categories have been identified.

Microassaults are attacks intended to convey discrimination and bias. The key to these dynamics is intentionality. Perpetrators foist blatant verbal, nonverbal, or environmental attacks at their victims. Perpetrators of microassaults try to conceal their actions as much as possible (Sue & Sue, 2012). Microinsults are unintentional actions and verbal communications. They indicate rudeness, insensitivity, or demeaning of a person's background. Embedded in microinsults are hidden messages that are insulting. Microinvalidations dismiss, negate, or exclude the victim's thoughts, feelings, or personal experience. They also are unintentional and occur outside of awareness.

Microaggressions in mentoring can be directed from trainers to trainees or from trainees to trainers. To check themselves for possible microaggressions, trainers should directly ask trainees if they have any concerns about the relationship. When they experience attacks from trainees, they should confront them on their behavior and use the experience as a developmental opportunity.

Becoming a Culturally Competent Trainer

Developing cultural competence is critical to trainers in using their power responsibly with trainees from diverse backgrounds. We argue that trainers who abuse their power preclude the possibility of their becoming culturally competent. Drawing on the work of Ridley, Mollen, and Kelly (2011) on counseling competence, we propose this definition of cultural competence in trainer-trainee relationships. Cultural competence is the deliberate incorporation of cultural data in the training relationship. The purpose of the incorporation is to determine, facilitate, evaluate, and sustain positive professional outcomes for the trainee. The outcomes include those that are behavioral, cognitive, and affective in nature. Five factors in particular enhance a trainer's cultural competence.

Create a Diversity-Welcoming Climate

One aspect of culturally competent education and training goes beyond the specific dynamics of trainer-trainee relationships. Trainees of color may find themselves challenged by covert racism and sometimes more blatant forms of bias. In addition, they may be challenged by the differences in the cultures of their communities of origin and the culture of academia (Alvarez, Blume, Cervantes, & Thomas, 2009). Culturally-competent trainers help to create environments that embrace diversity, operate as safe places where all trainees feel free to learn and develop, and encourage honest intellectual discourse but with respect to the varieties of perspectives students bring to the discourse. Along these lines, Davidson and Foster-Johnson (2001) state that "Successful mentoring of graduate students of color is fundamentally embedded within an organizational culture of diversity, empowerment, and valuing of differences" (p. 566).

To create a diversity-welcoming environment within academic departments and colleges, Davidson and Foster-Johnson (2001) cull from the literature several recommendations. Make diversity training mandatory for faculty, staff, and trainers in all settings. Prepare faculty to provide formal instruction and systematic supervision on diversity issues. Address diversity at all levels of the department by developing goals, benchmarking, and monitoring. Make formal or informal checks on trainer-trainee relationships. In this last recommendation, the goal is to ensure both parties' satisfaction with the training relationship and avoid harmful effects or negative experiences.

The preceding recommendations also are relevant to internships and postdoctoral residencies. A growing number of these training environments have an explicit diversity or multicultural focus as part of their training mission. Those that do not nevertheless can create a diversity-welcoming environment. The most important stance is for the leadership of a training site to agree on the importance of having this type of environment and determining which of the above suggestions are appropriate for implementing at the site.

Discuss Race and Racism

In that the denial and avoidance of race can be counterproductive to trainer-trainee relationships, taking the opposite approach potentially can yield positive outcomes. An APA mentoring program designed for African American, Asian American, Native American, and Latino/a American students who were applying to doctoral programs in psychology demonstrates how these outcomes could be achieved (Chan, 2008). The students were matched with mentors based on their research and clinical interests. The investigator uncovered a serendipitous finding that was significant: Trust and rapport were promoted through serious discussion about race, racism, and privilege.

The finding just mentioned parallels the importance of exploring race in multicultural counseling and therapy (Ridley, 2005). Although the suggestion does not fit for every training relationship, trainers can test its efficacy for each trainee. For instance, trainees may have deep-seated fears and anxieties stemming from their minority experience. Their fears and anxieties may serve as impasses to a constructive relationship. By initiating discussion about race and racism, demonstrating sensitivity to trainees' concerns, and making themselves vulnerable in these difficult conversations, trainers set the tone for students to lower their defenses, see cultural competence modeled for them, and take calculated risks to develop themselves personally and professionally.

Develop Cultural Self-Awareness

Cultural self-awareness has been a consistent professional dictum, and it clearly applies to the trainer-trainee relationship (Alvarez et al., 2009). Trainers need to determine if they harbor unexamined biases, prejudices, and attitudes that might interfere with a constructive relationship with their trainees. Alvarez and colleagues (2009) specifically asked graduate school mentors to reflect on these questions: "How do I think about myself racially and culturally? How have I been socialized and what assumptions do I make about my mentee's community? What is my understanding and experience with oppression?" (p. 185).

Cultural self-awareness is critical to trainers' capacity for competently engaging in discussions of race and racism. The process of becoming culturally self-aware normally is seldom easy. Airhihenbuwa (1995) made this point when he stated that the essence of multiculturalism is becoming comfortable with being uncomfortable. The most helpful step trainers can take is to seek out critical feedback from a professional who has expertise in multicultural issues.

Behave Ethically Relative to Multiculturalism

As indicated in the definition, cultural competence requires the incorporation of cultural data in the training relationship. Ethically appropriate trainers, then, have a *multicultural responsibility* in which they fuse "personal and professional commitments

to consider culture during all ethical encounters" (Ridley, Liddle, Hill, & Li, 2001, p. 176). This responsibility accords with Principle E: Respect for People's Rights and Dignity of the Ethical Principles of Psychologists and Code of Conduct of the American Psychological Association. "Psychologists are aware of and respect cultural, individual, and role differences…" (APA, 2010, p. 4). Among the various differences listed are race, ethnicity, and culture. On this subject, Schlosser and Foley (2008) discuss a number of ethical issues in multicultural trainer-trainee relationships. Four in particular are concerned with cultural considerations.

Multiple relationships. Some scholars contend that the effective training of trainees of color requires engaging them both within and outside of the training program (Brown et al., 1999). But interaction in nontraining venues carries an inherent ethical risk: the development of inappropriate multiple relationships. Trainers must be cautious at all times. On the one hand, they must consider the advantage of creating opportunities where trainees of color feel comfortable with the quantity and quality of interpersonal interactions (Johnson & Nelson, 1999). On the other hand, they must avoid making trainees feel exploited, crossing relationship boundaries, and participating in activities that impair their judgment.

Avoiding harm. Training in general can be intense. Both trainers and trainees can find intensity in these experiences. Perhaps, sexual attraction poses the most salient threat to trainers abusing their power, sexualizing a training relationship, and causing harm to a trainee. Ethical standards mandate that professionals do not have sexual intimacies (APA, 2010). However, the sexualizing of a training relationship is exacerbated by racial and cultural myths, fantasies, and media presentations. These dynamics increase the possibility of sexual attraction in cross-cultural trainer-trainee relationships.

Unfair discrimination. Trainees typically have one trainer, whereas trainers typically have many trainees. The sheer logistical imbalance opens the door for possible unequal access of trainees to trainers and favoritism. Nevertheless, unfair discrimination on the basis of cultural variables such as age, gender, race, religion, and ability status clearly is prohibited by the APA Ethics Code (APA, 2010). Several cultural issues have the potential of leading to unfair discrimination: (a) underperformance due to negative stereotypes (Steele, 1997), (b) training only of trainees who remind trainers of themselves (Blackburn, Chapman, & Cameron, 1981), and

(c) holding negative stereotypes about certain races (Schlosser, 2006).

Boundaries of competence. Due to some trainers' limited experiences with some racial groups, they may be seen as crossing boundaries of competence. This may pose an ethical dilemma for trainers. Their backgrounds may work against their cultural competence. However, their rationale for preferring homogeneous relationships may lead to unfair discrimination. To resolve this dilemma, trainers should obtain the essential training, experience, consultation, or supervision as mandated in Standard 2.01 of the APA Ethic Code.

Put Racial/Ethnic Matching into its Proper Perspective

Should trainers advise or supervise trainees with whom they share a racial, ethnic, or cultural background? An extension of the question is this: To what extent does training across race, ethnicity, and culture make a difference in the efficacy of the relationship? These questions underlie the matching model in trainer-trainee relationships.

The primary assumption underlying the matching model is that cultural competence is derived from the common sociocultural experiences, in this case those of the trainer and trainee (Mollen, Ridley, & Hill, 2003). It is further presumed that the common sociocultural experiences make it possible for trainers to identify and empathize with their trainees. Accordingly, such identification and empathy would be more difficult to achieve for trainers who are unmatched with their trainees. Two secondary assumptions logically follow. First, competence is independent of training. All trainers need is the common experience with trainees, something they acquire simply through living. Second, competence requires membership in trainee's racial, ethnic, or cultural group. By implication, competence is impossible to acquire in heterogeneous relationships.

Research on cultural matching is inconclusive. Chung, Bemak, and Talleyrand (2007) found that most of the minority graduate students in their study did not indicate a preference for the race or ethnicity in choosing a mentor. On the other hand, Blake-Beard et al. (2011) found that having a faculty mentor of one's race was somewhat important and that students reported receiving more help when they were matched. However, as previously noted, matching by race has still not been found to affect training outcomes (Blake-Beard et al., 2011).

Two People in a Relationship: Consequences of Trainees with Problems of Professional Competence in the Domain of Individual and Cultural Diversity

Sometimes trainees put a careful, culturally minded trainer in an uncomfortable position. Here race-related issues can be confused with issues of trainee development and performance. A trainee with problems of professional competence (TPPC) may exhibit a lag in the development of behaviors, attitudes, and skills for a healthy training relationship and adequate cultural competency (Elman & Forrest, 2007; Shen-Miller et al., 2012). However, as nonabusive trainers are mindful of wielding their power appropriately, confronting a competency-stunted trainee can be difficult when they are trying to respect power differentials and issues of race as well. This concluding comment briefly highlights the difficulties trainers might face when working with a trainee who exhibits poor cultural competency and steps trainers could take to ensure positive trainee outcomes.

The TPPC has no uniform identity. Trainees of any race, gender, sexual orientation, or religion can exhibit poor cultural competency and difficulty understanding how their backgrounds can affect the trainer-trainee relationship. A resulting challenge for the trainer is to understand how to address trainee incompetence in a culturally sensitive way without succumbing to a "walking on eggshells" emotional experience. In addition, trainers have reported that racial and ethnic differences between them and their trainees complicate evaluative decisions of trainees' performance (Shen-Miller et al., 2012; Gizara & Forrest, 2004; Vacha-Hasse, 1995). Methods to aid a trainer in this sensitive position are still debated. Many polarized arguments still exist on how to best address the TPPC.

Two such arguments, taken to their most extreme, include whether a trainer should take a culture-attentive approach or a colorblind approach. A culture-attentive approach may create discrimination or hyperattention toward trainees of different races, while a colorblind approach can result in over protection and an application of differing professional standards to trainees of color (Shen-Miller et al., 2012). Although a proper approach may lie somewhere in between the two extremes, trainers have reported that having an openness to explore cultures and identify biases between other trainers are helpful in "...covering for each other's blind spots'" (Shen-Miller et al., 2012, p. 1196). This demands a degree of vulnerability. By opening the door for race-power conversations, trainers risk exposing their deficits in multicultural awareness and competency to their colleagues.

Overall, trainers should not be surprised to one day encounter a TPPC whose difficulties are manifested vis-á -vis individual and cultural diversity, and although methods for raising cultural competency in the trainee are still developing, acknowledging racial differences remains crucial to both trainer and trainee growth. Trainers who do not develop their cultural awareness, develop their skill with multicultural populations, or increase their knowledge on inter-race interactions heighten the risk for ignoring the relevance of race when deciding how to approach the TPPC (Shen-Miller et al., 2012). Attention should be paid to the growing research on this topic because it highlights a problematic trainer-trainee dynamic that has yet to be fully resolved.

The Big Picture: Power, Diversity, and Student Outcomes

Although it is impossible to tell where any trainer-trainee relationship will "float," this chapter strongly emphasizes the role of proper power dynamics and cultural competency in how the metaphorical current flows. According to Creighton et al. (2008), graduating trainees frequently attribute their success and accomplishments to a healthy, positive trainer who facilitated personal, social, attitudinal, and scholarly development throughout their training program. Having a sense of support, acceptance and encouragement from a nonabusive trainer can greatly relieve trainee stress, provide them with confidence and encourage self-efficacy. Always remaining vigilant to differences in race between the trainer-trainee and taking active steps by both parties to enrich their cultural competency also allows for such positive outcomes to occur. Overall, power is a necessary component in the training relationship and can lead to high-quality productivity, work satisfaction, and interpersonal growth. To achieve these outcomes, trainers must use their power responsibly and with constant vigilance to invaluable cultural differences.

Note

1. To avoid awkward writing, we use the words *trainers* and *trainees* in this paper. We use the word *trainer* synonymously with the words *advisors, instructors, supervisors, professors, research directors*, and any other mentors. We use the word trainee synonymously with the words *students, advisees, trainees, supervisees, protégés, research assistants*, and other mentees.

References

Airhihenbuwa, C. O. (1995). *Health and culture: Beyond the western paradigm*. Thousand Oaks, California: Sage.

Allen, T. D., Day, E. L., & Lentz, E. (2005). The role of interpersonal comfort in mentoring relationships. *Journal of Career Development, 31*(3), 155–169. doi: 10.1177/ 089484530503100301

Allen, T. D., Schockley, K. M., Poteat, L. (2010). Protégé anxiety attachment and feedback in mentoring relationships. *Journal of Vocational Behavior, 77*(1), 73–80. http://dx.doi.org.lib-ezproxy.tamu.edu:2048/10.1016/j.jvb.2010.02.007

Alvarez, A. N., Blume, A. W., Cervantes, J. M., & Thomas, L. R. (2009). Tapping the wisdom tradition: Essential elements to mentoring students of color. *Professional Psychology: Research and Practice, 40*(2), 181–188. doi:10.1037/a0012256

American Psychological Association. (2002). *Guidelines on Multicultural Education, Training, Research, Practice, and Organizational Change for Psychologists*. Washington, DC: Author.

American Psychological Association. (2005). *Report of the 2005 Presidential Task Force on Evidence-Based Practice*. Washington, DC: Author.

American Psychological Association (2007). *Guidelines and principles for accreditation of programs in professional psychology*. Washington, DC: Author.

American Psychological Association, Office of Minority Affairs (2008). *A portrait of success and challenge—Progress report: 1997–2005*. Washington, DC: Author.

American Psychological Association. (2010). *Ethical principles of psychologists and code of conduct*. Washington, DC: Author.

Atkinson, D. E., Neville, H., & Casas, A. (1991). The mentorship of ethnic minorities in professional psychology. *Professional Psychology: Research and Practice, 22*, 336–338. doi:10.1037/0735–7028.22.4.336

Blackburn, R. T., Chapman, D. W., & Cameron, S. M. (1981). "Cloning" in academe: Mentorship and academic careers. *Research in Higher Education, 15*(4), 315–327. doi: 10.1007/BF00973512

Blake-Beard, S., Bayne, M. L., Crosby, F. J., & Muller, C. B. (2011). Matching by race and gender in mentoring relationships: Keeping our eyes on the prize. *Journal of Social Issues, 67*(3), 622–643. doi: 10.1111/j.1540–4560.2011.01717.x

Boyle, P. & Boice, B. (1998). *Best practices for enculturation: Collegiality, mentoring and structure*. Thousand Oaks, CA: Jossey-Bass.

Boysen, G. A., Vogel, D. L., Cope, M. A, & Hubbard, A. (2009). Incidents of bias in college classrooms: Instructor and student perceptions. *Journal of Diversity in Higher Education, 2*, 219–231. http://dx.doi.org.lib-ezproxy.tamu.edu:2048/10.1037/a0017538

Brown, R. (1965). *Social Psychology*. New York: Free Press.

Brown, R. T., Daly, B. P., & Leong, F. T. L. (2009). Mentoring in research: A developmental approach. *Professional Psychology: Research and Practice, 40*(3), 306–313. http://dx.doi.org.lib-ezproxy.tamu.edu:2048/10.1037/a0011996

Burnes, T. R., Wood, J., Inman, J., & Welikson, G. (2013). An investigation of process variables in feminist group clinical supervision. *The Counseling Psychologist, 41*(1), 86–109. doi:10.1177/0011000012442653

Castelfranchi, C. (2003). Available at SSRN: http://ssrn.com/abstract=1829901 or http://dx.doi.org/10.2139/ssrn.1829901.

Chan, A. W. (2008). Mentoring ethnic minority, pre-doctoral students: An analysis of key mentor practices. *Mentoring*

& *Tutoring: Partnership in Learning, 16*(3), 263–277. doi:10.1080/13611260802231633

Chung, R. C.-Y., Bemak, F., & Talleyrand, R. (2007). Mentoring within the field of counseling: A preliminary study of multicultural perspective. *International Journal for the Advancement of Counseling, 29*, 21–32.

Clark, R. A., Harden, S. L., & Johnson, W. B. (2000). Mentor relationships in clinical psychology doctoral training: Results of a national survey. *Teaching of Psychology, 27*(4), 262–268. doi:10.1207/S15328023TOP2704_04

Constantine, M. G., Smith, L., Redington, R. M., & Owens, D. (2008). Racial microaggressions against black counseling and counseling psychology faculty: A central challenge in the multicultural counseling movement. *Journal of Counseling & Development, 86*(3), 348–355. doi:10.1002/j.1556-6678.2008.tb00519.x

Creighton, T., Parks, D., & Creighton, L. (2008). *Mentoring doctoral students: The need for a pedagogy.* Retrieved from http://cnx.org/content/m14516/1.3/

Cynkar, A. (November, 2007). Clinch your graduate school acceptance. *gradPSYCH Magazine.* Retrieved from http://www.apa.org/gradpsych/2007/11/cover-acceptance.aspx

Davids, A. & Brenner, D. (1971). Competition and the premedical student. *Journal of Consulting and Clinical Psychology, 37*(1), 67–72. http://dx.doi.org.lib-ezproxy.tamu.edu:2048/10.1037/h0031307

Davidson, M. N. & Foster-Johnson, L. F. (2001). Mentoring in the preparation of graduate researchers of color. *Review of Educational Research, 71*(4), 549–574. doi:10.3102/00346543071004549

Deschamps, J. C. (1982). Social identity and relations of power between groups. In H. Tajfel (Ed.). *Social identity and intergroup relations* (pp. 85–98). New York: Cambridge University Press.

Dovidio, J. F. & Gaertner, S. L. (2000). Aversive racism and selection decisions: 1989–1999. *Psychological Science, 11*(4), 315–319. doi:10.1111/1467-9280.00262

Elman, N. S., & Forrest, L. (2007). From trainee impairment to professional competence problems: Seeking terminology that facilitates effective action. *Professional Psychology: Research and Practice, 38*(5), 501–509. http://dx.doi.org.lib-ezproxy.tamu.edu:2048/10.1037/0735-7028.38.5.501

Emerson, R. M. (1962). Power-dependence relations. *American Sociological Review, 27*(1), 31–41.

Falender, C. A., Burnes, T. R., & Ellis, M. V. (2013). Multicultural clinical supervision and benchmarks: Empirical support informing practice and supervision training. *The Counseling Psychologist, 41*(1), 8–27. doi:10.1177/0011000012438417

Fiske, S. T. (1993). Controlling other people: The impact of power on stereotyping. *American Psychologist, 48*(6), 621–628. http://dx.doi.org.lib-ezproxy.tamu.edu:2048/10.1037/0003-066X.48.6.621

Foo-Kune, N. W. R. & Rodolfa, E. R. (2013). Putting the benchmarks into practice: Multiculturally competent supervisors—effective supervision. *The Counseling Psychologist, 41*(1), 121–130. doi:10.1177/0011000012453944

Fouad, N. A., Grus, C. L., Hatcher, R. L., Kaslow, N. J. Hutchings, P. S., Madson, M.,...Crossman, R. E. (2009). Competency benchmarks: A developmental model for understanding and measuring competence in professional psychology. *Training and Education in Professional Psychology, 3*(4), S5–S26. doi: 10.1037/a0015832.

Friere, P. (2000). *Pedagogy of the oppressed* (30th anniversary ed.; M.B. Ramos, Trans.). New York: Continuum.

Gizara, S. S., & Forrest, L. (2004). Supervisors' experiences of trainee impairment and incompetence at APA-accredited internship sites. *Professional Psychology, 35*(2), 131–140. http://dx.doi.org.lib-ezproxy.tamu.edu:2048/10.1037/0735-7028.35.2.131

Gonzáez, C. (2006). When is a mentor like a monk? *Academe, 92*(3), 29–32.

Goodman, D. J. (2001). *Promoting diversity and social justice: Educating people from privileged groups.* Thousand Oaks, CA: Sage.

Greenhaus, J. H., & Parasuaman, S. (1993). Job performance attributions and career advancement prospects: An examination of gender and race effects. *Organizational Behavior and Human Decision Processes, 55*(2), 273–297. http://dx.doi.org.lib-ezproxy.tamu.edu:2048/10.1006/obhd.1993.1034

Hamilton, D. L. & Trolier, T. K. (1986). Stereotypes and stereotyping: An overview of the cognitive approach. In J. F. Dovidio & S. L. Gaertner (Eds.). *Prejudice discrimination, and racism* (pp. 127–163). Orlando, FL: Academic Press.

Helms, J. E. (1984). Toward a theoretical explanation of the effects of race on counseling: A Black and White model. *The Counseling Psychologist, 12*(4), 153–165. doi:10.1177/0011000084124013

Hoffer, T. B., Hess, M., Welch, V., & Williams, K. (2007). *Doctorate recipients from United States Universities: Summary Report 2006.* Chicago: National Opinion Research Center.

Johnson, W. B. (2002). The intentional mentor: Strategies and guidelines for the practice of mentoring. *Professional Psychology: Research and Practice, 33*(1), 88–96. http://dx.doi.org.lib-ezproxy.tamu.edu:2048/10.1037/0735-7028.33.1.88

Johnson, W. B. & Huwe, J. M. (2002). Toward a typology of mentorship dysfunction in graduate school. *Psychotherapy: Theory/Research/Practice/Training, 39*(1), 44–55.

Johnson, W. B. & Nelson, N. (1999). Mentoring relationships in graduate training: Some ethical concerns. *Ethics and Behavior, 9*, 189–210.

Kalbfleisch, P. J. (1997). Appeasing the mentor. *Aggressive Behavior, 23*, 389–403.

Kaslow, N. J., Borden, K. A., Collins, F. L., Jr., Forrest, L., Illfelder-Kaye, J., Nelson, P., & Rallo, J. S. (2004). Competencies conference: Future directions in education and credentialing in professional psychology. *Journal of Clinical Psychology, 60*(7), 699–712. doi:10.1002/jclp.20016

Katz, J. H. & Ivey, A. (1977). White awareness: The frontier of racism awareness training. *Personnel and Guidance Journal, 55*(8), 485–489. doi:10.1002/j.2164-4918.1977.tb04332.x

Keller, T. E. & Pryce, J. M. (2010). Mutual but unequal: Mentoring as a hybrid of familiar relationship roles. *New Directions for Youth Development, 2010*(126), 33–50. doi:0.1002/yd.348

King, J. E. (1991). Dysconscious racism: Ideology, identity, and the miseducation of teachers. *Journal of Negro Education, 60*(2), 133–146.

Manathunga, C. (2007). Supervision as mentoring: The role of power and boundary crossing. *Studies in Continuing Education, 29*(2), 207–221. doi:0.1080/01580370701424650

Mollen, D., Ridley, C. R., & Hill, C. L. (2003). Models of multicultural counseling competence: A critical evaluation. In D. Pope-Davis, H. L. Coleman, W. M. Lui, & R. L. Toprek (Eds.). *Handbook of multicultural counseling competencies* (pp. 21–37). Thousand Oaks, CA: Sage.

Noonan, M. J., Ballinger, R., Black, R. (2007). Peer faculty mentoring in doctoral education: Definitions, experiences, and expectations. *International Journal of Teaching and Learning in Higher Education, 19*(3), 251–262.

Pettigrew, T. F., & Martin, J. (1987). Shaping the organizational context for Black American inclusion. *Journal of Social Issues, 43*(1), 41–78. doi:10.1111/j.1540–560.1987.tb02330.x

Ragins, B. R. (1995). Diversity, power, and mentorship in organizations: A cultural, structural and behavioral perspective. In M. M. Chemers, M. A. Costanzo, & S. Oskamp (Eds.) *Diversity in organizations: New perspectives for a changing workplace* (pp. 91–132). Newbury Park, CA: Sage.

Ragins, B. R. (1997). Diversified mentoring relationships in organizations: A power perspective. *Academy of Management Review, 22*(2), 482–521. doi:10.5465/AMR.1997.9707154067

Ridley, C. R. (2005). *Overcoming unintentional racism in counseling and therapy: A practitioner's guide to intentional intervention* (2nd ed.). Thousand Oaks, CA: Sage.

Ridley, C. R., Liddle, M. C., Hill, C. L., & Li, L. C. (2001). Ethical decision making in multicultural counseling. In J. G. Ponterotto, J.M. Casas, L.A. Suzuki, & C.M. Alexander (Eds.). *Handbook of multicultural counseling* (2nd ed., pp.165–188). Thousand Oaks, CA: Sage.

Ridley, C. R., Mendoza, D. W., Kanitz, B. E. (1994). Multicultural training: Reexamination, operationalization, and integration. *The Counseling Psychologist, 22*(2), 227–289. doi:10.1177/0011000094222001

Ridley, C. R., Mollen, D., & Kelly, S. M. (2011). Beyond microskills: Toward a model of counseling competence. *The Counseling Psychologist, 39*(6), 825–864. doi:10.1177/0011000010378440

Ryan, W. (1971). *Blaming the victim.* New York: Pantheon.

Schlosser, L. Z. (2006). Affirmative psychotherapy for American Jews. *Psychotherapy: Theory, Research, Practice, Training, 43*(4), 424–435. doi:10.1037/0033–3204.43.4.424

Schlosser, L. Z., & Foley, P. F. (2008). Ethical issues in multicultural student—faculty mentoring relationships in higher education. *Mentoring & Tutoring: Partnership in Learning, 16*(1), 63–75. doi:10.1080/13611260701801015

Shen-Miller, D. S., Forrest, L., & Burt, M. (2012). Contextual influences on faculty diversity conceptualizations when working with trainee competence problems. *The Counseling Psychologist, 40*(8), 1181–1219. doi:10.1177/0011000011431832

Steele, C. M. (1997). A threat in the air: How stereotypes shape intellectual identity and performance. *American Psychologist, 52*, 613–629. http://dx.doi.org/10.1016/j.jesp.2007.07.005

Sue, D. W., Capodilupo, C. M., Torino, G. C. Bucceri, J. M., Holder, A. M. B., Nadal, K. L., & Esquilin, M. E.(2007). *Racial microaggressions in everyday life: Implications for clinical practice. American Psychologist, 62*, 271–286. doi: 10.1037/0003–066X.62.4.271

Sue, D. W., & Sue, D. (2012). *Counseling the culturally diverse: Theory and practice* (6th ed.). Hoboken, NJ: Wiley.

Tajfel, H., & Turner, J. C. (1985). The social identity theory of intergroup behavior. In S. Worchel & W. G. Austin (Eds.), *Psychology of intergroup relations* (pp. 7–24). Chicago: Nelson-Hall.

Thomas, D. A. (1990). The impact of race on managers' experiences of developmental relationships (mentoring and sponsorship): An intraorganizational study. *Journal of Organizational Behavior, 11*(6), 479–492.http://dx.doi.org.lib-ezproxy.tamu.edu:2048/10.1002/job.4030110608

Thomas, D. A. (1993). Racial dynamics in cross-race developmental relationships. *Administrative Science Quarterly, 38*(2), 169–194.

Vacha-Hasse, T. (1995). *Impaired graduate students in APA-accredited clinical, counseling, and school psychology programs* (Unpublished doctoral dissertation). Texas A&M University, College Station.

Webster, D. W., Sedlacek, W. E., & Miyares, J. (1979). A comparison of problems perceived by minority and White university students. *Journal of College Student Personnel, 20*(2), 165–170.

Wellman, D. (1977). *Portraits of White racism.* New York: Cambridge University Press.

Wong, L. C. J., Wong, P. T. P., & Ishiyama, F. I. (2013). What helps and what hinders in cross-cultural clinical supervision: A critical incident study. *The Counseling Psychologist, 41*(1), 66–85. doi:10.1177/0011000012442652

Sexual Identity Issues in Education and Training for Professional Psychologists

Joseph R. Miles *and* Ruth E. Fassinger

Abstract

Ethical and professional guidelines in psychology highlight the importance of psychologists having competence regarding issues related to sexual orientation and gender identity. Thus, sexual orientation and gender identity should be addressed in education and training in psychology just as are any other aspect of diversity (e.g., age, ethnicity, gender, race, religion, social class). This chapter reviews key terminology and conceptual issues regarding sexual orientation and gender identity, and then uses the framework of multicultural competence in psychology (e.g., Sue, et al. 1982; Sue, Arredondo, & McDavis, 1992) to examine how knowledge, skills, and attitudes about lesbian, gay, bisexual, and transgender (LGBT) individuals may be incorporated into education and training in psychology. It then discusses several administrative concerns related to LGBT issues in accredited programs in professional psychology, including "Footnote 4" and conscience clauses. It concludes with a discussion of additional training considerations, including the mentoring of LGBT students.

Key Words: bisexual, gay, gender identity, lesbian, sexual orientation, transgender

Introduction

Through their roles as scientists, practitioners, educators, and advocates, psychologists play central roles in producing knowledge about sexual orientation, gender identity, and mental health; developing public policies affecting lesbian, gay, bisexual, and transgender (LGBT) individuals and families; and providing mental health services for LGBT individuals. Therefore, like other aspects of diversity (e.g., [dis]ability, age, ethnicity, nationality, race, religion and spirituality, social class), sexual orientation and gender identity are significant considerations in the education and training of psychologists.

Ethical principles and other professional guidelines set forth by the American Psychological Association (APA), the largest professional organization for psychologists, underscore the importance of developing and maintaining competence with regard to sexual orientation and gender identity.

For example, APA's (2010) *Ethical Principles of Psychologists and Code of Conduct* (hereafter referred to as *Ethical Principles*) states:

> Where scientific or professional knowledge...establishes that an understanding of factors associated with age, gender, *gender identity*, race, ethnicity, culture, national origin, religion, *sexual orientation*, disability, language or socioeconomic status is essential for effective implementation of their services or research, psychologists have or obtain the training, experience, consultation or supervision necessary to ensure the competence of their services, or they make appropriate referrals, except as provided in Standard 2.02, Providing Services in Emergencies. (p. 5; emphasis added)

Similarly, *Guiding Principle E: Respect for People's Rights and Dignity* of the *Ethical Principles* (APA, 2010) states that psychologists should be "aware of and respect cultural, individual, and role differences," including those associated with gender identity and sexual orientation, and that psychologists should "try to eliminate the effect on their work of biases based on [these] factors, and they do not knowingly participate in or condone activities of others based upon such prejudices" (p. 4).

Regarding clinical practice, APA's Division 44 (the *Society for the Psychological Study of Lesbian, Gay, Bisexual, and Transgender Issues*) and the *Committee on Lesbian, Gay, and Bisexual Concerns Joint Task Force* (APA, 2012c) have developed guidelines for affirmative psychological practice with lesbian, gay, and bisexual (LGB) clients. The APA has also urged "all mental health professionals to take the lead in removing the stigma of mental illness that has long been associated with homosexual orientations," condemning public and private discrimination on the basis of sexual orientation (Conger, 1975, p. 633). In addition, an APA *Task Force on Psychotherapy Guidelines for Transgender and Gender Non-Conforming Clients* currently is working on similar guidelines for affirmative psychological practice with transgender and gender nonconforming clients (APA, 2012a).

These ethical and professional guidelines highlight the fact that "multicultural competence" in psychology (Sue, et al. 1982; Sue, Arredondo, & McDavis, 1992) has come to include knowledge, skills, and attitudes related to sexual orientation and gender identity (e.g., see Lowe & Mascher, 2001) in addition to other aspects of diversity (e.g., [dis] ability, age, ethnicity, gender, nationality, race, religion, and social class). As such, this chapter focuses on issues related to sexual orientation and gender identity in education and training in psychology. We begin by discussing important contextual issues related to sexual orientation and gender identity. We then explore the development of LGBT competence in terms of necessary knowledge, skills, and attitudes (Sue et al., 1982; Sue et al., 1992). Next, we discuss APA accreditation of professional programs in psychology as related to LGBT issues, and we conclude with a discussion of additional programmatic considerations in education and training.

We acknowledge at the outset of this chapter that the field of LGBT psychology is rapidly evolving. Within the past 40 years, great advances have been made within psychology regarding the knowledge, skills, and attitudes necessary for affirmative work with LGBT individuals (Garnets, 2007), and the status of LGBT issues in the public domain is rapidly changing. For example, the year preceding the writing of this chapter has seen the repeal of the "Don't Ask, Don't Tell" policy in the United States military (American Forces Press Service, 2011), the adoption of a constitutional amendment opposing same-sex marriage in North Carolina (Robertson, 2012), and the endorsement of same-sex marriage for the first time by a sitting president (Calmes & Baker, 2012) and the voting public (in Maine and Maryland; Eckholm, 2012). Therefore, as with any aspect of diversity, we encourage psychologists to maintain current knowledge of issues facing LGBT communities, and of the psychological research and theory on LGBT issues, in order to remain aware of state-of-the-art developments in this evolving field.

Contextual Issues Regarding Sexual Orientation and Gender Identity
Language and Language Use

Smith et al. (2012) pointed out that consideration of language around sexual orientation and gender identity is important because language is "not merely descriptive, but constitutive" (p. 387). That is, the language that psychologists use "reinforce[s] and 'write[s]' societal notions of appropriate roles and behaviors," and shapes our approach to research, teaching, clinical practice, and social justice advocacy relating to sexual minorities in both explicit and implicit ways (Fassinger, 2000; Smith et al., 2012). Smith et al. (2012) suggested that language use is an especially crucial consideration in clinical settings, due to the potential for psychologists, even those who identify as "LGBT affirming," to perpetuate heterosexist dominance through the enactment of *micro-aggressions* when working with LGBT clients (e.g., Sue, 2010; Sue et al., 2007). Micro-aggressions are "brief and commonplace daily verbal, behavioral, and environmental indignities, whether intentional or unintentional, that communicate hostile, derogatory, or negative slights and insults to the target group or person" (Sue, 2010, p. 191). In a recent study, self-identified lesbian, gay, bisexual, and queer individuals reported experiencing a variety of sexual orientation-related micro-aggressions in psychotherapy, including expressions of heteronormative bias (Shelton & Delgado-Romero, 2011). (Note that the term *queer* is often used as an umbrella term to describe sexual orientations and gender identities that transgress societal norms. For others, *queer* is a political term that denotes a rejection of traditional sexual identity categories and practices. Historically, this term was used derogatorily to refer to LGBT individuals, but has been reclaimed by many LGBT individuals with a sense of pride and political efficacy). Beyond clinical settings, psychologists may enact micro-aggressions in their research, education, and advocacy efforts through the language that they use. Therefore, appropriate and affirmative language use regarding sexual orientation and gender identity are important topics for education and training programs in psychology. We review here several of the most pertinent language issues in LGBT psychology.

Sexual orientation, as defined in the APA's *Guidelines for Psychological Practice with Lesbian, Gay, and Bisexual Clients*, "refers to the sex of those to whom one is sexually and romantically attracted" (APA, 2012c, p 11). Bohan (1996) notes an important caveat about the term *sexual orientation* is that, "while [it] emphasizes the sexual component of interpersonal relationships, in reality, any sexual orientation involves a wide range of feelings, behaviors, experiences, and commitments" (p. *xvi*). Definitional categories of sexual orientation typically include the discrete categories of *bisexual* women and men, *lesbian* women, *gay* men, and *heterosexual* women and men.

Gender identity is distinct from sexual orientation and refers to one's sense of oneself as a gendered individual (APA, 2011a). Categories of gender identity typically include woman, man, and the broad categories of *transgender* ("an umbrella term for persons whose gender identity, gender expression, or behavior does not conform to that typically associated with the sex to which they were assigned at birth" [APA, 2011a, p. 1) or *cisgender* (i.e., an individual whose gender assigned at birth, typically based on sex organs, is consistent with one's sense of oneself as a woman or man). In addition, some individuals decline to identify with binary categories altogether.

Collectively, LGBT individuals may be referred to as *sexual minorities* in that they share marginalized status in terms of gender identity or sexual orientation (or both). Fassinger and Arseneau (2007) observed that all LGBT people may be considered to be *gender-transgressive* in that they defy traditionally gendered roles, norms, and behaviors (i.e., lesbian, gay, and bisexual individuals transgress norms dictating the sex of intimate partner choices, whereas transgender people violate societal expectations regarding adherence to and expression of norms related to assigned/biological sex). However, there also are key differences between LGB and transgender individuals. The terms *lesbia, gay*, and *bisexual* refer to specific choices regarding intimate partners and claimed social identities that are same-sex oriented, whereas *transgender* refers to a particular expression of gendered roles and behaviors organized around a transgressive social identity that is gendered. The inclusion of T in the acronym LGBT (as reflected in the fairly recent addition of *Transgender* to the official name of Division 44 of the APA, now the *Society for the Psychological Study of Lesbian, Gay, Bisexual, and Transgender Issues*) may lead to the erroneous conflation of sexual orientation and gender identity, but it also reflects shared oppression related to status as gender transgressive sexual minorities (Fassinger & Arseneau, 2007). The *Guidelines for Psychological Practice with Lesbian, Gay, and Bisexual Clients* indicate that psychologists should "strive to *distinguish* issues of sexual orientation from those of gender identity when working with lesbian, gay, and bisexual clients" (emphasis added, APA, 2012c, p. 16). Education and training programs in psychology need to acknowledge both the commonalities and differences in experiences based on sexual orientation and gender identity, and help trainees learn the subtleties of gender transgression in claimed personal and social identities. The APA (2008, 2011a) also offers written materials created for a lay audience answering common questions about sexual orientation and gender identity. Educators and supervisors might also assign readings that explore the commonalities and differences in experience between sexual minorities (e.g., Fassinger & Arseneau, 2007), and strive to create a climate in which open conversation about issues related to sexual orientation and gender identity is encouraged and modeled. We also suggest that both trainers and trainees become familiar with their campus LGBT resource center, which may also offer educational materials or training.

Essentialism and Social Constructionism

Two competing epistemologies complicate the idea that the categories just described are necessary and sufficient for describing sexual orientations and gender identities, and who is represented in the "LGBT community." The first is that of *essentialism*. From an essentialist perspective, categories of sexual orientation and gender identity (as well as other aspects of identity, such as ethnicity and race) are core, "essential" parts of individuals' identities (Bohan, 1996). An essentialist perspective posits that sexual orientation and gender identity can be traced to inherent, immutable qualities of the individual, and assumes that the categories lesbian, gay, bisexual, heterosexual, transgender, cisgender, woman, and man are homogeneous, discrete, and distinguishable from one another, and that they exist across time and place, regardless of sociocultural context (Bohan, 1996; Fassinger, 2000; Fassinger & Arseneau, 2007; Smith et al., 2012). The search for a biological "cause" of sexual orientation (e.g., research focused on a "gay gene") likely would follow from an essentialist epistemology in that it assumes that there is something inherent or innate within an individual that accounts for a lesbian or gay identity. A significant challenge to the essentialist perspective that sexual orientation categories (i.e., bisexual, lesbian, gay, heterosexual) are homogenous, discreet, and distinguishable is posed by research that sheds significant doubt on the notion that sexual orientation is a dichotomous variable, with complete heterosexuality on the one hand, and complete homosexuality on the other (e.g., Kinsey, Pomeroy, & Martin, 1948; Kinsey, Pomeroy, Martin, & Gebhard, 1953).

An alternative to the essentialist epistemology is *social constructionism*. Social constructionism argues that sexual orientation and gender identity are the results of "particular historical and cultural understandings rather than being universal and immutable categories of human experience" (Bohan, 1996, p. *xvi*). From this perspective, sexual orientation and gender identity are not inherent traits or qualities of individuals that reflect core aspects of the individual, but, rather, they represent meaning assigned to certain experiences and behaviors within a particular social, historical, and cultural context. The social constructionist perspective acknowledges temporal and contextual influences on the definitions of sexual orientation and gender identity, and the categories used to label these identities. This suggests that sexual orientation and gender identity have been, are, and will be defined differently in varied social and historical contexts. This is evident in the fact that the origins of the modern label of *homosexuality* can be traced to the late 19th century (Bohan, 1996; Foucault, 1978). This does not imply that same-sex attractions and behaviors did not exist prior to this time, but rather, that at this time, same-sex attraction and behaviors came to denote aspects of *identity* rather than descriptors of behaviors. Similarly, Lev (2007) points out that the current use of the word *transgender* as an umbrella term that includes all gender-variant people (e.g., cross-dressers, transsexuals, male-to-female transsexuals, female-to-male transsexuals, drag queens, feminine gay men, butch lesbians, two-spirit, and intersex people) can be traced to the 1990s, even though gender-variant behavior and expression have been documented across cultures and historical contexts.

The contrasts between the essentialist and social constructionist perspectives have important implications. An essentialist perspective, as reflected, for instance, in song recently made popular in the United States by Lady Gaga, *Born this Way* (Gaga, 2011 track 2), suggests that sexual orientation and gender identity are innate, biological characteristics of individuals that merit the distinction of "protected class" in civil rights legislation (e.g., Fassinger & Arseneau, 2007). However, although most contemporary scholars acknowledge the possibility of some genetic or biological component to sexual orientation and gender identity (e.g., Fassinger & Arseneau), there is no agreement among scientists about the "causes" of *any* sexual orientation or gender identity (APA, 2008).

Alternatively, a social constructionist perspective suggests that, although our categories of sexual orientation and gender identity are ingrained in our beliefs about these identities, they do not represent a singular "truth" about individuals who have been placed in these categories. In advocating for this perspective, sociologist Jeffrey Weeks suggested that, "sexuality, like everything else, attains meaning only in culture" (Weeks, 2011, p. 18). He goes on to explain that:

> We cannot understand the subtleties and complexities of the sexual world if we try to reduce everything to imperatives of Nature, or a particular type of brain or a special gene for this or that behaviour…Even if there were a gay gene it could not possibly explain the varied historical patterning of homosexuality over time, or even within a single culture." (pp. 18–19)

A social constructionist perspective also differs from an essentialist perspective in that it addresses power and privilege associated with different sexual orientation and gender identity categories. That is, rather than representing inherent qualities of individuals who naturally find themselves grouped into different but value-neutral categories of sexual orientation and gender identity, these categories "are written into society and maintained by way of discourses that position individuals and groups in power relations with one another," thereby "promoting social privilege for dominant groups" (Smith et al., 2012, p. 387). By way of example, Bohan (1996) pointed out that there is little concern with "causation" of heterosexual or cisgender identities, as these are dominant social identities and represent the norms by which other sexual orientations and gender identities are judged. She suggested that the continued interest in essentialist "causes" of nondominant (same-sex) sexual orientation (and, we would add, non-conforming gender identity) relates to the maintenance of real differences in privilege and power that accompany these social identities and serve to oppress gender-transgressive sexual minorities. For a more detailed discussion of essentialist and social constructionist epistemologies, we refer readers to a theoretical model by Fassinger and Arseneau (2007) that conceptualizes sexual orientation and gender identity within a temporal context (i.e., age cohort and specific age) and that also incorporates individual differences and cultural orientations.

Psychology and the Social Construction of Sexual Orientation and Gender Identity

Historically, psychology and psychiatry have played important roles in the social construction of sexual orientation and gender identity in the United States. For example, the first publication of the American Psychiatric Association's (1952) *Diagnostic and Statistical Manual*, the field of psychiatry's official classification system of mental disorders, listed "homosexuality" as a mental disorder, reflecting the social and historical zeitgeist, and contributing to the pathologizing and oppression of sexual minorities. Pioneering research by Evelyn Hooker (1957) first began to dismantle the notion that homosexuality is pathological, as she found no discernible differences in psychological adjustment between the gay and heterosexual men drawn from the same well-functioning population (Previous research had sampled gay men from imprisoned and institutionalized populations, but heterosexual men from the general, wellfunctioning population). Hooker's research, and the research of others (e.g., Thompson, McCandless, & Strickland, 1971) led to the eventual removal of "homosexuality" from the *DSM* by the American Psychiatric Association in 1973. In 1975, the APA followed suit, issuing a resolution that supported the removal of "homosexuality" from the *DSM* and urged psychologists to work toward eradicating stigma and discrimination faced by LGB individuals (Conger, 1975). Given that the term *homosexuality* was long used as a diagnosis of mental illness, its ongoing use is problematic. As an alternative, Bohan (1996) suggested the use of the word *homophilic*, pointing out that this term also removes the specific focus on sexuality. The use of the terms *lesbian* and *gay man* are preferred to *homosexual* for similar reasons.

Although the American Psychiatric Association long ago removed "homosexuality" from its classification system for mental disorders, Gender Identity Disorder is still found in the *Diagnostic and Statistical Manual*, 4th edition, text-revision (*DSM-IV*; American Psychiatric Association, 2000). In addition, drafts of the next edition of the *Diagnostic and Statistical Manual (DSM-V)* available at the time of this writing (American Psychiatric Association, 2011) included three diagnoses of Gender Dysphoria (in children, in adolescents and adults, and unspecified). The American Psychiatric Association suggests that the use of the word *dysphoria* implies an "aversive emotional component" (American Psychiatric Association, 2011, Rationale section), and, thus, need not apply to all transgender or gender nonconforming individuals. This also likely will be reflected in the addition of a criterion in the *DSM-V* stating that, "The condition is associated with clinically significant distress or impairment in social, occupational, or other important areas of functioning, or with a significantly increased risk of suffering, such as distress or disability" (American Psychiatric Association, 2011, Proposed Revision section). However, as the APA (2011a) pointed out, gender identity disorder diagnoses are highly controversial. Some argue that gender identity diagnoses are necessary in order to ensure that transgender individuals will have access to care in a U.S. health-care system that often requires a diagnosis in order for services to be covered by insurance companies. However, a large number of psychologists, members of the transgender community, and professional organizations (e.g., World Professional Association for Trans Health [WPATH], 2012b) argue that the labels Gender Identity Disorder *and* Gender Dysphoria inappropriately pathologize gender variance. Although the APA has not articulated a stance against these gender identity disorders (as it did against the diagnosis of "homosexuality"), it has issued a resolution condemning discrimination against individuals on the basis of gender identity and gender expression (APA, 2008).

The revisions of the *DSM* provide clear examples of how psychiatry and psychology continue to play a major role in the social construction of "mental illness," and sexual orientation and gender identity. In order to train psychologists as competent researchers, educators, clinicians, and advocates for LGBT people, training programs must help students to explore and understand the implications of both essentialist and social constructionist perspectives on sexual orientation and gender identity, and their relationships to the perpetuation of a hierarchical status quo characterized by differing levels of social privilege and power. To do this, educators and trainers may consider assigning readings such as Bohan's (1996) *Psychology and Sexual Orientation: Coming to Terms*, or the theoretical model by Fassinger and Arseneau (2007), both of which deal extensively with the concepts of essentialism and social constructionism as related to sexual minority individuals. Additionally, educators and trainers should encourage and model open conversation around epistemologies related to social identities (including sexual orientation and gender identity).

Diverse and Intersecting Identities

Another crucial consideration regarding sexual orientation and gender identity is the diversity within the LGBT community, and the fact that these social identities intersect and interact with one another, as well as with other social identities such as ethnicity, race, and social class (Bieschke, Hardy, Fassinger & Croteau, 2008; Greene, 1997, 2007; Moradi, DeBlaere & Huang, 2010). Therefore, it is important for training and education programs in psychology to emphasize the diversity of identities and experiences within LGBT communities. For example, although both lesbian women and gay men may experience heterosexism on the basis of a homophilic sexual orientation, lesbian women also experience oppression on the basis of their gender (i.e., *sexism*), whereas gay men enjoy male privilege in a patriarchal, male-dominated society. For LGBT people of color, racism and White privilege are likely to compound prejudice related to sexual orientation and gender identity. The experiences of a Black lesbian should not be assumed to be similar to those of a White lesbian, for instance, despite a shared sexual orientation and gender. Bisexual individuals may share *with* lesbians and gay men the experience of oppression by heterosexuals on the basis of their sexual orientation (i.e., *biphobia*), but also may experience prejudice *from* lesbians and gay men, who may resent the ability of bisexual individuals to enjoy heterosexual privilege (Diehl & Ochs, 2000).

The conflation of sexual orientation and gender identity often obscures the fact that transgender individuals may be of any sexual orientation. Thus, transgender individuals may identify as lesbian, gay, bisexual, or as heterosexual. And, just as bisexual individuals can experience oppression from both within and outside of LGBT communities, transgender individuals, too, may experience oppression

based on their gender identity (i.e., *antitransgender prejudice*) from both heterosexual and LGB people because they so strongly challenge deeply socialized gender norms and roles. In addressing some of the similarities and differences among categories of sexual orientation and gender identity, the APA (2012c) *Guidelines for Psychological Practice with Lesbian, Gay, and Bisexual Clients* specifically have addressed the need for psychologists to attend to the unique experiences of bisexual individuals (*Guideline 5*), as well as to understand the important differences between sexual orientation and gender identity (*Guideline 6*).

Cole (2009) pointed out that psychologists have been slow to attend to *intersectionality*, or the "meaning and consequences of multiple categories of social identity group membership" (p. 170), including a critical examination of the hierarchical social structures and the systems of privilege and oppression that these structures reproduce. Similarly, many scholars have noted that, until recently, much of the psychological research on sexual minority individuals drew from White, male, middle-class, educated, able-bodied samples, and may not be generalizable to all LGB individuals (e.g., Bieschke et al., 2008; Moradi et al., 2010).

The APA (2012c) *Guidelines for Psychological Practice with Lesbian, Gay, and Bisexual Clients* exhort psychologists to strive to recognize and consider unique challenges, experiences, norms, values, and beliefs of LGB people of color (*Guideline 11*); LGB individuals from different religious and spiritual backgrounds (*Guideline 12*); LGB individuals from different age cohorts (*Guideline 13*); LGB youth (*Guideline 14*); LGB people with disabilities (*Guideline 15*), and LGB individuals from different socio-economic classes (*Guideline 17*). Also related to issues of diversity, the *Guidelines* state that psychologists should strive to recognize the impact of HIV/AIDS on LGB individuals and communities (*Guideline 16*).

The need to address intersections of sexual orientation, gender identity, and other social identities is reflected in other APA practice guidelines. The (2002) *Guidelines on Multicultural Education, Training, Research, Practice, and Organizational Change for Psychologists*, for example, which tend to focus on race and ethnicity, also acknowledge that "multiculturalism" and "diversity" encompass a wide scope of identities, including ability status, age, education, ethnicity, gender, language, nationality, race, religion/spirituality, social class, and sexual orientation; and that "to effectively help clients, to effectively train students to be most effective as agents of change and as scientists, psychologists are encouraged to be familiar with issues of these multiple identities within and between individuals" (APA, 2002, p. 10). Other practice guidelines to aid in competent clinical work across a number of multiple social identities include (but are not limited to) the *Guidelines for Psychological Practice with Girls and Women* (APA, 2007), the *Guidelines for Psychological Practice with Older Adults* (APA, 2004), and the *Guidelines for Assessment of and Intervention with Persons with Disabilities* (APA, 2012b).

Psychology training programs should help students understand that gender identity and sexual orientation represent only one part of LGBT individuals' complex social identities, and that other aspects of social identity (e.g., race, social class) shape the ways in which they experience their gender identity and/or sexual orientation. In order to accomplish this, readings may be assigned in psychology courses that examine the experiences of LGBT individuals of different ages, ethnicities, genders, nationalities, races, religions, and social classes to help students explore within and between group differences. In addition, we refer readers to an excellent introduction to the topic of *intersectionality* by Cole (2009). Again, educators and trainers should also encourage and model open and honest conversation about issues related to sexual orientation, gender identity, and other forms of diversity in courses and supervision.

Developing LGBT Competence through Education and Training in Psychology

Education and training pertaining to LGBT issues in psychology have been characterized as inadequate across several decades, despite fairly radical social change regarding LGBT issues (e.g., Buhrke & Douce, 1991; Croteau, Bieschke, Phillips, & Lark, 1998; Lyons, Bieschke, Dendy, Worthington, & Georgemiller 2010). This may be, in part, because the literature on multicultural counseling (which often focuses on racial and ethnic identities) and the literature on LGBT counseling have developed somewhat separately from one another (until fairly recently), and educators may feel forced into choices about what to include in already-cramped curricula (Israel & Selvidge, 2003). However, as Israel and Selvidge pointed out, models of multicultural competence and LGBT competence in psychology work well to complement one another. Multicultural competence in psychology typically is characterized as *knowledge*

(e.g., culture-specific knowledge about various cultural groups), *skills* (e.g., ability to respond verbally and nonverbally in manners appropriate to the cultures of one's clients), and *attitudes* (e.g., awareness of one's own cultural identities, values, beliefs, and biases) (Sue, et al. 1982; Sue, Arredondo, & McDavis, 1992), all of which are also elements of appropriate work with LGBT people. More recent conceptualizations of multicultural competence do, in fact, include LGBT issues as an important aspect of multicultural competence in psychology (e.g., Lowe & Mascher, 2001; Lyons et al., 2010), and (as noted earlier) the APA (2002) *Guidelines on Multicultural Education, Training, Research, Practice, and Organizational Change for Psychologists* reinforce the inclusion of a wide range of social identities as "multicultural."

Professional guidelines highlight the need for education and training programs in psychology to incorporate knowledge, skills, and attitudes relevant to LGBT issues into their curricula and training experiences, in order to train multiculturally competent and ethical psychologists. For example, in the APA's (2012c) *Guidelines for Psychological Practice with Lesbian, Gay, and Bisexual Clients*, *Guideline 19* states, "Psychologists strive to include lesbian, gay, and bisexual issues in professional education and training" (p. 25), and *Guideline 20* states, "Psychologists are encouraged to increase their knowledge and understanding of homosexuality and bisexuality through continuing education, training, supervision, and consultation" (p. 26). The *Guidelines* suggest that "key areas" with which psychologists should be familiar include: sexuality across the life span; the impact of social stigma; identity development and coming out; same-sex relationship dynamics; religious/spiritual issues for LGB individuals; family issues (i.e., family of origin and family of choice); career and work issues; and coping strategies. As noted previously, similar guidelines for psychological practice with transgender and gender nonconforming clients also are forthcoming (APA, 2012a), and will provide training programs with additional guidance in an area in which faculty and students may have little preparation or knowledge.

An in-depth review of the foundational elements needed for competent work in LGBT psychology is well beyond the scope of this chapter. However, in the following sections, we briefly highlight how *knowledge* of LGBT issues; *skills* in affirmative clinical work, research, and advocacy; and *attitudes* (including developing an awareness of one's own and societal heterosexism and transgender biases) may be incorporated into psychology education and training programs.

Knowledge

The first of the three aspects of multicultural competence in psychology, "knowledge" (Sue, et al. 1982; Sue, Arredondo, & McDavis, 1992), suggests that curricula in psychology should incorporate content knowledge on LGBT issues. This includes sexual and gender identity development and "coming out," as well as issues related to stigma, mental health, and well-being of LGBT individuals (e.g., the impacts of heterosexism and antitransgender prejudice on LGBT individuals). The APA (2012c) *Guidelines for Psychological Practice with Lesbian, Gay, and Bisexual Clients* provides an excellent "mini" literature review and many key references to the knowledge base in LGBT psychology, and should be consulted. We briefly review several of the most important concepts here.

LGBT development. Sexual and gender identity development are a natural starting place in education and training for several reasons. First, identity development is a critical part of the life experiences of those with whom psychology students will eventually work in a variety of roles (i.e., as therapists, educators, advocates, researchers). It also is imperative that educators and administrators of psychology training programs have a sense of the processes that LGBT students themselves may be experiencing. Research has shown that negotiation of sexual identity development consume emotional and cognitive resources, which may leave individuals at various stages of their identity development processes with fewer resources to negotiate other developmental tasks, such as education and career development (e.g., Hetherington, 1991; Schmidt & Nilsson, 2006). In addition, LGBT individuals may experience unique stressors as they negotiate their identities in educational settings and workplaces characterized by heterosexist/transphobic individuals and institutional policies. As members of marginalized and stigmatized social identity groups, LGBT students need positive role models and mentoring to help them negotiate their educational and career development in the context of a predominantly heterosexist and transphobic society. Role models and mentors can be well-informed faculty and/or supervisors of any sexual orientation or gender identity.

Stage models of sexual orientation identity development have been promulgated for more than three decades (e.g., Cass, 1980). Early models were based on racial identity development models, which focused on claiming and becoming proud of a stigmatized identity. However, these models have been criticized for being too confining and limited (e.g., Bohan, 1996; Fassinger & McCarn, 1996; Fassinger & Miller, 1996). Not all LGBT individuals pass through all the stages (and certainly not at the same time or in the same way), and stage models do not capture the fluid nature of sexual orientation (particularly for women; Fassinger & Arseneau, 2008). Moreover, the models assume that "coming out" is the "epitome of healthy identity development" (Bohan, 1996, p. 110), but public disclosure of identity is bound so strongly by cultural and contextual variables (e.g., ethnic communities, workplaces) that viewing it as a marker of developmental maturity is highly problematic (Fassinger & McCarn, 1996). Because sexual orientation and gender identity unfold within a context of social stigma, it is a stigma model (e.g., Herek, 2000; 2004) that offers an understanding of how sexual and gender identity unfold in contexts of heterosexism and transgender prejudice.

Stigma, mental health, and well-being. In the late 1960s, psychiatrist George Weinberg introduced the word *homophobia*, claiming that it is this antihomosexual bias, not pathology inherent in one's sexual orientation, that largely accounted for the problems he saw in his gay patients (Herek, 2004). Since that time, the term *homophobia* has been critiqued on the grounds that true phobias represent pathological, intense, and irrational fear responses to a stimulus (LGB individuals). In contrast, antihomosexual or antigay attitudes may better be characterized by anger and disgust, or the fear of being labeled or associated with homosexuality (rather than fear of LGB individuals themselves) (Herek, 2004). In order to address some of these critiques, Herek (2007) proposed a model of *sexual stigma*, including *enacted stigma* (i.e., overt behavioral expressions of sexual stigma, such as the use of antigay epithets), *felt stigma* (i.e., individuals' expectations that sexual stigma will be enacted, which may motivate people to modify their behavior in order to avoid stigma), *internalized stigma* (i.e., "an individual's personal acceptance of sexual stigma as a part of her or his own value system and self-concept," Herek, 2007, p. 910), and *heterosexism* (i.e., "a cultural ideology embodied in institutional practices that work to the disadvantage of sexual minority groups even in the absence of individual prejudice or discrimination," Herek, 2007, p. 907). Deeply ingrained societal heterosexism serves to perpetuate and legitimize sexual stigma, as well as the power and privilege differentials that exist between LGB and heterosexual individuals.

As we noted previously, APA has articulated a strong stance that lesbian, gay, and bisexual identities are not mental illnesses and has called upon psychologists to take a proactive stance in combating stigma associated with minority sexual identities (e.g., APA, 2012c; Conger, 1975). Moreover, the APA has issued resolutions and position statements, based on psychological research regarding sexual orientation and gender identity, supporting: child custody rights of LGBT individuals (Conger, 1977); rights of gay teachers (Abeles, 1981); samesex marriage (APA, 2011b; Paige, 2005); transgender, gender identity, and gender expression nondiscrimination (Anton, 2009); military service by sexual minorities (Paige, 2005); appropriate therapeutic responses to sexual orientation (Anton, 2010); and condemning hate crimes (Paige, 2005). Such resolutions represent an attempt at primary prevention by outlining basic rights of LGBT people, the absence of which supports discrimination leading to compromised health and well-being (e.g., Cochran & Mays, 2013; Herek, 2000; Herek & Garnets, 2007; Mays & Cochran, 2001).

Research indicates that LGBT individuals experience mental health problems at rates higher than their heterosexual and cisgender counterparts, largely due to the impacts of *minority stress* (e.g., Meyer, 2003). That is, mental health problems in LGBT individuals are related to "excess stress" (stigma, prejudice, discrimination) that they experience as members of a stigmatized minority group, rather than something inherent in themselves or their LGBT identities (Meyer, 2003, p. 675; also see Herek & Garnets, 2007; Mays & Cochran, 2001; Meyer & Frost, 2013). A sizeable body of research supports the link between mental health concerns among LGBT individuals and the oppression that they face (Cochran & Mays, 2013). For example, perceptions of discrimination among LGBT people have been found to be related to depressive symptoms, psychological distress, and risky sexual behaviors (e.g., Diaz, Ayala, & Bein, 2004; Huebner, Nemeroff, & Davis, 2005); and LGBT individuals have been found to be more likely than their heterosexual counterparts to report discrimination as an obstacle to a fulfilling life (Mays & Cochran, 2001).

In addition, LGBT individuals exist in a heterosexist and transphobic society in which their identities fall outside of the "mythical norm" (Lorde, 2007) of dominant heterosexual and cisgender identities. As such, they are consistently exposed to explicit and implicit negative messages about their identities, which may become internalized. *Internalized heterosexism* (e.g., Herek, 2007; Szymanski, Kashubeck-West, & Meyer, 2008) has been found to relate to a variety of negative mental and physical health outcomes (e.g., lower self-esteem, depression; for a review, see Szymanski, Kashubeck-West, & Meyer, 2008).

Therefore, developing knowledge in their students and trainees of both externalized and internalized heterosexism and antitransgender prejudice and their effects on LGBT individuals are important tasks for education and training programs in psychology. For example, educators and trainers may incorporate readings and discussion of the growing body of research on internalized heterosexism (e.g., Herek, 2007; Szymanski, Kashubeck-West, & Meyer, 2008). In addition, educators and supervisors should again encourage and model open conversation about the experiences of LGBT individuals. Students (and faculty) may also be encouraged to participate in formal intergroup dialogues or informal discussions that encourage exploration of personal experiences with various forms of privilege and oppression (including internalized heterosexism) on personal and interpersonal levels.

Strength and resilience. In addition to developing knowledge about the impact of prejudice and stigma on the mental and physical health and well-being of LGBT individuals, students in psychology programs also should learn about the strength and resilience of the LGBT community in the face of oppression. Although externalized and internalized oppression may be related to a variety of negative mental and physical health outcomes, the majority of LGBT individuals are high-functioning, healthy people. There are a variety of strengths and resources on which LGBT people draw to negotiate typical developmental processes (e.g., career development, formation of intimate relationships) and stressors associated with a sexual or gender minority status. For example, a growing body of research highlights the impact of social support on the lives of LGBT individuals (e.g., Gallor & Fassinger, 2010; Mustanski, Newcomb, & Garofalo, 2011; Sheets & Mohr, 2009).

Others have suggested that LGBT individuals may develop strengths specifically through their management of stigma. For example, Brown (1989) argued that lesbian and gay individuals are *bicultural* in that their development typically occurs in the context of a hetereosexual family and society, but must also expand beyond heterosexual culture and norms. Recent research on bicultural competence in racial and ethnic minority individuals supports the notion that bicultural competence may be a resource on which individuals who experience oppression may draw (e.g., Wei et al., 2010), and this is an area for future empirical study within LGBT psychology.

The concept of *crisis competence* also has been proposed to explain the resilience of sexual minority individuals (e.g., Friend, 1990a; Friend, 1990b; Kimmel, 1978). Crisis competence refers to skills that sexual minority individuals develop and use in their management of oppression across the life span, which are then useful in negotiating aging and late-life transitions.

Social support, bicultural competence, and crisis competence are psychological assets that those trained in clinical work can learn to examine and emphasize with their LGBT clients. Again, we encourage educators and trainers to incorporate readings and open conversation about the strength and resilience of LGBT individuals into their training.

Skills

In addition to development of knowledge about LGBT issues and people (including the impact of oppression, and strength and resilience), and awareness of one's own biases, it is important that psychology education and training programs equip students with the *skills* necessary to be LGBT-affirming clinicians, consultants, researchers, educators, and advocates in their future professional roles. We highlight here some of the skills necessary for successful LGBT-affirmative competence in several distinct work roles.

Clinical work. Matthews (2007) highlights some of the specific skills and considerations for affirmative clinical work with LGBT individuals. In the assessment of LGBT individuals for example, Matthews discusses the need for openness, the recognition that sexual orientation and gender identity are socially-constructed and fluid identities, and the awareness that standardized assessment tools may have a heterosexual bias. She also highlights some of the unique presenting concerns with which counselors and therapists working with LGBT individuals (and their friends and families) should be familiar, including the process of identity development and coming out, negotiating life as an LGBT individual (and managing associated stigma), and the importance of finding support in the LGBT community.

To this partial list, we would add the necessity for a thorough understanding of and comfort with sexuality and varied sexual behaviors, as well as a basic knowledge of world religious beliefs as they pertain to sexuality and gender.

Clinicians also must be educated regarding appropriate therapeutic methods for work with LGBT individuals, including recognition of the lack of empirical and professional support for sexual orientation change (or "conversion") efforts. In 2007, the APA established a task force to determine, based on the available psychological research, appropriate therapeutic approaches to sexual orientation (APA, 2009). This task force concluded that "enduring change in an individual's sexual orientation is uncommon" (p. 2), that claims of the effectiveness of sexual orientation change efforts are not supported, and that there is some evidence that sexual orientation change efforts may, in fact, be harmful to individuals. The task force also concluded that "adults perceive a benefit [from therapeutic treatments] when they are provided with client-centered, multicultural, evidence-based approaches that provide (a) acceptance and support, (b) assessment, (c) active coping, (d) social support, and (e) identity exploration and development" (p. 4). Thus, psychologists should learn and use affirmative, multiculturally competent treatments rather than potentially harmful sexual orientation change efforts, and are cautioned not to misrepresent the efficacy around sexual orientation change efforts to their clients (APA, 2009).

As previously mentioned, APA's (2012c) *Guidelines for Practice with Lesbian, Gay, and Bisexual Clients* provide an invaluable, broadly applicable resource to those providing therapy to LGB individuals. Until guidelines for psychological practice with transgender and gender nonconforming clients (APA, 2012a) are completed, psychologists working with transgender and gender nonconforming clients can be guided by the World Professional Association for Transgender Health's (2012a) *Standards of Care for the Health of Transsexual, Transgender, and Gender Nonconforming People*. We again remind readers that there are many other APA practice guidelines to aid in multiculturally competent clinical practice, and the *Ethical Principles of Psychologists and Code of Conduct* (APA, 2010) also can serve as important guides to developing skills in LGBT affirmative clinical work. Finally, the *Handbook of Counseling and Psychotherapy with Lesbian, Gay, Bisexual, and Transgender Clients (2nd Ed.)* (Bieschke, Perez, & DeBord, 2007) offers psychologists an accessible resource on affirmative treatment with LGBT individuals across a variety of life areas (including work and career, health, relationships and families, diversity, and legal and policy issues). Educators and trainers in psychology programs should ensure that trainees are exposed to all the relevant professional guidelines for competent multicultural practice. Supervisors should also encourage and promote open conversation about issues related to sexual orientation and gender identity (and all aspects of diversity) during supervision.

Research. Psychologists in training, particularly those in programs based on the Boulder *scientist-practitioner model*, learn about the important relationship between practice and research. Just as applied programs in psychology have a responsibility to train students to be competent clinicians regarding LGBT issues, students also should be trained to be competent researchers in, and informed consumers of, LGBT research. Research on LGBT populations is explicitly addressed in *Guideline 21* of the *Guidelines for Psychological Practice with Lesbian, Gay, and Bisexual Clients* (APA, 2012c), which states, "In the use and dissemination of research on sexual orientation and related issues, psychologists strive to represent results fully and accurately and to be mindful of the potential misuse or misrepresentation of research findings" (p. 27). Moradi, Mohr, Worthington, and Fassinger (2009) pointed out that research on LGBT populations may provide valuable information about human nature more broadly, a fact that often is overlooked. They suggest, for example, that research on LGBT individuals may provide an understanding of sexuality or relationships that extends beyond LGBT populations specifically.

In their recent article on the conceptual and methodological issues unique to LGBT research, Moradi et al. (2009) highlighted some of the important issues that should be considered by researchers and those who consume this research. They described, for example, the challenges in defining and sampling the population of interest due to language and labeling issues in these populations (see earlier); operationalizing constructs (e.g., "internalized heterosexism," "coming out"); addressing threats to internal validity (e.g., over-reliance on cross-sectional survey designs) and external and ecological validity (e.g., the underrepresentation of racial and ethnic minority participants); selecting measures (e.g., measures that do not contain heterosexist bias); and

resolving procedural problems (e.g., ensuring honesty of responses from a stigmatized group), to name a few of the challenges faced by researchers in this area of investigation.

Education and training programs in psychology should incorporate a discussion of these challenges into their research training component in order to ensure that future psychologists are able to be both critical consumers of LGBT research and ethical, informed scientists. A recent special edition of the *Journal of Counseling Psychology* has several articles that may be assigned to trainees in order to help increase their understanding of the issues related to LGBT research in psychology. For example, Moradi et al. (2009) provide an excellent broad overview of LGBT research issues, and Meyer and Wilson (2009) highlight the specific challenges in sampling associated with LGBT research.

Advocacy. Recently, there has been increased attention to the need to train psychologists as advocates for *social justice* (e.g., Toporek & McNally, 2006; Fouad, 2012a, 2012b, special sections of *The Counseling Psychologist, Volume 40, nos. 3 & 8*). Social justice includes "the notions of equity and liberty" (Speight & Vera, 2006, p. 54), and has as its goals "full and equal participation of all groups in a society that is mutually shaped to meet their needs. [It] includes a vision of society in which the distribution of resources is equitable and all members are physically and psychologically safe and secure" (Bell, 1997, p. 3, as cited in Speight & Vera, 2006, pp. 54–55). This involves the acknowledgement that not all problems that individuals face are intrapersonal, and that LGBT individuals exist in a society that is characterized by heterosexism and antitransgender stigma and bias. Therefore, psychologists need to be equipped to intervene at institutional and systemic levels to address injustices, and to help empower individuals from historically marginalized groups. We point to skills needed for such work, which may include training in consultation, organizational development and change, familysystems approaches, program development and evaluation, action research, leadership, grantwriting, and liberation pedagogy, all areas that likely are not a focus of most traditional counseling and clinical programs. Partnerships with colleagues in industrial-organizational (I/O), community, and health psychology, as well as those in management and public policy may offer promise in developing effective training for competence in the advocacy arena.

Attitudes

Affirmative clinical practice must begin with an acknowledgement of the powerful presence of heterosexism (in oneself, in clients, and in the environment) and a proactive commitment on the part of the clinician to overcome (or at least minimize) heterosexist assumptions and behaviors (e.g., Matthews, 2007). Therefore, a third critical aspect of multicultural competence is attitudes, including developing an awareness of one's own cultural attitudes, values, and biases. We suggest that this involves developing a *critical consciousness* (Freire, 2008), or a critical awareness and understanding of hierarchical (i.e., inequitable) social systems characterized by privilege and oppression, and the roles that society, institutions, and systems (e.g., psychology and its sub-disciplines), and individuals (including ourselves), play in perpetuating the oppressive status quo. This task may be one of the most challenging facing education and training programs in psychology, because it involves both trainers and trainees having to grapple with the difficult issues of privilege and oppression as they relate to one's own life. Specifically, those who are perceived to identify with dominant social identity groups (e.g., heterosexual and cisgender individuals) are endowed with privilege in society based on social group membership, rather than anything that they have done or failed to do (e.g., Johnson, 2006; McIntosh, 1998). Heterosexual individuals, for example, can depend on public and legal recognition of their relationships (Bohan, 1996), and cisgender individuals with access to health care can be reasonably confident that they will receive appropriate, timely, and nonintrusive treatment from most physicians (e.g., Feinberg, 2001). Exploration of one's access or lack of access to privilege can be a difficult process because it challenges the deeply held belief that we live in a meritocracy (i.e., a system in which effort is congruent with attainment) and fundamental acceptance of the importance of individualism. The necessity for psychologists to develop awareness around issues of power and privilege cannot be overstated, given that most psychologists will offer interventions, teach, conduct research, or work and live beside LGBT people or those connected with LGBT people.

In their introduction to the *Handbook of Counseling and Psychotherapy with Lesbian, Gay, Bisexual, and Transgender Clients* (2nd ed.), Bieschke, Perez, and DeBord (2007) pointed out that "the path to affirmation begins with the realization that as members of a heterosexist society, all of us, regardless of sexual orientation, bring our heterosexual biases into our work as counselors and therapists." (p. 5). A recent study by Shelton and Delgado-Romero (2011) also highlights the importance of counselors and therapists developing awareness around their (often implicit) assumptions and biases about LGB individuals (Note that this study examined sexual orientation micro-aggressions, specifically, and did not address microaggressions based on gender identity. Additional work is needed to better understand the experiences of micro-aggressions of transgender individuals). Specifically, self-identified LGB individuals in this study reported experiencing micro-aggressions related to sexual orientation in psychotherapy. Micro-aggressions described by the participants included therapists' identification of LGB sexual orientation as the source of the presenting problem, avoidance or minimization of the role of sexual orientation, over-identification with LGB clients, stereotypical assumptions, expression of heterosexist bias (e.g., therapist-provided literature referring only to heterosexual relationships), and the expressed belief that LGB clients *need* counseling. We note that these kinds of biases in therapy are still being reported 20 years after the groundbreaking study that first documented such bias in therapy (Committee on Lesbian and Gay Concerns, 1991) and prompted the development of practice guidelines related to sexual orientation. Prejudice related to sexual orientation and gender identity clearly permeates our society very deeply (even among those who choose to "help" others), and, therefore, we assert that the development of critical consciousness is imperative in training psychologists for a wide variety of professional roles.

Self-assessment is foundational in developing deeply critically conscious self-awareness and respectful and accepting attitudes toward self and others. In order to guide self-assessment, Worthington (cited in Lyons et al., 2010, p. 427) suggested that psychologists ask themselves the following questions: "Have my training and clinical experiences prepared me to see this client?" "Can I receive regular supervision or consultation with an expert in LGBT issues and individuals if I accept this client?" "What are my motivations to treat this client?" "Do my motivations conflict with or complement the client's?" "What are my own levels of sexual identity development?" "How well can I reflect on my countertransferential reactions to this case?" Worthington further challenged psychologists to ponder why, given the field's stated commitment to multicultural competence and social justice, there remains a consistent lack of competence regarding work with LGBT populations, a problem well-documented in research (e.g., Shelton & Delgado-Romero, 2011).

Recommendations for gay- and trans-affirmative education and training typically call for infusing LGBT issues into all aspects of training for psychologists (e.g., clinical work, multiculturalism, ethics, research methods), but psychologists in training also can explore their own experiences with, and assumptions and biases about, sexual orientation and gender identity in their own personal therapy. In addition, both faculty and students can be encouraged to participate in intergroup dialogues, an intervention designed to bring together individuals from social identity groups with a history of conflict, with the goals of building bridges across groups, developing awareness of hierarchical systems that perpetuate inequality, and developing capacities to work toward social justice (e.g., Zúñiga, Nagda, & Sevig, 2002).

APA Accreditation and Other Structural Issues

In addition to curricular and student development issues associated with building LGBT competence in psychology education and training programs, there are additional concerns for those administering APA-accredited doctoral, internship, and postdoctoral residency programs in professional psychology (e.g., clinical, counseling, school psychology). Among them are Footnote 4 of the APA Commission on Accreditation's (CoA) *Guidelines and Principles for Accreditation of Programs in Professional Psychology* (2007), and the related challenge of conscience clauses.

Footnote 4

In order to be eligible for accreditation according to the APA CoA's (2007) *Guidelines and Principles for Accreditation of Programs in Professional Psychology* (referred to in this section as *Guidelines and Principles*), a program must engage in "actions that indicate respect for and understanding of cultural and individual diversity" (p. 6). The *Guidelines and Principles* define, "cultural and individual diversity" as "diversity with regard to personal and demographic characteristics. These include, but are not limited to, age, disability, ethnicity, gender, *gender identity*, language, national origin, race, religion, culture, *sexual orientation*, and social economic

status" [emphasis added] (p. 6). Thus, faculty and supervisors from accredited programs in professional psychology are ethically and professionally compelled to convey respect and understanding regarding sexual orientation and gender identity.

The *Guidelines and Principles* include a section on "Cultural and Individual Differences and Diversity" (APA CoA, 2007, p. 10), which states that graduate programs in professional psychology must recognize "the importance of cultural and individual differences and diversity in the training of psychologists...[and have] made systematic, coherent, and long-term efforts to attract and retain students and faculty from differing ethnic, racial, and personal backgrounds into the program" (p. 10). Further, "Consistent with such efforts, [graduate programs in psychology act] to ensure a supportive and encouraging learning environment appropriate for the training of diverse individuals and the provision of training opportunities for a broad spectrum of individuals...and [avoid] any actions that would restrict program access on grounds that are irrelevant to success in graduate training" (p. 10).

However, a controversial footnote follows this last requirement in the *Guidelines and Principles*. Specifically, Footnote 4 states:

> This requirement does not exclude programs from having a religious affiliation or purpose and adopting and applying admission and employment policies that directly relate to this affiliation or purpose so long as: (1) public notice of these policies has been made to applicants, students, faculty, or staff before their application or affiliation with the program; and (2) the policies do not contravene the intent of other relevant portions of this document or the concept of academic freedom. These policies may provide a preference for persons adhering to the religious purpose or affiliation of the program, but they shall not be used to preclude the admission, hiring, or retention of individuals because of the personal and demographic characteristics described in Domain A, Section 5 of this document (and referred to as cultural and individual diversity). This footnote is intended to permit religious policies as to admission, retention, and employment only to the extent that they are protected by the U.S. Constitution. It will be administered as if the U.S. Constitution governed its application. (APA CoA, 2007, p. 10)

The implication of this footnote is that education and training programs in psychology that have a religious affiliation may discriminate against LGBT individuals in their admissions and hiring processes, when such discrimination is consistent with the religious affiliation. Footnote 4 highlights the complications that lie at the intersections of religion, sexual orientation, and gender identity, and has been the topic of extensive review and debate (e.g., Ladany, Kaduvettoor, & Soheilian, 2007).

In 2009, the APA CoA attempted to address some of the problems inherent in Footnote 4 in its *Implementing Regulations Frequently Used in Program Review* (*IR*; APA CoA, 2009). Specifically, IR section *C-22[a]: Review of programs invoking Footnote 4* points out that Footnote 4 is, in part, a response to the federal Higher Education Opportunity Act that requires accrediting agencies and associations to "consistently [apply] and [enforce] standards that respect the stated mission of the institution of higher education, including religious missions…" (p. 247, H.R. 4137, 2008). The IR explains that Footnote 4 is to be applied only to Domain D.1, which says that the program under review has:

> …made systematic, coherent, and long-term efforts to attract and retain students and faculty from differing ethnic, racial, and personal backgrounds into the program…. acts to ensure a supportive and encouraging learning environment appropriate for the training of diverse individuals and the provision of training opportunities for a broad spectrum of individuals… [and] avoids any actions that would restrict program access on grounds that are irrelevant to success in graduate training. (APA CoA, 2007, p. 10).

According to the IR, Footnote 4 is not to be applied to any other domain in the *Guidelines and Principles*, including Domain D.2, which states that the program:

> …has and implements a thoughtful and coherent plan to provide students with relevant knowledge and experiences about the role of cultural and individual diversity in psychological phenomena as they relate to the science and practice of professional psychology. (APA CoA, 2007, p. 10)

The IR further explains that all aspects of the self-study for a program invoking Footnote 4 will be reviewed in the same manner as any other program's self-study, which includes demonstrating that students are educated at the level required by the *Guidelines and Principles*. Thus, the clarification that the APA CoA has attempted to provide states that, although programs may have a religious affiliation and purpose that guides admission and hiring policies, thcsc programs must ensure that these policies are made clear. Moreover, they must adhere

to all other sections of the *Guidelines and Principles*, including Domain D.2, which requires that students gain multicultural competence in their education and training, and multicultural competence is defined clearly as including LGBT issues and populations.

Conscience Clauses

Regardless of general training standards put into place and monitored by accrediting bodies, training programs are made up of individuals, some of whom invoke a personal stance (generally on the basis of religious beliefs) declining to work with gender-transgressive sexual minority clients. Recent media attention to a number of court cases (e.g., *Keeton v. Anderson-Wiley*, 2010/2011; *Ward v. Willbanks*, 2010) has highlighted the question of whether students can be exempt from learning about LGBT issues and providing affirmative counseling to LGBT individuals. In *Keeton v. Anderson-Wiley* (2010/2011), Keeton, a master's student in school counseling in an ACA-accredited program was asked to complete a remediation plan when faculty perceived deficiencies in her ability to work with LGBT clients (i.e., she commented that she would try to change LGBT clients' behavior, or would refer them for "conversion therapy"). The program argued that Keeton's statements violated ACA's *Code of Ethics*, which the university is required to follow in order to maintain its accreditation through the ACA's Council for Accreditation of Counseling and Related Programs, and thus required remediation. Rather than completing the remediation plan, Keeton filed a lawsuit alleging that requiring her to complete the remediation plan would violate her First Amendment rights to free speech and free exercise (*Keeton v. Anderson-Wiley*, 2010/2011). In December 2011, the US Court of Appeals upheld the decision of a lower court in favor of the university, stating that it "has the authority to require all students enrolled in its clinical practicum, which involves one-on-one interaction with actual counselees, to adhere to a code of ethics" (*Keeton v. Anderson-Wiley*, 2010/2011, p. 36).

Another recent prominent case was *Ward v. Willbanks* (2010). In 2009, Ward, a master's student in an ACA-accredited counseling program asked a supervisor whether she should refer a gay client because she could not affirm the client's "homosexual behavior" based on her religious beliefs (Eastern Michigan University [EMU], n.d.). Her supervisor re-assigned the client, but brought Ward up for review by the faculty who, after a hearing, voted to dismiss Ward from the program because her actions violated the ACA *Code of Ethics*. Ward brought suit against the university, alleging that its actions violated her First and Fourteenth Amendment rights. The court granted a summary judgment in favor of the University, upholding the University and counseling program's right to establish their own curriculum (which includes conforming to professional codes of ethics that explicitly require nondiscriminatory practices). Ms. Ward appealed this decision, and the U.S. Court of Appeals for the Sixth District remanded the decision in January of 2012 (EMU, n.d.). EMU has petitioned for rehearing of the case, which is still pending as of this writing (EMU, n.d.).

These ongoing court cases, and their outcomes, have important implications for education and training programs in professional psychology. Following the *Ward v. Willbanks* (2010) case, for example, the Michigan House of Representatives passed the Julea Ward Freedom of Conscience Act (2011) forbidding public colleges and universities from "discriminating" against a student who "refuses to counsel a client as to goals, outcomes, or behaviors that conflict with sincerely held religious beliefs of the student," if the student refers the client to someone else who will provide service (pp. 1–2). Several other states (e.g., Arizona) have passed or are in the process of developing similar legislation. Because professional guidelines and ethics (e.g., APA 2010; APA, 2012c) make clear that training programs have an obligation to ensure that their trainees develop multicultural competence, including in the areas of gender identity and sexual orientation, it is crucial for training programs to keep abreast of enacted or proposed legislation aimed at overstepping the ethical codes that guide the profession. Moreover, they should articulate a clear and unambiguous stance on these issues on the part of the program, and anticipate and prepare for challenges from individual students. We also refer readers to a special section of *Training and Education in Professional Psychology* (Forrest, 2012) for an in depth discussion of educators' and trainers' legal and ethical responsibilities when personal beliefs collide with professional and ethical responsibilities.

Additional Training Considerations and Conclusion

The APA (2012c) *Guidelines for Psychological Practice with Lesbian, Gay, and Bisexual Clients* provide some help to practitioners (and those who train and supervise psychology students) in addressing anti-LGB bias when working with LGB clients. Consistent with the APA's (2010) *Ethical Principles*

of Psychologists and Code of Conduct, Principle E: Respect for People's Rights and Dignity, the *Guidelines* state that psychologists must "strive to evaluate their competencies and the limitations of their expertise, especially when offering assessment and treatment services to people who share characteristics that are different from their own [e.g., lesbian, gay, and bisexual clients]" (*Guideline 4*; p. 15). The *Guidelines* go on to describe how unexamined implicit or explicit biases against LGB individuals can impede treatment progress, and/or adversely affect the client. It is imperative that education and training programs encourage trainees' exploration of their assumptions, knowledge (or lack thereof), and biases regarding LGB(T) individuals. This recommendation is based on the conscious recognition of heterosexist biases that can be counteracted, and psychologists with anti-LGB biases are encouraged to "identify and ameliorate implicit and explicit biases about homosexuality and bisexuality" (p. 15, APA, 2012c) through the use of consultation, supervision, study, and continuing education.

Just as the APA (2012c) *Guidelines for Psychological Practice with Lesbian, Gay, and Bisexual Clients* urge psychologists to develop awareness of their own implicit and explicit anti-LGB biases, it is also important for training program faculty in psychology to examine *institutional heterosexism* and *institutional antitransgender prejudice*, or the ways in which the oppression of LGBT individuals may be perpetuated via institutional policies and practices. More specifically, the *Guidelines* (APA, 2012c) make an important point about "sexual orientation blind" approaches (p. 15). That is, just as clinicians must not ignore sexual orientation and gender identity in clinical work, educators and trainers in psychology run the risk of failing to address systemic or institutionalized inequities when they overlook these issues at the administrative level. Freeman (1979) and Betz (1989) discussed the problems associated with this type of "null [academic] environment" that "neither encourages nor discourages individuals" (Betz, p. 137). They noted that, given the overwhelming occurrence of negative messages directed toward marginalized populations (e.g., women, LGBT individuals) in society, academic programs and institutions that fail to proactively encourage students with marginalized identities (e.g., programs that are "gender blind" or "sexual orientation blind") are inherently discriminatory against these students because they fail to take into account—and try to counteract the effects of—the different external environments from which marginalized and dominant people come. The implication in regard to sexual orientation and gender identity is that training programs should take a proactive stance, clearly affirming these marginalized statuses.

Mentoring LGBT psychology students. The concept of the null environment has particular relevance to the topic of mentoring LGBT students. In a study of LGB mentorship in counseling psychology programs, for instance, Lark and Croteau (1998) found that null or negative environments provided LGB graduate students with fewer LGB faculty role models and fewer LGB-affirming heterosexual faculty members. This is noteworthy because research has shown that mentoring relationships in graduate school can have important implications for student productivity (e.g., Forehand, 2008; Hollingsworth & Fassinger, 2002; Tenenbaum, Crosby, & Gliner, 2001), and satisfaction with their schooling and career (e.g., Forehand, 2008; Tenenbaum et al., 2001). Mentors provide students with needed instrumental and psychosocial support, as well as networking opportunities, that help them to succeed. Research also has shown that members of underrepresented social identity groups (e.g., women and racial/ethnic minorities) may especially benefit from mentoring relationships, but that they may have different mentoring needs and differential access to mentoring relationships than do individuals in dominant social identity groups (e.g., men and White people) (e.g., Liang, Tracy, Kauh, Taylor, & Williams, 2006; Williams-Nickelson, 2009). Both researchers and practitioners have discussed the unique issues involved in LGBT mentorship (e.g., Lark & Croteau, 1998; Russell & Horne, 2009). For example, Russell and Horne highlighted the importance of attending to *sexual prejudice* (i.e., homophobia, heterosexism, biphobia, antitransgender prejudice) in mentoring relationships. They assume that all people (including LGBT individuals) are exposed to and learn sexual prejudice in the United States, and that sexual prejudice is often automatic. Thus, sexual prejudice and stigma need to be addressed explicitly in mentoring relationships. Mentors need to be ready and able to discuss the impacts of sexual prejudice on the lives of LGBT students, and need to have the capacities to serve as allies to LGBT students who are experiencing oppression. In addition, mentors of LGBT students need to examine their own attitudes toward LGBT individuals, and continually work toward developing competence in LGBT issues.

Lark and Croteau (1998) discussed unique mentoring needs and experiences of LGB students, and made recommendations for individuals who mentor LGB students. These researchers identified two major "contextual themes" that shape sexual minority students' experiences with mentoring: level of "outness" of the student, and perceived safety for LGB students within the psychology program. For example, students who reported being out for long periods of time prior to entering their graduate programs had expectations of affirmation of their LGB identities, and specifically sought out relationships with LGB mentors and/or openly LGB affirming heterosexual mentors. Lark and Croteau recommended that mentors of LGB students signal their affirmation, serve as "safe-havens" in null or negative training environments, directly address potential challenges in mentoring LGB students with more than one minority social identity, and be sensitive to personal boundaries concerning issues related to sexual orientation (e.g., like any student, LGBT students may not wish to discuss their sexual orientation, relationships, etc. with professional mentors). In addition, mentors need to remain aware of their position as role models and/or allies to LGBT communities.

Concluding Thoughts

The context in which training programs in professional psychology operate always has been bounded by legal, economic/marketplace, political, social, and professional association forces well beyond the local control of the individuals in those programs. But the current context is especially challenging, particularly in regard to fostering LGBT competence in trainees. For example, the current legal and political landscape is one in which LGBT rights can change (literally) overnight. Additionally, the economic recession and concomitant emphasis on efficiency often renders additions to curricula untenable; and the growing tendency of students-as-consumers to express dissatisfaction and exercise their rights (not only antigay or anti-trans "conscience" rights claims, but also the rights of LGBT students to a safe and supportive training environment) present additional challenges for educators and trainers in psychology in terms of both curriculum development and the creation of the "climate" of the program around LGBT issues. These challenges are compounded by marketplace forces (e.g., internship shortages, insurance reimbursements) that compel trainees to carve out specialized professional niches sooner and sooner in their training (and perhaps too early to have experienced the kinds of diversity that might open them to different career paths); and the lack of expertise and training that most faculty and supervisors in existing programs have personally experienced with regard to LGBT issues.

All of these forces conspire to put education and training programs in difficult situations when dealing with the need to train LGBT-competent psychologists. We would argue, however, that the only professionally defensible path through this maze of oft-competing demands is conversation, conversation, conversation. Education and training program personnel should continually discuss, consensually decide, articulate, and communicate program stances and policies regarding LGBT issues, and then be ready to engage in the entire process again and make accommodations as the context shifts. Waiting until an instance of a trainee's problems of professional competence emerges or antigay hostility arises can plunge a faculty or staff into confusion, at best, or warfare, at worst, and does not serve students well. Programs that take time to establish the program on a firm foundation of agreed-upon and communicated positions regarding LGBT issues are less likely to find themselves unprepared for sudden changes in society, local communities, higher education, and the needs of their own students, and they will be places where expectations are clear and trusted by all.

References

Abeles, N. (1981). Proceedings of the American Psychological Association, Incorporated, for the year 1980: Minutes of the Annual Meetings of the Council of Representatives. *American Psychologist, 36*, 552–586. doi:10.1037/h0078369

American Forces Press Service (2011). Obama: Americans no longer have to lie to serve. Retrieved July 23, 2013 from http://www.defense.gov/news/newsarticle.aspx?id=65381

American Psychiatric Association. (1952). *Diagnostic and statistical manual of mental disorders* (1st ed.) Washington, DC: Author.

American Psychiatric Association. (2000). *Diagnostic and statistical manual of mental disorders* (4th ed., text rev.). Washington, DC: Author.

American Psychiatric Association. (2011). *DSM-V Development: Proposed revisions: P 01 Gender Dysphoria in Adolescents or Adults*. Retrieved August 25, 2012 from http://www.dsm5.org/ProposedRevisions/Pages/proposedrevision.aspx?rid=482

American Psychological Association. (2002). *Guidelines on multicultural education, training, research, practice, and organizational change for psychologists*. Washington, DC: Author. Retrieved May 30, 2012 from http://www.apa.org/pi/oema/resources/policy/multicultural-guidelines.aspx

American Psychological Association. (2004). Guidelines for psychological practice with older adults. *American Psychologist, 59*, 236–260. doi:10.1037/0003-066X.59.4.236

American Psychological Association. (2007). *Guidelines for psychological practice with girls and women*. Washington, DC: Author. Retrieved July 23, 2013 from http://www.apa.org/practice/guidelines/girls-and-women.pdf

American Psychological Association. (2008). *Answers to your questions: For a better understanding of sexual orientation and homosexuality*. Washington, DC: Author. Retrieved July 23, 2013 from http://www.apa.org/topics/sexuality/sorientation.pdf

American Psychological Association. (2009). *Report of the American Psychological Association's Task Force on Appropriate Therapeutic Responses to Sexual Orientation*. Washington, DC: Author. Retrieved June 24, 2012 from http://www.apa.org/pi/lgbt/resources/therapeutic-response.pdf

American Psychological Association. (2010). *Ethical principles of psychologists and code of conduct: 2010 amendments*. Washington, DC: Author. Retrieved August 17, 2012 from http://www.apa.org/ethics/code/index.aspx?item=4

American Psychological Association. (2011a). *Answers to your questions about transgender people, gender identity, and gender expression*. Washington, DC: Author. Retrieved July 23, 2013 from http://www.apa.org/topics/sexuality/transgender.pdf

American Psychological Association. (2011b). *Resolution on marriage equality for same-sex couples*. Washington, DC: Author.

American Psychological Association. (2012a). *Atlanta meeting of the APA Task Force on Guidelines for Psychological Practice with Transgender and Gender Non-Conforming Clients*. Washington, DC: Author. Retrieved July 23, 2013 from http://www.apa.org/pi/lgbt/committee/atlanta-meeting.aspx

American Psychological Association. (2012b). Guidelines for assessment of and intervention with persons with disabilities. *American Psychologist, 67*, 43–62. doi:10.1037/a0025892

American Psychological Association. (2012c). Guidelines for psychological practice with lesbian, gay, and bisexual clients. *American Psychologist, 67*, 10–42. doi: 10.1037/a0024659

American Psychological Association Commission on Accreditation (2007). *Guidelines and principles for accreditation of programs in professional psychology*. Washington, DC: American Psychological Association. Retrieved June 5, 2012 from http://www.apa.org/ed/accreditation/index.aspx

American Psychological Association Commission on Accreditation (2009). *Implementing regulations frequently used in program review: C-22(a): Review of programs invoking Footnote 4*. Washington, DC: American Psychological Association. Retrieved June 5, 2012 from http://www.apa.org/ed/accreditation/about/policies/implementing-regulations.aspx?item=27

Anton, B. S. (2009). Proceedings of the American Psychological Association for the legislative year 2008: Minutes of the annual meeting of the Council of Representatives. *American Psychologist, 64*, 372–453. doi:10.1037/a0015932

Anton, B. S. (2010). Proceedings of the American Psychological Association for the legislative year 2009: Minutes of the annual meeting of the Council of Representatives and minutes of the meetings of the Board of Directors. *American Psychologist, 65*, 385–475. doi:10.1037/a0019553

Betz, N. E. (1989). Implications of the null environment hypothesis for women's career development and for counseling psychology. *The Counseling Psychologist, 17*, 136–144. doi:10.1177/0011000089171008

Bieschke, K. M., Hardy, J. A., Fassinger, R. E. & Croteau, J. M. (2008). Intersecting identities of gender-transgressive sexual minorities: Toward a new paradigm of affirmative psychology. In W. B. Walsh (Ed.), *Biennial review of counseling psychology* (pp. 177– 208). New York: Routledge.

Bieschke, K. J., Perez, R. M., & DeBord, K. A. (2007). Introduction: The challenge of providing affirmative psychotherapy while honoring diverse contexts. In K. J., Bieschke, R. M. Perez, & K. A. DeBord (Eds.), *Handbook of counseling and psychotherapy with lesbian, gay, bisexual, and transgender clients* (2nd ed., pp. 3–11). Washington, DC: American Psychological Association.

Bohan, J. S. (1996). *Psychology and sexual orientation: Coming to terms.* New York: Routledge.

Brown, L. S. (1989). New voices, new visions: Toward a lesbian/gay paradigm for psychology. *Psychology of Women Quarterly, 13*, 445–458. doi:10.1111/j.1471-6402.1989.tb01013.x

Buhrke, R. A., & Douce, L. A. (1991). Training issues for counseling psychologists in working with lesbian and gay men. *The Counseling Psychologist, 19*(2), 216–234. doi:10.1177/0011000091192006

Calmes, J., & Baker, P. (2012, May 9). Obama says same-sex marriage should be legal. *New York Times.* Retrieved July 23, 2013 from http://www.nytimes.com/2012/05/10/us/politics/obama-says-same-sex-marriage-should-be-legal.html?pagewanted=all

Cass, V. C. (1980). Homosexual identity formation: Testing a theoretical model. *The Journal of Sex Research, 20*, 143–167.

Cochran, S. D. & Mays, V. M. (2013). Sexual orientation and mental health. In C. J. Patterson & A. R. D'Augelli (Eds.), *Handbook of psychology and sexual orientation* (pp. 204–222). New York: Oxford University Press.

Cole, E. R. (2009). Intersectionality and research in psychology. *American Psychologist, 64*, 170–180. doi:10.1037/a0014564

Committee on Lesbian and Gay Concerns. (1991). *Bias in psychotherapy with lesbians and gay men.* Washington, DC: American Psychological Association.

Conger, J. J. (1975). Proceedings of the American Psychological Association, Incorporated, for the year 1974: Minutes of the annual meeting of the Council of Representatives. *American Psychologist, 30*, 620–651. doi:10.1037/h0078455

Conger, J. J. (1977). Proceedings of the American Psychological Association, Incorporated, for the year 1976: Minutes of the Annual Meeting of the Council of Representatives. *American Psychologist, 32*, 408–438. doi:10.1037/h0078511

Croteau, J. M., Bieschke, K. J., Phillips, J. C., & Lark, J. S. (1998). Moving beyond pioneering: Empirical and theoretical perspectives on lesbian, gay, and bisexual affirmative training. *The Counseling Psychologist, 26*, 707–711. doi:10.1177/0011000098265001

Diaz, R. M., Ayala, G., & Bein, E. (2004). Sexual risk as an outcome of social oppression: Data from a probability sample of Latino gay men in three U.S. cities. *Cultural Diversity and Ethnic Minority Psychology, 10*, 255–267.

Diehl, M., & Ochs, R. (2000). Biphobia. In M. Adams, W. J. Blumenfeld, R. Castañeda, H. W. Hackman, M. L. Peters, & Ximena Zúñiga (Eds.), *Readings for diversity and social justice: An anthology on racism, anti-Semitism, sexism, heterosexism, ableism, and classism* (pp. 276–280). New York: Routledge.

Eastern Michigan University (n.d.). Julea Ward case information re: American Counseling Association code of ethics. Retrieved July 23, 2013 from http://www.emich.edu/aca_case/

Eckholm, E. (2012, November 7). In Maine and Maryland, victories at the ballot box for same-sex marriage. Retrieved July 22, 2013 from http://www.nytimes.com/2012/11/07/us/politics/same-sex-marriage-voting-election.html?ref=us

Fassinger, R. E. (2000). Applying counseling theories to lesbian, gay, and bisexual clients: Pitfalls and possibilities. In R. M. Perez, K. A. DeBord, & K. J. Bieschke (Eds.), *Handbook of counseling and psychotherapy with lesbian, gay, bisexual clients* (pp. 107–131). Washington, DC: American Psychological Association.

Fassinger, R. E., & Arseneau, J. R. (2007). "I'd rather get wet than be under that umbrella": Differentiating the experiences and identities of lesbian, gay, bisexual, and transgender people. In K. J., Bieschke, R. M. Perez, & K. A. DeBord (Eds.), *Handbook of counseling and psychotherapy with lesbian, gay, bisexual, and transgender clients* (2nd ed., pp. 19–49). Washington, DC: American Psychological Association.

Fassinger, R. E. & Arseneau, J. R. (2008). Diverse women's sexualities. In F. L. Denmark & M. A. Paludi (Eds.)., *Psychology of women: A handbook of issues and theories* (pp. 484–505). Westport, CT: Praeger.

Fassinger, R. E. & McCarn, S. R. (1996). Re-visioning sexual minority identity formation: A new model of lesbian development and its implications for counseling and research. *The Counseling Psychologist, 24*, 508–534.

Fassinger, R. E. & Miller, B. A. (1996). Validation of an inclusive model of homosexual identity formation in a sample of gay men. *Journal of Homosexuality, 32* (2), 53–78.

Feinberg, L. (2001). Trans health crisis: For us it's life and death. *American Journal of Public Health, 91*, 897–900. doi:10.2105/AJPH.91.6.897

Forehand, R. L. (2008). The art and science of mentoring in psychology: A necessary practice to ensure our future. *American Psychologist, 63*, 744–755. doi:10.1037/0003-066X.63.8.744

Forrest, L. (2012). Educators' and trainers' responsibilities when trainees' personal beliefs collide with competent practice. *Training and Education in Professional Psychology, 6*(4), 187–188. doi:10.1037/a0030799

Fouad, N. A. (Ed.). (2012a). Multicultural competence and social justice. *The Counseling Psychologist, 40*(8), 1101–1180. (*Special section*).

Fouad, N. A. (Ed.). (2012b). Social justice advocacy. *The Counseling Psychologist, 40*(3), 326–408. (Special section).

Foucault, M. (1978). *The history of sexuality: An introduction, vol. I.* New York: Pantheon Books.

Freeman, J. (1979). How to discriminate against women without really trying. In J. Freeman (Ed.), *Women: A feminist perspective* (2nd ed., pp. 217–232). New York: McGraw Hill.

Freire, P. (2008). *Pedagogy of the oppressed.* New York: Continuum.

Friend, R. A. (1990a). Older lesbian and gay people: Responding to homophobia. *Marriage & Family Review, 14*, 241–263. doi:10.1300/J002v14n03_12

Friend, R. A. (1990b). Older lesbian and gay people: A theory of successful aging. *Journal of Homosexuality, 20*, 99–118. doi:10.1300/J082v20n03_07

Gaga, L. (2011). *Born this way. On Born this way [CD].* Santa Monica, CA: Interscope Records.

Garnets (2007). Foreword: The "coming of age" of lesbian, gay, bisexual, and transgender affirmative psychology. In K. J. Bieschke, R. M. Perez, & K. A. DeBord (Eds.), *Handbook of counseling and psychotherapy with lesbian, gay, bisexual, and transgender clients* (2nd ed., pp. xi–xvi). Washington, DC: American Psychological Association.

Gallor, S. M. & Fassinger, R. E. (2010). Social support, ethnic identity, and sexual identity of lesbians and gay men, *Journal of Gay & Lesbian Social Services, 22*(3), 287–304.

Greene, B. (1997). Ethnic minority lesbians and gay men: Mental health and treatment issues. In B. Greene (Ed.), *Ethnic and cultural diversity among lesbians and gay men* (pp. 216–239). Thousand Oaks, CA: Sage Publications.

Greene, B. (2007). Delivering ethical psychological services to lesbian, gay, and bisexual clients. In K. J. Bieschke, R. M. Perez, & K. A. DeBord (Eds.), *Handbook of counseling and psychotherapy with lesbian, gay, bisexual, and transgender clients* (2nd ed., pp. 181–200). Washington, DC: American Psychological Association.

Herek, G. M. (2000). The psychology of sexual prejudice. *Current Directions in Psychological Science, 9*, 19–22. doi: 10.1111/1467-8721.00051

Herek, G. M. (2004). Beyond "homophobia": Thinking about sexual stigma and prejudice in the twenty-first century. *Sexuality Research and Social Policy, 1*, 6–24.

Herek, G. M. (2007). Confronting sexual stigma and prejudice: Theory and practice. *Journal of Social Issues, 63*(4), 905–925. doi:10.1111/j.1540–4560.2007.00544.x

Herek, G. M. & Garnets, L. D. (2007). Sexual orientation and mental health. *Annual Review of Clinical Psychology, 3*, 353–375.

Hetherington, C. (1991). Life planning and career counseling with gay and lesbian students. In N. J. Evans & V. A. Wall (Eds.), *Beyond tolerance: Gays, lesbians, and bisexuals on campus* (pp. 131–145). Alexandria, VA: American College Personnel Association.

Higher Education Opportunity Act, H.R. 4137, 110th Cong. (2008).

Hollingsworth, M. A., & Fassinger, R. E. (2002). The role of faculty mentors in the research training of counseling psychology doctoral students. *Journal of Counseling Psychology, 49*, 324–330. doi: 10.1037/0022-0167.49.3.324

Hooker, E. E. (1957). The adjustment of the male overt homosexual. *Journal of Projective Techniques, 21*, 18–31. doi:10.10 80/08853126.1957.10380742

Huebner, D. M., Nemeroff, C. J., & Davis, M. C. (2005). Do hostility and neuroticism confound associations between perceived discrimination and depressive symptoms? *Journal of Social and Clinical Psychology, 24*, 723–740. doi:10.1521/jscp.2005.24.5.723

Israel, T., & Selvidge, M. M. D. (2003). Contributions of multicultural counseling to counselor competence with lesbian, gay and bisexual clients. *Journal of Multicultural Counseling and Development, 31*, 84–98. doi:10.1002/j.2161-1912.2003.tb00535.x

Johnson, A. G. (2006). *Privilege, power, and difference* (2nd ed., pp. 12–40). Boston: McGraw Hill.

Julea Ward Freedom of Conscience Act, Mi. House Bill 5040 (2012).

Keeton v. Anderson-Wiley, 733 F. Supp. 2d 1368 (S.D. Ga. 2010), aff'd, 664 F.3d 865 (11th Cir. 2011).

Kimmel, D. C. (1978). Adult development and aging: A gay perspective. *Journal of Social Issues, 34*, 113–130. doi:10.1111/j.1540-4560.1978.tb02618.x

Kinsey, A. C., Pomeroy, W. B., & Martin, C. E. (1948). *Sexual behavior in the human male*. Philadelphia: W. B. Saunders.

Kinsey, A. C., Pomeroy, W. B., Martin, C. E., & Gebhard, P. H. (1953). *Sexual behavior in the human female*. Philadelphia: W. B. Saunders.

Ladany, N., Kaduvettoor, A., & Soheilian, S. S. (2007, August). Footnote 4: APA sanctioned homophobia in psychology training. In M. V. Ellis and N. Ladany (Chairs), *Hot Topics in Supervision and Training 2007*. Roundtable conducted at the meeting of the American Psychological Association, San Francisco, CA.

Lark, J. S., & Croteau, J. M. (1998). Lesbian, gay, and bisexual doctoral students mentoring relationships with faculty in counseling psychology: A qualitative study. *The Counseling Psychologist, 26*, 754–776. doi: 10.1177/0011000098265004

Lev, A. I. (2007). Transgender communities: Developing identity through connection. In K. J. Bieschke, R. M. Perez, & K. A. DeBord (Eds.), *Handbook of counseling and psychotherapy with lesbian, gay, bisexual, and transgender clients* (2nd ed., pp. 147– 175). Washington, DC: American Psychological Association.

Liang, B., Tracy, A., Kauh, T., Taylor, C., & Williams, L. M. (2006). Mentoring Asian and Euro-American college women. *Journal of Multicultural Counseling and Development, 34*, 143–143. doi:10.1002/j.2161-1912.2006.tb00034.x

Lorde, A. (2007). Age, race, class, and sex: Women redefining difference. In A. Lorde, *Sister outsider: Essays and speeched by Audre Lorde* (pp. 114–123). New York: Crossing Press.

Lowe, S. M. & Mascher, J. (2001). The role of sexual orientation in multicultural counseling: Integrating bodies of knowledge. In J. G. Ponterotto, J. M. Casas, L. A. Suzuki, & C. M. Alexander (Eds.), *Handbook of multicultural counseling* (2nd. ed., pp.755–778). Thousand Oaks, CA: Sage Publications.

Lyons, H. Z., Bieschke, K. J., Dendy, A. K., Worthington, R. L., & Georgemiller, R. (2010). Psychologists' competence to treat lesbian, gay and bisexual clients: State of the field and strategies for improvement. *Professional Psychology: Research and Practice, 41*, 424–434. doi:10.1037/a0021121

Matthews, C. R. (2007). Affirmative lesbian, gay, and bisexual counseling with all clients. In

K. J., Bieschke, R. M. Perez, & K. A. DeBord (Eds.), *Handbook of counseling and psychotherapy with lesbian, gay, bisexual, and transgender clients* (2nd ed., pp. 201–219). Washington, DC: American Psychological Association.

Mays, V. M., & Cochran, S. D. (2001). Mental health correlates of perceived discrimination among lesbian, gay, and bisexual adults in the United States. *American Journal of Public Health, 91*, 1869–1876. doi:10.2105/AJPH.91.11.1869

McIntosh, P. (1998). White privilege and male privilege: A personal account of coming to see correspondences through work in women's studies. In M. L. Andersen, & P. H. Collins (Eds.), *Race, class, and gender: An anthology* (3rd ed. pp. 94–105). Belmont, CA: Wadsworth.

Meyer, I. H. (2003). Prejudice, social stress, and mental health in lesbian, gay, and bisexual populations: Conceptual issues and research evidence. *Psychological Bulletin, 129*, 674–697. doi:10.1037/0033-2909.129.5.674

Meyer, I. H. & Frost, D. M. (2013). Minority stress and the health of sexual minorities. In C. J. Patterson & A. R. D'Augelli (Eds.), *Handbook of psychology and sexual orientation* (pp. 252–266). New York: Oxford University Press.

Meyer, I. H., & Wilson, P. A. (2009). Sampling lesbian, gay, and bisexual populations. *Journal of Counseling Psychology, 56*(1), 23–31. doi:10.1037/a0014587

Moradi, B., DeBlaere, C., & Huang, Y. (2010). Centralizing the experiences of LGB people of color in counseling psychology. *The Counseling Psychologist, 38*(3), 322–330.

Moradi, B., Mohr, J. J., Worthington, R. L., & Fassinger, R. E. (2009). Counseling psychology research on sexual (orientation) minority issues: Conceptual and methodological challenges and opportunities. *Journal of Counseling Psychology, 56*, 5–22. doi: 10.1037/a0014572

Mustanski, B., Newcomb, M. E., & Garofalo, R. (2011). Mental health of lesbian, gay, and bisexual youths: A developmental resiliency perspective. *Journal of Gay & Lesbian Social Services, 23*, 204–225. doi:10.1080/10538720.2011.561474

Paige, R. U. (2005). Proceedings of the American Psychological Association, Incorporated, for the legislative year 2004. Minutes of the meeting of the Council of Representatives. *American Psychologist, 60*, 436–511. doi:10.1037/0003-066X.60.5.436

Robertson, C. (2012, May 8,). North Carolina voters pass same-sex marriage ban. *New York Times.* Retrieved July 23, 2013 from http://www.nytimes.com/2012/05/09/us/north-carolina-voters-pass-same-sex-marriage-ban.html

Russell, G. M., & Horne, S. G. (2009). Finding equilibrium: Mentoring, sexual orientation, and gender identity. *Professional Psychology: Research and Practice, 40*, 194–200. doi:10.1037/a0011860

Schmidt, C. K., & Nilsson, J. E. (2006). The effects of simultaneous developmental processes: Factors relating to the career development of lesbian, gay, and bisexual youth. *The Career Development Quarterly, 55*, 22–37.

Sheets, R. L. & Mohr, J. J. (2009). Perceived social support from friends and family and psychosocial functioning in bisexual young adult college students. *Journal of Counseling Psychology, 56*, 152–163. doi:10.1037/0022-0167.56.1.152.

Shelton, K. A., & Delgado-Romero, E. A. (2011). Sexual orientation microaggressions: The experience of lesbian, gay, bisexual, and queer clients in psychotherapy. *Journal of Counseling Psychology, 58*, 210–221. doi:10.1037/a0022251

Smith, L. C., Shin, R. Q., & Officer, L. M. (2012). Moving counseling forward on LGB and transgender issues: Speaking queerly on discourses and microaggressions. *The Counseling Psychologist, 40*, 385–408. doi:10.1177/0011000011403165

Speight, S. L., & Vera, E. M. (2006). Social justice and counseling psychology: A challenge to the profession. In S. D. Brown, & R. W. Lent (Eds.), *Handbook of counseling psychology* (4th ed., pp. 54–67). Hoboken, NJ: Wiley.

Sue, D. W. (2010). *Microaggressions in everyday life: Race, gender, and sexual orientation.* Hoboken, NJ: Wiley.

Sue, D. W., Arredondo, P., & McDavis, R. J. (1992). Multicultural counseling competencies and standards: A call to the profession. *Journal of Counseling & Development, 70*, 477–486. doi:10.1002/j.2161-1912.1992.tb00563.x

Sue, D. W., Bernier, J., Durran, M., Feinberg, L., Pedersen, P., Smith, E., & Vasquez-Nuttall, E. (1982). Position paper: Cross-cultural counseling competencies. *The Counseling Psychologist, 10*, 45–52.

Sue, D. W., Capodilupo, C. M., Torino, G. C., Bucceri, J. M., Holder, A. M. B., Nadal, K. L., & Esquilin, M. (2007). Racial microaggressions in everyday life: Implications for clinical practice. *American Psychologist, 62*, 271–286. doi:10.1037/0003-066X.62.4.271

Szymanski, D. M., Kashubeck-West, S., & Meyer, J. (2008). Internalized heterosexism: Measurement, psychosocial correlates, and research directions. *The Counseling Psychologist, 36*, 525–574. doi:10.1177/0011000007309489

Tenenbaum, H. R., Crosby, F. J., & Gliner, M. D. (2001). Mentoring relationships in graduate school. *Journal of Vocational Behavior, 59*, 326–341. doi:10.1006/jvbe.2001.1804

Thompson, N. L., McCandless, B. R., & Strickland, B. R. (1971). Personal adjustment of male and female homosexuals and heterosexuals. *Journal of Abnormal Psychology, 78*, 237–240. doi:10.1037/h0031990

Toporek, R. L., & McNally, C. J. (2006). Social justice training in counseling psychology. In R. L. Toporek, L. H. Gerstein, N. A. Fouad, G. Roysircar, & T. Israel (Eds.), *Handbook for social justice in counseling psychology: Leadership, vision, and action* (pp. 37–43). Thousand Oaks, CA: Sage.

Ward v. Wilbanks, No. 09-CV-112 37, 2010 U.S. Dist. Westlaw 3026428 (E. D. Michigan, July 26, 2010).

Weeks, J. (2011). The social construction of sexuality. In S. Seidman, N. Fischer, & C. Meeks (Eds.), *Introducing the new sexuality studies* (2nd ed., pp. 13–19). New York: Routledge.

Wei, M., Liao, K. Y.-H., Chao, R. C.-L., Mallinckrodt, B., Tsai, P.-C., & Botello-Zamarron, R. (2010, September 20). Minority stress, perceived bicultural competence, and depressive symptoms among ethnic minority college students. *Journal of Counseling Psychology.* Advance online publication. doi:10.1037/a0020790

Williams-Nickelson, C. (2009). Mentoring women graduate students: A model for professional psychology. *Professional Psychology: Research and Practice, 40*, 284–291. doi:10.1037/a0012450

World Professional Transgender Health Association (2012a). *Standards of Care for the Health of Transsexual, Transgender, and Gender Nonconforming People.* Minneapolis, MN: Author. Retrieved August 24, 2012 from http://www.wpath.org/documents/SOC%20V7%2003-17-12.pdf

World Professional Transgender Health Association (2012b). *WPATH De-Psychopatholisation Statement.* Retrieved July 23, 2013 from http://www.wpath.org/publications_public_policy.cfm

Zúñiga, X., Nagda, B. A. & Sevig, T. D. (2002). Intergroup dialogues: An educational model for cultivating engagement across differences. *Equity and Excellence in Education, 35*, 7–17.

Religion in Education and Training

Clark D. Campbell

Abstract

The religious distinctive doctoral programs that are accredited by the American Psychological Association (APA) provide a significant training niche in the landscape of professional psychology education. We live in a culture in which religion plays an important role in the everyday lives of people, and religion is particularly salient when people cope with trauma and emotional difficulties. Religion is a factor of cultural diversity, yet psychologists as a group have not embraced its role either personally or professionally. Although religious distinctive programs provide doctoral education to graduate students interested in working with spiritual and religious issues within the context of psychotherapy, these programs account for relatively few graduates annually. Within the scope of professional psychology training programs, the religious distinctive programs must address relevant training issues such as academic freedom and the role of Footnote 4 in the APA accreditation guidelines.

Key Words: religion, education, training, accreditation, Footnote 4

The Need for Competence in Addressing Religious Issues in Practice

Whenever I think of religion within the context of training professional psychologists, the words of Tina Turner's song comes to mind: "What's love got to do with it, got to do with it? What's love but a sweet old-fashioned notion?" What does religion have to do with educating and training professional psychologists? Of course this question was stated more eloquently several centuries ago by Tertullian when he asked, "What does Athens have to do with Jerusalem?" (cited in Dunn, 2004, p. 23). Simply stated, in contemporary scholarship and education, what does the Academy have to do with religion? Specifically, what does doctoral education and training in psychology have to do with religion?

To address this and related questions adequately, one has to look at the role of religion in society, in mental health, in mental illness, and in the psychotherapy process. Findings from these areas establish the need for psychologists who are competent to address the spiritual and religious issues that are intertwined in the lives of those who seek psychological help. The focus of this chapter will be on the religious distinctive model of training in religion for psychologists. This model will be described along with some of the strengths and associated controversies of the model within professional psychology.

Role of Religion in Society

There are hundreds of world and indigenous religions, and more than 2,800 religious organizations in North America alone (Melton, 2009). The number of religions and the terms used to describe religion speak to the complexity and diversity of religious beliefs and practices around the world. More recently the term spirituality has been used to describe the personal aspects of religion. Spirituality is a broader concept than religion and is described as a personal expression of faith and connection with the sacred without the traditional and institutional aspects of religion. Hill and colleagues (2000) describe spirituality as involving one's relationship to the transcendent as experienced in one's feelings, thoughts, and behaviors. Religion, on the other hand, is a more narrow construct that describes adhering to a particular worldview or core set of beliefs or doctrines, as well as exhibiting behaviors that are sanctioned by a religious community or tradition.

Worthington and Aten (2009) categorized four types of spirituality according to the object that is viewed as sacred: religious spirituality, humanistic spirituality, nature spirituality, and cosmos spirituality. According to this categorization, spirituality may or may not be religious. Over the last couple of decades, being "spiritual but not religious" is a phrase that has become increasingly popular (Fuller, 2001), and a national newspaper reported a survey in which 72% of 18- to 29-year-olds described themselves as more spiritual than religious (Grossman, 2010). However, Hill and colleagues (2000) reviewed the research in this area and reported that many people integrate both religion and spirituality into their lives and state that these "phenomena are inherently intertwined" (p. 72). Aten and Leach (2009) also cite several studies in which people describe themselves as both religious and spiritual. So, although it may be in vogue to describe oneself as spiritual rather than religious, "several researchers have cautioned against superficial separation between religion and spirituality" (Aten, Hall, Weaver, Mangis, & Campbell, 2012, p. 82). Given the significant overlap in these terms, spirituality and religion (or religious) will be used interchangeably in this essay.

Religion appears to have been in existence since humans began interacting, and religion, or some concept of the divine, is found in every culture. Some have described this as a reflection of an innate religious tendency within persons; yet one that finds various expressions across time and culture (Jung, 1958; 1964). This need to relate to some things or beings as sacred or transcendent, and to hold those things or beings in awe or worship, is common and has been described by anthropologists, sociologists, theologians, and psychologists for centuries (Meadow & Kahoe, 1984). Timpe (1999) describes the Latin origin of the word religion: "Hence religion is seen etymologically as a force that reconnects human disjointedness, restrains errant impulses, and gives uniqueness, identity, and integrity to the individual" (p. 1020). Religion, then, promotes identity, connection, reflective action, and integration.

The role of religion in American society has been studied for decades, and this research consistently indicates that religion is an important aspect of people's lives. Approximately 95% of Americans believe in God, and 40% attend religious services at least weekly (Gallup 2002; Gallup & Lindsay, 1999). The Pew Forum on Religion & Public Life (2008) reported a survey of 35,000 adults and found that 56% indicated that religion was very important in their daily lives. Approximately 85% of Americans identify as Christian (59% Protestant and 26% Catholic); 2% identify as Jewish; 3% identify as either Hindu, Muslim, or Buddhist; and 6% do not identify with a religious tradition. Religion plays a major role in the lives of most Americans.

The Role of Religion in Mental Health

Only a brief summary is offered here regarding the significant body of literature on the critical role of religion in well-being and mental health. Several surveys report a positive relationship between religious affiliation and mental and physical health, and Plante (2009) summarized some of these findings: "People who engage in religious-spiritual tradition tend to be healthier and happier, maintain better habits, and have more social support than those who do not engage in religious-spiritual activities, interests, and beliefs" (p. 14). Interestingly, religiously affiliated people live about seven years longer than people who are not religiously affiliated (Miller & Thoresen, 2003).

A Gallup poll of more than 500,000 Americans reported that very religious people reported higher levels of well-being even when demographic factors were controlled (Gallup Organization, 2010). Several findings on psychological well-being (including happiness, purpose, meaning, self-esteem, and marital satisfaction) were reported in the literature review of more than 850 studies by Moreira-Almeida, Neto, and Koenig (2006). Additionally, they reported that high levels of religiosity were generally associated with lower levels of depression, substance abuse, and suicidal behavior.

The Role of Religion in Mental, Social, and Health Problems

Religiosity has been associated with avoiding or rejecting needed medical and psychological services (Pargament, 1997; 2007). African American women may rely on religious coping and prayer rather than seeking medical help for breast cancer (Mitchell, Lannin, Mathews, & Swanson, 2002). Many psychologists have worked with delusional individuals who have incorporated strong religious themes into their delusions, or have worked with clients who use their religious beliefs to harm, oppress, and control others for their own advantage. Religion has been used to instill guilt and anxiety, and has been used in a manipulative manner by those in power against vulnerable individuals. Religious beliefs and practices have even been used as a rationale for war. Thus there are negative aspects to religious belief as well (Plante, 2009).

The Role of Religion in Psychotherapy

Many people use religious resources to cope with psychological difficulties. Moreira-Almedia and colleagues (2006) reported that the positive outcomes associated with religion were even more evident when stressful events were experienced. When facing disaster events, approximately 70% of Americans use their faith and faith community to cope (Weaver, Flannelly, Garbarino, Figley, & Flannelly, 2003). Additionally, Lindgren and Coursey (1995) found that two thirds of adults with serious mental illness wanted to discuss spiritual issues in psychotherapy, but most felt uncomfortable doing so. Similarly, Rose, Westefeld, and Ansley (2001) found that when clients were offered the option, they preferred to discuss spiritual and religious issues in therapy.

Whether or not psychologists are competent or comfortable addressing religious issues or using religious coping resources, it appears that most clients have an expectation that their religion will not be checked at the door of the psychotherapy office. Eck (2002) estimated that 80% to 90% of clients in psychotherapy are dealing with some kind of spiritual or religious issue in their lives. Sometimes the religious issues are crucial in the psychotherapy context. In a recent article on ethical issues related to religion in psychotherapy, Barnett and Johnson (2011) write, "It stands to reason that when clients present for psychotherapy, religious or spiritual concerns may occasionally play a crucial role in both the process and outcome of treatment" (p. 149).

Because religious issues are likely to be involved in psychotherapy encounters, it is important that psychologists become aware of their own religious beliefs as well as their clients' beliefs. Without this awareness the psychologist runs two risks—imposing his or her own religious beliefs on the client or being insensitive to important worldview issues of the client. "For just as there is the risk that religious counselors might impose their religious values on clients, however inadvertently, there is also the risk

that counselors who are nonreligious or religiously uninformed might be insensitive to important aspects of client experience" (Schulte, Skinner, & Claiborn, 2002, p. 120). Intentional training of psychologists to address religious issues in psychotherapy could lessen the likelihood of these risks.

Therapist behaviors are important when religious issues are discussed in psychotherapy. Sorenson (1997) studied religiously committed graduate students who sought personal growth psychotherapy. He found six therapist behaviors that facilitated the students' growth: (a) acknowledging their relationship with God as real; (b) a non-defensive and open approach to their faith; (c) connecting the student's experience to their parents, God, and the therapist; (d) viewing their relationship with God as positive and a potential resource; (e) expecting that issues of faith would be discussed in therapy; and (f) demonstrating a personal openness to the transcendent. Although this in-depth study pertained to graduate students as clients, the therapist behaviors are likely applicable to psychotherapy with non-student clients who want to have their faith integrated with therapy.

Religious beliefs are likely to have an impact on whether or not one seeks treatment, as well as on the treatment process and outcome (Eck, 2002). These findings point to the need for psychologists who are trained to understand religious issues in themselves and others, as well as the role these issues play in health and illness.

Religion and Psychologists

Unfortunately, psychologists as a group do not share religious beliefs and practices to the same extent as the general public. Although many of the founders of clinical psychology had significant religious influences in their development, several of them rejected the value of religion in the therapeutic process. For example, Freud described God as nothing more than a projected father image (see *The Future of an Illusion*, 1961; *Moses and Monotheism*, 1955; and *Totem and Taboo*, 1950.) Freud writes, "the defense against childish helplessness is what lends its characteristic features to the adult's reaction to the helplessness which he has to acknowledge—a reaction which is precisely the formation of religion" (1961, p. 24). In comparing Freud to C. S. Lewis' views on religion, Nicholi (2002) notes that Lewis turns Freud's argument on its head. Lewis' position is that the universal wish for a rescuer or father figure actually may be evidence for, not against, the existence of the rescuer.

Another famous psychologist, Albert Ellis, was also direct about his belief that religion did not have any place in psychotherapy (see *The Case Against Religion: A Psychotherapist's View and the Case Against Religiosity*, 1980.) He emphasized the negative aspects of religion and seemed to think of religion as an intellectual and emotional crutch.

In addition to leaders in the field having negative reactions to religion, most psychologists do not share religious beliefs to the same degree as the general population. "Relative to the general population, psychologists [are] more than twice as likely to claim no religion, three times more likely to describe religion as unimportant in their lives, and five times more likely to deny belief in God" (Delaney, Miller, & Bisono, 2007, p. 542). Bergin and Jensen (1990) found that 72% of the general population agreed with the statement "My whole approach to life is based on my religion," while only 33% of the psychologists surveyed agreed with this statement. Furthermore, Walker, Gorsuch, and Tan (2004) reviewed four studies involving more than 1,100 therapists and found that 82% of the therapists reported never or rarely discussing religious or spiritual issues in their training.

Shafranske (2000) found that 51% of the psychologists in his sample reported that religion was not important to them. Similarly, Delaney and colleagues (2007) found that half of the psychologists in their study indicated that religion was not important in their lives. There is also evidence that psychologists do not incorporate religious or spiritual issues into their treatment planning. Hathaway, Scott, and Garver (2004) surveyed 1,000 clinical psychologists in a national sample and found that psychologists believed that client religion or spirituality was an important area of functioning. However, most of these same psychologists reported that they did not address religion or spirituality in treatment planning. More recently, McMinn, Hathaway, Woods, and Snow (2009) surveyed APA division presidents and council representatives. They found that 37% of these leaders indicated that *religion* was not at all important, yet 61% indicated that *spirituality* was somewhat or very important to them. Perhaps this more recent survey suggests increasing interest in spirituality rather than religion among psychologists.

Education and Training in Religion Within Psychology Programs

As with psychologists, psychology training programs in general have not been affirming of religious topics in the curriculum. Few programs include religious or spiritual issues in the training of their graduate students (Hage, Hopson, Siegel, Payton, & DeFanti, 2006). This may be due to the lack of competence (or perceived lack of competence) in addressing religious diversity issues by the faculty in these programs (Hage, 2006). Early reports by Shafranske and Maloney (1990) indicated that fewer than 5% of clinical psychologists had religious or spiritual issues addressed in their professional training. Similarly, no internship programs offered training on these issues in a survey conducted by Lannert (1991). In a more comprehensive survey of directors of clinical training in APA-accredited clinical programs, Brawer, Handal, Fabricatore, Roberts, and Wajda-Johnston (2002) found that 17% of the programs covered religion or spirituality in the areas of course work, supervision, and research. Fifty-three percent of the programs covered this diversity topic in two of the three areas, but 16% of the programs did not cover these issues at all.

Russell and Yarhouse (2006) conducted a survey of training directors in psychology internship programs and found that 68% "never foresee religious/spiritual training being offered in their program" (p. 434). Although faculty members in doctoral programs appear open to classroom discussions and willing to supervise students on religious issues in psychotherapy (Brawer et al, 2002), they may lack competence to fully embrace these issues in training graduate students. Brawer and colleagues (2002) summarize their findings by stating, "Few psychologists have received professional training with regard to religion and spirituality, despite the public's overwhelming interest. Currently, the topic of religion/spirituality is being covered to some degree in most accredited clinical programs. However, a distinct minority of these programs approaches this education and training in a systematic fashion" (p. 203).

Given the prevalence of religious beliefs in the general population, the ways in which most people see religious issues involved in their everyday experiences, and especially issues related to suffering and coping, professional psychology training programs may be missing an important area of training for doctoral students. Hage (2006) stated this issue clearly: "the failure to integrate content related to spiritual and religious issues into psychology training may have significant consequences for the overall mental well-being of individuals and families" (p. 303).

In addition to the general lack of training to address religious issues in professional programs, there has been some evidence that programs are hesitant to admit overtly religious students. Gartner (1986) mailed identical admission applications, except for a brief statement that referred to the applicant's personal religious experience, to APA-accredited doctoral programs. Applicants who were considered to be evangelical fundamentalist Christians were significantly less likely to be admitted than were applicants who made no mention of religious experience. This study and the anecdotal reports of several students propelled the perspective that secular doctoral programs were not open to training students who wanted to maintain an open religious identity.

APA Ethics Code and Guidelines Related to Religion

In the last few decades religion has been recognized as an important area of human functioning and has been conceptualized as an area of diversity that should be respected and valued in research and practice. Principle E of the APA Ethics Code lists several aspects of diversity and states that psychologists "are aware of and respect...religion...and consider these factors when working with members of such groups" (APA, 2002, p. 1063). Thus, all members of the APA are supposed to show respect and awareness of the ways in which religious issues could be involved when providing psychological services. Similarly, Standard 3.01 states that psychologists may not "engage in unfair discrimination based on...religion" (p. 1064). Ethical psychologists respect religion and do not engage in unfair discrimination based on religious issues.

In addition to the APA Ethics Code, three guidelines provide assistance for work with religious persons and their presenting problems. The *APA Guidelines for Providers of Psychological Services to Ethnic, Linguistic, and Culturally Diverse Populations* (APA, 1993) state that "psychologists respect clients' religious and/or spiritual beliefs and values, including attributions and taboos since they affect worldview, psychological functioning, and expressions of distress" (p. 46). Similarly, the *APA Guidelines on Multicultural Education, Training, Research, Practice, and Organizational Change for Psychologists* (APA, 2005) affirm that all interpersonal interactions occur in a multicultural context and that religion is one aspect of that context that should be accommodated. More recently, Division 36 (Psychology of Religion) of APA published the *Preliminary Practice Guidelines for Working with Religious and Spiritual Issues* (Hathaway & Ripley, 2009). These 26 practice guidelines provide assistance with such issues as assessment, informed consent, respect, and self-awareness.

Approaches to Education on Religious Issues in Doctoral Programs

The Ethical Principles of Psychologists and Code of Conduct (APA, 2002) and the guidelines cited above make it clear that religion and spirituality are diversity issues that psychologists should consider to practice competently in our multicultural society. Yet, as stated earlier, relatively few programs train doctoral students explicitly in this area, and most psychologists do not hold personal religious beliefs that may provide the internal impetus to motivate this emphasis in training programs. Yarhouse and Fisher (2002) acknowledge that strides have been made in encouraging diversity education in religion, yet recognize that few programs offer substantial training in this area. They write, "there appears to be little evidence of widespread intention to train psychology students and existing practitioners in clinical service delivery to religious persons" (p. 173).

In an attempt to address this lack of training in professional psychology programs, Yarhouse and Fisher (2002) recommended a three-tier system that accommodates religious diversity training in doctoral programs. The three tiers describe training models for competency in the assessment and intervention of psychologically relevant religious issues, and the three models are hierarchically related to one another. The first two models could be incorporated into existing training programs, whereas the third model is distinct and involves more comprehensive training. The first model is called the *Integration-Incorporation Model*, which involves incorporating religious issues into several already existing classes in the curriculum. Yarhouse and Fisher (2002) suggest that relevant classes may be ethics, clinical interviewing, child, adult and family therapy, psychopathology, and assessment.

More recently, Worthington and colleagues (2009) elaborated a model for understanding spiritual and religious clients. This model, which could be incorporated into existing doctoral programs, involves facilitating comfort among graduate students in dealing with religious issues. The model then suggests movement from facilitating comfort to skill acquisition in areas such as taking a religious history, assessment of spiritual functioning, and working with the psychological meaning of significant spiritual experiences.

The second model described by Yarhouse and Fisher (2002) is called the *Certificate-Minor Model*, which involves the development of a track in which students can take some courses in working responsibly with religious issues. This model requires the addition of some elective courses and functions best in a system in which there are other tracks available as well.

The third model proposed by Yarhouse and Fisher (2002) is the *Religious Distinctive Model*, which "provides a full degree in clinical psychology through a doctoral program that is shaped by a specific religious tradition" (p. 174). Programs employing this model require faculty, and often students as well, to endorse a doctrinal or faith statement in order to teach or matriculate into the program. In addition to the typical curriculum required for an APA-accredited doctoral program, this model requires additional coursework (and sometimes an additional graduate degree) in theological studies. The religious distinctive model provides in-depth interaction between faculty and students on clinical and research topics in the context of a distinct religious worldview, which is seen as a major benefit of the model. This model seeks to train "clearly religious doctoral students from within a distinctively religious milieu for eventual service to the larger faith community" (Johnson, Campbell, & Dykstra, 1997, p. 265). Johnson and colleagues (1997) describe graduates of these programs as "faith identified psychologists."

Presently those training programs operating on the *Religious Distinctive Model* exist exclusively within the Christian religious tradition, and these programs will be discussed in the sections that follow. There is no reason, however, that other religious traditions could not develop similar programs designed to address the specific religious and psychological issues of their faith tradition.

Christian Universities and Religious Distinctive Programs

In order to understand the religious distinctive programs, it is helpful to view the current relationship between religion and training in professional psychology within the broader context of university education. The debate and controversy about the relationship between religion and higher education has been around for a long time and continues to be a matter of important discussion (Marsden, 1997; Sommerville, 2006). Part of the conflict revolves around the nature of religious dogma and the way that it has been taught within some institutions as a process of indoctrination rather than education. Thoughtful educators within the academy view education as a free expression of ideas in the marketplace of ideas, and not as a forum for indoctrination (Diekema, 2000). However, this is not the same as saying that there is no structure to the pursuit of truth or that there is not a worldview that directs the way these ideas are pursued and discussed (Holmes, 1987). Faculty members within Christian institutions approach the pursuit of truth from a Christian worldview (Huffman, 2011), which is an interpretive and conceptual scheme for viewing the world based on Scripture, tradition, reason, and experience.

The interface between religion and academic disciplines, or faith and reason, gets to the heart of the existence of universities. Newman (1960) wrote that universities begin with an idea, not brick and mortar, and therefore the nature of a university is to create, explore, explain, and teach knowledge that is unified in some coherent or cohesive way. Traditionally, universities engage a community of scholars who are dedicated to the creation and dissemination of knowledge (Kerr, 1963); further, universities provide a forum for exploring, understanding, and teaching what is true, good, and beautiful. From this perspective universities are always culturally embedded. The culture holds one or more moral visions (a worldview and ethos) about what is true, good, and beautiful, and the universities explore, develop, expand, and teach from that moral vision (Diekema, 2000).

All disciplines, including the sciences, are grounded in a moral vision, and this is particularly true of the social sciences. "Social science makes assumptions about the nature of persons, the nature of society, the relation between persons and society. It also, whether it admits it or not, makes assumptions about good persons and a good society and considers how far these assumptions are embedded in our actual society" (Bellah, Madsen, Sullivan, Swidler, & Tipton, 1985, p. 301). Professional education and training is a reflection of embedded assumptions, and religious distinctive programs attempt to be intentional about these assumptions.

The ways in which religious beliefs and psychology relate within Christian universities have often been described as the "integration of psychology and theology." The phrase itself may offend some psychologists, but it is an important concept for understanding how various universities within the Christian tradition approach relating faith issues with the science of psychology (Jones, 1994).

Carter and Narramore (1979) presented various models of relating psychology and theology that are based on the work of theologian Niebuhr (1951). The *Against Model* posits that psychology and religion cannot be integrated because they oppose each other and are fundamentally incompatible. The *Of Model* (psychology of religion) posits that these are two different disciplines that benefit each other when they evaluate the other discipline from the perspective of their own discipline. The *Parallels Model* posits that these are two separate disciplines with their own sources of data, goals, and methods. One gains a broader perspective on reality by respecting the other discipline, but there is little integration between the two disciplines. The *Integrates Model* posits that there is unity of truth and that truth can be known. Therefore, truth found in psychology is fundamentally compatible with truth found in Scripture. This model explores the congruency of truth between psychology and theology looking for how each discipline expands and clarifies the other.

These models represent various ways of understanding the association between psychology and theology at an academic level, and they have been informative in the development of the religious distinctive programs. Although there have been adherents to each of these models within the religious programs, the *Integrates Model* is the one to which many adhere and find meaning in their academic work.

Specific Religious Distinctive Programs

There are currently a few programs, probably fewer than a dozen, in universities that offer doctoral professional psychology education and training within a Christian context that are also accredited by the APA. There is no reason that other religious traditions cannot have similar programs, but at this point in time, all religious distinctive programs are founded on the Christian faith tradition. It is unclear just how many doctoral programs identify as religious distinctive, and that is one of the reasons that the APA required these programs to self-identify in their accreditation documentation (APA Commission on Accreditation, Implementing Regulations [C-22a], 2009a). This accreditation information, however, is not available to the public according to Commission on Accreditation policy, so one has to look at each accredited program website (where the information is publically available) to discern whether the program is religiously distinctive.

Using data from the APA Center for Work Force Studies, Kohut and Wicherski (2010) reported that there are roughly 3,000 students who obtain a doctoral degree annually in clinical or counseling psychology. It is difficult to know the actual number of graduates from religious distinctive programs, but it would be reasonable to estimate that, combined, these programs generate about 175 doctorates annually. This means that less than 6% of the annual professional psychology graduates are from religious distinctive programs, a percentage much smaller than represents the percentage of the population who endorse Christian faith.

For the sake of clarity, religious distinctive programs that are APA accredited are those that come under the Footnote 4 provisions of the *Guidelines and Principles for Accreditation of Programs in Professional Psychology*, known as the G&P (APA, 2009b). The implementation of this footnote will be discussed below, but it will be helpful to review the history that led to the development of the footnote. Campbell (2011) recently provided a summary of this history, and an abbreviated version of which follows.

In 1962, Fuller Theological Seminary in California was given a grant and a decision was made by its board of trustees to start a PhD program in clinical psychology. The seminary hired a respected clinical scientist as dean and assembled a distinguished faculty to begin this program. In 1965, students matriculated for the first class, and Dean Lee Travis wrote to the APA Education and Training Board to inquire about accreditation of the program. The first application for accreditation was made in 1972, but the Education and Training Board seemed unsure of what to do about accrediting a doctoral program housed within a seminary. After two site visits and correspondence, the APA awarded accreditation in 1974. Other programs in explicitly Christian institutions had similar difficulties with initial APA accreditation over the last three decades, which led Campbell (2011) to speculate about the possibility of unintentional bias in the accreditation process.

The concern over religious freedom led to the development of Footnote 3 in the accreditation guidelines, which allowed for APA-accredited programs to have specific religious distinctives consistent with their faith tradition (personal communication, Susan Zlotlow, 3/24/10). This footnote was revised in 1995 to be consistent with the First Amendment of the United States (U.S.) Constitution, and language was adopted from the American Bar Association. This rewritten footnote became Footnote 4 and allows religious institutions to exercise religious preferences in hiring employees and admitting students.

Although there are some similarities among the religious distinctive APA-accredited programs, there is also considerable variation. Some programs require students to endorse a faith statement or creed in order to matriculate. Others also require students to endorse a code of conduct or adhere to behavioral expectations in order to matriculate. Similarly, schools vary on the degree to which they require faculty to abide by such creeds and codes of conduct. Although the lack of uniformity in these requirements for matriculation or employment may be confusing to some, it is seen as a reflection of the religious diversity in America and within educational institutions, and therefore is consistent with an appropriately diverse approach to education.

For the most part, programs that invoke Footnote 4 are housed in protestant Christian universities that take their religious roots and commitments very seriously. It is inaccurate to think of religious distinctive programs as simply discriminating in hiring and admissions. Discrimination is considered to be prejudicial hiring or admission of individuals based on their group membership. In religious distinctive programs, preference is shown for those who endorse specific doctrinal statements and experiences, and agree to abide by behavioral standards regardless of their group status. Hiring and admissions are part of a broader approach to education in psychology that matches the overall integration of faith and learning that these schools attempt to achieve. Schools that invoke Footnote 4 are likely to have the following characteristics:

• The mission of the parent institution (university) has been developed from a recognized faith tradition, and its mission involves education and service to religious communities as well as the broader population as part of the underlying religious foundation of the institution.

• The goals of the psychology doctoral program include service to religious communities and/or research to enhance the understanding of how faith and belief relate in psychological practice.

• The goals of the doctoral program are consistent with the overall mission of the parent institution (university). This is a requirement of the accreditation G&P (APA, 2009b).

• Faculty and/or students may be hired or selected based on consistency with the mission and goals of the institution and the doctoral program.

• There are required courses in the curriculum that facilitate these goals and expand students' understanding of how religion impacts human behavior. These courses may include religion, theology, or an integration of psychology and theology.

• There are clinical training experiences that involve acquisition of knowledge, skills, and attitudes that prepare students to serve religious communities, and this training is consistent with the mission of the program and the university.

• Supervision of clinical experience and training is provided by a variety of supervisors, some of whom are employed by the university and hold similar religious beliefs, and many of whom are employed by the practicum and internship agencies and do not hold similar religious beliefs.

Some institutions may frame each of the foregoing features differently, but it is likely that those programs invoking Footnote 4 acknowledge these characteristics of their programs.

In describing why such programs exist, Johnson, Campbell, and Dykstra (1997) write, "Religious graduate programs in professional psychology exist for the purpose of training psychologists to serve the needs of the global religious community, including churches, parachurch organizations, and individuals" (p. 263). Johnson and McMinn (2003) succinctly describe the rationale for the existence of these programs: (a) the high endorsement of belief in God in the U.S. population and the related influence in people's lives; (b) many psychologists seeming uninterested and perhaps hostile to the religious beliefs of clients; (c) the bias against openly religious applicants to secular graduate programs in psychology; (d) the historic role of the church in providing care, including psychological care, for those in need; and (e) the frequency with which clients present clinically relevant religious beliefs. This rationale could be used to support the addition of many more programs to meet the psychological needs of those in the faith community, but there is recognition among the religious distinctive programs that quality education and training in psychology is expensive and requires substantial resources on the part of parent universities.

Religious distinctive programs attempt to expand students' understanding of the ways religious beliefs and psychological concepts interact rather than reinforce rigid religious beliefs, and many students find this deconstructive process to be challenging (Sorenson, 1997; Sorenson & Hales, 2002). This process further equips students to understand their own religious beliefs and not impose their beliefs on others in clinical practice. Worthington and colleagues (2009) commented that religious distinctive programs "provide special attention to dealing sensitively with clients who (a) are not of the spiritual or religious faith of most of the therapists, supervisors, and teachers in the program; (b) profess no faith; (c) are antagonistic to any faith tradition; or (d) consider themselves spiritual but not religious" (p. 268). Clearly, religious distinctive programs must prepare students for work with a broad range of clients who maintain a variety of religious beliefs.

Religious distinctive programs also produce similar professional outcomes as secular programs in terms of faculty and student publication rates and job placement. Student admission selectivity and internship placement rates also are similar between religious distinctive and secular programs (Johnson & McMinn, 2003; McMinn, Johnson, & Haskell, 2004).

Clinical Training in Religious Distinctive Programs

Clinical training in the religious distinctive programs is more similar to than different from clinical training in other APA-accredited clinical programs where the educational model is primarily designed to produce practitioners. Although considerable research training is provided in these programs, the focus has been on training practitioners. The training is sequential, cumulative, and graded in complexity, as is required by the G&P (APA. 2009b). Training begins with pre-practicum, where students learn foundational skills in an intensive lab situation that involves videotape and review of sessions with evaluative feedback by faculty. Some practicum placements may occur on campus, but most placements are off campus and utilize a variety of secular placements in community mental health centers, medical centers, college counseling centers, and forensic settings. These training experiences provide broad exposure to both clinical populations that are severe and those that are growth oriented and less severe. Licensed psychologists, most of whom are not employed by the clinical programs, provide supervision in practicum placements, and many of these psychologists do not have explicit religious affiliations.

The pre-practicum and practicum training prepares students for internship, which occurs in recognized training settings (primarily APA accredited or Association of Psychology Postdoctoral and Internship Centers affiliated). Although some nationally recognized internships are associated with religious organizations, very few have such an affiliation. Supervision in internship settings is therefore provided by licensed psychologists who are not employed by or affiliated with religious institutions. Religious distinctive programs recognize the need for students to have broad training with a variety of clients and supervisors, many of whom will not share their worldview, belief system, or behavioral expectations.

As in other APA-accredited clinical training programs, doctoral students in religious distinctive programs are expected to have training in evidence-based practices and to learn to track the outcomes of their therapeutic interventions, as required in the G&P (APA, 2009b). Thus in coursework, supervision, and clinical experience, students learn the competencies that are necessary for licensure and competent practice in the field.

What then is distinctive about these programs in terms of education and clinical training? Although there is variability between programs, students are required to complete courses in biblical studies (biblical literature, language studies, interpretation), theology (church doctrines and creeds), and religion (world religions and worldviews). They also complete required courses in the integration of psychology and theology (e.g., addressing religious issues in psychotherapy) so that they can understand and respond to some of the complex intersections of these fields of study. Finally, they receive instruction and supervision on some of the specific spiritual topics that are described in the psychotherapy literature, such as the use of religious language, prayer, Scripture, forgiveness, and religious imagery (Walker, Gorsuch, & Tan, 2005; Wade, Worthington, & Vogel, 2007).

Considerable attention is given to ethics (such as informed consent) and caution in using religious or spiritual interventions, so students likely learn about when to use and not use these interventions. Faculty also give considerable emphasis to discerning the meaning of these topics to clients, so that students use these interventions in psychologically sophisticated ways that benefit clients and are not simply a manifestation of transference or countertransference.

In general, students are taught to respond to religious issues in psychotherapy rather than to initiate discussion on religious topics. It is the ability to respond in a psychologically informed manner rather than avoid such topics that distinguishes the well-trained clinician who is from a religious distinctive program. Interestingly, Sorenson and Hales

(2002) found that religious therapists who graduated from secular programs used religious interventions more frequently than those who graduated from the religious distinctive programs. Perhaps the training provided in religious distinctive programs prepares students for more judicious use of such interventions. Walker, Gorsuch, and Tan (2005) found that it was the clinical training and not the course work, however, that most prepared therapists to use religious interventions competently. Thus supervision, workshops, and clinical practice with these interventions are the most salient components of developing competence in this area.

A survey of graduate students, alumni, and faculty in religious distinctive programs indicated that students were satisfied with their clinical training at these institutions (McMinn, Bearse, Heyne, & Staley, 2011). Interestingly, the alumni satisfaction ratings were higher than the student ratings, which the authors speculate may be due to graduates having more opportunity to compare their training with that of colleagues from other programs and thus retrospectively valuing their own training more highly. Student-faculty relationships were the primary strength identified in the survey, which suggests that the mentoring bond between students and faculty in these programs is very strong.

A recent special edition of the *Journal of Psychology and Christianity* (McMinn & Hill, 2011) was devoted to clinical training in explicitly Christian doctoral programs. The editors commented on four themes in the descriptions of the programs by the Directors of Clinical Training (DCTs): (a) although the programs had different emphases, each DCT was enthusiastic about the mission of his or her program; (b) the observed transformation of students in the second year of the programs, which appeared to be the result of students' diverse and challenging clinical work; (c) the intentional progress of training in which students seemed to uniformly embrace increasing professional responsibility; and (d) the varied meanings of "integration" in these programs, ranging from more conceptual to more practical emphases.

It is difficult to gauge the practices of the graduates of these programs because much of the research on religious interventions and practices involves "Christian counseling," a term that is broad, ill-defined, and involves practitioners from various professional backgrounds who are not necessarily psychologists (McMinn, Staley, Webb, & Seegobin, 2010). Wade, Worthington, and Vogel (2007) compared the practices of Christian counseling agencies and a secular agency and found that therapists in the Christian agencies used secular interventions as frequently as therapists in the secular agency, but the Christian therapists used religious interventions more frequently. They also found that clients with high religious commitment reported greater improvement in their presenting concerns when receiving religious interventions than the low religious commitment clients.

In a large meta-analysis involving more than 5,000 psychotherapists, Walker, Gorsuch, and Tan (2004) found that religious therapists discussed forgiveness in 42% of the cases, used Scripture or biblical concepts in 39% of the cases, confronted sin in 32% of the cases, and used religious imagery in 18% of the cases. In-session prayer was used in 29% of the cases. As suggested above, it is unclear whether these studies on the practices of religious or Christian counselors reflect the practices of psychologists who graduate from the religious distinctive programs. Given that the training of psychologists is more extensive and sophisticated than counselors in general, it may be that psychologists actually use these interventions less frequently than Christian counselors as a group.

Issues in Education and Training Relevant to Religious Distinctive Programs

As may be expected, any time minority programs deviate from accepted paradigms for professional preparation, there are issues with which to reckon. In describing APA accreditation site visits to Fuller Theological Seminary, Maloney (1995) writes, "Adequate academic freedom and diversity have had to be demonstrated every time" (p. 119). Specifically, religious distinctive programs have to repeatedly address issues of academic freedom and diversity, particularly as they relate to sexual orientation and the provisions of Footnote 4 in the G&P (APA, 2009b). Both of these issues are addressed here.

Academic Freedom

One of the important issues at religious distinctive programs relates to academic freedom. Do faculty have the freedom necessary to think, write, and speak on issues relevant to their work as academics? From the outside, it may appear that any faculty member who is required to endorse a faith statement or creed and to abide by certain behavioral expectations in order to maintain employment does not have academic freedom. However, this is not the typical insiders' perspective.

Academic freedom has been described traditionally as the freedom to pursue truth wherever that pursuit may lead (Diekema, 2000). This traditional view is both the freedom to teach and the freedom to learn, and Holmes (1987) writes of these freedoms, "together they amount to the freedom of a college really to be an educational institution rather than an indoctrination center or a political tool" (p. 62). Academic freedom, then, is "the freedom to pursue truth in a responsible fashion" (Holmes, 1987, p. 69). However, it is inaccurate and limited to view academic freedom as the right to speak and express oneself in any way one desires. Diekema (2000) writes, "academic freedom is no longer viewed in the traditional sense of searching for truth through intensive study and careful reflection in the academy…. Many fear that academic freedom has become nothing more than the expression of any sentiment, any impulse, or any desire" (p. 71).

Scholars in Christian universities view truth as consistent or unitary and believe that all truth comes from God. This is part of a Christian worldview. Thus academic freedom is the freedom to make sense of facts and experiences within this worldview, which leads to greater meaning in life. Christian scholarship, then, is about developing and enhancing an integrated worldview rather than a fragmented view of life. Holmes (1987) writes, "Liberty flourishes under neither totalitarianism nor anarchy, neither legalism nor license…. Academic freedom is valuable only when there is a prior commitment to the truth. And commitment to the truth is fully worthwhile only when that truth exists in One who transcends both the relativity of human perspectives and the fears of human concern" (p. 69). Thus academic freedom is quite active and appreciated on many Christian university campuses.

It is not unusual to hear that the faculties of many universities today do not value religious beliefs. Sometimes in overt ways, but often in powerful, subtle ways, religious bias is experienced on secular campuses as reported anecdotally by faculty who seek to work in religious institutions. Pargament (2007) described how psychology faculty and students had to keep their religious interests quiet in order not to be shunned by colleagues. He noted that some faculty delayed open discussion of their religious interests and research until attaining tenure for fear that tenure would not be granted. Anecdotally, several faculty members have expressed the freedom experienced in being able to research and pursue their scholarship in a supportive and open environment provided by religiously oriented institutions.

Footnote 4 Provisions

The provisions of G&P Footnote 4 present another issue relevant to religious distinctive programs (APA, 2009b). Footnote 4 provides implementation of the First Amendment (religious freedom and freedom of speech) of the U.S. Constitution by religiously owned and/or operated private institutions and universities. This provision allows private universities to hire faculty who are in agreement with the mission and tradition of the university. In other words, these private institutions can hire preferentially based on the religious beliefs and mission of the school. This allows Jewish schools to hire Jewish faculty and Muslim schools to hire Muslim faculty, as well as Christian schools to hire Christian faculty. This does not apply to public institutions, which cannot hire preferentially based upon religion.

Footnote 4 also applies to students who matriculate in the university. It allows private institutions to admit students who agree with the faith statement of the institution. As with faculty, it also allows private institutions to implement behavioral standards of conduct that are consistent with the religious tradition of the university. Private religious institutions can choose to admit and retain only students and faculty who agree with the religious beliefs and practices of the institution.

Implementing Regulation C-22a (APA, 2009a) requires Footnote 4 programs to state publically their hiring or admission policies and to provide notice of these policies to students, faculty, and staff before their affiliation with the program. This is an important aspect of the footnote and assures that students or faculty are not blindsided in the admission or hiring process. It provides an appropriate informed consent to those interested in affiliating with the program.

Footnote 4 does not allow accredited programs to avoid teaching and training students on all forms of diversity, including sexual diversity. Thus it is intended to protect the religious freedom of the private religious organization to hire and admit those who are in agreement with the institutions' mission, but not to avoid teaching issues that are professionally relevant even if those issues are at variance with the religious tradition of the university. All Footnote 4 programs have to teach and train students to be sensitive to and respectful of all forms of diversity listed in Domain A of the G&P. These include issues related to age, disability, ethnicity, gender, gender identity, language, national origin, race, religion, culture, sexual orientation, and social economic status.

Footnote 4 and Issues Relevant to Sexual Behavior

Since many religious traditions endorse beliefs related to appropriate sexual practices, religious distinctive programs that invoke Footnote 4 may have behavioral standards that prohibit certain sexual behaviors or expressions. For example, several Christian universities that have APA-accredited professional psychology programs have policies that prohibit faculty, staff, and students from engaging in sexual intimacy outside of marriage. Furthermore, marriage is often defined as between one man and one woman. Thus heterosexual behavior and homosexual behavior outside of marriage is discouraged and prohibited among those who choose to work and study at the institution. To be clear, these statements are directed at the behavior and not the sexual orientation of the persons involved. Faculty and students of all sexual orientations are likely to work and study at these universities. However, in keeping with the theological perspectives of these universities, sexual intimacy is limited to heterosexual expression within marriage while one is affiliated with these universities.

Many may legitimately ask how a religious distinctive program could train students to work effectively with sexual orientation issues if the programs do not have faculty actively advocating for lesbian, gay, bisexual, transgender, and questioning (LGBTQ) issues. It is up to the program to ensure that all students are provided appropriate experience and supervision in order to develop minimal thresholds of competence with sexually diverse populations. This is accomplished in the religious distinctive programs through required courses on the full range of diversity, supervision by LGBTQ supervisors in non-religious facilities, and through appropriate training experiences with clinical populations that represent LGBTQ clients. It may be that this is accomplished in the same way that non-religiously affiliated programs attempt to ensure that all students are appropriately educated and trained to work with religious issues in clinical populations.

These policies appear to concern some in the LGBTQ community who may see these policies as insensitive, discriminatory, and not based on science. The concern is that by implementing these policies, these programs could produce graduates that perpetuate beliefs about sexual behavior and orientation that are inaccurate, outdated, and unscientific. These graduates, it is thought, could harm clients and perpetuate discriminatory ideas in their roles as psychologists. Thus each time an accredited program comes up for re-accreditation, the program receives detailed and multi-paged comments and questions from APA Division 44 (Society for the Psychological Study of Lesbian, Gay, Bisexual and Transgender Issues). This is sanctioned the APA Commission on Accreditation policy on public comment available to all people to address concerns with accredited programs. The comments from Division 44 often address biblical passages, theological issues, scientific findings related to LGBTQ issues, and APA policies in this area. However, the program policies of concern in these public comments are directly linked to the mission, religious tradition, and faith commitments of the universities, and changing these policies would require a major shift in theology and mission for most of these schools.

It is unfortunate that Footnote 4, which allows programs to select students and faculty who are in agreement with the institutions' mission and theological perspective, is reduced to issues relevant only to sexual orientation. The theological perspectives are tied to the goals and objectives of the doctoral program and the university, so to change something so foundational would have broad implications for the program. It may seem rather simple to change a theological perspective, and certainly changes in theology have occurred over the last centuries, but to demand change seems to be a reaction based on perspectives and worldviews rather than data. Unfortunately, there are relatively little data on either side of this debate, so we are left with some anecdotal stories or narratives of mythic proportions.

One of the narratives perpetuated is that Footnote 4 programs teach reparative or conversion therapy to their students. The implication is that these students then go out and practice these dubious therapies on the public. (See Haldeman, 2002 and 2004, for a discussion of these therapies.) The author of this essay is familiar with the most conservative Footnote 4 programs and is not aware of any that teach or train students to practice reparative or conversion therapies. These therapies may be described so that doctoral students are aware of the terminology and what some in the Christian community may request, but these therapies are not taught in accredited programs. Furthermore, APA Division 36 (Society for the Psychology of Religion and Spirituality) was supportive of the *Report of the American Psychological Association Task Force on Appropriate Therapeutic Responses to Sexual Orientation* (APA, 2009c). Although there is no mechanism for individual doctoral programs to endorse this report, it is apparent that the leaders of religious distinctive programs are generally supportive of the report's findings.

Another narrative commonly heard is that students or faculty who come out and identify as gay in one of the Footnote 4 programs are treated badly, shunned, and dismissed from the program. Most likely there are LGBTQ students (and probably faculty) in each of the Footnote 4 programs, and some of these students and faculty may not feel affirmed in expressing their sexuality. Typically, students who identify as gay are allowed to stay in the program and continue through graduation, but these students likely do not express their orientation openly. There is a concern about gay and straight students who decide not to abide by the sexual behavior expectations of all students—that they refrain from sexual intimacy outside of heterosexual marriage. If students, both heterosexual and LGBTQ, decide not to abide by this code of conduct, then there is likely a compassionate response to encourage fidelity to the policy. If that fidelity cannot be maintained, then a student may be asked to leave the program. This, however, is a very rare event that occurs only after appropriate due process procedures are followed.

Some of these narratives are initiated or exacerbated by stories in the popular press about students in other mental health programs. There have been several stories over the last few years about trainees who refused to work with a gay student or a trainee who insisted upon using reparative therapies, among other examples. However, in reviewing these cases, the students are usually not psychology graduate students from APA-accredited programs. Rather, these students tend to come from counseling, marriage and family, or social work programs. (See Ward v. Wilbanks, 2010; *Ward v. Polite*, 2012; *Keeton v. Anderson-Wiley*, 2011 as examples of Master's level counseling students.) Unfortunately, these students and programs are conflated with the psychology doctoral students and programs that are religiously affiliated.

Although these may be strange bedfellows, it is likely that the best proponents of LGBTQ acceptance in the religious community are graduates of religious distinctive programs. The graduates of these programs are the ones who interact with and provide psychological services to Christian clients, some of whom may hold internalized toxic beliefs about the LGBTQ community. Compassionate and understanding responses that are so needed in the dialogue between religious and LGBTQ communities may come from these graduates. If graduates of these programs were not available, who would reach out to the religious communities with psychological expertise, and who within the psychological community would religiously oriented clients trust?

Conclusion

Many Americans hold strong religious beliefs that influence their daily lives, and the majority of these Americans endorse Christianity as their faith tradition. Those who experience psychological difficulties and hold religious beliefs would like to discuss their religious concerns within the context of psychotherapy. Psychologists, on the other hand, tend to be much less religious as a group, and at times have been hostile toward religious belief. There has been little training in understanding or addressing religious concerns in doctoral training programs, even though there are ethical and treatment guidelines that suggest the appropriateness of training in this area.

Religious distinctive programs have steadily developed, and several are now accredited by the APA. These programs play an important role in the overall landscape of education and training in professional psychology. These programs invoke the provisions of Footnote 4 in the G&P (APA, 2009b), which allows them to hire and admit faculty and students who endorse the publically stated faith statements and code of conduct that are consistent with the mission of the universities in which the programs are housed. These graduate students are required to obtain education and training in working with all forms of diversity, including LGBTQ issues. Graduates of these programs likely represent less than 6% of the annual doctorates received in APA-accredited programs in professional psychology, which is far less than representative of the Christian communities in which they practice.

Graduates of religious distinctive programs are likely in a strong position to help disseminate accurate information that will be helpful to both the religious and LGBTQ communities. These graduates should be particularly skilled at helping clients blend faith with mental health care, and can hopefully engage in constructive dialogue that will enhance empathy and understanding.

References

American Psychological Association. (1993). Guidelines for providers of psychological services to ethnic, linguistic, and culturally diverse populations. *American Psychologist, 48*, 45–48. doi: 10.1037/0003-066X.48.1.45

American Psychological Association. (2002). Ethical principles of psychologists and code of conduct. *American Psychologist, 57*, 1060–1072. doi: 10.1037/0003-066X.57.12.1060

American Psychological Association. (2005). *Guidelines on multicultural education, training, research, practice, and organizational change for psychologists*. Retrieved from: http://www.apa.org/pi/oema/resources/policy/multicultural-guideline.pdf

American Psychological Association. (2009a). Commission on Accreditation Implementing Regulations (C-22a). Retrieved from: http://www.apa.org/ed/accreditation/about/policies/implementing-guidelines.pdf

American Psychological Association. (2009b). *Guidelines and principles for accreditation of programs in professional psychology*. Retrieved from: http://www.apa.org/ed/accreditation/about/policies/guiding-principles.pdf

American Psychological Association. (2009c). *Report of the American Psychological Association Task Force on Appropriate Therapeutic Responses to Sexual Orientation*. Retrieved from http://www.apa.org/pi/lgbt/resources/therapeutic-response.pdf

Aten, J. D., Hall, P., Weaver, I., Mangis, M. W., & Campbell, C. D. (2012). Religion and rural mental health (pp. 79–96). In Smalley, Warren, and Rainer (Eds.) *Rural mental health*. New York: Springer.

Aten, J., & Leach, M. (2009). Spirituality and mental health research: A primer. In J. Aten, & M. Leach (Eds.), *Spirituality and the therapeutic process: A comprehensive resource from intake through termination* (pp. 9–24). Washington, DC: American Psychological Association.

Barnett, J. E. & Johnson, W. B. (2011). Integrating spirituality and religion into psychotherapy: Persistent dilemmas, ethical issues, and a proposed decision-making process. *Ethics & Behavior, 21*, 147–164. doi: 10.1080/10508422.2011.551471

Bellah, R. N., Madsen, R., Sullivan, W. M., Swidler, A., & Tipton, S. M. (1985). *Habits of the heart: Individualism and commitment in American life*. New York, NY: Harper & Row.

Bergin, A. E., & Jensen, J. (1990). Religiosity of psychotherapists: A national survey. *Psychotherapy, 27*, 3–7. doi: 10.1037/0033-3204.27.1.3

Brawer, P. A., Handal, P. J., Fabricatore, A. N., Roberts, R., & Wajda-Johnston, V. A. (2002). Training and education in religion/spirituality within APA-accredited clinical psychology programs. *Professional Psychology: Research and Practice, 33*, 203–206. doi: 10.1037/0735-7028.33.2.203

Campbell, C. D. (2011). APA Accreditation of doctoral psychology programs in Christian universities. *Journal of Psychology and Theology, 39*, 59–67.

Carter, J. D. & Narramore, B. (1979). *The integration of psychology and theology*. Grand Rapids, MI: Zondervan.

Delaney, H. D., Miller, W. R., Bisono, A. M. (2007). Religiosity and spirituality among psychologists: A survey of clinicians members of the American Psychological Association. *Professional Psychology: Research and Practice, 38*, 538–546. doi: 10.1037/0735-7028.38.5.538

Diekema, A. J. (2000). *Academic freedom and Christian scholarship*. Grand Rapids, MI: Eerdmans.

Dunn, G. D. (2004). *Tertullian*. New York, NY: Routledge.

Eck, B. (2002). An exploration of the therapeutic use of spiritual disciplines in clinical practice. *Journal of Psychology and Christianity, 21*, 266–280.

Ellis, A. (1980). *The case against religion: A psychotherapist's view and the case against religiosity*. Parsippany, NJ: American Atheist Press.

Freud, S. (1955). *Moses and monotheism*. New York, NY: Vintage.

Freud, S. (1961). *The future of an illusion*. New York, NY: W. W. Norton.

Freud, S. (1950). *Totem and taboo*. New York, NY: W. W. Norton.

Fuller, R. C. (2001). *Spiritual, but not religious: Understanding unchurched America*. New York, NY: Oxford University Press.

Gallup, G. H. (2002). *The Gallup poll: Public opinion 2001*. Wilmington, DE: Scholarly Resources.

Gallup, G., & Lindsay, D. M. (1999). *Surveying the religious landscape: Trends in U.S. beliefs*. Harrisburg, PA: Morehouse.

Gallup Organization. (2010). *Religion*. Retrieved from: http://www.gallup.com/poll/145379/Religious-Americans-Lead-Healthier-Lives.aspx

Gartner, J. D. (1986). Antireligious prejudice in admissions to doctoral programs in clinical psychology. *Professional Psychology: Research and Practice, 17*, 473–475. doi: 10.1037/0735-7028.17.5.473

Grossman, C. L. (2010, April 27). Survey: 72% of Millennials "more spiritual than religious." *USA TODAY*. Retrieved from: http://www.usatoday.com/news/religion/2010-04-27-1Amillfaith27_ST_N.htm

Hage, S. M. (2006). A closer look at the role of spirituality in psychology training programs. *Professional Psychology: Research and Practice, 37*, 303–310. doi: 10.1037/0735-7028.37.3.303

Hage, S. M., Hopson, A., Siegel, M., Payton, G., & DeFanit, E. (2006). Multicultural training in spirituality: An interdisciplinary review. *Counseling and Values, 50*, 217–235. doi: 10.1002/j.2161-007X.2006.tb00058.x

Haldeman, D. C. (2002). Gay rights, patient rights: The implications of sexual orientation conversion therapy. *Professional Psychology: Research and Practice, 33*, 260–264. doi: 10.1037/0735-7028.33.3.260

Haldeman, D. C. (2004). When sexual and religious orientation collide: Considerations when working with conflicted same-sex attracted male clients. *The Counseling Psychologist, 32*, 691–715. doi: 10.1177/0011000004267560

Hathaway, W. L., & Ripley, J. S. (2009). Ethical concerns around spirituality and religion in clinical practice. In J. D. Aten & M. M. Leach (Eds.), *Spirituality and the therapeutic process: A comprehensive resource from intake to termination* (pp. 25–52). Washington, DC: American Psychological Association.

Hathaway, W. L., Scott, S. Y., & Garver, S. A. (2004). Assessing religious/spiritual functioning: A neglected domain in clinical practice? *Professional Psychology: Research and Practice, 35*, 97–104. doi: 10.1037/0735-7028.35.1.97

Hill, P. C., Pargament, K. I., Hood, R.W., McCullough, M. E., Swyers, J. P., Larson, D. B., Zinnbauer, B. J. (2000). Conceptualizing religion and spirituality: Points of commonality, points of departure. *Journal for the Theory of Social Behaviour, 30*, 51–77. doi: 10.1111/1468-5914.00119

Holmes, A. F. (1987). *The idea of a Christian college*. Grand Rapids, MI: William B. Eerdmans Publishing Company

Huffman, D. S. (2011). *Christian contours: How a biblical worldview shapes the mind and heart*. Grand Rapids, MI: Kregel Publications.

Johnson, W. B., Campbell, C. D., & Dykstra, M. L. (1997). Professional training in religious institutions: Articulating models and outcomes. *Journal of Psychology and Theology, 25*, 260–271.

Johnson, W. B., & McMinn, M. R. (2003). Thirty years of integrative doctoral training: Historic developments, assessment of outcomes, and recommendations for the future. *Journal of Psychology and Theology, 31*, 83–96.

Jones, S. L. (1994). A constructive relationship for religion with the science and profession of psychology: Perhaps the boldest model yet. *American Psychologist, 49*, 184–199. Doi: 10.1037/0003-066X.49.3.184

Jung, C. G. (1958). *The undiscovered self*. New York, NY: New American Library.

Jung, C. G. (1964). *Man and his symbols*. New York: NY: Dell.

Keeton v. Anderson-Wiley. (2011). 664 F. 3d 865..

Kerr, C. (1963). *The uses of the university*. New York, NY: Harper and Row.

Kohut, J. & Wicherski (2010). *2011 Graduate Study in Psychology Snapshot: Applications, Acceptances, Enrollments, and Degrees Awarded to Master's- and Doctoral-Level Students in U.S. and Canadian Graduate Departments of Psychology: 2009-2010*. Retrieved from: http://www.apa.org/workforce/publications/11-grad-study/applications.pdf

Lannert, J. L. (1991). Resistance and countertransference issues with spiritual and religious clients. *Journal of Humanistic Psychology, 31*, 68–76. doi: 10.1177/0022167891314005

Lindgren, K. N., & Coursey, R. D. (1995). Spirituality and mental illness: A two-part study. *Psychosocial Rehabilitation Journal, 18*, 93–111.

Maloney, H. N. (1995). *Psychology and the cross. The early history of Fuller Seminary's School of Psychology*. Pasadena, CA: Fuller Seminary Press.

Marsden, G. M. (1997). *The outrageous idea of Christian scholarship*. New York, NY: Oxford University Press.

McMinn, M. R., Bearse, J. L, Heyne, L. K., & Staley, R. C. (2011). Satisfaction with clinical training in Christian psychology doctoral programs: Survey findings and implications. *Journal of Psychology and Christianity, 30*, 156–162.

McMinn, M. R., Hathaway, W. L., Woods, S. W., & Snow, K. N. (2009). What American Psychological Association leaders have to say about Psychology of Religion and Spirituality. *Psychology and Spirituality, 1*, 3–13. doi: 10.1037/a0014991

McMinn, M. R., & Hill, P. C. (2011). Clinical training in explicitly Christian doctoral programs: Introduction to the special issue. *Journal of Psychology and Christianity, 30*, 99–100.

McMinn, M. R., Staley, R. C., Webb, K. C., Seegobin, W. (2010). Just what is Christian counseling anyway? *Professional Psychology: Research and Practice, 41*, 391–397. doi: 10.1037/a0018584

McMinn, M. R., Johnson, W. B., & Haskell, J. S. (2004). Publication frequency among faculty in explicitly Christian doctoral programs. *Journal of Psychology and Christianity, 23*, 298–304.

Melton, J. G. (2009). *Melton's encyclopedia of American religions (8th ed.)*. Detroit, MI: Gale Research.

Meadow, M. J. & Kahoe, R. D. (1984). *Psychology of religion: Religion in individual lives*. New York, NY: Harper and Row.

Miller, W. R., & Thoresen, C. E. (2003). Spirituality, religion and health: An emerging research field. *American Psychologist, 58*, 24–35. doi: 10.1037/0003-066X.58.1.24

Mitchell, J., Lannin, D. R., Mathews, H. F., & Swanson, M. S. (2002). Religious beliefs and breast cancer screening. *Journal of Women's Health, 11*, 907–915. doi: 10.1089/154099902762203740

Moreira-Almeida, A., Neto, F., & Koenig, H. G. (2006). Religiousness and mental health: A review. *Revista Brasileira de Psiquiatria, 28*, 242–250. Doi: 10.1590/S1516-44462006005000006

Newman, J. H. (1960). *The idea of a university*. New York, NY: Holt, Rinehart, and Winston.

Nicholi, A. M. (2002). *The question of God: C. S. Lewis and Sigmund Freud debate God, love, sex, and the meaning of life*. New York, NY: Free Press.

Niebuhr, H. R. (1951). *Christ and culture*. New York, NY: Harper.

Pargament, K. I. (1997). *The psychology of religious coping: Theory, research, practice*. New York, NY: Guilford.

Pargament, K. I. (2007). *Spiritually integrated psychotherapy: Understanding and addressing the sacred*. New York, NY: Guilford Press.

The Pew Forum on Religion & Public Life. (2008). *U.S. religious landscape survey*. Retrieved from http://religions.pewforum.org/maps#

Plante, T. G. (2009). *Spiritual practices in psychotherapy: Thirteen tools for enhancing psychological health*. Washington, DC: American Psychological Association.

Rose, E. M., Westefeld, J. S., & Ansley, T. N. (2001). Spiritual issues in counseling: Clients' beliefs and preferences. *Journal of Counseling Psychology, 48*, 61–71. doi: 10.1037/1941-1022.S.1.18

Russell, S. R., & Yarhouse, M. A. (2006). Religion/spirituality within APA-accredited psychology predoctoral internships. *Professional Psychology: Research and Practice, 37*, 430–436. doi: 10.1037/0735-7028.37.4.430

Shafranske, E. P. (2000). Religious involvement and professional practices of psychiatrists and other mental health professionals. *Psychiatric Annals, 30*, 525–532.

Schulte, D. L., Skinner, T. A., & Claiborn, C. D. (2002). Religious and spiritual issues in counseling psychology training. *The Counseling Psychologist, 30*, 118–134. doi: 10.1177/0011000002301009

Shafranske, E. P., & Malony, H. N. (1990). Clinician psychologists' religious and spiritual orientations and their practice of psychotherapy. *Psychotherapy, 27*, 72–78. doi: 10.1037/0033-3204.27.1.72

Sommerville, J. C. (2006). *The decline of the secular university*. New York, NY: Oxford University Press.

Sorenson, R. L. (1997). Doctoral student's integration of psychology and Christianity: Perspectives via attachment theory and multidimensional scaling. *Journal For the Scientific Study of Religion, 36*, 530–548. doi: 10.2307/1387688

Sorenson, R., & Hales, S. (2002). Comparing evangelical Protestant psychologists trained at secular versus religiously affiliated programs. *Psychotherapy, 39*, 163–170. doi: 10.1037/0033-3204.39.2.163

Timpe, R. L. (1999). Religion and personality. In D. G. Benner & P. C. Hill (Eds.) *Baker Encyclopedia of Psychology & Counseling* (pp. 1020–1023). Grand Rapids, MI: Baker Books.

Wade, N. G., Worthington, E. L., & Vogel, D. L. (2007). Effectiveness of religiously tailored interventions in Christian therapy. *Psychotherapy Research, 17*, 91–105. doi: 10.1080/10503300500497388

Walker, D.F., Gorsuch, R.L., & Tan, S.Y. (2004). Therapists' integration of religion and spirituality in counseling:

A meta-analysis. *Counseling and Values, 49*, 69–80. doi: 10.1002/j.2161-007X.2004.tb00254.x

Walker, D.F., Gorsuch, R.L., & Tan, S.Y. (2005). Therapists' use of religious and spiritual interventions in Christian counseling: A preliminary report. *Counseling and Values, 49*, 107–119. doi: 10.1002/j.2161-007X.2005.tb00257.x

Ward v. Polite. (2012). 667 F. 3d 727.

Ward v. Wilbanks. (2010). No. 09-CV-112 37, 2010 U.S. Dist. WL 3026428 (E. D. Michigan, July 26, 2010).

Weaver, A. J., Flannelly, L. T., Garbarino, J., Figley, C. R., & Flannelly, K. J. (2003). A systematic review of research on religion and spirituality in the Journal of Traumatic Stress: 1990–1999. *Mental Health, Religion, & Culture, 6*, 215–228. doi: 10.1080/1367467031000088123

Worthington, E. L., Jr., & Aten, J. D. (2009). Psychotherapy with religious and spiritual clients: An introduction. *Journal of Clinical Psychology, 65*, 123–130. doi: 10.1002/jclp.20561

Worthington, E. L., Sandage, S. J., Davis, D. E., Hook, J. N., Miller, A. J., Hall, M. E. L., & Hall, T. W. (2009). Training therapists to address spiritual concerns in clinical practice and research. In J. Aten, & M. Leach (Eds.), *Spirituality and the therapeutic process: A comprehensive resource from intake through termination* (pp. 267–291). Washington, DC: American Psychological Association.

Yarhouse, M. A. & Fisher, W. (2002). Levels of training to address religion in clinical practice. *Psychotherapy: Theory, Research, Practice, and Training, 39*, 171-176. doi: 10.1037/0033-3204.39.2.171

PART 5

Emerging Trends in Education and Training

Professionalism: Professional Attitudes and Values in Psychology

Catherine L. Grus *and* Nadine J. Kaslow

Abstract

Professionalism is a multifaceted construct, making it difficult to develop a consensus definition of the term. This lack of an agreed-upon definition poses challenges to the development of this competency in psychology education and training, as well as to its assessment. Despite these barriers, development of professionalism in psychology trainees serves a critical societal function. This chapter describes the construct of professionalism in professional psychology and in the broader health professions context. Attention is paid to effective strategies for assessing and teaching professionalism. Consideration is given to addressing trainees with competence problems that are manifested in the professionalism domain. Future directions are offered with regard to defining, assessing, and training for this competency.

Keywords: professionalism, competence, education, training, trainees with problems of professional competence

Professionalism is a construct that for many years has received considerable attention in other health professions in North America and Europe (Passi, Doug, Peile, Thistlethwaite, & Johnson, 2010). It is only recently that professionalism has emerged as an independent construct and core competency within professional psychology. Professionalism is a necessary, albeit not sufficient, competency for effective and high-quality practice and the protection of the pubic in the twenty-first century (Lesser et al., 2010; Pellegrino, 2002). It is critical to psychologists' social contract with the public (Cruess, Cruess, & Steinert, 2009; Cruess, Cruess, & Steinert, 2010). More than an innate character trait or virtue, professionalism is a complex and multifaceted competency that incorporates a broad array of essential components. This competency can be taught, and it is imperative that psychologists make a lifelong commitment to refining this competency over the course of their professional development (Lesser et al., 2010). Further, the values that fall under the rubric of professionalism must be espoused and modeled in all educational and training endeavors as professionalism is context dependent and thus systems-level issues influence its manifestation and assessment (Lesser et al., 2010; Wear & Kuczewski, 2004). As professional psychologists, it is imperative that we create a culture of professionalism within our discipline.

This article represents one of the first systematic efforts to review the pertinent literature on professionalism for the professional psychology literature. Given the dearth of information about professionalism within psychology, most of what will be discussed will draw upon the literature from other health professions. Specifically, attention will be paid to the definitions and history of the construct of professionalism. Strategies for assessing professionalism will be reviewed. There will be a discussion of a variety of techniques for teaching and enhancing the professionalism competency.

In addition, approaches for addressing problems in the competency domain of professionalism will be shared. As the field of professional psychology evolves, the role of professionalism will shift, and thus consideration will be given to the ways in which this construct is relevant to psychologists' efforts to effectively address such shifts (e.g., social networking). Throughout the article, we will gear our comments to ways in which this literature can be applied within professional psychology.

Definitions

Professionalism is a multidimensional construct that includes interpersonal, intrapersonal, and public elements (Van de camp, Vernooij-Dassen, Grol, & Bottema, 2004). According to Merriam-Webster, professionalism is defined as "the conduct, aims, or qualities that characterize or mark a professional or a professional person" (Merriam-Webster Online Dictionary). Thus it is a way of acting, rather than a way of being (Cohen, 2007). Humanism, an overlapping and mutually enriching construct, is the term that refers to the associated way of being (Cohen, 2007; Swick, 2007). Despite the aforementioned dictionary definition, within the health professions broadly as well as individually, there is no consensus definition of professionalism (Hafferty, 2006). Rather the definitions of this construct vary according to the profession, underlying philosophical perspective, the culture, and the context. It is worth noting that discussion in the literature this competency's definition sometimes defines the construct and at other times offers descriptions of behavior that fall within the bounds of this construct.

Medicine Over the millennium and more specifically in the last decade, the concept of professionalism has undergone major changes within medicine (Van Mook, De Grave, Wass et al., 2009). As such, multiple definitions have been put forward. The following are some well-known examples. According to the Accreditation Council of Graduate Medical Education (ACGME) Outcomes Project, professionalism entails the demonstration of: compassion, integrity, and respect for others; responsiveness to patient needs that supersedes self-interest; respect for patient privacy and autonomy; accountability to patients, society, and the profession; excellence in ongoing professional development; adherence to ethical principles; and sensitivity and responsiveness to diverse patient populations, including but not limited to diversity in gender, age, culture, race, religion, disabilities, and sexual orientation (Swing, 2007).

A later definition of medical professionalism was proffered in 2000 by Swick, who stated that the construct was comprised of the following set of physician behaviors:

(1) subordinating own interests to the interests of others

(2) adhering to high ethical and moral standards

(3) responding to societal needs, with behaviors reflecting a social contract with the communities served

(4) evincing core humanistic values, including honesty and integrity, caring and compassion, altruism and empathy, respect for others, and trustworthiness

(5) exercising accountability for themselves and for their colleagues

(6) demonstrating continued commitment to excellence

(7) exhibiting a commitment to scholarship and to advancing their field

(8) dealing with high levels of complexity and uncertainty

(9) reflecting upon their actions and decision (Swick, 2000)

These behaviors were adopted by multiple groups (Hilton & Soutgate, 2007), including the Association of American Medical Colleges for their undergraduate medical student outcomes work (Medical School Objectives Writing Group, 1999), accreditation and reaccreditation processes, and the American Board of Internal Medicine in its *Project Professionalism* (American Board of Internal Medicine, 2001).

According to Stern, who edited the book, *Measuring Medical Professionalism* (Stern, 2006), "professionalism is "demonstrated through a foundation of clinical competence, community skills, and ethical and legal understanding, upon which is built the aspiration to and wise application of the principles of professionalism: excellence, humanism, accountability, and altruism" (p. 19).

The following are the key themes, listed alphabetically, that are associated with the definitions of the construct of professionalism within medicine: altruism, accountability, benevolence, caring and compassion, courage, ethical practice, excellence, honesty, honor, humanism, integrity, reflection/self-awareness, respect for others, responsibility and duty, service, social responsibility, team work, trustworthiness, and truthfulness (American Board of Internal Medicine, 2001; Hafferty, 2006; Hilton & Soutgate, 2007; Van Mook, Van Luijk, O'Sullivan, et al., 2009).

Other health professions. Within dentistry, professionalism has been defined by six value-based statements: competence, fairness, integrity, responsibility, respect, and service-mindedness (American Dental Education Association; ADEA, 2009). Descriptions and behaviors associated with each of these values are provided by the ADEA in their Statement on Professionalism in Dental Education.

Within nursing, "professionalism and professional values" are constructs that encompass fourteen behaviors such as: adhering to professional standards; being accountable; modeling the values and articulating the knowledge, skills, and attitudes of the nursing profession; demonstrating professionalism; appreciating the history of and contemporary issues in nursing; engaging in self-reflection; identifying risks that impact personal and professional choices and behaviors; communicating personal bias in difficult decisions to the health care team; recognizing the impact of attitudes, values, and expectations on the care of vulnerable populations; protecting privacy and confidentiality; using interprofessional and intraprofessional resources to resolve ethical and other practice dilemmas; acting to prevent unsafe, illegal, or unethical care practices; articulating the value of pursuing practice excellence, lifelong learning, and professional engagement; and valuing self-care (American Association of Colleges of Nursing, 2008). Using Q-methodology with nursing faculty and students, it was shown that individuals with different perspectives varied in the ways in which they defined professionalism (Akhtar-Danesh et al., 2013). For example, those classified as *humanists* highlighted the professional values associated with the construct, such as respect for human dignity, personal integrity, protection of patient privacy, and the protection of patients from harm. For those categorized as *portrayers*, professionalism was manifested by one's image, attire, and expression. For those termed *facilitators*, the construct incorporated standards and policies, as well as personal beliefs and values. Finally, those categorized as *regulators* asserted that professionalism is fostered in a work context in which suitable beliefs and standards are communicated, accepted, and implemented.

Psychology. Within professional psychology, professionalism as defined in the revised benchmarks model encompasses a number of specific competencies, one of which is professional attitudes and values (Hatcher et al., 2013). The specific competency of professional attitudes and values, which is the competency most germane to this article, has the following agreed upon definition within professional psychology: "behavior and comportment that reflect the values and attitudes of psychology" (Found et al., 2009; Hatcher et al., 2013). The essential components include: (1) integrity—honesty, personal responsibility, and adherence to professional values; (2) deportment; (3) accountability; (4) concern for the welfare of others; and (5) professional identity.

History of Professionalism

Medicine. The following is a brief recent history of efforts focused on professionalism within medicine (Kirk, 2007; Passi et al., 2010; Thistelethwaite & Spencer, 2008). In the mid-1990s, *Project Professionalism* was commissioned by the American Board of Internal Medicine. *Project Professionalism* was designed to promote integrity within the specialty of internal medicine, in the educational context, and among all internists and subspecialists within medicine. It defined six components of professionalism: altruism, accountability, excellence, duty, honor/integrity, and respect (American Board of Internal Medicine, 1995, 2001). A parallel process occurred in Canada, *CANMEDS*, which was sponsored by the Royal College of Physicians and Surgeons of Canada (Thistelethwaite & Spencer, 2008). *CANMEDS* articulated a competency-based framework and delineated roles that should define a competent specialist: medical expert, communicator, collaborator, manager, health advocate, scholar, and professional.

In 1999, the ACGME defined general competencies that each specialty within medicine is expected to impart to its residents during training; professionalism was listed as one of these six core competencies. In that same year, the American Board of Internal Medicine Foundation, in partnership with the American College of Physicians Foundation and the European Federation of Internal Medicine, initiated the Medical Professionalism Project. This effort resulted in the creation of a physician's charter published in 2002, entitled "Medical professionalism in the new millennium," which states, "Professionalism is the basis of medicine's contract with society. It demands placing the interests of patients above those of the physician, setting and maintaining standards of competence and integrity, and providing expert advice to society on matters of health" (Project of the ABIM Foundation, ACP-ASIM Foundation, & European Federation of Internal Medicine, 2002). The fundamental principles that undergird this charter are the primacy of patient welfare (altruism), respect for patient autonomy, and commitment to social justice (Smith, Saavedra, Raeke, & O'Donell, 2007). Based upon these principles, this charter delineates a set of professional responsibilities for the physician that serve as indicators of professionalism. The charter articulates ten commitments: professional competence, honesty with patients, patient confidentiality, maintaining appropriate relations with patients, improving quality of care, improving access to care, just distribution of finite resources, scientific knowledge, maintaining trust by managing conflicts of interest, and professional responsibilities. It also notes actions that physicians should take associated with each of these commitments.

In addition to the definition of professionalism and its attributes, recent years have witnessed a growing focus on assessing professionalism within medicine using multiple methodologies (Stern, 2006). This reflects the expectation by the accreditation body that graduate medical education and residency programs assess the attainment of professionalism, along with other core competencies. Further, attention has been paid to strategies for teaching professionalism, which also is an expectation of the accreditation process. Both topics are discussed in more detail later in this article.

There has been a burgeoning effort within medicine to promote the development and implementation of campus-wide efforts designed to apply the fundamental principles of the professionalism component of the Physician's Charter in order to ensure meaningful cultural change. Some but not all of these efforts were funded by grants from the Medical Professionalism Project to academic health centers. The following are some medical schools that recently have developed pertinent activities to promote professionalism in trainees and have implemented a program to transform the culture of their academic institution to one in which professionalism is central: Indiana University School of Medicine, University of Chicago Pritzker School of Medicine, University of Pennsylvania School of Medicine, University of North Dakota School of Medicine and Health Sciences, University of Texas Medical Branch at Galveston, University of

Washington School of Medicine (Brater, 2007; Christianson, McBride, Vari, Olson, & Wilson, 2007; Fryer-Edwards et al., 2007; Goldstein et al., 2006; Humphrey et al., 2007; Smith et al., 2007; Wasserstein, Brennan, & Rubenstein, 2007). We now summarize these strategies for promoting professionalism. Some of these approaches have targeted primarily medical students, whereas others have been more comprehensive and have focused on medical students, housestaff (i.e., residents), faculty, and staff. The key activities include: developing a value statement that incorporates professionalism; creating professionalism committees and vertically integrated advisory groups; focusing on various cultures (e.g., organizational, safety) within the system and instituting efforts to enhance the level of professionalism within these contexts; encouraging more effective community efforts (i.e., use of appreciative inquiry); evaluating their admissions criteria to ensure they were making selections in a fashion that valued professionalism; offering various educational programs and experiential workshops; developing and providing a professionalism curriculum for medical students and/or modifying their curriculum to be patient-centered; ensuring that professionalism was a component of the performance evaluation for trainees at all levels of professional development, faculty, and staff; instituting interdisciplinary rounds; implementing an informal and confidential intervention for students, staff, and faculty for whom there were concerns about professionalism; introducing mechanisms for reporting of unprofessional behavior; and recognizing, including in their compensation, individuals whose behavior reflects and/or promotes the values of professionalism. Many of the leaders of these institutional initiatives have offered thoughtful strategies for overcoming the challenges associated with such culture transformation.

The Mayo Clinic may be the academic health science center most regarded for the high degree of professionalism manifested by its health care professionals (Viggiano, Pawlina, Lindor, Olsen, & Cortese, 2007). Their core value is "putting the needs of the patient first," and this signifies their emphasis on professionalism and informs their approach to leadership, management, and day-to-day practice. All clinic staff embrace this core value in all of their efforts and interactions and view doing so as their "professionalism covenant"—that is, a collective, tacit agreement that each person who works at the institution will actively and sincerely collaborate to put the patients' needs and welfare at the forefront.

This covenant, which is part of the institution's mission statement, is shared with patients and trainees in two seminal documents, the *Mayo Clinic Model of Care* and the *Mayo Clinic Model of Education*.

One significant element of professionalism's history within medicine pertains to the ways in which this competency has been viewed as key to physicians' social contract with society (Cruess et al., 2010). Proponents of professionalism have argued that physicians need to reassert their professionalism in order to redefine their contract with society (Cruess, Cruess, & Johnston, 1999; Cruess & Cruess, 1997). Given cultural and societal differences, attention has begun to be paid in medical education to the ways in which professionalism should be taught and must be manifested with respect to local customs and values (Cruess et al., 2010).

Other health professions. Within dentistry, professionalism is one of six required competencies. The American Dental Education Association has argued that graduates must be competent to apply ethical and legal standards in the provision of dental care and practice within the scope of their competence and consult with or refer to professional colleagues when indicated (American Dental Education Association, 2009). In terms of nursing, professionalism is identified as one of ten competencies that will inform future nursing practice and curricula, although the focus is at the baccalaureate, rather than masters or doctoral, level (American Association of Colleges of Nursing, 2008). According to the American Association of Colleges of Nursing, the nurse of the future will demonstrate accountability for the delivery of standards-based nursing care that is consistent with moral, altruistic, legal, ethical, regulatory, and humanistic principles (American Association of Colleges of Nursing, 2008).

In 2011, a document was published that articulated the core competencies for interprofessional collaborative practice (Interprofessional Education Collaborative Expert Panel, 2011). Nursing, osteopathic and allopathic medicine, pharmacy, dentistry, and public health collaborated in this endeavor. Although professionalism as a term is not used to describe one of the four competency sets in this document, one of the competency sets clearly incorporates elements of professionalism and is entitled "values/ethics for interprofessional practice." In addition, growing attention has been paid to the importance for interprofessional education of teaching health care trainees about professionalism (McNair, 2005). Health care professionals in some countries have worked across health care specialties to collaboratively develop and implement models for evaluating and teaching professionalism (Van Luijk, Gorter, & Van Mook, 2010).

Psychology. In general, psychology has been slower than other health professions in identifying and agreeing upon core competencies. The 2002 Competencies Conference was first time in which professionalism was noted to be a competency within professional psychology (Kaslow, 2004; Kaslow et al., 2004; Rodolfa et al., 2005). It was conceptualized at that time as the outcome of professional development, which was conceived as being a foundational competency (Elman, Illfelder-Kaye, & Robiner, 2005). Attention was given to two elements of professionalism—interpersonal functioning and thinking like a psychologist. It was only more recently, as competency models evolved within professional psychology, that professionalism itself has been viewed as a core foundational competency. It was articulated as such for the first time in the Benchmarks document (Fouad et al., 2009). Recently, professionalism has been conceptualized more broadly as an overarching competency cluster that includes four specific competencies: (1) professional attitudes and values; (2) individual and cultural diversity; (3) ethical and legal standards and policy; and (4) reflective practice, self-assessment, and self-care (Hatcher et al., 2013).

Within professional psychology, steps have been taken to delineate strategies for the formative and summative assessment of this competence at multiple stages of professional development (Kaslow et al., 2009). Of note, although the Commission on Accreditation incorporates a competency-based focus to the accreditation process of graduate, internship, and post-doctoral residency programs, they have yet to focus on professional attitudes and values as one of the competencies on which they evaluate training programs' educational efforts or outcomes.

Assessment

Rationale for assessing professionalism. There are multiple reasons to assess professionalism in trainees. First, the assessment of this foundational competency is critical for providing meaningful and valuable formative and summative feedback that assists trainees in continuing to improve and grow developmentally in this domain. Second, evaluating professionalism can enable trainers to identify trainees with problems of professional competence. This is particularly important given the link between unprofessional behavior in school and future performance and disciplinary action, at least as shown to be the case in medicine (Murden, Way, Hudson, & Westman, 2004; Papadikis, Hodgson, Teherani, & Kohatsu, 2004; Papadikis et al., 2005; Teherani, Hodgson, Banach, & Papadakis, 2005). Third, an accurate and comprehensive assessment of professionalism can be useful to trainers in guiding the documentation and implementation of remediation efforts for trainees who evidence problems of professional competence related to professionalism. Fourth, when remediation efforts fail, assessment processes that yield specifics about ways in which the trainee's performance falls below benchmark expectations set by the program for this competency domain can be helpful in informing decision makers and gatekeepers. Finally, the assessment of this competency guarantees greater accountability of psychologists, which ensures quality service delivery, and as a result, protects and benefits the public.

Assessment approach. It is important that training programs employ both formative and summative assessments of professionalism (Kaslow et al., 2009; Van Mook, Van Luijk, O'Sullivan, et al., 2009). When assessing professionalism, multiple subjective and objective methods that provide complementary information should be utilized (Stern, 2006; Van Mook, Gorter, O'Sullivan, et al., 2009). For example and specific to psychology, the Competency Assessment Toolkit for Professional Psychology recommends that the following techniques be utilized for assessing the overall broad competency of professionalism: 360-degree evaluations, annual/rotation performance reviews, Competency Evaluation Rating Forms, client/patient process and outcome data, and consumer surveys (Kaslow et al., 2009). Evaluations should attend to the various components of the construct and should be based on observations within realistic contexts whenever possible. Such evaluations should focus not just on an understanding of professionalism and professional behavior, but also on the attitudes that underlie professionalism (Rees & Knight, 2007; Van Mook, Gorter, O'Sullivan, et al., 2009). It is advisable for numerous trainers to assess this construct in each trainee and that this construct be assessed longitudinally. It is essential that trainers be transparent to trainees that they are being evaluated on this domain of professional functioning.

The value of peer assessments of professionalism is a recent focus for trainers (Arnold, 2002; Arnold, Shue, Kritt, Ginsburg, & Stern, 2005; Ginsburg et al., 2000). There is some evidence that peer evaluations may provide useful information about trainees' professional behaviors (Arnold, 2002). There are mixed feelings among trainees vis-à-vis peer assessments (Arnold et al., 2005). A number of factors promote and/or discourage this process, including personal challenges with peer feedback, the nature of the assessment approach, and the context in which the evaluations take place. Trainees often are afraid to raise concerns about professionalism with a peer or other colleague. However, such assessment feedback can be invaluable if offered in a thoughtful, specific, and compassionate fashion. In general, effective peer assessment systems of professional attitudes and values are anonymous, offer input in a timely fashion, address both professional and unprofessional attitudes and behaviors, are part of a formative evaluation, and take place in a supportive context (Arnold et al., 2007).

There also is some evidence that patient ratings of professionalism are reliable and valid, including with psychiatrists, especially when used in the context of a 360-degree evaluation (Lelliott et al., 2008; Wood et al., 2004). However, not all studies have found these ratings to be reliable (Ginsburg et al., 2000). In addition, there are concerns about the use of patients to evaluate psychology trainees and psychologists. These concerns include power differentials, ways in which personality pathology might influence perceptions, and the nature of the transference relationship. Thus it may be more appropriate to use standardized patients to evaluate this competency (Ginsburg et al., 2000).

Assessment tools. A number of different instruments can be useful for assessing professionalism within health care (Lynch, Surdyk, & Eiser, 2004; Van Mook, Gorter, O'Sullivan, et al., 2009; Veloski, Fields, Boex, & Blank, 2005). Some of these tools offer a comprehensive assessment of the construct, whereas others assess one facet or a specific attribute(s) of the construct. The most commonly cited of these attributes are: ethics, ethical decision making, moral reasoning, and humanism. Additional components of this construct that may be assessed include multiculturalism, empathy, values, attitudes toward deception in patient relationships, care for the indigent, and trust.

Unfortunately, at present, there are no well-accepted or commonly used assessment devices for professionalism. Furthermore, few of the available instruments meet the minimal validity and reliability criteria to support their operational use for formative or summative assessments of for academic decision-making (Jha, Bekker, Duffy, & Roberts, 2007; Veloski et al., 2005). However, assessment tools have begun to appear in the literature to assess the fundamental concept of professionalism. Indeed, a 2007 paper found a total of 55 different measures of professionalism and related elements (Jha et al., 2007).

The following represent some of the most frequently used tools developed for use with physicians and medical students. The Evaluation of Professional Behavior in General Practice is a scale developed to assess professional behavior in primary care physicians (Van de camp, Vernooij-Dassen, Grol, & Bottema, 2006). The Nijmegen Professionalism Scale, which was developed to evaluate professional behavior in primary care physicians, has been used with trainers and trainees alike (Tromp, Vernooij-Dassen, Kramer, Grol, & Bottema, 2010). The Professionalism Mini-Evaluation Exercise is an assessment tool with some psychometric support in which trained faculty observe and rate behaviors associated with professionalism in medical students (Cruess, McIlroy, Cruess, Ginsburg, & Steinert, 2006). Recently, a tool was created to assess medical students' perceptions of professionalism in their learning environment, the Learning Environment for Professionalism Survey (Thrush, Spollen, Tariq, Williams, & Shorey, 2011). Until these tools are used either in their current format or in a revised format, their utility for psychologists is an empirical question.

Measures also have been created to assess professionalism in other health professions. For example, the nursing literature reports on assessment tools of professionalism, such as Hall's Professionalism Inventory Scale (Hall, 1968). Although developed more than 40 years ago, it is still used today (Wynd, 2003). One of the more commonly used scales to assess this construct in nursing has been the Professionalism in Nursing Behaviors Inventory (Adams & Miller, 2001; Miller, Adams, & Beck, 1993) that covers nine categories of behavior representing professionalism and is based on the model that is reflected in the Wheel of Professionalism in Nursing. The Professionalism and Environmental Factors in the Workplace Questionnaire encourages nurses to reflect upon their behavior; offers a framework for discussing, planning, and implementing strategies to encourage professionalism in practice; and is associated with productive work environments (Baumann & Kolotylo, 2009). Once again, the relevance of these tools for psychologists has yet to be determined.

Assessment challenges. There are myriad challenges associated with assessing professionalism. There is a general lack of consensus about the definition and manifestation of this construct. Our assessment armamentarium specific to this construct is weak to relatively nonexistent. Lapses in professionalism often are subtle, and trainees' behavior is not consistent across contexts. Factors such as these make the assessment of this competency questionable in terms of their reliability, validity, and fidelity (Schwartz, Kotwicki, & McDonald, 2009).

Teaching Professionalism

As far back as the Greek philosophers Plato and Socrates, the question of whether virtue can be taught has been debated. Socrates did not answer this question definitively. Today, trainers debate whether professionalism can be taught, and the answer appears to be both yes and no. We believe that there are three groups of trainees for whom professionalism can be taught. The first group is comprised of individuals with a high level of natural competence in professionalism. They developed this competency even before entering the formal psychology educational and training sequence, and thus simply require that it be honed and made more psychology-specific. The second group can be defined as "good-enough" trainees in the professionalism domain. These are people for whom solid training and experience can enable them to meet or exceed the benchmarks in this domain. The third group consists of the subgroup of trainees with problems of professional competence within the professionalism domain who are motivated to address these difficulties.

The following section offers a framework and strategies for teaching professionalism to these subgroups of trainees. For the teaching of this competency to be effective, professionalism must be treated carefully and comprehensively throughout the educational and training sequence within professional psychology (Ginsburg & Stern, 2004). An effective approach for teaching professionalism entails offering myriad learning opportunities for gaining experience in and reflecting upon professionalism (Passi et al., 2010). These opportunities should include a mixture of formal experiences and informal opportunities to examine issues related to professionalism (Stern & Papadakis, 2006; Van Mook, De Grave, Van Luijk, et al., 2009; Van Mook, Van Luijk, De Grave, et al., 2009). It is also optimal that the education and teaching of this construct be guided by relevant educational theory and principles of adult learning (Cruess et al., 2009).

Training the trainers. Trainer development is a prerequisite for the teaching of professionalism

(Cruess et al., 2009). Before trainers can teach professionalism to trainees they must themselves be trained and competent in this domain of functioning (Cruess et al., 2009). Systematic, integrated faculty development programs and workshops need to be created, disseminated, and implemented. Such programs must be devised in a manner that takes into account the institutional/organizational culture, targets diverse stakeholders, uses diverse formats and strategies that are guided by educational theory and principles of effective instructional design, and communicates in a transparent fashion its goals and priorities (Cruess et al., 2009). These programs must be evaluated in an ongoing fashion and revised in accord with the feedback and outcomes.

Faculty development programs optimally entail defining professionalism, focusing on its ecology, attending to the hidden curriculum (i.e., unintended problematic behaviors modeled in the culture), modeling professionalism, examining teaching strategies, evaluating professional behavior accurately and comprehensively with a high degree of fidelity, creating action plans associated with assessment outcomes, providing techniques for addressing competence problems in the professionalism domain, promoting reflection and self-awareness in trainers and trainees alike, and considering institutional responsibility for professionalism (Gabbard et al., 2012; Gaiser, 2009; Goldstein et al., 2006; Larkin, 2003; Stark, Korenstein, & Karani, 2008; Steinert, Cruess, Cruess, & Snell, 2005; Sutkin, Wagner, Harris, & Schiffer, 2008). In general, these programs should be experiential and discussion oriented in nature. Participation in such programs is associated with self-reported changes in teaching and practice and a perception that such programs serve as an instrument of change (Steinert, Cruess, Cruess, Boudreau, & Fuks, 2007; Steinert et al., 2005). In addition, training faculty in professionalism has a significant positive impact on the behavior and performance of trainees in this competency domain (Joyner & Vemulakonda, 2007). Trainers should be evaluated in this competency domain and given ongoing feedback to ensure attainment and maintenance of competence in professionalism (Larkin, 2003). Measurement tools to do so need to be created and evaluated.

It is important that we train the trainers to be attentive to indicators of professionalism in selecting trainees (Passi et al., 2010). It behooves trainers to avoid choosing those who appear to exhibit unprofessional personal characteristics that are likely to negatively impact their capacity to effectively carry out the functions of being a psychologist. In other words, the focus should be more on "de-selection," rather than selection (Passi et al., 2010). Unfortunately, there are limited empirical data with regard to the characteristics that are predictive of unprofessional behavior, as well as a lack of psychometrically sound measures to tap the capacity to develop and manifest professionalism. As psychologists, we may be particularly competent to develop such selection methods.

Creating a climate of professionalism. The first step that trainers must take when teaching this competency is to create a climate of professionalism. Such a climate fosters professional attitudes and values in the individuals within the culture (Ratanawongsa et al., 2006). This entails a number of steps. Trainers must convey to everyone what is expected and what is valued and underscore the point that professionalism is critical to effective practice and professional functioning. It is essential that they communicate that professionalism is a dynamic and lifelong practice that entails ongoing self-reflection and ethical engagement.

It is imperative that the training climate supports people in talking about their own lapses in professionalism, that they acknowledge such difficulties, and apologize for their errors. It is also is beneficial to the community if there are mechanisms in place for making complaints about the unprofessional behavior of colleagues and if such concerns are handled sensitively and seriously.

A climate of professionalism is one in which bidirectional feedback is commonplace. Trainers must be open to feedback about their own level of professionalism. It is important that trainees' views of their trainers' performance in this competency domain be solicited and that such information be considered seriously in trainers' evaluations and promotion/retention decisions. For example, teaching portfolios should include an assessment of the trainer's professionalism, as well as a philosophy and/or plan with regard to how they will maintain and enhance both their own and their trainee's level of professionalism (Seldin & Associates, 1993; Seldin & Miller, 2009; Seldin, Miller, & Seldin, 2010). Similarly, the climate should be one in which trainees welcome feedback from multiple people about their performance in the professionalism domain. Trainers should pass along feedback about trainees' levels of professionalism using a "forward feeding" process (Cleary, 2008; Cox, 2008; Pangaro, 2008). "Forward feeding" refers to the freely communicating information about trainees across all levels of the system, a process that is particularly crucial when there are concerns regarding the trainees' professionalism.

Finally, for a climate of professionalism to be pervasive within an educational system or organization, the community norms often need to be altered. The norms should be ones that reinforce appropriate social and subjective elements of professional attitudes and values throughout the institutional culture. Unfortunately, at the present time, deficiencies in our learning environments, which include unprofessional conduct by trainers, in conjunction with the subjective nature of the assessment of professional attitudes and values, often leaves trainees feeling vulnerable, confused, and unjustly evaluated and treated (Brainard & Brislen, 2007). As a result, trainees are less likely to exhibit developmentally normative levels of professional attitudes and values (Cruess & Cruess, 2006). A climate of professionalism is one that is transparent, has clear communication and expectations, treats trainees and trainers alike with respect and compassion, and includes trainers that model professional behavior (Brainard & Brislen, 2007).

Role modeling. One critical component of a culture of professionalism is role modeling, a process that involves both conscious and unconscious activities (Cruess et al., 2009). Positive role models are central to professional character development and serve as an effective means for imparting professional values, attitudes, and behaviors (Cruess, Cruess, & Steinert, 2008; Kenny, Mann, & MacLeod, 2003). Role models manifest positive professional behaviors and characteristics. As Aristotle said, "we learn by practice and the best practice is to follow the model of the virtuous person." Thus all trainers, from the most senior to the most junior, must serve as role models (Wear & Aultman, 2010).

There are a number of qualities associated with the effective role modeling of professionalism. These include, but are not limited to, clinical competence and the provision of quality care, teaching skills, capacity for and willingness to share their self-reflections, sensitivity to diversity, and personal attributes reflective of good character (Cruess et al., 2008; Weissman, Branch, Gracey, Haidet, & Frankel, 2006; Wright & Carrese, 2003). These trainers prioritize providing feedback and articulating what they are modeling (Wright, Kern, Kolodner, Howard, & Brancati, 1998). In addition, positive role models demonstrate a commitment to improving their competence as role models (Cruess

et al., 2008). Further, they have minimal tolerance for unprofessional behavior (Duff, 2004) and, when such behavior does occur, they address it promptly and with all seriousness.

Trainers must model professionalism, which entails working together collaboratively to establish group norms for professional behavior and to personally behave in accord with such standards (Larkin, 2003). With regard to teaching professionalism, role models need to exemplify virtue in their interactions with patients, trainees, colleagues, and the community at large; demonstrate a humanistic perspective; communicate honestly and directly with trainees, who get the message because the trainer's words come from the heart; and convey the value of self-reflection (Coulehan, 2005). They also need to be models for coping adaptively with the myriad stressors associated with professional practice (Mareiniss, 2004). Effective role modeling fosters professional attitudes and behaviors and serves a preventive function vis-à-vis inappropriate professional behavior (Mareiniss, 2004; Ratanawongsa et al., 2006). It is useful if mentoring systems are created to support trainers in developing as role models and teachers of professionalism. Clearly, we need virtuous psychologists as teachers and role models at every stage of the education and training sequence.

Devising and implementing a curriculum. A systematic curriculum should be implemented in professional psychology training programs. It is ideal if this curriculum is developmentally informed, multifaceted, and comprehensive and includes didactics and situational learning. Both the curriculum and the participants should be evaluated in an ongoing fashion (Verderk, de Bree, & Mourits, 2007).

For trainees, the didactics optimally include a combination of coursework, readings, lectures, discussions, vignettes, case presentations, skills trainings, and activities (Boenink, De Jonge, Smal, Oderwald, & Van Tilburg, 2005; Passi et al., 2010). Didactics programs should focus on a review of the history and literature related to professionalism, with attention paid to historical figures as role models; a discussion of professionalism knowledge, skills, and attitudes; an examination of pertinent ethics, morals, and human values; and a list of what and what not to do in clear behavioral terms (Archer, Elder, Hustedde, Milam, & Joyce, 2008; Eggly, Brennan, & Wiese-Rometsch, 2005; Ginsburg, Regehr, Stern, & Lingard, 2002).

While didactics are valuable and associated with positive changes in relationships with patients, cultural issues, ethics, humanism, and professional values (Jha et al., 2007), the most effective teaching of professionalism is based in both situational and experiential learning (Cruess & Cruess, 2006; Roberts, Hammond, Geppert, & Warner, 2004). There are a number of productive methods for situational teaching, including but not limited to case review and analysis, experiential training, self-awareness training, narrative competence development, collaborative interactions, community service activities, supervision and mentoring, individual or group coaching, peer supervision consultation, and Balint training.

Case review and analysis is an increasingly popular approach for teaching professionalism and typically should occur in small group discussions with trainers who serve as role models and who engage trainees in a Socratic dialogue (Duff, 2004; Stern, Frohna, & Gruppen, 2005). These efforts usually involve goal-directed problem solving and problem-based learning to increase the knowledge-skill-attitude link. In these small group discussions, the principles of professionalism should be tied to the cases being analyzed.

A variety of experiential exercises can be used to teach professionalism. These exercises afford trainers and trainees the opportunity to discuss and develop positive professionalism attitudes, as well as to describe, model, and practice professionalism (Archer et al., 2008; Eggly et al., 2005; Ginsburg et al., 2002). One activity that appears promising is using trigger films, a brief vignette depicting an interaction between a provider and a patient, to facilitate a discussion about various aspects of professional behavior (Ber & Alroy, 2002). A second exercise entails encouraging trainees to share observations of unprofessional behavior that they witnessed and having them compare the behavior to articulated principles of professionalism. A third activity includes asking trainees to discuss or write essays about their experiences with professional and unprofessional behavior (i.e., critical events), both their own and those of others. This affords them the opportunity to reflect upon the challenges of behaving in a professional fashion (Ginsburg, Regehr, & Lingard, 2003). Discussing these critical event analyses with a trainer can enhance the self-reflection process, particularly when the trainer provides a safe and nonjudgmental context, offers a framework for understanding the events and associated emotional reactions, underscores the fact that there often is no right or wrong way to engage in a significant event analysis, and shares his/her own significant event

analyses to model such exploration (Henderson, Berlin, Freeman, & Fuller, 2002; Stark, Roberts, Newble, & Bax, 2006). A fourth exercise is the establishment of an online professional development portfolio. The creation of such portfolios facilitates self-awareness, narrative competence, goal setting, and structured mentorship related to professionalism (Kalet et al., 2007).

Self-awareness training is critical to ensuring that psychologists engage in a process of self-reflection throughout the course of their careers. To begin this process, trainers must provide a training environment that is a safe venue for trainees to share their experiences; understand their own beliefs, feelings, attitudes, and response patterns; and engage in personal psychotherapy if desired (Coulehan, 2005). They must underscore the fact that self-assessment is critical to lifelong learning and ongoing performance enhancement (Duffy & Holmboe, 2006). There are multiple techniques for teaching enhanced self-assessment, such as mindful practice in action training (Epstein, 2003a, 2003b). One-on-one interviews with a faculty mentor are a particularly effective mechanism for eliciting personal reflections on professionalism (Baernstein & Fryer-Edwards, 2003).

One very important facet of professionalism competence is evidencing the capacity for narrative competence. To be competent in professionalism, the construct has to be meaningful to the individual, and this occurs through having the construct become personally relevant through the process of stories (i.e., narrative competence) (Coulehan, 2005). To assist trainees in narrative competence development, trainers should encourage trainees to acknowledge, absorb, interpret, and act on the stories and lives of others; place a value on clinical empathy in establishing and maintaining therapeutic relationships; connect with the stories and experiences of those persons not immediately known to them; and use their own life experiences, molded by positive role modeling and reflective practice, or through indirect experiences such as films and stories to develop personal narratives about professionalism.

Engaging in and giving back to the community is a key indicator of professionalism, especially if it comes from an altruistic place (Wear & Bickel, 2000). Thus it is essential that the curriculum include socially relevant, service-oriented learning efforts so that students view community service as integral to their professional role and responsibility (Coulehan, 2005). In addition, such curricula train people to respond to society's changing needs (Wear & Bickel, 2000).

A professional approach also can be inculcated in trainees through the process of engaging in productive collaborative endeavors with other trainees. Activities reflective of such collaboration include co-interviewing patients, co-therapy, and co-authorship.

Supervision related to professionalism is optimal when it capitalizes on the teaching moment (Coulehan, 2005). Supervision is an ideal venue to promote professionalism, as through the supervision process, trainers can assist trainees in connecting their knowledge, skills and attitudes to the experiences of their patients and promote awareness of relevant professional policies and organizations (Spruill & Benshoff, 1996). In addition, competency based supervisors can instill professional attitudes and values by offering the essential tools to ensure the attainment of continuous professional development and growth (Falender & Shafranske, 2007). In a related vein, coaching can occur in either an individual or a group format. Coaching sessions can be used to review feedback on trainees' performance related to professionalism with the trainee, raise awareness of their strengths and weaknesses, discuss both the costs and benefits of addressing their weaknesses, develop behavioral goals, and make plans to meet these goals (Brinkman et al., 2007). Mentoring, often a logical outgrowth of a supervisory or coaching relationship, also can be an effective way to promote reflective experiences and competence in professionalism (Wear & Aultman, 2010). Mentors assist trainees in identifying their personal calling or mission. Professionalism is fostered through the alignment of these identified interests and goals with one's work activities (Larkin, 2003).

Peer supervision and consultation can be helpful methods for learning professionalism (De Haan, 2005). Peer feedback is often very honest and direct with regard to professionalism, and trainees often are more open to input from their peers than from authority figures (Spruill & Benshoff, 1996). However, such feedback is valuable only if it occurs in a context that supports mutual learning and respect.

Balint training increasingly is used in residency training programs, particularly family medicine programs. It consists of a small group of individuals meeting together on a regular basis to reflect about their own interactions and relationships with their patients (Balint, 1957). The method involves exploring interactions with patient in depth in order to gain insight into one's own reactions to patients. Balint groups in medical training have been proposed as one vehicle for teaching professionalism through enhancing listening and observational skills; encouraging integrative, creative, and divergent perspectives; valuing empathy; and supporting the reflective process and ongoing self-assessment. Trainees who participate in such groups have found them to be useful tools for enhancing self-reflection and gaining insight into self- and patient-care issues (Adams, O'Reilly, Romm, & James, 2006).

Problems of Competence in the Professional Attitudes and Values Competency Domain

There may be subgroups of trainees for whom professional attitudes and values may not be teachable. Some are individuals who manifest serious problems in this competency domain overall and in one/or more of its essential components. Others are trainees with serious problems related to professional attitudes and values who also exhibit problems of professional competence in one or more other competency clusters or domains. Examples of competency problems related to professional attitudes and values may include an inability/unwillingness to self-reflect, acknowledge problems, and/or be open to formative and summative input including remediation plans. Unfortunately, at times, no matter how effective the educational and training system may be, it is not possible to assist the trainee in making the requite progress to meet developmentally appropriate benchmarks in this competency domain. However, there are other trainees with problems in this competency domain that can benefit from more focused remediation efforts.

A number of strategies have been recommended for addressing competency problems vis-à-vis professional attitudes and values. First, there needs to be an organized approach for monitoring and addressing unprofessional behavior that is clearly delineated and communicated to all parties (Papadakis, Loeser, & Healy, 2001). Second, it is necessary to acknowledge the importance and seriousness of the issue (Schwartz et al., 2009). Professional attitudes and values need to be addressed from the outset of any training experience or relationship and such attention must be ongoing. The threshold for attending to lapses in professionalism should be kept low (Van Mook et al., 2010). Links should be made between professional attitudes and values and patient care, as well as with disciplinary action.

Third, when giving feedback, problems of professional attitudes and values need to be linked to performance in the other competencies in the professionalism cluster, as well as to the specific competencies that fall under all of the other competency clusters. In this feedback process, the essential components of the professional attitudes and values competency that are of particular concern need to be clearly operationalized, with clear behavioral indicators of developmentally appropriate levels of performance. Such information should be included in a thoughtfully crafted remediation plan (Kaslow et al., 2007). The plan should incorporate goals, expectations, and strategies for meeting the goals; a timeline for review of progress; and information about when more severe actions will be taken (Cruess et al., 2009). Formative feedback should be provided related to this remediation plan, using multiple methods of assessment (Cruess et al., 2009). However, if at a summative evaluation point performance in this competency domain does not meet developmentally expected levels, gatekeeping efforts may be indicated.

Fourth, a trainee's competence problems related to professional attitudes and values must be conceptualized in the broader ecological system (Cruess et al., 2009; Forrest, Shen-Miller, & Elman, 2008). To this end, rather than just considering the individual trainee, trainers must examine problems related to professional attitudes and values that are manifested in the microsystem, mesosystem, exosystem, and macrosystem in which the individual trainee is embedded and, if such difficulties are noted, systemic strategies for addressing them must be implemented.

Finally, one of the most effective approaches for addressing problems of professional competence in the professionalism domain is prevention (Gabbard et al., 2012). Prevention efforts include selecting students based on their capacity for professionalism, providing role models who value professionalism, creating institutional policies related to all elements of professionalism, offering ongoing feedback regarding trainees' strengths and areas for improvement, and recognizing publically trainees who are high achievers in professionalism (Cruess et al., 2009; Gabbard et al., 2012; Van Mook et al., 2010; Wear & Aultman, 2010).

Concluding Comments

Professionalism is a core element of personal identity and character that develops over the course of one's professional life (Passi et al., 2010). The way that we desire others to experience us as psychologists and as human beings is the cornerstone of professionalism (Gabbard et al., 2012).

Professionalism is a complex construct, which has led to challenges vis-à-vis its definition, assessment, and teaching (Wear & Aultman, 2010). It is not just the definitions of this core competency that vary, but there are differences of opinion regarding its essential components. Such differences may reflect, at least in part, the various perspectives that individuals bring to bear in conceptualizing this multifaceted construct (Akhtar-Danesh et al., 2013). We recommend that a group of knowledgeable, interested parties within psychology collaboratively build upon the existing work on professional psychology competencies to craft a more comprehensive definition of professionalism and specify the essential components of this competency and how they should be manifested at various stages of professional development. This document should then go out for public comment, and the feedback received should be incorporated such that a final product can be created and shared with the education, training, practice, and credentialing communities. While it will be valuable to articulate the characteristics or behaviors that fall under the rubric of professionalism, a conceptualization of this construct must attend to the social, political, and economic contexts within which professionalism is embedded (Passi et al., 2010).

For the assessment of professionalism to be effective, clear and measureable standards need to be determined via consensus by the profession (Schwartz et al., 2009). In addition, there needs to be greater agreement with regard to clear benchmarks for performance in this competency domain for each developmental stage, as well as the behaviors and attitudes that reflect and underlie this construct (Ginsburg, Regehr, & Lingard, 2004; Rees & Knight, 2007). Once there is a clear definition of professionalism and corresponding essential components at various stages of the professional life cycle, psychologists must conduct in-depth psychometric evaluations of various available assessment tools to determine which ones are optimal for use and/or modification. Such determination will be based in part on their predictive validity of actual professional attitudes and behaviors and clinical outcomes (Epstein & Hundert, 2002; Lynch et al., 2004; Stern et al., 2005). We also need to create new tools that assess more comprehensively this complex and multidimensional construct (Hodges et al., 2011) and that do so specifically for psychologists. Ultimately, psychologists should create a professionalism toolkit for formative and summative evaluations that includes self- and other-rated scales (including multisource assessments or 360-degree evaluation methodologies), observational methodologies, high-fidelity simulations (e.g., clinical vignettes, Objective Structured Clinical Examinations, standardized patients, multiplayer/virtual games), critical incident reports, and portfolios (including self-reflections and journals) (Brinkman et al., 2007; Cruess et al., 2009; Epstein & Hundert, 2002; Kaslow et al., 2009; Passi et al., 2010; Van Mook, Gorter, O'Sullivan, et al., 2009; Veloski et al., 2005; Wilkinson, Wade, & Knock, 2009; Wood et al., 2004). This toolkit should include both quantitative and qualitative assessment methods, as the triangulation of such information is likely to be critical to the meaningful evaluation of this construct and the valuable provision of feedback with regard to this competency domain (Arnold, 2002; Van Mook, Gorter, O'Sullivan, et al., 2009; Van Mook, Van Luijk, O'Sullivan, et al., 2009). Measures in this toolkit must be set in real-life contexts so that we can observe trainees resolving relevant value conflicts associated with professionalism (Epstein & Hundert, 2002; Ginsburg et al., 2000; Van Mook, Van Luijk, O'Sullivan, et al., 2009). In addition, measures of professionalism in the learning environment need to be created (Baumann & Kolotylo, 2009; Thrush et al., 2011), as feedback on such tools can help guide improvements in the learning context, which in turn will result in psychology trainees and psychologists who exhibit high levels of professionalism. Until a state-of-the-art toolkit is established, combinations of the existing methodologies will need to suffice (Van Mook, Van Luijk, O'Sullivan, et al., 2009).

Further, there is a need to assess professionalism not only at the individual level, but also at the interpersonal and societal-institutional levels (Hodges et al., 2011). Training of those who will be conducting the assessment is also critical to ensuring the quality of the results (Van Mook, Gorter, O'Sullivan, et al., 2009). The ways in which this assessment data can be used to assist trainers in offering formative and summative feedback related to professionalism require greater delineation (Schwartz et al., 2009). Moreover, with growing attention to maintenance of competence within our profession, strategies for assessing professionalism over the lifespan need to be created, and formal implementation efforts need to get underway.

To date, there has been a dearth of empirical studies with regard to interventions that are effective for teaching professionalism (Jha et al., 2007).

The limited extant research has not yielded specific or promising protocols (Jha et al., 2007). Despite this, the data and conceptual literature shed light on a variety of promising teaching methods. It is essential that a wide array of approaches be integrated in the teaching of professionalism and that trainees be afforded multiple learning opportunities for gaining experience in and reflecting upon the concepts and principles of professionalism (Passi et al., 2010). These approaches should take into account the developmental stage of the trainee, diversity factors, and the context in which the training occurs (Cruess et al., 2009). In addition, the overall teaching of professionalism optimally will involve setting expectations, providing experiences, and evaluating outcomes (Stern & Papadakis, 2006).

One overarching framework for teaching professionalism within medicine is the *Professionalism Cycle* (Passi et al., 2010); this framework easily could be adopted for psychology. It includes four key components: (1) Professional action—knowledge, skills, and attitudes; (2) Component methods—problem-based learning, consultation, observation tools, case-based discussions, bedside teaching, videotaped consultations, role-playing exercises, and interactive lectures; (3) Tutor feedback—educational portfolios, one-on-one teaching, group teaching, and written feedback; and (4) Action plan—remediation plan to improve professionalism. This cycle also underscores the importance of lifelong learning and continuing professional development.

It is imperative that we create and disseminate best practices for addressing trainees or trainers who exhibit competency problems related to professional attitudes and values. Managing such difficulties in a systematic and respectful fashion is associated with more positive work environments, greater satisfaction and productivity among trainers and trainees alike, enhanced reputation of the educational/training program, and improved educational and patient-care outcomes (Hickson, Pichert, Webb, & Gabbe, 2007). New ways to frame problems in this competency domain may offer a fresh outlook, which appears to have occurred to some extent in the medical literature with the reframing of professionalism problems as a form of a medical error (Lucey & Souba, 2010). Indeed, strategies for dealing with medical errors may provide a useful template for efforts to address problems related to professional attitudes and values (Lucey & Souba, 2010).

As society evolves, the construct of professionalism can be a useful guide for addressing new trends. For example, social networking, commonly used by the current generation of trainees, along with other aspects of the cyber-revolution, presents psychologists with new ethical, legal, and professional dilemmas (Chretien, Greysen, Chretien, & Kind, 2009; Guesh II, Brendel, & Brendel, 2009; Thompson et al., 2008). Professionalism can help us frame our conceptualization of boundaries in cyberspace including e-mail, Google, social networking sites, blogs, and others. (Gabbard et al., 2012). Unfortunately, there are few formal guidelines or blueprints at present to inform decision making related to social media presence and the managing of cyberspace boundaries (Gabbard et al., 2012; Kind, Genrich, Sodhi, & Chretien, 2010). This is problematic given evidence of cyberspace-related unprofessional behavior by students, such as inappropriate online postings (Chretien et al., 2009). The development of such guidelines and policies should be informed by an appreciation of professionalism. In addition, our educational efforts related to the teaching of professionalism must include dialogues related to preparing future psychologists for appropriately engaging in cyberspace activities. These discussions should cover such topics as the challenges of applying principles of professionalism to the online environment, the potential impact of one's online content to patients and the public, the ways in which lapses in professional judgment or negligence in online postings reflects negatively on the institution and the profession, and the positive applications of social media for professional practice (Greysen, Kind, & Chretien, 2010).

In closing, a call for a culture of professionalism within professional psychology is vital and timely. Professionalism should be inculcated as a value within all of our training programs and should be viewed as relevant to trainers and trainees alike (Passi et al., 2010). A culture of professionalism involves clear and consistent messages within our community about the behaviors and attitudes that define highly professional psychologists (Papadakis, Arnold, Blank, Holmboe, & Lipner, 2008; Schwartz et al., 2009). Acting in a fashion that is reflective of professionalism would be considered a salient value within this culture. The assessment of professionalism would be considered integral to the evaluation of not only trainees, but also of practicing psychologists. This active transfer of professionalism self-assessment beyond the training years and into one's professional life would benefit not only the individual psychologist, but also those he/she serves, the institution in which he/she practices, and society (Van Mook, Gorter, de Grave,

et al., 2009). Individuals would engage in lifelong learning activities related to professionalism, just as they do with other competencies that define our profession. Moreover, individuals would not only be responsible for acting professionally themselves, but would assume a communitarian stance, such that they would feel responsible for ensuring that all members of our psychological community present themselves in a fashion indicative of a high level of professionalism (Johnson, Barnett, Elman, Forrest, & Kaslow, 2012). Finally, we would communicate to the public the high value placed on professionalism within our profession (Cruess et al., 2009).

References

Adams, D., & Miller, B. K. (2001). Professionalism in nursing behaviors of nurse practitioners. *Journal of Professional Nursing*, 17, 203–210. doi: 10.1053/jpnu.2001.25913

Adams, K. E., O'Reilly, M., Romm, J., & James, K. (2006). Effect of Balint training on resident professionalism. *American Journal of Obstetrics and Gynecology*, 195, 1431–1437. doi: 10.1016/j.ajog.2006.07.042

Akhtar-Danesh, N., Baumann, A., Kolotylo, C., Lawlor, Y., Tompkins, C., & Lee, R. (2013). Perceptions of professionalism among nursing faculty and nursing students. *Western Journal of Nursing Research*, 35, 248–271, doi: 10.1177/0193945911408623

American Association of Colleges of Nursing. (2008). *The essentials of baccalaureate education for professional nursing practice.* Washington DC: American Association of Colleges of Nursing.

American Board of Internal Medicine. (1995). *Project Professionalism.* Philadelphia: American Board of Internal Medicine.

American Board of Internal Medicine. (2001). *Project Professionalism.* Philadelphia: American Board of Internal Medicine.

American Dental Education Association. (2009). ADEA statement on professionalsim in dental education (as approved by the 2009 ADEA House of Delegates). Available at: www.adea.org.

Archer, R., Elder, W., Hustedde, C., Milam, A., & Joyce, J. (2008). The theory of planned behaviour in medical education: A model for integrating professionalism training. *Medical Education*, 42, 771–777. doi: 10.1111/j.1365-2923.2008.03130.x

Arnold, L. (2002). Assessing professional behavior: Yesterday, today, and tomorrow. *Academic Medicine*, 77, 502–515. doi: 10.1097/00001888-200206000-00006

Arnold, L., Shue, C. K., Kalishman, S., Prislin, M., Pohl, C., Pohl, H., et al. (2007). Can there be a single system for peer assessment of professionalism among medical students? A multi-institutional study. *Academic Medicine*, 82, 578–586. doi: 10.1097/ACM.0b013e3180555d4e

Arnold, L., Shue, C. K., Kritt, B., Ginsburg, S., & Stern, D. T. (2005). Medical students' views on peer assessment of professionalism. *Journal of General Internal Medicine*, 20, 819–824. doi: 10.1111/j.1525-1497.2005.0162.x

Baernstein, A., & Fryer-Edwards, K. (2003). Promoting reflection on professionalism: A comparison trial of educational interventions for medical students. *Academic Medicine*, 78, 742–747. doi: 10.1097/00001888-200307000-00018

Balint, M. (1957). *The doctor, his patient and the illness.* London: Pitman.

Baumann, A., & Kolotylo, C. (2009). The Professionalism and Environmental Factors in the Workplace Questionnaire: Development and psychometric properties. *Journal of Advanced Nursing*, 65, 2216–2228. doi: 10.1111/j.1365-2648.2009.05104.x

Ber, R., & Alroy, G. (2002). Teaching professionalism with the aid of trigger films. *Medical Teacher*, 24, 528–531. doi: 10.1080/0142159021000012568

Boenink, A. D., De Jonge, P., Smal, K., Oderwald, A., & Van Tilburg, W. (2005). The effects of teaching medical professionalism by means of vignettes: An exploratory study. *Medical Teacher*, 27, 429–432. doi: 10.1080/01421590500069983

Brainard, A. H., & Brislen, H. C. (2007). Learning professionalism: A view from the trenches. *Academic Medicine*, 82, 1010–1014. doi: 10.1097/01.ACM.0000285343.95826.94

Brater, D. C. (2007). Viewpoint: Infusing professionalism into a School of Medicine: Perspectives from the Dean. *Academic Medicine*, 82, 1094–1097. doi: 10.1097/ACM.0b013e3181575f89

Brinkman, W. B., Geraghty, S. R., Lanphear, B. P., Khoury, J. C., Gonzalez del Rey, J. A., DeWitt, T. G., et al. (2007). Effect of multisource feedback on resident communication skills and professionalism: A randomized controlled trial. *Archives of Pediatric Adolescent Medicine*, 161, 44–49. doi: 10.1001/archpedi.161.1.44

Chretien, K. C., Greysen, S. R., Chretien, J.-P., & Kind, T. (2009). Online postings of unprofessional content by medical students. *JAMA*, 302, 1309–1315. doi: 10.1001/jama.2009.1387

Christianson, C. E., McBride, R. B., Vari, R. C., Olson, L., & Wilson, H. D. (2007). From traditional to patient-centered learning: Curriculum change as an intervention for changing institutional culture and promoting professionalism in undergraduate medical education. *Academic Medicine*, 82, 1079–1088. doi: 10.1097/ACM.0b013e3181574a62

Cleary, L. (2008). "Forward feeding" about students' progress: The case for longitudinal, progressive, and shared assessment of medical students. *Academic Medicine*, 83, 800. doi: 10.1097/ACM.0b013e318181cfbc

Cohen, J. J. (2007). Linking professionalism to humanism: What it means, why it matters. *Academic Medicine*, 82, 1029–1032. doi: 10.1097/01.ACM.0000285307.17430.74

Coulehan, J. (2005). Today's professionalism: Engaging the mind but not the heart. *Academic Medicine*, 80, 892–898. doi: 10.1097/00001888-200510000-00004

Cox, S. M. (2008). "Forward feeding" about students' progress: Information on struggling medical students should not be shared among clerkship directors or with students' current teachers. *Academic Medicine*, 83, 801. doi: 10.1097/ACM.0b013e318181cfe6

Cruess, R. L., & Cruess, S. R. (2006). Teaching professionalism: General principles. *Medical Teacher*, 28, 205–208. doi: 10.1080/01421590600643653

Cruess, R. L., Cruess, S. R., & Johnston, S. E. (1999). Renewing professionalism: An opportunity for medicine. *Academic Medicine*, 74, 878–884. doi: 10.1097/00001888-199908000-00010

Cruess, R. L., Cruess, S. R., & Steinert, Y. (Eds.). (2009). *Teaching medical professionalism*. Cambridge: Cambridge University Press.

Cruess, R. L., McIlroy, J. H., Cruess, S. R., Ginsburg, S., & Steinert, Y. (2006). The professionalism mini-evaluation exercise: A preliminary investigation. *Academic Medicine*, 81 (10 Supplement), S74–S78. doi: 10.1097/00001888-200610001-00019

Cruess, S. R., & Cruess, R. L. (1997). Professionalism must be taught. *British Medical Journal*, 315, 1674–1677. doi: 10.1136/bmj.315.7123.1674

Cruess, S. R., Cruess, R. L., & Steinert, Y. (2008). Role modelling—Making the most of a powerful teaching strategy. *British Medical Journal*, 336, 718–721. doi: 10.1136/bmj.39503.757847.BE

Cruess, S. R., Cruess, R. L., & Steinert, Y. (2010). Linking the teaching of professionalism to the social contract: A call for cultural humility. *Medical Teacher*, 32, 357–359. doi: 10.3109/01421591003689272

De Haan, E. (2005). *Learning with colleagues: An action guide for peer consultation*. London: Palgrave Macmillan.

Duff, P. (2004). Teaching and assessing professionalism in medicine. *Obstetrics and Gynecology*, 104, 1362–1366. doi: 10.1097/01.AOG.0000146287.86079.d9

Duffy, F. D., & Holmboe, E. S. (2006). Self-assessment in life-long learning and improving performance in practice: Physician know thyself. *JAMA*, 296, 1137–1139. doi: 10.1001/jama.296.9.1137

Eggly, S., Brennan, S., & Wiese-Rometsch, W. (2005). "Once when I was on call...," Theory versus reality in training for professionalism. *Academic Medicine*, 80, 371–375. doi: 10.1097/00001888-200504000-00015

Elman, N., Illfelder-Kaye, J., & Robiner, W. (2005). Professional development: A foundation for psychologist competence. *Professional Psychology: Research and Practice*, 36, 367–375. doi: 10.1037/0735-7028.36.4.367

Epstein, R. M. (2003a). Mindful practice in action (1): Technical competence, evidence-based medicine, and relationship-centered care. *Families, Systems, & Health*, 21, 1–9. doi: 10.1037/h0089494

Epstein, R. M. (2003b). Mindful practice in action (ii): Cultivating habits of mind. *Families, Systems, & Health*, 21, 11–17. doi: 10.1037/h0089495

Epstein, R. M., & Hundert, E. M. (2002). Defining and assessing professional competence. *Journal of the American Medical Association*, 287, 226–235. doi: 10.1001/jama.287.2.226

Falender, C. A., & Shafranske, E. P. (2007). Competence in competency-based supervision practice: Construct and application. *Professional Psychology: Research and Practice*, 38, 232–240. doi: 10.1037/0735-7028.38.3.232

Forrest, L., Shen-Miller, D. S., & Elman, N. (2008). Psychology trainees with competence problems: From individual to ecological conceptualizations. *Training and Education in Professional Psychology*, 2, 183–192. doi: 10.1037/1931-3918.2.4.183

Fouad, N. A., Grus, C. L., Hatcher, R. L., Kaslow, N. J., Hutchings, P. S., Madson, M., et al. (2009). Competency benchmarks: A model for the understanding and measuring of competence in professional psychology across training levels. *Training and Education in Professional Psychology*, 3, S5–S26. doi: 10.1037/a0015832

Fryer-Edwards, K., Van Eaton, E., Goldstein, E. A., Kimball, H. R., Veith, R. C., Pellegrini, C. A., et al. (2007). Overcoming institutional challenges through continuous professionalism improvement: The University of Washington experience. *Academic Medicine*, 82, 1073–1078. doi: 10.1097/ACM.0b013e3181574b30

Gabbard, G. O., Roberts, L. W., Crisp-Han, H., Ball, V., Hobday, G., & Rachal, F. (2012). *Professionalism in psychiatry*. Washington D.C.: American Psychiatric Publishing.

Gaiser, R. R. (2009). The teaching of professionalism during residency: Why. *Anasthesia and Analgesia*, 108, 948–954. doi: 10.1213/ane.0b013e3181935ac1

Ginsburg, B. G., Regehr, G., & Lingard, L. (2004). Basing the evaluation of professionalism on observable behaviors: A cautionary tale. *Academic Medicine*, 79, S1–S4. doi: 10.1097/00001888-200410001-00001

Ginsburg, S., Regehr, G., Hatala, R., McNaughton, N., Frohna, A., Hodges, B., et al. (2000). Context, conflict, and resolution: A new conceptual framework for evaluating professionalism. *Academic Medicine*, 75, S6–S11. doi: 10.1097/00001888-200010001-00003

Ginsburg, S., Regehr, G., & Lingard, L. (2003). The disavowed curriculum: Understanding students' reasoning in professionally challenging situations. *Journal of General Internal Medicine*, 18, 1015–1022. doi: 10.1111/j.1525-1497.2003.21247.x

Ginsburg, S., Regehr, G., Stern, D., & Lingard, L. (2002). The anatomy of the professional lapse: Bridging the gap between traditional frameworks and students' perceptions. *Academic Medicine*, 77, 516–522. doi: 10.1097/00001888-200206000-00007

Ginsburg, S., & Stern, D. (2004). The professionalism movement: Behaviors are key to progress. *The American Journal of Bioethics*, 4, 14–15. doi: 10.1162/152651604323097637

Goldstein, E. A., Maestas, R. R., Fryer-Edwards, K., Wenrich, M. D., Oelschlager, A.-M. A., Baernstein, A., et al. (2006). Professionalism in medical education: An institutional challenge. *Academic Medicine*, 81, 871–876. doi: 10.1097/01.ACM.0000238199.37217.68

Greysen, S. R., Kind, T., & Chretien, K. C. (2010). Online professionalism and the mirror of social media. *Journal of General Internal Medicine*, 25, 1227–1229. doi: 10.1007/s11606-010-1447-1

Guesh II, J. S., Brendel, R. W., & Brendel, D. H. (2009). Medical professionalism in the age of online social networking. *Journal of Medical Ethics*, 35, 584–586. doi: 10.1136/jme.2009.029231

Hafferty, F. W. (2006). Definitions of professionalism: A search for meaning and identity. *Clinical Orthopaedics and Related Research*, 449, 193–204. doi: 10.1097/01.blo.0000229273.20829.d0

Hall, R. H. (1968). Professionalism and bureaucratization. *American Sociological Review*, 63, 92–104. doi: 10.2307/2092242

Hatcher, R. L., Fouad, N. A., Grus, C. L., Campbell, L., McCutcheon, S. R., & Leahy, K. K. (2013). Competency benchmarks: Practical steps toward a culture of competence. *Training and Education in Professional Psychology*, 7, 84–91, doi:10.1037/a0029401

Henderson, E., Berlin, A., Freeman, G., & Fuller, J. (2002). Twelve tips for promoting significant event analysis to enhance reflection in undergraduate medical students. *Medical Teacher*, 2, 121–124. doi: 10.1080/01421590220125240

Hickson, G. B., Pichert, J. W., Webb, L. E., & Gabbe, S. G. (2007). A complementary approach to promoting professionalism: Identifying, measuring, and addressing unprofessional behaviors. *Academic Medicine*, 82, 1040–1048. doi: 10.1097/ACM.0b013e31815761ee

Hilton, S., & Soutgate, L. (2007). Professionalism in medical education. *Teaching and Teacher Education*, 23, 265–279. doi: 10.1016/j.tate.2006.12.024

Hodges, B. D., Ginsburg, S., Cruess, R. L., Cruess, S. R., Delport, R., Hafferty, F. W., et al. (2011). Assessment of professionalism: Recommendations from the Ottawa 2010 Conference. *Medical Teacher*, 33, 354–363. doi: 10.3109/0142159X.2011.577300

Humphrey, H. J., Smith, K., Reddy, S., Scott, D., Madara, J. L., & Arora, V. M. (2007). Promoting an environment of professionalism: The University of Chicago "roadmap." *Academic Medicine*, 82, 1098–1107. doi: 10.1097/01.ACM.0000285344.10311.a8

Interprofessional Education Collaborative Expert Panel. (2011). *Core competencies for interprofessional collaborative practice: Report of an expert panel*. Washington D.C.: Interprofessional Education Collaborative.

Jha, V., Bekker, H. L., Duffy, S. R. J., & Roberts, T. E. (2007). A systematic review of studies assessing and facilitating attitudes towards professionalism in medicine. *Medical Education*, 41, 822–829. doi: 10.1111/j.1365-2923.2007.02804.x

Johnson, W. B., Barnett, J. E., Elman, N. S., Forrest, L., & Kaslow, N. J. (2012). The competent community: Toward a vital reformulation of professional ethics. *American Psychologist*. 67, 557–569, doi: 10.1037/a0027206

Joyner, B. D., & Vemulakonda, V. M. (2007). Improving professionalism: Making the implicit more explicit. *The Journal of Urology*, 177, 2287–2291. doi: 10.1016/j.juro.2007.01.149

Kalet, A. L., Sanger, J., Chase, J., Keller, A., Schwartz, M. D., Fishman, M. L., et al. (2007). Promoting professionalism through an online professional development portfolio: Successes, joys, and frustrations. *Academic Medicine*, 82, 1065–1072. doi: 10.1097/ACM.0b013e31815762af

Kaslow, N. J. (2004). Competencies in professional psychology. *American Psychologist*, 59, 774–781. doi: 10.1037/0003-066X.59.8.774

Kaslow, N. J., Borden, K. A., Collins, F. L., Forrest, L., Illfelder-Kaye, J., Nelson, P. D., et al. (2004). Competencies Conference: Future directions in education and credentialing in professional psychology. *Journal of Clinical Psychology*, 80, 699–712. doi: 10.1002/jclp.20016

Kaslow, N. J., Grus, C. L., Campbell, L. F., Fouad, N. A., Hatcher, R. L., & Rodolfa, E. R. (2009). Competency assessment toolkit for professional Psychology. *Training and Education in Professional Psychology*, 3, S27–S45. doi: 10.1037/a0015833

Kaslow, N. J., Rubin, N. J., Forrest, L., Elman, N. S., Van Horne, B. A., Jacobs, S. C., et al. (2007). Recognizing, assessing, and intervening with problems of professional competence. *Professional Psychology: Research and Practice*, 38, 479–492. doi: 10.1037/0735-7028.38.5.479

Kenny, N. P., Mann, K. B., & MacLeod, H. (2003). Role modeling in physicians' professional formation: Reconsidering an essential but untapped educational strategy. *Academic Medicine*, 78, 522–534. doi: 10.1097/00001888-200312000-00002

Kind, T., Genrich, G., Sodhi, A., & Chretien, K. C. (2010). Social media policies at US medical schools. *Medical Education Online*, 15, 5324. doi: 10.3402/meo.v15i0.5324

Kirk, L. M. (2007). Professionalism in medicine: Definitions and considerations for teaching. *Baylor University Medical Center Proceedings*, 20, 13–16. doi: Available at: http://www.baylorhealth.edu/Research/Proceedings/Pages/default.aspx

Larkin, G. L. (2003). Mapping, modeling, and mentoring: Charting a course for professionalism in graduate medical education. *Cambridge Quarterly of Healthcare Ethics*, 12, 167–177. doi: 10.1017/S0963180103122062

Lelliott, P., Williams, R., Mears, A., Andiappan, M., Owen, H., Reading, P., et al. (2008). Questionnaires for 360-degree assessment of consultant psychiatrists: Development and psychometric properties. *British Journal of Psychiatry*, 193, 156–160. doi: 10.1192/bjp.bp.107.041681

Lesser, C. S., Lucey, C. R., Egener, B., Braddock, C. H., Linas, S. L., & Levinson, W. (2010). A behavioral and systems view of professionalism. *JAMA*, 304, 2732–2737. doi: 10.1001/jama.2010.1864

Lucey, C. R., & Souba, W. (2010). The problem with the problem of professionalism. *Academic Medicine*, 85, 1018–1024. doi: 10.1097/ACM.0b013e3181dbe51f

Lynch,D. C., Surdyk, P. M., & Eiser, A. R. (2004). Assessing professionalism: A review of the literature. *Medical Teacher*, 26, 366–373. doi: 10.1080/01421590410001696434

Mareiniss, D. P. (2004). Decreasing GME training stress to foster residents' professionalism. *Academic Medicine*, 79, 825–831. doi: 10.1097/00001888-200409000-00003

McNair, R. P. (2005). The case for educating health care students in professionalism as the core content of interprofessional education. *Medical Education*, 39, 456–464. doi: 10.1111/j.1365-2929.2005.02116.x

Medical School Objectives Writing Group. (1999). Learning objectives for medical student education—Guidelines for medical schools: Report I of the Medical School Objectives Project. *Academic Medicine*, 74, 13–18. doi: Available at: http://journals.lww.com/academicmedicine/pages/default.aspx

Merriam-Webster. (Retrieved September 5, 2012). Professionalism. Available at: http://www.merriam-webster.com/dictionary/professionalism.

Miller, B. K., Adams, D., & Beck, L. (1993). A behavioral inventory for professionalism in nursing. *Journal of Professional Nursing*, 9, 290–295. doi: 10.1016/8755-7223 (93)90055-H

Murden, R. A., Way, D. P., Hudson, A., & Westman, J. A. (2004). Professionalism deficiencies in a first-quarter doctor-patient relationship course predict poor clinical performance in medical school. *Academic Medicine*, 79, S46–S48. doi: 10.1097/00001888-200410001-00014

Pangaro, L. (2008). "Forward feeding" about students' progress: More information will enable better policy. *Academic Medicine*, 83, 802. doi: 10.1097/ACM.0b013e318181d025

Papadakis, M. A., Arnold, G. K., Blank, L. L., Holmboe, E. S., & Lipner, R. S. (2008). Performance during internal medicine residency training and subsequent disciplinary action by state licensing boards. *Annals of Internal Medicine*, 148, 869–876. doi: Available at: www.annals.org

Papadakis, M. A., Loeser, H., & Healy, K. (2001). Early detection and evaluation of professionalism deficiencies in medical students: One school's approach. *Academic Medicine*, 76, 1100–1106. doi: 10.1097/00001888-200111000-00010

Papadikis, M. A., Hodgson, C. S., Teherani, A., & Kohatsu, N. D. (2004). Unprofessional behavior in medical school is associated with subsequent disciplinary action by state medical board. *Academic Medicine*, 79, 244–249. doi: 10.1097/00001888-200403000-00011

Papadikis, M. A., Teherani, A., Banach, M. A., Knettler, T. R., Rattner, S. L., Stern, D. T., et al. (2005). Disciplinary action by medical boards and prior behavior in medical school. *New England Journal of Medicine*, 353, 2673–2682. doi: 10.1056/NEJMsa052596

Passi, V., Doug, M., Peile, E., Thistlethwaite, J., & Johnson, N. (2010). Developing medical professionalism in future doctors: A systematic review. *International Journal of Medical Education*, 1, 19–29. doi: 10.5116/ijme.4bda.ca2a

Pellegrino, E. D. (2002). Professionalism, profession and the virtues of the good physician. *The Mount Sinai Journal of Medicine*, 69, 378–384. doi: Retrieved from http://onlinelibrary.wiley.com/journal/10.1002/(ISSN)1931-7581

Project of the ABIM Foundation, ACP-ASIM Foundation, & European Federation of Internal Medicine. (2002). Medical professionalism in the new millennium: A physician charter. *Annals of Internal Medicine*, 1136, 243–246. doi: Available at: http://www.annals.org/

Ratanawongsa, N., Bolen, S., Howell, E. E., Kern, D. E., Sisson, S. D., & Larriviere, D. (2006). Residents' perceptions of professionalism in training and practice: Barriers, promoters, and duty hour requirements. *Journal of General Internal Medicine*, 21, 758–763. doi: 10.1111/j.1525-1497.2006.00496.x

Rees, C. E., & Knight, L. V. (2007). The trouble with assessing students' professionalism: Theoretical insights from sociocognitive psychology. *Academic Medicine*, 82, 46–50. doi: 10.1097/01.ACM.0000249931.85609.05

Roberts, L. W., Hammond, K. A. G., Geppert, C. M. A., & Warner, T. D. (2004). The positive role of professionalism and ethics training in medical education: A comparison of medical student and resident perspectives. *Academic Psychiatry*, 28, 170–182. doi: 10.1176/appi.ap.28.3.170

Rodolfa, E. R., Bent, R. J., Eisman, E., Nelson, P. D., Rehm, L., & Ritchie, P. (2005). A cube model for competency development: Implications for psychology educators and regulators. *Professional Psychology: Research and Practice*, 36, 347–354. doi: 10.1037/0735-7028.36.4.347

Schwartz, A. C., Kotwicki, R. J., & McDonald, W. M. (2009). Developing a modern standard to define and assess professionalism in trainees. *Academy Psychiatry*, 33, 442–450. doi: 10.1176/appi.ap.33.6.442

Seldin, P., & Associates. (1993). *Successful use of teaching portfolios.* Bolton, MA: Anker Publishing Company.

Seldin, P., & Miller, J. E. (2009). *The academic portfolio: A practical guide to documenting teaching, research, and service.* San Francisco: Jossey-Bass.

Seldin, P., Miller, J. E., & Seldin, C. A. (2010). *The teaching portfolio: A practical guide to improved performance and promotion/tenure decisions (4th edition).* San Francisco: Jossey-Bass.

Smith, K. L., Saavedra, R., Raeke, J. L., & O'Donell, A. A. (2007). The journey to creating a campus-wide culture of professionalism. *Academic Medicine*, 82, 1015–1021. doi: 10.1097/ACM.0b013e318157633e

Spruill, D. A., & Benshoff, J. M. (1996). The future is now: Promoting professionalism among counselors-in-training. *Journal of Counseling & Development*, 74, 468–471, doi: 10.1002/j.1556-6676.1996.tb01894.x

Stark, P., Roberts, C., Newble, D., & Bax, N. (2006). Discovering professionalism through guided reflection. *Medical Teacher*, 28, e25–e31. doi: 10.1080/01421590600568520

Stark, R., Korenstein, D., & Karani, R. (2008). Impact of a 360-degree professionalism assessment on faculty comfort and skills in feedback delivery. *Journal of General Internal Medicine*, 23, 969–972. doi: 10.1007/s11606-008-0586-0

Steinert, Y., Cruess, R. L., Cruess, S. R., Boudreau, J. D., & Fuks, A. (2007). Faculty development as an instrument of change: A case study on teaching professionalism. *Academic Medicine*, 82, 1057–1064. doi: 10.1097/01.ACM.0000285346.87708.67

Steinert, Y., Cruess, S. R., Cruess, R. L., & Snell, L. (2005). Faculty development for teaching and evaluating professionalism: From programme design to curriculum change. *Medical Education, 39,* 127–136. doi: 10.1111/j.1 365-2929.2004.02069.x

Stern, D. T. (Ed.). (2006). *Measuring medical professionalism.* Oxford: Oxford University Press.

Stern, D. T., Frohna, A. Z., & Gruppen, L. D. (2005). The prediction of professional behaviour. *Medical Education, 39,* 75–82. doi: 10.1111/j.1365-2929.2004.02035.x

Stern, D. T., & Papadakis, M. A. (2006). The developing physician—Becoming a professional. *New England Journal of Medicine, 355,* 1794–1799. doi: 10.1056/NEJMra054783

Sutkin, G., Wagner, E. F., Harris, I., & Schiffer, R. (2008). What makes a good clinical teacher in medicine: A review of the literature. *Academic Medicine, 83,* 452–466. doi: 10.1097/ACM.0b013e31816bee61

Swick, H. M. (2000). Toward a normative definition of medical professionalism. *Academic Medicine, 75,* 612–616. doi: 10.1 097/00001888-200006000-00010

Swick, H. M. (2007). Professionalism and humanism beyond the academic health center. *Academic Medicine, 82,* 1022–1028.

Swing, S. R. (2007). The ACGME outcome project: Retrospective and prospective. *Medical Teacher, 29,* 648–654. doi: 10.1080/01421590701392903

Teherani, A., Hodgson, C. S., Banach, M., & Papadakis, M. A. (2005). Domains of unprofessional behavior during medical school associated with future disciplinary action by a state medical board. *Academic Medicine, 80,* S17–S20. doi: 10.10 97/00001888-200510001-00008

Thistelethwaite, J. E., & Spencer, J. (2008). *Professionalism in medicine.* Oxford: Radcliff Medical Press.

Thompson, L. A., Dawson, K., Ferdig, R., Black, E. W., Boyer, J., Coutts, J., et al. (2008). The intersection of online social networking with medical professionalism. *Journal of General Internal Medicine, 23,* 954–957. doi: 10.1007/s11606-008-0538-8

Thrush, C. R., Spollen, J. J., Tariq, S. G., Williams, K., & Shorey, J. M., II. (2011). Evidence for validity of a survey to measure the learning environment for professionalism. *Medical Teacher, 33,* e683–e688. doi: 10.3109/0142159X. 2011.611194

Tromp, F., Vernooij-Dassen, M. J. F. J., Kramer, A., Grol, R., & Bottema, B. J. A. M. (2010). Behavioural elements of professionalism: Assessment of a fundamental concept in medical care. *Medical Teacher, 32,* e161–e169. doi: 10.3109/01421590903544728

Van de camp, K., Vernooij-Dassen, M. J. F. J., Grol, R., & Bottema, B. J. A. M. (2006). Professionalism in general practice: Development of an instrument to assess professional behaviour in general practitioner trainees. *Medical Education, 40,* 43–50. doi: 10.1111/j.1365-2929.2005.023 46.x

Van de camp, K., Vernooij-Dassen, M. J. F. J., Grol, R. P. T. M., & Bottema, B. J. A. M. (2004). How to conceptualize professionalism: A qualitative study. *Medical Teacher, 26,* 696–702. doi: 10.1080/01421590400019518

Van Luijk, S. J., Gorter, R. C., & Van Mook, W. N. K. A. (2010). Promoting professional behaviour in undergraduate medical, dental and veterinary curricula in the Netherlands: Evaluation of a joint effort. *Medical Teacher, 32,* 733–739. doi: 10.3109/0142159X.2010.505972

Van Mook, W. N. K. A., De Grave, W. S., Van Luijk, S. J., O'Sullivan, H., Wass, V., Schuwirth, L. W., et al. (2009). Training and learning professionalism in the medical school curriculum: Current considerations. *European Journal of Internal Medicine, 29,* e96–e100. doi: 10.1016/j. ejim.2008.12.006

Van Mook, W. N. K. A., De Grave, W. S., Wass, V., O'Sullivan, H., Zwaveling, J. H., Schuwirth, L. W., et al. (2009). Professionalism: Evolution of the concept. *European Journal of Internal Medicine, 20,* e81–e84. doi: 10.1016/j. ejim.2008.10.005

Van Mook, W. N. K. A., Gorter, S. L., de Grave, W. S., Van Luijk, S. J., O'Sullivan, H., Wass, V., et al. (2009). Professionalism beyond medical school: An educational continuum. *European Journal of Internal Medicine, 2009,* e148–e152. doi: 10.1016/j.ejim.2009.09.009

Van Mook, W. N. K. A., Gorter, S. L., De Grave, W. S., Van Luijk, S. J., Wass, V., Zwaveling, J. H., et al. (2010). Bad apples spoil the barrel: Addressing unprofessional behavior. *Medical Teacher, 32,* 891–898. doi: 10.3109/0142159x.2010.497823

Van Mook, W. N. K. A., Gorter, S. L., O'Sullivan, H., Wass, V., Schuwirth, L. W. T., & Van der Vleuten, C. P. M. (2009). Approaches to professional behaviour assessment: Tools in the professionalism toolbox. *European Journal of Internal Medicine, 20,* e153–e157. doi: 10.1016/j.ejim.2009.07.012

Van Mook, W. N. K. A., Van Luijk, S. J., De Grave, W. S., O'Sullivan, H., Wass, V., Schuwirth, L. W. T., et al. (2009). Teaching and learning professional behavior in practice. *European Journal of Internal Medicine, 20,* e105–e111. doi: 10.1016/j.ejim.2009.01.003

Van Mook, W. N. K. A., Van Luijk, S. J., O'Sullivan, H., Wass, V., Zwaveling, J. H., Schuwirth, L. W., et al. (2009). The concepts of professionalism and professional behaviour: Conflicts in both definition and learning outcomes. *European Journal of Internal Medicine, 20,* e85–e89. doi: 10.1016/j.ejim.2008.10.006

Veloski, J. J., Fields, S. K., Boex, J. R., & Blank, L. L. (2005). Measuring professionalism: A review of studies with instruments reported in the literature between 1982 and 2002. *Academic Medicine, 80,* 366–370. doi: 10.109 7/00001888-200504000-00014

Verderk, M. A., de Bree, M. J., & Mourits, M. J. E. (2007). Reflective professionalism: Interpreting CanMEDS' "professionalism." *Journal of Medical Ethics, 33,* 663–666. doi: 10.1136/jme.2006.017954

Viggiano, T. R., Pawlina, W., Lindor, K. D., Olsen, K. D., & Cortese, D. A. (2007). Putting the needs of the patient first: Mayo Clinic's core value, institutional cultural, and professionalism covenant. *Academic Medicine, 82,* 1089–1093. doi: 10.1097/ACM.0b013e3181575dcd

Wasserstein, A. G., Brennan, P. J., & Rubenstein, A. H. (2007). Institutional leadership and faculty response: Fostering professionalism at the University of Pennsylvania School of Medicine. *Academic Medicine, 82,* 1049–1056. doi: 10.1097/ACM.0b013e31815763d2

Wear, D. M., & Aultman, J. M. (Eds.). (2010). *Professionalism in medicine: Critical perspectives.* New York: Springer.

Wear, D. M., & Bickel, J. (Eds.). (2000). *Educating for professionalism: Creating a culture of humanism in medical education.* Iowa City: University of Iowa Press.

Wear, D. M., & Kuczewski, M. G. (2004). The professionalism movement: Can we pause? *American Journal of Bioethics*, 4, 1–10. doi: 10.1162/152651604323097600

Weissman, P. F., Branch, W. T., Gracey, C. F., Haidet, P., & Frankel, R. M. (2006). Role modeling humanistic behavior: Learning bedside manner from the experts. *Academic Medicine*, 82, 661–667. doi: 10.1097/01.ACM. 0000232423.81299.fe

Wilkinson, T. J., Wade, W. B., & Knock, L. D. (2009). A blueprint to assess professionalism:. *Academic Medicine*, 84, 551–558. doi: 10.1097/ACM.0b013e31819fbaa2

Wood, J., Collins, J., Burnside, E. S., Albanese, M. A., Propeck, P. A., Kelcz, F., et al. (2004). Patient, faculty, and self-assessment of radiology resident performance. *Academic Radiology*, 11, 931–939. doi: 10.1016/j.acra.2004.04.016

Wright, S. M., & Carrese, J. A. (2003). Serving as a physician role model for a diverse population of medical learners. *Academic Medicine*, 78, 623–628. doi: 10.1097/ 00001888-200306000-00013

Wright, S. M., Kern, D. E., Kolodner, K., Howard, D. M., & Brancati, F. L. (1998). Attributes of excellent attending-physician role models. *New England Journal of Medicine*, 339, 1986–1993. doi: 10.1056/NEJM199812313392706

Wynd, C. A. (2003). Current factors contributing to professionalism in nursing. *Journal of Professional Nursing*, 5, 251–261. doi: 10.1016/S8755-7223(03)00104-2

Emerging Technologies and Innovations in Professional Psychology Training

Michael J. Constantino, Christopher E. Overtree, *and* Samantha L. Bernecker

Abstract

The most effective and ineffective facets of professional psychology training remain largely unknown, and many questions remain about the field's traditional training models and how such models can be improved, restructured, or refocused. The present chapter focuses on such questions and improvement efforts in the forms of emerging training technologies and innovations. Specifically, we address both technological advances and paradigmatic challenges to professional psychology training and their related implications, across four main sections: (1) direct technological innovations for training; (2) non-technology-based innovations; (3) promising technological innovations for direct psychological care, which, by extension, require training schemes on those technologies (training that is mostly absent in current paradigms); and (4) challenges to integrating technological innovations in professional training and direct practice. Finally, we offer several concluding comments on the state and future of training in professional psychology.

Key Words: psychotherapy training, technology, innovations, continuing education, distance learning, accreditation, training clinics, outcomes monitoring and management, common factors, therapist responsiveness

Introduction

The field of professional psychology, and psychotherapy in particular, appears to operate under an implicit assumption that long-standing education and training practices (e.g., didactics, supervision, skill-building, continuing education) are directly responsible for the effectiveness of psychological services. However, the most effective and ineffective aspects of professional psychology training, especially as they pertain to direct service in the form of psychotherapy and assessment, remain largely unknown, with little systematic training research to inform best practices (Boswell & Castonguay, 2007a; Eby, Chin, Rollock, Schwartz, & Worrell, 2011; Stein & Lambert, 1995). Thus, many questions remain about the field's traditional training models and how such models can be improved (from whatever their current baseline of relevance and importance). In this chapter, we highlight such questions and improvement efforts in the forms of emerging technological and conceptual innovations.

Professional psychology is embedded in a sociopolitical context rife with ongoing technological advancement. The upside of psychology-relevant technologies includes greater access to treatment, consultation, and training opportunities, as well as potentially greater efficiency and efficacy of psychological services and training on these services (Barnett, 2011; Kazdin & Blase, 2011. Increased access, in the form of technologies such as the Internet, video-conferencing, virtual reality, smart phones, and so forth, holds clear promise as an adjunct to, or even possible replacement for (in certain contexts), face-to-face contact among professionals, trainees, and consumers (Wolf, 2011).

For example, numerous psychotherapies already rely heavily on technology, and early research suggests that technology-centered or technology-enhanced treatments can be at least as effective as traditional therapies both in process (e.g., Sucala et al., 2012) and outcome (e.g., Barak, Hen, Boniel-Nissim, & Shapira, 2008). Although the data are less abundant for psychological assessment, there are certainly promising technological advances that may ultimately improve the reliability, validity, and/or practicality of such assessments (e.g., Garb, 2007; Piasecki, Hufford, Solhan, & Trull, 2007; Trull, 2007).

Although one could argue that psychology and technology historically have not been bedfellows, it seems clear that this relationship is changing dramatically. The age of rapid dissemination of information and services is upon us, and it is incumbent on the field to continue to adopt, develop, test, and implement cutting-edge technologies into its service, training, and research missions (Kazdin & Blase, 2011). Such innovations undoubtedly will force the field to scrutinize traditional training practices that have gone largely unchallenged for decades.

Of course, innovations are not restricted to digital technology. They also can represent a challenge to the status quo and the asking of difficult questions about what does and does not work with regard to psychology practice and training. Thus, in this chapter, we address both technological advances and paradigmatic challenges to professional psychology training, with a relative focus on clinical training and training in the practice of psychotherapy (an activity in which clinical psychologists spend the largest percentage of their time; Norcross & Karpiak 2012). In the first section, we outline direct technological innovations for training and their implications. In the second section, we address non-technology-based innovations and their associated implications. In the third section, we review current and promising technological innovations for direct care, which, by logical extension, require training on those technologies (training that is mostly absent in current paradigms and in some cases is hindered by current licensing and accreditation requirements). Finally, we offer several concluding comments on the state of psychotherapy training and visions for its responsive evolution in the face of promising technological and non-technology-based innovations.

Technology-Based Training Innovations

Information technologies are in constant flux: The world's capacity to communicate and store information is rapidly accelerating (Hilbert & López, 2011). Articles and books about technology often are outdated even before they make it to print. Therefore, instead of reviewing issues around specific hardware and software currently available, we focus on the implications of technologies more broadly. For example, in the case of streaming video for therapeutic, teaching, or mentoring purposes, there is a greater benefit to focusing on the clinical and pedagogical issues rather than the technological ones. The question is not whether online video quality and security levels are high enough for use in clinical, classroom, or administrative settings. Rather, the more relevant question is, assuming that online video quality and security is (or will shortly be) sufficient for clinical, classroom, and meeting use, what are the ethical, pedagogical, or practical issues that make this sustainable or unsustainable? Or, in other words, do new technological advances replace, improve, or serve as satisfactory substitutes for more traditional models of clinical service or training? Or even better, are there ways that technology can alter some of the core features of professional service and training that have not yet been envisioned? These questions serve as the foundation of this section on technology-based training innovations.

Real-time e-learning tools, such as text chat, have the potential to enhance important training components like counseling or psychotherapy supervision and teaching. Some research has supported the benefits of online peer supervision via text chat; for example, school counselor trainees undergoing such supervision evidenced higher counselor self-esteem and better case conceptualization skill than trainees with no online supervision (Butler & Constantine, 2006). Other research has demonstrated specific advantages (e.g., more positive perceptions of supervision quality) of hybrid supervision (e.g., integrating traditional face-to-face supervision with online text chat) over face-to-face supervision alone (Conn, Roberts, & Powell, 2009; Gammon, Sørlie, Bergvik, & Hoifodt, 1998).

Although text-based e-learning tools have shown promise, video conferencing may have added value in that it includes nonverbal cues in the supervisory experience (Abbass et al., 2011). Research has shown that the experiences of supervisees and supervisors are largely comparable in video conference-based supervision and face-to-face supervision (Reese et al., 2009; Sørlie, Gammon, Bergvik, & Sexton, 1999). Any limitations noted often were related to the contemporary limitations of the technology itself (e.g., connection issues) rather than its pedagogical or clinical utility (Sørlie et al., 1999). As we have suggested, technical limitations are virtually always temporary and need not be a prominent focal point.

Although participants may perceive the supervisory experience as equivalent in either Web-based or face-to-face formats, it is premature to assume that patient outcomes of trainees in these different formats will be equivalent. More research is needed to help professional psychology educators determine whether Web-based supervision can augment or even fully replace traditional face-to-face supervision, particularly as it pertains to patient outcomes (Abbass et al., 2011; Reese et al., 2009). And given that Web-conferencing originally was used as an occasional alternative to face-to-face meetings, rather than as a replacement for them, research is also needed to determine the optimal frequency and length of Web-based meetings.

As the technological barriers to Web conferencing decline, we should expect that broader adoption might lead to unexpected problems. For example, supervision relationships may occasionally (or often) occur exclusively in the Internet environment in order to take advantage of the opportunity to bridge long distances between supervisees and supervisors. Although this carries the obvious advantage of broadening collaboration opportunities, it also raises questions about whether direct personal contact is needed to foster an emotional connection and/or how frequently direct personal contact must be made to maintain connection even with ongoing Web supervision (Reese et al., 2009). Researchers must ask whether truly efficacious supervisory or therapeutic relationships can be developed or maintained exclusively online.

Of course, the potential benefits and challenges of the online environment are not restricted to supervision. E-learning tools also apply to other training elements like coursework, continuing education, and dissemination of treatment techniques. Although there are aspects of a face-to-face classroom that cannot be replicated online, there are surely unique advantages of an online course. For example, online work facilitates immediate multimedia access. Moreover, students may be less inhibited in their critical thinking/expression and more open in their dialogue (which might be inhibited in face-to-face settings). Students living on-site also would have greater access to instructors, perhaps even luminaries in the field, beyond those offering courses at their home institution. There might also be significant financial or time savings if travel is removed from the equation—savings that could take place not only when in training, but also when engaging in continuing education throughout one's career.

Information technology has implications for coursework in professional psychology beyond those involving distance learning. For example, instructors can easily exchange lesson plans, syllabi, exercises, and other course material, and use these resources to improve their own teaching. Many instructors already use presentation software like PowerPoint and use videos to provide examples in the classroom. Moreover, online textbooks are rising in popularity and offer enrichments impossible in paper textbooks like embedded videos and hyperlinks. Outside the classroom, students can thus have instant access to more information on any topics that intrigue or confuse them while they are reading, and they should be encouraged to use this access. In fact, because access to information is so instant, we argue that it is now just as important for students to learn how to find and evaluate sources and to synthesize new information as it is to memorize basic facts, if not more so. Instant access also allows future psychologists to keep current in a constantly changing science and to tailor their learning to their own interests and relevant areas of professional psychology.

Regarding continuing education and technique dissemination, one also can imagine the benefits of online video training or even training wikis. For example, researchers and clinicians could collaborate to develop an online catalogue of empirically supported treatment packages or individual strategies that includes text description, clinical transcripts, and video demonstrations. Armed with such clinical material, all relevant participants could continually update catalogue entries as the evidence base evolves (Barnett, 2011). A central benefit, of course, is that psychotherapists from around the world, at whatever training level, would have access to descriptions and demonstrations of the latest treatment techniques, which would help to keep them up-to-date and evidence-informed in their practice. Further, with clinicians' contributing to the wiki, science-practice integration would be inbuilt. A variety of strategies could be implemented to ensure the quality of wiki entries, including requiring certain types of empirical support before a technique may be included or establishing editorial oversight.

Technology also can powerfully affect the evaluation of clinical psychology training. For example, monitoring patients' outcomes with computer-, tablet-, or smartphone-based administration of core assessment measures can help to direct practice, training, patient-therapist matching, and other important administrative decision making. Such guidance is in the form of predictive analytics, or algorithm-driven and computer-assisted feedback. For example, in light of research demonstrating that some therapists provide little help to their average patients (Lambert, 2007), others actually harm their average patient (Okiishi, Lambert, Nielsen, & Ogles, 2003), and still others consistently produce positive change across their cases (Okiishi et al., 2003), Kraus, Castonguay, Boswell, Nordberg, and Hayes (2011) conducted a study to assess (a) the pervasiveness of helpful and harmful therapists and (b) the degree to which such effects are problem specific. In a naturalistic sample of 696 therapists with varying licenses, Kraus and colleagues (2011) analyzed reliable changes for 10 patients per therapist across 12 symptom and functional domains (e.g., depression, panic/anxiety, work functioning) as assessed by the Treatment Outcome Package (TOP; Kraus, Seligman, & Jordan, 2005) used in routine outcome monitoring across the represented clinics. The authors defined an "effective" therapist as one whose average patient reliably improved, an "unclassifiable/ineffective" therapist as one whose average patient neither reliably improved nor deteriorated, and a "harmful" therapist as one whose average patient reliably deteriorated. Results indicated a striking number of ineffective or harmful therapists (ranging from 33–65%) providing large negative effects on their patients. However, the results also showed marked variability of therapist effectiveness between symptom and functional domains, with 96% of therapists showing effectiveness in at least one domain and none demonstrating effectiveness across all 12 domains.

Kraus and colleagues (2011) highlighted the immense public-health and professional-training implications of their findings on therapist effects. First, and echoing Lambert (2010), they called for more widespread evaluation of patient outcomes as part of routine clinical care (including in training clinics)—a practice that remains underutilized at best and actively resisted at worst (Liptzin, 2009). Not only can outcome tracking and related statistical algorithms provide useful information about clinicians' global and domain-specific effectiveness, they can also provide valuable real-time feedback to help clinicians respond more effectively to potential blind spots. These blind spots appear prevalent, because research has demonstrated that most therapists overestimate their own effectiveness and are also poor prognosticators of their patients' likelihood of deteriorating across treatment (Hannan et al., 2005). Thus, outcome tracking may be reaching a level of ethical mandate. Second, the authors called for the use of outcome monitoring and computer-assisted feedback throughout training to inform general clinical evaluation, to guide the assessment of and supervision around negative therapist effects, and to advise important decisions around clinical placements, probations, and possible clinical training termination.

Youn, Kraus, and Castonguay (2012) further highlighted several possible uses and benefits of outcomes monitoring in training clinics. For example, baseline assessment of core outcome measures can assist clinicians with case formulation and discussion of treatment goals. Information from outcome measures can also provide additional insights into patients' intrapsychic and/or interpersonal functioning (especially when patients are reticent to disclose relevant clinical information verbally). With measurement across time, outcome data can help track progress and provide clinician alerts for patients at risk of deterioration or premature termination, which seems particularly important, considering that up to 58% of patients experience clinical deterioration on at least one clinical dimension (Kraus et al., 2005). Finally, and perhaps most importantly for broader application, a clinician or trainee engaging in outcomes monitoring might have a "corrective experience" that refutes prior worries about the burdens of data collection on patients and the treatment process.

The notion of using outcome monitoring in psychotherapy as a "lab test" (Hannan et al., 2005; Lambert, 2010) is further supported by data on clinical versus actuarial prediction, which convincingly has demonstrated the superiority of actuarial methods (Grove & Meehl, 1996). This research also highlights that clinical experience is uncorrelated with accuracy of clinical judgment. Yet, mental health practitioners still largely rely on intuition and experience in their decision making. As Lambert (2010) has reported, providing therapists with computer-assisted feedback about their clients' progress (or lack thereof), as well as additional information on alliance quality, the patient's readiness for change, and the patient's level of social support, can double the number of patients who experience adaptive and clinically significant change at post-treatment. We agree with Lambert that there is no longer a viable excuse "for failing to assist clients by using these methods. Certainly clients do not find being asked about their functioning inside and outside of psychotherapy to be a burden if the therapists discuss and use this information to make treatment more responsive to their needs" (p. 260).

The now-available outcome monitoring and predictive analytic technologies have even broader implications for traditional training models. If we use evidence to guide treatment decisions, then it would follow that we utilize evidence to guide aspects of training that have also traditionally been guided by intuition, judgment, and reputation. Keeping with outcomes monitoring, such data can inform how clinicians are doing relative to their training stage. Further, in addition to analyzing data by trainee, one could also imagine analyzing data by supervisor to inform the evaluation of supervisor effectiveness (which has typically either gone without evaluation or has occurred through far more subjective and biased means). Such data-informed evaluation would presumably go a long way toward anchoring our training practices to empirical evidence and providing an opportunity to contribute to the scant research base on effective training practices and characteristics (Boswell & Castonguay, 2007b). Unfortunately, few training programs are currently on the cutting edge of formally tracking patient progress and capitalizing on the predictive power of actuarial techniques (Lambert, 2010).

Technological innovations in training also have implications for clinical training accreditation standards. The American Psychological Association (APA) Commission on Accreditation (CoA) is recognized by both the United States (U.S.) Department of Education and the Council of Higher Education Accreditation as the national accrediting authority for professional education and training in psychology, and it maintains policies and procedures consistent with national standards and common understanding about the purpose and value of accreditation and periodic reviews. However, the accreditation process is not without controversy, nor are the promulgated standards ideally suited to the missions of all training institutions. The core of most arguments about the accreditation process is often related to pedagogy and the application of one's training mission. The techniques available for providing graduate education in professional psychology (e.g., clinical, counseling, school) are considerably more diverse in the age of increasing technological sophistication. Considering our discussion about Web-based coursework, supervision,

and mentoring, it may be useful to review specific accreditation challenges that early-adopters of enhanced e-learning might face in the current version of the APA-CoA (2009) standards, as well as ways in accreditation standards might be modified to consider more effectively education and training in the new technological climate.

Most of the accreditation standards are not generally impacted by technology and, in some cases, it is extremely clear that technology greatly enhances the educational process. Consider that access to all published research in psychology can be reviewed in the comfort of your office rather than in the stacks of a university library. Because the process of reviewing academic scholarship is a relatively independent process, the venue for one's research review seems irrelevant to the accumulation of published knowledge. However, when it comes to teaching, mentorship, peer interactions, clinical supervision, and supports, the venue suddenly becomes germane to the overall training experience. And, as would be expected, the APA-CoA (2009) accreditation standards are *currently* written in ways that could limit how fully technology might be integrated into the training experience without jeopardizing accreditation.

Regarding the appropriate setting for program *Eligibility* (Domain A), the APA-CoA (2009) states, "the program's purpose...must be pursued in an institutional setting appropriate for the doctoral education and training of professional psychologists" (p. 5). This statement leaves considerable ambiguity regarding programs that rely exclusively or heavily on distance learning, video supervision, or online or hybrid course content. With the presently nebulous notion of an appropriate institutional setting, it seems important that future iterations of the APA-CoA standards incorporate a clear statement on the appropriateness of programs that exist in many hybrid settings, such as those that straddle state or national boundaries or do not primarily employ a face-to-face classroom or face-to-face mentorship model. The APA-CoA also suggests that programs must have "students in sufficient number and the facilities necessary to ensure meaningful peer interaction, support and socialization" (pp. 5–6), and it requires students to spend at least one year in "full-time residence (or the equivalent thereof)" (p. 6). One can be certain that these standards were written with face-to-face assumptions in mind, even though many of the concepts and terms (e.g., *peer interactions, socialization, facilities,* or *appropriate settings*) have taken on new or expanded meanings in the Internet age. Many of us now have colleagues and friends with whom we interact exclusively online, and we would most likely deem this environment sufficient to ensure meaningful peer interactions, support, and socialization. But can this environment truly replace the learning experiences in face-to-face settings, and do so at a level of fidelity warranting full academic accreditation? Hybrid and exclusively online programs already exist in other fields, and receive accreditation, but how well will models of clinical training accommodate these advances? This is a key point, as future APA-CoA standards might need to focus less on the delivery mode (or location) of learning and more on the outcomes and utility of the pedagogical tools in use. And, to us, research should guide the revision of these standards.

Interestingly, one aspect of the APA-CoA Eligibility domain, that of providing for cultural and individual diversity, can actually be enhanced by more online or hybrid learning tools. Reducing the barriers to program development also can pave the way for students from underrepresented categories to complete graduate programs in clinical psychology. In the same way that telehealth has the potential to provide services to the underserved, e-learning has the potential to teach the undertaught.

Regarding Domain B of the accreditation standards, *Program Philosophies, Objectives, and Curriculum Plan*, the APA-CoA states that clinical psychology programs must have a "clearly specified philosophy of education and training" (p. 6), something that could easily incorporate e-learning goals and techniques. However, this domain also specifies that this philosophy must be appropriate to the "science and practice of psychology" (p. 6). In other words, if telehealth becomes a truly viable service-provision method, then delivering gold-standard training in this format will be closer to meeting this current standard. Perhaps more importantly, training in the provision of telehealth services might benefit from occurring in the same medium as the service delivered. This, of course, has yet to be tested, but it certainly holds exciting promise if research were to substantiate this notion and thus inform future revisions of APA-CoA standards.

Technology has an impact on other APA-CoA (2009) domains as well. For example, according to APA-CoA, a clinical psychology program "has, and appropriately utilizes, the additional resources it needs to achieve its training goals and objectives" (Domain C; p. 9), "recognizes the importance of cultural and individual differences in the training of psychologists" (Domain D; p. 10), operates in a context of "mutual respect and courtesy between students and faculty" (Domain E; p. 10), "demonstrates a commitment to excellence through self-study" (Domain F; p. 11), "demonstrates a commitment to public disclosure by providing written materials…that appropriately represent it to the relevant publics" (Domain G; p. 12), and "demonstrates its commitment to the accreditation process by fulfilling its responsibilities to the accrediting body" (Domain H; p. 12). In our reading, none of these domains possess language that would expressly (or accidentally) preclude the accreditation of programs that rely heavily on the online arena for teaching. However, the methods for meeting these standards would necessarily differ depending on the institution and its pedagogy. A graduate school program that seeks to use hybrid instruction methods must do so with great facility and integrity to seek accreditation in the same way as traditional programs. Perhaps more exciting, as technological advances become more fully integrated in clinical training, the manner in which programs respond to these domains can become more creative and sophisticated.

Non-Technology-Based Training Innovations

In addition to direct technology-based training innovations, we argue that the psychotherapy field in particular also could benefit from complementary conceptual and paradigmatic challenges to the training status quo. In this section, which is focused on psychotherapy, we offer several possible revisions to standard clinical training models that hold promise for advancing training practices, as well as science-practice-training integration.

Integrating Research Infrastructures into the Psychotherapy Training Mission

One potential innovation is the incorporation of research infrastructures into psychotherapy training/teaching clinics. Although science-practice assimilation has long been a primary agenda for professional psychology (as reflected in the dominant scientist-practitioner and clinical scientist training models), there has been strikingly little meaningful integration of science and practice into our training programs (Borkovec, 2004). To strengthen this link, Borkovec articulated a "dream" route to consequential science-practice integration that centers on the training clinic. The training clinic is a largely untapped resource that is well situated as an ecologically valid clinical setting, as well as an integral element of early clinical training. In addition to incorporating predictive analytic technology in the form of patient outcomes monitoring (as discussed earlier), training clinics hold promise for engaging an array of professionals, at different career stages, in the process of translational research and the application of evidence-based practice (Castonguay, 2011; Castonguay, Locke, & Hayes, 2011).

To elaborate on Borkovec's (2004) proposal, graduate trainees would observe and experience from the first day of their training the genuine integration of science and practice. Ideally this would take the form of intensive training in clinic protocols, including a comprehensive diagnostic evaluation that would allow for reliable diagnosis and the accumulation of invaluable assessment training and hours. Trainees also would complete therapist characteristic measures at strategic points in their training, which would allow for subsequent research on therapist variables. Thus, from the beginning, graduate students are clinicians *and* research participants. Further, when commencing psychotherapy training, graduate students ideally would be consumers of the literature and constantly attending to the empirical support for their interventions—support that could come from their own work (i.e., personal case studies) or from the extant research base. In this type of training clinic, patients would also complete clinically germane measures. As noted earlier, a core outcome measure like the TOP would allow for outcomes monitoring and therapist responsiveness to predictive analytics. The core battery would also allow for overall program evaluation or pointed evaluation at the clinic, service, supervisor, and/or clinician level. In addition to the core battery, patients can also complete other baseline and during-treatment measures for the purpose of informing treatment (e.g., a measure of therapeutic alliance quality), psychological assessment (e.g., ruling out a psychotic process), and/or answering specific research questions (e.g., how do patients' attachment styles relate to the course and outcome of psychotherapy?). In addition, sessions would be videotaped for purposes of intensive supervision and possible use in rigorous coding-based research. Finally, as the database evolves, both faculty and student researchers would have the opportunity to propose and conduct original, clinically relevant research based on the core infrastructure and possible study-specific add-on measures. And, with multiple clinics adopting the same infrastructure

and/or collaborating on specific research projects, a practice-research network (PRN) could be established that would allow for rigorous naturalistic research conducted by a larger number of clinicians and researchers on a larger sample of clinicians and patients (thereby increasing statistical power, sample diversity, and intellectual creativity).

PRNs, of course, are not limited to the training clinic. They can be developed between researchers and practitioners in community settings (Castonguay, 2011), leading to complementary research on practice-oriented questions that practitioners are most interested in having answered; that is, practitioners have a vested interest and active role in the research being conducted (Castonguay et al., 2010). The ultimate goal of PRNs, beginning at the training level, would be a lifelong learning process whereby clinicians witness and participate in the seamless and consequential blending of science and practice. Surrounding this process would be an evolving, large-scale database loaded with promise for answering various research questions of keen interest to the practicing community. Within this model of science-practice-training integration, the term *scientist-practitioner* would likely become synonymous with *clinical scientist* (Castonguay, 2011). Moreover, a telltale sign of the field's advancement might be when a trainee (or any clinician engaging in a PRN) is unaware about whether he or she is currently engaging in a clinical intervention or a research activity, as the two would be intimately, and appropriately, intertwined (Castonguay, 2011).

Related to research infrastructures and outcomes monitoring, Kraus et al. (2011) highlighted the potential utility of re-deploying the workforce toward practicing within one's clear competence domains, which would seemingly benefit all stakeholders. Capitalizing on the previously reviewed finding that most therapists are competent in at least one or a few domains, it may be that matching patient to therapist strength will become the quintessential "matching" variable. We would also argue that training, after large enough trainee work samples have been produced, might also begin to focus more on specialized tracks. This would help trainees (perhaps beginning as early as graduate school, but certainly at the internship and postdoctoral fellowship stages) become even stronger at what they are good at, which would translate to expertise carried into the workforce. This specialization would reflect a movement away from the long-standing predominant model of training generalists, which, to us, carries a higher likelihood of doing harm in some domains, with some patients, at some point in one's career. Specialist training also might help trainees to integrate more readily their research expertise into their specialized, and expertise-centered, clinical practice. This melding of science and practice expertise would likely go far in promoting adaptive treatment outcomes in clinical practice, which should have positive implications for therapists (e.g., less experience of incompetence), patients (e.g., improved quality of life), managed-care companies (e.g., lowered health-care costs), and training programs (e.g., producing high quality next generation psychologists). Of course, the notion of training specialization is not without challenges. For example, it is unclear if trainees would have large enough work samples to allow for reliable prediction of good outcome domains. Further, not all trainees would have access to population or treatment domains for which they are likely to be effective. Thus, the idea of training specialization remains in a conceptual stage and requires significant research.

Moving from Theory-Specific to Common Factors Psychotherapy Training

A second potential conceptual innovation relates to shifting the focus of current psychotherapy training from theory-specific treatment packages to more pantheoretical common factors (Boswell & Castonguay, 2007b; Stein & Lambert, 1995). This culture shift would be commensurate with the research literature, which strongly suggests that common treatment factors, or change principles, are instrumental in promoting psychotherapeutic change (e.g., Duncan, Miller, Wampold, & Hubble, 2010; Wampold, 2001). In fact, there is compelling evidence that common factors account for a significant portion of treatment outcome variance, perhaps even more so than the theory-specific packages and techniques that have been the dominant focus of training models to date (Norcross, 2011; Wampold, 2007). Despite this evidence, relatively scant attention has been paid to the direct implications of these findings for psychotherapy supervision and training (Castonguay, 2005). The innovation, then, would be for trainees to receive core competency training on the most empirically supported common factors. Ideally, this training would remain grounded in theory, which would provide the conceptual backdrop for the delivery of a coherent treatment rationale and the provision of rationale-consistent therapist behaviors. Not only is the provision of a theoretical rationale important for patient engagement (Ahmed & Westra, 2009),

but it also provides the framework that gives contextual meaning to the common factors (Anderson, Lunnen, & Ogles, 2010).

Of course, if training is going to shift toward a common factors focus, the most robust of these so-called relational and nonspecific variables need to be identified and systematized into a trainable form. Although there is currently no consensus on the most robust and important of the common factors, and many such factors require greater systematization for teaching and dissemination, we discuss here several possible heuristics as "food for innovative thought" (though the ideas will require empirical scrutiny and empirically informed evolution).

As one heuristic, Fauth, Gates, Vinca, Boles, and Hayes (2007) called for psychotherapy training to refocus on two interrelated "big ideas" (Binder, 2004), namely therapist responsiveness and therapist metacognitive skill development. In psychotherapy, responsiveness reflects participant behavior affected by emerging context, including the behaviors, perceptions, wishes, and characteristics of the participants (Stiles, Honos-Webb, & Surko, 1998). Thus, responsiveness involves dynamic and reciprocal feedback systems among its participants, which inevitably affect the psychotherapeutic process before it begins (e.g., treatment assignment), in the moment (e.g., a specific utterance based on the other participant's prior reaction), and/or across time (e.g., using multiple sessions to address an alliance rupture). To be responsive, therapists need to be attuned to the ongoing therapy process so that they can recognize important markers to which they need to be responsive. Such attunement and presence can be facilitated by therapist mindfulness or by sustained, nonjudgmental attention and awareness of one's momentary experience in the session (Bruce, Manber, Shapiro, & Constantino, 2010; Safran & Muran, 2000). Fauth et al. argued that mindfulness is a metacognitive therapist skill that can best be facilitated in training programs via experiential practice. Thus, in this heuristic, training programs would emphasize experiential exercises focused on mindfulness, empathic attunement, and salient pattern recognition (i.e., key therapeutic moments to which to respond).

To us, the notion of attunement can be expanded to another heuristic: a set of therapist competencies on marker-guided, empirically informed interventions, or what we have called context-responsive integration (Constantino, Boswell, Bernecker, & Castonguay, in press; Constantino, DeGeorge, Dadlani, & Overtree, 2009). The context would be comparable to Fauth et al.'s (2007) notion of pattern recognition or to what others have referred to as markers (e.g., Safran & Muran, 2000). Common factors also could be reframed as common situations that therapists encounter to which they need to be responsive in some way. Based on the research literature, we view at least four candidate common situations that all have empirically supported interventions from which to draw when the situation arises. The notion would be that therapists could be trained to both recognize these situations and to implement context-responsive interventions. The first reflects patients' low expectation for change; in this context, a therapist could reiterate or revise the therapeutic rationale (with an emphasis on sensitive, though skillful persuasion; Frank, 1961) and/or implement pointed expectancy-enhancing interventions (e.g., see Constantino, Ametrano, & Greenberg, 2012). The second situation reflects alliance ruptures, or problems in the patient-therapist bond or sense of coordinated collaboration. In this context, a therapist could implement specific alliance-rupture repair strategies (e.g., see Safran & Muran, 2000). The third situation involves a patient's change ambivalence. In this situation, a therapist might implement motivational interviewing strategies that have been shown to be effective in addressing and resolving ambivalence (e.g., see Arkowitz, Westra, Miller, & Rollnick, 2008). Finally, an alarming psychological "lab test," as detected in regular outcomes monitoring, could lead to therapist metacommunication—that is, a frank and open discussion with patients about their progress (Lambert, 2010), which might even reveal signs of lowered expectations, alliance tensions, and/or change ambivalence. Focusing training and practice on these context-responsive scenarios and interventions would not eliminate the need for theory-based practice. In fact, the main operating treatment frame could (and probably should) still be a specific psychotherapy model. Although all theories have flaws and most overlap in some ways, the delivery of the rationale in a coherent and genuinely confident manner also reflects an empirically supported stance or intervention (Anderson et al., 2010).

Although direct testing of structured responsiveness training remains in its infancy, there are some promising data that support its efficacy, especially with regard to the four elements outlined earlier: rationale delivery (e.g., Ahmed & Westra, 2009) and expectancy enhancement (e.g., Constantino, Klein, Smith-Hansen, & Greenberg,

2009), alliance development and rupture repair (e.g., Constantino et al., 2008), resolving ambivalence with motivational interviewing (e.g., Aviram & Westra, 2011), and drawing on clinical support options in the face of negative outcomes indicators (e.g., Harmon et al., 2007). We would argue that training programs would be well served to begin incorporating such trainings into their curriculum, as well as to contribute to the testing and advancement of trainings by ideally developing and drawing on their research infrastructures and PRNs as outlined earlier. As Boswell and Castonguay (2007b) argued, "training programs are likely to be more cohesive and lead to broader clinical skills if their primary focus is on general principles or models of change...as opposed to a list of variables or a series of empirically supported treatment (EST) manuals alone" (p. 379). Of course, this idea still requires direct and controlled testing (i.e., of the efficacy of principle-based, common factors training versus training that focuses solely on an EST manual); however, it reflects an empirically informed paradigmatic challenge to the current state of psychotherapy training.

Socializing Clinicians to Key Psychotherapeutic Processes

A third potential innovation relates to the former on responsiveness training. The idea would be to turn the role induction (RI) literature (e.g., see Walitzer, Dermen, & Connors, 1999) on its head: It is possible that therapists more than patients need to be socialized (perhaps especially during early training) to key psychotherapy processes (Johansen, Lumley, & Cano, 2011; Strassle, Borckardt, Handler, & Nash, 2011). In other words, therapists need to be trained to recognize contexts like alliance ruptures more than patients, as this will allow them to skillfully respond to these key therapeutic moments. This innovative notion is supported at least indirectly by several literatures.

First, recent findings suggest that preparing patients via video-based RI about potential alliance ruptures can actually have negative effects on early therapy process (Johansen et al., 2011). These authors argued that preparatory focus on potential relationship difficulties with their therapist might have led to greater apprehension in patients, which could have manifested in interpersonal distance that negatively disrupted early relational process. Although this study requires replication, it supports the notion that RI, or structured clinical training, may be better targeted at therapists versus patients (at least with regard to the alliance; see, for example, Hilsenroth, Ackerman, Clemence, Strassle, & Handler, 2002). Second, the pattern of RI findings over time is suggestive of a need to rethink RI strategies. Although early RI studies for patients generally supported the efficacy of this method for treatment engagement and outcomes (Walitzer et al., 1999), there was a long gap in RI research over the past 20 years (perhaps reflective of nonsignificant file drawer studies), as well as some recently published null findings (e.g., Johansen et al., 2011; Strassle et al., 2011). This pattern suggests a cohort effect in which patients today may be far more likely to have been exposed to therapy either in person and/or via the Internet and media, thus rendering them less in need of preparatory socialization. Third, therapist-effects research, though relatively limited, also points toward a possible shift in RI to focus more on the therapist. That is, another interpretation of more recent null findings for patient RIs is that such work failed to account for between-therapist variability in promoting adaptive process and outcome, irrespective of whether their patients received an RI. Not only do therapists account for substantial variance in process and outcome (e.g., Baldwin, Wampold, & Imel, 2007; Kim, Wampold, & Bolt, 2006), but such effects might also be able to be influenced by structured clinical trainings on therapist responsiveness to key therapy processes.

Another way to think about training is to follow the research base to develop a training flow to evidence-based practice. As Norcross and Wampold (2011) noted, elements of the psychotherapy relationship make substantial and consistent contributions to treatment outcomes, independent of the treatment type. Thus, practice and training guidelines need to focus explicitly on therapist behaviors, characteristics, and qualities that promote a helping relationship. Without this explicit focus, training might reasonably be considered seriously incomplete and potentially misguided; yet, very few programs have implemented structured training on therapeutic relationship development and negotiation (Constantino, Morrison, MacEwan, & Boswell, in press). Furthermore, research supports the notion that therapists need to adapt or tailor their relationship and their treatment approach to specific patient needs and characteristics (Norcross, 2011). In light of this, Norcross and Wampold outlined three specific training and continuing professional development recommendations: (1) programs should begin providing competency-based training

in the demonstrably and probably effective therapy relationship elements (e.g., alliance in individual, youth, and family therapies, cohesion in group therapy, empathy), and be prepared to enhance training on promising elements (e.g., repairing alliance ruptures, managing countertransference) if future support emerges; (2) programs should begin providing competency-based training in adapting psychotherapy to the individual patient in ways that likely enhance treatment efficacy (e.g., reactance/resistance level, preferences, culture), and be prepared to enhance training on promising adaptation elements (e.g., expectations, attachment style) if future support emerges; and (3) training program accreditation and certification bodies should develop criteria for evaluating the satisfactoriness of training in evidence-based therapy relationships.

Increase Direct Research on Psychotherapy Training

A fourth potential innovation was implied in those just discussed: conduct more rigorous research on psychotherapy training. Although there is a widespread assumption that because psychotherapy generally works then our training activities must work, this has yet to be borne out convincingly in empirical research (Boswell & Castonguay, 2007a; Stein & Lambert, 1995). Fauth et al. (2007) stated the following about traditional training practices that emphasize didactics, adherence to treatment manuals, and/or theory-guided supervision: "Although such trainings tend to demonstrably improve adherence to the psychotherapy model...they do not enhance psychotherapist competence or effectiveness beyond the training period... In fact, research indicates that traditional forms of psychotherapy training can even have unintended deleterious consequences at times (Henry et al., 1993)" (p. 384).

Ladany (2007) highlighted three central competency domains for psychotherapists: knowledge, self-awareness, and skills. He argued that traditional training models tend to focus predominantly on knowledge in the form of coursework and supervision. Although becoming more knowledgeable through these means might promote a solid foundation about psychotherapy theory and process, it does not automatically transfer to self-awareness, skills, and overall applied competency, though most training programs likely assume that such knowledge will spread to these other domains (i.e., the "germ myth" of psychotherapy training; Beutler, 1995). In light of this tenuous link between training models/activities and applied competence, graduate training programs in psychology, psychiatry, counseling, and social work all face continued challenges to demonstrate the direct efficacy of their models, that is, the direct association between specific training elements and clinicians' subsequent ability to foster positive outcomes and reduce negative outcomes in their patients (Stein & Lambert, 1995).

Researchers and clinicians also have begun to pay more attention, at least conceptually, to supervision competencies and supervisor/trainer effects. As Kaslow, Falender, and Grus (2012) have indicated, it is only recently that a movement toward establishing and evaluating supervision competencies has gained momentum (Falender et al., 2004; Fouad et al., 2009). This movement appears long overdue and necessary on at least two fronts. First, the supervision competence of many core training faculty and staff supervisors are likely inconsistent with evolving practice standards (Kaslow et al., 2012). Second, the sociopolitical reality is that master's-level therapists increasingly will be providing direct psychological services, whereas doctoral-level psychologists will increasingly find themselves in a supervisory role over master's-level providers (Eby et al., 2011). Thus, the traditional focus of doctoral students' training on the practice of individual psychotherapy may be misdirected. Instead, doctoral-level training may be most aligned with reality if it shifted its focus to the training of the next generation of competent supervisors (Fouad et al., 2009). Unfortunately, it remains unclear how well supervision can be taught, and the science behind this practice is meager (Eby et al., 2011).

The implications of shifting toward training/ supervision competencies have far-reaching implications for the inner workings of graduate training programs. For one, it seems that the days of the "guru" model of supervision need to end abruptly; simply passing on clinical wisdom accumulated over years of practice is vastly insufficient and potentially even harmful if one considers the previously reviewed research on therapist judgment and experience. Consonant with this shift is the need for supervisors and supervisees to be willing to open themselves up to close evaluation and constant scrutiny of their competence and impact. The idea would be to move from an input to an output model of competency assessment for all parties (Roe, 2002). In traditional input models, faculty and supervisors determine course content and training activity, as well as make subjective evaluations of how trainees are doing in these domains. In output models, constant attention would need to be paid

to evidence supported competencies of the supervisor and supervisee at every stage of the supervisee's training. Working from the aforementioned probability that not all supervisors and supervisees are created equal, it seems essential for programs to begin tracking patient outcomes data as a central indicator of clinical skill for *both* the clinician and the supervisor. Any consistent negative patterns will indicate a need to take action, be it through directed specialization or even counseling a student out of the program or the faculty member out of the supervisor role. Although this will likely be intimidating and unwelcome to some, establishing and evaluating competencies in this form will not only promote better patient care but will also model the importance of self-awareness and self-assessment (which seem to be consensus "good clinician" traits and states; Kaslow et al., 2012).

Technology-Based Treatment Innovations Requiring Technology Training

As discussed in the previous sections, innovations in information technology and other arenas can be applied to enhance the training of mental health professionals. Additionally, technologies have been developed to enhance mental health services (e.g., psychotherapy, psychological assessment) themselves, and these continue to proliferate and improve with astounding rapidity. Such technologies have the potential not only to improve the care of those already in treatment but also to help reach the substantial population that struggles with untreated mental illness (Kazdin & Blase, 2011). This level of unmet need is daunting; the current population of mental health professionals is inadequate both in number and in geographic distribution, and those currently practicing are not consistently able to relieve the symptoms of those who do present for treatment. Because of the capability of technological applications for psychotherapy to address some of these unmet needs, we believe that it is ethically imperative to test these interventions for efficacy and to implement those that can bring relief to our clients. However, there are numerous hurdles to overcome in adopting these tools: it is necessary that clinicians develop a level of personal comfort in incorporating information technologies into practice, that validated interventions be widely disseminated, and that clinicians be knowledgeable about how to use these tools with facility and fidelity. Training, therefore, has a vital role to play in making technological developments in psychotherapy available to those in need of them.

Incorporating these tools into training programs can acclimate future clinicians to the use of technology, act as a dissemination venue, and teach clinicians the skills necessary for implementation. This section describes some promising technologies, discusses strategies for incorporating them into training, and highlights related challenges.

Several applications of information technology to psychotherapy practice have been extensively researched and have shown considerable utility. Computer-aided psychotherapies are automated self-help systems that deliver behavioral, cognitive-behavioral, or psychoeducational interventions with minimal or no clinician support. They can be implemented on a variety of devices (e.g., personal computers, mobile devices, gaming machines; Marks, Cavanagh, & Gega, 2007), but typically are accessed via the Internet (Andersson & Cuijpers, 2009). They often include (a) information about the causes of a disorder, the rationale for interventions, or strategies for change, delivered by text, audio, or video; (b) various interactive exercises for identification of patient problem areas, cognitive restructuring, behavioral activation, and more; and (c) monitoring of and feedback on symptom change, though there are certainly no limits on their content (Marks & Cavanagh, 2009).

Computer-aided psychotherapies have been evidenced in meta-analyses to be more effective than waitlist and placebo conditions and largely comparable to face-to-face therapy for various anxiety disorders (e.g., Andrews, Cuijpers, Craske, McEvoy, & Titov, 2010; Cuijpers et al., 2009; Spek, Cuijpers, Nyclíček, Riper, Keyzer, & Pop, 2007), depression (e.g., Andersson & Cuijpers, 2009; Andrews et al., 2010; Spek et al., 2007), and health-related behaviors (Portnoy, Scott-Sheldon, Johnson, & Carey, 2008). Promising computer-aided treatments for drug and alcohol abuse and smoking cessation also have been developed (Newman, Szkodny, Llera, & Przeworski, 2011). Finally, computer-aided treatment systems that include minimal clinician support to promote adherence, whether in person or via phone or email, tend to outperform those that are completely self-guided (Andersson & Cuijpers, 2009; Spek et al., 2007).

Computer-aided psychotherapy's boon, as a treatment that is primarily self-help and can be optimally administered with only minimal contact from a therapist, is its ability to extend vastly the number of patients treated (Kazdin & Blase, 2011). Additionally, because it can be accessed in any location and at any time, computer-aided psychotherapy can reach those who are unable or unwilling to attend face-to-face treatments due to geographical location, issues with physical mobility or transportation, work schedules, the risk of stigma, agoraphobia, or social phobia, and so forth. Depending on the format, such therapies can also be less costly than traditional ones. Because it is not yet as well validated as face-to-face therapy, patients should be sensitively triaged between computer-aided psychotherapy and face-to-face psychotherapy, with the computer-aided variant ideal for those with milder symptoms and/or the limitations described earlier. Computer-aided interventions also may have utility as maintenance treatments following traditional therapy or as prepackaged and automated sets of homework assignments for inclusion in face-to-face therapy. Again, given the promise of computer-aided psychotherapy, it seems important for training programs to incorporate direct training on these treatment platforms.

Another well-studied application of technology to psychotherapy is telehealth. Traditional psychotherapy can be administered via telephone, videoconference, text chat, or e-mail (Barak et al., 2008). There is much evidence that such interventions can reduce depression (Mohr, Vella, Hart, Heckman, & Simon, 2008) and posttraumatic stress disorder (PTSD) symptoms (Sloan, Gallagher, Feinstein, Lee, & Pruneau, 2011), and can improve the psychosocial functioning of those with acquired physical disabilities (Dorstyn, Mathias, & Denson, 2011). Moreover, telephone quit lines are effective for smoking cessation (Lichtenstein, Zhu, & Tedeschi, 2010). Telehealth interventions have other successful applications, including to treat obsessive-compulsive disorder (Lovell et al., 2006), bulimia nervosa (Mitchell et al., 2008), panic (Rollman et al., 2005), substance abuse (McKay, Lynch, Shepard, & Pettinati, 2005), and oppositional-defiant, attention-deficit/hyperactivity, and anxiety disorders in children (McGrath et al., 2011), as well as to provide services to patients with dementia (Poon, Hui, Dai, Kwok, & Woo, 2005), schizophrenia (Sharp, Kobak, & Osman, 2011), and their caregivers (Haley et al., 2011). Additionally, psychiatric diagnosis and symptom assessment using high-bandwidth videoconference does not differ from face-to-face assessment (Hyler, Gangure, & Batchelder, 2005). Preliminary evidence also suggests that therapy via videoconference is often as effective as face-to-face therapy (García-Lizana & Muñoz-Mayorga, 2010) and can produce comparably strong alliances (Germain, Marchand, Bouchard, Guay, & Drouin, 2010). Like computer-aided treatment, teletherapy can reach those who are unable or unwilling to attend face-to-face therapy. Particularly when conducted via telephone, e-mail, or text chat, it may also engender more disinhibited self-disclosure (Rochlen, Zack, & Speyer, 2004); when communication is text-based, it provides greater opportunities for reflection and takes advantage of the therapeutic benefits of writing (Rochlen et al., 2004). Telehealth can also allow for the continuation of traditional therapy when the client or therapist moves out of the area and can be interwoven with traditional therapy or provided as a hybrid alternative to face-to-face treatment alone (Krupinski et al., 2002). Like computer-aided psychotherapies, then, it seems logical to extend professional training curriculum to cover telehealth applications (a curriculum that should flexibly evolve as new research illuminates best practices).

Technology has been put to myriad other uses in the field. In the area of assessment, technology has the potential to make administration and scoring of instruments more efficient with digital data collection (Hoyer, Ruhl, Scholz, & Wittchen, 2006) and computer-adaptive instruments (Fliege et al., 2009), to collect more ecologically valid data using in-vivo mobile assessments (Trull & Ebner-Priemer, 2009), and to increase diagnostic accuracy with the addition of neuroimaging and psychophysiological data (Brammer, 2009) and the use of artificially intelligent decision-making systems (Delavarian, Towhidkhah, Gharibzadeh, & Dibajnia, 2011). Communication technologies (e.g., telephone, e-mail, text message) can be used to maintain contact with patients between sessions in order to manage crises (Ben-Porath & Koons, 2005), provide appointment reminders, encourage homework completion, guide in-vivo exposure sessions, and more (Boschen & Casey, 2008); they can also facilitate collaboration among service providers and enable consultation with experts at a distance. Technology also has a vital role to play in promoting the services of mental health professionals on websites and social media (Johnson, 2011).

Technology-based components can also augment and enhance traditional therapies. Virtual reality exposure is effective for phobias, panic, and PTSD (Powers & Emmelkamp, 2008) and, thus, can be incorporated when a patient is unwilling to try in vivo exposure, when the appropriate in-vivo experience is inaccessible, or as a way to develop a customized exposure schedule suitable to patients' preferences and need. Computer-administered exercises can reliably improve cognitive and global

functioning in schizophrenia (Wykes, Huddy, Cellard, McGurk, & Czobor, 2011) and can reduce symptoms of inattention in children with Attention-Deficit/Hyperactivity Disorder (Rabiner, Murray, Skinner, & Malone, 2010). Multimedia tools can be used for educational purposes; for example, videos can instruct clients in new skills (Waltz et al., 2009). Video games may have utility in working with children and adolescents to strengthen the alliance and to facilitate exploration in play therapy (Ceranoglu, 2010). Certain online activities, such as blogging (Baker & Moore, 2008) and participating in Internet support groups (Griffiths, Calear, & Banfield, 2009), also may have therapeutic effects and could be assigned as homework.

From our review, it seems clear that currently available information technologies have the potential to improve the standard of care. Technologies for use in psychotherapy will only continue to grow in quality, number, and variety; within the next decade there are sure to be technological applications for psychotherapy that are now impossible to imagine. (If you doubt this, note the vast effects that social networking has had on business, research, the interpersonal landscape, even governance in the Middle East, and then realize that Facebook began in 2004, Twitter in 2006, and that these were only reliably available to people at all times with the onset of smartphones, which made Internet access and availability ubiquitous—the iPhone was released in 2007.) Clinicians being trained today will need to navigate this proliferation of technologies and select and apply those that will be most effective for their clients. Equally important, licensing and accrediting bodies will need to be apprised of new technologies, quick to adopt tested tools into accepted practice, and provide some form of vetting and guidance for training new users.

Challenges to Integrating Technologies in Professional Training and Practice

There are several challenges to be addressed before new technologies can be included in a professional training program. A primary obstacle is emotional resistance on the part of trainers and trainees. For example, many psychotherapists seem wary of technology, perhaps out of skepticism that technology can perform better than a human in a human service profession or, conversely, out of fear of being replaced by a computer (Nadelson, 1987). A more moderate position is probably warranted: Technology for psychotherapy is neither completely worthless nor is it powerful enough to replace human clinicians. As we have noted, it has been repeatedly demonstrated that algorithms can perform better than clinician judgment in some, though certainly not all, decision-making processes. Therapists, like all humans, are prone to a variety of biases and distortions (Lambert, 2011), and technology can correct some of these faults. On the other hand, the nuances of human capabilities extend far beyond those of computers. Note that even the most automated of the interventions described earlier, computer-assisted psychotherapy, requires some clinician interaction to be maximally effective and is confined to the treatment of a set of circumscribed problems of mild severity with a limited repertoire of techniques. We suggest viewing technologies as tools for extending our capabilities in the service of meeting patient needs; that is, computers will enhance, not replace us. In fact, if we fail to embrace innovations that can improve our efficiency, accessibility, and visibility to the public, psychotherapists run the risk of being replaced not by computers, but by other health-care providers (Bray, 2010) who utilize these tools to improve their own practice. Fortunately, we believe that comfort will vastly increase when therapists directly experience the nonthreatening nature of these technologies (beginning with the first step of the training process).

Other obstacles to the adoption of technologies in psychotherapy education and training are pragmatic. One is lack of awareness of what tools are available and knowledge about how to use them. Fortunately, many of the products and processes described earlier are user-friendly. We suggest that training clinic directors, supervisors, and trainees undertake the learning process together, experimenting with the application of technology to their work and educating each other collaboratively. Training programs also can facilitate learning through colloquia, by identifying and offering credit for relevant webinars and online training courses, and by connecting students with practica and internships in which technologies are already being implemented. The developers of technologies should endeavor to make their products as accessible as possible and should consider directing dissemination efforts toward trainees and organizations of trainers. Perhaps equally important, professional groups such as the APA should focus some of its own resources toward the production of technology that is specifically designed to enhance clinical treatment, training, and supervision. For example, applications that are designed expressly for these purposes could serve as a major new innovation in the clinical realm, and one that should be led by psychologists.

Lack of time and financial resources may be a concern. Although learning a new technology will require some initial time investment, many technologies are fairly intuitive and/or are extensions of traditional clinical practice, thus speeding the learning process, especially for today's trainees who grew up with computer access. Additionally, some technologies can make clinic operations more efficient, resulting in net time saving. To maximize gain from the training process, programs should focus on incorporating the most common, essential, and convenient technologies into everyday procedures for all students; programs should direct interested individuals to outside resources and should encourage and reward them for utilizing them. In some cases, little to no financial investment is required, because much of what we have described in this chapter uses equipment and programs that are already ubiquitous or that are inexpensive and easily obtained. However, when the cost for a given technology is prohibitive (e.g., virtual reality), we suggest that training programs direct interested students to practicum and internship opportunities that already have such technologies in place.

Finally, a number of ethical concerns must be addressed before many of these innovative ideas can be implemented in either training or in psychotherapy. First, although there is a dearth of evidence on whether current training practices are effective (Boswell & Castonguay, 2007b), and, therefore, it could be argued that there is no "standard" of training quality that new, technology-assisted techniques must meet or exceed, it would be best to test both current and proposed new practices to ensure that trainees are receiving the high-quality training in which they have invested and on which their future patients will rely. Applications of technology to psychotherapy itself will need the same empirical validation. Second, communication technologies make confidential messages vulnerable to interception by third parties. High-quality encryption can reduce this risk to negligible, but some risk does remain, especially if the sender of the message does not use the best security practices; the field, then, must decide what constitutes an acceptable level of risk. Telehealth raises some unique concerns: discovering and policing malpractice could be difficult given the anonymity afforded by the Internet, and interruptions in treatment could result from poor connections or malfunctions in equipment. Finally, psychologists must ensure that there is equal access to services across the population. Though owner-ship of communication devices is rapidly increasing in all groups, it remains unevenly distributed. Rural, low-income, and older Americans and those with less than a high school education are less likely to own smartphones (Rainie, 2012); one in five Americans does not use the Internet, and lack of Internet access is associated with lower educational attainment, lower income, older age, and non-White race or ethnicity (Zickuhr & Smith, 2012). In order to ethically apply technology to training, and then to treatment, the field will need to address these issues, remembering that there are also ethical pitfalls of traditional training and psychotherapy and recognizing that the benefits likely outweigh the risks. The benefits of applying information technologies to training and practice of professional psychology could be revolutionary. Although there are certainly obstacles, they are surmountable, and making the effort to train students has the potential to pay off in the forms of better treatments for larger populations and in a brighter future for the field.

Conclusion

We have reviewed direct technological innovations for training, non-technology-based training innovations, promising technological innovations for direct psychological care, and challenges and potential obstacles to incorporating technologies into training models and direct practice. We offer here several concluding thoughts stemming from our reviews in these domains and our relevant calls to action. Regarding technology, we acknowledge the vastness and immensely rapid growth of different platforms. Although many of these may be promising, it is also impossible to predict where technology will take us and exactly how it will affect the future of psychological practice. We still need to test various platforms more rigorously, appreciate and address potential ethical pitfalls, and assimilate technology more fully into our professional identity. However, advanced technology is ubiquitous, and any technologies that prove useful to our patients will need to be taught effectively in our training programs. As Eby et al. (2011) stated,

> As trainers and educators of future psychologists, we share a responsibility to ensure that those we train today will be equipped for practice tomorrow... It is our job to anticipate the future, knowing that our predictions will be imperfect. Therefore, because we hold no crystal ball, it is important that we provide tools to trainees with which they can steer

an ethical and optimal course through unpredictable circumstances. (p. 58)

Related to this statement, we argue that it is our job to use technology when it can help us make more accurate and reliable forecasts (e.g., predictive analytics), even if it challenges some of our most deeply held, yet often-inaccurate assumptions (e.g., that experience is positively correlated with wisdom and trainer competence). To us, then, there is a need for accreditation bodies to consider setting specific criteria (i.e., benchmarks) for competencies in professional psychology and for requiring trainees to "pass" these criteria (i.e., meet these benchmarks). As we outlined earlier, it is not necessary that every clinical psychology student pass as a generalist; some students might exceed all competency criteria, but only when working in a specialized domain. In other words, trainees need not be good at everything clinically; however, the idea is that they do need to be competent at something if they want to retain their practice credentials (i.e., a graduate with a degree in clinical psychology versus, for example, general or experimental psychology).

We would also argue that clinical and training practices should be adapted based on evidence as opposed to the more traditional guru model; we need to shift away from independent work, based predominantly on wisdom and charismatic influence, to accepting the predictive power and guidance of analytic tools. Without such reliance on science and actuarial methods, clinical practice amounts to guesswork (Eby et al., 2011), and it is incumbent on the field to halt the perpetuation of this guesswork approach. As just one manifestation of "following the data," trainers need to pay more attention to evidence-based practice. Although adopted as policy by APA's (2005) Council of Representatives, the use of evidence-based practice in psychology training continues to lag behind that of other health professionals (Spring, 2007). In a survey of 221 directors (or their designates) from various training programs in psychiatry, psychology, and social work, the percentage of psychology programs that did not require a didactic and supervision component in at least one evidence-based psychotherapy ranged from 43.8% to 67.3% (Weissman et al., 2006). Thus, a relatively low percentage of training programs have what might be considered a "gold-standard" protocol for training their students on empirically supported psychotherapies.

In sum, although we have presented several emerging technologies and innovations as potential tools or keys to improving the training of professional psychologists, we in no way mean to imply that there is a one-size-fits-all training model. However, there might be effective ways in which different models can interrelate, and such means might be enhanced via technology. Further, there might be common threads across most or all current models that could, and perhaps should, be discarded or seriously revised. In whatever forms, modern psychology training requires responsive evolution.

References

Abbass, A., Arthey, S., Elliott, J., Fedak, T., Nowoweiski, D., Markovski, J., & Nowoweiski, S. (2011). Web-conference supervision for advanced psychotherapy training: A practical guide. *Psychotherapy, 48*, 109–118. doi:10.1037/a0022427

Ahmed, M., & Westra, H. A. (2009). Impact of a treatment rationale on expectancy and engagement in cognitive behavioral therapy for social anxiety. *Cognitive Therapy and Research, 33*, 314–322. doi:10.1007/s10608-008-9182-1

American Psychological Association. (2005). Policy statement on evidence-based practice in psychology. Retrieved from http://www.apa.org/practice/resources/evidence/index.aspx on August 5, 2013.

American Psychological Association Commission on Accreditation. (2009). Guidelines and principles for accreditation of programs in professional psychology. Retrieved from http://www.apa.org/ed/accreditation/about/policies/guiding-principles.pdf on August 5, 2013.

Andersson, G., & Cuijpers, P. (2009). Internet-based and other computerized psychological treatments for adult depression: A meta-analysis. *Cognitive Behaviour Therapy, 38*, 196–205. doi: 10.1080/16506070903318960

Anderson, T., Lunnen, K. M., & Ogles, B. M. (2010). Putting models and techniques in context. In B. L. Duncan, S. D. Miller, B. E. Wampold, & M. A. Hubble (Eds.), *The heart and soul of change: Delivering what works in therapy* (2nd ed., pp. 143–166). Washington, DC US: American Psychological Association. doi:10.1037/12075-005

Andrews, G., Cuijpers, P., Craske, M. G., McEvoy, P., & Titov, N. (2010). Computer therapy for the anxiety and depressive disorders is effective, acceptable, and practical health care: A meta-analysis. *PLoS ONE, 5*, e13196. doi: 10.1371/journal.pone.0013196

Arkowitz, H., Westra, H. A., Miller, W. R., & Rollnick, S. (2008). *Motivational interviewing in the treatment of psychological problems*. New York: Guilford Press.

Aviram, A., & Westra, H. (2011). The impact of motivational interviewing on resistance in cognitive behavioural therapy for generalized anxiety disorder. *Psychotherapy Research, 21*, 698–708. doi:10.1080/10503307.2011.610832

Baker, J. R., & Moore, S. M. (2008). Blogging as a social tool: A psychosocial examination of the effects of blogging. *CyberPsychology & Behavior, 11*, 747–749. doi:10.1089/cpb.2008.0053

Baldwin, S. A., Wampold, B. E., & Imel, Z. E. (2007). Untangling the alliance-outcome correlation: Exploring the relative importance of therapist and patient variability in the alliance. *Journal of Consulting and Clinical Psychology, 75*, 842–852. doi:10.1037/0022-006X.75.6.842

Barak, A., Hen, L., Boniel-Nissim, M., & Shapira, N. (2008). A comprehensive review and a meta-analysis of the effectiveness of Internet-based psychotherapeutic interventions. *Journal of Technology in Human Services, 26*, 109–160. doi:10.1080/15228830802094429

Barnett, J. E. (2011). Utilizing technological innovations to enhance psychotherapy supervision, training, and outcomes. *Psychotherapy, 48*, 103–108. doi:10.1037/a0023381

Ben-Porath, D. D., & Koons, C. R. (2005). Telephone coaching in dialectical behavior therapy: A decision-tree model for managing inter-session contact with clients. *Cognitive and Behavioral Practice, 12*, 448–460. doi:10.1016/S1077-7229(05)80072-0

Beutler, L. E. (1995). The germ theory myth and the myth of outcome homogeneity. *Psychotherapy, 32*, 489–494. doi:10.1037/0033-3204.32.3.489

Binder, J. L. (2004). *Key competencies in brief dynamic psychotherapy: Clinical practice beyond the manual*. New York: Guilford Press.

Borkovec, T. D. (2004). Research in training clinics and practice research networks: A route to the integration of science and practice. *Clinical Psychology: Science and Practice, 11*, 211–215. doi:10.1093/clipsy/bph073

Boschen, M. J., & Casey, L. M. (2008). The use of mobile telephones as adjuncts to cognitive behavioral psychotherapy. *Professional Psychology: Research and Practice, 39*, 546–552. doi:10.1037/0735-7028.39.5.546

Boswell, J. F., & Castonguay, L. G. (2007a). Guest editors' introduction. *Psychotherapy, 44*, doi:10.1037/0033-3204.44.4.363

Boswell, J. F., & Castonguay, L. G. (2007b). Psychotherapy training: Suggestions for core ingredients and future research. *Psychotherapy, 44*, 378–383. doi:10.1037/0033-3204.44.4.378

Brammer, M. (2009). The role of neuroimaging in diagnosis and personalized medicine—current position and likely future directions. *Dialogues in Clinical Neuroscience, 11*, 389–396.

Bray, J. (2010). The future of psychology practice and science. *American Psychologist, 65*, 355–369. doi:10.1037/a0020273

Bruce, N. G., Manber, R., Shapiro, S. L., & Constantino, M. J. (2010). Psychotherapist mindfulness and the psychotherapy process. *Psychotherapy, 47*, 83–97. doi:10.1037/a0018842

Butler, S., & Constantine, M. G. (2006). Web-based peer supervision, collective self-esteem, and case conceptualization ability in school counselor trainees. *Professional School Counseling, 10*, 146–152.

Castonguay, L. G. (2005). Training issues in psychotherapy integration: A commentary. *Journal of Psychotherapy Integration, 15*, 384–391. doi:10.1037/1053-0479.15.4.384

Castonguay, L. G. (2011). Psychotherapy, psychopathology, research and practice: Pathways of connections and integration. *Psychotherapy Research, 21*, 125–140. doi:10.1080/10503307.2011.563250

Castonguay, L. G., Locke, B. D., & Hayes, J. A. (2011). The center for collegiate mental health: An example of a practice-research network in university counseling centers. *Journal of College Student Psychotherapy, 25*, 105–119. doi:10.1080/87568225.2011.556929

Castonguay, L. G., Nelson, D. L., Boutselis, M. A., Chiswick, N. R., Damer, D. D., Hemmelstein, N. A., & …Borkovec, T. D. (2010). Psychotherapists, researchers, or both? A qualitative analysis of psychotherapists' experiences in a practice research network. *Psychotherapy, 47*, 345–354. doi:10.1037/a0021165

Ceranoglu, T. A. (2010). Video games in psychotherapy. *Review of General Psychology, 14*, 141–146. doi: 10.1037/a0019439

Conn, S. R., Roberts, R. L., & Powell, B. M. (2009). Attitudes and satisfaction with a hybrid model of counseling supervision. *Educational Technology and Society, 12*, 298–306.

Constantino, M. J., Ametrano, R. A., & Greenberg, R. P. (2012). Clinician interventions and participant characteristics that foster adaptive patient expectations for psychotherapy and psychotherapeutic change. *Psychotherapy, 49*, 557-569. doi:10.1037/a0029440

Constantino, M. J., Boswell, J. F., Bernecker, S. L., & Castonguay, L. G. (in press). Context-responsive psychotherapy integration as a framework for a unified clinical science: Conceptual and empirical considerations. *Journal of Unified Psychotherapy and Clinical Science.*

Constantino, M. J., DeGeorge, J., Dadlani, M. B., & Overtree, C. E. (2009). Motivational interviewing: A bellwether for context-responsive psychotherapy integration. *Journal of Clinical Psychology, 65*, 1246–1253. doi:10.1002/jclp.20637

Constantino, M. J., Klein, R., Smith-Hansen, L., & Greenberg, R. (2009, October). *Augmenting cognitive therapy for depression with an Expectancy Enhancement module: Preliminary efficacy.* Paper presented at the meeting of the Canadian Chapter of the Society for Psychotherapy Research, Montreal, Canada.

Constantino, M. J., Marnell, M., Haile, A. J., Kanther-Sista, S. N., Wolman, K., Zappert, L., & Arnow, B. A. (2008). Integrative cognitive therapy for depression: A randomized pilot comparison [Special issue]. *Psychotherapy, 45*, 122–134. doi:10.1037/0033-3204.45.2.122

Constantino, M. J., Morrison, N. R., MacEwan, G., & Boswell, J. F. (in press). Therapeutic alliance researchers' perspectives on alliance-centered training practices. *Journal of Psychotherapy Integration.*

Cuijpers, P., Marks, I. M., Van Straten, A., Cavanagh, K., Gega, L., & Andersson, G. (2009) Computer-aided psychotherapy for anxiety disorders: A meta-analytic review. *Cognitive Behaviour Therapy, 38*, 66–82. doi: 10.1080/16506070802694776

Delavarian, M., Towhidkhah, F., Gharibzadeh, S., & Dibajnia, P. (2011). Automatic classification of hyperactive children: Comparing multiple artificial intelligence approaches. *Neuroscience Letters, 498*, 190–193. doi:10.1016/j.neulet.2011.03.012

Dorstyn, D. S., Mathias, J. L., & Denson, L. A. (2011). Psychosocial outcomes of telephone-based counseling for adults with an acquired physical disability: A meta-analysis. *Rehabilitation Psychology, 56*, 1–14. doi: 10.1037/a0022249

Duncan, B. L., Miller, S. D., Wampold, B. E., & Hubble, M. A. (Eds.). (2010). *The heart and soul of change: Delivering what works in therapy* (2nd ed.). Washington, DC: American Psychological Association. doi:10.1037/12075-000

Eby, M. D., Chin, J., Rollock, D., Schwartz, J. P., & Worrell, F. C. (2011). Professional psychology training in the era of a thousand flowers: Dilemmas and challenges for the future. *Training and Education in Professional Psychology, 5*, 57–68. doi:10.1037/a0023462

Falender, C. A., Cornish, J., Goodyear, R., Hatcher, R., Kaslow, N. J., Leventhal, G., & ...Grus, C. (2004). Defining competencies in psychology supervision: A consensus statement. *Journal of Clinical Psychology, 60*, 771–785. doi:10.1002/jclp.20013

Fauth, J., Gates, S., Vinca, M., Boles, S., & Hayes, J. A. (2007). Big ideas for psychotherapy training. *Psychotherapy, 44*, 384–391. doi:10.1037/0033-3204.44.4.384

Fliege, H., Becker, J., Walter, O. B., Rose, M., Bjorner, J. B., & Klapp, B. F. (2009). Evaluation of a computer-adaptive test for the assessment of depression (D-CAT) in clinical application. *International Journal of Methods in Psychiatric Research, 18*, 23–36. doi: 10.1002/mpr.274

Fouad, N. A., Grus, C. L., Hatcher, R. L., Kaslow, N. J., Hutchings, P., Madson, M. B., & ...Crossman, R. E. (2009). Competency benchmarks: A model for understanding and measuring competence in professional psychology across training levels. *Training and Education in Professional Psychology, 3*(4, Suppl), S5–S26. doi:10.1037/a0015832

Frank, J. D. (1961). *Persuasion and healing: A comparative study of psychotherapy.* Oxford England: Johns Hopkins University Press.

Gammon, D., Sørlie, T., Bergvik, S., & Hoifodt, T. S. (1998). Psychotherapy supervision conducted by videoconferencing: A qualitative study of users' experiences. *Journal of Telemedicine Telecare, 4*, 33–35. doi:10.1258/1357633981931353

Garb, H. N. (2007). Computer-administered interviews and ratings scales. *Psychological Assessment, 19*, 4–13. doi:10.1037/1040-3590.19.1.4

García-Lizana, F., & Muñoz-Mayorga, I. (2010). Telemedicine for depression: A systematic review. *Perspectives in Psychiatric Care, 46*, 119–126. doi:10.1111/j.1744-6163.2010.00247.x

Germain, V., Marchand, A., Bouchard, S., Guay, S., & Drouin, M.-S. (2010). Assessment of the therapeutic alliance in face-to-face or videoconference treatment for posttraumatic stress disorder. *Cyberpsychology, Behavior, and Social Networking, 13*, 29–35. doi:10.1089/cyber.2009.0139

Griffiths, K. M., Calear, A. L., & Banfield, M. (2009). Systematic review on Internet Support Groups (ISGs) and depression (1): Do ISGs reduce depressive symptoms? *Journal of Medical Internet Research, 11*, 1–20. doi:10.2196/jmir.1270

Grove, W. M., & Meehl, P. E. (1996). Comparative efficiency of informal (subjective, impressionistic) and formal (mechanical, algorithmic) prediction procedures: The clinical–statistical controversy. *Psychology, Public Policy, and Law, 2*, 293–323. doi:10.1037/1076-8971.2.2.293

Haley, C., O'Callaghan, E., Hill, S., Mannion, N., Donnelly, B., Kinsella, A., ...Turner, M. (2011). Telepsychiatry and carer education for schizophrenia. *European Psychiatry, 26*, 302–304. doi: 10.1016/j.eurpsy.2009.12.021

Hannan, C., Lambert, M. J., Harmon, C., Nielsen, S., Smart, D. W., Shimokawa, K., & Sutton, S. W. (2005). A lab test and algorithms for identifying clients at risk for treatment failure. *Journal of Clinical Psychology, 61*, 155–163. doi:10.1002/jclp.20108

Harmon, S., Lambert, M. J., Smart, D. M., Hawkins, E., Nielsen, S. L., Slade, K., & Lutz, W. (2007). Enhancing outcome for potential treatment failures: Therapist-client feedback and clinical support tools. *Psychotherapy Research, 17*, 379–392. doi:10.1080/10503300600702331

Henry, W. P., Strupp, H. H., Butler, S. F., Schacht, T. E., & Binder, J. L. (1993). Effects of training in time-limited dynamic psychotherapy: Changes in therapist behavior. *Journal of Consulting and Clinical Psychology, 61*, 434–440. doi:10.1037/0022-006X.61.3.434

Hilbert, M., & López, P. (2011). The world's technological capacity to store, communicate, and compute information. *Science, 332*(6025), 60–65. doi:10.1126/science.1200970

Hilsenroth, M. J., Ackerman, S. J., Clemence, A. J., Strassle, C. G., & Handler, L. (2002). Effects of structured clinician training on patient and therapist perspectives of alliance early in psychotherapy. *Psychotherapy, 39*, 309–323. doi:10.1037/0033-3204.39.4.309

Hoyer, J., Ruhl, U., Scholz, D., & Wittchen, H.-U. (2006). Patients' feedback after computer-assisted diagnostic interviews for mental disorders. *Psychotherapy Research, 16*, 357–363. doi:10.1080/10503300500485540

Hyler, S. E., Gangure, D. P., & Batchelder, S. T. (2005). Can telepsychiatry replace in-person psychiatric assessments? A review and meta-analysis of comparison studies. *CNS Spectrums, 10*, 403–413.

Johansen, A. B., Lumley, M., & Cano, A. (2011). Effects of video-based therapy preparation targeting experiential acceptance or the therapeutic alliance. *Psychotherapy, 48*, 163–169. doi:10.1037/a0022422

Johnson, L. (2011). Clients, connections, and social media. *Annals of the American Psychotherapy Association, 14*, 10–11.

Kaslow, N. J., Falender, C. A., & Grus, C. L. (2012). Valuing and practicing competency-based supervision: A transformational leadership perspective. *Training and Education in Professional Psychology, 6*, 47–54. doi:10.1037/a0026704

Kazdin, A. E., & Blase, S. L. (2011). Rebooting psychotherapy research and practice to reduce the burden of mental illness. *Perspectives on Psychological Science, 6*, 21–37. doi:10.1177/1745691610393527

Kim, D., Wampold, B. E., & Bolt, D. M. (2006). Therapist effects in psychotherapy: A random-effects modeling of the National Institute of Mental Health Treatment of Depression Collaborative Research Program data. *Psychotherapy Research, 16*, 161–172. doi:10.1080/10503300500264911

Kraus, D. R., Castonguay, L., Boswell, J. F., Nordberg, S. S., & Hayes, J. A. (2011). Therapist effectiveness: Implications for accountability and patient care. *Psychotherapy Research, 21*, 267–276. doi:10.1080/10503307.2011.563249

Kraus, D. R., Seligman, D. A., & Jordan, J. R. (2005). Validation of a behavioral health treatment outcome and assessment tool designed for naturalistic settings: The treatment outcome package. *Journal of Clinical Psychology, 61*, 285–314. doi:10.1002/jclp.20084

Krupinski, E., Nypaver, M., Poropatich, R., Ellis, D., Safwat, R., & Sapci, H. (2002). Clinical applications in telemedicine/telehealth. *Telemedicine Journal and E-Health, 8*, 13–34. doi:10.1089/15305620252933374

Ladany, N. (2007). Does psychotherapy training matter? Maybe not. *Psychotherapy, 44*, 392–396. doi:10.1037/0033-3204.44.4.392

Lambert, M. (2007). Presidential address: What we have learned from a decade of research aimed at improving psychotherapy outcome in routine care. *Psychotherapy Research, 17*, 1–14. doi:10.1080/10503300601032506

Lambert, M. J. (2010). "Yes, it is time for clinicians to routinely monitor treatment outcome." In B. L. Duncan, S. D. Miller, B. E. Wampold, & M. A. Hubble (Eds.), *The heart and soul of change: Delivering what works in therapy* (2nd ed., pp. 239–266). Washington, DC: American Psychological Association. doi:10.1037/12075-008

Lambert, M. J. (2011). What have we learned about treatment failure in empirically supported treatments? Some suggestions for practice. *Cognitive and Behavioral Practice, 18*, 413–420. doi:10.1016/j.cbpra.2011.02.002

Lichtenstein, E., Zhu, S.-H., & Tedeschi, G. J. (2010). Smoking cessation quitlines: An underrecognized intervention success story. *American Psychologist, 65*, 252–261. doi:10.1037/a0018598

Liptzin, B. (2009). Quality improvement, pay for performance, and "outcomes measurement": What makes sense? *Psychiatric Services, 60*, 108–111. doi:10.1176/appi.ps.60.1.108

Lovell, K., Cox, D., Haddock, G., Jones, C., Raines, D., Garvey, R., ...Hadley, S. (2006). Telephone administered cognitive behaviour therapy for treatment of obsessive compulsive disorder: Randomised controlled non-inferiority trial. *British Medical Journal, 333*(7574), 883. doi:10.1136/bmj.38940.355602.80

Marks, I., & Cavanagh, K. (2009). Computer-aided psychological treatments: Evolving issues. *Annual Review of Clinical Psychology, 5*, 121–141. doi:10.1146/annurev.clinpsy.032408.153538

Marks, I. M., Cavanagh, K., & Gega, L. (2007) Computer-aided psychotherapy: Revolution or bubble? *British Journal of Psychiatry, 191*, 471–473. doi: 10.1192/bjp.bp.107.041152

McGrath, P. J., Lingley-Pottie, P., Thurston, C., MacLean, C., Cunningham, C., Waschbusch, D. A., ...Chaplin, W. (2011). Telephone-based mental health interventions for child disruptive behavior or anxiety disorders: Randomized trials and overall analysis. *Journal of the American Academy of Child & Adolescent Psychiatry, 50*, 1162–1172. doi:10.1016/j.jaac.2011.07.013

McKay, J. R., Lynch, K. G., Shepard, D. S., & Pettinati, H. M. (2005). The effectiveness of telephone-based continuing care for alcohol and cocaine dependence: 24-month outcomes. *Archives of General Psychiatry, 62*, 199–207. doi: 10.1001/archpsyc.62.2.199

Mitchell, J. E., Crosby, R. D., Wonderlich, S. A., Crow, S., Lancaster, K., Simonich, H., ...Cook Meyers, T. (2008). A randomized trial comparing the efficacy of cognitive-behavioral therapy for bulimia nervosa delivered via telemedicine versus face-to-face. *Behaviour Research and Therapy, 46*, 581–592. doi:10.1016/j.brat.2008.02.004

Mohr, D. C., Vella, L., Hart, S., Heckman, T., & Simon, G. (2008). The effect of telephone-administered psychotherapy on symptoms of depression and attrition: A meta-analysis. *Clinical Psychology: Science and Practice, 15*, 243–253. doi:10.1111/j.1468-2850.2008.00134.x

Nadelson, T. (1987). The inhuman computer/the too-human psychotherapist. *American Journal of Psychotherapy, 41*, 489–498.

Newman, M. G., Szkodny, L. E., Llera, S. J., & Przeworski, A. (2011). A review of technology-assisted self-help and minimal contact therapies for drug and alcohol abuse and smoking addiction: Is human contact necessary for therapeutic efficacy? *Clinical Psychology Review, 31*, 178–186. doi:10.1016/j.cpr.2010.10.002

Norcross, J. (Ed.). (2011). *Psychotherapy relationships that work: Evidence-based responsiveness* (2nd ed.). New York: Oxford University Press.

Norcross, J. C., & Karpiak, C. P. (2012). Clinical psychologists in the 2010s: 50 years of the APA Division of Clinical Psychology. *Clinical Psychology: Science and Practice, 19*, 1–12. doi:10.1111/j.1468-2850.2012.01269.x

Norcross, J. C., & Wampold, B. E. (2011). Evidence-based therapy relationships: Research conclusions and clinical practices. In J. C. Norcross (Ed.), *Psychotherapy relationships that work: Evidence-based responsiveness* (2nd ed., pp. 423–430). New York: Oxford University Press.

Okiishi, J., Lambert, M. J., Nielsen, S. L., & Ogles, B. M. (2003). Waiting for supershrink: An empirical analysis of therapist effects. *Clinical Psychology and Psychotherapy, 10*, 361–373. doi:10.1002/cpp.383

Piasecki, T. M., Hufford, M. R., Solhan, M., & Trull, T. J. (2007). Assessing clients in their natural environments with electronic diaries: Rationale, benefits, limitations, and barriers. *Psychological Assessment, 19*, 25–43. doi:10.1037/1040-3590.19.1.25

Poon, P., Hui, E., Dai, D., Kwok, T., & Woo, J. (2005). Cognitive intervention for community-dwelling older persons with memory problems: telemedicine versus face-to-face treatment. *International Journal of Geriatric Psychiatry, 20*, 285–286. doi:10.1002/gps.1282

Portnoy, D. B., Scott-Sheldon, L. A., Johnson, B. T., & Carey, M P. (2008). Computer-delivered interventions for health promotion and behavioural risk reduction: A meta-analysis of 75 randomized controlled trials, 1988–2007. *Preventive Medicine, 47*, 3–16. doi:10.1016/j.ypmed.2008.02.014

Powers, M. B., & Emmelkamp, P. M. G. (2008). Virtual reality exposure therapy for anxiety disorders: a meta-analysis. *Journal of Anxiety Disorders, 22*, 561–569. doi:10.1016/j.janxdis.2007.04.006

Rabiner, D. L., Murray, D. W., Skinner, A. T., & Malone, P. S. (2010). A randomized trial of two promising computer-based interventions for students with attention difficulties. *Journal of Abnormal Child Psychology, 38*, 131–142. doi:10.1007/s10802-009-9353-x

Rainie, L. (September 11, 2012). Smartphone ownership update: September 2012. Retrieved from Pew Internet & American Life Project: http://pewinternet.org/Reports/2012/Smartphone-Update-Sept-2012.aspx

Reese, R. J., Aldarondo, F., Anderson, C. R., Lee, S., Miller, T. W., & Burton, D. (2009). Telehealth in clinical supervision: A comparison of supervision formats. *Journal of Telemedicine and Telecare, 15*, 356–361. doi:10.1258/jtt.2009.090401

Rochlen, A. B., Zack, J. S., & Speyer, C. (2004). Online therapy: Review of relevant definitions, debates, and current empirical support. *Journal of Clinical Psychology, 60*, 269–283. doi:10.1002/jclp.10263

Roe, R. A. (2002). What makes a competent psychologist? *European Psychologist, 7*, 192–202. doi:10.1027//1016-9040.7.3.192

Rollman, B. L., Belnap, B. H., Mazumdar, S., Houck, P. R., Zhu, F., Gardner, W., ...Shear, M. K. (2005). A randomized trial to improve the quality of treatment for panic and generalized anxiety disorders in primary care. *Archives of General Psychiatry, 62*, 1332–1341. doi:10.1001/archpsyc.62.12.1332

Safran, J. D., & Muran, J. (2000). *Negotiating the therapeutic alliance: A relational treatment guide.* New York: Guilford Press.

Sharp, I. R., Kobak, K. A., & Osman, D. A. (2011). The use of videoconferencing with patients with psychosis: A review of the literature. *Annals of General Psychiatry, 10*, 14. doi:10.1186/1744-859X-10-14

Sloan, D. M., Gallagher, M. W., Feinstein, B. A., Lee, D. J., & Pruneau, G. M. (2011). Efficacy of telehealth treatments for posttraumatic stress-related symptoms: A meta-analysis. *Cognitive Behaviour Therapy, 40*, 111–125. doi:10.1080/16506073.2010.550058

Sørlie, T., Gammon, D., Bergvik, S., & Sexton, H. (1999). Psychotherapy supervision face-to-face and by videoconferencing: A comparative study. *British Journal of Psychotherapy, 15*, 452–462. doi:10.1111/j.1752-0118.1999.tb00475.x

Spek, V., Cuijpers, P., Nyklíček, I., Riper, H., Keyzer, J., & Pop, V. (2007). Internet-based cognitive behavior therapy for symptoms of depression and anxiety: A meta-analysis. *Psychological Medicine, 37*, 319–328. doi: 10.1017/S0033291706008944

Spring, B. (2007). Evidence-based practice in clinical psychology: What it is, why it matters; What you need to know. *Journal of Clinical Psychology, 63*, 611–631. doi:10.1002/jclp.20373

Stein, D. M., & Lambert, M. J. (1995). Graduate training in psychotherapy: Are therapy outcomes enhanced? *Journal of Consulting and Clinical Psychology, 63*, 182–196. doi:10.1037/0022-006X.63.2.182

Stiles, W. B., Honos-Webb, L., & Surko, M. (1998). Responsiveness in psychotherapy. *Clinical Psychology: Science And Practice, 5*, 439–458. doi:10.1111/j.1468-2850.1998.tb00166.x

Strassle, C. G., Borckardt, J. J., Handler, L., & Nash, M. (2011). Video-tape role induction for psychotherapy: Moving forward. *Psychotherapy, 48*, 170–178. doi:10.1037/a0022702

Sucala, M., Schnur, J. B., Constantino, M. J., Miller, S. J., Brackman, E., & Montgomery, G. H. (2012). The therapeutic relationship in E-therapy for mental health: A systematic review. *Journal of Medical Internet Research, 14*:e110. URL: http://www.jmir.org/2012/4/e110/. doi:10.2196/jmir.2084.

Trull, T. J. (2007). Expanding the aperture of psychological assessment: Introduction to the special section on innovative clinical assessment technologies and methods. *Psychological Assessment, 19*, 1–3. doi:10.1037.1040-3590.19.1.1

Trull, T. J., & Ebner-Priemer, U. W. (2009). Using experience sampling methods/ecological momentary assessment (ESM/EMA) in clinical assessment and clinical research: Introduction to the special section. *Psychological Assessment, 21*, 457–462. doi: 10.1037/a0017653

Walitzer, K. S., Dermen, K. H., & Conners, G. J. (1999). Strategies for preparing clients for treatment: A review. *Behavior Modification, 23*, 129–151. doi:10.1177/0145445599231006

Waltz, J., Dimeff, L. A., Koerner, K., Linehan, M. M., Taylor, L., & Miller, C. (2009). Feasibility of using video to teach a Dialectical Behavior Therapy skill to clients with borderline personality disorder. *Cognitive and Behavioral Practice, 16*, 214–222. doi:10.1016/j.cbpra.2008.08.004

Wampold, B. E. (2001). *The great psychotherapy debate: Models, methods, and findings.* Mahwah, NJ: Erlbaum.

Wampold, B. E. (2007). Psychotherapy: The humanistic (and effective) treatment. *American Psychologist, 62*, 857–873. doi:10.1037/0003-066X.62.8.857

Weissman, M. M., Verdeli, H., Gameroff, M. J., Bledsoe, S. E., Betts, K., Mufson, L., &...Wickramaratne, P. (2006). National Survey of Psychotherapy Training in Psychiatry, Psychology, and Social Work. *Archives of General Psychiatry, 63*, 925–934. doi:10.1001/archpsyc.63.8.925

Wolf, A. W. (2011). Internet and video technology in psychotherapy supervision and training. *Psychotherapy, 48*, 179–181. doi:10.1037/a0023532

Wykes, T., Huddy, V., Cellard, C., McGurk, S. R., & Czobor, P. (2011). A meta-analysis of cognitive remediation for schizophrenia: Methodology and effect sizes. *American Journal of Psychiatry, 168*, 472–485. doi: 10.1176/appi.ajp.2010.10060855

Youn, S., Kraus, D. R., & Castonguay, L. G. (2012). The treatment outcome package: Facilitating practice and clinically relevant research. *Psychotherapy, 49*, 115–122. doi:10.1037/a0027932

Zickuhr, K., & Smith, A. (April 13, 2012). Digital differences. Retrieved from Pew Internet & American Life Project: http://pewinternet.org/Reports/2012/Digital-differences.aspx on August 5, 2013.

Professional Psychology Program Leaders: Competencies and Characteristics

Mary Beth Kenkel

Abstract

This chapter discusses the competencies needed by leaders of professional psychology education and training programs. The competencies are in domains similar to those endorsed for the education and training of all professional psychologists as noted in the Competency Cube Model (Rodolfa, et al., 2005). However, the knowledge, skills, and attitudes required for effective performance in the program director role are more specific and described here. This list of competencies clarifies the role and performance expectations of program leaders and can be used to recruit, screen, and develop candidates for program leader positions.

Key Words: psychology education, program leader, program director, competencies, job expectations

Introduction

Although much has been written about the training and education of professional psychologists, little literature has addressed the characteristics and competencies of the individuals responsible for the design and delivery of training programs. Who are these program leaders? What are their responsibilities and activities? What competencies must they have to insure the quality and effective functioning of training programs? Will new or different competencies be required to keep up with future challenges and opportunities for psychologists?

This chapter will attempt to answer these questions by drawing upon the scholarly literature in a number of areas. First, of course, is research in psychology especially that related to professional psychology, leadership, and organizational management. To lead educational or training programs, psychologists not only must know the discipline of psychology; they also must know "leadership," that is, how to lead, manage, organize and direct programs. Historically, professional psychology training programs did not teach those skills, although more recent training

models have included them as essential competencies for professional psychologists (Kenkel & Peterson, 2010, Rodolfa, et al., 2005). Therefore, many current program leaders must have acquired those skills in other ways, most often through on the job (OTJ) training (Picano & Blusewicz, 2003).

This chapter will discuss those competencies related to effective performance in the job as director of a professional psychology training program. These competencies have not been determined through research or a broad consensus-seeking process (Naquin & Holton III, 2006), but instead from the observations, experiences, and expectations of those who have held, supervised, or work with those in such positions. Identifying these competencies is key to preparing individuals to progress to and succeed in such positions (Charan, Drotter, & Noel, 2001). These leader competencies can clarify the role and performance expectation of the program director, aid in recruiting and screening potential applicants for the position, and identify goals for performance improvement and professional development (Garman & Johnson, 2006).

A wealth of literature in organizational psychology, business, and management outlines the characteristics of effective leaders and managers, and this chapter will discuss that research. However, professional psychology training and educational programs do not exist in isolation. Instead, they are in colleges, universities, medical schools, hospitals, and other settings that typically offer training programs for many other health professions as well. Psychology increasingly regards itself as a health profession, in contrast to a mental health profession, and the expectations, challenges, and opportunities for those other professions are increasingly relevant to psychology. Therefore, the expected competencies of leaders of other health professions' training programs might be instructive in describing the future roles and skills of psychology training program leaders. Thus, the literature bearing on training program leadership in the health professions will be used to inform the discussion here.

Neither education nor health care services are standing still. Much change is afoot in both arenas. Technological advances, changing markets, escalating costs and limited resources, are fueling major transformations in both fields. What are the implications of these changes for psychology education and training programs and the needed knowledge, skills, and attitudes of the individuals who lead them? This chapter will describe how effective program leaders can (actually must) foresee and address innovations in education and health care in their training programs.

Characteristics of Program Leaders

Three major levels of training exist within professional psychology education: doctoral academic programs, pre-doctoral internships, and postdoctoral residencies. The American Psychological Association's (APA) Commission on Accreditation accredits programs at each level. Each of these programs typically has a person leading/directing it, although titles for those individuals differ given the structure of the organization or the size of the program. In academic programs, common titles are program chair, director of clinical training, department chair, or dean. For internships, internship director or training director are often used. Since postdoctoral programs are typically small, most directors of those programs carry the "director" title in addition to other service-related titles.

In most programs, many individuals have responsibilities associated with training or educational functions, but typically, one person can

be identified as the person "in charge." The APA accreditation standards (American Psychological Association Commission on Accreditation, 2007) refer to this position as the "designated leader" or "director" who is a doctoral level psychologist and is primarily responsible for directing the program, and has the "credentials and expertise consistent with the program's mission and goals and with the substantive area of professional psychology in which the program provides training" (p. 8). For internship and postdoctoral residencies, the individual must be "appropriately credentialed (i.e. licensed, registered, or certified) to practice psychology in the jurisdiction in which the program is located" (p.15).

In this chapter, the terms *program leader, program director,* or *training director* are being used to refer to that individual with primary responsibility for program leadership, and the discussion will focus on that role. However, many of the competencies discussed here also are applicable to others holding major responsibilities for key elements of the training program. In addition, the terms *student, trainee, intern* or *postdoc* refer to those enrolled in the training program.

How many professional psychology program leaders are there? The short answer is "a lot." If we count only APA accredited programs in clinical, counseling, and school psychology in the U.S. and Canada at the end of 2011 (American Psychological Association, 2011a, 2011b), there are 367 accredited doctoral programs of which 237 are clinical, 60 are counseling, 62 are school, and 8 are combined professional—scientific. In addition, there are 469 accredited pre-doctoral internship programs and 30 accredited postdoctoral residency training programs.

Information on program directors is not collected on a consistent basis. However, a few surveys provide us with snapshots of the individuals holding these roles. In the 2011 annual surveys conducted by the Association of Psychology Postdoctoral and Internship Centers (APPIC, 2011a), 242 directors of APPIC member internships and 58 directors of postdoctoral fellowships provided their views of the internship/postdoctoral match process, as well as information on their own characteristics. Seventy-one percent of the internship directors held only that role, whereas 27% also were the director of a postdoctoral fellowship programs, and 2% were directing both an internship and an academic program. Fifty-two percent of the internship directors had been in that role at that site for less than five years; with another 26% held the position for five to ten years. When asked how many hours per week their organization allotted them for their role as internship training director, most directors (25%) indicated 20 hours or approximately half-time, 24% reported 8 or less hours (including 5% who indicated that they were allotted no time!) and another 33% reported between 9–19 hours. Therefore 82% of internship directors reported 20 hours or less are allotted for that role.

There was a wide distribution in years since initial licensure, from less than 1 year to over 36 years, with a median of 16 years. These internship directors were in a variety of settings with the highest percentages in university counseling centers (19%), followed by VA Medical Centers (13%), community mental health centers (12%), and state hospitals (11%).

Of the 58 directors of APPIC postdoctoral residencies who participated in the 2011 survey (APPIC, 2011b), 55% reported being the director of the postdoc program only, whereas 45% directed both a postdoctoral and an internship program. However, 72% of the postdoc directors reported that their site had an APPIC internship program as well. Not surprising then, the predominant sites for the postdoctoral residencies were similar to the internships, with VA Medical Centers being the most prevalent (28%), followed by university counseling centers (19%). Sixty-one percent of these postdoc directors had held the job for less than 5 years, and 87% had been in that role for 10 years or less.

These characteristics of program directors are similar to those found in other samples. Ko and Rodolfa (2005) in a survey of training directors' views on the appropriate number of practicum hours prior to internship, found that characteristics of their sample of training directors from academic, predoctoral, and postdoctoral programs directors did not differ, except in a few areas. Academic training directors were a bit older ($x = 51$ years) than predoctoral and postdoctoral directors (both $x = 48$ years) and were licensed longer (19.1 years versus 14.6 and 16.2). As a group, the training directors had held their positions for a mean of 7.4 years, were predominately male (63%) and European American (91%). In a survey of clinical psychology doctoral programs that were members of the Council of University Directors of Clinical Psychology (CUDCP), King (2002) found that directors reported a mean tenure of 6.4 years, with 36% in the role for 3 years or less, and only 21% in the role for more than 10 years, whereas in an

earlier study (Wisocki, Grebstein, & Hunt, 1994), the average tenure was shorter, at 4 years. In comparison to other studies, the directors in the 1994 survey (Wisocki et al., 1994) were younger with an average age of 45; almost all were Caucasian. The group overall were quite satisfied with their jobs as DCTs and felt that the most positive aspects of the position included contact with the students, making a positive contribution to the program's development, and the opportunity to influence the profession. DCTs overwhelmingly indicated that the most negative aspect of the job was the reduced time for personal work and research, followed by the amount of paperwork and administrative trivia, lack of support from faculty, and high levels of stress and burnout. A common complaint was that the job was "heavy in responsibility, but light in authority "(King, 2002, p. 420).

The benefits typically associated with the position of DCT include reduced teaching load, increased secretarial assistance, budgetary help, salary supplement, extra teaching/research assistants, and additional equipment (Wicherski, Mulvey, Hart, & Kohout, 2011; Wisocki, Grebstein, & Hunt, 1994). For 2010–2011, the median 9–10-month salary for a director of clinical training was $104,728 for full professors and $74,460 for associate professors.

In summary, leaders of professional psychology training programs tend to assume those positions in early midcareer, and most hold the position for less than 10 years. More men than women are among the ranks, and over 90% have a European American ethnicity. At any given time, over 30% of the leaders are relatively new in their jobs. Such turnover helps to bring in fresh perspectives, but also might lead to discontinuities and loss of leadership expertise in the training program. In addition, for academic training directors, longer tenure in jobs is related to greater satisfaction with the position and greater sense of power and influence (Wisocki et al., 1994). Interestingly, DCTS who spent more time engaged in administrative tasks (over 25%) had higher job satisfaction (Wisocki et al., 1994). This might have implications for other program leaders in psychology who often are allotted little time for their administrative and training roles.

Are the frequent turnovers an indication of inherent dissatisfactions or challenges with the job? In examining the selection process of DCTs, King (2002) reported that 20% of his DCT sample provided unprompted comments about the undesirability of the job and their eagerness to relinquish it to an interested colleague. For related fields,

Buckley and Rayburn (2010) found that chairs of departments of psychiatry remain in their positions for a longer period than psychology training leaders, but still less than 39% remained in their jobs after 10 years. The common frustrations and reasons for leaving include wanting to look for new opportunities, seeking retirement, disagreements with the strategic direction of the institution or superiors, not feeling effective because of too many obstacles, becoming burned out, having insufficient time for research, lack of explicit criteria for evaluating their job performance, and enormously time-consuming administrative tasks (Strickland, 1984).

Competencies in Professional Psychology

A competency-based model of education and training is gaining ground in professional psychology. In the 1980s, The National Council of Schools and Programs of Professional Psychology (NCSPP) was the first psychology training council to articulate competencies for professional psychology training programs. The NCSPP competency-based training model was further developed over the next 20 years (Peterson, Peterson, Abrams, & Stricker, 1997) and adopted by many of the clinical PsyD training programs. A slightly revised version of the NCSPP competencies were incorporated into the APA accreditation standards in 1996, thereby exposing a broader array of training programs to competency-based education and training.

A competency model for professional psychology gained widespread attention and endorsement through work at the Competencies Conference: Future Directions in Education and Credentialing in Professional Psychology, held in Scottsdale, Arizona, in 2002 (Kaslow, 2004; Kaslow, et al., 2004). A broad spectrum of psychology training constituencies and stakeholders participated in the conference, including APPIC which initiated the conference, APA, the Council of the Chairs of Training Councils (CCTC) representing doctoral training programs, credentialing and regulatory bodies, ethnic minority psychology organizations, and practitioner groups. With this broad and diverse representation, competency models could be considered by all levels of professional psychology training (doctoral programs, internships, postdoctoral residencies) as well as by licensure and certification groups. At the subsequent Benchmarks conference, participants specified proficiency levels for each competency at each level of training (Fouad et al., 2009). As a result of these conferences, a broad

base of psychology trainers found utility in using competency thinking and language to develop curriculum and to communicate to others the expected outcomes of that training. The competencies also provided a means for identifying the skills of a psychologist and for ensuring continuity across levels of training in the development of those skills.

Conference participants developed the *Competency Cube*, a schematic depiction of the competencies needed by professional psychologists (Rodolfa et al., 2005). The cube is a three-dimensional conceptual framework delineating (a) competencies that serve as the foundation for all professional psychology work (foundational competencies); (b) competencies that define what psychologists do (functional competencies); and (c) the stages of professional training and development, from doctoral academic training to continuing education. The domains of the foundational competencies include reflective practice and self-assessment; scientific knowledge and methods; relationships; ethical and legal standards and policy; individual and cultural diversity; and interdisciplinary systems. The domains of the functional competencies include assessment, diagnosis and case conceptualization, intervention, consultation, research and evaluation, supervision and teaching, and management and administration. The Competency Cube provides a common language and frame of reference for all the stakeholders involved in professional psychology education, credentialing, and regulation.

Since it so clearly delineates the competencies for professional psychologists, the Competency Cube is a natural starting point for discussing the competencies of training directors. In the initial publication of the Competency Cube (Rodolfa, et al., 2005), the authors discussed how different specialties within professional psychology, e.g., neuropsychology or forensic psychology, require the same foundational and functional competencies. However, the practice parameters of the specialty, such as the populations served or the practice setting, shape the required competencies. Therefore, while each specialty requires assessment competencies, the particular assessment tools used by each specialty might differ. A similar case can be made for psychologists holding different professional roles, including the position of program director. The role and its demands will shape the foundational and functional competencies and may even require additional competencies not listed in the cube.

Training directors design programs whereby graduate students, interns, or postdoctoral fellows acquire the competencies described in the Cube. In addition, they are assessing the attainment of the specific knowledge (K), skills (S), and attitudes (A) that comprise the competencies. Do program leaders need these same competencies to be effective in their roles? Does education based on the competency cube effectively prepare psychologists-in-training for positions as psychology training directors? The next section of this chapter addresses these questions.

Competencies of Psychology Program Leaders

In addition to leading the training program, most directors have a number of other job activities, such as teaching, research, clinical services, or administration. In fact, surveys (APPIC, 2011a) show most training directors spend less, or, at least, are allotted less, than halftime for training program activities. However, for this chapter, the focus is on program administration activities and the knowledge, skills, and attitudes (KSAs) required to perform them.

It is not surprising that many training directors feel overloaded. Their duties are substantial and typically include the following:

• Recruit, review, and select trainees (doctoral students, interns, or postdoctoral fellows).
• Orient, advise, and schedule/assign trainees.
• Monitor and evaluate trainees' progress.
• Develop and implement the training program/curriculum.
• Develop and administer program policies and procedures.
• Select, coordinate/supervise the training faculty and staff.
• Coordinate with other disciplines and departments associated with the program.
• Create and monitor the training climate/culture.
• Represent the training program to various internal and external constituencies.
• Prepare reports on the program for internal and external review bodies.
• Ensure sufficient resources for the program and its financial stability.
• Conduct short- and long-term program planning.
• Evaluate the program's achievements and effectiveness and make needed. adjustments.

Although a number of the above activities involve the entire faculty or training staff, the training director generally bears the primary responsibility for them, even if they are delegated to another individual or group.

To perform these activities, program directors, like psychologists in other roles, rely heavily on the *foundational* and *functional* competencies of the cube model (Rodolfa et al., 2005).

Effective program leaders have advanced levels of these *foundational* competencies, and that expertise allows them to better execute the *functional* competencies required of program leaders.

Table 30.1 provides a listing of some key foundational KSAs required of training directors given the duties specified above. Table 30.2 lists the functional competencies' KSAs and includes two additional competencies: leadership and advocacy. The lists are not exhaustive, but instead are meant to highlight some distinct KSAs required for the particular role of psychology training director.

The tables highlight the importance of key attitudes in the role of program director. When discussing the competencies of trainees, most educators concentrate on the required knowledge and skills, but fail to describe needed attitudes or how to inculcate them in students. Instead, the totality of attitudes is deemed to be taught by that vague process of "professional socialization" (Kenkel, 2009). In contrast, these tables attempt to be more specific in delineating these attitudes since they figure largely in the success and satisfaction of training directors.

Foundational Competencies

The foundational competencies are the "building blocks of what psychologists do" (Rodolfa et al., 2005, p.350). These competencies provide the groundwork for the subsequent acquisition of the psychology functional competencies. Interestingly, many aspects of this substratum are not unique to psychology. Research on leaders in health care, government, the military, and the corporate world reveal the value and importance of many of these KSAs, especially those related to the self-assessment and relationship competencies. For example, several of the KSAs are similar to the concept of Emotional Intelligence (EI) (Goleman, 1996). Emotional intelligence is generally defined as dealing effectively with one's own and others' emotions and includes such abilities as self-awareness, self-management, and empathy. Although disagreements continue over the definition and measurement of EI, research has shown that the higher up one goes in an organization, EI is more critical and contributes more to success, in some cases, even more so than IQ (Dulewicz, Young, & Dulewicz, 2005; Dulewicz, 2003; Walter, Cole, & Humphrey, 2011).

Table 30.1. Foundational competencies for psychology program leaders

Domain	Knowledge	Skills	Attitudes
Reflective Practice and Self-assessment	Accurate self-awareness. Knowledge of one's managerial style, preferences, strengths and weaknesses.	Self-management of emotions and workload. Self-direction Self-care strategies.	Open to feedback from colleagues, trainees, supervisors. Flexible. Persistent. Conscientious. Resilient. Self-confident.
Scientific Knowledge and Methods	Knowledge of the research skills and practices most useful in professional practice. Knowledge of evidence-based practices in professional psychology. Knowledge of local clinical scientist approach.	Ability to develop training curricula that incorporate evidence based practices. Ability to develop clinical training experiences requiring clinical outcome assessments.	Values the broad-base of knowledge and research in psychology. Committed to staying current with the research literature. Values research and evaluation in making programmatic changes and improvement. Values experimentation.
Relationships	Knowledge of self, personal strengths, limits, motives, and conflicts. Knowledge of personality styles and different world views. Knowledge of group dynamics. Knowledge of conflict management strategies.	Ability to connect quickly and meaningfully with others. Ability to adjust communication based on other's personal style/ needs. Ability to recognize, support, and show appreciation to others. Capable of building teams. Ability to read a group's emotional currents and power relationships. Ability to influence and negotiate effectively with others. Conflict management skills.	Values communication. Tolerates affect and disagreement. Willing to serve the needs of the "customer" (trainee, training staff) not just one's own. Open to diverse worldviews and personal styles. Generous with praise and appreciation. Flexible. Patient. Tough skinned.
Ethical and Legal Standards and Policy	Advanced knowledge of the ethical and legal standards pertinent to graduate education/ training and psychology practice.	Ability to develop policies and procedures for assessing whether trainees are practicing in accordance with ethical and legal standards and for intervening when they are not.	Committed to acting with integrity. Committed to ensuring the ethical conduct and moral character of trainees and colleagues.
Individual and Cultural Diversity	Knowledge of the scientific and application-based literature related to diversity. Knowledge of effective methods for diversity recruitment, retention, training, and service delivery.	Ability to develop recruitment and retention policies that promote diversity. Ability to create a training environment, procedures, and policies that respect and welcome diversity. Ability to design a training curriculum that has thorough and integrative coverage of diversity issues.	Courageous and willing to address biases, privilege, and discrimination in professional roles. Committed to increasing diversity of the profession and to ensuring all trainees are prepared to effectively provide services to diverse populations. Committed to ongoing examination of one's own biases. Committed to lifelong education in diversity issues.

(continued)

Table 30.1. (continued)

Domain	Knowledge	Skills	Attitudes
Interdisciplinary Systems	Advanced understanding of systems. Understanding of one's own professional role and the roles of other professionals. Knowledge of related disciplines and their common practices. Knowledge of team dynamics and group processes.	Abilxity to describe psychologists' roles, proficiencies, and norms. Ability to tailor interactions for different disciplines. Ability to resolve interprofessional conflict. Ability to engage in collaborative leadership.	Comfortable with identity as a psychologist. Appreciates and respects other disciplines. Willing to promote goal of the organization over own discipline's objective. Values the interdependence of the professions.

Table 30.2. Functional competencies for psychology program leaders

Competency	Knowledge	Skills	Attitudes
Assessment	Knowledge of methods for assessing student competencies. Knowledge of benchmarks for competency achievement at different levels of training.	Ability to develop sensitive, developmentally appropriate, and valid tools for measuring trainees' competencies. Ability to develop and implement a comprehensive system for assessing students'/interns' achievement of training objectives. Ability to share/convey assessment results to trainees in a manner that fosters growth and improvement. Ability to use assessment results to determine trainees' needs.	Commitment to ongoing formal assessment as the major way to measure trainees' progress in gaining competencies. Commitment to assessment as the major way to determine program's strengths and weaknesses.
Intervention	Knowledge of the benchmarks for competency at different levels of training. Knowledge of effective remediation strategies. Knowledge of due process requirements, and ethical and legal issues related to dealing with trainees with performance problems.	Ability to develop constructive and educative remediation plans. Ability to maintain alliance with trainee with performance problems while requiring remediation. Ability to determine when remediation is insufficient and trainee should be dismissed.	Desire to help trainees remediate competence problems. Sensitive to the tension between remediating trainees with competence problems and protecting the public. Appreciation of trainees' strengths and belief in trainees' ability to grow and remediate.
Research Evaluation	Knowledge of accreditation standards and requirements. Knowledge of program evaluation methods.	Ability to develop systems for collecting and analyzing data about student learning and program quality and effectiveness. Ability to use evaluation results to improve program quality	Commitment to program quality enhancement. Commitment to evaluation as means for improving training program.
Consultation	Knowledge of institutional procedures and practices. Knowledge of organizations relevant to psychology training and practice.	Problem-solving abilities. Coaching abilities. Ability to empower others.	Willing to provide guidance and advice. Confidence in one's ability to function in the role of consultant Interest in promoting others' growth and independence.

Table 30.2. (continued)

Competency	Knowledge	Skills	Attitudes
Supervision and Teaching	Knowledge of effective feedback strategies. Knowledge of developmental phases of professional psychology students/interns.	Ability to provide effective developmental feedback. Mentoring ability. Ability to maintain appropriate boundaries with mentees.	Concerned with others' professional and personal development. Willingness to invest time and energy in others' development. Willingness to engage in a reciprocal process with trainee. Trainee-focus.
Management and Administration	Basic knowledge of management theory and strategies, financial management. Knowledge of the structure, functions, policies and procedures of the training organization and associated agencies.	Planning ability. Organizing and delegating abilities. Coordinating abilities. Ability to make sound and timely decisions. Ability to manage and allocate program resources. Financial management abilities.	Willing to be accessible to students and faculty. Collaborative/team oriented. Focused on trainees, faculty/staff, program. Decisive. Patient. Enjoys multi-tasking/variety of tasks.
Leadership	Knowledge of projected trends and changes in higher education, professional psychology, and related fields. Knowledge of behavioural health workforce needs and projections.	Environmental scanning ability. Ability to develop and communicate a compelling vision for the training program. Ability to do strategic planning and goal-setting. Ability to influence, inspire, and motivate others. Team-building abilities. Ability to listen to others with empathy and curiosity.	Trustworthy. Creative/resourceful. Willing to take risks. Adaptable. Enthusiastic. Committed to continuous learning. Oriented to accomplishment.
Advocacy	Knowledge of policy issues relevant to professional psychology. Knowledge of effective advocacy strategies.	Ability to speak and write persuasively. Ability to build relationships with policy-makers. Coalition building ability. Ability to develop a long-term perspective and plan for accomplishing change. Ability to compromise.	Willing to take a stand/speak out. Persistent and perseverant. Patient. Committed to working with others to reach goal.

Competencies described for health-care leaders are similar to the foundational competencies for psychologists. Duberman (2011) succinctly described physician executive competencies as:

• Leading self—Self-awareness, self-management, self-development.

• Leading others—Building an effective team; developing, communicating, and inspiring.

• Leading change—Resiliency, courage and authenticity, change management.

• Leading for results—Decisiveness, systems thinking.

Additionally, in his guide for department chairs, Learning (2003) stated that the first lesson is for chairs to understand themselves: "Above all else, academic deans and department chairs—and all leaders—must come to terms with and accept who they are" (p. 1).

Therefore, fundamental competencies for leaders in many fields include *self-awareness, self- management, and relationship skills*. Perhaps these foundational competencies are even more important for psychology program leaders since they are dealing with colleagues and trainees very attuned to these skills and seeking to develop them further. In addition, training directors' competencies in these areas, that is, their emotional and relational styles, can dramatically affect a program's climate. A highly anxious, overly emotional director is more likely to have a hectic, stress-ridden organization than a calm, organized director. A warm, empathic director is more likely to create a positive and engaging climate, than a cool, aloof, or self-centered one. Such differences in program climates dramatically affect the satisfaction, participation, and learning of those involved.

Because of their roles, psychology program leaders need *advanced* self-management and relationship skills. They must have the ability to control their emotions, but because they are responsible for the leadership and continuity of programs, they also need persistence and perseverance to overcome obstacles and resilience to bounce back when setbacks occur. They must have good skills for relating to others on a one-to-one basis, but must go beyond those fundamental interpersonal skills, to be able to work with groups, teams, and people at multiple levels within an organization. They need to engender trust, build teams, manage conflict, influence others, and negotiate. They need patience for dealing with multiple demands and the frailties of human nature ("Yes, Dr. Jones, that form was due last Friday, not this Friday") and a thick skin to deal with the jibes, slights, and disagreements that inevitably will transpire.

An important part of self-awareness for program directors is the awareness of their managerial style. Not all program directors manage alike, nor should they. However, whatever their style, program directors must get the job done and do it in a way that emphasizes quality, involvement, and satisfaction. Program directors can learn what their styles are from assessment instruments, workshops, supervisor and/or subordinate feedback, or self-reflection over time. By doing so, they can determine how to organize their time, what to delegate to others, what prompts to use, and how to create and implement a successful professional development plan. For example, program directors who like to gather lots of information before making decisions, may need to set deadlines for making decisions in a timely way. Directors who prefer independent versus team work may need to intentionally establish work groups to deal with issues that would benefit from multiple and diverse inputs. Directors who are strongly "present-oriented" might want to delegate long-range planning functions to another individual or task force. In summary, by having accurate assessments of their managerial style and preferences, program directors can devise strategies for meeting program demands and responsibilities in ways that accommodate their preferences and strengths.

Scientific knowledge and methods, another foundational competency, undergird the functioning of all psychologists, including those holding the position of training director. Professional psychology program directors have a unique opportunity in this arena. They can be very instrumental in ensuring that the research-practice gap, so often described in the literature, (Kazdin, 2008; Kenkel, 2001; Teachman et al., 2012) is reduced in training programs and hopefully, through that training, in the future careers of the professional psychology graduates. One of the more effective ways to close the gap is by incorporating evidence-based treatments into clinical training. Efforts to do this have been increasing (Crits-Christoph, 1995; Maki & Syman, 1997)) since APA accreditation standards required all programs to provide students with training in empirically supported treatment (APA Commission on Accreditation, 2007). Additionally more attention has been on dissemination efforts and providing resources to help program directors accomplish this (American Psychological Association Presidential Task Force on Evidence-Based Practice, 2006; Hershenberg, 2012).

Additionally, trainees should be guided into, and learn about, methods by which they can consistently measure their effectiveness, for example, through ongoing assessment of clinical outcomes (Lambert, 2012; Wise, 2004; Youn, 2012) or the use of a local clinical scientist approach (Trierweiler, Stricker, & Peterson, 2010). Adoption of these practices by the program director and faculty/staff and their active engagement in applied research serve as potent models and motivators for students/interns as they pursue their professional careers.

An increasingly important foundational competency is the domain of *interdisciplinary systems*. Most psychologists have experience in working with other professionals in the mental health field, that is, psychiatrists, social workers, counselors. Depending on their specialty, they also may have worked with professionals in school, forensic, rehabilitation, or healthcare settings. However, many new opportunities are open to psychologists in the health care system envisioned in the Patient Protection and Affordable Care Act (2010), that is, health-care reform. The health-care system outlined in ACA has a strong consumer and population focus and promotes patient-centered medical homes that provide a consistent primary-care provider and seamless integrated care to patients. Health promotion and the management of chronic illnesses are emphasized, providing many opportunities for psychologists to practice their skills. Proving health care in this manner requires strong collaboration and a team approach among health care professionals. The Institute of Medicine (IOM) has issued several reports indicating that effective teams and redesigned systems are necessary for health care that is patient centered, safer, timelier, more effective, and more efficient (IOM, 2001). These developments have propelled many health-care professions to come together and develop competencies for interdisciplinary collaboration (Interprofessional Education Collaborative Expert Panel, 2011). As professional psychologists increasingly become integrated into these primary care and specialty health teams, they need skills for collaborating with partners beyond the traditional mental health providers. For that to happen, the curriculum needs to incorporate interdisciplinary collaboration skill training.

Other countries are ahead of the United States in these areas and have organizations dedicated to interprofessional education. For example, the Canadian Interprofessional Health Collaborative (http://www.cihc.ca) promotes collaboration in health and education, whereas the Centre for the Advancement of Interprofessional Education (http://www.caipe.org.uk/) promotes and develops interprofessional education in the UK and overseas.

Training in interprofessional collaboration is most effective when it starts early, but the "educational silos" of most professional training programs often do not permit it. To maximize the opportunity afforded to psychologists by these major changes in the health-care system, program leaders will need expanded competencies in interdisciplinary systems and will have to find ways to break down the educational silos (Kenkel, 2011). They will need to know about related professions in the settings where psychologists will be practicing, for example, health care, schools, forensic settings; how to work effectively with those groups, and how to design interprofessional educational experiences so that trainees can learn collaboration skills.

Though some may not want to acknowledge this aspect of their role, program directors are the moral and *ethical* leaders of their programs. As "actions speak louder than words," the training director's ethical behavior stands as a signpost for all others in the program. It is not only what training directors

say, but also what they do, attend to, and ignore. "A person with integrity" is a common description of an effective leader and refers to behaving in a manner consistent with one's values, principles, and commitments. It involves having the courage to say what needs to be said, and to do what needs to be done. As a role model for faculty, staff, and trainees, program leaders must be scrupulous in abiding by the profession's ethical code as well as the policies and regulations of the training institution. Bray (2008) investigated faculty's expectations regarding proscriptive norms for academic deans, that is, what they believed was unacceptable behavior, and found that one of the perceived "high crimes" was regulatory disdain, or the administrator's personal disregard of university rules and regulations as well as their failure to hold others accountable for following the rules. A second "high crime" was the inappropriate use of college funds, another violation of the rules. Faculty and trainees expect their leaders to be models for professional and ethical conduct and hold others to those same standards. They also expect their program leaders to "speak truth to power," that is, to voice concerns or opposing viewpoints to upper administration when an undesirable policy or initiative is proposed. Bray (2008) found another proscriptive norm for deans (in this case, a "minor felony") was bending to pressure, that is, not maintaining a stand with upper administration, parents, students, and so on, or bending the rules or covering up difficulties to avoid conflict or embarrassing situations. When they observe these failures of integrity, faculty, staff, and students lose faith and trust in their leaders. In studies of effective leadership in academic departments, researchers (Bryman, 2007; Murry & Stauffacher, 2001; & Trocchia & Andrus, 2003) have found that effective academic leaders are those faculty regard as trustworthy and having integrity. Additionally Barge and Musambira (1992) found that negative turning points in relationships between program leaders and their faculty were often associated with a change in the perceived trustworthiness of the program head. Acting with integrity is a fundamental competency for program leaders.

Training directors need to attend not only to their own ethical and professional behavior, but also to that of the trainees. Johnson and Campbell (2004) found that academic training directors were very concerned about the character and fitness (psychological health) of their students. They reported using a number of measures to assess these characteristics, including recommendation letters and interviews during the application process, and the students' clinical and personal behavior while they were in the program. Unlike the legal profession, psychology has no mandated or standard way to assess these student attributes (Johnson & Campbell, 2002); therefore, it is up to the individual programs to determine how to most effectively balance this training and gatekeeping requirement. Training directors must find ways to assess character and psychological fitness and develop clear policies and procedures for handling those times when trainees who evidence problems of professional competence in this arena (Elman & Forest, 2007; Kaslow et al., 2007b). It is probably the least favorite part of the job for training directors, but it also is the most critical in protecting the public who will be served by psychologists in the future. In determining means for assessing students' competence in ethical and professional behavior, program directors can draw on these best practices developed by a Council of Chairs of Training Councils' work group on student competence problems (Kaslow et al., 2007b):

> Best practices include constructing policies that delineate behavioral indicators of competence criteria, minimum acceptable standards of performance, and criteria signaling the need for remediation and/or dismissal and/or reporting to ethics committees or a licensing board. A well-prepared system provides clear expectations; presents criteria and procedures (i.e., due process) in recruitment and acceptance materials, operating handbooks, professional standards, codes of conduct, and licensing regulations; and educates relevant parties. Optimal systems articulate practices for assessing competence and delineate competency requirements, assessment procedures, and decision-making processes regarding the handling of competence problems (e.g., remediation, probation, and dismissal policies). Policies and procedures must be tailored to the needs of the program's faculty and supervisors, who are responsible for the quality of the professionals that they graduate or certify as competent. Yet they must also reflect the professional literature and best practices congruent with the APA Ethical Principles and Code of Conduct (i.e., the Ethics Code; APA, 2002b), APA's Accreditation Guidelines and Principles (APA, 2005), APA and Association of State and Provincial Psychology Boards (ASPPB) policies, state laws, and standards of practice. The system, prepared to act as a gatekeeper, ensures that trainees with competence problems do not move toward licensure and independent practice

without attention being given to issues that could affect the ability to practice safely. (Kaslow et al., 2007b, p. 482)

There continues to be a great mismatch between the demographics of professional psychologists and of clients needing services. Clearly, the need for more *diversity* within the field of psychology persists, and it will take the commitment of training directors to make it happen. Good intentions and lip service are not enough. Commitment must be followed by action: developing effective recruitment strategies to attract diverse trainees and retention policies to keep them, hiring diverse faculty and training staff, and designing and implementing an effective curriculum whereby trainees learn multicultural competencies. However, this process starts with the program's commitment to diversity, and the training director has a key role in leading the charge. Program directors may not be aware of effective strategies for recruiting diverse students, faculty, and staff, or may cite such obstacles as poor funding, lack of diverse faculty mentors, location in a geographical area with little diversity, etc. (Rogers & Molina, 2006; Vasquez et al., 2006). However, much can be learned from programs with "exemplary" records in diversity recruitment and retention (Rogers & Molina, 2006) and from the personal accounts of ethnic minority psychologists who had welcoming or isolating experiences as graduate students and faculty members (Vasquez et al., 2006). Additionally, the APA Commission on Ethnic Minority Recruitment, Retention, and Training in Psychology (1998, n.d.) and the APA Office of Minority Affairs (n.d.) have assembled useful guides to assist programs with recruitment and retention of diverse students and faculty.

In addition to recruiting and retaining diverse students/interns, faculty and staff, program directors have a central role in infusing multicultural competencies into the training curriculum and in building an organizational climate that supports multicultural learning. This requires the program director to be culturally self-aware to be better able to understand, empathize, and work with people from different cultural groups and to encourage faculty and staff to likewise develop cultural competence. The APA guidelines on multicultural education, and training (American Psychological Association, 2003) as well as a growing body of other resources provide a road map for this critical process (Roysircar, Dobbins, & Malloy, 2010; Sanchez-Hucles & Jones, 2005; Young, 2003).

Functional Competencies

In addition to the foundational competencies, effective program leaders demonstrate many of the *functional* competencies listed in the cube model. The functional competency domains include assessment, intervention, supervision/teaching, management/administration, research/evaluation, and consultation. In addition, there are two additional competencies needed to be most effective in the role of training director: leadership and advocacy. The key aspects of these competencies are listed in Table 30.2.

The program director's role in *assessment* is very important and can be quite creative. With the move to competency-based models in professional training (Kaslow, 2004; Kaslow et al., 2004; Kenkel & Peterson, 2010) and the emphasis on measuring educational outcomes by higher education accrediting bodies (APA Commission on Accreditation, 2007), competency assessment is an essential element in determining the effectiveness of professional education and training (Kenkel, 2009; Roberts, Borden, Christiansen, & Lopez, 2005). Standard tools for measuring professional psychology competencies are still in their infancy, though the methods and formats developed largely by other health professions and other psychology subfields hold potential (Kaslow, et al., 2009). This is the time for experimentation so that the tools that hold the most promise for cost-effectiveness and fidelity can be adopted more widely by training programs and perhaps be used for constructive program comparisons (Kenkel, 2009). To comprehensively assess trainees' competencies, program leaders can make use of the guiding principles developed by an APA task force (Kaslow et al., 2007a) that emphasize the use of multiple methods and the assessment of all elements of competencies, that is, the knowledge, skills, and *attitudes*. Programs seldom assess attitudes, but their attainment is integral to the demonstration of competence.

The *intervention* competency refers to a broader spectrum of activities than psychotherapy. It has been defined as "activities that promote, restore, sustain, and/or enhance positive functioning and a sense of well-being in clients through preventive, developmental, and/or remedial services" (Peterson, Peterson, Abrams, & Stricker, 1997, p. 380). One of the most critical times requiring program directors' proficiency in this competency is when they are dealing with trainees with professional competence problems (Elman & Forest, 2007; Kaslow et al., 2007b). In these situations, program directors do not, and should not, conduct psychotherapy or act as therapists. However, similar to psychotherapists, they attempt to restore or promote the trainee's well-being and positive functioning. In addressing problem students and interns, program directors, like psychotherapists, need knowledge of appropriate interventions and must have a realistic sense of what is possible. (Binder & Wechsler, 2010). They need skills in maintaining an alliance with the trainee while addressing the complex issues that are causing his or her poor performance. They must have the desire to help the trainee resolve the problems while appreciating the roles, responsibilities, and boundaries of their positions as program directors. They also must know the institutional, ethical, and legal requirements and guidelines relevant to these situations and the documentation that is required, especially in cases involving negative academic actions, such as unsatisfactory evaluations, probation, or termination (Kaslow, et al., 2007b). Clearly, in these situations, the program director's competency in intervention is seriously tested.

Program directors make great use of the *research/evaluation* functional competency. Accountability is the mantra within educational institutions as national, regional and specialty (e.g. APA) accrediting bodies require academic and training programs to show evidence of their effectiveness. Although many groan about this onus of accountability, this is not a new way of thinking for psychologists. Scientific training in psychology prepares program leaders to embrace and support the development of a culture of inquiry, evidence, and improvement (Western Association of Schools and Colleges, 2008) where questions are raised about the learning process, and data and assessment results are used to determine program performance and to make programmatic improvement.

In most psychology academic and training programs, the program director is responsible for the APA accreditation process. This involves being knowledgeable about accreditation principles, standards, and processes and being responsible for annual reviews, self-studies, site visits, and all communications with the Commission on Accreditation. Program directors' competency in program evaluation comes into play when they must set up systems for collecting, storing, and analyzing information on the program's students, faculty, processes, and outcomes and when they must develop an evaluation plan that collects information about program outcomes in a manner consistent with the accrediting body's format. The collected data should meaningfully convey whether the program is meeting its goals and objectives and should clearly indicate where improvements are needed (APA Commission on Accreditation, 2009). Of course, program directors cannot do this themselves. For the review to have real impact on program development, the program leader must engage others in the program-evaluation processes. When that happens, a culture of inquiry, evidence, and improvement takes hold and the education/training program is consistently concerned with, and committed to, quality and effectiveness.

Many program leaders have teaching or supervision responsibilities in addition to their jobs as directors. However, less formal aspects of *teaching, supervision,* and *consultation* are important for program leaders. For example, as they interact with trainees, faculty, and staff, program directors can promote desired performance (i.e., teach, model, shape) through feedback. Numerous studies have shown the great importance of feedback in improving learning and increasing motivation (London, 2003). Research in organizational psychology demonstrates that feedback-oriented work settings promote employee loyalty, courtesy, cooperation, and teamwork—traits highly desirable in training programs as well. However to be effective, feedback must be specific, timely, relevant, and provide information on ways to improve performance (London, 2003) and presented in a feedback-oriented culture in which individuals are comfortable giving and receiving feedback, and where feedback is an integral part of the learning process. Program directors can create this type of effective learning culture by providing more developmentally oriented feedback opportunities, by training individuals (including trainees) on how to provide constructive feedback, and by giving individuals opportunities to ask questions about the feedback they receive (Jacobs et al., 2011; London & Smither, 2002). In addition, program directors can act as role models for others by soliciting and using feedback from students/interns and faculty. This feedback-oriented culture will encourage all to engage in continuous learning and performance improvement.

Program leaders state that one of the most rewarding parts of the job is the ongoing contact with students/interns/postdoctoral residents (Wisocki, Grebstein, & Hunt, 1994). Program leaders spend much of their time guiding, advising, and counseling students/interns/postdoctoral residents, and trainees frequently seek them out for this help. In this capacity, program leaders often assume the role of mentors where they guide trainees into

becoming full members of the psychology profession and remain concerned with their professional development even after they leave the training program (Johnson, 2002, 2006, 2007). Program leaders also have valuable roles as mentors to junior faculty/staff by sharing with them institutional knowledge and assisting them with developmental goal setting and career planning (Kaslow & Mascaro, 2007).

In addition to understanding the workings of their own institutions, program leaders are knowledgeable about those professional psychology organizations concerned with education, training, credentialing, and practice, such as APA's accreditation commission, relevant directorates, and divisions, APPIC, Association of State and Provincial Psychology Boards (ASPPB), state psychological associations and licensing boards. Because of this knowledge, the program director often serves as a consultant to other faculty/staff providing counsel, suggestions, and advice on both programmatic and professional development issues. This often proves invaluable to those trying to navigate the multitude of groups involved with professional psychology training and practice.

In their day-to day activities, program directors exercise the functional competency of *management* and *administration* more than any other. They are performing the standard management functions of planning, organizing, coordinating, and directing. However, it is unlikely that program directors developed this competency in their psychology training programs, since historically little training has been provided on these skills (Hutchings, Lewis, & Bhargava, 2010; Malloy, Dobbins, Ducheny, & Winfrey, 2010). Many of the skills and attitudes associated with the other psychology competencies, such as those in relationships, self-reflection, research and evalaution, interdiciplinary systems, and so on are the elements, also, of good management (Reid & Silver, 2003; Veenhuis, 2003).

Systems thinking is a requisite for any manager (Hutchings, Lewis, & Bhargava, 2010; Veenhuis, 2003). A manager's success often depends on being aware of how one's program operates within the larger system and knowing the constructive ways to influence that system in order to accomplish programmatic goals. Additionally, a basic skill of all good managers is knowing how to put systems in place for planning, organizing, scheduling, and evaluating so those functions are carried out routinely and consistently. The manager's job, then, is keeping the wheels oiled and making adjustments and quick repairs when needed.

An effective professional psychology training program requires significant faculty/staff interdependence (Kenkel & Crossman, 2010). Faculty as a group must decide what and how competencies will be learned and who will be responsible for teaching and assessing trainees' acquisition of the competencies. These decisions require faculty to coordinate, collaborate, and commit to carrying out their respective roles. The program director's job is to guide them in that process, or as many program directors indicate, this is where they earn their pay by "herding cats." This exercise is often one of the most frustrating parts of a program director's job. University faculty and many individuals in professions expect and highly value autonomy and self-direction (Birnbaum, 1992). Relinquishing autonomy for programmatic goals may not occur enthusiastically. Most times, program directors manage faculty without "carrots or sticks," the common management tools, because university or institutional policies provide them with limited ability to grant (or deny) pay raises or other financial rewards, adjust workloads, or assign the bigger office. Additionally the leadership literature suggests that, in contrast to other occupational groups, professionals, such as faculty, need a more subtle form of management and supervision (Bryman, 2007). Rather than needing close supervision, professionals require a covert form of supervision that involves "protection and support" (Mintzberg, 1998, p. 146). In this form of managing, the program leader links the faculty/staff to important constituencies which are needed to support and advance the professional's and program's work, and helps manage the professional's autonomy (Raelin, 1995) by attending to the threats (busy work, administrative details, policy) impinging upon it. Most of all, the program director must be careful to avoid behaviors that undermine the professional's commitment and autonomy, such as being unfair, undermining collegiality or participation in decision-making, or any of the proscriptive norms outlined by Bray (2008). Managing this way, program directors must rely on components of the other competencies, such relationship skills, persuasion, negotiation, team building, and most importantly, the one to be discussed next: leadership.

A vast literature on the components of *leadership* exists, starting in the 1950s when researchers (Stogdill & Coons, 1957; Tannenbaum & Schmidt, 1958) identified two primary characteristics of a leader: (a) setting task and structure and (b) providing consideration and support. In keeping with the current zeitgeist favoring competency development, recent research has focused on describing and measuring the competency of leadership. One of the more recent assessment devices is the Leadership Competency Scale (Yoon, Song, Donahue, & Woodley, 2010). The scale was based on extensive leadership assessment work by the federal government's Office of Personnel Management (Flanders & Utterback, 1985; U.S. Office of Personnel Management, Human Resources Development, 1993) and validated on a sample of 323 managers in the health care industry. The scale has four factors: personal mastery, supervisory and managerial competencies, organizational leadership, and resource leadership.

The supervisory and management factor and the personal mastery factor overlap with competencies contained in the psychology *Competency Cube*. However, organizational leadership and resource leadership include skills that seem critical for program directors but not central to other roles of psychologists. Organizational leadership includes skills that pertain to visioning, external awareness, strategic planning, creativity, and leading change. If you are a leader, you need to keep your sights on the horizon. What are the opportunities and threats over that next hill? How will I prepare the group following me to meet those challenges? How can I get my team geared up to make best use of the opportunities that will be there? Leaders do not trudge along with their heads down; instead, they are always scanning the environment (Choo, 2001) and making plans and adjustments to meet new demands and opportunities. Perhaps the most challenging aspect of the psychology program leader's job is making sure the training program prepares today's trainees to meet tomorrow's needs and realities. That requires constant environmental scanning for trends, threats, and opportunities in psychology, education, health care, and related fields and the willingness and enthusiasm to the lead the change process in the program (Daft, Sormunen, & Parks, 1988; Subramanian, Fernandes, & Harper, 1993).

Leaders know that creating a vision for the program is a critical aspect of the change process. There are different types of leadership. Transactional leadership emphasizes a quid-proquo exchange relationship between the leader and followers, while transformational leadership emphasizes the inspirational aspects of the relationship between leaders and followers. Transactional leaders might tell followers what tasks are expected of them and what benefits they will receive upon completion, while transformational leaders use charisma, individual-ized attention, and intellectual stimulation to stir followers to go beyond their own self- interest for the good of the group and to reach the vision that they have presented (Bass, 1990). Transformational leaders are more effective than transactional lead-ers in higher education. The charismatic, relation-ship-oriented transformational leadership style is associated with faculty's perception of greater organizational effectiveness, satisfaction with super-vision, and willingness to expend greater effort (Brown & Moshavi, 2002). Therefore, effective program leaders must first have a vision, then use it to inspire others to action and cooperation, and, at the same time, through individual personal rela-tionships, describe for each follower their place and part in that vision.

One last, but extremely critical, competency for training directors is that of *advocacy*, meaning the ability to advocate both internally and externally for the training program and for the profession (Lating, Barnett, & Horowitz, 2010). Training directors must represent and advocate for the program in the larger organizational system, for example, the university, hospital, medical school, or community mental health center. In these tight economic times, failure to do so may result in cutbacks or even elimination of the training program. Researchers have found that engaging in advocacy, that is, championing the cause of the staff and program within and beyond the uni-versity, is associated with being perceived as an effec-tive academic leader (Benoit, 2005; Bryman, 2007; Creswell & Brown, 1992). To advocate effectively, directors should be prepared to show evidence of the program's achievements and its success in advancing the organization's mission and strategic objectives. Although formal mechanisms for doing this (e.g., annual reports or required program reviews) often exist, more frequent updates on recent successes can have many beneficial impacts. This is especially true if the program leader "shares the by-line" with oth-ers who had some role in the successful venture and uses the opportunity to express appreciation for sup-port provided by others in the university or training facility. Such recognition and appreciation go far in building support for the program and in enlisting others in the desire for it to excel. In advocating for the program, the director also should describe the major requirements of psychology training pro-grams, that is, what is needed for them to be effective and of high quality. The director must articulate how the training might require resources or accommoda-tions that are different from others in the institution

(Kenkel & Crossman, 2010), for example, time allocation in the workload for clinical supervision or interdisciplinary meetings. Internal advocacy is critical to garnering the resources and support needed for the program's continuance, growth, and improvement. This advocacy work is more effec-tive when emotional intelligence skills, such as social awareness, empathy, and assertion (Nelson & Low, 2003) are employed. Bryman (2007), in his literature review of research on effective leadership in higher education, found that advocacy was one of the 13 forms of leader behavior associated with departmental effectiveness. The effective behaviors are very similar to program directors' competencies enumerated in this chapter and include the follow-ing: having a clear sense of direction/strategic vision; preparing department arrangements to facilitate the direction set; treating academic staff fairly and with integrity; being trustworthy and having personal integrity; allowing the opportunity to participate in key decisions/encouraging open communication; communicating well about the direction the depart-ment is going; acting as a role model/having cred-ibility; creating a positive/collegial work atmosphere in the department; providing feedback on perfor-mance; providing resources for and adjusting work-loads to stimulate scholarship and research; making academic appointments that enhance department's reputation, and advancing the department's cause with respect to constituencies internal and external to the university and being proactive in doing so (p. 697).

As indicated by Bryman (2007), program leaders must engage not only in internal advocacy but also in a number of external advocacy activities. These activities are needed to not only preserve and build the training programs, but also to enhance others' recognition and valuing of psychological services, and ultimately the future of the psychology gradu-ates. At the local, state, or national level, the director might seek additional resources, such as practicum sites, service contracts or referrals, program fund-ing, or favorable policies. In all these cases, the director employs the advocate's skills of identifying the pressing societal need or problem, describing the consequences of not attending to the problem, explaining the ways in which that need could be addressed by the psychology training programs, and enumerating the benefits that would accrue from the program's actions.

External advocacy efforts sometimes require the director to collaborate with others with similar goals. In some cases, this may involve familiar partners, such as other psychologists or mental health providers. Increasingly, though, training programs' aims will require building coalitions with partners outside the traditional mental health fields and include those in health care, legal, and business fields. Proficiency with multidisciplinary collaboration, another program-director competency, is important in these activities. Some of the most effective advocacy efforts involve a coalition of professionals and consumers of psychology services or their family members. By telling of the needs and positive benefits in their own lives, consumers and their families often are the most convincing advocates for psychological services.

External advocacy effort requires skills in coalition building and maintenance, activities that often require long-term effort. Advocacy work also requires vision and commitment. In all, the advocate must practice the *five Ps*—persistence, patience, personal relationships, partnerships, and a long-term perspective (DeLeon, Kenkel, Oliveira Gray, & Sammons, 2011). The ultimate pay-off for the program, as well as the field of psychology, can be immense and long lasting.

Conclusion

This chapter has described the characteristics and competencies of leaders of professional psychology training programs. In many cases, program directors do not actively seek the role, but are "recruited" to it by their faculty colleagues or supervisor. However, whether the selection process involves strong-armed recruitment, formal application and review, or self-nomination, the competencies described in this chapter may help selection committees screen candidates and provide candidates themselves with a realistic preview of the knowledge, skills, and attitudes needed for the job. The competencies also suggest goals for professional development for those in, or aspiring to be in, program leadership positions.

How might psychologists develop these program leader competencies? Corporate America uses the 70-20-10 rule (Duberman, 2011). About 70% of leadership development should take place through on-the-job training by having to grapple with daily organizational problems and having special work assignments. Another 20% of the training should come from drawing upon the knowledge of those in the workplace through mentoring or coaching activities. The last 10% could be formal learning through courses, workshops, or online sessions. Some psychology organizations and training councils already are providing these training experiences for their

members, and many educational institutions are providing mentoring experiences for their program directors. The competencies described in this chapter can be used to identify the types of training and mentoring experiences needed to gain proficiency in the program director role. With more attention to the needed competencies for program directors and with expanded mentoring and training opportunities, psychology will ensure that a next generation of psychologists will be prepared to take on critical leadership roles in professional education and training.

References

American Psychological Association. (2003). Guidelines on multicultural education, training, research, practice, and organizational change for psychologists. *American Psychologist, 58*, 377–402. doi:10.1037/0003-066X.58.5.377

American Psychological Association. (2011a). Accredited doctoral programs in professional psychology: 2011. *American Psychologist, 66*, 884–898. doi:10.1037/a0026057

American Psychological Association. (2011b). Accredited internships and postdoctoral programs for training: 2011. *American Psychologist, 66*, 857–883. doi:10.1037/a0026059

American Psychological Association Commission on Accreditation. (2007). *Guidelines and principles for accreditation.* Washington, DC: APA.

American Psychological Association Commission on Accreditation. (2009). *Guidelines and principles for accreditation.* Washington, DC: APA. Retrieved July 10, 2013 from http://www.apa.org/ed/accreditation/about/policies/guiding-principles.pdf

American Psychological Association Commission on Ethnic Minority Recruitment, Retention and Training in Psychology. (1998, March). Resources for psychology training programs: Recruiting students of color. Retrieved July 10, 2013 from http://www.apa.org/education/undergrad/ethnic-minority.aspx

American Psychological Association Commission on Ethnic Minority Recruitment, Retention, and Training in Psychology. (n.d.). How to recruit and hire ethnic minority faculty. Retrieved July 10, 2013 from http://www.apa.org/pi/oema/resources/brochures/how-to.aspx

American Psychological Association Office of Minority Affairs. (n.d.). Model strategies for ethnic minority recruitment, retention, and training in higher education. Retrieved July 13, 2013 from http://www.apa.org/pi/oema/programs/recruitment/model-strategies.pdf

American Psychological Association Presidential Task Force on Evidence-Based Practice. (2006). Evidence-based practice in psychology. *American Psychologist, 61*, 271–285. doi:10.1037/0003-066X.61.4.271

Association of Psychology Postdoctoral and Internship Centers (APPIC). (2011a). 2011 survey of APPIC members with doctoral internships. Retrieved July 10, 2013 from http://www.zoomerang.com/Shared/SharedResultsSurveyResultsPage.aspx?ID=L26Q6VQ2V626

Association of Psychology Postdoctoral and Internship Centers (APPIC). (2011b). 2011 survey of APPIC members with postdoctoral programs. Retrieved July 10, 2013 from http://www.zoomerang.com/Shared/SharedResultsSurveyResultsPage.aspx?ID=L26Q6ZGVLLZ2

Barge, J. K., & Musambira, G. W. (1992). Turning points in chair–faculty relationships. *Journal of Applied Communication, 20*, 54–77.

Bass, B. M. (1990). From transactional to transformational leadership: Learning to share the vision. *Organizational Dynamics, 18*, 1931. doi:10.1016/0090-2616(90)90061-S

Benoit, P. (2005). Leadership excellence: Constructing the role of department chair. *Academic Leadership Journal, 3*(1). Retrieved July 10, 2013 from http://contentcat.fhsu.edu/cdm/compoundobject/collection/p15732coll4/id/124/rec/1

Binder, J. L., & Wechsler, F. S. (2010). The intervention competency. In M. B. Kenkel, & R. L. Peterson (Eds.), *Competency-based education for professional psychology* (pp. 105–123). Washington, DC: American Psychological Association. doi:10.1037/12068-006

Birnbaum, R. (1992). *How academic leadership works: Understanding success and failure in the college presidency.* San Francisco: Jossey Bass.

Bray, N. (2008). Proscriptive norms for academic deans: Comparing faculty expectations across institutional and disciplinary boundaries. *The Journal of Higher Education, 79*, 692–721.

Brown, F. W., & Moshavi, D. (2002). Herding academic cats: Faculty reactions to transformational and contingent reward leadership by department chairs. *Journal of Leadership Studies, 8*, 79–94. doi:10.1177/107179190200800307

Bryman, A. (2007). Effective leadership in higher education: A literature review. *Studies in Higher Education, 32*, 693–710.

Buckley, P. F., & Rayburn, W. F. (2010). The care and feeding of chairs of departments of psychiatry. *American Journal of Psychiatry, 167*, 376–378.

Charan, R., Drotter, S., & Noel, J. (2001). *The leadership pipeline.* San Francisco: Jossey-Bass.

Choo, C. W. (2001). Environmental scanning as information seeking and organizational learning. *Information Research, 7*(1). Retrieved July 10, 2013 from http://informationr.net/ir/7-1/paper112.html

Creswell, J. W., & Brown, M. L. (1992). How chairpersons enhance faculty research: A grounded theory study. *Review of Higher Education, 16*, 41–62.

Crits-Christoph, P. F. (1995). Training in empirically validated treatments: What are clinical students learning? *Professional Psychology: Research and Practice, 26*, 514–522. doi:10.1037/0735-7028.26.5.514

Daft, R. L., Sormunen, J. & Parks, D. (1988). Chief executive scanning, environmental characteristics, and company performance: an empirical study. *Strategic Management Journal, 9*, 123–139.

DeLeon, P. H., Kenkel, M. B., Oliveira Gray, J. M., & Sammons, M. T. (2011). Emerging policy issues for psychology: A key to the future of the profession. In D. H. Barlow (Ed.), *Oxford handbook of clinical psychology* (pp. 34–51). New York: Oxford University Press.

Duberman, T. (2011, September–October). Developing physician leaders today using the 70/20/10 rule. *Physician Executive Journal, 37* (5), 66–68.

Dulewicz, C., Young, M., & Dulewicz, V. (2005). The relevance of emotional intelligence for leadership performance. *Journal of General Management, 30*, 71–86.

Dulewicz, V. (2003). Leadership at the top: The need for emotional intelligence. *International Journal of Organizational Analysis, 11*, 193–210. doi:10.1108/eb028971

Elman, N. S., & Forest, L. (2007). From trainee impairment to professional competence problems: Seeking new terminology that facilitates effective action. *Professional Psychology: Research and Practice, 38*, 501–509. doi:10.1037/0735-7028.38.5.501

Flanders, L. R., & Utterback, D. (1985). The management excellence inventory: A tool for management development. *Public Administration Review, 45*, 403–410. doi:10.2307/3109968

Fouad, N. A., Grus, C. L., Hatcher, R. L., Kaslow, N. J., Hutchings, P. S., Madson, M. B.,...Crossman, R. E. (2009). Competency benchmarks: A model for the understanding and measuring of competence in professional psychology across training levels. *Training and Education in Professional Psychology, 4* (Suppl.), S5–S26. doi:10.1037/a0015832

Garman, A. N., & Johnson, M. P. (2006). Leadership competencies: An introduction. *Journal of Healthcare Management, 51*, 13–17.

Goleman, D. (1996). *Emotional intelligence: Why it can matter more than IQ.* London: Bloomsbury Publishing.

Hershenberg, R. D. (2012). How can graduate training programs bridge the clinical practice and research gap? *Psychotherapy, 49*, 123–134. doi:10.1037/a0027648

Hutchings, P. S., Lewis, D., & Bhargava, R. (2010). Management and administration. In M. Thomas, & M. Hersen (Eds.), *Handbook of clinical psychology competencies* (pp. 609–636). New York, NY: Springer Science + Business Media, LLC.

Institute of Medicine (IOM). (2001). *Crossing the quality chasm.* Washington, DC: National Academy Press.

Interprofessional Education Collaborative Expert Panel. (2011). *Core competencies for interprofessional collaborative practice: Report of an expert panel.* Washington, DC: Interprofessional Education Collaborative. Retrieved July 10, 2013 from https://www.aamc.org/download/ 186750/ data/core_competencies.pdf

Jacobs, S. C., Huprich, S. K., Grus, C. L., Cage, E. A., Elman, N. S., Forrest, L.,...Kaslow, N. J. (2011). Trainees with professional competency problems: Preparing trainers for difficult but necessary conversations. *Training and Education in Professional Psychology, 5*, 175–184. doi: 10.1037/a0024656

Johnson, W. B. (2002). The intentional mentor: Guidelines and strategies for the practice of mentoring. *Professional Practice: Research and Practice, 11*, 88–96. doi:10.1037/0735-7028.33.1.88

Johnson, W. B. (2006). *On being a mentor: A guide for higher education faculty.* Mahwah, NJ: Erlbaum.

Johnson, W. B. (2007). Transformational supervision: When supervisors mentor. *Professional Practice: Research and Practice, 38*, 259–267. doi:10.1037/0735-7028.38.3.259

Johnson, W. B., & Campbell, C. D. (2002). Character and fitness requirements for professional psychologists: Are there any? *Professional Psychology: Research and Practice, 33*, 46–53. doi:2002-10109-00710.1037//0735-7028.33.1.46

Johnson, W. B., & Campbell, C. D. (2004). Character and fitness requirements for professional psychologists: Training directors' perspectives. *Professional Psychology: Research and Practice, 35*, 405–411. doi:10.1037/0735-7028.35.4.405

Kaslow, N. J. (2004). Competencies in professional psychology. *American Psychologist, 59*, 774–781. doi:10.1037/0003–066X.59.8.774

Kaslow, N. J., & Mascaro, N. A. (2007). Mentoring interns and postdoctoral residents in academic health sciences centers. *Journal of Clinical Psychology in Medical Settings, 14*, 191–196. doi:10.1007/s10880–007–9070–y

Kaslow, N. J., Borden, K. A., Collins, F. L., Forest, L., Illfelder-Kaye, J., Nelson, P. D.,...Crossman, R. E. (2004). Competencies Conference: Future directions in educational and credentialing in professional psychology. *Journal of Clinical Psychology, 80*, 699–712. doi:10.1002/jclp.20016

Kaslow, N. J., Grus, C. L., Campbell, L. F., Fouad, N. A., Hatcher, R. L., & Rodolfa, E. R. (2009). Competency assessment toolkit for professional psychology. *Training and Education in Professional Psychology, 3* (Suppl), S527–S545. doi:10.1037/a0015833

Kaslow, N. J., Rubin, N. J., Bebeau, M., Leigh, I. W., Lichtenberg, J., Nelson, P. D.,...Smith, I. L. (2007a). Guiding principles and recommendations for the assessment of competence. *Professional Psychology: Research and Practice, 38*, 241–251. doi:10.1037/0735-7028.38.5.441

Kaslow, N. J., Rubin, N. J., Forest, L., Elman, N. S., Van Horne, B. A., Jacobs, S. C.,...Thorne, B. E. (2007b). Recognizing, assessing, and intervening with problems of professional competence. *Professional Psychology: Research and Practice, 38*, 479–492. doi:10.1037/0735-7028.38.5.479

Kazdin, A. E. (2008). Evidence-based treatment and practice: New opportunities to bridge clinical research and practice, enhance the knowledge base, and improve patient care. *American Psychologist, 63*, 146–159. doi:10.1037/0003-066X.63.3.146

Kenkel, M. B. (2001). Editorial: Research informing practice in Professional Psychology. *Professional Psychology: Research and Practice, 32*, 3–4. doi:10.1037//0735-7028.32.1.3

Kenkel, M. B. (2009). Adopting a competency model for professional psychology: Essential elements and resources. *Training and Education in Professional Psychology, 3* (Suppl), S859–S862. doi:10.1037/a0017037

Kenkel, M. B. (2011, January). Interprofessional collaboration. Presentation at the NCSPP Mid-Winter Conference: NCSPP 2025–Leap into the Future. San Juan, PR.

Kenkel, M. B., & Crossman, R. C. (2010). Faculty and administrators in professional psychology programs: Characteristics, roles, and challenges. In M. B. Kenkel, & R. L. Peterson (Eds.), *Competency-based education for professional psychology* (pp. 249–259). Washington, DC: American Psychological Association. doi:10.1037/12068–015

Kenkel, M. B., & Peterson, R. L. (Eds.). (2010). *Competency-based education for professional psychology*. Washington, DC: American Psychological Association.

King, A. R. (2002). Processes governing the selection of academic clinical training directors. *Professional Psychology: Research and Practice, 33*, 418–421. doi:10.1037/0735-7028.33.4.418

Ko, S. F., & Rodolfa, E. (2005). Psychology training directors' views of number of practicum hours necessary prior to internship application. *Professional Psychology: Research and Practice, 36*, 318–322. doi:10.1037/0735-7028.36.3.318

Lambert, M. (2012). Helping clinicians to use and learn from research-based systems: The OQ Analyst. *Psychotherapy, 49*, 109–114. doi:10.1037/a0027110

Lating, J. M., Barnett, J. E., & Horowitz, M. (2010). Creating a culture of advocacy. In M. B. Kenkel, & R. L. Peterson (Eds.), *Competency-based education for professional psychology* (pp. 201–208). Washington, DC: American Psychological Association. doi:10.1037/12068–011

Learning, D. R. (Ed.). (2003). *Managing people: A guide for department chairs and deans*. Williston, VT: Anker Publishing Co.

London, M. (2003). *Job feedback: Giving, seeking, and using feedback for performance improvement* (2nd ed.). Mahwah, NJ: Erlbaum.

London, M., & Smither, J. W. (2002). Feedback orientation, feedback culture, and the longitudinal performance management process. *Human Resources Management Review, 12*, 81–101. doi:10.1016/S1053–4822(01)00043-2

Maki, R. H., & Syman, E. M. (1997). Teaching of controversial and empirically validated treatments in APA- accredited clinical and counseling psychology programs. *Psychotherapy, 34*, 44–57.

Malloy, K. A., Dobbins, J. E., Ducheny, K., & Winfrey, L. L. (2010). The management and supervision competency: Current and future directions. In M. B. Kenkel, & R. L. Peterson (Eds.), *Competency-based education for professional psychology* (pp. 161–178). Washington, DC: American Psychological Association. doi:10.1037/12068-009

Mintzberg, H. (1998). Covert leadership: Notes on managing professionals. *Harvard Business Review, 76*, 140–147.

Murry, J. W. J., & Stauffacher, K. B. (2001). Department chair effectiveness: What skills and behaviors do deans, chairs, and faculty in research universities perceive as important? *Arkansas Educational Research & Policy Studies Journal, 1*, 62–75.

Naquin, S. S., & Holton III, E. F. (2006). Leadership and managerial competency models. *Advances in developing human resources, 8*, 144–165. doi:10.1177/1523422.305286152

Nelson, D. B., & Low, G. R. (2003). *Emotional intelligence: Achieving academic and career excellence*. Upper Saddle River, NJ: Prentice-Hall.

Patient Protection and Affordable Care Act, Pub. L. No. 111–148, §2702, 124 Stat. 119, 318–319 (2010).

Peterson, R. L., Peterson, D. R., Abrams, J. C., & Stricker, G. (1997). The National Council of Schools and Programs of Professional Psychology educational model. *Professional Psychology: Research and Practice, 28*, 337–386. doi:10.1037/0735-7028.28.4.373

Picano, J., & Blusewicz, M. (2003). Disciplinary foundations. Organization and administration of psychology services. In W. H. Reid, & S. B. Silver (Eds.), *Handbook of mental health administration and management* (pp. 192–205). New York: Brunner-Routledge.

Raelin, J. A. (1995). How to manage your local professor. *Academy of Management Proceedings, 1995* (1), 207–211. doi:10.5465/AMBPP.1995.17536478

Reid, W. H., & Silver, S. B. (Eds.). (2003). *Handbook of mental health administration and management*. New York, NY: Brunner-Routledge.

Roberts, M. C., Borden, K. A., Christiansen, M. D., & Lopez, S. J. (2005). Fostering a culture shift: Assessment of competence in the education and careers of professional psychologists. *Professional Psychology: Research and Practice, 36*, 355–361. doi:10.1037/0735-7028.36.4.355

Rodolfa, E., Bent, R., Eisman, E., Nelson, P., Rehm, L., & Ritchie, P. (2005). A cube model for competency development: Implications for psychology educators and regulators. *Professional Psychology: Research and Practice, 36*, 347–354. doi:10.1037/70735-7028.36.4.347

Rogers, M. R., & Molina, L. E. (2006). Exemplary efforts in psychology to recruit and retain graduate students of color. *American Psychologist, 61*, 143–156. doi: 10.1037/0003-066X.61.2.143

Roysircar, G., Dobbins, J. E., & Malloy, K. A. (2010). Diversity competence in training and clinical practice. In M. B. Kenkel, & R. L. Peterson (Eds.), *Competency-based education for professional psychology* (pp. 179–197). Washington, DC: American Psychological Association. doi:10.1037/12068-010

Sanchez-Hucles, J., & Jones, N. (2005). Breaking the silence around race in training, practice, and research. *The Counseling Psychologist, 33*, 547–558. doi:10.1177/0011000005276462

Stogdill, R. M., & Coons, A. E. (Eds.). (1957). *Leader behavior: Its description and measurement.* Columbus: Ohio State University College of Administrative Science.

Strickland, B. (1984). Psychologist as department chair. *Professional Psychology: Research and Practice, 15*, 730–740. doi:10.1037/0735–7028.15.5.730

Subramanian, R., Fernandes, N., & Harper, E. (1993). Environmental scanning in U.S. companies: Their nature and their relationship to performance. *Management International Review, 33*, 271–286.

Tannenbaum, R., & Schmidt, W. H. (1958). How to choose a leadership pattern. *Harvard Business Review, 36*, 95–101.

Teachman, B. A., Drabick, D. A., Hershenberg, R., Vivian, D., Wolfe, B. E., & Goldfried, M. A. (2012). Bridging the gap between clinical research and clinical practice: Introduction to the special section. *Psychotherapy, 49*, 97–100. doi:10.1037/a0027346

Trierweiler, S., Stricker, G., & Peterson, R. L. (2010). The research and evaluation competency: The local clinical scientist—Review, current status, future directions. In M. B. Kenkel, & R. L. Peterson (Eds.), *Competency-based education for professional psychology* (pp. 125–141). Washington, DC: American Psychological Association. doi:10.1037/12068–007

Trocchia, P. J. & Andrus, D. M. (2003). Perceived characteristics and abilities of an effective marketing department head. *Journal of Marketing Education, 25*, 5–15.

U.S. Office of Personnel Management, Human Resources Development. (1993). *Leadership effectiveness framework and inventory.* Washington, DC: Author.

Vasquez, M. J. T., Lott, B., García-Vaázquez, E., Grant, S. K., Iwamasa, G. Y., Molina, L. E.,...Vestal-Dowdy, E. (2006). Personal reflections: Barriers and strategies in increasing diversity in psychology. *American Psychologist, 61*, 157–172. doi: 10.1037/0003–066X.61.2.157

Veenhuis, P. E. (2003). Essential management functions. In Reid, W. H., & Silver, S. B. (Eds.), *Handbook of mental health administration and management* (pp. 101–110). New York: Brunner-Routledge.

Walter, F., Cole, M. S., & Humphrey, R. H. (2011). Emotional intelligence: Sine qua non of leadership or folderol? *Academy of Management Perspectives, 45*, 45–59. doi:10.5465/AMP.2011.59198449

Western Association of Schools and Colleges. (2008). *Handbook of accreditation 2008.* Retrieved July 10, 2013 from http://www.wascsenior.org/files/Handbook_of_Accreditation.pdf

Wicherski, M., Mulvey, T., Hart, B., & Kohout, J. (March 2011). 2010–2011 Faculty salaries in graduate departments of psychology. Retrieved July 9, 2013, from APA Center for Workforce Studies: http://www.apa.org/workforce/publications/11-fac-sal/report.pdf

Wise, E. A. (2004). Methods for analyzing psychotherapy outcomes: A review of clinical significance, reliable change, and recommendations for future directions. *Journal of Personality Assessment, 82*, 50–59. doi:10.1207/s15327752jpa8201_10

Wisocki, P. A., Grebstein, L. C., & Hunt, J. B. (1994). Directors of clinical training: An insider's perspective. *Professional Psychology: Research and Practice, 25*, 482–488. doi:0735–7028/94/$3.00

Yoon, H. J., Song, J. H., Donahue, W. E., & Woodley, K. K. (2010). Leadership Competency Inventory: A systematic process for developing and validating a leadership competency scale. *Journal of Leadership Studies, 4*, 39–50. doi:10.1002/jls.20176

Youn, S. J. (2012). The treatment outcome package: Facilitating practice and clinically relevant research. *Psychotherapy, 49*, 115–122. doi:10.1037/a0027932

Young, G. (2003). Dealing with difficult classroom dialogue. In P. Bronstein, & K. Quina (Eds.), *Teaching gender and multicultural awareness: Resources for the psychology classroom* (pp. 347–360). Washington, DC: American Psychological Association.

Employment Trends for Early Career Psychologists: Implications for Education and Training Programs in Professional Psychology and for Those Who Wish to Become Successful Early Career Psychologists

Ronald H. Rozensky

Abstract

This chapter highlights issues that can impact the success of Early Career Psychologists (ECP) by focusing on the academic and clinical preparation of professional psychologists throughout the education and training sequence. The evolving healthcare system is reviewed including psychologists' preparation for interprofessional, team-based practice, economic and reimbursement changes, team science, and how various training models in professional psychology can impact success. Licensure rates, job prospects, salaries, and student debt are discussed as measurable outcomes of education. Questions about professional psychology's doctoral education, internship training, postdoctoral experiences, and lifelong learning are offered in service of seeking answers that will help maximize the professional success of ECPs as well as ensuring a robust future for the field of professional psychology.

Key Words: early career psychologist, professional psychology, education and training, healthcare reform

If one advances confidently in the direction of one's dreams,
and endeavors to live the life which one has imagined,
one will meet with a success unexpected in common hours.

— *Henry David Thoreau*

The purpose of this chapter is to highlight issues that can impact the success of Early Career Psychologists (ECP). It relates those issues to the academic and clinical preparation of professional psychologists throughout the education and training sequence. Topics discussed related to the evolving healthcare system include psychologists' preparation for interprofessional, team-based practice, and new systems of reimbursement for services, team science, and the impact of various training models in professional psychology. Measurable outcomes of the education and training experience such as licensure rates, job prospects, salaries, and even student debt are described. Suggestions for curricular

components of doctoral education, internship training, postdoctoral experiences, and lifelong learning are offered that would assure that the educational sequence in psychology maximizes the professional success of individuals as well as enhances the overall growth and future robustness of the field of professional psychology.

The American Psychological Association (APA) (APA, 2006) defines an ECP as someone who is within seven years of having received his or her doctoral degree. However, one might consider first year graduate students in psychology, or even first year undergraduate psychology majors, to be "early career" in that they are embarking on a lifetime of ongoing preparation for successes within their chosen field. This might even apply to the high school senior taking an advanced placement course in psychology–a student who only now is discovering the rich scientific and applied aspects of, and career opportunities in, psychology and who is just beginning to formulate high hopes for a successful future as a psychologist.

Having a clear picture of outcome variables that reflect defined successes for postlicensure ECPs can be most helpful for those embarking on each step of the education and training ladder as they chart their own plan of study towards becoming a psychologist. These outcome variables also apply to those psychologists who, as academic faculty or staff in training programs, will shape education and training opportunities within and across those steps. As educators, their goal should be to concentrate on formulating curricula, educational objectives, and training opportunities that will maximize ultimate professional success for their students and trainees.

Trends both within and outside the field of psychology will have an impact on what is defined as professional success. Attention to trends in society, in the healthcare system, in scientific inquiry, and in the psychology workforce will help shape the content of education and assist in delineating the competencies needed to be successful (Rozensky, 2011). McFall (2006, p 37) underscored the importance of the field *adapting* to "…major forces operating outside of psychology, forces over which psychologists have little or no control. These forces are reshaping the world…" in which doctoral training in psychology is embedded. Before addressing those trends and the opportunities for the field to evolve, and maybe even influence those trends, developing a clear picture of what an "early career in psychology" might look like will be helpful.

Sources of Information

From their perspective as members of the APA's Early Career Psychologist Committee, Green and Hawley (2009) reviewed some of the data-based information that helps define the march toward becoming a professional psychologist including time in training, debt load, employment trajectories, and salary base for ECPs. The ECP Committee provides many resources for both ECPs (who may be at any step along the education and training sequence) as well as for those more senior members of the field who are helping to shape the professional lives of those in training by mentoring the newest members

of the professional workforce (e.g., http://www.apa. org/careers/early-career/index.aspx).

Source material that includes data describing the activities and attributes of the professional workforce in psychology in general, and early career colleagues more specifically, can be found at the APA's Center for Workforce Studies (CWS; http://www. apa.org/workforce/index.aspx). This site provides the most current information on salaries, demographic, and educational backgrounds of students moving through the educational pipeline in psychology. It also contains a growing focus on estimates of society's workforce need for psychologists across the employment spectrum.

For those considering a career in professional psychology, the APA's *Graduate Study in Psychology* (http://www.apa.org/pubs/books/4270096.aspx) provides comparative information regarding 660 graduate programs in psychology. Information presented that will inform the "consumer" of the education and training opportunities in professional psychology includes program acceptance rates, tuition costs, time to degree, and employment information regarding program graduates, among other information.

Finally, the APA's Commission on Accreditation (http://www.apa.org/ed/accreditation/about/ program-choice.aspx) provides a wealth of information concerning the importance of education and training within accredited institutions, how accreditation is designed to protect the public and guide students seeking quality graduate education towards programs meet predefined standards of education and training, and lists those programs in professional psychology that are indeed accredited. Understanding the context within which training takes place will help direct curricular development that meets the standards of accreditation, the expectation of quality education and training, and helps assure a competent start towards the professional success of program graduates.

A Picture of Early Psychologists in the Workforce

Data regarding the professional psychology workforce is collected and published routinely by the APA's CWS (e.g., Michalski & Kohout, 2011; Michalski, Kohout, Wicherski, & Hart, 2011). This information helps describe the employment environment toward which ECPs are headed or into which they have entered recently. It also can strategically guide those educators developing the curricula for preparing the next generation of psychologists so that they possess the competencies needed for the workplace venues where those psychologists will be employed now and in the future. Although Rozensky (2011) and Sweet, Meyer, Nelson, and Moberg (2011) have raised some concerns about the veridicality of the CWS data due to small samples, and the CWS itself offers appropriate caveats about sample size and generalizability of its own information, "...for the sake of the discussion,...this is an accurate snapshot of the field of psychology since these are the only specific data available on the employment locations of psychology's practice workforce" (Rozensky, 2011, p 798). It should be noted that Rozensky (2011) has raised similar concerns about the job data provided by the United States (U.S.) Bureau of Labor Statistics (2010) regarding the professional psychology workforce due to the Bureau's inclusion of individuals with masters and bachelor degrees in their definition of the psychology workforce.

The doctorate employment data for ECPs entering the professional workforce in 2009 (Michalski, et al, 2011), the most current information available, found that the median starting salary for recent graduates was $64,000 (average of $66,008; SD= $23,861). Women reported a median salary $8,000 lower than men ($62,000 versus $70,000), Although the median and mean salary reported by psychologists across various minority groups were similar to that of nonminorities. The majority of all salaries were between $50,000 and $70,000, which Michalski et al. noted was a slight downtick from two years earlier. Clinical psychologists working in the field of criminal justice reported the highest median starting salary ($80,500) and graduates working in applied psychology positions tended to have the highest median salaries overall ($73,332; which includes those in consulting firms at $75,000). ECP faculty members in academic departments, identified as departments "other than psychology," had the highest median 9–10 month salaries (as assistant professors; $60,000) reflecting higher salaries for those psychologists teaching within such professions as business, for example.

Of the 2009 cohort of new doctorates, 75% were women, an increase of 5% in 10 years and 18% over 20 years. The CWS reported that 10 years ago just over 83% of new graduates were White, whereas Hispanics/Latinos and Blacks/African Americans each comprised 5% of the new doctorates and Asians represented 7%. The number of new doctorates younger than 35 years has increased 13% from 58% to 71%. Of the respondents, 75% earned a PhD, whereas 24% were awarded a PsyD in 2009 (PsyDs comprised less than 8% of new doctorates during the mid-1980s). Michalski et al. noted that 63% of the new doctorates were employed full time, approximately 8% were employed part time, and 24% were working in postdoctorate positions. Nearly 6% were unemployed with nearly two thirds of those unemployed actively seeking employment. The proportion of those working full time has declined steadily (from 82% in 1986 and 69% in 1997). The number of new doctorates employed in postdoctoral positions has more than doubled from about 6% in 1986 to 20% in 2007. In all, 47% of 2009 doctorate recipients were engaged in or had completed postdoctoral study. According to Michalski et al., men were more likely than women to be employed full time (67% versus 62%). Ethnic minority psychologists reported full time employment at a slightly higher rate than White respondents (65% versus 62%), with minorities just as likely as Whites to have engaged in postdoctoral study. The highest rates of full time employment (70%) were reported by Asian psychologists.

Michalski et al. found that toward the end of the first decade of the 21st century, the overall unemployment rate remained relatively low among new psychologists (6% as noted earlier) despite the severity of the economic downturn that began in 2008. However, this does represent an increase from 2007 when approximately (only) 2% of new doctorates were unemployed. The largest single proportion of those seeking work (36%) indicated that they did not want to relocate and could find no suitable position in their geographic location. The rates of full time employment, part time employment, postdoctoral involvement, and unemployment did not vary substantially between graduates from health service provider training and those in research subfields when considered in the aggregate according to the CWS. Of those full time positions, 37% were in the human service sector; 32% were in academia, 21% were located in business, government, and other settings, and 8% could be found in schools and other educational settings.

Most of those employed in full time human service positions worked in organized care settings rather than individual or group private practices (31% versus 6%). Rozensky (2011) noted that, according to the CWS, across the general population of all psychologists (early career and more senior colleagues), there are *more* psychologists now employed in *institutional* settings than in independent practice. He went on to predict that this trend will continue to increase given the changes to the healthcare system brought on by the recent Affordable Care Act (Public Law No: 111–148, 111th Congress: Patient Protection and Affordable Care Act, 2010).

Almost 30% of newly employed psychologists began their current, primary employment within three months of completing their doctoral degree, 38% found a position before completion of their degree, and 6% had had the job when they began their graduate program. Nearly 75% of the newly hired psychologists stated that their general graduate training was closely related to their current employment, with 66% acknowledging that courses in their major subfield were closely related to their (new) job.

Looking at specific workplace venues, university settings and business, government, and other such settings each accounted for 21% of the employment sites, hospitals (predominantly VA medical centers) represented 14%, followed by other human service settings at 11% (including university/college counseling centers, outpatient clinics, and primary care offices or community health centers), Eight percent indicated schools and educational settings, slightly less than 6% indicated independent practice as their primary position, with another 6% working in managed care. Of note, "most new doctorates appeared to be fairly satisfied with their current positions" (Michalski et al., 2011, p. 6).

The CWS then looked at student funding and debt load of the newest graduates entering the field (in 2009) and found that almost 78% of the respondents used their own or family resources to help complete their graduate studies. Most *also* received support from an overlapping range of other funding sources at some point during their graduate education, including university-based funding (71%), student loans (56%), and nonuniversity grant support (15%). Ethnic minority and White graduates reported using their own earnings/family support in similar proportions (79% versus 75%) with little variance in the proportions of ethnic minority and White doctorates whose primary support were personal resources (12% and 17%, respectively). Michalski et al. go on to note "differential debt levels being assumed by those seeking PhDs versus PsyDs" (p. 9). PhD students (52%) indicated that they relied primarily on university sources of support, with 18% using loans and only 15% using their own resources. PsyD recipients, on the other hand, reported that (only) 4% of them had university sources as their primary means of

financial support, 65% utilized nonuniversity or federal loans, with 22% using personal or family financial support. Of all 2009 doctorates, 68% reported some level of debt upon receipt of the doctoral degree. Seventy-eight percent of health service provider trained graduates and 48% of those in research subfields reported carrying debt. Across all models of training, graduates in health, counseling, and clinical psychology reported the highest proportion of debt (94%, 81%, and 79% respectively). Almost half the health service provider graduates owed $80,000 with 11% having debt in excess of $160,000. According to Michalski et al., the median debt for those in the practice subfields was $80,000—more than double that for those in the research subfields ($32,000). Eighty-nine percent of PsyD recipients and 62% of PhD recipient reported some amount of debt. Those with a PsyD in clinical psychology reported a median debt load of $120,000 in 2009, up from $100,000 in 2007, $70,000 in 1999, and $53,000 in 1997. Clinical PhD recipients reported a median level of debt of $68,000, up from $55,000 in 2007. Those with PhDs in the research subfields had a median debt of $38,500. Almost 60% of PsyD graduates owed more than $100,000 compared to less than 17% of those with PhDs. Michalski et al. (2011) noted that "these debts have real implications for productivity and lifetime earnings among substantial segments of the doctoral population in psychology" (p. 10).

For that same cohort of new ECP graduates, Michalski et al. (2011) reported that the most utilized and most successful mechanism for job hunting by those in the human services area was through informational job search channels (69%) followed by electronic resources (32%), faculty advisors (29%), APA *Monitor on Psychology* ads (25%), and *Chronicle of Higher Education* advertisements and other classified ads in newspapers (15%). They noted that over the past decade the most successful job search strategies have shifted from print media to informal sources with electronic resources a distance second.

Trends Impacting the Psychology Workforce

Given the preceding picture of the personal issues impacting ECPs like debt load, salaries, job searches, and workplace settings, we will discuss next a range of trends that can impact the day-to-day activities of early career psychologists. We will look at trends within society in general, trends within healthcare, and then trends within the field of psychology. We then will relate those trends to current developments within graduate education in professional psychology as well as opportunities to adapt our education and training models and programs in anticipation of these evolving developments. First, however, we will review several outcome measures that reflect the attainment of success at work and across the span of one's career. Those outcomes can be used to further focus the discussion of the necessary components of education and training to assure the ultimate success of ECPs within the context of the trends presented. A series of questions will be presented regarding how to assure ECP success and then be summarized at the end of the article.

Personal Success

Judge and Hurst (2008) describe how a higher level of "core self-evaluations" are associated with both higher initial levels of work success and steeper work success trajectories with career success defined "as the real and perceived achievement individuals have accumulated as a result of their work experiences" (p. 850). Those authors suggest that early career successes help set individuals on a course for stronger career progress over time and that those with higher "self-evaluations might draw greater satisfaction from their extrinsic success" and be more "equipped psychologically to take increasing amounts of satisfaction and fulfillment from their work" (p. 851). Myers, Sweeney, Popick, Wesley, Bordfeld, and Fingerhut (2012) looked at graduate student self-care and found that "sleep hygiene, social support, emotion regulation, and acceptance within a mindfulness framework were significantly related to perceived stress" (p 55). A good question then for each ECP, and for every graduate education and training program and mentor is, how is this type of "self-assurance" addressed in the preparation of (early career) psychologists as they move through the sequence of steps in their education and ultimately embark on a career of success, growth, and fulfillment? Further, as Myers et al. (2012) suggest, how do graduate programs assist their students in developing self-care related competencies in order to better participate and learn from their education and training?

Programmatic Success

McFall (2006) warned that when making comparisons of various models of training or across programs in professional psychology it should be noted that there are no controlled studies—no random assignment of students to programs—and the majority of studies comparing programs and training models are correlational in nature. This caveat should apply to any discussion of outcomes in education and training in professional psychology.

However, McFall did note that "training models do seem to make a difference" (p. 37). For example, he highlights the workplace setting (outcome) data presented by Cherry, Messenger, and Jacoby (2000) that compared the most common workplace settings of graduates from the three prominent training models in clinical psychology: scientist-practitioners (medical center, 18%; CMHC, 15%; hospitals, 14%; postdoctoral training, 13%; and academic, 11%), scholar-practitioners (CMHC, 25%; other/multiple, 23%; and medical center, hospital, private practice, 12% each) and clinical scientists (academic, 29%; medical center, hospital, private practice, 13% each; and postdoc, 9%). Can these "outcome" data provide a measure of possible "steerage" or direction for those students choosing their graduate training (program) when they have a particular workplace venue as their ultimate goal? Do the graduate programs within these three general training models actually build specific workplace-related competencies into their curricula to assure high quality preparation for success in the venues toward which their graduates gravitate? Do these workplace choices actually reflect the program's defined competencies and thus graduates actually go to work where they are best prepared to succeed?

Sayette, Norcross, and Dimoff (2011) compared graduate programs in clinical psychology that were members of the Academy of Clinical Science (ACS) with programs that were university-based clinical programs but not members of the Academy and with programs that were located in "specialized schools" that did not provide academic programming beyond psychology or counseling. They conclude that, although there is a great deal of heterogeneity across training models in the field, those programs that are members of the ACS admit fewer students, provide more financial aid to students, and have very different theoretical orientations than those programs found within specialized institutions (the differences between ACS programs and university based graduate programs were considered by the authors as not significant). They raise the concern that "the programs with the least stringent admission criteria are admitting much larger proportions of applicants" (p. 10).

Graham and Kim (2011) reviewed predictors of success in professional psychology by looking at individual student characteristics as well as university and programmatic variables. They began their discussion by reiterating Peterson's (2003) defined purpose of graduate education in professional psychology as "the attainment and advance of excellence in the education and training of psychologists for illustrious careers in professional service" (p. 797). To evaluate this concept of "attainment and advance of excellence," Graham and Kim looked across types of graduate training programs in professional psychology and collected data on three outcome variables: number of students receiving an APA-accredited internship, graduates' scores on the national licensing exam in psychology, and the percentage of graduates becoming board certified (by the American Board of Professional Psychology; ABPP). They considered the licensing exam score to be a measure of the knowledge necessary for the *successful practice* of psychology; accredited internships were assumed to be a measure of *quality training*; and becoming board certified was consider as a measure of *peer-perceived quality of service*\practice. Graham and Kim concluded that "clinical PhD programs outperform clinical PsyD programs on the outcomes examined" (p. 349). Further, they reported that program type (PsyD versus PhD) and *not* size (number of students) or selectivity (incoming GRE scores, for example) accounted for the relative success of graduates from each training model-type program. These authors also argue that research university based programs have better outcomes than free standing professional programs, and this might be due to financial (grant funding) and increased research opportunities that may well account for these differences. Graham and Kim conclude that the focus on *scientific rigor* in doctoral-level training might be the best predictor of better professional outcomes as measured in their study (accredited internships, higher licensing examination scores, and higher likelihood of becoming board certified). How do graduate programs evaluate their 'scientific rigor' in their curricula and how is that 'rigor' operationalized for students so they may evaluate their programmatic choices?

Schaffer, Rodolfa, Owen, Lipkins, Webb, and Horn (2012) looked at 6,937 (94%) of the total number of doctoral level individuals who took the Examination for Professional Practice of Psychology (EPPP) national licensing examination between 2008 and 2010 considered by some as a viable outcome measure of ECP success. Some general findings suggest that women had a higher pass rate than men; the longer one waits to take the exam post degree the poorer the pass rate; and the more time one spends studying for the exam (to a point) the higher the pass rate. Schaffer and colleagues concluded that "those who were trained in PhD programs passed at a rate of 82%, while those trained in PsyD programs passed at the rate of 69%" (p<.001) (p. 3). Further, they found that those examinees from *accredited* doctoral programs (APA or CPA) passed the EPPP at a rate of 78% compared to only 58% for those from nonaccredited programs. For those who attended APA or CPA accredited (or Association of Psychology Postdoctoral and Internship Centers (APPIC) member programs) internships, the pass rate was 82% versus 68% for those who did not attend an accredited (or APPIC member) internship program. Schaffer et al. offered several recommendations to individuals as well as the field in general. Understanding a program's EPPP pass rates, they suggest, may well help students in choosing programs with a better success rate. For the field and future students, they recommend, that the "pass rate on the EPPP should be one important variable influencing whether a graduate program *receives* (italics added) APA or CPA accreditation" (p. 6). It is clear that pass rate is one of the (outcome) markers of successful students and successful programs, and, thus, understanding variables related to success is a key to helping prepare ECPs for their future. How are graduate programs and internships addressing the licensing pass rates of their graduates and assuring that a high standard of quality education and training is met?

Jaffe (2004) argued that professional psychology training programs have different selection criteria than academic psychology departments that might account for such differences. He opined that universities are looking for "intelligence, research capability, and a high level of competence as a scholar" and a free standing professional program looks for students who are "competent, dedicated, and capable professionals it can prepare to respond to the needs of society" (p. 648). For the individual student seeking to become a successful ECP, and for graduate programs that wish to maximize the professional and personal development of their new, soon to be successful professionals, success might be maximized by looking specifically at which training experiences, in which academic and training situations, will be most efficacious in developing those competencies needed to assure success (e.g., Collins, Callahan, & Klonoff, 2007).

The APA (APA, 2011a) Commission on Accreditation (CoA) stated in its 5-year summary report on accreditation in psychology that "ensuring the quality of education and training of students/ trainees is one of the ways we as a health care and mental health profession can best retain the trust of the public and of our colleagues in other professions, as well as assure our continued growth and development" (p. i). That report presents data submitted by all accredited programs at the doctoral, internship, and postdoctoral levels and across types of program (PsyD, PhD, clinical, counseling, school, combined, postdoctoral specialty). A range of metrics are presented by the CoA that include total number of students by program, percentage of student admitted to a program, gender and ethnicity of programs, time to degree, percentage of attrition, and annual financial support for interns and postdoctoral residents. Although accreditation may well be the ultimate benchmark indicating at least minimal quality (Boelen & Woollard, 2009) in professional psychology education and training (e.g, Rozensky, 2011, 2012), some of these programmatic variables might be useful for both the individual student seeking quality education and for programs themselves to consider when measuring their program's success or as variables that predict early career success. For example, programs with higher attrition rates may well be programs with either higher expectations of their students, and, thus, a more difficult curriculum and thus more students leaving the program—or they may be programs with low initial admission criteria with many students admitted who cannot make the grade and must leave the program. Such concrete measures of program performance can be useful prospective students in assessing program choice, thereby assuring a trajectory toward ECP success. How can the field assure that these issues are routinely included in outcome measurements of quality in education and training?

Trends That Will Influence Success of the Professional Psychology Workforce

Rozensky (2012a,b) has detailed a series of trends—patterns of change over time—that he believes have direct impact on society in general, the evolving healthcare system in the United States, and thereby, will impact the training and day-to-day activities of professional psychologists over the next several decades. Such trends should be reviewed as to their implications for the preparation of the next generation of psychologists who must work within our changed, and changing society.

Diversity and the changing population. The demographic picture of the United States is changing, the population is aging, and the number of those living with chronic diseases is increasing. The United States Census Bureau states that "between 2010 and 2050, the U Sis projected to experience rapid growth in its older population" (Vincent & Velkoff, 2010, p. 1) as the number of those over the age of 65 doubles from 40.2 million in 2010 to 88.5 million by 2050. Further, "an increase in the proportion of the older population that is Hispanic and an increase in the proportion that is a race other than White" (p. 8) also is projected to increase. The 2010 census (U.S. Census Bureau, 2011) reported that half of the growth in the U.S. population between 2000 and 2010 was due to an increase in the Hispanic population, which increased some 43%. Thirteen percent of the population was African American and 5% was Asian with a population growth of 43% in that group over those 10 years. Ortman and Guarneri (2009) state that the "racial and ethnic diversity of the U.S. population is shown to increase" well into the future with the percentage of White only population decreasing. Plaut (2010) acknowledged the impact of this changing picture of the U.S. population on healthcare disparities and access to healthcare.

The advent of these changes presents professional psychologists the opportunity to build on its strong commitment to multiculturalism as a core competency (e.g., Rogers, 2009). Further, through their education and training and a commitment to lifelong learning, ECPs should have an ongoing focus on these societal changes. The individual student, each ECP, and education and training program(s) in general should incorporate such resources as the APA's guidelines on aging, disabilities, multiculturalism, and lesbian, gay, and bisexual clients (APA 2002, 2004, 20011b, 2012) in their personal readings as well as formal curricula and as the basis of functional competencies that prepare the success ECP to work within the context of the changing demographics of our society.

Changing healthcare system. "Changes to the healthcare delivery system as detailed in the *Patient Protection and Affordable Care Act* (ACA; Public Law No: 111–148, Mar 23, 2010) focus on efficient, effective, and affordable quality healthcare, a transparent and accountable healthcare system, prevention of chronic diseases, expansion of eligibility for publically supported healthcare programs, patient involvement in their own care, and the expansion of the healthcare workforce that is educated, trained, and prepared to practice in an interprofessionally focused, team-based delivery system" (Rozensky, 2012, p. 5).

After over 100 years of attempts to transform the healthcare system in the United States, the ACA, and the various implementing regulations and rules that are promulgated to shape the day-to-day practice of healthcare, will have profound implications for patients, their families and for those who provide the clinical services within a truly comprehensive, integrated healthcare system. Professional psychology must be focused strategically on its own readiness for these changes—especially so in the academic and clinical preparation of those ECPs who will be entering the healthcare workforce as transformed by this legislation. How are programs and students preparing for these changes?

In 2001 the APA reaffirmed its commitment to being a broad healthcare profession, broader than its roots in mental health. This was accomplished by adding "health" to the APA bylaws (Rozensky, Johnson, Goodheart, & Hammond, 2004). Clearly an important statement given that in 2005, 133 million Americans had at least one chronic medical condition and this is predicted to increase to 157 million by 2020. At the same time those with multiple chronic illnesses numbered 63 million in 2005 with a predicted 81 million in 2020 (Bodenheimer, Chen, & Bennett; 2009). Although the aging population accounts for some of this increase in chronic illness, Bodenheimer et al. noted that behaviorally related risk factors, such as obesity and tobacco usage, are responsible for adding to this rate. Those authors are concerned about increased healthcare costs due to these multiple chronic healthcare problems and have asked if "robust public health measures" (p. 66) could flatten the healthcare cost curve by addressing and preventing many of the behavioral health risk factors. Psychology *is* the profession that should be addressing these behavioral health risk issues at the individual, family, and community levels (Rozensky, 2011, 2012). How are our ECPs being prepared to carrying out such population-based research, and evidence-based treatment research for these issues, and for ultimately providing the services needed to prevent or ameliorate these problems?

Rozensky (2012a) stated that, along with psychology's traditions of efficacy, effectiveness, and community-based research and treatment, the profession also should prepare some of its next generation of psychologists to engage in population-based approaches to the scientific study and treatment of the human condition. As our healthcare system evolves, this additional set of competencies will position psychology to use its critical thinking and research skills to bring important changes to the delivery system and, of course, highlight psychology's leading scientific and applied roles in understanding and positively influencing health behaviors (Rozensky, 2008). The U.S. Government's Healthy People 2010 and 2020 (U.S. Department of Health and Human Services; USDHHS, 2000) has long had a focus on the key role of health behaviors in health promotion, and the ACA, in its section Title IV—"Prevention of Chronic Disease and Improving Public Health," is looking for evidenced-based approaches to health promotion and a national disease prevention model for the public health. The *Advisory Committee on Interdisciplinary Community Base Linkages* (2012) of the USDHHS focused its 10th annual report to Congress and the Secretary of DHHS on building a robust interprofessional healthcare workforce prepared to address health behavior change in a cost-effective manner. How are health promotion, disease prevention, and population-based interventions infused in our curricula, and then, within the portfolio of scientific and clinical competencies of our new ECPs? How do our training programs assure those skills along with the already strong bedside treatment approaches for working with patients with various health and medical diagnoses (e.g., Johnson, Perry, & Rozensky, 2002)?

Accountability. Much of the focus on "accountability" in the ACA has to do with quality care, tracking clinical outcomes, building a financially accountable healthcare system, "pay for performance," (Rosenthal & Dudley, 2007), and otherwise containing healthcare costs. Much has been written on healthcare finances and healthcare reform, with some readings recommended as informative and entertaining (Reid, 2009; Gruber, 2011). But given the focus on *accountability* within ACA, professional psychology must use its scientific acumen to collect and publish outcome data to illustrate how psychological services are cost effective and produce cost savings across the healthcare system as well as having (clinical) effect sizes (e.g. Ferguson, 2009) that are equal to or surpass medical procedures–medical procedures where little question is raised about whether *those* treatments will be reimbursed within the changing healthcare system. This psychologically focused outcome information *must* include data regarding services for traditional mental health care, psychological services to those with medical illnesses, and disease prevention and health promotion approaches as well. Goodheart (2010) noted that psychology must make a strategic transformation regarding healthcare economics given the upcoming changes to the entire system. Where in the curriculum are our ECPs exposed to the acquisition of knowledge regarding healthcare economics and day-to-day implications of costs and cost containment for their involvement in patient care?

Evidence-based treatments and medical cost offset. The Institute of Medicine (2001) recommended in its classic *Crossing the Quality Chasm*, that successful healthcare outcomes can be best accomplished by the practice of evidenced-based healthcare. Psychology has embraced evidence-based practice (EBP) with its own set of conclusions that EBP "is the integration of the best available research with clinical experience in the context of patient characteristics, culture, and preferences" that assures effective psychological practice and enhances public health (APA, 2005; APA Presidential Task Force on Evidence-Based Practice, 2006; p. 280).

Although evidence-based psychological treatment outcome research provides robust data to support inclusion of psychological services within the evolving, integrated, interprofessional healthcare system, clinical outcomes that are *cost effective* and actually can contribute to cost savings in this accountable system will be expected and be beneficial to the field. Thus, are ECPs prepared for this type of data collection and program evaluation within the new healthcare system including the clinical use of EBP when appropriate? Are ECPs prepared to advocate for the use and reimbursement of EBP both locally and nationally? And, as Levant and Hasan (2008) have suggested, how are mentors and supervisors modeling the use of EBP for graduate students and ECPs and do trainees take the responsibility to ask for this level of training?

Continued collection of *medical cost offset* research data that supports psychological services (Chiles, Lambert, & Hatch, 1999; Tovian, 2004) should be built into routine program evaluation education of all of psychology's students. It should be a core competency taught to the next generation of healthcare psychologists. Treatment outcome research done by graduate students for their doctoral dissertations routinely should include *healthcare cost offset data* and that data should be reported routinely in the literature. This training will prepare a subset of ECPs to take a leadership role in evaluating the new healthcare system and provide data so that advocates for psychology can use that information in discussions with policy makers at the national, state and local services system levels (Rozensky, 2011).

Electronic healthcare records. The ACA is projected to lower healthcare expenditures by 0.5% (as part of the gross domestic product) and reduce the federal deficit by more than $100 billion over its first decade and then by $1 trillion between 2020 and 2030 (Orszag & Emanuel, 2010). Orszag and Emanuel go on to say that this decrement in costs will result from the establishment of "dynamic and flexible structures that can develop and institute policies that respond in real time to changes in the system in order to improve quality and restrain unnecessary cost growth" (p. 601). Some of this savings will be generated by more efficient information sharing via electronic health records through "greater integration" (p. 602) of care throughout the system (hospitals and outpatient services) and amongst providers (interprofessionalism). Richards (2009) attempted to strike a balance between professional psychology's focus on ethical responsibilities for maintaining patient confidentiality and the requirements of the Health Insurance Portability and Accountability Act (HIPAA) regarding the limitations of sharing of patients' personal health information (HIPAA, 1996). This is particularly important given the complications for psychologists working within an integrated, interprofessional healthcare work environment with medically ill patients where sharing information is key to quality care. How are ECPs being educated about the use of electronic healthcare records? Education and training programs should include literature in their curricula focused on the ethical, legal, regulatory and financial issues surrounding the evolving use of telehealth and electronic healthcare recordkeeping (e.g., Baker & Bufka, 2011). When possible, practicum opportunities that provide hands on use of direct services via telehealth technologies and direct exposure to the use of electronic healthcare records should be part of training. How else will ECPs be prepared for this component of the healthcare system?

Competency-based education. Continued preparation of the next generation of psychologists using competency-based education will be very important given a growing movement towards shared competencies in healthcare (Kaslow, Dunn, & Smith, 2008). Education and training programs and each individual ECP must have an appreciation of the issues surrounding development of a psychology workforce that will be responsive to evolving healthcare demands of the country. Roberts,

Borden, Christiansen, and Lopez, (2005) described the importance of this "culture of competency" in professional psychology and Fouad and colleagues (2009) highlighted the need for consistent, agreed upon, and measureable competencies in professional psychology. Measurable competencies will be key (D'Amour & Oandasan, 2005), given the focus on accountable care that must include a healthcare workforce with shared, interprofessional competencies. How does each education and training program in professional psychology incorporate defined and measurable foundational and functional competencies (Kaslow et al., 2002) in preparing our ECPs? Can each ECP innumerate the competencies they will need to successfully work within the (new) interprofessional, healthcare system? Does each psychologist have a clear picture of their own acquired competencies and those competencies they need to develop further?

Interprofessionalism. Possibly the most far reaching, functional change to healthcare is the ACA's focus on interprofessionalism. The history and current development of federal policy recommendations supporting "the integration of interprofessional education (IPE) into health professions education as a means of assuring a more collaborative health care workforce" has been described by Wilson, Rozensky, and Weiss (2010; p. 210). Interprofessionality "is defined as the development of a cohesive practice between professionals from different disciplines. It is the process by which professionals reflect on and develop ways of practicing that provides integrated and cohesive answers to the needs of the client/family/population" (D'Amour & Oandasan 2005, p. 9). The collaborative education of *all* health professionals for team-based care actually provides better clinical and financial performance while reducing clinician workload (Schuetz, Mann, & Evertt, 2010). Four shared competency domains—values and ethics, roles and responsibilities for collaborative practice, interprofessional communication, and team work and team-based care—form the basis of this interprofessional approach to healthcare (Interprofessional Education Collaborative, 2011; Interprofessional Education Collaborative Expert Panel, 2011).

The ACA clearly recognizes the value of interprofessional care and its impact on quality and cost savings in Section 3502, "Establishing Community Health Teams to Support the Patient Centered Medical Home." In Section 935, the Act recognizes provision of interprofessional, integrated disease prevention and health promotion services and provision of interprofessional treatment of chronic diseases. Section 747, "Primary Care Training and Enhancement," discusses clinical teaching settings and interprofessional models of health care including integration of physical and mental health services. How are ECPs being prepared for this interprofessional, team-based healthcare system? How are these interprofessional, team-based competencies built into the education and training system and graduate education curricula with real, practical opportunities to train ECPS to succeed in interprofessional teams (Scheutz, Mann, & Evertt, 2010)?

Structural changes and enhanced accountability in the healthcare system. The ACA describes the advent of structural changes to the healthcare system and enhanced expectations of accountability with the advent of accountable care organizations (ACO) and patient centered healthcare (medical) homes (PCMH) built on the foundation of interprofessionalism, interprofessional competencies, and team-based care. ACOs are designed to align financial incentives with accountability (quality-based outcomes) across the care continuum (Rittenhouse, Shortell, & Fisher, 2009), whereas PCMHs emphasizes strongly coordinated primary care services as the key to delivery system reforms. Fisher, Staiger, Bynum, and Gottlieb (2007) recommend that ACOs utilize an enhanced hospital medical staff model, in concert with hospitals themselves as the hub of the healthcare wheel. This structure will assure continuity of care designed to accomplish the mandates of the ACO concept—including performance measures that hold the healthcare professionals (the professional staff) in their community care and institutional roles and hospitals themselves accountable for quality, cost-effective care.

These hospital-based ACOs, most likely, will require enhanced accountability including the issues of measurable clinical and financial outcomes discussed earlier as well as explicit credentialing of providers. Credentialing of staff will assure that these systems of care only include the highest qualified providers as part of their system of care; an easily reviewable measure a priori. That is, credentialing will require *graduation from accredited education and training programs*, which, to many, suggests that providers have met (at least minimal) defined standards of training (Rozensky, 2011). There also will be an increasing expectation of specialty board certification—already routine expectations of hospital-based healthcare providers on the "professional staff"

(Rozensky, 2012). Robiner, Dixon, Miner, and Hong (2012) and Kaslow Graves, and Smith (2012) reinforce the importance of board certification for psychologists noting that, in medicine, board certification is a response to consumer desire for a measure of quality in healthcare and that patient prefer to see board certified providers.

These system-based expectations should stimulate professional psychology to review its training models, its commitment as a field to requiring universal accreditation of its training programs as a statement of quality assurance, and taking a hard look at the importance of both the general practice and specialized practice of psychology (Rozensky, 2011; 2012). This too requires the ECP to understand the credentialing requirements for participation in this evolving, accountable care system. How are the graduate programs preparing soon to be ECPs for the mechanics of seeking staff privileges, for understanding specialization and board certification, and assuring that they are preparing the next generation within only accredited education and training programs?

Nutting et al. (2011) describe PCMHs as a major improvement to primary care delivery with their focus on access, coordination, and comprehensive/integrated care, and the sustained (long- term) personal relationship between patient and a provider group, with patients actively engaged in this healthcare partnership. The Carter Center (2011) recommends that, in order to maximize the success of this enhanced primary care system, all health profession education and training programs should include education about the demographic, socioeconomic, financial, quality, political, and cultural issues affecting healthcare services, educate students about development of high functioning teams in primary care, and educate providers about the incidence and prevalence of behavioral conditions in primary care settings. How are professional psychology programs doing in following the Carter Center's recommendations so that ECPs demonstrate competencies in these areas and thus, can be viable members of the PCHM movement?

Are graduate training programs in professional psychology incorporating knowledge-based content and practical, clinical competencies for practice in the accountable care and primary care environments? Is the field of psychology, and each individual program making certain that ECPs are being trained in only accredited programs, given the increased demand for accountability in the evolving healthcare system (Rozensky, 2012)? How

are students being prepared to enter the healthcare system where specialization is a growing expectation and where lifelong learning might suggest specialization is even more pressing (Rozensky and Kaslow, 2012)?

Supply, demand, and the professional psychology workforce. Professional psychology must have an accurate accounting of the current psychology workforce (who is doing what and where are they working?) and an understanding of its readiness for the service demands based on the upcoming changes to the healthcare system (Rozensky 2011; 2012). We must have a clear picture of the future demands for psychological services (what *should* we be doing and in what work setting?) so the field can prepare the correct number of psychologists needed, with the requisite special(ist) skills\competencies required by healthcare reform. Do our graduates know what those demands will be so they can place themselves in jobs to meet those demands?

Some authors (e.g. Stedman, Schoenfeld, Caroll, & Allen, 2007) have raised concerns about a possible oversupply of psychologists, while others (Rozensky, Grus, Belar, Nelson, & Kohout, 2007) advocate for a systematic workforce analysis to provide a data-based approach in order to plan for the future of education and training programs in psychology–especially when the field must consider the number of graduate students seeking predoctoral internships. This becomes even more acute when that training only occurs within accredited programs. The CWS (APA, 2009) reported that the majority (54.5%) of psychologists work in a wide range of institutional work environments as their primary place of employmentwhile45.5% indicated their work setting was "private practice." It remains to be known if this is the appropriate number of psychologists and if they are working in the correct healthcare venues in anticipation of the evolving healthcare system demands. How are academic and clinical training programs using the available workforce data to help shape their training of the next, and next, cohorts of ECPs? How are the ECPs of tomorrow—whether beginning their education today, choosing their next training venue, or establishing their own lifelong learning plans—using available workforce data and available data on professional success to choose from which academic institutions they will seek their training, what competencies they will need to develop to succeed in their chosen career work setting, or whether they should consider additional, specialized training?

Preparation for Success in the World of Tomorrow: The Responsibilities of both Early Career Psychologists and Education and Training Programs in Professional Psychology

"America's health care system is methodically entering into the 21st century with society's leaders steadily developing the expectation of possessing an unprecedented availability for documented accountability" (DeLeon & Kazdin, 2010, p. 314). In order for ECPs to succeed in an environment of heightened accountability, each individual ECP must take responsibility for being accountable for their own preparation for success. But, more so, each graduate education and training program must be accountable for providing the highest quality of education and training necessary to prepare the next, and next, and next cohorts of successful ECPs. We will review briefly the trends identified earlier and make some recommendations for programs and students to maximize opportunities for success as ECPs.

Truth in Advertising, Student and Early Career Choices, and the Professional Psychology Workforce

The legal doctrine of *caveat emptor*—buyer beware (e.g., Garner, 2009)—suggests that the buyer cannot recover damages from the seller if the property in question has defects unless such defects are concealed or misrepresented. Further, the doctrine suggests that the buyer must examine or judge for themselves a given product that they are considering purchasing. However, in the majority opinion in one of the more notable, interesting, and entertaining legal cases on this topic (*Stambovsky v. Ackley*, 1991), the Court said that the "plaintiff, to his horror, discovered that the house he had recently contracted to purchase was widely reputed to be possessed by poltergeists" and he had *not been informed* of this information when purchasing the house. The court eventually ruled that when this "haunted house" was sold to this uninformed buyer "the seller not only takes unfair advantage of the buyer's ignorance but has created and perpetuated a condition about which he (the buyer) is unlikely even to inquire…" and that the buyer "cannot be expected to have any familiarity with the folklore" of the town where the house in question was located.

It is imperative that young psychologists in training take responsibility for understanding the education and training issues in the field into which they are entering. They should work directly with their faculty mentor on, but be responsible for their ownership of, their own plan of study, and they must take care to understand the trends and workforce issues in their new field. This would include choice of their educational and training programs, knowledge of emerging areas of practice, employment opportunities, and what continuing education responsibilities exist in order to remain current in both the broad and general and specialized practice areas in professional psychology.

However, it may be even more clear that the *providers* of education and training in professional psychology (that is, faculty, program administrators, and training staff members) have a responsibility to the next generation(s) they are educating; a responsibility *to inform the consumer* of the education and training system about all these issues including "product information" about the house they are about to enter. This might even be considered as explicit in the APA Ethics Code (APA, 2002) section 7.0 where those responsible for education and training programs "take responsible steps to ensure that there is a current and accurate description of the program content….., training goals and objectives, stipends and benefits…made readily available to all interested parties" (p. 1068). Graduate programs *must* be responsible for making programmatic information transparent to students who might well be naïve as to a broader range of variable leading to what makes a successful career (that folklore described in *Stambovsky*). Likewise, they must *communicate* those variables clearly, so when students choose an academic home for their own education, they can make an informed decision about their training options by understanding such variables as financial support, debt load, chances of passing the national licensing examination, internship match rates, initial salary expectations, and the ultimate (professional) trajectory of the program's graduates. Although program statistics do not necessarily speak directly to the success of any one individual student or trainee, clearly, program output—the ultimate success of program graduates—should be made as concrete to students as poltergeists are transparent to the unwary homebuyer.

With that in mind, programs routinely should publish and update, and potential students should review in detail, the type of programmatic outcome data suggested by Gaddy, Charlot-Swilley, Nelson, and Reich (1995; that is, student involvement in teaching, research, publications, and clinical work; time to degree, initial and subsequent employment); these data are part and parcel of the CoA information collected and are used to support the review of accredited programs and programs seeking accreditation (APA, 2011a). Gaddy et al. clearly state that educational programs "are obliged to establish systematic assessment procedures to account for the outcomes of their operation, including the types of outcomes that reflect faculty and student development, contributions of the program to its institution's mission, and the *achievements of its graduates* (italics added)" (p. 512).

Possibly the most pressing issue for many of those young colleagues working toward soon becoming ECPs is the ongoing question of "supply and demand" in both the number of students seeking doctoral internships and the question of the needed supply of psychologists to meet the service demands of the general population over the next epoch of healthcare in the United States (Rozensky, et al, 2007; Rozensky, 2011). Rodolfa et al. (2007) even suggested that it is an *ethical mandate* to address this issue and that graduate programs must report internship match rates, time to degree, and costs to students. Grus, McCutcheon, and Berry (2011) detailed the history of the internship imbalance and the Herculean efforts untaken to help manage that challenge. Callahan, Collins, and Klonoff (2010) found that the only significant variable that predicted whether given student is chosen for an internship (matching or not matching) was the number of invitations for interviews for internship with the participants in their study submitting an average of 14.47 applications for internship, obtaining an average of 7.81 interviews, and 85.2% of the total sample being chosen\matched with an internship. Is it possible that the number of interviews offered, however, reflects the overall quality of the application, while the many variables studied by Callahan et al. (gender, sexual orientation, ethnicity, socioeconomic status, geographic restrictions, having dependents, PsyD versus PhD, status of dissertation, etc.) are just parts of the gestalt that even their multivariant approach has not explicated? No matter what, Parent and Williamson (2010), in identifying the specific, relatively small number of graduate programs that contributed almost 30% of those students who did not find accredited internships, said, "Failure of programs to take action to improve internship match rates and to consider the impact of disparities in different demand curves that exist in psychology (student demand for graduate programs and market demand for psychologists) is a disservice to psychology as a profession, to students of psychology, to professionals, and to all the populations psychologists serve" (p 120). How adherent are programs to the concept of "truth in advertising," what information is routinely presented (and updated), how are undergraduates prepared to evaluate possible graduate programs in professional psychology wherein they are considering matriculating, and how do matriculated students participate with their faculty in reviewing program quality and outcome to assure success of graduates?

Recommendations for Those on the Way to Becoming ECPs and for the Programs Helping Them Achieve that Goal

Although predicting the future is not easy, studies by Prinstein (2012) and Taylor, Neimeyer, and Rozensky (2012 a,b) offer pictures of what rank-and-file members and experts in the field see as the evolution of professional psychology over the next 20 years. The APA CWS provides snapshots regarding current workforce issues in professional psychology like salaries and workplace settings. Individual, soon-to-be ECPs must avail themselves of as much information as they can to make the best choices they can as they construct their plans of study in preparation for their future. Graduate, internship, postdoctoral, and continuing education programs in professional psychology must use available data as part of their ongoing strategic planning efforts as they review and modify their curricula and seek contemporary training opportunities to assure they are preparing a competent workforce of (new) psychologists to enter the professional workforce of tomorrow.

Throughout this article, recommendations were embedded in the form of questions for ECPs and for the faculty and staff of education and training programs. These questions suggest topics for discussion when planning successful education and training programs and for soon-to-be ECPs to consider at various steps throughout their education and training sequence. Outcome data was presented that authors suggest relates to learning opportunities that will maximize the success of the next generation(s) of ECPs.

Table 31.1 brings together, rephrases, or expands some of those questions presented in this chapter. Table 31.1 can serve as a list of discussion points for faculty, for each student, for faculty and students together, and for national leaders in professional psychology. This list should be part of planning strategically for the field of professional psychology, for programmatic improvement and quality education

Table 31.1. Questions to Consider When Maximizing the Opportunity for the Future Success of ECPS

- **Programmatic Variables**

  - How are academic and clinical training programs using the available psychology workforce data to help shape their training of the next, and next, cohorts of ECPs?
  - How clearly are graduate programs making 'truth in advertising' information transparent (e.g., financial support, debt load, chances of passing the national licensing examination, initial salary expectations, ultimate (professional) trajectory of the program's graduates, accreditation status) to students who need that data to choose an academic home for their education? Is there similar information that internships, postdoctoral programs, and continuing education programs should share with potential students?
    1. How adherent are programs to the concept of 'truth in advertising,' what information is presented, and how often is it truly updated?
  - How are undergraduates who wish to become psychologists prepared to evaluate possible graduate programs? How do matriculated graduate students participate *with* their faculty in reviewing program quality and program outcomes to assure success of (future) graduates?
  - Do the graduate programs within each of the three general training models in professional psychology (clinical scientist, scientist practitioner, scholar-practitioner) actually build into their curricula specific, workplace-related competencies to assure preparation for success in the venues towards which their specific graduates gravitate?
    1. Do the workplace choices reflected by graduates of a given program actually reflect acquisition of those competencies and thus graduates go to work where they are best prepared to succeed?
  - Given that scientific rigor in doctoral-level training might be the best predictor of better professional outcomes (accredited internships, higher licensing examination scores, higher likelihood of becoming board certified), how do programs plan for, and then evaluate, the scientific focus and critical thinking competencies within their curriculum?
    1. Given the growing interprofessional healthcare environment, how are students acquainted with the concepts and competencies of successful team science (http://teamscience.net/about.html)?
  - Given higher pass rates on the EPPP for those examinees who graduated from *accredited* doctoral programs than those from non-accredited programs, what are non-accredited programs doing to enhance quality and seek and attain accreditation?
  - What academic and training situations (course work and practical training) are most efficacious in developing those competencies needed to assure success as an ECP? How are those competencies measured and evaluated by each program?
  - How is evidenced based treatment built into education & training experience of each soon to be ECP? How are those ECPs prepared to utilize that approach within the evolving healthcare system?
  - How has each education and training program in professional psychology incorporated defined and measurable competencies (foundational and functional; knowledge, skills and attitudes) into their knowledge and skills based curricula?
  - How are ECPs being prepared for the evolving, interprofessional, team-based healthcare system based upon the expectations of the Affordable Care Act?
    1. How are these interprofessional, team-based competencies built into the education and training system with real time, practical opportunities to train ECPS to succeed when working in interprofessional teams?
    2. How are the graduate programs and internships preparing soon to be ECPs for seeking staff privileges within accountable care organizations?
    3. Are graduate training programs in professional psychology incorporating knowledge-based content and practical, clinical team-based competencies for practice in the upcoming accountable care organization and primary care environments?
    4. How are students being prepared to enter the healthcare system where specialization (board certification) is a growing expectation as part of enhanced accountability and where lifelong learning might suggest specialization is even more pressing?
    5. Once again, are all programs accredited so as to provide the most face-valid, basic, entry level credential of quality education for each of its graduates who are joining healthcare workforce in the accountable care system?

- **Individual Student-Trainee-ECP variables**

  - How is the concept of "self assurance" addressed in the preparation of each ECP as they embark on their career of success, growth, and fulfillment?
  - How is the ECP prepared for managing the competency of "self care?"

(continued)

Table 31.1 (continued)

- Do healthcare workforce data and program outcome data provide a measure of possible 'steerage' or direction for those choosing their graduate training (program) especially when they have a particular workplace venue or specialty focus as their ultimate professional goal?
- How do we define quality education to those seeking training in professional psychology? How do students understand the importance of matriculating in an accredited training program as the first step towards quality training and ultimately maximizing successful outcomes from their training?
- How does each soon be ECP understand that it is imperative, as young psychologists in training, that they take responsibility for understanding the contemporary education and training issues of the field into which they are entering, that they work directly with their faculty mentor on–but be responsible for ownership of–their own plan of study, and they take care to understand the workforce issues in their new field? How do faculty maximize this positive interaction as part of their prescribed mentoring role?
- What does a soon to be ECP need to ask of his or her graduate program and mentor–whether beginning their education, choosing their next training venue, or establishing their own lifelong learning plans–in order to receive the guidance necessary to use available workforce data and available data on predictors of professional success, to choose which institutions they will seek their training and what competencies they must develop to succeed in their chosen career work setting?
- Can each ECP innumerate the competencies needed to successfully work within the (new) healthcare system? Does each individual have a clear picture of their own (current) acquired competencies and those competencies in need of further development?
- How does each individual ECP establish their own lifelong learning plan to assure ongoing success?
- How does each individual ECP determine whether they need additional preparation to practice within a specialty in professional psychology (e.g., http://www.apa.org/ed/graduate/specialize/crsppp.aspx) and whether they should seek board certification (e.g., http://www.abpp.org/i4a/pages/index.cfm?pageid=3285) to enhance their career success with the new, accountable healthcare system?

- **Societal Trends**

- How have programs incorporated awareness of society's demographic trends (diversity, aging, chronic illness) into their curricula? How do programs utilize available practice guidelines focused on diversity and cultural issues (e.g., http://www.apa.org/practice/guidelines/index.aspx) as part of the preparation of soon to be ECPs to enhance opportunities for success within our changing society?
- Given the changes to healthcare system based on the ACA, where in the preparation of ECPs do we find preparation for success given the following?
  1. Accountable care
  2. Team-based, interprofessional care & interprofessionalism
  3. Healthcare economics
  4. Evidence-based care
  5. Medical cost offset, program evaluation, cost effectiveness
  6. Electronic healthcare records and telehealth-based services including legal and ethical issues brought forth by this type of change to the healthcare system

---

- Psychology *is* the profession that should be addressing behavioral health risk issues at the individual, family and community levels. How are our ECPs being prepared for these services needs given their focus in the ACA (e.g., ACICBL, 2012; Healthy People 2020)?

---

and training at the local level, and for each individual student as they prepare for their own plan of study to become a successful ECP.

Conclusion

Foran-Tuller, Robiner, Breland-Noble, Otey-Scot, Wybork, King and Sanders (2012) presented the details of an "early career boot camp" (p 117) that took place as part of a professional conference. This intensive workshop engaged ECP participants in addressing strategic career goals including a focus on the domains of research, teaching/training/supervision, clinical service responsibilities, program development and evaluation, and professional issues such as work and personal life balance, departmental politics, keeping a job, networking, and involvement in professional organizations. Although this particular boot camp was focused on the immediate needs of ECPs, a similar type workshop could be conducted in any graduate department or training program, at any level of the education and training sequence, with doctoral students, interns, or postdoctoral fellows. Content could address similar domains, but be tailored to the current knowledge level and competencies of the attendees, with the ultimate goal of maximizing early career success.

Departments and programs could stipulate in their job expectations for faculty, a mentoring policy that includes *specific* expectations that mentoring include discussions of maximizing success for the soon-to-be ECPs. Faculty culture could include an expectation of directly discussing how mentoring skills (Forehand, 2008) could be enhanced with the goal of assuring alumni success. Honoring the accomplishments of program graduates (i.e., awards, publications, promotions, job changes, and personal individual and family activities) would assure that success is an explicitly acknowledged, discussed, and valued part of the education and training experience. Bringing back program alumni to speak about their scientific, scholarly, and applied accomplishments would introduce students and trainees to successful role models, offer a broader opportunity for students to ask questions about what brings about future success, and encourages program faculty to seek feedback about how they can maximize ECP accomplishment.

Using the questions listed in Table 31.1, faculty, those soon-to-be ECPs, and ECPs, can engage in a dialogue to assure that contemporary issues in society and the field of professional psychology are being addressed within each student's plan of study and within each education and training program's self-study and strategic plan for program development and growth. This will assure the success of the next generations of Early Career Psychologists and the continued vitality of the field of professional psychology.

You must live in the present,
Launch yourself on every wave,
Find your eternity in each moment.
– *Henry David Thoreau*

References

Advisory Committee on Interdisciplinary Community Based Linkages (ACICBL). (2012). *Preparing the interprofessional healthcare workforce to address health behavior change: Ensuring a high quality and cost-effective healthcare system (10th Annual Report to Congress and the Secretary of DHHS)*. Rockville, MD: Health.

American Psychological Association (2002). *Guidelines on multicultural education, training, research, practice and organizational change*. APA Author.

American Psychological Association (2002). Ethical principles of psychologists and code of conduct. *American Psychologist, 57*, 1060–1073.

American Psychological Association (2004). Guidelines for psychological practice with older adults. *American Psychologists, 59*, 236–260.

American Psychological Association (2005) Policy statement on evidence-based practice in psychology. Retrieved from http://www.apa.org/practice/guidelines/index.aspx

American Psychological Association. (2006). *Building bridges: Opportunities for learning, networking, and leadership*. Washington, DC: Author.

American Psychological Association. (2011a). *5 Year summary report: Commission on Accreditation*. Washington, DC: Author.

American Psychological Association (2011b). The guidelines for psychological practice with lesbian, gay, and bisexual Clients. Retrieved from http://www.apa.org/pi/lgbt/resources/guidelines.aspx

American Psychological Association (2012). Guidelines for assessment of and intervention with persons with disabilities. Retrieved from http://www.apa.org/pi/disability/resources/assessment-disabilities.aspx

American Psychological Association, Center for Psychology Workforce Analysis and Research. (2007). *2005 doctorate employment survey*. Washington, DC: Author.

APA Presidential Task Force on Evidence-Based Practice. (2006). Evidence-based practice in psychology. *American Psychologist, 61*, 271–285. doi:10.1037/0003-066X.61.4.271.

Deborah C. Baker & Lynn F. Bufka (2011). Preparing for the telehealth world: Navigating legal, regulatory, reimbursement, and ethical issues in an electronic age. *Professional Psychology: Research and Practice, 42*, 405–411. doi: 10.1037/a0025037

Bodenheimer, T., Chen, E., & Bennett, H. D. (2009). Confronting the growing burden of chronic disease: Can the US health care workforce do the job? *Health Affairs, 28*, 64–74. doi:10.1377/ hlthaff.28.1.64.

Boelen, C. & Woollard, B. (2009). Social accountability and accreditation: a new frontier for educational institutions. *Medical Education, 43*, 887–894 doi.org/10.1111/j.1365-2923.2009.03413.x

Baker, D. C. & Bufka, L.F. (2011). Preparing for the telehealth world: Navigating legal, regulatory, reimbursement and ethical issues in an electronic age. *Professional Psychology: Research and Practice, 42*, 405–411. doi: 10.1037/a0025037

Callahan, J. L., Collins, F. L., & Klonoff, E. A. (2010). An examination of applicant characteristics of successfully matched interns: Is the glass half full or half empty and leaking miserably? *Journal of Clinical Psychology, 66*, 1–16. doi: 10.1002/jclp

Carter Center. (2011). Five prescriptions for ensuring the future of primary care. *Proceedings from the Health Education Summit, October 5 and 6, 2010*. Retrieved from http://www.carter-center.org/news/pr/ReinvigoratingPrimaryCareSystem.html.

Cherry D. K., Messenger L. C. &, Jacoby, A. M. (2000). An examination of training model outcomes in clinical psychology programs. *Professional Psychology: Research and Practice, 31*, 562–568. doi 10.1037/0735-7028.31.5.562

Chiles, J. A., Lambert, M., & Hatch, A. L. (1999). The impact of psychological interventions on medical cost offset: A meta-analytic review. *Clinical Psychology: Science and Practice, 6*, 204–220. doi:10.1093/clipsy/6.2.204.

Collins, Jr., F. L., Callahan, J. L., & Klonoff, E. A. (2007). A scientist-practitioner perspective of the internship match and imbalance: The stairway to competence. *Training* and Education in Professional Psychology, 1, 267–275. doi 10.1037/1931-3918.1.4.267

D'Amour, D., & Oandasan, I. (2005). Interprofessionality as the field of interprofessional practice and interprofessional education: An emerging concept. *Journal of Interprofessional Care, 19, Suppl 1*, 8–20. doi:10.1080/13561820500081604

DeLeon, P. H. & Kazdin, A. E. (2010). Public Policy: Extending psychology's contributions to national priorities. *Rehabilitation Psychology, 55* 311–319. doi: 10.1037/a0020450

Fisher, E. S., Staiger, D. O., Bynum, J. P. W., & Gottlieb, D. J. (2007). Creating accountable care organizations: The extended hospitalmedical staff. *Health Affairs, 26*, w44–w57. doi:10.1377/hlthaff.26.1.w44.

Fouad, N. A., Grus, C. L., Hatcher, R. L., Kaslow, N. J., Hutchings, P. S., Madson, M. B., Collins, F. L., &Crossman, R. E. (2009). Competency benchmarks: A model for understanding and measuring competence in professional psychology across training levels. *Training and Education in Professional Psychology, 3*, S5–S26. doi:10.1037/a0015832.

Ferguson, C. J. (2009). An effect size primer: A guide for clinicians and researchers. *Professional Psychology: Research and Practice, 40*, 532–538. doi 10.1037/a0015808

Foran-Tuller, K, Robiner, W. H., Alfiee Breland-Noble, A. Otey-Scott, S., Wryobeck, J. King, C. & Sanders, K. (2012). Early career boot camp: A novel mechanism for enhancing early career development for psychologists in academic healthcare, *Journal of Clinical Psychology in Medical Settings, 19*, 117–125 doi 10.1007/s10880-011-9289-5

Forehand, R. L. (2008). The art and science of mentoring in psychology: A necessary practice to ensure our future. *American Psychologist, 63*, 744–755. doi: 10.1037/0003-066X.63.8.744

Gaddy, C. D., Charlot-Swilley, D., Nelson, P. D., & Reich, J. N. (1995). Selected outcomes of accredited programs. *Professional Psychology: Research and Practice, 26*, 507–513. doi: 10.1037/0735-7028.26.5.507

Garner, B. A. (Ed.). (2009). *Black's Law Dictionary, Deluxe 9th Edition*. St. Paul, MN: Thomas Reuters.

Goodheart, C. D. (2010). Economics and psychology practice: What we need to know and why. *Professional Psychology: Research and Practice, 41*, 189–195. DOI: 10.1037/a0019498

Green, A. G. & Hawley, G. C. (2009). Early career psychologists: Understanding, engaging, and mentoring tomorrow's leaders. *Professional Psychology: Research and Practice, 40*, 206–212, doi: 10.1037/a0012504

Grus, C. L., McCutcheon, S. T., & Berry, S. L. (2011). Actions by professional psychology education and training groups to mitigate the internship imbalance. *Training and Education in Professional Psychology, 5*, 193–201. doi: 10.1037/a0026101

Gruber, J. (2011). *Health Care Reform* New York: Farrar, Straus, & Giroux.

Health Insurance Portability and Accountability Act. (1996). P.L. 104–191, 42 U.S.C. 1320d.

Institute of Medicine. (2001). *Crossing the quality chasm: A new health system for the 21st Century.* Washington, DC: National Academies Press.

Interprofessional Education Collaborative. (2011). Team-based competencies: Building a shared foundation for education and clinical practice: Conference proceedings. Washington DC, February 16 and 17, 2011.

Interprofessional Education Collaborative Expert Panel. (2011). *Core competencies for interprofessional*

collaborative practice: Report of an expert panel. Washington, DC: Interprofessional Education Collaborative.

Johnson, S. B., Perry, N. W., & Rozensky, R. H. (2002) *Handbook of clinical health psychology: Medical disorders and behavioral applications. Volume 1.* Washington, DC: American Psychological Association.

Judge, T. A. & Hurst, C. (2008). How the rich (and happy) get richer (and happier): Relationship of core self-evaluations to trajectories in attaining work success. *Journal of Applied Psychology, 93*, 849–863. doi: 10.1037/0021-9010.93.4.849

Kaslow, N. J., Dunn, S. E., & Smith, C. O. (2008). Competencies for psychologists in academic health centers (AHCs) *Journal of Clinical Psychology in Medical Settings, 15*, 18–27, doi: 10.1007/s10880-008-9094-y

Kaslow, N. J., Graves, C. C., & Smith C. O. (2012). Specialization in psychology and health care reform. *Journal of Clinical Psychology in Medical Settings, 9*, 12–21, doi: 10.1007/s10880-011-9273-0

Levant, R. F. & Hasan, N. T. (2008). Evidence-based practice in psychology. *Professional Psychology: Research and Practice, 39*, 658–662. doi: 10.1037/0735-7028.39.6.658

McFall, R. (2006). Doctoral training in clinical psychology. *Annual Review of Clinical Psychology, 2*, 21–49. doi: 10.1146/annurev.clinpsy.2.022305.095245

Michalski, D.S. & Kohout, J.L. (2011). The state of psychology health service provider workforce. *American Psychologists, 66*, 825–834 DOI: 10.1037/a0026200

Michalski, D., Kohout, J., Wicherski, M. & Hart, B. (2011). *2009 doctorate employment survey.* Washington, DC: American Psychological Association.

Myers, S. B., Sweeney, A. C., Popick, V., Wesley, K., Bordfeld, A. & Fingerhut, R. (2012). Self-care practices and perceived stress levels among psychology graduate students. *Training and Education in Professional Psychology, 6*, 55–66 DOI: 10.1037/a0026534

Nutting, P. A., Crabtree, B. F., Miller, W. L., Stange, K. C., Stewart, E., & Jaen, C. (2011). Transforming physician practices to patient-centered medical homes: Lessons from the National Demonstration Project. *Health Affairs, 30*, 439–445. doi: 10.1377/hlthaff.2 010.0159.

Ortman, J. M., & Guarneri, C. E. (2009). United States population projections: 2000 to 2050. Retrieved from http://www.census.gov/population/www/porjections/analytical-document09.pdf.

Orszag, P. R. & Emanuel, E. J. (2010). Health care reform and cost control. *New England Journal of Medicine, 363*, 601–603. doi.org/10.1056/NEJMp1006571

Parent, M. C. & Williamson, J. B. (2010). Program disparities in unmatched internship applicants. *Training and Education in Professional Psychology, 4*, 116–120. doi: 10.1037/a0018216

Peterson, D. R. (2003). Unintended consequences: Ventures and misadventures in the education of professional psychologists. *American Psychologist, 58*, 791–800. doi. 10.1037/0003–066X.58.10.791

Plaut, V. C. (2010). Diversity science: Why and how difference makes a difference. *Psychological Inquiry, 21*, 77–99. doi 10.1080/10478401003676501

Prinstein, M. (2012). *Psychologists' and trainees' perceptiion of the future of clinical psychology.* Chapel Hill, NC: Author.

Public Law No: 111–148, 111th Congress: Patient Protection and Affordable Care Act. (2010). 124 STAT. 119. Retrieved from www.gpo.gov/fdsys/pkg/PLAW-111publ148/pdf/PLAW-111publ148.pdf.

Reid, T. R. (2009). *The healing of America: A global quest for better, cheaper, and fairer health care.* New York: Penguin Press.

Rittenhouse, D. R., Shortell, S. M., & Fisher, E. S. (2009). Primary care and accountable care—two essential elements of delivery system reform. *New England Journal of Medicine, 361,* 2301–2303. doi:10.1056/NEJMp0909327.

Robiner, W.N., Dixon, K.E., Miner, J.L. & Hong, B.A. (2012) Board certification in psychology: Insights from medicine and hospital psychology. *Journal of Clinical Psychology in Medical Settings, 19,* 30–40. doi 10.1007/s10880-011-9280-1

Rodolfa, E. R., Bell, D. J., Bieschke, K. J., Davis, C., & Peterson, R. L. (2007). The internship match: Understanding the problem–seeking solutions. *Training and Education in Professional Psychology, 1,* 225–228. doi: 10.1037/1931-3918.1.4.225

Rogers, M. (2009). Cultural competency training in professional psychology. In R. H. Dana & J. R. Allen (Eds.), *Cultural competency training in a global society* (pp. 157–173). New York: Springer. doi:10.1007/978-0-387-79822-6_9

Rosenthal, M. B., & Dudley, A. (2007). Pay-for-performance: Will the latest payment trend improve care? *JAMA, 297,* 740– 744. doi:10.1001/jama.297.7.740

Rozensky, R. H. (2008). Healthy People 2020: Good vision for psychology's future. *Independent Practitioner, 28,* 188–191.

Rozensky, R. H. (2011). The institution of the institutional practice of psychology: Healthcare reform and psychology's future workforce. *American Psychologist, 66,* 794–808. doi: 10.1037/a0024621

Rozensky, R. H. (2012a). Health care reform: preparing the psychology workforce. *Journal of Clinical Psychology in Medical Settings, 19,* 5–11. doi:10.1007/s10880-011-9287-7

Rozensky, R. H. (2012b). Psychology in academic health centers: A true healthcare home. *Journal of Clinical Psychology in Medical Settings, 19,* doi:10.1007/s10880-012-9312-5

Rozensky, R. H., Grus, C. L., Belar, C. D., Nelson, P. D., & Kohout, J. L. (2007). Using workforce analysis to answer questions related to the internship imbalance and career pipeline in professional psychology. *Training and Education in Professional Psychology, 1,* 238–248. doi:10.1037/1931-3918.1.4.238

Rozensky, R. H., Johnson, N. G., Goodheart, C. D., & Hammond, W. R. (2004). *Psychology builds a healthy world: Opportunities research and practice.* Washington, DC: American Psychological Association. doi:10.1037/10.

Sayette, M. A., Norcross, J. C., & Dimoff, J. D. (2011).The heterogeneity of clinical psychology Ph.D. programs and the distinctiveness of APCS programs. *Clinical Psychology: Science and Practice, 18,* 4–11. doi:org/10.1111/j.1468-2850.2010.01227.x

Schaffer, J. B., Rodolfa, E., Owen, J., Lipkins, R., Webb, C. & Horn, J. (2012). The examination for professional practice in psychology: New data–practical implications. *Training and Education in Professional Psychology, 6,* 1–7, doi: 10.1037/a0026823

Scheutz, B., Mann, E., & Evertt, W. (2010). Educating health professionals collaboratively for team-based primary care. *Health Affairs, 29,* 1476–1480. doi:10.1377/hlthaff.2010.00526 78–000

Stambovsky v. Ackley, 169 A.D.2d 254 (NY App. Div. 1991)

Stedman, J. M., Schoenfeld, L. S., Caroll, K., & Allen, T. F. (2007). The internship supply-demand crisis: Time for solution is now. *Training and Education in Professional Psychology, 3,* 135–139. doi:10.1037/a0016048.

Sweet, J. J., Meyer, D. G., Nelson, N. W., & Moberg, P. J. (2011). The TCN/AACN 2010 "salary survey": Professional practice, beliefs, and incomes of U.S. neuropsychologists. *The Clinical Neuropsychologist, 25,* 12–61. doi: 10.1080/13 854046.2010.544165

Taylor, J. M., Neimeyer, G. J., & Rozensky, R. H. (August 2012,). Crystal ball gazing: A Delphi poll of the half-life of knowledge in professional psychology. Poster session presented at the 2012 American Psychological Association Conference, Orlando, FL.

Tovian, S. (2004). Health services and health care economics: The health psychology marketplace. *Health Psychology, 23,* 138–141. doi:10.1037/0278-6133.23.2.138

U.S. Bureau of Labor Statistics. (2010). Psychologists. In *Occupational outlook handbook, 2010–2011 edition.* Retrieved from http://www.bls.gov/ooh/

U.S. Census Bureau. (2011). 2010 Census shows America's diversity. Retrieved from http://www.census.gov/2010census/

U.S. Department of Health and Human Services. (2000). *Healthy People 2020: Understanding and improving health.* Washington, DC: US Department of Health and Human Services, Government Printing Office.

Vincent, G. K., & Velkoff, V. A. (2010). *The next four decades, The older population in the United States: 2010 to 2050.* Current Population Reports (pp. 25–1138). Washington, DC: US Census Bureau.

Wilson, S. L., Rozensky, R. H., & Weiss, J. (2010). The Advisory Committee on Interdisciplinary Community-based linkages and the federal role in advocating for interprofessional education. *Journal of Allied Health, 39,* 210–215.

INDEX

competence (*Cont.*)
　conceptualizing and assessing,
　　221–223
　ethics, 350–352
　evaluating trainees with, problems,
　　265–266
　evaluation of, 351
　multiple factors of gender, 427
　principles for assessment, 253
　professional, and confidence, 276
　religious issues in practice, 472–474
　trainees with problems of professional
　　competence (TPPC), 266, 378
competence constellations, 11
competencies
　acquisition during practicum training,
　　137–139
　American Board of Professional
　　Psychology (ABPP), 128t, 129t
　assessment of, 316
　cultural, 439–440, 443–444
　"eddy effect", 443–444
　mentoring, 278–280
　professional psychology, 3–5, 69,
　　398–399, 532–533
　supervisor, 295–297
Competencies Conference, 55, 109–110,
　　135, 157, 176, 187, 222, 253, 320,
　　323, 532
Competency Assessment Toolkit for
　　Professional Psychology, 113
competency-based education and
　　training, 105–107
　ASPPB practice analysis, 114
　assessment toolkit, 113
　Benchmarks Competencies Model,
　　110–112
　challenges and vision for future,
　　115–116
　Competencies Conference, 109–110
　continuing professional development,
　　114–115
　doctoral-level initiatives, 109–113
　health professions, 107–108
　internship training, 166
　licensure, 113–114
　nondoctoral models in psychology,
　　108–109
　Pikes Peak Model, 112
　postdoctoral training, 181
　psychology workforce, 556–557
　Practicum Competencies Outline, 110
　recommendations, 115–116
　specialty-specific competency models,
　　112–113
Competency Benchmarks, 187, 398,
　　399t, 400
The Competency Benchmarks
　　Project, 363
Competency Benchmarks Work
　　Group, 222
Competency Conference, 315
Competency Cube, 532, 542

competency domains
　cognitive-behavioral orientation, 75
　humanistic-existential orientation, 77
　integrative training, 81–82
　psychodynamic orientation, 73
　systemic orientation, 79
Competency Evaluation Rating
　　Forms, 258
competency movement
　core curriculum, 54–55
　definition, 253–254
　evaluation, 252–253
　reactions to, 254–255
Competency Remediation Plan
　　Template, 363
computer-aided psychotherapies, 521
Conference of State Psychology
　　Associations, 202
confidence, mentoring, 276
confidentiality
　boundaries of trainee, 328–329, 331
　clinical internships, 368–369
　documents governing, 366–367
　duty to protect, 371–372
　HIPAA vs. FERPA, 367–368
　limits for supervisors, 369–370
　policy and procedure documents, 358
　relationships, 357
　remediation plans, 365–366
Connecticut, licensing act in
　　psychology, 202
consortia models, internship
　　governance, 161
consultation
　internships, 369
　practicum training, 138, 151
　psychology program leaders, 535t, 541
consumption, research findings, 188
content
　curricular assessment and gender, 423
　psychotherapy supervision, 422
context, 400
　core curriculum, 62–64
　exercise of privilege, 402–405
　identity status, 400–402
　privilege and oppression, 400–405
　training, 384–385, 388–389
continuing education
　best practices in, 220–221
　conceptualizing and assessing
　　competence, 221–223
　designating activities, 214–217
　developing infrastructure of, 229–230
　diminishing durability of professional
　　knowledge, 228–229
　evaluation, 224–226
　intersection between personal and
　　professional life, 223–224
　lifelong learning and, 214, 230–231
　mandating, 217–218
　measuring outcomes of, 218–220
　professional psychology, 114–115
　reflection, 224–226

　self-assessment, 224–226
　technology trends in, 226–228
continuing professional development
　　(CPD), 214–217
coping strategies, training trainees, 386
core competency, trainees with problems
　　of professional competence
　　(TPPC), 378
core curriculum, 52, 64
　broad and general education, 55,
　　58, 59–60
　cognitive and affective bases of
　　behavior, 61–62
　common and essential
　　knowledge, 53–54
　competency movement, 54–55
　drawbacks and possible risks, 64
　economics, 63
　emphasizing context, 62–64
　epistemology, 64
　essential courses for scientific
　　information, 60–61
　general argument for, 52–53
　history, 54
　licensure and accreditation
　　requirements, 59
　local cultures, 63
　social class, 63
The Core Curriculum in Professional
　　Psychology, Peterson, 54
core principle, 174
cost, professional training, 106
Council for Accreditation of Counseling
　　and Related Educational Programs
　　(CACREP), 29
Council of Chairs of Training Councils
　　(CCTC), 47, 110, 135, 222, 323, 539
　doctoral and internship training,
　　157–158
　internship toolkit, 164
　practicum, 141, 142
　professional practice, 176
Council of Counseling Psychology
　　Training Programs (CCPTP),
　　108, 320
Council of Graduate Departments of
　　Psychology, 60, 252
Council of Graduate Schools, 272
Council of Representatives (CoR),
　　134, 255
Council of Specialties (CoS), 124
Council of the Chairs of Training
　　Councils (CCTC), 532
Council of University Directors of
　　Clinical Psychology (CUDCP), 46,
　　48, 320
Council on Higher Education
　　Accreditation, 89, 106
Council on Higher Education
　　Accreditation (CHEA), 94–95, 99
Council on Medical Education and
　　Hospitals, 88
The Counseling Psychologist (journal), 295

E

Early Career Psychologist Committee, 549
early career psychologists (ECPs), 548–549, 562–563
  accountability, 555–556
  competence-based education, 556–557
  definition, 548–549
  diversity and changing population, 554
  electronic healthcare records, 556
  evidence-based treatments, 556
  healthcare system, 557–558
  healthcare system changes, 554–555
  interprofessionalism, 557
  medical cost offset, 556
  personal success, 552
  preparation for success, 559–560
  programmatic success, 552–554
  questions to consider for success of, 561t, 562t
  recommendations for, 560–562
  starting salaries, 550
  student funding and debt load, 551
  supply and demand of workforce, 558
  trends impacting workforce, 551–558
  trends influencing success for, 554–558
  workforce, 549–551
ecological model, 319
economics, professional psychology, 63
"eddy effect," cultural competency, 439f, 443–444
education and training. See also early career psychologists (ECPs); race
  academic integrity, 344–346
  benefits of internship program, 163
  boundary issues and relationships in, 346–350
  cognitive-behavioral orientation, 71t, 73–75
  culture and context, 7–8
  diversity-welcoming climate, 446
  due process, 360–361
  ethical and legal context, 143–145
  evidence-based practice, 82–83
  gender, 409
  graduate assistants, multiple roles and multiple relationships, 349–350
  history of multicultural, in psychology, 398–400
  humanistic-existential orientation, 71t, 75–77
  immigration, 409–410
  Individual and Cultural Diversity (ICD) competency, 405–406
  informed consent in, 343–344
  integrative trends in, 79–82
  intersections of identity, 405–406
  language, 410
  lesbian, gay, bisexual and transgender (LGBT) competence, 458–464
  plagiarism, 345–346
  psychodynamic orientation, 70–73, 71t
  psychology specialization, 2–3, 122–123
  publication credit, 345

race and ethnicity, 437, 446–447, 449
religion in psychology programs, 475–476
sex and gender, 419–420, 432–433
standards for independent practice, 209–210
systemic orientation, 71t, 77–79
trainees with problems of professional competence (TPPC), 378
theory in psychology, 68–70
Education Directorate, American Psychological Association (APA), 109–110, 112, 141
efficacy, mentoring, 286
e-learning
  continuing education, 221
  training innovations, 511–512
electronic communication, licensed psychologists, 210–212
eligibility, accreditation, 92
Ellis, Albert, 475
elucidation of common factors, psychotherapy, 80
emotional intelligence (EI), psychology program leaders, 533
employment. See also early career psychologists (ECPs)
  mentoring in, 285
  networking and initial, 276
  professional workforce, 549–551
enacted stigma, 459
English as a Second Language (ESL), 403
entitlement, attitude, 445
entrustability, clinical supervision, 293
epistemology, professional psychology, 64
essentialism, sexual orientation and gender identity, 454–455
essential tension, 123
Ethical Principles of Psychologists and Code of Conduct, 267, 300, 336, 337, 341, 398, 452, 476
ethics
  boundaries in academic setting, 346–347
  boundaries in clinical supervision, 346–347
  boundary issues and relationships in education and training, 346–350
  challenges of trainers, 383–384
  clinical supervision, 300
  competence and client welfare, 143–144
  competence issues, 350–352
  creating culture of, and ethical practice, 339–340
  decision making, 338–339
  evaluation of competence, 351
  faculty roles and relationships with students, 348
  gate keepers of profession, 351–352
  gender, 421–422
  graduate assistants, multiple roles and multiple relationships, 349–350
  informed consent in education and

training, 343–344
interns and post-doctoral fellows, 350
modeling self-care and wellness, 340–342
multiple relationships in academic setting, 347–348
multiple relationships in clinical supervision, 347–348
personal psychotherapy, 342–343
plagiarism, 345–346
practicum training, 136, 138, 143–145
professional relationships, 346–347
program directors, 538–539
promoting academic integrity, 344–346
publication credit, 345
religious or spiritual interventions, 480
technology-assisted techniques, 523–524
trainee evaluation, 264, 266–267
trainers, 337, 383–384
training, 6, 322–324, 337, 338
ethics acculturation, 338
Ethics Code, 143, 369
  confidentiality, 366–367
  problems of competence, 324, 328, 329
  religion, 476
  remedial interventions, 360–362
  training, 336–339, 343, 345
  unprofessional behavior, 373–374
ethics course, mandatory, 224
ethnicity. See also race
  intersections of identity, 408
  matching model, 448
  psychology workforce, 550, 554
European Federation of Internal Medicine, 493
evaluation. See also trainee evaluation
  clinical supervision, 301–302
  competence, 351
  continuing education, 224–226
  trainees, 5, 266
Evaluation of Professional Behavior in General Practice, 497
evidence-based practice (EBP)
  clinical supervision, 306–307
  education and training, 82–83
  functional competency, 150
  postdoctoral training, 181
  research findings, 188
Examination for Professional Practice in Psychology (EPPP), 3, 39, 59, 203, 204, 247, 553
exosystem, 385
exploitation, cloning and theoretical abuse, 383–384
external accountability, accreditation, 93
externships, practicum in doctoral programs, 139–140

F

Facebook, 522
face-to-face supervision, 511, 512
facilitative interpersonal skills (FIS), 5, 243–244

National Institute of Mental Health (NIMH), 22–25, 34
National Institutes of Health (NIH), Individual National Research Service Awards (NRSAs), 177
National Mental Health Act (NMHA), 22, 25
National Register of Health Service Providers in Psychology, 252
national standards, postdoctoral training, 173–175
National Standards for High School Psychology Curricula, 109
Native American Spirituality, 412
Neisser, Ulric, 59
nested systems, training context, 385
New York Psychiatrical Society, 20
New York State Association of Consulting Psychologists, 21
New York University, 27
Nijmegen Professional Scale, 497
noncisgender, 409
nondoctoral competency models, psychology, 108–109
non-formal learning, continuing education, 215–216, 217
Northwestern Conference, 26, 27, 186
notice, 359
nursing, professionalism, 493, 495

O

obesity, 408
Objective Structured Clinical Examinations, 258, 302
online education
    accreditation, 97–98
    continuing education, 226–228, 512
operational definitions, trainee evaluation, 262–264
oppression
    concept, 402, 404
    continuum of, 403t
    discrimination, 403
    exercise of privilege, 402–405
oral examination, psychology specialization, 128
organizational & business consulting psychology, specialty board, 125t
organizational structures, accreditation, 93–95
orientation and empathy, mentoring, 278–279
outcomes
    clinical supervision, 304
    measuring continuing education, 218–220
    research training, 192
outcomes monitoring
    lab test, 513, 518
    research, 516–517
    training clinics, 513–514

P

parallel process, concept, 149
parallels model, psychology and religion, 478
paraphilic coercive disorder, 421
Parsons, Frank, 19
past performance, reviewing, 225
patient centered healthcare (medical) homes (PCMH), 557–558
Patient Protection and Affordable Care Act (2010), 537–538, 554–555, 557–558. *See also* Affordable Care Act
Pedagogical Seminary (journal), 18
peers
    evaluation feedback, 262
    learning experience, 226
    problems with professional competence (PPC), 384
    professionalism, 496
    recommendations for addressing, 388
Penfield, Wilder, 61
Pennsylvania State University, 27
personal factors, clinical supervision, 299
personality pathology, trainees with problems of professional competence (TPPC), 379
personality psychology, education and training, 79–80
personal problems, competence, 328
personal psychotherapy, ethical training, 342–343
personal therapy, remediation, 328
Pew Forum on Religion & Public Life, 473
physical therapy, specialty, 121
Physician's Charter, 494
PICO mnemonic acronym, evidence-based practice, 150
Pikes Peak Model, 112
plagiarism, academic integrity, 345–346
Plato, 497
police & public safety psychology, specialty board, 125t
political, intersections of identity, 410–411
portrayers, 493
positive ethics, 338
post-doctoral fellows, boundary and relationship issues, 350
postdoctoral training, 171–172
    4 plus 2 model, 172
    advising and mentoring, 273–274
    benefits of, 178
    challenges to, 178–180
    content of, 175–177
    core principle, 174
    defining, 172
    development of national standards, 173–175
    formal vs. informal experiences, 177–178
    future directions, 180–181
    origins of, 172–173

practicum hours, 179
    recommendations, 180–181
    settings for, 175
postmodernist approaches, trainee evaluation, 255
power
    abusive trainers, 444
    blaming the victim, 444–445
    diversity and student outcomes, 449
    false generosity, 445
    nonabusive trainers, 438–439
    relationships, 437
    supervisory relationships, 428
power-down position, 443
A Practical Guidebook for the Competency Benchmarks, 363
practice, scientific endeavor, 188–189
practice-research network (PRN), 516–517
Practicum Competencies Outline, 110, 135–136, 137, 141
practicum training, 133–134
    background, 134–135
    competencies acquired during, 137–139
    doctoral programs, 139–141
    externships, 139–140
    foundational competencies, 137–138
    foundational competencies incorporation in, 143–149
    functional competencies, 138, 150–152
    future of, 152–153
    goals of, 135–139
    in-house training clinics, 139, 140
    length of, 134
    licensure, 134–135
    policies and procedures, 140–141
    postdoctoral, 179
    preparation for, 135–137
    quality standards for, 141–143
    scientific knowledge and methods, 137, 149–150
Practitioner Research Vertical Team (PRVT), 283
practitioner-scholar model, 38
    central characteristics, 37–38
    development, 37
    doctoral education in psychology, 91
    doctoral training, 33, 37–39
    evaluation of, 39
    implementation, 38–39
    internships, 45
    practice emphasis, 37–38
    professional psychology, 3
    research training, 186
    role of science and research, 38
    Vail Conference, 37
premenstrual dysphoric disorder, 421
pre-practicum group, case example, 424–425
Prince Edward Island, psychology licensing law, 202
Princeton University, 88